1,000
LOW-CALORIE
RECIPES

JACKIE NEWGENT, RD

WILEY

JOHN WILEY & SONS, INC.

For general information on our other products and services, or technical support, please contact our Customer Care Department within the United States at 800–762–2974, outside the United States at 317–572–3993 or fax 317–572–4002.

Wiley publishes in a variety of print and electronic formats and by print-on-demand. Some material included with standard print versions of this book may not be included in e-books or in print-on-demand. If this book refers to media such as a CD or DVD that is not included in the version you purchased, you may download this material at http://booksupport.wiley.com. For more information about Wiley products, visit www.wiley.com.

Library of Congress Cataloging-in-Publication Data

Newgent, Jackie.
  1,000 low-calorie recipes / Jackie Newgent, RD.
  Includes bibliographical references and index.
ISBN 978-1-118-44177-0 (hardback) (print)–ISBN 978-1-118-44177-0 (ebk.)–ISBN 978-1-118-44179-4 (ebk.)–ISBN 978-1-118-44180-0 (ebk.)–1. Low-calorie diet–Recipes. 2. Low-fat diet--Recipes. 3. Reducing diets–Recipes. I. Title. II. Title: One thousand low-calorie recipes.
  RM222.2
  641.5'63–dc23
                         2012035234

Decorative spot art © enderstse/iStockphoto.com

Printed in the United States of America

10 9 8 7 6 5 4 3 2 1

Publisher: Natalie Chapman

Senior Editor: Linda Ingroia

Production Editor: Margaret Vernon

Cover Designer: Jeffrey Faust

Interior Designer: Holly Wittenberg

Manufacturing Manager: Kevin Watt

Cover Illustrator: Gina Triplett

For my smart and spirited nephews, Aiden and Rhyus

Thank you for inspiring me to do all I can to make a better, healthier, and tastier future for all. Wishing you good health always.

Contents

Acknowledgments

I have so many to be appreciative of for their energy, time, and support of this decidedly heavy cookbook about eating light . . . and for helping me ultimately make a real difference.

I'm thankful to my:

dear Aunt Ceal, for passing on her cooking prowess to my mother—who then paid it forward to me.

food-loving sister, Rebecca, for her assistance in testing some of the book's recipes—and for having her friends and colleagues taste them to make sure they're delicious enough to print.

brilliant colleagues and friends Cynthia Sass, MPH, MA, RD; Ellie Krieger, MS, RD; Lisa Drayer, MA, RD; Patricia Bannan, MS, RD; Keri Gans, MS, RD; Bonnie Taub-Dix, MA, RD; Maye Musk, MS, RD; Rachel Begun, MS, RD; and Darren Smith and David Strumeyer for their encouragement and insights.

friendly neighbors Jennifer Sarkilahti, Steve Schwartz, Jessica Freeman, and Angela Nguyen, for letting me borrow their enthusiastic food- (and cocktail-!) loving palates, and making sure none of my recipe-testing leftovers ever went to waste.

amazing friends near and far, Amy Morse, Leah McLaughlin, Maureen Heritage, Alyssa Gelbard, and Jass Babin, for their gifts of friendship and for being so understanding when making this project my priority.

hard-working chef assistants Lindsay Stoulil, RD, and Kristy Lambrou, MS, RD, without whom I couldn't have completed this cookbook.

talented culinary and nutrition interns Courtney Yablonsky, Carissa Anderson, Stephanie Lang, Sandy Pagan, Gilda Mulero, Dara Yaffe, and Aylene Lambert, for their passion and skills.

business development partner Maureen Yarnon for her public relations and brand-building guidance.

spokesperson agent Beth Shepard, for keeping me on the right career path.

literary agent Michael Bourret of Dystel & Goderich Literary Management, for always believing in and looking out for me.

editors and the motivated behind-the-scenes talent at Wiley, especially Linda Ingroia, for providing me with the enormous opportunity to make a positive impact on the health, waistlines, and palates of so many. Emily Nolan helped shape this huge collection and Maggie Vernon in production kept the book on schedule. Thanks to Holly Wittenberg for her simple, modern book design and Gina Triplett for her unique cover illustration.

colleagues at the Academy of Nutrition and Dietetics (formerly the American Dietetic Association) and all the registered dietitians, dietetic technicians, health professionals, and other advocates who work brilliantly and tirelessly to fight our obesity epidemic.

Thank you so much to everyone!

Introduction

Delicious. Scrumptious. Mouthwatering. Those are some of the first words that will roll off your tongue when cooking and enjoying the recipes in *1,000 Low-Calorie Recipes.*

Yes, finally, an incredible cookbook in which eating healthfully and eating deliciously is now in your hands. In a nutshell, *1,000 Low-Calorie Recipes* features great-tasting "real" cuisine, **with each recipe providing less than 500 calories per serving.** Trying to lose weight? The compendium of dishes can be considered like a dieter's recipe "bible." It will support weight loss books, programs, and plans as a recipe resource. Trying to simply eat healthier? This cookbook is equally ideal for anyone desiring a fit lifestyle—even when weight loss is not a goal. You'll be able to serve these dishes to everyone.

Most of yesterday's calorie-conscious and healthy-weight cookbooks forgot nearly everything else that mattered to people. Often filled with nutrient-poor, unsatisfying ingredients, they lacked flavor appeal. I didn't want to create yet another cookbook with recipes whose main inspiration was that they be low in calories. My goal was to take a fresh approach and create recipes that are both exciting and taste good. In fact, deliciousness is the most important feature of *1,000 Low-Calorie Recipes.*

You'll have so many options, you will be able to focus on eating well to suit your palate.

As a natural culinary nutritionist, my philosophy is that if you prepare a nutritious recipe that's tasteless or otherwise unsatisfying, chances are you probably won't make it again. I want you to want to make these recipes again and again—to best help you stay fit and manage weight in the long run. You can and should expect your food to be enjoyable even when—and perhaps especially when—eating healthfully.

In addition to being high-flavored, the enticing, simple-to-follow dishes within *1,000 Low-Calorie Recipes* focus on filling ingredients with a contemporary edge. The recipes are not unrealistically low in calories, fat, or sodium, just cleverly lower in calories than you otherwise might expect. I prefer to call them "calorie friendly"! The health strategy is about adding nutritional richness. This is accomplished mainly by boosting nutrient-dense plant foods—fresh, vibrant, colorful, appealing plant foods. Meats, poultry, fish, and dairy products are featured smartly, in small quantities. The result is mouthwatering cuisine—naturally. You'll find absolutely nothing artificial in here!

1,000 Low-Calorie Recipes is about making food that's scrumptious while still keeping calories in check. It's about what you *can* have! It's about making sure portion sizes are satisfying and right-sized—not bigger than you really need or want and not too small. It's not about sacrificing. It's about balancing luscious ingredients with full-flavored lean ingredients to create wonderfully lean, calorie-friendly cuisine.

Beyond eating deliciously, it's important to remember why eating nutritious foods is so essential. The main reason is that we have an obesity epidemic in the United States. Yes, an epidemic! Today, according to data from the National Health and Nutrition Examination Survey, more than two-thirds of adults in the United States are overweight or obese. According to the Centers for Disease Control, about one-third of children and teens are, too. And unfortunately, this is a growing problem in far too many other regions of the world.

Facts and Figures

How do you know if you're obese or overweight? There's one measurement called the body mass index (BMI) that's a general guide to determining if you fit into either category. An adult is considered overweight if her or his BMI is 25 to 29.9 or obese if it's 30 or higher. The BMI isn't a direct measure of body fat, so athletes and other muscular individuals may need to rely on more specific measures of body fat. You can determine your BMI by entering your weight and height into the calculator at http://www.cdc.gov/healthyweight/.

How'd you do? If you fall into the category of healthy weight, great! If you find you fit into the overweight or obese category, you're not alone. I wish there was a magic recipe that I could whip up for everyone that would miraculously melt all those extra pounds away. But, alas, there's no such recipe. Trust me, if there were, I'd be whipping it up for myself, too!

No doubt, there's absolutely no simple solution to solving these weighty issues. But how you eat can definitely play a key role in your efforts to manage a healthy weight. And though there's no simple answer to the ideal eating plan to follow, the bottom line for maintaining a healthy weight comes down to this calorie equation: you need to balance calories in with calories out.

If you consume more calories than your body needs, you'll gain weight. If you consume fewer calories than your body needs, you'll lose weight. Though very simplified, that's the gist of it all. (Of course, being physically active can play an important role in calorie management, too.) And there's more. Besides quantity, the quality and even the timing of the calories you consume is essential to consider. I'll share how to make calories count a bit later on in this cookbook. In fact, you are what you eat!

How does this all translate into numbers within *1,000 Low-Calorie Recipes*? Here's the nutrition criteria per serving that applies to all the recipes:

> MAXIMUM OF:
>
> **500 calories; 20g total fat; 10g saturated fat; 800mg sodium**

These are maximums. Don't worry, most recipes will provide far less than these criteria. What's more, every recipe provides zero grams of trans fat.

There are two highlighted categories to help you decide which of the recipes fit best with your other needs. You'll see symbols with the recipes that identify these important nutrition features:

(S) = 250mg sodium or less per serving (and no more than 1mg sodium per calorie—so if a recipe has 200 calories, it has no more than 200mg sodium)

An easy-to-remember goal is to consume no more than 1mg sodium per calorie daily. So for a 1,500-calorie plan, consuming less than 1,500mg sodium is an excellent goal for health (1,500mg sodium is also the suggested maximum daily level if you are age 51 or older, if you're African-American, or if you have high blood pressure, diabetes, or chronic kidney disease). I used this as a guide for establishing "light in sodium" recipes.

(F) = 5g dietary fiber or more per serving

This level is meaningful since 5g is equivalent to 20 percent of the daily value for dietary fiber, which also means a particular food is an excellent source.

Many people feel that keeping within recommended quantities of calories and sodium or getting enough key nutrients, such as fiber and calcium, requires sacrifice. What better way to stay inspired and make it easy to eat well than to have a seemingly endless supply of recipes? No sacrifice required! Not only should you look to cook any of the 1,000 recipes here, you should consider this book also a guide to being creative in the kitchen and from which you can vary the dishes to suit your unique needs. In fact, I encourage you to truly make this a resource for any cooking needs. Even if you're following a gluten-free diet, vegan eating plan, or perhaps your very own diet, you'll be able to find endless ways to personalize and enjoy this recipe compendium. I hope that you, your family, and your friends will savor *1,000 Low-Calories Recipes* as much as I enjoyed putting it together. I'm sure you'll find these recipes will appeal to your senses and benefit your waistline for years to come.

What to Eat

My basic philosophy for eating well is this: Eat right-size amounts of real food—and relish it. *1,000 Low-Calorie Recipes* is designed for you to be able to do just that.

Here's a checklist that provides you with general guidelines for following this eating philosophy. The ultimate goal is to be able to check this list off daily (even if it's just a mental checklist).

Healthy Eating Daily Checklist

✓ **FOLLOW THE 5-HOUR RULE.** Healthy eating and weight management don't require starvation. And in fact, try not to go more than five waking hours without eating so your blood sugar stays level and metabolism stays revved up. Otherwise, you may be more likely to make poor food or drink choices to fulfill cravings.

✓ **REACH FOR REAL.** Increase whole foods and decrease overly processed foods. Keep "natural" ingredients in and artificial ingredients out. It will help keep flavors up and fillers out. It will help assure that your body is getting important nutrients it needs and not those it doesn't. It's the key aspect of a better eating plan.

✓ **BE PLANT FRIENDLY.** Focus your plate on plant foods, especially produce which naturally provides fiber and low-calorie goodness. (See Fill Up on Fiber, page xi.) It heightens volume and overall appeal of your meals while boosting satiety (makes you feel full). Select fresh seasonal produce often. It will be at its peak of ripeness, nutritional value, and flavor. Aim for five total cups of vegetables and fruits daily. Pick various colors, too, including red, orange, and dark-green produce. Every time you eat, plan to fill half of your plate with produce—especially veggies.

✓ **MAKE NUTRIENT-RICH CHOICES.** When you're losing weight, it's more important than ever to make every calorie count. Choose foods that have significant amounts of key nutrients, naturally. (See Nutrient Full, Calorie Friendly, page xii.) Limit "empty-calorie" foods that have significant caloric amounts of added sugars and saturated (solid) fats. Always go for zero trans fats. Select whole grains in place of refined grains whenever possible. (See What Counts as a Whole Grain?, page xiii.) When eating sweets, choose those naturally sweetened, such as with fruit, most often. When in doubt, choose real foods with the richest color.

✓ **GET THE RIGHT BALANCE.** Balance meals by selecting good carbs, adequate protein, and healthful fats. (See Getting the Right Balance, below.) Good carbs, like whole grains,

are essential for providing energy. Ensure that you're getting enough protein throughout the day, not just at lunch or dinnertime. Protein can help boost satiety (make you feel full) and maintain your lean tissue (muscle). Choose plant-based proteins, such as beans, more often than animal-based proteins. Include at least 2 teaspoons of healthful oils, such as extra-virgin olive oil, each day within your meals; it can improve health, nutrient absorption, and flavor. Don't forget other natural flavor enhancers, such as honey or sea salt—but just a drizzle or a pinch, respectively. (See A Note about Sodium, page xiv.)

✓ **DRINK RIGHT.** Calories can add up quickly when you're gulping them down. So, when

GETTING THE RIGHT BALANCE

What's the right mix of carbohydrates, proteins, and fats within a nutritious diet? Based on the current research available on healthy eating, my recommendations as a registered dietitian are below. *1,000 Low-Calorie Recipes* was planned for you to be able to meet these nutrition criteria. Use them as a guide.

40 TO 60 PERCENT CALORIES FROM CARBOHYDRATES

- Aim for higher fiber choices, little to no refined grains, and only small amounts of added unrefined sugars, including honey and turbinado sugar.
- Foods that provide healthful or "good" carbs include whole-grain foods and whole-grain food products (see What Counts as a Whole Grain?, page xiii) and fresh or frozen vegetables and fruits (not processed juices).
- If highly active, aim for closer to 60 percent.

20 TO 35 PERCENT CALORIES FROM FATS

- Aim for mostly healthful, unsaturated fats (monounsaturated and polyunsaturated).
- Foods that provide healthful, unsaturated or "good" fats include oils like canola, olive,

grapeseed, and peanut, and include foods naturally high in oils, such as nuts, avocados, and salmon.
- If following a Mediterranean-style eating plan rich in healthful fats, it's okay to aim for closer to 35 percent.

20 TO 35 PERCENT CALORIES FROM PROTEINS

- Aim for mostly plant-based proteins.*
- Foods that are healthful choices of proteins include plant-based foods, like beans, soybeans, nuts, and seeds, and include nutrient-rich animal-based foods, such as plain fat-free or low-fat Greek yogurt and whole eggs.
- Be sure to get proteins at every meal since the body needs a continual supply.

A vegan diet based on only plant-based proteins can be healthful when properly planned.

you're simply quenching thirst, sip calorie-free or very low calorie, better-for-you beverages—focusing on cold filtered fresh tap water or unsweetened tea. (Try the very low calorie beverage, Spa H$_2$0, on page 544.) Aim to drink at least six 8-ounce glasses daily of these, especially water like Spa H$_2$0. When choosing a beverage for enjoyment, make calories count by choosing nutrient-rich beverages, like real fruit smoothies; they do count as part of your fruit servings, after all. (Check out the nutrient-rich beverages beginning on page 541.) And, if you're able to consume alcohol, plan for the added calories within your meal plan. Generally, up to one drink a day for women or two for men can be included healthfully. What counts as a drink? A 12-fluid-ounce beer, 5-fluid-ounce glass of wine, or cocktail containing 1½ fluid ounces 80-proof spirits. Cocktails can provide a clever way to boost your fruit and vegetable intake. (Check out the cocktails beginning on page 554.)

✓ **BE REALISTIC.** You don't have to give up your favorites! But do try to make wiser, fresher, "cleaner" picks when you do. Look for the dishes that delight your palate the most. I bet you'll discover most, if not all, of your favorites here.

✓ **SAVOR SLOWLY.** How you eat is important, not just what you eat. So eat slowly—whenever possible, sit at a table, use silverware, plates, and bowls. You'll be able to truly appreciate your food.

✓ **KEEP IT DELICIOUS.** Always know that a tasty meal plan is one that's easiest to stick to. Enjoyment is key to following a good-for-you eating plan for the long term. So when it comes to dishes from *1,000 Low-Calorie Recipes* and beyond, relish them!

A Healthful Meal Plan

There's no one right meal plan for everyone. It's always best that it be individualized. That's where specialized advice from a registered dietitian (RD) can be especially helpful. (See Seeking RD Advice, page xv.)

But there's a general guide that can be followed as a baseline for balanced meal planning. The Dietary Guidelines for Americans provides science-based advice on how to eat for health. The guidelines encourage all Americans to eat a healthy diet and be physically active. By improving what you eat and being active, you help reduce your risk of chronic diseases, such as diabetes, heart disease, some cancers, and, yes, obesity.

When it comes to eating well, the guidelines provide basic "rules of thumb" to remember—which fit well within the philosophy of *1,000 Low-Calorie Recipes*. Try these three tips:

1. **FOR BALANCING CALORIES:** Enjoy your food, but eat less. That's the basic premise of this cookbook. Recipe portions are already adjusted for you, so simply enjoy.

2. **FOR FOODS TO INCREASE:** Make half your plate vegetables and fruits. Alternatively, just make half your dish veggies. In *1,000 Low-Calorie Recipes*, I generously incorporate produce into dishes to make this easy for you.

3. **FOR FOODS TO REDUCE:** Compare sodium in foods like soup, bread, and frozen meals—and choose the foods with the lowest sodium, for instance. Check out all the recipes with the Ⓢ symbol to help you lighten up on sodium without losing out on enjoyment.

For more details about how to plan a healthful plate, MyPlate was developed. It corresponds directly to the Dietary Guidelines for Americans, 2010. Check out http://www.DietaryGuidelines.gov and http://www.ChooseMyPlate.gov for more details.

HOW CAN YOU BE SURE YOU'LL BE SATISFIED?
Fill Up on Fiber

Dietary fiber is the part of plant foods that the body can't digest. Yet it's a vital part of a healthful eating plan. It adds bulk to your diet to help you feel fuller longer, which is a key for managing weight. By boosting high-fiber foods, you'll have less room for high-calorie nutrient-poor (aka "empty-calorie") foods, too. What's more, naturally fibrous foods generally take more time to chew, which may give your body more time to realize that you're satisfied, ultimately preventing you from overeating.

Dietary fiber also plays a key role in the digestion process, can help prevent constipation, and may play a beneficial role in managing blood cholesterol and blood sugar levels.

Most Americans don't consume enough dietary fiber, with averages of only 15 grams per day. For wholesome eating and a fit body, the Dietary Guidelines for Americans recommend a daily fiber intake of 25 grams for women and 38 grams for men. After age 50, daily fiber needs drop to 21 grams for women and 30 grams for men. A simpler tip: the National Fiber Council suggests an average of 32 grams of fiber per day for adults in general. Determine your specific daily fiber recommendation based on your gender and age by using the Fiber Calculator at http://www.nationalfibercouncil.org.

The best way to meet dietary fiber needs is by eating a variety of fiber-rich foods, including beans, whole grains, nuts, fruits, and vegetables. Beans are the best—and found liberally sprinkled throughout the recipes within *1,000 Low Caloric Recipes!* Keep in mind that it's advisable to boost fiber in your diet slowly since too much too quickly can contribute to gas, bloating, and cramps.

Discover the fiber-rich dishes in *1,000 Low-Calorie Recipes* by looking for the ⓕ next to the recipe titles.

Good Sources of Dietary Fiber

FOOD	PORTION	CALORIES IN PORTION	DIETARY FIBER IN PORTION (G)
Beans (navy, pinto, black, kidney, white, Great Northern, lima), cooked	½ cup	104–149	6.2–9.6
Split peas or lentils, cooked	½ cup	115	8.0
Artichoke, cooked	½ cup hearts	45	7.2
Pear	1 medium	103	5.5
Soybeans, mature, cooked	½ cup	149	5.2
Green peas, cooked	½ cup	67	4.4
Whole-wheat English muffin	1 muffin	134	4.4
Bulgur, cooked	½ cup	76	4.1
Mixed vegetables, cooked	½ cup	59	4.0
Raspberries	½ cup	32	4.0
Sweet potato, baked in skin	1 medium	103	3.8
Blackberries	½ cup	31	3.8
Soybeans, green, cooked	½ cup	127	3.8
Figs, dried	¼ cup	93	3.7

NUTRIENT FULL, CALORIE FRIENDLY

When foods are high in nutrients compared to the calories provided, they're considered to be nutrient-rich or nutrient-dense foods. (When especially nutrient rich, they may be called "superfoods.") These are the foods that are celebrated as ingredients within *1,000 Low-Calorie Recipes.*

Why are nutrient-rich foods key for you? Eating nutrient-rich foods means you're making your calories count, which is especially important when you're eating fewer calories. You need to pack as much nutrition into the calories you consume to keep your overall meal plan a good-for-you one—and one that provides the best boost for your healthy eating or weight loss goals.

Below are a dozen of my favorite nutrient-rich ingredients in *1,000 Low-Calorie Recipes:*

1. Garlic:
   - is one of the simplest ways to boost flavor
   - may be beneficial for reducing risk of heart disease
2. Onions:
   - provide texture, color, and an occasional touch of sweetness
   - may help maintain a healthy immune system and suppress unwanted inflammation
3. Beans:
   - impart a wonderful creaminess, especially when pureed into recipes
   - provide a sustained energy source with their coupling of plant-based protein and fiber
4. Mushrooms:
   - are rich in umami and provide savoriness, "meatiness," and earthiness
   - are the only natural food source of bone-friendly vitamin D in the produce aisle
5. Leafy greens:
   - add volume, crispness, freshness, color, taste, and more

   - are a nutritional powerhouse that may help to protect you from heart disease
6. Tomatoes:
   - come in many forms and nothing beats their rich redness
   - contain lycopene, which is associated with reduced risk of certain cancers
7. Fresh herbs:
   - are way more than garnishes and give dishes lovely aroma
   - count as veggies; can potentially help you use less salt in cooking
8. Spices:
   - offer an easy way to create intrigue and international flair; a pinch adds pow
   - have antioxidants; sweet spices can potentially help you use less sugar in baking
9. Avocado:
   - has a buttery texture that's unsurpassed
   - has heart-healthful fat; may reduce "bad" cholesterol levels
10. Nuts:
   - provide crunchiness, richness, and, of course, nuttiness
   - may reduce the risk of heart disease without causing weight gain
11. Plain almond milk:
   - can be used just like regular milk
   - has fewer calories than regular milk
12. Plain fat-free or low-fat Greek yogurt:
   - makes recipes creamy with distinct tang
   - its protein boosts satiety; its active cultures boosts the immune system

WHAT COUNTS AS A WHOLE GRAIN?

Whole grains contain all edible parts of the grain, including the bran, germ, and endosperm. Refined grains have been processed to remove the outer bran and inner germ—which removes many nutrients, including B vitamins, iron, and dietary fiber. So it's important to focus grain intake on whole grains for whole benefits.

Examples of whole grains include whole-wheat flour, brown rice, and whole-grain corn. Examples of refined grains include white flour, white rice, and degermed cornmeal.

Sometimes there's confusion about what's considered a whole grain. One example is wheat bread. Wheat bread is only made with the whole grain when it says "whole-wheat flour" on the ingredient list. Otherwise it simply means it was made with refined wheat flour—or white flour that simply isn't bleached. So look for the word "whole" often.

There are so many whole grains and whole-grain products available today. Some whole grains are actually ancient grains that have gained newfound popularity. Below is a sampling of the myriad whole grains you'll find in *1,000 Low-Calorie Recipes* along with why you should enjoy each. When you do enjoy, aim for no fewer than 3 servings of whole grains a day. A serving—or 1-ounce equivalent— counts as ½ cup cooked whole grain, such as brown rice or oatmeal, 3 cups popped popcorn, 1 cup whole-grain cereal flakes, or 1 slice whole-grain bread.

WHOLE GRAIN	HIGHLIGHTS
Amaranth	Creamy, mildly earthy flavor. Tiny seed yet packed with protein. Rich in phytosterols that are beneficial for a healthy heart and immune system.
Brown Rice	Light brown, nutty, and chewy grain. Excellent source of manganese, which helps you produce energy from protein and carbohydrates.
Buckwheat	Rich earthy flavor. Despite its name, it's not related to wheat; it's a seed of a fruit. Contains rutin, which acts as an antioxidant and anti-inflammatory.
Bulgur	Steamed, dried, crushed wheat kernels—from fine to coarse. Taste pleasantly nutty, like wheat, since it is wheat. Chewy yet tender and quick cooking.
Farro	Deep nutty flavor and extra chewy. Ancient whole grain that's a member of the wheat family and looks like spelt. Choose it for a satiating protein and fiber boost.
Millet	Tiny and round seed that's as much bird seed as it is people seed. Good source of magnesium, which can be beneficial for healthy bones and blood pressure.
Quinoa	Subtly nutty flavor. A seed that looks similar to sesame seed. A complete source of protein as it containing all essential amino acids. Cooks in 15 minutes.
Oats	Oat groats (steel-cut oats) and rolled oats (old-fashioned oats) provide beta-glucan, a soluble fiber that's beneficial for managing blood sugar and cholesterol.
Spelt	Mild nutty taste and extra chewy. Ancient whole grain that looks like farro. Rich in manganese and ultimately may help to fight free radicals.
Teff	Mildly molasses-like taste. Whole grain from the lovegrass plant group. Super tiny yet super nutritious. Especially notable for its calcium and iron.
Whole-grain barley	Nutty flavor and chewy texture. Loaded with dietary fiber to help maintain a healthy colon. Loaded with selenium, which has cancer preventative properties.
Whole-grain corn	Whole grain grown as "ears." Various colors, not just yellow. Yellow corn provides high concentrations of lutein and zeaxanthin, which are important for eye health.
Whole-wheat	Found in many foods. Can play key role in weight loss as it provides insoluble fiber, which provides bulk. High in gluten, which is why it works well in making bread.

Why Eat Nutritiously?

Reasons why you want to eat well may differ from someone else's reasons. Some people may want to lose weight to look better. Others may want to feel better. And yet others may need to eat right for management of a health condition.

However, for those who need extra motivation to stick to a nutritious eating plan for weight loss, here's info about obesity that is useful to know:

When obese, it means that you have so much body fat that it has a negative effect on your health, placing you at higher risk of developing several diseases, including type 2 diabetes, heart disease, hypertension (high blood pressure), some cancers, sleep apnea, and osteoarthritis. You also have a greater risk of dying younger than a non-obese person.

Yes, it is serious. So take a minute to digest.

Now, let's get back to the other kind of digestion. Whatever your reason for wanting to eat better, it's a valid reason—especially when it is that reason that motivates you to eat well. And when eating right, always remember this: While keeping it nutritious, make sure it's delicious. That's where this cookbook really comes into play. So start eating better today . . . there's no time like the present.

Healthy Weight Tips

Everyone has a personal calorie limit. Staying within the right calorie level for you can help you reach or maintain a healthy weight. Seek the advice of a registered dietitian (RD) to identify the specific calorie level and eating plan best for you. (See Seeking RD Advice, page xv.) You can also go to http://www.ChooseMyPlate.gov to find your daily calorie limit.

Or, try this tip. For losing weight, my easiest rule of thumb is to add a 0 to your weight (in pounds) and use that as a guideline (if you're moderately active). So if you weigh 160 pounds, then aim to eat 1,600 calories for an eating plan for weight loss. Going too far below that number may result in a greater loss of lean muscle tissue (muscle helps you burn calories!), it may not be sustainable, and it may not allow you to meet your overall nutritional needs. If you're focused on maintaining instead of losing weight, add about 400 to 500 calories per day to the "weight + 0" rule of thumb. Also, keep in mind, the more active you are, the more calories you'll need—even when losing weight. So the daily calorie level you follow will actually vary based on activity. One caveat: Be sure to not consume less than 1,000 calories daily—even if you're small-framed and say 90 pounds; it's important to assure basic nutrient needs are met.

A NOTE ABOUT SODIUM

When using this cookbook, know that all of the recipes are under 800mg sodium per serving. Most fall well under that mark. This sodium level is well within the daily recommendations for most people, 2,300mg sodium per day. What's more, the recipes that are especially light in sodium are indicated by the symbol: Ⓢ. Keep your eye out for them.

Keys to Weight-Management Success

Even if you know what to eat and how many calories to eat, weight management still provides many, many challenges. But knowing some of the keys to success—especially from people who have lost weight and kept it off—will help give you a greater chance at long-term weight management.

Habits of Highly Successful Losers

In addition to modifying food intake in some way to lose weight, being a successful loser (which also means keeping lost weight off), based on the majority of participants' habits within The National Weight Control Registry (NWCR), includes:

- Eating breakfast daily
- Weighing themselves at least once weekly
- Watching less than 10 hours of television weekly
- Exercising (especially walking), on average, about 1 hour daily (Hint: It can be broken up into increments, like 20 minutes three times daily.)

Three Rules to Remember

What about what goes onto your plate? There seems to be a new study every day touted by the media about what to eat for weight loss. Some of it gets downright confusing, especially when what was supposedly "good" yesterday is "bad" today, and vice versa. But filtering through all of the research, there are some common denominators that you can rely on to help you beat the battle of the bulge. Here are three rules to remember—and put into practice:

1. **DON'T EAT TOO MUCH.** Steer clear of portion distortion. Aim for just-right-size portions.

2. **DON'T EAT TOO OFTEN.** Have a plan of a snack, don't just give in to any snack attack.

3. **DO EAT NUTRIENT-RICH FOODS.** That means vegetables, fruits, whole grains, yogurt, and nuts.

SEEKING RD ADVICE

While the Dietary Guidelines can help to provide a framework for a balanced eating plan, you may need to follow a more specialized diet for weight loss or for other health reasons. This is where a registered dietitian (RD) can play a key role as a vital member of your health team. A dietitian can design an individualized meal plan to meet your specific needs—weight-wise, health-wise, taste-wise, lifestyle-wise, and otherwise. If you prefer to follow a popular diet, an RD can also help you appropriately utilize it and make it uniquely fit you. Popular diet approaches that are based on solid nutrition principles include the Mediterranean Diet (I'm a big fan of it!), the Dash Diet, and Weight Watchers. What's more, an RD can help you determine which recipes within this cookbook can be part of any meal plan. If you don't already have a dietitian, you can find one at http://eatright.org.

Counting Sheep

Besides eating right and moving around often, is there anything else that can help with weight loss efforts? Possibly! According to recent research, getting restful sleep may help. So count your sheep and aim for getting Zs 6 to 8 hours a night.

Diet Dos and Don'ts

In addition to the basic guidelines I've provided for eating right, weight loss takes additional tools, which eventually will become second nature to you. Being a dietitian for so many years, I've learned which dieting tips actually work for people. Below is a list of a handful of the most helpful—from the mainstream to the quirky. Pick a few that seem to speak to you if weight loss is your goal.

- **THINK BEFORE YOU BITE.** Count to three before you take your first bite. If you didn't plan for it, ask yourself this while counting: "Is this worth the calories?"

- **SLOW DOWN**. Enjoy every morsel of your healthful, high-flavor, homemade dishes from *1,000 Low-Calorie Recipes*. Faster eating seems to translate to greater weight. So savor flavors and focus only on your food when eating. One study finds that cutting up food into smaller pieces may lead to more satisfaction than eating one large piece. Another study even suggests that chewing each bite of food 40 times may be a key to eating less. That's a lot of savoring . . . but it may work for you!

- **DON'T LET THE CLOCK TELL YOU WHEN TO EAT.** Listen to your internal hunger cues. Follow this approach: Eat when you're hungry and stop when you're satisfied, not full. Also, consider using my 3 Hs: hungry, happy, or hurting. You should be hungry *before* you're satisfied; you're happy when you're satisfied (satiated); and you're hurting when you've eaten too much. The goal is to feel hunger and reach a happy place, while you avoid hurting as a result of overeating.

- **THINK "NEW PLATE SPECIAL."** Choose new, smaller plates when starting on your new and nutritious eating plan. Consider using a salad-size or a more petite-size dinner plate as your dish of choice (no more than 10 inches). When you pull out the "special" plate for each meal, it'll be a reminder of your better-for-you diet.

- **DON'T BE MATCHY-MATCHY.** Plate color can be key. The higher the contrast of the food you're eating to the color of the plate, the more likely it is that you'll eat less. So, basically, if your food is red, serve it on a white plate, not a red plate.

- **HAVE A GAME PLAN.** Lay out your own plan to win at weight loss. Store the plan in your hand-held device or use a mobile app. And be sure you have the foods on hand for your plan.

- **KEEP A COUNT.** Track what you're eating and drinking at mealtime—and everything in

ARE LOW-CARB APPROACHES HEALTHFUL?

For calorie reduction, eating plans that slightly reduce total carbs or suggest elimination of only refined carbohydrates, such as white rice and white bread, can be a good thing, especially if you're an over-avid carbohydrate consumer. I'd consider that to be a carb-friendly approach. However, approaches that come in and out of style that are considered either low-carbohydrate diets or high-protein diets, like the Dukan Diet or the original Atkins Diet, are not a good thing. Just because something is trendy and you hear a lot about it, that doesn't make it a beneficial approach to weight management. Low-carb diets may help you lose weight in the short run, mainly due to a low calorie level, but they're not ideal for weight management in the long run. A diet that is a temporary fix or that doesn't enable you to obtain all important nutrients through foods is never a healthful approach to good health. (A vitamin-mineral supplement does not replace the hundreds and hundreds of nutrients found naturally within plant foods, by the way.) And any diet plan that suggests you avoid healthful foods, like fruits or other plant foods, at any point, is not one that should be followed; it may ultimately have health-harming effects.

between. When you see what you're consuming, it can help you consume less.

- **DO THE MATH.** Check calories on food labels. And compare the serving size listed to the actual amount you'll consume. If you eat double the servings, you get double the calories. Simple, but effective.

- **EAT "SEE" FOOD.** Have good-for-you eats, like fresh seasonal produce, on hand for snack attacks. Place in plain sight so you'll reach for it instead of not-so-good treats. Research suggests that keeping unhealthful food out of sight may be a key to keeping your appetite in check.

- **DON'T SAY NEVER.** If you say you'll never eat something, it sets you up for problems when you actually do eat it. Rather, incorporate appropriate amounts of favorites into your fit eating plan from the get-go. Hint: If you want to eat a sweet, plan for it immediately after a workout or a walk where it'll do double-duty—please your palate and refuel your muscles.

- **EAT BREAKFAST—EVEN IF YOU DON'T HAVE TIME.** It helps rev up your metabolism for the day. You don't have to stick with "breakfast" food. How about a leftover veggie pizza slice? It takes only 30 seconds to reheat it in the microwave. Or top it with a poached egg and you've got a breakfast to boast about.

- **USE UTENSILS ANYWAY.** Even if it's something that you can pick up (think burger or burrito), use a fork and knife. You can then savor it slowly instead of gobbling it up mindlessly. You'll potentially be eating less while gaining satisfaction.

- **EAT BEFORE YOU EAT.** If you're headed to a fabulous dinner or festive food gathering where there will be an abundance of food, enjoy a piece of fruit or a small handful of nuts right before you go. Think mini-snack. It'll keep your appetite in check—and ultimately help you consume fewer overall calories.

- **DON'T STOP AT SKIM.** Switch from whole to 2 percent to 1 percent to skim (fat-free) milk. Then switch from skim milk to plain almond milk, unsweetened coconut milk beverage, light soy milk, or unsweetened sunflower beverage, at least from time to time. They tend to average around 50 calories a cup.

- **TRY LOOK-ALIKES.** Don't go fake. But do go for the fake-out on occasion. Try savory spaghetti squash instead of spaghetti. Enjoy summery strings of zucchini instead of linguine. Sink your teeth into a bodacious grilled portabella cap instead of a grilled burger.

- **SEE SHELLS.** You're likely to eat fewer nuts—and fewer calories—by choosing a snack-size portion of in-shell nuts, such as pistachios, instead of those already shelled. The visual cue provided by the empty shells, along with the extra time to shell the nuts, can help you realize you're satisfied.

- **BE BORING, IF NECESSARY.** Not in terms of flavor, but in terms of how many different recipes or dishes you try to eat or prepare. Sometimes the exciting array of too many dishes can cause the appetite to go into overdrive. So it's okay to stick to a handful of recipes for a period of time and repeat or vary them, at least to get you on the right track. But boring and bland don't go hand in hand.

- **(FOR LADIES ONLY!) PARTY IN STYLE.** These are shared a bit tongue in cheek but what you wear can impact how you eat. Think about wearing slimming shapewear and lip gloss! Shapewear, like Spanx, not only makes you appear slimmer, it's rather tight. That'll help keep you from overeating. Your glossy lips will keep you from eating anything crumbly that can stick to your lips. But it'll also remind you to keep kissable-ready.

What does the trick for one person doesn't always work perfectly for all. So if you find that one of these tips isn't working that well for you, choose another. I have no doubt you'll find that several of these strategies will boost your own efforts at successful weight management.

Stocking the Low-Cal Kitchen

Top Equipment Essentials

There are gadgets I use on a regular basis which make my calorie-conscious cooking efforts simpler, more satisfying, and more successful. Consider stocking your kitchen with these helpful tools.

HIGH-QUALITY CHEF'S KNIFE. Make sure your knife feels good as you hold it—and you're comfortable with the size. Since many dishes within *1,000 Low-Calorie Recipes* include plenty of fruits, veggies, and fresh herbs, it'll make chopping up fresh produce easier and more enjoyable. Keep your knife well sharpened, too.

NONSTICK OR STICK-RESISTANT PANS. Choose at least one large sauté pan or skillet and one stockpot. They brown well without sticking and without the need to add excess fat, which helps to keep calories in check. A nonstick pan isn't always required; but it's ideal for most recipes when significantly less oil or other fat is used in the cooking process. Look for PFOA-free nonstick pans, which don't contain the potentially harmful chemicals of the old Teflon-coated nonstick pans.

CAST IRON GRILL PAN. This pan cooks evenly and retains significant heat for incredible grill marks—indoors, all year round. Plus, the food is elevated on ribs, so extra grease collects between them for better lower-calorie cooking.

PANINI GRILL. No added fat calories are required when grilling—or panini-grilling. Grease drips away from food rather than sitting in it, too. A panini press evenly grills and toasts quickly since you're cooking both sides of the food at once. The cooking plates of the press adjust to the height of the food and the grill works especially well for quickly browning sandwiches, chicken, or fish. Browning means more taste without more calories.

12-CUP CAPACITY FOOD PROCESSOR. There's no other single piece of equipment that can chop, grate, and puree—and do it all well. It helps reduce prep time for dishes within *1,000 Low-Calorie Recipes*. Most importantly, it helps speed up prep of produce, making you want to cook with produce more often. And more produce means more volume and satisfaction . . . and fewer calories.

5-CUP CAPACITY BLENDER. It'll crush ice, blend smoothies, and puree soups and sauces until perfectly smooth, creating a rich texture. It works better than a food processor for liquid ingredients, too. I find the skinnier the container, the quicker and creamier the result. And that creamy consistency lends mouth-feel and enjoyment to low-cal cuisine. Choose a blender that has a clear container so you can see how well your food is being blended.

IMMERSION BLENDER. This handheld blender is an easy-to-use and convenient choice over a tall food and beverage blender, and ideal for blending hot ingredients. It purees soups and sauces into velvety, creamy concoctions (without heavy cream) in seconds—right in the pots or pans in which they're cooked. And no heavy cream means significantly fewer calories!

HINT: Let friends and family help build your culinary tool collection. It will benefit them, too! Add the essentials that you don't already have to your birthday, holiday, or other gift wish lists. Consider using an online universal gift registry.

SILICONE UTENSILS. Silicone or silicone-coated cooking utensils are versatile and can be used with very high heat without worry. Additionally, they easily scrape up food that sticks (without scraping the pan), which occasionally happens when using leaner foods or less added fat in cooking. What's more a silicone pastry brush is fabulous. Using it rather than a bristle brush ("mop") will help you more lightly baste or brush oil, melted butter, or sauces onto foods before toasting, oven-browning, or grilling, rather than mopping them on. Ideally, choose three sizes: short pastry brush, medium basting brush, and long barbecue brush.

GRATER/ZESTER. You'll love this tool for finely grating ingredients that add so much flavor appeal to healthful dishes, including citrus peels (for zest), fresh gingerroot, nutmeg, and Parmesan, Romano, or other hard cheeses. A little goes a long way.

COFFEE GRINDER. Actually, I recommend this not for grinding coffee beans, but for grinding spices. Buy whole spices, pan-toast until aromatic, then grind. You'll get the most flavor and fragrance from spices—and make low-cal cuisine that much tastier. Consider grinding nuts, seeds, or whole grains in a coffee grinder, too.

REAMER. The quickest and easiest way to juice a citrus fruit is by using a reamer. And when you only need to extract a small amount, it's the absolute best way. Lemon and lime juices are an essential ingredient in so many healthful recipes—including those in this cookbook. That makes this tool a definite must.

COOKING OIL SPRAY BOTTLE. Instead of using a commercial oil spray can with propellants, choose a spray bottle and fill with your heart-healthful oil of choice—especially one that best fits with the flavor profile of the recipe, such as extra-virgin olive oil for Italian dishes.

HOMEMADE COOKING SPRAY

When I suggest "homemade" cooking spray in *1,000 Low-Calorie Recipes,* filling a spray bottle with your cooking oil of choice is what I'm referring to. You'll be able to spritz the oil onto foods to help them brown whether prepared on the stovetop or in the oven—with a little rather than a lot of oil. I prefer the Misto oil bottle sprayer.

The Portion-Pleasing Pantry

Take this checklist over to your pantry. Check to be sure you have these staples on hand. They help make good-for-you cooking and baking—and preparing the properly portioned recipes in this cookbook—a breeze. These are foods that I recommend to help maintain or lose weight but also be your healthiest. That's why you don't see refined sugar and flour and other common pantry items. If you don't have all the ingredients below, try adding a few at a time from this collection so you can introduce variety and intriguing flavors to your everyday cooking:

- Sea salt
- Spices: cinnamon, nutmeg, turmeric, cumin seeds, cayenne, dried hot pepper flakes, and black peppercorns
- Dried herbs: oregano, rosemary, and sage
- Vinegars: brown rice, apple cider, red wine, aged balsamic, and white balsamic
- Oils: extra-virgin olive, unrefined peanut, canola, toasted sesame, and grapeseed
- Low-sodium broths: vegetable and chicken
- Pure extracts: vanilla, almond, peppermint, chocolate, and coconut
- Honey or agave nectar
- Flours: whole-wheat, whole-wheat pastry, and whole oat
- Garlic, onions (various), and shallots
- Whole grains: brown basmati rice, long- and short-grain brown rice, quinoa, bulgur wheat, and farro
- Tomato products: fresh tomatoes (especially cherry or grape tomatoes), sun-dried tomatoes, and canned tomato products, including tomato paste
- No-salt-added canned beans
- Pastas: whole-wheat couscous, whole-wheat orzo, and whole-grain spaghetti
- Nuts and seed: pistachios, almonds, walnuts, pine nuts, sunflower seeds, and sesame seeds
- Nut butters: natural peanut and almond

- Avocados
- Dried fruits: prunes (dried plums), black seedless raisins, figs, tart cherries, cranberries, and unsulfured apricots
- Hot pepper sauce
- Naturally brewed soy sauce
- Tea bags or loose tea

And don't forget the parchment paper and aluminum foil. Try to always use parchment paper that's unbleached and aluminum foil that's recycled for environmental friendliness.

The Friendly Fridge & Freezer

Be sure to keep most of these foods and ingredients at-the-ready to be able to whip up a healthful, calorie-friendly dish whenever you wish:

Fridge

- Colorful array of fresh seasonal vegetables, including mushrooms and leafy greens
- Colorful array of fresh seasonal fruit, including melons and mangoes
- Lemons and limes or bottled 100 percent fresh lemon or lime juice
- Real fruit spreads/jams
- No-sugar-added apple butter
- No-sugar-added applesauce
- Mustards
- Eggs
- Fat-free or low-fat plain Greek yogurt
- Fresh gingerroot
- Jalapeño peppers
- Pickled ingredients, including hot peppers
- Parmigiano-Reggiano and/or Pecorino Romano cheese
- Plain almond milk or other plant-based milk

Freezer

- Farm fresh chicken breasts and thighs
- Flash-frozen vegetables, including edamame and peas
- Flash-frozen fruits, including berries and cherries
- Frozen whole-grain breads

Calorie-Friendly Cooking Tips & Techniques

There's no need to slim down the taste of your food to keep your meals fit. Try this advice for good-for-you cooking that's big on taste, not calories. Focus on one new tip or technique at a time and before you know it, you'll be preparing calorie-conscious cuisine to please . . . with ease.

21 Flavor-Boosting, Calorie-Reducing Hints

Plan to incorporate these tasty concepts, in any order you wish, by using recipes from this cookbook as well as your own dishes and drinks.

1. **TURN UP THE VOLUME WITH SEASONAL VEGGIES.** When in season, vegetables are at their peak of ripeness, nutritional value, color, and flavor. If you're going to fall in veggie love, this is when it will happen. Go bigger and bolder often—veggies are one food category that most people need to boost. Luckily, they're naturally low in calories.

    Hint: Move veggie side dishes to the center of plate. Sometimes it's about presentation. Consider stacking veggies for eye appeal and entrée appeal. Check out Grilled Eggplant Stack with Feta and Fresh Basil (page 267); it's one way that a usual side dish—eggplant—transforms into an entrée stunner.

2. **TRY SWAPPING.** This is replacing some or all of a more fattening ingredient in a recipe with a healthier one. For example, you can replace some of the meat with mushrooms. It will reduce calories without compromising flavor, texture, moistness, or satisfaction. The swap can be small to start with—and can be increased in increments. The more mushrooms, the better, of course.

    Hint: One simple way to savor mushroom "swapability" is in burgers. For instance, you can replace a quarter of the ground beef in a burger with sautéed finely chopped mushrooms. The next time, consider swapping half. This technique fully realized can be found in savory "Swedish" Meatballs (page 80) and Breakfast Turkey Links (page 36). Or go for a total swap, like in Philly Cheesesteak-less (page 385).

3. **FAVOR THE SWEETNESS OF FRUITS.** Think outside the fruit bowl. There's so much more culinary exploration that can be done with seasonal and naturally sweet produce, such as using fruit as the main ingredient of a sundae or serving a fruit soup. Fruits, fruit butters, and jams can provide sweetness along with rich nutrition in place of added sugars, too.

    Hint: Enjoy a spiced fruit salsa or chutney in place of gravy or über-rich sauces, as you'll find in Grilled Curry Portobella "Steak" with Mango Chutney (page 268).

4. **DON'T FEAR SALT!** A little pinch of salt can bring out full flavors. That's especially important for healthful dishes—to keep desiring those healthful dishes. Use less if you like, but please don't eliminate it. It truly makes food taste better. Use a salt that you enjoy the taste of. Choose sea salt over regular iodized table salt. Have fleur de sel on hand, too; it's the loveliest of the sea salts.

    Hint: A pinch of sea salt can steal the show and highlight flavors in both savory and sweet foods. See how it's a star in savory foods, like Salt and Pepper Asparagus (page 439) and sweet foods, like Fleur de Sel Brownie Rounds (page 518).

5. **BEFRIEND HERBS.** Nutritious cuisine would be boring and bland without salt. But too much sodium can be problematic, especially for people with heart-health concerns. That's where a liberal use of herbs can play a helpful, healthful role. They add flavor intrigue,

freshness, and aroma. Grow your own fresh herbs—indoors all-year-round on your windowsill. Stick to fresh herbs for most dishes; use dried herbs for recipes with lengthy cooking times, such as stews, or if you prefer.

Hint: Don't just go for the grains; go for whole grains mixed robustly with fresh herbs, such as a farro, quinoa, or bulgur salad. The Blood Orange Bulgur Mint Salad (page 183) is an example of this fresh, flavorful approach.

6. **BE A SPICE FAN.** Spices add flavor pizzazz to plain foods and create aromatic intrigue to fit fare. Buy whole spices when possible; toast and grind them (use a coffee grinder or peppermill) for full release of flavor, as with cumin seeds. Use spices to add an inviting color accent to dishes, too. Turmeric adds rich yellow color and an earthiness that boosts flavor like no other! Add a pinch or two of one new spice at a time—from savories to sweets.

Hint: Add new life, even international intrigue, to cuisine just by swapping spices, such as using pumpkin pie spice or Chinese five-spice powder instead of cinnamon. Or simply add spice, period. Try Five-Spice Yam Frites (page 461) or Pumpkin Spice Coffee (page 552) and become a fan.

7. **PUMP UP THE "PLEASURABLE PAIN."** To create the effect of more taste depth, bring on the "heat" with a few drops of hot pepper sauce, a touch of curry paste, or a dash of cayenne pepper or wasabi powder to soups, sauces, dips, mixed dishes, and more—even desserts. A bonus: hot peppers contain an ingredient called capsaicin, which may provide a slight metabolism boost.

Hint: Instead of an oil-soaked tomato bruschetta topping, use a little less oil and a little more spice. A touch of Thai red curry paste

adds real global flair, such as in Red Curry Tomato Bruschetta (page 48).

8. **CREATE CUISINE DRAMA AND WHIMSY.** In addition to our sense of smell and taste, we do eat with our eyes. How you present a food or drink may seem to actually make it taste better. The more eye appealing, the more enticing a good-for-you recipe will be. So toss out the rule book and play with your food a little. Layer ingredients or deconstruct a dish. If it fits on a stick, stick it! Present in festive serving ware. Be artful and use your imagination. Let your surroundings inspire you.

Hint: Instead of arranging or tossing together a salad or side, layer it artfully for impressive effect, as in the spectacular Caprese Salad "Lasagna" (page 166). Or for family-friendly flair, blend fresh herbs into your food to make it unexpectedly green, as is deliciously done in "Green" Eggs and Ham (page 132).

9. **BE A LITTLE NUTTY (OR SEEDY).** Nuts and seeds provide rich taste, memorable texture, eye appeal, and excellent nutrition. Their protein and fiber can help you feel full longer. There are endless ways to incorporate their various satisfying forms into or onto cuisine. Enjoy them roasted or toasted for deeper flavor in every bite. Remember nut and seed butters, too.

Hint: Make savory or sweet foods appear richer by sprinkling nuts onto dishes instead of mixing them in when you can. Pick pistachios for their lively green accent, like for Rainforest Chocolate Muffins (page 535), which actually provides a "rainforest" appearance.

10. **ONE UP THE FLAVOR ANTE.** When in doubt, pick the higher flavor item. If it's a calorie-dense item, you can use less of it for the same full flavors—and potentially heightened flavor.

In some cases, going for the richer looking item, especially produce, may equate to more nutritional richness. When it works, pick sharp cheeses over mild cheeses. Plus, selectively choose naturally flavored ingredients, like truffle cheese and rosemary sea salt.

Hint: Go for groovier grains. Instead of typical white spaghetti, consider one of the many whole-grain pastas on the market today. Try whole-grain spinach spaghetti in Spaghetti a Cacio e Pepe (page 486). Or go for a black rice and truffle goat cheese instead of a refined grain and regular goat cheese, like in the divine Creamy Truffled Black Rice (page 480).

11. **SAVOR CREAMINESS WITHOUT THE CREAM.** There are good-for-you ways to create the mouth-feel of creaminess. Whirl or puree Greek yogurt, beans, tahini, silken tofu, banana, mangoes, avocado, or potatoes into soups, sauces, spreads, smoothies, and beyond. Greek yogurt creates tangy lusciousness in creamy salads, scrambled eggs, risottos, and fluffy frostings. No-salt-added white beans boost satiety while providing velvety texture when pureed into foods, and can marry so well with other flavors since they're so mild.

Hint: Create an intriguing creamy pasta sauce with the combination of pureed white beans, vegetable broth, and heavy cream instead of straight heavy cream, as in my inspired "Alfredo" Sauce (page 99). Or use pureed black beans as a clever creaming and binding agent in chocolaty baked goods, as Fudgy Superfood Brownies (page 516).

12. **COLOR YOUR PLATE HAPPY.** Vibrant naturally occurring colors make foods seem richer. They can turn a traditional food into a tantalizing dish. For instance, try blue or purple

potatoes or red quinoa instead of lighter versions at least some of the time. Look for some unusual color sources, like pickled turnip—it's fuchsia from beet juice! And consider creating color by incorporating various hued vegetables into otherwise bland-colored foods.

Hint: Opt for more colorful vegetable varieties to add interest. Pick purple produce whenever possible, as in Soft Scrambled Eggs with Purple Potato and Chives (page 116), Purple Potato Pancakes (page 162), and Asian Angel Hair with "Confetti" (page 289).

13. **DRINK AND COOK WITH TEA.** Tea contains flavonoids, naturally occurring compounds with health promoting antioxidant properties. It's virtually calorie-free, too—naturally. Though tea—black, green, or white, iced or hot—makes an ideal, economical, and delightful beverage, you don't always have to drink it; you can cook with it. Use it as a uniquely appealing poaching or simmering liquid. Or try in place of some oil. By the way, there is some research that suggests green tea contains plant nutrients called catechins which may promote weight loss.

Hint: Poach poultry in unsweetened tea to add flavor panache to a salad recipe, as Turkey and Fig Salad on Toasted Muffin (page 378). Or use it to replace some of the oil in a salad dressing, as in Seckel Pear and Green Tea Vinaigrette (page 147).

14. **BALANCE WITH ACID.** If you don't enjoy the bitterness of dark leafy greens or other "superfood" veggies, add a sassy splash of acid, like lemon juice or balsamic vinegar. It helps balance the bitters to boost taste appeal. Also, acid can provide a tangy boost of moistness for sautéing in place of adding extra butter or oil, as when sautéing shallots or onions.

Hint: Pair acid as you might pair wines to food. Pair a rich vinegar, like aged balsamic, with dark vegetables, like Brussels sprouts, (purple-red) beets, or leafy greens. See it work its magic on a bed of Balsamic Wilted Spinach (page 450).

15. **UP THE UMAMI.** Umami is the fifth sense of taste, imparting savoriness to cuisine. When you can, embrace ingredients that boast high amounts of umami along with low calories, like fully ripened tomatoes, shiitake mushrooms, naturally brewed soy sauce, and green tea. Be sure your tomatoes are fully ripened. That means don't refrigerate them! When it makes flavor and technique-sense in a recipe, add a splash of naturally brewed soy sauce instead of adding salt; you'll basically be getting umami with your "salt."

    Hint: Mushrooms are "meaty," versatile, nutrient rich, and aromatic. So give them a starring role and enjoy in place of meat, as in Smoky Portabella and Cheese Burger (page 396).

16. **REDUCE TO ENHANCE.** The technique of reduction—simmering to thicken a liquid—is meant to concentrate flavors and consistency. It's an ideal way to enrich flavors without increasing calories for stews, sauces, and more.

    Hint: Instead of relying on added sugar, use 100% real fruit juice to provide sweetness to a sauce; reduce it to concentrate the flavor and consistency, as in Cherry Balsamic Peppercorn Sauce (page 134).

17. **LET BREAD BE YOUR FRIEND.** When based on whole grains, bread is a friendly part of a healthful diet. To cut away excess calories, think thin when buying any form of bread. Use tortillas or wraps as a bread of choice often. When you prefer traditional sliced bread, buy it in loaf form, then cut into thin slices so the focus can be on the sandwich contents instead of the bread.

    Hint: Think thin most of the time for pizza crusts, not just bread-based sandwiches. Consider a tortilla or lavash as a pizza crust, which becomes crisp, fast—and provides significantly fewer calories than a deep doughy crust. Check out the crusts on Roasted Cauliflower Pizza (page 424).

18. **DO DRIZZLE WITH HEALTHFUL OIL.** Dietary fats are a good thing when they're mostly unsaturated. They add flavor and overall appeal, and help us better absorb key nutrients. When it works well with a recipe's ingredients or instructions, aim for extra-virgin olive oil, unrefined peanut oil, or other high-flavored oils. Sometimes just a drizzle or a spritz is all you need to pump up flavor. Use the best oil for the function, such as canola or grapeseed oil when sautéing onion at high heat or when you don't want the flavor to overpower mild-tasting dishes.

    Hint: Add a waft of wow with truffle oil—a little drizzle goes a long way, as in Mashed Purple Potatoes (page 462) or Grilled Steak Pizza (page 416).

19. **THINK AROMA.** The majority of flavor appeal begins with aroma. When food is full flavored and high calorie, the scent will allow you to be satisfied with smaller portions. When it's full flavored and low calorie, the scent will enhance your lean eating experience. So give food the sniff test. Keep these key terms in mind: stinky, strong, sharp, and smoky. Robiola is stinky; fresh ginger is strong; citrus is sharp; and smoked Gouda is smoky. Also, where it's an option, serve food at room temperature; generally the warmer the temperature, the more aroma.

Hint: Opt for smokiness; it adds no calories, just taste. So grill out. Or choose naturally smoked cheese or smoked turkey or tofu instead of their plain counterparts. Also consider a pinch of hickory-smoked sea salt. Try this double dose of smoky sensation: Smoky Mozzarella Grilled Portabellas (page 455).

20. **ADD A DROP OF EXCITEMENT WITH EXTRACTS.** Think flavor excitement way beyond vanilla. Pure extracts are ideal for use in baking. But they're not just for use in baked goods anymore. Extracts are available in so many flavors, including orange, lemon, coconut, almond, coffee, and chocolate. Befriend all the flavors and be sure they're pure. When cutting down on fat, sugar, or salt in a cuisine, extracts provide zero calories and can play a key flavor-boosting role.

Hint: For bonus nuttiness without using extra nuts, a couple drops of pure almond extract into a batter is delightful, such as in Double Squash Bread (page 537).

21. **USE THE REAL THING.** Even when rich, it's usually better to stick with the real ingredient than opt for an inferior or "fake" fat-free substitute. For instance, mayonnaise is divine—and rich in healthful fats. Simply use just a smear of it. Or try one of my "Mayos" (pages 123 to 124) for added meal appeal. This philosophy applies to other rich ingredients. For instance, if you want bacon or pepperoni without all the calories, don't go for "fake" bacon or pseudo-pepperoni; consider a focused, mindful use of the real thing—or use sun-dried tomatoes instead.

Hint: Try my "4-3-2-1 rule" for the perkiest potato salad dressing for two pounds of potatoes: 4 tablespoons real mayo; 3 tablespoons Dijon mustard; 2 tablespoons plain Greek yogurt; and 1 tablespoon white wine vinegar. This "rule" is used in Dijon Fingerling Potato Salad (page 160).

Low-Calorie Eating Outside Your Kitchen

Eating healthfully is a way of life. That includes when you're away from home. It's important and very doable to make nutrient-rich, low-calorie choices when eating in restaurants, at the homes of family and friends, and when traveling. Here are a few key tips for you to keep in mind:

- **BRING BETTER-FOR-YOU BITES.** Don't get stuck without something nutritious to snack on, like Nature Trail Mix (page 44). It'll help ensure you don't need to head to the nearest fast-food drive-thru, find a vending machine full of overly processed "junk" food, or otherwise reach for not-so-good-for-you eats.

- **ALWAYS BEGIN WITH BREAKFAST.** It's the most important meal of the day when following a healthful eating plan—wherever you are. Even if you're short on time, fruit and yogurt work fine.

- **PLAN MEALS INTO YOUR ITINERARY.** A happy tourist is a nourished tourist. So check restaurant menus online or healthydiningfinder.com in advance and include nutritious meal choices along with other travel sites to see and things to do.

- **ORDER WISELY.** Check for notations of healthful or calorie-friendly dishes on a menu. Or order from a lunch or "kids" menu instead of a dinner menu. Request steamed veggies instead of any fried side. And remember, it's okay to share or take home leftovers.

- **INCLUDE ACTIVITY AROUND YOUR DINING DECISIONS.** That can simply mean walking to and from a restaurant. It's enjoyable and can help with digestion, too.

10 "Clean" Cuisine Approaches

A low-calorie diet and healthy way of eating require thoughtful choices. Once you're actively thinking about the foods you cook and put in your body, you may also be interested in considering the environmental impact of producing and distributing food and how in turn that affects what you eat. Whenever possible I try to be eco-conscious when cooking. You can do the same for practically any recipe within *1,000 Low-Calorie Recipes*. The foods you choose, how you store them, and how you prepare them matter. Following a low-calorie and an "ecotarian" eating plan can go hand in hand. (See What Is an Ecotarian?, page xxviii.) Eating green—or "clean"—can mean eating more seasonal produce, more plant foods in general, and plenty of fresh, unprocessed ingredients when it's affordable, available, and convenient for you to do. Eating this way is something that you can feel good about—now and later.

There are already significant green influences throughout the recipes in this cookbook. But you can incorporate as many additional eco-strategies as you see fit. Implement these tips to go "clean" in your green kitchen—or to go green in your clean kitchen—whenever you can.

1. **GET REAL!** Aim to keep foods as fresh, whole, and "natural" or minimally processed as possible. I've already done this for you in *1,000 Low-Calorie Recipes*. But for your other food prep, if you're choosing foods that come with labels, read the ingredient list and pick those with ingredients that sound like something you'd find in a recipe, not a strange science experiment. Steer clear of the word "artificial," period. Don't worry about the ingredient list length; it's most important to focus on what the ingredients are rather than on how many there are. And when it comes to meat and poultry, the USDA has a specific definition of "natural" to help you out:

"A product containing no artificial ingredient or added color and is only minimally processed." "Minimal processing" means that the product was processed in a manner that does not fundamentally alter the product. The label must include a statement explaining the meaning of the term "natural" (such as "no artificial ingredients, minimally processed").

2. **CHOOSE LOCALLY WHEN LOGICAL.** To get foods to your table, shippers use fossil fuels, contributing to global climate change. When fresh food, namely produce, doesn't need to travel as far, there's a good chance it'll be fresher and therefore potentially more nutritious. Plus, when produce is local (or from your own garden!), that means it's picked closer to the stage of ripeness than if it were to travel a distance. So hit your local farmers market, choose a variety of fresh fruits and veggies, or focus just on a couple items. Then browse this cookbook and see what recipes work best with your local picks. But do keep in mind that not all produce grows locally to you. So balance local picks with the best of the rest.

3. **GO ORGANIC, IF POSSIBLE.** If you do have the option and the budget to go organic, make this choice when you can. It's an investment in your health—and the health of the planet. In many cases, it can be better for you overall. It means fewer pesticides and other possibly toxic chemicals end up in the food that you eat—and in the environment. It basically means an animal was given organic feed and not given hormones or antibiotics. In terms of produce, it means that farmers are rotating their crops, protecting sources of water, and not using pesticides, synthetic fertilizers, or bioengineering. In simpler terms, organic produce is grown in nutrient-rich soil that isn't weighted down by pesticides. Even though you don't see the term "organic" specifically listed for ingredients in

this cookbook's recipe lists, do take the initiative and go organic if you can for at least a selection of the ingredients. A good place to start is by choosing organic meat. That's on my "always" organic list. Finally, remember this: We are what we eat, and animals are what they eat, and plants are what they eat!

4. **EAT PLANTS.** Switching to veggies in place of meat just one day a week can make a significant, beneficial impact on the environment. The more you make the switch, the more significant the impact. Eating more veggies can translate to better success at weight management and provide a health-promoting boost, too. So consider preparing plant-based meals most often. That's going to be simple with *1,000 Low-Calorie Recipes* in tow, as the majority of recipes are plant based.

5. **KNOW THE DIRTY DOZEN AND CLEAN 15.** When something can be simplified to make the process of eating healthier easier, I'm a fan. So I'm a fan of the Environmental Working Group's rankings of fresh produce based on pesticide residue levels. The fruits and vegetables on the Dirty Dozen are highest in pesticides; those on the Clean 15 are lowest in pesticides. Plenty of Clean 15 produce is found throughout *1,000 Low-Calorie Recipes.*

   - **Dirty Dozen:** apples, celery, strawberries, peaches, spinach, nectarines (imported), grapes (imported), sweet bell peppers, potatoes, blueberries (domestic), lettuce, and kale/collard greens.

   - **Clean 15:** onions, sweet corn, pineapples, avocado, asparagus, sweet peas, mangoes, eggplant, cantaloupe (domestic), kiwi, cabbage, watermelon, sweet potatoes, grapefruit, and mushrooms.

   This list is especially helpful if you can only afford to go organic for a few produce items.

But remember this: The health and weight-management benefits associated with eating a diet rich in vegetables and fruits outweigh the risk of pesticide exposure. So eat fruits and veggies, period.

6. **SELECT SUSTAINABLY RAISED MEAT, POULTRY, AND FISH.** If you include fish, poultry, or meat in your meal plan, enjoy "clean" options.

   - Meat production is resource intensive, so consider these eco-conscientious strategies when savoring it. First, choose organic meat when possible. Look for "grass-fed," too. When you can, purchase from local farmers—look for them at your farmers' market. And keep it petite—or "green size" it. That obviously keeps calories lower, too.

   - Poultry is as an eco-friendlier option to red meats. However, it's still eco-friendliest to choose chicken, turkey, and eggs labeled "100 percent organic." Note that hormones aren't used in U.S. poultry (or pork) production.

   - Fish has health benefits, including heart-healthful attributes provided by omega-3s. Unfortunately, there are ecological issues that go along with enjoying seafood. Polychlorinated biphenyls (PCBs) and mercury both raise significant health concerns. Plus, there's currently an overfishing situation in many of the world's waters. Look for Marine Stewardship Council certification to help pinpoint what's not being overfished. Check the Super Green List produced by the Monterey Bay Aquarium Seafood Watch: http://www.seafoodwatch.org/cr/cr_seafoodwatch/sfw_health.aspx. It's a list of seafood that's good for your health and doesn't harm the oceans.

7. **BE CAUTIOUS OF BPA.** BPA is a chemical; its full name is bisphenol A. Some scientists suggest that it may disrupt regular hormone activity in the body. One place it can be found is in the lining of the canned foods that you eat. So be sure to choose BPA-free-lined cans whenever possible.

8. **MAKE LEFTOVERS LOVABLE.** First, some foods taste better the day after they're made. Second, using leftovers saves money! And third, it's eco-friendly. Using next-day eats is a "green" approach to help prevent food waste—and to prevent excess food from winding up in our landfills. Food waste in landfills releases methane, a potent greenhouse gas, into the atmosphere as it decomposes. Each year, American food waste represents the energy equivalent of 350 million barrels of oil, according to a study published in *Environmental Science and Technology*. It's estimated that at least 25 percent of food is wasted yearly! So get creative in your kitchen and whip up dishes with whatever may be left from your delicious *1,000 Low-Calorie Recipes* preparations.

9. **TRY OUT GREEN COOKING TECHNIQUES.** The recipes within *1,000 Low-Calorie Recipes* use mainly classic culinary techniques. But implement some green cooking concepts into any recipe you choose. It can reduce energy, save time, and be fun. Try these eco-cooking options:

   • **Hyperbaking.** Place foods, like cookies, into a nonpreheated oven, then turn on the heat and bake most of the way, then turn off the heat and continue to bake until done. This may take a couple tries for success. Or try this "cheaters" version: bake as instructed and simply turn off the oven 5 minutes ahead of schedule, keeping oven closed until done.

   • **Lid cooking.** Finish simmering or boiling a food on the stovetop by covering it tightly and "cooking" with just trapped heat. For instance, to lid cook whole-grain pasta, bring water to a boil, stir in pasta, bring back to a boil, put the lid on, and turn off the heat. (Note: Remove from burner if using an electric stove.) Let lid cook (cook covered without heat) for the exact time suggested on the package—or 1 minute less. It works perfectly with pasta.

10. **PICK PFOA-FREE PANS.** PFOA, or perfluoro-octanoic acid, is a chemical that has been used in the past in manufacturing Teflon. (Don't worry if you can't pronounce the full name; I can't either!) Unfortunately, it's likely to be a carcinogen, according to the U.S. Environmental Protection Agency (EPA). However, nonstick skillets are very helpful for preparing lower calorie cuisine as they help you use less excess fat. The solution: prepare in PFOA-free nonstick skillets. If you don't already have these skillets, try these other stick-resistant skillets in the meantime: hard anodized aluminum, ceramic enamel, or well-seasoned cast iron cookware.

For more detailed "clean" cooking advice and recipes, check out my previous book, *Big Green Cookbook: Hundreds of Planet-Pleasing Recipes & Tips for a Luscious, Low-Carbon Lifestyle* (Wiley, 2009).

WHAT IS AN ECOTARIAN?

An ecotarian is someone who eats a plant-based diet and chooses foods with environmental friendliness in mind. They may or may not eat small amounts of organic or sustainably raised animal products.

Healthful, Flavorful Makeovers

Taking a decadent high-calorie recipe, and then making a few substitutions to create a low-calorie recipe can turn into a total disaster—negatively affecting a recipe's taste, texture, appearance, or all of the above. Some changes may add preservatives and other not-so-real ingredients that your body clearly doesn't need. On the other hand, some adjustments can result in a dazzling dish that's better for you and potentially better tasting than the original. That was my goal in *1,000 Low-Calorie Recipes* when starting with a rich idea, like lasagna, quiche, or cake. And, naturally, a majority of the recipes in the cookbook were truly original and didn't require any ingredient swapping at all!

The philosophy behind the recipes I made over was not to have ingredients, such as mayonnaise or cheese, swapped out for very low calorie or fat-free versions. The philosophy was to innovatively adjust recipes to make them lower in calories than expected; and do so in a "real" way—focusing on boosting flavor lusciousness and nutritional richness, not taking it away. In many instances, only additions were made, such as stirring in seasonal vegetables or fruits, creating more volume and therefore creating fewer calories in the same-sized or larger portion. No fat-free mayo or fat-free cheese here, in any case! However, you will see fat-free Greek yogurt, as that's an ingredient that's 100 percent natural, as well as luscious-textured and nutritious. And you will actually still see creamy, rich, real mayo and high-flavored cheese used creatively in *1,000 Low-Calorie Recipes*!

I hope you'll find that the resulting dishes in this cookbook exceed your flavor expectations while helping you meet your healthful eating goals.

Savory and Sweet Substitutions

Below is a select sampling of high-flavored, simple, and "real" swaps to try at home. These calorie-cutting swaps—or creative versions of them—are already used within some of the recipes in *1,000 Low-Calorie Recipes*. Use these substitutions mainly to inspire makeovers for your own too-rich recipes. It's a starting point since adaptations are recipe dependent—basically meaning that what works with one recipe may not work as well with another.

Please use this chart as a guide and add to the list with other original, lusciously light swaps of your own as you go.

Savory and Sweet Substitutions Guide

INSTEAD OF	SWAP FOR	OPTIONAL FLAVOR ADD-INS
¼ cup sour cream (for savory food)	¼ cup plain fat-free or low-fat Greek yogurt	• Pinch of ground cayenne • Pinch of grated lemon zest or fresh gingerroot • Minced garlic, shallot, or scallion to taste • 2 teaspoons chopped fresh herb
2 tablespoons mayonnaise (for dip or creamy salad)	1 tablespoon mayonnaise + 1 tablespoon plain fat-free or low-fat Greek yogurt	• Pinch of grated lemon zest • Splash of hot pepper sauce • Pinch more spice or fresh herb already in recipe • Stone-ground or Dijon mustard to taste
2 tablespoons mayonnaise (on sandwiches)	2 tablespoons of one of the "Mayos" in this cookbook (pages 123 to 124) or 2 tablespoons tzatziki, hummus, bean dip, guacamole, or mashed avocado	• Freshly ground black pepper to taste • Splash of vinegar of choice or lemon juice • Minced sweet onion or caramelized onions to taste • Additional spicier or more peppery greens, such as baby arugula, on sandwich
2 tablespoons oil (for stir-frying, sautéing, or sweating)	1 tablespoon canola, grapeseed, or other heart-healthful oil with a high smoke point (for medium-high or high temperature cooking) or 1 tablespoon high-flavored heart-healthful oil, such as toasted sesame, extra-virgin olive oil, or unrefined peanut (for medium or lower temperature cooking)	• 2 teaspoons acid ingredient, such as white balsamic vinegar, lemon juice, or white wine (to be added with onion or other ingredient to be sautéed) • Sauté a minute or two longer than usual to aim for some/more caramelization to boost flavor (Note: Use a PFOA-free nonstick skillet to help prevent sticking when using less fat. Otherwise, if ingredients begin to stick due to too little fat, cover with the lid to trap moisture for a few minutes.)
½ cup butter (in baking)	¼ cup unsalted butter + 3 tablespoons no-sugar-added apple butter or plain fat-free Greek yogurt or mashed banana or (3 tablespoon) mixture of no-sugar-added apple butter and plain fat-free Greek yogurt	• ¼ teaspoon additional pure vanilla extract and/or other pure extract
1 cup sugar (in baking)	¾ cup to ⅞ cup turbinado sugar or coconut palm sugar	• Pinch of sweet spice, such as ground cinnamon or pumpkin pie spice • Pinch of intrigue, such as rosemary or cayenne pepper • ¼ teaspoon additional pure vanilla extract or other pure extract • 2 (or more) tablespoons mashed fruit or fruit spread (adjust other liquid in the recipe if needed)

INSTEAD OF	SWAP FOR	OPTIONAL FLAVOR ADD-INS
1 ounce regular mild cheese	¾ ounce sharp, stinky, or smoky cheese, such as extra-sharp Cheddar, Limburger, or smoked Gouda	• Sprinkle some on top of dish (if not already indicated in recipe) to provide appearance of more cheese • Stir in about 2 tablespoons plain fat-free Greek yogurt for additional creaminess in a recipe • Combine crumbled cheese with about 2 tablespoons crumbled tofu to "stretch" the cheese
1 cup milk	1 cup plain almond milk, light soy milk, unsweetened coconut milk beverage, or unsweetened sunflower beverage	• Use exactly like fat-free milk; no additions needed (Note: Just like fat-free milk in some cooked recipes, it may benefit from being whisked with a thickener, such as arrowroot, cornstarch, or whole oat flour, or blended with a handful of no-salt-added white beans.)
1 pound ground beef (for burgers)	12 ounces lean ground beef or poultry + 4 ounces sautéed finely chopped mushrooms or 8 ounces lean ground beef or poultry + 8 ounces sautéed finely chopped mushrooms	• Freshly ground black pepper to taste
1 cup bleached all-purpose flour	1 cup whole-wheat pastry flour	• Use exactly like all-purpose flour; no additions needed
1 teaspoon salt	¾ teaspoon sea salt or naturally flavored sea salt	• Boost (up to double) the amount of herbs or spices already in the recipe • Pinch of grated lemon or lime zest • Incorporate an ingredient with a salty essence, like sun-dried tomato
¼ cup vinaigrette (3 tablespoons oil + 1 tablespoon vinegar)	¼ cup vinaigrette (2 tablespoons oil + 2 tablespoons vinegar) or (¼ cup cubed fruit + 1 tablespoon oil + 1 tablespoon vinegar)	• 1 small minced shallot and/or small clove garlic, whisked or blended into vinaigrette • 2 tablespoons chopped English cucumber blended into vinaigrette • 1 or 2 tablespoons low-sodium vegetable broth or unsweetened green tea to "stretch" the vinaigrette • Puree with varying amounts of silken tofu, no-salt-added white beans, tahini, or avocado for a creamy dressing

Recipe Makeovers

When giving one of your own recipes a fit and flavorful makeover, I suggest making one adaptation at a time instead of a sweeping swap. Think of it as getting a first-rate nose job instead of a risky nose job, chin lift, butt tuck, Botox, and liposuction all at once. If the first change works well, then move onto the next. The goal is to have a successful new dish, not just a potentially scary looking low-cal one! To give you a better idea of how savory and sweet ingredient swaps were put into practice in dishes within *1,000 Low-Calorie Recipes*, check out these Before and After delights to use as behind-the-scenes insight. As you'll notice, I was ultimately able to make several swaps successfully.

Savory Makeover:

A highlight of this "After" dip is that the serving size is actually bigger!

BEFORE: Spinach Dip	AFTER: Fresh Spinach–Truffle Party Dip (PAGE 94)
Makes 16 servings: 3 tablespoons each	Makes 16 servings: ¼ cup (4 tablespoons) each
5 ounces cooked frozen chopped spinach, squeezed of excess liquid **1½ cups sour cream** **¾ cup mayonnaise** **3 scallions, chopped** **1 package vegetable recipe (soup/dip) mix**	**1 (5-ounce) package fresh baby spinach** **1¼ cups fat-free or low-fat plain Greek yogurt** **¾ cup mayonnaise** **¼ cup sour cream** **2 teaspoons white truffle oil or extra-virgin olive oil** **6 scallions, green and white parts, minced** **⅓ cup finely diced jicama or celery** **¼ cup finely diced orange bell pepper or grated carrot** **1 large garlic clove, minced** **¾ teaspoon sea salt, or to taste** **½ teaspoon ground cayenne, or to taste** **⅛ teaspoon freshly grated nutmeg**
Combine all ingredients and chill about 2 hours, and serve.	**1.** Add the spinach, yogurt, mayonnaise, sour cream, and oil to a large bowl and stir until well combined. Stir in the scallions, jicama, bell pepper, garlic, salt, cayenne, and nutmeg. Adjust seasoning. **2.** Chill for at least 4 hours or overnight to allow spinach to naturally wilt and flavors to blend. Remove from the refrigerator and serve immediately.
Per serving: 120 calories, 12g total fat, 4g saturated fat, 0g trans fat, 20mg cholesterol, 210mg sodium, 3g total carbohydrate, 1g dietary fiber, 1g sugars, 1g protein	Per serving: 110 calories, 10g total fat, 1.5g saturated fat, 0g trans fat, 5mg cholesterol, 200mg sodium, 3g total carbohydrate, 1g dietary fiber, 1g sugars, 2g protein

MY SWAPS:

1. Used fresh spinach instead of frozen, plus added jicama, for more volume and texture and fresher appeal.
2. Made 1½ cups mixture of fat-free Greek yogurt and sour cream instead of 1½ cups of straight sour cream to provide similar creamy texture and tang with fewer calories, naturally. Added truffle oil, cayenne pepper, and nutmeg for unique flavor boost.
3. Doubled the scallions for more flavor, volume, and color.
4. Created a vegetable mix with a similar flavor profile, no artificial ingredients, and less sodium by combining orange bell pepper, garlic, and sea salt.

Tip: If you were making your own swaps to an original ("before") recipe like the above, I suggest starting with one swap, such as the Greek yogurt and sour cream mixture instead of straight sour cream. Then on your next makeover of the recipe, add one additional swap. And so on.

Sweet Makeover:

The "After" banana bread tastes sweeter and nuttier.

BEFORE:
Mom's Old-Fashioned Banana Bread

20 servings: 1 slice each

½ cup + 3 tablespoons unsalted butter, melted
1⅓ cups sugar
2 large eggs, well beaten
2 cups all-purpose flour
1 teaspoon baking soda
½ teaspoon salt
½ teaspoon cream of tartar
3 large ripe bananas, mashed
1 teaspoon vanilla extract
½ cup chopped walnuts

In a large mixing bowl, cream melted butter and sugar well. Add beaten eggs; blend well. In a separate bowl, sift together dry ingredients; add sifted dry ingredients to the butter mixture. Blend on low speed, just until completely mixed. Add mashed bananas, vanilla extract, and nuts to the mixture. Stir until just mixed. Pour the batter into a well-greased and floured loaf pan. Bake at 350°F for 1 hour.

Per serving: 180 calories, 9g total fat, 4.5g saturated fat, 0g trans fat, 35mg cholesterol, 130mg sodium, 24g total carbohydrate, 1g dietary fiber, 12g sugars, 3g protein

AFTER:
Mom's New Banana Bread
(PAGE 536)

20 servings: 1 slice each

1¾ cups whole-wheat pastry flour
1 teaspoon baking soda
½ teaspoon sea salt
½ teaspoon cream of tartar
1 cup turbinado sugar
3 tablespoons unsalted butter, melted
2 teaspoons unrefined or roasted walnut or unrefined peanut oil
2 large eggs
4 large fully ripened bananas, mashed
1½ teaspoons pure vanilla extract
⅓ cup hulled millet
¼ cup walnuts, pan-toasted, chopped

1. Preheat the oven to 350°F. Lightly coat a 9 × 5-inch loaf pan with homemade cooking spray. Dust with 2 teaspoons of the flour.

2. Whisk together the remaining flour, baking soda, salt, and cream of tartar in a medium bowl. Set aside.

3. Blend together the sugar, butter, and walnut oil with an electric mixer on low speed in a large bowl until combined. Add the eggs and blend well. Add the flour mixture and blend until just combined. Add the bananas and vanilla extract and blend until just combined.

4. Stir in the millet and nuts until evenly combined.

5. Pour the batter into the loaf pan. Bake until browned, set, and a toothpick inserted in the center comes out clean, about 1 hour 10 minutes. Let cool completely in the pan on a wire rack. Cut into 20 slices and serve at room temperature, chilled, or semi-frozen.

Per serving: 150 calories, 4g total fat, 1.5g saturated fat, 0g trans fat, 25mg cholesterol, 130mg sodium, 27g total carbohydrate, 3g dietary fiber, 13g sugars, 3g protein

MY SWAPS:

1. Significantly reduced butter. Added another banana to replace the buttery moistness and boost sweetness.

2. Used whole-wheat pastry flour instead of all-purpose flour for heartier, richer color and more satisfying fiber. Added millet in place of a small amount of the flour for more texture.

3. Added turbinado sugar instead of white granulated sugar for a more natural product and more caramel-like flavor appeal.

4. Heightened sweet overall flavor by use of additional vanilla extract.

5. Replaced part of the nuts with nut oil so the walnut flavor would be in every bite of bread, not just in the nuts. Toasted the walnuts for more nuttiness. Plus, the crunchy millet created the effect of more nuts, even though less was used.

Tip: If you were making your own swaps to an original ("before") recipe like the above, I suggest starting with one swap, such as using whole-wheat pastry flour instead of all-purpose (white) flour. Then on your next makeover of the recipe, add one additional swap. And so on.

Following the Recipes

In *1,000 Low-Calorie Recipes*, I aim for the perfect balance of lusciousness and calorie friendliness to keep your palate pleased and your body healthy. The goal is not to go low on fat. The goal is to provide recipes that are lower in calories than you might expect while focusing on flavor and nutritional richness.

Ingredient Lists

Don't be intimidated by the number of ingredients in any of the recipes. Some are long and some are short. But in many cases the longer lists are due to the use of several spices or herbs to boost flavors—which actually only take seconds in the prep. Also, unlike many cookbooks, I list salt and pepper so you know how much is good for the recipes (you can always adjust to your taste after you first make it). What's more, nearly all ingredients should be easy to find in most major markets.

To Taste

What does "to taste" mean? It means you can add more, less, or possibly none of the ingredient at all. It's up to you and your taste buds and health goals. However, for the recipes in this book, it means that I recommend a specified amount of an ingredient for best results. For instance, if a recipes says "¼ teaspoon ground cinnamon, or to taste," I found that ¼ teaspoon resulted in the best-tasting dish. But if you're not a sweet-spice fan, you can instead use less, such as ⅛ teaspoon and vice versa. (See A Dash of Cinnamon, page xxxv.)

Salt

One of the ingredients that's most often listed as "to taste" in *1,000 Low-Calories Recipes* is sea salt. I specify sea salt instead of typical iodized table salt due to preferential taste, not due to sodium differences. I've kept all recipes at 800mg or less

sodium per serving, and most of them are significantly lower than that. (See How Much Sodium Is Okay?, above.) Keep an eye out for the recipes highlighted with low-sodium labels. Try your best not to add any more than the amount listed. If you desire more flavor, reach for extra amounts of other very low calorie ingredients in a recipe, such as herbs or spices. It's okay to use less salt in a recipe if that suits your palate or your dietary needs better. But do keep in mind that sodium adds flavor. And for healthy folks, taste rules!

Sweeteners

I use turbinado sugar or honey as the "sugar" of choice in *1,000 Low-Calorie Recipes* to keep it 100 percent real and delicious—but without overdoing it. I suggest agave nectar as an option for honey if you prefer to keep vegan. Though not listed in this cookbook, since not as readily available, I suggest coconut palm sugar as an option for turbinado sugar. Consider replacing part of the turbinado sugar with it, one for one. It may have less impact on blood sugar.

What about using naturally derived calorie-free sweeteners? They can obviously help reduce calories from sugar even further, if that's your goal. So if you prefer to try substituting sugar with 0-calorie stevia, check the package for instructions. I suggest replacing no more than half of the sugar with it. Too much stevia in a recipe can result in a slightly bitter taste. And if you're baking, know that you'll lose the baking qualities that real sugar provides, including bulk and caramelization. But here is a general guide to follow, based on packets:

1 tablespoon sugar is the equivalent of about 2 packets of stevia

1 cup sugar is the equivalent of about 20 packets of stevia

And be on the lookout as additional natural sugar replacers come to market, like no-calorie sweeteners made with monk fruit.

Milk

My recipes rely mainly on plant-based "milk" as the milk of choice. These include plain almond milk, unsweetened coconut milk beverage, light soy milk, and unsweetened sunflower beverage. Other plant-based "milks" appear to be on the horizon too, so keep your eyes open for them. These milk alternatives provide a bevy of nutrients and they're low in calories—many brands averaging around just 50 calories per cup. All of those saved calories add up. However, do know that most plant-based beverages (other than soy milk) do not naturally have nearly as much protein as

dairy milk? So if you prefer to keep your protein boost using a plant-based "milk," go with light soy milk. Look for a GMO free variety. Or check labels carefully and see if the plant-based "milk" has added protein. If you personally prefer to use dairy milk—whether cow, goat, or sheep—use the lowest fat options available. When possible and available, choose milk (and yogurt and cheese) from cows that were raised without the artificial growth hormone, *rBST*. Finally, when using any dairy milk in place of plant-based "milk" in this cookbook's recipes, remember that the calories per serving will be slightly higher.

Organic

As noted earlier (see 10 "Clean" Cuisine Approaches, page xxvi), I recommend going organic if you can. It's a vote for your health and the health of our planet. Though there is no scientifically proven connection between eating organic foods and weight loss, choosing organic foods may result in an overall healthier diet. And that may assist you with weight-loss efforts. In *1,000 Low-Calorie Recipes*, I leave the choice up to you regarding which organic items to choose. My suggested starting point is to select organic meats.

Flexitarians, Vegetarians, Vegans, and Ecotarians

What's for dinner? Beef? Chicken? Well, it used to be commonplace to have an entrée that was protein rich—and usually animal based. But it's definitely okay if your entrée is based on vegetables or whole grains. In fact, I recommend it!

- **FLEXITARIAN:** A flexitarian is basically an "almost" vegetarian—or someone who occasionally may eat small amounts of poultry, fish, or meat. The Main Dishes: Vegetarian and Flexitarian chapter (page 255) was designed with the flexitarian in mind. The recipes in the

---

A DASH OF CINNAMON

Cinnamon is a notable spice in *1,000 Low-Calorie Recipes* for a couple of reasons. First, I'm half Lebanese, so you'll see some of the signature influences of Middle Eastern cuisine in many of my recipes, including cinnamon. Also, cinnamon has been associated with helping to regulate blood sugar levels. This may be especially helpful for people with or at risk for diabetes.

---

chapter are all vegetarian; however, you'll see flexitarian options highlighted for every recipe, too. It'll help "beef" up the dishes. Many of these options can also be ideal if you're preparing a dish for both vegetarians and non-vegetarians, making it simple to fix one dish both ways. What's more, the flexitarian options can help you boost the protein content of the dish, if that's your goal. Otherwise, keep in mind that if you do choose one of the entrées that's relatively low in protein, balance it with a side dish that's higher in protein, like beans, tofu, or (for flexitarians) chicken.

- **VEGETARIAN:** A vegetarian doesn't eat any chicken, fish, or meat. The most common is a lacto-ovo vegetarian, who includes eggs and dairy in the diet. A vegan avoids all animal products. Other than the two main dish chapters based on animal foods, the majority of the book falls into the lacto-ovo vegetarianism category. So if you're a vegetarian who includes eggs and dairy, you'll find hundreds upon hundreds of recipes well suited for you in *1,000 Low-Calorie Recipes*. If you're a vegan or someone who desires to occasionally follow more of a vegan-style approach, there are hundreds of recipe options throughout this cookbook for you, too.

- **ECOTARIAN:** An ecotarian is a "green" eater. (See What Is an Ecotarian?, page xxviii.) Being mostly plant-based, *1,000 Low-Calorie Recipes* can easily fit within an ecotarian-style eating plan. (That's how I prefer to eat!) Fresh and natural ingredients are the focus. No overly processed ingredients will be found in the recipes, period. Plus, you can adapt the recipes to meet more specific environmentally conscious habits of your own choosing, such as selecting more organic foods or using energy-saving eco-cuisine cooking techniques. (See 10 "Clean" Cuisine Approaches on page xxvi for tips.)

Weight-Loss Diets

1,000 Low-Calorie Recipes is not designed to be a weight-loss diet by itself. Rather, it's a resource that will work well with your personal diet plan. Whether following a do-it-yourself diet, one of the many popular commercialized weight-loss approaches, or a dietitian-developed plan, you'll be able to find recipes to fit into your chosen weight-management approach. Do consult with your physician and/or registered dietitian before beginning any weight-loss plan.

Modifications

If you prefer to go even lower in calories, please use the recipes as a guide and experiment as you wish—one adjustment at a time. But do keep in mind that the lower in calories you go and the more substitutes you make, the more those changes will affect taste, texture, satisfaction, and overall appeal. And the goal for eating healthfully is to do so for the long run, not temporarily. So do make any changes wisely. Enjoyment is important.

Nutrition Analysis

The nutrition analysis is provided for every recipe to help guide you in selecting recipes to fit into your healthful eating plan. In the analysis, I include the specific amounts of ingredients actually used. So, for instance, if a marinade doesn't all get utilized in the recipe as served, only the actual amount of marinade in the final product is used for the analysis. If an ingredient is listed as optional, it's not included in the analysis. And the equivalent of ⅛ teaspoon oil per serving is included in the analysis for any recipe where cooking spray is used. Precise measurements were taken whenever possible to provide you with the most accurate nutrition information.

Special Diets

There are so many different types of diet-related needs that it's not possible to be the perfect cookbook for everyone. But since *1,000 Low-Calorie Recipes* does have one thousand recipes, you can almost guarantee it is likely to still have hundreds of recipes that can fit nearly anyone's special need or desired eating style, whether gluten-free, dairy-free, low-sodium, low-glycemic, vegan, or other. The recipes can also be incorporated into eating plans for chronic health conditions, such as diabetes and pre-diabetes, hypertension, hyperlipidemia, metabolic syndrome, and more. To determine which recipes may best meet your specific nutrition or health requirement, seek the individualized advice of a registered dietitian.

Sautéing

I often suggest sautéing at medium heat instead of the traditional medium-high. This is done for a couple of reasons: (1) the recipe may use an oil with a lower smoke point (one that's not meant to be used at high temps), such as extra-virgin olive oil, and (2) the recipe may benefit from "sweating" an item, especially onions, to bring out all the moisture and flavors. Classically, "sautéing" refers to cooking food quickly in a small amount of oil in a sauté pan or skillet over direct heat, usually at medium-high or higher heat. If done at a lower heat a little more slowly, it's classically called "sweating." But in *1,000 Low-Calorie Recipes* I simply use the term "sautéing" for both of these types of cooking to keep it simple.

Also, cooking at medium instead of medium-high heat works better when you don't have as much oil in the skillet, since cooking at too high temps can be drying, potentially causing ingredients to stick to the pan. One trick of mine is to add a splash of vinegar and a pinch of sea salt in this process, mainly when sautéing onions. It helps create extra moisture so you don't need as much oil during the sautéing process, which saves calories. Plus, the vinegar is an acidic ingredient that works to balance any bitterness from additional ingredients included in the dish. To prevent splattering, just remember to carefully add the vinegar or other acid ingredient with or after the ingredient that is to be sautéed, not with the oil. (Note: There was a recent animal study which suggested that vinegar may have a fat-burning role in the body. Though there is no decisive evidence yet that vinegar helps humans lose weight, a splash of vinegar here and there may be a good thing.)

I hope you love the taste of nutrient-rich, low-calorie cooking. There are enough recipes and ideas in *1,000 Low-Calorie Recipes* to last you a lifetime. But if you have comments or questions, please let me know: jnewgent@aol.com. And for more tips and recipe ideas, please visit:

Web site: http://jackienewgent.com

Recipe blog: http://jackienewgent.com/recipe-blog/

Twitter: @jackienewgent.

Facebook page: Jackie Newgent

Good-for-You Menus

Having 1,000 recipes to choose from translates to an endless number of menus that can be created to suit anyone's needs. Here's a sampling of several to get you started. Each ranges from 400 to 500 calories to easily fit into a healthful meal plan. Additionally, please do go ahead and add nonstarchy raw, steamed, or grilled seasonal vegetables, plus herbs and spices, as you wish. Consider them menu freebies that boost enjoyment and satisfaction.

SPRING MENUS

Lovely Ladies' Brunch (Vegetarian)

Homemade Citrus Soda (page 543): *70 calories*

Crustless Asparagus Quiche (page 26): *160 calories*

Fresh Herb Hash Browns (page 33): *200 calories*

TOTAL CALORIES: **430**

Italian Picnic al Fresco

Italian-Style Submarine (page 381): *270 calories*

Sweet Pea and Prosciutto Potato Salad (page 164): *180 calories*

TOTAL CALORIES: **450**

Backyard Asian Cookout

Spa H$_2$0 (page 544): *5 calories*

3-Ingredient Grilled Chicken Paillard (page 310): *170 calories*

Asian Angel Hair with "Confetti" (page 289): *300 calories*

TOTAL CALORIES: **475**

Springtime Farmers' Market Meal

Vichyssoise Shots (page 207): *35 calories*

Chicken Shawarma (page 387): *340 calories*

Artichoke Heart "Salsa" (page 438): *110 calories*

TOTAL CALORIES: **485**

Mediterranean Delight

Seed-Crusted Whole-Grain Bread (page 499): *90 calories*

Mediterranean Mussels (page 362): *375 calories*

Roasted Grape Tomatoes (page 470): *35 calories*

TOTAL CALORIES: **500**

Family-Friendly Fish Sticks Soiree

Creole Panko-Crusted Tilapia Sticks (page 350): *210 calories*

Fresh Tartar Sauce (page 129): *70 calories*

Broccoli Slaw (page 179): *100 calories*

Homemade Pretzel Puffs (page 73): *100 calories*

TOTAL CALORIES: **480**

Spring Salad Sampler (Vegan)

Salad for Every Season (page 159): *160 calories*

Spelt Tabbouleh Salad (page 183): *160 calories*

Smoked Tofu Chef Salad (page 172): *170 calories*

TOTAL CALORIES: **490**

SUMMER MENUS

AUTUMN MENUS

Breakfast in Bed (Vegetarian)

Soft Scrambled Eggs with Purple Potato
and Chives (page 16): *140 calories*

Freshly Squeezed Orange Float (page 547):
140 calories

Mom's Banana Bread (page 536): *150 calories*

TOTAL CALORIES: **430**

Fall Hiking Fare (Vegetarian)

Hot Spiced Apple Cider (page 544): *100 calories*

Cucumber and Caramelized-Onion Tea
Sandwiches (page 374): *200 calories*

Orzo with Greens, Feta, and Cranberries
(page 178): *200 calories*

TOTAL CALORIES: **500**

Pacific Pasta Party

Sardine Bruschetta-Style Pasta (page 366):
370 calories

Stewed Tomatoes Oregano (page 471):
70 calories

TOTAL CALORIES: **440**

Worldly Indian Curry (Vegetarian)

Tofu Curry with Coconut Rice (page 270):
300 calories

Cumin-Spiced Chickpea Raita (page 97):
40 calories

Dal Masala with Cilantro (page 490): *150 calories*

TOTAL CALORIES: **490**

Fun Fall Food (Vegan)

Hummus Pitza (page 426): *380 calories*

Semisweet Chocolate-Dipped Figs (page 525):
110 calories

TOTAL CALORIES: **490**

Middle Eastern-Inspired Comfort

Velvety Sweet Potato Soup (page 215):
100 calories

Sticky Lebanese Cinnamon Chicken and Rice
(page 337): *270 calories*

Mid-East Tomato-Stewed Beans (page 449):
90 calories

TOTAL CALORIES: **460**

Mexican Fiesta (Vegan)

California Guacamole Parfait (page 90):
260 calories

Grilled Sweet Potato Salad (page 165):
170 calories

TOTAL CALORIES: **430**

WINTER MENUS

Casual Celebration Breakfast

Blood Orange Mimosa (page 570): *45 calories*

Jackie's "Quiche" (page 431): *300 calories*

Anjou Chicken Breakfast Sausage Patties
(page 35): *80 calories*

TOTAL CALORIES: **425**

Soothing Fare for the Soul (Vegetarian)

Goat Cheese Medallions with Balsamic
Caramelized Onions (page 64): *130 calories*

Sunny-Side-Up Salad (page 156): *260 calories*

Fresh Herbal Polenta (page 492): *100 calories*

TOTAL CALORIES: **490**

Luscious Indian Pleasures (Vegan)

Delhi Coleslaw (page 172): *100 calories*

Creamy Seasonal Vegetable Korma (page 272):
270 calories

Sticky Ginger Rice (page 476): *130 calories*

TOTAL CALORIES: **500**

Savory & Sweet Aromatic Eats

Gingered Carrot Juice (page 544): *70 calories*

Turkey, Cheese, and Tart Apple Toastie (page
395): *330 calories*

Extra-Virgin Roasted Cauliflower (page 446):
90 calories

TOTAL CALORIES: **490**

Burgers & Fries (Vegan)

Roasted Winter Veggie Burgers (page 397):
260 calories

Spicy Skinny Fries (page 459): *150 calories*

Jamaican Bloody Mary Shots (page 558):
40 calories

TOTAL CALORIES: **450**

Truffle Lovers Get-Together (Vegetarian)

White Party Pizzette Platter (page 67):
120 calories

Truffle Purple Potato Soup (page 212):
130 calories

Creamy Truffled Black Rice (page 480):
170 calories

TOTAL CALORIES: **420**

Party Buffet Bites (Vegan)

Garlic-Tarragon Pita Chips (page 41):
120 calories

Edamame "Hummus" (page 88):
110 calories

Sweet Potato Guacamole (page 91):
60 calories

Jamaican Bean Salad (page 189):
120 calories

Ginger Tofu Chick'n Salad (page 170):
80 calories

TOTAL CALORIES: **490 calories**

Breakfasts and Brunches

Cereal

Banana-Nut Granola

Pure Maple Cinnamon Granola

Granola-Berry "Parfaitini"

Petite Granola-Peach Parfait

Creamy California Orange Oatmeal

Sweet Cherry–Almond Oatmeal

Cocoa Breakfast Cereal Bar

Pancakes, Crepes, Waffles, and French Toast

Mini-Pancakes with Mango Coulis

Oat Pancakes with Fruit Compote

Banana-Berry Buckwheat Pancakes

Raspberry-Laced Chocolate Chip Buttermilk Pancakes

Ham and Cheese Crepes

Caramelized Apple Cinnamon Crepes

Farmers' Market Almond Waffles

Strawberry-Pecan Waffle "Sundae"

Cinnamon Stix with Maple Crème

Flax French Toast with Fruit Salsa

Egg Dishes

Scrambled Huevos Rancheros with Fresh Salsa

Soft Scrambled Eggs with Purple Potato and Chives

Herb and Sweet Potato Soft Scramble

Madras-Style Scramble

Black Forest–Shiitake Scramble

West Coast Scramble

Irish-Inspired Breakfast

Truffled Egg Bruschetta

Burrito el Desayuno

Sunnyside-Up Pizza

Eggs Tatsoi Florentine

Skillet Omelet Baja

Omelet O'Brien

Punjabi Spinach Omelet

Egg Strata Florentine

Broccoli Bocconcini Strata

Roasted Vegetable Strata

Goat Cheese, Onion,
and Fingerling Frittata

Crustless Asparagus
"Quiche"

Spanish Manchego "Quiche"

Potato Hash
with Poached Egg

Sausage Hash
with Quail Eggs

Bean and Herb Eggs Tostada

Robiola Egg Muffin

Soft-Boiled Egg and Soldiers

Sunnyside-Up Jambalaya

"Green" Eggs and Ham

Vegetables and Fruits

Cheesy Grits

Fresh Herb Hash Browns

Cinnamon Apple Compote

Berry-Peach Compote

Other Breakfast and Brunch Dishes

Grecian Yogurt Sundae

Buttermilk Biscuits and Gravy

Anjou Chicken
Breakfast Sausage

Breakfast Turkey Links

Smoked Salmon
on Pumpernickel

Sunrise Vegan Burrito

Eating breakfast helps you obtain a diet that's balanced and nutrient-rich, boosts your energy levels, and potentially reduces hunger levels throughout the day.

It may be key for weight-management efforts. Studies show that breakfast skippers tend to weigh more than breakfast eaters. So, yes, breakfast is the most important meal of the day! I've included breakfast items that you know and love in this chapter so that you'll be enticed to eat breakfast regularly.

An important component of a healthful, sustaining breakfast is protein. Protein can help you feel full longer than either carbohydrates or fats. It helps you maintain muscle, which ultimately can help you burn calories. What's more, studies have found that eating eggs at breakfast time may play a valuable role in weight management, mainly due to the feeling of fullness they impart. That said, you'll see plenty of egg dishes in this chapter; eggs are rich in high-quality protein. And they're delicious.

It may surprise some to see many recipes use whole eggs, and not egg whites. Most health professionals agree that enjoying an egg a day can easily fit within a healthful diet. A whole egg is not a high-calorie food—it provides about 75 calories. Plus, most of the taste and nutrition is in the yolk. I encourage choosing organic eggs if you can; they're from pasture-raised hens and some studies suggest they may provide more omega-3s, vitamin E, and beta-carotene. They taste better to me, too.

But all eggs are nutrient rich. To prepare them, I use some culinary nutrition tricks. You'll see fat-free plain Greek yogurt or part-skim ricotta, which "stretches" eggs and makes them seem creamier in a calorie-friendly way. There are plenty of fresh herbs and spices for flavor and eye appeal, as in Herb and Sweet Potato Soft Scramble (page 17). A couple recipes, including Goat Cheese, Onion, and Fingerling Frittata (page 26), contain turmeric (which is rich in antioxidants!) to emphasize the golden yellow hue of the eggs. You'll even find a couple mouthwatering made-over versions of quiche—definitely try Spanish Manchego "Quiche" (page 127).

If you're very young or old, pregnant, or your immune system is compromised, cook eggs until fully done. For example, though the recipes for Soft Scrambled Eggs with Purple Potato and Chives (page 16) and Herb and Sweet Potato Soft Scramble (page 17) suggest to cook eggs only until custard-like, do prepare longer to meet your stricter needs for food safety. They're still going to taste good and be good for you.

But eggs aren't the only answer to a nutritious breakfast. Eating whole-grain cereal can be a beneficial part of a healthy diet and, potentially, a healthy weight. In this chapter, you'll find oatmeal recipes that have big flavors and use real fruits and crunchy granola filled with delicious, nutrient-rich ingredients to help you out. These granolas, granola parfaits, and fruity oatmeal recipes all contain whole grains from the oats. The fiber provided will be helpful for keeping you satisfied—and managing blood sugar and cholesterol. There's even a 250-calorie Cocoa Breakfast Cereal Bar (page 18) if you need to eat on the run—or need a chocolate fix.

You'll also find the comforting choices of pancakes, crepes, waffles, and French toast. They're all made with nutritious, flavorful flours: whole-wheat pastry flour, oat flour, or almond flour. Some are mixed with low-fat buttermilk, which tastes rich and tangy but is only 100 calories a cup. You'll also see plain almond milk, which is the "milk" of choice throughout *1,000 Low-Calorie Recipes*; a cup provides an average of only 50 calories!

There's an array of recipes from which to select, from the savory—Ham and Cheese Crepes (page 12)—to the sweet—Raspberry-Laced Chocolate Chip Buttermilk Pancakes (page 11).

The chapter is rounded out by some fruit and veggie-based sides, such as Berry-Peach Compote (page 34) and Fresh Herb Hash Browns (page 33), as well as some specialty recipes, like Sunrise Vegan Burrito (page 37). You can round out some of your main breakfast dishes with some of the produce-pleasing sides. Actually, you can complete any breakfast meal with a fruit or vegetable. In many cases, I've already done that for you; where veggies are mixed into the egg dish or fruit is served atop a whole-grain dish. Fresh fruit or vegetable juice can count, too. When pairing your breakfast meal with a glass of 100% fruit juice, go with a 6-ounce not 16-ounce, serving to keep calories in check.

But please don't feel that you must eat "breakfast food" in the morning. The most important thing is to eat breakfast, period. That means if you prefer a veggie burger or chicken salad, go for it. Just be sure it's still nutrient rich and fits within your eating plan.

Calorie range in this chapter: 45 to 470 calories.

Low-calorie pick: Berry-Peach Compote, 45 calories (page 34).

Cereal

Banana-Nut Granola Ⓢ

Makes 6 servings: ½ cup each

One of the best ways to start the day is with a boost of good nutrition. Granola is loaded with it—including immune-boosting zinc and vitamin B$_6$. This fruity version is baked with a banana to make it naturally sweet and flavor laden, too.

1½ cups old-fashioned oats
⅓ cup puffed millet, kamut, or brown rice cereal
⅓ cup coarsely chopped walnuts or Brazil nuts
3 tablespoons raw wheat germ
2 tablespoons raw sunflower seeds
1 teaspoon ground cinnamon
1 small fully ripened banana, well mashed

1. Preheat the oven to 325°F.

2. Stir together the oats, cereal, walnuts, wheat germ, sunflower seeds, and cinnamon in a medium bowl. Add the banana and stir until well combined.

3. Spread the mixture evenly into a parchment paper–lined large baking tray. Bake until toasted and crisp, about 35 minutes, stirring once halfway through the baking. Remove from the oven and let the granola cool on a rack on the baking tray. (Granola can be stored in an airtight container at room temperature for several days.)

Per serving: 170 calories, 8g total fat, 1g saturated fat, 0g trans fat, 0mg cholesterol, 0mg sodium, 22g total carbohydrate, 4g dietary fiber, 3g sugars, 5g protein

Pure Maple Cinnamon Granola Ⓢ

Makes 6 servings: ⅓ rounded cup each

The combination of rich maple syrup, pure apple butter, and cinnamon adds an interesting sweetness to this granola that's a sure taste winner. The addition of puffed whole-grain cereal lightens it up so you get a little bit bigger serving than a traditional version. That makes this sweet and nutty granola a win-win.

1½ cups old-fashioned oats
⅓ cup puffed millet, kamut, or brown rice cereal
3 tablespoons raw wheat germ
3 tablespoons slivered almonds
2 tablespoons coarsely chopped pecans
2 tablespoons raw sunflower seeds
1½ teaspoons ground cinnamon
3 tablespoons no-sugar-added apple butter
1½ tablespoons pure maple syrup

1. Preheat the oven to 325°F.

2. Stir together the oats, cereal, wheat germ, almonds, pecans, sunflower seeds, and cinnamon in a medium bowl.

3. Stir together the apple butter and maple syrup in a small bowl. Add the apple butter mixture to the granola mixture and stir to combine.

4. Spread the mixture evenly into a parchment paper–lined large baking tray. Bake until toasted and crisp, about 30 minutes, stirring once halfway through the baking. Remove from the oven and let the granola cool on a rack on the baking tray. (Granola can be stored in an airtight container at room temperature for several days.)

Per serving: 170 calories, 7g total fat, 0.5g saturated fat, 0g trans fat, 0mg cholesterol, 0mg sodium, 24g total carbohydrate, 4g dietary fiber, 7g sugars, 5g protein

Granola-Berry "Parfaitini" Ⓢ Ⓕ

Makes 4 servings: 1 parfait each

For an eye-opening start to your day, simply serve your yogurt parfait in a martini glass and enjoy with a spoon. This fresh strawberry-studded "parfaitini" is the perfect light morning meal. Enjoy it "straight up"—before and after noon.

1½ cups fat-free or low-fat plain yogurt
    (not Greek yogurt)

1 tablespoon apricot or peach 100% fruit spread

¼ teaspoon pure vanilla extract

1½ cups Banana-Nut Granola (page 6)

1⅓ cups thinly sliced fresh strawberries

4 whole large fresh strawberries

1. Stir together the yogurt, fruit spread, and vanilla extract in a small bowl until well combined.

2. Layer the granola, yogurt mixture, and sliced strawberries into four martini or other beverage glasses. Top each with a whole strawberry, and serve.

Per serving: 210 calories, 6g total fat, 0.5g saturated fat, 0g trans fat, 0mg cholesterol, 70mg sodium, 31g total carbohydrate, 5g dietary fiber, 15g sugars, 10g protein

Petite Granola-Peach Parfait Ⓢ Ⓕ

Makes 4 servings: 1 parfait each

For a light yet fully pleasing breakfast in the summertime, try this parfait filled with fresh seasonal fruit, creamy yogurt, and crunchy granola. It's a perfect choice for keeping calories in check while appealing to your sweet tooth. And for added pizzazz, grill the peaches before dicing.

1½ cups fat-free or low-fat plain yogurt
    (not Greek yogurt)

1 tablespoon apricot or peach 100% fruit spread

¼ teaspoon pure vanilla extract

1½ cups Pure Maple Cinnamon Granola (page 6)

2 large yellow or white peaches or nectarines,
    pitted and diced

1. Stir together the yogurt, fruit spread, and vanilla extract in a small bowl until well combined.

2. Layer the granola, yogurt mixture, and peaches into four beverage glasses, and serve.

Per serving: 260 calories, 7g total fat, 1g saturated fat, 0g trans fat, 0mg cholesterol, 75mg sodium, 41g total carbohydrate, 5g dietary fiber, 22g sugars, 11g protein

Creamy California Orange Oatmeal Ⓕ

Makes 4 servings: 1 rounded cup each

This creamy citrus-spiked oatmeal is a tasty meal in a bowl. The soluble fiber from the oats makes it exceptionally satisfying. You'll love its appealing texture, fragrant aroma, and refreshing taste.

2 cups fresh-squeezed orange juice

1 teaspoon ground cinnamon

½ teaspoon sea salt

¼ teaspoon pure vanilla extract

2 cups old-fashioned oats

1 cup fat-free or low-fat plain yogurt
    (not Greek yogurt)

1 tablespoon no-sugar-added apple butter

2 tablespoons sliced natural almonds, toasted,
    or chopped unsalted dry-roasted pistachios

1. Bring the juice, 1 cup water, cinnamon, salt, and vanilla extract just to a boil in a medium saucepan over medium-high heat.

2. Stir in the oats and return to a boil. Reduce heat to medium-low. Cook 5 minutes, stirring occasionally.

3. Stir in the yogurt and apple butter and continue cooking while stirring until the oatmeal mixture is heated through, about 2 minutes.

4. Spoon the oatmeal into four cereal bowls. Top with the nuts, and enjoy while hot.

Per serving: 260 calories, 5g total fat, 0.5g saturated fat, 0g trans fat, 0mg cholesterol, 340mg sodium, 47g total carbohydrate, 5g dietary fiber, 18g sugars, 10g protein

Sweet Cherry–Almond Oatmeal Ⓕ

Makes 4 servings: 1¼ cups each

When sweet cherries are in season, I love incorporating them into cuisine for a pop of excitement. The pairing of cherries with the pleasant nutty flavor and delicate crunch of sliced almonds in this delightful bowl of oatmeal transforms it from simple to scrumptious.

1¾ cups 100% unsweetened apple juice

1 teaspoon ground cinnamon

½ teaspoon sea salt

¼ teaspoon pure vanilla extract

¼ teaspoon pure almond extract

2 cups old-fashioned oats

1 cup fat-free or low-fat plain yogurt
    (not Greek yogurt)

¾ cup sweet Bing or Rainier cherries, pitted and
    sliced, or 3 tablespoons dried tart cherries

2 tablespoons sliced natural almonds, toasted

1. Bring the juice, 1¼ cups water, cinnamon, salt, vanilla extract, and almond extract just to a boil in a medium saucepan over medium-high heat.

2. Stir in the oats and return to a boil. Reduce heat to medium-low. Cook 5 minutes stirring occasionally.

3. Stir in the yogurt and cherries and continue cooking while stirring until the oatmeal mixture is heated through, about 2 minutes.

4. Spoon the oatmeal into four cereal bowls. Top with the almonds, and enjoy while hot.

Per serving: 270 calories, 4.5g total fat, 0.5g saturated fat, 0g trans fat, 0mg cholesterol, 340mg sodium, 50g total carbohydrate, 5g dietary fiber, 19g sugars, 9g protein

Cocoa Breakfast Cereal Bar

Makes 10 servings: 1 bar each

I wish I had invented this chewy-chocolaty recipe when I was in elementary school. This cereal bar would have been like a dream back then. But, even today, it's still dreamy. One of my secrets is that I love these straight from the freezer like a dessert.

⅔ cup (about 10–12) pitted dried plums (prunes)

2 tablespoons unrefined peanut or canola oil

1¼ teaspoons pure vanilla extract

4 ounces unsweetened chocolate, coarsely chopped

¾ cup turbinado sugar

1 teaspoon sea salt

3 large eggs, lightly beaten

1¾ cups whole-grain cereal flakes, coarsely crushed

½ cup old-fashioned oats

¼ cup chopped pecans, peanuts, walnuts,
    or mixture

1. Line an 8-inch square baking pan with parchment paper. Set aside.

2. Add the plums, oil, and vanilla extract to a food processor. Cover and pulse into a paste. Set aside.

3. Preheat the oven to 350°F.

4. Bring 1 inch of water to a simmer in a medium saucepan; reduce heat to low. Add the chocolate to a heatproof bowl and set over the saucepan. Stir occasionally just until chocolate is melted. Remove from heat.

5. Add the chocolate, plum paste, sugar, and salt to a large mixing bowl. Stir until combined. Add the eggs and stir until well combined. Fold in the cereal and oats until well combined. Spread the batter in the pan. Sprinkle with the nuts

6. Bake until springy to the touch about 2 inches around edges, about 25 minutes. Cool on a rack.

7. Cut into 10 bars and enjoy at room temperature or chilled. Store in the freezer for up to 1 month.

Per serving: 250 calories, 13g total fat, 4.5g saturated fat, 0g trans fat, 55mg cholesterol, 280mg sodium, 35g total carbohydrate, 4g dietary fiber, 19g sugars, 5g protein

Pancakes, Crepes, Waffles, and French Toast

Mini Pancakes with Mango Coulis Ⓕ

Makes 2 servings: 6 pancakes each

Fluffy pancakes can absolutely fit into a calorie-friendly eating plan. So go ahead, make these satisfying mini pancakes; you can have six! Then top with a delightfully fresh and fruity topping instead of syrup—to help cut back on calories from added sugar. The pleasurable result will amaze your eyes and taste buds.

½ cup whole-wheat pastry flour

1 teaspoon baking powder

¼ teaspoon sea salt

¼ teaspoon ground cinnamon

2 teaspoons cold unsalted butter, cut into pieces

1½ teaspoons honey or agave nectar

1 large egg

½ cup plain almond milk or unsweetened coconut milk beverage

¼ teaspoon pure vanilla extract

⅓ cup Mango Coulis, warm (page 537)

1. Combine the flour, baking powder, salt, cinnamon, butter, and honey into a fine crumbled mixture with a pastry blender or potato masher in a medium bowl.

2. Whisk together the egg, almond milk, and vanilla extract in a large bowl until well combined. Add the flour mixture and whisk until well combined. Let stand for 5 minutes.

3. Lightly coat a large nonstick skillet or stick-resistant griddle with cooking spray (preferably homemade, page xix) and place over medium heat. Spoon the batter onto the hot surface—roughly 1 rounded tablespoon per pancake. Cook the pancakes in batches until lightly browned, about 1 minute on the first side and 30 seconds on the flip side. Transfer the pancakes after cooked to a heatproof platter. Keep warm in a 200°F oven, if necessary, until ready to serve.

4. Serve the pancakes topped with the coulis. Sprinkle with additional cinnamon, if desired.

Per serving: 240 calories, 7g total fat, 3g saturated fat, 0g trans fat, 105mg cholesterol, 660mg sodium, 38g total carbohydrate, 5g dietary fiber, 13g sugars, 7g protein

Oat Pancakes with Fruit Compote

Makes 3 servings: 2 pancakes each

These vanilla lover's pancakes taste devilishly good. The fresh fruit compote that's served on top is angelically sweet. Together they create a most memorable mouthful—especially since each tasty serving is a surprisingly low 200 calories.

½ cup whole-grain oat flour

3 tablespoons whole-wheat pastry flour

1 teaspoon baking powder

¼ teaspoon sea salt

2 teaspoons cold unsalted butter, cut into pieces

1 teaspoon honey or agave nectar

1 large egg

½ cup low-fat buttermilk

½ teaspoon pure vanilla extract

¾ cup Berry-Peach Compote, at room temperature (page 341)

1. Combine the flours, baking powder, salt, butter, and honey into a fine crumbled mixture with a pastry blender or potato masher in a medium bowl.

2. Whisk together the egg, buttermilk, and vanilla extract in a large bowl until well combined. Add the flour mixture and whisk until well combined. Let stand for 5 minutes.

3. Lightly coat a large nonstick skillet or stick-resistant griddle with cooking spray (preferably homemade, page xix) and place over medium heat. Spoon the batter onto the hot surface–about ¼ scant cup per pancake. Cook the pancakes in batches until lightly browned, about 2 minutes per side. Transfer the pancakes after cooked to a heatproof platter. Keep warm in a 200°F oven, if necessary, until ready to serve.

4. Serve the pancakes topped with the compote.

Per serving: 200 calories, 7g total fat, 3g saturated fat, 0g trans fat, 70mg cholesterol, 450mg sodium, 28g total carbohydrate, 4g dietary fiber, 10g sugars, 7g protein

Banana-Berry Buckwheat Pancakes Ⓕ

Makes 3 servings: 2 pancakes each

The vivid blueberries and creamy bananas stuffed into these buckwheat pancakes add so much flavor and palate appeal. When you can, enjoy with wild instead of cultivated blueberries for a more intense, tangy-sweet taste and more powerful antioxidants. And don't forget to finish with toasty nuts—it'll win you over.

½ cup buckwheat flour

1 teaspoon baking powder

¼ teaspoon sea salt

¼ teaspoon ground cinnamon

2 teaspoons cold unsalted butter, cut into pieces

1 teaspoon honey or agave nectar

1 large egg

½ cup plain almond milk or unsweetened coconut milk beverage

¼ teaspoon pure vanilla extract

⅛ teaspoon pure almond extract

2 medium fully ripened bananas

⅓ cup fresh or frozen blueberries, thawed

2 tablespoons coarsely chopped toasted walnuts

1. Combine the flour, baking powder, salt, cinnamon, butter, and honey into a fine crumbled mixture with a pastry blender or potato masher in a medium bowl.

2. Whisk together the egg, almond milk, vanilla extract, and almond extract in a large bowl until well combined. Add the flour mixture and whisk until well combined. Let stand for 5 minutes. Mash one banana with a fork until smooth; set aside. Very thinly slice the other banana. Stir the banana slices and blueberries into the batter.

3. Lightly coat a large nonstick skillet or stick-resistant griddle with cooking spray (preferably homemade, page xix) and place over medium heat. Spoon the batter, about ¼ cup per pancake, onto the hot surface and spread to flatten slightly with the back of the spoon or ladle or by shaking pan. Cook the pancakes in batches until lightly browned, about 2 minutes per side. Transfer the pancakes after cooked to a heatproof platter. Keep warm in a 200°F oven, if necessary, until ready to serve.

4. Top the pancakes with the mashed banana and the walnuts, and serve.

Per serving: 230 calories, 9g total fat, 2.5g saturated fat, 0g trans fat, 70mg cholesterol, 380mg sodium, 34g total carbohydrate, 6g dietary fiber, 14g sugars, 6g protein

Raspberry-Laced Chocolate Chip Buttermilk Pancakes Ⓕ

Makes 2 servings: 2 pancakes each

These are the richest of all of my pancakes . . . but they're oh so worth it! You can never go wrong with chocolate, right? Especially since the flavonoids in chocolate have some heart-health benefits. Then, the perfect complement, fresh raspberries offer a sweet-tart kick to each bite of these chocolate-spiked pancakes.

½ cup fresh raspberries

1 teaspoon pure maple syrup

½ cup whole-wheat pastry flour

1 teaspoon baking powder

¼ teaspoon sea salt

2 teaspoons cold unsalted butter, cut into pieces

1 teaspoon honey or agave nectar

1 large egg

½ cup low-fat buttermilk

¼ teaspoon pure vanilla extract

⅛ teaspoon pure almond extract

⅓ cup semisweet chocolate chips

1. Combine the raspberries and maple syrup in a small bowl and mash with a fork. Set aside.

2. Combine the flour, baking powder, salt, butter, and honey into a fine crumbled mixture with a pastry blender or potato masher in a medium bowl.

3. Whisk together the egg, buttermilk, vanilla extract, and almond extract in a large bowl until well combined. Add the flour mixture and whisk until well combined. Let stand for 5 minutes. Stir in the chocolate chips.

4. Lightly coat a large nonstick skillet or stick-resistant griddle with cooking spray (preferably homemade, page xix) and place over medium heat. Spoon the batter onto the hot surface—roughly ¼ cup per pancake. Cook the pancakes in batches until lightly browned, about 2 minutes on the first side and 1 minute on the flip side. Transfer the pancakes after cooked to a heatproof platter. Keep warm in a 200°F oven, if necessary, until ready to serve.

5. Serve the pancakes warm topped with the raspberry mixture.

Per serving: 380 calories, 16g total fat, 8g saturated fat, 0g trans fat, 105mg cholesterol, 590mg sodium, 53g total carbohydrate, 8g dietary fiber, 24g sugars, 10g protein

Ham and Cheese Crepes

Makes 4 servings: 2 crepes each

Here, fragrant rosemary is added to the buckwheat crepe batter to create extra herbaceous goodness. Then the filling of full-flavored Swiss cheese and Black Forest ham, coupled with the naturally sweet Bosc pear, creates an unforgettable crepe-eating experience.

¾ cup plain almond milk or light soy milk

1 large egg

¾ teaspoon chopped fresh rosemary, or to taste

¼ teaspoon sea salt

½ cup buckwheat flour

2 teaspoons unsalted butter, melted

1 cup grated Appenzeller, Gruyère, or other aged Swiss cheese

8 (½-ounce) thin slices Black Forest or Virginia baked ham

1 medium Bosc pear, cored, quartered, and very thinly sliced

½ teaspoon freshly ground black pepper, or to taste

1. Add the almond milk, egg, rosemary, salt, and flour to a covered container. Shake vigorously until the mixture is very smooth, about 1 minute. Let the batter stand for 15 minutes. Add the melted butter, cover and shake until combined.

2. Coat a stick-resistant crepe pan with cooking spray (preferably homemade, page xix) and place over medium heat. Spoon or pour about 2 rounded tablespoons of the batter into the pan, tilting the pan to make a thin circular crepe. Cook until the crepe is lightly browned on the bottom, about 1 minute. Flip over, top with the cheese, ham, pear, and pepper, and cook until lightly browned on the bottom, about 1 minute. Roll up and arrange on a heatproof platter. Repeat the process with remaining batter to make 8 crepes. Keep warm in a 200°F oven, if necessary.

3. Garnish the crepes with additional fresh rosemary, if desired, and serve.

Per serving: 270 calories, 14g total fat, 7g saturated fat, 0g trans fat, 95mg cholesterol, 590mg sodium, 20g total carbohydrate, 4g dietary fiber, 7g sugars, 17g protein

Caramelized Apple Cinnamon Crepes Ⓕ

Makes 4 servings: 2 crepes each

These crepes offer the essence of apple pie. The use of almond milk and yogurt instead of regular milk and whipped cream creates crepes that are light yet still a little lavish with an unforgettable and voluminous caramel apple filling. It's a truly satisfying autumn pleasure.

¾ cup plain almond milk or unsweetened coconut milk beverage

1 large egg

¼ teaspoon ground cinnamon

¼ teaspoon sea salt

½ cup buckwheat flour

2 teaspoons unsalted butter, melted

2 cups Cinnamon Apple Compote (page 33)

3 tablespoons fat-free or low-fat plain Greek yogurt

1. Add the almond milk, egg, cinnamon, salt, and flour to a covered container. Shake vigorously until the mixture is very smooth, about 1 minute. Let the batter stand for 15 minutes. Add the melted butter, cover and shake until combined.

2. Coat a stick-resistant crepe pan with cooking spray (preferably homemade, page xix) and place over medium heat. Spoon or pour about 2 rounded tablespoons of the batter into the pan, tilting the

pan to make a thin circular crepe. Cook until the crepe is lightly browned on the bottom, about 1 minute. Spread the compote down the center of the crepe, and cook until lightly browned on the bottom, about 1 minute. Roll up and arrange on a heatproof platter. Repeat the process with remaining batter to make 8 crepes. Keep warm in a 200°F oven, if necessary.

3. Top each crepe with about a teaspoon of the yogurt. Sprinkle with additional cinnamon, if desired, and serve.

Per serving: 210 calories, 5g total fat, 2.5g saturated fat, 0g trans fat, 55mg cholesterol, 260mg sodium, 35g total carbohydrate, 7g dietary fiber, 21g sugars, 5g protein

Farmers' Market Almond Waffles Ⓕ

Makes 7 servings: 1 (6½-inch round) waffle with ¼ cup topping each

These waffles are a celebration of the almond. The almond flour and almond milk provide "superfood" benefits, including vitamin E. The pure almond extract, which has virtually no calories, helps keep these waffles calorie friendly—and enhance the lovely almond flavor. The fresh fruit topping makes them extra delightful.

1 cup whole-wheat pastry flour

1 cup almond flour or whole-grain oat flour

1 tablespoon baking powder

1 teaspoon ground cinnamon

⅛ teaspoon sea salt

1 tablespoon unsalted butter, melted

1 cup plain almond milk or light soy milk

½ cup low-fat buttermilk

2 large eggs, lightly beaten

2 tablespoons honey or agave nectar

½ teaspoon pure almond extract, or to taste

¼ teaspoon pure vanilla extract

1 cup Farmers' Market Strawberry and Stone Fruit Spread (page 132) or other fruit topping

1. Lightly coat the cooking surface of a waffle maker with cooking spray (preferably homemade, page xix) and heat to medium-high (or #3 of a 5-setting waffle maker).

2. Whisk together the flours, baking powder, cinnamon, and salt in a medium bowl.

3. Whisk together the melted butter, almond milk, buttermilk, eggs, honey, almond extract, and vanilla extract in a small bowl until smooth. Add the liquid mixture to the dry mixture and stir until just combined.

4. Pour ½ cup batter into the center of the hot waffle cooking surface, close the waffle lid, and cook until golden brown, about 3 minutes. Repeat with remaining batter.

5. Keep warm in a single layer on baking sheets in a 200°F oven, if desired. For crispier waffles, place in a 300°F oven until desired crispness. Serve the waffles warm topped with the fruit spread.

Per serving: 210 calories, 5g total fat, 2g saturated fat, 0g trans fat, 60mg cholesterol, 360mg sodium, 35g total carbohydrate, 5g dietary fiber, 10g sugars, 6g protein

Strawberry-Pecan Waffle "Sundae"

Makes 8 servings: 1 (6½-inch round) waffle with 2 tablespoons topping and 1 strawberry each

There's a touch of elegance to these waffles. The bits of strawberries and pecans inside create interest while boosting flavor and nutrition. The dollop of creamy yogurt—and the ruby strawberry on top—turn these good-for-you waffles into a dessert-style dish.

1 cup whole-wheat pastry flour
1 cup almond flour or whole-grain oat flour
2 tablespoons finely chopped pecans
1 tablespoon baking powder
1 teaspoon ground cinnamon
⅛ teaspoon sea salt
1 cup plain almond milk or light soy milk
½ cup low-fat buttermilk
2 large eggs, lightly beaten
2 tablespoons honey or agave nectar
¾ teaspoon pure vanilla extract
⅔ cup finely diced fresh strawberries
1 tablespoon unsalted butter, melted
1 cup low-fat strawberry yogurt or Chantilly Vanilla Yogurt (page 540)
8 large fresh strawberries

1. Lightly coat the cooking surface of a waffle maker with cooking spray (preferably homemade, page xix) and heat to medium-high (or #3 of a 5-setting waffle maker).

2. Whisk together the flours, pecans, baking powder, cinnamon, and salt in a medium bowl. Whisk together the almond milk, buttermilk, eggs, honey, and vanilla extract in a small bowl, then stir in the strawberries and melted butter until combined.

Add the liquid mixture to the dry mixture and stir until just combined.

3. Pour ½ cup batter into the center of the hot waffle cooking surface, close the waffle lid, and cook until golden brown, about 3 minutes. Repeat with remaining batter.

4. Keep warm in a single layer on baking sheets in a 200°F oven, if desired. For crispier waffles, place in a 300°F oven until desired crispness. Serve the waffles warm topped with the yogurt. Top with 1 fresh strawberry each.

Per serving: 210 calories, 6g total fat, 2g saturated fat, 0g trans fat, 50mg cholesterol, 260mg sodium, 33g total carbohydrate, 4g dietary fiber, 12g sugars, 7g protein

Cinnamon Stix with Maple Crème

Makes 4 servings: 10 toast stix and about 2 tablespoons crème each

This fun version of French toast is kid and adult friendly. The syrup is skipped and instead the toast strips are drizzled with a velvety yogurt and maple syrup crème—making the topping lighter, yet seemingly more indulgent.

3 large eggs
1 cup plain almond milk or light soy milk
1 tablespoon unsalted butter, melted
2 tablespoons pure maple syrup
¾ teaspoon ground cinnamon
¼ teaspoon pure vanilla extract
¼ teaspoon sea salt, or to taste
8 slices day-old whole-grain bread, each cut into 5 strips
½ cup fat-free or low-fat plain yogurt, at room temperature
2 tablespoons chopped walnuts, toasted

1. Whisk together the eggs, almond milk, melted butter, 1 tablespoon of the maple syrup, ½ teaspoon of the cinnamon, the vanilla extract, and salt until well blended. Pour the egg mixture into two 9 × 13-inch baking pans, about ⅞ cup each.

2. Arrange the bread slices in a single layer in both pans. Soak the slices for 10 minutes, turning once halfway through soaking. (Note: Most of the liquid should be absorbed by the bread.)

3. Stir together the yogurt and the remaining 1 tablespoon of maple syrup in small bowl until smooth. Set aside.

4. Heat a large nonstick skillet or stick-resistant griddle over medium-high heat. Transfer the soaked bread slices in batches to the skillet using a slotted spatula and cook until browned, about 1½ minutes per side. Repeat with remaining bread slices. Keep warm in a 200°F oven, if necessary, until ready to serve. Dust with the remaining ¼ teaspoon cinnamon.

5. Arrange the French toast stix on a platter or individual plates while hot. Drizzle with the maple syrup crème, sprinkle with the walnuts, and serve immediately.

Per serving: 300 calories, 12g total fat, 3.5g saturated fat, 0g trans fat, 150mg cholesterol, 480mg sodium, 35g total carbohydrate, 4g dietary fiber, 13g sugars, 14g protein

Flax French Toast with Fruit Salsa Ⓕ

Makes 4 servings: 2 toasts each

Almond milk lightens up this updated take on French toast just right. The finishing touch is a fresh summery fruit salsa that's a lovely pairing with the flaxseeds of the bread.

3 large eggs

1 cup plain almond milk or light soy milk

1 tablespoon unsalted butter, melted

1 tablespoon honey or agave nectar

¼ teaspoon + ⅛ teaspoon sea salt, or to taste

1½ teaspoons fresh lemon juice

2 medium ripe nectarines, pitted and sliced

8 slices day-old flaxseed or other seeded whole-grain bread

⅛ teaspoon ground cinnamon

1. Whisk together the eggs, almond milk, melted butter, honey, and ¼ teaspoon of the salt until well blended. Pour the egg mixture into two 9 × 13-inch baking pans, about ⅞ cup each.

2. Meanwhile, add the lemon juice, nectarines, and the remaining ⅛ teaspoon salt to a food processor. Cover and pulse to desired lumpy or smooth consistency. Pour into a small bowl. Set aside.

3. Arrange the bread in a single layer in both pans. Soak the bread for 10 minutes, turning once halfway through soaking.

4. Heat a large nonstick skillet or stick-resistant griddle over medium-high heat. Transfer the bread slices in batches to the skillet using a slotted spatula and cook until browned, about 2 minutes per side. Repeat with remaining bread slices. Keep warm in a 200°F oven, if necessary, until ready to serve.

5. Arrange the French toast on a platter or individual plates while hot. Top with the nectarine salsa, dust with the cinnamon, and serve immediately.

Per serving: 280 calories, 10g total fat, 3.5g saturated fat, 0g trans fat, 145mg cholesterol, 530mg sodium, 37g total carbohydrate, 5g dietary fiber, 15g sugars, 13g protein

Egg Dishes

Scrambled Huevos Rancheros with Fresh Salsa

Makes 4 servings: ½ rounded cup each

Eggs aren't fattening . . . they're only about 75 calories each. By making just a few small nutritious changes and keeping portion size in check, this great-tasting rancheros-style dish is a perfect pick as a protein-pleasing start to the day. Round it out with a side of Southwestern Pinto Beans (page 487) to create a meal that'll wake up your palate.

4 large eggs

2 tablespoons plain almond milk or light soy milk

¼ teaspoon sea salt, or to taste

¼ teaspoon freshly ground white or black pepper, or to taste

1½ teaspoons unrefined peanut or canola oil

¼ cup part-skim ricotta cheese, at room temperature

¼ cup shredded dry Jack cheese, at room temperature

1 small jalapeño pepper, with or without some seeds, minced

12 blue corn tortilla chips

½ Hass avocado, pitted, peeled, and diced

¼ cup Spicy Raw Tomatillo Salsa (page 114) or other salsa verde

¼ cup fat-free or low-fat plain Greek yogurt

½ teaspoon lime zest

1 tablespoon chopped fresh cilantro

1. Whisk together the eggs, almond milk, salt, and pepper in a small bowl.

2. Heat the oil in a medium nonstick skillet over medium heat. Pour in the egg mixture and cook while scrambling until no longer runny, about 3 minutes. Remove from heat and immediately stir in the ricotta, Jack cheese, jalapeño, and chips. Adjust seasoning.

3. Transfer the egg mixture to a platter. Top with the avocado, salsa, yogurt, lime zest, and cilantro, and serve.

Per serving: 200 calories, 13g total fat, 4.5g saturated fat, 0g trans fat, 195mg cholesterol, 320mg sodium, 8g total carbohydrate, 2g dietary fiber, 2g sugars, 12g protein

Soft Scrambled Eggs with Purple Potato and Chives

Makes 4 servings: ½ cup each

This inviting entrée teams hash browns and scrambled eggs in a creative way. The purple potato adds volume, texture, and eye appeal plus the herbs add fresh flavor. It's so satisfying.

8 ounces baby purple or red creamer potatoes, unpeeled and scrubbed

4 large eggs

2 tablespoons plain almond milk or light soy milk

¼ teaspoon + ⅛ teaspoon sea salt, or to taste

¼ teaspoon freshly ground black pepper, or to taste

1½ teaspoons unrefined peanut oil

1 large shallot, minced

3 tablespoons chopped fresh chives

1 tablespoon chopped fresh tarragon

1. Place the potatoes in a microwave-safe dish, cover with parchment paper, and microwave on high until done, about 2½ minutes. Carefully slice into ¼-inch-thick coins. Set aside.

2. Whisk together the eggs, almond milk, ¼ teaspoon of the salt, and the pepper in a small bowl.

3. Heat the oil in a large nonstick skillet over medium heat. Add the shallot and sauté until softened, about 3 minutes. Stir in the potato and the remaining ⅛ teaspoon salt. Reduce heat to medium-low. Pour in the egg mixture and cook while scrambling until custard-like, about 3 minutes.

4. Remove from heat and immediately stir in the chives and tarragon. Adjust seasoning, and serve.

Per serving: 140 calories, 7g total fat, 2g saturated fat, 0g trans fat, 185mg cholesterol, 300mg sodium, 12g total carbohydrate, 1g dietary fiber, 1g sugars, 8g protein

Herb and Sweet Potato Soft Scramble

Makes 4 servings: ½ cup each

Here's a stunning egg dish that helps you deliciously get more veggies into your day. How I luckily stumbled upon its creation was simply by having leftover cooked sweet potatoes. And since sweet potatoes are so rich in health-promoting beta-carotene, I encourage enjoying including them regularly in cuisine—including at breakfast time.

4 large eggs

2 tablespoons plain almond milk or light soy milk

¼ teaspoon sea salt, or to taste

¼ teaspoon freshly ground white or black pepper, or to taste

1½ teaspoons unsalted butter or unrefined peanut oil

1 large shallot, minced

1 large cooked sweet potato, unpeeled, scrubbed, and diced

2 tablespoons chopped fresh flat-leaf parsley

2 tablespoons chopped fresh chives

1 tablespoon chopped fresh tarragon

1. Whisk together the eggs, almond milk, salt, and pepper in a small bowl. Set aside.

2. Melt the butter in a large nonstick skillet over medium heat. Add the shallot and sauté until softened, about 3 minutes. Stir in the sweet potato.

3. Reduce heat to medium-low. Pour in the egg mixture and cook while scrambling until custard-like, about 3 minutes.

4. Remove from heat and immediately stir in the parsley, chives, and tarragon. Adjust seasoning, and serve.

Per serving: 140 calories, 6g total fat, 2.5g saturated fat, 0g trans fat, 190mg cholesterol, 240mg sodium, 12g total carbohydrate, 2g dietary fiber, 5g sugars, 8g protein

Madras-Style Scramble

Makes 4 servings: ⅔ cup each

If you love Indian food and you're big on breakfast, you'll adore this enticing egg entrée. The authentic Indian spices, plentiful veggies, and fresh cilantro provide provocative flavors.

4 large eggs

¼ cup fat-free or low-fat plain Greek yogurt

½ teaspoon sea salt, or to taste

¼ teaspoon hot Madras curry powder

¼ teaspoon ground cumin

¼ teaspoon ground coriander

¼ teaspoon freshly ground black pepper, or to taste

1½ teaspoons unrefined peanut or canola oil

1 large Idaho potato, unpeeled, scrubbed, and finely diced

1 medium white onion, finely diced

2 teaspoons white wine vinegar

1 plum tomato, pulp removed and finely diced

2 tablespoons chopped fresh cilantro

1. Whisk together the eggs, yogurt, ¼ teaspoon of the salt, the curry powder, cumin, coriander, and pepper in a small bowl. Set aside.

2. Heat the oil in a large nonstick skillet over medium heat. Stir in the potato, onion, vinegar, and the remaining ¼ teaspoon salt, cover, and cook until the potato is just tender and both the potato and onion are lightly caramelized, about 15 minutes, stirring occasionally. Remove the lid. Stir in the tomato and sauté for 2 minutes.

3. Pour in the egg mixture and cook while scrambling until the eggs are no longer runny, about 3 minutes. Immediately stir in the cilantro. Adjust seasoning.

4. Transfer the egg mixture to a platter or four individual plates, and serve.

Per serving: 180 calories, 7g total fat, 2g saturated fat, 0g trans fat, 185mg cholesterol, 230mg sodium, 20g total carbohydrate, 2g dietary fiber, 3g sugars, 10g protein

Black Forest–Shiitake Scramble

Makes 4 servings: ½ cup each

Juicy grape tomatoes and rich, earthy shiitake mushrooms mingle with aromatic rosemary and smoky ham to create a luscious and lean dish. Fluffiness is cleverly enhanced with tangy Greek yogurt. For an ultimate meal experience, enjoy this full-flavored scramble as the highlight in the Irish-Inspired Breakfast (page 19).

4 large eggs

¼ cup fat-free or low-fat plain Greek yogurt

¼ teaspoon freshly ground black pepper, or to taste

⅛ teaspoon sea salt, or to taste

1½ teaspoons unsalted butter

3 ounces Black Forest ham, diced or chopped

12 grape tomatoes, quartered lengthwise

½ cup very thinly sliced fresh shiitake mushroom caps or cremini (baby bella) mushrooms

½ teaspoon chopped fresh rosemary or ¼ teaspoon crushed dried rosemary

1. Whisk together the eggs, yogurt, pepper, and salt in a small bowl.

2. Melt the butter in a large nonstick skillet over medium heat. Add the ham, tomatoes, mushrooms, and rosemary and sauté until the mushrooms are fully softened, about 5 minutes.

3. Pour in the egg mixture and cook while scrambling until the eggs are no longer runny, about 3 minutes. Adjust seasoning.

4. Transfer the egg mixture to a platter or four individual plates, and serve.

Per serving: 120 calories, 7g total fat, 2.5g saturated fat, 0g trans fat, 200mg cholesterol, 380mg sodium, 3gtotal carbohydrate, 0g dietary fiber, 2g sugars, 11g protein

West Coast Scramble

Makes 4 servings: 1 cup each

Here's my refreshing, savory, sweet, and slightly pungent version of a California-style scrambled egg dish, inspired by one of my L.A. food experiences. You'll fall for all of its flavor character.

2 teaspoons extra-virgin olive oil

1 large sweet onion, very thinly sliced

Juice and zest of ½ small lemon (1 tablespoon juice)

½ teaspoon sea salt, or to taste

1 large garlic clove, minced

1 (3-ounce) link cooked Italian-style poultry sausage, cut crosswise into ⅛-inch slices

4 large eggs

2 tablespoons plain almond milk or light soy milk

¼ teaspoon freshly ground black pepper, or to taste

¼ cup part-skim ricotta cheese, at room temperature

5 cups packed fresh baby spinach

1 tablespoon freshly grated Parmigiano-Reggiano or other Parmesan cheese

⅛ teaspoon dried hot pepper flakes (optional)

1. Heat the oil in a large nonstick skillet over medium heat. Add the onion, lemon juice, and ¼ teaspoon of the salt and cook, while stirring occasionally, until lightly caramelized, about 25 minutes. Add the garlic and sausage and sauté until the sausage is fully heated through, about 3 minutes.

2. Meanwhile, in a medium bowl, whisk together the eggs, almond milk, pepper, and the remaining ¼ teaspoon salt.

3. Pour the egg mixture onto the onion-sausage mixture and scramble until nearly done, about 2 minutes. Add the ricotta cheese and lemon zest and scramble for 1 minute more.

4. Add the spinach by the large handful and cook while stirring until fully wilted, about 3 minutes. Transfer to a platter or individual plates, sprinkle with the Parmigiano-Reggiano cheese and dried hot pepper flakes (if using), and serve.

Per serving: 200 calories, 11g total fat, 3.5g saturated fat, 0g trans fat, 210mg cholesterol, 590mg sodium, 12g total carbohydrate, 2g dietary fiber, 5g sugars, 14g protein

Irish-Inspired Breakfast Ⓕ

Makes 4 servings: ¼ breakfast each

Whenever I arrange a hearty, fresh, flavorful, and full breakfast like this, I dream of being in one of my favorite travel destinations, Ireland. There, beans, potatoes, sausage, and eggs are the morning norm. Except for the eggs, all of these recipes can be made in advance and simply reheated.

2 cups Black Forest–Shiitake Scramble, freshly prepared (page 18), or other egg preparation

2 cups Fresh Herb Hash Browns, warm (page 33), or other potato preparation

4 patties Anjou Chicken Breakfast Sausage, (page 35), or other sausage, warm

2 cups whole-grain corn grits or polenta or 4 squares Baked Polenta with Swiss Chard (page 493), warm

2 cups baked beans (preferably unsalted), warm

Arrange the ingredients on four individual plates, and serve.

Per serving: 470 calories, 12g total fat, 4g saturated fat, 0g trans fat, 220mg cholesterol, 710mg sodium, 65g total carbohydrate, 10g dietary fiber, 15g sugars, 25g protein

Truffled Egg Bruschetta

Makes 4 servings: 1 bruschetta each

Eating healthfully, even dieting, allows for indulgence; here it means simply including exotic flavors in your food. Instead of spending $100 for a bitty bite of fresh truffle, you can incorporate truffles in a price-friendly way with variations of foods that are already part of the ingredient list, as in this bruschetta-style recipe's sea salt and goat cheese. Cypress Grove's Chevre Truffle Tremor goat cheese is one of my favorites, but see what's available near you. This dish will impress.

4 medium asparagus spears, ends trimmed,

4 thick slices whole-grain bread, toasted, crusts trimmed or untrimmed

4 large eggs

2 tablespoons plain almond milk or light soy milk

¼ teaspoon truffle salt or sea salt, or to taste

¼ teaspoon freshly ground black pepper, or to taste

1½ teaspoons unsalted butter

1 ounce crumbled soft goat cheese with truffles or plain goat cheese, at room temperature

1. Preheat a panini grill or a grill pan on medium-high. Grill the asparagus spears until cooked through yet al dente (about 3 minutes in a panini grill or 6 minutes on a grill pan). Slice on the diagonal (¼ inch thick) and set aside.

2. Whisk together the eggs, almond milk, salt, and pepper in a small bowl.

3. Melt the butter in a large nonstick skillet over medium-low heat. Pour in the egg mixture and cook while scrambling until no longer runny, about 3 minutes. Turn off the heat and immediately stir in the cheese.

4. Spoon the egg mixture on top of each toast (about ⅓ cup each), sprinkle with the asparagus, adjust seasoning, and serve.

Per serving: 180 calories, 9g total fat, 3.5g saturated fat, 0g trans fat, 195mg cholesterol, 360mg sodium, 13g total carbohydrate, 2g dietary fiber, 2g sugars, 12g protein

Burrito el Desayuno Ⓕ

Makes 4 servings: 1 burrito each

Burritos are one of my favorite foods! Here you'll use aged, intensely flavored cheese—like dry Jack instead of Monterey Jack cheese—so a little provides a lot of flavor. Then roll everything into a tortilla that's perfectly sized to fit all the ingredients and savor the flavors.

4 large eggs

¼ cup fat-free or low-fat plain Greek yogurt

¼ teaspoon sea salt, or to taste

¼ teaspoon freshly ground white or black pepper, or to taste

¼ teaspoon adobo or Mexican seasoning (optional)

1½ teaspoons unrefined peanut or canola oil

2 scallions, green and white parts, thinly sliced

1 (15-ounce) can pinto beans, drained

½ cup Vine-Ripened Pico de Gallo (page 114) or other fresh chunky salsa, drained of excess liquid

4 (8-inch) whole-wheat tortillas

¼ cup shredded dry Jack cheese, at room temperature

½ Hass avocado, pitted, peeled, and diced

Juice and zest of ½ lime (1 tablespoon juice)

2 tablespoons chopped fresh cilantro

1. Whisk together the eggs, yogurt, salt, pepper, and adobo seasoning (if using) in a small bowl. Set aside.

2. Heat the oil in a medium nonstick skillet over medium heat. Add the white part of the scallions and sauté until the scallions begins to caramelize, about 2 minutes.

3. Add the beans, green part of the scallions, and egg mixture, and cook while scrambling until the eggs are no longer runny, about 4 minutes. Remove from heat and stir in the pico de gallo. Adjust seasoning.

4. Transfer the egg mixture to the tortillas, about ⅔ cup each. Sprinkle with the cheese, avocado, lime juice and zest, and cilantro. Tightly roll up each tortilla into a burrito (no need to fold in sides), secure closed with a toothpick, if necessary, and serve.

Per serving: 380 calories, 14g total fat, 3.5g saturated fat, 0g trans fat, 195mg cholesterol, 610mg sodium, 42g total carbohydrate, 9g dietary fiber, 4g sugars, 19g protein

Sunnyside-Up Pizza

Makes 4 servings: 1 pizza each

Pizza for breakfast? This voluptuous breakfast version, using English muffins for the "crust" and topped with a sunny side-up egg with two types of cheese, is my favorite version of pizza in the morning. It's 200 calories worth of pure pleasure. If you plan for it, two full servings can fit into a healthful breakfast, too!

2 whole-grain English muffins, split

¼ cup Bell Pepper Marinara (page 182) or other marinara sauce

¼ cup crumbled soft goat cheese or feta cheese

¼ cup shredded part-skim mozzarella cheese

1½ teaspoons extra-virgin olive oil

4 large eggs

⅛ teaspoon sea salt, or to taste

⅛ teaspoon freshly ground black pepper, or to taste

1 tablespoon thinly sliced fresh basil leaves

1. Arrange the muffin halves, cut side up, on a toaster oven baking tray. Spread halves with the marinara and top with 1 tablespoon each of the goat cheese and mozzarella. Bake in the toaster oven at 425°F until the muffin bottoms are lightly toasted and the cheese is bubbly and lightly browned, about 8 minutes.

2. Meanwhile, heat the oil in a large nonstick skillet over medium heat. Crack the eggs into the skillet and cook until the bottom of the eggs are firm, about 3 minutes. (Prepare in batches, if necessary.) Cover, and continue to cook until the eggs are lightly browned on the bottom and the egg yolks are desired firmness, about 3 minutes. Add the salt and pepper.

3. Top each muffin half with an egg, sprinkle with the basil, and serve.

Per serving: 200 calories, 10g total fat, 3.5g saturated fat, 0g trans fat, 195mg cholesterol, 460mg sodium, 15g total carbohydrate, 3g dietary fiber, 4g sugars, 12g protein

Eggs Tatsoi Florentine

Makes 6 servings: 1 topped muffin with 1 rounded tablespoon sauce each

Increasing your veggie intake can help you decrease your weight. But breakfast is usually the meal in which the fewest vegetables are eaten. You can change that by way of tatsoi—an Asian salad green. Or substitute it with Swiss chard or spinach, if you like, in this flavorful and surprisingly low-calorie version of Eggs Florentine. It's drizzled with a mouthwatering madeover Hollandaise sauce for the grand finale.

5 cups packed fresh baby spinach

4 cups packed tatsoi or other leafy green

¼ teaspoon sea salt, or to taste

⅛ teaspoon freshly grated nutmeg

3 whole-grain English muffins, split and toasted

6 large eggs, poached (right)

6 rounded tablespoons Silky Hollandaise-Style Sauce (page 134), warm

⅛ teaspoon smoked paprika or ground cayenne (optional)

1. Add the spinach and tatsoi to a large nonstick skillet over medium heat. Cover and steam until all greens are fully wilted, about 6 minutes, stirring occasionally. (Note: The greens will wilt down to about 1½ cups.) Add the salt and nutmeg.

2. Top each toasted muffin half with the greens, 1 poached egg, and 1 rounded tablespoon of the sauce. Sprinkle with the paprika (if using), and serve immediately.

Per serving: 170 calories, 6g total fat, 1.5g saturated fat, 0g trans fat, 185mg cholesterol, 510mg sodium, 19g total carbohydrate, 4g dietary fiber, 3g sugars, 11g protein

POACHING EGGS

Bring about 3 inches of water to boil over high heat in a large shallow sauté pan. Turn off the heat and add eggs at once by breaking eggs directly into the water. Immediately cover the pan with a tight-fitting lid. Allow the eggs to cook undisturbed until desired doneness, about 4 minutes. Remove the eggs with a perforated spatula or large slotted spoon. Further drain on paper towels, if desired.

Skillet Omelet Baja Ⓕ

Makes 4 servings: ¼ open-face omelet each

If you're an "egg-whites only" person, here's a taste-tempting recipe for your eating enjoyment. The fat-free evaporated milk adds creaminess sans cream. The serrano pepper and garlic provide plenty of pep for your palate. And the avocado and beans create bonus appeal and satisfaction.

1½ teaspoons extra-virgin olive oil

1 small garlic clove, minced

1 small serrano pepper with some seeds, minced

⅓ cup fat-free evaporated milk

½ teaspoon sea salt, or to taste

¼ teaspoon freshly ground white or black pepper, to taste

2 medium vine-ripened tomatoes, pulp removed and diced

1½ teaspoons unsalted butter

1 (15-ounce) can black beans or black soybeans, drained

12 large egg whites, lightly beaten, or 1½ cups pasteurized 100% egg whites

1 Hass avocado, pitted, peeled, and diced

1. Heat the oil in a small saucepan over medium heat. Add the garlic and serrano and sauté for 30 seconds. Add the milk, salt, and black pepper and bring to a simmer. Reduce heat to low and stir in the tomatoes.

2. Melt the butter in a large nonstick skillet over medium heat. Add the beans and sauté for 30 seconds. Pour in the egg whites and cook, scraping edges inward to let uncooked egg run underneath, until fully set, about 6 minutes.

3. Sprinkle the omelet with the avocado. Pour the tomato mixture on top and let cook for 1 minute more. Adjust seasoning.

4. Remove from the heat and serve directly from the skillet. Spoon into four bowls, and serve.

Per serving: 240 calories, 9g total fat, 2g saturated fat, 0g trans fat, 5mg cholesterol, 600mg sodium, 24g total carbohydrate, 7g dietary fiber, 8g sugars, 19g protein

Omelet O'Brien

Makes 4 servings: ¼ of 12-inch omelet with side of ⅓ cup potatoes each

For some Western-style flair, this veggie-stuffed omelet has a healthful dose of O'Brien-style potatoes inside. You'll get to enjoy them as a side dish here, too!

1 tablespoon unrefined peanut or canola oil

1 large white onion, finely diced

1 large russet potato, unpeeled, scrubbed, and cut into ⅓-inch cubes

1 large red bell pepper, cut into ⅓-inch pieces

1 large green bell pepper, cut into ⅓-inch pieces

1 small jalapeño pepper with some seeds, minced

2 teaspoons apple cider vinegar

2 teaspoons finely chopped fresh oregano

1 teaspoon finely chopped fresh thyme

¾ teaspoon sea salt, or to taste

4 large eggs

¼ cup fat-free or low-fat plain Greek yogurt

1½ teaspoons unsalted butter

½ cup shredded extra-sharp Cheddar cheese

¼ teaspoon freshly ground black pepper, or to taste

1. Heat the oil in a large nonstick skillet over medium heat. Add the onion, potato, bell peppers, jalapeño, and vinegar, stir to coat, cover, and cook until the potato is tender and onion is caramelized, about 15 minutes, stirring occasionally. Stir in 1 teaspoon of the oregano, the thyme, and ½ teaspoon of the salt. Transfer mixture to a bowl, cover, and set aside.

2. Meanwhile, whisk together the eggs, yogurt, and the remaining 1 teaspoon oregano and remaining ¼ teaspoon salt in a medium bowl.

3. Melt the butter in the large skillet over medium heat. Pour in the egg mixture. Tilt the pan slightly and use a silicone spatula to lift the edges of the omelet, allowing uncooked egg to run underneath. Cook until the omelet is nearly set, about

4 minutes. Sprinkle the entire surface of the omelet with the cheese and black pepper. Cover and turn off the heat. Let stand until the omelet is fully cooked and set, yet still moist, about 3 minutes. Shake the pan or use the spatula to gently loosen the omelet to ensure it's not sticking to the pan.

4. Top half of the omelet with about half of the potato mixture. Slide the omelet out of the pan onto a platter, while using the edge of the pan to help fold the unfilled side over the potato filling. Cut the omelet into four portions and serve immediately with the remaining potato mixture on the side.

Per serving: 290 calories, 15g total fat, 5g saturated fat, 0g trans fat, 205mg cholesterol, 620mg sodium, 26g total carbohydrate, 4g dietary fiber, 6g sugars, 14g protein

Punjabi Spinach Omelet

Makes 3 servings: ⅓ of 12-inch omelet each

The turmeric makes this omelet deliciously golden as if extra egg yolks are used. The yogurt provides a lovely, creamy texture and tang. And the spinach and chickpea mixture makes it unforgettable, with the distinctive flavors of India.

4 large eggs
¼ cup fat-free or low-fat plain Greek yogurt
¼ teaspoon sea salt, or to taste
¼ teaspoon ground turmeric
1½ teaspoons grapeseed or canola oil
¼ teaspoon freshly ground black pepper,
**   or to taste**
1 cup Punjabi Baby Spinach with Chickpeas
**   (page 452), warm, or other spinach**
**   preparation**

1. Whisk together the eggs, yogurt, salt, and turmeric in a medium bowl.

2. Heat the oil in a large nonstick skillet over medium heat. Pour in the egg mixture. Tilt the pan slightly and use a silicone spatula to lift the edges of the omelet, allowing uncooked egg to run underneath. Cook until the omelet is nearly set, about 4 minutes. Cover and turn off the heat. Let "lid cook" (see page xxviii) until the omelet is fully cooked and set, yet still moist, about 3 minutes. Shake the pan or use the spatula to gently loosen the omelet to assure it's not sticking to the pan. Sprinkle with the pepper.

3. Top half of the omelet with the spinach mixture. Slide the omelet out of the pan onto a platter, while using the edge of the pan to help fold the unfilled side over the vegetable filling. Cut the omelet into three portions, adjust seasoning, and serve immediately.

Per serving: 160 calories, 8g total fat, 2g saturated fat, 0g trans fat, 250mg cholesterol, 490mg sodium, 11g total carbohydrate, 3g dietary fiber, 3g sugars, 12g protein

Egg Strata Florentine

Makes 10 servings: 2½ × 4½-inch portion each

It's utterly surprisingly how low in calories this strata is yet how rich it tastes. The spices and Dijon mustard punch up the flavors. But the trio of high-flavored cheeses is what truly makes this dish burst out as a cuisine idol. Amazingly tasty!

1½ teaspoons unsalted butter

2 medium white onions, finely chopped

Juice of 1 small lemon (2 tablespoons)

1¼ teaspoons sea salt, or to taste

1 large garlic clove, minced

½ teaspoon freshly ground black pepper, or to taste

¼ teaspoon freshly grated nutmeg

¼ teaspoon dried hot pepper flakes

10 ounces fresh baby spinach

9 ounces whole-grain bread, cut into 1-inch cubes

1 cup shredded Appenzeller, Gruyère,
    or other aged Swiss cheese

4 ounces crumbled soft goat cheese or feta cheese

½ cup shredded Parmigiano-Reggiano
    or other Parmesan cheese

6 large eggs

2½ cups plain almond milk or light soy milk

1½ teaspoons Dijon mustard

1. Melt the butter in a large skillet over medium heat. Add the onions, 1 tablespoon of the lemon juice, and ¼ teaspoon of the salt, cover, and cook until the onions begin to caramelize, about 12 minutes, stirring occasionally. Uncover, add the garlic, ½ teaspoon of the salt, the black pepper, nutmeg, and hot pepper flakes and sauté for 1 minute. Add the spinach in batches and sauté until all the spinach is fully wilted. Set aside.

2. Lightly coat a 9 × 13-inch baking dish with cooking spray (preferably homemade, page xix). Spread half of the bread cubes in the dish. Top with half of the spinach mixture and half of each of the cheeses. Repeat.

3. Whisk together the eggs, almond milk, mustard, remaining lemon juice, and the remaining ½ teaspoon salt in a medium bowl and pour evenly over the strata. Let stand for 30 minutes.

4. Preheat the oven to 400°F.

5. Bake the strata, uncovered, until cooked through and golden brown, about 35 to 40 minutes. Remove from oven and let stand 10 minutes to complete the cooking process.

6. Cut into 10 rectangular portions, and serve.

Per serving: 260 calories, 13g total fat, 6g saturated fat, 0g trans fat, 135mg cholesterol, 720mg sodium, 19g total carbohydrate, 4g dietary fiber, 5g sugars, 16g protein

Broccoli Bocconcini Strata

Makes 10 servings: 2½ × 4½-inch portion each

This recipe celebrates my admiration for broccoli—and it's a wonderful comfort food that's light on calories. Bocconcini are small fresh mozzarella balls that, along with Romano, offer a great pop of cheesy flavor to this delightful dish. It's a win-win combination, even if you're not broccoli obsessed like me.

1½ teaspoons unsalted butter

2 medium white onions, finely chopped

4 cups chopped broccoli florets and tender stems

2 teaspoons white balsamic vinegar

1¼ teaspoons sea salt, or to taste

½ teaspoon freshly ground black pepper,
    or to taste

¼ teaspoon freshly grated nutmeg

¼ teaspoon dried hot pepper flakes

9 ounces whole-grain bread, cut into 1-inch cubes

8 ounces unsalted bocconcini, sliced,
    or fresh mozzarella, cubed

½ cup grated Pecorino Romano or other
    Romano cheese

6 large organic eggs

2½ cups plain almond milk or light soy milk

1½ teaspoons Dijon mustard

1. Melt the butter in a large skillet over medium heat. Add the onions, broccoli, vinegar, and ¼ teaspoon of the salt, cover, and cook until the onions are fully softened and broccoli is al dente, about 15 minutes, stirring occasionally. Uncover, add ½ teaspoon of the remaining salt, the pepper, nutmeg, and hot pepper flakes and sauté for 1 minute. Set aside.

2. Lightly coat a 9 × 13-inch baking dish with cooking spray (preferably homemade, page xix). Spread half of the bread cubes in the dish. Top with half of the broccoli mixture and half of each of the cheeses. Repeat.

3. Whisk together the eggs, almond milk, mustard, and remaining ½ teaspoon salt in a medium bowl and pour evenly over the strata. Let stand for 30 minutes.

4. Preheat the oven to 400°F.

5. Bake the strata, uncovered, until cooked through and golden brown, about 35 to 40 minutes. Remove from oven and let stand 10 minutes to complete the cooking process.

6. Cut into 10 rectangular portions, and serve.

Per serving: 240 calories, 11g total fat, 5g saturated fat, 0g trans fat, 130mg cholesterol, 580mg sodium, 18g total carbohydrate, 3g dietary fiber, 5g sugars, 17g protein

Roasted Vegetable Strata

Makes 10 servings: 2½ × 4½-inch portion each

The rich root vegetables add so much heartiness to this comforting strata. And the mixture of aged Gouda and tangy goat cheese adds just the right amount of sharpness and creaminess. Serve for brunch or any other time of day.

1½ teaspoons unsalted butter

2 medium white onions, finely chopped

3 medium Yukon Gold potatoes, unpeeled, scrubbed, and cut into ½-inch cubes (about 3 cups)

1 medium sweet potato, unpeeled, scrubbed, and cut into ½-inch cubes (about 1 cup)

2 teaspoons apple cider vinegar

1¼ teaspoons sea salt, or to taste

1½ teaspoons finely chopped fresh rosemary

½ teaspoon freshly ground black pepper, or to taste

9 ounces whole-grain bread, cut into 1-inch cubes

1 cup shredded extra-aged Gouda or aged goat cheese

4 ounces crumbled soft goat cheese

6 large eggs

2½ cups plain almond milk or light soy milk

1½ teaspoons Dijon mustard

1. Melt the butter in a large skillet over medium heat. Add the onions, potatoes, sweet potatoes, vinegar, and ¼ teaspoon of the salt, cover, and cook until the onions are softened and root vegetables are firm yet tender, about 20 minutes, stirring occasionally. Uncover and add the rosemary, ½ teaspoon of the remaining salt, and the pepper and sauté for 1 minute. Set aside.

2. Lightly coat a 9 × 13-inch baking dish with cooking spray (preferably homemade, page xix). Spread half of the bread cubes in the dish. Top with half of the vegetable mixture and half of each of the cheeses. Repeat.

3. Whisk together the eggs, almond milk, mustard, and the remaining ½ teaspoon salt in a medium bowl and pour evenly over the strata. Let stand for 30 minutes.

4. Preheat the oven to 400°F.

5. Bake the strata, uncovered, until cooked through and golden brown, about 40 minutes. Remove from oven and let stand 10 minutes to complete the cooking process.

6. Cut into 10 rectangular portions, and serve.

Per serving: 260 calories, 11g total fat, 5g saturated fat, 0g trans fat, 130mg cholesterol, 640mg sodium, 26g total carbohydrate, 4g dietary fiber, 6g sugars, 14g protein

Goat Cheese, Onion, and Fingerling Frittata

Makes 4 servings: 1 wedge of frittata

A frittata is an Italian-style omelet with ingredients mixed together instead of stuffed inside. It's actually easier to make than a typical omelet. The caramelization of the fingerling potatoes, along with the prominent truffle flavor from the goat cheese and touch of oil, will amaze you.

4 large eggs

¼ cup fat-free or low-fat plain Greek yogurt

2 teaspoons finely chopped fresh sage

¾ teaspoon sea salt, or to taste

¼ teaspoon ground turmeric

1½ teaspoons white truffle oil

1 medium red onion, halved, thinly sliced

8 ounces fingerling potatoes, unpeeled, scrubbed, and cut into ¼-inch slices

¼ cup low-sodium vegetable broth or Vegetable Stock (page 103)

2 teaspoons white balsamic vinegar

1 garlic clove, minced

3 ounces crumbled goat cheese with truffles or soft goat cheese

1. Whisk together the eggs, yogurt, sage, ½ teaspoon of the salt, and the turmeric in a medium bowl until combined. Set aside.

2. Heat the oil in a large nonstick skillet over medium-high heat. Add the onion, potatoes, broth, vinegar, and remaining ¼ teaspoon salt, cover, and cook until the onion is fully softened and the potatoes are just tender and lightly caramelized, about 12 minutes, stirring occasionally. Reduce heat to medium. Add the garlic and sauté for 1 minute.

3. Spread the potato mixture evenly in the pan. Sprinkle with the cheese. Pour the egg mixture over the cheese and potato mixture. Shake the pan slightly to allow the egg mixture to fully settle. Cook until the eggs are fully set around the edges, about 5 minutes. (Note: Halfway through the cooking process, tilt the pan and let any uncooked egg on top run to the underside of the frittata.)

4. Cover and remove from heat. Let stand covered until the eggs are completely set, about 3 minutes. Adjust seasoning.

5. Slide the frittata onto a plate, place another plate on top, then invert so the caramelized side is up. Slice into four wedges and serve.

Per serving: 210 calories, 11g total fat, 5g saturated fat, 0g trans fat, 195mg cholesterol, 610mg sodium, 13g total carbohydrate, 2g dietary fiber, 3g sugars, 13g protein

Crustless Asparagus "Quiche"

Makes 8 servings: 1 wedge each (⅛ of 9-inch round)

Who needs crust? Fortunately this nontraditional version of quiche tastes rich without the traditional cream and pastry shell. It's the pungent cheese bubbling on top that makes this aromatic dish deceivingly decadent.

1½ teaspoons grapeseed or canola oil

1 large white onion, diced

Juice of ½ small lemon (1 tablespoon)

1 teaspoon sea salt, or to taste

7 large eggs

⅓ cup fat-free or low-fat plain Greek yogurt

¼ cup plain dry whole-wheat breadcrumbs

3 tablespoons plain almond milk or light soy milk

1 teaspoon finely chopped fresh tarragon

¼ teaspoon freshly ground black pepper, or to taste

1 pound asparagus spears, ends trimmed and cut into ¼-inch slices

¼ cup diced or crumbled Robiola, Taleggio, or other soft, ripened cow's milk cheese

¼ cup diced or crumbled smoked Gouda cheese

1. Heat the oil in a large skillet over medium-high heat. Add the onion, lemon juice, and ¼ teaspoon of the salt, and sauté until softened and lightly caramelized, about 8 minutes. Set aside.

2. Preheat the oven to 400°F. Lightly coat a 9-inch deep-sided pie pan with cooking spray (preferably homemade, page xix).

3. Whisk together the eggs, yogurt, breadcrumbs, almond milk, tarragon, pepper, and remaining ¾ teaspoon salt. Set aside.

4. Layer the asparagus and then the onion into the pan. Ladle the egg mixture evenly over the onion. Sprinkle with the cheeses.

5. Bake until the eggs are set and cheese is golden brown, about 25 minutes. Let stand for 10 minutes to complete the cooking process. Slice and serve.

Per serving: 160 calories, 10g total fat, 4g saturated fat, 0g trans fat, 180mg cholesterol, 470mg sodium, 6g total carbohydrate, 1g dietary fiber, 2g sugars, 11g protein

Spanish Manchego "Quiche"

Makes 8 servings: 1 wedge each (⅛ of 9-inch round)

This inspired take on quiche will not disappoint. It's filled with full-flavored, vibrant-colored, aromatic ingredients that are sure to be a hit with any expectant palate.

1½ teaspoons extra-virgin olive oil

2 large shallots, finely chopped

1 teaspoon sea salt, or to taste

1 packed cup very thinly sliced radicchio

1 large garlic clove, minced

1 large freshly roasted red bell pepper (right), chopped

1½ teaspoons aged red wine vinegar

7 large eggs

¼ cup fat-free or low-fat plain Greek yogurt

¼ cup dry plain whole-wheat breadcrumbs

3 tablespoons plain almond milk or light soy milk

1 teaspoon finely chopped fresh oregano

½ teaspoon freshly ground black pepper, or to taste

⅓ cup shredded aged Manchego or mildly stinky sheep's milk cheese

3 large pitted Spanish olives, thinly sliced (optional)

1. Heat the oil in a large skillet over medium heat. Add the shallots and ¼ teaspoon of the salt and sauté until softened, about 3 minutes. Add the radicchio and garlic and sauté until the radicchio is softened, about 2 minutes. Stir in the bell pepper and vinegar, and sauté for 1 minute. Set aside.

2. Preheat the oven to 400°F. Lightly coat a 9-inch deep-sided pie pan with cooking spray (preferably homemade, page xix).

3. Whisk together the eggs, yogurt, breadcrumbs, almond milk, oregano, black pepper, and the remaining ¾ teaspoon salt in a medium bowl.

4. Evenly spread the radicchio mixture into the pan. Ladle the egg mixture evenly over the radicchio mixture. Sprinkle with the cheese and the olives (if using).

5. Bake until the eggs are set and cheese is golden brown, about 25 minutes. Let stand for 10 minutes to complete the cooking process, and serve.

Per serving: 140 calories, 9g total fat, 3.5g saturated fat, 0g trans fat, 175mg cholesterol, 450mg sodium, 5g total carbohydrate, 1g dietary fiber, 2g sugars, 10g protein

FRESHLY ROASTED BELL PEPPER

Stand the pepper and cut down each side, creating 4 large, wide pieces. Slice off the bottom of the pepper, creating another piece. Discard the stem and seeds. Line a baking sheet with aluminum foil and arrange the pepper slices in a single layer, skin side up. Broil about 3 inches from the heat source, until the skins are well charred. (Alternatively, carefully char the whole pepper over an open flame, such as a gas burner flame.) Transfer the well-charred pepper to a bowl, cover, and let stand to complete the cooking process, about 10 minutes. Rub off all or most of the charred skin. (Use this recipe for sweet bell peppers or poblano peppers.)

Potato Hash
with Poached Egg

Makes 5 servings: 1 rounded cup hash and 1 egg each

Use a dramatic mixture of red, white, and blue potatoes to make this the main attraction. The poached egg creates a culinary focal point. But the surprise twist to this dish is the sun-dried tomato, adding a salty, smoky quality, only more intriguing.

1½ teaspoons hot chili oil or unrefined peanut oil

24 ounces baby creamer potatoes, unpeeled, scrubbed, and cut into ¼-inch slices

2 medium white onions, finely diced

2 teaspoons apple cider vinegar

¾ teaspoon sea salt, or to taste

¼ teaspoon freshly ground black pepper, or to taste

¼ cup plain almond milk or light soy milk

1 large garlic clove, minced

8 sun-dried tomatoes, very thinly sliced

1 teaspoon finely chopped fresh rosemary

⅓ cup roughly chopped fresh flat-leaf parsley

5 large eggs, poached (page 21)

1. Heat the oil in a large nonstick skillet over medium-high heat. Add the potatoes, onions, vinegar, salt, and pepper, cover, and cook until the onions are fully softened, about 15 minutes, stirring occasionally. Uncover, increase heat to medium-high, add the almond milk, and sauté until the potatoes and onions are caramelized and the potatoes are fully cooked, about 8 minutes. Add the garlic, sun-dried tomatoes, and rosemary and sauté for 1 minute. Remove from heat and stir in half of the parsley.

2. Transfer the hash to a platter or individual plates, top with the eggs, and adjust seasoning. Sprinkle with the remaining parsley, and serve.

Per serving: 210 calories, 7g total fat, 2g saturated fat, 0g trans fat, 185mg cholesterol, 510mg sodium, 29g total carbohydrate, 3g dietary fiber, 5g sugars, 10g protein

Sausage Hash
with Quail Eggs Ⓕ

Makes 4 servings: 1 cup with 2 eggs each

Here, hash is given a first-class healthful upgrade partly by using the skillet lid to trap in moist heat during the beginning stages of cooking, to ultimately require less overall oil—cutting excess calories. Plus, the poultry sausage, sweet potatoes, and leafy greens add dramatic culinary flair while still being calorie conscious.

1½ teaspoons extra-virgin olive oil

1 large (12-ounce) sweet potato, unpeeled, scrubbed, and cut into ¼-inch dice, or 12 ounces fingerling sweet potatoes, unpeeled, scrubbed, and cut into ¼-inch coins

1 large red onion, diced

4 teaspoons white balsamic vinegar

¾ teaspoon sea salt, or to taste

½ teaspoon freshly ground black pepper, or to taste

8 patties Anjou Chicken Breakfast Sausage (page 135)

2 cups packed tatsoi, mâche, or baby spinach

8 quail eggs or 4 medium eggs

1 teaspoon finely chopped fresh rosemary

1. Heat the oil in large nonstick skillet over medium heat. Add the sweet potato, onion, 2 teaspoons of the vinegar, and ¼ teaspoon each of the salt and pepper, cover, and cook for 10 minutes. Stir the potato mixture and add the sausage, cover, and cook until the sweet potato is tender and onion is lightly caramelized, about 5 minutes. Uncover and sauté until the onion and sweet potato are fully caramelized, about 5 minutes. Top with the tatsoi, remaining 2 teaspoons vinegar, and ¼ teaspoon of the remaining salt, cover, and set aside until the tatsoi is wilted, about 3 minutes.

2. Meanwhile, break each egg into a separate small dish or cup. Fill a large, deep skillet with 2 inches of water and bring to a boil over high heat. Remove from the heat and add eggs to the water. Cover, and poach until the eggs whites turn opaque, about 2 minutes. Gently remove the eggs from the saucepan with a slotted spoon.

3. Divide the hash among individual plates, and top with the eggs. Sprinkle with rosemary and the remaining ¼ teaspoon salt and ¼ teaspoon pepper, and serve from the skillet.

Per serving: 200 calories, 6g total fat, 1.5g saturated fat, 0g trans fat, 190mg cholesterol, 720mg sodium, 25g total carbohydrate, 5g dietary fiber, 6g sugars, 12g protein

Bean and Herb Eggs Tostada Ⓕ

Makes 4 servings: 1 topped tortilla each

If you need to impress anyone, this flavor-popping tostada takes the cake for presentation. All of the enticing ingredients—eggs, black beans, salsa, and avocado—are stacked high atop a crisp corn tortilla. What's more, the finishing cumin-lime yogurt sauce will make converts out of sour cream devotees.

½ cup fat-free or low-fat plain Greek yogurt

½ teaspoon fresh lime zest

¼ teaspoon ground cumin

4 (6-inch) soft corn tortillas

4 large eggs

2 tablespoon finely chopped fresh cilantro

1 teaspoon finely chopped fresh oregano

½ teaspoon sea salt, or to taste

¼ teaspoon freshly ground black pepper,
   or to taste

1½ teaspoons unrefined peanut or canola oil

1 (15-ounce) can black beans, drained and well rinsed

¼ cup shredded dry Jack cheese, at room temperature

½ cup Vine-Ripened Pico de Gallo (page 114)
   or ¼ cup other salsa

½ Hass avocado, pitted, peeled, and diced

1. Preheat the oven to 475°F. Mix together ¼ cup of the yogurt, the zest, and cumin until well combined. Set aside.

2. Lightly coat both sides of the tortillas with cooking spray (preferably homemade, page xix). Place on a baking sheet and bake until crisp and lightly browned, about 4 minutes per side. Remove from oven and let cool on pan.

3. Whisk together the eggs, remaining ¼ cup yogurt, 1 tablespoon of the cilantro, the oregano, salt, and pepper in a small bowl.

4. Heat the oil in a large nonstick skillet over medium heat. Add the beans and egg mixture and scramble until the eggs are no longer runny, about 4 minutes. Remove from heat and immediately stir in the cheese. Adjust seasoning.

5. Spoon the egg mixture (about ½ rounded cup) on top of each crisp tortilla. Top each with the pico de gallo, avocado, reserved yogurt mixture, and remaining 1 tablespoon cilantro. Serve with lime wedges on the side, if desired, and enjoy immediately.

Per serving: 300 calories, 13g total fat, 4g saturated fat, 0g trans fat, 190mg cholesterol, 450mg sodium, 29g total carbohydrate, 7g dietary fiber, 5g sugars, 17g protein

Robiola Egg Muffin Ⓕ

Makes 4 servings: 1 muffin each

Looking for a sophisticated sandwich that you can serve at sunrise? This farm-fresh egg muffin will bring glory to any morning. The little bit of Robiola, a strong-tasting cheese, provides a lot of flavor. And the pairing with lemony dressed peppery greens makes it scrumptious.

4 whole-grain English muffins, split

3 ounces Robiola or creamy, mildly pungent
      cheese, thinly sliced, at room temperature

1½ cups packed baby arugula

2 teaspoons fresh lemon juice

1½ teaspoons unsalted butter

4 large eggs

¼ teaspoon freshly ground black pepper,
      or to taste

⅛ teaspoon sea salt, or to taste

1. Toast the English muffins. Immediately top all of the halves with the cheese. Set aside.

2. Toss the arugula with the lemon juice in a small bowl. Set aside.

3. Melt the butter in a large nonstick skillet over medium heat. Break the eggs into the skillet, add the pepper and salt, and cook until the undersides of the eggs are firm, about 3 minutes. Gently flip the eggs over and cook until the whites are firm and the yolks are still soft, about 1 minute.

4. Place one egg on top of the bottom portion of each English muffin half. Top with the arugula. Place top portion of each muffin half onto the arugula, and serve.

Per serving: 300 calories, 14g total fat, 6g saturated fat, 0g trans fat, 210mg cholesterol, 710mg sodium, 28g total carbohydrate, 5g dietary fiber, 6g sugars, 17g protein

Soft-Boiled Egg and Soldiers

Makes 1 serving: 1 egg and 5 toast pieces

"Soldiers" are toast pieces—which you can line up like soldiers. To keep them body-friendly, you'll be spreading them with a calorie-friendlier mixture of ricotta and butter, rather than straight butter. The tarragon provides memorable flavor flair. To enjoy, just dip into the egg and savor this British-inspired bite.

2 teaspoons part-skim ricotta cheese,
      at room temperature

½ teaspoon unsalted butter, at room temperature

¼ teaspoon finely chopped fresh tarragon

1 large egg

1 slice whole-grain bread

Pinch of sea salt

1. Mix together the cheese, butter, and half of the tarragon. Set aside.

2. Place the egg into a small saucepan. Cover with cold water, about ½ inch above the egg. Place over high heat and bring just to a boil. Cover, remove from heat, and let stand for 4 minutes.

3. Meanwhile, toast the bread until fully crisp. Immediately spread with the cheese mixture and cut into 5 strips.

4. Place the soft-cooked egg into an egg cup. Immediately slice off the top with an egg cutter or knife. Sprinkle with remaining tarragon.

5. Sprinkle the egg and toast with the salt and serve the egg with the toast strips (soldiers) on the side for dipping.

Per serving: 170 calories, 9g total fat, 3.5g saturated fat, 0g trans fat, 195mg cholesterol, 340mg sodium, 12g total carbohydrate, 2g dietary fiber, 2g sugars, 11g protein

Sunnyside-Up Jambalaya Ⓕ

Makes 4 servings: 1⅓ cups jambalaya and 1 egg each

I was enjoying jambalaya one evening and decided to continue enjoying it for my Sunday brunch—which inspired this tasty recipe. It has everything you'll desire for morning-time jambalaya—with breakfast links, Creole rice, and colorful veggies topped with an egg. Plus, it's made in a pressure cooker to save time.

1½ tablespoons grapeseed or canola oil

2 scallions, green and white parts, thinly sliced

1 large red bell pepper, thinly sliced into
    2- to 3-inch strips

1 large green bell pepper, thinly sliced into
    2- to 3-inch strips

6 frozen vegetarian breakfast "sausages," partially
    thawed, cut into ⅓-inch slices on the diagonal

2 cups long-grain brown rice

1 teaspoon Creole seasoning (page 31), or to taste

½ teaspoon sea salt, or to taste

⅓ cup chopped fresh flat-leaf parsley

4 large eggs

1. Stir the oil, scallions, peppers, and "sausage" in a pressure cooker without the lid over high heat for 1 minute.

2. Stir in 4 cups water, the brown rice, Creole seasoning, and ¼ teaspoon of the salt. Close the pressure cooker lid and turn to the high pressure setting. Once the pressure cooker hisses, adjust the heat as necessary to maintain high pressure with gentle hissing, and cook for 18 minutes, or until the rice is fully cooked. Turn off the heat and gradually release the pressure cooker lid. Let stand covered about 5 minutes before serving. Stir three-fourths of the parsley into the jambalaya.

3. Meanwhile, break the eggs onto a large non-stick skillet or griddle over medium heat and cook until the whites are firm and the yolks begin to firm, about 1 minute, or to desired doneness.

4. Spoon the jambalaya onto a platter or four individual plates. Top with the eggs, sprinkle with the remaining ¼ teaspoon salt and remaining parsley, and serve.

Per serving: 300 calories, 13g total fat, 2.5g saturated fat, 0g trans fat, 185mg cholesterol, 690mg sodium, 32g total carbohydrate, 5g dietary fiber, 5g sugars, 16g protein

MAKE YOUR OWN CREOLE SEASONING

Mix together 1 tablespoon each sweet paprika, garlic powder, onion powder, cayenne pepper, dried oregano, dried thyme, sea salt, and freshly ground black pepper. Store in a sealed and labeled jar. Makes ½ cup. (Although Creole and Cajun food are not identical, this can also be used when a recipe calls for Cajun seasoning.)

"Green" Eggs and Ham

Makes 4 servings: ½ cup eggs and 1½-ounce ham slice each

Dr. Seuss made this famous but I've brought it into the modern era—in the culinary sense. The generous aromatic herb mixture provides the fresh green hue. And if you use organic eggs and ham, these delightful ingredients provide another kind of "greenness."

1 large garlic clove, chopped

½ cup loosely packed fresh basil leaves

¼ cup loosely packed fresh flat-leaf parsley leaves

⅛ cup loosely packed fresh tarragon leaves

4 large eggs

3 tablespoons part-skim ricotta cheese

2 tablespoons plain almond or light soy milk

2 teaspoons fresh lemon juice

½ teaspoon sea salt, or to taste

¼ teaspoon freshly ground black pepper, or to taste

2 (3-ounce) extra-thick slices deli baked ham,
    cut in half

1½ teaspoons unsalted butter

1. Add the garlic, basil, parsley, tarragon, eggs, cheese, almond milk, lemon juice, salt, and pepper to a blender. Cover and blend on low speed until the egg mixture is smooth. Set aside.

2. Heat a grill pan or panini grill over medium-high heat. Add the ham and cook until grill marks form, about 2 minutes per side in a grill pan (or 2 minutes total in a panini grill). Remove from heat and cover to keep warm.

3. Melt the butter in a large nonstick skillet over medium heat. Pour in the egg mixture and cook while scrambling until the eggs are no longer runny, about 5 minutes. Adjust seasoning.

4. Serve the eggs aside or on top of the ham. If desired, garnish with additional fresh basil, parsley, or tarragon.

Per serving: 150 calories, 9g total fat, 4g saturated fat, 0g trans fat, 210mg cholesterol, 750mg sodium, 4g total carbohydrate, 0g dietary fiber, 1g sugars, 16g protein

Vegetables and Fruits

Cheesy Grits

Makes 7 servings: ½ cup each

I think of grits like a comforting breakfast version of mashed potatoes. This recipe has just a hint of butter, not a stick! It uses two cheeses—ricotta for creaminess and an extra-sharp cheese for high flavor in a petite amount. The almond milk keeps it light while letting the full sweet and savory corn flavor shine through. And the microgreens add a nice fragrant herbal finish.

1¼ cups plain almond milk or light soy milk

¾ teaspoon sea salt, or to taste

1 cup stone-ground yellow corn grits (not polenta)

¼ cup part-skim ricotta cheese, at room
    temperature

1 teaspoon unsalted butter, at room temperature

¼ cup finely shredded extra-sharp Cheddar cheese

¼ cup loosely packed microgreens or 2 tablespoons
    minced fresh chives

1. Bring 2 cups water, the almond milk, and salt to a boil in a large saucepan over high heat. Slowly stir in the grits until thoroughly combined, and return to a boil. Reduce heat to low, and cook while stirring until thickened, about 4 minutes. Remove from heat.

2. Stir in the ricotta cheese and butter. Adjust seasoning.

3. Transfer the grits to individual bowls, sprinkle with the Cheddar cheese and microgreens, and serve immediately.

Per serving: 130 calories, 3.5g total fat, 1.5g saturated fat, 0g trans fat, 10mg cholesterol, 320mg sodium, 21g total carbohydrate, 1g dietary fiber, 1g sugars, 4g protein

Fresh Herb Hash Browns

Makes 4 servings: 1 cup each

Changing something as simple as the color of an ingredient can refresh even a classic dish. The purple color of these hash browns will dazzle. Leaving the peel on the potatoes boosts flavor, texture, nutrients, and color contrast. And the trio of aromatic herbs creates fresh appeal along with more eye-appealing delight. It's a winning side dish for the senses.

2 teaspoons unsalted butter

1 tablespoon extra-virgin olive oil

1½ pounds baby purple or red creamer potatoes, unpeeled, scrubbed, halved and thinly sliced

3 large shallots, chopped

1 serrano pepper with some seeds, minced

2 teaspoons apple cider vinegar

¾ teaspoon sea salt, or to taste

2 scallions, green and white parts, minced

2 large garlic cloves, minced

1 teaspoon finely chopped fresh mint

1 teaspoon finely chopped fresh rosemary

¼ cup chopped fresh flat-leaf parsley

1. Melt the butter with the oil in a large nonstick skillet over medium-high heat. Add the potatoes, shallots, serrano, vinegar, and ¼ teaspoon of the salt. Stir to combine. Cover and cook until the shallots are softened, about 8 minutes, stirring once halfway through the cooking.

2. Remove the lid and sauté until the potatoes are cooked through yet al dente and lightly browned, about 4 minutes. Add the scallions, garlic, mint, rosemary, and the remaining ½ teaspoon salt and sauté for 1 minute.

3. Turn off the heat, cover, and let stand until the potatoes are tender, about 5 minutes.

4. Stir in the parsley, adjust seasoning, and serve immediately.

Per serving: 200 calories, 6g total fat, 2g saturated fat, 0g trans fat, 5mg cholesterol, 450mg sodium, 34g total carbohydrate, 3g dietary fiber, 3g sugars, 4g protein

Cinnamon Apple Compote Ⓢ

Makes 10 servings: ¼ cup each

This is my take on an apple side dish for breakfast. The fruity sweet-spiced cubes are quite versatile, too. Serve warm or cool as a breakfast side dish or topped with a scoop of low-fat frozen yogurt. Or enjoy in Caramelized Apple Cinnamon Crepes (page 12) for a wow-worthy entrée.

4 medium Empire or other crisp apples, cored, quartered, and cut into 1-inch chunks

Juice and zest of 1 small lemon (2 tablespoons juice)

2 tablespoons 80-proof brandy

½ teaspoon ground ginger

½ teaspoon ground cinnamon

¼ teaspoon ground allspice (optional)

¼ teaspoon pure vanilla extract

⅛ teaspoon sea salt, or to taste

1½ teaspoons unsalted butter

1. Toss together the apples, lemon juice and zest, brandy, ginger, cinnamon, allspice (if using), vanilla extract, and salt in a medium bowl.

2. Melt the butter in a large nonstick skillet over medium heat. Add the apple mixture and sauté until the apples are softened and fully caramelized, about 25 minutes.

3. Remove the apple mixture from the heat, let cool slightly, and serve.

Per serving: 60 calories, 0.5g total fat, 0g saturated fat, 0g trans fat, 0mg cholesterol, 30mg sodium, 13g total carbohydrate, 2g dietary fiber, 9g sugars, 0g protein

Berry-Peach Compote

Makes 10 servings: ¼ cup each

Try this quick-cooking version of compote that's ideal when berries and peaches are at their peak in late spring and summer. Its seasonally vibrant colors and naturally sweet flavors will dazzle. Delicious served warm or cool, as a pancake topping, as a dessert, or just as is at breakfast time.

3 large or 4 medium peaches, pitted and cut into
    ½-inch chunks
Juice and zest of 1 small lemon (2 tablespoons
    juice)
2 tablespoons 80-proof brandy
¼ teaspoon ground ginger
¼ teaspoon sea salt, or to taste
1½ teaspoons unsalted butter
½ cup fresh blueberries
½ cup finely diced fresh strawberries

1. Toss together the peaches, lemon juice, brandy, ginger, and salt in a medium bowl.

2. Melt the butter in a large nonstick skillet over medium heat. Add the peach mixture and gently sauté until fully heated, about 5 minutes. Stir in the blueberries and strawberries and sauté for 1 minute, being careful not to smash the fruit.

3. Remove the fruit mixture from the heat, let cool slightly, stir in desired amount of the lemon zest, and serve.

Per serving: 45 calories, 1g total fat, 0g saturated fat, 0g trans fat, 0mg cholesterol, 60mg sodium, 8g total carbohydrate, 1g dietary fiber, 6g sugars, 1g protein

Other Breakfast and Brunch Dishes

Grecian Yogurt Sundae

Makes 1 serving: 1 sundae each

This marvelously simple breakfast will be sure to delight. Do try the orange extract and rosemary salt additions; they're truly transforming. They provide an intriguing blend of fruity and salty elements to the nutty, sweet, tangy components of the rest of the sundae.

1 cup fat-free or low-fat plain Greek yogurt,
    well chilled
⅛ teaspoon pure orange extract or pinch of
    orange zest (optional)
2 tablespoons sliced natural almonds, toasted,
    or chopped unsalted dry-roasted pistachios
1 tablespoon honey or agave nectar
⅛ teaspoon rosemary sea salt (optional)

1. Stir together the yogurt and the orange extract (if using). Transfer to a chilled parfait or other dessert dish.

2. Sprinkle with the almonds, honey, and salt (if using), and enjoy.

Per serving: 250 calories, 6g total fat, 0g saturated fat, 0g trans fat, 0mg cholesterol, 85mg sodium, 29g total carbohydrate, 1g dietary fiber, 27g sugars, 23g protein

Buttermilk Biscuits and Gravy

Makes 10 servings: 1 biscuit with ¼ cup gravy each

If you've never baked homemade biscuits before, know that they're so much easier to make then you might realize. So give it a try. Smothered in gravy, this heartier whole-grain variety makes a luscious-tasting dish that's actually light in calories.

1 cup whole oat flour

⅔ cup + 3 tablespoons whole-wheat pastry flour

2 teaspoons baking powder

½ teaspoon sea salt

1½ teaspoons turbinado sugar

5 tablespoons unsalted butter, chilled and diced

½ cup low-fat buttermilk

¼ cup fat-free or low-fat plain Greek yogurt

2½ cups Sweet Italian Turkey Sausage Gravy (page 113) or Country Bean Gravy (page 112), heated

5 fresh sage leaves, thinly sliced

1. Preheat the oven to 400°F.

2. Sift together the oat flour, ⅔ cup of the whole-wheat pastry flour, the baking powder, and salt in a medium bowl. Stir in the sugar.

3. Cut in the butter using a pastry blender until crumbly.

4. Whisk together the buttermilk and yogurt in a liquid measuring cup and gradually add to the crumbly mixture, stirring until a soft dough forms. Turn out the dough onto a lightly floured surface, using only as much of the remaining 3 tablespoons whole-wheat pastry flour as needed.

5. Roll out the dough to about ¾-inch thickness. Cut with a 2½-inch floured biscuit cutter into 10 biscuits. Bake on a parchment paper–lined baking sheet until light golden brown and cooked through, about 22 to 25 minutes.

6. Cut or split the biscuits in half to form two rounds. Ladle the gravy (¼ cup each) over the biscuit halves, sprinkle with the sage, and serve.

Per serving: 150 calories, 8g total fat, 3.5g saturated fat, 0g trans fat, 20mg cholesterol, 330mg sodium, 14g total carbohydrate, 2g dietary fiber, 1g sugars, 5g protein

Anjou Chicken Breakfast Sausage

Makes 10 servings: 2 patties each

Some sausages can contain excess fat, salt, fillers, and preservatives. But not this one! It starts with lean poultry and is joined with fresh ingredients, including four types of herbs and Anjou pear. Enjoy these pretty patties anytime you want savory sausage.

12 ounces ground chicken breast

1 Anjou or other pear, cored and coarsely grated

⅔ cup old-fashioned oats

⅓ cup coarsely grated red onion

¼ cup chopped fresh flat-leaf parsley

1 tablespoon finely chopped fresh sage

1 teaspoon finely chopped fresh rosemary

1 teaspoon finely chopped fresh thyme

1 teaspoon freshly ground black pepper, or to taste

¾ teaspoon sea salt, or to taste

1 large egg, lightly beaten

1. Combine all the ingredients by hand in a large bowl. Portion the mixture into 20 loosely formed balls, about 2 tablespoons each.

2. Place a large nonstick skillet over medium heat. Add the sausage balls, in batches, to the skillet, flattening each to a 2½-inch diameter patty with a spatula or your fingers as you add each to the skillet. Cook, turning over once until well done and browned, about 3 minutes per side.

3. Remove cooked patties to plate and keep covered until all patties are done. Serve while warm.

Per serving: 80 calories, 1.5g total fat, 0g saturated fat, 0g trans fat, 35mg cholesterol, 200mg sodium, 7g total carbohydrate, 1g dietary fiber, 2g sugars, 8g protein

Note: Keep food safety in mind when handling raw poultry.

Breakfast Turkey Links

Makes 6 servings: 2 links each

Shiitake mushrooms—prized for their earthiness—add body, moistness, and even elegance to this savory morning treat. Plus they make the breakfast links seem meatier. If you're like me, you may never want to go back to those frozen sausage links in a box again.

1 pound ground turkey (about 94% lean)

½ cup finely chopped fresh shiitake mushroom caps or crimini (baby bella) mushrooms

⅓ cup dry whole-wheat breadcrumbs

2 tablespoons 100% unsweetened apple juice

1 teaspoon sea salt, or to taste

½ teaspoon freshly ground black pepper, or to taste

½ teaspoon ground sage

¼ teaspoon crushed dried thyme

⅛ teaspoon ground ginger

⅛ teaspoon ground allspice

1. Add all ingredients to a large bowl. Mix well by hand until well combined. Form into 12 (5-inch-long) links, about 3 tablespoons each. For best results, chill in the refrigerator at least 4 hours or overnight to allow flavors to blend; let stand about 30 minutes at room temperature before cooking.

2. Cook the sausage in two batches (6 links each) in a large nonstick skillet over medium heat until well browned on all sides and fully cooked, about 9 to 10 minutes per batch, and serve.

Per serving: 130 calories, 5g total fat, 1.5g saturated fat, 0g trans fat, 45mg cholesterol, 450mg sodium, 5g total carbohydrate, 1g dietary fiber, 1g sugars, 16g protein

Smoked Salmon on Pumpernickel

Makes 4 servings: 3 pieces each

These delights look like appetizers. But when you plate several finger foods together, they can be considered an entrée. That's exactly what these savory salmon bites are—which are pleasing to bite into at breakfast time and offer a balanced way to begin your day.

⅓ cup Neufchâtel cream cheese, at room temperature

3 tablespoons minced red onion

2 teaspoons tiny capers, well drained

2 teaspoons fresh lime juice

1 tablespoon chopped fresh dill, plus garnish

3 long slices European-style whole-grain pumpernickel bread, halved, then cut on the diagonal to make 12 triangular slices

2 ounces gravlax or Scottish smoked salmon, cut into 12 pieces

1. Stir together the Neufchâtel, onion, capers, lime juice, and dill in a small bowl until well combined. Dollop or spread about 2 teaspoons of the mixture evenly on each bread slice.

2. Top each slice with the salmon, garnish with additional fresh dill, if desired, and serve.

Per serving: 280 calories, 8g total fat, 3.5g saturated fat, 0g trans fat, 20mg cholesterol, 610mg sodium, 41g total carbohydrate, 3g dietary fiber, 5g sugars, 11g protein

Sunrise Vegan Burrito Ⓕ

Makes 4 servings: 1 burrito each

Even if you're not a tofu lover, you must try this breakfast-style burrito. The recipe provides one of the most succulent ways to start enjoying tofu, since its chameleon-like nature takes on all of the amazing flavors of the other ingredients with which it's prepared.

1½ teaspoons unrefined peanut or grapeseed oil

2 scallions, green and white parts, thinly sliced

1 medium zucchini, and finely diced

1 small jalapeño pepper with some seeds, minced

14 ounces extra-firm tofu, drained, gently
    squeezed dry, and diced or crumbled

¾ teaspoon sea salt, or to taste

½ teaspoon ground cumin

¼ teaspoon chili powder

¼ teaspoon freshly ground black pepper,
    or to taste

¾ cup grape tomatoes, halved lengthwise

1 tablespoon finely chopped fresh cilantro

½ cup Tomatillo-Avocado "Crème" Sauce
    (page 133) or guacamole of choice

4 (8-inch) whole-wheat flour tortillas

1. Heat the oil in a large nonstick skillet over medium-high heat. Add the scallions, zucchini, and jalapeño and sauté for 2 minutes. Add the tofu, salt, cumin, chili powder, and pepper and sauté until the zucchini is tender, about 6 minutes. Stir in the tomatoes and sauté until the tomatoes are hot, about 2 minutes. Remove from heat and stir in the cilantro. Adjust seasoning.

2. Spread half of the sauce over the entire surface of each tortilla (1 tablespoon each). Spoon the tofu mixture down the center of each tortilla (about 1 cup each). Tightly roll up the tortillas without tucking in the sides. Secure each with a toothpick, if necessary.

3. Arrange the burritos onto a platter or individual plates and dollop with remaining sauce (1 tablespoon each). Garnish with additional fresh cilantro, if desired, and serve warm or at room temperature.

Per serving: 300 calories, 12g total fat, 1.5g saturated fat, 0g trans fat, 0mg cholesterol, 640mg sodium, 31g total carbohydrate, 6g dietary fiber, 5g sugars, 16g protein

Small Plates, Finger Foods, and Snacks

Chips, Nuts, and Snack Mixes

Hint-of-Lime Tortilla Chips

Garlic-Tarragon Pita Chips

Cumin-Dusted Naan Chips

Crystallized Almonds

Chinese Five-Spice Walnuts

Creole Spiced Pecans

Sweet-n-Savory Snack Mix

Nature Trail Mix

Dark Chocolate Trail Mix

Crostini and Bruschetta

Extra-Virgin Grilled Zucchini Crostini

Caramelized Pear and Gorgonzola Crostini

Ham and Havarti Crostini

Smoky Baba Ghanoush Crostini

Masala Pea Bruschetta

Artichoke, White Bean and Roasted Bell Pepper Bruschetta

Red Curry Tomato Bruschetta

Ricotta, Fig, and Honey-Nut Bruschetta

Fresh Mango–Scallion Crab Bruschetta

Creamy Almond Hummus Canapés

Tzatziki Chicken Nugget Canapés

Fresh Spinach–Truffle Dip Canapés

Mini Frittatas, Flans, Quiches, Wonton Cups, and Tarts

Parsley, Sage, Rosemary, and Thyme Frittata Bites

Grecian Zucchini Frittata Pie

Southwestern Couscous Flan Minis

Jasmine Tea Chicken Salad in Wonton Cups

Shrimp Salad in Parmesan-Wonton Cups

Vegetable Fajita Tartlets

Pesto-Glazed Sirloin Tarts

Skewered Hors d'Oeuvres

Asian Sesame Grilled Zucchini Ribbon Picks

Grilled Vegetable Antipasto Skewers

Cucumber Satay with Peanut Sauce

Dilly Egg Pop

Thai-Inspired Chicken Satay

Teriyaki Pineapple-Pork Kebabs

Tzatziki Shish Kebabs

Grilled Bistec Palomilla Pops

Other Finger Foods: Vegetarian

Platanos with Fleur de Sel

Hummus in Red and Yellow Cherry Tomatoes

Herbed Goat Cheese–Dressed Figs

Grilled Jalapeño Poppers

Purple Potato Pancakes

Wasabi-Charred Green Beans

"Buffalo Wing" Yellow Squash

Panko-Crusted Zucchini Nuggets with Marinara

Goat Cheese Medallions with Caramelized Onions

Roasted Cauliflower Goat Cheese Toasts

Monterey Bean Nachos

Black and White Nachos

White Party Pizzette Platter

Herb Rice–Stuffed Grape Leaves

Tijuana Tortilla Pinwheels

Hoisin Broccoli and Cauliflower Dumplings

South Asian Potato and Spring Pea Samosas

Southwestern Egg Rolls

Shrimp Spring Rolls

Farmers' Market Stuffed Russet Skins

Devilish Spiced Eggs

Homemade Pretzel Puffs

Other Finger Foods: Poultry, Fish, Shellfish, and Meat

Turkey Sliders

Tequila Turkey Cocktail Meatballs

Slim Chicken Nachos

Wild Peruvian Chicken Wings

Flash-Fried Adobo Chicken Fingers

Smoked Salmon Pâté Canapés

Sassy Shrimp Cocktail

Chutney-Dressed Crab Cakes

Broiled Sardines Oregano

Bok Choy, Scallion, and Pork Dumplings

"Swedish" Meatballs

Cinnamon-Spiced Lamb Meatballs

When well planned, snacking is a good thing—and can help you stick to a healthful eating plan.

Fruits, veggies, and yogurt are always a good foundation for excellent snacks. Ideally, aim for whole foods that contain some fiber and protein so your snack keeps you full and energized for a while.

Even though there are lots of ready-made snacks on the market, many of the calorie-controlled snack packs are overly processed, unsatisfying, nutrient poor, and not so tasty. This is what inspired some of the recipes in this chapter—to provide you with calorie-friendly snacks and small plates that are satisfying, nutritious, and tasty.

My other inspiration came from my passion for hosting gatherings for my friends and family—and serving petite party fare. Popular appetizers can be high in calories and low in nutrition. So another goal was to make sure you have an entire array of finger foods you can serve for parties that not only taste good but are good for you. These apps can also serve as the perfect "bites" before a meal to help curb a ravenous appetite.

Whether a snack, small plate, or other finger food, they can be mixed and matched as you wish. Typical hors d'oeuvres can be served as snacks and vice versa. You'll have dozens and dozens of recipes from which to choose in the chapter.

The chapter begins with high-flavored munchies that provide whole grains or nuts—or both, including Sweet-n-Savory Snack Mix (page 43). It's followed by delights served atop toasts or veggies, such as Ricotta, Fig, and Honey-Nut Bruschetta (page 49), Tzatziki Chicken Nugget Canapés (page 50), and Ham and Havarti Crostini (page 46).

Next you'll find a mélange of party fare including mini-frittatas and flans, stuffed wonton cups, and savory tarts with plenty of international flair. And if you're a fan of food served on sticks, the recipes that follow will provide you with many skewered picks. These recipes tend to be easy to make and fun to eat. Try the Dilly Egg Pop (page 57) for an afterschool treat or the Thai-Inspired Chicken Satay (page 58) for people into "heat."

Last, but certainly not least, you'll find other true finger foods. Vegetarians will fancy a bevy of bites from dumplings to samosas, including the comforting, like Purple Potato Pancakes (page 62) and Roasted Cauliflower Goat Cheese Toasts (page 65), and the festive, such as Grilled Jalapeño Poppers (page 61) and Homemade Pretzel Puffs (page 73). And meat lovers will have no problem finding something that will satisfy—including three clever cocktail-style meatballs!

Is it time for your snack? Remember the golden rule: Don't let more than 5 waking hours go by without eating. Your body requires a steady stream of energy. So if you eat lunch at noon and dinner's at eight, you'll want to plan a snack or other small plate in between so you're not "running on empty." It's a healthy thing—and can actually help weight-management efforts since it'll keep your metabolism running well. And don't worry if you're not always near your kitchen to whip up one of these delights. Keep a small stash of nuts nearby—or have one of the trail mixes (page 44) on hand—when you need a grab-and-go nibble.

Calorie range in this chapter: 35 to 260 calories.

Low-calorie pick: Asian Sesame Grilled Zucchini Ribbon Picks, 35 calories (page 56).

Chips, Nuts, and Snack Mixes

Hint-of-Lime Tortilla Chips

Makes 3 servings: 8 chips each

Enjoy these extra-large baked chips that really deliver on crunch. You'll love the lovely lime essence that adds perkiness to these snappy chips. They're the ideal companion for dip, salsa, or guacamole of choice, such as Grilled Fig Guacamole (page 90) or Sweet Pea "Guacamole" (page 91).

Juice of 1 lime (2 tablespoons)
2 teaspoons peanut or grapeseed oil
¼ teaspoon sea salt, or to taste
¼ teaspoon chili powder (optional)
6 (6-inch) stone-ground or sprouted corn tortillas

1. Preheat the oven to 400°F.

2. Whisk together the lime juice, oil, salt, and chili powder (if using) until well combined. Rub the lime vinaigrette with your fingers or brush with a pastry brush onto the entire surface of both sides of the tortillas, using all the vinaigrette. Cut the tortillas each into 4 wedges.

3. Place the tortilla wedges in a single layer on a large baking sheet. Bake until just crisp, about 12 minutes. Remove from the oven and let finish cooling and crisping on a rack.

4. Serve at room temperature. The chips will keep in an airtight container for up to 1 week.

Per serving: 120 calories, 4.5g total fat, 0.5g saturated fat, 0g trans fat, 0mg cholesterol, 200mg sodium, 20g total carbohydrate, 2g dietary fiber, 0g sugars, 2g protein

Garlic-Tarragon Pita Chips

Makes 4 servings: 8 chips each

Vegetable broth replaces most of the oil to make these crispy chips friendlier for your hips. Then the tarragon and garlic work together to create a savory, sophisticated bite. Dip them into Caramelized Maui Onion Dip (page 96) or Edamame "Hummus" (page 88), or serve as an accompaniment to Littleneck Clam Stew with Turkey Sausage (page 244).

¼ cup low-sodium vegetable broth or Vegetable Stock (page 203)
1 tablespoon extra-virgin olive oil
1 tablespoon finely chopped fresh tarragon or 1 teaspoon dried tarragon
1 large garlic clove, minced
¼ teaspoon sea salt, or to taste
2 (8-inch) whole-grain pita breads, split and cut into 8 wedges

1. Preheat the oven to 375°F.

2. Whisk together the broth, oil, tarragon, garlic, and salt in a liquid measuring cup until well combined. Add the individual pita wedges to a large bowl. Drizzle with the broth mixture and gently toss by hand to coat.

3. Arrange the pita wedges in a single layer on a large baking sheet. Bake until slightly crisp, about 12 minutes. Turn the oven off, rotate tray, and let the pita chips finish crisping in the off oven with the residual heat, about 18 minutes. Remove from the oven and let finish cooling on a rack.

4. Serve at room temperature. The chips will keep in an airtight container for up to 1 week.

Per serving: 120 calories, 4.5g total fat, 0.5g saturated fat, 0g trans fat, 0mg cholesterol, 320mg sodium, 18g total carbohydrate, 2g dietary fiber, 0g sugars, 3g protein

Cumin-Dusted Naan Chips

Makes 4 servings: 6 chips each

These thick, earthy-spiced chips are super satisfying and sturdy enough for the goopiest of dips, like Sweet Pea "Guacamole" (page 91) or Zesty Lemon Soybean Hummus (page 87). You'll find many other accompaniments for these international bites, including salads, soups, and chilis.

¼ cup low-sodium vegetable broth
　　or Vegetable Stock (page 203)
1 tablespoon extra-virgin olive oil
½ teaspoon ground cumin
¼ teaspoon sea salt, or to taste
2 (3-ounce) whole-grain naan or pocketless pitas,
　　each cut into 12 pieces

1. Preheat the oven to 350°F.

2. Whisk together the broth, oil, cumin, and salt in a liquid measuring cup until well combined. Add the individual naan pieces to a large bowl. Drizzle with the broth mixture and gently toss by hand to coat.

3. Arrange the naan pieces in a single layer on a large baking sheet. Bake until slightly crisp, about 18 minutes. Rotate the tray, turn the oven off, and let the naan chips finish crisping in the off oven with the residual heat, about 18 minutes. Remove from the oven and let finish cooling on a rack.

4. Serve at room temperature. The chips will keep in an airtight container for up to 1 week.

Per serving: 160 calories, 7g total fat, 1.5g saturated fat, 0g trans fat, 0mg cholesterol, 360mg sodium, 21g total carbohydrate, 3g dietary fiber, 2g sugars, 4g protein

Crystallized Almonds

Makes 6 servings: about 3 tablespoons each

Nuts are a helpful part of weight management due mostly to their satiety value. So it's okay to value these nutty treats that have just the perfect touch of sweetness. Toss these babies onto a salad for a decidedly different crunch, such as Peach Bellini Salad (page 152). Or enjoy as a little snack.

1 tablespoon honey or agave nectar
1 teaspoon unsalted butter
½ teaspoon sea salt, or to taste
1 cup natural dry-roasted almonds
1 tablespoon turbinado sugar

1. Preheat the oven to 375°F.

2. Combine the honey, butter, and salt in a small saucepan. Place over medium heat and bring mixture to a boil while stirring occasionally. Add the almonds and stir until well coated, about 1 minute.

3. Transfer the almond mixture to a parchment paper–lined 9 × 13-inch baking dish. Spread out to a single layer and sprinkle with the sugar. Stir and spread out again into a single layer.

4. Bake for 15 minutes. Let cool on a rack until fully crisp. When completely cooled, break apart any nuts that are sticking together.

5. Serve at room temperature. The nuts will keep in an airtight container for up to 2 weeks.

Per serving: 160 calories, 12g total fat, 1.5g saturated fat, 0g trans fat, 0mg cholesterol, 190mg sodium, 10g total carbohydrate, 3g dietary fiber, 6g sugars, 5g protein

Chinese Five-Spice Walnuts Ⓢ

Makes 4 servings: ¼ cup walnuts each

Need a super-quick hunger helper or lickety-split party fare? These uniquely spiced nuts make a zippy snack or party nibble on the fly. Or create surprising crunch by sprinkling on a salad, such as Pear and Walnut Field Green Salad (page 155) or Layered Waldorf Salad (page 157).

1 cup walnut halves
1½ teaspoons walnut or peanut oil
1½ tablespoons turbinado sugar
¼ teaspoon Chinese five-spice powder
¼ teaspoon cayenne pepper
¼ teaspoon sea salt, or to taste

1. Toss the walnuts with the oil in a small microwave-safe bowl until fully coated.

2. Stir together the sugar, five-spice powder, cayenne, and salt in another small bowl. Sprinkle over the walnuts and gently toss until just coated. Microwave on high for 1½ minutes.

3. Serve warm or at room temperature. The nuts will keep in an airtight container for up to 2 weeks.

Per serving: 190 calories, 18g total fat, 1.5g saturated fat, 0g trans fat, 0mg cholesterol, 150mg sodium, 5g total carbohydrate, 2g dietary fiber, 2g sugars, 4g protein

Creole Spiced Pecans Ⓢ

Makes 5 servings: 3 tablespoons (about 12 pecans) each

Take your salad to another level by tossing on these kicked-up pecans. They're especially delectable in autumn or winter when paired with a salad containing apples or pears, such as Jasmine Green Tea and Pear-Dressed Mesclun (page 155). Or savor as a little snack.

1 cup Georgia pecan halves
1½ teaspoons peanut or grapeseed oil
1 teaspoon Creole seasoning (page 31)
1 teaspoon turbinado sugar

1. Toss the pecans with the oil in a small microwave-safe bowl until fully coated.

2. Stir together the Creole seasoning and sugar in another small bowl. Sprinkle over the pecans and gently toss until just coated. Microwave on high for 1½ minutes.

3. Serve warm or at room temperature. The nuts will keep in an airtight container for up to 2 weeks.

Per serving: 150 calories, 16g total fat, 1.5g saturated fat, 0g trans fat, 0mg cholesterol, 110mg sodium, 4g total carbohydrate, 2g dietary fiber, 2g sugars, 2g protein

Sweet-n-Savory Snack Mix Ⓢ

Makes 7 servings: ½ cup each

When planned, snacks can be a healthy thing. Fix this mix for the whole family or get the kids involved with the measuring and mixing. Crunch on it as an afterschool snack, movie munchie, or travel-friendly finger food.

2 tablespoons low-sodium vegetable broth
    or Vegetable Stock (page 203)
1 tablespoon unsalted butter, melted
1 garlic clove, creamed or minced
1 teaspoon chili powder
½ teaspoon ground cumin
1½ cups bite-size whole-wheat cheese crackers
3 cups fresh air-popped popcorn or natural
    prepopped popcorn
⅓ cup lightly salted peanuts or cashews
½ cup black seedless raisins

1. Preheat the oven to 325°F.

2. Stir together the broth, butter, garlic, chili powder, and cumin in a liquid measuring cup.

3. Stir together the crackers, popcorn, and peanuts in a large bowl. Drizzle with the broth mixture and toss until well coated. Arrange in a single layer in a large baking pan.

4. Bake until the snack mix is fully crisp, about 15 minutes, stirring twice during baking. Remove from the oven, stir in the raisins, and cool on a rack.

5. Serve at room temperature as a snack. The mix will keep in an airtight container for up to 2 weeks.

Per serving: 190 calories, 9g total fat, 2g saturated fat, 0g trans fat, 5mg cholesterol, 170mg sodium, 24g total carbohydrate, 3g dietary fiber, 8g sugars, 5g protein

Nature Trail Mix Ⓢ

Makes 10 servings: ⅓ cup each

Munch on this mix as a nutrition-rich between meal fix. Take it on a hike . . . or on your bike. Or sprinkle it on yogurt. One-third cup is the ideal size for a quick energy lift.

1 cup black seedless raisins

1 cup lightly salted peanuts

1 cup granola cereal without fruit

⅓ cup dried tart cherries, dried cranberries, or finely chopped unsulfured dried apricots

3 tablespoons lightly salted sunflower seeds

1. Toss together the raisins, peanuts, granola, dried cherries, and sunflower seeds in a large bowl.

2. Divide the trail mix among 10 cups or small lidded containers and serve at room temperature as a snack. The mix will keep in an airtight container for up to 2 weeks.

Per serving: 200 calories, 9g total fat, 1.5g saturated fat, 0g trans fat, 0mg cholesterol, 75mg sodium, 26g total carbohydrate, 4g dietary fiber, 13g sugars, 6g protein

Dark Chocolate Trail Mix Ⓢ

Makes 12 servings: ¼ cup each

Recipes don't get much simpler than this. Just toss and taste. It's a perfect party food in a pinch—especially when chocolate lovers are on the guest list. Or if you're an avid exerciser, it's a swift and scrumptious energy fix post workout.

1 cup semisweet chocolate chunks

1 cup lightly salted peanuts

1 cup whole-grain cereal clusters, pillows, squares, or loops

1. Toss together the chocolate, peanuts, and cereal in a medium bowl.

2. Serve in a bowl party style or divide the trail mix among 12 cups or small lidded containers and serve at room temperature as a snack. The mix will keep in an airtight container for up to 2 weeks.

Per serving: 180 calories, 12g total fat, 4g saturated fat, 0g trans fat, 0mg cholesterol, 60mg sodium, 17g total carbohydrate, 3g dietary fiber, 11g sugars, 5g protein

Crostini and Bruschetta

Extra-Virgin Grilled Zucchini Crostini Ⓢ

Makes 12 servings: 2 crostini each

In Italian, *crostini* refers to "little toasts." The toasted thinly sliced bread is just the vehicle with which to dazzle with practically any savory topper.

24 (⅓-inch-thick) slices whole-grain baguette

2 tablespoons extra-virgin olive oil

⅛ teaspoon dried hot pepper flakes, or to taste

3 medium zucchini, each cut lengthwise into 8 thin slices

1 tablespoon white balsamic vinegar

1 large garlic clove, minced

¼ teaspoon sea salt, or to taste

3 tablespoons pine nuts, toasted

2 tablespoons thinly sliced fresh basil leaves or 2 teaspoons chopped fresh oregano

1. Preheat the oven to 400°F. Arrange the baguette slices in a single layer on a large baking sheet, then lightly brush the top of all the slices with ½ tablespoon of the oil and sprinkle with the hot pepper flakes. Bake until toasted, about 12 minutes. Cool on a rack.

2. Prepare an outdoor or indoor grill, or a grill pan. Brush the zucchini slices with the remaining 1½ tablespoons oil. Grill the slices over medium-high heat until just cooked through, about 3 minutes per side. Grill in batches, if necessary.

3. Place the grilled zucchini in a large rimmed dish. Immediately add the vinegar, garlic, and salt. Gently toss to coat using tongs. Adjust seasoning.

4. Arrange each zucchini slice in accordion-like manner on top of each toast. Or dice the zucchini and mound upon each toast. Sprinkle with the pine nuts and basil, and serve at room temperature.

Per serving: 80 calories, 4.5g total fat, 0.5g saturated fat, 0g trans fat, 0mg cholesterol, 55mg sodium, 7g total carbohydrate, 1g dietary fiber, 2g sugars, 3g protein

Caramelized Bosc Pear and Gorgonzola Crostini

Makes 6 servings: 2 crostini each

If you like a little bit of everything all in one bite—sweet, savory, crispy, juicy, sharp, and herbal—this crostini takes the cake. You'll be amazed at the big flavor and your big smile after you slowly savor every little mouthful of these morsels.

2 teaspoons apple cider vinegar

2 teaspoons pure maple syrup, chestnut honey, or agave nectar

1 teaspoon finely chopped fresh rosemary

1 Bosc pear, cored and halved lengthwise

12 (⅓-inch-thick) slices whole-grain baguette

1 teaspoon extra-virgin olive oil

1½ ounces creamy Gorgonzola cheese, crumbled and at room temperature

¼ teaspoon freshly ground black pepper, or to taste

1. Stir together the vinegar, maple syrup, and rosemary in a medium bowl.

2. Cut each pear half crosswise into about 18 thin slices, no more than ¼ inch thick. Toss the pear slices with the vinegar mixture until well coated. Let marinate for about 15 to 20 minutes.

3. Preheat the oven to 400°F. Arrange the baguette slices in a single layer on a large baking sheet, then lightly brush the top of each slice with the oil. Bake until lightly toasted, about 7 minutes.

4. Immediately sprinkle the warm toasts with the cheese and spread it like you're buttering toast.

5. Preheat the broiler. Drain and discard the excess marinade from the pear slices. Arrange about 3 pear slices on each toast. Broil the crostini until the pear slices are softened and lightly browned, about 2½ minutes. Add the pepper.

6. Arrange the crostini on a platter. Serve warm or at room temperature.

Per serving: 90 calories, 3.5g total fat, 1.5g saturated fat, 0g trans fat, 10mg cholesterol, 120mg sodium, 11g total carbohydrate, 2g dietary fiber, 5g sugars, 3g protein

Ham and Havarti Crostini

Makes 12 servings: 1 crostini each

If you like grilled cheese sandwiches, you'll adore these "topless" oven-crisped, ham and melted-cheese crostini. What's more, this elegant snack or party fare contains high-flavored ingredients, like fig jam and fresh tarragon, creating a real treat for the taste buds.

12 thin slices whole-grain bread

¼ cup fig jam or 100% fruit spread of choice

1 tablespoon unsalted butter, at room temperature

1½ teaspoons finely chopped fresh tarragon or thyme

¼ teaspoon sea salt, or to taste

12 (1-ounce) slices turkey ham, Black Forest ham, or smoked turkey breast

12 (1-ounce) slices Havarti cheese

12 fresh tarragon leaves or thyme sprigs

1. Preheat the oven to 400°F. Arrange the bread in a single layer on two large baking sheets. Bake until lightly toasted, about 7 minutes. Remove from the oven and immediately cut each slice into a round with a large (3-inch) biscuit or cookie cutter. (Reserve the toast trimmings for other uses, such as a soup topping.)

2. Stir together the jam, butter, tarragon, and salt in a small bowl until very well combined. Spread the jam mixture on top of each toast piece.

3. Cut the ham and cheese slices into the same size rounds as the toast pieces. (Reserve the trimmings for other uses.) Place one ham slice, then one cheese slice, onto each toast.

4. Place crostini onto a large baking sheet and bake at 400°F until the cheese is melted, about 6 minutes. Remove from the oven, place crostini onto a large platter, top each with a tarragon leaf, and enjoy while warm.

Per serving: 140 calories, 7g total fat, 4g saturated fat, 0g trans fat, 20mg cholesterol, 300mg sodium, 12g total carbohydrate, 2g dietary fiber, 3g sugars, 7g protein

Smoky Baba Ghanoush Crostini

Makes 16 servings: 3 crostini each

Baba Ghanoush, a tantalizing Middle Eastern eggplant dip, can be enjoyed in a variety of ways, such as a sandwich condiment or a thick sauce for whole-grain pasta. Served as a topping in this pita crostini recipe, it creates a truly wow-worthy presentation. They're great bites when you have a houseful of guests.

1 large eggplant

3 tablespoons tahini (sesame seed paste)

Juice of 1 lemon (3 tablespoons)

3 tablespoons extra-virgin olive oil

3 garlic cloves, 2 cloves minced and 1 clove cut in half crosswise

¼ teaspoon sea salt, or to taste

⅛ teaspoon ground cumin, or to taste

8 (7-inch) whole-grain pocketless pitas, cut into 6 wedges each

¼ cup roughly chopped fresh flat-leaf parsley

1. Grill or broil the eggplant on a charcoal grill or under the broiler, turning occasionally, until just charred, about 6 minutes. Then bake uncovered in 375°F oven until fully cooked, about 45 minutes.

2. Meanwhile, whisk together the tahini, lemon juice, 1 tablespoon of the olive oil, the minced garlic, the salt, and cumin in a medium bowl until well combined.

3. Cool eggplant slightly and cut into small bite-size cubes. (Note: Keep the charred skin on for flavor, texture, and color.) Add the eggplant cubes and any collected juices to the bowl with the tahini mixture and stir to combine. Chill in the refrigerator for at least 2 hours to allow flavors to blend. (The eggplant mixture holds well in the fridge for 3 days.)

4. Preheat the oven to 375°F. Arrange the pita wedges on two large baking sheets. Lightly rub or brush the top surface of the wedges with the remaining 2 tablespoons oil. Bake until just crisp, about 22 minutes, rotating tray halfway through the baking process. Remove from oven and immediately rub the surface of each crisp with the garlic halves.

5. Just before serving, adjust seasoning of the eggplant mixture. Top each pita crisp with 1 table-spoon of the eggplant mixture, sprinkle with the parsley, and serve at room temperature.

Per serving: 160 calories, 5g total fat, 1g saturated fat, 0g trans fat, 0mg cholesterol, 250mg sodium, 26g total carbohydrate, 4g dietary fiber, 2g sugars, 5g protein

Masala Pea Bruschetta

Makes 8 servings: 4 bruschetta each

When peas are fresh and in-season, my culinary creative juices start flowing with ideas for how to serve them other than as a side dish. Here I've whipped them up into a bruschetta topping for pita or naan chips—or even wasabi rice crackers—creating a beautiful finger food that's loaded with veggie goodness and vivid eye appeal.

1 tablespoon extra-virgin olive or grapeseed oil

3 scallions, green and white parts, thinly sliced

1 pound fresh or frozen peas

3 tablespoons chopped fresh cilantro

1 teaspoon fresh lemon juice or brown rice vinegar, or to taste

½ teaspoon garam masala

¾ teaspoon sea salt, or to taste

32 whole-grain pita chips sprinkled with ground cumin, or Cumin-Dusted Naan Chips (page 42)

Cilantro leaf or lemon zest, for garnish (optional)

1. Heat the oil in a large saucepan over medium heat. Add the white part of the scallions and sauté until beginning to caramelize, about 4 minutes. Stir in the peas, green part of the scallions, and the chopped cilantro, cover, and cook for 3 minutes. Remove from heat and keep covered until the peas are tender, about 3 minutes.

2. Add the pea mixture to a food processor along with the lemon juice, garam masala, and salt. Cover and pulse to desired consistency. Chill in the refrig-erator until ready to serve. Adjust seasoning.

3. Top each with 1 tablespoon of the pea mixture. Garnish each with a cilantro leaf or lemon zest, if desired. Serve at room temperature.

Per serving: 110 calories, 4g total fat, 0g saturated fat, 0g trans fat, 0mg cholesterol, 370mg sodium, 14g total carbohydrate, 4g dietary fiber, 3g sugars, 4g protein

Artichoke, White Bean, and Roasted Bell Pepper Bruschetta Ⓕ

Makes 8 servings: 3 bruschetta each

Beans create creaminess. Herbs and zest provide flavor flair. Put them together and generously top it onto toasts and you have a fabulous finger food.

1 (15-ounce) can no-salt-added cannellini or other white beans, drained

2 large garlic cloves, minced

2 teaspoons extra-virgin olive oil

Juice and zest of 1 lemon (3 tablespoons juice)

¾ teaspoon sea salt, or to taste

⅛ teaspoon dried hot pepper flakes (optional)

1 (9-ounce) package frozen artichoke hearts, thawed and chopped

1 teaspoon chopped fresh oregano

1 large freshly roasted red bell pepper (page 27) or drained jarred red bell pepper, diced

1 (8-inch) portion whole-grain French baguette, cut diagonally into 24 (about ⅓-inch-thick) slices

2 tablespoons thinly sliced fresh basil leaves or chopped fresh flat-leaf parsley

1. Stir together the beans, garlic, oil, 1 tablespoon of the lemon juice, the lemon zest, ¼ teaspoon of the salt, and hot pepper flakes (if using) in a medium bowl.

2. Pour half of the bean mixture into a food processor along with the artichokes, oregano, remaining lemon juice, and remaining ½ teaspoon salt. Cover and pulse until a smooth paste forms. Adjust seasoning and set aside.

3. Stir the roasted pepper into the remaining half of the bean mixture in the medium bowl. Adjust seasoning and set aside.

4. Preheat the oven to 400°F. Arrange the bread slices in a single layer on a large baking sheet, then spread 1 tablespoon of the artichoke-bean mixture onto each baguette slice. Bake until the bean mixture is hot and the bottom of the toasts are crisp, about 12 minutes. Cool on a rack.

5. When the toasts are slightly cool, arrange on a platter and press a spoonful of the bean-bell pepper mixture on top of each toast. Sprinkle with the basil and serve at room temperature.

Per serving: 140 calories, 3g total fat, 0g saturated fat, 0g trans fat, 0mg cholesterol, 360mg sodium, 22g total carbohydrate, 6g dietary fiber, 3g sugars, 7g protein

Red Curry Tomato Bruschetta

Makes 8 servings: 3 bruschetta each

When tomatoes are fully ripe and seasonal, the umami taste of the tomatoes makes them delectable in this fusion bruschetta recipe. For worldly flair, red curry paste takes it to another flavor level. If you can stand the heat, go ahead and add more red curry paste!

1 (8-inch) portion whole-grain Italian baguette, cut diagonally into 24 (about ⅓-inch-thick) slices

3 large garlic cloves, peeled

2 teaspoons extra-virgin olive oil

1 teaspoon aged red wine vinegar

¾ teaspoon red curry paste, or to taste

½ teaspoon sea salt, or to taste

¼ teaspoon freshly ground black pepper, or to taste

3 large heirloom or beefsteak tomatoes, diced

⅓ cup thinly sliced or chopped fresh basil

1. Preheat the oven to 400°F. Arrange the bread slices in a single layer on two large baking sheets. Bake until toasted, about 12 minutes. Cut one of the garlic cloves in half and immediately rub the top side of each toast while warm with the cut end of the garlic. Cool on a rack.

2. Mince the 2 remaining garlic cloves and add to a medium bowl along with the oil, vinegar, curry paste, salt, and pepper. Stir to combine. Add the tomatoes and basil and stir to combine. Adjust seasoning.

3. Serve the tomato mixture in a small serving bowl surrounded by the garlic toasts. Or, just before serving, arrange the toasts on a platter, top each with about 2 rounded tablespoons of the tomato mixture, and serve immediately.

Per serving: 100 calories, 2.5g total fat, 0g saturated fat, 0g trans fat, 0mg cholesterol, 290mg sodium, 16g total carbohydrate, 3g dietary fiber, 4g sugars, 5g protein

Ricotta, Fig, and Honey-Nut Bruschetta Ⓢ

Makes 12 servings: 2 bruschetta each

Fresh figs definitely are among my top ten favorite foods. So I love creating clever ways in which to enjoy them. The fresh cheese and slightly nutty pairing in this finger food lets the fig shine in a scrumptiously sweet and savory way. But please be creative and top this with other fresh seasonal fruits, too: try 2 plums or apricots cut into 12 wedges each.

24 slices raisin-pecan or other fruit-nut bread (about ⅓ inch thick)

1 cup part-skim ricotta cheese

3 large fresh Black Mission figs, stems removed, cut into 8 wedges each

2 tablespoons honey or agave nectar

1½ teaspoons fresh thyme leaves or finely chopped fresh rosemary, or 1 tablespoon minced fresh chives

¼ teaspoon sea salt, or to taste

¼ teaspoon freshly ground black pepper, or to taste

1. Preheat the oven to 400°F. Arrange the bread slices in a single layer on a large baking sheet. Bake until toasted, about 12 minutes. Cool on a rack.

2. Arrange the toasts on a large platter. Onto each toast dollop or spread 2 teaspoons of the ricotta cheese, position a fig piece, drizzle with ¼ teaspoon of the honey, and sprinkle with the thyme, salt, and pepper. Serve at room temperature.

Per serving: 110 calories, 3g total fat, 1g saturated fat, 0g trans fat, 5mg cholesterol, 75mg sodium, 18g total carbohydrate, 1g dietary fiber, 8g sugars, 3g protein

Fresh Mango–Scallion Crab Bruschetta

Makes 10 servings: 3 large or 6 small bruschetta each

These cute little crab lover's bites with sweet heat will delight all parts of your palate. It's a party pleaser for sure. This mango-spiked crab topping is tasty served beyond bruschetta, too. Skip the chips or crackers and stuff into a pita to create a refreshing sandwich or stir into chilled quinoa or whole-wheat couscous to make a sensational salad.

2 tablespoons orange marmalade

Juice of ½ lemon (1½ tablespoons)

Juice of ½ lime (1 tablespoon)

1 small jalapeño pepper with some seeds, minced

½ teaspoon sea salt, or to taste

¼ teaspoon freshly ground black pepper

1 tablespoon unrefined peanut or flaxseed oil

1 pound fresh premium wild lump crabmeat, picked over and separated into chunks

1 mango, peeled, pitted, and finely diced

3 scallions, green and white parts, minced

2 tablespoons dry-roasted sunflower seeds

30 large tortilla chips or 60 brown rice crackers

1. Whisk together the orange marmalade, lemon and lime juices, jalapeño, salt, and black pepper in a medium bowl. Whisk in the oil until well combined. Stir in the crabmeat, mango, and scallions until well combined. Keep chilled until ready to serve. Stir in 1 tablespoon of the sunflower seeds and adjust seasoning.

2. Arrange the tortilla chips on platters, top each chip with about 2 tablespoons of the crab salad (1 tablespoon each if using rice crackers), sprinkle with the remaining 1 tablespoon sunflower seeds, and serve at room temperature.

Per serving: 120 calories, 4.5g total fat, 0.5g saturated fat, 0g trans fat, 40mg cholesterol, 280mg sodium, 11g total carbohydrate, 1g dietary fiber, 6g sugars, 10g protein

Creamy Almond Hummus Canapés Ⓢ

Makes 12 servings: 3 canapés each

Serving zippy hummus atop veggies rather than chips or bread is an even tastier way to enjoy it. Plus, it can help reduce your overall calorie intake without losing an ounce of enjoyment. So have fun with healthful food—and your company will, too.

1 recipe Creamy Almond Hummus (page 88) or 2 cups of your favorite hummus

1 large English cucumber, unpeeled and cut into 36 (⅓-inch-thick) coins or diagonal slices

36 fresh flat-leaf parsley leaves (1 small bunch)

1. Fill a pastry bag (using a plain or star tip) with the hummus and pipe about 1 tablespoon hummus onto each cucumber slice. Alternatively, dollop the hummus onto each cucumber slice using a spoon.

2. Garnish each with a parsley leaf and serve as pop-into-your-mouth savory treats.

Per serving: 130 calories, 9g total fat, 1g saturated fat, 0g trans fat, 0mg cholesterol, 105mg sodium, 10g total carbohydrate, 2g dietary fiber, 1g sugars, 4g protein

Tzatziki Chicken Nugget Canapés

Makes 1 serving: 3 canapés each

What do I make when trying to impress my adorably finicky nephews—and my foodie brother and sister-in-law? This is a winner. The tzatziki is a garlicky yogurt-cucumber dip that works beautifully with salty, crunchy breaded chicken. It's semi-homemade so it's actually a perfect recipe when you need to whip up a clever bite in minutes. This recipe serves one—so you can adjust it as needed.

3 (⅓-inch-thick) slices (coins) English cucumber

1 tablespoon Mint Tzatziki (page 95) or other cucumber yogurt dip

3 cooked frozen natural chicken nuggets, warm

Pinch of freshly ground black pepper

3 small fresh mint sprigs

1. Top each cucumber slice with 1 teaspoon of the tzatziki, then the chicken nugget. Sprinkle with the pepper.

2. Insert a small bamboo skewer into each, if desired, garnish with the mint, and serve immediately.

Per serving: 90 calories, 4.5g total fat, 0.5g saturated fat, 0g trans fat, 15mg cholesterol, 110mg sodium, 7g total carbohydrate, 1g dietary fiber, 1g sugars, 6g protein

Fresh Spinach–Truffle Dip Canapés

Makes 16 servings: 2 canapés each

A big bowl of dip can be a bit too tempting to keep dipping into. By putting just one tablespoon onto a petite piece of pumpernickel, you'll be able to have your dip and eat it, too—two canapés for a just-right 100 calories. This dip can be used for a special dinner party—or even an "Oscar" party. Topping with truffle is a show-stopper but sliced carrots offer beautiful contrast in flavor and color anytime.

16 slices extra-firm European-style pumpernickel or rye bread

2 cups Fresh Spinach–Truffle Party Dip (page 94) or other spinach dip

24 small pieces shaved fresh black truffle or carrot

1. Cut two 2-inch circles or squares using a cookie cutter or knife from each bread slice to make 32 total pieces. (Reserve remaining bread scraps for other uses, such as making croutons.)

2. Arrange the bread slices on a platter. Top each slice with 1 tablespoon of the dip. Top with the truffle piece, and serve at cool room temperature.

Per serving: 100 calories, 5g total fat, 1g saturated fat, 0g trans fat, 0mg cholesterol, 210mg sodium, 10g total carbohydrate, 2g dietary fiber, 1g sugars, 3g protein

Mini-Frittatas, Flans, Quiches, Wonton Cups, and Tarts

Parsley, Sage, Rosemary, and Thyme Frittata Bites

Makes 12 servings: 3 cubes each

A frittata is usually something that you'd see at breakfast or brunch. But since I'm a party girl, I get a kick out of turning favorites into finger foods. I've incorporated couscous, not cream, as a key ingredient to provide body for these herbaceous breakfast-inspired bites.

2 teaspoons canola or grapeseed oil

1 large red or Spanish onion, finely diced

2 teaspoons white balsamic vinegar

4 large eggs

4 large egg whites

½ cup plain almond milk or light soy milk

¾ teaspoon sea salt, or to taste

¼ teaspoon freshly ground black pepper, or to taste

½ cup finely shredded extra-sharp Cheddar cheese

⅓ cup whole-wheat couscous

3 tablespoons finely chopped fresh parsley

1 tablespoon finely chopped fresh sage
    or 1 teaspoon ground sage

1 teaspoon finely chopped fresh rosemary

1 teaspoon finely chopped fresh thyme

1. Preheat the oven to 350°F. Line the bottom of an 8-inch square baking dish with parchment paper. Coat the pan sides with cooking spray (preferably homemade, page xix).

2. Heat the oil in a large nonstick skillet over medium heat. Add the onion and vinegar and sauté until fully softened and just beginning to caramelize, about 10 minutes. Set aside.

3. Whisk together the eggs, egg whites, almond milk, salt, and pepper in a medium bowl until well combined. Add the cheese, couscous, parsley, sage, rosemary, and thyme and stir until combined. Add the cooked onion and stir until combined.

4. Pour the egg mixture into the prepared dish. Bake until the mixture has set, about 35 minutes. Cool on a rack.

5. Fully trim around the outside edges. Turn out onto a cutting board. Cut into 36 squares using a bread knife. Serve warm or at room temperature with toothpicks.

Per serving: 90 calories, 4.5g total fat, 1.5g saturated fat, 0g trans fat, 65mg cholesterol, 230mg sodium, 6g total carbohydrate, 1g dietary fiber, 1g sugars, 5g protein

Grecian Zucchini Frittata Pie

Makes 12 servings: 1 slice each

When is pie better than a pie? When it's a caramelized frittata pie—and when it's brimming with a lovely summery veggie, like zucchini. The farm-fresh whole eggs hold it all together and the cheese adds zing. Enjoy a deceptively luscious sliver (or two!) as an appetizer, snack, side dish, or whatever part of the meal you desire.

6 large eggs

1 teaspoon finely chopped fresh oregano
    or ½ teaspoon dried oregano

1 teaspoon sea salt, or to taste

½ teaspoon finely chopped fresh rosemary
    or ¼ teaspoon crushed dried rosemary

¼ teaspoon freshly ground black pepper, or to taste

2 teaspoons extra-virgin olive oil

1 medium white onion, finely diced

1½ teaspoons fresh lemon juice or white wine vinegar

2 medium zucchini, unpeeled and very thinly sliced
    crosswise

1 garlic clove, minced

⅓ cup finely crumbled feta or goat cheese

1. Whisk together the eggs, oregano, ¾ teaspoon of the salt, the rosemary, and pepper. Set aside.

2. Heat the oil in a large nonstick skillet over medium heat. Add the onion and lemon juice and sauté until the onion is softened, about 5 minutes. Add the zucchini and remaining ¼ teaspoon salt, cover, and cook, stirring occasionally, until the zucchini are softened, about 10 minutes. (Note: It's okay if some of the zucchini or onion is slightly caramelized.) Add the garlic and sauté for 1 minute.

3. Spread the zucchini mixture evenly in the skillet. Sprinkle with the cheese. Pour the egg mixture over the cheese-zucchini mixture. Shake the pan slightly to allow the egg mixture to fully settle. Cover and cook until the eggs are fully set, about 7 minutes. (Note: Halfway through the cooking, tilt the pan and use a silicon spatula to lift the edges and let any uncooked egg run underneath.)

4. Remove from the heat and let stand, covered, until the eggs are completely set, about 5 minutes. Adjust seasoning.

5. Slide the frittata onto a cutting board. (Note: Any moisture on top should evaporate within a couple minutes.) Place another board or platter on top, then invert so the caramelized side is up. Slice into 12 wedges using a bread knife, and serve warm or at room temperature.

Per serving: 60 calories, 4g total fat, 1.5g saturated fat, 0g trans fat, 95mg cholesterol, 280mg sodium, 2g total carbohydrate, 0g dietary fiber, 1g sugars, 4g protein

Southwestern Couscous Flan Minis

Makes 12 servings: 3 mini flans each

Flan is usually a sweet custard dessert. But here it's turned into a cheesy, peppery, savory hors d'oeuvre with a Southwestern flair, thanks to the peppers and cilantro! If you want to make 12 individual flans, use a regular-size cupcake or muffin tin and bake for about 22 minutes.

2 tablespoons unsalted butter, at room temperature

¾ cup cooked whole-wheat couscous,
    at room temperature

¾ cup shredded extra-sharp Cheddar cheese

⅓ cup finely diced red bell peppers

⅓ cup finely diced green bell peppers

1 serrano or small jalapeño pepper with seeds,
    minced

2 tablespoons finely chopped fresh cilantro

6 large eggs

6 large egg whites

¾ cup plain almond milk or light soy milk

1 teaspoon sea salt, or to taste

¼ teaspoon freshly ground black pepper,
    or to taste

1. Using your fingers, rub the butter to coat 36 of the cups of 2 or 3 mini muffin tins.

2. Divide the couscous evenly among the buttered cups, 1 teaspoon per muffin cup. Sprinkle the cheese, bell peppers, serrano, and cilantro evenly over the couscous.

3. Preheat the oven to 350°F.

4. Whisk the eggs, egg whites, almond milk, salt, and black pepper in a medium bowl. (Makes about 3 cups egg mixture.) Spoon the egg mixture into the tins, about 1 tablespoon per mini-muffin cup. Wiggle and tap the tray against the counter to assure the couscous absorbs some of the egg mixture.

5. Bake until the flans are set, about 18 minutes. Remove from the oven and cool on rack for 10 to 15 minutes.

6. Remove the flans by carefully going around the entire inside cup of each tin with a butter knife to loosen the flans. Arrange on platters, and serve warm or at room temperature.

Per serving: 110 calories, 7g total fat, 3.5g saturated fat, 0g trans fat, 105mg cholesterol, 310mg sodium, 4g total carbohydrate, 1g dietary fiber, 1g sugars, 7g protein

Jasmine Tea Chicken Salad in Wonton Cups

Makes 18 servings: 2 stuffed wonton cups each

Jasmine green tea is an intriguingly flavored, calorie-free poaching liquid for poultry. It provides a magical quality to this sweet and nutty chicken salad. Stuffed into crispy wonton cups, it's a perky little party starter.

36 square whole-wheat wonton wrappers

1 tablespoon canola or grapeseed oil

1 pound boneless skinless chicken breast, cut into ⅓-inch cubes

1 teaspoon sea salt, or to taste

2 tea bags jasmine green tea or tea of choice

2 celery stalks, finely diced

1 large shallot, minced

½ cup Sassy "Mayo" (page 123)

½ cup red or black seedless grapes, quartered lengthwise

¼ teaspoon freshly ground black pepper, or to taste

¼ cup walnut or pecan halves, toasted and coarsely chopped

2 teaspoons poppy seeds

1. Preheat the oven to 350°F. Very lightly rub or brush both sides of the wonton wrappers with the oil. Press a wonton wrapper into each of 36 cups of 2 or 3 mini muffin tins. Bake until golden brown and crisp, about 15 minutes; rotate tray(s) halfway through baking. Cool on a rack. (Note: Store wonton shells in an airtight container at room temperature for up to 1 week or in the freezer for up to 1 month.)

2. Add the chicken to a medium saucepan. Add enough cold water to cover the chicken and ½ teaspoon of the salt. Place over medium-high heat. Bring just to a boil, reduce heat to medium-low, add the tea bags, cover, and cook until the chicken is just cooked through, about 6 minutes. Remove from heat and let sit for 5 minutes to steep further. Remove the tea bags and drain the chicken. Set aside the chicken to cool slightly, about 15 minutes. (Reserve the chicken cooking liquid for other use, if desired.)

3. Gently combine the tea-poached chicken cubes, the celery, shallot, and Sassy "Mayo" in a large bowl. Gently stir in the grapes. Add the pepper and remaining ½ teaspoon salt. Chill in the refrigerator until ready to serve.

4. Just before serving, stir in the walnuts. Adjust seasoning. Arrange the wonton cups on platters, stuff each cup with about 1 rounded tablespoon of the chicken salad, sprinkle with the poppy seeds, and serve.

Per serving: 110 calories, 4.5g total fat, 0.5g saturated fat, 0g trans fat, 15mg cholesterol, 250mg sodium, 11g total carbohydrate, 1g dietary fiber, 1g sugars, 7g protein

Shrimp Salad in Parmesan-Wonton Cups

Makes 12 servings: 3 stuffed wonton cups each

When this hors d'oeuvre is stuffed into crisp wonton cups, no utensils are required. The crisp lettuce creates so much freshness and the kicked-up dressing adds flavor drama. These cups are perfect for a summer soiree.

36 square whole-wheat wonton wrappers

1 tablespoon canola or grapeseed oil

¼ cup grated Parmigiano-Reggiano or other Parmesan cheese

4½ cups finely chopped romaine lettuce

1 recipe "Caliente" Caesar Dijon Dressing (page 148) or ¾ cup other salad dressing

36 cooked peeled shrimp, chilled

¾ teaspoon freshly ground black pepper, or to taste

1. Preheat the oven to 350°F. Very lightly rub or brush both sides of 36 wonton wrappers with the oil. Sprinkle the entire surface of the top of each wonton wrapper with the cheese. Press a wonton wrapper into each of 36 cups of 2 or 3 mini muffin tins. Bake until golden brown and crisp, about 15 minutes; rotate tray(s) halfway through baking. Cool on a rack.

2. Just before serving, toss the lettuce with half of the dressing in a medium bowl. Stuff each wonton cup with the lettuce, top with 1 shrimp, and sprinkle with the pepper. Drizzle with the remaining dressing or serve on the side.

Per serving: 130 calories, 3.5g total fat, 0.5g saturated fat, 0g trans fat, 30mg cholesterol, 260mg sodium, 16g total carbohydrate, 1g dietary fiber, 1g sugars, 7g protein

Vegetable Fajita Tartlets

Makes 12 servings: 2 tartlets each

These tartlets are basically very little tostadas. Or think of this Mexican appetizer as an extreme version of chips and salsa. But don't overthink; enjoy simply eating them.

12 (6-inch) stone-ground corn tortillas

2 teaspoons peanut or grapeseed oil

1 large green bell pepper, diced

1 large red or orange bell pepper, diced

Juice of ½ lime (1 tablespoon)

½ teaspoon ground cumin

½ teaspoon chili powder

½ teaspoon sea salt, or to taste

1 (15-ounce) can black beans or black soybeans, drained

1½ cups finely shredded romaine lettuce

1 Hass avocado, pitted, peeled, and finely diced

⅓ cup Spicy Raw Tomatillo Salsa (page 114) or other tomatillo salsa

½ cup loosely packed small fresh cilantro sprigs

1. Preheat the oven to 350°F. Cut each tortilla into two 3-inch rounds each using a biscuit or cookie cutter. (Reserve the remaining tortilla scraps for other use.) Lightly spray both sides of the rounds with cooking spray (preferably homemade, page xix). Place the tortilla rounds on a large baking sheet. Place another baking sheet on top to keep the tortilla rounds flat. Bake (in batches, if necessary) until golden brown and crisp, about 12 minutes. Cool on a rack.

2. Heat the oil in a large nonstick skillet over medium-high heat. Add the bell peppers and sauté until crisp tender, about 4 minutes. Stir in the lime juice, cumin, chili powder, and ¼ teaspoon of salt and sauté for 30 seconds. Add the beans and cook while stirring until warm, about 30 seconds.

3. Top each tortilla round with 1 tablespoon of the lettuce, then top with the bean mixture, avocado, and salsa. Sprinkle with the remaining ¼ teaspoon salt. Top with the cilantro, and serve at room temperature.

Per serving: 90 calories, 3g total fat, 0g saturated fat, 0g trans fat, 0mg cholesterol, 140mg sodium, 13g total carbohydrate, 3g dietary fiber, 2g sugars, 3g protein

Pesto-Glazed Sirloin Tarts

Makes 12 servings: 1 tart each

These savory shells will knock your socks off. With so many layers of flavors and textures, it's a true delight that these tarts are only 100 calories. Have all ingredients ready to go and whip these up for your next get-together—and watch all of your guests be wowed, too.

6 (2½-ounce) crusty whole-grain rolls

1 (12-ounce) lean boneless beef sirloin or shell steak (about ½ inch thick)

2 tablespoons Enlightened Fresh Basil Pesto (page 117) or other pesto

¼ teaspoon sea salt, or to taste

¼ teaspoon freshly ground black pepper, or to taste

1 cup packed baby arugula or torn arugula

1 teaspoon extra-virgin olive oil

1 teaspoon aged red wine vinegar

1 medium vine-ripened tomato, cut into 12 thin slices

⅛ cup very thinly sliced red onion

2 tablespoons Garlic "Mayo" or other "Mayo" (pages 123–124)

1. Cut the rolls in half and scoop out all the doughy bread to create 12 small bread bowls (tart shells). Set aside. (Reserve the doughy bread scraps for other uses, such as in Sunnyside-Up Salad, page 156, or Tuscan-Style Ribollita, page 236.)

2. Rub the entire surface of the steak with the pesto sauce. Cook the steak in a large nonstick skillet or stick-resistant grill pan over medium-high heat until medium-rare or desired doneness, about 2½ minutes per side. Remove to a cutting board and let stand for 15 minutes. Thinly slice the steak against the grain on a diagonal. Add the salt and pepper.

3. Gently toss the arugula with the oil and vinegar in a small bowl to very lightly coat the leaves.

4. Evenly divide the tomato, arugula, steak, and onion among the tart shells. Drizzle each with ½ teaspoon "Mayo." Adjust seasoning and serve at room temperature.

Per serving: 100 calories, 3.5g total fat, 1g saturated fat, 0g trans fat, 10mg cholesterol, 160mg sodium, 9g total carbohydrate, 2g dietary fiber, 2g sugars, 8g protein

Skewered Hors d'Oeuvres

Asian Sesame Grilled Zucchini Ribbon Picks

Makes 8 servings: 3 picks each

Satay is usually marinated, skewered grilled poultry or meat. But the same can be done with veggies. Securing zucchini onto skewers in a ribbon-like manner provides the essence of a meaty satay, but with shockingly few calories!

1 tablespoon naturally brewed soy sauce

2 teaspoons toasted sesame oil

2 teaspoons brown rice vinegar

1 large garlic clove, minced

1 teaspoon freshly grated gingerroot

1 teaspoon honey or agave nectar

3 medium zucchini, cut lengthwise into 8 thin slices

3 medium scallions, green and white parts, minced

1 tablespoon sesame seeds, toasted

1. Whisk together the soy sauce, oil, vinegar, garlic, ginger, and honey in a small bowl. Add the zucchini to a large rimmed dish, drizzle with the soy sauce mixture, and toss until all zucchini slices are lightly coated. Let stand for 15 minutes.

2. Prepare an outdoor or indoor grill or a grill pan. Grill the zucchini slices over medium-high heat until cooked through, about 3 to 3½ minutes per side. (Alternatively, cook in a panini grill over medium-high heat for 3½ minutes.) Place grilled zucchini back into the dish and let cool for at least 15 minutes.

3. Arrange the zucchini in ribbon-like fashion onto 24 (8-inch) bamboo or reusable skewers. Firmly dip each zucchini pick into the scallions, arrange scallion-coated side down on a platter, and sprinkle with the sesame seeds. Sprinkle with any remaining scallions, if desired, and serve at room temperature.

Per serving: 35 calories, 2g total fat, 0g saturated fat, 0g trans fat, 0mg cholesterol, 120mg sodium, 4g total carbohydrate, 1g dietary fiber, 3g sugars, 1g protein

Grilled Vegetable Antipasto Skewers

Makes 12 servings: 2 skewers each

Antipasto is traditionally an Italian first course. Here these skewers can be served to start the meal or just as stand-alone hors d'oeuvres. But actually, toss out the rules. These are veggies. So eat them any time—and often.

1 medium yellow squash, cut lengthwise in half and each half cut into 12 half-moons

1 medium zucchini, cut lengthwise in half and each half cut into 12 half-moons

1 (9-ounce) package frozen artichoke hearts, thawed, cut, if necessary, into 24 bite-size pieces

24 large grape tomatoes

2 tablespoons extra-virgin olive oil

1 tablespoon aged red wine vinegar

1 large garlic clove, minced

¼ teaspoon sea salt, or to taste

¼ teaspoon freshly ground black pepper, or to taste

24 fresh basil leaves

6 ounces ready-to-eat Italian tofu, Robiola cheese, or fresh mozzarella cheese, cut into 24 cubes

24 large pitted Kalamata olives, other brine-cured black olives, or pickled vegetable pieces

1. Prepare an indoor or outdoor grill. Toss the yellow squash, zucchini, artichoke hearts, and tomatoes with the oil, vinegar, garlic, salt, and pepper in a medium bowl until coated. Secure the vegetables on 24 (8-inch) water-soaked bamboo or reusable skewers, placing one piece of yellow squash, zucchini, artichoke heart, and tomato on each, leaving about ⅛-inch gap between vegetables.

2. Grill over medium-high heat until cooked through, about 3 to 3½ minutes per side. Let stand to cool to room temperature. (Note: Vegetables can be grilled up to 2 days in advance and chilled in the refrigerator.)

3. Add 1 basil leaf, 1 tofu cube, and 1 olive to the end of each skewer and serve at room temperature.

Per serving: 90 calories, 6g total fat, 1g saturated fat, 0g trans fat, 0mg cholesterol, 220mg sodium, 5g total carbohydrate, 2g dietary fiber, 1g sugars, 5g protein

Cucumber Satay with Peanut Sauce

Makes 10 servings: 2 satay each

The best part of Thai satay to me is the peanut sauce. So make the sauce the standout star, as in this crisp raw cucumber satay. It's a refreshing change of taste from the traditional grilled skewers.

1 large English cucumber, unpeeled
½ cup Peanut Sauce (page 108) or Asian peanut satay sauce, chilled
¼ cup honey-roasted peanuts, finely chopped
2 tablespoons chopped fresh cilantro

1. Cut the cucumber in half crosswise. Cut each half lengthwise into 10 slices. Secure each slice lengthwise onto one of 20 (8-inch) bamboo or reusable skewers. Spread one entire side of each cucumber skewer with about 1 rounded teaspoon of the peanut sauce. (Note: These can be served without skewers, too. Just leave a small portion of each cucumber sauce-free for picking up with fingers.)

2. Arrange the cucumbers on a platter, sauce side up. Sprinkle with the peanuts and cilantro, and serve at room temperature.

Per serving: 50 calories, 3.5g total fat, 0.5g saturated fat, 0g trans fat, 0mg cholesterol, 110mg sodium, 3g total carbohydrate, 1g dietary fiber, 1g sugars, 2g protein

Dilly Egg Pop

Makes 1 serving: 1 pop with about 1 tablespoon dip each

Stick it to 'em. When you can eat food on a bamboo skewer, do it. It's fun—and makes the food seem even more flavorful. It's a whimsical way to turn the protein-rich egg into a great-tasting snack. NOTE: Make sure the egg yolk is not overcooked; when "just cooked" through yet still moist, the yolk will hold together better. But eat over a plate, just in case.

1½ teaspoons mayonnaise
1 teaspoon fat-free or low-fat plain Greek yogurt
¼ teaspoon minced fresh dill
Pinch of sea salt
1 large hard-cooked egg, peeled (page 377)

1. Stir together the mayonnaise, yogurt, dill, and salt in a small bowl.

2. Insert a thick bamboo skewer into the egg.

3. Serve the egg with the dip.

Per serving: 130 calories, 11g total fat, 2.5g saturated fat, 0g trans fat, 190mg cholesterol, 270mg sodium, 1g total carbohydrate, 0g dietary fiber, 1g sugars, 7g protein

Thai-Inspired Chicken Satay

Makes 12 servings: 2 satays each

This chicken satay has the tastes of Thai food, but you'll save a tremendous number of calories using almond milk (less than 50 calories a cup) instead of traditional coconut milk (450 calories a cup!).

2 cups plain almond milk or unsweetened coconut milk beverage

⅓ cup unsweetened applesauce

⅓ cup naturally brewed soy sauce

¼ cup honey or agave nectar

6 large garlic cloves, quartered or smashed

1 tablespoon Thai red curry paste

1½ teaspoons pure coconut extract

24 fresh cilantro sprigs

2 pounds boneless skinless chicken breast, sliced lengthwise into 24 strips

½ teaspoon sea salt, or to taste

½ cup unsalted mixed nuts, such as peanuts, almonds, and cashews, finely chopped

1. Add the almond milk, applesauce, soy sauce, honey, garlic, curry paste, coconut extract, and cilantro to a large saucepan. Place over medium-high heat and bring to a boil, stirring occasionally. Reduce heat to medium-low and simmer for 5 minutes, stirring occasionally. Remove from the heat, pour the sauce into a medium bowl, and cool completely. Once cool, add the chicken pieces, cover, and let marinate for at least 4 hours or overnight.

2. Preheat the oven to 400°F. Thread the chicken onto 24 (10-inch) water-soaked bamboo or reusable skewers and divide among two 9×13-inch baking pans, placing skewer handles in the center. Drizzle just the chicken with ½ cup of the marinade and sprinkle with ¼ teaspoon of the salt. Sprinkle with the nuts and the remaining ¼ teaspoon salt. Discard remaining marinade.

3. Bake until fully cooked, about 13 to 15 minutes and serve warm.

Per serving: 60 calories, 2.5g total fat, 0g saturated fat, 0g trans fat, 20mg cholesterol, 125mg sodium, 2g total carbohydrate, 0g dietary fiber, 1g sugars, 8g protein

Teriyaki Pineapple-Pork Kebabs

Makes 8 servings: 2 kebabs each

If you're a devotee of sweet and savory combinations, these kebabs will be a culinary hit. They're best enjoyed by eating a piece of bell pepper, pineapple, and pork in every bite. Turn this into an entrée by serving four kebabs on a bed of brown basmati rice.

8 ounces pork tenderloin, cut into 32 (¼-ounce) cubes

1 small or ½ large pineapple, peeled, cored,* cut into 32 cubes (about 2 rounded cups)

1 large red bell pepper, cut into 32 squares

½ cup + 2 tablespoons Tangy Teriyaki Sauce (page 135) or other teriyaki sauce

¼ teaspoon freshly ground black pepper, or to taste

1. Add the pork, pineapple, bell pepper, the ½ cup teriyaki sauce, and the black pepper to a large bowl. Toss to combine. Let sit for 30 minutes, stirring twice.

2. Meanwhile, prepare an outdoor or indoor grill. Arrange two pieces of pork, pineapple, and bell pepper onto each of 16 (6- to 8-inch) water-soaked bamboo or reusable skewers. Discard leftover marinade.

3. Grill over medium-high heat until the pork is at medium doneness, about 5 minutes. Remove the skewers from the grill, brush or drizzle with the remaining 2 tablespoons teriyaki sauce, and adjust seasoning.

4. Arrange the skewers on a platter and serve warm.

Leave a bit of the core on each pineapple piece so it holds up better when skewered and grilled.

Per serving: 60 calories, 1g total fat, 0g saturated fat, 0g trans fat, 15mg cholesterol, 170mg sodium, 8g total carbohydrate, 1g dietary fiber, 6g sugars, 6g protein

Tzatziki Shish Kebabs

Makes 6 servings: 1 beef and 1 veggie skewer each

I adore this recipe right off the grill. But I also secretly love to make this recipe intentionally for leftovers. I serve the grilled and chilled kebabs thinly sliced and stuffed in pitas with the remaining tzatziki. Try it!

1½ pounds boneless top butt beef sirloin or tenderloin, or boneless leg of lamb, trimmed, cut into 36 (1-inch) cubes

½ teaspoon sea salt, or to taste

1½ cups Mint Tzatziki (page 95) or other tzatziki dip

2 large green bell peppers, cut into 18 pieces each

1 medium red onion, cut into quarters and separated

1 tablespoon extra-virgin olive oil

1. Season the meat cubes with ¼ teaspoon of the salt, then toss with ¾ cup of the tzatziki in a medium bowl and let sit for 30 to 45 minutes. Toss the bell peppers, onion, oil, and the remaining ¼ teaspoon salt in a separate medium bowl and let sit for 30 to 45 minutes. (Note: Cut the largest onion pieces in half, if desired.)

2. Prepare an outdoor or indoor grill. Arrange onto 12 (8-inch) water-soaked bamboo or reusable skewers the beef, bell peppers, and onion. (Note: For best results, arrange beef on separate skewers from the veggies. Alternatively, grill the vegetables unskewered, in a grill basket.) Discard leftover marinade.

3. Grill the kebabs over medium-high heat until the meat is medium-rare and vegetables are desired doneness, about 4 to 5 minutes. Adjust seasoning.

4. Serve the kebabs over the grilled vegetables with the remaining ¾ cup tzatziki on the side.

Per serving: 200 calories, 8g total fat, 2g saturated fat, 0g trans fat, 40mg cholesterol, 300mg sodium, 6g total carbohydrate, 1g dietary fiber, 3g sugars, 25g protein

Grilled Bistec Palomilla Pops

Makes 12 servings: 2 pops each

Bistec Palomilla is traditionally a fried steak popular in Cuba. In this lively preparation, the tenderloin is used for ideal tenderness—and leanness. I call them pops simply because it's more fun that way!

4 large garlic cloves, smashed

1 medium yellow onion, quartered

Juice and zest of 2 limes (¼ cup juice)

2 teaspoons extra-virgin olive oil

¾ teaspoon sea salt

½ teaspoon freshly ground black pepper

1½ pounds lean beef tenderloin, cut into 24 long thin strips

1 teaspoon finely chopped fresh rosemary or 2 tablespoons chopped fresh flat-leaf parsley

1. Add the garlic, onion, lime juice, ½ of the lime zest, oil, salt, and pepper to a food processor. Cover and pulse until the onion is fully grated. Pour the onion mixture into a medium bowl. Add the beef strips and toss to coat. Cover and marinate in the refrigerator for 1 to 2 hours.

2. Prepare an outdoor or indoor grill.

3. Insert each beef strip in a ribbon-like manner onto 24 (8-inch) water-soaked sturdy bamboo or reusable skewers. Discard leftover marinade. Grill over medium-high heat until desired doneness, about 1 minute per side for medium-rare. Adjust seasoning.

4. Arrange the skewers onto a platter, sprinkle with the rosemary and remaining lime zest, and serve.

Per serving: 120 calories, 8g total fat, 3g saturated fat, 0g trans fat, 35mg cholesterol, 170mg sodium, 2g total carbohydrate, 0g dietary fiber, 0g sugars, 11g protein

Other Finger Foods: Vegetarian

Platanos with Fleur de Sel

Makes 4 servings: about 10 pieces each

These extra-sweet and slightly savory Cuban delights made with a banana relative are traditionally fried—sometimes even sugar coated and fried in lard. You'll still get all their flavorful goodness without all the calorie excess by simply roasting in the oven until they're caramelized. Sometimes the best things come in simple preparations. Savor their pleasures as is—or pair them with black bean, rice, or roasted chicken dishes.

2 large very ripe yellow plantains (well spotted to nearly blackened), unpeeled

¼ teaspoon + ⅛ teaspoon fleur de sel, or to taste

½ lime, cut into 4 wedges

1. Preheat the oven to 450°F.

2. Cut the ends off of each plantain and peel. Cut each plantain on the diagonal into about 20 slices, about ⅓ inch thick. Arrange in a single layer on a parchment paper–lined large baking sheet. Spray the top of each plantain slice with cooking spray (preferably homemade, page xix). Sprinkle with ⅛ teaspoon of the fleur de sel, making sure a few granules are sprinkled onto each slice.

3. Bake for 12 minutes, flip the plantain slices over using a spatula, spray the tops with cooking spray, and sprinkle with another ⅛ teaspoon of the fleur de sel. Bake until tender and deep golden brown, about 15 minutes.

4. Transfer to a serving platter, sprinkle with the remaining ⅛ teaspoon fleur de sel, and serve with the lime wedges.

Per serving: 140 calories, 1g total fat, 0g saturated fat, 0g trans fat, 0mg cholesterol, 180mg sodium, 36g total carbohydrate, 3g dietary fiber, 17g sugars, 1g protein

Hummus in Red and Yellow Cherry Tomatoes

Makes 4 servings: 6 stuffed cherry tomato halves each

Veggie dips and bean dips, especially hummus, are more popular than ever. That's a good thing because dips are vehicles through which you can get more vegetables. Hummus counts as a veggie, too. Plus, by using a pastry bag for serving the dip, a dazzlingly delicious presentation is the result. If you don't have a pastry bag, fill a plastic bag with a tiny corner snipped off.

6 red cherry tomatoes

6 yellow cherry tomatoes

1 cup Zesty Lemon Soybean Hummus (page 87) or other hummus, chilled

24 small fresh parsley or other herb leaves

1. Cut the tomatoes in half crosswise and scoop out the pulp of each using a ¼ teaspoon measuring spoon or melon baller, creating cups. Place upside down on a clean kitchen towel or paper towel to drain.

2. Place tomatoes cut side up on a platter. (Note: If necessary, cut a very thin sliver off the bottom of tomato cups that are too rounded to stand.)

3. Add the hummus to a pastry bag fitted with a star tip and pipe 2 teaspoons into each tomato half. Alternatively add a dollop of the hummus into each using a small spoon.

4. Insert an herb leaf on top of each, and serve at room temperature.

Per serving: 140 calories, 8g total fat, 1g saturated fat, 0g trans fat, 0mg cholesterol, 180mg sodium, 11g total carbohydrate, 3g dietary fiber, 3g sugars, 9g protein

Herbed Goat Cheese–Dressed Figs

12 servings: 2 stuffed fig halves each

Dips and spreads not only provide an opportunity to boost veggie intake; they can also help you boost your fruit servings. Here a Boursin-like goat cheese spread is a lovely companion to figs and makes for an elegant hors d'oeuvre—or even dessert.

¾ cup Herbed Goat Cheese Spread, chilled
    (page 132)
12 fresh or lightly grilled medium Black Mission
    or Calimyrna figs, stems removed and halved
    lengthwise, at room temperature
24 tiny sprig leaf tops of fresh thyme (optional)

1. Add the cheese spread to a pastry bag fitted with a star tip and pipe ½ tablespoon onto the cut surface of each fig. Alternatively, smear the cheese spread onto each using a butter knife.

2. Arrange the stuffed figs on a platter. Garnish with the thyme, if using.

Per serving: 70 calories, 1.5g total fat, 1g saturated fat, 0g trans fat, 0mg cholesterol, 80mg sodium, 12g total carbohydrate, 2g dietary fiber, 8g sugars, 2g protein

Grilled Jalapeño Poppers

Makes 4 servings: 3 poppers each

Usually the jalapeño poppers you see in restaurants are fried. Here they're grilled and stuffed with a flavorful filling of beans and just the right touch of sharp cheese—they're irresistible.

½ cup drained canned no-salt-added black or pinto
    beans
¼ cup shredded dry Jack cheese
1 tablespoon Roasted Green Tomato Salsa
    (page 114) or other thick salsa verde
1 teaspoon finely chopped fresh cilantro
¼ teaspoon sea salt, or to taste
12 large jalapeño peppers with stems
1 teaspoon unrefined peanut or grapeseed oil
½ small lime, cut into 12 small wedges

1. Mash together with a fork the beans (make sure they're well drained), cheese, salsa, cilantro, and ⅛ teaspoon of the salt until just combined into an extra-thick paste. (Makes about ¾ cup bean stuffing.) Roll the stuffing into 12 logs about the length of the peppers.

2. Prepare an outdoor or indoor grill. Slice each pepper from tip to stem without cutting completely in half. Do not remove stem. Gently squeeze the sides of each pepper and scoop out seeds and veins with a grapefruit spoon or small spoon, or very carefully with a paring knife.

3. Stuff (don't overstuff) each pepper with the bean mixture. Insert each jalapeño popper onto a water-soaked toothpick, if desired. Brush each popper with the oil. Grill the poppers over medium-high heat, about 5 minutes per side.

4. Remove from the grill, add the remaining ⅛ teaspoon salt, and serve while warm with the lime wedges.

Per serving: 80 calories, 3.5g total fat, 1.5g saturated fat, 0g trans fat, 5mg cholesterol, 190mg sodium, 8g total carbohydrate, 3g dietary fiber, 2g sugars, 4g protein

Purple Potato Pancakes

Makes 14 servings: 1 pancake each

These vivid potato pancakes are fried and can still fit into your eating plan. Just remember to thoroughly enjoy one of these generous appetizer bites, not a plateful. The rich hue of the purple potatoes makes the pancakes seem special, but if you can't find them, these pancakes are still delicious with gold or red potatoes.

4 large purple potatoes or 2 pounds purple
    baby creamer potatoes, unpeeled and scrubbed

1 large sweet onion, peeled

3 large eggs, lightly beaten

4 scallions, white and green parts, very thinly sliced

½ cup whole-wheat pastry flour

¼ cup finely chopped fresh flat-leaf parsley

1¼ teaspoons sea salt, or to taste

½ teaspoon freshly ground black pepper, or to taste

½ teaspoon finely chopped fresh rosemary
    or ¼ teaspoon crushed dried rosemary

⅛ teaspoon ground cayenne, or to taste

¼ cup unrefined peanut or grapeseed oil

⅔ cup fat-free or low-fat plain Greek yogurt

1. Quarter the potatoes if large and add to a food processor. Cover and pulse to coarsely grate. Transfer to a large clean kitchen towel. (Note: The purple potatoes can stain.) Quarter the onion, coarsely grate, and transfer to the towel with the potatoes. Squeeze the mixture well in the towel over the sink to remove excess liquid.

2. Transfer the mixture to a large bowl and add the eggs, scallions, flour, parsley, salt, pepper, rosemary, and cayenne and stir gently to combine.

3. Form the potato mixture into 14 packed balls, about ¼ rounded cup each. Heat 2 tablespoons of the oil in a large nonstick skillet over medium heat. Place 7 of the balls into the pan and gently flatten into about 2½-inch disks. Cook, gently flipping only once, until well browned on both sides, about 9 minutes on the first side and 6 minutes on the second side. Transfer to paper towels to drain. If desired, keep the first batch of potato pancakes warm in a 200°F oven. Cook remaining pancakes with the remaining oil. Adjust seasoning.

4. Serve warm topped with a dollop of the yogurt. Garnish with additional sliced scallion or tiny fresh rosemary sprigs, if desired.

Per serving: 120 calories, 5g total fat, 1g saturated fat, 0g trans fat, 40mg cholesterol, 230mg sodium, 16g total carbohydrate, 2g dietary fiber, 2g sugars, 4g protein

Wasabi-Charred Green Beans

Makes 5 servings: 1 cup each

Playing with food can add new life to dishes that you feel have lost their luster. So move over raw veggies and dip. There are charred veggies on the loose. Just remember to opt for this snack when you don't mind getting your fingers a little messy.

1 tablespoon naturally brewed soy sauce

1 tablespoon turbinado sugar

2 teaspoons brown rice vinegar

2 teaspoons toasted sesame oil

1 large garlic clove, minced

¾ teaspoon wasabi powder, or to taste

¼ teaspoon sea salt, or to taste

1½ pounds green beans, trimmed

¾ cup Creamy Cucumber Dipping Sauce (page 98)

1. Stir together the soy sauce, sugar, vinegar, oil, garlic, wasabi powder, and salt in a small bowl. Set aside.

2. Heat a large stick resistant skillet or wok over high heat. Add the green beans and 3 tablespoons water, cover, and cook, stirring once, until the green beans are nearly crisp-tender, about 3 minutes.

3. Add the soy sauce mixture and stir-fry until the sauce coats the beans and the beans are slightly charred, about 3 minutes. Serve beans on a platter with the dipping sauce on the side.

Per serving: 100 calories, 3.5g total fat, 0.5g saturated fat, 0g trans fat, 0mg cholesterol, 370mg sodium, 14g total carbohydrate, 4g dietary fiber, 6g sugars, 5g protein

"Buffalo Wing" Yellow Squash Ⓕ

Makes 5 servings: 4 "wings" and 3 tablespoons sauce each

These are a crispier and healthier take on Buffalo wings since they're baked till crisp and made from fresh summery squash. Don't forget the flavorful dipping sauce; it makes these fun and hearty veggie "wings" extra special when served as an appetizer. And for an extra special entrée, enjoy them in Crispy "Buffalo Wing" Squash Pizza (page 413).

2 medium yellow squash

1¼ cups low-fat buttermilk

1 teaspoon sea salt, or to taste

½ teaspoon hot pepper sauce, or to taste

½ teaspoon freshly ground black pepper, or to taste

1¼ cups stone-ground whole-wheat flour

2 large eggs

1¾ cups whole-wheat panko breadcrumbs

½ teaspoon garlic powder, or to taste

¼ teaspoon ground cayenne, or to taste

1 recipe Rosemary Ranch-Style Dipping Sauce (page 98) or 1 cup other dip

1. Cut the squash into 10 strips each, about 4 inches long, 2 inches wide, and ½ inch thick. (Reserve any remaining squash for another purpose.)

2. Preheat the oven to 450°F.

3. Add the buttermilk, ½ teaspoon of the salt, the hot pepper sauce, and black pepper to a medium bowl. In a second medium bowl, add the flour. In a third medium bowl, whisk the eggs with 2 tablespoons cold water and ¼ teaspoon of the salt. In a fourth bowl, add the panko.

4. Dip each squash strip into the buttermilk, then the flour, the egg mixture, and the panko, gently shaking off excess between each. (Note: You'll likely only use up to half each of the buttermilk mixture and flour, but it's helpful to use the amount suggested to allow for proper coating of the squash. Also, try to keep one hand as the "dry" one and one as the "wet" hand during the breading process.)

5. Place the coated yellow squash strips onto two large baking sheets. Coat with cooking spray (preferably homemade, page xix). Sprinkle with the garlic powder, cayenne, and remaining ¼ teaspoon salt. Bake until the squash is cooked through and the coating is crisp and golden, about 22 minutes, rotating trays about halfway through baking. Adjust seasoning. Drizzle with additional hot pepper sauce, if desired.

6. Serve the "wings" on a platter with the dipping sauce on the side.

Per serving: 260 calories, 7g total fat, 3g saturated fat, 0g trans fat, 85mg cholesterol, 530mg sodium, 39g total carbohydrate, 6g dietary fiber, 6g sugars, 13g protein

Panko-Crusted Zucchini Nuggets with Marinara

Makes 8 servings: 5 nuggets with ⅛ cup marinara each

You're never too old to enjoy dunking nuggets into something saucy. Since these crispy coins start with zucchini and never see the deep fryer, you'll never need to feel guilty about eating an appetizing plateful of them.

1¼ cups low-fat buttermilk

2 large garlic cloves, minced

1 teaspoon finely chopped fresh oregano
 or ½ teaspoon crushed dried oregano

1 teaspoon sea salt, or to taste

½ teaspoon freshly ground black pepper, or to taste

1¼ cups stone-ground whole-wheat flour

2 large eggs

¼ teaspoon ground cayenne, or to taste

1¾ cups whole-wheat panko breadcrumbs

2 medium zucchini, each cut into 20 coins

½ teaspoon garlic powder, or to taste

1 cup Fresh Marinara (page 101) or other marinara
 sauce, warm

1. Stir together the buttermilk, minced garlic, oregano, ½ teaspoon of the salt, and the black pepper in a medium bowl. In a second bowl, add the flour. In a third bowl, whisk the eggs with 2 tablespoons cold water, the cayenne, and ¼ teaspoon of the salt. In a fourth bowl, add the panko.

2. Preheat the oven to 450°F.

3. Dip each zucchini coin into the buttermilk, then the flour, the egg mixture, and the panko, gently shaking off excess between each. (Note: You'll likely only use up to half each of the buttermilk mixture and flour, but it's helpful to use the amount suggested to allow for proper coating of the squash. Also, try to keep one hand as the "dry" one and one as the "wet" hand during the breading process.)

4. Place the coated zucchini cubes onto two large baking sheets. Coat with cooking spray (preferably homemade, page xix). Sprinkle with the garlic powder and remaining ¼ teaspoon salt. Bake until the squash is cooked through and the coating is crisp and golden, about 22 minutes, rotating trays about halfway through baking. Adjust seasoning.

5. Serve the nuggets on a platter while warm with the marinara sauce on the side.

Per serving: 160 calories, 3g total fat, 1g saturated fat, 0g trans fat, 50mg cholesterol, 410mg sodium, 27g total carbohydrate, 4g dietary fiber, 5g sugars, 7g protein

Goat Cheese Medallions with Caramelized Onions

Makes 8 servings: 1 medallion each

If there is a food heaven, this dish, known as *queso de cabra con miel,* certainly is an angel. Though I usually say I love all my recipes equally but differently, this taste-bud tantalizer is one of my favorite small plates recipes.

2 teaspoons extra-virgin olive oil

1 large sweet onion, halved and very thinly sliced

2 teaspoons aged balsamic vinegar

½ teaspoon sea salt, or to taste

½ cup whole-wheat panko breadcrumbs

¼ teaspoon freshly ground black pepper, or to taste

1 (8-ounce) log soft goat cheese, at room
 temperature, sliced into 8 rounds

2 teaspoons honey, white truffle honey,
 or agave nectar

1 tablespoon chopped fresh flat-leaf parsley

1. Heat the oil in a large nonstick skillet over medium heat. Stir in the onion, vinegar, and ¼ teaspoon of the salt, cover, and cook until the onion is fully softened, about 8 minutes. Uncover, and cook while stirring occasionally, until the onion is fully caramelized, about 15 minutes. Cover and set aside.

2. Preheat the oven to 475°F. Combine the panko, pepper, and remaining ¼ teaspoon salt in a small bowl. Firmly dip each goat cheese round into the panko to fully coat the top, bottom, and sides. Place coated goat cheese rounds into an attractive baking dish. Coat with cooking spray (preferably homemade, page xix).

3. Bake until the coating is crisp and golden and cheese is warm, but not runny, about 10 minutes.

4. Remove from the oven. Pile 1 rounded tablespoon of the cooked onion on top of each medallion, drizzle each with ¼ teaspoon of the honey, sprinkle with the parsley, and serve while warm.

Per serving: 130 calories, 8g total fat, 4.5g saturated fat, 0g trans fat, 15mg cholesterol, 260mg sodium, 9g total carbohydrate, 1g dietary fiber, 4g sugars, 6g protein

Roasted Cauliflower Goat Cheese Toasts

Makes 8 servings: about ⅓ cup pâté with sauce and 3 toast slices each

A popular tapas dish to share is goat cheese baked with tomato sauce that's then spread onto garlic toasts, though it's easy to eat a little too much of it. My addition of roasted cauliflower whirled into the goat cheese makes this version extra flavorful and seem extra cheesy—and one that's all right to eat a little more of!

6 ounces small cauliflower florets (about 2 cups)
2 teaspoons extra-virgin olive oil
6 ounces soft goat cheese
¼ teaspoon sea salt, or to taste
1¼ cups Bell Pepper Marinara (page 102)
 or tomato-basil marinara sauce of choice
1 (8-ounce) whole-grain baguette, cut into
 24 slices on the diagonal
1 large garlic clove, halved

1. Preheat the oven to 375°F.

2. Toss the cauliflower florets with the oil, spread in a single layer on a parchment paper–lined baking pan, and roast in the oven until tender and lightly caramelized, about 30 minutes. Let cool slightly.

3. Add the roasted cauliflower, goat cheese, and salt to a food processor. Cover and puree until smooth. Pat the cheese-cauliflower mixture into a 1-inch-thick round pâté-like mound and place in a shallow 2-quart (10-inch) round baking dish.

4. Ladle the marinara sauce into the dish around the cheese-cauliflower mixture (not on top of it), to come about ¾ inch up the sides of the round.

5. Bake, uncovered, until the sauce begins to bubble around the edges and the mixture is hot, about 30 minutes. During the last 15 minutes arrange the bread slices in a single layer on a baking sheet, and toast in the oven until crisp. Rub each slice of toast with the cut end of the garlic.

6. Garnish the pâté-like mixture with fresh basil leaves, if desired, and serve while hot. Savor by generously spreading each toast with the cheese mixture and sauce.

Per serving: 180 calories, 8g total fat, 4g saturated fat, 0g trans fat, 10mg cholesterol, 440mg sodium, 19g total carbohydrate, 4g dietary fiber, 6g sugars, 9g protein

Monterey Bean Nachos

Makes 6 servings: 4 nachos each

This refined, bean-based version of nachos has all of the fun essence without all the grease. You might enjoy them so much that you'll double your portion and dive into it as your dinner entrée (as I did after I developed this recipe)!

½ cup fat-free or low-fat plain Greek yogurt

Juice of ½ lime (1 tablespoon)

1 (15-ounce) can no-salt-added black or pinto beans, drained

3 tablespoons Spicy Raw Tomatillo Salsa (page 114), salsa verde, or other salsa

¼ teaspoon chili powder, or to taste

⅛ teaspoon sea salt, or to taste

24 Hint-of-Lime Tortilla Chips (page 41) or other large tortilla chips

¾ cup shredded Monterey Jack cheese

24 fresh cilantro leaves

12 grape tomatoes, cut in half vertically

1. Combine the yogurt and lime juice in a small bowl and set aside.

2. Add the beans, salsa, chili powder, and salt to a large nonstick skillet over medium-high heat. Cook while stirring until the beans are hot and have absorbed the salsa, about 2 minutes.

3. On three large microwave-safe plates, arrange 8 tortilla chips each. Top each chip with 1 tablespoon of the bean mixture and a pinch of the cheese. Microwave each plate of nachos on high just until the cheese melts, about 30 seconds.

4. Top each individual nacho with 1 teaspoon of the yogurt–lime juice mixture, a cilantro leaf, and a grape tomato half. Serve while warm.

Per serving: 180 calories, 7g total fat, 3g saturated fat, 0g trans fat, 15mg cholesterol, 250mg sodium, 22g total carbohydrate, 5g dietary fiber, 2g sugars, 10g protein

Black and White Nachos

Makes 6 servings: 4 nachos each

This is what I consider an elegant nacho recipe since the toppings look rather artful instead of heavily plopped onto tortilla chips. It'll still be a palate-pleasing hit—and a party favorite. It's fit for a black-tie affair, an ultra casual soiree, or just as a starter for a fun family meal. Feel free to use all white or black beans, if you prefer.

½ (15-ounce) can black beans, drained

½ (15-ounce) can cannellini or other white beans, drained

⅓ cup finely diced white onion

1 small jalapeño pepper with some seeds, minced

2 tablespoons finely chopped fresh cilantro

Juice of 1 lime (2 tablespoons)

¼ teaspoon sea salt, or to taste

⅛ teaspoon ground cumin, or to taste

⅛ teaspoon chili powder (optional)

2 teaspoons grapeseed or canola oil

6 (6-inch) white corn tortillas

¾ cup shredded Monterey Jack cheese

1. Stir together the beans, onion, jalapeño, cilantro, 1 tablespoon of the lime juice, ⅛ teaspoon of the salt, cumin, and chili powder (if using) in a medium bowl. (Alternatively, stir together all of these ingredients except the beans. Divide into two bowls. Stir the black beans into one bowl and the white beans into the other.) Adjust seasoning. Set aside the bean-salsa mixture.

2. Preheat the oven to 400°F.

3. Whisk together the remaining 1 tablespoon lime juice, oil, and the remaining ⅛ teaspoon salt until well combined. Rub or brush the lime vinaigrette onto the entire surface of both sides of the tortillas, using all the vinaigrette. Cut the tortillas into 4 wedges each.

4. Place the tortilla wedges in a single layer on a large baking sheet. Bake until nearly crisp, about 12 minutes, rotating the tray halfway through the baking process.

5. Top each tortilla chip with ½ tablespoon of the cheese and bake until the cheese melts, about 5 minutes. Remove from the oven and let stand for 5 minutes to crisp further.

6. Place the tortilla chips on a large platter. Stir the prepared bean-salsa mixture, then top each chip with about 1 tablespoon of the mixture, and serve.

Nutrition info: 170 calories, 6g total fat, 3g saturated fat, 0g trans fat, 15mg cholesterol, 250mg sodium, 21g total carbohydrate, 5g dietary fiber, 3g sugars, 8g protein

White Party Pizzette Platter

Makes 8 servings: 1 piece each

I can't live without pizza. There, I said it! How about you? Here you don't even need to wait for dinner since you can have it as an app. This winter white version is so amazingly aromatic that you might just decide to have it for your entrée, too. Go ahead . . . plan for it!

6 ounces bite-size cauliflower florets
    (about 1½ cups)

1 tablespoon extra-virgin olive oil

1½ teaspoons white truffle oil or extra-virgin olive oil

1 large garlic clove, minced

2 teaspoons minced fresh chives (optional)

½ teaspoon finely chopped fresh rosemary

⅛ teaspoon sea salt or truffle salt, or to taste

⅛ teaspoon freshly ground black or white pepper,
    or to taste

⅛ teaspoon dried hot pepper flakes, or to taste

2 (7-inch) whole-grain pocketless pitas or
    soft flatbreads

3 ounces provolone cheese, thinly sliced

1 tablespoon freshly grated Parmigiano-Reggiano
    or other Parmesan cheese

1 tablespoon coarsely chopped fresh flat-leaf parsley

1. Preheat the oven to 450°F.

2. Toss the cauliflower with the olive oil, truffle oil, garlic, chives (if using), rosemary, salt, black pepper, and hot pepper flakes in a medium bowl.

3. Top the entire surface of each pita with equal amounts of the provolone, cauliflower mixture, and Parmigiano-Reggiano cheese.

4. Place both pizzettes on a large baking sheet and bake until the cauliflower is tender and beginning to caramelize and the crust is crisp, about 16 minutes.

5. Remove from the oven. Let stand for 5 minutes to complete the cooking process. Adjust seasoning. Sprinkle with the parsley. Cut each pizzette in quarters, arrange pieces on a platter, and serve immediately.

Nutrition info: 120 calories, 6g total fat, 2.5g saturated fat, 0g trans fat, 10mg cholesterol, 250mg sodium, 12g total carbohydrate, 2g dietary fiber, 1g sugars, 5g protein

Herb Rice–Stuffed Grape Leaves

Makes 8 servings: 4 stuffed leaves each

These Middle Eastern delights are not like the mushy, oily stuffed grape leaves you sometimes find in cans or on salad bars. That's a good thing as this is a much less oily, more flavorful whole-grain twist on a traditional recipe that my Lebanese mother taught me years ago. Thanks, Mom.

1⅓ cups brown basmati rice

3 large shallots, minced

⅓ cup finely chopped fresh mint

¼ cup finely chopped fresh flat-leaf parsley

3 tablespoons dried Zante currants or chopped black seedless raisins

2 large garlic cloves, minced

1¼ teaspoons sea salt, or to taste

¾ teaspoon freshly ground black pepper

½ teaspoon ground cinnamon

¼ teaspoon ground allspice

32 large fresh grape leaves, lightly blanched, or grape leaves from jar, soaked in water, rinsed well, and drained

2 lemons

2 tablespoons extra-virgin olive oil

1 cup fat-free or low-fat plain Greek yogurt

1. Combine the rice, shallots, mint, parsley, currants, garlic, salt, pepper, cinnamon, and allspice in a medium bowl. Add ¼ cup water and stir to combine. Set aside. (Makes about 2¾ cups rice mixture.)

2. Lay the grape leaves individually, dull (or vein) side up, on paper towels. Snip off any long stems. Place about 1 rounded tablespoon of the rice mixture across the center of each leaf. Roll each leaf tightly by folding the bottom end of each leaf over the filling, folding the edges over the filling, then rolling toward the leaf point, until they look like mini green burritos.

3. After rolling each leaf, place seam side down in a large, heavy-duty skillet, firmly packing them

in a single layer. Pour water over the rolls until just covered (about 3 cups).

4. Cut one of the lemons into small wedges and set aside. Cut the other lemon in half and squeeze it. Add lemon juice and 1 tablespoon of the oil over the stuffed grape leaves.

5. Place a heavy, heatproof plate onto the stuffed leaves to keep them from opening up during cooking. Place the skillet over high heat and bring to boil. Cover, reduce heat to low, and cook until the rice is nearly tender, about 55 minutes. Turn off heat and keep covered. Let stand until the rice is fully cooked and the leaves are tender, about 20 minutes. Remove the lid and plate.

6. Arrange the stuffed grape leaves with the reserved lemon wedges and yogurt on a platter, drizzle the grape leaves with the remaining 1 tablespoon oil, and serve while warm or at room temperature.

Per serving: 180 calories, 5g total fat, 0.5g saturated fat, 0g trans fat, 0mg cholesterol, 380mg sodium, 31g total carbohydrate, 3g dietary fiber, 6g sugars, 6g protein

Tijuana Tortilla Pinwheels

Makes 12 servings: 3 roll-ups each

When you need a party hors d'oeuvres that's both kid and adult friendly, these pop-in-your-mouth tortilla pinwheels are a perfect pick. They kind of look like Mexican sushi rolls. But instead of being fishy, they're fresh and zesty.

4 ounces Neufchâtel (light cream cheese), at room temperature

3 tablespoons Roasted Green Tomato Salsa (page 114) or other salsa, drained of excess liquid

1 small jalapeño pepper with seeds, minced

2 scallions, green and white parts, minced

2 tablespoons finely chopped fresh cilantro

1 teaspoon finely chopped fresh oregano

½ teaspoon grated lime zest (optional)

¼ teaspoon ground cumin

6 (8-inch) stone-ground whole-wheat or sprouted grain tortillas

1 (15-ounce) can pinto or red kidney beans, drained

36 whole fresh cilantro leaves

1. Add the Neufchâtel, salsa, jalapeño, scallions, chopped cilantro, oregano, lime zest (if using), and cumin to a medium bowl and stir until well combined.

2. Spread about 2 rounded tablespoons of the Neufchâtel mixture on one entire side of each tortilla. Sprinkle the entire surface of each tortilla with about 3 tablespoons of the beans. Tightly roll up. Chill in the refrigerator for at least 30 minutes.

3. Slice about ½ inch off each end of the rolled tortillas. Then slice each rolled tortilla into 6 equal pieces.

4. Stand each pinwheel piece on a cut edge and garnish the top with 1 cilantro leaf. Chill in the refrigerator until ready to serve.

Per serving: 120 calories, 3.5g total fat, 1g saturated fat, 0g trans fat, 5mg cholesterol, 150mg sodium, 16g total carbohydrate, 3g dietary fiber, 2g sugars, 4g protein

Hoisin Broccoli and Cauliflower Dumplings

Makes 12 servings: 3 dumplings each

This veggie-loaded steamed dumpling rendition may become a new tradition—they're better for you and taste great. Take delight in these dumplings as is or dip into Szechuan Sesame-Ginger Soy Sauce (page 130).

½ cup drained canned no-salt-added chickpeas
 (garbanzo beans)

1 large egg

1 tablespoon hoisin sauce (at right)

1¼ teaspoons naturally brewed soy sauce

2 teaspoons toasted sesame oil

½ teaspoon sea salt, or to taste

¼ teaspoon dried hot pepper flakes

½ cup finely chopped broccoli florets

½ cup finely chopped cauliflower florets

⅓ cup coarsely grated carrots

2 scallions, green and white parts, minced

2 teaspoons freshly grated gingerroot

1 tablespoon finely chopped fresh cilantro

36 square whole-wheat wonton or
 round dumpling wrappers

1. Add the chickpeas, egg, hoisin sauce, soy sauce, sesame oil, salt, and hot pepper flakes to a food processor. Cover and puree until smooth. Pour into a medium mixing bowl and stir in the broccoli, cauliflower, carrots, scallions, ginger, and cilantro until combined.

2. Keep the wonton wrappers covered with a damp clean kitchen towel. One at a time, lightly brush the edges of each wrapper with fresh cold water. Place 1½ teaspoons of the vegetable mixture in the center of the wrapper, join the corners in the middle over the filling, and pinch firmly to form a purse. (If using round wrappers, form dumplings into half-moons.) Work in four batches of 9 dumplings each and stir the mixture before filling each wrapper.

3. Preheat the oven to 200°F.

4. Bring about 1 inch of water to a simmer in a large saucepan over medium heat. Spray a steamer basket with cooking spray (preferably homemade, page xix), if necessary, to help prevent sticking. Place 9 of the dumplings (or as many dumplings as can fit) into the steamer without touching. Cover and steam until dumpling wrappers and filling are cooked through, about 15 minutes. Remove the dumplings from the steamer to a heatproof platter and place in the oven to keep warm. Repeat until all of the dumplings are steamed, adding additional water for simmering between batches, if necessary. Serve warm.

Per serving: 100 calories, 1.5g total fat, 0g saturated fat, 0g trans fat, 20mg cholesterol, 300mg sodium, 17g total carbohydrate, 1g dietary fiber, 1g sugars, 4g protein

HOISIN-STYLE SAUCE

If desired, you can make your own preservative-free, hoisin-style sauce. Mix together 2 tablespoons naturally brewed soy sauce, 1 tablespoon natural peanut or almond butter, 1½ teaspoons honey or agave nectar, 1½ teaspoons brown rice vinegar, and 1 teaspoon toasted sesame oil. Makes about ¼ cup.

South Asian Potato and Spring Pea Samosas

Makes 24 servings: 1 samosa each

Phyllo dough is the secret to the flakiest finger foods. It's easier to work with than you might think. And it's the secret to making these samosas a new favorite. For extra enjoyment, pair these warm, aromatic bites with Fresh Mint Chutney (page 119) or chutney or raita of choice.

1 tablespoon unrefined peanut or grapeseed oil

½ cup finely chopped white onion

1½ teaspoons freshly grated gingerroot

2 teaspoons brown rice vinegar

½ cup fresh or frozen spring peas, thawed

1 tablespoon ground coriander

1 teaspoon ground cumin

1 teaspoon grated lemon zest

½ teaspoon garam masala or freshly ground black pepper

½ teaspoon sea salt, to taste

¼ teaspoon chili powder

1 pound Yukon gold potatoes, unpeeled, scrubbed, baked, and smashed

¼ cup chopped fresh cilantro

2 tablespoons unsalted butter, melted, or unrefined peanut oil

2 tablespoons tahini (sesame seed paste)

1 teaspoon Dijon mustard

24 sheets whole-wheat or spelt phyllo dough, thawed if frozen

1. Heat the oil in a large skillet over medium-high heat. Add the onion, ginger, and vinegar and sauté for 3 minutes. Add the peas, coriander, cumin, lemon zest, garam masala, salt, and chili powder and sauté for 2 minutes. Add the potatoes and cilantro and sauté for 2 minutes. Adjust seasoning. Transfer to a bowl and set aside.

2. Whisk together the butter, tahini, mustard, and 3 tablespoons water until smooth. Set aside. (If mixture gets too thick as it sits, add extra water by the teaspoon.)

3. Preheat the oven to 400°F.

4. Unroll and cover the phyllo sheets with a damp clean kitchen towel. One at a time, lay a phyllo sheet flat on a clean surface and very lightly brush with the melted butter mixture. Fold in one-third of the phyllo lengthways toward the middle. Very lightly brush again with the butter mixture and fold in the other side to make a long triple-layered rectangle. (Note: If you prefer smaller hors d'oeuvre-size rather than appetizer-size samosas, fold in the phyllo lengthwise completely, then brush, then fold again to form a 4-layer sheet instead of a 3-layer sheet.)

5. Place 1 rounded tablespoon of the vegetable mixture at one end of the long rectangle, leaving about a 1-inch border. Take the right corner and fold diagonally to the left, encasing the filling and forming a triangle. Then fold along the upper crease of the triangle, and continue folding in this manner until you reach the end of the long rectangle. Place on a parchment paper–lined baking sheet and very lightly brush the outer surface with the remaining butter mixture.

6. Bake in the oven until crisp and golden brown, about 25 minutes, rotating halfway through the baking process.

7. Place the samosas onto a large platter and serve.

Per serving: 110 calories, 3g total fat, 1g saturated fat, 0g trans fat, 5mg cholesterol, 160mg sodium, 19g total carbohydrate, 2g dietary fiber, 1g sugars, 3g protein

Southwestern Egg Rolls Ⓕ

Makes 6 servings: 1 roll and 2 tablespoons dipping sauce each

This recipe is sort of a cross between a burrito and an egg roll. Whatever you want to call these rolls, the most important thing is that they're tasty and super hearty. Add the dipping sauce for super satisfaction.

1 (15-ounce) can no-salt-added black beans, drained

⅓ cup fat-free or low-fat plain Greek yogurt

Juice of 1 lime (2 tablespoons)

½ teaspoon ground cumin

¾ teaspoon sea salt, or to taste

8 ounces Swiss chard with tender stems, chopped, steamed, and drained, if necessary

3 scallions, green and white parts, minced

3 tablespoons finely chopped fresh cilantro

1 small jalapeño pepper with some seeds, minced

6 (8-inch) stone-ground whole-wheat or sprouted grain tortillas

1 large egg

1 tablespoon finely chopped pumpkin seeds

¾ cup Avocado-Ranch Dipping Sauce (page 98) or salsa, or to taste

1. Add the beans, yogurt, 1 tablespoon of the lime juice, the cumin, and ¼ teaspoon of the salt to a food processor. Cover and puree. Set aside.

2. Preheat the oven to 475°F.

3. Add the chard, scallions, cilantro, jalapeño, remaining 1 tablespoon lime juice, and remaining ½ teaspoon salt to a medium bowl and stir to combine.

4. Spread about 3 rounded tablespoons of the bean filling down the center of each tortilla, then top with about 3 rounded tablespoons of the chard mixture (leaving about 1 inch on each end untopped). Tightly roll up each tortilla to form a long skinny log. Place seam side down onto a parchment paper–lined 9 × 13-inch baking pan.

5. Whisk the egg with 1 tablespoon of cold water. Brush the entire surface of each roll with the egg wash. Sprinkle the top of each roll evenly with the pumpkin seeds. Bake until the ends are crisp and fully browned, about 9 minutes.

6. Cut each roll in half diagonally with a serrated knife. Serve rolls warm with the dipping sauce on the side.

Per serving: 260 calories, 7g total fat, 1g saturated fat, 0g trans fat, 10mg cholesterol, 610mg sodium, 37g total carbohydrate, 7g dietary fiber, 3g sugars, 12g protein

Shrimp Spring Rolls

Makes 12 servings: 1 roll each

Spring rolls are an Asian appetizer that are sometimes fresh and sometimes fried. Mine are somewhat of a hybrid between fresh and fried and somewhat Asian fusion. But there's nothing "somewhat" about their taste; they're 100 percent sumptuous, especially when paired with Szechuan Sesame-Ginger Soy Sauce (page 130).

1 tablespoon canola or grapeseed oil

1 cup coleslaw mix or shredded green cabbage

½ cup finely diced baby bok choy or celery

1 small or ½ large red bell pepper, finely diced

1 pound cooked small shrimp, chilled and peeled

¼ cup thinly sliced crosswise canned or frozen baby corn, thawed

2 scallions, green and white parts, thinly sliced

2 tablespoons finely chopped fresh basil

2 tablespoons naturally brewed soy sauce

2 teaspoons freshly grated gingerroot

1 large garlic clove, minced

12 sheets whole-wheat or spelt phyllo dough, thawed if frozen

1. Preheat the oven to 425°F.

2. Heat the oil in a large skillet over medium-high heat. Add the coleslaw mix, bok choy, and bell pepper and sauté until crisp-tender, about 3 minutes.

3. Add the sautéed vegetables to a medium bowl along with the shrimp, baby corn, scallions, basil, soy sauce, ginger, and garlic. Stir until combined.

4. Unroll and cover the phyllo sheets with a damp clean kitchen towel. One at a time, lay a phyllo sheet flat on a clean surface. Spray with cooking spray (preferably homemade, page xix) and fold the sheet in half to form a long rectangle (about 6 × 17 inches); spray again. Place the short side of the rectangle toward you. Working with one sheet at a time, place ¼ cup of the filling near the bottom of the sheet, leaving about 1 to 1½ inches unfilled

at both sides of the sheet. Fold the bottom flap up over the filling, then the full side edges in, and spray again. Gently roll up tightly (like a burrito) to form a short stubby roll. Place seam side down, and spray again. Repeat with the remaining phyllo and filling. Place the rolls onto a large parchment paper–lined baking sheet.

5. Bake the rolls until golden and flaky, about 15 minutes. Let stand for 5 minutes. Serve whole or cut in half diagonally.

Per serving: 140 calories, 3g total fat, 0g saturated fat, 0g trans fat, 55mg cholesterol, 310mg sodium, 17g total carbohydrate, 1g dietary fiber, 1g sugars, 10g protein

Farmers' Market Stuffed Russet Skins

Makes 8 servings: 1 stuffed skin each

Have a hankering for comfort food? These very-stuffed veggie potato skins are filling, flavorful, and fully comforting. Want still more comfort? Serve with additional Greek yogurt.

4 large russet potatoes, unpeeled and scrubbed

6 large garlic cloves

1½ teaspoons extra-virgin olive oil

1 teaspoon sea salt, or to taste

¼ teaspoon freshly ground black pepper

1½ cups diced, roasted, or steamed vegetables of choice, such as broccoli and cauliflower

½ cup fat-free or low-fat plain Greek yogurt

4 scallions, green and white parts, thinly sliced

2 tablespoons chopped fresh flat-leaf parsley

¼ teaspoon ground cayenne

¾ cup shredded extra-sharp Cheddar cheese

1. Preheat the oven to 450°F. Prick the potatoes a few times with a fork and bake the potatoes on a rack in the middle of the oven until skin is crisp and flesh is tender, about 1 hour. Position a baking sheet on the rack below to catch any drippings, if desired. Meanwhile, place the garlic cloves on aluminum foil, drizzle with the oil, wrap, place in

the oven next to the potatoes, and roast until tender, about 20 minutes. Remove the potatoes and garlic from oven and let cool slightly.

2. Reduce oven temperature to 400°F.

3. Cut each potato lengthwise in half. Scoop out the centers into a medium bowl, leaving about ½-inch-thick rim. Place the skins, skin side down, on a baking sheet. Add ¼ teaspoon of the salt and the pepper.

4. Smash the garlic. Add the garlic, vegetables, yogurt, three-fourths of the scallions, the parsley, cayenne, and remaining ¾ teaspoon salt to the bowl with the potato filling. Stir until just combined. Stuff the vegetable mixture into the skins. Sprinkle with the cheese. Bake until the filling is hot and cheese is melted, about 15 minutes.

5. Transfer the skins to a platter. Sprinkle with remaining scallions and serve.

Per serving: 210 calories, 4.5g total fat, 2.5g saturated fat, 0g trans fat, 10mg cholesterol, 390mg sodium, 35g total carbohydrate, 4g dietary fiber, 3g sugars, 8g protein

Devilish Spiced Eggs

Makes 4 servings: 2 stuffed egg halves each

You don't have to worry about getting a devilish surprise when you bite into these deviled eggs. The sprinkling of spice on top of each gives it away so you can choose your favorite to delight!

4 large hard-cooked eggs, peeled and cut in half
    lengthwise (page 377)
1 tablespoon fat-free or low-fat plain Greek yogurt
1 tablespoon mayonnaise
¾ teaspoon Dijon mustard
Pinch of sea salt
Pinch each of different spices, such as paprika,
    cayenne, black pepper, white pepper, ground
    cumin, ground coriander, curry powder, and
    chili powder

1. Remove the egg yolks to a small bowl and mash well with a fork. Add the yogurt, mayonnaise, mustard, and salt and stir well until creamy.

2. Fill the empty egg white shells with the egg yolk mixture with a fork or use a piping bag for a more elegant presentation. Chill in the refrigerator until ready to eat.

3. Sprinkle the top of each egg half with a different spice and serve.

Per serving: 100 calories, 8g total fat, 2g saturated fat, 0g trans fat, 185mg cholesterol, 180mg sodium, 1g total carbohydrate, 0g dietary fiber, 0g sugars, 7g protein

Homemade Pretzel Puffs

Makes 24 servings: 1 pretzel puff each

You'll amaze yourself when you try these aromatically enticing bites that you've created. Serve them just-baked from the oven. Got mustard?

1½ cups warm (115°F) water
1½ teaspoons mild honey or agave nectar
1 (¼-ounce) envelope active dry yeast
4⅓ cups whole-wheat pastry flour
1½ teaspoons sea salt
3 tablespoons unsalted butter, melted
1 teaspoon extra-virgin olive oil
6 tablespoons baking soda
1 large egg
¾ teaspoon fleur de sel or kosher salt

1. Combine the water with the honey in a large liquid measuring cup. Sprinkle the yeast on top and gently stir. Allow to stand for 5 minutes or until the mixture begins to foam.

2. Add 4 cups of the flour and the salt to a large mixing bowl and stir to combine. Make a well in the center of the flour mixture. Add the warm yeast liquid to the flour mixture along with the butter, and stir until well combined.

continues on next page

3. Knead the dough on a lightly floured surface (using only as much of the remaining ⅓ cup flour as needed) until the dough is just smooth and springy, about 7 to 8 minutes. Rub the dough ball with the oil, place into a clean bowl, cover and let stand in a warm place until the dough doubles in size, about 45 minutes.

4. Preheat the oven to 425°F. Line two large baking sheets with parchment paper. Set aside.

5. Divide the dough into four portions. Roll each portion into 6 balls, placing 12 of the balls onto each baking sheet.

6. Meanwhile, bring 1½ quarts (6 cups) water and the baking soda to a rolling boil in a medium saucepan.

7. Using a slotted spoon, gently dunk the pretzel balls into the boiling water (no more than 3 balls at a time), for about 30 seconds. Then place back onto the baking sheet.

8. Whisk the egg with 1 tablespoon cold water. Brush the top of each pretzel ball with the egg wash and sprinkle with the fleur de sel. (Note: You will not use all of the egg wash.)

9. Bake until the pretzels are a rich golden brown and have a distinctive crackled appearance, about 15 minutes, rotating trays halfway through the baking process. Transfer to a rack to cool for at least 5 minutes, and serve.

Per serving: 100 calories, 2g total fat, 1g saturated fat, 0g trans fat, 10mg cholesterol, 290mg sodium, 17g total carbohydrate, 3g dietary fiber, 0g sugars, 2g protein

Other Finger Foods: Poultry, Fish, Shellfish, and Meat

Turkey Sliders

Makes 8 servings: 1 slider each

You'll find condiments inside this turkey burger instead of just on top—which creates a super tasty and moist bite. The avocado topping adds that ideal touch of an indulgent component. And on that occasion you'd prefer to go bun-free and enjoy these burgers as "pancakes," they're only 110 calories a pop!

12 ounces ground turkey (about 94% lean)
⅔ cup finely chopped fresh spinach or other leafy green
½ cup grated red or white onion
⅓ cup old-fashioned oats
3 tablespoons ketchup
1 teaspoon finely chopped fresh oregano
¾ teaspoon sea salt, or to taste
½ teaspoon grated lemon zest (optional)
¼ teaspoon freshly ground black pepper, or to taste
1 Hass avocado, pitted, peeled, and cubed
2 teaspoons fresh lemon juice
1 medium vine-ripened tomato, cut into 8 slices
8 small (1¾-ounce) whole-grain rolls, split

1. Add the turkey, spinach, onion, oats, ketchup, oregano, ½ teaspoon of the salt, the lemon zest (if using), and pepper to a medium bowl. Gently mix by hand and form into 8 balls, about ⅓ cup each. Set aside.

2. Add the avocado, lemon juice, and remaining ¼ teaspoon salt to a small bowl and mash with a fork. Set aside.

3. Heat a large nonstick skillet over medium heat. Add 4 of the turkey balls, patting down to form 3½-inch patties with the back of a spatula, and cook until well done, about 5 to 6 minutes per side (flip using a separate spatula that didn't touch the raw turkey mixture). Repeat with the remaining turkey balls. Adjust seasoning.

4. Place a tomato slice, then a turkey patty on the bottom half of each roll, spread 1 tablespoon of the avocado mixture onto the top half of each roll, form into burgers, and enjoy while warm.

Per serving: 240 calories, 8g total fat, 1.5g saturated fat, 0g trans fat, 25mg cholesterol, 520mg sodium, 29g total carbohydrate, 6g dietary fiber, 6g sugars, 16g protein

Tequila Turkey Cocktail Meatballs

Makes 8 servings: 3 meatballs with 3 tablespoons sauce

Who doesn't love a good meatball? And good is exactly what you'll be saying about this mini toothpick-ready turkey adaptation. These sweet-n-savory bites are just right for a summer gathering or Labor Day party.

3 medium or 2 large vine-ripened tomatoes, coarsely chopped

2 medium or 2 large ripe blood plums, pitted and quartered

1 teaspoon sea salt, or to taste

¼ cup 80-proof tequila, such as 4 Copas

12 ounces ground turkey (about 94% lean)

2 large poblano peppers, roasted or grilled, charred skin removed, and finely chopped

½ cup plain dry whole-grain breadcrumbs

¼ cup grated white onion

1 large egg, lightly beaten

Juice of ½ lime (1 tablespoon)

½ teaspoon freshly ground black pepper, or to taste

1. Add the tomatoes to a blender. Cover and blend on low until just pureed. Add the plums and ½ teaspoon of the salt. Cover and blend on low until just combined. Pour into a large saucepan, stir in the tequila, and place over medium-high heat.

2. Combine the turkey, poblanos, breadcrumbs, onion, egg, lime juice, black pepper, and remaining ½ teaspoon salt in a medium bowl. Form the mixture into 24 meatballs, about 1½ tablespoons each.

3. When the tomato-plum mixture reaches a boil, reduce heat to medium, very carefully add the meatballs one by one, and cover. Cook until done, about 10 minutes, stirring once halfway through the cooking process. Turn off heat. Let "lid cook" (see page xxviii) until the meatballs have absorbed some sauce, about 10 minutes.

4. Transfer the meatballs with a slotted spoon to a small saucepan or serving dish, cover, and set aside.

5. Bring the sauce in the large saucepan to a boil over medium-high heat. Let continue to boil, while stirring occasionally, until reduced to about 1½ cups, about 5 minutes. Pour the sauce reduction over the meatballs.

6. Insert toothpicks into each meatball and serve warm with the sauce.

Per serving: 170 calories, 6g total fat, 1.5g saturated fat, 0g trans fat, 65mg cholesterol, 440mg sodium, 12g total carbohydrate, 2g dietary fiber, 5g sugars, 13g protein

Slim Chicken Nachos

Makes 6 servings: 4 nachos each

Kids and adults will love these hip, highly flavored nachos. Using ground chicken breast makes these satisfying yet slim. Who would ever think nachos could be considered slimming?

½ cup fat-free or low-fat plain Greek yogurt
2 teaspoons fresh lime juice
10 ounces ground chicken breast
¼ teaspoon chili powder, or to taste
¼ teaspoon sea salt, or to taste
3 tablespoons Vine-Ripened Pico de Gallo
    (page 114) or thick salsa of choice
24 Hint-of-Lime Tortilla Chips (page 41)
    or other large tortilla chips
¾ cup shredded Monterey Jack cheese
24 fresh cilantro leaves
12 grape tomatoes, cut in half vertically

1. Combine the yogurt and lime juice in a small bowl and set aside.

2. Heat a large nonstick skillet over medium-high heat. Add the chicken, chili powder, and salt; cook while stirring until chicken is done and crumbled, about 5 minutes. Stir in the salsa. Cook until the salsa is absorbed by the chicken, about 1 minute.

3. On three separate large microwave-safe plates, arrange 8 tortilla chips. Top each with 1 tablespoon of the chicken mixture and a pinch of the cheese. Microwave each serving on high for 30 seconds, or just until cheese is just melted.

4. Top each with 1 teaspoon of the yogurt mixture, a cilantro leaf, and a grape tomato half. Serve warm.

Per serving: 180 calories, 8g total fat, 3.5g saturated fat, 0g trans fat, 40mg cholesterol, 320mg sodium, 12g total carbohydrate, 1g dietary fiber, 2g sugars, 16g protein

Wild Peruvian Chicken Wings

Makes 8 servings: 3 wings each

If you have a craving for chicken with the skin, here's your culinary ticket to enjoyment. The Peruvian flair is the key to their memorable flavor.

1 (15-ounce) can Great Northern or other
    white beans, drained
Juice and zest of 1 lime (2 tablespoons juice)
2 tablespoons honey or agave nectar
2 tablespoons naturally brewed soy sauce
2 teaspoons chili-garlic paste
1½ teaspoons toasted sesame oil
24 split chicken wings with skin
⅛ teaspoon sea salt, or to taste

1. Add the beans, lime juice, honey, soy sauce, chili-garlic paste, and oil to a blender. Cover and puree. Pour the bean sauce into a bowl, add the chicken, and toss to coat. Cover and place in the refrigerator to marinate for 2 to 4 hours. Remove chicken and discard excess marinade.

2. Preheat the oven to 475°F.

3. Place the marinated chicken on a parchment paper–lined baking sheet. Sprinkle with the salt. Bake until the chicken is done and skin is fully caramelized and slightly crisp, about 20 minutes, rotating the tray halfway through the baking process. Remove from the oven and let stand for 5 minutes. Adjust seasoning.

4. Place the chicken on a serving platter, sprinkle with the lime zest, and serve while warm.

Per serving: 220 calories, 13g total fat, 3.5g saturated fat, 0g trans fat, 55mg cholesterol, 250mg sodium, 6g total carbohydrate, 1g dietary fiber, 3g sugars, 19g protein

ADOBO-STYLE SEASONING

Mix together ½ teaspoon onion powder, ¼ teaspoon ground cumin, and ¼ teaspoon crushed, dried oregano leaves. Makes 1 teaspoon.

Flash-Fried Adobo Chicken Fingers

Makes 6 servings: 2 fingers each

This recipe uses my flash-frying technique, so only a little oil (about 2 tablespoons) actually winds up in these scrumptious, super-moist bites. Licking your fingers will be required.

1 pound boneless, skinless chicken breasts, sliced into 12 long strips ("fingers")

¾ cup low-fat buttermilk

2 large garlic cloves, minced

1 teaspoon sea salt, or to taste

¾ cup plain dry whole-wheat breadcrumbs

1 teaspoon adobo seasoning (page 76)

½ teaspoon fresh ground black pepper

½ teaspoon ground cayenne

⅛ teaspoon ground cinnamon

2 cups grapeseed or peanut oil

1. Add the chicken, buttermilk, garlic, and ½ teaspoon of the salt to a medium bowl. Let marinate for 30 to 45 minutes. (If longer than 1 hour, marinate covered in the refrigerator.)

2. Preheat the oven to 425°F.

3. Stir together the breadcrumbs, adobo seasoning, pepper, cayenne, cinnamon and remaining ½ teaspoon salt in a large bowl. One at a time, remove a chicken strip from the buttermilk marinade, shake off the excess, and thoroughly coat the chicken fingers with the breadcrumb mixture. Discard leftover marinade.

4. Heat the oil in a large skillet over high heat. Once hot (but not smoking), add the chicken (in two batches of 6 fingers each) and fry until the coating is browned yet chicken is not fully cooked, about 1 minute. For best results, make sure the chicken is fully immersed in the oil so there's no need to flip each piece. Place each finger onto a rack to drain.

5. Place the flash-fried chicken fingers on a baking sheet and bake until the chicken is fully cooked, about 7 minutes. Let stand on the sheet on a rack for at least 5 minutes before serving.

6. Serve the chicken fingers while warm or at room temperature, with or without a dipping sauce of choice. Enjoy with a fork and knife.

Per serving: 170 calories, 7g total fat, 1g saturated fat, 0g trans fat, 40mg cholesterol, 360mg sodium, 8g total carbohydrate, 1g dietary fiber, 1g sugars, 17g protein

Smoked Salmon Pâté Canapés

Makes 6 servings: 3 pieces each

Some Scottish cuisine is unsurpassed in the world. Their salmon is one of those foods—and it's the highlight of these cucumber canapés. Adding cucumber to Neufchâtel creates a naturally lighter topping that's full of interest.

1 large English cucumber, unpeeled

¼ cup Neufchâtel (light cream cheese)

1 teaspoon grated lemon zest

⅛ teaspoon salt, or to taste

⅛ teaspoon freshly ground black pepper, or to taste

¼ cup finely chopped red onion

8 ounces thinly sliced Scottish smoked salmon, cut into 18 pieces

1 tablespoon minced fresh chives or scallion

½ teaspoon chopped fresh dill

1. Finely mince one-fourth of the cucumber. Cut the other three-fourths of the cucumber into 18 slices on the diagonal, about ⅓ inch thick.

2. Stir together the Neufchâtel, minced cucumber, lemon zest, salt, and pepper in a small bowl until well combined.

3. Pat both sides of each cucumber slice dry with paper towels. Top each cucumber slice with 2 teaspoons of the Neufchâtel mixture. Sprinkle with the onion. Top each with one piece of the salmon. Arrange on a platter. Sprinkle with the chives and dill, and serve immediately.

Per serving: 80 calories, 4g total fat, 2g saturated fat, 0g trans fat, 15mg cholesterol, 390mg sodium, 3g total carbohydrate, 0g dietary fiber, 1g sugars, 8g protein

Sassy Shrimp Cocktail

Makes 4 servings: about 8 shrimp each

Shrimp cocktail doesn't have to be plain shrimp served with a side of cocktail sauce. This globally inspired version is so much more interesting. And presented in a martini glass, it is so much more party worthy. Or for quirkier style, serve in grapefruit-peel halves and garnish with additional fresh cilantro.

1 cup fresh-squeezed pink grapefruit
    or blood orange juice

¼ cup ketchup

3 tablespoons 80-proof tequila, such as 4 Copas

Juice of 1 lime (2 tablespoons)

2 tablespoons honey or agave nectar

2 teaspoons Asian garlic-chili sauce

2 tablespoons unrefined peanut oil or flaxseed oil

1 pound gently cooked chilled peeled or thawed
    frozen large shrimp with tail (about 32 shrimp)

¼ cup very thinly sliced red onion

½ cup finely chopped fresh cilantro

1. Combine the grapefruit juice, ketchup, tequila, lime juice, honey, and garlic-chili sauce in a large bowl. Whisk in the oil. Stir in the shrimp, onion, and cilantro.

2. Cover and refrigerate for about 2 hours (and no more than 4 hours).

3. Place individual servings in martini glasses or arrange the shrimp and onion on a platter. Drizzle each portion with about 1 tablespoon of the marinade and serve.

Per serving: 140 calories, 2.5g total fat, 0.5g saturated fat, 0g trans fat, 220mg cholesterol, 290mg sodium, 4g total carbohydrate, 0g dietary fiber, 2g sugars, 24g protein

Chutney-Dressed Crab Cakes

Makes 8 servings: 2 crab cakes each

The spices in these crab cakes and the zingy chutney topping will be sure to intrigue. The crispy bites will transport your taste buds to India.

4½ tablespoons canola or grapeseed oil

½ cup finely chopped red onion

2 teaspoons brown rice vinegar

1 teaspoon freshly grated gingerroot

½ teaspoon ground coriander

½ teaspoon ground cumin

¼ teaspoon ground turmeric

⅛ teaspoon freshly ground black pepper, or to taste

1 pound fresh premium wild lump crabmeat,
    picked over and separated into chunks

3 large eggs, lightly beaten

1¾ cups whole-wheat panko breadcrumbs

1 tablespoon chopped fresh cilantro

¼ teaspoon sea salt, or to taste

½ cup Tamarind Fresh Fig Chutney (page 121)
    or Major Grey's chutney

1. Heat 1½ teaspoons of the oil in a large nonstick skillet over medium heat. Add the onion, vinegar, ginger, coriander, cumin, turmeric, and pepper and sauté until the onion is softened, about 5 minutes. Transfer to a large bowl. Stir in the crabmeat, eggs, 1 cup of the panko, and the cilantro. Form the crab mixture into 16 cakes (about ¼ cup each), about ¾ inch thick.

2. Carefully dredge the cakes in the remaining ¾ cup panko, coating completely.

3. Heat 2 tablespoons of the remaining oil in the skillet over medium-high heat. Gently transfer 8 of the cakes to the skillet with a spatula. Cook until crisp, browned, and cooked through, about 1½ minutes per side. (Hint: When placing crab cakes in the skillet, arrange in a clockwise manner so that you know which one needs to be flipped over first.) Transfer to a platter. Repeat with remaining 2 tablespoons oil and crab cakes. Add the salt.

4. Serve each crab cake topped with 1½ teaspoons of the chutney. Garnish with additional cilantro, if desired.

Per serving: 250 calories, 11g total fat, 1.5g saturated fat, 0g trans fat, 120mg cholesterol, 350mg sodium, 21g total carbohydrate, 3g dietary fiber, 8g sugars, 17g protein

Broiled Sardines Oregano

Makes 2 servings: 4 fillet halves each

You're just minutes away from a savory, mouthwatering treat. I promise, you'll be delighted by these cute little fishies, especially in this Mediterranean-inspired recipe.

1 (4.375-ounce) can oil-packed wild sardines, drained and halved lengthwise
1 small shallot, minced
⅛ teaspoon freshly ground black pepper, or to taste
⅛ teaspoon dried hot pepper flakes
1 large garlic clove, minced
½ teaspoon finely chopped fresh oregano
2 lemon wedges

1. Preheat the broiler.

2. Place sardines, skin side down, in a 9×13-inch or similar-size baking dish. Sprinkle with the shallot, black pepper, and hot pepper flakes. Broil about 6 inches from the heat source for 2 minutes. Sprinkle with the garlic and continue to broil until the sardines are fully heated and garlic is lightly caramelized, about 1 minute. Adjust seasoning.

3. Transfer the sardines to serving plates or leave in the baking dish, sprinkle with the oregano, and serve with the lemon wedges.

Per serving: 130 calories, 9g total fat, 1g saturated fat, 0g trans fat, 25mg cholesterol, 290mg sodium, 3g total carbohydrate, 0g dietary fiber, 1g sugars, 11g protein

Bok Choy, Scallion, and Pork Dumplings

Makes 12 servings: 3 dumplings each

Though nearly every culture has a dumpling that it's known for, Chinese dumplings—or *jiaozi* (also known as *gyoza* in Japan)—may be the best known of them all. At fewer than 50 calories each, these high-flavored steamed pork and veggie dumplings may become the best known in your kitchen. Enjoy them dipped into Szechuan Sesame-Ginger Soy Sauce (page 130) or other sauce of choice for extra palate pizzazz.

½ cup drained canned no-salt-added chickpeas (garbanzo beans)
1 large egg
2 teaspoons hoisin sauce (page 67)
1¼ teaspoons naturally brewed soy sauce
2 teaspoons toasted sesame oil
¼ teaspoon sea salt, or to taste
¼ teaspoon dried hot pepper flakes
8 ounces ground lean pork
½ cup finely chopped bok choy, baby bok choy, or green cabbage
3 scallions, green and white parts, minced
1 tablespoon finely chopped fresh cilantro
2 teaspoons freshly grated gingerroot
36 square wonton or round dumpling wrappers (preferably whole-wheat)

1. Add the chickpeas, egg, hoisin sauce, soy sauce, oil, salt, and hot pepper flakes to a food processor. Cover and puree. Pour into a medium bowl with the pork, bok choy, scallions, cilantro, and ginger. Mix by hand until combined.

2. Keep the wonton wrappers covered with a damp clean kitchen towel. One at a time, lightly brush the edges of each wrapper with fresh cold water. Place about 1 tablespoon of the filling in the center of the wrapper, join the corners in the

continues on next page

middle over the filling, and pinch firmly to form a square purse. (If using round wrappers, form dumplings into half-moons.) Place on a baking sheet and cover with another damp clean kitchen towel. Repeat until all the filling is used.

3. Preheat the oven to 200°F.

4. Bring about 1 inch of water to a simmer in a large saucepan over medium heat. Spray a steamer basket with cooking spray (preferably homemade, page xix), if necessary, to help prevent sticking. Place 9 of the dumplings (or as many dumplings as can fit) into the steamer without touching. Cover and steam until dumpling wrappers and filling are cooked through, about 15 minutes. Remove the dumplings from the steamer to a heatproof platter and place in the oven to keep warm. Repeat until all of the dumplings are steamed, adding additional water for simmering between batches, if necessary. Serve warm.

Per serving: 140 calories, 4.5g total fat, 1.5g saturated fat, 0g trans fat, 30mg cholesterol, 260mg sodium, 17g total carbohydrate, 1g dietary fiber, 0g sugars, 7g protein

"Swedish" Meatballs
Makes 12 servings: 3 meatballs and 3 tablespoons gravy each

My first experience with Swedish meatballs was in a frozen dinner back in the seventies. Believe it or not, I have fond memories of them. Now I create new memories with a fresher, body-friendlier version. I incorporated shiitake mushrooms to boost volume, nutrition, and taste. I'm even fonder of this sumptuous, saucy recipe than the ones from the past.

2 slices fresh whole-wheat bread, torn or chopped into tiny bite-size pieces
¼ cup plain almond milk or light soy milk
2 tablespoons unsalted butter
2½ teaspoons grapeseed or canola oil
⅔ cup finely chopped white or red onion
1½ cups finely chopped fresh shiitake mushroom caps or cremini (baby bella) mushrooms
2 teaspoons white wine vinegar
1½ teaspoons sea salt, or to taste
1 pound ground turkey (about 94% lean)
8 ounces lean ground beef sirloin
1 large egg, lightly beaten
¾ teaspoon freshly ground black pepper, or to taste
½ teaspoon ground allspice
¼ cup whole-oat or soy flour
3 cups low-sodium beef or chicken broth
¼ cup fat-free evaporated milk
¼ teaspoon freshly grated or ground nutmeg, or to taste

1. Add the bread to a small mixing bowl. Drizzle with the almond milk and toss to combine. Set aside.

2. Melt 1 tablespoon of the butter with 1 teaspoon of the oil in a large nonstick skillet over medium heat. Add the onion, mushrooms, vinegar, and ¼ teaspoon of the salt and sauté until the onion is softened, about 8 minutes. Remove from heat, transfer to a platter, and let cool for 15 to 30 minutes.

3. Add the bread mixture, turkey, beef, egg, pepper, allspice, onion mixture, and ¾ teaspoon of salt to a large mixing bowl. Thoroughly combine by hand.

4. From the mixture into 36 meatballs, about 1 rounded tablespoon (1 ounce) each.

5. Preheat the oven to 300°F.

6. Heat 1½ teaspoons (½ tablespoon) of the butter and ¾ teaspoon of the oil in the skillet over medium heat. Add half of the meatballs and sauté until just brown on all sides, about 8 to 10 minutes. Transfer the meatballs using tongs or a slotted spoon to a 9×13-inch or other ovenproof dish. Repeat with the remaining butter, oil, and meatballs.

7. Bake the meatballs until fully cooked, about 25 minutes.

8. Meanwhile, add the flour to the remaining bits and grease in the meatball skillet over medium heat. Stir continuously for about 1 minute. Whisk in the broth, about ¼ cup at a time, until fully incorporated. Increase heat to medium-high and stir frequently until the sauce begins to thicken, about 12 minutes. Reduce heat to medium, add the evaporated milk, nutmeg, and remaining ½ teaspoon salt, and continue to cook while stirring until the gravy is desired thickened consistency, about 5 minutes. Adjust seasoning.

9. Remove the meatballs from the oven. Pour the gravy over the meatballs. Sprinkle with additional nutmeg or allspice, if desired, and serve.

Per serving: 140 calories, 7g total fat, 2.5g saturated fat, 0g trans fat, 50mg cholesterol, 380mg sodium, 6g total carbohydrate, 1g dietary fiber, 2g sugars, 14g protein

Cinnamon-Spiced Lamb Meatballs

Makes 8 servings: 3 meatballs each

Kibbeh, a traditional Lebanese dish usually consisting of ground lamb, bulgur wheat, and spices, was my inspiration for this nontraditional, internationally inspired recipe in which I added a pinch of Greek and Italian flair and then, of course, formed into meatballs. For extra lusciousness, dunk them into Greek yogurt or Rosemary Ranch-Style Dipping Sauce (page 98). Or for a surprise twist, try them in Cinnamon-Spiced Meatball Pizzette (page 422).

3 tablespoons fat-free or low-fat plain
    Greek yogurt
1 tablespoon tomato paste
12 ounces lean ground lamb
½ cup plain dry whole-wheat breadcrumbs
½ cup grated white onion
¼ cup finely chopped fresh mint
1 teaspoon chopped fresh oregano
¾ teaspoon sea salt, or to taste
¾ teaspoon ground cinnamon
¼ teaspoon freshly ground black pepper
¼ teaspoon ground allspice

1. Preheat the oven to 500°F.

2. Stir together the yogurt and tomato paste in a large bowl until well combined. Add the lamb, breadcrumbs, onion, mint, oregano, salt, cinnamon, pepper, and allspice and mix with your hands until just combined. Form into 24 meatballs, about 1 rounded tablespoon each.

3. Place the meatballs onto a parchment paper–lined 9×13-inch dish and bake until cooked through and brown, about 10 minutes.

4. Serve warm on toothpicks. Garnish with additional fresh mint, if desired.

Per serving: 90 calories, 3.5g total fat, 1g saturated fat, 0g trans fat, 25mg cholesterol, 260mg sodium, 6g total carbohydrate, 1g dietary fiber, 1g sugars, 8g protein

Dips, Salsas, and Sauces

Hummus

Tahini Chickpea Hummus

Sun-Dried Tomato
Pesto Hummus

Zesty Lemon
Soybean Hummus

Creamy Almond Hummus

Edamame "Hummus"

Guacamole

3-Ingredient Guacamole

Indian Guacamole

California Guacamole Parfait

Grilled Fig Guacamole

Sweet Potato Guacamole

Sweet Pea "Guacamole"

Green and White Asparagus
"Guacamole"

Dips

2-Ingredient Pinto Bean Dip

Tuxedo Black and White
Bean Dip

Layered Baja Bean Dip

Roasted Garlic-Spiked
Great Northern "Fondue"

Romesco-Style Dip

Fresh Spinach–Truffle Party Dip

Avocado "Mousse"

Mint Tzatziki

Caramelized Maui Onion Dip

Creamy Scallion Veggie Dip

Baked Artichoke Heart Dip

Cucumber Raita

Cumin-Spiced Chickpea Raita

Creamy Cucumber
Dipping Sauce

Rosemary Ranch-Style
Dipping Sauce

Avocado–Ranch
Dipping Sauce

Pasta Sauces

"Alfredo" Sauce

Lemony Pasta Cream Sauce

Zesty Lemon-Thyme
Pasta Sauce

Creamy Lime Santa Fe Sauce

Raw Diced Tomato
Basil Sauce

Fresh Marinara

Triple Tomato Marinara Sauce

Fennel Turkey Pasta Sauce

Bell Pepper Marinara

80-Proof Vodka Sauce

Squash Pasta Sauce

Barbecue Sauces

Home-Style Barbecue Sauce

Ancho Chili Barbecue Sauce

Pineapple-Serrano
Barbecue Sauce

Tangy Apricot Barbecue Sauce

Apple Cider Barbecue Sauce

Fig Barbecue Sauce

Nut and Seed Sauces

Peanut Sauce

Gingery Peanut-Almond Sauce

Creamy Tahini Sauce

Harissa Lemon-Tahini Sauce

Pistachio Plum Sauce

Gravies

Savory Carrot-Shallot Gravy

Rosemary Sweet Potato Gravy

Roasted Chestnut Gravy

Shiitake Gravy

Farmers' Market Summer
Squash Gravy

Country Bean Gravy

Home-Style Chicken Gravy

Sweet Italian Turkey Sausage
Gravy

Salsas

Roasted Green Tomato Salsa

Spicy Raw Tomatillo Salsa

Vine-Ripened Pico de Gallo

Fresh Sicilian Salsa

Roasted Beet-Nectarine
Salsa

Sweet-n-Savory Melon Salsa

Strawberry Mojito Salsa

Tropical Fruit and Cucumber
Salsa

Black Bean Salsa

Pestos, Chutneys, and Tapenades

Enlightened Fresh
Basil Pesto

Arugula Pesto

Swiss Chard Pesto

Sun-Dried Tomato Pesto

Fresh Mint Chutney

Cilantro-Mint Chutney

Vine-Ripened Tomato
Chutney

Mango Chutney

Tamarind and Fresh Fig Chutney

Olive–Bell Pepper Tapenade

Sun-Dried Tomato Tapenade

Grilled Onion Tapenade

Condiments

Sassy "Mayo"

Garlic "Mayo"

Bourbon "Mayo"

Lemon-Caper "Mayo"

Cilantro-Jalapeño "Mayo"

Balsamic-Basil "Mayo"

Blue Cheese Tofunnaise

Dijon Tofunnaise

Herbal Tofunnaise

 = Low-Sodium   = Fiber-Rich

Zesty Lime Avocado Spread

Creamy Herbes de Provence Sandwich Spread

Tuscan Basil White Bean Spread

All-Natural Ketchup

Banana-Guava Ketchup

Pickled Jalapeño Mustard

Raspberry Mustard

"Hot" Honey Dijon Sauce

Pickled Red Onion–Jalapeño Relish

Fresh Tartar Sauce

Fresh Rémoulade Sauce

Szechuan Sesame-Ginger Soy Sauce

Wasabi-Spiked Soy Sauce

Seasonal Cranberry Sauce

Raw Cranberry–Tangerine Sauce

Papaya Puree

Other Bread Spreads and Savory Sauces

Farmers' Market Strawberry and Stone Fruit Spread

Fresh Fig Fruit Spread

Herbed Goat Cheese Spread

Silken Scallion Bagel Spread

Tomatillo-Avocado "Crème" Sauce

Silky Hollandaise-Style Sauce

Cherry Balsamic Peppercorn Sauce

Rosemary Grill Sauce

Merlot Sauce

Tangy Teriyaki Sauce

Roasted Red Bell Pepper Sauce

Sweet-n-Sour Tomato Sauce

Cantonese Garlic Sauce

Lemon-Dill Yogurt Sauce

Blood Orange–Shallot Sauce

Margarita Serving Sauce

Aged Balsamic Reduction

One of my favorite ways to make a healthful food extra tasty is to serve accompaniments that add flavor, like salsas, dips, and sauces.

It helps dress up foods and adds another layer of flavor. And as my philosophy goes, if your nutritious food is tasty, you'll be more likely to keep following a healthful meal plan. Simple roasted turkey is so much tastier with rosemary sweet potato gravy drizzled over it. Instead of plain grilled chicken breast, bathing it with a tangy apricot barbecue sauce gives it flavor that'll make you go "wow."

Dips can provide that little "something on the side" to enhance the natural flavors of foods. Serving veggies or fruits with dips boosts kids' produce intake, too. The same can apply for adults, especially those who find meeting vegetable or fruit goals challenging. Plus, pairing produce with dips that contain some "good" fat can actually help you better absorb some of its beneficial antioxidants.

You'll be impressed by the sheer number of dips, salsas, sauces, and other condiments this chapter contains—over 100! You'll never be at a loss for something to dress up a dish.

Kicking off the chapter are satisfying recipes that are ideal for snacking along with veggies or tortilla chips or for spreading onto sandwiches and beyond. They consist of popular traditional and creative nontraditional hummus, guacamoles, and dips. They use edamame, beans, spicy blends, and other high-flavored ingredients.

You'll be excited by the array of enticing pasta, barbecue, and nut and seeds sauces. Some are creamy and others are chunky. There's an innovative "Alfredo" Sauce (page 99) that's made calorie-friendly without giving up taste by way of pureed cannellini beans. The barbecue sauces are high in flavor as you'd expect, but the addition of fruits to most of them naturally creates intriguing sweetness, such as in Pineapple-Serrano Barbecue Sauce (page 105). And you'll discover that there's more to nut sauces than just peanuts . . . try Pistachio Plum Sauce (page 109).

Gravies come next. The coolest part about the gravies in *1,000 Low-Calorie Recipes* is that they can also be enjoyed as soups. All you'll need to do is add a little more broth if you wish and adjust seasonings. And if you have any smooth gravy leftover, such as Roasted Chestnut Gravy (page 111), it can be frozen, simmered, and whisked again until creamy.

Next up is salsa. Though you might normally dip into salsas with tortilla chips, I encourage you to think outside the box (or chip bag) and use salsas to garnish entrées, top sandwiches, or pair with pilafs. The salsas here aren't just made with tomatoes; they include bean and fruit-based salsas, too, such as Strawberry Mojito Salsa (page 116). For added interest, grill large pieces of the fruits or veggies for use in the recipes. You can even try that with melon slices for Sweet-n-Savory Melon Salsa (page 116)!

Rounding out the chapter are a host of pestos, chutneys, tapenades, condiments, and other savory spreads and sauces. Pestos are kicked up with extra garlic, and then beans or tofu give them creamy body. Chutneys cover all categories: herbal, fruity, and tomato-based. The herb chutneys are sweetened with apple juice instead of sugar. And there are three extra-tasty tapenade recipes with which to experiment. Make sure to use the best-quality ingredients, including olives, for the best-tasting results.

Instead of reaching for a low-cal mayo, which may contain ingredients that your body doesn't need, I suggest using real natural mayonnaise with a twist in my lovely "mayo" recipes. That twist includes plain Greek yogurt, vinegar, and a touch of honey and citrus zest. You'll find tofunnaise recipes, too, which are made with tofu, of course. Discover out-of-the-ordinary spreads, ketchups, mustards, and more that use creative ingredients, like guava or herb blends to make them unique. And I'll let you in on one of my culinary secrets that makes many of the spreads special: beans, which you'll find are one of my favorite ingredients throughout *1,000 Low-Calorie Recipes*. Pureed and added to dips, sauces, or other spreads, they lend creamy body while blending in and carrying the other flavors. The coupling of protein and fiber from the beans help keep you satisfied, too.

Calorie range in this chapter: 5 to 260 calories.

Low-calorie picks: Spicy Raw Tomatillo Salsa, 5 calories (page 114) and Wasabi-Spiked Soy Sauce, 5 calories (page 130).

Hummus

Tahini Chickpea Hummus

Makes 7 servings: ¼ cup each

A little Greek yogurt provides a tangy twist to traditional hummus Serve it traditionally—or nontraditionally—with fresh whole-wheat pita wedges, Cumin-Dusted Naan Chips (page 42), or raw seasonal vegetables.

1 (15-ounce) can no-salt-added chickpeas (garbanzo beans), drained

¼ cup tahini (sesame seed paste)

⅓ cup fat-free or low-fat plain Greek yogurt

Juice of 1 lemon (3 tablespoons)

1 large garlic clove, chopped, or to taste

½ teaspoon sea salt, or to taste

¼ teaspoon ground cumin, or to taste

⅛ teaspoon ground cayenne or smoked paprika (optional)

2 tablespoons chopped fresh flat-leaf parsley

1. Set aside ¼ cup of the chickpeas and 1 tablespoon of the tahini. Add the remaining chickpeas, tahini, yogurt, the lemon juice, garlic, salt, cumin, and cayenne (if using) to a food processor or blender. Cover and puree. Adjust seasoning.

2. Spoon into a serving bowl and top with the reserved 1 tablespoon tahini, reserved ¼ cup chickpeas, and the parsley. Chill until ready to serve.

Per serving: 120 calories, 5g total fat, 0.5g saturated fat, 0g trans fat, 0mg cholesterol, 190mg sodium, 14g total carbohydrate, 3g dietary fiber, 1g sugars, 6g protein

Sun-Dried Tomato Pesto Hummus

Makes 8 servings: ¼ cup each

Make a nontraditional hummus that has an unexpected accent. The sun-dried tomato pesto gives this sexier version a pop of flavor. For extra pep, puree in additional rehydrated sun-dried tomatoes. It'll dazzle as a dip.

1 (15-ounce) can no-salt-added chickpeas (garbanzo beans), drained

6 tablespoons Sun-Dried Tomato Pesto (page 119)

⅓ cup fat-free or low-fat plain Greek yogurt

Juice of 1 small lemon (2 tablespoons)

1 large garlic clove, chopped, or to taste

¼ teaspoon sea salt, or to taste

⅛ teaspoon ground cayenne (optional)

2 tablespoons chopped fresh flat-leaf parsley or basil

1. Add the chickpeas, pesto, yogurt, lemon juice, garlic, salt, and cayenne (if using) to a food processor or blender. Cover and puree. Adjust seasoning.

2. Spoon into a serving bowl and sprinkle with the parsley. Chill until ready to serve.

Per serving: 90 calories, 3.5g total fat, 0g saturated fat, 0g trans fat, 0mg cholesterol, 170mg sodium, 11g total carbohydrate, 2g dietary fiber, 1g sugars, 4g protein

Zesty Lemon Soybean Hummus

Makes 6 servings: ¼ cup each

Soybeans create delicious hummus with punched-up protein to create extra satisfaction. Scoop up its thick, creamy pleasures with raw seasonal vegetables or Cumin-Dusted Naan Chips (page 42).

1 (15-ounce) can soybeans, drained

3 tablespoons tahini (sesame seed paste)

Juice and zest of 1 large lemon (¼ cup juice)

1 large garlic clove, chopped, or to taste

¼ teaspoon ground cumin, or to taste

¼ teaspoon ground cayenne, or to taste

¼ teaspoon sea salt, or to taste

⅛ teaspoon freshly ground black or white pepper, or to taste

1. Add the soybeans, tahini, lemon juice, garlic, cumin, cayenne, salt, and pepper to a food processor or blender. Cover and puree. Adjust seasoning.

2. Spoon into a serving bowl and sprinkle with lemon zest as desired. Chill until ready to serve.

Per serving: 130 calories, 8g total fat, 1g saturated fat, 0g trans fat, 0mg cholesterol, 180mg sodium, 9g total carbohydrate, 2g dietary fiber, 2g sugars, 8g protein

Creamy Almond Hummus Ⓢ

Makes 12 servings: 3 tablespoons each

Put a little spin on a regular dip to add pizzazz. Change one or two ingredients at a time. Here a generous amount of almond butter is used instead of tahini for a unique-tasting hummus. Serve it in style on cucumber slices in Creamy Almond Hummus Canapés (page 50) or use in Grilled Veggie Burgers (page 396). Or simply spoon into a serving bowl and scoop up with raw seasonal vegetables or fresh whole-wheat pita wedges.

1 (15-ounce) can no-salt-added chickpeas (garbanzo beans), drained
⅔ cup no-salt-added creamy raw almond butter
1 large garlic clove, chopped, or to taste
Juice of 1 lemon (3 tablespoons)
½ teaspoon sea salt, or to taste
¼ teaspoon ground cumin
¼ teaspoon ground cayenne or smoked paprika

1. Add the chickpeas, almond butter, garlic, lemon juice, salt, cumin, and cayenne to a food processor or blender. Cover and puree. Adjust seasoning.

2. Spoon into a serving bowl. Chill until ready to serve.

Per serving: 130 calories, 9g total fat, 1g saturated fat, 0g trans fat, 0mg cholesterol, 105mg sodium, 10g total carbohydrate, 2g dietary fiber, 0g sugars, 4g protein

Edamame "Hummus"

Makes 6 servings: ⅓ cup each

Technically this isn't hummus. But the chickpea dip is what inspired this tasty twist on the recipe. Edamame provides a gorgeous green color. Enjoy it as a party dip with fresh whole-grain pita wedges or as a distinctive sandwich condiment. Or go for an extra taste twist by serving with Garlic-Tarragon Pita Chips (page 41) or Cumin-Dusted Naan Chips (page 42).

1 (10-ounce) bag frozen shelled edamame
Juice of 1 large lemon (¼ cup)
3 tablespoons tahini (sesame seed paste)
1 large garlic clove, chopped, or to taste
¾ teaspoon sea salt, or to taste
2 tablespoons chopped fresh flat-leaf parsley

1. Bring 4 cups of water to a boil in a medium saucepan over high heat. Add the edamame and boil according to package directions or until tender, about 5 minutes. Drain and reserve ½ cup of the cooking liquid.

2. Add the edamame, lemon juice, tahini, garlic, salt, and 6 tablespoons of the reserved cooking liquid to a food processor. Cover and blend until desired consistency, adding additional cooking liquid only if needed. Adjust seasoning.

3. Spoon into a serving bowl, sprinkle with or stir in the parsley, and serve.

Per serving: 110 calories, 6g total fat, 0.5g saturated fat, 0g trans fat, 0mg cholesterol, 310mg sodium, 8g total carbohydrate, 3g dietary fiber, 1g sugars, 6g protein

Guacamole

3-Ingredient Guacamole

Makes 4 servings: ¼ cup each

The avocado is one of my all-time favorite foods—that includes guacamole. If you ever need a quick guacamole fix like me, here's one of the fastest ways to be appetizingly gratified. A ¼-cup serving of it is just enough—and it's only 60 calories. Serve with fresh lime wedges and tortilla chips, if you like. By the way, I'm not officially counting salt as an ingredient here, just in case you're counting!

1 Hass avocado, pitted, peeled, and cubed

¼ cup well-drained Vine-Ripened Pico de Gallo (page 114) or other medium or spicy pico de gallo or chunky salsa

2 tablespoons finely chopped fresh cilantro

⅛ teaspoon sea salt, or to taste

Gently stir all ingredients together in a medium bowl until just combined. Serve as a dip at room temperature.

Per serving: 60 calories, 5g total fat, 0.5g saturated fat, 0g trans fat, 0mg cholesterol, 190mg sodium, 4g total carbohydrate, 2g dietary fiber, 1g sugars, 1g protein

Indian Guacamole

Makes 10 servings: ¼ cup each

Mexico meets India? When flavors work well together, why not? This unique version of guacamole is saucy and sassy with distinctive Indian flavors. Be sure to not overmix it so you'll be able to see and savor the lusciously appealing cubes of avocado. Dip into its lusciousness with Hint of Lime Tortilla Chips (page 41) or enjoy it in Punjabi Avocado and Bean Torte (page 259).

¼ cup fat-free or low-fat plain Greek yogurt

Juice of ½ lemon (1½ tablespoons), or to taste

Juice of ½ lime (1 tablespoon), or to taste

1 small jalapeño pepper with seeds, minced

1 large garlic clove, minced

1 teaspoon freshly grated gingerroot

½ teaspoon ground turmeric

½ teaspoon ground cumin

½ teaspoon ground coriander

¼ teaspoon sea salt, or to taste

2 Hass avocados, pitted, peeled, and cubed

½ cup grape tomatoes, thinly sliced lengthwise

⅓ cup diced white onion

2 tablespoons chopped fresh cilantro

Stir together the yogurt, lemon juice, lime juice, jalapeño, garlic, ginger, turmeric, cumin, coriander, and salt in a medium bowl until well combined. Add the avocados, tomatoes, onion, and cilantro and gently stir until just combined. Adjust seasoning. Serve as a dip at room temperature.

Per serving: 60 calories, 4.5g total fat, 0.5g saturated fat, 0g trans fat, 0mg cholesterol, 65mg sodium, 4g total carbohydrate, 2g dietary fiber, 1g sugars, 1g protein

California Guacamole Parfait

Makes 4 servings: 1 parfait each

Give guacamole a fresh new look. Serve it deconstructed in a martini glass. The beans layered in the parfait add enough heartiness and good-for-you fiber that you won't need to pair it with tortilla chips. Simply dig in with a spoon. ¡Olé!

1 pint grape tomatoes, thinly sliced lengthwise
Juice of 1 lime (2 tablespoons)
¼ teaspoon sea salt, or to taste
2 Hass avocados, pitted, peeled, and diced
1 small jalapeño pepper with seeds, minced
¼ teaspoon ground cumin
1 (15-ounce) can black or pinto beans, drained
⅓ cup finely diced white onion
3 tablespoon chopped fresh cilantro

1. Gently stir together the tomatoes, half the lime juice, and ⅛ teaspoon of the salt in a medium bowl. Set aside.

2. Very gently stir together the avocados, remaining lime juice, jalapeño, cumin, and the remaining ⅛ teaspoon salt in another medium bowl.

3. In four martini or other beverage glasses, layer the avocado mixture, beans, onion, tomato mixture (drain first, if desired), and cilantro, pressing slightly on the avocado mixture, bean, and onion layers to flatten while layering. Enjoy immediately with a spoon.

Per serving: 260 calories, 15g total fat, 2g saturated fat, 0g trans fat, 0mg cholesterol, 270mg sodium, 29g total carbohydrate, 12g dietary fiber, 7g sugars, 8g protein

Grilled Fig Guacamole Ⓢ

Makes 10 servings: ¼ cup each

How I wish fresh figs were available all year round. The smoky, sweet addition of the grilled figs creates a mouthwatering guacamole. But, if you want to prepare this recipe during cooler months, simply use 4 or 5 finely diced dried figs instead—there's no grilling required.

9 medium fresh Black Mission or other figs, stem removed and halved lengthwise
2 Hass avocados, pitted, peeled, and cubed
Juice of 1 lime (2 tablespoons), or to taste
⅓ cup diced white onion
2 tablespoons chopped fresh cilantro
1 small jalapeño pepper with some seeds, minced
¼ teaspoon ground cumin
¼ teaspoon ground coriander
¼ teaspoon sea salt, or to taste

1. Prepare an outdoor or indoor grill or grill pan. Spritz the cut surface of each fig half with cooking spray (preferably homemade, page xix). Grill over medium-high heat on the cut side only until well caramelized, about 3 to 3½ minutes. Set aside to cool.

2. Gently stir together the avocados, lime juice, onion, cilantro, jalapeño, cumin, coriander, and salt in a medium bowl until just combined. Dice the figs and gently stir into the guacamole. Adjust seasoning. Serve as a dip at room temperature.

Per serving: 90 calories, 5g total fat, 0.5g saturated fat, 0g trans fat, 0mg cholesterol, 60mg sodium, 12g total carbohydrate, 3g dietary fiber, 8g sugars, 1g protein

Sweet Potato Guacamole

Makes 8 servings: ½ cup each

I think of this as guacamole gone wild. Sweet potatoes are added to create sweet-savory interest. Plus, you'll be able to eat twice as much for a serving. Dig in with whole-grain chips or take delight in it at breakfast time as a scrambled egg topping.

2 medium sweet potatoes, unpeeled and scrubbed
½ cup diced white onion
¼ cup chopped fresh cilantro
1 small jalapeño pepper with some seeds, minced
1 Hass avocado, pitted, peeled, and cubed
Juice and zest of 1 lime, or to taste
    (2 tablespoons juice)
½ teaspoon sea salt, or to taste
¼ teaspoon freshly grated nutmeg, or to taste

1. Poke holes with a fork in the sweet potatoes to vent steam. Place potatoes in a microwave-safe dish. Cover well with parchment paper. Microwave on high until potatoes are nearly fork-tender yet still slightly firm in the center, about 5 minutes. Let the potatoes cool at room temperature for about 30 to 45 minutes and cut into ½-inch cubes.

2. Add the cubed potatoes to a medium serving bowl. Gently stir (do not mash) in the onion, cilantro, jalapeño, avocado, lime juice, salt, and nutmeg until just combined. Adjust seasoning. Top with desired amount of lime zest to serve

Per serving: 60 calories, 2.5g total fat, 0g saturated fat, 0g trans fat, 0mg cholesterol, 160mg sodium, 9g total carbohydrate, 2g dietary fiber, 2g sugars, 1g protein

Sweet Pea "Guacamole"

Makes 12 servings: ¼ cup each

For the essence of guacamole in a slimmer style, consider veggies in place of avocado. Springy peas make a vivid green dip that's still perfect paired with chips. Try it with Hint-of-Lime Tortilla Chips (page 41) or Cumin-Dusted Naan Chips (page 42).

20 ounces frozen peas, thawed and patted dry
1 small or ½ large white onion, finely diced
1 small jalapeño pepper with seeds, minced
1 garlic clove, minced
Juice of ½ lime (1 tablespoon)
2 teaspoons fresh lemon juice
¼ cup chopped fresh cilantro
¾ teaspoon sea salt, or to taste
½ teaspoon chili powder, or to taste

1. Add the peas to a food processor. Cover and pulse until desired consistency.

2. Transfer the peas to a medium bowl. Stir in the onion, jalapeño, garlic, lime and lemon juices, cilantro, salt, and chili powder. Adjust seasoning. Chill until ready to serve.

Per serving: 40 calories, 0g total fat, 0g saturated fat, 0g trans fat, 0mg cholesterol, 200mg sodium, 7g total carbohydrate, 2g dietary fiber, 3g sugars, 3g protein

Green and White Asparagus "Guacamole"

Makes 4 servings: ½ cup each (¼ cup green; ¼ cup white)

Plating two versions of a recipe side by side creates a dramatic palette. And when it tastes just like guacamole, it creates drama for your palate. For a simpler version, double the green asparagus; it's less impressive visually, but still so delicious.

8 ounces (2-inch) white asparagus pieces
8 ounces (2-inch) green asparagus pieces
1 small jalapeño pepper with some seeds, halved
1 garlic clove, halved
Juice of ½ lime (1 tablespoon)
Juice of ½ small lemon (1 tablespoon)
¼ teaspoon sea salt, or to taste
¼ cup finely diced white or red onion
2 tablespoons chopped fresh cilantro

1. Place the white and green asparagus pieces in separate saucepans. Pour ½ cup cold water into each pan. Cover, place over medium heat, and cook until the asparagus is very tender, about 10 minutes. Drain both well of any remaining liquid.

2. Add the white asparagus to a food processor with half each of the jalapeño, garlic, lime juice, lemon juice, and salt. Cover and blend until nearly smooth, scraping down the sides as needed. Transfer to a small bowl.

3. Add the green asparagus to the food processor with remaining jalapeño, garlic, lime juice, lemon juice, and salt. Cover and blend until nearly smooth, scraping down the sides as needed. Transfer to another small bowl.

4. Stir half of the onion and cilantro into each bowl of pureed asparagus. Adjust seasoning. Serve the guacamoles cool or at room temperature.

Per serving: 30 calories, 0g total fat, 0g saturated fat, 0g trans fat, 0mg cholesterol, 160mg sodium, 6g total carbohydrate, 2g dietary fiber, 2g sugars, 3g protein

Dips

2-Ingredient Pinto Bean Dip

Makes 6 servings: ¼ cup each

Simple recipes can taste as delightful as complex recipes—and save so much time. So when you need a dip in a jiff, this effortless, no-fail pinto bean pleaser will become a popular pick. Garnish it with sliced scallions and serve with fresh seasonal vegetables or baked tortilla chips.

1 (15-ounce) can no-salt-added pinto or red kidney beans, well drained

½ cup Vine-Ripened Pico de Gallo (page 114), spicy pico de gallo, or thick salsa

Sea salt to taste (optional)

1. Add the beans and pico de gallo to a food processor. Cover and puree. Add salt to taste, if desired.

2. Spoon the dip into a serving bowl. Chill until ready to serve.

Per serving: 60 calories, 0g total fat, 0g saturated fat, 0g trans fat, 0mg cholesterol, 135mg sodium, 11g total carbohydrate, 4g dietary fiber, 1g sugars, 4g protein

Tuxedo Black and White Bean Dip Ⓕ

Makes 10 servings: ¼ cup each (2 tablespoons black; 2 tablespoons white)

Try this festive appetizer dip with other color beans, too. No matter what the color, all beans are antioxidant rich and provide protein and fiber. That's a win-win for weight management. And it's a win-win for your palate when served with vine-ripened cherry tomatoes or blanched, chilled asparagus spears.

1 (15-ounce) can no-salt-added Great Northern, navy, or other white beans, well drained

2 large garlic cloves, chopped

¼ cup no-salt-added creamy raw almond butter

Juice of 1 small lemon (2 tablespoons)

½ teaspoon ground cumin, or to taste

½ teaspoon sea salt, or to taste

¼ teaspoon ground cayenne or ground coriander, or to taste

1 (15-ounce) can no-salt-added black beans, well drained

Juice of 1 lime (2 tablespoons)

1 tablespoon sliced natural almonds, toasted (optional)

2 tablespoons fresh parsley or cilantro leaves

1. Add the white beans, 1 garlic clove, 2 tablespoons of the almond butter, the lemon juice, ¼ teaspoon of the cumin, ¼ teaspoon of the salt, and ⅛ teaspoon of the cayenne to a blender or food processor. Cover and puree. Add cold water by the teaspoon only if necessary for blending. Adjust seasoning. Spoon into a bowl. Set aside.

2. Add the black beans, the remaining garlic clove, the remaining 2 tablespoons almond butter, the lime juice, the remaining ¼ teaspoon cumin, and the remaining ¼ teaspoon salt to a blender or food processor. Cover and puree. Add cold water by the teaspoon only if necessary for blending. Adjust seasoning.

3. Spoon the two dips side by side into a serving bowl. Sprinkle with the almonds (if using) and parsley. Chill until ready to serve.

Per serving: 110 calories, 4g total fat, 0g saturated fat, 0g trans fat, 0mg cholesterol, 135mg sodium, 15g total carbohydrate, 5g dietary fiber, 0g sugars, 5g protein

MEXICAN SEASONING

Make your own Mexican seasoning if you like. Mix together ½ teaspoon each chili powder, onion powder, garlic powder, and ground cumin.

Layered Baja Bean Dip

Makes 18 servings: ¾ cup each

Layered bean dip is a request of my friend, Alyssa, at every one of my friendly gatherings. She says this Latin-inspired version is her favorite one yet. Not only is it a taste hit, it's a nutrition hit as it is filled with plant-based goodness in every bite. Pair it with grilled jumbo shrimp for extra protein.

1 (16-ounce) can spicy refried black beans
    or 1¾ cups Spicy Un-fried Beans (page 487)

2 Hass avocados, peeled, pitted, and diced

3 tablespoons finely chopped fresh cilantro

Juice and zest of 1 lime (2 tablespoons juice)

¼ teaspoon sea salt, or to taste

¾ cup fat-free or low-fat plain Greek yogurt

2 teaspoons chili powder or Mexican seasoning
    (page 92)

1½ cups shredded extra-sharp Cheddar cheese
    or Chihuahua or Monterey jack cheese

1 pint cherry tomatoes, thinly sliced and patted dry

6 scallions, green and white parts, minced

⅓ cup finely diced fresh mango, patted dry

1. Spread the beans in a 9 × 13-inch serving dish or on a large platter.

2. Stir together the avocados, cilantro, 1 tablespoon of the lime juice, and the salt in a medium bowl and spread on top of the beans.

3. Stir together the yogurt, chili powder, and remaining 1 tablespoon lime juice in a small bowl and spread on top of the avocados.

4. Top with the cheese, tomatoes, scallions, mango, and desired amount of lime zest. Serve at room temperature.

Per serving: 100 calories, 6g total fat, 2.5g saturated fat, 0g trans fat, 10mg cholesterol, 140mg sodium, 7g total carbohydrate, 3g dietary fiber, 1g sugars, 5g protein

Roasted Garlic-Spiked Great Northern "Fondue"

Makes 8 servings: ¼ cup "fondue"

This no-cook "fondue" is so flavorful that you may never go back to that ultra-cheesy kind. It's velvety with the mellow but distinct taste of roasted garlic, citrusy tang from lemon, and nutty richness from almond butter finished by a delightful rosemary aroma. Serve it fondue-style along with skewers and an 8-ounce fresh whole-grain baguette cut into cubes—about 8 cubes per ounce.

5 large garlic cloves, peeled

1 tablespoon extra-virgin olive oil

1 (15-ounce) can no-salt-added Great Northern,
    navy, or cannellini beans, drained

⅓ cup low-sodium vegetable broth or
    Vegetable Stock (page 203)

¼ cup no-salt-added creamy raw almond butter

Juice and zest of 1 small lemon (2 tablespoons
    juice)

2 tablespoons unsweetened green tea or water

¾ teaspoon sea salt, or to taste

½ teaspoon finely chopped fresh rosemary
    or thyme leaves

⅛ teaspoon ground cayenne, or to taste

1. Preheat the oven to 450°F. Place the garlic cloves on aluminum foil, drizzle with 1 teaspoon of the oil, wrap, and roast until tender, about 20 minutes.

2. Pinch the roasted garlic out of the bulb and into a blender. Add the beans, broth, almond butter, lemon juice and half of the zest, tea, salt, rosemary, cayenne, and remaining 2 teaspoons oil. Cover and puree on high speed until smooth and creamy. Adjust seasoning.

3. Pour the bean dip into a deep bowl and garnish with remaining lemon zest. Serve fondue style, at room temperature.

Per serving: 120 calories, 7g total fat, 0.5g saturated fat, 0g trans fat, 0mg cholesterol, 240mg sodium, 11g total carbohydrate, 4g dietary fiber, 1g sugars, 3g protein

Romesco-Style Dip

Makes 12 servings: 2 tablespoons each

A traditional Catalonian roasted red bell pepper and garlic dip is known as Romesco sauce. You'll enjoy that this skinny version is big on flavor. And beyond the taste, the texture provided by almonds will make this a standout sauce that can stand up to grilled poultry and shellfish, crusty bread, and more.

½ cup natural almonds, toasted

2 large roasted red bell peppers (page 27)

1 tablespoon low-sodium vegetable broth
   or Vegetable Stock (page 203)

1 tablespoon extra-virgin olive oil

2 teaspoons aged red wine or sherry vinegar

6 fresh mint leaves

1 large garlic clove, chopped, or 3 large roasted
   garlic cloves

½ teaspoon grated lemon zest, or to taste

½ teaspoon sea salt, or to taste

⅛ teaspoon freshly ground black pepper,
   or to taste

1. Add the almonds to a food processor. Cover and pulse until finely chopped. Add the peppers, broth, oil, vinegar, mint, garlic, lemon zest, salt, and black pepper and puree until just combined. Adjust seasoning.

2. Transfer to a small serving bowl. Chill until ready to serve. Remove from the refrigerator about 20 minutes prior to serving.

Per serving: 50 calories, 4g total fat, 0g saturated fat, 0g trans fat, 0mg cholesterol, 100mg sodium, 3g total carbohydrate, 1g dietary fiber, 1g sugars, 2g protein

Fresh Spinach–Truffle Party Dip

Makes 16 serving: ¼ cup each

Serve this fitter, more "natural" twist on classic spinach dip at a special occasion. No packaged dried dip mix is required to make this fresher, spinach-packed flavor-brimming version. Enjoy scooping it up from a bowl with small pumpernickel bread slices or mini-rounds. Or go for an eye-opening upgrade and serve a dollop of the dip on top of the bread or jicama slices and attractively arrange several on a platter, such as in Fresh Spinach–Truffle Dip Canapés (page 50).

1 (5-ounce) package fresh baby spinach

1¼ cups fat-free or low-fat plain Greek yogurt

¾ cup mayonnaise

¼ cup sour cream

2 teaspoons white truffle oil or extra-virgin olive oil

6 scallions, green and white parts, minced

⅓ cup finely diced jicama or celery

¼ cup finely diced orange bell pepper
   or grated carrot

1 large garlic clove, minced

¾ teaspoon sea salt, or to taste

½ teaspoon ground cayenne, or to taste

⅛ teaspoon freshly grated nutmeg

1. Add the spinach, yogurt, mayonnaise, sour cream, and truffle oil to a large bowl and stir until well combined. Stir in the scallions, jicama, bell pepper, garlic, salt, cayenne, and nutmeg. Adjust seasoning.

2. Chill for at least 4 hours or overnight to allow spinach to naturally wilt and flavors to blend. Remove from the refrigerator and serve immediately.

Per serving: 110 calories, 10g total fat, 1.5g saturated fat, 0g trans fat, 5mg cholesterol, 200mg sodium, 3g total carbohydrate, 1g dietary fiber, 1g sugars, 2g protein

Avocado "Mousse"

Makes 10 servings: ¼ cup each

I used to make a super-rich version of this versatile dip that was weighted down with cream cheese. Now, it's lightened up by the addition of beans and yogurt while remaining smooth and silky. I prefer this velvety mousse-like version, which is full of flavor, not "bad" fat. Serve it with sweet red pepper strips or Hint-of-Lime Tortilla Chips (page 41). Or smear it onto sandwiches as a super creamy condiment.

1 (15-ounce) can no-salt-added cannellini
    or other white beans, drained

1 garlic clove or 2 roasted garlic cloves, smashed

1 Hass avocado, pitted, peeled, and cubed

3 tablespoons fat-free or low-fat plain Greek yogurt

Juice of ½ lime (1 tablespoon)

Juice of ½ small lemon (1 tablespoon)

4 ounces Neufchâtel (light cream cheese),
    at room temperature

¼ cup mayonnaise

¼ teaspoon sea salt, or to taste

⅛ teaspoon ground cayenne

Add the beans, garlic, avocado, yogurt, lime and lemon juices, Neufchâtel, mayonnaise, salt, and cayenne to a food processor. Cover and pulse until velvety smooth and fluffy. Adjust seasoning. Spoon the dip into a serving bowl. Chill until ready to serve.

Per serving: 130 calories, 9g total fat, 2.5g saturated fat, 0g trans fat, 0mg cholesterol, 150mg sodium, 8g total carbohydrate, 3g dietary fiber, 1g sugars, 4g protein

Mint Tzatziki

Makes 8 servings: ¼ cup each

Tzatziki is a Greek dip, condiment, or sauce featuring yogurt, cucumbers, and garlic. I've doubled the mint and included just enough oil to provide richness and tradition in this tangy version while letting all the other flavors shine. Add extra intrigue by using two different types of mint, like peppermint and spearmint. Try the dip as an accompaniment for Tzatziki Chicken Nugget Canapés (page 150), Tzatziki Shish Kebabs (page 159), or Vegetarian Gyro with Double-Mint Tzatziki (page 373).

1 tablespoon extra-virgin olive oil

Juice of ½ small lemon (1 tablespoon)

1 large garlic clove, minced

1 cup fat-free or low-fat plain Greek yogurt

1 cup finely diced unpeeled English cucumber

2 tablespoons chopped fresh mint

¼ teaspoon sea salt, or to taste

⅛ teaspoon freshly ground black pepper, or to taste

Whisk together the oil, lemon juice, garlic, and yogurt in a medium bowl until well combined. Stir in the cucumber, mint, salt, and pepper. Adjust seasoning. Chill until ready to serve.

Per serving: 35 calories, 2g total fat, 0g saturated fat, 0g trans fat, 0mg cholesterol, 85mg sodium, 2g total carbohydrate, 0g dietary fiber, 1g sugars, 3g protein

Caramelized Maui Onion Dip

Makes 15 servings: ¼ cup each

I created this onion-overloaded dip that's the ideal balance of sweet to savory and delicious to nutritious to replace traditional French onion dip; it provides a whopping two-thirds fewer calories! The culinary trick is to caramelize the onions to a rich deep golden brown. Serve as a dip with Garlic-Tarragon Pita Chips (page 41). Or enjoy a dollop on Farmers' Market Stuffed Russet Skins (page 72).

1 tablespoon extra-virgin olive or grapeseed oil

2 large Maui or other sweet onions, quartered lengthwise and very thinly sliced crosswise

¼ cup Sauvignon Blanc or dry (brut) sparkling wine

1 teaspoon sea salt, or to taste

1½ cups fat-free or low-fat plain Greek yogurt

½ cup sour cream

1 medium celery stalk, minced

1 large garlic clove, minced

¼ teaspoon freshly ground black pepper, or to taste

1. Heat the oil in a large nonstick skillet over medium heat. Add the onions, 1 tablespoon of the wine, and ¼ teaspoon of the salt, stir to coat, cover, and cook, stirring twice, until the onions are fully softened, about 15 minutes. Remove cover, increase heat to medium-high, and sauté until fully caramelized, about 7 to 10 minutes. Pour in the remaining 3 tablespoons wine and sauté for 1 minute. Transfer the caramelized onions to a medium bowl and let cool for 30 minutes.

2. Add the yogurt, sour cream, celery, garlic, pepper, and the remaining ¾ teaspoon salt to the onions and stir until well combined. Adjust seasoning. Chill until ready to serve.

Per serving: 50 calories, 2g total fat, 1g saturated fat, 0g trans fat, 5mg cholesterol, 170mg sodium, 5g total carbohydrate, 0g dietary fiber, 3g sugars, 3g protein

Creamy Scallion Veggie Dip

Makes 24 servings: 2 tablespoons each

This is a refreshing party dip that makes fresh, crisp veggies extra enticing. You'll wind up eating more veggies—and loving them. Dip into it with a variety of fresh seasonal vegetables. Or enjoy it with Balsamic Roasted Beet Fries (page 440).

1¼ cups low-fat cottage cheese

¾ cup mayonnaise

½ cup fat-free or low-fat plain Greek yogurt

4 scallions, green and white parts, minced

2 large garlic cloves, minced

1 teaspoon fresh lemon juice

½ teaspoon vegetarian Worcestershire sauce

¼ teaspoon sea salt, or to taste

¼ teaspoon freshly ground black pepper, or to taste

⅛ teaspoon freshly grated nutmeg

Add all the ingredients to a medium bowl and stir until well combined. Adjust seasoning. Chill until ready to serve.

Per serving: 60 calories, 6g total fat, 1g saturated fat, 0g trans fat, 5mg cholesterol, 115mg sodium, 1g total carbohydrate, 0g dietary fiber, 1g sugars, 2g protein

Baked Artichoke Heart Dip

Makes 20 servings: about ¼ cup each

This is a gooey, cheesy, decadent dip for times when you plan for the extra richness. It provides maximum mouthwatering pleasure in every bite, while one serving is only 100 very worthwhile calories. This dip is easy to throw together and heat up, particularly in a toaster oven. Savor your serving with whole-grain toasts or crackers.

1 (12-ounce) jar marinated artichoke hearts, well drained and chopped

1 (15-ounce) can Great Northern or other white beans, drained

1 cup shredded part-skim mozzarella cheese

¾ cup freshly grated Parmigiano-Reggiano or other Parmesan cheese

½ cup mayonnaise

⅓ cup fat-free or low-fat plain Greek yogurt

⅓ cup chopped fresh chives

1 garlic clove, minced (optional)

¾ teaspoon freshly ground black pepper, or to taste

¼ cup sliced natural almonds

1. Stir together the artichoke hearts, beans, both cheeses, mayonnaise, yogurt, half of the chives, the garlic (if using), and pepper in a 6½ × 8½-inch or similar size toaster oven pan. Firmly spread the mixture into the pan. Wipe clean the pan rims. Scatter the almonds on top of the dip.

2. Bake in a 375°F toaster oven (or preheated conventional oven) until the cheeses are fully melted and bubbly around the edges and almonds are golden brown, about 25 minutes. Remove from the oven and sprinkle with the remaining chives. Let stand at least 5 minutes to complete the cooking process. Serve warm.

Per serving: 100 calories, 8g total fat, 2g saturated fat, 0g trans fat, 10mg cholesterol, 180mg sodium, 5g total carbohydrate, 2g dietary fiber, 1g sugars, 5g protein

Cucumber Raita

Makes 8 servings: ¼ cup each

The use of fresh cilantro and ground cumin are the secrets to this condiment's distinctive cultural panache. It has a practical purpose, too—to cool down your palate when paired with something spicy. Try it with Cumin-Dusted Naan Chips (page 42), Vegetable Biryani (page 272), Red Curry Chicken Breasts (page 313), or Madras Naan Burger (page 400).

½ large English cucumber, unpeeled

1½ cups fat-free or low-fat plain Greek yogurt

2 tablespoons finely chopped fresh cilantro

1 tablespoon finely chopped fresh mint

1 garlic clove, minced

1 teaspoon brown rice vinegar

½ teaspoon sea salt, or to taste

⅛ teaspoon ground cumin or garam masala, or to taste

1. Coarsely grate the cucumber. Drain well of excess liquid.

2. Add the grated cucumber, yogurt, cilantro, mint, garlic, vinegar, salt, and cumin to a medium bowl and stir until well combined. Adjust seasoning. Chill until ready to serve, at least 30 minutes.

Per serving: 25 calories, 0g total fat, 0g saturated fat, 0g trans fat, 0mg cholesterol, 160mg sodium, 3g total carbohydrate, 0g dietary fiber, 2g sugars, 4g protein

Cumin-Spiced Chickpea Raita

Makes 10 servings: ¼ cup each

The pan-toasted cumin seeds give this raita a lingering, earthy fragrance. But don't feel that you need to couple this condiment with strictly Indian dishes. It can add authenticity and complexity to a variety of savory and simple dishes. It's a highlight when paired with fresh whole-grain naan or Tofu Curry with Coconut Rice (page 270).

½ large English cucumber, unpeeled

1½ cups fat-free or low-fat plain Greek yogurt

¾ cup drained canned chickpeas (garbanzo beans)

2 tablespoons finely chopped fresh cilantro

1 scallion, green and white part, minced

1 teaspoon brown rice vinegar

½ teaspoon sea salt, or to taste

½ teaspoon cumin seeds, toasted

1. Coarsely grate the cucumber. Drain well of excess liquid.

2. Add the grated cucumber, yogurt, chickpeas, cilantro, scallion, vinegar, salt, and cumin seeds to a medium bowl and stir until well combined. Adjust seasoning. Chill until ready to serve, at least 30 minutes.

Per serving: 40 calories, 0g total fat, 0g saturated fat, 0g trans fat, 0mg cholesterol, 150mg sodium, 5g total carbohydrate, 1g dietary fiber, 2g sugars, 4g protein

Creamy Cucumber Dipping Sauce

Makes 6 servings: ¼ cup each

This cucumber lover's recipe is versatile. It can be enjoyed like a saucy dip. It can also be a marinade for grilled veggies, poultry, or shellfish. It makes an intriguing dipping sauce for Wasabi-Charred Green Beans (page 62) or partnered with fish in place of tartar sauce.

1 cup fat-free or low-fat plain Greek yogurt

½ cup sliced or chopped unpeeled English cucumber

1 tablespoon extra-virgin olive or flaxseed oil

Juice of ½ small lemon (1 tablespoon)

1 teaspoon freshly grated gingerroot

¼ teaspoon sea salt, or to taste

⅛ teaspoon freshly ground black pepper, or to taste

1 teaspoon finely chopped fresh cilantro (optional)

Add the yogurt, cucumber, oil, lemon, ginger, salt, and pepper to a blender or food processor. Cover and puree. Stir in the cilantro, if using. Adjust seasoning. Chill until ready to serve.

Per serving: 40 calories, 2.5g total fat, 0g saturated fat, 0g trans fat, 0mg cholesterol, 110mg sodium, 2g total carbohydrate, 0g dietary fiber, 2g sugars, 3g protein

Rosemary Ranch-Style Dipping Sauce

Makes 5 servings: about 3 tablespoons each

Instead of a bottled ranch dressing that provides 150 calories for a 2-tablespoon serving, whip up this fresh, full-flavored, ranch-style dipping sauce and serve it with anything you wish, especially seasonal vegetables. You'll whittle away 100 unnecessary calories a serving. And you'll add flair when teamed with "Buffalo Wing" Yellow Squash (page 63), Cinnamon-Spiced Lamb Meatballs (page 191), grilled chicken, or a baked potato or sweet potato.

⅓ cup fat-free or low-fat plain Greek yogurt

⅓ cup sour cream

2 scallions, green and white parts, minced

1 shallot, minced

1 large garlic clove, minced

2 teaspoons fresh lemon juice

¾ teaspoon finely chopped fresh rosemary
    or ½ teaspoon crushed dried rosemary

¼ teaspoon vegetarian Worcestershire sauce

¼ teaspoon freshly ground black pepper, or to taste

⅛ teaspoon sea salt, or to taste

Stir together all ingredients in a small bowl. Chill until ready to serve.

Per serving: 50 calories, 2.5g total fat, 2g saturated fat, 0g trans fat, 10mg cholesterol, 75mg sodium, 4g total carbohydrate, 0g dietary fiber, 2g sugars, 2g protein

Avocado–Ranch Dipping Sauce

Makes 10 servings: 2 tablespoons each

This thick, lively condiment is a lively blend of ranch dressing and avocado. It's deceptively rich and will add pizzazz to sandwiches, wraps, and more, like Southwestern Egg Rolls (page 71).

1 Hass avocado, pitted, peeled, and cubed

Juice of ½ lemon (1½ tablespoons)

⅓ cup fat-free or low-fat plain Greek yogurt

3 tablespoons sour cream

2 scallions, green and white parts, minced

1 tablespoon finely chopped fresh cilantro
    or flat-leaf parsley

1 large garlic clove, minced

¼ teaspoon vegetarian Worcestershire sauce

¼ teaspoon sea salt, or to taste

¼ teaspoon freshly ground black pepper, or to taste

Add the avocado and lemon juice to a medium bowl and mash until well combined and nearly smooth. Add the yogurt, sour cream, scallions, cilantro, garlic, Worcestershire sauce, salt, and pepper and stir until well combined. Chill until ready to serve.

Per serving: 35 calories, 3g total fat, 0.5g saturated fat, 0g trans fat, 0mg cholesterol, 65mg sodium, 2g total carbohydrate, 1g dietary fiber, 1g sugars, 1g protein

Pasta Sauces

"Alfredo" Sauce

Makes 4 servings: ¼ cup each

I've created a dreamier and more calorie-friendly "cream" sauce for pasta. My version saves about 15 grams of saturated fat by pureeing white beans with just ¼ cup heavy cream. Now you can indulge in fettuccine "Alfredo" regularly instead of rarely. So indulge—in Veggie Fettuccine "Alfredo" with Garlic Chips (page 292). Or simply enjoy this sauce with your favorite whole-grain pasta or "ribbons" of steamed zucchini.

½ cup drained canned no-salt-added cannellini
    or other white beans
⅓ cup low-sodium vegetable broth
    or Vegetable Stock (page 203)
¼ cup heavy cream
2 teaspoons freshly grated Parmigiano-Reggiano
    or other Parmesan cheese
2 teaspoons unsalted butter, melted
¼ teaspoon sea salt, or to taste
¼ teaspoon freshly ground black pepper, or to taste
Pinch of freshly grated nutmeg

Add all the ingredients to a blender. Cover and puree on low speed for 1 minute, then on high speed until emulsified and smooth, about 1 minute. Adjust seasoning. Heat to serve in recipe of choice.

Per serving: 100 calories, 8g total fat, 5g saturated fat, 0g trans fat, 25mg cholesterol, 190mg sodium, 5g total carbohydrate, 1g dietary fiber, 0g sugars, 2g protein

Lemony Pasta Cream Sauce

Makes 5 servings: ¼ cup each

Love a creamy sauce but want a zippy burst of freshness? This recipe will be a hit for your taste buds. Think Alfredo sauce, but a lemony, still velvety version that won't add inches to your waistline. It's a versatile sauce for pasta, poultry, or fish. You'll adore it with Luscious Lemony Linguine (page 291).

½ cup drained canned no-salt-added cannellini
    or other white beans
⅓ cup low-sodium vegetable broth
    or Vegetable Stock (page 203)
¼ cup heavy cream
Juice of 1 lemon (3 tablespoons)
2 teaspoons freshly grated Parmigiano-Reggiano
    or other Parmesan cheese
2 teaspoons unsalted butter, melted
¼ teaspoon sea salt, or to taste
¼ teaspoon freshly ground black pepper, or to taste
Pinch of freshly grated nutmeg

Add all the ingredients to a blender. Cover and puree on low speed for 1 minute, then on high speed until emulsified and smooth, about 1 minute. Adjust seasoning. Heat to serve in recipe of choice.

Per serving: 80 calories, 6g total fat, 4g saturated fat, 0g trans fat, 20mg cholesterol, 150mg sodium, 5g total carbohydrate, 1g dietary fiber, 1g sugars, 2g protein

Zesty Lemon-Thyme Pasta Sauce

Makes 5 servings: ¼ cup each

Want to toss your pasta with a savory sauce that'll knock your socks off? This recipe provides the perfect balance of saucy to creamy. And the lemon-herb combination is delicious in Lemony-Thyme Mushroom Tagliatelle (page 292). Actually, it'll likely knock your socks off as a sauce for nearly any pasta, poultry, fish, or pork dish.

½ cup drained canned no-salt-added cannellini
    or other white beans
⅓ cup low-sodium vegetable broth
    or Vegetable Stock (page 203)
¼ cup heavy cream
Juice and zest of 1 lemon (3 tablespoons juice)
2 teaspoons freshly grated Parmigiano-Reggiano
    or other Parmesan cheese
2 teaspoons unsalted butter, melted
½ teaspoon fresh thyme leaves, or to taste
¼ teaspoon sea salt, or to taste
¼ teaspoon freshly ground black pepper,
    or to taste
¼ teaspoon ground cayenne, or to taste

Add the beans, broth, cream, lemon juice, cheese, butter, thyme, salt, pepper, and cayenne to a blender. Cover and puree on low speed for 1 minute, then on high speed until emulsified and smooth, about 1 minute. Stir in desired amount of lemon zest. Adjust seasoning. Heat to serve in recipe of choice.

Per serving: 80 calories, 6g total fat, 4g saturated fat, 0g trans fat, 20mg cholesterol, 150mg sodium, 5g total carbohydrate, 1g dietary fiber, 1g sugars, 2g protein

Creamy Lime Santa Fe Sauce

Makes 4 servings: ¼ cup each

A divine cream sauce is created by using a puree of beans and broth in place of more than half of the heavy cream. Fresh lime juice is added to create a unique and zingy Southwestern flair. Perfect for Creamy Santa Fe Pappardelle (page 293), Tequila Turkey Pasta (page 342), or as a sauce for poultry or fish of choice.

½ cup drained canned no-salt-added cannellini
    or other white beans
⅓ cup heavy cream
2 tablespoons low-sodium vegetable broth
    or Vegetable Stock (page 203)
Juice of 1 lime (2 tablespoons)
¼ teaspoon sea salt, or to taste
¼ teaspoon freshly ground black pepper,
    or to taste

Add all the ingredients to a blender. Cover, puree until smooth. Adjust seasoning. Heat to serve in recipe of choice.

Per serving: 100 calories, 8g total fat, 4.5g saturated fat, 0g trans fat, 25mg cholesterol, 170mg sodium, 6g total carbohydrate, 1g dietary fiber, 0g sugars, 2g protein

Raw Diced Tomato Basil Sauce

Makes 4 servings: ¾ cup each

This sauce requires only a few minutes of chopping and no cooking. It's like pico de gallo, but an Italian-inspired take on it that uses the skins, seeds, and all of the tomatoes. It's the fresh-faced star in Caprese Quesadilla (page 427), Spaghetti with Tomato and Basil Sauce (page 290), or Tomato-Basil Spaghetti Squash (page 469) And it's equally enjoyable as a bruschetta topping or omelet filling.

1 tablespoon extra-virgin olive oil

1 teaspoon aged balsamic vinegar

1 large garlic clove, minced

¼ teaspoon sea salt, or to taste

4 medium vine-ripened tomatoes, finely diced

8 large or 12 medium fresh basil leaves, thinly sliced

Whisk the oil, vinegar, garlic, and salt in a medium bowl until well combined. Stir in the tomatoes and basil. Adjust seasoning and serve.

Per serving: 50 calories, 4g total fat, 0.5g saturated fat, 0g trans fat, 0mg cholesterol, 150mg sodium, 5g total carbohydrate, 2g dietary fiber, 3g sugars, 1g protein

Fresh Marinara

Makes 7 servings: ½ cup each

Got juicy ripe tomatoes? Then make this sauce. It can be enjoyed like a traditional marinara, such as in Fresh Spaghetti and Meatballs (page 344), or as a condiment. It's not thick like a jarred sauce, so keep that in mind when pairing it with dishes. Also keep in mind that it has lycopene from the vibrant red tomatoes . . . which means it's pretty good for the heart, not just your palate.

4 large vine-ripened tomatoes, pulp removed and quartered

2 large garlic cloves, minced

1 tablespoon extra-virgin olive oil

1 teaspoon balsamic vinegar

½ teaspoon sea salt, or to taste

8 large or 12 medium fresh basil leaves, finely chopped

Add the tomato, garlic, oil, vinegar, and salt to a food processor or blender. Cover and pulse until a thick, slightly lumpy sauce forms. Stir in the basil. Adjust seasoning and serve.

Per serving: 40 calories, 2g total fat, 0g saturated fat, 0g trans fat, 0mg cholesterol, 170mg sodium, 5g total carbohydrate, 1g dietary fiber, 3g sugars, 1g protein

Triple Tomato Marinara Sauce

Makes 10 servings: ½ cup each

This recipe will awaken your senses. The layering of the fresh, crushed, and sun-dried tomatoes creates a distinctly different tomato taste. You can freeze this sauce for later, too. Make it your go-to marinara for pastas and pizzas, including Roasted Vegetable Rigatoni (page 296) and Superfood Veggie Stuffed Pizza (page 419).

2 teaspoons extra-virgin olive oil

1 medium red onion, diced

½ cup Merlot or other red wine

1¼ teaspoons sea salt, or to taste

2 large garlic cloves, minced

1 (28-ounce) can no-salt-added crushed tomatoes

6 sun-dried tomato halves (not oil-packed), very thinly sliced

⅓ cup chopped fresh flat-leaf parsley

½ teaspoon freshly ground black pepper, or to taste

⅛ teaspoon dried hot pepper flakes, or to taste

1 medium vine-ripened tomato, pulp removed, finely chopped

1 tablespoon chopped fresh basil

1 teaspoon chopped fresh oregano

1. Heat the oil in a large skillet or saucepan over medium heat. Add the onion, 1 tablespoon of the wine, and ¼ teaspoon of the salt and sauté until the onion is softened, about 5 minutes. Add the garlic and sauté for 1 minute.

2. Slowly pour in the remaining wine, increase heat to high, and continue to cook until the onion mixture is moist yet no runny liquid remains, about 3 minutes.

3. Stir in the canned tomatoes, sun-dried tomatoes, half of the parsley, the black pepper, hot pepper flakes, and the remaining 1 teaspoon salt. Cover, reduce heat to low, and simmer for 20 minutes. Stir in the fresh tomato, basil, oregano, and remaining parsley. Adjust seasoning. Serve.

Per serving: 60 calories, 1g total fat, 0g saturated fat, 0g trans fat, 0mg cholesterol, 320mg sodium, 7g total carbohydrate, 2g dietary fiber, 4g sugars, 2g protein

Fennel Turkey Pasta Sauce

Makes 12 servings: ⅔ cup each

I set out to develop a meat sauce where the only thing out of the ordinary was the extraordinary taste. Using turkey and fennel instead of beef keeps it slim and savory. A lively combination of herbs and citrus juice makes it sumptuous, especially in Fennel-Turkey Spaghetti Bolognese (page 342).

1 tablespoon extra-virgin olive oil

1 pound ground turkey (about 94% lean)

1 fennel bulb, diced (about 1½ cups)

1 large white onion, chopped

½ cup Merlot or other red wine

1½ teaspoons sea salt, or to taste

3 large garlic cloves, minced

1 teaspoon dried oregano

½ teaspoon ground sage

1 (28-ounce) can no-salt-added crushed tomatoes

½ cup fresh-squeezed orange juice

½ cup unsweetened green tea or water

⅓ cup chopped fresh parsley

½ teaspoon freshly ground black pepper, or to taste

1 teaspoon finely chopped fresh oregano

1. Heat ½ tablespoon of the oil in large skillet or saucepan over medium-high heat. Add the turkey and cook, stirring, until fully cooked, about 5 minutes. Transfer the turkey to a plate.

2. Heat the remaining ½ tablespoon of the oil in the skillet. Add the fennel, onion, 1 tablespoon of the wine, and ¼ teaspoon of the salt and sauté until the onion is softened, about 5 minutes. Stir in the garlic, dried oregano, and sage and continue cooking for 30 seconds. Slowly pour in the remaining wine, scrape up any browned bits in the pan, and cook while stirring for 1 minute.

3. Return the turkey to the skillet and add the tomatoes, orange juice, tea, half of the parsley, the pepper, and the remaining 1¼ teaspoons salt.

4. Cover, reduce heat to medium-low, and simmer for 25 minutes.

5. Stir in the oregano and remaining parsley. Adjust seasoning and serve.

Per serving: 100 calories, 2g total fat, 0g saturated fat, 0g trans fat, 15mg cholesterol, 320mg sodium, 7g total carbohydrate, 2g dietary fiber, 4g sugars, 11g protein

Bell Pepper Marinara

Makes 12 servings: ½ cup each

Looking for a thick, hearty sauce that can stand up to hearty pasta shapes as well as a variety of other entrées? This green bell pepper–spiked pick with plenty of flavor will pair nicely when you want to branch out from true Italian cuisine with some Spanish panache. It transforms these dishes: Sunnyside-Up Pizza (page 20), Crisped Zucchini Stacks (page 466), Roasted Cauliflower Goat Cheese Toasts (page 65), and more.

2 teaspoons extra-virgin olive oil

2 large green bell peppers, chopped

1 medium yellow onion, diced

½ cup Merlot or other red wine

1¼ teaspoons sea salt, or to taste

2 large garlic cloves, minced

1 (28-ounce) can no-salt-added crushed tomatoes

1 (14.5-ounce) can no-salt-added diced tomatoes (with liquid)

¼ cup chopped fresh flat-leaf parsley

½ teaspoon ground sage (optional)

½ teaspoon freshly ground black pepper, or to taste

¼ teaspoon dried hot pepper flakes, or to taste

2 tablespoons chopped fresh basil

1 teaspoon chopped fresh oregano

1. Heat the oil in a large skillet or saucepan over medium heat. Add the bell pepper, onion, 1 tablespoon of the wine, and ¼ teaspoon of the salt and sauté until the bell pepper and onion are softened, about 10 minutes. Add the garlic and sauté for 1 minute.

2. Slowly pour in the remaining wine, increase heat to high, and continue to cook until the bell pepper mixture is moist yet no runny liquid remains, about 5 minutes.

3. Stir in the crushed and diced tomatoes with liquid, parsley, sage (if using), black pepper, hot pepper flakes, and the remaining 1 teaspoon salt. Cover, reduce heat to low, and simmer until desired sauce consistency and flavor are reached, about 25 minutes. Stir in the basil and oregano. Adjust seasoning and serve.

Per serving: 60 calories, 1g total fat, 0g saturated fat, 0g trans fat, 0mg cholesterol, 250mg sodium, 8g total carbohydrate, 2g dietary fiber, 4g sugars, 2g protein

80-Proof Vodka Sauce

Makes 10 servings: ½ cup each

The subtle addition of vodka along with a velvety bean puree creates a pasta sauce that's a bit more glamorous and, well, spirited than a traditional vodka sauce. Luckily, this skinny sauce has bodacious flavor. Taste it for yourself in Penne alla Vodka (page 290) or Vodka Chicken Fettuccine (page 339).

½ cup drained canned no-salt-added cannellini
     or other white beans
⅓ cup low-sodium vegetable broth
     or Vegetable Stock (page 203)
3 tablespoons heavy cream
1 tablespoon extra-virgin olive oil
1 large shallot, minced
2 large garlic cloves, minced
1 (28-ounce) can no-salt-added crushed tomatoes
1 teaspoon aged balsamic vinegar
1 teaspoon sea salt, or to taste
¼ teaspoon dried hot pepper flakes, or to taste
½ cup unsweetened green tea or water
¼ cup 80-proof vodka
2 tablespoons chopped fresh flat-leaf parsley
2 tablespoons chopped fresh basil (optional)

1. Add the beans, broth, and cream to a blender. Cover and puree on low speed for 1 minute, then on high speed until emulsified, about 1 minute. Set aside.

2. Heat the oil in a large skillet or saucepan over medium heat. Add the shallot and sauté until softened and fragrant, about 1 minute. Add the garlic and sauté until fragrant, about 1 minute. Add the tomatoes, vinegar, salt, hot pepper flakes, and tea and increase heat to medium-high, and bring to a boil. Slowly pour in the vodka and let cook for 1 minute. Reduce heat to low, pour in the bean mixture, and stir until creamy and fully heated. Stir in the parsley and basil (if using). Adjust seasoning and serve.

Per serving: 80 calories, 3g total fat, 1g saturated fat, 0g trans fat, 5mg cholesterol, 240mg sodium, 7g total carbohydrate, 2g dietary fiber, 3g sugars, 2g protein

Squash Pasta Sauce

Makes 4 servings: ⅔ cup each

This is a wonderful, hearty sauce in colder months. Golden kabocha or butternut squash, rich in both color and flavor, create uniqueness here. The sauce, with a touch of butter and olive oil for richness, is worthy of pairing with any whole-grain pasta. Enjoy it in Gemelli Pasta with Squash and Herbs (page 288). Go beyond pasta and consider serving this special recipe as gravy for roasted poultry, too.

1 pound peeled cubed kabocha or butternut squash

2 cups low-sodium vegetable broth
   or Vegetable Stock (page 203)

2 teaspoons unsalted butter

2 teaspoons extra-virgin olive oil

1 large shallot, minced

2 large garlic cloves, minced

2 tablespoons finely chopped fresh flat-leaf parsley

¾ teaspoon sea salt, or to taste

¼ teaspoon freshly ground black pepper, or to taste

1. Add the squash to a medium saucepan with the broth. If necessary, add cold water so squash is fully immersed in liquid. Place over medium heat, cover, and simmer until the squash is fully softened, about 35 minutes. Drain the squash and reserve the cooking liquid. Add the squash cubes to a medium bowl and mash with a potato masher until smooth.

2. Melt the butter with the oil in a medium saucepan over medium heat. Add the shallot and sauté until softened and fragrant, about 1 minute. Add the garlic and sauté until fragrant, about 1 minute. Stir in the mashed squash, the parsley, salt, and pepper and cook until fully heated. Stir in the reserved cooking liquid and cook until fully heated. Adjust seasoning and serve.

Per serving: 90 calories, 4.5g total fat, 1.5g saturated fat, 0g trans fat, 5mg cholesterol, 510mg sodium, 14g total carbohydrate, 4g dietary fiber, 3g sugars, 1g protein

Barbecue Sauces

Home-Style Barbecue Sauce

Makes 24 servings: 2 tablespoons each

There's an interesting note of sweetness from the turbinado sugar and molasses and a lovely bit of homemade texture provided by the onions in this highly flavored, lower-calorie sauce. Slather it onto grilled chicken or tofu or use in California Boneless BBQ Ribs (page 319) or Brooklyn Lager Baked Beans (page 488).

1 tablespoon unrefined peanut or grapeseed oil

1 large red onion, minced

3 tablespoons red wine vinegar

½ teaspoon sea salt, or to taste

2 large garlic cloves, minced

1 cup low-sodium vegetable broth
   or Vegetable Stock (page 203)

¾ cup no-salt-added tomato sauce

3 tablespoons unsulfured molasses

3 tablespoons Dijon mustard

3 tablespoons turbinado sugar

2 tablespoons tomato paste

2 tablespoons vegetarian Worcestershire sauce

Juice of 1 small lemon (2 tablespoons)

½ teaspoon chili powder

½ teaspoon smoked paprika

½ teaspoon freshly ground black pepper, or to taste

1. Heat the oil in a large saucepan over medium heat. Add the onion, 1 tablespoon of the vinegar, and ¼ teaspoon of the salt and sauté until the onion is fully softened, about 8 minutes. Add the garlic and sauté 1 minute.

2. Stir in the broth, tomato sauce, molasses, mustard, sugar, tomato paste, Worcestershire sauce, lemon juice, chili powder, paprika, pepper, the remaining 2 tablespoons vinegar, and the remaining ¼ teaspoon salt and bring to a boil over medium-high heat. Reduce heat to low and simmer uncovered, stirring occasionally, until the mixture is desired consistency, about 12 minutes. Adjust seasoning. Use immediately or store in the refrigerator for up to 1 week or freezer for up to 1 month

Per serving: 30 calories, 0.5g total fat, 0g saturated fat, 0g trans fat, 0mg cholesterol, 125mg sodium, 6g total carbohydrate, 0g dietary fiber, 4g sugars, 0g protein

Ancho Chili Barbecue Sauce

Makes 28 servings: 2 tablespoons each

If you prefer a hint of smoky heat in your barbecue sauce, this recipe is for you. It'll amaze you how much vibrancy it will add to your plate. Serve the sauce in Barbecued Seitan Sandwich (page 385), Barbecued Chicken Pizza (page 419), or with grilled chicken, pork, or tofu.

1 tablespoon unrefined peanut or grapeseed oil

1 large red onion, minced

1 poblano pepper, minced

3 tablespoons apple cider vinegar

½ teaspoon sea salt, or to taste

2 large garlic cloves, minced

1 cup low-sodium vegetable broth
    or Vegetable Stock (page 203)

¾ cup no-salt-added tomato sauce

3 tablespoons unsulfured molasses

3 tablespoons Dijon mustard

2 tablespoons turbinado sugar

2 tablespoons tomato paste

2 tablespoons vegetarian Worcestershire sauce

Juice of 1 small lemon (2 tablespoons)

1 teaspoon ancho chili powder

½ teaspoon smoked paprika

½ teaspoon freshly ground black pepper, or to taste

1. Heat the oil in a large saucepan over medium heat. Add the onion, poblano, 1 tablespoon of the vinegar, and ¼ teaspoon of the salt and sauté until the onion and poblano are fully softened, about 10 minutes. Add the garlic and sauté 1 minute.

2. Stir in the broth, tomato sauce, molasses, mustard, sugar, tomato paste, Worcestershire sauce, lemon juice, chili powder, paprika, black pepper,

the remaining 2 tablespoons vinegar, and the remaining ¼ teaspoon salt and bring to a boil over medium-high heat. Reduce heat to low and simmer uncovered, stirring occasionally, until the mixture is desired consistency, about 12 minutes. Adjust seasoning. Use immediately or store in the refrigerator for up to 1 week or freezer for up to 1 month.

Per serving: 25 calories, 0.5g total fat, 0g saturated fat, 0g trans fat, 0mg cholesterol, 110mg sodium, 5g total carbohydrate, 0g dietary fiber, 3g sugars, 0g protein

Pineapple-Serrano Barbecue Sauce

Makes 28 servings: 2 tablespoons each

The pineapple juice in this perky sauce will add a slightly tropical touch to your barbecue. It'll be marvelous slathered onto nearly anything you choose to cook on the grill, especially chicken, pork, or poultry. Try it in Pineapple-Serrano BBQ Pork Sandwich (page 389). Consider grilling a side of fresh pineapple wedges or cubes to serve alongside your barbecued dish, too.

1 tablespoon unrefined peanut or grapeseed oil

1 large red onion, minced

2 serrano peppers with seeds, minced

3 tablespoons apple cider vinegar

½ teaspoon sea salt, or to taste

1 large garlic clove, minced

¾ cup 100% pineapple juice

½ cup low-sodium vegetable broth
    or Vegetable Stock (page 203)

½ cup no-salt-added tomato sauce

3 tablespoons unsulfured molasses

3 tablespoons Dijon mustard

3 tablespoons tomato paste

2 tablespoons turbinado sugar

2 tablespoons vegetarian Worcestershire sauce

Juice of 1 small lemon (2 tablespoons)

½ teaspoon chili powder

¼ teaspoon smoked paprika, or to taste

¼ teaspoon freshly ground black pepper, or to taste

continues on next page

1. Heat the oil in a large saucepan over medium heat. Add the onion, serrano, 1 tablespoon of the vinegar, and ¼ teaspoon of the salt and sauté until the onion and peppers are fully softened, about 10 minutes. Add the garlic and sauté 1 minute.

2. Stir in the pineapple juice, broth, tomato sauce, molasses, mustard, tomato paste, sugar, Worcestershire sauce, lemon juice, chili powder, paprika, black pepper, the remaining 2 table-spoons vinegar, and the remaining ¼ teaspoon salt and bring to a boil over medium-high heat. Reduce heat to low and simmer uncovered, stir-ring occasionally, until the mixture is desired con-sistency, about 12 minutes. Adjust seasoning. Use immediately or store in the refrigerator for up to 1 week or freezer for up to 1 month.

Per serving: 25 calories, 0.5g total fat, 0g saturated fat, 0g trans fat, 0mg cholesterol, 110mg sodium, 5g total carbohydrate, 0g dietary fiber, 4g sugars, 0g protein

Tangy Apricot Barbecue Sauce

Makes 28 servings: 2 tablespoons each

If you adore a sweet barbecue sauce, this one is for you. It blends sweet-tart accents into all the amazing savoriness that you expect from a barbe-cue sauce. It's tantalizing in Apricot BBQ Chicken Legs (page 308).

1 tablespoon unrefined peanut or grapeseed oil

1 large sweet onion, minced

¼ cup white balsamic or champagne vinegar

½ teaspoon sea salt, or to taste

2 large garlic cloves, minced

1 cup low-sodium vegetable broth
    or Vegetable Stock (page 203)

¾ cup no-salt-added tomato sauce

½ cup apricot 100% fruit spread or jam

3 tablespoons Dijon mustard

2 tablespoons unsulfured molasses

2 tablespoons tomato paste

2 tablespoons vegetarian Worcestershire sauce

Juice of 1 small lemon (2 tablespoons)

½ teaspoon chili powder

¼ teaspoon smoked paprika, or to taste

¼ teaspoon freshly ground black pepper, or to taste

1. Heat the oil in a large saucepan over medium heat. Add the onion, 1 tablespoon of the vinegar, and ¼ teaspoon of the salt and sauté until the onion is fully softened, about 8 minutes. Add the garlic and sauté 1 minute.

2. Stir in the broth, tomato sauce, fruit spread, mustard, molasses, tomato paste, Worcester-shire sauce, lemon juice, chili powder, paprika, pepper, the remaining 3 tablespoons vinegar, and the remaining ¼ teaspoon salt and bring to a boil over medium-high heat. Reduce heat to low and simmer uncovered, stirring occasionally, until the mixture is desired consistency, about 12 minutes. Adjust seasoning. Use immediately or store in the refrigerator for up to 1 week or freezer for up to 1 month.

Per serving: 30 calories, 0.5g total fat, 0g saturated fat, 0g trans fat, 0mg cholesterol, 110mg sodium, 6g total carbohydrate, 0g dietary fiber, 4g sugars, 0g protein

Apple Cider Barbecue Sauce

Makes 32 servings: 2 tablespoons each

Choose this sauce if you want the essence of apple to shine. The layering of the flavors of apple cider vinegar, fresh apple cider, and apple butter creates an indescribable autumn palate pleaser. Try it in Apple Cider Barbecue Beans (page 489); it's a side of savory, slow-cooked goodness.

1 tablespoon unrefined peanut or grapeseed oil

1 large red onion, minced

¼ cup apple cider vinegar

½ teaspoon sea salt, or to taste

1 large garlic clove, minced

¾ cup no-salt-added tomato sauce

½ cup fresh apple cider

½ cup low-sodium vegetable broth
    or Vegetable Stock (page 203)

½ cup no-sugar-added apple butter

3 tablespoons unsulfured molasses

3 tablespoons Dijon mustard

2 tablespoons tomato paste

2 tablespoons vegetarian Worcestershire sauce

Juice of 1 small lemon (2 tablespoons)

½ teaspoon chili powder

½ teaspoon smoked paprika

½ teaspoon freshly ground black pepper, or to taste

1. Heat the oil in a large saucepan over medium heat. Add the onion, 1 tablespoon of the vinegar, and ¼ teaspoon of the salt and sauté until fully softened, about 8 minutes. Add the garlic and sauté 1 minute.

2. Stir in the tomato sauce, cider, broth, apple butter, molasses, mustard, tomato paste, Worcestershire sauce, lemon juice, chili powder, paprika, pepper, the remaining 3 tablespoons vinegar, and the remaining ¾ teaspoon salt and bring to a boil over medium-high heat. Reduce heat to low and simmer uncovered, stirring occasionally, until the mixture is desired consistency, about 12 minutes. Adjust seasoning. Use immediately or store in the refrigerator for up to 1 week or freezer for up to 1 month.

Per serving: 25 calories, 0g total fat, 0g saturated fat, 0g trans fat, 0mg cholesterol, 95mg sodium, 5g total carbohydrate, 0g dietary fiber, 4g sugars, 0g protein

Fig Barbecue Sauce

Makes 28 servings: 2 tablespoons each

I'm a big fig fan. And since they're only seasonal for such a short time, I take full advantage of dried figs wherever possible—for year-round delight. They add texture and fruitiness to this rich sauce, making it an intriguing match for nearly any meat . . . tofu, too.

1 tablespoon unrefined peanut or grapeseed oil

1 large red onion, minced

3 tablespoons red wine or fig balsamic vinegar

½ teaspoon sea salt, or to taste

2 large garlic cloves, minced

1 cup low-sodium vegetable broth
    or Vegetable Stock (page 203)

¾ cup no-salt-added tomato sauce

12 dried Black Mission figs, minced

3 tablespoons unsulfured molasses

3 tablespoons Dijon mustard

2 tablespoons tomato paste

2 tablespoons vegetarian Worcestershire sauce

Juice of 1 small lemon (2 tablespoons)

½ teaspoon chili powder

¼ teaspoon smoked paprika, or to taste

¼ teaspoon freshly ground black pepper, or to taste

1. Heat the oil in a large saucepan over medium heat. Add the onion, 1 tablespoon of the vinegar, and ¼ teaspoon of the salt and sauté until fully softened, about 8 minutes. Add the garlic and sauté 1 minute.

2. Stir in the broth, tomato sauce, figs, molasses, mustard, tomato paste, Worcestershire sauce, lemon juice, chili powder, paprika, pepper, the remaining 2 tablespoons vinegar, and the remaining ¼ teaspoon salt and bring to a boil over medium-high heat. Reduce heat to low and simmer uncovered, stirring occasionally, until the mixture is desired consistency, about 12 minutes. Adjust seasoning. Use immediately or store in the refrigerator for up to 1 week or freezer for up to 1 month.

Per serving: 35 calories, 0.5g total fat, 0g saturated fat, 0g trans fat, 0mg cholesterol, 110mg sodium, 8g total carbohydrate, 1g dietary fiber, 6g sugars, 0g protein

Nut and Seed Sauces

Peanut Sauce

Makes 8 servings: 2 tablespoons each

The secret to this slim satay-like sauce is apple-sauce—which also provides a hint of natural sweetness to balance the nuttiness. It provides rich Asian appeal when dipped into or tossed with noodles, cucumbers, zucchini, poultry, and so much more. Take your taste buds on a culinary adventure; try it with Lime-Peanut Zucchini Noodles (page 263) and Thai Turkey Pizza (page 416).

⅓ cup + 1 tablespoon no-sugar-added apple sauce

3 tablespoons no-salt-added creamy natural peanut butter

2 tablespoons naturally brewed soy sauce

1 teaspoon brown rice vinegar

1½ teaspoons toasted sesame oil

½ teaspoon freshly grated gingerroot

½ teaspoon Asian garlic-chili sauce

2 scallions, green and white parts, minced

Stir together all the ingredients in a small bowl until well combined. Use immediately or store in the refrigerator for up to 1 week.

Per serving: 50 calories, 4g total fat, 0.5g saturated fat, 0g trans fat, 0mg cholesterol, 240mg sodium, 3g total carbohydrate, 1g dietary fiber, 2g sugars, 2g protein

Gingery Peanut-Almond Sauce

Makes 6 servings: 2 tablespoons each

I'm head over heels in love with this nutty Asian-inspired sauce where all of my favorite flavors are joined in culinary matrimony. It'll be sure to wow your taste buds, too. Try it in these tempters: Thai Sesame Summer Squash (page 265) and Take-Away Thai Chicken Wrap (page 403). Or enjoy as a zingy dip for carrots or sauce for soba noodles or grilled shrimp.

2 tablespoons no-salt-added creamy natural peanut butter

2 tablespoons no-salt-added creamy roasted or raw almond butter

2 tablespoons naturally brewed soy sauce

1 tablespoon freshly grated gingerroot

1 tablespoon honey or agave nectar

1 teaspoon brown rice vinegar

1½ teaspoons toasted sesame oil

½ teaspoon Asian garlic-chili sauce

2 scallions, green and white parts, minced

Stir together all the ingredients until well combined. Use immediately or store in the refrigerator for up to 1 week.

Per serving: 90 calories, 7g total fat, 1g saturated fat, 0g trans fat, 0mg cholesterol, 330mg sodium, 6g total carbohydrate, 1g dietary fiber, 4g sugars, 3g protein

Creamy Tahini Sauce

Makes 14 servings: 2 tablespoons each

If you take a hummus recipe and swap the beans for more tahini, the result is a thick tahini sauce. Use it like a different kind of mayo for a change of taste. It's an intriguing condiment for lean sandwiches and burgers, including Moroccan "Burger-Dog" (page 401).

¾ cup tahini (sesame seed paste)

⅔ cup unsweetened green tea or water

Juice of 1 large or 2 small lemons (¼ cup)

1 tablespoon extra-virgin olive oil

1 garlic clove, chopped

¼ teaspoon sea salt, or to taste

⅛ teaspoon ground cumin

Add the tahini, tea, lemon juice, oil, garlic, salt, and cumin to a blender. Cover and puree. Adjust tea and seasoning, if necessary. Use immediately or store in the refrigerator for up to 2 weeks.

Per serving: 90 calories, 8g total fat, 1g saturated fat, 0g trans fat, 0mg cholesterol, 55mg sodium, 3g total carbohydrate, 1g dietary fiber, 0g sugars, 2g protein

Harissa Lemon-Tahini Sauce Ⓢ

Makes 16 servings: 2 tablespoons each

Delight your taste buds by drizzling this smooth sauce over nearly any veggie or into a falafel or veggie-stuffed sandwich, like Edamame Salad Shawarma (page 383). The contrast of the sesame and lemon along with the kick of heat from the harissa sauce are magical together, adding pow to plain and not-so-plain veggies.

¾ cup tahini (sesame seed paste)
⅔ cup unsweetened green tea or water
Juice of 2 lemons (6 tablespoons)
1 tablespoon extra-virgin olive oil
1 tablespoon harissa sauce
1 garlic clove, chopped
¼ teaspoon sea salt, or to taste
⅛ teaspoon ground cumin

Add the tahini, tea, lemon juice, oil, harissa, garlic, salt, and cumin to a blender. Cover and puree. Adjust tea and seasoning, if necessary. Use immediately or store in the refrigerator for up to 2 weeks.

Per serving: 90 calories, 8g total fat, 1g saturated fat, 0g trans fat, 0mg cholesterol, 55mg sodium, 3g total carbohydrate, 1g dietary fiber, 0g sugars, 2g protein

Pistachio Plum Sauce Ⓢ

Makes 12 servings: 2 tablespoons each

So fruity and so much more . . . you'll love the hint of pistachio and the Asian flair that make this sweet-n-savory sauce extra special. It's ideally used as a marinade and basting grill sauce. The natural fruit sugars provide flavor-enhancing caramelization during the grilling process that'll wow you in recipes like Pistachio-Plum Glazed Chicken (page 308).

12 ounces plum or cherry 100% fruit spread or jam
3 tablespoons apple cider vinegar
2 tablespoons no-salt-added pistachio
    or other nut butter
1 tablespoon naturally brewed soy sauce
1 large garlic clove, minced
1 teaspoon freshly grated gingerroot
¼ teaspoon dried hot pepper flakes
1 tablespoon finely chopped unsalted dry-roasted
    pistachios

Add the jam, vinegar, pistachio butter, soy sauce, garlic, ginger, hot pepper flakes, and 1 tablespoon water to a saucepan over medium-high heat. Bring to a full boil while stirring. Remove from heat. Stir in the pistachios. Chill. Store in the refrigerator for up to 1 week. Bring to room temperature before using in a recipe.

Per serving: 80 calories, 1.5g total fat, 0g saturated fat, 0g trans fat, 0mg cholesterol, 75mg sodium, 16g total carbohydrate, 0g dietary fiber, 12g sugars, 1g protein

Gravies

Savory Carrot-Shallot Gravy

Makes 22 servings: ¼ cup each

Here, beans create silkiness and carrots add an orange hue and sweet savoriness. It's a veggie-friendly gravy for nearly everything.

2 teaspoons extra-virgin olive or grapeseed oil

2 large shallots, finely chopped

2 teaspoons apple cider vinegar

1½ teaspoons sea salt, or to taste

12 ounces large carrots, finely chopped

1 (15-ounce) can no-salt-added cannellini
    or other white beans, drained

1 bay leaf

½ teaspoon freshly ground black pepper, or to taste

½ teaspoon ground sage

1 (32-ounce) carton low-sodium vegetable broth
    or 4 cups Vegetable Stock (page 203)

1 cup plain almond milk

½ teaspoon finely chopped fresh thyme

½ teaspoon finely chopped fresh marjoram or dill

1. Heat the oil over medium heat in a large sauce-pan. Add the shallots, vinegar, and ¼ teaspoon of the salt and sauté until slightly softened, about 5 minutes.

2. Add the carrots, beans, bay leaf, pepper, sage, broth, and the remaining 1¼ teaspoons salt. Increase heat to high and bring to a boil.

3. Reduce heat to medium, cover, and cook until the carrots are fully softened, about 35 minutes. Remove from heat and remove the bay leaf.

4. Fully puree using a hand immersion blender or in batches in a blender. Stir in the almond milk, thyme, and marjoram and adjust seasoning. Bring back to a simmer, if necessary, and serve while hot.

Per serving: 35 calories, 0.5g total fat, 0g saturated fat, 0g trans fat, 0mg cholesterol, 210mg sodium, 6g total carbohydrate, 1g dietary fiber, 2g sugars, 1g protein

Rosemary Sweet Potato Gravy

Makes 22 servings: ¼ cup each

The key to a low-cal, yet luscious gravy is to begin with a base of vegetables. Yes, you can boost your veggie intake with gravy. Here the sweet potatoes provide color, creaminess, and nutrition, becoming a delightful companion to Sage Turkey Tenders with Gravy (page 316).

2 teaspoons extra-virgin olive or grapeseed oil

1 medium red or white, onion, finely chopped

2 teaspoons apple cider vinegar

1½ teaspoons sea salt, or to taste

1 large sweet potato, unpeeled, scrubbed, and diced

1 (15-ounce) can no-salt-added cannellini
    or other white beans, drained

1 bay leaf

½ teaspoon freshly ground black pepper,
    or to taste

½ teaspoon ground sage

1 (32-ounce) carton low-sodium vegetable broth
    or 4 cups Vegetable Stock (page 203)

1 teaspoon minced fresh rosemary

1. Heat the oil over medium heat in a large sauce-pan. Add the onion, vinegar, and ¼ teaspoon of the salt and sauté until slightly softened, about 5 minutes.

2. Add the sweet potato, beans, bay leaf, pepper, sage, broth, and the remaining 1¼ teaspoons salt. Increase heat to high and bring to a boil.

3. Reduce heat to medium, cover, and cook until the sweet potato is fully softened, about 20 minutes. Remove from heat and remove the bay leaf.

4. Fully puree using a hand immersion blender or in batches in a blender. Stir in the rosemary and adjust seasoning. Bring back to a simmer, if necessary, and serve while hot.

Per serving: 40 calories, 0.5g total fat, 0g saturated fat, 0g trans fat, 0mg cholesterol, 200mg sodium, 8g total carbohydrate, 2g dietary fiber, 2g sugars, 1g protein

Roasted Chestnut Gravy

Makes 32 servings: ¼ cup each

This holiday-inspired recipe is ideal for a large festive gathering and divine over roasted turkey. If you can't find raw chestnuts, just use 15 ounces of packaged or jarred roasted peeled chestnuts and skip step 1.

1½ pounds raw European chestnuts

2 teaspoons canola or grapeseed oil

1 large sweet onion, chopped

2 teaspoons white balsamic vinegar

1¼ teaspoons sea salt, or to taste

2 bay leaves

¼ teaspoon freshly ground white pepper, or to taste

⅛ teaspoon ground allspice

2 (32-ounce) cartons low-sodium vegetable broth or 8 cups Vegetable Stock (page 203)

½ cup plain almond or light soy milk

1 teaspoon honey or agave nectar, or to taste

3 tablespoons minced fresh chives

1. Preheat the oven to 450°F. Slice an "X" across each chestnut using a sharp knife. Place chestnuts in a single layer in a large baking pan and pour in ¼ cup water. Roast in the oven for 10 minutes. When cool enough to handle, shell and peel the chestnuts.

2. Heat the oil over medium-high heat in a stockpot or large saucepan. Add the onion, vinegar, and ¼ teaspoon of the salt and sauté until slightly caramelized, about 8 minutes.

3. Add the roasted chestnuts, the bay leaves, pepper, allspice, broth, and the remaining 1 teaspoon salt. Increase heat to high and bring to a boil.

4. Reduce heat to medium-low and simmer uncovered for 1 hour. Remove from heat and remove the bay leaves.

5. Fully puree using a hand immersion blender or in batches in a blender. Stir in the almond milk, honey, and chives and adjust seasoning. Bring back to a simmer, if necessary, and serve while hot.

Per serving: 40 calories, 0.5g total fat, 0g saturated fat, 0g trans fat, 0mg cholesterol, 130mg sodium, 8g total carbohydrate, 1g dietary fiber, 2g sugars, 0g protein

Shiitake Gravy

Makes 14 servings: ¼ cup each

This earthy gravy is loaded with shiitakes. Savor it over potatoes, chicken, or roast beef.

2 cups low-sodium vegetable broth or Vegetable Stock (page 203)

3 tablespoons whole-wheat pastry flour

2 teaspoons extra-virgin olive or grapeseed oil

6 scallions, green and white parts, minced

3 large garlic cloves, minced

Juice of ½ small lemon (1 tablespoon)

¾ teaspoon sea salt, or to taste

1 pound fresh shiitake mushrooms, stems removed and sliced

1 tablespoon naturally brewed soy sauce

½ cup Chardonnay or other dry white wine

½ teaspoon freshly ground black pepper, or to taste

2 tablespoons finely chopped fresh flat-leaf parsley

½ teaspoon fresh thyme or oregano leaves

1. Whisk the flour and broth in a medium bowl or large measuring cup until smooth. Set aside.

2. Heat the oil in a large skillet over medium heat. Add the scallions, garlic, lemon juice, and ¼ teaspoon of the salt and sauté until the scallions are softened, about 3 minutes. Increase heat to medium-high, add the mushrooms and soy sauce, and sauté until the mushrooms are softened and excess liquid is absorbed, about 8 minutes.

3. Add the wine and cook until the liquid is evaporated, about 5 minutes.

4. Increase heat to high, stir the reserved broth mixture into the mushroom mixture along with the pepper and the remaining ½ teaspoon salt, and bring to a boil while stirring. Reduce heat to medium-low and cook while stirring for 2 minutes.

5. Stir in the parsley and thyme. Adjust seasoning. Serve while hot.

Per serving: 35 calories, 1g total fat, 0g saturated fat, 0g trans fat, 0mg cholesterol, 210mg sodium, 5g total carbohydrate, 1g dietary fiber, 0g sugars, 1g protein

Farmers' Market Summer Squash Gravy

Makes 28 servings: ¼ cup each

I developed this fragrant, fresh take on gravy specifically for spring and summer dishes. Serve it with poultry or pilaf.

2 teaspoons extra-virgin olive or grapeseed oil

2 large shallots, finely chopped

2 teaspoons white balsamic vinegar

1¾ teaspoons sea salt, or to taste

1 large zucchini, unpeeled and chopped

1 large yellow squash, unpeeled and chopped

1 (15-ounce) can no-salt-added cannellini or other white beans, drained

1 bay leaf

¾ teaspoon freshly ground black pepper, or to taste

1 (32-ounce) carton low-sodium vegetable broth or 4 cups Vegetable Stock (page 203)

2 tablespoons finely chopped fresh chives

1 tablespoon finely chopped fresh basil

½ teaspoon finely chopped fresh oregano

1. Heat the oil in a large saucepan over medium heat. Add the shallots, vinegar, and ¼ teaspoon of the salt and sauté until softened, about 5 minutes.

2. Add the zucchini, yellow squash, beans, bay leaf, pepper, broth, and the remaining 1½ teaspoons salt. Increase heat to high and bring to a boil.

3. Reduce heat to medium-low, cover, and cook until the zucchini and yellow squash are fully softened, about 18 minutes. Remove from heat and remove the bay leaf.

4. Puree to desired consistency using a hand immersion blender or in batches in a blender. Stir in the chives, basil, and oregano and adjust seasoning. Reheat, if necessary, and serve while hot.

Per serving: 25 calories, 0.5g total fat, 0g saturated fat, 0g trans fat, 0mg cholesterol, 170mg sodium, 4g total carbohydrate, 1g dietary fiber, 1g sugars, 1g protein

Country Bean Gravy

Makes 28 servings: ¼ cup each

This textured gravy can be your culinary trick to a tantalizing meal. Using two different beans along with the ham adds flavor intrigue, too.

2 teaspoons extra-virgin olive or grapeseed oil

1 medium white or yellow onion, finely chopped

1 medium green bell pepper, finely chopped

4 ounces baked ham, finely chopped

2 teaspoons apple cider vinegar

1 (15-ounce) can no-salt-added lima or navy beans, drained

1 (15-ounce) can no-salt-added pinto or red kidney beans, drained

1 bay leaf

1¼ teaspoons sea salt, or to taste

½ teaspoon freshly ground black pepper, or to taste

½ teaspoon ground sage

1 (32-ounce) carton low-sodium chicken broth or 4 cups Chicken Stock (page 203)

½ teaspoon minced fresh oregano

½ teaspoon minced fresh rosemary

1. Heat the oil in a large saucepan over medium heat. Add the onion, bell pepper, ham, and vinegar, increase heat to medium-high, and sauté until the onion is softened, about 8 minutes.

2. Add the beans, bay leaf, salt, black pepper, sage, and broth. Increase heat to high and bring to a boil.

3. Reduce heat to medium-low, cover, and cook until the bell peppers are fully softened, about 15 minutes. Remove from heat and remove the bay leaf.

4. Puree to desired consistency using a hand immersion blender or in batches in a blender. Stir in the oregano and rosemary and adjust seasoning. Bring back to a simmer, if necessary, and serve while hot.

Per serving: 35 calories, 0.5g total fat, 0g saturated fat, 0g trans fat, 0mg cholesterol, 160mg sodium, 5g total carbohydrate, 1g dietary fiber, 0g sugars, 2g protein

Home-Style Chicken Gravy

Makes 7 servings: ¼ cup each

If you're a gravy traditionalist, this one's for you. It's simple to prepare. It has pep from a generous amount of freshly ground black pepper. The golden color is enriched by turmeric. And the home-style effect is created by shallot. The texture, taste, and aroma remind me of home . . . good old-fashioned comforting gravy. Want a double-dose of comfort? Enjoy it with Montreal-Inspired Poutine (page 461).

1 tablespoon unsalted butter

2 teaspoons grapeseed or canola oil

1 large shallot, minced

3 tablespoons whole-wheat pastry flour

1¾ cups low-sodium chicken broth
   or Chicken Stock (page 203)

¾ teaspoon freshly ground black pepper, or to taste

½ teaspoon sea salt, or to taste

⅛ teaspoon paprika

⅛ teaspoon ground turmeric

1. Heat the butter and oil in a medium saucepan over medium heat. Once the butter melts, add the shallot and sauté until fully softened and begins to caramelize, about 5 minutes.

2. Stir in the flour and cook while stirring for 1 minute. Pour in the broth and add the pepper, salt, paprika, and turmeric. Cook while stirring until desired thickened gravy consistency, about 8 minutes. Adjust seasoning and serve while hot.

Per serving: 45 calories, 3g total fat, 1g saturated fat, 0g trans fat, 5mg cholesterol, 180mg sodium, 4g total carbohydrate, 1g dietary fiber, 0g sugars, 1g protein

Sweet Italian Turkey Sausage Gravy

Makes 12 servings: ¼ cup each

After you pop biscuits from the oven, you'll want to have this tasty gravy piping hot and ready for pairing with your fresh-baked delights. The turkey sausage gives the gravy meal-worthy appeal and the sage provides a special herbal accent. Partake of these pleasures with Buttermilk Biscuits & Gravy (page 35). The gravy is delightful spooned over turkey or potatoes, too.

1 tablespoon extra-virgin olive or grapeseed oil

6 ounces sweet Italian turkey or chicken sausage,
   removed from casings

1 large shallot, minced

3 tablespoons whole-wheat pastry flour

2 cups low-sodium chicken or vegetable broth
   or Chicken Stock (page 203)

¼ teaspoon sea salt, or to taste

¼ teaspoon freshly ground black pepper, or to taste

¼ teaspoon ground sage

1. Heat the oil in a medium saucepan over medium heat. Add the sausage and shallot and sauté until the sausage is fully cooked and finely crumbled, about 5 minutes.

2. Stir in the flour and cook while stirring for 1 minute. Add the broth, salt, pepper, and sage and cook while stirring, scraping up any browned bits from the bottom of the pan, until thickened and bubbling, about 6 minutes. Adjust seasoning and serve while hot.

Per serving: 40 calories, 2.5g total fat, 0g saturated fat, 0g trans fat, 10mg cholesterol, 150mg sodium, 1g total carbohydrate, 0g dietary fiber, 0g sugars, 3g protein

Salsas

Roasted Green Tomato Salsa

Makes 12 servings: 2 tablespoons each

Roasting brings depth of flavor to tart green tomatoes or tomatillos. They're spectacular when transformed into this salsa. Enjoy it anywhere you normally enjoy its red counterpart. Its bright taste adds deliciousness to Avocado and White Bean Salad (page 190), Deep Dish Green Enchilada (page 262), or Tijuana Turkey "Lasagna" Verde (page 344)

3 medium green tomatoes or 10 tomatillos, husks removed, rinsed, and diced

1 small or ½ large white onion, diced

1 small jalapeño pepper with some seeds, minced

1½ teaspoons unrefined peanut or grapeseed oil

1 large garlic clove, minced

Juice of ½ lime (1 tablespoon)

1 tablespoon chopped fresh cilantro

⅛ teaspoon sea salt, or to taste

1. Preheat the oven to 400°F. Add the tomatoes, onion, and jalapeño to a medium bowl. Drizzle with the oil and toss to coat the vegetables. Transfer to a single layer on a parchment paper–lined large baking sheet. Roast until the tomatoes are softened, about 18 minutes. Stir in the garlic and roast until the onion is softened and garlic is fully fragrant, about 10 minutes. Remove from the oven.

2. Transfer the salsa mixture to a medium bowl. Stir in the lime juice, cilantro, and salt. Adjust seasoning and chill until ready to serve.

Per serving: 15 calories, 0.5g total fat, 0g saturated fat, 0g trans fat, 0mg cholesterol, 30mg sodium, 2g total carbohydrate, 0g dietary fiber, 2g sugars, 0g protein

Spicy Raw Tomatillo Salsa

Makes 22 servings: 2 tablespoons each

This fresh Mexican green tomato salsa isn't cooked, so it's considered salsa cruda. When food is robust, this tangy, summery salsa can provide a refreshing balance. It'll also give a spicy kick to Avocado and White Bean Salad (page 190) or Scrambled Huevos Rancheros with Fresh Salsa (page 16).

8 tomatillos, husks removed, rinsed, and quartered

½ large sweet onion, chopped

¼ cup packed fresh cilantro leaves

1 serrano pepper with some seeds

1 large garlic clove

Juice of ½ lime (1 tablespoon)

¼ teaspoon sea salt, or to taste

Add the tomatillos, onion, cilantro, serrano, garlic, lime juice, and salt to a food processor. Cover and pulse to desired consistency. (It's okay if there are still some lumps.) Adjust seasoning and serve.

Per serving: 5 calories, 0g total fat, 0g saturated fat, 0g trans fat, 0mg cholesterol, 25mg sodium, 1g total carbohydrate, 0g dietary fiber, 1g sugars, 0g protein

Vine-Ripened Pico de Gallo

Makes 10 servings: ¼ cup each

When tomatoes are in season, be sure you make this fresh and vibrant version of salsa. Sure, you can dunk tortilla chips into it. But also create vivid cuisine with it, like Roasted Poblano, Black Beans, and Rice (page 285) and Burrito el Desayuno (page 20).

2 large or 3 medium vine-ripened tomatoes, pulp removed and finely diced

1 small or ½ large white onion, finely diced

1 serrano pepper with some seeds, minced

1 tablespoon finely chopped fresh cilantro

½ teaspoon sea salt, or to taste

Juice of ½ lime (1 tablespoon)

Stir all ingredients together in a medium bowl. Adjust seasoning and serve.

Per serving: 10 calories, 0g total fat, 0g saturated fat, 0g trans fat, 0mg cholesterol, 120mg sodium, 2g total carbohydrate, 1g dietary fiber, 1g sugars, 0g protein

Fresh Sicilian Salsa

Makes 8 servings: 2 tablespoons each

Salsa is usually considered a Mexican sauce. But by changing a few ingredients, it can have the spirit of nearly any world cuisine. This salsa is Sicilian-inspired by way of the pepperoncini, capers, herbs, and balsamic vinegar. In Eggplant Parmesan Sliders (page 384), it's a show-stopping sandwich topping.

2 teaspoons aged balsamic vinegar

2 teaspoons extra-virgin olive oil

1 medium vine-ripened tomato, diced

¼ cup finely diced white or red onion

2 tablespoons minced pepperoncini or hot pepper rings

1 garlic clove, minced

1 tablespoon finely chopped fresh basil

1 teaspoon minced drained capers or minced black olives

½ teaspoon chopped fresh oregano

⅛ teaspoon freshly ground black pepper, or to taste

Whisk together the vinegar and oil in a small bowl until combined. Stir in the tomato, onion, pepperoncini, garlic, basil, capers, oregano, and black pepper. Adjust seasoning. Just before serving, drain excess liquid.

Per serving: 15 calories, 1g total fat, 0g saturated fat, 0g trans fat, 0mg cholesterol, 85mg sodium, 1g total carbohydrate, 0g dietary fiber, 1g sugars, 0g protein

Roasted Beet-Nectarine Salsa

Makes 8 servings: ½ cup each

A salsa can be whipped up with various veggies or fruits. Roasted beets coupled with fresh nectarines create a vibrant, colorful salsa with a hint of natural sweetness. It's versatile, too. The white balsamic provides tangy taste without darkening the salsa but you can use regular balsamic vinegar, too. Pair it with whole-grain pilaf or goat cheese, or enjoy as is like a salad, if you prefer.

2 medium golden or candy-striped beets, greens trimmed, roasted (below)

1 medium red beet, greens trimmed, roasted

1 medium nectarine or navel orange, seeded and diced

2 large shallots, minced

3 tablespoons finely chopped fresh mint

2 tablespoons extra-virgin olive or flaxseed oil

1 tablespoon white balsamic vinegar

1 teaspoon minced fresh rosemary

½ teaspoon sea salt, or to taste

¼ teaspoon freshly ground black pepper, or to taste

1. Peel the beets. Cut into ¼- to ⅓-inch dice, separating the golden and red beets.

2. Add the golden beets, nectarine, shallots, and mint to a medium serving bowl.

3. Whisk together the oil, vinegar, rosemary, salt, and pepper in a small bowl or measuring cup.

4. Stir the vinaigrette into the golden beet mixture. Gently stir in the red beets. Adjust seasoning and serve at room temperature.

Per serving: 60 calories, 3.5g total fat, 0.5g saturated fat, 0g trans fat, 0mg cholesterol, 170mg sodium, 7g total carbohydrate, 1g dietary fiber, 4g sugars, 1g protein

COOKING BEETS TWO WAYS

To roast medium-size beets, individually wrap unpeeled beets in aluminum foil. Roast in a 375°F conventional or toaster oven until beets can be easily pierced with a knife, about for 1 hour. Unwrap, and when cool enough to handle, rub or peel off the skins with a paring knife.

To cook in the microwave oven, cover well with parchment paper and place in a microwave-safe dish. Cook on high until the beets can be easily pierced with a knife, about 6 minutes for 1 beet; about 10 minutes for 3 beets. (Do not overcook.) Keep covered and set aside until cool enough to handle. Peel off the skins with a paring knife.

Sweet-n-Savory Melon Salsa

Makes 16 servings: ¼ cup each

Have an abundance of seasonal fruit on hand? Nearly any fruit can make a sensational salsa. Here a mélange of sweet melons makes a fresh salsa with the perfect accent of heat and intrigue from serrano and ginger. It's memorable when served over grilled chicken or fish, like Pan-Blacked Mahi Mahi (page 353) or Grilled Tuna with Fruit Salsa (page 358).

3 cups diced melon, such as cantaloupe, honeydew, and seedless watermelon

½ large English cucumber, unpeeled and diced

½ cup diced red onion

3 tablespoons finely chopped fresh mint

1 tablespoon finely chopped fresh basil

1 serrano pepper without seeds, minced

Juice and zest of 1 lime (2 tablespoons juice)

1 teaspoon freshly grated gingerroot

1½ teaspoons honey or agave nectar

½ teaspoon sea salt, or to taste

Gently stir together the melons, cucumber, onion, mint, basil, serrano, lime juice, ginger, honey, and salt in a medium serving bowl. Stir in desired amount of lime zest. Adjust seasoning and serve chilled or at room temperature.

Per serving: 15 calories, 0g total fat, 0g saturated fat, 0g trans fat, 0mg cholesterol, 75mg sodium, 4g total carbohydrate, 0g dietary fiber, 3g sugars, 0g protein

Strawberry Mojito Salsa

Makes 8 servings: ¼ cup each

If a mojito could be a spiked salsa instead of a spirited cocktail, this would be it. The juicy strawberries make it magical—along with providing a bevy of antioxidants, including vitamin C. Serve it over grilled chicken or fish.

1½ cups finely chopped fresh strawberries

⅓ cup finely chopped white onion

1 serrano pepper with some seeds, minced

2 tablespoons finely chopped fresh cilantro

1 tablespoon finely chopped fresh mint

Juice of ½ lime (1 tablespoon)

1 tablespoon 100-proof spiced rum or 80-proof dark rum

1 teaspoon turbinado sugar

¼ teaspoon sea salt, or to taste

Stir all ingredients together in a medium bowl. Adjust seasoning and serve at room temperature.

Per serving: 20 calories, 0g total fat, 0g saturated fat, 0g trans fat, 0mg cholesterol, 75mg sodium, 4g total carbohydrate, 1g dietary fiber, 2g sugars, 0g protein

Tropical Fruit and Cucumber Salsa

Makes 16 servings: ¼ cup each

The celestial sweetness of this salsa comes from mango and peach. And the hint of ginger completes it with a brilliant touch of the tropics. It's delightful as an accompaniment to Jerk Cornish Game Hens (page 311), baked tortilla chips, or grilled fish.

1 medium mango, peeled, pitted, and finely diced

1 large yellow or white peach, pitted and finely diced

1 medium vine-ripened tomato, finely diced

½ cup finely diced unpeeled English cucumber

¼ cup finely diced red onion

2 tablespoons chopped fresh cilantro

Juice and zest of 1 lime (2 tablespoons juice)

½ teaspoon freshly grated gingerroot, or to taste

¼ teaspoon sea salt, or to taste

Gently stir together the mango, peach, tomato, cucumber, onion, cilantro, lime juice, ginger, and salt in a medium serving bowl until well combined. Stir in the lime zest to taste. Adjust seasoning and serve chilled or at room temperature.

Per serving: 15 calories, 0g total fat, 0g saturated fat, 0g trans fat, 0mg cholesterol, 35mg sodium, 4g total carbohydrate, 1g dietary fiber, 3g sugars, 0g protein

Black Bean Salsa

Makes 7 servings: ¼ cup each

The pinch of cumin gives depth of flavor to this satisfying salsa. And if you love a good kick in the palate, all of the jalapeño seeds will definitely do the trick. It's like a treat with "heat" in Papaya and Goat Cheese Quesadilla (page 407), Blackened Tilapia Tacos with Papaya (page 405), or other Mexican or Latin dishes.

1 (15-ounce) can black beans, drained
⅓ cup finely diced red onion
1 small jalapeño pepper with seeds, minced
2 tablespoons finely chopped fresh cilantro
Juice and zest of 1 lime (2 tablespoons juice)
¼ teaspoon sea salt, or to taste
⅛ teaspoon ground cumin

Stir together the beans, onion, jalapeño, cilantro, lime juice, salt, and cumin in a medium bowl. Stir in desired amount of lime zest. Adjust seasoning and serve at room temperature.

Per serving: 50 calories, 0g total fat, 0g saturated fat, 0g trans fat, 0mg cholesterol, 150mg sodium, 10g total carbohydrate, 3g dietary fiber, 3g sugars, 3g protein

Pestos, Chutneys, and Tapenades

Enlightened Fresh Basil Pesto

Makes 20 servings: 2 tablespoons each

Prepare this garlicky pesto and you'll save 85 calories compared to a 2-tablespoon helping of traditional Italian basil pesto. It has a creamy, satisfying consistency thanks to the cannellini. Most importantly, it's delicious. The six cloves of garlic are no doubt the secret! Toss it into pasta recipes and so much more, including Pesto-Glazed Sirloin Tarts (page 55).

¼ cup pine nuts, toasted
¼ cup walnut halves, toasted
6 large garlic cloves
5 cups packed fresh basil leaves
1 (15-ounce) can no-salt-added cannellini
    or other white beans, drained
¼ cup low-sodium vegetable broth
    or Vegetable Stock (page 203)
2 teaspoons fresh lemon juice
¾ teaspoon sea salt, or to taste
⅓ cup extra-virgin olive oil

1. Add the pine nuts, walnuts, and garlic to a food processor. Cover and pulse until just combined. Add the basil, beans, broth, lemon juice, and salt. Cover and pulse until just combined.

2. Slowly pour in the oil through the feed tube with the processor running and puree until desired consistency. Adjust seasoning. Use immediately or store in the refrigerator or freezer with very thin lemon slices on top to help prevent browning.

Per serving: 70 calories, 6g total fat, 0.5g saturated fat, 0g trans fat, 0mg cholesterol, 95mg sodium, 4g total carbohydrate, 1g dietary fiber, 0g sugars, 2g protein

Arugula Pesto

Makes 16 servings: 2 tablespoons each

This lively pesto will make you say "wow." Instead of basil, its distinctive color and peppery bite are from the fresh arugula. Tofu and goat cheese provide creaminess and body. And a definite pow is provided by several cloves of garlic. It's the star ingredient in Pesto, Tomato, and Mozzarella Panini (page 392) and Pesto Chicken Pizzette (page 423). If not serving right away, before storing, top with very thin lemon slices to help prevent browning.

¼ cup pine nuts, pan-toasted

¼ cup walnut halves, pan-toasted

5 large garlic cloves, peeled

3 cups packed fresh arugula, baby or wild preferred

4 ounces soft tofu, drained

¼ cup low-sodium vegetable broth
    or Vegetable Stock (page 203)

2 ounces soft goat cheese

Juice of ½ small lemon (1 tablespoon)

¾ teaspoon sea salt, or to taste

¼ teaspoon freshly ground black pepper, or to taste

¼ cup extra-virgin olive oil

2 tablespoons freshly grated Parmigiano-Reggiano
    or other Parmesan cheese

1. Add the pine nuts, walnuts, and garlic to a food processor. Cover and pulse until just combined. Add the arugula, tofu, broth, goat cheese, lemon juice, salt, and pepper. Cover and pulse until just combined.

2. Slowly pour in the oil through the feed tube with the processor running and puree until desired consistency. Stir in the cheese and adjust seasoning. Serve immediately or store in the refrigerator or freezer.

Per serving: 80 calories, 7g total fat, 1.5g saturated fat, 0g trans fat, 0mg cholesterol, 135mg sodium, 1g total carbohydrate, 0g dietary fiber, 0g sugars, 2g protein

Swiss Chard Pesto

Makes 14 servings: 2 tablespoons each

If you ever find yourself with extra leafy greens on hand, preparing a fresh pesto with them is a surefire fix. The pinches of hot pepper flakes and nutmeg in this Swiss chard version provide a little punch of intrigue. It's garlicky good, too! Whirl it up for Swiss Chard Pesto Couscous (page 476); your taste buds will surely give it thumbs up.

¼ cup pine nuts, toasted

¼ cup walnut halves, toasted

5 large garlic cloves, peeled

3 cups packed torn fresh Swiss chard leaves

4 ounces soft tofu, drained

¼ cup low-sodium vegetable broth
    or Vegetable Stock (page 203)

Juice of ½ small lemon (1 tablespoon)

¾ teaspoon sea salt, or to taste

¼ teaspoon dried hot pepper flakes, or to taste

⅛ teaspoon freshly grated nutmeg

¼ cup extra-virgin olive oil

2 tablespoons freshly grated Parmigiano-Reggiano
    or other Parmesan cheese

1. Add the pine nuts, walnuts, and garlic to a food processor. Cover and pulse until just combined. Add the chard, tofu, broth, lemon juice, salt, hot pepper flakes, and nutmeg. Cover and pulse until just combined.

2. Slowly pour in the oil through the feed tube with the processor running and puree until desired consistency. Stir in the cheese and adjust seasoning. Use immediately or store in the refrigerator or freezer with very thins lemon slices on top to help prevent browning.

Per serving: 70 calories, 7g total fat, 0g saturated fat, 0g trans fat, 0mg cholesterol, 150mg sodium, 1g total carbohydrate, 0g dietary fiber, 0g sugars, 2g protein

Sun-Dried Tomato Pesto

Makes 12 servings: 2 tablespoons each

Sun-dried tomatoes provide a distinct saltiness and slight smokiness, as well as a deep orange instead of green color in this flavor-bursting herb-free pesto. Savor it as a bold sandwich condiment or a surprising spread atop grilled or roasted poultry or fish. Or savor the full flavors in Sun-Dried Tomato Pesto Hummus (page 87) or Sun-Dried Tomato Pesto Pasta with Tuna (page 368).

12 sun-dried tomato halves (not oil-packed), rehydrated

¼ cup pine nuts, toasted

5 large garlic cloves

4 ounces soft tofu, drained

¼ cup low-sodium vegetable broth or Vegetable Stock (page 203)

Juice of ½ small lemon (1 tablespoon)

¾ teaspoon sea salt, or to taste

¼ teaspoon freshly ground black pepper, or to taste

⅓ cup extra-virgin olive oil

2 tablespoons freshly grated Parmigiano-Reggiano or other Parmesan cheese

1. Add the sun-dried tomatoes, pine nuts, and garlic to a food processor. Cover and pulse until just combined. Add the tofu, broth, lemon juice, salt, and pepper. Cover and pulse until just combined.

2. Slowly pour in the oil through the feed tube with the processor running and puree until desired consistency. Stir in the cheese and adjust seasoning. Use immediately or store in the refrigerator with very thin lemon slices on top to help prevent browning.

Per serving: 90 calories, 9g total fat, 1g saturated fat, 0g trans fat, 0mg cholesterol, 200mg sodium, 2g total carbohydrate, 0g dietary fiber, 1g sugars, 2g protein

Fresh Mint Chutney

Makes 5 servings: 2 tablespoons each

Chutney can come in so many forms—from mild to spicy, fruity to herbal, creamy to chunky, and more. This fresh and intriguing mint adaptation makes a delicious accompaniment to South Asian Potato and Spring Pea Samosas (page 70) or for shrimp, scallops, or lamb.

1 cup packed fresh mint leaves

2 medium shallots, peeled

1 green serrano pepper without seeds

1 large garlic clove, chopped

2 tablespoons brown rice vinegar

Juice of ½ lime (1 tablespoon)

1 tablespoon 100% unsweetened apple juice

1 teaspoon freshly grated gingerroot

½ teaspoon ground cumin, or to taste

½ teaspoon sea salt, or to taste

⅛ teaspoon ground cinnamon or Chinese five-spice powder, or to taste

Add all ingredients to a food processor. Cover and pulse to desired consistency. Adjust seasoning. If you desire a thinner consistency, add additional apple juice by the teaspoonful. Serve at room temperature.

Per serving: 20 calories, 0g total fat, 0g saturated fat, 0g trans fat, 0mg cholesterol, 240 mg sodium, 5g total carbohydrate, 1g dietary fiber, 2g sugars, 1g protein

Cilantro-Mint Chutney

Makes 5 servings: 2 tablespoons each

If you can't decide between cilantro or mint in your chutney, now you don't have to. Both fresh herbs are equally whirled into this recipe. Enjoy this chutney as an impressionable culinary accessory to fish, such as Cilantro-Mint Chutney Seared Halibut (page 351), shellfish, or lamb.

½ cup packed fresh cilantro leaves
½ cup packed fresh mint leaves
2 medium shallots, peeled
1 green serrano pepper without seeds
1 large garlic clove, chopped
2 tablespoons brown rice vinegar
Juice of ½ lime (1 tablespoon)
1 tablespoon 100% unsweetened apple juice
½ teaspoon ground cumin, or to taste
½ teaspoon sea salt, or to taste

Add all ingredients to a food processor. Cover and pulse to desired consistency. Adjust seasoning. If you desire a thinner consistency, add additional apple juice by the teaspoonful. Serve at room temperature.

Per serving: 20 calories, 0g total fat, 0g saturated fat, 0g trans fat, 0mg cholesterol, 240mg sodium, 4g total carbohydrate, 0g dietary fiber, 2g sugars, 1g protein

Vine-Ripened Tomato Chutney

Makes 12 servings: 2 tablespoons each

Here's a zippy tomato chutney that's pure satisfaction. The tangy excitement is from concentrated flavor due to the culinary technique of reduction. It stands up as a condiment next to rich flavors, like grilled wild salmon, and adds drama to mild flavors, like chicken breast.

½ cup aged red wine vinegar
⅓ cup turbinado sugar
Juice of 2 limes (¼ cup)
1 teaspoon freshly grated gingerroot
½ teaspoon sea salt, or to taste
¼ teaspoon freshly ground black pepper, or to taste
¼ teaspoon dried hot pepper flakes, or to taste
12 ounces vine-ripened tomatoes, pulp removed and diced
1 large red bell pepper, finely chopped
1 large shallot, minced

1. Add the vinegar, sugar, lime juice, ginger, salt, black pepper, and hot pepper flakes to a medium saucepan over medium-high heat and bring to a boil while stirring occasionally.

2. Stir in the tomatoes, bell pepper, and shallot. Reduce heat to medium-low and simmer the mixture, uncovered, stirring occasionally, until desired thick consistency, about 1 hour. Adjust seasoning, and chill for at least 1 hour. Serve at room temperature.

Per serving: 35 calories, 0g total fat, 0g saturated fat, 0g trans fat, 0mg cholesterol, 100mg sodium, 8g total carbohydrate, 1g dietary fiber, 7g sugars, 0g protein

Mango Chutney

Makes 12 servings: ¼ cup each

This nontraditional chutney is sweet and savory. Use a fully ripened mango for sweeter, juicier chutney or a slightly unripened mango for a more savory, textured version. It makes a winning dish out of Grilled Curry Portabella "Steak" with Mango Chutney (page 269) and Curried Veggie and Chickpea Stir-Fry (page 279).

1 large mango, peeled, pitted, and minced
½ cup minced unpeeled English cucumber
⅓ cup minced red onion
1 small jalapeño pepper without seeds, minced
Juice of 1 lime (2 tablespoons)

3 tablespoons chopped fresh cilantro

3 tablespoons chopped fresh mint leaves

2 teaspoons apple cider vinegar

1½ teaspoons freshly grated gingerroot

¾ teaspoon ground cumin

¼ teaspoon ground coriander

¼ teaspoon ground turmeric

¼ teaspoon sea salt, or to taste

Stir all ingredients together in a medium bowl. Adjust seasoning and chill for at least 2 hours to allow flavors to blend. Serve chilled or at room temperature.

Per serving: 20 calories, 0g total fat, 0g saturated fat, 0g trans fat, 0mg cholesterol, 50mg sodium, 6g total carbohydrate, 1g dietary fiber, 4g sugars, 0g protein

Tamarind and Fresh Fig Chutney

Makes 16 servings: 1 tablespoon each

This chutney looks like jam but is a little less sweet and has a little more tartness and "heat." It's one of my favorite ways to enjoy fresh, seasonal figs. The sourness from the tamarind, a tropical fruit, along with the various spices, add international flavor intrigue served atop Chutney-Dressed Crab Cakes (page 78).

1 tablespoon Thai tamarind concentrate

3 tablespoons turbinado sugar

1 tablespoon unsulfured molasses

2 teaspoons freshly grated gingerroot

¾ teaspoon ground cumin

½ teaspoon ground coriander

¼ teaspoon ground anise

¼ teaspoon chili powder (preferably hot), or to taste

¼ teaspoon sea salt, or to taste

1½ cups finely chopped stemmed fresh figs, such as 5 large Brown Turkey figs

Add the tamarind concentrate, ⅓ cup water, the sugar, molasses, and ginger to a medium saucepan over medium heat. Cook while stirring until the sugar is dissolved, about 2 minutes. Stir in the cumin, coriander, anise, chili powder, and salt until combined. Stir in the figs and cook while stirring on occasion until desired jam-like consistency, about 18 minutes. Adjust seasoning and chill for at least 1 hour. Serve at room temperature.

Per serving: 30 calories, 0g total fat, 0g saturated fat, 0g trans fat, 0mg cholesterol, 40mg sodium, 7g total carbohydrate, 1g dietary fiber, 6g sugars, 0g protein

Olive–Bell Pepper Tapenade

Makes 10 servings: 2 tablespoons each

Tapenade is a thick condiment containing ripe olives and fresh herbs, originally from the Provence region of France. What's perhaps most glorious to some, though, is that one large olive provides only 6 surprising calories! Serve this flavor-bursting recipe with crudités or grilled veggies, atop goat cheese or grilled fish, or as a sandwich condiment.

1 cup pitted brine-cured black olives

1 large roasted red bell pepper (page 27)

1 small shallot

Juice of ½ lemon (1½ tablespoons)

1 tablespoon extra-virgin olive oil

1 tablespoon drained capers

1 large garlic clove, chopped

1½ teaspoons fresh thyme leaves

½ teaspoon fresh oregano leaves

½ teaspoon anchovy paste (optional)

¼ teaspoon freshly ground black pepper, or to taste

⅛ teaspoon sea salt, or to taste

Add the olives, bell pepper, shallot, lemon juice, oil, capers, garlic, thyme, oregano, anchovy paste (if using), black pepper, and salt to a food processor. Cover and pulse until just combined into a paste. Adjust seasoning and serve at room temperature.

Per serving: 35 calories, 3g total fat, 0g saturated fat, 0g trans fat, 0mg cholesterol, 170mg sodium, 3g total carbohydrate, 1g dietary fiber, 1g sugars, 0g protein

Sun-Dried Tomato Tapenade

Makes 9 servings: 2 tablespoons each

Sun-dried tomatoes have a concentrated tomato flavor—creating extra intensity in this recipe. My favorite way to enjoy this tapenade is tossed with pasta, such as Ziti with Sun-Dried Tomato Tapenade and Arugula (page 287). But it's equally tantalizing as a sandwich condiment or paired with goat cheese, polenta, or grilled vegetables.

¾ cup pitted brine-cured black olives

15 large sun-dried tomato halves (not oil-packed), rehydrated

1 small shallot

1 tablespoon extra-virgin olive oil

1 tablespoon aged balsamic vinegar

1 tablespoon drained capers

1 large garlic clove, chopped

2 tablespoons fresh parsley leaves

1 teaspoon fresh oregano or thyme leaves

½ teaspoon anchovy paste (optional)

¼ teaspoon freshly ground black pepper, or to taste

Add the olives, tomatoes, shallot, oil, vinegar, capers, garlic, parsley, oregano, anchovy paste (if using), and pepper to a food processor. Cover and pulse until just combined into a paste. Adjust seasoning and serve at room temperature.

Per serving: 40 calories, 3g total fat, 0g saturated fat, 0g trans fat, 0mg cholesterol, 200mg sodium, 4g total carbohydrate, 1g dietary fiber, 2g sugars, 1g protein

Grilled Onion Tapenade

Makes 8 servings: 2 tablespoons each

When I have the grill on, I often try to grill whatever I have on hand. Sometimes that means I wind up with lots of extras. This recipe was developed when I had way too many grilled onions. It's sensational as a spread on any burger.

1 medium red or white onion, cut into 6 round slices

2 teaspoons extra-virgin olive oil

¾ cup pitted brine-cured black olives

Juice of ½ of lemon (1½ tablespoons)

1 tablespoon drained capers

1 large garlic clove, chopped

1½ teaspoons fresh thyme leaves

½ teaspoon fresh oregano leaves

½ teaspoon anchovy paste (optional)

¼ teaspoon freshly ground black pepper, or to taste

⅛ teaspoon sea salt, or to taste

1. Prepare an outdoor or indoor grill. Brush or rub the onion slices with the oil. Grill over medium-high heat until caramelized, about 4 minutes per side, keeping the onion in 6 whole rounds during grilling.

2. Add the grilled onion, olives, lemon juice, capers, garlic, thyme, oregano, anchovy paste (if using), pepper, and salt to a food processor. Cover and pulse until just combined into a paste. Adjust seasoning and serve at room temperature.

Per serving: 30 calories, 2.5g total fat, 0g saturated fat, 0g trans fat, 0mg cholesterol, 180mg sodium, 3g total carbohydrate, 1g dietary fiber, 1g sugars, 0g protein

Condiments

Sassy "Mayo"

Makes 9 servings: 1 tablespoon each

I adore real mayonnaise. But when trying to cut calories, I whip up this thoroughly modern "mayo." Use it anywhere you normally would use regular mayonnaise, as in Farm-Fresh Egg Salad Pita Sandwich (page 377). It provides fewer than half the calories of regular mayo—and perhaps twice the flavor.

⅓ cup fat-free or low-fat plain Greek yogurt

3 tablespoons mayonnaise

1½ teaspoons apple cider or white wine vinegar

½ teaspoon honey or agave nectar

¼ teaspoon grated lemon zest

¼ teaspoon sea salt, or to taste

⅛ teaspoon ground cayenne

Stir all the ingredients together in a small bowl until smooth. Adjust seasoning. Cover and chill for at least 30 minutes. Store in the refrigerator for up to 2 weeks.

Per serving: 40 calories, 3.5g total fat, 0.5g saturated fat, 0g trans fat, 0mg cholesterol, 100mg sodium, 1g total carbohydrate, 0g dietary fiber, 1g sugars, 1g protein

Garlic "Mayo"

Makes 10 servings: 1 tablespoon each

When you want the mouth-feel of mayo yet you want a flavor kick, stir up this recipe. It's all about the garlic, so toss in two cloves instead of one if you don't have to kiss anyone anytime soon. (Or if you both love garlic!) And consider other uses for this "mayo" other than as a traditional condiment. Check out how it's cleverly used in "BLT" Pizza (page 414).

⅓ cup fat-free or low-fat plain Greek yogurt

3 tablespoons mayonnaise

1½ teaspoons white balsamic or white wine vinegar

½ teaspoon honey or agave nectar

1 to 2 large garlic cloves, minced

¼ teaspoon grated lemon zest

¼ teaspoon sea salt, or to taste

⅛ teaspoon ground cayenne

Stir all the ingredients together in a small bowl until smooth. Adjust seasoning. Cover and chill for at least 30 minutes. Store in the refrigerator for up to 2 weeks.

Per serving: 35 calories, 3.5g total fat, 0g saturated fat, 0g trans fat, 0mg cholesterol, 90mg sodium, 1g total carbohydrate, 0g dietary fiber, 1g sugars, 1g protein

Bourbon "Mayo"

Makes 9 servings: 1 tablespoon each

Sometimes all it needs to take a recipe from bland to bold is a few drops of a spirit. Here, very spirited bourbon adds a burst of flavor to an already flavorful condiment. Thank you, Kentucky. And a double thank-you will be in order when it is served with comforting Spicy Skinny Fries (page 459) or in Philly-Inspired Cheesesteak (page 388).

⅓ cup fat-free or low-fat plain Greek yogurt

3 tablespoons mayonnaise

2 teaspoons 80- or 90-proof bourbon

½ teaspoon honey or agave nectar

¼ teaspoon sea salt, or to taste

¼ teaspoon freshly ground black pepper, or to taste

⅛ teaspoon ground cayenne, or to taste

Stir all the ingredients together in a small bowl until smooth. Adjust seasoning. Cover and chill. Store in the refrigerator for up to 2 weeks.

Per serving: 40 calories, 3.5g total fat, 0.5g saturated fat, 0g trans fat, 0mg cholesterol, 100mg sodium, 1g total carbohydrate, 0g dietary fiber, 1g sugars, 1g protein

Lemon-Caper "Mayo"

Makes 9 servings: 1 tablespoon each

The double whammy of lemon juice and lemon zest makes this a brilliant "mayo." And the studs of capers are bits of salty surprise. Tuna lovers . . . this "mayo" might quickly become your fave. Sandwich lovers . . . sink your teeth into it in the Smoked Gouda-Artichoke Club Sandwich (page 375).

⅓ cup fat-free or low-fat plain Greek yogurt

3 tablespoons mayonnaise

2 teaspoons fresh lemon juice

1½ teaspoons finely chopped drained capers

½ teaspoon grated lemon zest

½ teaspoon honey or agave nectar

⅛ teaspoon sea salt, or to taste

Stir all the ingredients together in a small bowl until smooth. Adjust seasoning. Cover and chill. Store in the refrigerator for up to 2 weeks.

Per serving: 40 calories, 3.5g total fat, 0.5g saturated fat, 0g trans fat, 0mg cholesterol, 80mg sodium, 1g total carbohydrate, 0g dietary fiber, 1g sugars, 1g protein

Cilantro-Jalapeño "Mayo"

Makes 10 servings: 1 tablespoon each

Salsa or guacamole creates Mexican flair for entrées or sandwiches. But now there's another option for mayo aficionados. This "mayo" with its heat and cilantro will add Mexican-style culinary thrill to your repertoire. It's especially enticing on a BLT. Ready to be enticed? Add the Applewood-Smoked BLT Baguette (page 382) to your menu.

⅓ cup fat-free or low-fat plain Greek yogurt

3 tablespoons mayonnaise

½ small jalapeño pepper with seeds, minced

1½ teaspoons apple cider or white wine vinegar

½ teaspoon honey or agave nectar

1 teaspoon finely chopped fresh cilantro

¼ teaspoon grated lime zest

¼ teaspoon sea salt, or to taste

Stir all the ingredients together in a small bowl until smooth. Adjust seasoning. Cover and chill. Store in the refrigerator for up to 1 week.

Per serving: 35 calories, 3.5g total fat, 0g saturated fat, 0g trans fat, 0mg cholesterol, 90mg sodium, 1g total carbohydrate, 0g dietary fiber, 1g sugars, 1g protein

Balsamic-Basil "Mayo"

Makes 20 servings: 1 tablespoon each

I think this may be my favorite of all of my "mayo" recipes, mostly because I'm a balsamic vinegar devotee. If you're a balsamic buff like me, then you've gotta give this zippy, creamy condiment a go. My suggestion: Taste it on Roasted Veggie Roti (page 384) or Italian-Style Submarine Sandwich (page 381).

⅔ cup fat-free or low-fat plain Greek yogurt

6 tablespoons mayonnaise

2 tablespoons finely chopped fresh basil

2 large garlic cloves, minced

1 tablespoon aged balsamic vinegar

1 teaspoon honey or agave nectar

½ teaspoon sea salt, or to taste

¼ teaspoon freshly ground black pepper

Stir all the ingredients together in a small bowl until well combined. Adjust seasoning. Cover and chill. Store in the refrigerator for up to 1 week.

Per serving: 35 calories, 3.5g total fat, 0g saturated fat, 0g trans fat, 0mg cholesterol, 90mg sodium, 1g total carbohydrate, 0g dietary fiber, 1g sugars, 1g protein

Blue Cheese Tofunnaise

Makes 5 servings: 2 tablespoons each

This is one of the most lip-smacking sandwich spreads in this cookbook. The marriage of blue cheese and balsamic vinegar creates the vibrant and distinctive taste and the tofu makes it silky. It'll seem sinful how sumptuous it is when slathered in the PLT Sandwich with Avocado (page 374).

4 ounces silken tofu, drained (about ½ cup)

1 ounce Stilton or other blue cheese

10 large fresh basil leaves

2 teaspoons white balsamic or aged balsamic vinegar

1 small garlic clove, chopped

¼ teaspoon freshly ground black pepper, or to taste

⅛ teaspoon sea salt, or to taste

Add all the ingredients to a blender. Cover and puree. Store in the refrigerator for up to 1 week.

Per serving: 35 calories, 2g total fat, 1g saturated fat, 0g trans fat, 5mg cholesterol, 140mg sodium, 1g total carbohydrate, 0g dietary fiber, 0g sugars, 2g protein

Dijon Tofunnaise

Makes 6 servings: 2 tablespoons each

Sometimes mustard is the answer. Sometimes mayonnaise is. But sometimes the combination is the best bet. This versatile sandwich spread tastes like a creamy Dijon mustard—or dijonnaise—yet it seems more luscious!

4 ounces silken tofu, drained (about ½ cup)

2 tablespoons Dijon mustard

2 tablespoons pine nuts, toasted, or chopped unsalted dry-roasted cashews

2 teaspoons white balsamic vinegar

1 large garlic clove, chopped

Add all the ingredients to a blender. Cover, puree, and serve. Store in the refrigerator for up to 1 week.

Per serving: 35 calories, 2.5g total fat, 0g saturated fat, 0g trans fat, 0mg cholesterol, 120mg sodium, 2g total carbohydrate, 0g dietary fiber, 0g sugars, 1g protein

Herbal Tofunnaise

Makes 5 servings: 2 tablespoons each

The lovely, fresh herbal aroma along with the natural springy green color will cause love at first site. Then when you taste this velvety spread with its pesto-esque appeal, it will be love at first bite. So take a bite and fall for it in New-Age Hero with Herbal Tofunnaise (page 380).

4 ounces silken tofu, drained (about ½ cup)

2 tablespoons pine nuts, toasted, or chopped unsalted dry-roasted cashews

2 teaspoons white balsamic vinegar

1 large garlic clove, chopped

12 large fresh basil leaves

1 teaspoon fresh oregano leaves

½ teaspoon fresh thyme leaves

¼ teaspoon sea salt, or to taste

Add all the ingredients to a blender. Cover and puree. Store in the refrigerator for up to 1 week.

Per serving: 35 calories, 3g total fat, 0g saturated fat, 0g trans fat, 0mg cholesterol, 115mg sodium, 1g total carbohydrate, 0g dietary fiber, 0g sugars, 2g protein

Zesty Lime Avocado Spread

Makes 16 servings: 2 tablespoons each

Beans provide an unmistakable creaminess to nearly anything, including this recipe. Plus their combination of fiber and protein provides satiety. So savor its full satisfaction as a sandwich condiment of choice, as in California Smoked Turkey Wrap (page 404) or Smokin' Salmon "Dog" (page 400).

1 (15-ounce) can no-salt-added cannellini or other white beans, drained

1 Hass avocado, pitted and peeled

¼ cup mayonnaise

Juice and zest of 1 lime (2 tablespoons juice)

1 large garlic clove, minced

½ teaspoon sea salt, or to taste

⅛ teaspoon ground cayenne, or to taste

Add the beans, avocado, mayonnaise, lime juice, garlic, salt, and cayenne to a food processor. Cover and puree. Stir in the lime zest to taste. Adjust seasoning. Chill until ready to serve. Store in the refrigerator for up to 4 days.

Per serving: 60 calories, 4.5g total fat, 0.5g saturated fat, 0g trans fat, 0mg cholesterol, 105mg sodium, 4g total carbohydrate, 2g dietary fiber, 0g sugars, 1g protein

Creamy Herbes de Provence Sandwich Spread

Makes 12 servings: 2 tablespoons each

I was inspired to create this recipe after a memorable trip to southern France. I returned with herbes de Provence—a fragrant combination of basil, marjoram, rosemary, thyme, and lavender, among other dried herbs. Luckily, you don't need to travel to France to enjoy this . . . try it in Ciabatta Provencale (page 382) or a sandwich favorite of yours. It'll make it memorable.

1 (15-ounce) can no-salt-added cannellini
    or other white beans, drained

3 tablespoons mayonnaise

Juice of 1 small lemon (2 tablespoons)

2 teaspoons extra-virgin olive oil

1 large garlic clove, chopped

1½ teaspoons herbes de Provence

¼ teaspoon sea salt, or to taste

⅛ teaspoon freshly ground black pepper,
    or to taste

Add all ingredients to a food processor. Cover and puree. Adjust seasoning. Chill until ready to serve. Store in the refrigerator for up to 1 week.

Per serving: 60 calories, 4g total fat, 0g saturated fat, 0g trans fat, 0mg cholesterol, 80mg sodium, 5g total carbohydrate, 1g dietary fiber, 0g sugars, 2g protein

Tuscan Basil White Bean Spread

Makes 13 servings: 2 tablespoons each

You'll take pleasure in this basil-lover's spread that adds a hint of Italian flair and creamy freshness to sandwiches, like 7-Veggie Sandwich on 7-Grain (page 376). It can also be served as a sauce for cooked veggies or as a dip for crudités. Any way you decide to enjoy it, your palate will be saying "grazie!"

2 large garlic cloves

1 (15-ounce) can no-salt-added cannellini
    or other white beans, drained

⅓ cup fat-free or low-fat plain Greek yogurt

¼ cup chopped or thinly sliced fresh basil leaves

Juice of ½ lemon (1 tablespoons)

1 tablespoon extra-virgin olive oil

2 teaspoons white balsamic vinegar

½ teaspoon sea salt, or to taste

Add the garlic to a food processor. Cover and blend until finely chopped. Add the beans, yogurt, basil, lemon juice, oil, vinegar, and salt. Cover and puree until velvety smooth. Adjust seasoning. Chill until ready to serve. Store in the refrigerator for up to 1 week.

Per serving: 40 calories, 1.5g total fat, 0g saturated fat, 0g trans fat, 0mg cholesterol, 100mg sodium, 5g total carbohydrate, 1g dietary fiber, 1g sugars, 2g protein

All-Natural Ketchup

Makes 32 servings: 2 tablespoons each

This ketchup seems a bit like a cross between ketchup and marinara sauce. I find it balances flavors rather than covers them up, making it a bit more useful. But it's still okay to enjoy it just like traditional ketchup; dip Spicy Skinny Fries (page 459) into it. Delicious!

2 teaspoons extra-virgin olive oil

1 medium white onion, finely chopped

⅓ cup aged red wine vinegar

¼ teaspoon sea salt, or to taste

1 (28-ounce) can roasted crushed tomatoes

⅓ cup honey or agave nectar

1 tablespoon tomato paste

2 teaspoons unsulfured molasses

1 bay leaf

1. Heat the oil in a large saucepan over medium heat. Add the onion, 2 teaspoons of the vinegar, and the salt and sauté until softened, about 6 minutes.

Add the tomatoes, honey, tomato paste, molasses, bay leaf, and the remaining vinegar, reduce heat to medium-low, and simmer, uncovered, stirring occasionally, until thick, about 45 minutes. Remove the bay leaf.

2. Puree the ketchup using an immersion blender. (Alternatively, puree the ketchup in a blender in batches using the hot fill line as a guide.) Adjust seasoning and chill. Store in the refrigerator for up to 2 weeks or the freezer for up to 2 months.

Per serving: 25 calories, 0g total fat, 0g saturated fat, 0g trans fat, 0mg cholesterol, 85mg sodium, 5g total carbohydrate, 0g dietary fiber, 4g sugars, 0g protein

Banana-Guava Ketchup

Makes 32 servings: 2 tablespoons each

This unique ketchup is for those who have a sweet tooth. It's tomato-less and tropically transforming! You'll be delighted by the texture of it—try it with the Jerk Chicken Sandwich (page 386) or with turkey burgers.

2 teaspoons canola or grapeseed oil

1 large sweet onion, finely diced

2 tablespoons apple cider vinegar

½ teaspoon sea salt, or to taste

5 large extra-ripe bananas, sliced

1¾ cups 100% guava or peach nectar

3 tablespoons no-sugar-added apple butter

1 tablespoon hot Madras curry powder, or to taste

Juice of 2 limes (¼ cup)

¼ teaspoon freshly ground black pepper, or to taste

1. Heat the oil in a large skillet over medium heat. Add the onion, 1 tablespoon of the vinegar, and ¼ teaspoon of the salt and sauté until slightly softened, about 5 minutes. Add the bananas and cook while stirring for 5 minutes.

2. Stir in the guava nectar, apple butter, curry powder, and the remaining 1 tablespoon vinegar. Bring

to a boil over high heat. Reduce heat to medium-low and simmer uncovered, stirring occasionally and smashing any large banana pieces with the back of a spoon, until it reaches an applesauce-like consistency, about 25 minutes.

3. Remove from heat and stir in the lime juice, pepper, and the remaining ¼ teaspoon salt. Adjust seasoning, cover, and chill. Store in the refrigerator for up to 1 week.

Per serving: 35 calories, 0g total fat, 0g saturated fat, 0g trans fat, 0mg cholesterol, 40mg sodium, 9g total carbohydrate, 1g dietary fiber, 6g sugars, 0g protein

Pickled Jalapeño Mustard

Makes 12 servings: 1 tablespoon each

This is a taste-bud thriller. It will seem scandalous how much flavor you can get from 10 calories. Think mustard with more tang, more "heat," and more sweetness. You'll definitely come back for more. Try it in Tomato-Glazed Mini Meatloaves (page 327).

1 small jalapeño pepper with seeds, minced

1 shallot, minced

3 tablespoon apple cider vinegar

1 teaspoon turbinado sugar

½ cup stone-ground mustard

2 tablespoons Dijon mustard

⅛ teaspoon sea salt, or to taste

1. Add the jalapeño, shallot, vinegar, and sugar to a small saucepan. Place over medium heat and simmer uncovered, stirring occasionally, until the jalapeño and shallot are fully softened and vinegar is fully reduced, about 8 minutes. Remove from heat and stir in both mustards and the salt. Adjust seasoning.

2. Transfer to a small container or bowl, cover, and chill. Store in the refrigerator for up to 1 week.

Per serving: 10 calories, 0g total fat, 0g saturated fat, 0g trans fat, 0mg cholesterol, 210mg sodium, 2g total carbohydrate, 0g dietary fiber, 0g sugars, 0g protein

Raspberry Mustard

Makes 16 servings: 1 tablespoon each

I'm always stocked with fresh raspberries when they're in season. And when I'm overstocked, here's one of the recipes I love to whirl them into. The result is zingy mustard with fruity sweetness. It'll add eye-opening appeal to even the leanest of burgers and lightest of sandwiches.

½ cup fresh or frozen raspberries, thawed

1 shallot, minced

3 tablespoons raspberry balsamic or apple cider vinegar

1 teaspoon turbinado sugar

½ cup coarse-grain Dijon or stone-ground mustard

2 tablespoons Dijon mustard

⅛ teaspoon sea salt, or to taste

1. Add the raspberries, shallot, vinegar, and sugar to a small saucepan. Place over medium heat and simmer uncovered, stirring occasionally, until the shallot is fully softened, the raspberries are mashed, and the liquid is almost fully reduced, about 8 minutes. Remove from heat and stir in both mustards and the salt. Adjust seasoning.

2. Transfer to a small container or bowl, cover, and chill. Store in the refrigerator for up to 1 week.

Per serving: 10 calories, 0g total fat, 0g saturated fat, 0g trans fat, 0mg cholesterol, 160mg sodium, 2g total carbohydrate, 0g dietary fiber, 1g sugars, 0g protein

"Hot" Honey Dijon Sauce

Makes 6 servings: 2 tablespoons each

Dijon mustard may have originated in France, but this version originated from my kitchen in Brooklyn. The tangy, sweet, and spicy characters you'll find in this sauce—just like the folks you find in my neighborhood—will enchant your palate. Slather it onto grilled Honey-Dijon Turkey Breast (page 310) for entrée enchantment.

⅓ cup Dijon mustard

3 tablespoons honey or agave nectar

3 tablespoons fat-free or low-fat plain Greek yogurt

1 tablespoon no-sugar-added apple butter

¼ teaspoon ground cayenne, or to taste

Mix together all the ingredients in a small bowl until well combined. Chill for at least 1 hour, and serve. Store in the refrigerator for up to 2 weeks.

Per serving: 50 calories, 0g total fat, 0g saturated fat, 0g trans fat, 0mg cholesterol, 320mg sodium, 13g total carbohydrate, 0g dietary fiber, 10g sugars, 1g protein

Pickled Red Onion–Jalapeño Relish

Makes 4 servings: 1 ½ tablespoons each

This kicky oniony relish is simply lovely—and kind of preppy looking, as the red onions turn a slight pink upon pickling. Relish never looked or tasted so fresh. It's delightful on a Chi-Chi Chicken Hot Dog (page 401) or with practically any sandwich you can concoct.

½ cup finely chopped red onion

½ small jalapeño pepper with seeds, minced

¼ cup low-sodium vegetable broth or Vegetable Stock (page 203)

1 tablespoon sherry wine vinegar

¼ teaspoon sea salt, or to taste

1. Heat a small nonstick skillet over medium heat. Add the onion, jalapeño, broth, vinegar, and salt, cover, and simmer until the onion is fully softened, about 6 minutes.

2. Uncover and sauté until the liquid is evaporated, about 2 minutes. Adjust seasoning, and cool. Serve at room temperature. Store in the refrigerator for up to 1 week.

Per serving: 10 calories, 0g total fat, 0g saturated fat, 0g trans fat, 0mg cholesterol, 160mg sodium, 2g total carbohydrate, 0g dietary fiber, 1g sugars, 0g protein

Fresh Tartar Sauce

Makes 12 servings: 2 tablespoons each

This tangy, bottle-free version of tartar sauce made with mayo and Greek yogurt is as delightful with fish sticks as it is with veggies. The parsley and tarragon provide fresh fragrant appeal that you simply can't find in a jarred version—and for 50 fewer calories a serving. Though slimmer, it adds succulence to whatever you pair it with, like Cornmeal-Breaded Catfish Bites (page 348) or Creole Panko-Crusted Tilapia Sticks (page 350).

½ cup mayonnaise

½ cup fat-free or low-fat plain Greek yogurt

2 scallions, green and white parts, minced

3 tablespoons minced gherkins or cornichons

Juice of ½ small lemon (1 tablespoon)

1 tablespoon finely chopped fresh flat-leaf parsley

2 teaspoons finely chopped fresh tarragon

1 teaspoon spicy brown mustard

¼ teaspoon sea salt, or to taste

¼ teaspoon freshly ground white or black pepper, or to taste

Stir together all the ingredients in a medium bowl until well combined. Adjust seasoning. Chill until ready to serve. Store in the refrigerator for up to 1 week.

Per serving: 70 calories, 7g total fat, 1g saturated fat, 0g trans fat, 5mg cholesterol, 180mg sodium, 1g total carbohydrate, 0g dietary fiber, 0g sugars, 1g protein

Fresh Rémoulade Sauce

Makes 18 servings: 2 tablespoons each

Rémoulade is a traditional French sauce served as an accent for chilled meat, fish, and shellfish. I successfully created a fresher, lighter yet luscious version without losing its true essence—a savoriness or horseradish-spiked zing. Enjoy it as an accompaniment for any food of choice, such as in Baked Potato Salad Rémoulade (page 161), with grilled shrimp, or on a sandwich.

⅔ cup mayonnaise

½ cup fat-free or low-fat plain Greek yogurt

4 scallions, green and white parts, minced or very thinly sliced

⅓ cup finely chopped fresh flat-leaf parsley

1 medium celery stalk, minced

3 tablespoons minced gherkins or cornichons

3 tablespoons ketchup

2 tablespoons horseradish mustard or stone-ground mustard

2 large garlic cloves, minced

Juice of ½ small lemon (1 tablespoon)

2 teaspoons vegetarian Worcestershire sauce

½ teaspoon smoked Spanish paprika, or to taste

¼ teaspoon ground cayenne, or to taste

¼ teaspoon freshly ground black pepper, or to taste

Stir together all the ingredients in a medium bowl until well combined. Adjust seasoning. Chill until ready to serve. Store in the refrigerator for up to 1 week.

Per serving: 70 calories, 7g total fat, 1g saturated fat, 0g trans fat, 5mg cholesterol, 160mg sodium, 2g total carbohydrate, 0g dietary fiber, 1g sugars, 1g protein

Szechuan Sesame-Ginger Soy Sauce

Makes 18 servings: 1½ teaspoons each

This sauce is a tastier version of traditional soy sauce while providing about half the sodium. Please adjust the recipe ingredients as you wish. For instance, when I want ginger to be the star, I increase the grated gingerroot to 1 tablespoon. It's a must-have for me as a dipping sauce for Hoisin Broccoli and Cauliflower Dumplings (page 69) or Bok Choy, Scallion, and Pork Dumplings (page 79). It's delicious just drizzled over steamed brown rice or veggies, too.

5 tablespoons naturally brewed soy sauce

2 tablespoons brown rice vinegar

2 teaspoons freshly grated gingerroot, or to taste

1 large garlic clove, minced

1½ teaspoons toasted sesame oil

1½ teaspoons honey or agave nectar

⅛ teaspoon dried hot pepper flakes

Whisk all the ingredients together in a small bowl or liquid measuring cup. Chill in the refrigerator. Store in the refrigerator for up to 2 weeks.

Per serving: 10 calories, 0g total fat, 0g saturated fat, 0g trans fat, 0mg cholesterol, 260mg sodium, 1g total carbohydrate, 0g dietary fiber, 1g sugars, 1g protein

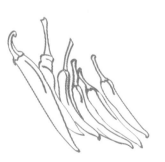

Wasabi-Spiked Soy Sauce

Makes 10 servings: 1½ teaspoons each

Soy sauces come in several varieties—from light to dark—and can be called shoyu or tamari. Whichever one you choose, make sure it's naturally brewed to get the brightest, purest taste. And when you want soy sauce with a spicy kick, try this one. It adds pep to Asian Asparagus and Basmati Rice Soup (page 217), Wok Veggie Fried Rice (page 275), steamed brown rice, or any stir-fry.

¼ cup naturally brewed soy sauce

1 tablespoon brown rice vinegar

½ teaspoon wasabi powder, or to taste

Whisk all the ingredients together in a small bowl or liquid measuring cup. Chill in the refrigerator. Store in the refrigerator for up to 2 weeks.

Per serving: 5 calories, 0g total fat, 0g saturated fat, 0g trans fat, 0mg cholesterol, 370mg sodium, 0g total carbohydrate, 0g dietary fiber, 0g sugars, 1g protein

Seasonal Cranberry Sauce Ⓢ

Makes 20 servings: 2 tablespoons each

Cranberry sauce is easier to fix than you might think. And this lovely version is sure to be tastier and healthier than anything from your holiday table of yesterday. It starts with fresh tart cranberries—which is one of nature's "superfoods." And the secret to its distinctive taste is fresh, aromatic rosemary—which provides a lot of health-promoting antioxidants in a little pinch.

¾ cup turbinado sugar

1 tablespoon unsulfured molasses

1 (12-ounce) package fresh whole cranberries

¾ teaspoon finely chopped fresh rosemary

1 teaspoon stone-ground mustard

½ teaspoon grated orange zest

⅛ teaspoon sea salt, or to taste

1. Add the sugar, molasses, and ¾ cup water to a medium saucepan over medium-high heat. Bring to a boil while stirring occasionally until the sugar dissolves, about 2 minutes.

2. Add the cranberries, reduce heat to medium, and simmer while stirring occasionally until the berries burst open, about 10 minutes.

3. Remove from heat and stir in the rosemary, mustard, zest, and salt. Adjust seasoning and chill. Store in the refrigerator for up to 1 week.

Per serving: 40 calories, 0g total fat, 0g saturated fat, 0g trans fat, 0mg cholesterol, 20mg sodium, 10g total carbohydrate, 1g dietary fiber, 8g sugars, 0g protein

Raw Cranberry–Tangerine Sauce

Makes 6 servings: 2 tablespoons each

Be on the lookout for fresh cranberries when they're available in late autumn through early winter. You won't want to miss out on the opportunity to enjoy the seasonal tastes and textures of this no-cook recipe.

1 cup whole fresh cranberries

Juice of 1 tangerine or 2 tablespoons fresh-squeezed orange juice

1 small shallot

1 tablespoon apple cider vinegar

1 tablespoon honey or agave nectar

2 teaspoons stone-ground mustard

¼ teaspoon freshly ground black pepper

⅛ teaspoon sea salt, or to taste

Add all the ingredients to a food processor or blender. Cover and pulse to desired consistency, such as a thick applesauce-like texture. Adjust seasoning. Chill until ready to serve. Store in the refrigerator for up to 1 week.

Per serving: 25 calories, 0g total fat, 0g saturated fat, 0g trans fat, 0mg cholesterol, 70mg sodium, 6g total carbohydrate, 1g dietary fiber, 4g sugars, 0g protein

Papaya Puree

Makes 6 servings: ¼ cup each

The papaya is a semitropical fruit, loaded with vitamin C. Its silky, creamy texture is perfect for pureeing into sauces, smoothies, and fruit soups. It lends sweet-tart balance to this sauce—ideal for fish, poultry, or rice. Serve it in Nut-Crusted Barramundi with Papaya Puree (page 348). Or, enjoy it on its own as an out-of-the-ordinary pudding.

1 medium fully ripened papaya, peeled, seeded, and cubed

½ cup Riesling, Pinot Grigio, or other fruity white wine

¾ teaspoon freshly grated gingerroot, or to taste

¼ cup plain almond milk or unsweetened coconut milk beverage

Juice of 1 lime (2 tablespoons)

¼ teaspoon sea salt, or to taste

1. Place the papaya, wine, and ginger into a medium saucepan over medium heat and simmer, reducing the volume by about three-fourths, about 12 minutes. Stir in the almond milk and bring just to a boil over high heat. Reduce the heat to medium-low and simmer for 5 minutes.

2. Transfer the mixture to a blender. Add the lime juice and salt. Cover and puree. Adjust seasoning. Serve immediately. Or cover and chill until ready to serve. Store in the refrigerator for up to 1 week.

Per serving: 40 calories, 0g total fat, 0g saturated fat, 0g trans fat, 0mg cholesterol, 105mg sodium, 6g total carbohydrate, 1g dietary fiber, 3g sugars, 0g protein

Other Bread Spreads and Savory Sauces

Farmers' Market Strawberry and Stone Fruit Spread

Makes 8 servings: ¼ cup each

You'll love this fresh version of jam that's loaded with a variety of fruity tastes and textures. I love it on pancakes and waffles, like Farmers' Market Almond Waffles (page 13). But I also fancy it straight from the bowl with a spoon!

8 large fresh strawberries, finely diced
1 medium ripe nectarine, pitted, or ⅔ cup frozen peaches, thawed, finely diced
1 medium ripe peach, pitted, or ⅔ cup frozen peaches, thawed, finely diced
1 medium extra-ripe banana, sliced
2 teaspoons fresh lemon juice
⅛ teaspoon sea salt, or to taste

Add all the ingredients to a medium bowl and stir while slightly mashing with a fork until desired consistency. Cover and chill until ready to use. Serve at room temperature. Store in the refrigerator for up to 3 days.

Per serving: 30 calories, 0g total fat, 0g saturated fat, 0g trans fat, 0mg cholesterol, 35mg sodium, 8g total carbohydrate, 1g dietary fiber, 5g sugars, 1g protein

Fresh Fig Fruit Spread

Makes 10 servings: 2 tablespoons each

You'll jump for joy with this jammy delight. It takes just minutes to prepare yet will give you endless flavor memories. For a perfect pairing, enjoy this intriguingly sweet fresh fig jam with pungent cheese or prosciutto. It's deserving of a standing ovation in Prosciutto and Provolone Ciabatta with Fig Jam (page 383).

10 medium fresh Black Mission or other figs, stems removed and finely diced
1 tablespoon no-sugar-added apple butter
2 teaspoons fresh lemon juice
¼ teaspoon sea salt, or to taste
⅛ teaspoon freshly ground black pepper, or to taste.

Add all the ingredients to a medium bowl and stir while slightly mashing with a fork until desired consistency. Adjust seasoning. Chill until ready to serve. Store in the refrigerator for up to 3 days.

Per serving: 40 calories, 0g total fat, 0g saturated fat, 0g trans fat, 0mg cholesterol, 60mg sodium, 10g total carbohydrate, 2g dietary fiber, 9g sugars, 0g protein

Herbed Goat Cheese Spread

Makes 16 servings: 2 tablespoons each

Whipping white beans and Greek yogurt into soft goat cheese will broaden the flavor and sharp creaminess of goat cheese, but will cut the calories. You'll find this velvety spread is more captivating to your palate, too. It's kind of like Boursin cheese. Smear it onto a bagel in place of cream cheese at 40 percent fewer calories for every serving. Or pipe it onto fruit as in the elegant Herbed Goat Cheese-Dressed Figs (page 61).

1 (15-ounce) can no-salt-added cannellini or other white beans, drained
6 ounces soft goat cheese, at room temperature
⅓ cup fat-free or low-fat plain Greek yogurt
1½ tablespoons finely chopped fresh herbs, such as mint, rosemary, and thyme
1 tablespoon champagne or white balsamic vinegar
1½ teaspoons extra-virgin olive oil
¾ teaspoon sea salt, or to taste
¾ teaspoon freshly ground black pepper, or to taste

Add all the ingredients to a food processor. Cover and puree until very smooth. Adjust seasoning. Serve at room temperature. Store in the refrigerator for up to 1 week.

Per serving: 60 calories, 3g total fat, 1.5g saturated fat, 0g trans fat, 5mg cholesterol, 160mg sodium, 4g total carbohydrate, 1g dietary fiber, 0g sugars, 4g protein

Silken Scallion Bagel Spread

Makes 9 servings: 3 tablespoons each

I'm a New Yorker, so I've lost count of the number of bagels that I've eaten—delicious, but the creamy spreads can often add a diet-busting calorie wallop. This is one of my preferred choices for topping them—it's half the calories of cream cheese and has a lovely velvety texture and distinctly nutty taste all its own. Try it with your favorite or mine—a whole-grain "everything" bagel.

1 (1-pound) package silken tofu, well drained
2 tablespoons no-salt-added creamy natural cashew or peanut butter
Juice of ½ small lemon (1 tablespoon)
1 teaspoon toasted sesame oil
1 teaspoon sea salt, or to taste
½ teaspoon mild honey or agave nectar
3 scallions, green and white parts, minced

1. Add the tofu, cashew butter, lemon juice, oil, salt, and honey to a food processor. Cover and puree, scraping down the sides as necessary. Add the scallions and briefly pulse a few times, just until incorporated.

2. Chill in the refrigerator at least 4 hours or overnight to let flavors blend. Adjust seasoning. Store in the refrigerator for up to 1 week.

Per serving: 60 calories, 3.5g total fat, 0.5g saturated fat, 0g trans fat, 0mg cholesterol, 260mg sodium, 3g total carbohydrate, 0g dietary fiber, 1g sugars, 3g protein

Tomatillo-Avocado "Crème" Sauce Ⓢ

Makes 16 servings: 2 tablespoons each

The "crème" in this thick, velvety sauce is from the avocado. It's super tangy, too. That means it'll perk up anything you pair it with. Start by dolloping it onto a burrito, including the Sunrise Vegan Burrito (page 37). Then expand your flavor pairing adventure from there.

2 teaspoons unrefined peanut or grapeseed oil
10 tomatillos, husks removed, rinsed, and coarsely chopped
1 medium white onion, chopped
1 small jalapeño pepper with some seeds, minced
Juice of 1 lime (2 tablespoons), or to taste
⅛ teaspoon sea salt, or to taste
1 Hass avocado, pitted and peeled

1. Heat the oil in a large nonstick skillet over medium-high heat. Add the tomatillos, onion, jalapeño, lime juice, and salt and sauté until the onion is fully softened and the tomatillos are a mushy consistency, about 10 minutes. Remove from heat and let stand for at least 10 minutes to slightly cool before blending.

2. Add the tomatillo mixture to a blender or food processor along with the avocado. Cover and puree until velvety smooth. Adjust seasoning. Serve at room temperature. Store in the refrigerator for up to 4 days.

Per serving: 30 calories, 2g total fat, 0g saturated fat, 0g trans fat, 0mg cholesterol, 20mg sodium, 3g total carbohydrate, 1g dietary fiber, 1g sugars, 0g protein

Silky Hollandaise-Style Sauce

Makes 6 servings: 2 rounded tablespoons each

A hollandaise-style sauce at 25 calories per serving? Yes, it's a reality. That's a whopping 115 calories less than the same amount of traditional hollandaise sauce. And there are no corners cut in flavor with this recipe. In fact, I think this version is zestier and more flavorful. Try it with Eggs Tatsoi Florentine (page 21) or drizzled over freshly roasted asparagus or simple poached eggs.

4 ounces silken tofu, drained (about ½ cup)

Juice of 1 small lemon (2 tablespoons)

2 tablespoons almond milk or light soy milk

2 teaspoons tahini (sesame seed paste)

1½ teaspoons Dijon mustard

1 teaspoon vegetarian Worcestershire sauce

¼ teaspoon sea salt, or to taste

⅛ teaspoon ground turmeric, or to taste

⅛ teaspoon ground cayenne, or to taste

1. Add all the ingredients to a blender. Cover and puree.

2. Pour the tofu mixture into a small saucepan and place over medium-low heat. Simmer uncovered, stirring occasionally, until fully heated, about 5 minutes. Adjust seasoning. Serve while hot.

Per serving: 25 calories, 1.5g total fat, 0g saturated fat, 0g trans fat, 0mg cholesterol, 140mg sodium, 2g total carbohydrate, 0g dietary fiber, 0g sugars, 1g protein

Cherry Balsamic Peppercorn Sauce

Makes 5 servings: 3 tablespoons each

This sauce is bursting with deep, rich, sweet flavor from cherries and apple juice along with nice savory notes from the shallot, vinegar, black pepper, and rosemary. But it's the technique of reduction that makes all the tastes provide that extra wow.

2 teaspoons canola or grapeseed oil

1 large shallot, very thinly sliced

1½ cups sweet cherries, pitted, or frozen pitted dark sweet cherries, thawed

½ cup 100% unsweetened apple juice

¼ cup aged balsamic vinegar

1 teaspoon freshly cracked black peppercorns, or to taste

¼ teaspoon sea salt, or to taste

¼ teaspoon finely chopped fresh rosemary, or to taste

1. Heat the oil in a skillet over medium-high heat. Add the shallot and cherries and sauté until fully softened, about 6 minutes.

2. Reduce heat to medium, stir in the apple juice, vinegar, peppercorns, salt, and rosemary, and cook, stirring occasionally, until the liquid reduces by one-third or to desired consistency. Adjust seasoning. Serve warm. Store in the refrigerator for up to 1 week.

Per serving: 80 calories, 2g total fat, 0g saturated fat, 0g trans fat, 0mg cholesterol, 120mg sodium, 14g total carbohydrate, 1g dietary fiber, 10g sugars, 1g protein

Rosemary Grill Sauce

Makes 9 servings: 2 tablespoons each

Sometimes I want to slather on a sauce during grilling but I don't want something as über distinctive as barbecue sauce. This roasted red bell pepper-based grill sauce provides a tantalizing taste while helping to showcase the grilled item. Marry it with poultry, such as Grilled Rosemary Turkey Patties (page 310), and you'll see what I'm talking about.

1 large freshly roasted (page 27) or jarred red bell pepper, drained

1 small or ½ large red onion, chopped

1 large garlic clove, chopped

¼ cup apple cider vinegar

¼ cup low-sodium vegetable broth or Vegetable Stock (page 203)

1 tablespoon naturally brewed soy sauce

2 teaspoons honey or agave nectar

1½ teaspoons chopped fresh rosemary

½ teaspoon freshly ground black pepper, or to taste

⅛ teaspoon sea salt, or to taste

1. Add all the ingredients to a blender. Cover and puree.

2. Pour the sauce into a medium saucepan and place over medium-high heat. Cook, stirring occasionally, until the sauce just begins to boil. Reduce heat to medium-low and simmer until the sauce is desired consistency, about 8 minutes. Adjust seasoning. Store in the refrigerator for up to 1 week.

Per serving: 20 calories, 0g total fat, 0g saturated fat, 0g trans fat, 0mg cholesterol, 140mg sodium, 4g total carbohydrate, 1g dietary fiber, 2g sugars, 1g protein

Merlot Sauce

Makes 4 servings: 2 tablespoons each

For a white tablecloth–style sauce, this recipe brings out every flavor nuance of the steak you serve with it. Make the heavenly Filet Mignon with Merlot Sauce (page 319) and you'll see what I mean. The savory broth and full-bodied red wine are concentrated to create amazing depth of flavor, the hint of butter provides a just-right sheen and richness, and the fresh thyme provides an aromatic herbal accent to complete this luxurious sauce.

1 teaspoon unsalted butter

1 teaspoon extra-virgin olive oil

1 large scallion, green and white parts, minced

1 large garlic clove, minced

1 teaspoon finely chopped fresh thyme or rosemary

¾ cup Merlot or other full-bodied red wine

½ cup low-sodium beef broth

¼ teaspoon sea salt, or to taste

¼ teaspoon freshly ground black pepper, or to taste

Add the butter and oil to a small saucepan over medium heat. Once the butter is melted, add the scallion, garlic, and thyme and sauté for 30 seconds. Add the wine, broth, salt, and pepper, increase heat to high, and cook while stirring until the sauce is reduced by about half, or desired consistency, about 4 minutes. Serve hot.

Per serving: 60 calories, 2.5g total fat, 1g saturated fat, 0g trans fat, 5mg cholesterol, 160mg sodium, 2g total carbohydrate, 0g dietary fiber, 0g sugars, 1g protein

Tangy Teriyaki Sauce

Makes 18 servings: 1 tablespoon each

If you read the ingredient label of some of the popular teriyaki sauces in your supermarket, you may not like what you see . . . ingredients like high-fructose corn syrup, succinic acid, or sodium benzoate. But it's easy to make your own, as I did below. Its distinctive sweetness comes naturally from pineapple juice and molasses. And it's this sauce that turns the Teriyaki Pineapple-Pork Kebabs (page 58) into a culinary hit.

⅓ cup naturally brewed soy sauce

⅓ cup dry sherry

⅓ cup 100% pineapple or unsweetened apple juice

2 large garlic clove, minced

1 tablespoon freshly grated gingerroot

1 teaspoon unsulfured molasses

Add the soy sauce, sherry, pineapple juice, garlic, ginger, and molasses to a medium saucepan and bring to a boil over medium-high heat, stirring constantly. Allow to boil for 1 minute. (Note: If using the sauce immediately, it's not necessary to cook it.) Store in the refrigerator for up to 1 week.

Per serving: 10 calories, 0g total fat, 0g saturated fat, 0g trans fat, 0mg cholesterol, 320mg sodium, 2g total carbohydrate, 0g dietary fiber, 1g sugars, 0g protein

Roasted Red Bell Pepper Sauce

Makes 10 servings: ¼ cup each

If I had my way, I'd probably try to slather this sauce on everything! It's versatile enough to harmonize with so many foods—from veggies to grains to poultry and eggs. So ad-lib with this sauce and find your favorite pairings. And for one of the most artful pairings, try it in this: Chicken Roulade with Bell Pepper Sauce (page 315).

2 teaspoons extra-virgin olive oil

2 large shallots, finely chopped

1 teaspoon aged red wine vinegar

¼ teaspoon sea salt, or to taste

2 freshly roasted red bell peppers, chopped
    (page 27), or jarred, drained

1 cup low-sodium vegetable broth
    or Vegetable Stock (page 203)

3 ounces soft goat cheese

⅛ teaspoon freshly ground black pepper,
    or to taste

1. Heat the oil in a medium saucepan over medium heat. Add the shallots, vinegar, and salt and sauté until the shallots just begin to caramelize, about 5 minutes.

2. Add the sautéed shallots along with the roasted peppers, broth, cheese, and black pepper to a blender. Cover and puree.

3. Pour the bell pepper sauce back into the saucepan. Bring to a boil over medium-high heat. Reduce heat to medium-low and simmer, uncovered, stirring occasionally, to concentrate flavors and slightly thicken sauce, about 15 minutes. Remove from heat, and adjust seasoning. Serve warm.

Per serving: 50 calories, 3g total fat, 1.5g saturated fat, 0g trans fat, 5mg cholesterol, 105mg sodium, 4g total carbohydrate, 1g dietary fiber, 2g sugars, 2g protein

Sweet-n-Sour Tomato Sauce

Makes 20 servings: ¼ cup each

Yum! I'm mad about this taste-tempting tomato-based sauce, especially for cabbage rolls, as in Sweet-n-Sour Stuffed Cabbage (page 273). It's also brilliant lightly brushed onto grilled poultry or a poultry burger or sprinkled into a stir-fry to create a nontraditional entrée.

1 (28-ounce) can peeled Italian plum tomatoes
    (with liquid)

1 (15-ounce) can no-salt-added tomato sauce

⅓ cup packed dark brown sugar

3 tablespoons apple cider vinegar
    or juice of 1 lemon

½ teaspoon sea salt, or to taste

½ teaspoon freshly ground black pepper, or to taste

Stir together all the ingredients in a large saucepan. Place over medium-high heat and bring just to a boil while stirring occasionally and smashing the tomatoes with the back of a spoon or spatula. Reduce heat to medium-low, cover, and simmer for 10 minutes. Adjust seasoning. Use immediately or store in the refrigerator for up to 1 week or freezer for up to 1 month.

Per serving: 30 calories, 0g total fat, 0g saturated fat, 0g trans fat, 0mg cholesterol, 150mg sodium, 7g total carbohydrate, 1g dietary fiber, 6g sugars, 1g protein

Cantonese Garlic Sauce

Makes 5 servings: 3 tablespoons each

When I crave a stir-fry, it's this slightly salty and slightly sweet sauce that I desire. It's a touch spicy and, of course, it's garlicky, as the title gives away. Plus, it packs a punch promptly as it takes only minutes to prepare. Try it with Garlic Chicken and Snow Pea Stir-Fry (page 329); it's delightful.

2 teaspoons unrefined peanut or grapeseed oil

1 teaspoon toasted sesame oil

4 large garlic cloves, minced

1 tablespoon whole-wheat pastry flour

⅔ cup low-sodium vegetable or chicken broth
or Vegetable Stock (page 203)

2 tablespoons naturally brewed soy sauce

1 tablespoon honey or agave nectar

2 teaspoons brown rice vinegar

⅛ teaspoon dried hot pepper flakes, or to taste

1. Heat the peanut and sesame oils in a small saucepan over medium heat. Add the garlic and sauté until fragrant, about 45 seconds. Stir in the flour and sauté for 30 seconds.

2. Add the broth, soy sauce, honey, vinegar, and hot pepper flakes, increase heat to medium-high, and bring to a boil while stirring, cooking until sauce slightly thickens. Remove from heat. Chill until ready to use in a recipe. Store in the refrigerator for up to 1 week.

Per serving: 50 calories, 3g total fat, 0.5g saturated fat, 0g trans fat, 0mg cholesterol, 390mg sodium, 6g total carbohydrate, 0g dietary fiber, 4g sugars, 1g protein

Lemon-Dill Yogurt Sauce

Makes 4 servings: 3 rounded tablespoons each

When you want to take a dish from good to great, this silky smooth, yogurt-based sauce is one of the simplest ways to do so. The lemon and dill provide unmistakably Greek flavor. It adds delicious flair when drizzled onto salmon. And as a creamy dressing, beans go from good to great, like in Lemony Dill-Dressed Garbanzos (page 489).

¾ cup fat-free or low-fat plain Greek yogurt

2 teaspoons extra-virgin olive or flaxseed oil

2 teaspoons mayonnaise

2 teaspoons fresh lemon juice

2 teaspoons chopped fresh dill

½ teaspoon grated lemon zest

¼ teaspoon sea salt, or to taste

¼ teaspoon freshly ground black pepper, or to taste

Whisk together all the ingredients in a small bowl until combined. Let stand 30 minutes to allow flavors to develop. Adjust seasoning. Store in the refrigerator for up to 1 week.

Per serving: 60 calories, 4g total fat, 0.5g saturated fat, 0g trans fat, 0mg cholesterol, 170mg sodium, 2g total carbohydrate, 0g dietary fiber, 2g sugars, 4g protein

Blood Orange–Shallot Sauce

Makes 9 servings: 2 tablespoons each

The blood orange is a bit tarter than the navel orange and typically in season beginning in late autumn and all through the winter season. It adds a bit more tang to sauces and other concoctions in which you want a sweet-tartness instead of just sweetness. It adds intrigue as a sauce for poultry or fish. Try it in Black and White Sesame Salmon (page 350). If you like, use a navel orange—different but still tasty.

¾ cup fat-free or low-fat plain Greek yogurt

3 tablespoons fresh-squeezed or bottled
100% blood orange juice

2 teaspoons extra-virgin olive or flaxseed oil

2 teaspoons mayonnaise

1 small shallot, minced

½ teaspoon grated blood or navel orange zest,
or to taste

¼ teaspoon sea salt, or to taste

⅛ teaspoon freshly ground black pepper, or to taste

Whisk together all the ingredients in a small bowl until combined. Adjust seasoning. Store in the refrigerator for up to 1 week.

Per serving: 30 calories, 2g total fat, 0g saturated fat, 0g trans fat, 0mg cholesterol, 80mg sodium, 2g total carbohydrate, 0g dietary fiber, 1g sugars, 2g protein

Margarita Serving Sauce

Makes 9 servings: 2 tablespoons each

Slather this "over twenty-one" sauce onto grilled poultry or fish, such as Blackened Margarita Catfish (page 352), and it'll transport your taste buds. It's a real beauty.

½ cup no-sugar-added applesauce

½ cup sliced unpeeled English cucumber

3 tablespoons 80-proof agave tequila

Juice of 1 lime (2 tablespoons)

1 tablespoon Cointreau, Triple Sec,
    or fresh-squeezed orange juice

2 teaspoons canola or flaxseed oil

2 teaspoons mild honey or agave nectar

¼ teaspoon sea salt, or to taste

Add all the ingredients to a blender or food processor. Cover and puree. Adjust seasoning. Chill until ready to serve. Store in the refrigerator for up to 1 week.

Per serving: 30 calories, 1g total fat, 0g saturated fat, 0g trans fat, 0mg cholesterol, 65mg sodium, 3g total carbohydrate, 0g dietary fiber, 3g sugars, 0g protein

Aged Balsamic Reduction Ⓢ

Makes 10 servings: 1 tablespoon each

True Italian balsamic vinegar is made from barrel-aged white Trebbiano grapes. It is distinctly dark, richly pungent, and slightly sweet. When you reduce it, the vinegar becomes a little more deliciously viscous and every one of its characteristics gets more potent. (For best results, select balsamic vinegar that's aged about 8 to 10 years.) And when you add a few pinches of sugar to it, this sauce becomes almost addictive. Find out for yourself by drizzling it over goat cheese, grilled vegetables, or the Caramelized Pear, Roquefort, and Prosciutto Quesadilla (page 408).

1¼ cups aged balsamic vinegar

1 tablespoon turbinado sugar

1. Bring the vinegar and sugar to a boil in a small saucepan over high heat. Reduce heat to medium-low and simmer until the vinegar reduces by half, about 20 minutes, or to desired consistency.

2. The sauce will slightly thicken as it cools. Store in the refrigerator for up to 2 weeks.

Per serving: 35 calories, 0g total fat, 0g saturated fat, 0g trans fat, 0mg cholesterol, 5mg sodium, 7g total carbohydrate, 0g dietary fiber, 6g sugars, 0g protein

Salads

Salad Dressings and Vinaigrettes

Fresh Herb and Shallot Vinaigrette

Dijon Balsamic Vinaigrette

Jalapeño Honey Vinaigrette

Bloody Mary Vinaigrette

Creamy Basil Vinaigrette

Minty Balsamic Vinaigrette

Syrian Vinaigrette

Garden Lemon Vinaigrette

Zesty Lime Vinaigrette

Tart Cherry Vinaigrette

Fresh Raspberry Vinaigrette

Seckel Pear and Green Tea Vinaigrette

Tart Apple Vinaigrette

"Caliente" Caesar Dijon Dressing

Peach Bellini Salad Dressing

Silky Lemon Dressing

Fresh-Squeezed Lemon-Dill Dressing

Spicy Roasted Pepper Dressing

Avocado Ranch Dressing

Exotic Papaya Dressing

Creamy Peppercorn Dressing

Winter White French Dressing

Tahini Za'atar Dressing

Mandarin Miso Dressing

Leafy Salads

Hearts of Romaine Salad

Avocado Ranch Corn Cobb Salad

Peach Bellini Salad

Mod Caesar Salad with Homemade Croutons

Leafy Greek Island Salad

Bibb-n-Blue Chopped Salad

"Trail Mix" Salad

Jasmine Green Tea and Pear-Dressed Mesclun

Pear and Walnut Field Green Salad

Soulful Taco Salad

Sunnyside-Up Salad

12-Layer Salad

Layered Waldorf Salad

Minty Strawberry Arugula Salad

Sunflower Raspberry Watercress Salad

Spicy Citrus Endive Salad

Salad for Every Season

Fattoush

Potato Salads

New American Potato Salad

Dijon Fingerling Potato Salad

Baked Potato Salad Rémoulade

Patriotic Potato Salad

Berlin Blue Potato Salad

Yukon Gold Potato Salad Deconstructed

Dilly Avocado Potato Salad

Hash Brown Potato Salad

Roasted Potato and Red Pepper Salad

Sweet Pea and Prosciutto Potato Salad

Jalapeño Corn and Potato Salad

Grilled Sweet Potato Salad

Tomato Salads

Tomatoes with Avocado Ranch Dressing

Caprese Salad "Lasagna"

Heirloom Tomato Salad

BLT-Stuffed Tomatoes

Athenian Caramelized Tomato Salad

Tomato "Carpaccio" Salad

Drunken Grilled Harvest Salad

Slaws and Assorted Vegetable Salads

Delhi Coleslaw

East Meets Napa Cabbage Salad

Asian Cabbage Salad with Red Onion and Mint

Broccoli Slaw

Artichoke Salad with Manchego and Tart Cherries

Beet and Fuji Apple Coleslaw

Warm Grilled Vegetable Salad

Retro Broccoli Layered Salad

Beet and Goat Cheese Salad

Tofu Salads

Turkish Tofu Salad

Ginger Tofu Chick'n Salad

Pan-Seared Tofu and Cucumber Salad

Curried Tofu and Pomegranate Salad

Grilled Tofu Baby Greens Salad

Smoked Tofu Chef Salad

Pasta and Noodle Salads

Bow-Tie Salad with Basil

Eco-Elbow Macaroni Salad

Creamy Cavatappi Salad with Ham

Herbed Goat Cheese
and Green Tea Orzo Salad

Orzo with Greens,
Feta, and Cranberries

Orecchiette and Arugula
Salad with Sausage

Pistachio-Kissed
Couscous Bowls

Ginger Spaetzle Salad

Thai Peanut Noodle Salad

Pesto Pasta and Spinach
Salad

Italian Eggplant Penne Salad

Whole-Grain Salads

Blood Orange
Bulgur Mint Salad

Spelt Tabbouleh Salad

Sesame Red Quinoa and Kale

Edamame and Frizzled Leek
Quinoa Salad

Fresh Fig and Red Quinoa
Salad with Pistachios

Curry Squash and Rice Salad

Orange Basmati Salad
with Almonds

French Green Bean–Barley
Salad

Barley, Corn, and Spinach
Salad with Feta

Garden Fresh Millet Salad

Roasted Veggie Farro Salad

Bean Salads

Jamaican Bean Salad

"Wild" White Bean Salad

Heirloom Bean Salad

Avocado and White Bean
Salad

Mediterranean Chickpea
Salad

Cuban Black Bean Salad

Cowgirl Caviar Salad

Poultry, Fish, Shellfish, and Meat Salads

Rotisserie Chicken
Cobb Salad

Luncheon Chef Salad

English Poached Egg Salad

Calypso Grilled Chicken Salad

Blackened Apricot
Chicken Salad

Spice-Rubbed Barramundi
Salad

Wild Yellowfin Salad Niçoise

Seared Salmon Salad

Salad with Sesame-Crusted
Tuna

Grilled Calamari-Cucumber
Salad

Polynesian Pork and
Pineapple Grilled Salad

Portabella and Peppercorn
Chophouse Salad

Cuban Mojo Steak Salad

Salads are often believed to be low-calorie dishes, but far too often they can be weight-management traps—with excess calories found in rich dressings and calorie-dense toppings.

Not here. However, I'm not one to compromise on taste, especially when it comes to salads, since they're such a refreshing way to boost veggies. So the outcome here is great-tasting salads and salad dressings that you can feel good about eating.

But before you reach for that salad bowl, remember this tip. Contrary to popular diet advice, I usually suggest not serving the dressing on the side of leafy tossed salads. You actually may eat more dressing by ultimately pouring it all on at the table—or by dipping your fork tongs into it for each salad bite. Rather, lightly yet thoroughly toss your salad with about half of the amount of dressing you think it needs, then serve the rest on the side. When your entire salad is lightly dressed, you'll likely find you enjoy it as is and won't need the remaining dressing . . . or extra calories. Of course, there are some exceptions to this rule, as in composed salads for which use of the exact amount of dressing is planned.

Kicking off this chapter are two dozen fresh and intriguing salad dressings and vinaigrettes. They're all 90 calories or less per serving, with a few chiming in at only 25 calories. That's far less than what you'll find bottled up—commercial varieties are often 120 to 150 calories per serving.

Dressings range from fruity, like the Peach Bellini Salad Dressing (page 148), to savory and creamy, as in Avocado Ranch Dressing (page 150); vinaigrettes include Bloody Mary Vinaigrette (page 145)—which actually uses a shot of vodka—to

those that use intriguing fruit and tea, like Seckel Pear and Green Tea Vinaigrette (page 147).

Don't think you have to give up creamy dressing when eating low calorie. I share many techniques to make them extra nutritious as well as delicious. Creaminess in these dressings is created in various ways, including by pureeing the dressing ingredients with avocado or other fruits, white beans, silken tofu, plain yogurt, tahini, and cooked chilled potatoes. For vinaigrettes, you'll find cucumber and shallots are often used to add body and help "stretch" them in a fresh, flavorful way. A splash of low-sodium vegetable broth replaces part of the oil in some cases, too. But I do still use oil—just in the right amount. Salad dressings and vinaigrettes that contain plant-based oils or other ingredients with healthful fats, like avocado, actually boost antioxidant benefits of the salad—and heighten enjoyment!

You'll find a variety of leafy salads with which to enjoy these dressings and vinaigrettes. Many of these recipes are salad makeovers of what you might find at your favorite restaurant, including Mod Caesar Salad with Homemade Croutons (page 153) and Leafy Greek Island Salad (page 154). There are also new homespun classics, found with the 12-Layer Salad (page 157).

Salads aren't just green salads, so I've included a dozen potato salads, using colorful potato varieties and various cooking methods. There's some evidence that cooked, cooled potatoes (like those in potato salad) may potentially help manage your appetite because they contain an ingredient called resistant starch, which acts a little bit like fiber. Plus, research finds the purple potato in particular may play a role in managing blood pressure without causing weight gain. What should you dress them with? One of the "secrets" to a perky dressing that I use in *1,000 Low-Calories Recipes* is my "4-3-2-1" rule: For 2 pounds potatoes use a mixture of 4 tablespoons mayo, 3 tablespoons mustard, 2 tablespoons Greek yogurt, and 1 tablespoon vinegar. I vary this recipe idea, too.

I went beyond the usual with the other vegetable-based salads to keep your taste buds enticed. There's a show-stopping fresh caprese-style salad that's layered like lasagna and a salad version of a BLT sandwich. The internationally inspired tofu salads, like Ginger Tofu Chick'n Salad (page 170), will definitely surprise your palate—even if only a tofu liker, not lover. The slaws can be especially exciting—they don't always start with cabbage, as in the Beet and Fuji Apple Coleslaw (page 174).

Whole-grain based salads are next, including pasta and noodle salads. If you're looking for comfort, you've got it. Try the Creamy Cavatappi Salad with Ham (page 177) or Pesto Pasta and Spinach Salad (page 181). Rather than taking anything out of these recipes to make them healthful, extra satisfaction is created by adding popular produce. The whole-grain salads take advantage of the growing availability of unique and "ancient" grains, including Spelt Tabbouleh Salad (page 183) and Roasted Veggie Farro Salad (page 188). They keep well in the fridge so you can enjoy them for lunch for days.

Boosting beans by way of salad is delightful—and helps you feel full. Bean salads in this chapter have a global flair and use various types of beans—all of which you can prepare quickly using canned varieties. If any recipe calls for a partial can of beans, use up whatever is remaining in a soup, or whip up a batch of hummus, or sprinkle them onto an entrée as a purposeful nutritional garnish. And do know that you can use cooked dried beans instead of the canned variety any time you like (see Preparing Dried Beans, page 436).

Of course, salads aren't just for vegetarians. This refreshing, veggie-rich chapter concludes with protein-rich salads prepared with poultry, fish, shellfish, and meat. Do be conscientious with your selections, such as choosing grass-fed beef and eco-friendly fish, when possible. These savory salads can be served as entrées. And the Rotisserie Chicken Cobb Salad (page 191) is ideal as an entire meal.

Enjoying salads is one of the simplest ways to boost your veggie intake. A greater vegetable intake can lead to a healthier weight.

Calorie range in this chapter: 25 to 400 calories.

Low-calorie picks: "Caliente" Caesar Dijon Dressing, (page 148), Spicy Roasted Pepper Dressing, (page 149), and Avocado Ranch Dressing, (page 150), 25 calories each.

Salad Dressings and Vinaigrettes

Fresh Herb and Shallot Vinaigrette

Makes 7 servings: 2 tablespoons each

A traditional vinaigrette is three parts oil to one part vinegar. I reduce the ratio to lighten this fine dining–style vinaigrette. I add shallot and fresh herbs for flavor depth—so you might say this simple version seems richer. It's as delightful in green salads, like Leafy Greek Island Salad (page 154), as nonleafy ones, such as Grilled Sweet Potato Salad (page 165) and "Wild" White Bean Salad (page 189).

¼ cup extra-virgin olive or flaxseed oil

¼ cup white wine vinegar

¼ cup sliced or chopped unpeeled English cucumber

1 large shallot

1 teaspoon honey or agave nectar

1 teaspoon chopped fresh oregano or rosemary

¼ teaspoon sea salt, or to taste

¼ teaspoon freshly ground black pepper, or to taste

Add all the ingredients to a blender. Cover and puree. Adjust seasoning. Use immediately or store covered in the refrigerator for up to 1 week.

Per serving: 80 calories, 8g total fat, 1g saturated fat, 0g trans fat, 0mg cholesterol, 85mg sodium, 2g total carbohydrate, 0g dietary fiber, 1g sugars, 0g protein

Dijon Balsamic Vinaigrette

Makes 6 servings: 2 tablespoons each

Whisk up this flavor-bursting vinaigrette and you'll be amazed at the speed at which it'll disappear. It's perfect for Pear and Walnut Field Green Salad (page 155), Portobella and Peppercorn Chophouse Salad (page 197), or really any leafy green salad.

¼ cup extra-virgin olive or flaxseed oil

¼ cup aged balsamic vinegar

¼ cup sliced or chopped unpeeled English cucumber

1 small shallot, peeled

2 teaspoons Dijon mustard

¼ teaspoon sea salt, or to taste

¼ teaspoon freshly ground black pepper, or to taste

Add all the ingredients to a blender. Cover and puree. Adjust seasoning. Use immediately or store covered in the refrigerator for up to 1 week.

Per serving: 90 calories, 9g total fat, 1.5g saturated fat, 0g trans fat, 0mg cholesterol, 140mg sodium, 3g total carbohydrate, 0g dietary fiber, 2g sugars, 0g protein

Jalapeño Honey Vinaigrette Ⓢ

Makes 9 servings: 2 tablespoons each

Beyond the sweet heat, perhaps the coolest part of this recipe is the cucumber; it provides freshness while reducing the need for excess oil. It'll please your palate when paired with Spicy Citrus Endive Salad (page 158) or Soulful Taco Salad (page 156).

½ cup sliced or chopped unpeeled English cucumber

¼ cup canola or flaxseed oil

2 tablespoons white wine vinegar

Juice of 1 lime (2 tablespoons)

1 shallot

1 small jalapeño pepper with some seeds

1 tablespoon honey or agave nectar

1 tablespoon fresh cilantro leaves (optional)

¼ teaspoon sea salt, or to taste

¼ teaspoon freshly ground black pepper, or to taste

Add all the ingredients to a blender. Cover and puree. Adjust seasoning. Use immediately or store covered in the refrigerator for up to 1 week.

Per serving: 70 calories, 6g total fat, 0g saturated fat, 0g trans fat, 0mg cholesterol, 65mg sodium, 3g total carbohydrate, 0g dietary fiber, 2g sugars, 0g protein

Bloody Mary Vinaigrette

Makes 18 servings: 2 tablespoons each

Here's a dressing inspired by a drink. It has many of the same aromatic, eye-opening ingredients as the classic cocktail—including vodka. So make sure to card anyone who wants to experience this spirited vinaigrette. It's a vivacious addition to fish or a spinach salad, like Sunnyside-Up Spinach Salad (page 156).

1 fully ripened Bosc, Comice, or Anjou pear, cored and coarsely chopped

1 cup low-sodium tomato or vegetable juice

Juice of 1 lemon (3 tablespoons)

3 tablespoons extra-virgin olive or flaxseed oil

3 tablespoons 80-proof vodka or low-sodium vegetable broth

¼ cup sliced or chopped unpeeled English cucumber

2 teaspoons freshly grated horseradish

½ teaspoon sea salt, or to taste

½ teaspoon freshly ground black pepper, or to taste

½ teaspoon hot pepper sauce, or to taste

¼ teaspoon vegetarian Worcestershire sauce

Add all the ingredients to a blender container. Cover and puree. Adjust seasoning. Use immediately or store covered in the refrigerator for up to 1 week.

Per serving: 35 calories, 2.5g total fat, 0g saturated fat, 0g trans fat, 0mg cholesterol, 80mg sodium, 3g total carbohydrate, 0g dietary fiber, 2g sugars, 0g protein

Creamy Basil Vinaigrette

Makes 11 servings: 2 tablespoons each

This herbal white wine vinaigrette gets its velvety rich mouth feel from white beans. Its creaminess provides a tempting contrast to the textures of Rotisserie Chicken Cobb Salad (page 191), Warm Grilled Vegetable Salad (page 175), and Salad for Every Season (page 159).

½ cup drained canned no-salt-added cannellini or other white beans

⅓ cup sliced or chopped unpeeled English cucumber

¼ cup white wine vinegar

¼ cup extra-virgin olive oil

8 large fresh basil leaves

1 shallot

1 large garlic clove, chopped

½ teaspoon pure maple syrup, mild honey, or agave nectar

½ teaspoon freshly ground black pepper, or to taste

¼ teaspoon sea salt, or to taste

Add all the ingredients to a blender. Cover and puree. Adjust seasoning. Use immediately or store covered in the refrigerator for up to 1 week.

Per serving: 60 calories, 5g total fat, 0.5g saturated fat, 0g trans fat, 0mg cholesterol, 55mg sodium, 2g total carbohydrate, 1g dietary fiber, 0.5g sugars, 1g protein

Minty Balsamic Vinaigrette

Makes 8 servings: 2 tablespoons each

When you don't want to overpower a leafy salad that showcases seasonal fruit, this white balsamic vinaigrette will allow the fresh fruit to shine brightly. The mint will provide added fragrance and a pop of sweet-peppery goodness, especially noteworthy in Minty Strawberry Arugula Salad (page 158).

½ cup sliced or chopped unpeeled English cucumber

¼ cup extra-virgin olive or flaxseed oil

¼ cup white balsamic vinegar

2 tablespoons chopped fresh mint

1 large shallot

¼ teaspoon sea salt, or to taste

¼ teaspoon freshly ground black pepper, or to taste

Add all the ingredients to a blender. Cover and puree. Adjust seasoning. Use immediately or store covered in the refrigerator for up to 1 week.

Per serving: 70 calories, 7g total fat, 1g saturated fat, 0g trans fat, 0mg cholesterol, 75mg sodium, 2g total carbohydrate, 0g dietary fiber, 0g sugars, 0g protein

Syrian Vinaigrette

Makes 6 servings: 2 tablespoons each

Here's an ultra tangy vinaigrette that's not meant for meek palates. There's nothing gentle about its lemony jolt—which is actually what makes the bread salad Fattoush (page 159) a standout. You might find that you want less of it than other vinaigrettes . . . which cuts calories, of course.

Juice of 1 large lemon (¼ cup)

¼ cup extra-virgin olive oil

2 tablespoons low-sodium vegetable broth

2 scallions, green and white parts, minced

1 small garlic clove, minced

½ teaspoon ground sumac (optional)

¼ teaspoon sea salt, or to taste

¼ teaspoon freshly ground black pepper, or to taste

Whisk together the lemon juice, oil, broth, scallions, garlic, sumac (if using), salt, and pepper in a small bowl. Use immediately or store covered in the refrigerator for up to 1 week.

Per serving: 90 calories, 9g total fat, 1.5g saturated fat, 0g trans fat, 0mg cholesterol, 100mg sodium, 2g total carbohydrate, 0g dietary fiber, 0g sugars, 0g protein

Garden Lemon Vinaigrette

Makes 6 servings: 2 tablespoons each

This vinaigrette has a fresh green appearance from the unpeeled cucumber. Its lovely lemony flavor will provide the ideal accent for a multitude of salads, including the Seared Salmon Salad (page 195) and English Poached Egg Salad (page 192).

½ cup sliced or chopped unpeeled English cucumber

¼ cup extra-virgin olive or flaxseed oil

2 tablespoons white balsamic vinegar

Juice and zest of 1 small lemon (2 tablespoons juice)

1 shallot

¼ teaspoon sea salt, or to taste

¼ teaspoon freshly ground black pepper, or to taste

Add all the ingredients to a blender. Cover and puree. Adjust seasoning. Use immediately or store covered in the refrigerator for up to 1 week.

Per serving: 90 calories, 1.5g total fat, 0g saturated fat, 0g trans fat, 0mg cholesterol, 95mg sodium, 2g total carbohydrate, 0g dietary fiber, 0g sugars, 0g protein

Zesty Lime Vinaigrette

Makes 9 servings: 2 tablespoons each

The flavors here are lively and refreshing without being overwhelming. And it's just the right vinaigrette for pairing with so many salads, including those with Caribbean, Mexican, or Asian flavors. Try it in Drunken Grilled Harvest Salad (page 169) and Jamaican Bean Salad (page 189).

½ cup sliced or chopped unpeeled English cucumber

¼ cup canola or flaxseed oil

¼ cup white wine vinegar

3 tablespoons 100% unsweetened apple juice

1 shallot

½ small jalapeño pepper with seeds

½ teaspoon lime zest

¼ teaspoon sea salt, or to taste

¼ teaspoon freshly ground black pepper, or to taste

Add all the ingredients to a blender. Cover and puree. Adjust seasoning. Use immediately or store covered in the refrigerator for up to 1 week.

Per serving: 60 calories, 6g total fat, 0g saturated fat, 0g trans fat, 0mg cholesterol, 65mg sodium, 2g total carbohydrate, 0g dietary fiber, 1g sugars, 0g protein

Tart Cherry Vinaigrette

Makes 7 servings: 2 tablespoons each

By pureeing dried tart cherries into this fruity and tangy vinaigrette, there's a bit of sweet-tart taste in every bite of the salad which it dresses. And you can sprinkle extra dried fruit onto your salad for a double fruity sensation. Give it a taste in "Trail Mix" Salad (page 155) and Artichoke Salad with Manchego and Tart Cherries (page 174).

¼ cup canola or flaxseed oil

¼ cup champagne vinegar

¼ cup dried tart cherries

2 tablespoons 100% unsweetened apple juice
    or tart cherry juice

1 tablespoon pure maple syrup

1 shallot

1½ teaspoons Dijon mustard

¼ teaspoon sea salt, or to taste

¼ teaspoon freshly ground black pepper, or to taste

Add all the ingredients to a blender. Cover and puree. (Note: Some flecks of the dried cherries will remain.) Adjust seasoning. Use immediately or store covered in the refrigerator for up to 1 week.

Per serving: 70 calories, 4g total fat, 0g saturated fat, 0g trans fat, 0mg cholesterol, 110mg sodium, 8g total carbohydrate, 1g dietary fiber, 4g sugars, 0g protein

Fresh Raspberry Vinaigrette Ⓢ

Makes 10 servings: 2 tablespoons each

Raspberry lovers will be thrilled with the intense burst of raspberry flavor here. Or you can vary this vinaigrette with any favorite berry depending on the season—or your mood. Enjoy its fresh fruity burst in Sunflower Raspberry Watercress Salad (page 158).

6 ounces fresh raspberries

1 large shallot, minced

3 large or 6 small fresh basil or mint leaves,
    finely chopped (optional)

Juice of ½ small lemon (1 tablespoon)

¼ teaspoon freshly ground black pepper,
    or to taste

⅛ teaspoon sea salt, or to taste

¼ cup sunflower, canola, or flaxseed oil

1. Add the raspberries to a medium bowl. Fully mash with a fork.

2. Stir in the shallot, basil (if using), lemon juice, pepper, and salt. Whisk in the oil. Adjust seasoning. Use immediately or store covered in the refrigerator for up to 3 days.

Per serving: 60 calories, 6g total fat, 0.5g saturated fat, 0g trans fat, 0mg cholesterol, 30mg sodium, 3g total carbohydrate, 1g dietary fiber, 1g sugars, 0g protein

Seckel Pear and Green Tea Vinaigrette

Makes 12 servings: 2 tablespoons each

For impressing dinner guests, this elegant vinaigrette will not let you down. The low calorie count will impress, too. The green tea provides a special flavor nuance that'll have people trying to guess your secret. What's no secret is how lovely it makes Jasmine Green Tea and Pear-Dressed Mesclun (page 155).

2 small Seckel pears or 1 medium Anjou pear,
    cored and chopped

⅓ cup unsweetened jasmine or ginger-peach
    green tea (brewed with 1 tea bag), chilled

3 tablespoons canola or flaxseed oil

3 tablespoons white wine vinegar

1 shallot

¼ teaspoon sea salt, or to taste

¼ teaspoon freshly ground black pepper,
    or to taste

Add all the ingredients to a blender. Cover and puree. Adjust seasoning. Use immediately or store covered in the refrigerator for up to 1 week.

Per serving: 40 calories, 3.5g total fat, 0g saturated fat, 0g trans fat, 0mg cholesterol, 50mg sodium, 3g total carbohydrate, 0g dietary fiber, 2g sugars, 0g protein

Tart Apple Vinaigrette Ⓢ

Makes 12 servings: 2 tablespoons each

This autumnal vinaigrette is loaded with Granny Smith apple enchantment . . . a terrific way to take advantage of the best the season has to offer. It's the pairing of choice for Bibb-n-Blue Chopped Salad (page 154).

1 large Granny Smith apple, cored and chopped

¼ cup canola or flaxseed oil

¼ cup apple cider vinegar

2 tablespoons low-sodium vegetable broth

2 teaspoons pure maple syrup

1 shallot

¼ teaspoon sea salt, or to taste

¼ teaspoon freshly ground black pepper, or to taste

⅛ teaspoon ground cinnamon

Add all the ingredients to a blender. Cover and puree. Adjust seasoning. Use immediately or store covered in the refrigerator for up to 1 week.

Per serving: 60 calories, 4.5g total fat, 0g saturated fat, 0g trans fat, 0mg cholesterol, 50mg sodium, 4g total carbohydrate, 0g dietary fiber, 3g sugars, 0g protein

"Caliente" Caesar Dijon Dressing

Makes 6 servings: 2 tablespoons each

At just 25 calories a serving, this zippy dressing is sure to please your need for spice while staying svelte. Enjoy in salads, like Mod Caesar Salad with Homemade Croutons (page 153), and in unique salad preparations, like Shrimp Salad in Parmesan-Wonton Cups (page 54) and Grilled Caesar Salad Pizza (page 416). Savor as a vivid dip for raw veggies, too.

4 ounces silken tofu, drained (about ½ cup)

1 (2-ounce) can anchovies in oil (about 3 anchovies), well drained (optional)

1 small jalapeño pepper with seeds

2 large garlic cloves, chopped

2 tablespoons Dijon mustard

1½ tablespoons vegetarian Worcestershire sauce

1 tablespoon freshly grated Parmigiano-Reggiano or other Parmesan cheese (optional)

1½ teaspoons extra-virgin olive or flaxseed oil

Add all the ingredients to a blender. Cover and puree. Adjust seasoning. Use immediately or store covered in the refrigerator for up to 3 days.

Per serving: 25 calories, 1.5g total fat, 0g saturated fat, 0g trans fat, 0mg cholesterol, 105mg sodium, 1g total carbohydrate, 0g dietary fiber, 0g sugars, 1g protein

Peach Bellini Salad Dressing

Makes 6 servings: 3 tablespoons each

When life hands you peaches, make peach salad dressing! It's sweet and sexy with the benefits of both a fresh juicy peach and a peachy shot! Toss it with the leafy salad in its namesake, Peach Bellini Salad (page 152).

1 medium ripe peach, pitted and sliced

3 tablespoons extra-virgin olive or flaxseed oil

3 tablespoons champagne vinegar or white balsamic vinegar

2 tablespoons peach schnapps

½ teaspoon freshly ground black pepper, or to taste

¼ teaspoon sea salt, or to taste

Add all the ingredients to a blender. Cover and puree. Adjust seasoning. Use immediately or store covered in the refrigerator for up to 1 week.

Per serving: 80 calories, 7g total fat, 1g saturated fat, 0g trans fat, 0mg cholesterol, 95mg sodium, 4g total carbohydrate, 0g dietary fiber, 3g sugars, 0g protein

Silky Lemon Dressing

Makes 6 servings: 2½ tablespoons each

This smooth dressing brings a balanced lemony flavor and a bright freshness to cuisine. Use it to dress Layered Waldorf Salad (page 157), Spice-Rubbed Barramundi Salad (page 194), or leafy salad greens of choice.

3 ounces silken tofu, drained

3 tablespoons fat-free or low-fat plain yogurt
    or soy yogurt

2 tablespoons extra-virgin olive or flaxseed oil

Juice and zest of 1 lemon (3 tablespoons juice)

1 small shallot

1 teaspoon honey or agave nectar

¼ teaspoon sea salt, or to taste

¼ teaspoon freshly ground black pepper,
    or to taste

Add all the ingredients to a blender. Cover and puree. Adjust seasoning. Use immediately or store covered in the refrigerator for up to 1 week.

Per serving: 60 calories, 5g total fat, 0.5g saturated fat, 0g trans fat, 0mg cholesterol, 100mg sodium, 2g total carbohydrate, 0g dietary fiber, 2g sugars, 1g protein

Fresh-Squeezed Lemon-Dill Dressing Ⓢ

Makes 18 servings: 2 tablespoons each

A potato is sometimes tossed with dressing, but here it's part of the dressing! The cooked, cooled potato helps create creaminess. The vegetable broth flavorfully replaces part of the oil, too, to lighten it up. Lucky for our hearts, this mono-unsaturated fat-rich salad dressing also provides rich Mediterranean diet benefits. It's delicious, especially in French Green Bean–Barley Salad (page 186).

1 baked medium Yukon Gold potato, unpeeled,
    chilled, and diced

¾ cup extra-virgin olive or flaxseed oil

Juice of 3 lemons (about ½ cup)

6 tablespoons low-sodium vegetable broth

1 large shallot

1 tablespoon chopped fresh dill

¼ teaspoon sea salt, or to taste

¼ teaspoon freshly ground black pepper, or to taste

Add all the ingredients to a blender. Cover and puree. Adjust seasoning. Use immediately or store covered in the refrigerator for up to 1 week.

Per serving: 90 calories, 9g total fat, 1.5g saturated fat, 0g trans fat, 0mg cholesterol, 35mg sodium, 3g total carbohydrate, 0g dietary fiber, 0g sugars, 0g protein

Spicy Roasted Pepper Dressing

Makes 18 servings: 2 tablespoons each

Your taste buds will celebrate the smoky, sweet, and spicy goodness of this dressing with your next salad . . . and the next . . . and the next. It makes Roasted Potato and Red Pepper Salad (page 164) and Edamame and Frizzled Leek Quinoa Salad (page 184) extra special.

2 large freshly roasted red bell peppers (page 27),
    or drained jarred peppers

1 small jalapeño pepper with some seeds, chopped

¼ cup no-sugar-added applesauce

3 tablespoons fat-free or low-fat plain yogurt

Juice of 1 lemon (3 tablespoons)

2 tablespoons flaxseed or unrefined peanut oil

½ teaspoon sea salt, or to taste

¼ teaspoon freshly ground black pepper, or to taste

Add all the ingredients to a blender. Cover and puree. Adjust seasoning. Use immediately or store covered in the refrigerator for up to 1 week.

Per serving: 25 calories, 1.5g total fat, 0g saturated fat, 0g trans fat, 0mg cholesterol, 65mg sodium, 2g total carbohydrate, 0g dietary fiber, 1g sugars, 0g protein

Avocado Ranch Dressing

Makes 16 servings: 2 tablespoons each

This buttery smooth dressing tastes just like the recipe name suggests—like an avocado-infused ranch dressing. And at only 25 calories per serving, you'll likely be reaching for this righteous version of ranch often.

1 Hass avocado, pitted and peeled

2 large garlic cloves, chopped

1 shallot, halved

½ cup low-sodium vegetable broth

¼ cup white wine vinegar

3 tablespoons sour cream or soy-based sour cream

3 tablespoons fat-free or low-fat plain yogurt

¼ teaspoon vegetarian Worcestershire sauce, or to taste

½ teaspoon freshly ground black pepper, or to taste

¼ teaspoon sea salt, or to taste

Add all the ingredients to a blender. Cover and puree. Adjust seasoning. Use immediately or store covered in the refrigerator for up to 1 week.

Per serving: 25 calories, 2g total fat, 0g saturated fat, 0g trans fat, 0mg cholesterol, 45mg sodium, 2g total carbohydrate, 1g dietary fiber, 0g sugars, 0g protein

Exotic Papaya Dressing

Makes 10 servings: 2 tablespoons each

This perfumed, sweet papaya dressing has a tropical aroma and a lusciously creamy mouthfeel. Enjoy its delights in Cuban Black Bean Salad (page 190) or with leafy salad greens of choice.

1 cup fresh papaya cubes

2 teaspoons fresh papaya seeds (optional)

¼ cup canola or flaxseed oil

Juice and zest of lime (2 tablespoons juice)

2 tablespoons apple cider vinegar or raspberry vinegar

1 small shallot

½ teaspoon sea salt, or to taste

¼ teaspoon freshly ground black pepper, or to taste

Add all the ingredients to a blender. Cover and puree. Adjust seasoning. Note: For a thinner dressing, whisk in 100% fruit juice of choice about 1 teaspoon at a time until desired consistency. Use immediately or store covered in the refrigerator for up to 1 week.

Per serving: 60 calories, 6g total fat, 0g saturated fat, 0g trans fat, 0mg cholesterol, 115mg sodium, 2g total carbohydrate, 0g dietary fiber, 1g sugars, 0g protein

Creamy Peppercorn Dressing

Makes 16 servings: 2 tablespoons each

Here's a full-flavored dressing that's whirled with white beans to create its memorable creaminess. The peppercorns give it an exciting kick, too, for a burst of enjoyment in 12-Layer Salad (page 157), Hearts of Romaine Salad (page 152), and Peppercorn Beef and Brie on Bread Ends (page 380).

1 (15-ounce) can no-salt-added cannellini or other white beans, drained

½ cup low-sodium vegetable broth

¼ cup aged balsamic or white balsamic vinegar

2 tablespoons extra-virgin olive or flaxseed oil

2 large garlic cloves, chopped

¾ teaspoon coarsely cracked black pepper, or to taste

½ teaspoon sea salt, or to taste

Add all the ingredients to a blender. Cover and puree. Adjust seasoning. Use immediately or store covered in the refrigerator for up to 10 days.

Per serving: 40 calories, 2g total fat, 0g saturated fat, 0g trans fat, 0mg cholesterol, 85mg sodium, 4g total carbohydrate, 1g dietary fiber, 1g sugars, 1g protein

Winter White French Dressing

Makes 16 servings: 2 tablespoons each

I developed this dressing per the request of my sister-in-law, Sandi. It's quite versatile and nicely balanced with a lively tang and hint of sweetness. It's the dressing of choice for Luncheon Chef Salad (page 192). Try it simply with leafy mixed salad greens, too.

1 baked medium Yukon Gold potato, unpeeled, chilled, and sliced

¾ cup low-sodium vegetable broth

¼ cup white balsamic vinegar

2 tablespoons canola or flaxseed oil

2 tablespoons no-sugar-added applesauce

1 shallot, halved

1 large garlic clove, chopped

2 teaspoons honey or agave nectar

1½ teaspoons Dijon mustard

½ teaspoon sea salt, or to taste

¼ teaspoon celery seeds (optional)

Add all the ingredients to a blender. Cover and puree. Adjust seasoning. Use immediately or store covered in the refrigerator for up to 1 week.

Per serving: 30 calories, 2g total fat, 0g saturated fat, 0g trans fat, 0mg cholesterol, 90mg sodium, 4g total carbohydrate, 0g dietary fiber, 1g sugars, 0g protein

Tahini Za'atar Dressing Ⓢ

Makes 7 servings: 2 tablespoons each

Now you can get an exquisite taste of the Middle East in a lively, velvety salad dressing. The creamy tahini makes it so full-bodied that you may forget all about über-rich ranch dressing.

3 tablespoons green tea or water

Juice of 1 small lemon (2 tablespoons)

1 large shallot, minced

2 tablespoons finely chopped fresh mint

2 large garlic cloves, minced

½ teaspoon dried za'atar or crushed dried oregano

¼ teaspoon freshly ground black pepper, or to taste

¼ teaspoon sea salt, or to taste

2 tablespoons canola or extra-virgin olive oil

¼ cup tahini (sesame seed paste)

Stir together the tea, lemon juice, shallot, mint, garlic, za'atar, pepper, and salt in a medium bowl until combined. Whisk in the oil, then the tahini. Adjust seasoning. Use immediately or store covered in the refrigerator for up to 1 week.

Per serving: 90 calories, 9g total fat, 1g saturated fat, 0g trans fat, 0mg cholesterol, 85mg sodium, 4g total carbohydrate, 0g dietary fiber, 0g sugars, 2g protein

Mandarin Miso Dressing

Makes 8 servings: 2 tablespoons each

Here you'll get to experience the sweet tangy taste of freshly squeezed mandarin orange (or tangerine or clementine) juice in an inventive way. Combined with miso and ginger, you'll find this dressing provides a truly unforgettable Asian flair to salads.

½ cup fresh-squeezed mandarin orange juice or orange juice

2 tablespoons white or yellow miso

1 large shallot, minced

1 large garlic clove, minced

1 teaspoon freshly grated gingerroot, or to taste

¼ cup sunflower, canola, or flaxseed oil

Stir together the mandarin orange juice, miso, shallot, garlic, and ginger in a medium bowl until combined. Whisk in the oil. Adjust seasoning. Use immediately or store covered in the refrigerator for up to 1 week.

Per serving: 80 calories, 7g total fat, 1g saturated fat, 0g trans fat, 0mg cholesterol, 135mg sodium, 4g total carbohydrate, 1g dietary fiber, 2g sugars, 1g protein

Leafy Salads

Hearts of Romaine Salad

Makes 4 servings: ½ Romaine heart bunch

A recipe doesn't get much simpler than this. Take pure delight in this crisp salad with its pleasingly sharp bite from the blue cheese.

2 romaine heart bunches, halved lengthwise,
    or 16 romaine lettuce leaves
¾ cup Creamy Peppercorn Dressing (page 150)
    or other creamy dressing
¼ cup crumbled blue cheese

1. Place each halved romaine heart bunch (or 4 stacked leaves) on a plate.

2. Drizzle with the dressing, sprinkle with the cheese, and serve.

Per serving: 100 calories, 6g total fat, 2g saturated fat, 0g trans fat, 5mg cholesterol, 250mg sodium, 9g total carbohydrate, 3g dietary fiber, 2g sugars, 5g protein

Avocado Ranch Corn Cobb Salad

Makes 4 servings: 2½ cups each

You'll be amazed by the little bits of sun-dried tomatoes that are downright bacon-like . . . but better. One of the tastiest salads you'll ever have with fewer than 200 calories!

6 cups packed mixed baby salad greens
2 medium ears corn, grilled or boiled,
    kernels cut from cobs
3 medium vine-ripened tomatoes, pulp removed
    and diced
⅓ cup crumbled blue cheese
2 large hard-cooked eggs, cut into 6 wedges each
    (page 377)

⅓ cup finely diced red onion
⅓ cup finely chopped sun-dried tomatoes
    (not oil packed), rehydrated, if necessary
½ cup Avocado Ranch Dressing (page 150)
    or other ranch dressing
½ teaspoon finely chopped fresh rosemary (optional)
½ teaspoon freshly ground black pepper,
    or to taste

1. Arrange the salad greens on a platter or four plates. Top with the corn, tomatoes, cheese, eggs, onion, and sun-dried tomato.

2. Drizzle with the dressing or serve it on the side. Sprinkle with the rosemary (if using) and pepper, and serve.

Per serving: 190 calories, 9g total fat, 3.5g saturated fat, 0g trans fat, 105mg cholesterol, 370mg sodium, 22g total carbohydrate, 5g dietary fiber, 9g sugars, 10g protein

Peach Bellini Salad Ⓢ

Makes 4 servings: about 2 cups each

A Bellini is an apéritif that's a mixture of Champagne and peach nectar. It inspired this simply lovely salad with its peachy dressing. It's refreshing, summery, and elegant.

8 cups packed mixed field greens or mesclun
¼ cup chopped fresh mint
¾ cup Peach Bellini Salad Dressing (page 148)
    or fruit vinaigrette of choice
⅔ cup Crystallized Almonds (page 42)
    or whole dry-roasted almonds

1. Toss together the salad greens, mint, and half of the dressing in a large bowl just before serving.

2. Arrange the salad on a platter or four plates. Top with the almonds, and serve with remaining dressing on the side.

Per serving: 260 calories, 20g total fat, 2.5g saturated fat, 0g trans fat, 0mg cholesterol, 200mg sodium, 16g total carbohydrate, 4g dietary fiber, 10g sugars, 6g protein

Mod Caesar Salad with Homemade Croutons

Makes 4 servings: 2½ cups each

The Caesar salad is believed to have originated in Tijuana, Mexico. That's what sparked me to make a version with a bit more bite to it. You'll be hot for my modern take on the traditional tangy pleasure.

8 cups chopped romaine lettuce

½ cup "Caliente" Caesar Dijon Dressing (page 148) or other Caesar dressing

¼ teaspoon freshly ground black pepper, or to taste

4 servings Homemade Croutons (at right)

1 orange or red hot Jamaican or small jalapeño pepper, very thinly sliced crosswise (optional)

1. Toss together the lettuce, dressing, black pepper, and half of the croutons in a large bowl just before serving.

2. Arrange the salad on a platter or four plates. Top with the hot pepper (if using) and the remaining croutons, and serve.

Per serving: 160 calories, 8g total fat, 1g saturated fat, 0g trans fat, 0mg cholesterol, 390mg sodium, 17g total carbohydrate, 4g dietary fiber, 3g sugars, 6g protein

HOMEMADE CROUTONS

Makes 4 servings (9 croutons each)

1½ tablespoons extra-virgin olive oil

½ teaspoon herbes de Provence

¼ teaspoon sea salt, or to taste

⅛ teaspoon freshly ground black pepper, or to taste

¼ teaspoon garlic powder (optional)

3 slices fresh whole-grain bread

1. Whisk together the oil, herbes de Provence, salt, pepper, and garlic powder (if using) in a small bowl.

2. Coat both sides of the bread slices with the oil mixture using a pastry brush, stirring the mixture with the brush before each use. Cut the bread into 12 cubes per slice using a bread knife. Arrange the cubes in a single layer on a large baking sheet.

3. Place the sheet in the oven (do not preheat). Turn the oven to 375°F and bake until the croutons are just crisp on the outside, about 12 to 15 minutes. Turn off the oven and let the croutons fully crisp in the oven with remaining heat, about 15 minutes. Remove to a cooling rack. Keep stored in a sealed container at room temperature for up to 1 week or in the freezer for up to 1 month.

Per serving: 130 calories, 6g total fat, 1g saturated fat, 0g trans fat, 0mg cholesterol, 280mg sodium, 14g total carbohydrate, 2g dietary fiber, 2g sugars, 4g protein

Leafy Greek Island Salad Ⓕ

Makes 6 servings: about 3 cups each

My sister told me that this salad reminded her of a memorable restaurant salad she once had—only tastier. It has an array of contrasting textures and tastes . . . salty olives, tangy feta, sharp onions, sweet tomatoes, mild creamy beans, and fresh crisp garden veggies. The lemon zest provides a flavorful finishing touch.

4 cups chopped romaine lettuce

4 cups packed fresh baby spinach

1 large English cucumber, unpeeled and thinly sliced or cubed

1 cup grape tomatoes, halved lengthwise

¾ cup pitted Kalamata or other brine-cured black olives

½ cup drained canned chickpeas (garbanzo beans)

½ cup crumbled feta cheese

⅓ cup very thinly sliced or diced red onion

1 (8-inch) whole-wheat pita, split into two rounds, toasted or grilled, and broken into bite-size pieces

¾ cup Fresh Herb and Shallot Vinaigrette (page 144) or other vinaigrette

2 teaspoons grated lemon zest

1. Toss together the lettuce, spinach, cucumber, tomatoes, olives, chickpeas, cheese, onion, pita pieces, and half of the vinaigrette in a large bowl just before serving.

2. Arrange the salad on a platter or four plates. Top with the lemon zest, and serve with the remaining vinaigrette on the side.

Per serving: 200 calories, 13g total fat, 3.5g saturated fat, 0g trans fat, 10mg cholesterol, 480mg sodium, 18g total carbohydrate, 5g dietary fiber, 4g sugars, 6g protein

Bibb-n-Blue Chopped Salad Ⓕ

Makes 4 servings: 2½ cups each

You'll be enamored of this salad's fruitiness, cheesiness, and nuttiness. And if that wasn't enough, its charismatic balance of sweetness and sharpness will charm your palate beyond autumn, when tart apples and pecans are traditionally enjoyed.

4 cups packed torn Bibb or Boston lettuce

4 cups chopped romaine lettuce

¾ cup chilled cooked shelled edamame or drained canned butter beans

½ cup Georgia pecan halves, toasted

⅓ cup finely diced sweet onion

⅓ cup black seedless raisins or dried tart cherries

½ cup Tart Apple Vinaigrette (page 148)

¼ teaspoon sea salt, or to taste

¼ cup crumbled Gorgonzola or other blue cheese

¼ teaspoon freshly ground black pepper, or to taste

1. Toss together the lettuces, edamame, pecans, onion, raisins, half of the vinaigrette, and the salt in a large bowl just before serving.

2. Arrange the salad on a platter or four plates. Sprinkle with the cheese and pepper, and serve with the remaining vinaigrette on the side.

Per serving: 270 calories, 18g total fat, 3.5g saturated fat, 0g trans fat, 10mg cholesterol, 340mg sodium, 23g total carbohydrate, 5g dietary fiber, 13g sugars, 8g protein

"Trail Mix" Salad Ⓢ Ⓕ

Makes 4 servings: 2¼ cups each

The trail mix of my childhood usually consisted of a mysterious jumble of cereal, nuts, and dried fruit. Here, I've exchanged grains for greens but kept the nutty and dried fruit goodness, which makes this salad supremely satiating—no real hiking on trails required.

8 cups packed mixed salad greens or baby arugula

½ cup dried tart cherries or other fruit bits

½ cup unsalted dry-roasted mixed nuts

½ cup Tart Cherry Vinaigrette (page 147)

1. Toss together the salad greens, dried cherries, nuts, and half the vinaigrette in a large bowl just before serving.

2. Arrange the salad on a platter or four plates, and serve with the remaining vinaigrette on the side.

Per serving: 230 calories, 13g total fat, 1.5g saturated fat, 0g trans fat, 0mg cholesterol, 120mg sodium, 26g total carbohydrate, 8g dietary fiber, 12g sugars, 5g protein

Jasmine Green Tea and Pear-Dressed Mesclun

Makes 4 servings: 2½ cups each

Fall and winter provide their own seasonal ingredients, like the petite and blissfully sweet and spicy Seckel pear. It creates idyllic salads and salad dressings that are to be enjoyed during cooler days. And pecans are an ideal accompaniment.

8 cups packed mesclun or mixed salad greens

1 cup red or black seedless grapes, quartered lengthwise

⅓ cup very thinly sliced red onion

½ cup Seckel Pear and Green Tea Vinaigrette (page 147) or other fruit vinaigrette

⅛ teaspoon sea salt, or to taste

6 tablespoons Cajun Spiced Pecans (page 43) or 24 dry-roasted pecan halves

1. Toss together the mesclun, grapes, onion, half the vinaigrette, and the salt in a large bowl just before serving.

2. Arrange the salad on a platter or four plates. Top with the pecans and serve with the remaining vinaigrette on the side.

Per serving: 160 calories, 12g total fat, 1g saturated fat, 0g trans fat, 0mg cholesterol, 190mg sodium, 14g total carbohydrate, 3g dietary fiber, 9g sugars, 2g protein

Pear and Walnut Field Green Salad Ⓢ Ⓕ

Makes 4 servings: about 2¼ cups each

My all-time favorite way to enjoy pears, especially delectable Bosc pears, is tossed into salads. You'll be pleased by the wintry sweet-tart appeal—plus the generous, spiced-up accent of crunchy, heart-friendly walnuts.

8 cups packed field greens or baby arugula

2 Bosc pears, cored, halved, and thinly sliced

½ cup Dijon Balsamic Vinaigrette (page 144) or other vinaigrette

⅓ cup very thinly sliced red onion

½ cup Chinese Five-Spice Walnuts (page 43) or toasted walnuts

1. Toss together the greens, pears, and half the vinaigrette in a large bowl just before serving.

2. Arrange the salad on a platter or four plates. Top with the onion and walnuts, and serve with the remaining vinaigrette on the side.

Per serving: 260 calories, 19g total fat, 2g saturated fat, 0g trans fat, 0mg cholesterol, 230mg sodium, 22g total carbohydrate, 5g dietary fiber, 13g sugars, 4g protein

Soulful Taco Salad Ⓕ

Makes 4 servings: about 3 cups each

I think soul food when I think of collard greens. Here I took the liberty of keeping the greens raw and adding some heat. The result: a fresh, spicy, and satisfying salad. It's decidedly different with a Southwestern flair, but it's still got soul.

4 cups very thinly sliced collard green leaves

½ cup Jalapeño Honey Vinaigrette (page 144)

¼ teaspoon sea salt, or to taste

4 cups chopped romaine lettuce

1 (15-ounce) can black beans, black-eyed peas, or hominy (posole), drained

12 cherry tomatoes, quartered

1 medium green bell pepper, diced

½ cup shredded or finely diced Monterey Jack cheese

2 tablespoons chopped fresh cilantro

24 blue corn tortilla chips or 16 Hint-of-Lime Tortilla Chips (page 41)

1. Toss together the collard greens with ¼ cup of the vinaigrette and the salt in a large bowl. Let stand for up to 1 hour to allow leaves to slightly wilt.

2. Just before serving, add the lettuce, beans, tomatoes, bell pepper, cheese, cilantro, the remaining ¼ cup vinaigrette, and half of the chips and toss with the collard greens.

3. Arrange the salad on a platter or four plates. Top with the remaining chips, and serve.

Per serving: 290 calories, 14g total fat, 3.5g saturated fat, 0g trans fat, 15mg cholesterol, 440mg sodium, 32g total carbohydrate, 8g dietary fiber, 8g sugars, 11g protein

Sunnyside-Up Salad Ⓕ

Makes 4 servings: 1½ cups salad and 1 egg each

Here's a quirky salad that's a little breakfast inspired, a little cocktail influenced, and very satisfying. Instead of nibbling on toast with eggs, you'll be dicing the toast as salad croutons and serving the egg as the main highlight atop the salad. Rather than sipping a Bloody Mary, you'll be dressing the salad with its essence. It all comes together on the plate in nutrient-rich, uniquely delicious style.

5 cups packed fresh baby spinach

4 slices whole-grain bread, toasted, and diced

2 ounces part-skim mozzarella cheese, diced

¾ cup Bloody Mary Vinaigrette (page 145)

4 sunnyside-up fried (in nonstick skillet lightly spritzed with cooking spray) or poached large eggs

8 sun-dried tomato halves (not oil-packed), rehydrated and thinly sliced

¼ teaspoon smoked sea salt, or to taste

¼ teaspoon freshly cracked black pepper, or to taste

1. Toss together the spinach, bread, cheese, and half of the vinaigrette in a large bowl just before serving.

2. Arrange the salad on a platter or four plates. Top with the eggs and sun-dried tomatoes. Sprinkle with the salt and pepper, and serve with the remaining vinaigrette on the side.

Per serving: 260 calories, 12g total fat, 3.5g saturated fat, 0g trans fat, 195mg cholesterol, 640mg sodium, 22g total carbohydrate, 5g dietary fiber, 6g sugars, 15g protein

12-Layer Salad

Makes 8 servings: 2 cups each

Chances are you've been treated to or made your own version of the classic seven-layer salad at a family gathering or friendly celebration. Unfortunately, the traditional version isn't a treat for anyone's health, as it's commonly layered with an entire pound of bacon, a heaping cup of mayo, and way too much cheese. So I recreated it to be friendlier for all, focusing on right-size portions of high-flavored ingredients. Move over seven-layer salad, there's a new salad in town—an amped-up twelve-layer one!

5 cups torn or chopped escarole or romaine lettuce

4 plum tomatoes, pulp removed and diced

1½ cups finely chopped broccoli florets, raw or blanched and chilled

½ cup shredded carrot

1½ cups packed baby arugula or chopped arugula

4 large hard-cooked eggs, sliced (page 377)

1 cup chilled cooked or thawed frozen green peas

1 cup thinly sliced cremini (baby bella) or white button mushrooms

½ cup very thinly sliced sweet onion

1 cup shredded aged Cheddar cheese

1 cup Creamy Peppercorn Dressing (page 150) or other ranch-style dressing

2 scallions, green and white parts, thinly sliced

6 slices applewood-smoked uncured bacon, cooked until crisp and finely chopped, or 6 tablespoons sun-dried tomato bits

1. One at a time, layer the escarole, tomatoes, broccoli, carrot, arugula, eggs, peas, mushrooms, onion, and cheese in a large (16-cup) trifle bowl.

2. Drizzle all the dressing evenly on top to cover the cheese. Chill overnight, up to 24 hours. Sprinkle with the scallions and bacon and serve.

Per serving: 200 calories, 12g total fat, 5g saturated fat, 0g trans fat, 110mg cholesterol, 380mg sodium, 13g total carbohydrate, 4g dietary fiber, 4g sugars, 12g protein

Layered Waldorf Salad

Makes 6 servings: about 2½ cups each

Apples, celery, and mayonnaise were the only ingredients found in the original Waldorf salad, but I've updated this classic by replacing the mayo dressing with a lighter, silkier lemony one. I added flavor interest and boosted health-promoting nutrients with a mélange of fruits, including dried tart cherries and fresh grapes. And for more interest, you can include three different varieties of apples. It's now a better tasting, better-for-you classic.

1 head Boston lettuce, cored, leaves separated, and large leaves torn

3 medium apples, such as Gala, Granny Smith, and/or Fuji, cored, halved lengthwise, and thinly sliced crosswise

1 cup Silky Lemon Dressing (page 149)

1 cup seedless green or red grapes, halved lengthwise

2 medium celery stalks with leaves, very thinly sliced on the diagonal

½ cup dried tart cherries or black seedless raisins

1 cup Chinese Five-Spice Walnuts (page 43) or chopped toasted walnuts

1. Arrange the lettuce on a platter or individual plates.

2. Toss together all the apples and half of the dressing in a medium bowl.

3. Arrange the apples on top of the lettuce. Top with the grapes, celery, dried cherries, and walnuts, and serve with the remaining dressing on the side.

Per serving: 290 calories, 17g total fat, 2g saturated fat, 0g trans fat, 0mg cholesterol, 210mg sodium, 33g total carbohydrate, 7g dietary fiber, 22g sugars, 5g protein

Minty Strawberry Arugula Salad Ⓕ

Makes 4 servings: about 2¾ cups each

This elegant salad tastes dreamy with the complementary tastes of sweet and salty; the bright flavors of fruits and nuts; and the contrasting textures of buttery and crunchy.

8 cups packed baby arugula or coarsely chopped arugula
1½ cups fresh wild strawberries or sliced large strawberries
⅓ cup diced hearts of palm
¼ cup finely diced red onion
1 tablespoon chopped fresh mint, or to taste
¾ cup Minty Balsamic Vinaigrette (page 145) or other vinaigrette
1 Hass avocado, pitted, peeled, and diced
⅛ teaspoon sea salt, or to taste
2 tablespoons sliced natural almonds, toasted
⅛ teaspoon freshly ground black pepper, or to taste

1. Toss together the arugula, strawberries, hearts of palm, onion, mint, and half of the vinaigrette just before serving. Gently toss in the avocado and salt.

2. Arrange the salad on a platter or four plates. Sprinkle with the almonds and pepper, and serve with the remaining vinaigrette on the side.

Per serving: 180 calories, 14g total fat, 2g saturated fat, 0g trans fat, 0mg cholesterol, 220mg sodium, 13g total carbohydrate, 5g dietary fiber, 5g sugars, 4g protein

Sunflower Raspberry Watercress Salad

Makes 4 servings: 2 cups each

Gorgeous, simply gorgeous! If your plate were a canvas, this would be art. It's as palate pleasing as it is eye-catching. More importantly, it's health pleasing; it's an excellent source of vitamins C, E, and K . . . all for only 130 calories.

8 cups packed watercress, coarse stems removed
¾ cup diced hearts of palm
⅓ cup finely diced red onion
2 tablespoons thinly sliced fresh basil leaves
½ cup Fresh Raspberry Vinaigrette (page 147)
¼ cup salted dry-roasted sunflower seeds
¼ teaspoon freshly ground black pepper, or to taste

1. Gently toss together the watercress, hearts of palm, onion, basil, and half of the vinaigrette just before serving.

2. Arrange the salad on a platter or four plates. Sprinkle with the remaining vinaigrette, the sunflower seeds, and pepper. Adjust seasoning and serve.

Per serving: 130 calories, 10g total fat, 1g saturated fat, 0g trans fat, 0mg cholesterol, 200mg sodium, 8g total carbohydrate, 3g dietary fiber, 2g sugars, 4g protein

Spicy Citrus Endive Salad Ⓢ Ⓕ

Makes 4 servings: 1¼ cups each

The intriguing textures and distinctive bitter notes from Belgian endive shine here in a sensational citrus and pomegranate-laced salad. To help balance bitterness, drizzle on a teaspoon of honey if you wish—it only adds about 20 calories. Otherwise, simply savor the high-flavored nuances (and the high-fiber goodness!) of this calorie-friendly salad.

3 (5-ounce) Belgian endive, cored and thinly sliced
1 large pink grapefruit, segmented
¼ cup finely diced red onion
2 tablespoons thinly sliced fresh mint leaves

½ cup Jalapeño Honey Vinaigrette (page 144) or fruit vinaigrette of choice

1 Hass avocado, pitted, peeled, and diced

⅛ teaspoon sea salt, or to taste

3 tablespoons pomegranate seeds (arils)

1. Toss together the endive, grapefruit, onion, mint, and half of the vinaigrette just before serving. Gently toss in the avocado and salt.

2. Arrange the salad on a platter or four plates. Sprinkle with the pomegranate seeds, and serve with the remaining vinaigrette on the side.

Per serving: 180 calories, 12g total fat, 1g saturated fat, 0g trans fat, 0mg cholesterol, 140mg sodium, 19g total carbohydrate, 7g dietary fiber, 10g sugars, 2g protein

Salad for Every Season

Makes 4 servings: 3 cups each

I developed this recipe so it can be enjoyed any time of year with any seasonal veggie and nut, such as roasted eggplant and pistachios. The generous sprinkling of tangy goat cheese makes this salad crave-worthy since it's an ideal culinary pairing for an array of nuts, roasted or grilled veggies, and the fresh basil of the vinaigrette.

8 cups chopped salad greens of choice

2 cups bite-size chilled roasted or grilled seasonal vegetables of choice

½ cup Creamy Basil Vinaigrette (page 145) or other vinaigrette

¼ teaspoon sea salt, or to taste

½ cup crumbled soft goat cheese or drained firm tofu

3 tablespoons toasted nuts or seeds of choice

¼ teaspoon freshly ground black pepper, or to taste

1. Gently toss together the salad greens, vegetables, half of the vinaigrette, and salt just before serving.

2. Arrange the salad on a platter or four plates. Sprinkle with the cheese, nuts, and pepper, and serve with the remaining vinaigrette on the side.

Per serving: 160 calories, 11g total fat, 3g saturated fat, 0g trans fat, 5mg cholesterol, 260mg sodium, 10g total carbohydrate, 4g dietary fiber, 3g sugars, 6g protein

Fattoush Ⓕ

Makes 4 servings: 3½ cups each

Many cultures have a salad or soup dish that's created specifically for a delicious use of their day-old bread. That's how this Middle Eastern salad with pita "croutons" came to be. The generous amount of herbs makes this a fresh and fragrant standout. And if you use the sumac (a pleasantly sour-tart spice), it'll be an extra tangy taste-bud temptress.

6 ounces romaine lettuce, torn

2 medium vine-ripened tomatoes, chopped

1 large English cucumber, unpeeled and chopped

1 small or ½ large white onion, diced

½ packed cup fresh flat-leaf parsley leaves

½ packed cup fresh mint leaves

2 (8-inch) whole-wheat pitas, split, toasted, and broken into bite-size pieces

½ cup Syrian Vinaigrette (page 146) or other lemon vinaigrette

⅛ teaspoon sea salt, or to taste

⅛ teaspoon freshly ground black pepper, or to taste

⅛ teaspoon ground sumac, or to taste (optional)

1. Toss together the lettuce, tomatoes, cucumber, onion, parsley, mint, and pita in a large bowl.

2. Drizzle the vinaigrette over the salad mixture. Add the salt, pepper, and sumac (if using), and toss well. Adjust seasoning and serve.

Per serving: 210 calories, 11g total fat, 1.5g saturated fat, 0g trans fat, 0mg cholesterol, 360mg sodium, 27g total carbohydrate, 6g dietary fiber, 5g sugars, 5g protein

Potato Salads

New American Potato Salad

Makes 6 servings: 1 cup each

Potato salad can be decadent without being rich in calories. Greek yogurt helps to lighten it up naturally and mustard gives it a pungent punch. In this recipe, toss the potatoes with the dressing while warm; the potatoes will absorb flavor more quickly. That makes each bite more luscious.

2 pounds baby creamer potatoes, unpeeled, scrubbed, and halved

1 teaspoon sea salt, or to taste

¼ cup mayonnaise

3 tablespoons stone-ground mustard

2 tablespoons fat-free or low-fat plain Greek yogurt

1 tablespoon apple cider vinegar

3 scallions, green and white parts, thinly sliced

1 tablespoon chopped fresh tarragon
   or 1½ teaspoons dried tarragon

2 teaspoons chopped fresh dill or 1 teaspoon dried dill

¼ teaspoon ground cayenne or Cajun seasoning, or to taste

½ cup finely diced fennel bulb or thinly sliced celery

1. Add the potatoes to a large saucepan or stockpot and cover with cold water. Add ¾ teaspoon of the salt. Bring to a boil over high heat. Cover and reduce heat to medium-low. Cook until the potatoes are just tender, about 10 minutes.

2. Meanwhile, stir together the mayonnaise, mustard, yogurt, vinegar, scallions, tarragon, dill, cayenne, and the remaining ¼ teaspoon salt in a large serving bowl.

3. Drain the potatoes. Add the warm potatoes along with the fennel to the mayonnaise mixture and stir gently to combine. Adjust seasoning, chill, and serve at room temperature or slightly chilled.

Per serving: 180 calories, 8g total fat, 1g saturated fat, 0g trans fat, 5mg cholesterol, 420mg sodium, 26g total carbohydrate, 3g dietary fiber, 2g sugars, 4g protein

Dijon Fingerling Potato Salad

Makes 6 servings: 1 cup each

I used one of my quirky culinary tips to develop this dill- and rosemary-accented fingerling recipe. It's my "4-3-2-1 rule" for a perky dressing that's perfect for 2 pounds of potatoes: 4 tablespoons (¼ cup) mayo, 3 tablespoons mustard, 2 tablespoons Greek yogurt, and 1 tablespoon vinegar.

2 pounds small banana fingerling potatoes, unpeeled and scrubbed

¾ teaspoon sea salt, or to taste

¼ cup mayonnaise

3 tablespoons Dijon mustard

2 tablespoons fat-free or low-fat plain Greek yogurt

1 tablespoon white wine vinegar

3 scallions, green and white parts, thinly sliced

1 tablespoon chopped fresh dill or 1½ teaspoons dried dill

1 teaspoon finely chopped fresh rosemary
   or ½ teaspoon dried crushed rosemary

¼ teaspoon ground cayenne, or to taste

1 large celery stalk, thinly sliced,
   or ⅓ cup finely diced jicama

1. Add the potatoes to a large saucepan or stockpot and cover with cold water. Add ½ teaspoon of the salt. Bring to a boil over high heat. Cover and reduce heat to medium-low. Cook until the potatoes are just tender, about 12 minutes.

2. Meanwhile, stir together the mayonnaise, mustard, yogurt, vinegar, scallions, dill, rosemary, cayenne, and the remaining ¼ teaspoon salt in a large serving bowl.

3. Drain the potatoes. Let cool slightly at room temperature, about 15 minutes. Slice into ¼-inch rounds.

4. Add the warm potato slices along with the celery to the mayonnaise mixture and stir gently to combine. Adjust seasoning, chill, and serve at room temperature or slightly chilled.

Per serving: 190 calories, 8g total fat, 1g saturated fat, 0g trans fat, 5mg cholesterol, 450mg sodium, 27g total carbohydrate, 3g dietary fiber, 2g sugars, 4g protein

Baked Potato Salad Rémoulade

Makes 2 servings: ¾ rounded cup each

Have leftover baked potatoes or roasted root veggies? Have a leftover sauce or salad dressing? Combine 'em and see what you get. This simple, yet standout potato salad is the epitome of fast and fabulous kitchen creativity.

1 large baked russet potato, chilled
2 tablespoons Fresh Rémoulade Sauce (page 129), or to taste
⅛ teaspoon sea salt, or to taste
⅛ teaspoon freshly ground black pepper, or to taste

Cut the potato into large bite-size cubes. Add to a medium bowl with the rémoulade sauce, salt, and pepper and gently stir until very lightly coated with the sauce. Adjust seasoning. Serve at room temperature or slightly chilled.

Per serving: 180 calories, 3.5g total fat, 0.5g saturated fat, 0g trans fat, 5mg cholesterol, 240mg sodium, 33g total carbohydrate, 4g dietary fiber, 2g sugars, 4g protein

Patriotic Potato Salad

Makes 6 servings: 1 rounded cup each

Three different colors of potatoes—red, white, and blue—combine in a perfect potato salad that blends creaminess with some crunch and spice for an Independence Day or any-other-day picnic.

12 ounces small red creamer potatoes, unpeeled, scrubbed, and halved
12 ounces small white creamer potatoes, unpeeled, scrubbed, and halved
12 ounces small blue creamer potatoes, unpeeled, scrubbed, and halved
1 teaspoon sea salt, or to taste
¼ cup mayonnaise
2 tablespoons Dijon mustard
2 tablespoons fat-free or low-fat plain Greek yogurt
Juice of ½ lemon (1½ tablespoons)
½ teaspoon freshly ground black pepper, or to taste
¼ cup finely diced red onion
¼ cup finely diced sweet onion
1 small jalapeño pepper with some seeds, minced
2 tablespoons minced fresh chives (optional)

1. Add all the potatoes to a large saucepan or stockpot and cover with cold water. Add ¾ teaspoon of the salt. Bring to a boil over high heat. Cover and reduce heat to medium-low. Cook until the potatoes are just tender, about 10 minutes.

2. Meanwhile, stir together the mayonnaise, mustard, yogurt, lemon juice, black pepper, and the remaining ¼ teaspoon salt in a large serving bowl.

3. Drain the potatoes. Add the warm potatoes along with the red and sweet onions, and jalapeño to the mayonnaise mixture and stir gently to combine. Adjust seasoning.

4. Chill, sprinkle with the chives (if using), and serve at room temperature or slightly chilled.

Per serving: 200 calories, 8g total fat, 1g saturated fat, 0g trans fat, 5mg cholesterol, 440mg sodium, 30g total carbohydrate, 3g dietary fiber, 3g sugars, 4g protein

Berlin Blue Potato Salad

Makes 6 servings: 1 cup each

Yes, you can have your bacon and eat it, too. There's less than one slice per serving in this salad. But when it's sprinkled on the top, as in this updated German potato salad, it'll seem extra indulgent.

2 pounds medium blue or red potatoes, unpeeled, scrubbed, and cut in half lengthwise, and then cut into ¼-inch slices crosswise

1 teaspoon sea salt, or to taste

4 slices uncooked applewood-smoked uncured bacon, chopped

½ cup finely diced red onion

⅓ cup apple cider vinegar

2 tablespoons honey mustard

2 tablespoons chopped fresh dill

½ teaspoon ground black pepper, or to taste

1. Add the potatoes to a large saucepan or stockpot and cover with cold water. Add ¾ teaspoon of the salt. Bring to a boil over high heat. Cover and reduce heat to medium-low. Cook until the potatoes are nearly tender, about 7 minutes. Remove from heat, drain, and cover to retain heat.

2. Meanwhile, sauté the bacon in a large skillet over medium heat until fully browned, about 8 to 9 minutes. Using a slotted spoon, transfer the bacon to paper towels to drain. Add the onion to remaining bacon drippings in the skillet and sauté until just softened, about 2 minutes. Whisk in the vinegar and mustard and simmer until the mixture is slightly reduced, about 3 minutes. Remove from heat.

3. Add the potatoes, dill, pepper, and the remaining ¼ teaspoon salt to the skillet and gently toss to coat. Adjust seasoning.

4. Transfer the potato salad to a platter, sprinkle with the bacon pieces, and serve warm.

Per serving: 190 calories, 7g total fat, 2.5g saturated fat, 0g trans fat, 10mg cholesterol, 430mg sodium, 28g total carbohydrate, 3g dietary fiber, 2g sugars, 5g protein

Yukon Gold Potato Salad Deconstructed

Makes 5 servings: about 2 cups each

Yukon Gold potatoes actually give a richer essence to a potato salad due to their golden hue and buttery creaminess. This luscious recipe is an upscale version of a classic potato salad, deconstructed so you can appreciate every intriguing ingredient.

2 pounds large Yukon Gold potatoes, unpeeled, scrubbed, and cut into ¼-inch slices

1¼ teaspoons sea salt, or to taste

¼ cup mayonnaise

3 tablespoons fat-free or low-fat plain yogurt (not Greek yogurt)

2 tablespoons Dijon mustard

Juice of ½ lemon (1½ tablespoons)

1 garlic clove, minced

¼ teaspoon ground cayenne, or to taste

3 scallions, green and white parts, thinly sliced on the diagonal

6 small red radishes, thinly sliced

1 large celery stalk, thinly sliced on the diagonal

1 tablespoon chopped fresh dill

1 tablespoon chopped fresh tarragon

1. Add the potatoes to a large saucepan or stockpot and cover with cold water. Add ¾ teaspoon of the salt. Bring to a boil over high heat. Cover and reduce heat to medium-low. Cook until the potatoes are just tender, about 7 minutes. Drain and chill the potatoes. Add the remaining ½ teaspoon salt.

2. Meanwhile, stir together the mayonnaise, yogurt, mustard, lemon juice, garlic, and cayenne in a small bowl or liquid measuring cup. Adjust seasoning.

3. Arrange on individual plates in three alternating layers the potatoes, mayonnaise mixture (drizzle it), scallions, radishes, celery, dill, and tarragon, and serve at room temperature or slightly chilled.

Per serving: 230 calories, 9g total fat, 1.5g saturated fat, 0g trans fat, 5mg cholesterol, 540mg sodium, 33g total carbohydrate, 4g dietary fiber, 3g sugars, 4g protein

Dilly Avocado Potato Salad Ⓕ

Makes 6 servings: 1 cup each

If you prefer a mayo-free salad, this will be your pick. The marriage of avocado and potato is blissful. You'll get a kick out of this lighter but highly flavorful mix.

2 pounds baby red creamer potatoes, unpeeled, scrubbed, and quartered

1 teaspoon sea salt, or to taste

1 Hass avocado, pitted, peeled, and diced

Juice of 1 small lemon (2 tablespoons)

2 tablespoons fat-free or low-fat plain Greek yogurt

2 scallions, green and white parts, thinly sliced

1 small hot Jamaican or jalapeño pepper with or without seeds, minced

1 garlic clove, minced

1 tablespoon chopped fresh dill or 1½ teaspoons dried dill

2 teaspoons chopped fresh cilantro or 1 teaspoon dried cilantro

⅓ cup finely diced jicama

1. Add the potatoes to a large saucepan or stockpot and cover with cold water. Add ¾ teaspoon of the salt. Bring to a boil over high heat. Cover and reduce heat to medium-low. Cook until the potatoes are just tender, about 10 minutes. Drain the potatoes and chill.

2. Mash together with a fork the avocado with the lemon juice until nearly smooth in a large bowl. Add the yogurt, scallions, hot pepper, garlic, dill, cilantro, and the remaining ¼ teaspoon salt and stir to combine.

3. Add the chilled potatoes along with the jicama to the avocado mixture and stir gently to combine. Adjust seasoning, and serve at room temperature or slightly chilled.

Per serving: 150 calories, 3.5g total fat, 0.5g saturated fat, 0g trans fat, 0mg cholesterol, 260mg sodium, 28g total carbohydrate, 5g dietary fiber, 2g sugars, 4g protein

Hash Brown Potato Salad

Makes 3 servings: ¾ cup each

This rich-tasting recipe came about when I got carried away making hash browns and had extras in my fridge calling out for culinary attention. It's an appetizing preparation of leftovers. Feel free to be creative with leftovers: You may just be thrilled by the results.

1 tablespoon mayonnaise

1 tablespoon fat-free or low-fat plain Greek yogurt

1½ teaspoons stone-ground mustard

1½ teaspoons apple cider vinegar

1 scallion, green and white part, minced

1 tablespoon finely chopped fresh flat-leaf parsley

⅛ teaspoon sea salt, or to taste

2 cups Fresh Herb Hash Browns (page 33) or other hash browns, chilled

¼ cup finely diced red bell pepper

1. Stir together the mayonnaise, yogurt, mustard, vinegar, scallion, parsley, and salt in a large serving bowl.

2. Chop the hash browns into bite-size pieces, if necessary. Add the hash browns and bell pepper to the mayonnaise mixture and stir until just combined.

3. Adjust seasoning, and serve at room temperature or slightly chilled.

Per serving: 170 calories, 8g total fat, 1.5g saturated fat, 0g trans fat, 5mg cholesterol, 470mg sodium, 24g total carbohydrate, 3g dietary fiber, 3g sugars, 4g protein

Roasted Potato and Red Pepper Salad

Makes 5 servings: 1 cup each

Roasting potatoes presents them with a new outlook—and deeper taste. Dressing them lightly like a leafy salad will let all the roasted goodness play the starring role. Any leftovers? Simply freshen up the chilled potato salad by tossing with a tad more dressing before serving.

2 pounds baby purple or other baby creamer potatoes, unpeeled, scrubbed, and quartered

1 large red bell pepper, finely diced

1 tablespoon extra-virgin olive or grapeseed oil

1 garlic clove, minced

1 teaspoon finely chopped fresh rosemary or ½ teaspoon dried rosemary

½ teaspoon sea salt, or to taste

3 scallions, green and white parts, thinly sliced

¼ cup Spicy Roasted Pepper Dressing (page 149) or other salad dressing

1. Preheat the oven to 400°F. Add the potatoes and bell pepper to a parchment paper–lined large baking pan. Sprinkle with the oil, garlic, rosemary, and ¼ teaspoon of the salt. Roast until the potatoes are tender and bell pepper is caramelized, about 40 minutes, stirring halfway through the roasting process. Remove from oven and let cool slightly.

2. Add the roasted potatoes and bell pepper along with the scallions to a large bowl and stir gently to combine. Sprinkle with the dressing and the remaining ¼ teaspoon salt and gently stir until lightly coated. Adjust seasoning, and serve at room temperature or slightly chilled.

Per serving: 180 calories, 4g total fat, 0.5g saturated fat, 0g trans fat, 0mg cholesterol, 270mg sodium, 32g total carbohydrate, 4g dietary fiber, 4g sugars, 4g protein

Sweet Pea and Prosciutto Potato Salad

Makes 7 servings: 1 cup each

The pairing of prosciutto and peas adds a deliciously Italian touch to dishes. By adding potatoes, you'll get a scrumptious, summery potato salad with a fresh European twist. *Buono!*

2 pounds large russet potatoes, unpeeled, scrubbed, and cut into ½-inch cubes

1 teaspoon sea salt, or to taste

1 cup fresh or thawed frozen sweet peas

3 tablespoons mayonnaise

2 tablespoons fat-free or low-fat plain Greek yogurt

2 tablespoon stone-ground mustard

Juice of ½ small lemon (1 tablespoon)

3 scallions, green and white parts, thinly sliced

¼ teaspoon freshly ground black pepper, or to taste

2 ounces thinly sliced prosciutto or country ham, finely chopped

1 tablespoon finely chopped fresh mint or basil

2 teaspoons chopped fresh dill

1. Add the potatoes to a large saucepan or stockpot and cover with cold water. Add ¾ teaspoon of the salt. Bring to a boil over high heat. Cover and reduce heat to medium-low. Cook until the potatoes are nearly tender, about 5 minutes. Add the peas, cover, and continue to cook for 1½ minutes.

2. Meanwhile, stir together the mayonnaise, yogurt, mustard, lemon juice, scallions, pepper, and the remaining ¼ teaspoon salt in a large serving bowl.

3. Drain the potatoes and peas. Add the warm potatoes and peas to the mayonnaise mixture and stir gently to combine. Chill.

4. Stir in the prosciutto, mint, and dill. Adjust seasoning, and serve at room temperature or slightly chilled.

Per serving: 180 calories, 6g total fat, 1g saturated fat, 0g trans fat, 10mg cholesterol, 530mg sodium, 27g total carbohydrate, 3g dietary fiber, 2g sugars, 7g protein

Jalapeño Corn and Potato Salad

Makes 6 servings: 1 cup each

When summer is in full swing with abundant fields of sweet corn . . . there are also barbecues ready to grill it. Since the prep of this peppery corn and potato salad takes place on a grill, it's perfect backyard party fare. You can also turn this party-worthy recipe into a vegetarian entrée by adding dark red kidney beans. Either way, it's unforgettable.

1½ pounds large Idaho potatoes, unpeeled, scrubbed, and cut crosswise into ½-inch slices

2 medium ears yellow corn, husks removed

1 jalapeño pepper with seeds

1 tablespoon peanut or grapeseed oil

¾ teaspoon sea salt, or to taste

3 tablespoons mayonnaise

2 tablespoons stone-ground mustard

2 tablespoons fat-free or low-fat plain Greek yogurt

1 tablespoon white wine vinegar

Juice of ½ lime (1 tablespoon)

3 scallions, green and white parts, thinly sliced

¼ teaspoon freshly ground black pepper, or to taste

2 tablespoons chopped fresh flat-leaf parsley

1 tablespoon chopped fresh cilantro

1. Prepare an outdoor or indoor grill. Lightly rub or brush the potatoes, corn, and jalapeño with the oil. Grill over medium-high heat until moderately charred and cooked through, turning only as needed, about 12 minutes over medium-high or 20 minutes over medium heat. Remove from heat and add ½ teaspoon of the salt. Set aside to slightly cool.

2. Stir together the mayonnaise, mustard, yogurt, vinegar, lime juice, scallions, black pepper, and the remaining ¼ teaspoon salt in a medium-large serving bowl.

3. When cool enough to handle, dice the potatoes, mince the jalapeño, and cut the kernels off the corncobs. Add the potatoes, jalapeño, and corn kernels to the mayonnaise mixture and stir gently to combine. Chill.

4. Stir in the parsley and cilantro, adjust seasoning, and serve at room temperature or slightly chilled.

Per serving: 200 calories, 8g total fat, 1.5g saturated fat, 0g trans fat, 5mg cholesterol, 420mg sodium, 28g total carbohydrate, 2g dietary fiber, 3g sugars, 4g protein

Grilled Sweet Potato Salad

Makes 6 servings: 1 cup each

Sweet potatoes are simply sensational when grilled and served at an outdoor gathering. They provide a vibrant orange color, unique sweetness, and flavor depth when transformed into a potato salad. Here, their coupling with mildly spiced poblano creates a perfectly balanced culinary match. This salad is then dressed with fresh herbal flair for a fragrant finish.

2 pounds large sweet potatoes, unpeeled, scrubbed, and cut into ½-inch slices

2 large (½-inch-thick) slices peeled red onion

1 large or 2 small fresh poblano peppers

1 tablespoon peanut or grapeseed oil

½ teaspoon sea salt, or to taste

½ cup Fresh Herb and Shallot Vinaigrette (page 144) or other vinaigrette

3 tablespoons minced fresh chives

1 tablespoon finely chopped fresh cilantro

1. Prepare an outdoor or indoor grill. Lightly rub or brush the potatoes, onion, and poblano with the oil. Grill over medium-high heat (in batches, if necessary) until lightly charred and cooked through, turning only as needed, about 15 total minutes. Remove from heat and add the salt. Set aside to slightly cool.

2. When cool enough to handle, dice the potatoes, onion, and poblano, removing the pepper stem and seeds. Add to a large bowl along with the vinaigrette, chives, and cilantro and stir gently to combine.

3. Adjust seasoning, chill, and serve at room temperature or slightly chilled.

Per serving: 170 calories, 8g total fat, 1.5g saturated fat, 0g trans fat, 0mg cholesterol, 280mg sodium, 23g total carbohydrate, 4g dietary fiber, 8g sugars, 2g protein

Tomato Salads

Tomatoes with Avocado Ranch Dressing

Makes 4 servings: 12 tomato wedges each

When fresh tomatoes are fully ripened, there's almost nothing that can compare. Their flavor is at its peak, not just their color and ripeness. This simple salad showcases the tomato with delicious adornments such as creamy goat cheese and a rich-tasting avocado dressing.

4 medium vine-ripened tomatoes, cut into
    12 wedges each
4 very thin slices medium red onion, halved and
    separated
⅛ teaspoon sea salt, or to taste
⅛ teaspoon freshly ground black pepper, or to taste
¼ cup Avocado Ranch Dressing (page 150)
    or other dressing
¼ cup crumbled soft goat cheese
2 tablespoons pine nuts, toasted
1 tablespoon roughly chopped fresh flat-leaf
    parsley, basil, or cilantro, or to taste

1. Arrange the tomatoes and onion on a platter or four plates. Add the salt and pepper.

2. Drizzle with the dressing. Sprinkle with the cheese, pine nuts, and parsley, and serve.

Per serving: 90 calories, 6g total fat, 2g saturated fat, 0g trans fat, 5mg cholesterol, 140mg sodium, 7g total carbohydrate, 2g dietary fiber, 4g sugars, 4g protein

Caprese Salad "Lasagna"

Makes 6 servings: about 3×4-inch portion each

When summertime gives you an abundance of yellow squash, use them like pasta. Very thinly slice the squash lengthwise so they look like long flat noodles. They're delightful in this fresh layered "lasagna" salad. No baking necessary.

2 large yellow summer squash, very thinly sliced
    lengthwise
2¼ teaspoons sea salt, or to taste
2 large vine-ripened tomatoes, very thinly sliced
2 tablespoons aged balsamic vinegar
1 large garlic clove, minced
1 cup fresh basil leaves
14 ounces lightly salted fresh mozzarella, thinly sliced
2 tablespoons extra-virgin olive oil
2 tablespoons pine nuts, toasted and minced
¼ teaspoon freshly ground black pepper, or to taste

1. Arrange the squash in layers in a large baking pan, sprinkling the layers with 2 teaspoons of the salt. Let sit at room temperature for about 1 hour to soften and flavor the squash. Place the squash into a colander, gently rinse, and drain.

2. Meanwhile, arrange the tomatoes in layers on another large baking pan, sprinkling the layers with the balsamic vinegar, the remaining ¼ teaspoon salt, and the garlic. Let sit at room temperature for about 30 minutes to marinate. Separately from the squash, place the tomatoes into a colander and drain. (Do not rinse.)

3. Onto a large platter, arrange in layers, in about a 6×12-inch rectangle, one-third each of the marinated squash, marinated tomatoes, basil leaves, and cheese. Repeat twice.

4. Drizzle the lasagna with the oil. Sprinkle with the pine nuts and pepper. Cut with a bread knife into 6 portions. Serve at room temperature.

Per serving: 280 calories, 22g total fat, 10g saturated fat, 0g trans fat, 55mg cholesterol, 530mg sodium, 8g total carbohydrate, 2g dietary fiber, 5g sugars, 13g protein

Heirloom Tomato Salad

Makes 4 servings: ¼ recipe each

Heirloom tomatoes are produced from older, open-pollinated varieties whose seeds have been passed down through generations. Many people prize heirlooms for their unique flavors and colors. Here, heirloom tomatoes shine in all of their glory when dressed with a lively vinaigrette and paired with sweet onion and dynamic touches of blue cheese and pistachios.

4 large heirloom tomatoes of various colors, thinly sliced

4 extra-thin slices large sweet onion, separated into rings

2 tablespoons extra-virgin olive oil

2 tablespoons aged balsamic vinegar

2 teaspoons no-sugar-added apple butter

1 garlic clove, minced

¼ teaspoon sea salt, or to taste

⅛ teaspoon freshly ground black pepper, or to taste

3 tablespoons crumbled Gorgonzola or other blue cheese

2 tablespoons coarsely chopped unsalted dry-roasted pistachios

1 tablespoon minced fresh chives

1. On individual plates, arrange the tomatoes and onions.

2. Whisk together the oil, vinegar, apple butter, garlic, salt, and pepper in a small bowl. Drizzle over the tomato salad.

3. Sprinkle the salad with the cheese, pistachios, and chives, and serve.

Per serving: 170 calories, 11g total fat, 3g saturated fat, 0g trans fat, 10mg cholesterol, 260mg sodium, 14g total carbohydrate, 4g dietary fiber, 9g sugars, 5g protein

BLT-Stuffed Tomatoes

Makes 4 servings: 1 stuffed tomato each

The BLT is a classic sandwich that's been around for over 100 years. This breadless BLT is a fun, creative Jackie-style salad that's brand new. It's not technically a classic; but I hope it will become one through the years. No doubt the tomatoes could make those years healthful by way of their lycopene—a naturally occurring pigment that protects your cells.

4 large beefsteak tomatoes

2 cups finely chopped curly endive or escarole

⅓ cup finely diced sweet onion

½ cup Creamy Peppercorn Dressing (page 150) or other creamy salad dressing

6 slices applewood-smoked uncured bacon, cooked until crisp and chopped

⅛ teaspoon sea salt, or to taste

1 tablespoon thinly sliced fresh basil leaves

⅛ teaspoon freshly ground black pepper, or to taste

1. Cut about ½ inch off the top of each tomato. Scoop out each tomato, leaving about a ¼-inch rimmed "cup." Reserve the tomato tops and filling. Turn the "cups" upside down on a paper towel to drain.

2. Dice the tomato filling and tomato tops, and add to a medium bowl. Add the endive, onion, dressing, and half of the bacon, and gently toss.

3. Turn the tomato "cups" upright, sprinkle with the salt. Stuff each with the salad. Sprinkle with the basil, remaining bacon, and pepper, and serve.

Per serving: 150 calories, 7g total fat, 2g saturated fat, 0g trans fat, 15mg cholesterol, 450mg sodium, 15g total carbohydrate, 4g dietary fiber, 8g sugars, 8g protein

Athenian Caramelized Tomato Salad

Makes 4 servings: 1 cup each

This versatile Greek-inspired salad makes a great snack served with pita or pita chips. Stir the salad into chilled whole-wheat couscous to make a more bountiful salad. Or stuff into a pita with a veggie or turkey burger . . . it's delish!

1 pint grape tomatoes

1½ teaspoons canola or grapeseed oil

Juice of ½ lemon (1½ tablespoons)

1½ tablespoons extra-virgin olive oil

1 large garlic clove, minced

½ teaspoon sea salt, or to taste

¼ teaspoon ground cumin, or to taste

¼ teaspoon freshly ground black pepper, or to taste

½ large English cucumber, unpeeled, halved or quartered lengthwise and thinly sliced crosswise

⅔ cup drained canned chickpeas (garbanzo beans)

10 small pitted Kalamata or other brine-cured black olives, thinly sliced

1 tablespoon finely chopped fresh mint or ½ tablespoon finely chopped fresh oregano

1. Toss the tomatoes with the canola oil in a medium bowl. Add to a large nonstick skillet over medium-high heat and sauté until just caramelized, about 3½ minutes. Transfer to a bowl; set aside.

2. Whisk together the lemon juice, olive oil, garlic, salt, cumin, and pepper in a large bowl.

3. Stir the cucumber, chickpeas, olives, and mint into the dressing. Gently stir in the tomatoes.

4. Adjust seasoning, and serve at room temperature.

Per serving: 130 calories, 9g total fat, 1g saturated fat, 0g trans fat, 0mg cholesterol, 410mg sodium, 12g total carbohydrate, 3g dietary fiber, 4g sugars, 3g protein

Tomato "Carpaccio" Salad

Makes 4 servings: ¼ recipe each

Enjoy a vegetable carpaccio by very thinly slicing a vivid tomato or roasted beet, and voilà! A mandoline or serrated bread knife can help you cut the tomatoes almost paper thin. This plum tomato version is a stunning appetizer salad that'll excite the palate with its contrasts of creamy avocado, piquant capers, and pinch of "heat."

6 plum tomatoes, very thinly sliced

1 Hass avocado, halved and pitted

Juice of 1 lime (2 tablespoons)

¼ teaspoon sea salt, or to taste

1 small shallot, minced

1 tablespoon chopped fresh cilantro

1 tablespoon drained tiny capers

⅛ teaspoon dried hot pepper flakes

1. Arrange the tomato slices on a platter.

2. Using a small melon baller, scoop the avocado halves to form several balls each and scatter on top of the tomato slices.

3. Sprinkle with the lime juice, salt, shallot, cilantro, capers, and hot pepper flakes, and serve.

Per serving: 80 calories, 5g total fat, 1g saturated fat, 0g trans fat, 0mg cholesterol, 220mg sodium, 9g total carbohydrate, 4g dietary fiber, 3g sugars, 2g protein

Drunken Grilled Harvest Salad

Makes 11 servings: ½ cup each

Queso de Murcia is a semisoft goat cheese that's soaked in red wine for a couple of days—which is why "drunken" is in the title! It provides a slightly sweet and tangy accent for a mélange of grilled vegetables in this multicolored summer salad. If you can't find it, add a little wine to the dressing.

1 pint grape tomatoes

8 ounces baby zucchini or 1 medium
    lengthwise-quartered zucchini

2 medium ears corn, husks removed

1 tablespoon peanut or grapeseed oil

½ teaspoon sea salt, or to taste

1 (15-ounce) can black beans, drained

1 teaspoon finely chopped fresh oregano
    or ½ teaspoon dried oregano

6 tablespoons Zesty Lime Vinaigrette (page 146)

3 ounces queso de Murcia, feta cheese, or queso
    fresco, diced or coarsely crumbled (¾ cup)

1. Prepare an outdoor or indoor grill. Insert the tomatoes onto water-soaked bamboo or reusable skewers. Lightly brush the tomatoes, zucchini, and corn with the oil. Grill, in batches if needed, over medium-high heat until all vegetables are lightly charred and just tender, turning only as needed, about 8 to 10 total minutes. Remove from heat and add the salt. Let cool slightly. Cut the zucchini into ½-inch coins.

2. Stir together the beans, oregano, and vinaigrette in a medium bowl.

3. Cut the corn kernels off the cobs. Add the corn kernels and zucchini to the bean mixture and stir. Add the tomatoes and half the cheese and very gently stir. Adjust seasoning.

4. Arrange the salad on a platter or individual plates. Sprinkle with the remaining cheese, and serve.

Per serving: 110 calories, 6g total fat, 2g saturated fat, 0g trans fat, 5mg cholesterol, 210mg sodium, 11g total carbohydrate, 2g dietary fiber, 3g sugars, 5g protein

Slaws and Assorted Vegetable Salads

Delhi Coleslaw

Makes 10 servings: 1 cup each

The only thing that people agree on about coleslaw is that it is made with cabbage. From there, anything goes. So I use a taste of India in this recipe. You'll be smitten with the contrasting sweet-heat nuances that make this a standout among slaws. And when served alongside Creole Panko-Crusted Tilapia Sticks (page 350), you'll have a mouthwatering family-friendly meal.

¼ cup apple cider vinegar

2 tablespoons honey or agave nectar

2 teaspoons stone-ground mustard

1 teaspoon freshly grated gingerroot

¾ teaspoon sea salt, or to taste

½ teaspoon freshly ground black pepper, or to taste

¼ teaspoon hot Madras curry powder

2 tablespoons canola or flaxseed oil

1 medium head green cabbage, cored, quartered,
    and very thinly sliced

1 large sweet onion, quartered lengthwise
    and very thinly sliced crosswise

½ cup finely diced pitted Medjool dates

¼ cup shredded carrot

1. Whisk together the vinegar, honey, mustard, ginger, salt, pepper, and curry powder in a very large bowl. Whisk in the oil.

2. Add the cabbage, onion, dates, and carrot, and toss with the apple cider vinaigrette. Adjust seasoning, and serve.

Per serving: 100 calories, 3g total fat, 0g saturated fat, 0g trans fat, 0mg cholesterol, 210mg sodium, 19g total carbohydrate, 3g dietary fiber, 14g sugars, 2g protein

East Meets Napa Cabbage Salad

Makes 5 servings: 1 cup each

When I was a recent college grad living in Chicago, it seemed nearly every Saturday my friend Mary Ann and I would wind up at the restaurant Houston's, enjoying the crunchy, sweet, and savory Asian chicken salad. Those irresistible flavor memories inspired this zestful slaw—now chicken free. Enjoy!

3 tablespoons honey or agave nectar

Juice of 1 lime (2 tablespoons)

1 tablespoon no-salt-added creamy natural peanut butter

1 tablespoon naturally brewed soy sauce

2 teaspoons stone-ground mustard

2 teaspoons unrefined peanut oil

1 teaspoon freshly grated gingerroot

1 teaspoon Asian garlic-chili sauce

5 cups shredded napa cabbage (about ½ head cored napa cabbage)

1 medium red bell pepper, cut into matchstick-size strips

2 scallions, green and white parts, thinly sliced on diagonal

2 tablespoons chopped fresh cilantro

⅓ cup salted dry-roasted peanuts, coarsely chopped

1. Whisk together the honey, lime juice, peanut butter, soy sauce, mustard, oil, ginger, and garlic-chili sauce in a large bowl.

2. Add the cabbage, bell pepper, scallions, and cilantro and toss to coat. Add the peanuts, toss, and serve.

Per serving: 160 calories, 8g total fat, 1.5g saturated fat, 0g trans fat, 0mg cholesterol, 360mg sodium, 18g total carbohydrate, 3g dietary fiber, 12g sugars, 5g protein

Asian Cabbage Salad with Red Onion and Mint

Makes 2 servings: 1½ cups each

If you fancy almonds, you'll be fond of this crunchy coleslaw. It has a slight sweetness along with its minty hint of Asian flair. Double or triple this alluring recipe if you're a party of three or more.

Juice of 1 lime (2 tablespoons)

2 teaspoons canola or peanut oil

2 teaspoons honey or agave nectar

1 teaspoon teriyaki sauce

3 cups packed shredded green cabbage

⅓ cup very thinly sliced red onion

3 tablespoons roughly chopped fresh mint

⅛ teaspoon freshly ground black pepper, or to taste

1 tablespoon sliced natural almonds, toasted, or chopped dry-roasted cashews

1. Whisk together the lime juice, oil, honey, and teriyaki sauce in a medium bowl. Add the cabbage, onion, mint, and pepper and toss to coat.

2. Divide the mixture among individual plates, sprinkle with the almonds, and serve.

Per serving: 130 calories, 6g total fat, 0g saturated fat, 0g trans fat, 0mg cholesterol, 140mg sodium, 17g total carbohydrate, 3g dietary fiber, 11g sugars, 2g protein

Broccoli Slaw

Makes 6 servings: ¾ cup each

I love broccoli. I created a snappy and simple way to fill my fancy for it. I'm sure you'll find this crunchy raw slaw to be quite appetizing . . . maybe lovable.

3 tablespoons apple cider vinegar

2 tablespoons canola or flaxseed oil

2 tablespoons honey or agave nectar

¼ teaspoon sea salt, or to taste

1 (12-ounce) bag broccoli slaw or shredded
    mixture of 3 cups broccoli, ½ cup carrots,
    and ½ cup red cabbage

2 scallions, green and white parts, minced

2 tablespoons dry-roasted sunflower seeds

1. Whisk together the vinegar, oil, honey, and salt in a large bowl. Add the slaw and scallions and toss to combine. Adjust seasoning.

2. Let stand for 30 minutes to allow flavors to blend. Toss again.

3. Sprinkle with the sunflower seeds and serve.

Per serving: 100 calories, 6g total fat, 0.5g saturated fat, 0g trans fat, 0mg cholesterol, 120mg sodium, 11g total carbohydrate, 2g dietary fiber, 7g sugars, 2g protein

Artichoke Salad with Manchego and Tart Cherries Ⓕ

Makes 4 servings: 2½ cups each

When I set out to create this heavenly salad, I was aiming to mingle several of the tastiest salad-friendly ingredients possible. So, I present one of the most scrumptious salads that I know— it's salty and sweet, tangy and tart.

1 (9 ounce) package thawed frozen artichoke
    hearts, well drained and thinly sliced

⅛ teaspoon sea salt, or to taste

4 cups packed baby arugula

1½ ounces thinly sliced serrano ham, coarsely
    chopped

¼ cup finely diced red onion

2 ounces Manchego or Asiago cheese, shaved

¼ cup dried tart cherries

¼ cup dry-roasted pistachios

½ teaspoon freshly ground black pepper, or to taste

½ cup Tart Cherry Vinaigrette (page 147)

1. Toss together the artichoke hearts with the salt in a medium bowl.

2. Arrange the arugula on a platter or four plates. Top with the artichoke hearts, ham, onion, cheese, dried cherries, pistachios, and pepper. Drizzle with half of the dressing, adjust seasoning, and serve with the remaining dressing on the side.

Per serving: 260 calories, 14g total fat, 3.5g saturated fat, 0g trans fat, 20mg cholesterol, 680mg sodium, 27g total carbohydrate, 10g dietary fiber, 11g sugars, 11g protein

Beet and Fuji Apple Coleslaw

Makes 4 servings: 1 cup each

Beets are delightful in a variety of preparations. In this one the beets are kept raw and mingle with a sweet apple and a bit of ginger to really bring out flavors. This sweet and savory recipe will likely even win over those of you who are a bit beet shy.

3 tablespoons apple cider vinegar

½ teaspoon sea salt, or to taste

⅛ teaspoon freshly ground black pepper, or to taste

2 teaspoons canola or flaxseed oil

1 teaspoon freshly grated gingerroot

2 medium beets, peeled and coarsely grated

1 medium Fuji or other crisp-sweet apple,
    cored, and coarsely grated

2 scallions, green and white parts, thinly sliced

1 teaspoon chopped fresh tarragon, or to taste

Whisk together the vinegar, salt, and pepper in a medium bowl. Whisk in the oil. Add the ginger, beets, apple, scallions, and tarragon and gently stir. Adjust seasoning, and serve.

Per serving: 90 calories, 2.5g total fat, 0g saturated fat, 0g trans fat, 0mg cholesterol, 350mg sodium, 16g total carbohydrate, 3g dietary fiber, 10g sugars, 2g protein

Warm Grilled Vegetable Salad

Makes 4 servings: 2 cups each

Think ruby red, garden green, lovely yellow, and vivid purple along with juicy, crisp, tender, and crunchy. This grilled vegetable salad is such a combination of colors and textures . . . like contemporary art on your dinner table. Plus, it'll make your taste buds pop. Actually, that makes this salad pop art!

2 medium Belgian endive

1 small head radicchio, halved

2 medium yellow squash, cut crosswise into
    ¾-inch cubes or half-moons

20 cherry tomatoes

12 asparagus spears, ends trimmed

½ cup Creamy Basil Vinaigrette (page 145)
    or other vinaigrette

¼ teaspoon sea salt, or to taste

¼ teaspoon freshly ground black pepper,
    or to taste

2 tablespoons thinly sliced fresh basil leaves

1. Prepare an outdoor or indoor grill. Add the endive, radicchio, squash, tomatoes, and asparagus to a large bowl or baking pan. Drizzle with half the vinaigrette and gently toss to coat. Add the salt and pepper.

2. Place the squash and tomatoes on several water-soaked bamboo or reusable skewers or into a grill basket. Grill the endive, radicchio, squash, tomatoes, and asparagus (in batches, if necessary) until lightly charred and just tender over medium-high heat, turning only as needed, about 8 total minutes. Return all the vegetables to the bowl.

3. Cut the endive in half lengthwise, cut out the core, then separate the endive leaves. Cut out the radicchio core and chop the leaves into 1-inch pieces. Remove the squash and tomatoes from the skewers. Cut the asparagus into 1-inch pieces.

4. Arrange the grilled vegetables on a platter or individual plates. Adjust seasoning. Drizzle with the remaining vinaigrette, top with the basil, and serve while slightly warm.

Per serving: 100 calories, 6g total fat, 1g saturated fat, 0g trans fat, 0mg cholesterol, 220mg sodium, 12g total carbohydrate, 4g dietary fiber, 5g sugars, 4g protein

Retro Broccoli Layer Salad

Makes 8 servings: about 1 cup each

Here's a salad packed with not only great taste but also vitamin C. There's 100 percent of the daily value in each serving of this brilliantly displayed salad. Every bite with its myriad textures, colors, and flavors will absolutely delight.

5 cups bite-size pieces broccoli florets

½ large sweet onion, halved again and very
    thinly sliced

1 medium red bell pepper, finely diced

⅔ cup shredded extra-sharp Cheddar
    or smoked Gouda cheese

½ cup black seedless raisins or dried blueberries

⅓ cup salted dry-roasted peanuts or cashews

¾ cup fat-free or low-fat plain yogurt

2 tablespoons white balsamic or champagne vinegar

2 tablespoons mayonnaise

2 tablespoons honey or agave nectar

5 slices applewood-smoked uncured bacon,
    cooked until crisp and finely chopped,
    or 2 tablespoons sun-dried tomato bits

1. Layer the broccoli, onion, bell pepper, cheese, raisins, and peanuts in alternating layers in a 7- to 8-cup glass trifle or other serving bowl.

2. Whisk together the yogurt, vinegar, mayonnaise, and honey in a small bowl. Pour half of the dressing evenly over the layered broccoli salad. Chill.

3. Sprinkle the broccoli salad with the bacon, and serve with the remaining dressing on the side.

Per serving: 200 calories, 10g total fat, 3g saturated fat, 0g trans fat, 15mg cholesterol, 240mg sodium, 20g total carbohydrate, 3g dietary fiber, 14g sugars, 8g protein

Beet and Goat Cheese Salad Ⓕ

Makes 4 servings: 1⅓ cups each

Beets with goat cheese are just one of those culinary marriages that make you go "mmm." And the addition of gorgeous pistachios, sweet cherries, and fragrant mint will make you go "mmm, mmm, mmm!"

2 tablespoons extra-virgin olive oil

2 tablespoons aged red wine vinegar

¼ teaspoon freshly ground black pepper, to taste

⅛ teaspoon sea salt, or to taste

4 medium beets, roasted (page 27), peeled, and thinly sliced

¾ cup crumbled soft goat cheese

⅓ cup fresh or thawed frozen Bing cherries, pitted and thinly sliced

2 tablespoons unsalted dry-roasted pistachios

1 tablespoon finely chopped fresh mint

1. Whisk together the oil, vinegar, pepper, and salt in a medium bowl. Add the beets and toss to coat.

2. Arrange the beets on a platter or four plates. Sprinkle with the cheese, cherries, pistachios, and mint. Adjust seasoning and serve.

Per serving: 240 calories, 14g total fat, 4.5g saturated fat, 0g trans fat, 10mg cholesterol, 320mg sodium, 25g total carbohydrate, 5g dietary fiber, 19g sugars, 9g protein

Tofu Salads

Turkish Tofu Salad

Makes 6 servings: 1 cup each

Today, there's an exciting array of tofu choices. One of the tastiest is baked ready-to-eat tofu that's available in various vibrant flavors. Here it's tossed with fresh veggies and a lemony vinaigrette to create a lovely Middle Eastern–style salad.

3 tablespoons extra-virgin olive oil

Juice of 1 small lemon (2 tablespoons)

2 large garlic cloves, minced

2 tablespoons finely chopped fresh mint or 1½ teaspoons dried crushed mint

1 teaspoon finely chopped fresh oregano or ½ teaspoon dried oregano

¾ teaspoon sea salt, or to taste

½ teaspoon freshly ground black pepper, or to taste

8 ounces garlic-herb, lemon-pepper, or Italian ready-to-eat baked tofu, diced

2 medium vine-ripened tomatoes, pulp removed and diced

½ large English cucumber, unpeeled and diced

½ cup finely diced pickled turnip or beet

⅓ cup finely diced red onion

3 tablespoons chopped fresh flat-leaf parsley

1. Whisk together the oil, lemon juice, garlic, mint, oregano, salt, and pepper in a large bowl. Add the tofu, tomatoes, cucumber, pickled turnip, onion, and parsley and gently stir. Cover and chill in the refrigerator for at least 2 hours to allow flavors to blend.

2. Adjust seasoning, and serve at room temperature or slightly chilled.

Per serving: 170 calories, 11g total fat, 1.5g saturated fat, 0g trans fat, 0mg cholesterol, 460mg sodium, 9g total carbohydrate, 2g dietary fiber, 4g sugars, 10g protein

Ginger Tofu Chick'n Salad

Makes 7 servings: ½ cup each

Tofu is the chick'n in this highly flavored Asian salad. Enjoy it as is or try it on brown rice crackers. Betcha people who like chicken will become fans of this chick'n salad, too.

2½ tablespoons naturally brewed tamari soy sauce

2 tablespoons brown rice vinegar

2 large garlic cloves, minced

1 tablespoon freshly grated gingerroot

2 teaspoons honey or agave nectar

2 teaspoons toasted sesame oil

1 (14-ounce) package firm tofu, well drained, gently squeezed dry, and finely diced

1 large red or orange bell pepper, finely diced

⅓ cup finely diced Cubanelle pepper or bok choy

2 scallions, green and white parts, very thinly sliced or minced

1 tablespoon chopped fresh cilantro

1. Whisk together the soy sauce, vinegar, garlic, ginger, honey, and oil in a large bowl. Gently stir in the tofu and let sit for 15 minutes.

2. Gently stir the bell pepper, Cubanelle, scallions, and cilantro into the tofu mixture.

3. Adjust seasoning, and serve at room temperature or slightly chilled.

Per serving: 80 calories, 4g total fat, 0g saturated fat, 0g trans fat, 0mg cholesterol, 360mg sodium, 5g total carbohydrate, 1g dietary fiber, 3g sugars, 6g protein

Pan-Seared Tofu and Cucumber Salad

Makes 4 servings: 1 cup each

This is a curiously captivating salad. You slightly "cook" the cucumber! Enjoy it with chopsticks.

1 large English cucumber, unpeeled and very thinly sliced crosswise

Juice of 1 lemon (3 tablespoons)

2 tablespoons peanut or grapeseed oil

¾ teaspoon salt, or to taste

½ teaspoon freshly ground black pepper, or to taste

1 (14-ounce) package firm tofu, well drained, gently squeezed dry, and cut into ⅓-inch cubes

2 tablespoons whole-wheat pastry flour

1 large shallot, minced

2 tablespoons pine nuts, toasted

1 scallion, green and white part, minced

1. Toss the cucumber with the lemon juice, 1 tablespoon of the oil, ½ teaspoon of the salt, and the pepper in a medium bowl. Set aside.

2. Toss the tofu with the flour in a medium bowl. Shake off excess flour.

3. Heat the remaining 1 tablespoon oil in a large nonstick skillet over medium-high heat. Add the tofu and sauté until lightly browned, about 2 minutes. Reduce heat to medium, add the shallot and the remaining ¼ teaspoon salt, and sauté until the tofu is golden brown and shallot is caramelized, about 3 minutes. Remove from heat.

4. Add the cucumber mixture (along with all liquid in the bowl) to the skillet with the tofu and stir together in the hot skillet until just combined, about 20 seconds. Transfer the tofu-cucumber mixture back into the bowl, chill, and adjust seasoning.

5. Arrange the cool tofu-cucumber salad on a platter or individual plates, sprinkle with the pine nuts and scallion, and serve.

Per serving: 210 calories, 14g total fat, 2g saturated fat, 0g trans fat, 0mg cholesterol, 440mg sodium, 12g total carbohydrate, 2g dietary fiber, 3g sugars, 11g protein

Curried Tofu and Pomegranate Salad

Makes 7 servings: ½ cup each

There are so many textures and rich Indian flavors in this recipe. The pop of pomegranate is truly special.

⅓ cup fat-free or low-fat plain Greek yogurt

3 tablespoons Major Grey's mango chutney

2 tablespoon mayonnaise

2 tablespoon hot Madras curry powder

1 tablespoon mango or peach nectar

1 teaspoon freshly grated gingerroot

½ teaspoon sea salt, or to taste

1 (14-ounce) package extra-firm tofu, well-drained, gently squeezed dry, and diced

½ cup fresh pomegranate seeds (arils) or thinly sliced red grapes

1 medium celery stalk, thinly sliced

⅓ cup walnut halves, toasted and chopped

2 tablespoons chopped fresh cilantro

Stir together the yogurt, chutney, mayonnaise, curry powder, nectar, ginger, and salt until smooth. Gently stir in the tofu, pomegranate seeds, celery, walnuts, and cilantro. Adjust seasoning and serve at room temperature or slightly chilled.

Per serving: 150 calories, 0g total fat, 1g saturated fat, 0g trans fat, 0mg cholesterol, 210mg sodium, 9g total carbohydrate, 2g dietary fiber, 5g sugars, 8g protein

Grilled Tofu Salad with Baby Greens

Makes 4 servings: ¼ recipe each

Mizuna is a delicate, peppery Japanese green. Look for it at a farmers' market. Try this salad with other tender baby greens available, too. Peppered with grilled tofu and vegetables and lightly dressed with homemade Asian vinaigrette, this salad is fit for a queen—or king.

18 white pearl onions

⅓ cup brown rice vinegar

3 tablespoons naturally brewed soy sauce

2 tablespoons mild honey or agave nectar

2 scallions, green and white parts, minced

1 tablespoon freshly grated gingerroot

1 tablespoon toasted sesame oil

2 teaspoons Asian garlic-chili sauce

7 ounces firm tofu, drained, gently squeezed dry, and cut into 1-inch cubes

1 large red bell pepper, cut into ¾-inch cubes

6 cups packed baby lettuce, such as mizuna or tatsoi and mâche

2 tablespoons chopped fresh cilantro

1 tablespoon toasted sesame seeds

1. Bring 3 cups of water to a boil in a saucepan over high heat. Add the pearl onions to the water and boil for 2½ minutes. Transfer to a bowl of ice-cold water to cool, then drain and peel.

2. Whisk together the vinegar, soy sauce, honey, scallions, ginger, oil, and garlic-chili sauce in a large bowl. Add the tofu, bell pepper, and onions. Marinate, stirring occasionally, for 30 minutes.

3. Prepare an indoor or outdoor grill. Insert the tofu, bell pepper, and onions onto separate water-soaked bamboo or reusable skewers. Reserve the marinade. Grill over medium-high heat until lightly charred and the pepper and onions are just tender, turning only as needed, about 8 total minutes. Remove from the grill.

4. Arrange the lettuces on a platter. Scatter the grilled tofu, bell pepper, and onions onto the lettuces. Drizzle with about half of the reserved marinade. Sprinkle with the cilantro and sesame seeds, and serve at room temperature.

Per serving: 170 calories, 8g total fat, 1g saturated fat, 0g trans fat, 0mg cholesterol, 430mg sodium, 18g total carbohydrate, 2g dietary fiber, 10g sugars, 7g protein

Smoked Tofu Chef Salad

Makes 4 servings: 2½ cups each

Savor this vegan chef salad that makes a super-satisfying side salad. Or, if you prefer, turn it into an entrée salad by adding slices of hard-cooked egg or additional smoked tofu.

2 cups chopped radicchio

2 cups chopped frisée

2 cups packed baby arugula or chopped arugula

½ cup Winter White French Dressing (page 151)
    or other salad dressing

4 ounces ready-to-eat smoked tofu, cut into
    matchstick-size strips

1 cup grape tomatoes, halved lengthwise

½ cup shredded carrot

5 small red radishes, thinly sliced

1 medium yellow bell pepper or 1 roasted
    bell pepper, diced

⅓ cup finely diced red onion

3 tablespoons salted dry-roasted sunflower
    or shelled pumpkin seeds

3 tablespoons black seedless raisins or dried
    currants

1. Toss the radicchio, frisée, and arugula with ¼ cup of the dressing. Arrange on a platter or four plates.

2. Top with the tofu, tomatoes, carrot, radishes, bell pepper, onion, sunflower seeds, and raisins, and serve with the remaining dressing on the side.

Per serving: 170 calories, 7g total fat, 1g saturated fat, 0g trans fat, 0mg cholesterol, 210mg sodium, 22g total carbohydrate, 4g dietary fiber, 12g sugars, 8g protein

Pasta and Noodle Salads

Bow-Tie Salad with Basil

Makes 6 servings: 1¼ cups each

I'm crazy about the iconic Caprese salad with its juicy vine-ripened tomatoes, fragrant Italian basil, and fresh buffalo mozzarella cheese. That's what influenced the creation of this tangy bow-tie pasta salad. It's easy to fix and it's delish.

10 ounces whole-wheat or other whole-grain
    farfalle (bow-tie) pasta

2 tablespoons aged balsamic or white balsamic
    vinegar

2 tablespoons extra-virgin olive oil

1 large garlic clove, minced

½ teaspoon sea salt, or to taste

¼ teaspoon dried hot pepper flakes, or to taste

¾ cup grape tomatoes, halved or quartered
    lengthwise

3 ounces part-skim mozzarella cheese, diced

¼ cup finely diced red onion

¼ cup thinly sliced fresh basil leaves

1. Cook the pasta according to package directions. Drain the pasta, toss or stir the pasta in the sauce-pan with several ice cubes to cool, and drain again.

2. Whisk together the vinegar, oil, garlic, salt, and hot pepper flakes in a large bowl.

3. Add the cooked pasta, tomatoes, cheese, onion, and basil and stir until well combined. Adjust sea-soning and serve.

Per serving: 250 calories, 8g total fat, 2g saturated fat, 0g trans fat, 10mg cholesterol, 290mg sodium, 37g total carbohydrate, 4g dietary fiber, 3g sugars, 11g protein

Eco-Elbow Macaroni Salad Ⓢ

Makes 6 servings: ¾ rounded cup each

Here you'll enjoy an earthier, prettier dish of macaroni salad than the usual. It's lightly dressed with a flavorful mixture of mayo and brown rice vinegar. And the vivid additions of roasted red bell pepper, scallions, and eggs take this recipe from picnic table to a formal table.

8 ounces whole-wheat or other whole-grain elbow macaroni

3 tablespoons mayonnaise

2 tablespoons brown rice vinegar

¼ teaspoon hot, smoked, or sweet paprika

¼ teaspoon sea salt, or to taste

2½ tablespoons sweet pickle relish

1 large freshly roasted red bell pepper (page 27), or drained jarred pepper, diced

3 scallions, green and white parts, very thinly sliced

2 large hard-cooked eggs, diced (page 377)

1. Cook the pasta according to package directions. Drain the pasta, toss or stir the pasta in the saucepan with several ice cubes to cool, and drain again.

2. Meanwhile, whisk together the mayonnaise, vinegar, paprika, and ⅛ teaspoon of the salt in a large bowl. Stir in the relish.

3. Add the cooked pasta, roasted pepper, and scallions to the mayonnaise mixture and stir until well combined. Sprinkle with or gently stir in the eggs and the remaining ⅛ teaspoon salt. Adjust seasoning and serve.

Per serving: 220 calories, 8g total fat, 1.5g saturated fat, 0g trans fat, 65mg cholesterol, 220mg sodium, 33g total carbohydrate, 4g dietary fiber, 5g sugars, 8g protein

Creamy Cavatappi Salad with Ham

Makes 6 servings: 1 cup each

Macaroni salad gets an extreme makeover here using cavatappi pasta—which is a double spiral shape—cubes of smoky ham, and remarkably fragrant fresh rosemary. Plus, the pops of piquant flavor from the cornichons and sweetness from the bell pepper take it to the top of the macaroni-salad class.

8 ounces whole-wheat or other whole-grain cavatappi or other shaped pasta

3 tablespoons mayonnaise

1 tablespoon apple cider vinegar

1½ teaspoons Dijon mustard

¾ teaspoon finely chopped fresh rosemary

¼ teaspoon sweet or smoked paprika

4 ounces hickory-smoked heritage or baked ham, diced

12 cornichons, sliced into very thin coins

1 small or ½ large roasted yellow or orange bell pepper, finely diced (page 27)

3 tablespoons finely diced red onion

⅛ teaspoon sea salt, or to taste

1. Cook the pasta according to package directions. Drain the pasta, toss or stir the pasta in the saucepan with several ice cubes to cool, and drain again.

2. Meanwhile, whisk together the mayonnaise, vinegar, mustard, rosemary, and paprika in a large bowl.

3. One at a time, stir in the pasta, ham, cornichons, bell pepper, and onion until well combined. Add the salt, adjust seasoning, and serve.

Per serving: 200 calories, 7g total fat, 1g saturated fat, 0g trans fat, 10mg cholesterol, 330mg sodium, 29g total carbohydrate, 3g dietary fiber, 2g sugars, 9g protein

Herbed Goat Cheese and Green Tea Orzo Salad

Makes 7 servings: about 1 cup each

The green tea–infused orzo creates flavor drama and boosts the health profile of this intriguing salad. The generous potpourri of fresh herbs adds so much bright and aromatic freshness. Hope you'll be intrigued.

4 green or jasmine green tea bags

8 ounces whole-wheat orzo

Juice of 1 lemon (3 tablespoons)

3 tablespoons extra-virgin olive oil

2 garlic cloves, minced

¾ teaspoon sea salt, or to taste

¼ teaspoon freshly ground black pepper, or to taste

1 cup grape tomatoes, quartered or halved lengthwise

3 scallions, green and white parts, thinly sliced

½ cup finely diced fennel bulb or celery

½ cup chopped fresh flat-leaf parsley

⅓ cup chopped fresh basil

¼ cup chopped fresh mint

2 teaspoons chopped fresh thyme

4 ounces crumbled soft goat cheese

3 tablespoons pine nuts, toasted

1. Bring a large saucepan with 4 cups of water to a boil over high heat. Add the green tea and let steep for 5 minutes. Remove the tea bags.

2. Bring the green tea to a boil, stir in the orzo, and cook according to package directions (in the green tea instead of water). Drain.

3. Meanwhile, whisk together the lemon juice, oil, garlic, salt, and pepper in a large bowl.

4. Add the hot orzo to the lemon vinaigrette in the large bowl and toss to coat. Set aside to cool for about 30 minutes, stirring occasionally to prevent sticking. Then chill in the refrigerator.

5. When the dressed orzo is cool, add the tomatoes, scallions, fennel, parsley, basil, mint, and thyme and stir until well combined. Then gently stir in the cheese and pine nuts. Adjust seasoning.

6. Arrange the orzo salad on a platter or individual plates or bowls, and serve at room temperature.

Per serving: 240 calories, 12g total fat, 3.5g saturated fat, 0g trans fat, 5mg cholesterol, 320mg sodium, 27g total carbohydrate, 4g dietary fiber, 2g sugars, 9g protein

Orzo with Greens, Feta, and Cranberries

Makes 8 servings: 1 cup each

The mélange of ingredients in this orzo salad recipe creates flavor magic. The combination of peppery arugula, toasty nuts, salty feta, and fresh mint and basil will put a spell on your taste buds.

1¼ cups whole-wheat orzo

2 lemons

2 tablespoons extra-virgin olive oil

½ teaspoon sea salt, or to taste

½ teaspoon freshly ground black pepper, or to taste

4 cups packed baby arugula or tatsoi

½ cup dried cranberries or other fruit bits

⅓ cup walnuts, toasted and coarsely chopped

⅓ cup finely crumbled feta or soft goat cheese

3 tablespoons finely chopped fresh basil

2 tablespoon finely chopped fresh mint

1. Cook the orzo according to package directions. Drain.

2. Meanwhile, cut one of the lemons into 8 wedges; set aside. Juice and zest the remaining lemon and add to a large bowl. Whisk in the oil, salt, and pepper until combined.

3. Add the hot orzo to the lemon vinaigrette and stir to coat. Set aside to cool for about 30 minutes, stirring occasionally to prevent sticking. Then chill in the refrigerator.

4. When the dressed orzo is cool, gently stir in the arugula, cranberries, walnuts, cheese, basil, and mint. Adjust seasoning.

5. Arrange the orzo salad on a platter or individual plates or bowls, and serve at room temperature with the lemon wedges on the side.

Per serving: 200 calories, 8g total fat, 2g saturated fat, 0g trans fat, 5mg cholesterol, 220mg sodium, 29g total carbohydrate, 3g dietary fiber, 6g sugars, 6g protein

Orecchiette and Arugula Salad with Sausage

Makes 6 servings: 1⅓ cups each

If not already, you'll fall in love with the cute little ear-shaped orecchiette pasta. You'll also be enchanted by the amazing flavors in this salad—pleasing every taste bud. The joining of orecchiette with fresh herbs and arugula, juicy sweet tomatoes, and tangy cheese, along with the surprising inclusion of savory poultry sausage, is simply terrific.

8 ounces whole-wheat or other whole-grain orecchiette pasta
Juice of 1 small lemon (2 tablespoons)
2 tablespoons extra-virgin olive oil
½ teaspoon herbs de Provence
½ teaspoon sea salt, or to taste
2 (3-ounce) refrigerated precooked chicken or turkey sausage links
2 cups packed baby arugula, fresh spinach, or tatsoi
8 ounces cherry tomatoes, sliced
⅓ cup finely diced red onion
¼ cup thinly sliced fresh basil leaves
2 tablespoons finely chopped fresh mint
3 tablespoons finely crumbled feta cheese
2 tablespoons pine nuts, toasted

1. Cook the pasta according to package directions. Drain.

2. Meanwhile, whisk together the lemon juice, oil, herbs de Provence, and salt in a large bowl.

3. Add the hot pasta to the lemon vinaigrette and toss to coat. Set aside to cool, stirring occasionally to prevent sticking.

4. Heat the sausage according to package directions. Thinly slice into coins, toss into the pasta, and chill.

5. When the pasta mixture is cool, toss with the arugula, tomatoes, onion, basil, and mint. Adjust seasoning.

6. Arrange the pasta salad on a platter or individual plates. Top with the cheese and pine nuts, and serve.

Per serving: 260 calories, 11g total fat, 2.5g saturated fat, 0g trans fat, 30mg cholesterol, 420mg sodium, 32g total carbohydrate, 4g dietary fiber, 3g sugars, 12g protein

Pistachio-Kissed Couscous Bowls Ⓕ

Makes 5 servings: 1 rounded cup each

Couscous is probably one of the easiest foods to prepare, so it's a staple in my pantry. But when I have 20 minutes to spare rather than my usual 2, couscous becomes the base for an endless array of interesting culinary creations. This is one of those creations. The best part: the sprinkles of dry-roasted pistachios and the edible burgundy radicchio bowl.

1 small head radicchio

1 tablespoon extra-virgin olive oil

1 medium orange or yellow bell pepper
    or yellow squash, finely diced

¾ cup finely chopped fresh shiitake
    or portobella mushroom caps

1 large garlic clove, minced

1⅔ cups low-sodium vegetable broth
    or Vegetable Stock (page 203)

1 cup fresh or thawed frozen petite peas

1 teaspoon finely chopped fresh rosemary

¾ teaspoon sea salt, or to taste

1 cup whole-wheat couscous

2 teaspoons finely chopped fresh oregano (optional)

1½ tablespoons aged balsamic vinegar

¼ cup finely chopped fresh basil leaves

⅓ cup salted dry-roasted pistachios, chopped

1. Carefully remove 5 leaves from the head of radicchio and chill until ready to use. Core and finely chop the remaining radicchio.

2. Heat the oil in an extra-large saucepan over medium heat. Add the chopped radicchio, the bell pepper, mushrooms, and garlic and sauté until the radicchio is fully softened, about 8 minutes. Increase heat to high and add the broth, peas, rosemary, and salt. Bring to a boil.

3. Stir in the couscous, cover, and remove from heat. Let stand for 7 minutes, covered. Remove the lid and stir in the oregano (if using). Chill at least 1 hour.

4. Fluff the chilled couscous with a fork while stirring in the vinegar, basil, and pistachios, and adjust seasoning. Serve in the reserved radicchio leaves.

Per serving: 240 calories, 4.5g total fat, 0.5g saturated fat, 0g trans fat, 0mg cholesterol, 440mg sodium, 42g total carbohydrate, 9g dietary fiber, 6g sugars, 10g protein

Ginger Spaetzle Salad

Makes 7 servings: 1 cup each

Spaetzle is a small German egg noodle often served as a warm side dish. Here, it's the "pasta" and highlight of a salad. The flavors of Asia and these popular noodles form a duet that's melodically marvelous. The textural bell peppers create a harmonious, colorful finale.

1 (8.8- to 9-ounce) package whole spelt,
    whole-wheat, or spinach spaetzle

¼ cup brown rice vinegar

3 tablespoons naturally brewed tamari soy sauce

2 tablespoons honey or agave nectar

1 large shallot, minced

1½ tablespoon freshly grated gingerroot

2 teaspoons Asian garlic-chili sauce, or to taste

1 tablespoon toasted sesame oil

3 medium bell peppers, mixed variety of colors,
    finely diced

2 tablespoons chopped fresh cilantro

1. Cook the spaetzle according to package directions. Drain.

2. Meanwhile, whisk together the vinegar, soy sauce, honey, shallot, ginger, and garlic-chili sauce in a small bowl. Set aside.

3. Add the spaetzle into a large mixing bowl, sprinkle with the oil, and toss to coat. Then pour in the vinegar mixture and toss again. Set aside to cool for 30 minutes, stirring occasionally to help prevent sticking. Then chill in the refrigerator.

4. When the spaetzle mixture is cool, stir in the bell peppers. Serve in a large bowl or individual bowls, sprinkle with the cilantro, and serve.

Per serving: 190 calories, 3.5g total fat, 0.5g saturated fat, 0g trans fat, 0mg cholesterol, 510mg sodium, 34g total carbohydrate, 4g dietary fiber, 8g sugars, 7g protein

Thai Peanut Noodle Salad

Makes 8 servings: 1 rounded cup each

This nutty noodle recipe is ideal for a gathering of folks who know how to enjoy fun, flavorful food. It has a little kick and crunch to it for extra interest. It keeps well for a few days . . . so savor it again and again.

1 (12.7-ounce) package 100% buckwheat soba
    noodles or 12 ounces whole-wheat linguine

⅓ cup brown rice vinegar

¼ cup naturally brewed soy sauce

3 tablespoons honey or agave nectar

2 tablespoons freshly grated gingerroot

1 tablespoon no-salt-added creamy natural
    peanut butter

1 tablespoon Asian garlic-chili sauce

2 tablespoons toasted sesame oil

1 medium head baby bok choy, cored and
    very thinly sliced

1 large yellow or orange bell pepper, thinly sliced

3 scallions, green and white parts, thinly sliced

3 tablespoons chopped fresh cilantro or Thai basil

3 tablespoons chopped unsalted dry-roasted peanuts

1. Cook the noodles for 1½ minutes less than indicated on package directions. Drain (do not rinse).

2. Meanwhile, whisk together the vinegar, soy sauce, honey, ginger, peanut butter, and garlic-chili sauce in a small bowl. Set aside.

3. Add the noodles to a large mixing bowl, sprinkle with the oil, and toss to coat. Then pour in the vinegar mixture and toss again. Set aside to cool for 30 minutes, tossing with tongs occasionally to help prevent sticking. Then chill in the refrigerator.

4. When the noodle mixture is cool, add the bok choy, bell pepper, and scallions and toss to combine.

5. Arrange on a deep platter or individual bowls, sprinkle with the cilantro and peanuts, and serve. Enjoy with chopsticks.

Per serving: 270 calories, 7g total fat, 1g saturated fat, 0g trans fat, 0mg cholesterol, 560mg sodium, 46g total carbohydrate, 4g dietary fiber, 11g sugars, 8g protein

Pesto Pasta and Spinach Salad Ⓕ

Makes 12 servings: 1 cup each

Savor this simple, comforting pasta salad, dressed in pesto and adorned with walnuts and fresh baby spinach. It's well suited for a side dish, appetizer, or entrée at a luncheon or dinner party—for everyone.

1 pound whole-wheat radiatore or other short pasta

1 cup Enlightened Fresh Basil Pesto (page 119)

¾ teaspoon sea salt, or to taste

5 cups packed fresh baby spinach

⅓ cup coarsely chopped walnuts, toasted

1 teaspoon lemon zest, or to taste

1. Cook the pasta according to package directions. Drain, toss or stir the pasta in the saucepan with several ice cubes to cool, and drain again.

2. Toss the cool pasta with the pesto sauce and salt in a large bowl. Gently toss with the spinach. Adjust seasoning.

3. Arrange the salad onto a platter or individual plates, sprinkle with walnuts and zest, and serve.

Per serving: 300 calories, 10g total fat, 1g saturated fat, 0g trans fat, 0mg cholesterol, 350mg sodium, 47g total carbohydrate, 7g dietary fiber, 2g sugars, 11g protein

Italian Eggplant Penne Salad 🄵

Makes 6 servings: 1 rounded cup each

Goodness, this is good. Using roasted Italian egg-plant boosts this penne pasta salad's authentic-ity and richness. The combo of sun-dried cherry tomatoes and baby mozzarella will make you hum with pleasure. It's like a culinary dream.

2 tablespoons extra-virgin olive oil

½ cup finely diced red onion

1 medium Italian (baby) eggplant, unpeeled and finely diced

⅓ cup sun-dried cherry tomatoes or sliced sun-dried tomatoes (not oil-packed), not rehydrated

2 large garlic cloves, finely chopped

Juice of 1 lemon (3 tablespoons)

¾ teaspoon sea salt, or to taste

½ teaspoon freshly ground black pepper, or to taste

12 ounces dry whole-wheat or other whole-grain penne pasta

3 tablespoons chopped fresh flat-leaf parsley

3 tablespoons chopped fresh basil

2 ounces fresh bocconcini or ciliegine mini mozzarella, thinly sliced (optional)

2 teaspoons drained tiny capers (optional)

1. Heat the oil in a large skillet over medium heat. Add the onion and sauté for 3 minutes. Stir in the eggplant, sun-dried tomatoes, garlic, lemon juice, ½ teaspoon of the salt, and the pepper to a large skillet, and cover. Cook until the eggplant is fully cooked, about 12 minutes, stirring occasionally. Transfer to a large serving bowl; set aside.

2. Cook the pasta according to package directions. Drain the pasta, toss or stir the pasta in the sauce-pan with several ice cubes to cool, and drain again.

3. Stir the drained pasta into the eggplant mix-ture along with the remaining ¼ teaspoon salt and 1½ tablespoons each of the parsley and basil. Chill, if desired.

4. Toss with the cheese and capers (if using). Adjust seasoning. Sprinkle with the remaining 1½ table-spoons each of the parsley and basil, and serve.

Per serving: 260 calories, 6g total fat, 1g saturated fat, 0g trans fat, 0mg cholesterol, 360mg sodium, 48g total carbohydrate, 6g dietary fiber, 4g sugars, 9g protein

Whole-Grain Salads

Blood Orange Bulgur Mint Salad Ⓕ

Makes 4 servings: ¾ cup each

If the most distinctive of Middle Eastern and Sicilian cuisines were to meet, this spectacular salad might be the result. The warm spices and blood orange juice infuse the bulgur to make it quite memorable. The mint creates a burst of aromatic freshness that completes it. You can use regular orange juice, if you like.

1 cup fresh-squeezed blood orange juice
1 cup medium (#2) bulgur wheat
¾ cup finely chopped fresh mint
3 tablespoons extra-virgin olive oil
1 large shallot, minced
1 large garlic clove, minced
¾ teaspoon sea salt, or to taste
¼ teaspoon freshly ground black pepper, or to taste
⅛ teaspoon ground cinnamon
⅛ teaspoon ground cardamom
¼ cup slivered almonds or husked halved hazelnuts, toasted

1. Pour the blood orange juice over the bulgur in a medium bowl. Cover and chill in the refrigerator at least 4 hours, or overnight.

2. Stir in the mint, oil, shallot, garlic, salt, pepper, cinnamon, and cardamom. Chill for about 1 hour to allow the flavors to blend.

3. Adjust the seasoning, stir in the almonds, and serve.

Per serving: 290 calories, 14g total fat, 2g saturated fat, 0g trans fat, 0mg cholesterol, 440mg sodium, 37g total carbohydrate, 8g dietary fiber, 5g sugars, 6g protein

Spelt Tabbouleh Salad

Makes 4 servings: 1 cup each

Instead of the traditional bulgur wheat, this tasty twist on tabbouleh is made with spelt. It adds just enough textural intrigue to this salad that's peppered with juicy tomato, crunchy cucumber, and fresh herbs.

¾ cup spelt
Juice of 1 small lemon (2 tablespoons)
1 tablespoon extra-virgin olive oil
1 large garlic clove, minced
¾ teaspoon sea salt, or to taste
1 medium vine-ripened tomato, pulp removed and finely diced
3 scallions, green and white parts, thinly sliced
¾ cup finely diced unpeeled Persian or English cucumber
⅓ cup finely chopped fresh flat-leaf parsley
2 tablespoons finely chopped fresh mint
¼ teaspoon freshly ground black pepper, or to taste

1. Add the spelt and 2½ cups water to a medium saucepan. Place over high heat and bring to a boil. Reduce heat to medium-low, cover, and simmer until the spelt is chewy, yet tender, about 1 hour 10 minutes. Remove from heat and let stand about 5 minutes while covered to complete the cooking process.

2. Meanwhile, whisk together the lemon juice, oil, garlic, and ½ teaspoon of the salt in a medium bowl. Add the cooked spelt, and chill.

3. Stir the tomato, scallions, cucumber, parsley, mint, pepper, and the remaining ¼ teaspoon salt into the spelt. Adjust seasoning, and serve.

Per serving: 160 calories, 5g total fat, 0.5g saturated fat, 0g trans fat, 0mg cholesterol, 440mg sodium, 28g total carbohydrate, 4g dietary fiber, 3g sugars, 5g protein

Sesame Red Quinoa and Kale

Makes 5 servings: 1 cup each

From the red quinoa to the deep green leafy kale and the tropically sweet pineapple, there's nothing ordinary about this full-flavored salad.

2 cups low-sodium vegetable broth
    or Vegetable Stock (page 203)
1 cup red quinoa, rinsed and drained
1½ tablespoons freshly grated gingerroot
1 large garlic clove, minced
1 pound kale, thick stems removed and
    leaves very thinly sliced
½ cup finely diced fresh pineapple
1½ tablespoons brown rice vinegar
2 teaspoons honey or agave nectar
1½ teaspoons naturally brewed soy sauce
2 teaspoons toasted sesame oil
2 tablespoons toasted sesame seeds
¾ teaspoon sea salt, or to taste

1. Bring the broth to a boil in a large saucepan over high heat. Stir in the quinoa, ginger, and garlic, then top with the kale. Cover, reduce heat to medium-low, and cook until the quinoa is nearly tender, about 22 minutes. Remove from heat and let stand covered for 5 minutes to complete the cooking process.

2. Stir the pineapple into the quinoa-kale mixture, and set aside for about 30 minutes to cool, stirring occasionally to prevent sticking. Then chill in the refrigerator.

3. Whisk together the vinegar, honey, and soy sauce in a small bowl, then whisk in the oil. Stir the vinaigrette into the chilled quinoa along with 1 tablespoon of the sesame seeds and the salt.

4. Adjust seasoning, sprinkle with the remaining 1 tablespoon sesame seeds, and serve.

Per serving: 210 calories, 6g total fat, 0.5g saturated fat, 0g trans fat, 0mg cholesterol, 520mg sodium, 34g total carbohydrate, 4g dietary fiber, 6g sugars, 7g protein

Edamame and Frizzled Leek Quinoa Salad

Makes 5 servings: ¾ rounded cup each

Edamame are immature soybeans with a lovely green hue. By plopping these delightful beans into a few dishes, you'll add style, substance, and notable protein. It's just one of the highlights of this quinoa salad with its luscious caramelized leeks and sprightly dressing.

1 cup quinoa, rinsed and drained
½ cup frozen shelled edamame
1 tablespoon peanut or grapeseed oil
1 large leek, white and light green parts,
    thinly sliced and well rinsed
½ cup Spicy Roasted Pepper Dressing (page 149)
⅓ cup chopped fresh flat-leaf parsley leaves
¾ teaspoon sea salt, or to taste

1. Bring the quinoa and 2 cups of water to a boil in a medium saucepan over high heat. Cover and reduce heat to medium-low, and cook until the quinoa is nearly tender, about 22 minutes. Remove from heat and let stand covered for 5 minutes to complete the cooking process.

2. Cook the edamame according to package directions. Drain.

3. Combine the cooked quinoa and edamame in a bowl and chill, stirring occasionally to help prevent sticking.

4. Heat the oil in a large skillet over medium-high heat. Add the leek and sauté until lightly caramelized, about 5 minutes. Stir the leek into the quinoa mixture.

5. Stir the dressing, parsley, and salt into the quinoa mixture, and serve.

Per serving: 200 calories, 7g total fat, 1g saturated fat, 0g trans fat, 0mg cholesterol, 410mg sodium, 28g total carbohydrate, 4g dietary fiber, 4g sugars, 7g protein

Fresh Fig and Red Quinoa Salad with Pistachios

Makes 6 servings: ¾ cup each

Throughout the summer and early autumn, fresh figs are in season. They're divine as is when fresh and add dazzle to dishes, like this red quinoa salad. The nutty accent from the roasted pistachios makes an exquisite flavor companion for the figs.

2 teaspoons extra-virgin olive oil

2 large shallots, finely chopped

1 cup red quinoa, rinsed and drained

4 large Calimyrna or other fresh figs, stems removed and diced

¼ cup unsalted dry-roasted pistachios, chopped

1¾ cups low-sodium vegetable broth or Vegetable Stock (page 203)

½ teaspoon sea salt, or to taste

½ teaspoon freshly ground black pepper, or to taste

3 tablespoons finely chopped or thinly sliced fresh basil leaves

Juice of ½ lemon (1½ tablespoons)

3 tablespoons finely crumbled soft goat cheese (optional)

1. Heat the oil in a large saucepan over medium heat. Add the shallots and sauté for 2 minutes. Add the quinoa, half the figs, and half the pistachios and sauté 1 minute.

2. Increase heat to high. Add the broth, salt, and pepper and bring to a boil. Reduce heat to medium-low, cover, and simmer until the liquid is absorbed and quinoa is chewy, yet tender, about 22 minutes. Remove from heat and let stand covered for 5 minutes to complete the cooking process. Transfer to a bowl, and chill.

3. Stir in the basil, lemon juice and the remaining figs. Adjust seasoning. Sprinkle with the cheese (if using) and the remaining pistachios, and serve.

Per serving: 190 calories, 6g total fat, 0.5g saturated fat, 0g trans fat, 0mg cholesterol, 240mg sodium, 31g total carbohydrate, 4g dietary fiber, 10g sugars, 6g protein

Curry Squash and Rice Salad

Makes 5 servings: ¾ rounded cup each

The nubby-sized brown rice is one of the best features of this recipe—along with the caramelized acorn squash. What's more, the exotic flavors from the curry and chutney make it out of this world!

¾ cup short-grain brown rice

2 teaspoons canola or peanut oil

1 cup finely diced acorn squash

3 tablespoons fat-free or low-fat plain yogurt

2 tablespoons mango chutney

1½ tablespoons mayonnaise

2 teaspoons hot Madras curry powder, or to taste

½ teaspoon sea salt, or to taste

¼ cup chopped sweet onion

2 tablespoons coarsely chopped unsalted dry-roasted cashews

2 tablespoons dried currants or chopped black seedless raisins

2 tablespoons chopped fresh cilantro

1. Cook the rice according to package directions. Transfer to a large bowl and set aside to cool for about 30 minutes, stirring occasionally to help prevent sticking. Then chill in the refrigerator.

2. Heat the oil in a large nonstick skillet over medium-high heat. Add the squash and sauté until lightly caramelized and tender, about 5 minutes. Transfer to a small bowl and chill.

3. Stir together the yogurt, chutney, mayonnaise, curry powder, and salt in a small bowl.

4. Add the squash, onion, cashews, currants, and cilantro to the rice and stir to combine. Add the yogurt mixture and stir to combine. Adjust seasoning, and serve. Garnish with additional fresh cilantro, if desired.

Per serving: 210 calories, 8g total fat, 1g saturated fat, 0g trans fat, 0mg cholesterol, 280mg sodium, 32g total carbohydrate, 2g dietary fiber, 5g sugars, 4g protein

Orange Basmati Salad with Almonds

Makes 4 servings: 1 cup each

This lovely salad begins with lightly fragrant, nutty basmati rice, which gets grace and freshness from orange zest and basil. A sprinkling of delicately sweet almonds provides a pleasing textural accent to complete the salad in style.

1 cup brown basmati rice

2 teaspoons grated orange zest

2 tablespoons fat-free or low-fat plain yogurt

1 tablespoon mayonnaise

½ teaspoon sea salt, or to taste

⅓ cup chopped red onion

¼ cup thinly sliced fresh basil leaves

3 tablespoons sliced natural almonds, toasted

1. Cook the rice according to package directions. Transfer to a medium bowl, stir in the zest, and set aside to cool for about 30 minutes, stirring occasionally to help prevent sticking. Then chill in the refrigerator.

2. Stir together the yogurt, mayonnaise, and salt in a small bowl.

3. Add the onion, basil, and almonds to the chilled rice and stir to combine. Add the yogurt mixture and stir to combine. Adjust seasoning, and serve. Garnish with additional fresh basil, if desired.

Per serving: 200 calories, 6g total fat, 0.5g saturated fat, 0g trans fat, 0mg cholesterol, 320mg sodium, 34g total carbohydrate, 3g dietary fiber, 2g sugars, 5g protein

French Green Bean–Barley Salad Ⓕ

Makes 4 servings: ¾ cup each

The chewy, nutty barley is a standout among whole grains, and it stands up well with the al dente textures of the freshly roasted carrots, haricot verts (thin green beans), and pearl onions. It's a must-try salad.

½ cup whole hulled barley (not pearled barley), rinsed

½ teaspoon sea salt, or to taste

¾ teaspoon freshly ground black pepper, or to taste

18 pearl onions, whole, or 3 ounces cipollini onions, quartered

2 large carrots, very thinly sliced crosswise (about ⅛ inch thick)

4 ounces fresh haricots verts, ends trimmed

1 tablespoon extra-virgin olive oil

¼ cup Fresh-Squeezed Lemon-Dill Dressing (page 149)

1. Bring the barley and 2¼ cups water to a boil in a medium saucepan over high heat. Reduce heat to medium-low, cover, and simmer until the barley is chewy, yet tender, about 45 minutes. Remove from heat and let stand for 10 minutes, covered. Drain excess liquid, transfer the barley to a bowl, season with ¼ teaspoon each of the salt and pepper, and chill.

2. Preheat the oven to 450°F.

3. Bring 3 cups water to a boil in a large saucepan over high heat. Add the pearl onions to the water and boil for 2½ minutes. Transfer to a bowl of ice cold water to cool, then drain and peel. (To peel, cut the root end of each to squeeze out the onion toward the cut end.)

4. Add the onions, carrots, and haricots verts to a large baking pan. Drizzle with the oil and toss to coat. Roast until the vegetables are just tender and lightly caramelized, about 12 minutes. Add ¼ teaspoon of the pepper and the remaining ¼ teaspoon salt.

5. Add the roasted vegetables, the dressing, and the remaining ¼ teaspoon pepper to the barley and stir to combine. Adjust seasoning, and serve.

Per serving: 200 calories, 9g total fat, 1g saturated fat, 0g trans fat, 0mg cholesterol, 340mg sodium, 26g total carbohydrate, 6g dietary fiber, 3g sugars, 4g protein

Barley, Corn, and Spinach Salad with Feta

Makes 6 servings: about 1½ cups each

Take pleasure in this baby spinach and barley salad, which takes full advantage of summer's fresh corn on the cob and seasonal tomatoes. The salty tang from feta cheese is the perfect final touch.

½ cup whole hulled barley (not pearled barley), rinsed

6 cups packed fresh baby spinach

2 grilled or boiled medium ears corn, kernels cut from cobs and chilled

¾ cup grape tomatoes, halved lengthwise

⅓ cup chopped fresh chives

3 tablespoons aged red wine vinegar

2 tablespoons extra-virgin olive oil

1 large shallot, minced

1 teaspoon finely chopped fresh oregano

¼ teaspoon sea salt, or to taste

¼ teaspoon freshly ground black pepper, or to taste

⅓ cup crumbled feta cheese

1. Bring the barley and 2¼ cups water to a boil in a medium saucepan over high heat. Reduce heat to medium-low, cover, and simmer until the barley is chewy, yet tender, about 45 minutes. Remove from heat and let stand for 10 minutes, covered. Drain excess liquid, transfer the barley to a bowl, and chill.

2. Stir the spinach, corn, tomatoes, and chives into the barley.

3. Whisk together the vinegar, oil, shallot, oregano, salt, and pepper in small bowl, pour over the barley mixture, and stir to combine. Adjust seasoning.

4. Stir in the cheese. Garnish with additional chives or oregano, if desired, and serve.

Per serving: 170 calories, 7g total fat, 2g saturated fat, 0g trans fat, 5mg cholesterol, 240mg sodium, 23g total carbohydrate, 5g dietary fiber, 3g sugars, 5g protein

Garden Fresh Millet Salad

Makes 10 servings: 1 cup each

I particularly enjoy the dried tart cherries and nuts in this confetti-like millet salad. Try it.

2 cups millet

¼ cup extra-virgin olive oil

2 tablespoons Dijon mustard

2 tablespoons white balsamic vinegar

1½ teaspoons sea salt, or to taste

4 scallions, green and white parts, thinly sliced

½ cup finely diced unpeeled English cucumber

⅓ cup coarsely shredded carrot

⅓ cup finely chopped fresh herbs of choice, such as basil, mint, and/or cilantro

⅓ cup dried tart cherries or cranberries

⅓ cup toasted walnut halves, coarsely chopped

1. Add the millet to a medium bowl, cover with cold water, and soak overnight in the refrigerator. Rinse and drain well.

2. Heat 1 tablespoon of the oil over medium-high heat in a large saucepan. Add the millet and cook, stirring frequently, until it makes rapid popping sounds and begins to turn golden, about 7 minutes. Add 4 cups water and bring to a boil over high heat. Reduce heat to low, cover, and cook until the water is absorbed and millet is softened, about 18 minutes.

3. Transfer the millet to a large bowl and fluff with a fork. Set aside to cool for about 30 minutes while fluffing and stirring occasionally to help prevent sticking. Then chill in the refrigerator.

4. Whisk together the mustard, vinegar, and salt in a small bowl. Drizzle in the remaining 3 tablespoons oil while whisking until smooth and thickened.

5. Stir the vinaigrette into the cooled millet. Add the scallions, cucumber, carrot, herbs, dried cherries, and walnuts and stir. Adjust seasoning, and serve at room temperature.

Per serving: 240 calories, 9g total fat, 1.5g saturated fat, 0g trans fat, 0mg cholesterol, 350mg sodium, 34g total carbohydrate, 5g dietary fiber, 3g sugars, 5g protein

Roasted Veggie Farro Salad (F)

Makes 8 servings: ¾ cup each

Farro is an ancient, highly textured, chewy whole grain with nut-like flavor. It provides plenty of satisfaction along with its fiber, protein, and whole-grain goodness. When the farro is tossed with a bevy of highly flavored roasted veggies and fresh herbs, there's plenty of reason to want to prepare this outstanding salad over and over again.

1½ cups whole farro, rinsed and drained

1¾ teaspoons sea salt, or to taste

12 ounces grape tomatoes

1 medium white onion, diced

1 small Italian eggplant or ½ large eggplant, cut into ¾-inch cubes

3 tablespoons extra-virgin olive oil

2 teaspoons finely chopped fresh rosemary

½ teaspoon freshly ground black pepper, or to taste

2 tablespoons aged red wine vinegar

1 large garlic clove, minced

¼ cup finely chopped fresh Italian parsley

¼ cup chopped fresh chives

1. Preheat the oven to 425°F.

2. Combine 5 cups water, the farro, and 1½ teaspoons of the salt in a medium saucepan and bring to a boil over high heat. Reduce the heat to medium-low, cover, and simmer until the farro is desired tenderness, about 40 minutes (cooking time varies). Drain well. Transfer to a large bowl and set aside to slightly cool for about 20 minutes, stirring occasionally. Then cool in the refrigerator while roasting the vegetables.

3. While the farro is cooling, add the tomatoes, onion, and eggplant to a medium bowl. Drizzle with 1 tablespoon of the oil and toss to coat. Add the rosemary, pepper, and the remaining ¼ teaspoon salt and toss to coat. Spread the vegetables onto a parchment paper–lined large tray and roast until the vegetables are cooked through and caramelized, about 40 minutes.

4. Whisk together the vinegar, garlic, and the remaining 2 tablespoons oil in a small bowl or liquid measuring cup.

5. Add the roasted vegetables, parsley, chives, and vinaigrette to the cooled farro, and gently toss to combine. Adjust seasoning, and serve at room temperature.

Per serving: 190 calories, 6g total fat, 1g saturated fat, 0g trans fat, 0mg cholesterol, 300mg sodium, 30g total carbohydrate, 5g dietary fiber, 5g sugars, 6g protein

Bean Salads

Jamaican Bean Salad F

Makes 10 servings: ½ cup each

Beans are one of the most satisfying foods mostly because they're superb sources of both protein and fiber. Fortunately, satisfying can be full-flavored, too. This brilliant bean salad will do so with a captivatingly spicy Jamaican flair!

3 (15-ounce) cans beans, such as red kidney, white, and black, drained

1 large red bell pepper, finely diced

½ cup finely diced red onion

5 tablespoons Zesty Lime Vinaigrette (page 146)

1 small hot Jamaican pepper with seeds, minced

¼ cup chopped fresh cilantro

½ teaspoon sea salt, or to taste

¼ teaspoon ground allspice, or to taste

1. Add the beans, bell pepper, onion, vinaigrette, hot pepper, cilantro, salt, and allspice to a large bowl and stir to combine. Let stand for 30 minutes to allow flavors to blend.

2. Stir, adjust seasoning, and serve.

Per serving: 120 calories, 1.5g total fat, 0g saturated fat, 0g trans fat, 0mg cholesterol, 270mg sodium, 21g total carbohydrate, 6g dietary fiber, 4g sugars, 7g protein

"Wild" White Bean Salad F

Makes 2 servings: ¾ cup beans plus ½ packed cup greens each

This stunning, yet simple bean recipe has quite complex flavors from the wild green topping. Make it with ready-made vinaigrette and it's ready to charm your palate in two minutes—or less!

1 (15-ounce) can cannellini or other white beans, drained

3 tablespoons Fresh Herb and Shallot Vinaigrette (page 144) or other vinaigrette

1 cup packed wild field greens or baby arugula

⅛ teaspoon freshly cracked black pepper, or to taste

1. Add the beans and 1½ tablespoons of the vinaigrette to a small bowl and stir to combine. Divide the beans among two salad plates or bowls.

2. Top each with the greens, drizzle with the remaining 1½ tablespoons vinaigrette, sprinkle with the pepper, and serve.

Per serving: 230 calories, 6g total fat, 1g saturated fat, 0g trans fat, 0mg cholesterol, 300mg sodium, 33g total carbohydrate, 10g dietary fiber, 4g sugars, 12g protein

Heirloom Bean Salad

Makes 4 servings: ¾ cup each

This lovely Tuscan-inspired bean salad marries heirloom beans with a rich-tasting vinaigrette, juicy tomatoes, and crunchy onion. Even if you use a variety of canned beans, it's still lovely.

3 tablespoons extra-virgin olive oil

2 tablespoons aged balsamic vinegar

½ teaspoon sea salt, or to taste

¼ teaspoon freshly ground black pepper, or to taste

2 cups cooked zolfini, borlotti, pavoni, or other heirloom beans, chilled

1 medium vine-ripened tomato, pulp removed and diced

¼ cup finely diced red onion

¼ cup finely diced celery

1 scallion, green and white parts, minced

2 tablespoons chopped fresh flat-leaf parsley

1. Whisk together the oil, vinegar, salt, and pepper in a medium bowl.

2. Add the beans, tomato, onion, celery, scallion, and parsley and stir until well combined. Let stand for 30 minutes to allow flavors to blend. Stir, adjust seasoning, and serve.

Per serving: 210 calories, 12g total fat, 1.5g saturated fat, 0g trans fat, 0mg cholesterol, 340mg sodium, 21g total carbohydrate, 6g dietary fiber, 3g sugars, 7g protein

Avocado and White Bean Salad Ⓕ

Makes 6 servings: ½ rounded cup each

The onion is an integral part of this avocado lover's salad. Since it's sweet, it's delicious to eat it raw in generous quantities. It helps keep calories down and satisfaction up in this 100-calorie recipe. The creaminess of the heart-healthful avocado, coupled with salsa and lime zest, eliminates the need for salad dressing.

1 (15-ounce) can Great Northern or other white beans, drained

½ large sweet onion, diced

⅓ cup Spicy Raw Tomatillo Salsa (page 114), Roasted Green Tomato Salsa (page 114), or other salsa verde

3 tablespoons chopped fresh cilantro

1 Hass avocado, pitted, peeled, and diced

1 teaspoon lime zest

½ teaspoon sea salt, or to taste

Add the beans, onion, salsa, and cilantro to a medium bowl and stir to combine. Very gently stir in the avocado, lime zest, and salt, and serve.

Per serving: 100 calories, 3.5g total fat, 0g saturated fat, 0g trans fat, 0mg cholesterol, 290mg sodium, 15g total carbohydrate, 5g dietary fiber, 3g sugars, 5g protein

Mediterranean Chickpea Salad Ⓕ

Makes 4 servings: 1 cup each

The cheerful chickpea—also known as a garbanzo bean or ceci—is highlighted whole in this marvelous Mediterranean salad. Think of it like a glammed-up, deconstructed version of hummus. Just dive into this delight with a fork

3 tablespoons Garden Lemon Vinaigrette (page 146) or other lemony vinaigrette

3 tablespoons fat-free or low-fat plain Greek yogurt

½ teaspoon ground cumin, or to taste

¼ teaspoon sea salt, or to taste

1 (15-ounce) can chickpeas (garbanzo beans), drained

1 small yellow or red bell pepper, diced

6 cherry tomatoes, quartered lengthwise

6 Kalamata olives, pitted and quartered lengthwise

¼ cup finely crumbled feta cheese

2 tablespoons chopped fresh flat-leaf parsley

1 tablespoon chopped fresh marjoram or tarragon

1 tablespoon chopped fresh mint

½ teaspoon lemon zest (optional)

1. Whisk together the vinaigrette, yogurt, cumin, and salt in a medium bowl.

2. Add the chickpeas, bell pepper, tomatoes, olives, cheese, parsley, marjoram, mint, and lemon zest (if using), and stir until well combined. Let stand for 30 minutes to allow flavors to blend.

3. Stir, adjust seasoning, and serve.

Per serving: 170 calories, 8g total fat, 2g saturated fat, 0g trans fat, 10mg cholesterol, 470mg sodium, 18g total carbohydrate, 5g dietary fiber, 4g sugars, 8g protein

Cuban Black Bean Salad Ⓕ

Makes 3 servings: 1 cup each

This colorful bean salad will thrill your taste buds with its textures and tropical appeal. It's versatile, too. Prepare it with other beans or serve it as a salsa rather than a salad. It's up to you.

¼ cup Exotic Papaya Dressing (page 150)

1 garlic clove, minced

¼ teaspoon ground cumin, or to taste

¼ teaspoon sea salt, or to taste

1 (15-ounce) can black beans, drained

1 small red bell pepper, diced

1 small yellow or orange bell pepper, diced

3 tablespoons diced red onion

2 tablespoons chopped fresh cilantro (optional)

1 teaspoon finely chopped fresh oregano

1. Whisk together the dressing, garlic, cumin, and salt in a medium bowl.

2. Add the beans, bell peppers, onion, cilantro (if using), and oregano and stir until well combined. Let stand for 30 minutes to allow flavors to blend.

3. Stir, adjust seasoning, and serve.

Per serving: 170 calories, 4g total fat, 0g saturated fat, 0g trans fat, 0mg cholesterol, 430mg sodium, 27g total carbohydrate, 7g dietary fiber, 7g sugars, 7g protein

Cowgirl Caviar Salad

Makes 10 servings: ½ cup each

So flavorful, there's no need for oil to dress this salad. If you have extra time, grill the jalapeño and corn—2 medium ears—for a flavor explosion. Savor it as a hearty salsa or side dish, too.

1 (15-ounce) can black beans, drained

1 (15-ounce) can black-eyed peas or pinto beans, drained

1 medium vine-ripened tomato, pulp removed and diced

1 cup chilled cooked or thawed frozen yellow corn kernels

2 scallions, green and white parts, thinly sliced

1 small jalapeño pepper with seeds, minced

Juice of 1 lime (2 tablespoons)

1 tablespoon finely chopped fresh cilantro

⅛ teaspoon sea salt, or to taste

1. Add all the ingredients to a large bowl and stir. Let stand for 30 minutes to allow flavors to blend.

2. Stir, adjust seasoning, and serve.

Per serving: 70 calories, 0g total fat, 0g saturated fat, 0g trans fat, 0mg cholesterol, 270mg sodium, 15g total carbohydrate, 4g dietary fiber, 3g sugars, 5g protein

Poultry, Fish, Shellfish, and Meat Salads

Rotisserie Chicken Cobb Salad Ⓕ

Makes 4 servings: about 3 cups each

Partially homemade can still be a good thing. Rotisserie chicken that you can pick up fresh from a market is suggested here to create an outstanding salad that's a satisfying one-plate meal.

6 cups packed mesclun or mixed salad greens

½ cup Creamy Basil Vinaigrette (page 145) or other vinaigrette

12 ounces rotisserie chicken breast meat, chopped

3 medium vine-ripened tomatoes, pulp removed and diced

⅓ cup crumbled blue cheese

⅓ cup finely diced red onion

5 slices applewood-smoked uncured bacon, cooked until crisp and finely chopped, or 2 tablespoons sun-dried tomato bits

2 large hard-cooked eggs, cut into 6 wedges (page 377)

1 Hass avocado, pitted, peeled, and diced

2 teaspoons fresh lemon juice

1 tablespoon finely chopped fresh tarragon or basil, or to taste

½ teaspoon freshly ground black pepper, or to taste

¼ teaspoon sea salt or rosemary sea salt, or to taste

1. Toss the mesclun with half the vinaigrette and arrange on a platter or four plates.

2. Top with the chicken, tomatoes, cheese, onion, bacon, eggs, and avocado. Drizzle the lemon juice over the avocado. Sprinkle the salad with the tarragon, pepper, and salt, and serve with the remaining vinaigrette on the side.

Per serving: 400 calories, 22g total fat, 6g saturated fat, 0g trans fat, 175mg cholesterol, 680mg sodium, 13g total carbohydrate, 5g dietary fiber, 4g sugars, 38g protein

Luncheon Chef Salad

Makes 4 servings: 3 cups each

You can enjoy this chef salad any time. It's a deliciously balanced bite that can be a lovely entrée salad at lunchtime or a side salad at dinnertime.

1 medium head red leaf lettuce, cored and leaves
   torn or chopped

½ cup Winter White French Dressing (page 151)

1 cup grape tomatoes

1 cup thinly sliced unpeeled English cucumber

¾ cup diced extra-sharp Cheddar cheese

½ cup cubed smoked turkey breast

½ cup cubed roasted or smoked uncured ham

½ cup thinly sliced celery

½ cup finely diced red onion

2 large hard-cooked eggs, sliced (page 377)

½ teaspoon freshly ground black pepper, or to taste

1. Toss the lettuce with half of the dressing and arrange on a platter or four plates.

2. Top with the tomatoes, cucumber, cheese, turkey, ham, celery, onion, and eggs. Sprinkle with the pepper, and serve with the remaining dressing on the side.

Per serving: 220 calories, 12g total fat, 6g saturated fat, 0g trans fat, 130mg cholesterol, 570mg sodium, 11g total carbohydrate, 2g dietary fiber, 5g sugars, 16g protein

English Poached Egg Salad

Makes 4 servings: 1¾ packed cups and 1 egg each

Eggs Florentine meets the iconic English muffin breakfast sandwich and turns into a salad. The poached egg nestled atop this salad with its English muffin "croutons" add intrigue to breakfast time . . . or lunch, dinner, or snack time.

5 cups packed baby arugula

4 large fresh sage leaves, thinly sliced

2 ounces aged Gouda or Cheddar cheese, diced

1 whole-grain English muffin, split, well toasted,
   and cubed

½ cup Garden Lemon Vinaigrette (page 146)

3 ounces smoked uncured ham or cooked
   Canadian-style bacon, diced

4 large eggs, poached (page 21)

¼ teaspoon freshly ground black pepper, or to taste

⅛ teaspoon sea salt or rosemary sea salt, or to taste

1. Add the arugula, sage, cheese, and English muffin to a bowl with half of the vinaigrette and toss to lightly coat.

2. Place the dressed arugula salad on individual plates. Sprinkle with the ham and top with the eggs. Add the pepper and salt, and serve with the remaining vinaigrette on the side.

Per serving: 190 calories, 10g total fat, 4.5g saturated fat, 0g trans fat, 205mg cholesterol, 570mg sodium, 10g total carbohydrate, 2g dietary fiber, 3g sugars, 16g protein

Calypso Grilled Chicken Salad Ⓕ

Makes 4 servings: 3 cups each

The Caribbean-inspired ingredients in this leafy chicken recipe create liveliness . . . like Calypso music for the palate. Serve it as a refreshing, savory, and satisfying entrée that offers plenty of natural sweetness and vitamins A, C, and E.

8 ounces boneless skinless chicken breast

2 teaspoons grapeseed or canola oil

½ teaspoon ground ginger

½ teaspoon sea salt, or to taste

½ teaspoon freshly ground black pepper, or to taste

⅛ teaspoon ground allspice

8 cups packed mixed baby salad greens

1 (15-ounce) can black beans, drained

2 small navel oranges, segmented

1 Hass avocado, pitted, peeled, and diced

½ cup hearts of palm, sliced into ¼-inch rounds or chopped

⅓ cup finely diced red onion

3 tablespoons chopped fresh cilantro

½ cup Zesty Lime Vinaigrette (page 146)

1. Preheat an outdoor or indoor grill, or a panini press. Rub or brush the chicken with the oil and season with the ginger, ¼ teaspoon of the salt, ¼ teaspoon of the pepper, and the allspice. Grill the chicken over direct medium-high heat until well done, about 10 minutes on a grill or 6 minutes in a panini press. Remove from the grill and let cool slightly. Cut into very thin slices.

2. Arrange the salad greens on a platter or individual plates. Top with the beans, grilled chicken, oranges, avocado, hearts of palm, onion, and cilantro. Drizzle with half of the vinaigrette and sprinkle with the remaining ¼ teaspoon salt and ¼ teaspoon pepper. Serve with the remaining vinaigrette on the side.

Per serving: 330 calories, 16g total fat, 2g saturated fat, 0g trans fat, 30mg cholesterol, 590mg sodium, 30g total carbohydrate, 9g dietary fiber, 10g sugars, 19g protein

Blackened Apricot Chicken Salad

Makes 4 servings: 1 chicken thigh with about 1½ cups salad each

Chicken thighs are more luscious than the breasts, yet still a lean pick—especially when skinless. Here you'll simply marinate them in a vibrant fruity-spicy puree and blacken them on a grill. They'll add drama to this fresh summery salad that'll become a regular go-to when grilling.

1 small white or yellow onion, coarsely chopped

2 serrano peppers with seeds, stem removed

2 tablespoons apricot 100% fruit spread

5 fresh apricots, halved and pitted

⅓ cup thinly sliced fresh basil

¼ cup grapeseed or canola oil

1 teaspoon sea salt, or to taste

4 (4-ounce) boneless skinless chicken thighs

4 packed cups fresh watercress, thick stems removed

1 small red bell pepper, sliced into thin rings

2 teaspoons aged red wine vinegar

1. Add the onion, serranos, apricot fruit spread, 3 of the apricots (6 halves), half of the basil, 2 tablespoons of the oil, and ¾ teaspoon of the salt to a food processor or blender. Cover and puree. Pour the apricot mixture over the chicken in a medium bowl or baking dish. Let marinate for 30 to 45 minutes.

2. Prepare an outdoor or indoor grill, or a panini press. Grill the chicken over direct high heat until well done, about 10 minutes on a grill or 6 minutes in a panini press. Remove from the grill and let cool slightly. Sprinkle with the remaining ¼ teaspoon salt.

3. Arrange the watercress, bell pepper, and remaining 4 apricot halves on a large platter. Drizzle with the vinegar and the remaining 2 tablespoons oil. Top with the grilled chicken while still warm. Adjust seasoning. Sprinkle with the remaining basil, and serve with additional red wine vinegar on the side, if desired.

Per serving: 290 calories, 19g total fat, 3.5g saturated fat, 0g trans fat, 75mg cholesterol, 450mg sodium, 9g total carbohydrate, 1g dietary fiber, 6g sugars, 22g protein

Spice-Rubbed Barramundi Salad

Makes 4 servings: 1 fillet and about 1¼ cups mesclun each

Barramundi farmed in the U.S. is an eco-friendly choice, so you can feel good about eating it. Here it's dusted with a unique mixture of Moroccan spices and then broiled until it flakes. If barramundi is not yet available near you, look for wild halibut.

4 (4-ounce) skinless barramundi or wild halibut fillets

½ teaspoon sea salt, or to taste

½ teaspoon freshly ground black pepper, or to taste

½ teaspoon ground ginger

½ teaspoon ground turmeric

⅛ teaspoon ground cinnamon (optional)

5 cups packed mesclun salad greens

⅓ cup shredded carrot

½ cup Silky Lemon Dressing (page 149)

2 tablespoons roughly chopped fresh cilantro

1. Preheat the broiler. Season the barramundi with the salt, pepper, ginger, turmeric, and cinnamon (if using) on all sides. Lightly coat with cooking spray (preferably homemade, page xix).

2. Broil the barramundi about 4 inches away from the heat source until well browned and the center flakes and is just slightly translucent in the center, about 5 total minutes.

3. Toss the mesclun and carrot with half the dressing in a large bowl. Arrange the salad on individual plates. Top with the cooked barramundi and cilantro. Serve with the remaining dressing on the side.

Per serving: 180 calories, 7g total fat, 1g saturated fat, 0g trans fat, 60mg cholesterol, 480mg sodium, 5g total carbohydrate, 1g dietary fiber, 3g sugars, 26g protein

Wild Yellowfin Salad Niçoise Ⓕ

Makes 4 servings: 1 tuna steak with ¼ of the salad

"Niçoise" describes a mixture of black olives, capers, garlic, tomatoes, and lemon juice. That inspired this aromatic grilled tuna salad.

12 ounces fingerling potatoes, unpeeled and scrubbed

12 ounces fresh green beans, trimmed

¾ teaspoon sea salt, or to taste

2 (5-ounce) yellowfin tuna steaks (preferably wild; about 1 inch thick)

½ cup Fresh-Squeezed Lemon-Dill Dressing (page 149) or other salad dressing or vinaigrette

6 cups packed fresh watercress, thick stems discarded, or mixed salad greens

½ cup pitted Niçoise or Kalamata olives

½ cup halved cherry tomatoes

2 hard-cooked large eggs, sliced (page 377)

2 tablespoons chopped fresh tarragon, or to taste

1 tablespoon drained tiny capers

½ teaspoon freshly cracked black pepper, or to taste

1. Place the potatoes in a large microwave-safe dish, cover with parchment paper, and microwave on high for 3 minutes. Add the green beans, recover, and microwave on high for 2½ minutes, or until the vegetables are just tender. Add ¼ teaspoon of the salt. Set aside to cool.

2. Prepare an outdoor or indoor grill. Brush the tuna with 1 tablespoon of the dressing. Grill the tuna over high heat until medium-rare, 1½ minutes per side. Add ¼ teaspoon of the salt.

3. Arrange the watercress on four plates. Thinly slice the potatoes. Arrange the potatoes, green beans, olives, tomatoes, and eggs over the greens.

4. Thinly slice the tuna and arrange over the salads. Drizzle with the remaining dressing, sprinkle with the remaining ¼ teaspoon salt, the tarragon, capers, and pepper, and serve.

Per serving: 330 calories, 15g total fat, 2.5g saturated fat, 0g trans fat, 125mg cholesterol, 770mg sodium, 28g total carbohydrate, 5g dietary fiber, 4g sugars, 25g protein

Seared Salmon Salad

Makes 4 servings: 1 small salmon filet with 1½ cups packed salad

This pan-seared wild salmon recipe is fully satisfying. It's an ideal light luncheon salad that's taste-tempting with its bits of sweetness from figs, pungency from capers, and freshness from mint.

2 (5-ounce) Alaskan sockeye salmon fillets
 with skin, cut in half to make 4 small fillets
½ teaspoon sea salt, or to taste
¾ teaspoon freshly ground black pepper
2 tablespoons whole-wheat flour
1 tablespoon unsalted butter
½ cup Garden Lemon Vinaigrette (page 146)
4 cups packed fresh baby spinach
½ large English cucumber, unpeeled and
 thinly sliced crosswise
2 dried Black Mission figs, finely chopped
2 tablespoons chopped fresh mint, or to taste
1 tablespoon drained tiny capers

1. Season the salmon with ¼ teaspoon each of the salt and pepper, then dust with the flour, shaking off the excess.

2. Melt the butter in a large nonstick skillet over medium-high heat. Add the salmon, skin side up, and cook until the bottom is browned, about 3 minutes. Add 3 tablespoons of the vinaigrette to the skillet, flip over the salmon, and cook until browned, about 3 minutes. Place the cooked salmon onto a platter.

3. Toss together the spinach, cucumber, figs, and the remaining vinaigrette, remaining ¼ teaspoon salt, and ¼ teaspoon pepper in a large bowl.

4. Arrange the spinach salad on a platter or individual plates. Top with the salmon. Sprinkle with the mint and capers, and serve.

Per serving: 270 calories, 17g total fat, 4g saturated fat, 0g trans fat, 45mg cholesterol, 530mg sodium, 15g total carbohydrate, 3g dietary fiber, 5g sugars, 16g protein

Salad with Sesame-Crusted Tuna

Makes 4 servings: 1 steak on about 1¼ cup arugula

The savory Asian flavors in this umami-rich salad will tantalize your taste buds.

3 tablespoons brown rice vinegar
1½ tablespoons naturally brewed soy sauce
1 tablespoon honey mustard
1½ teaspoons freshly grated gingerroot
½ teaspoon toasted sesame oil
1 garlic clove, minced
4 (4-ounce) yellowfin tuna steaks (preferably
 wild; about 1 inch thick)
¼ teaspoon sea salt, or to taste
¼ cup black sesame seeds
5 cups packed baby arugula
2 ounces fresh enoki or oyster mushrooms
⅓ cup shredded carrot or minced orange bell pepper
2 scallions, green and white parts, very thinly sliced

1. Whisk together the vinegar, soy sauce, mustard, ginger, oil, and garlic in a small bowl. Brush the entire surface of the tuna steaks with 2 tablespoons of the vinaigrette.

2. Heat a large nonstick skillet over medium-high heat. Sprinkle the tuna with the salt. Pour the sesame seeds on a plate and dip each tuna steak into the seeds to coat all sides. Lightly coat steaks with cooking spray (preferably homemade, page xix) and cook until medium-rare or desired doneness, about 1½ to 2 minutes per side.

3. Toss the arugula with 2 tablespoons of the vinaigrette. Slice the tuna on the bias (angle).

4. Arrange the arugula, mushrooms, and carrot on individual plates and top each with the tuna. Drizzle with the remaining vinaigrette, sprinkle with the scallions, and serve.

Per serving: 220 calories, 7g total fat, 1g saturated fat, 0g trans fat, 50mg cholesterol, 590mg sodium, 10g total carbohydrate, 3g dietary fiber, 3g sugars, 31g protein

Grilled Calamari–Cucumber Salad

Makes 4 servings: 1½ cups each

The mild, sweet squid known as calamari is commonly fried. Not here. This Vietnamese-style recipe shows off marinated and grilled calamari in a salad that's bursting with flavor from fish sauce, fresh lime juice, jalapeño, and a bouquet of fresh herbs.

1 pound whole calamari, cleaned

¾ cup roughly chopped fresh cilantro

Juice of 4 limes (½ cup)

1 large garlic clove, minced

1 small jalapeño pepper with seeds, minced

1 tablespoon peanut or canola oil

¼ teaspoon sea salt, or to taste

2 tablespoons Vietnamese or Thai fish sauce

1 tablespoon honey or agave nectar

1 large English cucumber, unpeeled and very thinly sliced crosswise

½ cup very thinly sliced red onion

½ cup loosely packed fresh parsley leaves

½ cup loosely packed fresh mint leaves

2 tablespoons chopped fresh basil (preferably Thai basil)

¼ cup unsalted dry-roasted cashew halves or pieces or dry-roasted peanuts

1. Toss together the calamari, 2 tablespoons of the cilantro, 2 tablespoons of the lime juice, the garlic, ½ of the jalapeño, the oil, and ⅛ teaspoon of the salt in a medium bowl. Let marinate for 45 minutes to 1 hour.

2. Prepare an outdoor or indoor grill.

3. Grill the calamari over direct medium-high heat (in batches, if necessary), turning once, just until firm, about 3 minutes. Slice the grilled calamari into ¼-inch-thick rings.

4. Whisk together the fish sauce, honey, and the remaining 2 tablespoons lime juice in a large bowl until combined. Add the cucumber, onion, parsley, mint, basil, and the remaining cilantro and jalapeño half and toss to combine. Add the grilled calamari slices and the remaining ⅛ teaspoon salt and toss to combine. Adjust seasoning.

5. Arrange the salad on individual plates or bowls, sprinkle with the cashews, and serve at room temperature or chilled.

Per serving: 200 calories, 6g total fat, 1g saturated fat, 0g trans fat, 265mg cholesterol, 790mg sodium, 18g total carbohydrate, 1g dietary fiber, 7g sugars, 21g protein

Polynesian Pork and Pineapple Grilled Salad

Makes 4 servings: about 3 cups each

Pineapple and pork is a popular pairing. Marinate with lively ingredients like ginger and soy sauce, add red onion and bell pepper, and grill—it transforms into extra-tasty kebabs with tropical appeal. They're simply scrumptious served here as the main feature of this salad.

½ fresh pineapple

1 medium red onion, cut into about 20 wedges

1 medium red bell pepper, cut into about 20 pieces

¼ cup chopped fresh basil

¼ cup chopped fresh cilantro

1 small jalapeño pepper with some seeds, minced

1 teaspoon freshly grated gingerroot

2 tablespoons naturally brewed soy sauce

Juice of 1 lime (2 tablespoons)

1 teaspoon honey or agave nectar

1 large garlic clove, minced

12 ounces trimmed lean pork tenderloin, cut into about 20 cubes

6 cups packed mixed salad greens

1. Peel, core, and cut the pineapple half into about 20 cubes. Reserve 2 tablespoons of the pineapple juice left from preparation. Place the pineapple cubes, the onion, bell pepper, basil, cilantro, jalapeño, ginger, and 1 tablespoon of the soy sauce in a large bowl. Set aside.

2. Whisk together the reserved 2 tablespoons pineapple juice, the lime juice, the remaining 1 tablespoon soy sauce, the honey, and garlic in a liquid measuring cup. Drizzle 2 tablespoons of the juice mixture over the pineapple-vegetable mixture and stir to combine. Drizzle the remaining juice mixture over the pork in a medium bowl and stir to combine. Let sit for up to 1 hour to marinate.

3. Prepare an outdoor or indoor grill.

4. Insert the pineapple, onion, bell pepper, and pork on water-soaked bamboo or reusable skewers. (For best results, place like ingredients on the same skewers.) Reserve the juices from the pineapple-vegetable mixture. Discard any remaining marinade used for the pork.

5. Grill the kebabs over direct medium-high heat, turning only as needed, until lightly charred and just cooked through, about 10 minutes.

6. Arrange the salad greens on a platter. Top with the grilled pineapple, onion, bell pepper, and pork. Drizzle with the reserved juices from the pineapple-vegetable mixture, and serve.

Per serving: 190 calories, 2.5g total fat, 1g saturated fat, 0g trans fat, 45mg cholesterol, 510mg sodium, 23g total carbohydrate, 4g dietary fiber, 16g sugars, 19g protein

Portabella and Peppercorn Chophouse Salad

Makes 4 servings: 2 cups salad with 1 cup vegetables and about 3 ounces steak each

You don't need to go to a steakhouse to enjoy a steakhouse-style salad. This grilled beef tenderloin steak salad is every bit as succulent. In fact, the addition of caramelized onions and sautéed portobellas, along with the finishing accent of feta, makes this extra delicious!

1 tablespoon peanut or canola oil

2 (6-ounce) lean beef tenderloin steaks, about 1 inch thick

1 teaspoon freshly cracked black pepper, or to taste

½ teaspoon sea salt, or to taste

1 large red onion, halved and thinly sliced

2 teaspoons aged balsamic vinegar

8 ounces sliced portobella mushroom caps

1 pint grape tomatoes

4 cups packed torn romaine lettuce leaves

4 cups packed torn curly endive leaves or baby arugula

½ cup Dijon Balsamic Vinaigrette (page 144) or other vinaigrette

3 tablespoons finely crumbled feta cheese

1. Heat 1½ teaspoons of the oil in a large nonstick skillet over medium-high heat. Add the steaks and cook until medium rare, about 3½ minutes per side. Remove the steaks with tongs to a plate and let rest for about 10 minutes. Sprinkle with ½ teaspoon of the pepper and ¼ teaspoon of the salt.

2. Meanwhile, heat the remaining 1½ teaspoons oil along with any remaining grease in the skillet over medium-high heat. Add the onion, vinegar, ¼ teaspoon of the pepper, and the remaining ¼ teaspoon salt and sauté for 2 minutes. Add the mushrooms and sauté until the onion and mushrooms are softened, about 3 minutes. Add the tomatoes and sauté until the tomatoes are softened and onion is lightly caramelized, about 3 minutes. Remove from heat. Adjust seasoning.

3. Thinly sliced the steak against the grain.

4. Toss the romaine and endive with half of the vinaigrette. Arrange the salad on individual plates. Top with the sautéed vegetables and steak. Sprinkle with the cheese and the remaining ¼ teaspoon pepper, and serve with the remaining vinaigrette on the side.

Per serving: 340 calories, 22g total fat, 6g saturated fat, 0g trans fat, 60mg cholesterol, 560mg sodium, 14g total carbohydrate, 4g dietary fiber, 8g sugars, 22g protein

Cuban Mojo Steak Salad

Makes 4 servings: ¼ salad each

The vivacious flavor essence of Cuban cuisine is found here. It's the generous and lively garlic and citrus notes of this panini-grilled flank steak salad that are so exhilarating. Enjoy with some salsa music to complete the experience.

¼ cup extra-virgin olive oil

6 large garlic cloves, very thinly sliced

⅓ cup fresh-squeezed orange juice

Juice of 2 limes (¼ cup)

½ teaspoon ground cumin

¾ teaspoon sea salt, or to taste

¼ teaspoon freshly ground black pepper, or to taste

2 teaspoons chopped fresh oregano

12 ounces lean grass-fed flank steak

6 cups packed torn green or red leaf lettuce

½ large English cucumber, unpeeled and
  very thinly sliced crosswise

1. Heat the oil in a medium saucepan over medium heat. Add the garlic and sauté until fragrant, about 1 minute. Carefully add the orange juice, lime juice, cumin, ½ teaspoon of the salt, the pepper, and 1 teaspoon of the oregano. Bring to a full rolling boil over high heat. Remove from heat to cool. Then chill this sauce, called mojo, in the refrigerator.

2. Reserve half of the mojo to dress the salad. Marinate the steak in the remaining half of the fully chilled mojo for 2 to 3 hours in a covered container in the refrigerator. Discard the mojo used for marinating the beef after use.

3. Prepare a panini press. Grill the steak in the panini press on high heat until medium rare, about 5 minutes. Let the steak rest for about 10 minutes, then very thinly slice against the grain.

4. Toss the greens and cucumber with the reserved mojo. Arrange the salad on a platter. Top with the steak while still warm. Sprinkle with the remaining ¼ teaspoon salt and 1 teaspoon oregano. Adjust seasoning, and serve.

Per serving: 250 calories, 17g total fat, 4g saturated fat, 0g trans fat, 30mg cholesterol, 410mg sodium, 7g total carbohydrate, 1g dietary fiber, 3g sugars, 19g protein

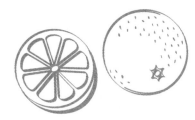

Soups, Stews, and Chilis

Stocks and Broths

Vegetable Stock

Chicken Stock

Chilled Soups

Creamy Carrot-Ginger Soup

Cool Mint–English Cucumber Soup

Verde Gazpacho Blanco

Heirloom Gazpacho

Garden Green Tea Gazpacho

Velvety Avocado Soup

Vichyssoise Shots

Sparkling Strawberry Soup

Tropical Fruit Soup Trio

Pineapple-Cucumber Chilled Soup

Vegetable Soups

Fall Country Vegetable Soup

Summer Squash Soup

Cajun Veggie Gumbo

Vegetarian Vietnamese Pho with Fresh Basil and Lime

Caramelized Red, White, and Yellow Onion Soup

Mashed Red Potato Soup

Truffle Purple Potato Soup

Leek and Yukon Gold Potato Chowder

Poblano Corn Chowder

Buttercup Squash Potage

Velvety Sweet Potato Soup

Puree of Broccoli Soup

Elegant White Asparagus Soup

Grain Soups

Asian Asparagus and Basmati Rice Soup

Cayenne Winter Squash-Speckled Orzo Soup

Minestrone

Fusilli e Fagioli

Exotic Mushroom and Barley Soup

Veggie Couscous Soup

Bean Soups

Red Bean and Blue Corn
Tortilla Soup

Roasted Italian Tomato
and Green Bean Soup

Creamy Butter Bean Soup

Peppery Five Bean Soup

Garlic Spinach
and White Bean Soup

Jamaican Red Bean Soup

Chili-Lime Black Bean Soup

Moroccan-Style Split Pea
Soup

Red Lentil Coconut
Curry Soup

Lentil and Greens Soup
with Poached Egg

Hoppin' John Soup
with Basmati Rice

Poultry, Fish, Shellfish, and Meat Soups

Egg Ribbon Soup

Avgolemono with Orzo
and Chicken

Pan-Asian Chicken
Udon Soup

Tarragon Chicken
and Black Quinoa Soup

Turkey Sausage Gumbo

Tunisian-Style Herbed
Cod Soup

Fresh Littleneck
Clam Chowder

Brooklyn Clam Chowder

Italian Tomato, Basil,
and Meatball Soup

Beef "Carpaccio"
and Shirataki Soup

Vegetarian Stews

Winter Root Vegetable Stew

Spring Vegetable Stew
with Fresh Tarragon

Turkish Vegetable Stew

Tuscan-Style Ribollita

North African Peanut Stew

Roasted Asian Eggplant
Stew

Irish Vegetable Stew

Herb and Spice Tomato
Chickpea Stew

White Bean Cassoulet
with Garlic Toast

Curry Lentil Stew
with Spinach

Poultry, Fish, Shellfish, and Meat Stews

Provencal-Style Poultry Stew with Fresh Basil

Creole Chicken and Okra Stew

Harissa Moroccan Chicken Amaranth Stew

Rotisserie Chicken Stew with Couscous, Carrots and Thyme

Adobo Chicken and Pepper Stew

Tropical Chicken and Shrimp Stew

Littleneck Clam Stew with Turkey Sausage

California Cioppino

Irish Beef Stew

Sonoma Bean and Pork Cassoulet

Spring Lamb Stew with Peas and Mint

Chilis

7-Veggie Chili

Black-n-White Chili Bowl

Superfood Soybean Chili

Chocolate Stout Chili

Cincinnati-Style Turkey Chili

5-Spice Turkey Chili

California Chicken Chili

Spanish Red Bean Chili with Chorizo

Secret-Ingredient Pasilla Chili Con Carne

Game Day Chili

Not only can soups and stews be satisfying and comforting or incredibly refreshing, but there are definite benefits to sipping soup when it comes to maintaining a healthy weight.

You can fill a soup with lots of nutrient-rich, low-calorie, satisfying ingredients. And if soup isn't intended as part of your main menu, you can enjoy a cup of soup before a meal to help curb hunger. You'll get to savor great flavors, feel nourished, and still have room for a balanced meal.

One of the not-so-good things about soup can be the sodium content. Too much salt can make you bloated and contribute to heart-health issues. So in this chapter, I focus on the ingredients within soups that provide flavor without the sodium, like onions, herbs, and spices. When I cook and create recipes, I include salt only after incorporating flavor-rich, nutrient-rich ingredients. I prefer sea salt for its more natural flavor. You'll find the recipes in this chapter taste delicious without tipping the sodium scales. But, of course, as you cook, adjust the amount of salt to meet your personal health or taste needs.

The chapter kicks off with a couple of stocks. They'll add much more flavor to soups than if you use water. Stocks can be frozen for a couple months; so make them in advance and freeze in pint-size containers. If you prefer, simply use cartons of low-sodium broth in the recipes.

Soups don't always have to be piping hot. Some of my favorites are meant to be served cool. The chilled soups and gazpachos in this chapter provide a refreshing way to enjoy seasonal fruits and vegetables—or both, such as in Pineapple-Cucumber Chilled Soup (page 208). They're ideal in summertime when produce is plentiful.

The vegetarian soups are the focal point of the chapter. They provide some of the simplest, slimmest, and most scrumptious ways to boost veggie intake anytime. Some of the soups are creamy—which is easily done by pureeing the soups in a blender. No actual cream is required! If you're into worldly cuisine, you'll find some international flair, too. The grain-based soups are a memorable marriage of whole grains and vegetables. Whole grains provide body to a soup and can be served as a substantial side dish; just include a simple entrée and that's it. And if you want something a little more filling, try one of the high-flavored bean soups. You can use canned beans to save time without giving up taste.

If you're an aficionado of poultry, fish, shellfish, or meat, you don't need to make that your entrée; it can be part of your soup. Want something a bit unusual? Try Tarragon Chicken and Black Quinoa Soup (page 229). Or enjoy Beef "Carpaccio" Shirataki Soup (page 233). The shirataki tofu noodles are exceptionally low in calories—just 20 calories for a 4-ounce serving. Pair these soups with a plant-based entrée for a wholesome meal.

But a hearty soup or stew can be the main focus of a meal, too. There's a stew for everyone in this chapter, from homestyle to fanciful. And there's a chili for everyone, too—there are ten to choose from. One of the secrets to great-tasting chili is to use more than just chili powder; you'll love the hint of cinnamon, cocoa powder, turmeric, or Chinese five-spice powder in these recipes. Beer can add unique depth of flavor and orange juice often brightens all the flavors it melds with for a pleasant balance. And if you want savory stew-like chili in minutes instead of hours, a pressure-cooker creates culinary magic.

Calorie range in this chapter: 15 to 380 calories.

Low-calorie picks: Vegetable Stock, 15 calories (page 203) and Chicken Stock, 15 calories (page 203).

Stocks and Broths

Vegetable Stock Ⓢ

Makes 10 servings: 1 cup each

Vegetable stock is one of the most important staples of healthful cooking. This recipe makes a garden-fresh, rich-tasting stock—adding great flavor to vegetarian cuisine. Use it in non-plant-based recipes, too.

1 tablespoon grapeseed or canola oil

3 large yellow onions, sliced

Juice of ½ small lemon (1 tablespoon)

4 large carrots, unpeeled, scrubbed, and sliced

1 fennel bulb, halved and sliced

3 large celery stalks, sliced

2 leeks, white and light green parts only, sliced and well rinsed

8 ounces portobella mushrooms, chopped

16 sprigs fresh thyme or parsley

4 garlic cloves, chopped

2 bay leaves

½ teaspoon black peppercorns

1. Heat the oil in a large stockpot over high heat. Add the onions and lemon juice and sauté until partially caramelized and nearly blackened in spots, about 8 minutes.

2. Add the remaining ingredients and 5 quarts cold water to the stockpot and bring just to a boil. Reduce heat to medium-low and simmer uncovered, stirring occasionally, until desired concentrated flavor, about 3½ to 4 hours.

3. Strain the stock through a fine-mesh strainer. Compost or discard inedible solids. Cool and refrigerate the stock. Store in the refrigerator for up to 5 days. Or store in 2-cup containers in the freezer for up to 3 months.

Per serving: 15 calories, 1.5g total fat, 1.5g saturated fat, 0g trans fat, 0mg cholesterol, 0mg sodium, 1g total carbohydrate, 0g dietary fiber, 0g sugars, 0g protein

Chicken Stock Ⓢ

Makes 14 servings: 1 cup each

Stock is basically a broth that doesn't have added salt. So it allows you to season the food to your taste—and you won't have to work around the high levels of sodium from broth. Use chicken stock in recipes that have poultry or other animal products already included. But if you do use it for plant-based dishes, be sure to alert any vegetarians!

1 tablespoon grapeseed or canola oil

3 large yellow onions, sliced

Juice of ½ small lemon (1 tablespoon)

1 (3½- to 4-pound) whole chicken, cut into 8 pieces, including necks and giblets

4 large carrots, unpeeled, scrubbed, and sliced

1 fennel bulb, sliced

2 leeks, white and light green parts only, sliced and well rinsed

2 large celery stalks, sliced

8 ounces portobella mushrooms, chopped

16 sprigs fresh thyme or parsley

4 garlic cloves, chopped

2 bay leaves

½ teaspoon black peppercorns

1. Heat the oil in a large stockpot over high heat. Add the onions and lemon juice and sauté until partially caramelized and nearly blackened in spots, about 8 minutes.

2. Add the remaining ingredients and 5 quarts cold water to the stockpot and bring just to a boil. Reduce heat to medium-low and simmer uncovered, skimming froth as needed, until desired concentrated flavor, about 3½ to 4 hours.

3. Strain the stock through a fine-mesh strainer. Compost or discard inedible solids. Cool and refrigerate the stock. Store in the refrigerator for up to 3 days. Or store in 2-cup containers in the freezer for up to 1 month.

Per serving: 15 calories, 1g total fat, 0g saturated fat, 0g trans fat, 0mg cholesterol, 0mg sodium, 1g total carbohydrate, 0g dietary fiber, 0g sugars, 1g protein

Chilled Soups

Creamy Carrot-Ginger Soup

Makes 11 servings: 1 cup each

Carrots and ginger unite in this smooth soup with Asian flair. It gets its creaminess from pureeing the veggies in the soup, which includes Yukon Gold potatoes. Cashews provide a little nuttiness along with extra creaminess. I actually use water instead of straight stock here to allow the pure carrot flavor in this specific recipe to stand out. You can enjoy this soup cool or hot.

1 tablespoon extra-virgin olive oil

1¼ pounds carrots, sliced, or 1 pound baby carrots

2 large celery stalks, chopped

1 large sweet onion, sliced

2 tablespoons freshly grated gingerroot

⅓ cup unsalted dry-roasted cashews

2 teaspoons apple cider vinegar

2 teaspoons sea salt, or to taste

1 pound Yukon Gold potatoes, unpeeled, scrubbed, and sliced

1 (32-ounce) carton low-sodium vegetable broth or 4 cups Vegetable Stock (page 203)

1½ teaspoons pure coconut extract (optional)

1 teaspoon freshly ground white pepper, or to taste

¼ teaspoon ground cayenne, or to taste

¼ teaspoon paprika, or to taste

2 tablespoons chopped fresh chives

1. Heat the oil in a large stockpot over medium-low heat. Add the carrots, celery, onion, ginger, cashews, vinegar, and ¼ teaspoon of the salt. Cover and sweat, stirring occasionally, for 10 minutes.

2. Add the potatoes, broth, extract (if using), white pepper, cayenne, paprika, the remaining 1¾ teaspoons salt, and 3 cups cold water. Cover and bring to a boil.

3. Reduce heat to medium-low and simmer, uncovered, until the potatoes and carrots are very tender, about 30 minutes.

4. Add in batches to a blender using the hot fill line as a guide; puree. (Alternatively, if you prefer a texture that's less creamy and more potage-like, puree in the pot using an immersion blender.) Adjust seasoning. Chill until ready to serve.

5. Divide the soup among individual soup bowls or cups, top with the chives, and serve.

Per serving: 100 calories, 3.5g total fat, 0.5g saturated fat, 0g trans fat, 0mg cholesterol, 520mg sodium, 16g total carbohydrate, 3g dietary fiber, 5g sugars, 2g protein

Cool Mint–English Cucumber Soup

Makes 4 servings: 1 cup each

This lovely minted cucumber recipe should be at the top of the list when looking for a delightful chilled soup. Its bright flavors and creamy tang are refreshing.

1 large English cucumber, unpeeled and coarsely grated

½ cup fat-free or low-fat plain Greek yogurt

¼ cup sour cream

3 tablespoons chopped fresh mint leaves

1 teaspoon chopped fresh dill

1 large garlic clove, minced

¾ teaspoon sea salt, or to taste

¼ teaspoon freshly ground white or black pepper, or to taste

¾ cup low-sodium vegetable broth or Vegetable Stock (page 203), or to taste

1. Stir together all of the ingredients in a medium bowl. Add additional broth for thinner consistency, if desired. Adjust seasoning. Chill until ready to serve.

2. Divide the soup among individual small soup bowls or cups. Serve topped with small fresh mint or dill sprigs, if desired.

Per serving: 60 calories, 2.5g total fat, 1.5g saturated fat, 0g trans fat, 5mg cholesterol, 480mg sodium, 6g total carbohydrate, 1g dietary fiber, 3g sugars, 3g protein

Verde Gazpacho Blanco

Makes 4 servings: 1 cup each

The velvety white gazpacho at Dovetail restaurant in New York City was the inspiration for this cool and lovely soup. My version is a little greener—from the cucumber skin that I include— and a little lighter than Dovetail's. But it still promises to provide pure delectableness.

2 tablespoons extra-virgin olive oil

1 small leek, white part only, thinly sliced and well rinsed

2 cups chopped unpeeled English cucumbers

2 slices whole-grain bread, crusts removed

15 white seedless grapes

3 tablespoons sliced natural almonds

2 tablespoons fat-free or low-fat plain Greek yogurt

1½ tablespoons white balsamic vinegar

1 teaspoon sea salt, or to taste

1½ cups unsweetened white tea or water, chilled

2 teaspoons chopped fresh dill or basil

1. Heat the oil in a small skillet over medium heat. Add the leek and sauté until softened, about 2½ minutes. Chill for 10 minutes.

2. Combine the chilled leek, the cucumbers, bread, grapes, almonds, yogurt, vinegar, and salt in a large bowl.

3. Add half of the leek mixture to a blender with ¾ cup of the tea; cover and puree; transfer to a pitcher or bowl. Repeat with the remaining leek mixture and the remaining ¾ cup of tea.

4. Strain the mixture through a fine-mesh strainer. Adjust seasoning. Chill soup, if desired, 1 hour.

5. Ladle the soup into small bowls or tea cups, top with the dill, and serve.

Per serving: 150 calories, 10g total fat, 1.5g saturated fat, 0g trans fat, 0mg cholesterol, 640mg sodium, 13g total carbohydrate, 2g dietary fiber, 5g sugars, 4g protein

Heirloom Gazpacho

Makes 5 servings: 1 cup each

I love to showcase all the unique characteristics, particularly the colors, of heirloom tomatoes when they're available. But at the end of the day, their most important culinary attribute is taste. And this gazpacho is overflowing with tastiness. Of course, use fresh, ripe regular tomatoes, if you like.

3 large fully ripened heirloom tomatoes, pulp removed and chopped

½ large English cucumber, unpeeled and chopped

1 large yellow bell pepper, chopped

1 large green bell pepper, chopped

½ cup finely diced red onion

1 serrano pepper with or without seeds, stem removed

1 small garlic clove, chopped

2 tablespoons extra-virgin olive oil

2 tablespoons white balsamic vinegar

1 teaspoon sea salt, or to taste

¼ teaspoon freshly ground black pepper, or to taste

½ cup low-sodium vegetable broth or Vegetable Stock (page 203), or to taste

1. Add the tomatoes, cucumber, bell peppers, ¼ cup of the onion, the serrano, garlic, oil, vinegar, salt, black pepper, and broth to a food processor. Cover and pulse until nearly smooth with some small lumps remaining. Add additional broth for thinner consistency, if desired. Adjust seasoning.

2. Pour into individual small bowls or martini glasses. Top with the remaining ¼ cup onion, and serve at room temperature.

Per serving: 100 calories, 6g total fat, 1g saturated fat, 0g trans fat, 0mg cholesterol, 490mg sodium, 12g total carbohydrate, 3g dietary fiber, 6g sugars, 2g protein

Garden Green Tea Gazpacho

Makes 5 servings: 1 cup each

This is an inspired gazpacho. Its golden-green hue gives it a fresh modern edge. And the unique addition of green tea gives it a hint of mystery. Mostly, you'll be delighted by the light garden freshness of this cool soup.

½ cup brewed green tea, chilled (made with 1 tea bag)

½ large English cucumber, unpeeled and chopped

1 medium green bell pepper, chopped

1 medium yellow bell pepper, chopped

Juice of 1 lemon (3 tablespoons)

2 medium vine-ripened yellow tomatoes, chopped

1 small jalapeño pepper, ½ chopped and ½ sliced crosswise

1 large shallot, chopped

1 small garlic clove, chopped

2 teaspoons extra-virgin olive oil

¾ teaspoon sea salt, or to taste

¼ teaspoon freshly ground black or white pepper, or to taste

1. Add the green tea, cucumber, and bell peppers to a blender. Cover and blend until smooth. Pour into a pitcher.

2. Add the lemon juice, tomatoes, chopped jalapeño, shallot, garlic, oil, salt, and black pepper to the blender. Cover and blend until smooth. Pour into the pitcher.

3. Stir the mixtures together in the pitcher, and adjust seasoning.

4. Pour into bowls, garnish each with a jalapeño slice, and serve.

Per serving: 50 calories, 2g total fat, 0g saturated fat, 0g trans fat, 0mg cholesterol, 360mg sodium, 8g total carbohydrate, 2g dietary fiber, 4g sugars, 1g protein

Velvety Avocado Soup Ⓕ

Makes 3 servings: about 1 cup each

There are so many culinary possibilities with avocados! Here their velvety texture and buttery flavor shine brightly; surely no one will realize how wonderfully nutritious this soup is. You can serve it in any bowls or cups, of course, but showcasing the soup in teacups is a super-simple way to make the presentation special and the soup even more inviting.

1 Hass avocado, pitted and peeled

Juice of ½ lemon (1½ tablespoons), or to taste

Juice of ½ lime (1 tablespoon), or to taste

1 cup low-sodium vegetable broth or Vegetable Stock (page 203)

¾ cup low-fat buttermilk or plain almond milk

½ teaspoon sea salt, or to taste

⅛ teaspoon ground cumin

⅛ teaspoon ground coriander

⅛ teaspoon hot pepper sauce, or to taste

2 teaspoons finely chopped fresh cilantro

1. Add all the ingredients to a blender or food processor. Cover and blend until smooth. Adjust seasoning.

2. Transfer the soup to a pitcher or bowl and cool in the refrigerator, covered, until well chilled, about 2 hours.

3. Pour the soup into teacups. Garnish with fresh small cilantro sprigs, if desired, and serve chilled.

Per serving: 140 calories, 10g total fat, 2g saturated fat, 0g trans fat, 0mg cholesterol, 510mg sodium, 10g total carbohydrate, 5g dietary fiber, 4g sugars, 3g protein

Vichyssoise Shots

Makes 20 servings: ¼ cup each

Vichyssoise is a classic cool, creamy, soothing soup made with potatoes, leeks, and, heavy cream. Here, a bit of butter along with creamy Greek yogurt provide all the silky richness you need sans cream. Then, instead of getting weighted down by eating a big bowlful, you'll get a terrific burst of flavors and textures from an espresso cup—a scrumptious 35-calorie shot of comfort.

1 tablespoon unsalted butter

2 large leeks, white and light green parts only, thinly sliced and well rinsed

2 teaspoons white balsamic vinegar

1 teaspoon sea salt

1 large Yukon Gold potato, unpeeled, scrubbed, and chopped

2½ cups low-sodium chicken broth or Chicken Stock (page 203)

1 cup plain almond milk or light soy milk

¼ teaspoon freshly ground white pepper, or to taste

½ cup fat-free or low-fat plain Greek yogurt

1 tablespoon minced fresh chives

1. Melt the butter in a large saucepan over medium heat. Add the leeks, vinegar, and ¼ teaspoon of the salt and sauté until softened, about 5 minutes. Then increase heat to medium-high and sauté until caramelized, about 10 more minutes.

2. Reduce heat to medium-low, add the potato, broth, and the remaining ¾ teaspoon salt, cover, and simmer until the potatoes are very soft, about 30 minutes.

3. Blend until smooth using an immersion blender. (Alternatively, puree in a blender in batches using the hot fill line as a guide; return to the saucepan over medium-low heat.)

4. Add the almond milk and pepper and bring to a simmer. Remove from heat and cool. Chill in the refrigerator at least 2 hours or overnight.

5. When ready to serve, whisk in the yogurt. Adjust seasoning and, if desired, add additional broth for a thinner consistency. Pour into espresso cups or juice glasses. Sprinkle with chives, and serve.

Per serving: 35 calories, 1g total fat, 0g saturated fat, 0g trans fat, 0mg cholesterol, 140mg sodium, 5g total carbohydrate, 1g dietary fiber, 1g sugars, 1g protein

Sparkling Strawberry Soup Ⓢ

Makes 3 servings: 1 cup each

You'll get a tickle out of the fizz in this brilliant strawberry red soup—it's sparkling wine. You can serve this as an elegant starter or a flirty dessert.

1 cup 100% pomegranate juice or pomegranate juice blend

2½ cups sliced fresh or frozen strawberries, thawed

¾ cup sparkling wine, Champagne, or sparkling fruit juice of choice

3 small sprigs fresh mint

1. Add the juice and half of the strawberries to a blender or food processor. Cover and blend until smooth. Add the remaining strawberries, cover, and blend until very smooth.

2. Pour into a pitcher and chill.

3. When ready to serve, stir the wine into the soup. Gently pour the soup into individual bowls, cups, or wide-rimmed beverage glasses. Garnish with the mint, and serve.

Per serving: 140 calories, 0.5g total fat, 0g saturated fat, 0g trans fat, 0mg cholesterol, 10mg sodium, 24g total carbohydrate, 3g dietary fiber, 17g sugars, 1g protein

Tropical Fruit Soup Trio (F)

Makes 6 servings: 1½ cups each

Simply beautiful! Eating fruit has never been more fun or flavorful. This recipe is actually three cool tropical fruit soups served together. You'll see each of the luminous green, perky orange, and vivid red soups all in one bowl. It'll absolutely make a lasting impression!

3 cups chopped honeydew melon

1 small banana, sliced

¼ cup 100% pear or peach nectar

Juice of 1 lime (2 tablespoons), or to taste

¼ teaspoon + ⅛ teaspoon sea salt, or to taste

2 cups chopped cantaloupe

2 cups chopped mango

¼ cup 100% apricot or peach nectar

2 cups chopped papaya

2 cups sliced strawberries

¼ cup 100% guava or peach nectar

6 small fresh mint sprigs

1. Add the honeydew, banana, pear nectar, 2 teaspoons of the lime juice, and a pinch of the salt to a blender. Cover and puree. Adjust the lime juice or salt, if necessary. Pour into a pitcher or large liquid measuring cup, and chill.

2. Add the cantaloupe, mango, apricot nectar, 2 teaspoons of the lime juice, and a pinch of the salt to a blender. Cover and puree. Adjust the lime juice or salt, if necessary. Pour into a separate pitcher or large liquid measuring cup, and chill.

3. Add the papaya, strawberries, guava nectar, 2 teaspoons of the lime juice, and a pinch of the salt to a blender. Cover and puree. Adjust the lime juice or salt, if necessary.

4. Pour ½ cup of each fruit soup into one of the bowls at the same time, pouring from 2, 6, and 10 o'clock positions. (Get someone to help you pour or just do two first, then follow with the third.)

Repeat with the remaining soup and bowls. Top each with the mint, and serve.

Per serving: 150 calories, 0.5g total fat, 0g saturated fat, 0g trans fat, 0mg cholesterol, 170mg sodium, 38g total carbohydrate, 5g dietary fiber, 30g sugars, 2g protein

Pineapple-Cucumber Chilled Soup

Makes 4 servings: 1 cup each

When there's an abundance of seasonal produce available to you, why not mix things up a bit? Here, fresh pineapple with an accent of ginger for zing makes for a vibrant and sumptuous summertime gazpacho-style soup.

2 cups finely diced fresh pineapple

2 cups finely diced unpeeled English cucumber

1 cup 100% pineapple juice

1 small jalapeño pepper with some seeds, stem removed

Juice of ½ lime (1 tablespoon)

1 tablespoon macadamia nut, avocado, or flaxseed oil

1 teaspoon freshly grated gingerroot

¼ teaspoon sea salt, or to taste

¼ cup finely diced sweet onion

3 tablespoons chopped fresh cilantro

1. Add 1½ cups of the pineapple, 1½ cups of the cucumber, the pineapple juice, jalapeño, lime juice, oil, ginger, and salt to a blender. Cover and puree. Pour the mixture into a large bowl.

2. Add the remaining ½ cup pineapple, ½ cup cucumber, the onion, and 2 tablespoons of the cilantro and stir. Chill.

3. Adjust seasoning. Ladle the soup into individual serving bowls or cups. Top with the remaining 1 tablespoon cilantro, and serve.

Per serving: 120 calories, 3.5g total fat, 0g saturated fat, 0g trans fat, 0mg cholesterol, 150mg sodium, 22g total carbohydrate, 2g dietary fiber, 17g sugars, 1g protein

Vegetable Soups

Fall Country Vegetable Soup

Makes 9 servings: 1 cup each

The chunky root veggies in this soup will be so tempting; you just know it's going to be hearty and flavorful! The herbal hint of rosemary and earthy sweet spice of cinnamon will provide aromatic happiness. Cook up a batch of this satisfying soup on one of those chilly, rainy days of autumn; it'll make you feel toasty warm all over.

1 tablespoon extra-virgin olive oil

1 medium red onion, finely diced

2 teaspoons apple cider vinegar

1½ teaspoons sea salt, or to taste

2 medium turnips or 1 large rutabaga, peeled and cut into ¾-inch pieces

1 large carrot, unpeeled, scrubbed, and cut into ¾-inch pieces

1 medium parsnip, unpeeled, scrubbed, and cut into ¾-inch pieces

1 medium sweet potato, unpeeled, scrubbed, and cut into ¾-inch cubes

1 teaspoon finely chopped fresh rosemary

½ teaspoon hot pepper sauce, or to taste

½ teaspoon freshly ground black pepper, or to taste

¼ teaspoon ground cinnamon, or to taste

6 cups low-sodium vegetable broth, Vegetable Stock (page 203), or Chicken Stock (page 203)

2 cups chopped fresh kale leaves

¼ cup chopped fresh flat-leaf parsley

1. Heat the oil in a large saucepan or stockpot over medium heat. Add the onion, vinegar, and ¼ teaspoon of the salt and sauté until slightly caramelized, about 10 minutes.

2. Add the turnips, carrot, parsnip, sweet potato, rosemary, hot pepper sauce, black pepper, cinnamon, broth, and the remaining 1¼ teaspoons salt. Increase heat to high and bring to a boil. Reduce heat to medium-low and simmer, uncovered, for 12 minutes. Add the kale and simmer until all the vegetables are tender, about 12 additional minutes. Adjust seasoning.

3. Stir the parsley into the soup, ladle into individual bowls, and serve.

Per serving: 70 calories, 2g total fat, 0g saturated fat, 0g trans fat, 0mg cholesterol, 520mg sodium, 14g total carbohydrate, 3g dietary fiber, 5g sugars, 1g protein

Herb-Infused Summer Squash Soup

Makes 11 servings: 1 cup each

The potatoes are the base of this soup's satisfying taste and texture. But it's the seasonal zucchini that add the essence of summer and impart its lovely garden fresh allure here. The herbs provide aromatic charm. For a different approach, you can puree the soup for a tantalizing, creamy texture.

1 tablespoon extra-virgin olive oil

1 large white onion, chopped

2 teaspoons fresh lemon juice

1¼ teaspoons sea salt, or to taste

2 large garlic cloves, finely chopped

2 teaspoons finely chopped fresh rosemary or mixture of fresh rosemary and oregano

6 cups low-sodium vegetable broth or Vegetable Stock (page 203)

1½ pounds baby Dutch yellow potatoes, unpeeled, scrubbed, and thinly sliced

¼ teaspoon freshly ground black pepper, or to taste

4 medium zucchini or yellow summer squash, unpeeled and thinly sliced crosswise

1 tablespoon finely chopped fresh mint or cilantro

2 tablespoons finely chopped fresh chives or basil

1. Heat the oil in a stockpot or extra-large saucepan over medium heat. Add the onion, lemon juice, and ¼ teaspoon of the salt and sauté until softened, about 8 minutes. Stir in the garlic and rosemary and sauté until fragrant, about 1 minute. Increase heat to high. Add the broth, potatoes, pepper, and the remaining 1 teaspoon salt and bring to a boil. Reduce heat to medium-low and

continues on next page

simmer, uncovered, for 8 minutes. Stir in the zucchini, cover, and simmer until the zucchini and potatoes are tender, about 12 additional minutes. Stir in the mint and adjust seasoning.

2. Ladle the soup into individual serving bowls. Sprinkle with the chives, and serve.

Per serving: 80 calories, 1.5g total fat, 0g saturated fat, 0g trans fat, 0mg cholesterol, 350mg sodium, 15g total carbohydrate, 3g dietary fiber, 4g sugars, 2g protein

Cajun Veggie Gumbo

Makes 8 servings: 1 cup each

If you've ever been to New Orleans, you know about the oh-so-rich gumbo. The depth of flavors of the stew-like Creole treat is unsurpassed. This jazzy vegan version with its rich forest green hue shouts of healthfulness—especially when served over brown rice. And its ingredients are buzzing of deliciousness.

10 ounces dark leafy greens, such as kale, chicory, mustard or collard greens, soaked, drained, and coarsely chopped

1¼ teaspoons sea salt, or to taste

¼ cup unrefined peanut or canola oil

¼ cup whole oat or soy flour

1 large Spanish or yellow onion, diced

1 large green bell pepper, diced

3 large celery stalks, very thinly sliced or diced

2 large garlic cloves, minced

1 small jalapeño pepper with seeds, minced

2 teaspoons apple cider vinegar

2 cups low-sodium vegetable broth or Vegetable Stock (page 203)

1 tablespoon Creole seasoning (page 31), or Cajun seasoning, to taste

½ teaspoon freshly ground black pepper, or to taste

¼ teaspoon ground allspice

⅛ teaspoon ground cloves

1½ teaspoons finely chopped fresh thyme or oregano

4 scallions, green and white parts, thinly sliced or minced

1. Add the greens to a large saucepan or stockpot with 3 cups water and 1 teaspoon of the salt over medium-high heat. Bring to a simmer, cover, and reduce heat to medium-low. Cook until the leaves are wilted, about 15 minutes. Remove the greens from the cooking liquid, strain the greens, reserving the liquid.

2. Add the greens to a food processor and puree until smooth. Set aside.

3. Heat the oil in a stockpot or Dutch oven over medium heat. Add the flour and continuously whisk for 5 minutes.

4. Add the onion, bell pepper, celery, garlic, jalapeño, vinegar, and the remaining ¼ teaspoon salt and sauté over medium-high heat until the mixture begins to caramelize and the onion is softened, about 8 minutes. Add the reserved greens cooking liquid, the broth, Creole seasoning, black pepper, allspice, cloves, and half of the thyme, reduce heat to medium, and bring to a simmer, uncovered, stirring frequently, until the soup is thickened, about 12 minutes.

5. Stir in the scallions and the pureed greens, cover, and simmer, uncovered, until desired gumbo consistency, about 8 minutes. Adjust seasoning. Garnish with the remaining thyme and serve.

Per serving: 110 calories, 8g total fat, 1.5g saturated fat, 0g trans fat, 0mg cholesterol, 640mg sodium, 11g total carbohydrate, 3g dietary fiber, 2g sugars, 2g protein

Vegetarian Vietnamese Pho with Fresh Basil and Lime Ⓕ

Makes 5 servings: 2 cups each

The distinct lime accent is just one of the beautiful nuances of this slightly tangy, hearty noodle soup brimming with mushrooms, fresh herbs, and Asian flavors. It can be served as a main dish. Slurping (politely) is expected!

1 cup frozen shelled edamame

1 tablespoon unrefined peanut or canola oil

1 large white onion, diced

2 teaspoons brown rice vinegar

¾ teaspoon sea salt, or to taste

2 large garlic cloves, minced

2 teaspoons freshly grated gingerroot

6 cups low-sodium vegetable broth or
    Vegetable Stock (page 203)

1½ cups bite-size broccoli florets

1½ cups fresh maitake, stemmed shiitake,
    or oyster mushrooms, thinly sliced

1½ teaspoons naturally brewed soy sauce

½ teaspoon freshly ground black pepper, or to taste

½ teaspoon Asian garlic-chili sauce, to taste

¼ teaspoon ground cinnamon or Chinese
    five-spice powder

3 scallions, green and white parts, thinly sliced

1 lime, ½ juiced, ½ cut into wedges

6 ounces brown rice noodles or soba noodles

¼ cup thinly sliced fresh basil or mixture of
    fresh basil, cilantro, and mint leaves

1. Cook the edamame according to package directions. Set aside.

2. Heat the oil in a stockpot over medium heat. Add the onion, vinegar, and ¼ teaspoon of the salt and sauté until softened, about 8 minutes. Add the garlic and ginger and sauté for 2 minutes. Add the broth, broccoli, mushrooms, soy sauce, pepper, garlic-chili sauce, cinnamon, and the remaining ½ teaspoon salt and bring to a boil. Reduce heat to medium-low, and simmer, uncovered, until the broccoli is just tender, about 8 minutes. Stir in the scallions and lime juice. Adjust seasoning.

3. Meanwhile, cook the noodles according to package directions.

4. Divide the noodles and cooked edamame among individual bowls. Ladle the soup on top. Top with the basil, and serve with the lime wedges. Enjoy with chopsticks and a spoon.

Per serving: 240 calories, 5g total fat, 0.5g saturated fat, 0g trans fat, 0mg cholesterol, 660mg sodium, 41g total carbohydrate, 7g dietary fiber, 7g sugars, 9g protein

Caramelized Red, White, and Yellow Onion Soup

Makes 8 servings: about 1 cup each

Sautéing onions until they're caramelized—browned, soft, and slightly sweet—imparts a deep, rich taste and texture. In this soup, the layering of flavor from three varieties of caramelized onions creates incredible lusciousness.

1 tablespoon extra-virgin olive oil

1 large red onion, halved, very thinly sliced

1 large white onion, halved, very thinly sliced

1 large yellow or Spanish onion, halved,
    very thinly sliced

2 teaspoons white balsamic vinegar

1¼ teaspoons sea salt, or to taste

2 large garlic cloves, minced

1 serrano pepper with seeds, minced

2 teaspoons finely chopped fresh thyme

1 (32-ounce) carton low-sodium vegetable
    or chicken broth or 4 cups Vegetable Stock
    (page 203)

1½ teaspoons naturally brewed soy sauce

½ teaspoon freshly ground black pepper,
    or to taste

1. Heat the oil in a stockpot over medium heat. Add the onions, vinegar, and ¼ teaspoon of the salt, cover, and cook, stirring occasionally, for 15 minutes. Remove cover, increase heat to medium-high, and sauté until the onions are caramelized, about 12 minutes. Add the garlic, serrano, and thyme and sauté 1 minute.

2. Add the broth, soy sauce, black pepper, and the remaining 1 teaspoon salt, increase heat to high, and bring to a boil, scraping up and stirring into broth any browned bits from pot. Reduce heat to low and simmer for 5 minutes.

3. Adjust seasoning, and serve.

Per serving: 50 calories, 2g total fat, 0g saturated fat, 0g trans fat, 0mg cholesterol, 490mg sodium, 7g total carbohydrate, 2g dietary fiber, 3g sugars, 1g protein

Mashed Red Potato Soup

Makes 4 servings: 1 cup each

Perhaps one of the few dishes more comforting than mashed potatoes is the spuds whipped into a soul-soothing soup. But comfort food certainly doesn't have to be bad for you; here, the skin is left on the potatoes for the goodness of fiber and earthier texture. The fragrantly distinguished spices and just a petite pat of butter in each serving stlll make this a culinary dream.

2 large red potatoes, unpeeled, scrubbed, and cut into ½-inch cubes

½ cup plain almond milk or light soy milk, at room temperature

2 teaspoons unsalted butter, at temperature, or extra-virgin olive oil

1 large garlic clove, minced

⅓ cup minced fresh chives or scallions

1¾ cups low-sodium chicken or Vegetable broth or Vegetable Stock (page 203)

¾ teaspoon sea salt, or to taste

½ teaspoon freshly ground black pepper, or to taste

⅛ teaspoon ground coriander, or to taste

⅛ teaspoon ground turmeric, or to taste

1. Place the potatoes in a large microwave-safe bowl. Cover well with parchment paper. Microwave on high until fork-tender, about 6 to 7 minutes. Let sit covered in the microwave oven to allow the potatoes to steam and further soften, about 5 minutes. Carefully remove parchment paper.

2. Add the almond milk, butter, and garlic and smash with a potato masher until nearly smooth. Stir in the chives, broth, salt, pepper, coriander, and turmeric.

3. Microwave on high, uncovered, until steaming hot, about 3½ to 4 minutes. Adjust seasoning, ladle into individual bowls, and serve.

Per serving: 130 calories, 2.5g total fat, 1.5g saturated fat, 0g trans fat, 5mg cholesterol, 490mg sodium, 25g total carbohydrate, 3g dietary fiber, 2g sugars, 4g protein

CLEAN YOUR PRODUCE

Be sure to scrub potato skins very well to remove pesticide residues. Consider using a vegetable wash, like Veggie Wash. Or make your own produce rinse by very carefully mixing 1 cup each fresh water and vinegar and 2 tablespoons each fresh lemon juice and baking soda; store in a spray bottle in the fridge. Also, when possible, pick organic produce when you plan on enjoying the skin so as to steer clear of chemical pesticides.

Truffle Purple Potato Soup

Makes 8 servings: 1 cup each

Yes, this soup is actually purple! It's out of the ordinary—in a good way, particularly with the addition of intoxicating truffle oil. To make it even more impressive, turn this soup into a silky lavender consommé by straining it through a fine-mesh strainer to serve.

1 head garlic

½ teaspoon extra-virgin olive oil

2 pounds large purple or Yukon Gold potatoes, unpeeled, scrubbed, and cut into 1-inch cubes

1 tablespoon unsalted butter, at room temperature

¾ cup plain almond milk or light soy milk

1 (32-ounce) carton low-sodium chicken broth or 4 cups Chicken Stock (page 203)

1 tablespoon white truffle oil

1¼ teaspoons sea salt, or to taste

1. Cut top portion off the garlic to expose all the cloves. Rub the cut surface of the exposed cloves with the olive oil. Wrap in aluminum foil. Bake in a toaster oven (or preheat conventional oven) at 400°F until fully softened, about 30 minutes.

2. Meanwhile, add the potatoes to a large saucepan or stockpot, cover with water, and bring to a boil over high heat. Reduce heat to medium-low and simmer until the potatoes are very soft, about 25 minutes. Drain the potatoes and place into a large bowl. Smash the potatoes with the butter in a large bowl using a potato masher until smooth.

3. Squeeze the roasted garlic cloves from their skins onto the potatoes and mash. Add the almond milk and mash until the mixture is creamy.

4. Add the mashed potatoes to a large saucepan with the broth, truffle oil, and salt over medium-high heat. Bring to a boil while stirring. Reduce heat to medium-low and simmer, uncovered, stirring occasionally, until desired consistency is reached, about 20 minutes. Adjust seasoning.

5. Ladle into individual bowls, and serve.

Per serving: 130 calories, 4g total fat, 1g saturated fat, 0g trans fat, 5mg cholesterol, 420mg sodium, 20g total carbohydrate, 2g dietary fiber, 2g sugars, 4g protein

Leek and Yukon Gold Potato Chowder

Makes 6 servings: 1 cup each

Today, if it's a thick, rich, chunky soup, it can be considered chowder. Here's a tasty lightened version. You'll love the confetti of fresh chives that'll provide a terrific accent. And to add a palate-pleasing, soul-satisfying element to your chowder, the smoky bacon bits add only 30 calories per serving.

1 tablespoon extra-virgin olive oil

2 teaspoons unsalted butter or unrefined peanut oil

4 medium leeks, white and light green parts only, halved lengthwise, sliced crosswise ½ inch thick and well rinsed

1 pound Yukon Gold potatoes, unpeeled, scrubbed, and diced

2 cups low-sodium chicken or vegetable broth or Vegetable Stock (page 203)

1 teaspoon sea salt, or to taste

½ teaspoon ground sage

3 tablespoons whole oat or soy flour

2 cups plain almond milk or light soy milk

¼ cup chopped fresh flat-leaf parsley

¼ cup chopped fresh chives

4 slices applewood-smoked uncured bacon, cooked until crisp and crumbled (optional)

1. Heat the oil and butter in a large saucepan over medium-high heat. Once the butter melts, add the leeks and sauté until softened, about 8 minutes.

2. Add the potatoes, broth, salt, and sage. Cover and cook until the potatoes are nearly tender, about 12 minutes.

3. Whisk together the flour and ¼ cup of the almond milk in a liquid measuring cup or small bowl into smooth.

4. Stir it, along with the remaining 1¾ cups almond milk, into the potato-leek mixture. Reduce heat to medium and cook, uncovered, until slightly thickened, stirring occasionally, about 5 to 6 minutes.

5. Remove from heat. Stir in the parsley and half of the chives. Adjust seasoning.

6. Ladle into individual cups or small serving bowls, sprinkle with the remaining chives and bacon (if using), and serve.

Per serving: 160 calories, 5g total fat, 1.5g saturated fat, 0g trans fat, 5mg cholesterol, 480mg sodium, 26g total carbohydrate, 3g dietary fiber, 5g sugars, 4g protein

Poblano Corn Chowder

Makes 9 servings: 1 cup each

Though there's no cream in this savory, good-for-you chowder, it's surprisingly decadent.

2 teaspoons unsalted butter

1 medium yellow onion, cut into ¼-inch dice

2 large poblano peppers, cut into ¼-inch dice

1 large red potato, unpeeled, scrubbed,
    and cut into ½-inch cubes

1 medium red bell pepper, cut into ½-inch cubes

1 small jalapeño pepper with seeds, halved
    vertically and thinly sliced crosswise

2 teaspoons apple cider vinegar

½ teaspoon ground cumin

1¼ teaspoons sea salt, or to taste

¼ cup whole oat or soy flour

1 (12-ounce) can fat-free evaporated milk

3 cups low-sodium chicken or vegetable broth
    or Vegetable Stock (page 203)

1 pound frozen yellow corn kernels, thawed

3 tablespoons finely chopped fresh cilantro

1. Melt the butter in a stockpot over medium heat. Add the onion, poblanos, potato, bell pepper, jalapeño, vinegar, cumin, and ¼ teaspoon salt, cover, and cook, stirring occasionally, until the potatoes and peppers are nearly tender, about 20 minutes.

2. Whisk together the flour and ½ cup of the evaporated milk in a small bowl until smooth. Add it along with the remaining milk, the broth, and the remaining 1 teaspoon salt into the potato mixture, increase heat to high, bring just to a boil, uncovered, stirring occasionally while scraping up any browned bits stuck to the pot. Reduce heat to medium, stir in the corn, and cook until the potatoes are tender, about 5 minutes.

3. Ladle the soup into individual bowls, top with the cilantro, and serve.

Per serving: 140 calories, 2g total fat, 0.5g saturated fat, 0g trans fat, 5mg cholesterol, 400mg sodium, 26g total carbohydrate, 3g dietary fiber, 9g sugars, 7g protein

Buttercup Squash Potage

Makes 6 servings: 1 cup each

Potage is a French term for a soup that's usually pureed, like this lovable buttercup squash recipe. Puree in a tall multi-speed blender for a creamier soup or with an immersion blender for a more textured potage. Either way, don't forget the dash of cinnamon for that special sweet-spicy note to properly finish the golden potage.

1 tablespoon unsalted butter or extra-virgin olive oil

1 large white onion, chopped

2 teaspoons apple cider vinegar

1 teaspoon sea salt, or to taste

4 cups buttercup or butternut squash cubes

1 (32-ounce) carton low-sodium chicken
    or vegetable broth or 4 cups Vegetable Stock
    (page 203)

½ teaspoon freshly ground black pepper, or to taste

⅛ teaspoon ground cinnamon or freshly grated
    nutmeg

1. Melt the butter in a stockpot over medium heat. Add the onion, vinegar, and ¼ teaspoon of the salt and sauté until softened, about 8 minutes. Add the squash, increase heat to medium-high, and sauté for 5 minutes.

2. Add the broth, pepper, cinnamon, and the remaining ¾ teaspoon salt and bring to a boil over high heat. Reduce heat to medium-low and simmer, uncovered, until the squash is tender, stirring occasionally, about 18 minutes.

3. Blend until smooth using an immersion blender. (Alternatively, puree in a blender in batches using the hot fill line as a guide; return to the saucepan over low heat.) Adjust seasoning.

4. Ladle into individual bowls, and serve. If desired, sprinkle with roasted buttercup squash seeds or insert a cinnamon stick into each bowl at serving.

Per serving: 70 calories, 2g total fat, 1g saturated fat, 0g trans fat, 5mg cholesterol, 440mg sodium, 12g total carbohydrate, 3g dietary fiber, 3g sugars, 2g protein

Velvety Sweet Potato Soup Ⓕ

Makes 7 servings: 1 cup each

This effortless soup is grand enough to serve at the Thanksgiving table. It'll make a lovely starter for any winter meal. And if you like, do plan to use the butter; it adds only 10 calories per cup and provides the just-right hint of richness and sheen to this festive soup.

1 large sweet potato, unpeeled, scrubbed, and finely diced

1 medium white or yellow onion, finely diced

1 (15-ounce) can no-salt-added Great Northern or butter beans, drained

¾ teaspoon finely chopped fresh rosemary, or to taste

½ teaspoon ground sage

6 cups low-sodium vegetable broth or Vegetable Stock (page 203)

1¼ teaspoons sea salt, or to taste

½ teaspoon freshly ground black pepper, or to taste

⅛ teaspoon ground cayenne, or to taste

2 teaspoons unsalted butter (optional)

1. Add all the ingredients except the butter to a large saucepan or stockpot. Bring to a boil over high heat. Reduce heat to medium and simmer, uncovered, stirring occasionally, until the potato and onion are fully softened, about 25 minutes.

2. Blend until smooth using an immersion blender. (Alternatively, puree in a blender in batches using the hot fill line as a guide; return to the saucepan over low heat.) Adjust seasoning and, stir in the butter (if using).

3. Ladle into individual bowls, and serve. If desired, garnish with fresh rosemary or sage.

Per serving: 100 calories, 0.5g total fat, 0g saturated fat, 0g trans fat, 0mg cholesterol, 570mg sodium, 20g total carbohydrate, 6g dietary fiber, 5g sugars, 3g protein

Puree of Broccoli Soup

Makes 9 servings: 1 cup each

This is nothing like you find in a can. It's appetizingly light and luscious.

2 tablespoons unsalted butter

1 large white onion, chopped

1 small jalapeño pepper with some seeds, minced

2 teaspoons fresh lemon juice

1¼ teaspoons sea salt, or to taste

⅓ cup whole oat or soy flour

3½ cups plain almond milk or light soy milk

1 (32-ounce) carton low-sodium chicken or vegetable broth or 4 cups Vegetable Stock (page 203)

1 pound roughly chopped broccoli florets with tender stems

½ teaspoon freshly ground black pepper, or to taste

¼ teaspoon freshly grated nutmeg, or to taste

1. Melt the butter in a stockpot over medium heat. Add the onion, jalapeño, lemon juice, and ¼ teaspoon of the salt and sauté until the onion is softened, about 8 minutes.

2. Whisk together the flour and ½ cup of the almond milk in a liquid measuring cup or small bowl into smooth.

3. Stir the flour-milk mixture, along with the remaining 3 cups almond milk, and the broth into the onion mixture. Add the broccoli, pepper, nutmeg, and the remaining 1 teaspoon salt and bring just to a boil over medium-high heat. Reduce heat to medium-low, and simmer, uncovered, until the broccoli is very tender, about 22 minutes.

4. Blend until smooth using an immersion blender.

5. Adjust seasoning, ladle into individual bowls, and serve.

Per serving: 100 calories, 4.5g total fat, 2g saturated fat, 0g trans fat, 5mg cholesterol, 430mg sodium, 13g total carbohydrate, 3g dietary fiber, 4g sugars, 4g protein

Elegant White Asparagus Soup

Makes 4 servings: 1 cup each

Europeans prefer white asparagus to the green variety. Which is your preference? Any kind of fresh asparagus will taste enticing here; but the more elegant white asparagus creates a sexy, silky soup that's fit for fine dining.

2 teaspoons unsalted butter

2 teaspoons extra-virgin olive oil

1 medium Vidalia or other sweet onion, chopped

Juice of 1 small lemon (2 tablespoons)

¾ teaspoon sea salt, to taste

1 pound white asparagus, ends trimmed and cut into 1-inch pieces

1 large garlic clove, minced

1 (32-ounce) carton low-sodium chicken or vegetable broth or 4 cups Vegetable Stock (page 203)

¼ teaspoon freshly ground black or white pepper, to taste

2 tablespoons minced fresh chives

1. Heat the butter and oil in a large saucepan over medium heat. Once the butter melts, add the onion, lemon juice, and ¼ teaspoon of the salt and sauté until softened, about 5 minutes. Add all the asparagus except the tips (heads), increase heat to medium-high, and sauté for 5 minutes. Add the garlic and sauté for 30 seconds.

2. Add the broth, 3½ cups water, the pepper, and the remaining ½ teaspoon salt and bring to a boil. Continue to boil until the asparagus is soft, about 35 minutes.

3. Puree the soup in a blender in batches using the hot fill line as a guide; return to the saucepan. (Note: This soup will not puree well using an immersion blender.)

4. Add the reserved asparagus tips to the pureed soup and simmer, stirring occasionally, over medium heat until the tips are just tender, about 10 minutes. Remove from heat and adjust seasoning.

5. Ladle the soup into individual bowls, top with the chives, and serve.

Per serving: 100 calories, 4.5g total fat, 1.5g saturated fat, 0g trans fat, 5mg cholesterol, 520mg sodium, 11g total carbohydrate, 3g dietary fiber, 5g sugars, 5g protein

NOT SIMPLY SOUP

The creamy soups in this chapter can not only be served in a bowl and enjoyed by spoon, they can also be drizzled onto cuisine as gravy.

Grain Soups

Asian Asparagus and Basmati Rice Soup

Makes 8 servings: 1½ cups each

I love this recipe! This is one of those soups that keeps well in the fridge for a few days. Quickly reheat and it makes a delicious go-to snack or satisfying accompaniment to meals in a minute. The flavors are distinctly Asian and decidedly fantastic. Serve with additional Wasabi-Spiked Soy Sauce on the side for extra pep.

1 tablespoon peanut or canola oil

2 teaspoons toasted sesame oil

1 large white onion, diced

2 cups finely chopped cauliflower florets
    and tender stems

2 teaspoons brown rice vinegar

¾ teaspoon sea salt, or to taste

2 large garlic cloves, minced

2 teaspoons freshly grated gingerroot

1 scallion, green and white part, thinly sliced

2 (32-ounce each) cartons low-sodium vegetable
    broth or 8 cups Vegetable Stock (page 203)

3 tablespoons Wasabi-Spiked Soy Sauce (page 130)
    or naturally brewed soy sauce

½ teaspoon freshly ground black pepper, or to taste

1 cup brown basmati rice

1½ pounds green asparagus, ends trimmed and
    cut into 1-inch pieces

1. Heat the oils in a stockpot or Dutch oven over medium-high heat. Add the onion, cauliflower, vinegar, and ¼ teaspoon of the salt and sauté until the onion begins to caramelize, about 8 minutes. Add the garlic, ginger, and white part of the scallion, and sauté for 1 minute.

2. Add the broth, soy sauce, pepper, and the remaining ½ teaspoon salt and bring to a boil over high heat. Stir in the rice, reduce heat to low, cover, and simmer for 30 minutes. Add the asparagus, cover, and simmer until the rice and asparagus are softened, about 20 more minutes. Adjust seasoning.

3. Ladle into individual bowls and top with the green part of the scallion.

Per serving: 140 calories, 4g total fat, 0.5g saturated fat, 0g trans fat, 0mg cholesterol, 650mg sodium, 24g total carbohydrate, 4g dietary fiber, 5g sugars, 4g protein

Cayenne Winter Squash–Speckled Orzo Soup Ⓕ

Makes 10 servings: 1 cup each

Once you've prepped the ingredients, this is a simple soup to make. You can even save some time and effort and purchase precut squash from the market. But don't let the simplicity fool you. The appearance is eye-catching and flavor is complex—with a definite kick from the cayenne.

6 cups low-sodium vegetable or chicken broth
    or Vegetable Stock (page 203)

1½ teaspoons sea salt, or to taste

¼ teaspoon + ⅛ teaspoon ground cayenne,
    or to taste

4 cups cubed butternut squash

1½ cups whole-wheat orzo

1 cup plain almond milk or light soy milk,
    at room temperature

3 tablespoons finely chopped fresh chives

3 tablespoons sliced natural almonds, toasted

1. Bring the broth, salt, and ¼ teaspoon of the cayenne to a boil in a stockpot over high heat. Add the squash, reduce heat to medium-low, and simmer, covered, until the squash is nearly tender, about 15 minutes. Stir in the orzo and almond milk and simmer, covered, until the orzo is al dente and squash is tender, about 8 minutes. Adjust seasoning.

2. Ladle into bowls, top with the chives, almonds, and the remaining ⅛ teaspoon cayenne, and serve.

Per serving: 140 calories, 1.5g total fat, 0g saturated fat, 0g trans fat, 0mg cholesterol, 450mg sodium, 29g total carbohydrate, 5g dietary fiber, 3g sugars, 5g protein

Minestrone F

Makes 8 servings: 1 cup each

Minestrone actually refers to a "big soup" of blended ingredients. This version is naturally nutritious and full of satisfying flavors—as you expect from Italian cooking. But instead of sticking with the traditional topping of grated Parmesan cheese at serving, you'll instead enjoy the bright and lively touch of lemon zest here. Soak up some the minestrone broth with a piece of crusty whole-wheat Italian bread; you'll be in carb-lovers paradise.

1 (14-ounce) can whole peeled tomatoes (with liquid)

1 tablespoon extra-virgin olive oil

1 small or ½ large red onion, diced

¾ cup finely diced carrot or very thinly sliced carrot rounds

1 medium red potato, unpeeled, scrubbed, and cut into ⅓-inch cubes

Juice and zest of 1 small lemon (2 tablespoons juice)

1¾ teaspoons sea salt, or to taste

2 large garlic cloves, minced

1 (32-ounce) carton low-sodium chicken or vegetable broth or 4 cups Vegetable Stock (page 203)

2 ounces dry whole-grain ditalini or elbow macaroni pasta

¾ teaspoon freshly ground black pepper, or to taste

½ teaspoon dried marjoram leaves

1 medium zucchini, finely diced

½ cup drained canned cannellini or borlotti beans

2 teaspoons chopped fresh marjoram or oregano, or to taste

4 cups packed fresh baby spinach

1. Add the tomatoes with liquid to a medium bowl and smash the whole tomatoes with a fork or squash by hand into very small pieces. Set aside.

2. Heat the oil in a large saucepan over medium-high heat. Add the onion, carrot, potato, 1 tablespoon of the lemon juice, and ¼ teaspoon of the salt and sauté until the onion is lightly caramelized, about 8 minutes. Add the garlic and sauté for 1 minute.

3. Add the smashed tomatoes with liquid, the broth, pasta, pepper, dried marjoram, and the remaining 1½ teaspoons salt and simmer, stirring frequently, until the carrot and pasta are nearly al dente, about 7 minutes.

4. Add the zucchini, beans, and fresh marjoram, stirring occasionally, and simmer until the zucchini is just tender, about 3 minutes. Stir in the spinach and the remaining lemon juice and let cook for 1 minute. Adjust seasoning.

5. Ladle the soup into bowls, top with the lemon zest, and serve. If desired, garnish with additional fresh marjoram.

Per serving: 200 calories, 2.5g total fat, 0g saturated fat, 0g trans fat, 0mg cholesterol, 680mg sodium, 40g total carbohydrate, 5g dietary fiber, 3g sugars, 8g protein

Fusilli e Fagioli F

Makes 6 servings: 1 cup each

You'll be smitten by this classic Italian soup that has it all—body, balance, and bold flavors. The duet of pasta and beans makes this melodious soup almost meal-like. Enjoy dipping into it with a piece of crusty whole-wheat Italian bread for extra satisfaction.

2 teaspoons extra-virgin olive oil

1 large red onion, diced

2 teaspoons aged balsamic vinegar

1 teaspoon sea salt, or to taste

2 garlic cloves, minced

1 large carrot, diced

1 large celery stalk, diced

1 (14-ounce) can no-salt-added diced tomatoes (with liquid)

1 (32-ounce) carton low-sodium vegetable broth or 4 cups Vegetable Stock (page 203)

1 teaspoon freshly ground black pepper, or to taste

1 teaspoon finely chopped fresh oregano

¼ teaspoon dried hot pepper flakes, or to taste

4 ounces dry whole-wheat or other whole-grain fusilli pasta

1 (15-ounce) can no-salt-added cannellini or other white beans, drained

10 cherry tomatoes, thinly sliced

3 tablespoons chopped fresh flat-leaf parsley

1 tablespoon freshly grated Parmigiano-Reggiano or other Parmesan cheese (optional)

1. Heat the oil in a stockpot over medium heat. Add the onion, vinegar, and ¼ teaspoon of the salt and sauté until slightly caramelized, about 8 minutes. Add the garlic and sauté for 1 minute. Add the carrot, celery and canned tomatoes with liquid and simmer for 12 minutes.

2. Add the broth, black pepper, oregano, hot pepper flakes, and the remaining ¾ teaspoon salt. Increase heat to high and bring to a boil. Stir in the pasta and beans and reduce heat to medium. Simmer until the pasta is al dente, about 10 to 12 minutes. Stir in the cherry tomatoes and parsley. Adjust seasoning.

3. Ladle the soup into bowls, top with the cheese (if using), and serve. If desired, garnish with additional fresh oregano.

Per serving: 140 calories, 2.5g total fat, 0g saturated fat, 0g trans fat, 0mg cholesterol, 530mg sodium, 25g total carbohydrate, 6g dietary fiber, 7g sugars, 6g protein

Exotic Mushroom and Barley Soup Ⓕ

Makes 9 servings: 1 cup each

The best part of this pleasantly filling, mushroom-and barley-packed soup is the exotic flavor provided by various mushrooms. Be adventurous by choosing a number of fresh seasonal mushrooms from your local market. There are so many different types to play with—all with distinctive tastes, textures, and appearances. Mushrooms feature what the Japanese call umami flavor—a rich, salty, almost-meaty taste that is the secret to this soup's deliciousness.

1 tablespoon extra-virgin olive oil

1 large white onion, halved lengthwise and sliced crosswise

2 teaspoons aged balsamic vinegar

1½ teaspoons sea salt, or to taste

2 large garlic cloves, minced

2 (32-ounce) cartons low-sodium beef or chicken broth or 8 cups Chicken Stock (page 203)

1 cup whole hulled barley (not pearled barley)

¼ teaspoon freshly ground black pepper, or to taste

10 ounces fresh mushroom blend, such as shiitake caps, shimeji, abalone, and field mushrooms, thinly sliced

1 medium zucchini, finely diced

1 medium yellow summer squash, finely diced

1 teaspoon finely chopped fresh rosemary, or to taste

3 tablespoons chopped fresh parsley

1. Heat the oil in a stockpot over medium heat. Add the onion, vinegar, and ¼ teaspoon of the salt and sauté until softened, about 5 minutes. Add the garlic and sauté for 1 minute.

2. Add the broth, 1 cup water, the barley, pepper, and the remaining 1¼ teaspoons salt. Increase heat to high and bring to a boil. Reduce heat to medium-low, cover, and cook until the barley is nearly tender, about 1 hour.

3. Add the mushrooms, zucchini, yellow squash, and rosemary and cook, covered, until the vegetables and barley are tender, about 12 minutes. Adjust seasoning.

4. Ladle into individual bowls, sprinkle with the parsley, and serve.

Per serving: 150 calories, 3.5g total fat, 0.5g saturated fat, 0g trans fat, 0mg cholesterol, 460mg sodium, 21g total carbohydrate, 5g dietary fiber, 3g sugars, 9g protein

Veggie Couscous Soup Ⓕ

Makes 12 servings: 1 cup each

Here's an especially simple soup to prepare—ideal for nearly any style of gathering, from a festive birthday party to a light ladies luncheon. The couscous adds body and the herbs provide fresh fragrance. Pops of spring peas and other vegetables make it a soup that's lovely to savor in the spring or summertime.

1 tablespoon extra-virgin olive oil

2 to 3 large garlic cloves, minced

9 cups low-sodium vegetable broth or Vegetable Stock (page 203), or to taste

Juice of ½ small lemon (1 tablespoon)

2 medium zucchini, diced

1 large red bell pepper, finely diced

½ cup shredded carrot

1¾ cups whole-wheat couscous

2 cups fresh or frozen petite peas, thawed

2¾ teaspoons sea salt, or to taste

½ cup thinly sliced fresh basil leaves

1 tablespoon finely chopped fresh oregano

½ teaspoon finely chopped fresh rosemary

1. Heat the oil in a stockpot over medium heat. Add the garlic and sauté for 1 minute. Add the broth, lemon juice, zucchini, bell pepper, and carrot. Increase heat to high and bring to a boil.

2. Pour in the couscous, peas, and salt and stir. Cover, remove from heat, and let sit until the couscous is desired texture, about 6 minutes. Stir in the basil, oregano, and rosemary. Adjust seasoning and broth, if necessary.

3. Ladle into bowls, and serve. If desired, garnish with additional fresh oregano.

Per serving: 150 calories, 1.5g total fat, 0g saturated fat, 0g trans fat, 0mg cholesterol, 670mg sodium, 30g total carbohydrate, 6g dietary fiber, 5g sugars, 6g protein

Bean Soups

Red Bean and Blue Corn Tortilla Soup Ⓕ

Makes 6 servings: 1 cup each

This Mexican-style soup is one that I find irresistible because it offers something for all the senses. It's an anytime soup, including right after you roll out of bed in the morning—if you have an adventurous palate! Top it with a poached egg for an enticing breakfast or brunch entrée.

1 (32-ounce) carton low-sodium vegetable or chicken broth or 4 cups Vegetable Stock (page 203)

1 (14.5-ounce) can crushed fire-roasted tomatoes

1 small jalapeño pepper with some seeds, minced

2 large garlic cloves, minced

½ teaspoon sea salt, or to taste

¼ teaspoon freshly ground black pepper, or to taste

1 (15-ounce) can red kidney beans, drained

3 scallions, green and white parts, thinly sliced

¼ cup chopped fresh cilantro

Juice and zest of 1 lime (2 tablespoons juice)

15 medium-size blue corn tortilla chips, broken into bite-size pieces

½ Hass avocado, pitted, peeled, and diced

1. Add the broth, tomatoes, jalapeño, garlic, salt, and black pepper to a stockpot or large saucepan over high heat and bring to a boil. Reduce heat to medium and simmer 5 minutes.

2. Stir in the beans and scallions. Simmer for 2 minutes.

3. Remove from heat. Stir in the cilantro and lime juice. Adjust seasoning.

4. Ladle into bowls, top with tortilla chips, avocado, and desired amount of lime zest, and serve.

Per serving: 130 calories, 3g total fat, 0g saturated fat, 0g trans fat, 0mg cholesterol, 540mg sodium, 23g total carbohydrate, 6g dietary fiber, 6g sugars, 6g protein

Roasted Italian Tomato and Green Bean Soup Ⓕ

Makes 6 servings: 1 cup each

Green beans can be a nutritious side dish. But I prefer to make them the star of a dish, as in this fragrant, flavorful, Italian-inspired soup. The roasted tomatoes and fresh green beans marry to become a dynamic duo.

1 tablespoon extra-virgin olive oil

1 small or ½ large red onion, finely diced

Juice and zest of ½ small lemon (1 tablespoon juice)

¾ teaspoon sea salt, or to taste

1 or 2 large garlic cloves, minced

1 (32-ounce) carton low-sodium vegetable broth or 4 cups Vegetable Stock (page 203)

1 (14.5-ounce) can crushed fire-roasted tomatoes

6 ounces fresh green beans, trimmed and cut on diagonal into ¾-inch pieces

1 teaspoon chopped fresh thyme

¼ teaspoon freshly ground black pepper, or to taste

1 (15-ounce) can no-salt-added cannellini or other white beans, drained

¼ cup chopped fresh flat-leaf parsley

¼ cup chopped fresh basil

1. Heat the oil to a large saucepan over medium heat. Add the onion, lemon juice, and ¼ teaspoon of the salt and sauté until softened, about 5 minutes. Add the garlic and sauté for 1 minute.

2. Add the broth, tomatoes, green beans, thyme, pepper, and the remaining ½ teaspoon salt. Increase heat to high and bring to a boil. Reduce heat to medium, and cook, stirring occasionally for 15 minutes. Stir in the cannellini beans and cook, stirring occasionally, until the green beans are tender, about 15 minutes. Stir in the parsley and basil, and adjust seasoning.

3. Ladle into individual bowls, sprinkle with the lemon zest, and serve.

Per serving: 120 calories, 3g total fat, 0g saturated fat, 0g trans fat, 0mg cholesterol, 580mg sodium, 20g total carbohydrate, 6g dietary fiber, 6g sugars, 5g protein

Creamy Butter Bean Soup Ⓕ

Makes 5 servings: 1 cup each

This vegan butter bean soup has a hummus-like essence. Dunk Cumin-Dusted Naan Chips (page 42) into it for added delight.

2 teaspoons extra-virgin olive oil

1 medium white onion, finely chopped

Juice of 1 small lemon (2 tablespoons)

¾ teaspoon sea salt, or to taste

1 large garlic clove, minced

1½ tablespoons tahini (sesame seed paste) or no-salt-added creamy almond butter

1 (32-ounce) carton low-sodium vegetable broth or 4 cups Vegetable Stock (page 203)

1 (15-ounce) can no-salt-added butter beans or cannellini beans, drained

½ teaspoon freshly ground black pepper, or to taste

¼ teaspoon ground cumin, or to taste

¼ teaspoon ground cinnamon, or to taste

2 tablespoons chopped fresh parsley

1 tablespoon chopped fresh mint

1. Heat the oil in a large saucepan over medium heat. Add the onion, 1 tablespoon of the lemon juice, and ¼ teaspoon of the salt and sauté until softened, about 5 minutes. Add the garlic and sauté for 1 minute. Add the tahini and stir until well combined.

2. Add the broth, beans, pepper, cumin, cinnamon, and the remaining lemon juice and remaining ½ teaspoon salt. Bring to a boil over high heat. Reduce the heat to medium-low and simmer, covered, stirring occasionally, for 15 minutes.

3. Puree in a blender in small batches using the hot fill line as a guide; return to the saucepan over medium-low heat. (Note: For a thicker soup, continue to simmer to desired consistency.) Adjust seasoning.

4. Ladle into individual bowls, sprinkle with the parsley and mint, and serve.

Per serving: 130 calories, 5g total fat, 0.5g saturated fat, 0g trans fat, 0mg cholesterol, 490mg sodium, 18g total carbohydrate, 5g dietary fiber, 3g sugars, 5g protein

Peppery 5-Bean Soup Ⓕ

Makes 15 servings: 1 cup each

It's so simple to fix this delish soup that's enjoyable for large gatherings of friends or family. It will please even persnickety palates.

1 tablespoon extra-virgin olive oil

1 large white onion, finely diced

1 extra-large or 2 medium green bell peppers, finely diced

1 medium red bell pepper, finely diced

2 teaspoons aged balsamic vinegar

1½ teaspoons sea salt, or to taste

3 large garlic cloves, minced

2 (32-ounce) cartons low-sodium vegetable broth or 8 cups Vegetable Stock (page 203)

5 (15-ounce) cans of beans, such as cannellini, red kidney, black, pinto, and chickpeas (garbanzo beans)

1 teaspoon freshly ground black pepper, or to taste

½ teaspoon hot pepper sauce, or to taste

¼ cup chopped fresh basil, parsley, or cilantro

1 lemon or lime, cut into 12 wedges

1. Heat the oil in a stockpot over medium heat. Add the onion, bell peppers, vinegar, and ¼ teaspoon of the salt and sauté until the onion and peppers are softened, about 10 minutes. Add the garlic and sauté for 1 minute.

2. Add the broth, beans, black pepper, hot pepper sauce, and the remaining 1¼ teaspoons salt. Bring to a boil over high heat. Reduce the heat to medium and simmer uncovered, stirring occasionally, until the peppers are fully softened and flavors are well combined, about 8 minutes. Adjust seasoning.

3. Ladle into individual bowls, sprinkle with the basil, and serve with the lemon wedges. Squirt the lemon into the soup to enjoy.

Per serving: 140 calories, 1.5g total fat, 0g saturated fat, 0g trans fat, 0mg cholesterol, 470mg sodium, 25g total carbohydrate, 7g dietary fiber, 5g sugars, 7g protein

Garlic, Spinach, and White Bean Soup Ⓕ

Makes 7 servings: 1 cup each

When spinach, garlic, and lemon unite, it's a glorious thing for the palate. The same goes for this soup with its special zing from grated lemon zest. But to me, it's really the garlic that causes this soup to stand up and be noticed. Garlic lovers, rejoice.

1 tablespoon extra-virgin olive oil

1 medium yellow onion, halved and thinly sliced

Juice and zest of 1 small lemon (2 tablespoons juice)

1 teaspoon sea salt, or to taste

6 cups packed fresh baby spinach

3 large garlic cloves, minced

5½ cups low-sodium vegetable broth or Vegetable Stock (page 203)

1 (15-ounce) can cannellini or other white beans, drained

½ teaspoon minced fresh rosemary or ¼ teaspoon crushed dried rosemary

¼ teaspoon freshly ground black pepper, or to taste

¼ teaspoon hot pepper sauce, or to taste

1. Heat the oil in a stockpot over medium heat. Add the onion, 1 tablespoon of the lemon juice, and ¼ teaspoon of the salt and sauté until the onion is fully softened, about 8 minutes. Add the spinach and garlic and sauté until the spinach is wilted, about 2 minutes.

2. Add the broth, beans, rosemary, black pepper, hot pepper sauce, and the remaining lemon juice and remaining ¾ teaspoon salt. Increase the heat to high and bring just to a boil. Adjust seasoning.

3. Ladle into individual bowls, sprinkle with the lemon zest, and serve.

Per serving: 100 calories, 2g total fat, 0g saturated fat, 0g trans fat, 0mg cholesterol, 550mg sodium, 16g total carbohydrate, 5g dietary fiber, 3g sugars, 4g protein

Jamaican Red Bean Soup

Makes 7 servings: 1 cup each

This red bean soup is every bit as spicy and tasty as you might hope. Most notable are the "heat" from the hot pepper and curry powder along with the sweet spiciness from fresh ginger and allspice. There's something for every taste bud.

1 tablespoon extra-virgin olive oil

1 large white onion, finely diced

1 large red or yellow bell pepper, finely diced

1 large green bell pepper, finely diced

⅓ cup fresh-squeezed orange juice

1 teaspoon sea salt, or to taste

1 large garlic clove, minced

2 teaspoons freshly grated gingerroot

1 Scotch bonnet or hot Jamaican pepper with some seeds, minced

1 (32-ounce) carton low-sodium vegetable broth or 4 cups Vegetable Stock (page 203)

1 (15-ounce) can red kidney beans, drained

1 teaspoon chopped fresh thyme

½ teaspoon freshly ground black pepper, or to taste

¼ teaspoon hot Madras curry powder

¼ teaspoon ground allspice

1 scallion, green and white parts, minced

1. Heat the oil in a stockpot over medium heat. Add the onion, bell peppers, 2 tablespoons of the orange juice, and ¼ teaspoon of the salt and sauté until the onion and bell peppers are softened, about 10 minutes. Add the garlic, ginger, and Scotch bonnet and sauté for 1 minute.

2. Add the broth, beans, thyme, black pepper, curry powder, allspice, and the remaining orange juice and remaining ¾ teaspoon salt. Bring to a boil over high heat. Reduce the heat to medium and simmer, uncovered, stirring occasionally, until the bell peppers are fully softened, about 8 minutes. Stir in the scallion. Adjust seasoning.

3. Ladle into individual bowls, and serve.

Per serving: 100 calories, 2g total fat, 0g saturated fat, 0g trans fat, 0mg cholesterol, 480mg sodium, 17g total carbohydrate, 4g dietary fiber, 6g sugars, 4g protein

Chili-Lime Black Bean Soup

Makes 8 servings: 1 cup each

I'm passionate about this perfect 100-calorie soup—it's loaded with veggie delight and full-bodied flavors. Hint: Top with a dollop of guacamole for extra culinary charm.

1 tablespoon unrefined peanut or canola oil

1 large sweet onion, finely diced

1 large red or orange bell pepper, finely diced

1 large green bell pepper, finely diced

Juice and zest of 1 lime (2 tablespoons juice)

1 teaspoon sea salt, or to taste

3 large garlic cloves, minced

1 small jalapeño pepper with some seeds, minced

1 (32-ounce) carton low-sodium vegetable broth or 4 cups Vegetable Stock (page 203)

1 (15-ounce) can black beans, drained

1 (14½-ounce) can stewed tomatoes

½ teaspoon freshly ground black pepper, or to taste

½ teaspoon ground ancho chili powder

¼ cup chopped fresh cilantro

1. Heat the oil in a stockpot over medium heat. Add the onion, bell peppers, 1 tablespoon of the lime juice, and ¼ teaspoon of the salt and sauté until the onion and bell peppers are softened, about 10 minutes. Add the garlic and jalapeño and sauté for 1 minute.

2. Add the broth, beans, tomatoes, black pepper, chili powder, and the remaining 1 tablespoon lime juice and remaining ¾ teaspoon salt. Bring to a boil over high heat. Reduce the heat to medium and simmer, uncovered, stirring occasionally while breaking up any large tomato pieces, until the bell peppers are fully softened, about 8 minutes. Adjust seasoning.

3. Ladle into individual bowls, sprinkle with the cilantro and desired amount of lime zest, and serve.

Per serving: 100 calories, 2g total fat, 0g saturated fat, 0g trans fat, 0mg cholesterol, 540mg sodium, 18g total carbohydrate, 4g dietary fiber, 7g sugars, 4g protein

Moroccan-Style Split Pea Soup Ⓕ

Makes 8 servings: 1 cup each

Split peas are field peas that are split and dried. But unlike many common dried beans, split peas don't require presoaking. Just simmer them. Then savor this sensationally aromatic soup that becomes a memorable one with its mélange of fresh herbs and distinctive Moroccan spices.

1 tablespoon extra-virgin olive oil

1 large white onion, chopped

1 large carrot, unpeeled, scrubbed, and finely diced

2 teaspoons brown rice vinegar

1½ teaspoons sea salt, or to taste

2 large garlic cloves, minced

1½ teaspoons freshly grated gingerroot

2 (32-ounce) cartons low-sodium vegetable broth or 8 cups Vegetable Stock (page 203)

1¼ cups dried green split peas, rinsed and drained

½ teaspoon freshly ground black pepper, or to taste

½ teaspoon ground cinnamon

¼ teaspoon ground cumin

¼ teaspoon ground turmeric

¼ cup chopped fresh flat-leaf parsley

¼ cup chopped fresh cilantro

1. Heat the oil in a stockpot over medium heat. Add the onion, carrot, vinegar, and ¼ teaspoon of the salt and sauté until the onion is softened, about 8 minutes. Add the garlic and ginger and sauté for 1 minute.

2. Add the broth, split peas, pepper, cinnamon, cumin, turmeric, and the remaining 1¼ teaspoons salt and bring the soup to a boil over high heat. Reduce the heat to medium-low and simmer, uncovered, for 1 hour 15 minutes, stirring occasionally.

3. Stir in half of the parsley and cilantro. Adjust seasoning.

4. Ladle into individual bowls, sprinkle with the remaining parsley and cilantro, and serve.

Per serving: 150 calories, 2g total fat, 0g saturated fat, 0g trans fat, 0mg cholesterol, 590mg sodium, 25g total carbohydrate, 10g dietary fiber, 6g sugars, 8g protein

Red Lentil Coconut Curry Soup Ⓕ

Makes 8 servings: 1 cup each

Lentils are popular in European, Middle Eastern, and Indian cooking. This may start out as an exotic recipe, but I have no doubt that you'll be embracing this remarkable red lentil recipe with its deep orange color, exotic spike of coconut, and velvety texture. It's rich on taste and light on calories. And if you want to go extra light, simply use 14 ounces of fat-free evaporated milk plus ½ teaspoon pure coconut extract in place of the coconut milk.

1 tablespoon unrefined peanut or canola oil

1 large white onion, chopped

1½ cups bite-size cauliflower florets or 1 parsnip, unpeeled, scrubbed, and finely diced

1 large carrot, unpeeled, scrubbed, and finely diced

2 teaspoons brown rice vinegar

1¼ teaspoons sea salt, or to taste

2 large garlic cloves, minced

2 teaspoons freshly grated gingerroot

1 (32-ounce) carton low-sodium vegetable broth or 4 cups Vegetable Stock (page 203)

1 cup dried red lentils, rinsed and drained

1 (14-ounce) can light coconut milk

2 teaspoons hot Madras curry powder

½ teaspoon freshly ground black pepper, or to taste

⅓ cup roughly chopped fresh cilantro

1. Heat the oil in a large saucepan over medium-high heat. Add the onion, cauliflower, carrot, vinegar, and ¼ teaspoon of the salt and sauté until the onion begins to caramelize, about 12 minutes. Add the garlic and ginger and sauté for 30 seconds.

2. Add the broth, lentils, coconut milk, curry powder, pepper, and the remaining 1 teaspoon salt and bring to a boil. Reduce heat to medium-low, and simmer, partially covered, until the lentils are tender, about 20 minutes.

3. Blend until smooth using an immersion blender. (Alternatively, for a creamier consistency, puree in a blender in batches using the hot fill line as a guide; return to the saucepan over low heat.) Adjust seasoning.

4. Ladle into individual bowls, sprinkle with the cilantro, and serve.

Per serving: 160 calories, 5g total fat, 3g saturated fat, 0g trans fat, 0mg cholesterol, 460mg sodium, 21g total carbohydrate, 5g dietary fiber, 4g sugars, 8g protein

Lentil and Greens Soup with Poached Egg Ⓕ

Makes 10 servings: 1 cup each

Serve this classy cup of comfort at your next brunch. The poached-egg topping makes this recipe unique and impressive, or you can skip the egg and just add a dollop of plain fat-free or low-fat Greek yogurt instead.

1 tablespoon extra-virgin olive oil
1 large yellow onion, diced
1 large carrot, unpeeled, scrubbed, and finely diced
1 large celery stalk, finely diced
Juice and zest of ½ lemon (1½ tablespoons juice)
1½ teaspoons sea salt, or to taste
2 large garlic cloves, minced
2 (32-ounce) cartons low-sodium vegetable broth or 8 cups Vegetable Stock (page 203)
1⅔ cups dried French green lentils, rinsed and drained
½ teaspoon freshly ground black pepper, or to taste
½ teaspoon ground cumin
⅛ teaspoon freshly grated nutmeg
8 cups packed fresh baby spinach
10 large poached eggs (page 21)

1. Heat the oil in a stockpot over medium heat. Add the onion, carrot, celery, lemon juice, and ¼ teaspoon of the salt and sauté until the onion is softened, about 10 minutes. Add the garlic and sauté for 1 minute.

2. Add the broth, lentils, pepper, cumin, nutmeg, and the remaining 1¼ teaspoons salt and bring to a boil over high heat. Reduce heat to medium-low and simmer, uncovered, until the lentils are tender, about 25 to 28 minutes. Stir in the spinach until wilted, about 2 minutes. Adjust seasoning.

3. Ladle into individual bowls, top with the poached eggs, sprinkle with the zest, and serve.

Per serving: 230 calories, 7g total fat, 2g saturated fat, 0g trans fat, 185mg cholesterol, 580mg sodium, 27g total carbohydrate, 6g dietary fiber, 4g sugars, 17g protein

Hoppin' John Soup with Basmati Rice Ⓕ

Makes 10 servings: 2 cups each

Tradition says that eating hoppin' John on New Year's Day brings good luck, so it's worth a try. This is a recipe that seems even tastier the next day. Serve a crowd or two, or make this main-dish soup to enjoy at several meals.

12 ounces black-eyed peas, rinsed and drained

2 smoked ham hocks (optional)

2 bay leaves

1 tablespoon grapeseed or canola oil

1 large white onion, finely diced

⅔ cup finely diced applewood-smoked or Berkshire ham

2 large garlic cloves, minced

1 large jalapeño pepper with seeds, minced

2 tablespoons apple cider or brown rice vinegar

12 ounces chopped collard leaves

2 (32-ounce) cartons low-sodium vegetable broth or 8 cups Vegetable Stock (page 203)

2¼ teaspoons sea salt, or to taste

½ teaspoon finely chopped fresh thyme

½ teaspoon freshly ground black pepper, or to taste

4 cups cooked brown basmati rice or whole-wheat couscous, warm

1 cup grape tomatoes, quartered lengthwise, or cherry tomatoes, thinly sliced

1. Add the black-eyed peas (do not presoak), ham hocks (if using), bay leaves, and 8 cups water to a stockpot over high heat and bring to a boil. Reduce heat to low and simmer, covered, without stirring, until the peas are just tender, about 35 minutes. Remove the bay leaves. Drain the peas, reserving the ham hocks and 2 cups of the cooking liquid. Set aside.

2. Heat the oil in the dry stockpot over medium heat. Add the onion, diced ham, garlic, jalapeño, and 1 tablespoon of the vinegar and sauté until the onion is softened, about 10 minutes.

3. Add the reserved cooking liquid, black-eyed peas, collard greens, ham hocks (if using), broth, salt, thyme, and black pepper. Bring to a boil over high heat. Reduce heat to low, and simmer, covered, without stirring, for 20 minutes. Remove cover and continue to simmer until the greens are tender, about 20 minutes. Remove and discard the ham hocks. Stir in the remaining 1 tablespoon vinegar and adjust seasoning.

4. Add the rice and tomatoes to individual bowls. Ladle the soup over or around the rice and tomatoes. Serve with a bottle of hot pepper sauce on the side.

Per serving: 260 calories, 3.5g total fat, 0g saturated fat, 0g trans fat, 5mg cholesterol, 790mg sodium, 46g total carbohydrate, 7g dietary fiber, 3g sugars, 13g protein

Poultry, Fish, Shellfish, and Meat Soups

Egg Ribbon Soup

Makes 4 servings: 1 cup each

I enjoy this home-prepared, chicken broth–based soup considerably more than the one in a takeout container from my nearby Chinese restaurant. I can ensure that it features the freshest ingredients. I call it "Egg Ribbon" instead of "Egg Drop" to highlight the lovely ribbon-like texture created by the eggs.

1 teaspoon toasted sesame oil

2 scallions, green and white parts, minced

2 teaspoons freshly grated gingerroot

1 (32-ounce) carton low-sodium chicken broth
    or 4 cups Chicken Stock (page 203)

2½ teaspoons naturally brewed soy sauce

½ teaspoon sea salt, or to taste

⅛ teaspoon freshly ground white or black pepper,
    or to taste

1 tablespoon cornstarch

2 large eggs, lightly beaten

1. Heat the oil in a large saucepan over medium-high heat. Add the white part of the scallions and the ginger and sauté until fragrant, about 1 minute.

2. Add 3¾ cups of the broth, the soy sauce, salt, and pepper, and bring to a boil over high heat.

3. Meanwhile, whisk together the cornstarch and the remaining broth in a small bowl or liquid measuring cup until smooth. Set aside.

4. Very slowly pour the eggs in a steady stream into the soup while stirring the soup clockwise with a fork for about 1 minute to create a ribbon-like texture. Reduce heat to medium and gradually stir in the broth-cornstarch mixture, while continuing to stir until slightly thickened, about 1 minute. Adjust seasoning.

5. Ladle into individual bowls, sprinkle with the green part of the scallions, and serve.

Per serving: 70 calories, 3.5g total fat, 1g saturated fat, 0g trans fat, 95mg cholesterol, 590mg sodium, 3g total carbohydrate, 0g dietary fiber, 0g sugars, 6g protein

Avgolemono with Orzo and Chicken

Makes 8 servings 1 cup each

Avgolemono is a Mediterranean soup made with egg and lemon juice mixed with broth, heated until it thickens. The orzo, egg, and chicken breast additions make this silky, citrus-tinged soup fully satisfying.

6 cups low-sodium chicken broth or Chicken Stock
    (page 203)

1¼ teaspoons sea salt, or to taste

¼ teaspoon freshly ground white or black pepper,
    or to taste

1 cup whole-wheat orzo

10 ounces boneless skinless chicken breast,
    very thinly sliced crosswise

2 large eggs

Juice and zest of 1 large lemon (¼ cup juice)

1½ teaspoons chopped fresh dill

1. Add the broth, salt, and pepper to a large saucepan over high heat. Bring to a boil. Stir in the orzo and reduce heat to medium-low. Simmer, uncovered, until the orzo is al dente, about 8 minutes.

2. Add the chicken and simmer until the chicken is done, about 3 minutes.

3. Whisk together the eggs and lemon juice in a liquid measuring cup or small bowl. Pour the egg mixture into the soup while whisking continuously until well combined, about 1 minute. Adjust seasoning.

4. Ladle into individual bowls, sprinkle with the dill and desired amount of the lemon zest, and serve.

Per serving: 150 calories, 2.5g total fat, 0.5g saturated fat, 0g trans fat, 65mg cholesterol, 450mg sodium, 18g total carbohydrate, 2g dietary fiber, 1g sugars, 14g protein

Pan-Asian Chicken Udon Soup

Makes 10 servings: 1 cup each

If Mom's chicken soup is for the soul, then this Asian-style chicken and noodle soup is for the soul as well as all of your senses. If you like, follow tradition and (courteously) slurp up the noodles with chopsticks. Then sip the rest with a spoon or pick up the bowl and take a few swigs—no utensil required.

2 teaspoons unrefined peanut or canola oil

1 teaspoon toasted sesame oil

3 large shallots, diced

3 scallions, green and white parts, thinly sliced on the diagonal

2 teaspoons brown rice vinegar

1¼ teaspoons sea salt, or to taste

1 cup small bite-size pieces broccoli florets

1 cup small bite-size pieces cauliflower florets

1 medium orange or red bell pepper, finely diced

1½ teaspoons freshly grated gingerroot

7 cups low-sodium chicken broth or Chicken Stock (page 203)

1 teaspoon naturally brewed soy sauce, or to taste

½ teaspoon Asian garlic-chili sauce, or to taste

10 ounces whole-grain udon noodles, broken into thirds

8 ounces boneless skinless chicken breast, very thinly sliced crosswise

1 teaspoon toasted sesame seeds

2 limes, cut into wedges

1. Heat the oils in a stockpot over medium heat. Add the shallots, white part of the scallions, vinegar, and ¼ teaspoon of the salt and sauté until the shallots are softened, about 8 minutes. Add the broccoli, cauliflower, bell pepper, and ginger, increase heat to high, and sauté until the shallots begin to caramelize, about 3 minutes.

2. Add the broth, soy sauce, garlic-chili sauce, and the remaining 1 teaspoon salt and bring to a boil over high heat.

3. Stir in the noodles and chicken and reduce heat to medium-low. Simmer until the vegetables, noodles, and chicken are done, about 8 minutes. Adjust seasoning.

4. Ladle into individual bowls, sprinkle with the green part of the scallions and the sesame seeds, and serve with lime wedges.

Per serving: 170 calories, 2.5g total fat, 0g saturated fat, 0g trans fat, 15mg cholesterol, 440mg sodium, 26g total carbohydrate, 2g dietary fiber, 2g sugars, 11g protein

Tarragon Chicken and Black Quinoa Soup

Makes 6 servings: 1⅔ cups each

Kick the can of plain ol' chicken and rice soup. You'll be captivated by this extreme makeover. The black quinoa creates intrigue and a pleasant texture. The touch of tarragon provides a distinct sweet anise-like freshness. And the hit of pure almond butter imparts a surprising richness.

1 tablespoon extra-virgin olive oil

1 large red onion, chopped

Juice and zest of 1 lemon (3 tablespoons juice)

1½ teaspoons sea salt, or to taste

1 large carrot, finely diced or cut into short matchstick-size strips

1 medium celery stalk, finely diced or cut into short matchstick-size strips

2 large garlic cloves, minced

1 tablespoon no-salt-added creamy roasted or raw almond butter

2 (32-ounce) cartons low-sodium chicken broth or 8 cups Chicken Stock (page 203)

¼ teaspoon freshly ground black pepper, or to taste

1 cup black or red quinoa, rinsed and drained

10 ounces boneless skinless chicken breast, very thinly sliced crosswise

2 tablespoons finely chopped fresh tarragon

1. Heat the oil in a stockpot over medium heat. Add the onion, 1 tablespoon of the lemon juice, and ¼ teaspoon of the salt and sauté until the onion is softened, about 8 minutes. Add the carrot and celery and sauté until the onion is nearly translucent, about 5 minutes. Add the garlic and almond butter and sauté for 1 minute.

2. Add the broth, pepper, and the remaining lemon juice and remaining 1¼ teaspoons salt and bring to a boil over high heat. Stir in the quinoa, reduce heat to medium-low, and simmer for 10 minutes. Stir in the chicken and continue to simmer until the vegetables, quinoa, and chicken are done, about 5 to 8 minutes. Stir in half of the tarragon and desired amount of the zest. Adjust seasoning.

3. Ladle into individual bowls, sprinkle with the remaining tarragon, and serve.

Per serving: 230 calories, 7g total fat, 1g saturated fat, 0g trans fat, 25mg cholesterol, 720mg sodium, 26g total carbohydrate, 3g dietary fiber, 2g sugars, 17g protein

Turkey Sausage Gumbo

Makes 8 servings: 1 cup gumbo and ½ cup rice each

The zesty turkey sausage here takes a great-tasting gumbo and punches it up another notch. You'll find this savory stew-like dish is an entrée when served with brown rice.

2 teaspoons peanut or canola oil

8 ounces Italian turkey sausage or smoked chicken andouille sausage links, casings removed

1 medium red onion, chopped

1 large green bell pepper, chopped

1 large red or orange bell pepper, chopped

1 cup sliced fresh or frozen okra, thawed

2 large garlic cloves, minced

3 tablespoons whole oat or soybean flour

3 cups low-sodium chicken broth or Chicken Stock (page 203)

1 (14.5-ounce) can diced tomatoes (with liquid)

1½ teaspoons chopped fresh thyme
or ¾ teaspoon dried thyme

1 teaspoon Creole seasoning (page 31) or Cajun seasoning, or to taste

1 teaspoon sea salt, or to taste

¼ teaspoon freshly ground black pepper, or to taste

4 cups cooked long-grain brown rice, warm

1. Heat the oil in a stockpot over medium-high heat. Add the sausage, onion, bell peppers, and okra and sauté until the sausage is done and crumbled and the onion and bell peppers are softened, about 8 minutes. Add the garlic and sauté for 30 seconds. Add the flour and cook while stirring for 1 minute.

2. Stir in the broth, tomatoes with liquid, thyme, Creole seasoning, salt, and black pepper, scraping up any browned bits in the pan. Bring to a boil over high heat. Reduce heat to low, cover, and simmer until the flavors are well blended, stirring occasionally, about 15 minutes. (Alternatively, for a thicker gumbo, simmer uncovered to desired consistency.) Adjust seasoning.

3. Add the rice to individual bowls, ladle the gumbo on top of or around the rice, and serve. If desired, garnish with additional fresh thyme leaves.

Per serving: 210 calories, 5g total fat, 0g saturated fat, 0g trans fat, 15mg cholesterol, 660mg sodium, 32g total carbohydrate, 4g dietary fiber, 4g sugars, 10g protein

Tunisian-Style Herbed Cod Soup

Makes 9 servings: 1 cup each

Cod, a popular, mild, moderately firm-fleshed fish, gets spiced up here in a worldly soup. Its finish is what I find most memorable with the aroma of fresh mint, the eye-opening zing of lemon zest, and the earthy fragrance of cumin. A stunner of a soup.

1 tablespoon extra-virgin olive oil

1 small or ½ large red onion, diced

Juice and zest of 1 small lemon (2 tablespoons juice)

1½ teaspoons sea salt, or to taste

2 large garlic cloves, minced

1 (32-ounce) carton low-sodium vegetable broth or 4 cups Vegetable Stock (page 203)

1 pound baby blue, red, or white creamer potatoes, unpeeled, scrubbed, and quartered

¾ teaspoon ground cumin

¼ teaspoon dried hot pepper flakes

¼ teaspoon freshly ground black pepper

1 pound wild cod (scrod) fillets, about ¾ inch thick, cubed

1 (15-ounce) can chickpeas (garbanzo beans), drained

2 cups cherry tomatoes, halved or quartered

½ cup chopped fresh flat-leaf parsley

3 tablespoons chopped fresh cilantro

2 tablespoons chopped fresh mint

1. Heat the oil in a stockpot over medium heat. Add the onion, 1 tablespoon of the lemon juice, and ¼ teaspoon of the salt and sauté until softened, about 5 minutes. Add the garlic and sauté for 1 minute.

2. Add the broth, potatoes, ½ teaspoon of the cumin, the hot pepper flakes, black pepper, remaining lemon juice, and remaining 1¼ teaspoons salt. Bring to a boil over high heat. Reduce heat to medium-low, cover, and simmer until the potatoes are nearly tender, about 12 to 15 minutes. Add the cod, chickpeas, and tomatoes and simmer until the fish is cooked through, about 7 minutes. Stir in the parsley, cilantro, and 1 tablespoon of the mint. Adjust seasoning.

3. Ladle into individual bowls, sprinkle with the remaining ¼ teaspoon cumin, remaining 1 tablespoon mint, and the lemon zest, and serve.

Per serving: 150 calories, 3g total fat, 0g saturated fat, 0g trans fat, 20mg cholesterol, 540mg sodium, 19g total carbohydrate, 4g dietary fiber, 4g sugars, 13g protein

Fresh Littleneck Clam Chowder

Makes 4 servings: 1 rounded cup each

Littleneck clams ("quahogs") are briny, sweet babies of the clam family. All two inches of them are bursting with flavor (and iron!) and the most tender. They'll delight you in this lightened-up, yet luscious clam chowder. (Use a similar locally available clam if needed for best freshness and flavor.)

30 littleneck clams, well scrubbed and rinsed

1 tablespoon extra-virgin olive oil

2 large or 3 medium leeks, white and light green parts only, very thinly sliced and well rinsed

1 large garlic clove, minced

1 pound Russian banana fingerling potatoes or baby creamer potatoes, unpeeled, scrubbed, and cut into ½-inch-thick slices

1 teaspoon sea salt, or to taste

½ teaspoon ground sage

¼ teaspoon freshly ground black or white pepper, or to taste

¾ cup half-and-half

¾ teaspoon finely chopped fresh rosemary or thyme

¼ cup chopped fresh flat-leaf parsley

2 teaspoons unsalted butter, cut into 4 pieces

1. Place the clams in a stockpot, and add cold water to cover the clams by about 1 inch. Cover and bring to a boil over high heat. Turn the heat to low, and cook the clams another 30 seconds. Remove from heat. Transfer all the opened clams to a bowl using a slotted spoon. If any clams remain unopened, place back over heat, cover, and cook for 1 additional minute. Transfer any additional opened clams to the bowl; discard any unopened clams.

2. Pour the clam cooking liquid through a mesh strainer; set aside. (Note: You'll need 3 cups of broth. If you have extra, reduce it to make 3 cups. If you have too little clam broth, add some bottled clam juice or low-sodium vegetable broth to make 3 cups total.)

3. Heat the oil in a large saucepan over medium heat. Add the leeks and sauté until softened, about 5 minutes. Add the garlic and sauté for 1 minute.

4. Increase the heat to high. Add the potatoes, reserved clam broth, the salt, sage, and pepper and bring to a boil. Cover, reduce the heat to medium, and cook until the potatoes are nearly tender, about 10 minutes. Uncover and continue to cook until the broth is thickened, about 8 to 10 minutes.

5. While the chowder is cooking, detach three-fourths of the clams from their shells and roughly chop. Add the chopped clams and the other opened clams in their shell, along with the half-and-half and ½ teaspoon of the rosemary to the chowder. Reduce heat to low and simmer until the clams are heated through. Stir in the parsley. Adjust seasoning.

6. Ladle into individual bowls, top with the butter and the remaining ¼ teaspoon rosemary, and serve.

Per serving: 290 calories, 12g total fat, 5g saturated fat, 0g trans fat, 50mg cholesterol, 670mg sodium, 32g total carbohydrate, 3g dietary fiber, 4g sugars, 16g protein

Brooklyn Clam Chowder

Makes 6 servings: 1 cup each

People say that Brooklyn is the "new" Manhattan, so a "new" borough means a new clam chowder. This is made with cherrystone clams, which have a bigger flavor than littlenecks. It's loaded with veggies for added flair. And it has an overall boldness about it . . . just like my neighboring Brooklynites.

16 cherrystone clams, well scrubbed and rinsed
1 tablespoon extra-virgin olive oil
1 medium white onion, finely diced
1 medium green bell pepper, diced
1 medium red bell pepper, diced
1 medium celery stalk, diced
2 teaspoons aged red wine vinegar
¾ teaspoon sea salt, or to taste
2 large garlic cloves, minced
1 large Yukon Gold potato, unpeeled, scrubbed, and cubed
1 (14.5-ounce) can diced tomatoes (with liquid)
½ teaspoon freshly ground black pepper, or to taste
½ teaspoon hot pepper sauce, or to taste
¼ cup chopped fresh flat-leaf parsley
2 tablespoons thinly sliced fresh basil leaves

1. Place the clams in a stockpot, and add cold water to cover the clams by about 1 inch. Cover and bring to a boil over high heat. Cook the clams 2½ to 3 minutes. Remove from heat. Transfer all the opened clams to a bowl using a slotted spoon. If any clams remain unopened, place back over heat, covered, and cook for 1 additional minute. Transfer additional opened clams to the bowl; discard any unopened clams.

2. Pour the clam cooking liquid through a mesh strainer; set aside. (Note: You'll need 2 cups of broth. If you have extra, reduce it to make 2 cups. If you have too little clam broth, add some bottled clam juice or low-sodium vegetable broth to make 2 cups total.)

continues on next page

3. Heat the oil in a large saucepan over medium heat. Add the onion, bell peppers, celery, vinegar, and ¼ teaspoon of the salt and sauté until softened, about 5 minutes. Add the garlic and sauté for 1 minute.

4. Stir in the potato, reserved clam broth, tomatoes with liquid, black pepper, hot pepper sauce, and the remaining ½ teaspoon salt. Reduce heat to medium-low, cover, and simmer until the potato is tender, about 15 minutes.

5. While the chowder is cooking, detach the clams from their shells and chop. Add the chopped clams to the chowder. Reduce heat to low and simmer until the clams are heated through. Stir in the parsley and 1 tablespoon of the basil. Adjust seasoning.

6. Ladle into individual bowls, top with the remaining 1 tablespoon basil, and serve.

Per serving: 130 calories, 3g total fat, 0g saturated fat, 0g trans fat, 15mg cholesterol, 490mg sodium, 19g total carbohydrate, 3g dietary fiber, 5g sugars, 7g protein

Italian Tomato, Basil, and Meatball Soup

Makes 8 servings: 1 cup plus ½ large meatball each

When tomatoes are in season, whenever possible, I try to enjoy their full flavors when fresh—right off the vine. But this recipe provides one way that vine-ripened tomatoes can be improved upon—roasting until they become sweeter and more savory. This freshly roasted tomato soup with a meatball in the middle is memorable.

3 pounds vine-ripened plum tomatoes,
**   halved lengthwise**
1¼ teaspoons sea salt, or to taste
¼ teaspoon freshly ground black pepper, or to taste
2 tablespoons extra-virgin olive oil

1 shallot, minced
2 large garlic cloves, minced
6 cups low-sodium chicken broth or Chicken Stock
**   (page 203)**
1 teaspoon aged balsamic vinegar
1 teaspoon finely chopped fresh rosemary
**   or ½ teaspoon crushed dried rosemary**
¼ teaspoon dried hot pepper flakes
⅓ cup thinly sliced fresh basil leaves
4 fully cooked large meatballs or Bodacious Turkey
**   and Fennel Meatballs (page 317), warm**

1. Preheat the oven to 425°F. Place tomatoes, cut side up, on a large baking sheet. Sprinkle with the salt and pepper and drizzle with 1½ tablespoons of the oil. Roast until the tomatoes are soft and caramelized on the bottom, about 45 minutes. Let cool slightly. Transfer the tomatoes and accumulated juices to a food processor. Cover and pulse until the tomatoes are well combined, but not smooth.

2. Heat the remaining ½ tablespoon oil in a stockpot or large saucepan over medium heat. Add the shallot and sauté for 1 minute. Add the garlic and sauté for 1 minute. Stir in the roasted tomatoes, the broth, vinegar, rosemary, and hot pepper flakes, increase heat to high, and bring to a boil. Reduce heat to medium-low and simmer, uncovered, until the soup thickens slightly, about 18 minutes. Add the meatballs and ¼ cup of the basil and simmer until the meatballs are heated through and soup is desired consistency, about 8 minutes. Adjust seasoning.

3. Cut the meatballs in half. Place a meatball half, rounded side up, into each of four small bowls. Ladle the soup over or around the meatball halves, sprinkle with the remaining basil, and serve.

Per serving: 120 calories, 5g total fat, 1g saturated fat, 0g trans fat, 25mg cholesterol, 460mg sodium, 10g total carbohydrate, 2g dietary fiber, 5g sugars, 8g protein

Beef "Carpaccio" and Shirataki Soup

Makes 6 servings: 1 cup each

It's difficult to pinpoint what makes this highly flavored Asian-influenced recipe so absolutely mouthwatering. I believe it must have something to do with . . . well, every ingredient! You can find shirataki tofu noodles in the refrigerated section of your grocery with other fresh Asian-style noodles; ask the butcher to cut the beef into thin strips for you.

¼ cup brown rice vinegar

1½ tablespoons naturally brewed soy sauce, or to taste

2 scallions, green and white parts, thinly sliced on the diagonal

2 large garlic cloves, minced

2 teaspoons toasted sesame oil

2 teaspoons honey or agave nectar

2 teaspoons freshly grated gingerroot

⅛ teaspoon dried hot pepper flakes

10 ounces lean beef tenderloin or sirloin, shaved or cut into 12 or more extra-thin "carpaccio-style" strips

1 (32-ounce) carton low-sodium beef broth

1 cup thinly sliced stemmed fresh shiitake mushrooms or cremini (baby bella) mushrooms

1 (8-ounce) package shirataki tofu noodles, rinsed and drained

¾ teaspoon toasted sesame seeds

¼ cup chopped fresh mint

1. Whisk together the vinegar, soy sauce, scallions, garlic, oil, honey, ginger, and hot pepper flakes in a medium bowl. Add the beef and toss to coat. Set aside to marinate up to 30 minutes. Remove the beef to a bowl or plate; reserve the marinade.

2. Add the broth, mushrooms, and 1½ tablespoons of the reserved marinade (discard any remaining marinade) to a large saucepan over high heat. Bring to a boil. Reduce heat to medium, stir in the noodles and beef, and simmer until the beef is gently cooked, about 1 minute. Adjust seasoning.

3. Ladle into individual bowls, top with the sesame seeds and mint, and serve. Enjoy with chopsticks and a spoon.

Per serving: 140 calories, 6g total fat, 2g saturated fat, 0g trans fat, 30mg cholesterol, 420mg sodium, 5g total carbohydrate, 1g dietary fiber, 3g sugars, 15g protein

Vegetarian Stews

Winter Root Vegetable Stew Ⓕ

Makes 9 servings: 1 cup each

We know potatoes, carrots, and sweet potatoes quite well. But this heartwarming stew will provide an easy "meet, greet, and eat" with the less well known root vegetables like rutabaga and parsnips.

1 tablespoon extra-virgin olive oil

1 large red onion, chopped

1 cup Fumé Blanc or other white wine

1½ teaspoons sea salt, or to taste

4 large garlic cloves, minced

2 tablespoons chopped fresh oregano

1½ tablespoons finely chopped fresh rosemary
     or 1½ teaspoons crushed dried rosemary

1 pound baby red potatoes, unpeeled, scrubbed,
     and quartered

4 medium carrots, cut into ⅓-inch rounds

1 small rutabaga or 2 medium turnips,
     peeled and cut into 1-inch pieces

2 medium parsnips, cut into ⅓-inch rounds

1 large sweet potato, unpeeled, scrubbed,
     and cut into ½-inch cubes

1 (32-ounce) carton low-sodium vegetable broth
     or 4 cups Vegetable Stock (page 203)

½ teaspoon freshly ground black pepper, or to taste

¼ teaspoon ground cinnamon

1. Heat the oil in a stockpot over medium heat. Add the onion, 1 tablespoon of the wine, and ¼ teaspoon of the salt and sauté until the onion is softened and begins to caramelize, about 10 minutes. Add the garlic and sauté 1 minute.

2. Add the remaining wine, 1½ tablespoons of the oregano, and the rosemary and simmer until the liquid evaporates, about 8 minutes. Add the potatoes, carrots, rutabaga, parsnips, sweet potato, broth, pepper, cinnamon, and the remaining 1¼ teaspoons salt. Cover and bring to a boil over high heat. Reduce heat to low and simmer, covered, until the vegetables are tender, about 20 minutes.

3. Transfer 1½ cups of the vegetables and 1 cup of the broth to a blender. Cover and blend until smooth. Stir back into the stew. Adjust seasoning.

4. Ladle the stew into bowls, sprinkle with the remaining ½ tablespoon oregano, and serve.

Per serving: 160 calories, 2g total fat, 0g saturated fat, 0g trans fat, 0mg cholesterol, 490mg sodium, 28g total carbohydrate, 6g dietary fiber, 9g sugars, 3g protein

Spring Vegetable Stew with Fresh Tarragon

Makes 6 servings: 1⅔ cups each

Head to the farmers' market in springtime, pick a basket of the seasonal highlights, and you'll have most of what you need for this beautiful stew. What makes this out of this world is the earthy morels; they're springtime mushrooms that impart smoky and almost nut-like nuances.

1 tablespoon extra-virgin olive oil

1 large white onion, chopped

Juice of 1 small lemon (2 tablespoons)

1½ teaspoons sea salt, or to taste

2 large garlic cloves, thinly sliced

1 cup Sauvignon Blanc or other white wine

1 medium fennel bulb, cored and shredded
     or finely diced

1 pound fingerling or baby gold creamer potatoes,
     unpeeled, scrubbed, and very thinly sliced

1 large orange bell pepper, finely chopped

1 (32-ounce) carton low-sodium vegetable broth
     or 4 cups Vegetable Stock (page 203)

¼ teaspoon freshly ground black pepper, or to taste

1 cup small fresh morels or sliced mushroom blend

1 pound thin green asparagus, ends trimmed
     and cut into 1-inch pieces

1 cup fresh or frozen peas, thawed

3 tablespoons chopped fresh tarragon

1. Heat the oil in a stockpot over medium heat. Add the onion, 1 tablespoon of the lemon juice, and ¼ teaspoon of the salt and sauté until slightly caramelized, about 8 minutes. Add the garlic and sauté 1 minute.

2. Add the wine and simmer until the liquid evaporates, about 10 minutes. Add the fennel, potatoes, bell pepper, broth, black pepper, and the remaining 1¼ teaspoons salt. Cover and bring to a boil over high heat. Reduce heat to medium-low and simmer, covered, until the vegetables are tender, about 15 minutes.

3. Blend until smooth using an immersion blender. (Alternatively, puree in a blender in batches using the hot fill line as a guide; return to the saucepan.)

4. Stir the morels and asparagus into the pureed stew and cook, covered, over medium heat, until the asparagus is nearly tender, about 12 to 15 minutes. Reduce heat to low and remove cover. Stir in the peas, 2 tablespoons of the tarragon, and the remaining 1 tablespoon lemon juice and cook while stirring for 2 minutes. Adjust seasoning.

5. Ladle the stew into bowls, sprinkle with the remaining 1 tablespoon tarragon, and serve.

Per serving: 110 calories, 1.5g total fat, 0g saturated fat, 0g trans fat, 0mg cholesterol, 430mg sodium, 17g total carbohydrate, 4g dietary fiber, 4g sugars, 3g protein

Turkish Vegetable Stew Ⓕ

Makes 8 servings: 1 cup stew and ⅓ cup couscous each

Once you've prepped all the ingredients, this becomes a quick-fix stew. It's prepared in the microwave oven, which I call "micro-stewing." Generally, you'll get more depth of flavor if you stew for lengthier times on the stovetop or in the oven. So to boost intensity here, the fresh herbs and spices become fundamental flavor enhancers while providing Turkish flair.

2½ cups low-sodium vegetable broth or Vegetable Stock (page 203)
3 medium carrots, unpeeled, scrubbed, and thinly sliced crosswise
2 large celery stalks, thinly sliced
1 large or 2 small yellow or red onions, halved and sliced
1 medium vine-ripened tomato, diced
2 large garlic cloves, thinly sliced
1 tablespoon extra-virgin olive oil
1 (15-ounce) can chickpeas (garbanzo beans), drained
1 medium red potato, unpeeled, scrubbed, and cut into ½-inch cubes
1 medium eggplant, cut into ½-inch cubes
⅓ cup chopped fresh mint
2 tablespoons dried currants or chopped dried Black Mission figs
1 tablespoon ground cumin
¼ teaspoon ground cinnamon
1¾ teaspoons sea salt, or to taste
¾ teaspoon freshly ground black pepper, or to taste
2⅔ cups cooked whole-wheat couscous, warm
2 tablespoons chopped fresh cilantro (optional)
2 tablespoons pine nuts, toasted
1 small lemon, cut into 6 wedges

1. Add the broth, carrots, celery, onion, tomato, and garlic to a large microwave-safe dish. Drizzle with the oil and toss to coat. Cover with parchment paper and cook in the microwave on high until the onion is softened, about 5 minutes.

2. Add the chickpeas, potato, eggplant, half of the mint, the currants, cumin, cinnamon, salt, and pepper to the vegetables and stir well. Cover with parchment paper and microwave on high until the vegetables are nearly tender, about 12 minutes, stirring twice. Adjust seasoning.

3. Place couscous in individual bowls. Ladle the stew on top, sprinkle with the remaining mint, the cilantro (if using), and pine nuts, and serve with the lemon wedges.

Per serving: 200 calories, 4.5g total fat, 0g saturated fat, 0g trans fat, 0mg cholesterol, 630mg sodium, 36g total carbohydrate, 6g dietary fiber, 7g sugars, 7g protein

Tuscan-Style Ribollita (F)

Makes 12 servings: 1 cup each

I became captivated by *ribollita,* a traditional Tuscan bread soup, on a trip to Fattoria di Castiglionchio, a twelfth-century rustic farm outside of Florence. It was a hearty bowlful of inviting textures, rich seasonal vegetables, and fresh herbal aromas drizzled with a burst of fruity olive oil. At the table, a bottle of extra-virgin olive oil was passed around for extra drizzling. Here I've created my own version to help transport your palate to the Italian countryside anytime.

1½ tablespoons extra-virgin olive oil

3 medium carrots, unpeeled, scrubbed, and chopped

2 large celery stalks, sliced

1 large red onion, chopped

2 to 3 large garlic cloves, minced

2 teaspoons aged balsamic vinegar

2½ teaspoons sea salt, or to taste

2 (15-ounce) cans no-salt-added cannellini or other white beans, drained

6 cups low-sodium vegetable or Vegetable Stock (page 203)

5 cups (12 ounces) chopped savoy cabbage, kale, or Swiss chard leaves

1 (14.5-ounce) can diced tomatoes (with liquid)

¾ teaspoon freshly ground black pepper, or to taste

¼ teaspoon dried hot pepper flakes, or to taste

8 ounces thick-sliced day-old whole-wheat ciabatta or Italian bread, cut into 1-inch cubes

1 cup chopped fresh flat-leaf parsley

3 tablespoons chopped fresh basil

1 tablespoon finely chopped fresh thyme or 1½ teaspoons finely chopped fresh rosemary

3 tablespoons freshly grated Parmigiano-Reggiano or other Parmesan cheese

1. Heat the oil in a stockpot over medium-low heat. Add the carrots, celery, onion, garlic, vinegar, and ¼ teaspoon of the salt and cook, stirring occasionally, until the celery is softened, about 20 minutes.

2. Meanwhile, add 1 can of the beans and 1 cup of the broth to a food processor or blender. Cover and blend until smooth.

3. Add the bean puree, the cabbage, remaining 5 cups of broth, tomatoes with liquid, black pepper, hot pepper flakes, and remaining 2¼ teaspoons salt and bring to a boil over high heat. Reduce heat to medium-low and simmer, uncovered, until the vegetables are cooked through and broth has thickened, about 30 minutes. Stir in the remaining can of beans, the bread, ¾ cup of the parsley, the basil, and thyme, and simmer for 5 minutes. Adjust seasoning.

4. Ladle into individual bowls, sprinkle with the cheese and the remaining ¼ cup parsley, and serve. For an extra special touch, place individual servings in the oven and bake until bubbling, then serve.

Per serving: 160 calories, 3.5g total fat, 0.5g saturated fat, 0g trans fat, 0mg cholesterol, 790mg sodium, 25g total carbohydrate, 7g dietary fiber, 6g sugars, 8g protein

North African Peanut Stew

Makes 10 servings: 1 cup stew and ⅓ cup rice each

A gastronomic delight, this interesting stew lends itself to many traditional North African flavors. From spicy gingerroot to sweet roasted peanuts, it offers full-bodied complexity that will excite every taste bud and leave you wanting more.

1 tablespoon extra-virgin olive oil

1 medium red onion, finely chopped

1 medium green bell pepper, finely chopped

½ cup chopped carrot

½ cup chopped celery

2 teaspoons brown rice vinegar

1¾ teaspoons sea salt, or to taste

2 large garlic cloves, minced

2 tablespoons freshly grated gingerroot

1 tablespoon hot Madras curry powder

1 (14.5-ounce) can diced tomatoes (with liquid)

1 (32-ounce) carton low-sodium vegetable broth or 4 cups Vegetable Stock (page 203)

1 large sweet potato, unpeeled, scrubbed, and cut into ½-inch cubes

⅓ cup no-salt-added creamy natural peanut
or raw almond butter

¼ teaspoon freshly ground black pepper, or to taste

1½ cups frozen shelled edamame, thawed

5 cups packed fresh baby spinach

⅓ cup chopped fresh cilantro

3⅓ cups cooked brown basmati rice, warm

3 tablespoons chopped unsalted dry-roasted peanuts

1. Heat the oil in a large saucepan over medium heat. Add the onion, bell pepper, carrot, celery, vinegar, and ¼ teaspoon of the salt and sauté until the onion is softened, about 5 minutes.

2. Add the garlic, ginger, and curry powder and sauté until fragrant, about 1 minute.

3. Add the tomatoes with liquid and cook uncovered until the tomatoes are slightly reduced, about 5 minutes.

4. Add the broth, sweet potato, peanut butter, black pepper, and the remaining 1½ teaspoons salt and bring to a boil over high heat. Reduce heat to low and simmer uncovered, gently stirring on occasion, until the sweet potato is tender and broth is slightly thickened, about 12 to 15 minutes.

5. Stir in the edamame, spinach, and about three-fourths of the cilantro and cook for 3 minutes. Adjust seasoning.

6. Add the rice to individual bowls. Ladle the stew around or over the rice, sprinkle with the peanuts and the remaining cilantro, and serve.

Per serving: 230 calories, 9g total fat, 1.5g saturated fat, 0g trans fat, 0mg cholesterol, 610mg sodium, 31g total carbohydrate, 6g dietary fiber, 6g sugars, 8g protein

Roasted Asian Eggplant Stew ⓕ

Makes 3 servings: 1 cup stew and ½ cup rice each

Hot and sour sets the tone for this exciting bowl of Asian goodness. While eggplant is the star of this stew, the peanut and lime accents will delight. Here the eggplant soaks up the vibrant essences of citrus, soy, and sesame, accompanied by a fresh punch of cilantro in every bite.

4 Asian eggplants or 1 medium quartered
eggplant

2 teaspoons toasted sesame oil

1 large shallot, very thinly sliced

2 scallions, green and white parts, thinly sliced

1 large garlic clove, very thinly sliced

3 cups low-sodium vegetable broth or
Vegetable Stock (page 203)

Juice of 1 lime (2 tablespoons)

2 teaspoons Asian garlic-chili sauce, or to taste

2 teaspoons naturally brewed soy sauce

½ teaspoon sea salt, or to taste

3 tablespoons chopped fresh cilantro

1½ cups cooked brown basmati or short-grain
brown rice, warm

1½ teaspoons honey or agave nectar

3 tablespoons coarsely chopped unsalted
dry-roasted peanuts

1. Preheat the oven to 425°F. Wrap each eggplant in aluminum foil. Roast until fully cooked, about 25 minutes. Let cool slightly. Cut into 1-inch cubes; discard stems.

2. Heat the oil in a large saucepan over medium heat. Add the shallot, white parts of the scallions, and the garlic and sauté for 1 minute.

3. Add the eggplant cubes, the broth, lime juice, garlic-chili sauce, soy sauce, salt, and half of the cilantro and bring to a boil over high heat. Reduce heat to medium and let simmer until stew-like consistency, about 30 minutes. Stir in the green parts of the scallion. Adjust seasoning.

4. Add the rice to individual bowls. Ladle the stew over or around the rice, sprinkle with the honey, peanuts, and the remaining cilantro, and serve.

Per serving: 200 calories, 6g total fat, 1g saturated fat, 0g trans fat, 0mg cholesterol, 670mg sodium, 33g total carbohydrate, 7g dietary fiber, 7g sugars, 5g protein

Irish Vegetable Stew Ⓕ

Makes 9 servings: 1 cup each

You don't have to travel to Ireland to enjoy this heartwarming pub fare. With a splash of stout, every taste will have you singing a Celtic tune. A vegan-friendly stew, full of traditional Irish staples like cabbage and potatoes, this provides depth of flavor and the perfect bite for warming you from the inside out. Enjoy it along with the same stout that you use in the recipe.

1½ tablespoons extra-virgin olive oil

1 large yellow onion, quartered and sliced

¾ cup Irish dry stout or lager

1¼ teaspoons sea salt, or to taste

2 large garlic cloves, minced

¾ teaspoon caraway or fennel seeds

1 (32-ounce) carton low-sodium vegetable broth or 4 cups Vegetable Stock (page 203)

1 tablespoon naturally brewed soy sauce

½ cup dried red lentils, rinsed and drained

½ medium head green cabbage, shredded

3 large russet potatoes, unpeeled, scrubbed, and diced

2 cups medium baby carrots, halved lengthwise, or whole small baby carrots

1½ cups thinly sliced white button mushrooms

1 large celery stalk, thinly sliced

1 teaspoon freshly ground black pepper, or to taste

2 teaspoons finely chopped fresh thyme

2 scallions, green and white parts, minced, or ⅓ cup minced fresh chives

⅓ cup chopped fresh flat-leaf parsley

1. Heat the oil in a stockpot over medium heat. Add the onion, 1 tablespoon of the stout, and ¼ teaspoon of the salt and sauté until softened, about 5 minutes. Add the garlic and caraway seeds and sauté for 1 minute.

2. Add the remaining stout and cook for 1 minute. Add the broth and soy sauce and bring to a boil over high heat. Add the lentils, reduce heat to medium-low, cover, and simmer for 10 minutes.

Add the cabbage, potatoes, carrots, mushrooms, celery, pepper, 1 teaspoon of the thyme, and the remaining 1 teaspoon salt, cover, and simmer until the vegetables and lentils are done, about 25 minutes. Stir in the scallions, the remaining 1 teaspoon thyme, and half the parsley. Adjust seasoning.

3. Ladle into individual bowls, sprinkle with the remaining parsley, and serve.

Per serving: 220 calories, 3g total fat, 0g saturated fat, 0g trans fat, 0mg cholesterol, 530mg sodium, 40g total carbohydrate, 6g dietary fiber, 7g sugars, 8g protein

Herb and Spice Tomato Chickpea Stew Ⓕ

Makes 8 servings: 1 cup each

The combination of Middle Eastern herbs and spices is so pleasing to the palate, it's simply irresistible. Cinnamon and cumin take center stage in seasoning this hearty dish, while fresh and aromatic mint enhance the flavor vibrancy. It's an enjoyable eating experience for all of the senses. Serve with whole-wheat pita bread or over whole-wheat couscous or bulgur.

1 tablespoon extra-virgin olive oil

2 medium white onions, halved and thinly sliced

Juice of 1 lemon (3 tablespoons)

1¼ teaspoons sea salt, or to taste

3 large garlic cloves, minced

½ teaspoon cumin seeds

1 (28-ounce) can crushed roasted tomatoes

3 cups low-sodium vegetable broth or Vegetable Stock (page 203)

1 large russet potato, unpeeled, scrubbed, and cut into ½-inch cubes

8 ounces fresh green beans, trimmed and cut in half on the diagonal (about 2 cups)

¾ teaspoon freshly ground black pepper, or to taste

¾ teaspoon ground cinnamon

½ teaspoon ground cumin

1 (15-ounce) can no-salt-added chickpeas (garbanzo beans), drained

¼ cup finely chopped fresh flat-leaf parsley

3 tablespoons chopped fresh mint

1. Heat the oil in a stockpot over medium heat. Add the onions, 1 tablespoon of the lemon juice, and ¼ teaspoon of the salt and sauté until softened, about 10 minutes. Add the garlic and cumin seeds and sauté for 1 minute.

2. Add the tomatoes, broth, potato, green beans, pepper, cinnamon, ground cumin, and the remaining 2 tablespoons lemon juice and remaining 1 teaspoon salt and bring to a boil over high heat. Reduce heat to medium-low, partially cover, and simmer for 40 minutes. Stir in the chickpeas and simmer, partially covered, until the potatoes and green beans are fully cooked and stew has reached desired consistency, about 40 minutes. Stir in the parsley and half the mint. Adjust seasoning.

3. Ladle into individual bowls, sprinkle with the remaining mint, and serve.

Per serving: 170 calories, 2.5g total fat, 0g saturated fat, 0g trans fat, 0mg cholesterol, 680mg sodium, 33g total carbohydrate, 6g dietary fiber, 8g sugars, 6g protein

White Bean Cassoulet with Garlic Toast Ⓕ

Makes 9 servings: 1 cup each

This simple, satisfying, French-style dish is incredibly rich and earthy with vegetable goodness. Here I've given it a fresh makeover with baby zucchini. Though, my favorite part is the buttery, melt-in-your-mouth quality from the white beans.

3 tablespoons extra-virgin olive oil

1 large white onion, chopped

2 teaspoons aged red wine vinegar

1¼ teaspoons sea salt, or to taste

4 large garlic cloves, very thinly sliced

¼ teaspoon dried hot pepper flakes, or to taste

1 (14.5-ounce) can diced tomatoes (with liquid)

3 (15-ounce) cans no-salt-added cannellini or other white beans, drained

8 ounces medium baby carrots, thinly sliced into coins or quartered lengthwise (about 2 cups)

2 large celery stalks, cut into 1-inch pieces

8 ounces baby zucchini, quartered lengthwise, or 1 medium zucchini, sliced into coins

1½ teaspoons finely chopped fresh thyme

⅓ cup chopped fresh flat-leaf parsley

1¾ cups low-sodium vegetable broth or Vegetable Stock (page 203)

9 thin slices whole-grain baguette, well toasted, and rubbed with half garlic clove

3 tablespoons chopped fresh basil (optional)

1. Preheat the oven to 400°F.

2. Heat 1½ tablespoons of the oil in a large skillet over medium heat. Add the onion, vinegar, and ¼ teaspoon of the salt and sauté until softened, about 8 minutes. Add the garlic and hot pepper flakes and sauté for 1 minute. Add the tomatoes with liquid and cook while stirring for 1 minute.

3. Add the tomato mixture to a cassoulet pot or 2½-quart baking dish. Stir in the beans, carrots, celery, zucchini, thyme, ¼ cup of the parsley, and the remaining 1 teaspoon salt. Pour the broth evenly over the mixture. Bake until the carrots are cooked through and the cassoulet is caramelized, about 1 hour 10 minutes. Adjust seasoning.

4. Top with the garlic toasts, drizzle with the remaining 1½ tablespoons oil, sprinkle with the basil (if using), and the remaining parsley, and serve from the baking dish.

Per serving: 230 calories, 7g total fat, 1g saturated fat, 0g trans fat, 0mg cholesterol, 580mg sodium, 33g total carbohydrate, 9g dietary fiber, 6g sugars, 10g protein

Curry Lentil Stew with Spinach Ⓕ

Makes 7 servings: 1 cup each

With so much punch it's no wonder curry is a worldwide crowd pleaser. It certainly heightens flavors in this tomatoey lentil stew—complementing the fragrant coconut and tangy gingerroot. It was lust at first whiff—and love at first bite for me.

1 tablespoon coconut oil or extra-virgin olive oil

1 large white onion, diced

2 teaspoons aged red wine vinegar

1½ teaspoons sea salt, or to taste

2 large garlic cloves, minced

2 teaspoons freshly grated gingerroot

1½ tablespoons hot Madras curry powder

1 (32-ounce) carton low-sodium vegetable broth or 4 cups Vegetable Stock (page 203)

1 cup dried red lentils, rinsed and drained

2 teaspoons pure coconut extract

½ teaspoon freshly ground black pepper, or to taste

3 medium vine-ripened tomatoes, pulp removed and diced

8 ounces fresh baby spinach

1. Heat the oil in a stockpot over medium heat. Add the onion, vinegar, and ¼ teaspoon of the salt and sauté until softened, about 8 minutes. Add the garlic, ginger, and curry powder and sauté for 1 minute.

2. Add the broth, lentils, coconut extract, pepper, and the remaining 1¼ teaspoons salt and bring to a boil over high heat. Reduce heat to medium-low, partially cover, and simmer until the lentils are nearly done, about 22 minutes. Stir in the tomatoes and simmer, uncovered, until the lentils are done, about 3 minutes. Stir in the spinach until completely wilted. Adjust seasoning.

3. Ladle into bowls, and serve.

Per serving: 160 calories, 3g total fat, 2g saturated fat, 0g trans fat, 0mg cholesterol, 640mg sodium, 26g total carbohydrate, 7g dietary fiber, 4g sugars, 9g protein

Poultry, Fish, Shellfish, and Meat Stews

Provençal-Style Poultry Stew with Fresh Basil

Makes 12 servings: 1 cup each

Stews aren't just for wintertime; spring and summertime stews can be truly delightful. It's a great time for enjoying light, fresh flavors. This Provençal-style stew captures the soft, alluring aromas of fresh rosemary, basil, and thyme. Enjoy it with crusty whole-grain bread and a refreshing glass of Sauvignon Blanc for extra satisfaction.

1 tablespoon extra-virgin olive oil

1 large red or white onion, cut into large dice

Juice of 1 lemon (3 tablespoons)

2¼ teaspoons sea salt, or to taste

1 pound boneless skinless chicken breast, cut into thin 2-inch long strips

3 large garlic cloves, minced

1 teaspoon ground sage

1 (14.5-ounce) can diced tomatoes (with liquid)

1 (32-ounce) carton low-sodium chicken broth or 4 cups Chicken Stock (page 203)

1 pound baby red or purple creamer potatoes, unpeeled, scrubbed, and sliced ¼ inch thick

2 cups small baby carrots, or halved medium baby carrots

1 medium red bell pepper, cut into 1-inch dice

1 teaspoon freshly ground black pepper, or to taste

1 large yellow summer squash or zucchini, quartered lengthwise and cut into 1-inch pieces crosswise

1 (15-ounce) can no-salt-added cannellini or other white beans, drained

2 teaspoons finely chopped fresh rosemary

1 teaspoon finely chopped fresh thyme

⅓ cup thinly sliced fresh basil

1. Heat the oil in a stockpot over medium heat. Add the onion, 1 tablespoon of the lemon juice, and ¼ teaspoon of the salt and sauté until softened, about 8 minutes. Increase heat to medium-high, add the chicken, and sauté until no longer pink on the outside, about 3 minutes. Add the garlic and sage and sauté for 30 seconds.

2. Add the tomatoes with liquid and broth and bring to a boil over high heat. Reduce heat to low, cover, and simmer for 15 minutes. Add the potatoes, carrots, bell pepper, black pepper, and the remaining 2 tablespoons lemon juice and 2 teaspoons salt, and simmer, uncovered, for 15 minutes. Stir in the squash, beans, rosemary, and thyme and simmer, fully covered, until all the vegetables are tender, about 1 hour. Uncover, and simmer until desired consistency, about 15 minutes. Stir in half of the basil. Adjust seasoning.

3. Ladle into individual bowls and sprinkle with the remaining basil. Garnish with fresh lemon zest, if desired, and serve.

Per serving: 140 calories, 2.5g total fat, 0g saturated fat, 0g trans fat, 20mg cholesterol, 580mg sodium, 18g total carbohydrate, 4g dietary fiber, 4g sugars, 12g protein

Creole Chicken and Okra Stew Ⓕ

Makes 9 servings: 1 cup stew and ½ cup rice each

Creole cooking is known for being down-home and downright delicious. And what would Southern cooking be without okra? Well, not Southern! This hearty, savory chicken thigh and okra stew captures the essence of slow food. It's sure to capture the heart—and taste buds—of whomever you serve this to, including you.

4 teaspoons peanut or canola oil
1 pound boneless skinless chicken thighs, cut into 1-inch cubes
1 large white onion, cut into large dice
1 large green bell pepper, cut into large dice
1 large celery stalk, sliced on the diagonal
2 teaspoons aged red wine vinegar
1½ teaspoons sea salt, or to taste
2 large garlic cloves, minced
1 (28-ounce) can crushed roasted tomatoes
1 pound fresh or frozen cut okra, thawed
1 cup low-sodium chicken broth or Chicken Stock (page 203)
1½ teaspoons Creole seasoning (page 31)
2 teaspoons finely chopped fresh thyme or oregano
1 (15-ounce) can no-salt-added red kidney beans, drained
4½ cups cooked long-grain brown rice, warm

1. Heat 2 teaspoons of the oil in a stockpot over medium-high heat. Add the chicken and sauté until just cooked through and beginning to brown, about 6 minutes. Transfer to a bowl using a slotted spoon.

2. Add the remaining 2 teaspoons oil to the stockpot. Add the onion, bell pepper, celery, vinegar, and ¼ teaspoon of the salt and sauté until the onion is lightly caramelized, while scraping up any browned chicken bits, about 8 minutes. Add the garlic and sauté for 30 seconds.

3. Stir in the chicken with any accumulated juices, the tomatoes, okra, broth, Creole seasoning, 1½ teaspoons of the thyme, and the remaining 1¼ teaspoons salt and bring to a boil over high heat. Reduce heat to low, stir in the beans, cover, and simmer until the chicken is tender, about 40 minutes. Adjust seasoning.

4. Add the rice to individual bowls. Ladle the stew over the rice and sprinkle with the remaining ½ teaspoon thyme. If desired, serve with hot pepper sauce on the side.

Per serving: 300 calories, 7g total fat, 1.5g saturated fat, 0g trans fat, 35mg cholesterol, 730mg sodium, 42g total carbohydrate, 7g dietary fiber, 7g sugars, 16g protein

Harissa Moroccan Chicken Amaranth Stew Ⓕ

Makes 7 servings: 1 cup each

The exotic, piquant flavors of Moroccan food are so addicting that this recipe may just become a family favorite. The traditional Moroccan pairing of cinnamon with turmeric, cumin, and cilantro is mouthwatering and memorable. Serve the stew over a bed of steamed spinach or other dark leafy greens, if you like.

2 teaspoons grapeseed or canola oil

1 pound boneless skinless chicken thighs, cut into 1-inch cubes

2 teaspoons extra-virgin olive oil

1 large sweet onion, cut into large dices

Juice and zest of 1 lemon (3 tablespoons juice)

1¼ teaspoons sea salt, or to taste

2 large garlic cloves, minced

2 teaspoons freshly grated gingerroot

1 (14.5-ounce) can diced tomatoes (with liquid)

3 cups low-sodium chicken broth or Chicken Stock (page 203)

1 (15-ounce) can no-salt-added chickpeas (garbanzo beans), drained

2 teaspoons harissa sauce or ¼ teaspoon dried hot pepper flakes

1 teaspoon ground cinnamon

½ teaspoon ground cumin

½ teaspoon freshly ground black pepper, or to taste

¾ cup whole-grain amaranth

⅓ cup fat-free or low-fat plain Greek yogurt

⅛ teaspoon ground turmeric

3 tablespoons sliced natural almonds, toasted

3 tablespoons chopped fresh cilantro

1. Heat the grapeseed oil in a stockpot over medium-high heat. Add the chicken and sauté until just cooked through and beginning to brown, about 6 minutes. Transfer to a bowl using a slotted spoon.

2. Reduce heat to medium. Add the olive oil to the stockpot. Add the onion, 1 tablespoon of the lemon juice, and ¼ teaspoon of the salt and sauté until the onion is softened, while scraping up any browned chicken bits, about 8 minutes. Add the garlic and ginger and sauté for 1 minute.

3. Add the tomatoes, broth, chickpeas, harissa, cinnamon, cumin, pepper, the lemon zest, remaining lemon juice, and remaining 1 teaspoon salt and bring to a boil over high heat. Vigorously stir in the amaranth. Stir in the chicken with any accumulated juices. Reduce heat to low, cover, and simmer for 20 minutes. Then partially cover and continue to simmer until the chicken is tender and the stew is desired consistency, about 20 minute. Remove from heat. Adjust seasoning.

4. Whisk together the yogurt and turmeric in a small bowl.

5. Ladle the stew into individual bowls, dollop with the yogurt mixture, sprinkle with the almonds and cilantro, and serve.

Per serving: 320 calories, 11g total fat, 2g saturated fat, 0g trans fat, 40mg cholesterol, 640mg sodium, 34g total carbohydrate, 5g dietary fiber, 6g sugars, 21g protein

Rotisserie Chicken Stew with Couscous, Carrots, and Thyme Ⓕ

Makes 9 servings: 1 cup each

Looking for a light and lovely meal with flair that you won't have to wait for? Your wish is granted! The beauty of this French-inspired stew is the time you'll save by using rotisserie chicken. (You can also use your own leftover roasted chicken, if you happen to have it on hand.) This completely satisfying stew with fresh thyme and rosemary is an excellent choice for a week-night delight.

1 tablespoon extra-virgin olive oil

1 large red onion, cut into large dice

Juice of 1 small lemon (2 tablespoons)

1¾ teaspoons sea salt, or to taste

5 cups low-sodium chicken broth or Chicken Stock (page 203)

¾ teaspoon freshly ground black pepper, or to taste

1 pound medium baby carrots, halved, or small baby carrots, whole

1 teaspoon minced fresh rosemary

⅔ cup whole-wheat couscous

1 (15-ounce) can cannellini or other white beans, drained

2 cups large shreds rotisserie chicken white meat without skin

1 cup large shreds rotisserie chicken dark meat without skin

1½ teaspoons finely chopped fresh thyme, or to taste

1. Heat the oil in a large saucepan over medium heat. Add the onion, 1 tablespoon of the lemon juice, and ¼ teaspoon of the salt and sauté until the onion begins to caramelize, about 12 minutes. Stir in the remaining 1 tablespoon lemon juice and cook while stirring for 1 minute.

2. Add the broth, pepper, carrots, rosemary, and remaining 1½ teaspoons salt and bring to a boil over high heat. Reduce heat to low, cover, and simmer until the carrots are al dente (cooked through yet still firm), about 15 minutes. Stir in the couscous, then stir in the beans, chicken, and 1 teaspoon of the thyme, cover, and simmer until the carrots are tender and couscous is fully cooked, about 8 minutes. Adjust seasoning.

3. Ladle into individual bowls, sprinkle with the remaining ½ teaspoon thyme, and serve.

Per serving: 200 calories, 3.5 g total fat, 0.5g saturated fat, 0g trans fat, 35mg cholesterol, 610mg sodium, 24g total carbohydrate, 6g dietary fiber, 4g sugars, 18g protein

Adobo Chicken and Pepper Stew

Makes 4 servings: 1 chicken breast with 1 cup stew each

The intriguing sharp tang of this dish can be attributed to the unique adobo cooking style. Adobo refers to a simmering technique native to the Philippines. In this version, you'll sauté poultry in soy sauce and vinegar. Adding bell peppers ramps up the deliciousness. Serve over brown basmati rice for a worldly dinner experience.

4 (8-ounce) split bone-in chicken breasts, skin removed

1 large white onion, cut into 1-inch dice

7 ounces apple cider vinegar

4 large garlic cloves, minced

½ teaspoon freshly ground black pepper, or to taste

2 bay leaves

2 cups low-sodium chicken broth or Chicken Stock (page 203)

2 tablespoons + 2 teaspoons naturally brewed soy sauce

1 large red bell pepper, cut into 1-inch cubes

1 large green bell pepper, cut into 1-inch cubes

1. Add the chicken, onion, vinegar, garlic, black pepper, bay leaves, and broth to a large saucepan. Bring to a boil over high heat. Reduce heat to low, cover, and simmer for 45 minutes. Add the soy sauce and bell peppers and simmer, covered, until the chicken is nearly falling off of the bone, an additional 45 minutes. Transfer the chicken to a plate and carefully remove the bones from the chicken; cover to keep warm.

2. Increase heat to high and boil the remaining bell pepper mixture until it's slightly reduced, about 10 minutes. Remove and discard the bay leaves. Check the mixture for any bones and discard, if any.

3. Pour the bell pepper mixture over the chicken, and serve.

Per serving: 250 calories, 4g total fat, 1g saturated fat, 0g trans fat, 85mg cholesterol, 730mg sodium, 17g total carbohydrate, 2g dietary fiber, 4g sugars, 35g protein

Tropical Chicken and Shrimp Stew Ⓕ

Makes 8 servings: 1 cup stew plus 1 chicken thigh and ½ cup quinoa each

Bursting with flavor, this tropical stew is sure to give you island fever. The sweetness of pineapple dances with the bite of fresh ginger. A generous pour of crisp, white wine infuses the wild rock shrimp. An array of fresh flavors your senses will surely thank you for.

1 tablespoon extra-virgin olive oil

8 (4-ounce) skinless bone-in chicken thighs

2 medium white onions, diced

1 large red bell pepper, diced

1 large orange or yellow bell pepper, diced

1 large green bell pepper, diced

1 cup Pinot Grigio or other white wine

1½ teaspoons sea salt, or to taste

5 large garlic cloves, minced

1 serrano pepper with seeds, minced

2 teaspoons freshly grated gingerroot

2 teaspoons dried thyme leaves

1 (28-ounce) can roasted diced tomatoes (with liquid)

2 cups low-sodium chicken broth or Chicken Stock (page 203)

½ teaspoon freshly ground black pepper, or to taste

1¼ cups finely diced fresh pineapple

8 ounces peeled deveined rock shrimp (about 40)

4 cups cooked quinoa, whole-wheat couscous, or sticky short-grain brown rice, warm

½ teaspoon chopped fresh thyme

1. Heat the oil in a stockpot over medium-high heat. Pat the chicken dry and add to the stockpot. Cook on all sides until golden brown, about 8 minutes. (Note: Chicken may not be fully cooked at this point.) Transfer to a bowl with tongs.

2. Add the onions, bell peppers, 1 tablespoon of the wine, and ¼ teaspoon of the salt to the stockpot and sauté until the onions are lightly caramelized, about 10 minutes. Add the garlic, serrano, ginger, and dried thyme and sauté for 1 minute.

3. Return the chicken and any accumulated juices to the stockpot. Stir in the remaining wine and cook for 1 minute. Stir in the tomatoes with liquid, broth, pepper, and the remaining 1¼ teaspoons salt and bring to a boil over high heat. Reduce heat to low, cover, and simmer until chicken is fully cooked, about 20 minutes.

4. Remove the cover, add 1 cup of the pineapple and simmer until a stew-like consistency and chicken is very tender, about 30 minutes. Add the shrimp and simmer just until cooked through, about 3 minutes. Adjust seasoning.

5. Spoon the quinoa into individual bowls; season to taste. Ladle the stew over the quinoa, sprinkle with the remaining ¼ cup pineapple and the fresh thyme, and serve.

Per serving: 380 calories, 11g total fat, 2g saturated fat, 0g trans fat, 100mg cholesterol, 780mg sodium, 36g total carbohydrate, 6g dietary fiber, 10g sugars, 28g protein

Littleneck Clam Stew with Turkey Sausage

Makes 4 servings: 1½ cups each

The marriage of fresh, sweet clams and spicy turkey sausage makes for an enchanting, well-balanced stew. Add the boldness of the aromatic French favorite, tarragon, coupled with the mildly sweet and lovely licorice-like taste of fennel, and it's sure your senses will take notice. For added attention, enjoy it with Garlic-Tarragon Pita Chips (page 41) or whole-grain country bread and a glass of Pinot Grigio.

1 tablespoon extra-virgin olive oil

1 large sweet onion, diced

1 large red or orange bell pepper, cut into matchstick-size strips

1 large fennel bulb, cut into matchstick-size strips and feathery fronds chopped

12 ounces spicy Italian turkey sausages,
casings removed

½ cup Pinot Grigio or other white wine

1½ cups low-sodium vegetable broth or
Vegetable Stock (page 203)

2 teaspoons dried tarragon

¼ teaspoon sea salt, or to taste

½ teaspoon freshly ground black pepper, or to taste

24 littleneck clams, well scrubbed and rinsed

2 teaspoons unsalted butter

1. Heat the oil in a large, deep skillet over medium-high heat. Add the onion, bell pepper, fennel strips, and sausage and sauté until the sausage is fully cooked and crumbled and vegetables are just tender, about 10 minutes. Stir in the wine, increase heat to high, and sauté for 2 minutes. Add the broth, tarragon, salt, and black pepper and bring to a boil. Add the clams, reduce heat to medium, cover, and cook just until clams open, about 7 minutes. Remove any unopened clams. Stir in the butter until melted. Adjust seasoning.

2. Ladle the stew into individual bowls, sprinkle with desired amount of the fennel fronds, and serve.

Per serving: 310 calories, 13g total fat, 3.5g saturated fat, 0g trans fat, 85mg cholesterol, 770mg sodium, 17g total carbohydrate, 4g dietary fiber, 7g sugars, 25g protein

California Cioppino

Makes 8 servings: 1 cup each

Cioppino, which sounds very Mediterranean, actually had its birthplace in San Francisco. Historically, this fish stew was made from the catch of the day, stewed with tomatoes in a wine sauce. Here the wild turbot—my suggested catch—will nearly melt in your mouth. Then to do it like the health-seeking San Franciscans, serve with whole-grain sourdough bread. A Californian treasure—now your own.

1½ tablespoons extra-virgin olive oil

1 large fennel bulb, cut into matchstick-size strips
and reserve feathery fronds chopped

1 medium white onion, diced

1 cup Chardonnay or other dry white wine

1 teaspoon sea salt, or to taste

3 large garlic cloves, minced

1 small jalapeño pepper with seeds, minced

1 (28-ounce) can crushed roasted tomatoes

2½ cups low-sodium vegetable broth or
Vegetable Stock (page 203)

¾ teaspoon freshly ground black pepper,
or to taste

¾ teaspoon dried crushed rosemary

12 ounces skinless wild turbot or halibut fillets,
cut into thick 2-inch long strips

16 mussels, well scrubbed and debearded

1. Heat the oil in a stockpot over medium heat. Add the fennel strips, onion, 1 tablespoon of the wine, and ¼ teaspoon of the salt and sauté until the fennel and onion are softened, about 10 minutes. Add the garlic and jalapeño and sauté for 1 minute. Stir in the remaining wine, increase heat to high, and sauté for 2 minutes.

2. Add the tomatoes, broth, black pepper, rosemary, and the remaining ¾ teaspoon salt and bring to a boil. Reduce heat to medium, cover, and simmer until the vegetables are fully tender, about 10 minutes. Add the turbot and mussels and cook, uncovered, until the fish is just cooked through and the mussels open, about 3 minutes. Discard any unopened mussels. Adjust seasoning.

3. Ladle the stew into individual bowls, sprinkle with the desired amount of fennel fronds, and serve.

Per serving: 170 calories, 4.5g total fat, 1g saturated fat, 0g trans fat, 30mg cholesterol, 750mg sodium, 15g total carbohydrate, 3g dietary fiber, 6g sugars, 13g protein

Irish Beef Stew

Makes 12 servings: 1 cup each

This robust stew is definitively Irish. Tender bites of succulent beef, sweet carrots, and earthy potatoes create a hearty meal that's sure to soothe the soul. Even with all the beefy flavor, it's a great way to boost your vegetable intake.

1 tablespoon grapeseed or canola oil

2 teaspoons unsalted butter

18 ounces stew beef, cut into 1-inch cubes

1 large sweet onion, cut into 1-inch cubes

6 large garlic cloves, minced

1 cup Shiraz or other red wine

2 tablespoons tomato paste

2 (32-ounce) cartons low-sodium beef broth

1 tablespoon Worcestershire sauce

2 ¼ teaspoons sea salt, or to taste

1½ teaspoons freshly ground black pepper, or to taste

2 teaspoons crushed dried rosemary

1½ teaspoons crushed dried thyme

1 pound baby carrots

2¾ pounds baby red or tricolor creamer potatoes, unpeeled, scrubbed, and quartered lengthwise

¼ cup chopped fresh flat-leaf parsley

1. Heat the oil and butter in a stockpot over medium-high heat. Once the butter melts, add the beef and onion and sauté until the beef is brown on all sides and onion begins to caramelize, about 10 minutes. Add the garlic and sauté for 30 seconds. Stir in the wine and tomato paste and cook while stirring for 2 minutes.

2. Add the broth, Worcestershire sauce, salt, pepper, rosemary, and thyme and bring to a boil over high heat. Reduce heat to low, cover, and simmer, stirring occasionally, until the beef is nearly tender, about 1 hour.

3. Increase heat to medium-low, add the carrots and simmer, uncovered, for 20 minutes. Add the potatoes and simmer, uncovered, until the beef is very tender and vegetables are softened, gently stirring a few times, about 2 hours. Adjust seasoning.

4. Ladle the stew into individual bowls, sprinkle with the parsley, and serve.

Per serving: 230 calories, 7g total fat, 2.5g saturated fat, 0g trans fat, 30mg cholesterol, 570mg sodium, 23g total carbohydrate, 3g dietary fiber, 4g sugars, 14g protein

Sonoma Bean and Pork Cassoulet Ⓕ

Makes 10 servings: 1 cup each

This cassoulet has so much depth and complexity that it'll take center stage on any table—from casual to classy. Robust pork sausage coupled with creamy white beans, along with a distinct hint of sharpness from the Parmesan cheese make it a true culinary treasure.

2 teaspoons grapeseed or canola oil

10 ounces spicy Italian-style pork sausage links

2 medium carrots, thinly sliced crosswise

2 cups cauliflower florets and tender stems, sliced

1 large celery stalk, sliced crosswise

1 large Spanish or yellow onion, chopped

1 cup Sauvignon Blanc or other dry white wine

3 large garlic cloves, minced

3 (15-ounce) cans Great Northern or other white beans, drained

1 (28-ounce) can roasted diced tomatoes (with liquid)

1 teaspoon sea salt, or to taste

1 teaspoon dried thyme

½ teaspoon freshly ground black pepper, or to taste

¾ cup whole-wheat panko breadcrumbs

3 tablespoons freshly grated Parmigiano-Reggiano or other Parmesan cheese

1 tablespoon extra-virgin olive oil

3 tablespoons chopped fresh flat-leaf parsley

1. Heat the grapeseed oil in a Dutch oven or oven-safe stockpot over medium heat. Add the sausage and sauté until brown on all sides and cooked through, about 12 minutes. Transfer to a bowl. When cool enough to handle, cut into thin diagonal slices.

2. Add the carrots, cauliflower, celery, onion, and 1 tablespoon of the wine and sauté until the onion is nearly softened, about 5 minutes. Add three-fourths of the garlic and sauté for 1 minute. Stir in the remaining wine, increase heat to high, and sauté for 2 minutes.

3. Add the sliced sausages and any accumulated juices, the beans, tomatoes with juices, salt, thyme, and pepper and bring to a boil. Reduce heat to medium-low and simmer, covered, for 30 minutes. Adjust seasoning.

4. Preheat the broiler. Sprinkle the top of the stew with the panko, the remaining garlic, the cheese, and olive oil. Place under the broiler and cook until the topping is golden brown, about 1 minute. Remove from the oven, sprinkle with the parsley, let stand for 15 minutes, and serve.

Per serving: 250 calories, 7g total fat, 2g saturated fat, 0g trans fat, 10mg cholesterol, 770mg sodium, 32g total carbohydrate, 8g dietary fiber, 6g sugars, 13g protein

Spring Lamb Stew with Peas and Mint

Makes 7 servings: 1 cup each

When spring is in the air, it's warm enough to wake the perennials, yet still chilly enough to summon a hearty stew. The seasonal lamb with fresh peas, rich balsamic, and a sassy mint finish create the perfect ensemble for a delish dish. Try it over whole-wheat couscous, too.

14 ounces lean boneless lamb shoulder, cut into 1-inch cubes
1½ tablespoons whole-wheat pastry flour
1 tablespoon extra-virgin olive oil
1 large white onion, halved, sliced
2 teaspoons aged balsamic vinegar
1¼ teaspoons sea salt, or to taste
2 large garlic cloves, minced
3 cups low-sodium vegetable broth or Vegetable Stock (page 203)
1 (14.5-ounce) can crushed roasted tomatoes
8 ounces fresh pattypan squash or halved baby zucchinis
1½ cups small fresh morels or sliced shiitake mushroom caps
1 cup fresh or frozen petite peas, thawed
⅓ cup finely chopped fresh mint

1. Toss the lamb cubes with the flour in a medium bowl.

2. Heat the oil in a large, deep skillet or stockpot over medium-high heat. Add the lamb, onion, vinegar, and ¼ teaspoon of the salt and sauté until the lamb is brown on all sides and onion is lightly caramelized, about 8 minutes. Add the garlic and sauté for 30 seconds.

3. Stir in the broth, tomatoes, and the remaining 1 teaspoon salt, while scraping up the browned bits from the bottom of the skillet, and bring to a boil over high heat. Reduce heat to low, cover, and simmer for 1 hour. Stir in the squash and morels, cover, and simmer until the lamb and squash are tender, about 20 minutes. Stir in the peas and ¼ cup of the mint and simmer, uncovered, until peas are just cooked through and stew is at desired consistency, about 5 minutes. Adjust seasoning.

4. Ladle into individual bowls, sprinkle with the remaining mint, and serve.

Per serving: 200 calories, 10g total fat, 3.5g saturated fat, 0g trans fat, 40mg cholesterol, 660mg sodium, 14g total carbohydrate, 4g dietary fiber, 7g sugars, 14g protein

Chilis

7-Veggie Chili ⓕ

Makes 8 servings: 1 cup each

A robust bowl of chili is an all-time American favorite, and an excellent choice for gatherings. This recipe offers sweetness from roasted tomatoes and sweet potato, paired with a kick from jalapeño and chili powder, plus aromatic interest from a hint of cinnamon spice and a cilantro finish. Yum!

1 tablespoon unrefined peanut or canola oil

1 medium red onion, finely diced

1 cup fresh or frozen corn kernels, thawed

2 teaspoons aged red wine vinegar

1 teaspoon sea salt, or to taste

1 medium sweet potato, unpeeled, scrubbed, and coarsely grated

1 large green bell pepper, diced

1 large red bell pepper, diced

1 small jalapeño pepper with seeds, minced

2 large garlic cloves, minced

1 tablespoon no-salt-added creamy cashew or almond butter

1 teaspoon vegetarian Worcestershire sauce

1 (14.5-ounce) can crushed roasted tomatoes

3 cups low-sodium vegetable broth or Vegetable Stock (page 203)

1½ tablespoons chili powder, or to taste

¼ teaspoon ground cinnamon

1 (15-ounce) can red kidney beans, drained

¼ cup chopped fresh cilantro or flat-leaf parsley

1 cup shredded extra-sharp Cheddar cheese (optional)

1. Heat the oil in a large saucepan over medium heat. Add the onion, corn, vinegar, and ¼ teaspoon of the salt and sauté until the onion is softened, about 8 minutes. Increase heat to medium-high, add the sweet potato, bell peppers, and jalapeño, and sauté for 3 minutes. Add the garlic, cashew butter, and Worcestershire sauce and sauté for 1 minute.

2. Stir in the tomatoes, broth, chili powder, cinnamon, and the remaining ¾ teaspoon salt and bring to a boil over high heat. Reduce heat to medium-low, stir in the beans, and simmer, uncovered, until the sweet potato is tender and chili is thickened, about 20 minutes. Stir in 3 tablespoons of the cilantro. Adjust seasoning.

3. Ladle into individual bowls, sprinkle with the cheese (if using), and the remaining 1 tablespoon cilantro, and serve.

Per serving: 150 calories, 3.5g total fat, 0.5g saturated fat, 0g trans fat, 0mg cholesterol, 560mg sodium, 25g total carbohydrate, 6g dietary fiber, 8g sugars, 6g protein

Black-n-White Chili Bread Bowl ⓕ

Makes 7 servings: 1 cup chili and 1¾ ounces bread each

Here's a veggie chili to comfort anyone anytime! It starts lean and becomes luscious with every sharp shred of cheese—so good, you simply can't resist. The bread bowl makes this a show-stopping one-dish meal.

1 (1-pound) whole-wheat or sourdough bread boule (round loaf)

1 tablespoon unrefined peanut or canola oil

1 large sweet onion, finely diced

1 tablespoon apple cider vinegar

½ + ⅛ teaspoon sea salt, or to taste

2 large garlic cloves, minced

1 (14.5-ounce) can crushed roasted tomatoes

2 cups low-sodium vegetable broth or Vegetable Stock (page 203)

1 tablespoon pure maple syrup

4 teaspoons chili powder, or to taste

½ teaspoon unsweetened cocoa powder

¼ teaspoon freshly ground black pepper

⅛ teaspoon dried hot pepper flakes, or to taste

1 (15-ounce) can black beans, drained

1 (15-ounce) can Great Northern or other white beans, drained

¾ cup shredded sharp Cheddar or Monterey Jack cheese (3 ounces)

2 tablespoons sour cream (optional)

1. Cut off the top of the bread loaf about 2 inches from the top. Remove inside of bread to create a bowl from the base of the loaf, leaving about a ½-inch thickness throughout. (Note: You'll have a 12-ounce bread bowl, including the top. Reserve the removed bread pieces for other use.)

2. Heat the oil in a large saucepan over medium heat. Add the onion, vinegar, and ⅛ teaspoon of the salt and sauté until the onion is softened, about 8 minutes. Add the garlic and sauté for 1 minute.

3. Stir in the tomatoes, broth, maple syrup, chili powder, cocoa powder, black pepper, hot pepper flakes, and the remaining ½ teaspoon salt and bring to a boil over high heat. Reduce heat to medium-low, stir in the beans, and simmer, uncovered, until desired consistency, about 12 minutes. Adjust seasoning.

4. Ladle as much of the chili as will fit into the bread bowl and serve the remaining chili in separate bowls. Sprinkle with the cheese and add a dollop of the sour cream (if using). Enjoy tearing and eating the bread bowl as you're eating the chili.

Per serving: 350 calories, 9g total fat, 3.5g saturated fat, 0g trans fat, 15mg cholesterol, 790mg sodium, 55g total carbohydrate, 10g dietary fiber, 12g sugars, 15g protein

Superfood Soybean Chili Ⓕ

Makes 8 servings: 1 cup each

This chili has pizzazz and a Middle-Eastern flair that will leave your taste buds very happy. Its big tastes and appealing textures are sure to satisfy even the biggest appetite. And for extra satisfaction, savor it along with the same lager-style beer as in the chili.

1 tablespoon unrefined peanut or roasted walnut oil

1 large red onion, finely diced

1 jalapeño pepper with seeds, minced

½ cup lager-style beer or low-sodium vegetable broth

1¾ teaspoons sea salt, or to taste

2 large garlic cloves, minced

1 tablespoon no-salt-added creamy almond butter

10 ounces extra-firm tofu, drained and diced

1 (15-ounce) can no-salt-added black soybeans or black beans, drained

1 (14.5-ounce) can crushed roasted tomatoes

2 cups low-sodium vegetable broth or Vegetable Stock (page 203)

1 tablespoon Major Grey's chutney

1½ tablespoons chili powder, or to taste

½ teaspoon freshly ground black pepper, or to taste

¼ teaspoon ground cinnamon

¼ teaspoon ground turmeric

10 ounces frozen shelled edamame, thawed

¼ cup chopped fresh cilantro or flat-leaf parsley

1. Heat the oil in a large saucepan over medium heat. Add the onion, jalapeño, 1 tablespoon of the beer, and ¼ teaspoon of the salt and sauté until the onion is softened, about 8 minutes. Add the garlic and sauté for 1 minute. Stir in remaining beer and the almond butter and sauté for 1 minute.

2. Stir in the tofu, soybeans, tomatoes, broth, chutney, chili powder, black pepper, cinnamon, turmeric, and remaining 1½ teaspoons salt and bring to a boil over high heat. Reduce heat to medium-low and simmer, partially covered, for 10 minutes. Stir in the edamame and simmer, partially covered, until desired chili consistency, about 8 minutes. Stir in 3 tablespoons of the cilantro. Adjust seasoning.

3. Ladle into individual bowls, sprinkle with the remaining 1 tablespoon cilantro, and serve.

Per serving: 200 calories, 9g total fat, 1g saturated fat, 0g trans tat, 0mg cholesterol, 720mg sodium, 18g total carbohydrate, 7g dietary fiber, 5g sugars, 13g protein

Chocolate Stout Chili Ⓕ

Makes 5 servings: about 1 cup each

I'm keen on the deep, rich, and yes, chocolaty (but not sweet) flavor that the chocolate stout infuses into this exciting vegetarian chili with Mexican mole essence. It's a cup of double comfort. Sip a glass of the stout along with it, if you like.

1 tablespoon unrefined peanut or canola oil

1 medium red onion, finely diced

¾ cup chocolate stout or other dark beer

½ teaspoon sea salt, or to taste

1 small jalapeño pepper with seeds, minced

2 large garlic cloves, minced

1 (14.5-ounce) can crushed roasted tomatoes

1½ tablespoons chili powder, or to taste

¼ teaspoon ground cinnamon

2 (15-ounce) cans red kidney beans, drained

½ cup shredded dry Jack or Monterey Jack cheese (optional)

2 tablespoons roughly chopped fresh cilantro or flat-leaf parsley

1. Heat the oil in a large saucepan over medium heat. Add the onion, 1 tablespoon of the stout, and ¼ teaspoon of the salt and sauté until the onion is softened, about 5 minutes. Add the jalapeño and garlic and sauté for 2 minutes. Stir in the remaining stout and sauté for 1 minute.

2. Stir in the tomatoes, chili powder, cinnamon, and remaining ¼ teaspoon salt and bring to a boil over high heat. Reduce heat to medium-low and simmer, uncovered, for 5 minutes. Stir in the beans, cover, and simmer for 5 minutes. Adjust seasoning.

3. Ladle into individual bowls, sprinkle with the cheese (if using) and cilantro, and serve.

Per serving: 210 calories, 3g total fat, 0.5g saturated fat, 0g trans fat, 0mg cholesterol, 650mg sodium, 35g total carbohydrate, 9g dietary fiber, 8g sugars, 11g protein

Cincinnati-Style Turkey Chili Ⓕ

Makes 6 servings: ¾ cup chili with 1⅓ cups pasta each

Here's an update on this Ohio classic—lightened up with turkey while keeping the spices just right. I still include a sneaky bit of unsweetened chocolate, like the original, because it adds an unmistakable depth of flavor. Serving the chili over pasta is known as a two-way. If you prefer, go for a three-way (with shredded Cheddar), four-way (with red beans or diced onions), or five-way (with red beans and diced onions)!

1 tablespoon grapeseed or canola oil

1 pound ground turkey (about 94% lean)

1 large sweet onion, finely diced

1 large garlic clove, minced

1 tablespoon Worcestershire sauce

1 tablespoon apple cider vinegar

1 (15-ounce) can no-salt-added tomato sauce

1 cup low-sodium vegetable broth, Vegetable Stock (page 203), or water

½ ounce unsweetened chocolate, finely chopped or 1½ tablespoons unsweetened cocoa powder

2½ teaspoons chili powder

1½ teaspoons ground cinnamon

1 teaspoon ground cumin

1 teaspoon sea salt

¾ teaspoon ground allspice

½ teaspoon ground cayenne

½ teaspoon dried oregano

1 teaspoon chopped fresh oregano

1 pound whole-wheat spaghetti or linguine

1. Heat the oil in a large skillet over medium-high heat. Add the turkey and onion and sauté until the onion is softened and turkey is crumbled and just cooked through, about 5 minutes. Reduce heat to medium, add the garlic, and sauté 1 minute. Stir in the Worcestershire sauce and vinegar and sauté for 1 minute.

2. Stir in the tomato sauce, broth, chocolate, chili powder, cinnamon, cumin, salt, allspice, cayenne, and dried oregano and bring to a boil over high heat. Reduce heat to low and simmer, uncovered, until desired thickness, about 1 hour. Stir in the fresh oregano. Adjust seasoning.

3. Meanwhile, cook the spaghetti according to package directions. Drain.

4. Transfer the spaghetti to individual serving plates or bowls. Ladle the chili over the spaghetti, and serve.

Per serving: 290 calories, 9g total fat, 2.5g saturated fat, 0g trans fat, 0mg cholesterol, 520mg sodium, 34g total carbohydrate, 6g dietary fiber, 8g sugars, 21g protein

5-Spice Turkey Chili Ⓕ

Makes 6 servings: 1 cup each

Prefer a chili that's rather meaty? This is it. It has intriguing flavor notes from five-spice powder and fresh ginger. Everything works together—"east meets west" style—into a spicy turkey chili with a balancing splash of citrusy sweetness.

1 tablespoon grapeseed or peanut oil

1 pound ground turkey (about 94% lean)

1 large red onion, chopped

1 medium green bell pepper, finely chopped

1 serrano or small jalapeño pepper with seeds, minced

1 teaspoon freshly grated gingerroot

2 large garlic cloves, minced

1 cup fresh-squeezed orange juice

1 tablespoon brown rice vinegar

2 cups low-sodium chicken broth or Chicken Stock (page 203)

1 (14.5-ounce) can crushed roasted tomatoes

2 tablespoons chili powder

1 teaspoon Chinese five-spice powder, or to taste

¾ teaspoon sea salt, or to taste

1 (15-ounce) can butter beans or Great Northern beans, drained

¼ cup chopped fresh cilantro

2 medium scallions, green and white parts, thinly sliced on the diagonal

1. Heat the oil in a stockpot over medium-high heat. Add the turkey, onion, bell pepper, serrano, and ginger and sauté until the onion is softened and turkey is cooked through and crumbled, about 8 minutes. Add the garlic and sauté for 30 seconds, Add the orange juice and vinegar and sauté for 1 minute.

2. Add the broth, tomatoes, chili powder, five-spice powder, and salt and bring to a boil over high heat. Reduce heat to medium-low, partially cover, and simmer, stirring occasionally, until the chili is near desired consistency, about 30 to 35 minutes. Stir in the beans, cilantro, and white part of the scallions and simmer, uncovered, until desired consistency, about 5 minutes. Adjust seasoning.

3. Spoon chili into bowls, top with the green part of the scallions, and serve.

Per serving: 250 calories, 8g total fat, 1.5g saturated fat, 0g trans fat, 45mg cholesterol, 640mg sodium, 26g total carbohydrate, 6g dietary fiber, 10g sugars, 21g protein

California Chicken Chili ⓕ

Makes 8 servings: 1 cup each

You'll find sweet satisfaction in every bite of this chili with its vine-ripened tomatoes, fresh cilantro, twist of lime, and finishing buttery avocado accent. The pressure-cooking makes the lean poultry so moist it'll practically melt in your mouth. If you don't have a pressure-cooker, don't worry. Just follow the instructions, cover, and simmer the chili until stew-like, at least 30 minutes.

1 tablespoon grapeseed or canola oil

1 pound ground chicken breast

2 large white onions, finely diced

1 large jalapeño pepper with some seeds, minced

4 large garlic cloves, minced

Juice of 1 lime (2 tablespoons)

2 (15-ounce) cans Great Northern or other white beans, drained

4 medium vine-ripened tomatoes, chopped

2½ tablespoons chili powder

1½ teaspoons sea salt, or to taste

1 teaspoon ground cumin

½ teaspoon freshly ground black pepper, or to taste

3 tablespoons chopped fresh cilantro

1 Hass avocado, pitted, peeled, and diced

1. Heat the oil in a stockpot or deep extra-large skillet over medium-high heat. Add the chicken, onions, and jalapeño and sauté until the chicken is cooked through and onions are softened, about 7 minutes. Stir in the garlic and 1½ tablespoons of the lime juice and sauté for 1 minute. Remove from heat.

2. Stir the beans, tomatoes, chili powder, salt, cumin, and black pepper into the chicken mixture, then transfer the mixture and any juices to a pressure-cooker. Close the pressure-cooker lid and turn to the high pressure setting. Turn the burner heat to high. Once the pressure-cooker hisses, adjust the heat as necessary to maintain high pressure with gentle hissing and cook for 8 minutes, or until stew-like.

3. Remove the pressure-cooker from the heat—or turn off the pressure-cooker. Carefully release the pressure and remove the lid. Stir in half of the cilantro. Adjust seasoning.

4. Ladle the chili into bowls. Sprinkle with the avocado and the remaining lime juice and cilantro, and serve.

Per serving: 220 calories, 6g total fat, 1g saturated fat, 0g trans fat, 30mg cholesterol, 610mg sodium, 25g total carbohydrate, 8g dietary fiber, 5g sugars, 19g protein

Spanish Red Bean Chili with Chorizo ⓕ

Makes 7 servings: 1 cup each

The smoky chorizo is an absolute showstopper in this Spanish-inspired dish. It's so rich and bold, yet well balanced, with a certain lightness brought to you by the cauliflower. Simply add a splash of red wine and a shaving of aged sheep's milk cheese, if you wish, and you have all the makings of a palate pleaser. And for extra pleasure, enjoy with a whole-grain baguette.

2 teaspoons extra-virgin olive oil

3½ ounces hot chorizo sausage, casings removed

1 medium red onion, finely diced

1½ cups finely chopped cauliflower florets and tender stems

2 large garlic cloves, minced

¾ cup Rioja or other dry red wine

1 (14.5-ounce) can crushed roasted tomatoes

½ cup low-sodium vegetable broth or Vegetable Stock (page 203)

1½ tablespoons chili powder, or to taste

½ teaspoon sweet paprika

½ teaspoon sea salt, or to taste

2 (15-ounce) cans no-salt-added red kidney beans, drained

⅓ cup chopped fresh flat-leaf parsley

⅓ cup shredded aged hard Manchego or other hard sheep's milk cheese (optional)

1. Heat the oil in a stockpot or large saucepan over medium heat. Add the chorizo and onion and sauté until the onion is softened and chorizo is cooked through and crumbled, about 8 minutes. Add the cauliflower and garlic and sauté for 1 minute. Stir in the wine and sauté for 1 minute.

2. Stir in the tomatoes, broth, chili powder, paprika, and salt and bring to a boil over high heat. Reduce heat to low and simmer, covered, for 15 minutes. Stir in the beans and ¼ cup of the parsley and simmer, covered, until the cauliflower is tender, about 10 minutes. Adjust seasoning.

3. Ladle into individual bowls, sprinkle with the cheese (if using) and the remaining parsley, and serve.

Per serving: 230 calories, 7g total fat, 2.5g saturated fat, 0g trans fat, 10mg cholesterol, 530mg sodium, 26g total carbohydrate, 12g dietary fiber, 5g sugars, 13g protein

Secret-Ingredient Pasilla Chili Con Carne

Makes 8 servings: 1 cup each

No beans about it! This captivating beef lover's chili gets extra savoriness from sweet potatoes and peppers and portrays the very essence of autumn with flavors of cinnamon, clove, ginger, nutmeg, and allspice with the clever use of a spice made for pies. For added appeal, garnish with diced avocado and savor every last bite along with whole-wheat sourdough bread.

2 teaspoons unrefined peanut or canola oil

1 pound ground lean beef sirloin

1 large red onion, finely diced

1 large green bell pepper, finely chopped

1 pasilla pepper with seeds or fresh poblano pepper without seeds, finely chopped

2 large garlic cloves, minced

2 tablespoons aged red wine vinegar

2½ cups low-sodium beef broth

1 (14.5-ounce) can crushed roasted tomatoes

3 tablespoons tomato paste

1 medium sweet potato, unpeeled, scrubbed, and finely diced

2 tablespoons chili powder

1¼ teaspoons pumpkin pie spice, or to taste

1¼ teaspoons sea salt, or to taste

¼ cup chopped fresh cilantro

1. Heat the oil in a stockpot over medium-high heat. Add the beef, onion, bell pepper, and pasilla and sauté until the onion is softened and beef is cooked through and crumbled, about 8 minutes. Add the garlic and vinegar and sauté for 1 minute.

2. Add the broth, crushed tomatoes, tomato paste, sweet potato, chili powder, pumpkin pie spice, and salt and bring to a boil over high heat. Reduce heat to low, cover, and simmer, stirring occasionally, for 30 minutes. Remove cover, and continue to simmer until desired consistency, about 10 to 12 minutes. Stir in half of the cilantro, and adjust seasoning.

3. Spoon chili into bowls, top with the remaining cilantro, and serve.

Per serving: 150 calories, 4.5g total fat, 1.5g saturated fat, 0g trans fat, 20mg cholesterol, 570mg sodium, 13g total carbohydrate, 3g dietary fiber, 6g sugars, 15g protein

Game Day Chili Ⓕ

Makes 8 servings: 1 cup each

Where fans gather, good food must follow. That's why this fabulous, no-frills chili con carne is a sure way to gear up—packed with extra heartiness from two types of beans and just enough serrano chiles to give it that winning quality. So cheer on your team with a bowl of this sporty chili, sourdough bread and hot pepper sauce on the side.

1 tablespoon peanut or canola oil

1 pound ground lean beef sirloin

1 large red onion, diced

1 medium green bell pepper, finely chopped

1 to 2 serrano peppers with seeds, minced

2 large garlic cloves, minced

1½ tablespoons aged red wine vinegar

3 cups low-sodium beef broth

1 (14.5-ounce) can crushed roasted tomatoes

1½ tablespoons chili powder

¾ teaspoon ground cinnamon

1 teaspoon sea salt, or to taste

1 (15-ounce) can black beans, drained

1 (15-ounce) can red kidney beans, drained

¼ cup chopped fresh cilantro

1. Heat the oil in a stockpot over medium-high heat. Add the beef, onion, bell pepper, and serrano and sauté until the beef is cooked through and crumbled, about 6 minutes. Stir in the garlic and vinegar and sauté for 1 minute.

2. Add the broth, tomatoes, chili powder, cinnamon, and salt and bring to a boil over high heat. Reduce heat to low, cover, and simmer, stirring occasionally, for 45 minutes. Stir in the beans and 2 tablespoons of the cilantro and simmer, uncovered, over low heat, stirring occasionally, until desired consistency, about 20 minutes. Adjust seasoning.

3. Spoon chili into bowls, top with the remaining cilantro, and serve.

Per serving: 210 calories, 4.5g total fat, 1.5g saturated fat, 0g trans fat, 20mg cholesterol, 600mg sodium, 23g total carbohydrate, 6g dietary fiber, 6g sugars, 20g protein

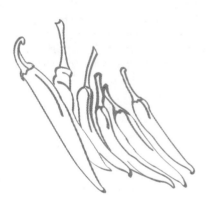

Main Dishes: Vegetarian and Flexitarian

Cool Dishes

Eco-Burrito Bowl

Punjabi Avocado and Bean Torte

Hummus Trio Martini

Lettuce Cups with Smoked Tofu

Tortilla Veggie Roll

Microwave-Cooked Dishes

Curried Eggplant "Steak"

Lime-Peanut Zucchini Noodles

Cheesy Broccoli-Couscous Crock

Deep Dish Green Enchilada

Basil Pesto Beans and Quinoa

Grilled Dishes

Ricotta with Grilled Figs and Honey

Thai Sesame Summer Squash

Vegetarian "Bangers"

Vegetable Souvlaki

Grilled Eggplant Stack with Feta and Fresh Basil

Grilled Curry Portabella "Steak" with Mango Chutney

Ginger Tofu Filets

Stovetop, Slow-Cooked, and Pressure-Cooked Dishes

Pesto Zucchini "Fettuccine"

Asparagus Shiitake "Paella"

Black Quinoa and Fava "Risotto"

Tofu Curry with Coconut Rice

West African Vegetarian Jollof Rice

Creamy Seasonal Vegetable Korma

Vegetable Biryani

Sweet-n-Sour Stuffed Cabbage

Southwestern Beans and Rice

Cajun Beans and Couscous

Stir-Fries

Wok Veggie Fried Rice

Pineapple Stir-Fried Rice

Szechuan Sesame
Baby Bok Choy

Garlic Eggplant Stir-Fry

Asparagus-Shiitake Tempeh

Sizzling Seasonal Stir-Fry
Veggie Fajitas

Southwestern Vegetable
Tortilla Stack

Curried Veggie and Chickpea
Stir-Fry

Oven-Cooked Dishes

Eggplant Parmesan
with Basil

Crispy Stacked Veggie
Parmigiana

Goat Cheese Roasted Beet
Torte

Stuffed Spaghetti Squash

Asparagus and Basmati Rice
Casserole

Eggplant Moussaka

Roasted Poblano,
Black Beans and Rice

Herb Couscous–Stuffed
Beefsteaks

Shepherd's Pie
with Smashed Blues

Pasta

Ziti with Sun-Dried Tomato
Tapenade and Arugula

Spicy Orecchiette
with Baby Spinach

Fusilli with Broccoli Raab
and Cherries

Gemelli Pasta
with Squash and Herbs

Artichoke Heart Spaghettini

Asian Angel Hair
with "Confetti"

Spaghetti with Tomato and
Basil Sauce

Penne Alla Vodka

Pesto Bow-Tie
Vegetable Primavera

Farfalle with Bell Pepper
Marinara and Goat Cheese

Luscious Lemony Linguine

Lemony-Thyme Mushroom
Tagliatelle

Veggie Fettuccine "Alfredo"
with Garlic Chips

Asparagus Radiatore Alfredo

Creamy Santa Fe
Pappardelle

Capellini Tahini

Mac and Cheese Ramekins

Greek Sticky Orzo

Baked Penne with Greens

Roasted Vegetable Rigatoni

Greens and Ricotta
Cannelloni

3-Cheese Lasagna
with Fresh Basil

Noodles and Risotto

Gingery Thai Udon Noodles

Smoky Butternut Noodles
with Pistachios

Soba with Greens
and Nectarine

Seasonal Veggie Chow Fun

Farmers' Market Shirataki

Rosemary Squash Risotto

Beet and Goat Cheese
Risotto over Greens

Spring Pea Risotto

Whether you're vegetarian or just trying to eat more vegetarian meals, this chapter is for you.

What makes the recipes here unique is that each one begins as a vegetarian recipe. Then there's a simple way to add poultry, fish, or meat if you choose. That's where the "Flexitarian Option" comes into play. A flexitarian is a flexible eater—someone who generally eats vegetarian meals, but may eat small amounts of poultry, fish, or meat from time to time. Having this option is also helpful if you're serving vegetarians and nonvegetarians; you can fix a recipe both ways at once in many cases.

The goal is that you'll begin thinking of vegetables, whole grains, beans, and tofu as entrées. Stir-fried veggies can be a main dish, for instance. It's a healthful way to eat—and may boost weight-management efforts since you'll be filling up first on voluminous vegetables and other plant-based foods that are rich in nutrients, not calories. When it's a vegetable- or grain-based recipe served as the main dish, you'll simply pair it with a protein-rich side to create a complete and balanced meal.

When it's not so cool outside, you may want to pick one of the cool dishes. Due to their beans, tofu, or Neufchâtel, they're proof that it's still possible to eat heartily even without "cooking." But if an oven-prepared dish is your pick, there are inventive, eye-catching, and internationally homespun recipes from which to choose.

Want something that's relatively quick to fix? You'll be pleasantly surprised by the array of quick and memorable microwave-cooked, grilled, pressure-cooked, and stir-fried entrées, including a luscious layered enchilada prepared in the microwave and a nontraditional Mexican-style stir-fry.

Grilled dishes go beyond veggies. Because tofu is made from protein-rich soybeans, it can be served kind of like a steak; try the Ginger Tofu Fillets (page 268). Fruit is turned into an entrée by serving it on a bed of ricotta in Ricotta with Grilled Figs and Honey (page 265). These grilled recipes can be prepared outdoors or indoors—some on a panini grill, which saves more time.

If you're a pasta lover, you're in luck. There are over twenty recipes from which to choose. You'll be using whole-wheat or other whole-grain pastas for their nutrient-rich benefits, including fiber and antioxidants. Try new types for added interest, like spelt and kamut pastas. Comfort food fits here, too, with two different Alfredo recipes from which to choose. Check out the Veggie Fettuccine "Alfredo" with Garlic Chips (page 292); it's made with a unique "Alfredo" sauce that's especially creamy from cannellini beans. Or savor the Asparagus Radiatore Alfredo (page 293); it's made more in the traditional sense, but without drowning the pasta in an overly rich sauce!

Beyond pasta, whole-grain international noodles are a scrumptious option, including udon, soba, brown rice noodles, and tofu shirataki noodles. Their use in this chapter will wow your taste buds with a recipe for every one of them: sweet, salty, sour, bitter, and umami. The Farmer's Market Shirataki (page 301) recipe showcases the shirataki noodles—they provide only 20 calories in a 4-ounce serving!

More of a rice fan? The three risotto dishes are made using short-grain brown rice, which provides a distinctive chewy texture and slightly nutty taste. It also allows you to use a simplified, not standard, risotto cooking technique to save time—and achieve a successful result every time.

NOTE The Flexitarian Options in this chapter are simply ideas and the ingredients are not calculated in the nutrition analysis.

Calorie range in this chapter: 130 to 440 calories.

Low-calorie pick: Thai Sesame Summer Squash, 130 calories (page 265).

Cool Dishes

Eco-Burrito Bowl Ⓕ

Makes 4 servings: 1½ cups each

This family-friendly recipe is ideal for a cool summertime main dish—no oven required. It's like a chopped-up burrito—including the tortilla—that you'll eat from a bowl.

1½ cups packed shredded romaine lettuce

1 (15-ounce) can black or kidney beans, drained

¾ cup Spicy Raw Tomatillo Salsa (page 114) or other spicy salsa verde

¼ cup chopped fresh cilantro

2 (8-inch) whole-wheat tortillas, finely diced

2 scallions, green and white parts, very thinly sliced on diagonal

1 cup grape tomatoes, quartered lengthwise

1 Hass avocado, pitted, peeled, and diced

¼ teaspoon sea salt, or to taste

1. Divide the lettuce among four individual serving bowls.

2. Toss together the beans, ¼ cup of the salsa, and 2 tablespoons of the cilantro in a medium bowl and transfer to the serving bowls.

3. Toss together the diced tortillas, ¼ cup of the salsa, and the remaining 2 tablespoons cilantro and arrange on top of the beans in the serving bowls.

4. Sprinkle with the scallions, grape tomatoes, avocado, salt, and the remaining ¼ cup salsa, and serve.

FLEXITARIAN OPTION: Dice Zesty Lime Grilled Chicken (page 308) or grilled lean steak and sprinkle into each bowl in step 4.

Per serving: 230 calories, 7g total fat, 1g saturated fat, 0g trans fat, 0mg cholesterol, 480mg sodium, 36g total carbohydrate, 9g dietary fiber, 8g sugars, 9g protein

Punjabi Avocado and Bean Torte Ⓕ

Makes 6 servings: 1 wedge each

This layered pleaser can be sliced into 16 wedges and served as an appetizer, but I prefer it as an entrée. Want more Indian punch? Add a pinch each of ground coriander, cumin, turmeric, and freshly grated gingerroot to the refried black beans. You can add these same spices to store-bought guacamole if you like, too.

3 (8-inch) whole-wheat tortillas

1 (15.4-ounce) can refried black beans, chilled

1 recipe Indian Guacamole (page 89) or freshly prepared store-bought guacamole, chilled

2 tablespoons fat-free or low-fat plain Greek yogurt

½ teaspoon grated lime zest

1. Lay out the tortillas on a large surface or cutting board. For each tortilla, spread the entire surface with the beans, like you're frosting a cake. Then gently spread the entire surface with the guacamole.

2. Place the three prepared tortillas on top of each other to form one stack, like a layered cake. Chill until ready to serve.

3. Top the center with the yogurt and lime zest, and serve whole. Alternatively, cut into 6 wedges with a bread knife, top each wedge with the yogurt and lime zest, and serve.

FLEXITARIAN OPTION: Place 1 ounce of very thinly sliced smoked salmon on top of each wedge in step 3.

Per serving: 230 calories, 9g total fat, 1g saturated fat, 0g trans fat, 0mg cholesterol, 290mg sodium, 28g total carbohydrate, 9g dietary fiber, 2g sugars, 8g protein

Hummus Trio Martini

Makes 1 serving: 1 martini

There are three distinct layers of delicious hummus here, creating a somewhat different entrée that let's you enjoy the different flavors combined. Serving it in a martini glass makes it fun to eat, but you can always simplify the presentation. Enjoy this with raw seasonal vegetables or fresh whole-wheat pita wedges.

½ cup + 2 tablespoons Tahini Chickpea Hummus (page 87) or other hummus

1½ tablespoons Enlightened Fresh Basil Pesto (page 117) or other basil pesto

1½ tablespoons Sun-Dried Tomato Pesto (page 119) or sun-dried tomato paste, to taste

¼ cup microgreens, alfalfa sprouts, or baby greens

1 small lemon wedge

1. Divide the hummus among three small bowls. Stir the basil pesto into one of the bowls until well combined. Stir the sun-dried tomato pesto into one of the other bowls until well combined.

2. Spoon the plain hummus into a martini glass in an even layer. Add the basil pesto hummus on top in an even layer. Then add the sun-dried tomato hummus on top in an even layer.

3. Top with the greens and a lemon wedge, and serve.

FLEXITARIAN OPTION: Top the filled martini glass with one of the Flash-Fried Adobo Chicken Fingers (page 77) or place cooked shrimp around the glass rim.

Per serving: 420 calories, 24g total fat, 3g saturated fat, 0g trans fat, 0mg cholesterol, 700mg sodium, 40g total carbohydrate, 9g dietary fiber, 4g sugars, 17g protein

Lettuce Cups with Smoked Tofu

Makes 2 servings: 2 large or 3 medium stuffed lettuce cups each

The smokiness from the tofu, the velvety richness from the avocado, and the perky piquancy from the pepperoncini create an intriguing harmony of ingredients all encompassed in a Bibb lettuce cup. It's a fresh deli-like delight.

4 large or 6 medium Bibb or Boston lettuce leaves

8 ounces ready-to-eat smoked tofu, diced

1 medium vine-ripened tomato, diced

½ Hass avocado, pitted, peeled, and diced

½ small red onion, finely diced

1 ounce chopped pepperoncini or pickled jalapeño pepper, or to taste

1½ tablespoons Dijon mustard, or to taste

¼ teaspoon freshly ground black pepper, or to taste

1. Stuff each lettuce leaf with the tofu, tomato, avocado, onion, and pepperoncini.

2. Dollop with the mustard. Sprinkle with the black pepper, and serve.

FLEXITARIAN OPTION: Try cubes of smoked turkey instead of smoked tofu.

Per serving: 250 calories, 11g total fat, 2g saturated fat, 0g trans fat, 0mg cholesterol, 730mg sodium, 19g total carbohydrate, 6g dietary fiber, 9g sugars, 18g protein

Tortilla Veggie Roll

Makes 1 serving: 6 to 8 slices

No cooking is required for this fresh, tasty, and zesty pinwheel-style roll. The mix of vegetable adds a nice crunch to this "finger-food" lunch. Perfect for a picnic. Multiply the recipe as you desire.

3 tablespoons Neufchâtel (light cream cheese)

1 tablespoon spicy stone-ground mustard

1 (8-inch) whole-wheat tortilla

⅓ cup coarsely grated carrot

⅓ cup finely diced or coarsely grated raw zucchini, broccoli, or cauliflower

1 scallion, green and white part, minced

1. Mix together the Neufchâtel and mustard in a small bowl until well blended.

2. Spread the entire surface of the tortilla with the Neufchâtel mixture. Sprinkle with the carrot, zucchini, and scallion, leaving about ½-inch rim. Tightly roll up. Chill in the refrigerator for at least 30 minutes.

3. Slice about ½ inch off each end of the rolled tortilla using a bread knife. Slice the rolled tortilla into 6 to 8 equal-size pieces. Stand each pinwheel piece on a cut edge, and serve.

FLEXITARIAN OPTION: Very finely dice up to ⅓ cup smoked turkey or chicken and sprinkle onto the cream cheese mixture in step 2. Secure closed with toothpicks, if necessary.

Per serving: 280 calories, 14g total fat, 7g saturated fat, 0g trans fat, 35mg cholesterol, 570mg sodium, 29g total carbohydrate, 4g dietary fiber, 4g sugars, 10g protein

Microwave-Prepared Dishes

Lime-Peanut Zucchini Noodles Ⓕ

Makes 1 serving: 2½ cups each

Dig into oodles of Thai peanut-inspired "noodles." This zucchini turned al dente "pasta" is pleasing to the palate and fit for the hips. The extra crunch provided by the peanuts and burst of tingly freshness from the cilantro complete the dish.

2 medium zucchini, cut lengthwise into thin, spaghetti-like strips

3 tablespoons Asian peanut satay sauce or Peanut Sauce (page 108)

Juice of ½ lime (1 tablespoon)

⅛ teaspoon sea salt, or to taste

2 tablespoons chopped fresh cilantro

2 tablespoons chopped unsalted dry-roasted peanuts

1. Add the zucchini to a 2-quart microwave-safe dish.

2. Stir together the peanut sauce, lime juice, and salt in a small bowl until smooth. Pour the sauce over the zucchini and toss to coat.

3. Cover the dish with parchment paper and cook in the microwave on high until the zucchini is al dente, about 4½ minutes, stirring once during cooking. Let stand covered for 5 minutes. Adjust seasoning.

4. Sprinkle with the cilantro and peanuts, and serve.

FLEXITARIAN OPTION: Serve two or three skewers of Thai-Inspired Chicken Satay (page 58) or other grilled poultry skewers on top.

Per serving: 290 calories, 17g total fat, 2g saturated fat, 0g trans fat, 0mg cholesterol, 520mg sodium, 26g total carbohydrate, 5g dietary fiber, 16g sugars, 12g protein

Curried Eggplant "Steak"

Makes 2 servings: 2 "steaks" each

For those who need a little heat, or just enjoy the exotic flavors of Thai cuisine, this curried eggplant combines red curry and piquant cilantro that carry exciting and elusive flavors. The confetti-like veggies on top create exciting eye appeal, too.

1 (1-pound) medium eggplant, cut into 4 thick
    slices lengthwise

2 teaspoons unrefined peanut or canola oil

1 large red onion, diced

1 large carrot, finely diced

1 large celery stalk, thinly sliced

1 large beefsteak tomato, pulp removed and diced

1 cup low-sodium vegetable broth or Vegetable
    Stock (page 203)

1½ teaspoons vegetarian red curry paste, or to taste

¼ teaspoon + ⅛ teaspoon sea salt, or to taste

½ teaspoon freshly ground black pepper, or to taste

3 tablespoons chopped fresh cilantro

1½ tablespoons finely chopped salted,
    dry-roasted peanuts

1 small lime, cut into 4 wedges

1. Lightly rub or brush the eggplant with the oil. Place the eggplant in two layers into a large microwave-safe dish, cover with parchment paper, and microwave on high until nearly cooked through, about 4 minutes. Remove to a plate.

2. Add the onion, carrot, celery, and tomato to the dish, cover with the parchment paper, and cook in the microwave on high until all vegetables are soft, about 4 minutes, stirring halfway through the cooking.

3. Whisk together the broth, curry paste, salt, and pepper in a medium bowl. Add the cooked onion, carrot, and celery to the curry mixture and stir to combine.

4. In two batches, transfer the cooked eggplant to the large dish in a single layer. Smother with the curry mixture. Cover with the parchment paper and microwave on high until the eggplant is fully cooked, about 2 minutes. Adjust seasoning.

5. Sprinkle with the cilantro and peanuts. Serve each with a lime wedge, for squirting onto the "steak."

FLEXITARIAN OPTION: Top with Tandoori Shrimp (page 359) or other shrimp when serving.

Per serving: 240 calories, 9g total fat, 2g saturated fat, 0g trans fat, 0mg cholesterol, 730mg sodium, 38g total carbohydrate, 10g dietary fiber, 16g sugars, 6g protein

Cheesy Broccoli-Couscous Crock

Makes 6 servings: 1 ramekin each

The mushrooms add meatiness, the yogurt creates creaminess, and the finishing pinch of nutmeg provides that extra-special something. All together, this single-serve couscous crock is fully appetizing as an entrée anytime of the year.

2 teaspoons unsalted butter, at room temperature

2 cups finely chopped broccoli florets and
    tender stems

1 small shallot, minced

1¼ cups low-sodium vegetable broth or Vegetable
    Stock (page 203)

1 cup whole-wheat couscous

½ cup fat-free or low-fat plain Greek yogurt

½ cup finely chopped cremini (baby bella)
    mushrooms

½ cup finely shredded extra-sharp Cheddar cheese

¼ cup freshly grated Parmigiano-Reggiano
    or other Parmesan cheese

¾ teaspoon sea salt, or to taste

¼ teaspoon freshly ground black pepper

⅛ teaspoon freshly grated nutmeg

1. Lightly grease six (8- to 10-ounce) microwave-safe ramekins with the butter. Set aside.

2. Add the broccoli, shallot, broth, couscous, yogurt, mushrooms, half of the Cheddar cheese, the Parmesan, salt, pepper, and nutmeg to a medium bowl and stir until well combined.

3. Spoon the broccoli mixture into each of the ramekins. Sprinkle with the remaining Cheddar. Cook the ramekins (in batches, if necessary) in the microwave on high until the broccoli is fully cooked and couscous is tender, about 4 minutes. (Alternatively, bake in a preheated 450°F oven until the top is golden brown and broccoli is al dente, about 15 minutes.)

4. Let stand for 5 minutes, and serve.

FLEXITARIAN OPTION: Add 1½ cups of finely cubed, precooked (or leftover) rotisserie chicken breast meat to the broccoli mixture, along with 1 tablespoon additional Greek yogurt and sea salt and freshly ground black pepper to taste.

Per serving: 210 calories, 6g total fat, 4g saturated fat, 0g trans fat, 15mg cholesterol, 450mg sodium, 29g total carbohydrate, 5g dietary fiber, 2g sugars, 10g protein

Deep-Dish Green Enchilada Ⓕ

Makes 6 servings: 1 wedge (⅙ of 10-inch round) each

This fast and family-friendly enchilada recipe is so simple, so scrumptious, and oh-so-satisfying, you'll be amazed that it's calorie friendly, too. Its lasagna-like layers are made from fresh corn tortillas and filled with hearty beans, high-flavored veggies, and, of course, real cheese.

1 cup spicy salsa verde or Roasted Green Tomato
    Salsa (page 114)

1 (15-ounce) can black beans, drained

1 large poblano pepper, chopped

½ large sweet onion, chopped

½ teaspoon finely chopped fresh oregano

½ teaspoon ground cumin

¼ teaspoon sea salt, or to taste

8 (6-inch) soft corn tortillas, halved

4 cups packed fresh baby spinach

1¼ cups shredded Monterey Jack cheese
    or mixed Mexican cheeses

2 tablespoons chopped fresh cilantro

1 lime, cut into 6 wedges

1. Stir together the salsa, beans, poblano, onion, oregano, cumin, and salt in a medium bowl. Set aside.

2. Arrange in layers in a 10-inch round microwave-safe dish the following: 4 of the tortilla halves, 1 cup of the spinach, one-fourth of the bean mixture, and ¼ cup of the cheese. Repeat three times while packing down layers. Top with the remaining ¼ cup of the cheese.

3. Cook in the microwave on high until the pepper and onion are fully cooked and the cheese is melted and bubbly, about 7 to 8 minutes.

4. Remove from the microwave, sprinkle with the cilantro, and let stand for about 5 minutes. Slice into 6 wedges, and serve with the lime wedges.

FLEXITARIAN OPTION: Arrange 8 ounces shredded roasted pork loin between the layers in step 2. Season with sea salt and ground cumin to taste.

Per serving: 230 calories, 8g total fat, 4.5g saturated fat, 0g trans fat, 20mg cholesterol, 490mg sodium, 30g total carbohydrate, 7g dietary fiber, 7g sugars, 12g protein

Basil Pesto Beans and Quinoa Ⓕ

Makes 5 servings: 1 rounded cup each

This quinoa and bean casserole-style dish is simple, yet has flavor complexity from garlic, shallot, and tomatoes. A memorable kiss of pesto brings it all together into one enticing entrée with sass.

1½ teaspoons extra-virgin olive oil

1 large shallot, thinly sliced

2 large garlic cloves, minced

1 cup quinoa, rinsed and drained

1 (14.5-ounce) can diced tomatoes (with liquid)

3 cups low-sodium vegetable broth or Vegetable Stock (page 203), hot

1 (15-ounce) can cannellini or other white beans, drained

¼ cup Enlightened Fresh Basil Pesto (page 117) or other pesto

¼ teaspoon sea salt, or to taste

10 large fresh basil leaves, thinly sliced

1 tablespoon pine nuts, toasted

1. Add the oil to a 2-quart deep-sided stoneware dish or large microwave-safe bowl. Stir in the shallot and garlic, and cook in the microwave on high until softened, about 1 minute.

2. Stir in the quinoa, tomatoes, and broth. Cover with parchment paper and cook on high until the quinoa is just cooked through, about 22 minutes, stirring halfway through cooking.

3. Stir in the beans, pesto, and salt. Cover and cook on high for 1 minute. Let stand covered for 5 minutes. Adjust seasoning.

4. Spoon into individual dishes or keep in the stoneware dish, sprinkle with the basil and pine nuts, and serve.

FLEXITARIAN OPTION: Top each serving with a Tuscan-Grilled Pacific Halibut steak (page 357) or grilled sardines.

Per serving: 280 calories, 7g total fat, 1g saturated fat, 0g trans fat, 0mg cholesterol, 520mg sodium, 43g total carbohydrate, 8g dietary fiber, 5g sugars, 11g protein

Grilled Dishes

Ricotta with Grilled Figs and Honey

Makes 1 serving: 1 bowl

Grilled Calimyrna figs served on a cloud of creamy ricotta look like a dessert, but this is actually a fully satisfying and refreshingly sweet main dish for anytime. Drizzle it with a unique honey, like chestnut honey, for a taste twist. Serve with small, thin slices of fruit-nut bread. It's simply dreamy.

2 large fresh Calimyrna or other figs,
    stems removed and halved lengthwise
⅔ cup part-skim ricotta cheese
1 teaspoon honey or agave nectar
½ teaspoon fresh thyme leaves
⅛ teaspoon sea salt, or to taste
⅛ teaspoon freshly ground black pepper,
    or to taste

1. Prepare an outdoor or indoor grill or a grill pan. Spritz the cut surface of each fig half with cooking spray (preferably homemade, page xix). Grill over medium-high heat on the cut side until well caramelized, about 3 minutes, then on the flip side until grill marks form, about 1 minute. Set aside to cool.

2. Spoon the ricotta into a bowl or spread on a plate. Top with the figs, drizzle with the honey, and sprinkle with the thyme, salt, and pepper.

FLEXITARIAN OPTION: Arrange about ¼ ounce very thinly sliced prosciutto onto each fig after drizzling with the honey.

Per serving: 350 calories, 14g total fat, 8g saturated fat, 0g trans fat, 50mg cholesterol, 500mg sodium, 39g total carbohydrate, 4g dietary fiber, 27g sugars, 20g protein

Thai Sesame Summer Squash

Makes 2 servings: 6 squash slices each

Grilled veggies play the starring role on the plate. The lively satay-style sauce provides Asian panache to these squash "filets." Try them showcased in Gingery Thai Udon Noodles (page 299), too.

2 medium yellow squash, ends trimmed and
    cut lengthwise into 6 slices each
¼ cup Gingery Peanut-Almond Sauce (page 108)
    or Asian peanut satay sauce of choice
1 large garlic clove, minced
⅛ teaspoon sea salt, or to taste
1 tablespoon chopped fresh basil or cilantro

1. Preheat the panini or other grill to medium-high heat.

2. Place the squash slices into a 9-inch or larger dish. Add 2 tablespoons of the sauce and the garlic and toss until the slices are fully coated.

3. Grill the squash slices, in two batches, until cooked through, about 3½ minutes per batch in a panini grill. Add the salt.

4. Arrange the slices in a stack on individual plates. Sprinkle with the remaining sauce and the basil, and serve.

FLEXITARIAN OPTION: Arrange the squash in clocklike fashion and sprinkle with remaining sauce. Place Shrimp Pad Thai Noodles (page 368) in the center. Sprinkle the entire dish with fresh basil and cilantro, and serve.

Per serving: 130 calories, 7g total fat, 1g saturated fat, 0g trans fat, 0mg cholesterol, 480mg sodium, 13g total carbohydrate, 3g dietary fiber, 8g sugars, 5g protein

Vegetarian "Bangers"

Makes 8 servings: 1 banger each

"Bangers" is the British term for sausages. These vegetarian bangers get their body from tofu, breadcrumbs, and broccoli and their savoriness from portabellas, almond butter, soy sauce, and spices. Relish them in Stuffed Vegetarian Banger Wrap (page 402). Or enjoy as bangers-n-mash on a bed of mashed potatoes ladled with gravy.

2 tablespoons unrefined peanut oil

1 cup finely chopped broccoli florets and tender stems

1 cup finely chopped portabella mushroom caps

1 large shallot, minced

2 large garlic cloves, minced

2 large eggs

2 tablespoons no-salt-added creamy raw almond butter or natural peanut butter

1 tablespoon turbinado sugar

2 teaspoons naturally brewed soy sauce

1¼ teaspoons sea salt, or to taste

1 teaspoon ground sage

¾ teaspoon freshly ground black pepper, or to taste

¾ teaspoon fennel seeds

¼ teaspoon ground cayenne

1 (14-ounce) package firm tofu, well drained and gently squeezed dry

1 cup plain dry whole-wheat or other whole-grain breadcrumbs

1. Heat 1 tablespoon of the oil in a large skillet over medium heat. Add the broccoli and stir to coat with the oil. Cover and cook until al dente, about 3 minutes. Stir in the mushrooms, shallot, and garlic. Cover, and cook until the shallot is softened, about 3 minutes. Remove from heat and keep covered.

2. Preheat the oven to 450°F.

3. Whisk the eggs in a large mixing bowl. Stir in the almond butter, sugar, soy sauce, salt, sage, black pepper, fennel, and cayenne until combined. Finely crumble and stir in the tofu. Stir in the breadcrumbs until combined. Stir in the broccoli mixture until well combined.

4. Very firmly form the mixture into 8 balls, ½ cup each. Place each onto a parchment paper-lined large baking sheet. Then shape each into about a 6-inch-long log.

5. Bake the bangers until cooked through and firm, about 20 minutes. Remove from the oven and let stand for at least 15 minutes.

6. Rub or drizzle the remaining 1 tablespoon oil onto the bangers. Cook the bangers, 4 at a time, in a large nonstick skillet over medium-high heat until well-browned on all sides, about 4 to 5 minutes total. Adjust seasoning and serve.

FLEXITARIAN OPTION: Serve the bangers on mashed potatoes and drizzle with Sweet Italian Turkey Sausage Gravy (page 113) or other meaty gravy.

Per serving: 180 calories, 11g total fat, 1.5g saturated fat, 0g trans fat, 45mg cholesterol, 470mg sodium, 13g total carbohydrate, 2g dietary fiber, 2g sugars, 8g protein

Vegetable Souvlaki Ⓕ

Makes 6 servings: 4 skewers and ¾ cup rice each

Souvlaki is popular Greek street fare made of grilled meat and veggie pieces on skewers. Here the souvlaki is served meat-free with hearty, colorful veggies. These skewers then transform into a stunning entrée when served over rice.

Juice of 1 large lemon (¼ cup)

⅓ cup low-sodium vegetable broth or Vegetable Stock (page 203)

1½ tablespoons extra-virgin olive oil

¼ cup pine nuts, toasted

3 large garlic cloves

1 tablespoon fresh oregano leaves

1 tablespoon fresh mint leaves

1 teaspoon sea salt, or to taste

2 large white onions, cut into 16 wedges each

32 cherry tomatoes

24 medium cremini (baby bella) mushrooms

1 medium zucchini, unpeeled, cut into quarters lengthwise, and cut into 6 slices crosswise

4½ cups steamed brown rice or Minted Pine Nut Pilaf (page 478)

1. Add the lemon juice, broth, oil, 2 tablespoons of the pine nuts, the garlic, oregano, mint, ½ teaspoon of the salt, 8 of the onion wedges, and 8 of the cherry tomatoes to a blender. Cover and puree into a smooth marinade.

2. Add the remaining onion wedges, and cherry tomatoes, the mushrooms, and zucchini to a large dish or bowl. Drizzle with all of the marinade and toss to coat. Marinate for 2 to 4 hours in the refrigerator.

3. Prepare an outdoor or indoor grill. Thread the vegetable pieces in an alternating fashion onto 24 small or 12 large reusable or water-soaked bamboo skewers. Grill over medium-high heat until the vegetables are cooked through and charred as desired, about 12 minutes.

4. Serve the vegetable skewers on the rice along with any remaining marinade on the side. Sprinkle with the remaining ½ teaspoon salt and the remaining 2 tablespoons pine nuts and, if desired, garnish with additional fresh mint.

FLEXITARIAN OPTION: Serve the skewers on Sticky Lebanese Cinnamon Chicken and Rice (page 337) instead of steamed rice.

Per serving: 290 calories, 9g total fat, 1g saturated fat, 0g trans fat, 0mg cholesterol, 420mg sodium, 48g total carbohydrate, 6g dietary fiber, 8g sugars, 8g protein

Grilled Eggplant Stack with Feta and Fresh Basil Ⓕ

Makes 4 servings: 1 stack (6 eggplant slices) each

Eggplant does a phenomenal job of soaking up the tangy marinade in this eye-catching stack. The dramatic presentation pops with excitement from the zingy feta mixture and vibrant color provided by the basil leaves.

½ cup low-sodium vegetable broth or
    Vegetable Stock (page 203)
¼ cup aged balsamic vinegar

1 tablespoon extra-virgin olive oil
6 fully ripened cherry tomatoes
2 large shallots
3 large garlic cloves
28 large fresh basil leaves
¾ teaspoon sea salt, or to taste
¼ teaspoon dried hot pepper flakes, or to taste
2 (1-pound) medium eggplants, cut crosswise into
    12 slices each
1 (14-ounce) package firm tofu, well drained and
    gently squeezed dry, crumbled
4 ounces crumbled feta cheese

1. Add the broth, 2 tablespoons of the vinegar, the oil, tomatoes, shallots, garlic, 4 of the basil leaves, the salt, and hot pepper flakes to a blender. Cover and blend into a smooth marinade. Pour ⅓ cup of the marinade into a medium bowl; set aside.

2. Pour the remaining marinade into a large dish or bowl. Add the eggplant slices and toss to coat. Marinate for 2 to 4 hours in the refrigerator.

3. Meanwhile, add the tofu to the reserved marinade in the medium bowl and toss to coat. Add the cheese and toss to coat. Marinate for 2 to 4 hours in the refrigerator. Adjust seasoning.

4. Prepare an outdoor or indoor grill. Grill the eggplant slices, in batches if necessary, over medium-high heat until fully cooked and rich grill marks form, about 4 minutes per side. Adjust seasoning.

5. Onto each of 4 individual plates, arrange in stacks as follows: 1 eggplant slice, 2 tablespoons of the tofu-feta mixture, 1 basil leaf (allow each leaf to peek out); repeat 5 times.

6. Drizzle with the remaining 2 tablespoons vinegar or serve it on the side. Enjoy at room temperature.

FLEXITARIAN OPTION: Add thinly sliced grilled striped bass or sardines between eggplant layers along with the tofu-feta mixture when stacking.

Per serving: 300 calories, 14g total fat, 5g saturated fat, 0g trans fat, 25mg cholesterol, 780mg sodium, 29g total carbohydrate, 6g dietary fiber, 12g sugars, 16g protein

Grilled Curry Portabella "Steak" with Mango Chutney

Makes 2 servings: 2 caps each

Portabellas are prized for their "meatiness." That's one reason they work so well here—grilled just like you might a steak. They're slathered with an Indian-inspired sauce and topped with spicy, sweet, and savory chutney, creating a portabella "steak" entrée with pizzazz.

2 tablespoons fat-free or low-fat plain yogurt or soy yogurt

1 tablespoon no-salt-added creamy almond or cashew butter

1 teaspoon hot Madras curry powder

¼ teaspoon sea salt, or to taste

4 large portabella mushroom caps, stemmed

1 cup Mango Chutney (page 120) or ½ cup other chutney

1 tablespoon finely chopped fresh cilantro (optional)

1. Prepare an outdoor or indoor grill.

2. Stir together the yogurt, almond butter, curry powder, and salt until well combined. Brush or rub the chutney mixture onto both sides of each mushroom cap.

3. Grill the mushrooms over medium-high heat until just tender and grill marks form, about 3 minutes per side. Adjust seasoning.

4. Transfer to a platter or individual plates, top with the chutney and cilantro (if using), and serve warm or at room temperature.

FLEXITARIAN OPTION: Place one or two Sea Salt and Pepper Scallops (page 361) or other grilled scallops onto each mushroom cap.

Per serving: 150 calories, 6g total fat, 0.5g saturated fat, 0g trans fat, 0mg cholesterol, 420mg sodium, 22g total carbohydrate, 5g dietary fiber, 15g sugars, 7g protein

Ginger Tofu Fillets

Makes 3 servings: 3 filets and ¾ cup greens each

This is one of my favorite ways to enjoy tofu as an entrée. The tantalizing combination of Asian flavors, especially the sweet honey and zesty ginger, is delectably dreamy. Turn it into a taste-tempting meal by pairing it with grilled bell peppers and steamed brown rice.

3 tablespoons naturally brewed soy sauce

1 tablespoon brown rice vinegar

1 scallion, green and white parts, minced

1 tablespoon freshly grated gingerroot

2 teaspoons toasted sesame oil

2 teaspoons honey or agave nectar

¼ teaspoon dried hot pepper flakes

1 (14-ounce) package extra-firm tofu, well drained and squeezed dry, cut crosswise into 9 slices

2¼ cups wilted or steamed baby spinach, tatsoi, or other greens

1 tablespoon finely chopped fresh cilantro

1. Whisk together the soy sauce, vinegar, scallion, ginger, oil, honey, and hot pepper flakes in a small bowl. Pour into a 9 × 13-inch or slightly smaller dish, add tofu slices in a single layer, and marinate 10 minutes per side.

2. Preheat a panini grill or a grill pan over medium-high heat. Transfer each tofu slice to the grill using tongs, reserving the marinade. Grill until rich grill marks form on both sides and tofu is fully cooked, about 3 minutes in a panini grill (5½ minutes on a grill pan).

3. Arrange the tofu fillets on a bed of the greens and sprinkle with the cilantro. Drizzle with about half of the remaining marinade or serve it on the side.

FLEXITARIAN OPTION: Dice and sprinkle the tofu fillets onto Thai Turkey Pizza (page 416) along with some cilantro.

Per serving: 200 calories, 9g total fat, 1.5g saturated fat, 0g trans fat, 0mg cholesterol, 730mg sodium, 12g total carbohydrate, 6g dietary fiber, 4g sugars, 19g protein

Stovetop, Slow-Cooked, and Pressure-Cooked Dishes

Pesto Zucchini "Fettuccine" Ⓢ

Makes 2 servings: 1 cup each

This dish doesn't actually contain fettuccine; rather, fettuccine-like zucchini strips are created with a vegetable peeler. They're like green pasta . . . but with fewer calories and fresher flavor.

2 teaspoons extra-virgin olive oil

1 large shallot, thinly sliced

1 large garlic clove, minced

2 medium zucchini, sliced into thin, fettuccine-like strips using a vegetable peeler

¼ teaspoon freshly ground black pepper, or to taste

⅛ teaspoon sea salt, or to taste

2 tablespoons Enlightened Fresh Basil Pesto (page 117) or other pesto

1 tablespoon pine nuts, toasted

4 large fresh basil leaves, thinly sliced

1. Heat the oil in a large skillet over medium heat. Add the shallot and sauté over medium heat until softened and lightly caramelized, about 3 minutes. Add the garlic and sauté for 1 minute.

2. Stir in the zucchini, pepper, and salt and cook while covered, stirring gently once, until the zucchini are just cooked through, yet still slightly firm, about 6 to 7 minutes. Stir in the pesto. Adjust seasoning.

3. Arrange in individual bowls, sprinkle with the pine nuts and basil, and serve warm.

FLEXITARIAN OPTION: Serve Oven-Fried Veal Parmigiana (page 325) over a bed of the "fettuccine." Or toss with cooked, chilled shrimp.

Per serving: 150 calories, 11g total fat, 1.5g saturated fat, 0g trans fat, 0mg cholesterol, 210mg sodium, 13g total carbohydrate, 3g dietary fiber, 5g sugars, 4g protein

Asparagus Shiitake "Paella" Ⓕ

Makes 4 servings: 1½ cups each

Ready for a flavor adventure? This very different paella will take your taste buds on one.

1 tablespoon extra-virgin olive oil

1 large white onion, finely diced

2 teaspoons white balsamic vinegar

¾ teaspoon sea salt, or to taste

2 cups chopped fresh shiitake mushroom caps

4 large garlic cloves, minced

1 pound asparagus, ends trimmed and cut into 1-inch pieces,

1½ cups long-grain brown rice

3 cups low-sodium vegetable broth or Vegetable Stock (page 203)

¼ cup finely diced sun-dried tomatoes (not oil-packed)

½ teaspoon freshly ground black pepper, to taste

¼ teaspoon saffron threads

½ cup shaved Manchego or hard sheep's milk cheese

3 tablespoons thinly sliced fresh basil leaves

1 lemon, cut into wedges

1. Heat the oil in a paella pan or large nonstick skillet over medium heat. Add the onion, vinegar, and ¼ teaspoon of the salt and sauté for 3 minutes. Add the mushrooms and garlic and sauté for 3 minutes. Add the asparagus, rice, broth, ⅔ cup water, the sun-dried tomatoes, pepper, saffron, and remaining ½ teaspoon salt and bring to a boil over high heat. Reduce heat to medium, cover, and cook until the rice is done and bottom is crisped and browned, about 45 minutes (do not stir).

2. Remove from the heat, sprinkle with the cheese and basil, and serve from the pan with the lemon.

FLEXITARIAN OPTION: Toss several slices of warm chorizo onto the paella before the cheese.

Per serving: 240 calories, 9g total fat, 3g saturated fat, 0g trans fat, 15mg cholesterol, 790mg sodium, 33g total carbohydrate, 6g dietary fiber, 7g sugars, 9g protein

Black Quinoa and Fava "Risotto" Ⓕ

Makes 4 servings: ¾ cup each

This risotto-style dish (made with ultra-hip black quinoa!) is full of inviting colors, textures, flavors, and ingredients. It's a must-try for early summertime when fava beans are bountiful.

1 pound fresh unshelled or 5 ounces shelled
    fava beans

2 tablespoons unsalted butter

1 large shallot, finely chopped

¼ cup Chardonnay or other dry white wine

1 cup black quinoa, rinsed and drained

1½ cups low-sodium vegetable broth
    or Vegetable Stock (page 203)

¾ teaspoon sea salt, or to taste

2 tablespoons freshly grated Pecorino Romano
    or other Romano cheese

1½ tablespoons minced fresh cilantro

1. Bring a small saucepan of water to a boil over high heat. Meanwhile, shell the fava beans and discard the pods. Boil the shelled favas until al dente, about 4 minutes. Drain and immediately stir into ice water and let cool for about 4 minutes. Drain and squeeze the fava beans from their skins.

2. Set aside about ¼ cup of the fava beans. Add the remaining fava beans to a food processor. Cover and pulse into a paste. Set aside.

3. Melt 1 tablespoon of the butter in a large saucepan over medium heat. Add the shallot and sauté until softened, about 3 minutes. Add the wine, increase heat to high, and cook while stirring for 1 minute. Add the quinoa and cook, while stirring, for 1 minute. Add the broth and bring just to a boil.

4. Cover, reduce heat to low, and cook until the quinoa is al dente and the broth is just absorbed, about 20 minutes, while only partially covering during the final 5 minutes.

5. Stir the pureed favas, the salt, and remaining 1 tablespoon butter into the quinoa over low heat until combined and butter is melted, about 1 minute. Add the whole fava beans and stir for about 1 minute.

6. Remove from heat and stir in the cheese and cilantro. Adjust seasoning, and serve.

FLEXITARIAN OPTION: Nestle some Roasted Artichoke–Stuffed Mussels (page 364) or other mussels on each serving.

Per serving: 360 calories, 11g total fat, 4.5g saturated fat, 0g trans fat, 20mg cholesterol, 570mg sodium, 52g total carbohydrate, 11g dietary fiber, 2g sugars, 17g protein

Tofu Curry with Coconut Rice Ⓕ

Makes 4 servings: 1 cup curry and ½ cup rice each

The distinctive Indian aromas, contrasting textures, and bold flavors, especially from the hot Madras curry powder, provide pure excitement for your taste buds. Served with fragrant rice, this dish will wow you in every way. Cumin-Spiced Chickpea Raita (page 97) makes a lovely accompaniment.

1 tablespoon coconut or grapeseed oil

1 large sweet onion, diced

2 teaspoons brown rice vinegar

½ teaspoon sea salt, or to taste

1 tablespoon freshly grated gingerroot

1 large garlic clove, minced

1½ teaspoons cumin seeds

1 (14-ounce) package firm tofu, well drained,
    gently squeezed dry and cut into ½-inch cubes

3 medium vine-ripened tomatoes, pulp removed
    and finely chopped

1 tablespoon hot Madras curry powder, or to taste

2 teaspoons naturally brewed soy sauce, or to taste

½ teaspoon ground turmeric

1 cup fresh or frozen peas, thawed

¼ cup chopped fresh cilantro

2 cups Coconut-Spiked Basmati Rice (page 477),
    or steamed brown basmati rice, warm

1. Heat the oil in a wok or large nonstick skillet over medium-high heat. Add the onion, vinegar, and ¼ teaspoon of the salt and sauté until the onion is slightly softened, about 3 minutes. Add the ginger, garlic, and cumin seeds and sauté until fragrant, about 1 minute. Add the tofu and sauté until the tofu is golden brown and onion is lightly caramelized, about 10 to 12 minutes. Add the tomatoes, curry powder, soy sauce, turmeric, and remaining ¼ teaspoon salt and sauté for 2 minutes. Add the peas and half of the cilantro and sauté until the peas are heated through, about 1 minute. Adjust seasoning.

2. Spoon the rice into individual bowls. Top with the tofu curry and the remaining cilantro, and serve.

FLEXITARIAN OPTION: Top with Red Curry Chicken Breasts (page 313). Or prepare with diced chicken thigh instead of tofu.

Per serving: 300 calories, 12g total fat, 6g saturated fat, 0g trans fat, 0mg cholesterol, 670mg sodium, 38g total carbohydrate, 7g dietary fiber, 11g sugars, 15g protein

West African Vegetarian Jollof Rice Ⓕ

Makes 8 servings: 1¼ cups each

Jollof rice, traditionally a mixture of spiced rice, meat, and tomatoes, is an essential and delicious part of the West African diet. I've updated the recipe here to make it vegetarian. The result is a fragrant all-in-one entrée with modern appeal.

1 tablespoon grapeseed or coconut oil
3 large white onions, finely chopped
3 large green bell peppers, finely chopped
1 large red bell pepper, finely chopped
3 large carrots, finely chopped
1 tablespoon aged red wine vinegar
1 cup fresh chopped trimmed haricots verts or string green beans
4 medium vine-ripened tomatoes, chopped
2 teaspoons sea salt, or to taste
1 teaspoon freshly ground black pepper, or to taste
1 teaspoon ground cumin, or to taste
¼ teaspoon freshly grated nutmeg, or to taste
¼ teaspoon ground cayenne, or to taste
4 cups cooked brown basmati rice, chilled
¾ cup fresh or frozen green peas, thawed
½ cup tomato paste
¼ cup low-sodium vegetable broth or Vegetable Stock (page 203)
2 teaspoons pure coconut extract (optional)
1 teaspoon finely chopped fresh thyme

1. Heat the oil in a stockpot over medium-high heat. Add the onions, bell peppers, carrots, and vinegar and sauté until the onions begin to caramelize, about 20 minutes. Add the beans, tomatoes, salt, black pepper, cumin, nutmeg, and cayenne, cover and cook, stirring occasionally, until the beans are just cooked through, about 8 minutes.

2. Stir together the rice, peas, tomato paste, broth, coconut extract (if using), and thyme in a medium bowl. Stir into the stockpot, and simmer uncovered, until the vegetables are fully softened and rice is hot.

3. Adjust seasoning, and serve.

FLEXITARIAN OPTION: Stir in spicy or smoked lean poultry sausage or grilled shrimp.

Per serving: 200 calories, 3g total fat, 0g saturated fat, 0g trans fat, 0mg cholesterol, 700mg sodium, 40g total carbohydrate, 7g dietary fiber, 9g sugars, 6g protein

Creamy Seasonal Vegetable Korma Ⓕ

Makes 4 servings: 1 rounded cup each

Fresh vegetables do a phenomenal job of sopping up all the creaminess in this dish, while complementing the robust ginger and curry flavors. Enjoy with rice.

2 teaspoons unrefined peanut or coconut oil

1 medium white or red onion, minced

2 teaspoons apple cider vinegar

1 teaspoon sea salt, or to taste

2 tablespoons no-salt-added creamy almond, cashew, or pistachio butter

2 large garlic cloves, minced

2 teaspoons freshly grated gingerroot

1 (15-ounce) can no-salt-added tomato sauce

1 tablespoon garam masala curry paste

2 teaspoons ground coriander

½ teaspoon ground turmeric

3 cups bite-size pieces fresh seasonal vegetables, such as cauliflower, broccoli, bell pepper, and/or stemmed fresh shiitake mushrooms

1 large Yukon Gold potato, unpeeled, scrubbed, and cut into ½-inch cubes

⅓ cup black seedless raisins

⅔ cup unsweetened coconut milk beverage

1 teaspoon pure coconut extract, or to taste

2 tablespoons chopped fresh cilantro

1. Heat the oil in a large, deep skillet over medium heat. Add the onion, vinegar, and ¼ teaspoon of the salt and sauté until softened, about 8 minutes. Add the almond butter, garlic, and ginger and stir for 1 minute. Add the tomato sauce, curry paste, coriander, and turmeric and cook while stirring until the mixture begins to bubble, about 3 minutes.

2. Add the vegetables, potato, raisins, coconut milk beverage, coconut extract, and the remaining ¾ teaspoon salt and bring to a boil over high heat. Reduce heat to medium-low, and simmer, covered, until the vegetables are tender, stirring occasionally, about 20 minutes. Adjust seasoning.

3. Ladle the korma into a large serving bowl, sprinkle with the cilantro, and serve.

FLEXITARIAN OPTION: Stir in cooked, sliced Bombay Chicken Thighs (page 313) or rotisserie chicken about 5 minutes before the end of the simmering process in step 2.

Per serving: 270 calories, 9g total fat, 2g saturated fat, 0g trans fat, 0mg cholesterol, 770mg sodium, 45g total carbohydrate, 7g dietary fiber, 18g sugars, 8g protein

Vegetable Biryani Ⓕ

Makes 6 servings: 1 rounded cup each

Biryani is a rice-based dish popular in South Asia. I've recreated it for a pressure-cooker to keep great taste while saving time. Raita is nice on the side.

1 tablespoon coconut or unrefined peanut oil

1 small or ½ large white onion, diced

2 teaspoons apple cider vinegar

1 teaspoon sea salt, or to taste

2 large garlic cloves, minced

1 tablespoon freshly grated gingerroot

1 tablespoon garam masala curry paste

1½ cups brown basmati rice

3 cups coarsely chopped fresh seasonal vegetables, such as cauliflower, carrots, and green beans

3⅛ cups low-sodium vegetable broth, Vegetable Stock (page 203), or water

1 cup fresh or frozen peas, thawed

¼ cup chopped fresh cilantro

1. Heat the oil in an uncovered pressure-cooker on medium-high heat. Add the onion, vinegar, and ¼ teaspoon of the salt and sauté until the onion is softened, about 3 minutes. Add the garlic, ginger, and curry paste and sauté for 1 minute. Add the rice and vegetables and sauté for 1 minute. Add the broth and the remaining ¾ teaspoon salt.

2. Close the pressure-cooker lid and turn to the high-pressure setting. Once the pressure-cooker hisses, adjust the heat as necessary to maintain high pressure with gentle hissing, and cook until the rice is fully cooked, about 18 minutes. Turn off the heat and gradually release the pressure-cooker lid.

3. Stir in the peas and half of the cilantro, cover, and let stand for at least 5 minutes before serving. Adjust seasoning.

4. Spoon the biryani onto a platter, sprinkle with the remaining cilantro, and serve.

FLEXITARIAN OPTION: Top with thin slices of Bison Tenderloin with Raita (page 322).

Per serving: 210 calories, 4g total fat, 2g saturated fat, 0g trans fat, 0mg cholesterol, 580mg sodium, 40g total carbohydrate, 5g dietary fiber, 5g sugars, 5g protein

Sweet-n-Sour Stuffed Cabbage Ⓕ

Make 8 servings: 2 large stuffed leaves each

These plump cabbage rolls are packed with ample veggie-stuffed quinoa filling. Once assembled, these beauties slow-cook to tender perfection and fill the air with an enticing aroma. It's true comfort food.

1 tablespoon extra-virgin olive oil

1 large yellow onion, chopped

Juice of 1 lemon (3 tablespoons)

1¼ teaspoons sea salt, or to taste

2 large garlic cloves, minced

1½ cups finely chopped cremini (baby bella) mushrooms

1 medium green bell pepper, diced

1 cup finely chopped cauliflower florets and tender stems

2 medium vine-ripened tomatoes, pulp removed and chopped

1½ cups quinoa, rinsed and drained

2¾ cups low-sodium vegetable broth or Vegetable Stock (page 203)

½ teaspoon freshly ground black pepper, or to taste

1 large head green cabbage

1 large egg, beaten

3 tablespoons freshly grated Parmigiano-Reggiano or other Parmesan cheese

1 teaspoon chopped fresh thyme or oregano, or to taste

4 cups Sweet-n-Sour Tomato Sauce (page 136), at room temperature

1. Heat the oil in a large saucepan over medium heat. Add the onion, 1 tablespoon of the lemon juice, and ¼ teaspoon of the salt and sauté until softened, about 8 minutes. Add the garlic and sauté for 1 minute. Add the mushrooms, bell pepper, and cauliflower and sauté for 1 minute. Stir in the remaining 2 tablespoons lemon juice and sauté for 1 minute. Add the tomatoes, quinoa, broth, black pepper, and remaining 1 teaspoon salt and bring to a boil over high heat. Cover, reduce heat to low, and cook until the quinoa is tender and liquid is absorbed, about 22 minutes. Remove from heat and let stand at least 30 minutes before stuffing the leaves.

2. Meanwhile, core the bottom of the cabbage. Place the whole head of cabbage in boiling water until leaves start falling off of the head, removing them one by one to a plate, and rotating the cabbage head in the water as needed. Set aside 16 large leaves for rolls. Cut out just the thickest part of the vein from each leaf.

3. Stir the egg, cheese, and thyme into quinoa mixture until well combined.

4. Overlap each leaf slightly to cover up the portion of the leaf in which the vein was removed. Place about ½ cup of quinoa stuffing onto each cabbage leaf on the overlapping portion. Fold in the sides of each leaf, then roll up like a burrito to completely enclose the filling.

5. Pour 1 cup of the Sweet-n-Sour Sauce into a 3-quart or larger slow-cooker. Place the cabbage rolls in alternating layers into the cooker and cover with the remaining 3 cups sauce. Cover and cook on high heat for 1½ hours or low heat for 3 hours.

6. Serve the rolls topped with the sauce while hot.

FLEXITARIAN OPTION: Replace the mushrooms with 12 ounces raw lean ground beef sirloin in step 1.

Per serving: 230 calories, 5g total fat, 1g saturated fat, 0g trans fat, 25mg cholesterol, 610mg sodium, 38g total carbohydrate, 6g dietary fiber, 12g sugars, 9g protein

Southwestern Beans and Rice (F)

Makes 1 serving: 1 cup beans and ⅔ cup rice

Rice and beans is a classic pairing found in a variety of world cuisines. It's one of the most satisfying combinations and also provides protein and fiber. Here, the fresh flair of cilantro and zing of lime will please your palate, too. For more global appeal, swap the pinto bean recipe with Cuban Beans with Lime (page 490) or Dal Masala with Cilantro (page 490); try various herbs and lemon, too.

⅔ cup steamed long-grain brown rice
    or brown basmati rice, warm
1 cup Southwestern Pinto Beans (page 487), warm
1 teaspoon finely chopped fresh cilantro
1 lime wedge

1. Arrange the rice in the center of a plate or bowl. Spoon the beans around the rice.

2. Sprinkle with the cilantro, and serve with the lime wedge.

FLEXITARIAN OPTION: Top the rice with Zesty Lime Grilled Chicken (page 308) or roasted chicken strips, then the beans.

Per serving: 420 calories, 7g total fat, 1.5g saturated fat, 0g trans fat, 0mg cholesterol, 700mg sodium, 73g total carbohydrate, 18g dietary fiber, 5g sugars, 17g protein

Cajun Beans and Couscous (F)

Makes 3 servings: 1 cup bean mixture and
¾ cup couscous each

This comforting veggie entrée gives a bit of a Moroccan twist to traditional Cajun red beans and rice. It's served on whole-wheat couscous instead of rice—which makes it a quicker fix. But it's the taste that's tops—with its "heat," garlicky accent, and richly fragrant mélange of thyme, parsley, chili powder, and cayenne.

1 tablespoon extra-virgin olive oil
1 medium yellow onion, diced
1 large green bell pepper, diced
2 teaspoons aged red wine vinegar
3/4 teaspoon sea salt, or to taste
3 large garlic cloves, finely chopped
1 (15-ounce) can red kidney beans, drained
½ cup low-sodium vegetable broth
    or Vegetable Stock (page 203)
1 large vine-ripened or beefsteak tomato, diced
½ teaspoon fresh thyme leaves
½ teaspoon chili powder
¼ teaspoon ground cayenne
¾ cup whole-wheat couscous
¼ cup chopped fresh flat-leaf parsley

1. Heat the oil in a large saucepan or deep skillet over medium heat. Add the onion, bell pepper, vinegar, and ¼ teaspoon of the salt and sauté until the onion is softened, about 8 minutes. Add the garlic and sauté for 1 minute.

2. Stir in the beans, broth, tomato, thyme, chili powder, cayenne, and ¼ teaspoon of the salt. Cook while gently stirring on occasion until the bean mixture is nearly thickened, about 5 minutes, cover, and turn off the heat. Let stand for 10 minutes. Adjust seasoning.

3. Bring 1¼ cups water to a boil over high heat in a small saucepan. Stir in the couscous, cover, and turn off the heat. Let stand for 7 minutes. Stir in the remaining ¼ teaspoon salt and half of the parsley while fluffing with a fork.

4. Serve the couscous in individual bowls or on a platter, top with the bean mixture, and sprinkle with the remaining parsley.

FLEXITARIAN OPTION: Top with slices of Blackened Cajun Duck Breast (page 311) or other cooked poultry.

Per serving: 300 calories, 5g total fat, 0.5g saturated fat, 0g trans fat, 0mg cholesterol, 770mg sodium, 52g total carbohydrate, 12g dietary fiber, 7g sugars, 13g protein

Stir-Fries

Wok Veggie Fried Rice Ⓕ

Makes 4 servings: 1 cup each

Here's a tasty way to include various veggies that you have on hand. Use my recipe, or turn it into your own. You can prepare it without the eggs, too, if you prefer.

1 tablespoon peanut or canola oil

2 teaspoons toasted sesame oil

3 scallions, green and white parts, thinly sliced

1 tablespoon freshly grated gingerroot

1 cup mung bean sprouts or ½ cup finely chopped yellow bell pepper

¾ cup coarsely grated carrot

½ cup finely chopped cremini (baby bella) mushrooms

1 large garlic clove, very thinly sliced

2½ cups cooked long-grain brown rice, chilled

½ cup fresh or frozen peas, thawed

3 tablespoons Wasabi-Spiked Soy Sauce (page 130) or naturally brewed soy sauce

2 large eggs, lightly beaten

1. Heat the peanut and sesame oils in a wok or large skillet over high heat. Add the white part of the scallions and the ginger and stir-fry for 30 seconds. Add the sprouts, carrot, mushrooms, and garlic and stir-fry for 2 minutes. Add the chilled rice, peas, soy sauce, and the green part of the scallions and stir-fry for 3 minutes, or until the rice is steaming hot.

2. Slowly stir the eggs into the rice and cook until the eggs are scrambled and the rice begins to crisp, about 3 to 4 minutes.

3. Serve immediately with extra soy sauce on the side, if desired.

FLEXITARIAN OPTION: Finely dice any leftover cooked poultry or fish and add in step 2 just before the eggs.

Per serving: 270 calories, 9g total fat, 2g saturated fat, 0g trans fat, 95mg cholesterol, 620mg sodium, 36g total carbohydrate, 5g dietary fiber, 4g sugars, 10g protein

Pineapple Stir-Fried Rice Ⓕ

Makes 5 servings: 1 cup each

It's still possible to have something "fried" even when trying to keep calories in check. You'll love the plentiful bits of juicy pineapple that you'll get in every memorable bite of this fried rice.

1½ tablespoons peanut or vegetable oil

6 ounces extra-firm tofu, drained and gently squeezed dry, diced

1 medium white onion, finely chopped

1 large red or orange bell pepper, finely diced

1 cup bite-size pieces broccoli florets

3 large garlic cloves, minced

1 serrano pepper with some seeds, minced

1¼ cups finely diced fresh pineapple, drained

3 cups cooked brown basmati rice, chilled

1 tablespoon ketchup or tomato puree

¾ teaspoon sea salt, or to taste

2 scallions, green and white parts, thinly sliced

¼ cup chopped fresh cilantro

3 tablespoons chopped unsalted dry-roasted cashews

1. In a wok or large nonstick skillet, heat the oil over medium-high heat. Add the tofu and onion and stir-fry until golden brown, about 6 minutes. Add the bell pepper, broccoli, garlic, and serrano and stir-fry for 2 minutes. Add the pineapple, rice, ketchup, and salt, mixing well and stir-fry until the rice begins to caramelize and crisp, about 8 to 10 minutes. Stir in the scallions and cilantro and stir-fry for 2 minutes.

2. Adjust seasoning (or enjoy with naturally brewed soy sauce on the side, if desired). Sprinkle with the cashews, and serve.

FLEXITARIAN OPTION: Serve Teriyaki Pineapple-Pork Kebabs (page 58) on top—or stir in diced roasted pork loin.

Per serving: 280 calories, 10g total fat, 1.5g saturated fat, 0g trans fat, 0mg cholesterol, 410mg sodium, 42g total carbohydrate, 5g dietary fiber, 8g sugars, 9g protein

Szechuan Sesame Baby Bok Choy Ⓕ

Makes 2 servings: 1½ cups stir fry and ½ cup rice each

This spicy, brothy Asian entrée brings a produce-rich side to the center of the plate. Complement this high-flavored bok choy and rice with a protein-rich side, like Asian grilled tofu.

2 teaspoons naturally brewed soy sauce

2 teaspoons brown rice vinegar

1 teaspoon honey or agave nectar

½ teaspoon Asian chili-garlic paste, or to taste

2 teaspoons canola or peanut oil

2 teaspoons toasted sesame oil

1½ teaspoons freshly grated gingerroot

2 large garlic cloves, very thinly sliced

4 bunches baby bok choy, stalks thinly sliced and leaves kept whole

1 teaspoon toasted sesame seeds

1 cup Sticky Ginger Rice (page 476) or steamed whole grain of choice, warm

1. Whisk together the soy sauce, vinegar, honey, and chili-garlic paste in a liquid measuring cup or small bowl. Set aside.

2. Heat the oils in a wok or large skillet over high heat. Add the ginger and garlic slices and stir-fry until the garlic is lightly browned, about 15 to 30 seconds. Add the bok choy stalks and stir-fry until the stalks are crisp tender, about 30 seconds. Add the bok choy leaves and stir-fry until the leaves are just wilted, about 1 minute. Remove from heat, add the soy sauce mixture, and toss to coat.

3. Transfer to a serving dish, sprinkle with the sesame seeds, and serve with the rice.

FLEXITARIAN OPTION: Place Wild Peruvian Chicken Wings (page 76) or rotisserie roasted chicken leg on top of the rice.

Per serving: 290 calories, 12g total fat, 1.5g saturated fat, 0g trans fat, 0mg cholesterol, 530mg sodium, 41g total carbohydrate, 6g dietary fiber, 9g sugars, 9g protein

Garlic Eggplant Stir-Fry Ⓕ

Makes 2 servings: 1 cup stir fry and ½ cup rice each

The eggplant is wonderfully absorbant of the mix of flavors in this dish. The sesame-lover's recipe uses a technique that's more like a "steam-stir" rather than a "stir-fry" to minimize the amount of oil used while bringing out all of the eggplant's deliciousness. Pair with a protein-rich side, like grilled seitan, to make it a meal with rich flavor and satisfaction.

1 tablespoon naturally brewed soy sauce

1½ teaspoons honey or agave nectar

⅛ teaspoon dried hot pepper flakes

¾ cup low-sodium vegetable broth or Vegetable Stock (page 203)

2 teaspoons toasted sesame oil

2 large garlic cloves, very thinly sliced

1 medium eggplant, cut into ½-inch cubes

½ teaspoon toasted sesame seeds

1 cup Sticky Ginger Rice (page 476) or other steamed whole grain, warm

1. Whisk together the soy sauce, honey, and hot pepper flakes in a liquid measuring cup or small bowl. Set aside.

2. Bring the broth and oil to a boil in a wok or large skillet over high heat. Add the garlic slices and eggplant and cook while stirring until the liquid is fully evaporated and eggplant is fully cooked, adding more broth if necessary, about 4 minutes. Add the soy sauce mixture and toss to coat.

3. Transfer to a serving dish, sprinkle with the sesame seeds, and serve with the rice.

FLEXITARIAN OPTION: Serve grilled lamb brochettes on top.

Per serving: 250 calories, 6g total fat, 1g saturated fat, 0g trans fat, 0mg cholesterol, 530mg sodium, 47g total carbohydrate, 6g dietary fiber, 11g sugars, 5g protein

Asparagus-Shiitake Tempeh

Makes 4 servings: 1½ cups each

The pairing of tempeh and shiitakes provides a savory meatiness to this asparagus-spiked stir-fry to make it hearty and satisfying. The combination of sweet, salty, and hot Asian ingredients creates amazing taste appeal.

2 teaspoons toasted sesame oil

1 serrano pepper with seeds, minced

1½ teaspoons freshly grated gingerroot

1 cup low-sodium vegetable broth or
    Vegetable Stock (page 203)

¼ cup ketchup

5 teaspoons naturally brewed soy sauce

2 tablespoons turbinado sugar

1 tablespoon brown rice vinegar

⅛ teaspoon sea salt, or to taste

2 teaspoons peanut or canola oil

1 pound tempeh, cut crosswise into 2½-inch-long
    and ¼-inch-wide strips

1 medium red onion, cut into large dices

1 pound thin asparagus, ends trimmed and cut
    crosswise into 1-inch pieces on a diagonal

2 large garlic cloves, minced

2 cups thinly sliced fresh shiitake mushroom caps
    or mushrooms of choice

3 scallions, green and white parts, cut into 1-inch
    pieces on a diagonal

¼ cup finely chopped unsalted dry-roasted peanuts

1. Heat the sesame oil in a small saucepan over medium heat. Add the serrano and ginger and sauté until fragrant, about 1 minute. Add the broth, ketchup, soy sauce, sugar, vinegar, and salt and simmer over medium-low heat until reduced by about one-third. Set aside.

2. Heat the peanut oil in a wok or large skillet over high heat. Add the tempeh and onion and stir-fry until the tempeh is golden on edges. Add the asparagus and garlic and stir-fry for 1 minute. Add the mushrooms and scallions and stir-fry for 1 minute. Add the sauce mixture and toss to combine. If necessary, continue to stir-fry until the asparagus is crisp-tender. Adjust seasoning.

3. Transfer the stir-fry to a platter, sprinkle with the peanuts, and serve.

FLEXITARIAN OPTION: Replace the tempeh with equal amounts of uncooked chicken, pork, beef, shrimp, or squid, and cook to appropriate doneness.

Per serving: 400 calories, 21g total fat, 4g saturated fat, 0g trans fat, 0mg cholesterol, 750mg sodium, 32g total carbohydrate, 4g dietary fiber, 14g sugars, 27g protein

Sizzling Seasonal Stir-Fry Veggie Fajitas Ⓕ

Makes 6 servings: 1 fajita each

This is a fiesta-worthy way to get your veggies. I've created this entrée-size fajita version, filled with peppers, seitan, and onion. Topped with zesty salsa, gauc, and lime-cilantro yogurt, it's delicioso!

½ cup fat-free or low-fat plain Greek yogurt

Juice of ½ lime (1 tablespoon), or to taste

2 tablespoons chopped fresh cilantro

1 tablespoon peanut or canola oil

1 medium white or red onion, halved, sliced

2 medium red bell peppers, thinly sliced

2 cups bite-size seasonal vegetable(s) of choice
    or thinly sliced green bell peppers

8 ounces cubed seitan, cut into thin slices

½ teaspoon ground cumin, or to taste

¼ teaspoon sea salt, or to taste

6 (8-inch) whole-wheat or other whole-grain
    flour tortillas, warm

½ cup Spicy Raw Tomatillo Salsa (page 114),
    salsa verde, or other salsa

½ cup 3-Ingredient Guacamole (page 89)
    or other guacamole

1. Whisk together the yogurt and 1½ teaspoons of the lime juice in a small bowl. Stir in the cilantro. Set aside.

2. Heat the oil in a wok or large, deep skillet over medium-high heat. Add the onion and sauté for 2 minutes. Add the bell peppers, vegetables, seitan, cumin, salt, and remaining 1½ teaspoons lime juice and sauté for 3 minutes. Increase heat to high and stir-fry until the onion and seitan begin to caramelize and the peppers and vegetables are cooked through, about 5 minutes. Adjust seasoning. Transfer to a dish.

3. Serve the vegetable mixture, tortillas, salsa, guacamole, and reserved yogurt mixture family-style, where each person fills his or her tortilla as desired. Enjoy while the vegetables and tortillas are warm.

FLEXITARIAN OPTION: Replace the seitan with equal amounts of uncooked chicken, pork, or shrimp, and cook to appropriate doneness. Or simply serve grilled chicken strips family-style alongside the vegetable mixture and other tortilla toppers.

Per serving: 280 calories, 7g total fat, 0.5g saturated fat, 0g trans fat, 0mg cholesterol, 740mg sodium, 38g total carbohydrate, 6g dietary fiber, 9g sugars, 18g protein

Southwestern Vegetable Tortilla Stack Ⓕ

Makes 6 servings: 1 stack (1 cup vegetable mixture,
⅓ cup cheese mixture, and 2 tortillas) each

The extra moisture (steam) created from "steam-stirring" the veggies here means you won't need excess oil to cook them or bring out their full flavors. Another unique technique is that the tofu "stretches" the cheese to make this appealing dish seem extra rich. However, the most enticing part may be the presentation; it's stacked, creating a dramatic plate.

1 cup crumbled firm tofu, gently squeezed dry

½ cup crumbled Cotija or feta cheese

½ cup shredded Monterey Jack cheese

1 tablespoon peanut or canola oil

1 large blue or red potato, unpeeled, scrubbed,
    and finely diced

1 large red bell pepper, finely diced

1½ cups fresh sweet corn (from 2 large ears)

1 large red onion, diced

1 small jalapeño pepper with some seeds, minced

Juice of 1 lime (2 tablespoons)

1¼ teaspoons sea salt, or to taste

2 medium zucchini or yellow summer squash,
    finely diced

4 scallions, green and white parts, thinly sliced

2 large garlic cloves, minced

1 large beefsteak tomato, pulp removed, diced

½ teaspoon freshly ground black pepper

⅓ cup chopped fresh cilantro

12 (6-inch) stone-ground corn tortillas,
    grilled or baked till crisp

¾ cup 3-Ingredient Guacamole (page 89)
    or other guacamole (optional)

1. Combine the tofu and cheeses in a small bowl. Set aside.

2. Heat the oil in a wok or large skillet over medium-high heat. Add the potato and bell pepper and stir-fry until the bell pepper is softened, about 5 minutes. Add the corn, onion, jalapeño, 1 tablespoon of the lime juice, and ¼ teaspoon of the salt and stir-fry until the onion is softened, about 5 minutes. Add the zucchini, scallions, and garlic and stir-fry until the zucchini are tender, about 5 minutes. Add the tomato, black pepper, and remaining 1 tablespoon lime juice and 1 teaspoon salt, increase heat to high, and stir-fry until the tomato is cooked through, about 2 minutes. Stir in half of the cilantro. Remove from heat and adjust seasoning.

3. Place six of the tortillas on a large platter or individual plates. Top each with about ½ cup of the vegetable mixture and about 2 rounded tablespoons of the cheese mixture. Top with the remaining tortillas. Top with the remaining vegetable and cheese mixtures. Dollop with the guacamole (if using), sprinkle with the remaining cilantro, and serve immediately.

FLEXITARIAN OPTION: In step 3, top each of the 12 tortillas with a slice of deli smoked turkey breast before topping as directed.

Per serving: 330 calories, 11g total fat, 4g saturated fat, 0g trans fat, 15mg cholesterol, 670mg sodium, 47g total carbohydrate, 7g dietary fiber, 7g sugars, 15g protein

Curried Veggie and Chickpea Stir-Fry Ⓕ

Makes 4 servings: 1½ cups each

This is one satisfying 200-calorie dish. The chickpeas scrumptiously create a feeling of fullness. Toss in the bevy of veggies and the layers of pleasing spice and you've got one sensational stir-fry. Enjoy with Sticky Ginger Rice (page 476) or other steamed whole grains for extra satisfaction.

1 tablespoon unrefined peanut or coconut oil

1 medium white onion, chopped

1 large green bell pepper, diced

1 large red or orange bell pepper, diced

1 cup finely chopped cauliflower florets and tender stems

1 serrano pepper with seeds, minced (optional)

2 tablespoons aged red wine vinegar

½ teaspoon sea salt, or to taste

1 (15-ounce) can diced tomatoes (with liquid)

1 (15-ounce) can chickpeas (garbanzo beans), drained

½ cup Mango Chutney (page 120) or ¼ cup other chutney

1½ teaspoons hot Madras curry powder

1 teaspoon ground cumin

1 teaspoon ground coriander or turmeric

1. Heat the oil in a wok or large skillet over medium-high heat. Add the onion, bell peppers, cauliflower, serrano (if using), vinegar, and ¼ teaspoon of the salt and stir-fry until the cauliflower and onion begin to caramelize, about 8 minutes.

2. Add the tomatoes with liquid, chickpeas, chutney, curry powder, cumin, coriander, and the remaining ¼ teaspoon salt and stir to combine. Cook while stirring until the mixture is bubbling hot and the vegetables are just tender, about 3 minutes.

3. Ladle into individual bowls and serve.

FLEXITARIAN OPTION: Stir in 8 ounces fresh premium lump crabmeat (picked over and separated into chunks) at the end of step 2.

Per serving: 200 calories, 6g total fat, 1g saturated fat, 0g trans fat, 0mg cholesterol, 610mg sodium, 31g total carbohydrate, 9g dietary fiber, 12g sugars, 8g protein

Oven-Prepared Dishes

Eggplant Parmesan with Basil

Makes 6 servings: 2 eggplant rounds each

Feast your eyes—this layered eggplant Parmesan creates a bolder version of an Italian classic that's sure to hit the spot. The combination of silky mozzarella and sharp Parmesan add an indulgence to the crispy baked eggplant rounds. The sweetly fresh Italian basil creates fragrant appeal for an ideal finishing touch. Serve with a side of spaghetti—it's amore!

1 large Italian eggplant, cut into 12 rounds

1 teaspoon sea salt, or to taste

⅔ cup stone-ground whole-wheat or other
    whole-grain flour

½ teaspoon freshly ground black pepper, or to taste

2 large eggs

⅔ cup plain dry whole-wheat or other whole-grain
    breadcrumbs

⅓ cup freshly grated Parmigiano-Reggiano
    or other Parmesan cheese

1 large garlic clove, minced

12 (¾-ounce) slices part-skim mozzarella cheese

1½ cups Triple Tomato Marinara Sauce (page 101)
    or other marinara sauce, hot

3 tablespoons thinly sliced fresh basil leaves

1. Sprinkle the eggplant slices with ½ teaspoon of the salt. Place in a colander set over the sink or a bowl. Let sit for about 30 minutes.

2. Preheat the oven to 425°F.

3. Stir together the flour, pepper, and ¼ teaspoon of the salt in a shallow bowl. Lightly beat the eggs with 2 tablespoons of cold water in a second shallow bowl. Stir together the breadcrumbs, Parmesan cheese, and garlic in a third shallow bowl. (Note: You will have some leftover flour, egg, and breadcrumb mixtures.)

4. Working with 1 slice at a time, dredge the eggplant in the flour, shaking off excess, then dip in the egg mixture, letting excess drip off, and dredge in the breadcrumb mixture until evenly coated. Transfer the eggplant to a large baking sheet. Spray both sides of the eggplant rounds with cooking spray (preferably homemade, page xix) and sprinkle with the remaining ¼ teaspoon salt.

5. Bake the eggplant until crisp, golden brown, and just cooked through, about 20 minutes, rotating the tray halfway through the cooking process.

6. Increase oven temperature to 475°F.

7. Top each eggplant round with the mozzarella. Bake until the cheese is melted and begins to brown, about 5 minutes. Adjust seasoning.

8. Ladle ¼ cup of the marinara sauce onto each of six individual plates. Arrange 2 eggplant rounds onto each plate, sprinkle with the basil, and serve immediately.

FLEXITARIAN OPTION: Place one well-drained, oil-packed anchovy fillet on each eggplant round after the cheese and before baking in step 7.

Per serving: 220 calories, 10g total fat, 5g saturated fat, 0g trans fat, 70mg cholesterol, 770mg sodium, 16g total carbohydrate, 3g dietary fiber, 4g sugars, 16g protein

Crispy Stacked Veggie Parmigiana ⓕ

Makes 4 servings: 1 stack each

This tall, highly flavored dish looks as impressive as it tastes. The thick and crispy slices of baked eggplant make it a good thing. When those slices are layered with Italian cheeses, roasted zucchini and sweet bell pepper, it's a great thing.

1 medium eggplant, cut into 12 rounds

½ teaspoon sea salt, or to taste

⅔ cup stone-ground whole-wheat or other whole-grain flour

¼ teaspoon freshly ground black pepper, or to taste

¼ teaspoon dried hot pepper flakes, or to taste

2 large eggs

⅔ cup plain dry whole-wheat or other whole-grain breadcrumbs

¼ cup freshly grated Parmigiano-Reggiano or other Parmesan cheese

2 large red bell peppers, cut into 4 pieces each

1 large zucchini, cut in half crosswise, each half cut into 4 slices lengthwise

¾ cup shredded part-skim mozzarella cheese

3 tablespoons shredded aged provolone cheese

¾ cup Triple Tomato Marinara Sauce (page 101) or other marinara sauce, warm

¼ cup fresh basil leaves, thinly sliced

1. Sprinkle the eggplant slices with ¼ teaspoon of the salt. Place in a colander set over the sink or a bowl. Let sit for about 30 minutes.

2. Preheat the oven to 425°F.

3. Stir together the flour, black pepper, hot pepper flakes, and ⅛ teaspoon salt in a shallow bowl. Lightly beat the eggs with 2 tablespoons of cold water in a second shallow bowl. Stir together the breadcrumbs and Parmesan cheese in a third shallow bowl.

4. Working with 1 slice at a time, dredge the eggplant in the flour, shaking off excess, then dip in the egg mixture, letting excess drip off, and dredge in the breadcrumb mixture until evenly coated. (Note: You will have some leftover flour mixture.) Transfer the eggplant to a large baking sheet. Spray both sides of each eggplant round with cooking spray (preferably homemade, page xix). Set aside.

5. Arrange the bell peppers and zucchini on a separate large baking sheet. Spray both sides of the bell peppers and zucchini with cooking spray (preferably homemade, page xix) and sprinkle with the remaining ⅛ teaspoon salt.

6. Bake the eggplant, bell peppers, and zucchini until the eggplant is crisp, golden brown, and just cooked through and the zucchini and bell peppers are just tender, about 25 minutes, rotating trays halfway through the cooking process.

7. Increase oven temperature to 475°F. Using the baking sheet with the eggplant, create four stacks as follows: 1 piece eggplant, 1 piece bell pepper, 1 piece zucchini, 1 piece eggplant, 3 tablespoons of the mozzarella cheese, 1 piece bell pepper, 1 piece zucchini, 1 piece eggplant, and about 2 teaspoons provolone cheese. Bake until the cheeses are melted and begin to brown, about 5 minutes. Adjust seasoning.

8. Serve each stack on individual plates. Ladle the sauce evenly over each stack, sprinkle with the basil, and serve.

FLEXITARIAN OPTION: Add one or two Flash-Fried Adobo Chicken Fingers (page 77) or a chicken patty within the layers to make a towering stack.

Per serving: 380 calories, 13g total fat, 6g saturated fat, 0g trans fat, 120mg cholesterol, 795mg sodium, 48g total carbohydrate, 10g dietary fiber, 12g sugars, 22g protein

Goat Cheese Roasted Beet Torte

Makes 6 servings: 1 wedge each

This torte is elegant and velvety, with a deceptive rustic richness thanks to the creamy potato, beans, and goat cheese. Enjoy a generous slice of this stunning and scrumptious dish packed with contrasting layers of tangy and mellow flavors.

3 medium beets, peeled, and very thinly sliced

1 tablespoon aged balsamic vinegar

1 teaspoon finely chopped fresh rosemary

1 teaspoon sea salt, or to taste

1 large Yukon Gold potato, unpeeled, scrubbed, and very thinly sliced

1 (15-ounce) can no-salt-added cannellini or other white beans, drained

4 ounces soft goat cheese

4 large egg whites

2 teaspoons extra-virgin olive oil

1 large garlic clove, minced (optional)

½ teaspoon freshly ground black pepper, or to taste

1. Lightly coat a 9½- or 10-inch round or oval baking dish with cooking spray (preferably homemade, page xix). Evenly arrange half the beets in the baking dish and sprinkle with ½ tablespoon of the vinegar, and ¼ teaspoon of the rosemary and ¼ teaspoon of the salt.

2. Layer all the potato slices on top of the beet layer and sprinkle with ¼ teaspoon of the rosemary and ¼ teaspoon of the salt.

3. Preheat the oven to 400°F.

4. Add the beans, cheese, egg whites, oil, garlic (if using), and pepper, and ¼ teaspoon of the salt to a blender. Cover and blend until very smooth.

5. Evenly pour half of the goat cheese puree on top of the potato layer. Top with a layer of the remaining beets, and sprinkle with the remaining ½ tablespoon vinegar and ¼ teaspoon salt and ¼ teaspoon of the rosemary.

6. Evenly pour the remaining goat cheese puree on top of the beet layer and sprinkle with the remaining ¼ teaspoon rosemary.

7. Bake until the beets and potatoes are fully softened and top is crisp and golden brown, about 1 hour 10 minutes.

8. Remove from oven and let stand for about 15 minutes, slice into 6 wedges, and serve while warm. Garnish each with a small sprig of fresh rosemary, if desired.

FLEXITARIAN OPTION: Serve thin slivers of rosemary roasted chicken or a poached egg on top of each wedge.

Per serving: 200 calories, 7g total fat, 3g saturated fat, 0g trans fat, 10mg cholesterol, 550mg sodium, 24g total carbohydrate, 5g dietary fiber, 5g sugars, 11g protein

Stuffed Spaghetti Squash

Makes 4 servings: ½ of a stuffed squash half each (1½ cups stuffing each)

Butter beans provide velvety indulgence while mushrooms add savoriness to every bite of this entrée. It's truly comfort food for the soul—and the heart. Share it with someone you love.

1 small spaghetti squash, halved lengthwise, seeded

1 tablespoon extra-virgin olive oil

1 large white onion, diced

2 teaspoons white balsamic vinegar

¾ teaspoon sea salt, or to taste

1 large green bell pepper, finely diced

2 cups very thinly sliced cremini (baby bella) mushrooms

2 large garlic cloves, minced

1 (15-ounce) can butter beans or Great Northern beans, drained

1 cup Fresh Marinara (page 101) or other marinara sauce

1 teaspoon chopped fresh oregano, or to taste

¼ teaspoon freshly ground black pepper, or to taste

3 tablespoons freshly grated Pecorino Romano or Parmesan cheese (optional)

1. Preheat the oven to 350°F. Brush or rub the squash halves with 1½ teaspoons of the oil. Place them, cut side down, on a large baking sheet and roast until tender, about 1 hour.

2. Meanwhile, heat the remaining 1½ teaspoons oil in a large, deep skillet or extra-large saucepan over medium heat. Add the onion, vinegar, and ¼ teaspoon of the salt and sauté until the onion is softened, about 8 minutes. Add the bell pepper and mushrooms and sauté until the bell pepper is softened, about 12 minutes. Add the garlic and sauté for 1 minute. Stir in the beans, marinara sauce, ¾ teaspoon of the oregano, and the black pepper and sauté until the sauce is fully heated and is no longer runny, about 3 minutes. Set aside.

3. Increase the oven temperature to 400°F. Pull out squash strands from the shells using a fork while leaving the shells intact. Mix squash strands with the remaining ½ teaspoon salt into the vegetable mixture. Adjust seasoning. Spoon about 3 cups of the filling into each squash shell, forming a mound in each.

4. Arrange the stuffed squash halves on the baking sheet. Sprinkle each with the cheese, if using. Bake uncovered until fully heated, about 12 minutes. Sprinkle with the remaining oregano, and serve.

FLEXITARIAN OPTION: Nestle several Roasted Artichoke–Stuffed Mussels (page 364) or cooked shrimp on top of the squash halves when serving.

Per serving: 220 calories, 5g total fat, 1g saturated fat, 0g trans fat, 0mg cholesterol, 680mg sodium, 38g total carbohydrate, 10g dietary fiber, 11g sugars, 9g protein

Asparagus and Basmati Rice Casserole

Makes 6 servings: 1⅓ cups each

Casseroles are convenient since everything is combined into one home-style dish and can be served for several meals. This contemporary casserole gets its succulence from asparagus, basmati rice, and cremini mushrooms. Eggs provide richness while blending everything together. And the bubbly, golden cheese creates a delicious topping.

2 teaspoons extra-virgin olive oil

1 large white onion, chopped

Juice of ½ small lemon (1 tablespoon)

1 teaspoon sea salt, or to taste

3 large garlic cloves, minced

½ cup Chardonnay or other dry white wine

2 cups low-sodium vegetable broth or Vegetable Stock (page 203)

1 cup brown basmati rice

4 ounces cremini (baby bella) mushrooms, chopped

3 large eggs, beaten

1 pound asparagus, ends trimmed and cut into 1½-inch pieces

3 tablespoons pine nuts, toasted

½ teaspoon freshly ground black pepper, or to taste

1 teaspoon unsalted butter, softened

¼ cup finely shredded part-skim mozzarella cheese

1. Heat the oil in a large saucepan over medium heat. Add the onion, lemon juice, and ¼ teaspoon of the salt and sauté until the onion begins to caramelize, about 10 minutes. Add the garlic and sauté for 1 minute. Add the wine and sauté for 1 minute.

2. Add the broth and bring to a boil over high heat, then stir in the rice, mushrooms, and the remaining ¾ teaspoon salt. Return to a boil, cover, reduce heat to medium-low, and simmer for 35 minutes.

3. Preheat the oven to 375°F.

4. Vigorously stir the eggs into the rice mixture until well combined. Stir in the asparagus, pine nuts, and pepper. Remove from heat. Adjust seasoning.

5. Lightly grease a 9-inch round baking dish with the butter. Evenly add the rice mixture to the dish. Sprinkle with the cheese. Bake until the rice is fully cooked and the cheese is golden brown, about 20 minutes. Let stand for about 10 minutes, and serve.

FLEXITARIAN OPTION: When serving, top with a thin slice smoked salmon or Pan-Seared Sea Scallops (page 362) and lemon zest, to taste.

Per serving: 240 calories, 9g total fat, 2g saturated fat, 0g trans fat, 100mg cholesterol, 510mg sodium, 30g total carbohydrate, 4g dietary fiber, 4g sugars, 9g protein

Eggplant Moussaka Ⓕ

Makes 12 servings: 3¼-inch × 3-inch piece

Moussaka is a traditional Greek dish that is like eggplant lasagna. This memorably spiced recipe is comforting from the cheese and touch of butter. But it's the cinnamon, allspice, and nutmeg that are the flavor stars.

3 medium eggplants, unpeeled, cut into ½-inch rounds

2 teaspoons sea salt, or to taste

2½ tablespoons extra-virgin olive oil

2 medium white onions, diced

½ cup Pinot Noir or other dry red wine

2 cups baby carrots or 8 ounces unpeeled scrubbed carrots, coarsely grated

1 large celery stalk, thinly sliced crosswise

4 or 5 large garlic cloves, minced

1 (28-ounce) can crushed tomatoes

⅓ cup chopped fresh flat-leaf parsley

1 teaspoon dried oregano

1 teaspoon ground cinnamon, or to taste

¾ teaspoon freshly ground black pepper, or to taste

¼ teaspoon ground allspice

¾ cup grated kefalotyri, Pecorino, or Romano cheese

¼ cup unsalted butter

¼ cup whole oat or soybean flour

2¾ cups plain almond milk or light soy milk

3 large egg yolks, lightly beaten

⅛ teaspoon freshly ground white pepper, or to taste

¼ teaspoon freshly grated nutmeg

1 teaspoon chopped fresh oregano (optional)

1. Line three baking sheets with paper towels. Lightly sprinkle both sides of the eggplant with 1 teaspoon of the salt and arrange in a single layer on the towels. Let stand for 45 minutes.

2. Preheat the oven to 400°F. Pat the eggplant dry and discard the paper towels. Lightly brush the eggplant with 2 tablespoons of the oil and arrange in a single layer on the baking sheets. Roast until cooked through and lightly caramelized, about 30 minutes, rotating halfway through the roasting.

3. Heat the remaining ½ tablespoon oil in a large deep skillet or stockpot over medium heat. Add the onions, 1 tablespoon of the wine, and ½ teaspoon of the salt and sauté until the onion is softened, about 10 minutes. Increase heat to medium-high, add the carrots and celery, and sauté until the onions are lightly caramelized, about 12 minutes. Add the garlic and sauté for 1 minute. Add the remaining wine and sauté for 1 minute. Add the tomatoes, parsley, oregano, cinnamon, pepper, and allspice and cook until no runniness remains, about 8 minutes.

4. Lightly coat a 9×13-inch baking dish with homemade cooking spray. Arrange half of the eggplant rounds evenly in the dish; spoon half of the tomato mixture evenly over the eggplant; and sprinkle with 1½ tablespoons of the cheese. Repeat. Firmly pack down the layers.

5. Melt the butter in a small saucepan over medium heat. Whisk in the flour and stir for 2 minutes. Gradually whisk in the almond milk and stir until slightly thickened, about 10 minutes. One at a time, gradually whisk in ½ cup of the cheese, the egg yolks, white pepper, and remaining ½ teaspoon salt. Pour the sauce evenly over the moussaka. Sprinkle with the remaining 1 tablespoon cheese.

6. Bake in the 400°F oven until hot, bubbly, and rich golden brown, about 1 hour. Sprinkle with the nutmeg and the fresh oregano (if using), and let stand for 10 to 15 minutes. Cut into 12 pieces, and serve.

FLEXITARIAN OPTION: Bake two smaller moussakas, one with meat. Use two 8-inch square or 9-inch deep round baking pans. In the meat version, sprinkle 6 ounces gently cooked and crumbled ground lamb between the eggplant layers in step 4. Season the lamb with additional cinnamon and pepper to taste. Bake for about 45 minutes.

Per serving: 210 calories, 11g total fat, 4.5g saturated fat, 0g trans fat, 65mg cholesterol, 680mg sodium, 24g total carbohydrate, 6g dietary fiber, 10g sugars, 6g protein

Roasted Poblano, Black Beans, and Rice Ⓕ

Makes 6 servings: 1 rounded cup each

The deep, distinctive flavors of Mexican cuisine, including two tantalizing types of peppers, are on taste display in this aromatic dish.

⅔ cup fat-free or low-fat plain Greek yogurt
⅓ cup sour cream
Juice of 1 lime (2 tablespoons)
¾ teaspoon sea salt, or to taste
¼ teaspoon ground cumin
2 cups unsalted cooked long-grain brown rice, chilled
1½ cups Vine-Ripened Pico de Gallo (page 114) or other pico de gallo, drained of excess liquid
1 (15-ounce) can black beans, drained
2 roasted poblano peppers, diced
12 blue corn tortilla chips, coarsely crushed
2 scallions, green and white parts, thinly sliced
¾ cup shredded dry Jack cheese
1 small jalapeño pepper, very thinly sliced crosswise

1. Preheat the oven to 375°F. Spray a 9- to 10-inch round baking dish with cooking spray (preferably homemade, page xix).

2. Stir together the yogurt, sour cream, lime juice, salt, and cumin in a large bowl until well combined. Stir in the rice, pico de gallo, beans, poblanos, tortilla chips, scallions, and half the cheese. Transfer to a baking dish and press to form an even layer. Bake until fully heated, about 20 minutes.

3. Top with the remaining cheese and the jalapeño, and bake until the cheese is fully melted and the edges are golden brown, about 20 minutes. Let stand for about 10 minutes, spoon into bowls, and serve while warm.

FLEXITARIAN OPTION: Add 8 ounces cooked crumbled ground turkey (about 94% lean) to the yogurt. Season to taste and squirt with lime.

Per serving: 250 calories, 8g total fat, 4g saturated fat, 0g trans fat, 20mg cholesterol, 590mg sodium, 33g total carbohydrate, 5g dietary fiber, 6g sugars, 12g protein

Herb Couscous–Stuffed Beefsteaks Ⓕ

Makes 3 servings: 2 stuffed tomatoes each

These delicate yet decadent stuffed tomatoes are treasures, especially in summer or early fall.

6 large fully ripened beefsteak tomatoes
Juice of 1 small lemon (2 tablespoons)
2 tablespoons extra-virgin olive oil
1 large garlic clove, minced
½ teaspoon sea salt
¼ teaspoon ground black pepper
⅛ teaspoon dried hot pepper flakes
2 cups cooked unseasoned whole-wheat couscous, chilled
2 scallions, green and white parts, thinly sliced
¼ cup chopped fresh flat-leaf parsley
3½ ounces crumbled feta cheese
2 tablespoons chopped fresh mint

1. Slice ½ inch off each tomato top, dice the top, and reserve. Scoop out the tomato cores and seeds, dice the cores, and reserve. Cut a tiny sliver off the bottom of each hollowed-out tomato to help it stand, if necessary. Arrange the tomatoes in three individual baking dishes.

2. Preheat the oven to 425°F. Whisk together the lemon juice, oil, garlic, salt, pepper, and hot pepper flakes in a medium bowl. Stir in the couscous, reserved tomato, scallions, parsley, half of the cheese, and 1 tablespoon of the mint. Adjust seasoning.

3. Mound the mixture into the tomatoes. Sprinkle the tops with the remaining cheese.

4. Bake until the tomatoes are softened, about 30 minutes. Let stand for 10 minutes. Sprinkle with the remaining mint, and serve while warm.

FLEXITARIAN OPTION: Serve Garlic Grilled Shrimp (page 360) or other cooked shrimp on top.

Per serving: 360 calories, 17g total fat, 6g saturated fat, 0g trans fat, 30mg cholesterol, 790mg sodium, 42g total carbohydrate, 6g dietary fiber, 12g sugars, 12g protein

Shepherd's Pie with Smashed Blues

Makes 8 servings: ¼ pie each

A celebration of veggies, this colorful, British-inspired shepherd's pie calls for a fresh assortment of produce that's seasoned with rosemary and topped with creamy potatoes. You'll be delighted by how light it is. So light, in fact, that you can sink your fork into two servings if you like.

1 tablespoon + 2 teaspoons extra-virgin olive oil

1 medium white onion, finely chopped

2 teaspoons apple cider vinegar

¾ teaspoon sea salt, or to taste

2 large garlic cloves, minced

1 large beefsteak tomato, pulp removed and finely chopped

1 large red bell pepper, finely chopped

1 medium zucchini, finely chopped

1 cup finely chopped cremini (baby bella) mushrooms

1 cup fresh or frozen corn kernels, thawed

½ cup low-sodium vegetable broth or Vegetable Stock (page 203)

2 teaspoons chopped fresh rosemary or 1 tablespoon chopped fresh tarragon

2 tablespoons whole-wheat pastry flour

1 cup frozen lima beans, thawed, or drained canned butter beans

1 cup fresh or frozen peas, thawed

1 teaspoon naturally brewed soy sauce

½ teaspoon freshly ground black pepper, or to taste

3½ cups Fluffy Buttermilk Blues (page 462) or other mashed potatoes

⅓ cup finely shredded Irish Cheddar or sharp Cheddar cheese (optional)

1. Preheat the oven to 450°F.

2. Heat 1 tablespoon of the oil in a stockpot over medium heat. Add the onion, vinegar, and ¼ teaspoon of the salt and sauté until slightly softened, about 5 minutes. Add the garlic and sauté for 1 minute. Add the tomato and sauté for 1 minute.

3. Add the bell pepper, zucchini, mushrooms, corn, broth, rosemary, and remaining ½ teaspoon salt and bring to a boil over high heat. Reduce heat to medium-low and cook until vegetables are nearly tender, about 5 minutes. Sprinkle with the flour and stir until well mixed. Stir in the beans, peas, soy sauce, and pepper, and adjust seasoning.

4. Brush or rub two (8- or 9-inch) pie pans with the remaining 2 teaspoons oil. Add the vegetable stew mixture to each. Spread the mashed potatoes on top. Sprinkle with the cheese (if using).

5. Bake until the potatoes form a browned crust and the vegetable mixture is thickened, about 25 to 30 minutes. Let stand for 10 minutes. Garnish with additional rosemary, if desired, and serve.

FLEXITARIAN OPTION: Add 12 ounces ground turkey (about 94% lean), cooked, crumbled, and seasoned with salt, pepper, and rosemary, to taste, to 9-inch deep pie pans or 10-inch round baking pans before the vegetable stew mixture in step 4. Alternatively, add 6 ounces turkey mixture to just one of the pans.

Per serving: 160 calories, 4.5g total fat, 1g saturated fat, 0g trans fat, 5mg cholesterol, 540mg sodium, 27g total carbohydrate, 4g dietary fiber, 6g sugars, 5g protein

Pasta

Ziti with Tomato Tapenade and Arugula

Makes 4 servings: 2 cups each

You'll be keen on this ziti pasta dish of bold tastes and textures. The smoky and bright tapenade, fresh peppery greens, and sharp tangy cheese are delicious individually and out of this world altogether.

10 ounces whole-wheat or other whole-grain ziti or penne pasta

½ cup Sun-Dried Tomato Tapenade (page 122) or other tapenade

1 tablespoon extra-virgin olive oil

¼ teaspoon sea salt, or to taste

4 cups packed baby or wild arugula

½ cup freshly shaved aged Asiago or Parmesan cheese

1. Cook the pasta according to package directions. Drain the pasta, reserving 1 cup cooking liquid.

2. Return the pasta to the dry pot over medium heat, add the tapenade, oil, and salt, and stir until just combined. Add the reserved cooking liquid, and toss to coat, cooking for 1 minute. Adjust seasoning.

3. Transfer the pasta to a serving platter, toss with the arugula, top with the cheese, and serve immediately.

FLEXITARIAN OPTION: Toss thin slices of Tuscan-Style T-Bone (page 320) or other lean steak along with the arugula in step 3.

Per serving: 370 calories, 12g total fat, 3.5g saturated fat, 0g trans fat, 10mg cholesterol, 520mg sodium, 57g total carbohydrate, 7g dietary fiber, 5g sugars, 15g protein

Spicy Orecchiette with Baby Spinach

Makes 3 servings: 2 cups each

Speziato means "spicy" in Italian. That's a fitting word for this orecchiette pasta dish. You'll get the hit of heat but also all of the other intriguing layers of flavors. The slight bitterness of the spinach is the ideal counterpoint to the sweetness of the tomatoes—with the balsamic vinegar working its balancing act on both.

1 tablespoon extra-virgin olive oil

2 large garlic cloves, minced

½ teaspoon dried hot pepper flakes, or to taste

2 cups cherry tomatoes, thinly sliced

¼ cup sun-dried tomatoes (not oil-packed), thinly sliced (not rehydrated)

1 teaspoon white balsamic vinegar

½ teaspoon sea salt, or to taste

10 ounces whole-wheat or other whole-grain orecchiette pasta

5 cups packed fresh baby spinach

2 tablespoons freshly grated Pecorino Romano cheese (optional)

1. Heat the oil in a large skillet over medium heat. Add the garlic and hot pepper flakes and sauté for 1 minute. Add the cherry tomatoes, sun-dried tomatoes, vinegar, and salt, reduce heat to low, and simmer covered for 10 minutes.

2. Meanwhile, cook the pasta according to package directions. Drain.

3. Add the pasta to the skillet, increase heat to medium-high, and toss to coat. Add the spinach and stir until the spinach just wilts.

4. Transfer to individual bowls, top with the cheese (if using), and serve.

FLEXITARIAN OPTION: Add cooked, sliced Italian poultry sausage or cooked shrimp along with the spinach in step 3.

Per serving: 410 calories, 6g total fat, 1g saturated fat, 0g trans fat, 0mg cholesterol, 570mg sodium, 81g total carbohydrate, 11g dietary fiber, 6g sugars, 17g protein

Fusilli with Broccoli Raab and Cherries Ⓕ

Makes 4 servings: 2 cups each

This fusilli pasta dish is rich and filling and can be served as a complete meal. It has it all—bitter greens, sweet fruit, salty cheese, fragrant herbs, and toasty nuts.

10 ounces whole-wheat or other whole-grain fusilli pasta

1½ tablespoons extra-virgin olive oil

3 large garlic cloves, minced

½ cup low-sodium vegetable broth or Vegetable Stock (page 203)

Juice and zest of 1 lemon (3 tablespoons juice)

1 pound broccoli raab, stems trimmed and leaves chopped, (about 8 cups)

½ cup dried sweetened cherries or cranberries

½ teaspoon sea salt, or to taste

¼ teaspoon dried hot pepper flakes, or to taste

½ cup fresh grated Parmigiano-Reggiano or other Parmesan or Romano cheese

¼ cup thinly sliced fresh basil leaves

3 tablespoons pine nuts or chopped walnuts, toasted

1. Cook the pasta according to package directions. Drain.

2. Meanwhile, heat the oil in a large skillet over medium-high heat. Add the garlic and sauté for 30 seconds. Add the broth, lemon juice, broccoli raab, dried cherries, salt, and hot pepper flakes and sauté until the broccoli raab is crisp-tender, about 5 minutes.

3. Add the pasta to the skillet and toss to coat. Add the cheese and toss to coat. Adjust seasoning.

4. Transfer to a platter, sprinkle with the basil, pine nuts, and desired amount of the zest, and serve.

FLEXITARIAN OPTION: Add cooked sliced Italian poultry sausage of choice along with the broccoli raab in step 2.

Per serving: 450 calories, 14g total fat, 3g saturated fat, 0g trans fat, 10mg cholesterol, 490mg sodium, 70g total carbohydrate, 12g dietary fiber, 10g sugars, 18g protein

Gemelli Pasta with Squash and Herbs Ⓕ

Makes 4 servings: 1⅔ cups each

Clever pasta sauces can be created from any vegetable of your choosing. Winter squash yields a velvety, golden sauce that's rather rich-tasting and a lovely match tossed together with any short or squatty pasta shape. The finish of fresh basil and toasty pine nuts creates a special ending.

10 ounces whole-wheat or other whole-grain gemelli, radiatore, or rotini pasta

2⅔ cups Squash Pasta Sauce (page 104), warm or room temperature

¼ teaspoon sea salt, or to taste

¼ cup finely chopped fresh chives

3 tablespoons finely chopped fresh basil

¼ cup pine nuts or chopped walnuts, toasted

1. Cook the pasta according to package directions. Drain the pasta, reserving 1 cup cooking liquid.

2. Return the pasta to the dry pot over medium heat, add the pasta sauce, salt, and desired amount of the reserved cooking liquid, and toss to coat, cooking for 1 minute. Adjust seasoning.

3. Transfer the pasta to a serving platter, top with the chives, basil, and pine nuts, and serve.

FLEXITARIAN OPTION: Toss in mini turkey meatballs at the end of step 2.

Per serving: 390 calories, 11g total fat, 2g saturated fat, 0g trans fat, 5mg cholesterol, 660mg sodium, 66g total carbohydrate, 9g dietary fiber, 5g sugars, 13g protein

Artichoke Heart Spaghettini Ⓕ

Makes 2 servings: 2 cups each

Tangy artichoke heart salsa provides a refreshing and fragrant accessory for pasta. It provides so much fiber, too! No doubt that this skinny pasta will be fully satisfying.

5 ounces whole-wheat or other whole-grain spaghettini (thin spaghetti)

1½ cups Artichoke Heart "Salsa" (page 438), warm or at room temperature

¼ teaspoon sea salt, or to taste

3 tablespoons freshly shredded or shaved Parmigiano-Reggiano or other Parmesan cheese (optional)

2 tablespoons thinly sliced fresh basil leaves

2 lemon wedges

1. Cook the pasta according to package directions. Drain, reserving ½ cup cooking liquid.

2. Return the pasta to the dry pot over medium heat, add the salsa, reserved cooking liquid, and salt, and toss to coat, cooking for 1 minute. Adjust seasoning.

3. Transfer the pasta to a serving platter, sprinkle with the cheese (if using), and basil, and serve with the lemon wedges.

FLEXITARIAN OPTION: Toss finely chopped pieces of thinly sliced prosciutto into the pasta along with the artichoke hearts in step 2.

Per serving: 410 calories, 13g total fat, 1.5g saturated fat, 0g trans fat, 0mg cholesterol, 670mg sodium, 67g total carbohydrate, 17g dietary fiber, 3g sugars, 15g protein

Asian Angel Hair with "Confetti" Ⓕ

Makes 4 servings: 1½ cups (1 cup pasta and ½ cup vegetables) each

This is one of my go-to recipes—for myself and for guests. The full-on Asian sensation of sweet heat turns angel hair into a high-flavored entrée topped with a confetti of crisp veggies. The cilantro finishes it with fresh aromatic appeal.

8 ounces whole-wheat or other whole-grain angel hair or capellini pasta

3 tablespoons brown rice vinegar

1½ tablespoons naturally brewed soy sauce

1½ tablespoons honey or agave nectar

1 tablespoon freshly grated gingerroot

1 serrano pepper with seeds, minced

1 large garlic clove, minced

1½ tablespoons toasted sesame oil

3 scallions, green and white parts, thinly sliced

1 cup snow peas, ends trimmed, thinly sliced lengthwise

½ cup matchstick-size sliced purple or white cauliflower or jicama

¼ cup chopped fresh cilantro

1. Cook the pasta according to package directions.

2. Meanwhile, whisk together the vinegar, soy sauce, honey, ginger, serrano, and garlic in a liquid measuring cup or small bowl. Set aside.

3. Drain the pasta, add to a large bowl, drizzle with the oil, and toss till coated. Add the sauce mixture and scallions and toss again.

4. Just before serving, top with the snow peas, cauliflower, and cilantro. Serve warm, at room temperature, or chilled.

FLEXITARIAN OPTION: Top with thinly sliced 3-Ingredient Grilled Chicken Paillard (see page 310) before the snow peas in step 4.

Per serving: 300 calories, 6g total fat, 1g saturated fat, 0g trans fat, 0mg cholesterol, 350mg sodium, 55g total carbohydrate, 9g dietary fiber, 12g sugars, 10g protein

Spaghetti with Tomato and Basil Sauce Ⓕ

Makes 2 servings: 2 cups each

When I lived in an apartment my last year of college, I existed mainly on this, a simple dish called *spaghetti alla checca*. I'm still a fan of it. You can prepare the fresh sauce ahead of time and this will become a lovely meal for two in minutes. Or, if you're in more of a rush, a fully ripened diced tomato and minced garlic clove does the trick instead.

5 ounces whole-wheat or other whole-grain spaghetti

1½ cups Raw Diced Tomato Basil Sauce (page 100)

3 ounces part-skim mozzarella cheese, diced

⅛ teaspoon sea salt, or to taste

1 tablespoon thinly sliced fresh basil leaves, or to taste

1. Cook the pasta according to package directions. Drain the pasta, return to the pot, and toss with the sauce, cheese, and salt. Adjust seasoning.

2. Divide the pasta between two bowls, top with the basil, and serve warm or at room temperature.

FLEXITARIAN OPTION: Dice 14 Garlic Grilled Shrimp (page 360) or other cooked shrimp and toss along with the sauce in step 1.

Per serving: 400 calories, 12g total fat, 5g saturated fat, 0g trans fat, 25mg cholesterol, 570mg sodium, 58g total carbohydrate, 10g dietary fiber, 5g sugars, 22g protein

Penne alla Vodka Ⓕ

Makes 4 servings: about 1½ cups each

Serving pasta with a sauce that contains vodka always seems to make it taste richer. You'll find this penne dish with its lightly tipsy sauce to be tasty. The sprinkling of basil and pine nuts provides appetizing flair to complete the dish.

10 ounces whole-wheat or other whole-grain penne or cavatelli

1½ cups 80-Proof Vodka Sauce (page 103) or other pasta sauce

½ teaspoon sea salt, or to taste

3 tablespoons thinly sliced fresh basil leaves

1½ tablespoons pine nuts, toasted

1. Cook the pasta according to package directions. Drain the pasta, reserving ½ cup cooking liquid.

2. Return the pasta to the dry pot over medium heat, add the sauce, desired amount of the reserved cooking liquid (if any), salt, and half of the basil and toss to coat, cooking for 1 minute. Adjust seasoning.

3. Transfer the pasta to a serving platter, sprinkle with the pine nuts and the remaining basil, and serve.

FLEXITARIAN OPTION: Shred pieces of rotisserie chicken and toss with the pasta at the end of step 2.

Per serving: 320 calories, 6g total fat, 1.5g saturated fat, 0g trans fat, 5mg cholesterol, 480mg sodium, 57g total carbohydrate, 7g dietary fiber, 4g sugars, 12g protein

Makes 4 servings: 2 cups each

Pesto Bow-Tie Vegetable Primavera Ⓕ

Makes 4 servings: 1¾ cups each

Here's an elegant pesto pasta dish that celebrates white veggies. All you need to do is cook the vegetables together with the pasta. It's simple and scrumptious.

1½ teaspoons sea salt, or to taste

10 ounces whole-wheat veggie farfalle (bow-tie pasta) or other whole-grain pasta

12 medium white or green asparagus spears, stems removed and sliced crosswise into ¼-inch-thick coins

1 cup bite-size pieces cauliflower florets and tender stems

1 small white onion, quartered and thinly sliced

3 large garlic cloves, thinly sliced

½ cup Enlightened Fresh Basil Pesto (page 117) or other pesto

Zest of 1 small lemon (optional)

1. Bring at least 2 quarts of water to a boil in a large pot. Stir in 1 teaspoon of the salt and the pasta and return to a boil. Stir in the asparagus, cauliflower, onion, and garlic and gently cook until the pasta and vegetables are fully cooked, about 12 minutes. Drain well.

2. Pour the drained pasta and veggies into a large serving bowl. Add the pesto and the remaining ½ teaspoon salt and toss well to coat. Adjust seasoning. Sprinkle with the zest (if using), and serve while warm.

FLEXITARIAN OPTION: Slice Sea Salt and Pepper Scallops (page 361) or cooked shrimp and toss into the pasta along with the pesto in step 2.

Per serving: 330 calories, 7g total fat, 1g saturated fat, 0g trans fat, 0mg cholesterol, 690mg sodium, 60g total carbohydrate, 8g dietary fiber, 4g sugars, 14g protein

Farfalle with Bell Pepper Marinara and Goat Cheese Ⓕ

Makes 4 servings: 1¾ cups each

Try this fun pasta dish. Using farfalle pasta adds a glee factor because of its bow-tie shape. And using soft goat cheese adds joyous flavor.

10 ounces whole-wheat or other whole-grain
    farfalle (bowtie pasta) or cavatelli
2 cups Bell Pepper Marinara (page 102)
    or other marinara sauce
⅓ cup crumbled soft goat cheese or feta cheese
2 tablespoons thinly sliced fresh basil leaves
2 tablespoons pine nuts, toasted

1. Cook the pasta according to package directions. Drain the pasta, reserving ½ cup cooking liquid.

2. Return the pasta to the dry pot over medium heat, add the marinara sauce, and toss to coat, cooking for 1 minute. Add the reserved cooking liquid for thinner consistency, if desired. Adjust seasoning.

3. Transfer the pasta to a serving platter, sprinkle with the cheese, basil, and pine nuts, and serve.

FLEXITARIAN OPTION: Prepare Grilled Calamari over Balsamic Spinach (page 356). Slice calamari into rings and toss with the pasta in step 2. If desired, add the spinach to the dish.

Per serving: 350 calories, 7g total fat, 2g saturated fat, 0g trans fat, 5mg cholesterol, 290mg sodium, 60g total carbohydrate, 8g dietary fiber, 6g sugars, 15g protein

Luscious Lemony Linguine Ⓕ

Makes 4 servings: 1½ cups each

The light lemony taste of this creamy, refreshing pasta provides a lovely contrast to the tangy cheese. The accent of fresh parsley is the ideal finishing pairing, all coming together in one simply unforgettable dish.

10 ounces whole-wheat or other whole-grain
    linguine
2 scallions, green and white parts, minced
2 teaspoons unsalted butter
½ teaspoon sea salt, or to taste
¼ teaspoon freshly ground black or white pepper,
    or to taste
1 cup Lemony Pasta Cream Sauce (page 99)
3 tablespoons freshly grated Parmigiano-Reggiano
    or other Parmesan cheese
⅓ cup chopped fresh flat-leaf parsley

1. Cook the pasta according to package directions. Drain.

2. Return the pasta to the dry pot over medium-high heat and toss with the scallions, butter, salt, and pepper until coated. Stir in the sauce, and toss to coat, cooking for 1 minute. Adjust seasoning.

3. Pour the pasta into a serving bowl. Sprinkle with the cheese and parsley and serve.

FLEXITARIAN OPTION: Toss Sea Salt and Pepper Scallops (page 361) or cooked shrimp along with the lemon cream sauce in step 2.

Per serving: 360 calories, 10g total fat, 6g saturated fat, 0g trans fat, 30mg cholesterol, 510mg sodium, 57g total carbohydrate, 10g dietary fiber, 2g sugars, 14g protein

Lemony-Thyme Mushroom Tagliatelle Ⓕ

Makes 4 servings: 1½ cups each

A blend of earthy mushrooms and the lemony thyme sauce in this pasta recipe will captivate your taste buds. Try it with a unique mixture of mushrooms, such as woodsy maitake, delicate oyster, and nutty beech mushrooms, to provide a spectrum of savory flavors.

10 ounces whole-wheat or other whole-grain tagliatelle or fettuccine

1 tablespoon extra-virgin olive oil

2 large shallots, minced

1½ cups thinly sliced mixed fresh mushrooms

2 large garlic cloves, minced

¾ teaspoon sea salt, or to taste

1 cup Zesty Lemon-Thyme Pasta Sauce (page 100)

2 tablespoons grated Parmigiano-Reggiano or other Parmesan cheese

½ teaspoon fresh thyme leaves

1. Cook the pasta according to package directions.

2. Meanwhile, heat the oil in a large pot or skillet over medium heat. Add the shallots and sauté until fully softened, about 4 minutes. Add the mushrooms and sauté for 1 minute. Add the garlic and ¼ teaspoon of the salt and sauté until fragrant, about 1 minute. Set aside.

3. Drain the pasta and add it with the sauce and the remaining ½ teaspoon salt to the mushroom mixture. Place over medium-high heat and toss until heated and well combined, about 30 seconds. Adjust seasoning.

4. Pour onto a platter or into four bowls, top with cheese and thyme, and serve.

FLEXITARIAN OPTION: Serve Broiled Sardines Oregano (page 79) on each portion. Or toss with small cubes of roasted chicken.

Per serving: 390 calories, 12g total fat, 5g saturated fat, 0g trans fat, 25mg cholesterol, 630mg sodium, 62g total carbohydrate, 10g dietary fiber, 4g sugars, 14g protein

Veggie Fettuccine "Alfredo" with Garlic Chips Ⓕ

Makes 4 servings: 1⅔ cups each

Here's one way to enjoy Alfredo-style fettuccine that's not considered unhealthful. What's more, the summery mix of veggies along with the cara-melized garlic creates punch, taking plain pasta to savory meal-in-a-bowl perfection.

1 tablespoon unsalted butter

3 large garlic cloves, very thinly sliced

10 ounces whole-wheat or other whole-grain fettuccine or linguine

1 large zucchini, halved lengthwise and thinly sliced crosswise

1 large yellow squash, halved lengthwise and thinly sliced crosswise

½ teaspoon sea salt, or to taste

¼ teaspoon freshly ground black or white pepper, or to taste

½ cup fresh or frozen peas, thawed

1 cup "Alfredo" Sauce (page 99) or other pasta sauce

1. Melt 1 teaspoon of the butter in a large skillet over medium heat. Add the garlic and sauté until lightly caramelized, about 3½ minutes. Remove to a small plate using a slotted spoon. Set aside.

2. Cook the pasta according to package directions in a large pot. Drain the pasta, reserving 1 cup cooking liquid. Return the pasta to the dry pot, toss with 1 teaspoon of the butter, and set aside.

3. Melt the remaining 1 teaspoon butter in the skil-let, add the zucchini, yellow squash, ¼ teaspoon of the salt, and the pepper, cover, and cook until nearly al dente, about 4 minutes, stirring once. Uncover, stir in the peas, and sauté for 1 minute. Add the pasta, pasta sauce, and the remaining ¼ teaspoon salt and toss to coat, cooking for 1 minute. Toss with desired amount of reserved cooking liquid, if necessary. Adjust seasoning.

4. Serve immediately topped with the garlic chips.

FLEXITARIAN OPTION: Sauté ⅓ cup of finely diced pancetta over medium heat until crisped. Remove to a paper towel to drain. Use the pancetta drippings in place of the butter in step 3. Garnish the pasta with the cooked pancetta.

Per serving: 410 calories, 12g total fat, 7g saturated fat, 0g trans fat, 35mg cholesterol, 490mg sodium, 65g total carbohydrate, 13g dietary fiber, 7g sugars, 16g protein

Asparagus Radiatore Alfredo Ⓕ

Makes 4 servings: 1½ cups each

Sometimes you just have to have something rich. To achieve a balance of richness and nutrition, incorporate a generous amount of veggies into indulgent dishes like this perfectly dressed Alfredo. For extra interest, it's made with quinoa radiatore pasta—though the shape is sometimes referred to as pagoda. Savor it slowly.

10 ounces quinoa radiatore or other whole-grain pasta

1 pound asparagus spears, stems trimmed and cut into 4 pieces each

1½ teaspoons sea salt, or to taste

⅔ cup heavy cream

¼ cup unsalted butter

1 large garlic clove, minced

½ teaspoon freshly ground black pepper, or to taste

⅛ teaspoon ground cayenne, or to taste

⅛ teaspoon freshly grated nutmeg, or to taste

⅓ cup grated Parmigiano-Reggiano or other Parmesan cheese

1 teaspoon grated lemon zest

1. Add 2 quarts of water to a large pot and bring to a boil over high heat. Stir in the pasta, asparagus, and 1 teaspoon of the salt, bring back to a boil, and cook according to pasta package directions, or until pasta is al dente and asparagus is cooked through. Drain.

2. Meanwhile, add the cream, butter, and garlic to a large pot or skillet and bring to a simmer over medium-low heat. Reduce heat to low and stir in the pepper, cayenne, nutmeg, and remaining ½ teaspoon salt.

3. Stir the cheese and drained pasta and asparagus into the sauce. Toss until the pasta is fully coated. Adjust seasoning.

4. Transfer to a platter or individual bowls, sprinkle with the zest, and serve.

FLEXITARIAN OPTION: Drain a can of sardines and break apart with a fork. Stir into the cream sauce at the end of step 2 before adding salt. Adjust seasoning.

Per serving: 420 calories, 19g total fat, 10g saturated fat, 0g trans fat, 60mg cholesterol, 710mg sodium, 54g total carbohydrate, 8g dietary fiber, 6g sugars, 15g protein

Creamy Santa Fe Pappardelle Ⓕ

Makes 4 servings: 2 cups each

This velvety, intriguing meal-in-one pasta dish is uniquely wonderful! The sauce is super creamy—mostly from beans. Then, the heat from the jalapeno seeds pairs with the tang of the fresh lime juice to create fascinating flavor.

10 ounces dry whole-wheat spinach pappardelle or other whole-grain spinach pasta

2 teaspoons unsalted butter

1½ tablespoons extra-virgin olive oil

1 medium red onion, halved, thinly sliced

1 lime, ½ juiced, ½ cut into 4 wedges

½ teaspoon sea salt, or to taste

2 large garlic cloves, minced

1 small jalapeño pepper with seeds, minced

2 medium red or orange bell peppers, or a mixture of both, thinly sliced

1 recipe Creamy Lime Santa Fe Sauce (page 100), warm or at room temperature

¼ cup chopped fresh cilantro

1. Cook the pasta according to package directions. Drain the pasta, reserving 1 cup cooking liquid.

continues on next page

2. Meanwhile, melt the butter with the oil in a large, deep skillet over medium heat. Add the onion, lime juice, and ¼ teaspoon of the salt and cook while stirring for 3 minutes; add the garlic and jalapeño and cook while stirring for 3 minutes; add the bell peppers and cook while stirring for 3 minutes.

3. Add the cooked pasta and the remaining ¼ teaspoon salt and toss to coat. Add the sauce and cilantro, toss to combine, and continue to cook for 1 minute. Toss with the desired amount of reserved cooking liquid, if necessary. Adjust seasoning.

4. Transfer the pasta to a serving bowl or individual bowls and serve with the lime wedges.

FLEXITARIAN OPTION: Add sliced Zesty Lime Grilled Chicken (page 309) along with the cooked pasta in step 3.

Per serving: 440 calories, 16g total fat, 7g saturated fat, 0g trans fat, 30mg cholesterol, 470mg sodium, 67g total carbohydrate, 12g dietary fiber, 7g sugars, 13g protein

Capellini Tahini Ⓕ

Makes 4 servings: 2 cups each

Tahini is the rich, creamy sesame seed sauce that is often stirred into hummus. It's as satisfying as creamy peanut butter and so easy to incorporate into many dishes. As a hummus and tahini enthusiast, here I highlight their attributes in this unique capellini dish.

10 ounces whole-wheat or other whole-grain capellini

1 tablespoon extra-virgin olive oil

1⅓ cups grape tomatoes

2 large garlic cloves, thinly sliced

½ teaspoon + ⅛ teaspoon sea salt, or to taste

1 cup Tahini Chickpea Hummus (page 87) or other hummus

2 tablespoons chopped fresh flat-leaf parsley

2 tablespoons finely diced red onion

1½ tablespoons pine nuts, toasted

1 lemon, cut into 4 wedges (optional)

1. Cook the pasta according to package directions. Drain the pasta, reserving 1 cup cooking liquid.

2. Meanwhile, heat the oil in a small skillet over medium heat. Add the tomatoes and sauté until the tomatoes start to blister, about 3 minutes. Add the garlic and ⅛ teaspoon of the salt and sauté until fragrant, about 1 minute. Set aside.

3. Return the pasta to the dry pot over medium heat, add the hummus, desired amount of reserved cooking liquid, and the remaining ½ teaspoon salt and toss to coat, cooking for 1 minute. Adjust seasoning.

4. Transfer the pasta to a serving platter, top with the tomato mixture, the parsley, onion, and pine nuts, and serve immediately. Serve with lemon wedges on the side (if using).

FLEXITARIAN OPTION: Top the pasta with a grilled cumin-rubbed wild yellowfin tuna steak, then top with the tomato mixture.

Per serving: 430 calories, 12g total fat, 1.5g saturated fat, 0g trans fat, 0mg cholesterol, 560mg sodium, 70g total carbohydrate, 12g dietary fiber, 5g sugars, 17g protein

Mac and Cheese Ramekins

Makes 8 servings: 1 ramekin each (¾ cup)

High-flavor cheeses blended with the golden potato creates the effect of extra cheesiness of this comforting classic. The cremini mushrooms add flavor and body with few calories. Serving it in a ramekin allows you to enjoy a proper portion. With the hit of truffle oil you will feel decadent, but leave it out if you like. Savor all of its comfort as an entrée along with a generous side of leafy greens.

2 cups plain almond milk or light soy milk

1 large baked Yukon Gold potato, diced

1½ teaspoons sea salt, or to taste

8 ounces whole-wheat elbow macaroni

1½ cups sliced cremini (baby bella) mushrooms

1 tablespoon unsalted butter

3 scallions, green and white parts, minced

1½ teaspoons white truffle oil

¾ teaspoon freshly ground black or white pepper, or to taste

⅛ teaspoon freshly grated nutmeg

5 ounces crumbled soft goat cheese

¾ cup shredded extra-sharp Cheddar cheese

⅔ cup shredded provolone or Gruyère cheese

3 tablespoons whole-wheat panko breadcrumbs

1. Add the almond milk and potato to a blender. Cover and blend until smooth. Set aside.

2. Bring 4 cups water and 1 teaspoon of the salt to a boil in a large pot. Stir in the macaroni and mushrooms and gently cook until the pasta is just al dente, about 1 minute less than package directions. Drain well.

3. Preheat the oven to 450°F.

4. Meanwhile, melt the butter in a medium saucepan. Add the scallions and sauté for 1 minute. Add the potato mixture, the oil, remaining ½ teaspoon salt, the pepper, and nutmeg while stirring constantly. Bring to a simmer, stir in the cheeses until melted, about 1 minute.

5. Stir the cooked macaroni mixture into the cheese mixture. Adjust seasoning. Place eight (6-ounce) ramekins on a baking tray and spoon the macaroni and cheese into each. Sprinkle with the panko. Bake until the top is golden brown, about 10 to 12 minutes, rotating the tray halfway through the baking process.

6. Remove from oven, let stand for 5 minutes, and serve.

FLEXITARIAN OPTION: Stir 1 cup cooked lobster meat into the macaroni mixture in step 5 before spooning into the ramekins.

Per serving: 300 calories, 13g total fat, 8g saturated fat, 0g trans fat, 30mg cholesterol, 550mg sodium, 33g total carbohydrate, 3g dietary fiber, 3g sugars, 14g protein

Greek Sticky Orzo Ⓕ

Makes 3 servings: 1 cup each

If you love risotto but are impatient during the preparation process, this versatile orzo dish with its straightforward cooking style will win you over. It's a lemony, creamy, risotto-like main dish that can be served warm or cool. It's stunning to look at and scrumptious to eat.

2 tablespoons fresh lemon juice, or to taste

2 tablespoons fat-free or low-fat plain Greek yogurt

4 teaspoons extra-virgin olive oil

1 garlic clove, minced

½ teaspoon sea salt, or to taste

½ teaspoon freshly ground black pepper, or to taste

1 cup dry whole-wheat or other whole-grain orzo

⅓ cup finely crumbled feta cheese

1 cup thinly sliced cherry tomatoes

¼ cup chopped fresh flat-leaf parsley

3 tablespoons finely chopped fresh mint
    + 3 sprigs fresh mint

½ teaspoon finely chopped fresh oregano or dill

3 tablespoons pine nuts, toasted

1. Whisk together the lemon juice, yogurt, oil, garlic, salt, and pepper in a medium bowl until smooth. Set aside.

2. Cook the orzo until softened, about 1 minute longer than indicated on package directions. Drain the orzo and immediately stir into the lemon-yogurt mixture along with the cheese until well combined and creamy. (It's okay if the cheese doesn't fully melt.) Stir in the tomatoes, parsley, chopped mint, the oregano, and half of the pine nuts. Adjust seasoning.

3. While still warm, firmly pack the orzo into a 1-cup dry measure, then invert to plate to serve; repeat twice. Garnish with the remaining pine nuts and mint sprigs and serve warm or cool.

FLEXITARIAN OPTION: Serve Santorini Chicken Breast Skewers (page 308) atop the orzo mounds.

Per serving: 350 calories, 16g total fat, 4g saturated fat, 0g trans fat, 15mg cholesterol, 590mg sodium, 44g total carbohydrate, 5g dietary fiber, 4g sugars, 13g protein

Baked Penne with Greens Ⓕ

Makes 10 servings: 1 (2½- × 4½-inch) portion each

Hooray! A luscious layered pasta dish that's good for you. Preparing it with the penne rigate and frozen greens makes it easy. Integrating the cauliflower florets makes it seem extra cheesy.

10 ounces frozen chopped spinach or other leafy greens, thawed

16 ounces whole-wheat or other whole-grain penne rigate

1 teaspoon extra-virgin olive oil

1 large egg

1½ cups finely chopped cauliflower florets and tender stems

24 ounces part-skim ricotta cheese

2 cups shredded part-skim mozzarella cheese

⅓ cup finely chopped fresh basil

Juice of 1 small lemon (2 tablespoons)

1 teaspoon chopped fresh oregano

¾ teaspoon sea salt, or to taste

½ teaspoon freshly ground black pepper, or to taste

¼ teaspoon freshly grated nutmeg (optional)

4 cups Triple Tomato Marinara Sauce (page 101) or other tomato-based pasta sauce

1. Squeeze the spinach of excess liquid through a fine-mesh strainer. Set aside.

2. Preheat the oven to 350°F.

3. Cook the pasta 2 minutes less than suggested on package directions. Drain the pasta and toss with the oil in the dry pan. Set aside.

4. Meanwhile, whisk the egg in a large bowl. Add the cauliflower, ricotta, 1 cup of the mozzarella, the drained spinach, ¼ cup of the basil, the lemon juice, oregano, salt, pepper, and nutmeg (if using).

5. Spread one-third of the sauce in a 9 × 13-inch baking dish. Then layer as follows: half of the pasta, half of the spinach mixture, one-third of the sauce, half of the pasta, half of the spinach mixture, and one-third of the sauce. Sprinkle with the remaining 1 cup mozzarella.

6. Bake until the layers are fully cooked and cheese is fully browned, about 1 hour 10 minutes. Remove from oven and let stand for 10 minutes to complete the cooking process.

7. Cut into 10 rectangular portions, sprinkle with the remaining basil, and serve.

FLEXITARIAN OPTION: Sprinkle with cooked crumbled or thinly sliced sweet or spicy Italian poultry sausage.

Per serving: 330 calories, 9g total fat, 4.5g saturated fat, 0g trans fat, 40mg cholesterol, 620mg sodium, 43g total carbohydrate, 6g dietary fiber, 5g sugars, 19g protein

Roasted Vegetable Rigatoni Ⓕ

Makes 8 servings: 1 (3¼-inch × 4½-inch) portion each

What better way to get your vegetables than to have them roasted to full-flavored glory in a pasta dish laced with Italian cheeses? Try this lasagna-style rigatoni recipe and taste for yourself how rich and delicious eating healthfully can be.

1 tablespoon extra-virgin olive oil

1 medium red onion, diced

1½ cups finely diced broccoli florets and tender stems

1½ cups finely diced cauliflower florets and tender stems

2 teaspoons white balsamic vinegar

¾ teaspoon sea salt, or to taste

2 large garlic cloves, minced

⅛ teaspoon freshly grated nutmeg

1 pound whole-wheat or other whole-grain rigatoni

3 cups Triple Tomato Marinara Sauce (page 101) or other marinara sauce

⅔ cup freshly grated Parmigiano-Reggiano or other Parmesan cheese

8 ounces fresh mozzarella, diced

1. Preheat the oven to 375°F.

2. Heat the oil in a large skillet over medium heat. Add the onion, broccoli, cauliflower, vinegar, and ¼ teaspoon of the salt and sauté for 2 minutes. Increase heat to medium-high and sauté until the onion is fully softened, about 8 minutes. Add the garlic, nutmeg, and remaining ½ teaspoon salt and sauté for 1 minute. Set aside.

3. Meanwhile, cook the pasta according to package directions. Drain.

4. Layer the ingredients in a 9 × 13-inch baking dish as follows: half each of the sauce, pasta, vegetable mixture, and cheeses; then the remaining half each of the pasta, sauce, vegetable mixture, and cheeses.

5. Bake until golden brown, about 25 minutes. Let stand for 10 minutes, and serve.

FLEXITARIAN OPTION: Slice each meatball from Bodacious Turkey and Fennel Meatballs (page 317) in half. Firmly position each, rounded side up, on top of the baked rigatoni immediately after removing from the oven in step 5.

Per serving: 370 calories, 12g total fat, 6g saturated fat, 0g trans fat, 30mg cholesterol, 590mg sodium, 50g total carbohydrate, 7g dietary fiber, 5g sugars, 18g protein

Greens and Ricotta Cannelloni

Makes 8 servings: 1 cannelloni each

Cannelloni refers to tube-shaped pasta that's stuffed and baked in a sauce. To make cannelloni here, you'll fill softened lasagna noodles with a luscious cheese and leafy green mixture, then roll up and bake in marinara. Some of the filling may ooze out of the stuffed pasta, making it even more tempting.

2 cups packed fresh baby spinach, pan-wilted or steamed, drained, and finely chopped

2 cups packed fresh torn Swiss chard leaves, pan-wilted or steamed, drained, and finely chopped

2 cups part-skim ricotta cheese

½ cup freshly grated Parmigiano-Reggiano or other Parmesan cheese

¼ cup + 2 tablespoons finely chopped or thinly sliced fresh basil leaves

1 teaspoon grated lemon zest

½ teaspoon sea salt, or to taste

½ teaspoon freshly ground black pepper, or to taste

8 whole-wheat or other whole-grain lasagna noodles

2½ cups Triple Tomato Marinara Sauce (page 101) or other marinara sauce

1. Stir together the spinach, chard, ricotta, ¼ cup of the Parmesan, ¼ cup of the basil, the zest, salt, and pepper in a medium bowl. Set aside.

2. Preheat the oven to 375°F.

3. Boil lasagna according to package directions. Drain.

4. Lay out each sheet on a cutting board. Place about ⅓ cup of the filling in the center of each lasagna noodle and roll into a cylinder.

5. Spread 1 cup of the sauce in a 9 × 13-inch or 2-quart baking dish, place the cannelloni on top of the sauce, spread with remaining sauce, and sprinkle with the remaining Parmesan.

6. Bake until cooked through and bubbling, about 30 minutes. Let stand for 10 minutes, sprinkle with the remaining 2 tablespoons basil, and serve.

FLEXITARIAN OPTION: Skewer Pan-Seared Sea Scallops (page 362) atop cannelloni after letting the cannelloni stand for 10 minutes in step 6.

Per serving: 210 calories, 8g total fat, 4g saturated fat, 0g trans fat, 25mg cholesterol, 520mg sodium, 21g total carbohydrate, 4g dietary fiber, 3g sugars, 13g protein

3-Cheese Lasagna with Fresh Basil

Makes 12 servings: 1 (3- × 3¼-inch) portion each

By mixing three cheeses together, you'll be creating a luscious flavor combination that you can't get from just one. The addition of cauliflower boosts its creaminess. Couple this with the layering of a vibrant tomato taste and the result is full-flavored, cheesy satisfaction in every forkful of this comforting Italian delight.

8 ounces whole-wheat or other whole-grain lasagna noodles

1 large egg

2 cups finely chopped cauliflower florets and tender stems

24 ounces part-skim ricotta cheese

1½ cups shredded part-skim mozzarella cheese

4 ounces crumbled soft goat cheese

⅓ cup finely chopped fresh basil + 12 sprigs fresh basil

Juice of ½ lemon (1½ tablespoons)

1 teaspoon chopped fresh oregano

¾ teaspoon sea salt, or to taste

½ teaspoon freshly ground black pepper, or to taste

3 cups Triple Tomato Marinara Sauce (page 101) or other tomato-based pasta sauce

1 cup thinly sliced cherry tomatoes

¼ teaspoon dried hot pepper flakes, or to taste

1. Fill a large bowl with hot water. Add the noodles and allow them to sit in the water for 20 minutes. Drain.

2. Preheat the oven to 350°F.

3. Whisk the egg in a large bowl. Add the cauliflower, ricotta, ½ cup of the mozzarella, the goat cheese, chopped basil, lemon juice, oregano, salt, and pepper and stir until well combined.

4. Stir together the marinara sauce and tomatoes in a medium bowl.

5. Spread one-third of the sauce mixture in a 9 × 13-inch glass baking dish. Then layer as follows: half of the noodles, half of the cauliflower mixture, one-third of the sauce mixture, half of the noodles, half of the cauliflower mixture, and one-third of the sauce mixture. Sprinkle with the remaining 1 cup mozzarella and the hot pepper flakes.

6. Bake until the lasagna is fully cooked and cheese is fully browned, about 1 hour 15 minutes. Remove from oven and let stand for 10 minutes to complete the cooking process.

7. Cut into 12 squares. Garnish with the fresh basil sprigs, and serve.

FLEXITARIAN OPTION: In step 5, divide 10 ounces cooked, crumbled, seasoned ground chicken or lean beef between the cauliflower and sauce layers.

Per serving: 250 calories, 10g total fat, 6g saturated fat, 0g trans fat, 45mg cholesterol, 510mg sodium, 21g total carbohydrate, 4g dietary fiber, 4g sugars, 17g protein

Noodles and Risotto

Gingery Thai Udon Noodles Ⓕ

Makes 1 serving: 2 cups

Treat yourself to this refreshing noodle dish with tasty Thai appeal. It's designed for one—but can easily be doubled or tripled.

2½ ounces brown rice or other whole-grain udon noodles

1 serving Thai Sesame Summer Squash (page 265), sliced into thin diagonal strips

½ teaspoon naturally brewed soy sauce, or to taste

2 teaspoons thinly sliced or chopped fresh basil leaves

2 teaspoons sliced natural almonds, toasted

1. Cook the noodles according to package directions. Drain (do not rinse) the noodles and transfer to a serving bowl.

2. Immediately toss the warm noodles with the squash and soy sauce. Sprinkle with the basil and almonds, and serve. Enjoy warm or at room temperature.

FLEXITARIAN OPTION: Top with Thai-Inspired Chicken Satay (page 58) or toss with cubes of rotisserie chicken.

Per serving: 410 calories, 12g total fat, 1g saturated fat, 0g trans fat, 0mg cholesterol, 730mg sodium, 63g total carbohydrate, 7g dietary fiber, 9g sugars, 17g protein

Smoky Butternut Noodles with Pistachios Ⓕ

Makes 4 servings: 1½ cups each

The smoky tofu, sweet butternut squash, fragrant basil, and perky roasted pistachios combine to create a savory, showstopping noodle dish.

1 cup low-sodium vegetable broth or Vegetable Stock (page 203)

1½ tablespoons naturally brewed soy sauce, or to taste

1 tablespoon no-salt-added creamy pistachio or almond butter

⅛ teaspoon dried hot pepper flakes, or to taste

2 teaspoons grapeseed or peanut oil

1 large white onion, sliced

2 teaspoons apple cider vinegar

¼ teaspoon sea salt, or to taste

2½ cups diced peeled butternut squash

1 cup diced ready-to-eat smoked tofu

8 ounces buckwheat soba noodles

¼ cup thinly sliced fresh basil leaves

3 tablespoons unsalted dry-roasted pistachios

1. Whisk together the broth, soy sauce, pistachio butter, and hot pepper flakes in a liquid measuring cup or small bowl. Set aside.

2. Heat the oil in a large, deep skillet over medium-high heat. Add the onion, vinegar, and salt and sauté until softened and lightly caramelized, about 5 minutes. Stir in the squash, cover, and cook until the squash is nearly tender, about 5 minutes. Stir in the broth mixture and tofu. Reduce heat to low, cover, and simmer until broth is slightly thickened, about 8 minutes. Remove from heat.

3. Meanwhile, cook the noodles about 1 minute less than indicated on package directions. Drain (do not rinse).

4. Add the noodles to the squash mixture along with 3 tablespoons of the basil, toss, and adjust seasoning.

5. Transfer to a serving bowl, sprinkle with the pistachios and the remaining basil, and serve while warm.

FLEXITARIAN OPTION: Try cubes of smoked turkey instead of the smoked tofu.

Per serving: 380 calories, 9g total fat, 1g saturated fat, 0g trans fat, 0mg cholesterol, 620mg sodium, 61g total carbohydrate, 8g dietary fiber, 8g sugars, 15g protein

Soba with Greens and Nectarine Ⓕ

Makes 4 servings: 1½ cups each

This intriguing dish is a summer special—featuring Asian noodles with greens and juicy, fragrant nectarine. It's a refreshing dish flourishing with citrusy appeal, along with a lovely contrast of toasty nuts and tangy cheese.

2 teaspoons extra-virgin olive oil

2 large garlic cloves, minced

¾ cup low-sodium vegetable broth
   or Vegetable Stock (page 203)

Juice of 1 lemon (3 tablespoons)

6 cups thinly sliced Swiss chard leaves

1 medium ripe nectarine, pitted and finely diced,
   or ¾ cup finely diced mango

½ teaspoon sea salt, or to taste

¼ teaspoon dried hot pepper flakes, or to taste

10 ounces buckwheat or other whole-grain
   soba noodles

¼ cup crumbled soft goat cheese

3 tablespoons pine nuts or chopped walnuts,
   toasted

1. Heat the oil in a large skillet over medium-high heat. Add the garlic and sauté for 30 seconds. Add the broth, lemon juice, chard, nectarine, salt, and hot pepper flakes and sauté until the chard is tender, about 5 minutes.

2. Meanwhile, cook the noodles about 1 minute less than indicated on package directions. Drain (do not rinse) the noodles.

3. Add the noodles to the skillet and toss to coat. Adjust seasoning.

4. Transfer to a platter, sprinkle with the cheese and pine nuts, and serve.

FLEXITARIAN OPTION: Toss Garlic Grilled Shrimp (page 360) or other cooked shrimp into the skillet along with the noodles in step 3.

Per serving: 370 calories, 10g total fat, 2g saturated fat, 0g trans fat, 5mg cholesterol, 450mg sodium, 62g total carbohydrate, 6g dietary fiber, 7g sugars, 12g protein

Seasonal Veggie Chow Fun

Makes 4 servings: 1 rounded cup each

This fresher veggie version of the popular noodle dish, Chow Fun, might take longer than one minute to order up, but I promise that you'll enjoy every minute that you get to savor it. Make it extra fresh and nutrient rich with just-picked seasonal veggies from the farmers' market.

½ cup low-sodium vegetable broth or Vegetable
   Stock (page 203)

2 tablespoons naturally brewed soy sauce,
   or to taste

1 teaspoon honey or agave nectar

8 ounces flat short and wide brown rice noodles

2 tablespoons peanut or canola oil

2 large garlic cloves, minced

1½ teaspoons freshly grated gingerroot

2 cups chopped vegetables of choice, such as
   cauliflower, broccoli, or bell pepper

1 cup mung bean sprouts, shredded cabbage,
   or coleslaw mix

¾ cup thinly sliced portabella or fresh shiitake
   mushroom caps

4 scallions, green and white parts, thinly sliced
   on the diagonal

1 small celery stalk, very thinly sliced on the
   diagonal

1. Whisk together the broth, soy sauce, and honey in a liquid measuring cup or small bowl. Set aside.

2. Prepare the noodles according to package directions. Drain the noodles and transfer to a medium serving bowl.

3. Heat 1 tablespoon of the oil in a wok or large skillet over high heat. Add the cooked noodles and stir-fry for 1 minute. Add half the soy sauce mixture and stir to evenly coat noodles. Transfer the noodles back to the serving bowl.

4. Replace the wok over high heat and add the remaining 1 tablespoon oil. Add the garlic and ginger and stir-fry for 30 seconds. Add the vegetables, sprouts, mushrooms, scallions, and celery and stir-fry until the vegetables are crisp-tender, about 2 to 2 ½ minutes.

5. Return the noodles to the wok along with the remaining soy sauce mixture and toss to coat while cooking until fully heated and combined, about 1 minute. Adjust seasoning.

6. Transfer to the serving bowl. Serve while hot with additional soy sauce on the side, if desired.

FLEXITARIAN OPTION: Cut Teriyaki New York Strip Steak (page 320) into thin, short pieces. Add to the pan along with the noodles in step 5.

Per serving: 300 calories, 7g total fat, 1g saturated fat, 0g trans fat, 0mg cholesterol, 500mg sodium, 57g total carbohydrate, 3g dietary fiber, 4g sugars, 4g protein

Farmers' Market Shirataki Ⓕ

Makes 2 servings: 2 cups each

Tofu shirataki noodles are super low in calories—just 20 calories for a 4-ounce serving! You can find them in most grocery stores, in the refrigerated product section with other fresh Asian-style noodles. Here they're transformed into a generous 2-cup Italian-style savory eat for under 250 calories. Now that's a treat.

2 teaspoons extra-virgin olive oil

1 small or ½ large red onion, diced

2 teaspoons white balsamic vinegar

¼ teaspoon + ⅛ teaspoon sea salt, or to taste

1½ cups diced or sliced mixed seasonal vegetables of choice, such as zucchini, yellow squash, or bell peppers

1 cup cherry tomatoes, quartered

1 large garlic clove, minced

2 teaspoons drained capers

1 (8-ounce) package shirataki tofu noodles

¼ cup thinly sliced fresh basil leaves

2 ounces part-skim mozzarella cheese, diced

1½ tablespoons pine nuts, toasted

1. Heat the oil in a large skillet over medium heat. Add the onion, vinegar, and ⅛ teaspoon of the salt and sauté until fully softened, about 8 minutes. Add the vegetables, cover, and cook until nearly tender, about 6 minutes. Add the tomatoes, garlic, capers, and remaining ¼ teaspoon salt and sauté until the tomato becomes fully softened, about 5 minutes.

2. Meanwhile, rinse and prepare the shirataki noodles according to package directions and drain. Add the hot noodles and half of the basil to the skillet and toss until well combined. Adjust seasoning.

3. Transfer a serving bowl, sprinkle with the cheese, pine nuts, and remaining basil, and serve.

FLEXITARIAN OPTION: Finely dice a grilled chicken breast, toss with 1 minced garlic clove, then toss into the tomato mixture at the end of step 1.

Per serving: 230 calories, 15g total fat, 4g saturated fat, 0g trans fat, 20mg cholesterol, 720mg sodium, 15g total carbohydrate, 5g dietary fiber, 6g sugars, 12g protein

Rosemary Squash Risotto Ⓕ

Makes 5 servings: 1 cup each

Use short-grain brown rice for an excellent and easy nontraditional risotto dish. Extra tang and creaminess is created here with Greek yogurt. The trio of butternut squash, rosemary, and Gorgonzola lends unforgettable flavor when paired with the nutty rice.

3½ cups low-sodium vegetable broth or Vegetable Stock (page 203)

1½ cups short-grain brown rice or brown Arborio rice

1 teaspoon sea salt, or to taste

2 teaspoons unsalted butter

2 teaspoons extra-virgin olive oil

1 medium white onion, finely diced

1½ cups cubed peeled butternut squash

2 teaspoons apple cider vinegar

1 teaspoon finely chopped fresh rosemary or sage, or to taste

3 tablespoons fat-free or low-fat plain Greek yogurt

3 tablespoons freshly grated Pecorino Romano or Parmigiano-Reggiano cheese

2 tablespoons finely crumbled Gorgonzola or other blue cheese

1. Bring the broth, rice, and ½ teaspoon of the salt to a boil in a medium saucepan over high heat. Cover, reduce heat to low, and simmer until the rice is cooked through yet slightly chewy, about 45 minutes.

2. Meanwhile, melt the butter with the oil in a large skillet over medium-high heat. Add the onion, squash, vinegar, rosemary, and remaining ½ teaspoon salt and sauté until the onion and squash are lightly caramelized, about 8 minutes. Cover, reduce heat to low, and cook until the squash is fork-tender, stirring once, about 4 minutes.

3. Add the cooked rice to the skillet with the squash along with the yogurt and half each of the Pecorino and Gorgonzola cheeses, and gently stir. Adjust seasoning.

4. Spoon onto individual plates, sprinkle with the remaining cheeses, and serve.

FLEXITARIAN OPTION: Stir up to 2 ounces of finely diced country ham into the cooked rice and squash in step 3.

Per serving: 310 calories, 7g total fat, 2.5g saturated fat, 0g trans fat, 10mg cholesterol, 660mg sodium, 55g total carbohydrate, 5g dietary fiber, 3g sugars, 8g protein

Beet and Goat Cheese Risotto over Greens Ⓕ

Makes 6 servings: 1 cup risotto plus greens each

Here's a risotto-style stunner. It has a vivid magenta color created by the beets. And the flavor . . . you can never go wrong with the blissful duo of beets and goat cheese. Served on a bed of wilted beet greens, it's like a culinary masterpiece.

4 small red beets with greens

2 teaspoons extra-virgin olive oil

1 medium red or white onion, finely diced

1 tablespoon aged balsamic vinegar

1¼ teaspoons sea salt, or to taste

2 large garlic cloves, minced

1½ cups short-grain brown rice or brown Arborio rice

3½ cups low-sodium vegetable broth or Vegetable Stock (page 203)

1 teaspoon finely chopped fresh rosemary, or to taste

¼ teaspoon freshly ground black pepper, or to taste

4 ounces crumbled soft goat cheese

1. Trim the greens from the beets, keeping them whole; rinse well. Peel and dice the beets into ⅓-inch cubes. Set aside.

2. Heat the oil in a large saucepan over medium heat. Add the onion, vinegar, and ¼ teaspoon of the salt and sauté until nearly softened, about 6 minutes. Add the garlic and sauté for 1 minute. Stir in the diced beets and sauté for 1 minute. Add the rice, broth, rosemary, pepper, and ¾ teaspoon

of the salt, increase heat to high, and bring to a boil. Cover, reduce heat to low, and simmer for 40 minutes. Add the beet greens and the remaining ¼ teaspoon salt to the rice mixture (do not stir them in), cover, and simmer until the rice is cooked through yet slightly chewy, about 10 minutes.

3. Transfer the greens to individual plates.

4. Stir about three-fourths of the cheese into the rice mixture and adjust seasoning.

5. Spoon the rice mixture on top of the cooked greens, sprinkle with the remaining cheese, and serve. Garnish with additional fresh rosemary, if desired.

FLEXITARIAN OPTION: Grill a turkey burger patty that's seasoned with rosemary. Serve the greens and rice mixture on top of the patty.

Per serving: 290 calories, 7g total fat, 3g saturated fat, 0g trans fat, 10mg cholesterol, 740mg sodium, 49g total carbohydrate, 5g dietary fiber, 6g sugars, 9g protein

Spring Pea Risotto

Makes 6 servings: 1 cup each

This streamlined risotto recipe lets the tender green pea flavor and freshness shine with splendor. The garden green colors will pop on your plate and the spring-like tastes will please your palate.

2 teaspoons extra-virgin olive oil

1 medium white onion, finely diced

2 teaspoons fresh lemon juice

1¼ teaspoons sea salt, or to taste

1½ cups short-grain brown rice or brown Arborio rice

3½ cups low-sodium vegetable broth
    or Vegetable Stock (page 203)

¼ teaspoon freshly ground black pepper, or to taste

16 ounces fresh or frozen peas, thawed

2 teaspoons unsalted butter

2 tablespoons freshly grated Parmigiano-Reggiano
    or Parmesan cheese

1 tablespoon finely chopped fresh mint, or to taste

1 cup microgreens or alfalfa sprouts, chilled

1. Heat the oil in a large saucepan over medium heat. Add the onion, lemon juice, and ¼ teaspoon of the salt and sauté until softened, about 8 minutes. Stir in the rice, 3 cups of the broth, the pepper, and the remaining 1 teaspoon salt, increase heat to high, and bring to a boil. Cover, reduce heat to low, and simmer for 30 minutes. (The rice will not be fully cooked.)

2. Meanwhile, add the peas and the remaining ½ cup broth to a blender. Cover and puree.

3. Stir the pea puree into the rice mixture, cover, and simmer over low heat until the rice is cooked through yet still slightly chewy, about 22 to 25 minutes.

4. Stir in the butter, cheese, and mint. Adjust seasoning.

5. Spoon onto individual plates or bowls, top with the microgreens, and serve.

FLEXITARIAN OPTION: Top with a few Sea Salt and Pepper Scallops (page 361) or grilled shrimp before the microgreens in step 5.

Per serving: 280 calories, 4.5g total fat, 1.5g saturated fat, 0g trans fat, 5mg cholesterol, 640mg sodium, 52g total carbohydrate, 7g dietary fiber, 5g sugars, 9g protein

Main Dishes:
Poultry, Meat, and Game

Grilled Poultry

Santorini Chicken Breast
Skewers

Pistachio-Plum
Glazed Chicken

Apricot BBQ Chicken Legs

Peach Grilled Chicken Breast

Zesty Lime Grilled Chicken

3-Ingredient Grilled
Chicken Paillard

Honey-Dijon Turkey Breast

Rosemary Turkey Patties

Jerk Cornish Game Hens

Blackened Creole
Duck Breast

Baked, Roasted,
or Broiled Poultry

Almond-Crusted Chicken

Cayenne Kentucky-Style
Flash-Fried Chicken

Red Curry Chicken Breasts

Bombay Chicken Thighs

Chicken Chimichurri

Roasted Pollo Buono
with Potatoes

Chicken Roulade
with Bell Pepper Sauce

Cheesy Chicken-Asparagus
Roulade

Sage Turkey Tenders
with Gravy

Roasted Summer Turkey

Turkey and Fennel Meatballs

Root Veggie-Turkey Meatloaf

Cran-Citrus Duck Skewers

Grilled Meat
and Wild Game

California Boneless BBQ Ribs

Filet Mignon with Merlot Sauce

Tuscan-Style T-Bone

Teriyaki New York Strip

Asian Butterhead Steak Bowls

Lebanese Lamb
and Fig Kebabs

Grilled Lamb Chops
with Fresh Mint Chutney

Bison Tenderloin with Raita

Grilled Venison with Cherry
Balsamic Peppercorn Sauce

Baked, Braised,
Roasted, or Broiled
Meat and Game

Tart Apple–Stuffed Pork Loin

Flash-Fried Pork Loin Chops

Caramelized Onion Salisbury
Steak with Shiitake Gravy

Oven-Fried Veal Parmigiana

Pinot Grigio Osso Buco

Cocoa-Dusted Lamb Loin

Tomato-Glazed
Mini Meatloaves

Roasted Bison Meatloaves

Stir-Fried or Sautéed Poultry and Meat

Ginger Chicken, Broccoli and Oyster Mushroom Stir-Fry

Garlic Chicken and Snow Pea Stir-Fry

Peppery Kung Pao Chicken

Citrus Chicken Stir-Fry with Peppers and Pine Nuts

Szechuan Chicken and Asparagus

Mongolian Flank Steak Stir-Fry

Cantonese Broccoli and Beef Tenderloin

Herb-Infused Steak Destiny

Meatballs Romano

Papaya Pork

Petite Apricot Ham Steak

Lamb and Eggplant Stir-Fry

Wok-Charred Turkish Lamb with Grape Tomatoes

Slow-Cooked and Pressure-Cooked Poultry and Meat

Shiitake Chicken Cacciatore

Coq au Vin Cabernet

Pulled Chicken Mole

Sticky Lebanese Cinnamon Chicken and Rice

Beef Brisket with Squash

Poultry and Meat Pastas and One-Dish Meals

Asparagus Chicken Linguine

Vodka Chicken Fettuccine

Grilled Chicken Fusilli Marinara

Chicken Fajita Bowl

Lemon Chicken and Broccoli Casserole

Garlic Chicken Bucatini and Herbs

Tequila Turkey Pasta

Fennel-Turkey Spaghetti Bolognese

Turkey Sausage Lasagna

Tijuana Turkey "Lasagna" Verde

Fresh Spaghetti and Meatballs

When it comes to eating poultry, meat, or game, the simple keys for including it in low-calorie cooking is to start with a lean cut, keep it portioned to no more than one-fourth of the plate, and prepare it in a healthful way.

This *1,000 Low-Calorie Recipes* chapter provides you with dozens of ways to do that, scrumptiously.

The leanest beef and pork cuts are those generally labeled "loin" or "round," such as round steak, tenderloin, or sirloin. For ground meat or poultry recipes, aim to choose options that say at least "90 percent lean." But you don't need to hunt for "99 percent"! If you go with cuts that are lean, you may wind up with a dish that's too dry. Boneless skinless chicken breasts and turkey cutlets are the leanest poultry choices, but generally all poultry can be included in a calorie-friendly plan. Even eating the skin can be an option from time to time—if you properly plan it into your meal.

I personally choose organic poultry and organic, grass-fed meats. I look at it as an investment in health; it has a better chance of being better for me overall. For instance, one study found that organic chicken contained 38 percent more heart-healthy omega-3 fatty acids than conventionally raised chicken. Organic chicken may contain less salt and other additives, too. When it comes to meat, grass-fed selections are likely lower in total calories and lower in saturated fat than conventional choices. What's more, meat from pastured cattle generally provides more omega-3 fats, which decrease inflammation in the body; it can be up to four times higher in vitamin E, an important antioxidant; and it can be significantly higher in conjugated linoleic acid (CLA), a nutrient associated with lower risk of heart disease and other chronic diseases. The bottom line: Grass-fed meat is leaner and more nutrient rich than grain-fed meat, which is why I recommend it.

The choice up to you. I realize selecting organic meat and poultry is not always an option, due to cost and/or availability.

No matter what your meat or poultry selection, you can make most picks delicious on the grill. Grilling is a lean-cooking technique since it doesn't require extra oil. If you're pressed for time or your grill is covered up for the season, many of the grilled recipes here can also be prepared on an indoor grill or a grill pan, or in a panini grill. Using a panini grill will be quicker since you're grilling both sides at once, so adjust the timing accordingly. Also, adjust timing if you prefer to prepare a panini-grilled recipe on a grill or grill pan. Something else you'll find in *1,000 Low-Calorie Recipes* is a naturally sweet ingredient, such as fruit, in some marinades; it can enhance grilling by creating delectable caramelization—and amazing grill marks.

If you prefer savory roasted goodness, you'll have dishes that run the spectrum, even classics like Salisbury steak, veal Parmigiana, osso buco, and meatloaf. If you fancy fried food, there's something special here for you, too. One clever way to "fry" is by using my flash-frying technique that's used for Cayenne Kentucky-Style Flash-Fried Chicken (page 312) and Flash-Fried Pork Loin Chops (page 324). Fry the chicken or pork briefly in very hot oil, just to get a crisp coating and rich color, and then bake it the rest of the way. The result is a delicate and crispy coating with all the fried flavor appeal with fewer calories than the traditional fried version.

If you're a fan of small appliances, check out the slow-cooker and pressure-cooker recipes. Slow-cooking transforms chicken and beef into melt-in-your-mouth dishes—without your having to pay attention to them during the process. Pressure-cooking does the same thing . . . just super quickly, under pressure. They're terrific cooking techniques to use for leaner cuisine.

The stir-fried and sautéed recipes, as well as the pastas and one-dish meals in this chapter, use meats to complement the other ingredients while providing excellent and delicious ways to include more veggies and whole grains in your eating routine. You'll savor comforting dishes like lasagna and spaghetti and meatballs, too.

Finally, remember when cooking with raw meat and poultry, keep it safe. Check out the safe cooking temperature chart (page 572) for details.

Calorie range in this chapter: 110 to 495 calories.

Low-calorie pick: Petite Apricot Ham Steak, 110 calories (page 334).

Grilled Poultry

Santorini Chicken Breast Skewers

Makes 3 servings: 4 skewers each

A tangy herb dip doubles as a marinade in this chicken recipe—taking chicken skewers from fine to fantastic.

1¼ cups low-fat plain yogurt
2 tablespoons extra-virgin olive oil
Juice of ½ lemon (1½ tablespoons)
2 large garlic cloves, minced
1 tablespoon finely chopped fresh mint
½ teaspoon finely chopped fresh oregano
½ teaspoon sea salt, or to taste
¼ teaspoon freshly ground black pepper, or to taste
12 ounces boneless skinless chicken breast, cut into 12 long thin strips
1 teaspoon drained tiny capers

1. Whisk together the yogurt, oil, lemon juice, garlic, mint, oregano, salt, and pepper in a medium bowl. Place half of the yogurt mixture in a small serving bowl and chill in the refrigerator until ready to serve as the dip.

2. Add the chicken to remaining yogurt mixture. Stir to coat and marinate for 30 to 45 minutes.

3. Preheat a panini grill or a grill pan. Insert each marinated chicken strip onto an 8- or 10-inch reusable or water-soaked bamboo skewer. Discard the yogurt marinade. Place the chicken skewers in the panini grill on high heat and cook until well done, about 2½ to 3 minutes. Prepare in batches, if necessary. Adjust seasoning.

4. Transfer the warm chicken skewers to a platter, sprinkle with the capers, and serve with the reserved dip.

Per serving: 270 calories, 14g total fat, 3g saturated fat, 0g trans fat, 70mg cholesterol, 540mg sodium, 9g total carbohydrate, 0g dietary fiber, 7g sugars, 28g protein

Pistachio-Plum Glazed Chicken Ⓢ

Makes 4 servings: 1 thigh each

The perky plum sauce provides natural fruit sugar that creates a rich glaze. The pistachios provide crunch. And using the dark thigh meat means it will be moist. This is where having plump juicy thighs is a great thing!

4 boneless skinless chicken thighs
¼ cup + 1 tablespoon Pistachio Plum Sauce (page 109)
⅛ teaspoon sea salt, or to taste
1 tablespoon coarsely chopped unsalted dry-roasted pistachios

1. Place the chicken in a medium bowl or dish. Toss or rub the chicken with ¼ cup of the sauce. Let marinate for 30 to 45 minutes.

2. Preheat a panini grill. Remove the chicken from the marinade and discard leftover marinade. Cook the chicken in the panini grill on medium-high heat until fully cooked, about 7 minutes. Brush with the remaining 1 tablespoon sauce. Add the salt.

3. Transfer the chicken to a platter, sprinkle with the pistachios, and serve immediately.

Per serving: 150 calories, 7g total fat, 1.5g saturated fat, 0g trans fat, 50mg cholesterol, 150mg sodium, 7g total carbohydrate, 0g dietary fiber, 5g sugars, 14g protein

Apricot BBQ Chicken Legs Ⓢ

Makes 4 servings: 2 legs each

Go ahead; leave the skin on . . . sometimes. You can still keep calories in check. The skin is part of what makes these sweet and tangy chicken legs extra succulent. An easy pleasing surprise, for sure!

¾ cup + 2 tablespoons Tangy Apricot Barbecue Sauce (page 106)
8 chicken drumsticks with skin
Pinch of sea salt, or to taste

1. Place the chicken in a large bowl or baking pan. Toss or rub the chicken with ¾ cup of the barbecue sauce. Let marinate for 30 to 45 minutes.

2. Prepare an outdoor or indoor grill.

3. Remove the chicken from the marinade and discard leftover marinade.

4. Grill the chicken over medium heat until fully cooked, turning the chicken only as needed, about 18 minutes total. Brush the chicken with the remaining 2 tablespoons sauce. Add the salt.

5. Transfer the chicken to a platter, and serve.

Per serving: 270 calories, 17g total fat, 4.5g saturated fat, 0g trans fat, 105mg cholesterol, 230mg sodium, 5g total carbohydrate, 0g dietary fiber, 3g sugars, 23g protein

Peach Grilled Chicken Breast

Makes 4 servings: 1 breast each

This slightly fruity, slightly spicy, slightly nutty recipe is scrumptious to grill at a cookout when peaches are in season. Pair it alongside grilled peach halves for extra fruity sensation.

1 large peach, pitted and halved, or 1 cup frozen sliced peaches, thawed
1 small or ½ large white onion, coarsely chopped
1 small jalapeño pepper, stem removed
3 tablespoons sliced natural almonds, toasted
2 tablespoons 100% peach or apricot jam
1 tablespoon grapeseed or canola oil
1 tablespoon apple cider vinegar or white wine vinegar
¾ teaspoon sea salt, or to taste
4 (5-ounce) boneless chicken breasts with skin

1. Add the peach, onion, jalapeño, almonds, jam, oil, vinegar, and ½ teaspoon of the salt to a blender or food processor. Cover and blend until smooth.

2. Place the chicken in a large bowl or baking pan. Pour the peach mixture over the chicken. Let marinate for 30 to 45 minutes.

3. Prepare an outdoor or indoor grill.

4. Remove the chicken from the marinade and discard leftover marinade. Grill chicken over direct medium-high heat until fully cooked and rich grill marks form, turning the chicken only as needed, about 5 to 6 minutes per side. Add the remaining ¼ teaspoon salt to taste.

5. Transfer the chicken to a platter, and serve.

Per serving: 210 calories, 10g total fat, 2.5g saturated fat, 0g trans fat, 80mg cholesterol, 270mg sodium, 4g total carbohydrate, 1g dietary fiber, 3g sugars, 25g protein

Zesty Lime Grilled Chicken

Makes 3 servings: 3 chicken strips each

This is one of my go-to grilled picks when I plan to add poultry to other recipes. The addition of fresh lime juice and zest takes chicken from plain to pizzazz. Try these versatile grilled strips in Creamy Santa Fe Pappardelle (page 293), Eco-Burrito Bowl (page 259), or other Southwestern or Mexican-inspired dishes.

1 pound boneless skinless chicken breasts, patted dry and cut into 9 long pieces
1 tablespoon extra-virgin olive oil or canola oil
Juice and zest of ½ lime (1 tablespoon juice)
¼ teaspoon sea salt, or to taste
¼ teaspoon freshly ground black pepper, or to taste

1. Rub the chicken with the oil, drizzle with the lime juice, and season with the salt and pepper. Let marinate for 30 to 45 minutes.

2. Prepare an outdoor or indoor grill.

3. Cook the chicken over direct medium-high heat until fully cooked and grill marks form, about 2½ to 3 minutes per side. Adjust seasoning.

4. Sprinkle with the zest, and serve.

Per serving: 200 calories, 8g total fat, 1.5g saturated fat, 0g trans fat, 85mg cholesterol, 270mg sodium, 1g total carbohydrate, 0g dietary fiber, 0g sugars, 31g protein

3-Ingredient Grilled Chicken Paillards

Makes 4 servings: 1 chicken breast each

The combination of maple syrup and an Asian sauce might seem odd . . . until you taste it. What a delicious duo it is. Who knew something so simple could be so tantalizing. Transform it into a memorable meal with Asian Angel Hair with "Confetti" (page 289).

4 teaspoons pure maple syrup

2 teaspoons Asian garlic-chili sauce

¼ teaspoon sea salt, or to taste

4 (5-ounce) boneless skinless chicken breasts, patted dry and pounded evenly to ⅓-inch thickness

1. Prepare an outdoor or indoor grill.

2. Whisk together the maple syrup, garlic-chili sauce, and salt in a medium bowl. Add the chicken and toss until all breasts are well coated with the maple syrup mixture.

3. Grill the chicken over direct medium-high heat until fully cooked, turning the chicken only as needed, about 2½ to 3 minutes per side. Adjust seasoning.

4. Transfer the chicken to a platter and serve hot or chilled.

Per serving: 170 calories, 3.5g total fat, 1g saturated fat, 0g trans fat, 80mg cholesterol, 330mg sodium, 5g total carbohydrate, 0g dietary fiber, 4g sugars, 29g protein

Honey-Dijon Turkey Breast

Makes 4 servings: 1 cutlet each

The high point of this extra lean grilled turkey "steak" recipe is the companion sweet and spicy mustard sauce, which is full of zing. Serve it as a dipping sauce on the side for even more juicy flavor.

12 ounces boneless skinless turkey breast, patted dry and cut into 4 (½-inch-thick) fillets

½ cup "Hot" Honey Dijon Sauce (page 126)

⅛ teaspoon sea salt, or to taste

⅛ teaspoon freshly ground black pepper, or to taste

1. Prepare an outdoor or indoor grill.

2. Add the turkey and ¼ cup of the sauce to a medium bowl and toss until all cutlets are coated. Let stand to marinate for 30 to 45 minutes. Discard residual marinade in bowl.

3. Grill the turkey over direct medium-high heat until fully cooked and rich grill marks form, flipping the turkey only once, about 4 minutes per side. Add the salt and pepper.

4. Let the turkey stand for at least 5 minutes before serving. Arrange the turkey on a platter or individual plates. Serve hot or chilled with the remaining ¼ cup sauce on the side.

Per serving: 140 calories, 0.5g total fat, 0g saturated fat, 0g trans fat, 55mg cholesterol, 430mg sodium, 13g total carbohydrate, 0g dietary fiber, 10g sugars, 21g protein

Rosemary Turkey Patties

Makes 4 servings: 1 patty each

Bored with burgers? This grilled recipe is a twist on a bunless turkey burger. It's slathered with a high-flavored rosemary grilling sauce. Create a special cookout by pairing it with a blue cheese-freckled salad, like Bibb-n-Blue Chopped Salad (page 154).

12 ounces ground turkey (about 94% lean)

½ cup Rosemary Grill Sauce (page 134), at room temperature

¾ teaspoon finely chopped fresh rosemary

½ teaspoon sea salt, or to taste

¼ teaspoon freshly ground black pepper, or to taste

1 medium sweet onion, cut into 8 rounds

1. Prepare an outdoor or indoor grill.

2. Add the turkey, 2 tablespoons of the sauce, the rosemary, ¼ teaspoon of the salt, and the pepper to a medium bowl. Gently combine by hand and form mixture into 4 oval patties, about ½ inch thick each. Set aside.

3. Grill the onion rounds (do not separate) over medium-high heat until cooked through and caramelized, about 3 minutes per side, brushing with 2 tablespoons of the remaining sauce during grilling. Add the remaining ¼ teaspoon salt.

4. Grill the turkey over medium heat until well done, about 3½ minutes per side.

5. Arrange the onions (as rounds or separated) on a platter. Place the turkey on the onions. Adjust seasoning. Drizzle with the remaining ¼ cup sauce, and serve.

Per serving: 150 calories, 5g total fat, 1.5g saturated fat, 0g trans fat, 50mg cholesterol, 490mg sodium, 9g total carbohydrate, 1g dietary fiber, 5g sugars, 17g protein

Jerk Cornish Game Hens

Makes 4 servings: ½ game hen each

Cornish game hen is deliciously juicy, and this preparation of it is no exception. The perky jerk seasoning rub makes the hen memorably flavorful, too. It's a definite must-try when grilling out. The nutrition analysis assumes you will be enjoying the skin; if you prefer, trim down calories by not eating all of it.

**2 Cornish game hens (petit poulet),
    about 1 to 1⅓ pounds each**

1 tablespoon jerk seasoning rub, or to taste (page 311)

⅛ teaspoon sea salt, or to taste

1. Remove and discard the fat just inside the body cavities of each game hen. Remove the giblets (if any); reserve for another use. Rinse the hens well, then drain and pat fully dry, inside and out, with paper towels. Cut each hen in half lengthwise with poultry shears. Place into a large, deep baking dish or bowl.

2. Rub the hens with the seasoning. Let flavors blend at least 4 hours or overnight, covered, in the refrigerator, turning the hens occasionally.

3. Prepare an outdoor grill.

4. Drain the hens of any excess liquid. Then grill, skin side down, over direct medium heat for about 18 minutes. Flip hens over, and grill until fully cooked and slightly charred, about 12 to 15 more minutes. Add the salt.

5. Transfer the hens to a platter, and serve.

Per serving: 280 calories, 20g total fat, 5g saturated fat, 0g trans fat, 140mg cholesterol, 350mg sodium, 0g total carbohydrate, 0g dietary fiber, 0g sugars, 24g protein

HOMEMADE JERK SEASONING RUB

Combine ¾ teaspoon sea salt, ¾ teaspoon freshly ground black pepper, ½ teaspoon onion powder, ½ teaspoon dried crushed thyme, ⅛ teaspoon cayenne pepper, ⅛ teaspoon allspice, ⅛ teaspoon ground ginger, and ⅛ teaspoon ground cinnamon in small bowl. Makes 1 tablespoon.

Blackened Creole Duck Breast

Makes 4 servings: about 3½ ounces grilled breast each

This duck dish is gorgeous when sliced and served. There will be noticeably indulgent fat from the skin. But not to worry, it's edible and factored into the nutrition analysis. Go ahead, indulge in this entrée on occasion. It's a show-stopper served over Tart Cherry-Speckled Spinach (page 451).

1 tablespoon Worcestershire sauce

2 teaspoons Creole seasoning (page 31), or to taste

1½ teaspoons turbinado sugar

**1 (1-pound) boneless Moulard duck breast half
    with skin**

1. Whisk together the Worcestershire sauce, Creole seasoning, and sugar in a medium bowl. Add the duck and toss well to coat. Let marinate 30 to 45 minutes.

2. Prepare an outdoor or indoor grill.

3. Grill the duck, skin side down, over direct medium-high heat until the skin is blackened and crisp, about 3 minutes. Then turn over the duck breast and grill over medium heat until blackened and just cooked through, about 10 minutes.

4. Let duck stand for at least 10 minutes. Thinly slice the duck and serve while warm.

Per serving: 250 calories, 17g total fat, 6g saturated fat, 0g trans fat, 0mg cholesterol, 380mg sodium, 2g total carbohydrate, 0g dietary fiber, 2g sugars, 20g protein

Baked, Roasted, or Broiled Poultry

Almond-Crusted Chicken

Makes 4 servings: 1 chicken breast each

This sweet and nutty recipe gives new life to the tried-and-true chicken breast. The end result is an inviting contrast of textures—juicy on the inside and crunchy on the outside.

¼ cup plain almond milk or unsweetened
    coconut milk beverage

1 large garlic clove, minced

1 teaspoon brown rice vinegar

¾ teaspoon sea salt, or to taste

4 (5-ounce) boneless skinless chicken breasts

¼ cup sliced natural almonds, chopped

¼ cup whole-wheat panko breadcrumbs

1 tablespoon turbinado sugar

1. Whisk together the almond milk, garlic, vinegar, and ¼ teaspoon of the salt in a medium bowl. Add the chicken and toss to coat. Let marinate for 30 to 45 minutes. Discard excess marinade.

2. Preheat the oven to 400°F.

3. Stir together the almonds, panko, sugar, and ¼ teaspoon of the salt in a small bowl. Pour the almond mixture onto a plate.

4. Dredge both sides of each chicken breast in the almond mixture. Arrange chicken on a parchment paper-lined baking sheet. If any excess almond mixture, pat it onto the chicken breasts. Sprinkle with the remaining ¼ teaspoon salt.

5. Bake until the chicken is fully cooked and the coating is crisp and adheres to the chicken, about 18 to 20 minutes. (Do not flip chicken over during baking process.) Let stand for at least 5 minutes, adjust seasoning, and serve.

Per serving: 220 calories, 6g total fat, 1g saturated fat, 0g trans fat, 80mg cholesterol, 440mg sodium, 8g total carbohydrate, 1g dietary fiber, 4g sugars, 31g protein

Cayenne Kentucky-Style Flash-Fried Chicken Ⓢ

Makes 4 servings: 1 chicken breast each

Fried chicken can be a reality even in the world of weight management with my par-fry technique. What you do is fry the chicken ever so briefly, just to get a crisp coating and rich color, then you bake it the rest of the way. The result is a delicate and crunchy surface even though the breasts are skinless. Plus, you're only coating the top part of the breasts—so you save calories there, too.

1 cup whole-wheat pastry flour

1⅛ teaspoons sea salt, or to taste

½ teaspoon freshly ground black pepper, or to taste

½ teaspoon + ⅛ teaspoon ground cayenne,
    or to taste

1 cup plain almond milk or unsweetened
    coconut milk beverage

1 large garlic clove, minced

4 (7-ounce) bone-in skinless chicken breasts,
    patted dry

2 cups peanut or canola oil

1. Combine the flour, 1 teaspoon of the salt, the black pepper, and ½ teaspoon of the cayenne in a medium bowl. Combine the almond milk and garlic in another medium bowl.

2. Dredge the flesh side (where skin would be) of each chicken breast in the flour mixture, dip into the milk mixture and allow excess to drip off, then dredge the flesh side again in the flour mixture and shake off excess flour. Set aside.

3. Preheat the oven to 350°F.

4. Heat the oil over high heat. Once hot (but not smoking), add two of the chicken breasts, flesh side down, and fry only the one side until the coating is crisp and golden, about 2½ minutes. Remove the chicken and place coated side up in a 9×13-inch baking pan. Repeat with the remaining chicken breasts. Sprinkle with the remaining ⅛ teaspoon salt and ⅛ teaspoon cayenne.

5. Bake the chicken uncovered until fully cooked and the coating is deep golden brown, about 30 minutes. Let stand about 10 minutes before serving, adjust seasoning, and serve.

Per serving: 290 calories, 14g total fat, 3.5g saturated fat, 0g trans fat, 90mg cholesterol, 230mg sodium, 6g total carbohydrate, 1g dietary fiber, 0g sugars, 33g protein

Red Curry Chicken Breasts

Makes 4 servings: 1 chicken breast and 1 cup sauce each

With all of the amazing flavors combined with the creaminess from the yogurt and tomato, no one will ever suspect how light this stewed chicken breast really is. The aroma of curry alone will win you over. Enjoy over steamed quinoa or whole-wheat couscous for a blissful meal in a bowl.

2 teaspoons unrefined peanut or coconut oil

1 large white onion, finely chopped

2 teaspoons apple cider vinegar

1 teaspoon sea salt, or as needed

1 tablespoon freshly grated gingerroot

2 large garlic cloves, minced

1 cup low-sodium chicken broth or Chicken Stock (page 203)

1 cup fat-free or low-fat plain yogurt

1 (6-ounce) can tomato paste

1 tablespoon turbinado sugar

1 tablespoon hot Madras curry powder, or to taste

½ teaspoon ground cumin, or to taste

½ teaspoon pure coconut extract

4 (7-ounce) bone-in skinless chicken breasts

2 tablespoons chopped fresh cilantro

1. Preheat the oven to 350°F.

2. Heat the oil in a Dutch oven over medium-high heat. Add the onion, vinegar, and ¼ teaspoon of the salt and sauté until softened and beginning to caramelize, about 8 minutes. Add the ginger and garlic and sauté for 1 minute. Remove from heat.

3. Stir in the broth, yogurt, tomato paste, sugar, curry powder, cumin, coconut extract, and the remaining ¾ teaspoon salt until well combined. Add the chicken, bone side up, and cover.

4. Place the Dutch oven into the oven and bake until the chicken is fully cooked and tender, about 2½ hours. Remove from oven and let stand covered for 15 minutes. Adjust seasoning.

5. Transfer the chicken to a platter, drizzle with the sauce from the Dutch oven, sprinkle with the cilantro, and serve.

Per serving: 310 calories, 6g total fat, 1.5g saturated fat, 0g trans fat, 90mg cholesterol, 750mg sodium, 21g total carbohydrate, 3g dietary fiber, 13g sugars, 38g protein

Bombay Chicken Thighs

Makes 4 servings: 2 thighs each

These chicken thighs are extra flavorful and gorgeous, redolent with Indian spices. You'll be especially pleased that not one, but two thighs is a portion size here.

½ cup fat-free or low-fat plain yogurt

Juice of ½ small lemon (1 tablespoon)

2 teaspoons extra-virgin olive oil

1 large garlic clove, minced

2 teaspoons freshly grated gingerroot

2 teaspoons paprika

2 teaspoons chili powder

¾ teaspoon sea salt

½ teaspoon ground cayenne

¼ teaspoon ground cinnamon

⅛ teaspoon ground cardamom

8 (4-ounce) bone-in skinless chicken thighs

1. Whisk together the yogurt, lemon juice, oil, garlic, ginger, paprika, chili powder, salt, cayenne, cinnamon, and cardamom in a medium bowl or baking pan. Add the chicken and toss to coat. Cover and marinate in the refrigerator at least 4 hours or overnight.

2. Preheat the broiler. Discard any remaining marinade.

3. Place the chicken on a broiler pan and broil about 4 inches from the heat until fully cooked and lightly charred, about 6 minutes per side. Serve immediately.

Per serving: 300 calories, 16 total fat, 4g saturated fat, 0g trans fat, 115mg cholesterol, 590mg sodium, 5g total carbohydrate, 1g dietary fiber, 3g sugars, 33g protein

Chicken Chimichurri

Makes 5 servings: 2 thighs (sliced) and 2½ tablespoons sauce each

Chimichurri is a thick Argentinian herb sauce that's typically served with steak. But the fragrant pesto-like sauce goes equally well with this extra-juicy chicken thigh dish. All together, it's delectable.

10 boneless skinless chicken thighs
    (about 2 pounds), patted dry

1 teaspoon sea salt

½ teaspoon ground cumin

½ teaspoon ground coriander

½ teaspoon freshly ground black pepper

2 large garlic cloves

1½ cups fresh cilantro leaves and tender stems

1½ cups fresh flat-leaf parsley leaves and
    tender stems

¼ cup low-sodium vegetable broth
    or Vegetable Stock (page 203)

1½ tablespoons aged red wine vinegar
    or sherry vinegar

1 tablespoon extra-virgin olive oil

⅛ teaspoon ground cayenne, or to taste

1. Preheat the broiler.

2. Stir together ¾ teaspoon of the salt, the cumin, coriander, and black pepper in a small bowl. Sprinkle the seasoning mixture onto the chicken. Place the chicken on a broiler pan and broil about 4 inches from the heat until well done, about 6 minutes per side. Transfer to a cutting board and let stand 5 minutes. Adjust seasoning.

3. Add the garlic to a food processor and pulse until chopped. Add the cilantro, parsley, broth, vinegar, oil, cayenne, and the remaining ¼ teaspoon salt, then pulse until herbs are finely chopped. Adjust seasoning.

4. Thinly slice the chicken into long strips against the grain, arrange onto a platter, and top with half of the sauce. Serve with the remaining sauce on the side.

Per serving: 300 calories, 17g total fat, 4g saturated fat, 0g trans fat, 120mg cholesterol, 590mg sodium, 2g total carbohydrate, 1g dietary fiber, 0g sugars, 33g protein

Roasted Pollo Buono with Potatoes

Makes 8 servings: 1 piece chicken with ¾ cup vegetables each

Savor the wonderfully crisp, luscious Italian-style chicken that's kissed by rosemary. You remove the skin from the bottom of the chicken that will sit on the potatoes as it roasts. This helps to reduce calories. Plus, that bottom portion of the skin won't brown anyway due to the steam from the potatoes.

1 (4-pound) whole chicken, giblets removed,
    excess fat trimmed, skin removed from
    bottom side, and patted dry

3 small fresh rosemary sprigs + 1 tablespoon
    finely chopped fresh rosemary

1 head garlic, halved crosswise

2 teaspoons extra-virgin olive oil

2 teaspoons unsalted butter, melted

1¼ teaspoons sea salt, or to taste

¾ teaspoon freshly ground black pepper, or to taste

2 large sweet potatoes, unpeeled, scrubbed,
    and cut into 1-inch cubes

2 large russet potatoes, unpeeled, scrubbed,
    and cut into 1-inch cubes

1 large red onion, cut into thick slices

1. Preheat the oven to 425°F.

2. Stuff the chicken cavity with the rosemary sprigs and garlic.

3. Tie the chicken legs together with kitchen twine or a silicone band and tuck the wing tips underneath the chicken.

4. Stir together the oil, butter, 2 teaspoons of the chopped rosemary, 1 teaspoon of the salt, and

½ teaspoon of the pepper in a small bowl. Rub or brush the outside of the chicken with the oil mixture.

5. Place the potatoes and onion in a roasting pan and add the remaining 1 teaspoon chopped rosemary, ¼ teaspoon salt, and ¼ teaspoon pepper. Position the chicken on the potato mixture.

6. Place in the oven and roast until the chicken and vegetables are fully cooked, about 1 hour 30 minutes, stirring the vegetables twice during the roasting process. Remove from the oven and loosely cover with aluminum foil to finish the cooking process, about 15 minutes. Adjust seasoning.

7. Cut the chicken into 8 parts: 2 wings, 2 legs, 2 thighs, and 2 breasts. Serve the chicken with the roasted vegetables.

Per serving: 390 calories, 17g total fat, 5g saturated fat, 0g trans fat, 95mg cholesterol, 480mg sodium, 27g total carbohydrate, 4g dietary fiber, 5g sugars, 32g protein

Chicken Roulade with Bell Pepper Sauce

Makes 4 servings: 1 roulade with ⅔ cup sauce each

The bright, peppery, pleasantly bitter taste of arugula brings balance to the other savory and slightly sweet elements of this vibrant chicken dish. It'll inspire the artist in you when plating the roulades with the vivid sauce.

1 large egg

1 tablespoon extra-virgin olive oil

2 teaspoons fresh lemon juice

¾ teaspoon sea salt, or to taste

½ teaspoon freshly ground black pepper, or to taste

4 ounces soft goat cheese, chilled

1 cup finely chopped baby arugula
    or fresh baby spinach

⅓ cup whole-wheat couscous

4 (4-ounce) boneless skinless chicken breasts,
    pounded to ¼-inch thickness

1½ cups Roasted Red Bell Pepper Sauce, warm
    (page 136)

1. Add the egg, 2 teaspoons of the oil, the lemon juice, ½ teaspoon of the salt, and ¼ teaspoon of the pepper to a medium bowl and whisk until lightly beaten. Add the cheese, arugula, and couscous and combine the mixture by hand until well blended. Form the mixture into 4 (4-inch-long) logs. (Note: The logs will be very soft, but will firm when cooked.)

2. Preheat the oven to 350°F.

3. Lay the chicken breasts out on a cutting board. Add the remaining ¼ teaspoon salt and ¼ teaspoon pepper. Top each with a cheese log, and firmly roll the chicken around the cheese. If necessary, secure with water-soaked toothpicks. Lightly rub the chicken with the remaining 1 teaspoon oil.

4. Place the roulades on a parchment paper–lined baking sheet. Cover with aluminum foil. Bake until the chicken and filling are fully cooked through, about 25 minutes. Let stand for 5 minutes to complete the cooking process.

5. Cut each roulade into 5 slices, arrange cut side up on the sauce, and serve immediately.

Per serving: 380 calories, 18g total fat, 8g saturated fat, 0g trans fat, 130mg cholesterol, 770mg sodium, 19g total carbohydrate, 3g dietary fiber, 4g sugars, 35g protein

Cheesy Chicken-Asparagus Roulade

Makes 4 servings: 1 roulade each

If you desire a spectacular, succulent entrée for a special meal, this chicken roulade recipe will not disappoint. The plated presentation of the roulades is stunning. No one will guess that the preparation is actually quite simple.

1 teaspoon grapeseed or canola oil

20 thin green asparagus spears, ends trimmed

1 teaspoon fresh lemon juice

¼ teaspoon + ⅛ teaspoon sea salt, or to taste

4 (4-ounce) boneless skinless chicken breasts, pounded to ¼-inch thickness

¼ teaspoon freshly ground black pepper, or to taste

4 (1-ounce) thin slices aged Swiss or Gruyère cheese

2 tablespoons freshly grated Asiago cheese

4 thin slices prosciutto or country ham

1. Heat the oil in a large skillet over medium-high heat. Add the asparagus and sauté until the asparagus is lightly caramelized, but still firm, about 1 minute. Add the lemon juice and ⅛ teaspoon of the salt. Remove from heat.

2. Preheat the oven to 400°F.

3. Lay the chicken breasts out on a cutting board. Add the remaining ¼ teaspoon salt and the pepper. Top each with 1 slice Swiss, ½ tablespoon Asiago, and 5 asparagus spears. Roll up each as tightly as possible. Then wrap a piece of prosciutto around each. If necessary, secure with water-soaked toothpicks.

4. Place the roulades on a parchment paper–lined baking sheet. Bake until the chicken is fully cooked through, about 18 to 20 minutes. Serve whole or sliced.

Per serving: 310 calories, 16g total fat, 7g saturated fat, 0g trans fat, 110mg cholesterol, 780mg sodium, 3g total carbohydrate, 1g dietary fiber, 1g sugars, 37g protein

Sage Turkey Tenders with Gravy

Makes 4 servings: 1 turkey tenderloin portion with ¼ cup gravy each

Thanksgiving to me always conjures up comforting, delicious dishes that I like to enjoy more than once a year. If we can't change our holiday calendar, at least we can have a taste of Thanksgiving anytime. This turkey tenderloin and sweet potato gravy recipe will transport you to your holiday table—in under 30 minutes!

1 large shallot, minced

2 teaspoons extra-virgin olive oil

2 teaspoons unsalted butter, melted

2 teaspoon ground sage

½ teaspoon sea salt, or to taste

¼ teaspoon freshly ground black pepper, or to taste

1 pound turkey tenderloin, cut into 4 portions

2 teaspoons finely chopped fresh sage

1 cup Rosemary Sweet Potato Gravy (page 110) or other gravy, warm

1. Preheat the oven to 400°F.

2. Stir together the shallot, oil, butter, ground sage, salt, and pepper in a medium bowl. Add the turkey and toss to coat.

3. Place the tenderloin pieces on a parchment paper–lined baking pan. Sprinkle with the fresh sage. Roast in the oven until fully cooked, about 15 minutes. Adjust seasoning.

4. Arrange turkey on individual plates, ladle the gravy on top, and serve.

Per serving: 210 calories, 6g total fat, 1.5g saturated fat, 0g trans fat, 50mg cholesterol, 560mg sodium, 10g total carbohydrate, 2g dietary fiber, 2g sugars, 30g protein

Roasted Summer Turkey

Makes 8 servings: 4 ounces turkey with ¼ cup gravy each

For a celebratory warm-weather meal, try a boneless roasted turkey breast with a summer squash gravy. For extra succulence, roast with the skin on; it creates especially moist turkey. You can remove the skin before eating, if you choose. If you can't find a boneless turkey breast, ask your butcher to debone one and tie it up with twine for you.

1 (2¾-pound) boneless turkey breast with skin

2 large garlic cloves, minced

1 large shallot, minced

Juice of 1 small lemon (2 tablespoons)

1 tablespoon extra-virgin olive oil

1 tablespoon ground sage

2 teaspoons finely chopped fresh oregano

2 teaspoons finely chopped fresh rosemary

1½ teaspoons sea salt, or to taste

1 teaspoon freshly ground black pepper, or to taste

2 cups low-sodium vegetable broth or Vegetable Stock (page 203)

1 cup Chardonnay or other dry white wine

2 cups Farmers' Market Summer Squash Gravy (page 112) or other gravy, warm

1. Preheat the oven to 350°F.

2. Tie the turkey with kitchen twine and place it, skin side up, on a rack in a roasting pan.

3. Stir together the garlic, shallot, lemon juice, oil, sage, oregano, rosemary, salt, and pepper in a small bowl to make a paste. Pat the paste over the top portion of the turkey breast. Pour the broth and wine into the roasting pan.

4. Roast the turkey until an instant-read thermometer registers 165°F when inserted into the thickest part, about 2 hours 15 minutes, while basting the turkey with the pan juices about every 30 minutes during the roasting process. Remove from oven, cover with foil, and let stand for about 15 to 20 minutes to complete the cooking process. Remove the twine. Slice as desired. Adjust seasoning.

5. Arrange the turkey slices on individual plates, ladle the gravy on top, and serve. Alternatively, serve with any remaining pan juices.

Per serving: 310 calories, 11g total fat, 3g saturated fat, 0g trans fat, 90mg cholesterol, 720mg sodium, 7g total carbohydrate, 1g dietary fiber, 2g sugars, 37g protein

Turkey and Fennel Meatballs

Makes 6 servings: 1 large meatball each

It's possible to have a luscious lean meatball by beginning with ground turkey. Freshly grated fennel bulb takes these large meatballs to a new level of intrigue that's sure to satisfy. If you prefer smaller meatballs, simply form them into 12 balls and roast for 25 to 30 minutes.

½ cup whole-wheat panko breadcrumbs

1 cup coarsely grated or finely minced fennel bulb

1 small or ½ large red onion, grated

⅓ cup packed finely chopped fresh basil

⅓ cup freshly grated Parmigiano-Reggiano or other Parmesan cheese

2 large eggs, lightly beaten

2 large garlic cloves, minced

1 pound ground turkey (about 94% lean)

1 teaspoon sea salt, or to taste

½ teaspoon freshly ground black pepper, or to taste

½ teaspoon dried hot pepper flakes, or to taste

1. Preheat the oven to 450°F. Stir together the panko, fennel, and onion in a medium bowl. Let stand for at least 5 minutes to allow the breadcrumbs to become fully moistened.

2. One at a time, stir in the basil, cheese, eggs, garlic, turkey, salt, black pepper, and hot pepper flakes until just combined.

3. Form mixture into 6 large balls (about 5 ounces each) and place on a parchment paper–lined 9 × 13-inch baking pan. Roast until well done and browned about 35 to 40 minutes. Serve immediately.

Per serving: 180 calories, 8g total fat, 2.5g saturated fat, 0g trans fat, 110mg cholesterol, 550mg sodium, 8g total carbohydrate, 2g dietary fiber, 1g sugars, 20g protein

Root Veggie-Turkey Meatloaf

Makes 6 servings: 2 slices each (⅙ loaf each)

Go rustic with autumn-inspired turkey meatloaf. It's "beefed" up with plenty of onions and root vegetables—which also make the meatloaf exceptionally moist. The herbs and spices are what make this comfort food exceptionally memorable.

2 large eggs

½ cup ketchup

3 tablespoons stone-ground mustard

2 large garlic cloves, minced

1 teaspoon finely chopped fresh rosemary

1¼ teaspoons freshly ground black pepper, or to taste

1 teaspoon sea salt, or to taste

⅛ teaspoon ground cinnamon or Chinese five-spice powder, or to taste

1 pound ground turkey (about 94% lean)

1¼ cups coarsely grated raw root vegetable mixture, such as carrot, sweet potato, potato, parsnip, turnip, and/or taro root

1 medium red onion, minced or coarsely grated

½ cup old-fashioned oats

1. Preheat the oven to 400°F.

2. Whisk together the eggs, 3 tablespoons of the ketchup, 2 tablespoons of the mustard, the garlic, rosemary, pepper, salt, and cinnamon until well combined in a medium bowl. Add the turkey, root vegetables, onion, and oats and combine well with your hands. Sculpt the mixture into a football-shaped loaf, about 1¾ inches in height. Place on a parchment paper–lined baking pan.

3. Stir the remaining 5 tablespoons ketchup and 1 tablespoon mustard together in a small bowl. Rub the ketchup mixture over the top and sides of the loaf.

4. Bake until the loaf is cooked through, the root vegetables are tender, and a crust forms, about 1 hour to 1 hour and 10 minutes. Remove from the oven and let stand for at least 5 minutes. Cut into 12 slices crosswise—or cut 6 slices crosswise and then lengthwise down the center.

5. Serve the meatloaf slices while warm. If desired, garnish with additional rosemary.

Per serving: 200 calories, 7g total fat, 2g saturated fat, 0g trans fat, 105mg cholesterol, 750mg sodium, 15g total carbohydrate, 2g dietary fiber, 6g sugars, 18g protein

Cran-Citrus Duck Skewers

Makes 4 servings: 3 skewers each

If you haven't prepared plump duck breast much, know that it's quite versatile and more forgiving than leaner types of poultry. Sliced, marinated in a fruity sauce, broiled, and then served with more of the fresh sauce brings out the best in these duck skewers.

12 ounces boneless skinless duck breast, cut into 12 long thin strips

½ cup Raw Cranberry–Tangerine Sauce (page 131) or other cranberry sauce

⅛ teaspoon sea salt, or to taste

⅛ teaspoon freshly ground black pepper, or to taste

1. Place the duck in a medium bowl. Add 5 tablespoons of the cranberry sauce and toss to coat. Let marinate for 30 to 45 minutes

2. Preheat the broiler.

3. Thread the duck onto 12 (8-inch or longer) metal skewers. Discard the excess marinade. Broil the duck skewers until desired doneness, about 1½ minutes per side. (Do not overcook.) Add the salt and pepper.

4. Arrange the skewers on a platter or individual plates, and serve with the remaining 3 tablespoons cranberry sauce.

Per serving: 120 calories, 3.5g total fat, 1g saturated fat, 0g trans fat, 65mg cholesterol, 170mg sodium, 5g total carbohydrate, 1g dietary fiber, 3g sugars, 17g protein

Grilled Meat and Wild Game

California Boneless BBQ Ribs

Makes 4 servings: 3½ ounces sliced spareribs each

No bones about it: With these country-style hearty ribs you get flavorful pork sparerib slices with 100 percent barbecue goodness. Savor slowly . . . with a fork and knife.

1 teaspoon smoked paprika

1 teaspoon onion powder

1 teaspoon garlic powder

¾ teaspoon crushed dried rosemary

½ teaspoon sea salt, or to taste

½ teaspoon freshly ground black pepper, or to taste

4 (3½-ounce portions) boneless country-style lean pork spareribs

½ cup Home-style Barbecue Sauce (page 109) or other barbecue sauce

1. Prepare an outdoor or indoor grill.

2. Mix together the paprika, onion powder, garlic powder, rosemary, salt, and pepper in a small bowl. Rub the seasoning mixture onto each rib portion until fully coated.

3. Place on the grill over direct medium-high heat and grill until medium doneness, about 5 minutes per side. Pour the barbecue sauce into a grill-safe pan or dish, add the ribs, and toss to coat. Cover well and return the pan to the grill over low heat to finish the cooking process, about 20 minutes. Remove from grill (or oven) and let stand covered about 10 minutes.

4. Very thinly slice the ribs against the grain. Transfer the slices back to pan to coat with the sauce. Adjust seasoning. Plate the rib slices, top with the remaining sauce from the pan, and serve.

Per serving: 190 calories, 10g total fat, 3.5g saturated fat, 0g trans fat, 0mg cholesterol, 440mg sodium, 7g total carbohydrate, 1g dietary fiber, 4g sugars, 18g protein

Filet Mignon with Merlot Sauce

Makes 4 servings: 1 steak each

Filet mignon is from the beef tenderloin, prized for being the most tender, succulent cut that's considered lean. Grill it until just medium-rare, and it's delicious with nothing more than a pinch of sea salt and freshly ground black pepper. But pair it with full-bodied red wine sauce and it becomes heavenly.

1 pound lean beef tenderloin, well trimmed and sliced into 4 steaks about 1¼ inch thick

¼ teaspoon sea salt, or to taste

¼ teaspoon freshly ground black pepper, or to taste

1 recipe Merlot Sauce (page 135), warm

1. Prepare an indoor or outdoor grill.

2. Spray the steaks on all sides with cooking spray (preferably homemade, page xix). Add the salt and pepper. Grill the steak over medium-high heat until desired doneness, about 3½ minutes per side for medium-rare.

3. Pour the sauce over the steaks. Serve immediately. Garnish with fresh thyme or rosemary, if desired.

Per serving: 230 calories, 9g total fat, 4g saturated fat, 0g trans fat, 55mg cholesterol, 350mg sodium, 2g total carbohydrate, 0g dietary fiber, 0g sugars, 24g protein

Tuscan-Style T-Bone

Makes 4 servings: about 4 ounces each

If you start with a quality cut of beef, you don't need much more. Add a few pinches of fresh herbs when you're in the occasional mood for a little more flavor drama. It's what takes this steak from classically simple to simply intriguing. Serve with sautéed greens for extra intrigue.

2 teaspoons chopped fresh rosemary

1 teaspoon chopped fresh sage

¾ teaspoon sea salt, or to taste

½ teaspoon chopped fresh thyme

½ teaspoon freshly ground black pepper, or to taste

1 (1½-pound) lean T-bone steak, about 1½ inches thick, well-trimmed

1 teaspoon extra-virgin olive oil

1. Preheat an outdoor or indoor grill.

2. Mix together the rosemary, sage, salt, thyme, and pepper in a small bowl. Rub the steak with the oil. Then coat with the rosemary mixture.

3. Place the steak on the grill over direct medium-high heat and grill until desired doneness, about 5 minutes per side for medium-rare. Transfer to a cutting board and let stand for at least 5 minutes to complete the cooking process.

4. Cut the strip steak and the filet portion of the steak from the bone, then slice. Adjust seasoning.

5. Divide the steak slices among individual plates and serve.

Per serving: 300 calories, 21g total fat, 7g saturated fat, 0g trans fat, 70mg cholesterol, 510mg sodium, 0g total carbohydrate, 0g dietary fiber, 0g sugars, 27g protein

Teriyaki New York Strip

Makes 4 servings: 3½ ounces each

The tender New York strip cut goes by many other names depending on where you live, such as Kansas City steak. No matter the name, this grilled steak preparation is easy to fix and easy to love. The Asian flair makes it unforgettable, especially when enjoyed in Asian Butterhead Steak Bowls (page 321) or with Asian Cabbage Salad with Red Onion and Mint (page 173).

1 tablespoon teriyaki sauce or Tangy Teriyaki Sauce (page 135)

Juice of ½ lime (1 tablespoon)

2 teaspoons canola or peanut oil

2 teaspoons honey or agave nectar

1 teaspoon freshly grated gingerroot

½ teaspoon freshly ground black pepper, or to taste

¼ teaspoon sea salt, or to taste

1 pound well-trimmed boneless New York strip steak, about 1¼ inches thick

1. Whisk together the teriyaki sauce, lime juice, oil, honey, ginger, pepper, and salt in a small bowl or liquid measuring cup. Place the steak into a 9 × 13-inch pan, drizzle with the teriyaki sauce mixture, and rub to fully coat. Let marinate about 45 minutes.

2. Prepare an outdoor or indoor grill.

3. Grill the steak over direct medium-high heat until desired doneness, about 4 minutes per side for medium-rare. Transfer the steak to a cutting board, let stand for at least 5 minutes to complete the cooking process. Adjust seasoning. Slice, if desired.

4. Divide the steak among individual plates and serve.

Per serving: 200 calories, 8g total fat, 2.5g saturated fat, 0g trans fat, 55mg cholesterol, 360mg sodium, 4g total carbohydrate, 0g dietary fiber, 4g sugars, 26g protein

Asian Butterhead Steak Bowls

Makes 4 servings: 2 stuffed lettuce bowls each

Satisfy your hankering for the savory succulence of grilled steak with this dish showcasing Asian flavors. Here, the steak is paired with crisp veggies, garlic-chili sauce for extra kick, and a distinctive cilantro highlight, and displayed in delicate lettuce leaf bowls.

8 large leaves butterhead or Boston lettuce

1 recipe Teriyaki New York Strip (page 320) or 14 ounces grilled New York strip steak (brushed with teriyaki sauce), thinly sliced against the grain

1 cup fresh cilantro sprigs, thick stems removed

12 baby carrots, halved lengthwise and then very thinly sliced lengthwise

6 radishes, thinly sliced

3 scallions, green and white parts, thinly sliced on the diagonal

1½ tablespoons Asian chili-garlic sauce, or to taste

1. Arrange on a platter separate piles of the lettuce leaves, steak, cilantro, carrots, radishes, and scallions.

2. Serve family style. Enjoy all of the ingredients stuffed into the lettuce and sprinkled with the sauce. Wrap and enjoy by hand, if desired.

Per serving: 230 calories, 8g total fat, 3g saturated fat, 0g trans fat, 55mg cholesterol, 650mg sodium, 11g total carbohydrate, 2g dietary fiber, 6g sugars, 27g protein

Lebanese Lamb and Fig Kebabs

Makes 6 servings: 1 kebab each

When you combine grilled figs, onions, and lamb, the flavors are outstanding—a little bit sweet, a little bit savory, and a lot of scrumptiousness. If figs aren't in season, enjoy these gorgeous lamb kebabs using a dozen cherry tomatoes instead. Serve over steamed brown rice or Minted Pine Nut Pilaf (page 478) alongside Greek yogurt for a delicious meal. Any leftovers? You'll love them in Lebanese Grilled Lamb Burrito (page 406).

Juice of 1 small lemon (2 tablespoons)

1 tablespoon extra-virgin olive oil

2 large garlic cloves, minced

1 teaspoon sea salt, or to taste

½ teaspoon freshly ground black pepper, or to taste

½ teaspoon ground cinnamon

1 pound lean leg of lamb or lamb loin, cut into 1½-inch cubes

¼ cup chopped fresh mint

1 large red onion, cut into 1½-inch wedges and separated

6 medium fresh Kadota, Tiger, or other figs

1. Whisk together the lemon juice, oil, garlic, salt, pepper, and cinnamon in a medium bowl. Add the lamb and toss to coat. Add 2 tablespoons of the mint and toss to coat. Add the onion and toss to coat. Cover and marinate in the refrigerator at least 2 hours.

2. Prepare an outdoor or indoor grill.

3. Arrange the meat, onion, and figs on six (10- to 12-inch) reusable or water-soaked bamboo skewers. Discard any remaining marinade. Grill the kebabs over direct medium-high heat until lamb is desired doneness, about 10 total minutes for medium-rare. Adjust seasoning.

4. Sprinkle the kebabs with the remaining 2 tablespoons mint and serve.

Per serving: 160 calories, 6g total fat, 1.5g saturated fat, 0g trans fat, 45mg cholesterol, 420mg sodium, 13g total carbohydrate, 2g dietary fiber, 9g sugars, 15g protein

Grilled Lamb Chops with Fresh Mint Chutney

Makes 4 servings: 1 chop and 2 tablespoons chutney each

Consider grilling lamb chops instead of beef for your next cookout—especially in the springtime. It's a marvelous alternative to beef. It stands up well to various spices, lending to its surprising versatility in cuisine. Plus it pairs especially well with mint. Serving these chops with fresh mint chutney adds international intrigue—and a fun factor.

1 tablespoon brown rice vinegar

1 tablespoon extra-virgin olive oil

1 small white or yellow onion, minced or coarsely grated

2 large garlic cloves, minced

1 teaspoon freshly grated gingerroot

¾ teaspoon sea salt, or to taste

½ teaspoon freshly ground black pepper

½ teaspoon ground cumin

¼ teaspoon dried hot pepper flakes

4 (4-ounce) lean lamb loin chops (about 1½ inch thick)

½ cup Fresh Mint Chutney (page 119)

1. Mix together the vinegar, oil, onion, garlic, ginger, salt, black pepper, cumin, and hot pepper flakes in a large bowl. Add the lamb and toss to coat. Cover and marinate in refrigerator for at least 2 hours.

2. Prepare an outdoor or indoor grill.

3. Discard any remaining onion marinade mixture. Grill the chops (it's okay if still coated with some of the onion) over direct medium-high heat to desired doneness, about 4 minutes per side for medium-rare. Alternatively, broil the chops for about 2 minutes per side. Adjust seasoning.

4. Serve the chops immediately with the chutney on the side.

Per serving: 170 calories, 8g total fat, 2g saturated fat, 0g trans fat, 45mg cholesterol, 710mg sodium, 8g total carbohydrate, 1g dietary fiber, 3g sugars, 15g protein

Bison Tenderloin with Raita

Makes 4 servings: 1 steak and ¼ cup raita each

Have no fear; bison meat is tender, lean, and tastes like beef. The tenderloin cut can be grilled just as you might filet mignon. Because it's so lean, it's best when cooked until medium-rare. For further razzle-dazzle, the flavorful side of Indian raita will make this bison serving succulent.

4 (4½-ounce) bison or beef tenderloin steaks (about 1 inch thick)

1 tablespoon extra-virgin olive oil

1 large garlic clove, minced

1 teaspoon grated lime zest

1 teaspoon sea salt, or to taste

½ teaspoon freshly ground black pepper, or to taste

2 tablespoons chopped fresh cilantro

1 cup Cumin-Spiced Chickpea Raita (page 97) or other raita

1. Prepare an outdoor or indoor grill.

2. Rub the steaks with the oil, garlic, and zest. Add the salt and pepper.

3. Grill the steaks over direct medium-high heat until desired doneness, about 3½ minutes per side for medium-rare. Adjust seasoning. Let stand for about 10 minutes. Thinly slice, if desired.

4. Transfer the whole or thinly sliced steaks to individual plates, sprinkle with the cilantro and serve with the raita on the side.

Per serving: 240 calories, 9g total fat, 3g saturated fat, 0g trans fat, 85mg cholesterol, 790mg sodium, 5g total carbohydrate, 1g dietary fiber, 2g sugars, 32g protein

Grilled Venison with Cherry Balsamic Peppercorn Sauce

Makes 4 servings: 3½ ounces grilled venison slices with 1½ tablespoons sauce each

The venison in this preparation has naturally mysterious intrigue while the savory sauce has surprising sweetness. Though you can prepare it with beef tenderloin, do try the venison for a change of taste. It's exceptionally rich in iron, too.

¾ cup Cherry Balsamic Peppercorn Sauce
(page 134), at room temperature)
1 large garlic clove, minced
1 teaspoon finely chopped fresh rosemary
½ teaspoon sea salt, or to taste
½ teaspoon freshly ground black pepper, or to taste
2 (8-ounce) venison or lean beef tenderloin steaks
(about 1 inch thick)

1. Prepare an outdoor or indoor grill.

2. Stir together 6 tablespoons of the sauce, the garlic, rosemary, salt, and ¼ teaspoon of the pepper. Rub over the steaks to coat. Let marinate 30 to 45 minutes. Shake off excess marinade and discard marinade.

3. Grill the steaks over direct medium-high heat until desired doneness, about 4 minutes per side for medium-rare. Add the remaining ¼ teaspoon pepper and adjust seasoning. Let stand for at least 5 minutes. Thinly slice against the grain.

4. Transfer the sliced venison to individual plates, top with the remaining 6 tablespoons sauce, and serve.

Per serving: 190 calories, 3.5g total fat, 1g saturated fat, 0g trans fat, 75mg cholesterol, 430mg sodium, 11g total carbohydrate, 1g dietary fiber, 8g sugars, 26g protein

Baked, Braised, Roasted, or Broiled Meat and Game

Tart Apple–Stuffed Pork Loin

Makes 10 servings: about 1-inch thick slice each

When you need an entrée to impress a table full of guests, this fruity stuffed pork loin is a showstopper! The caramelized sweet onion and tart apple filling create a succulently moist, mildly sweet stuffing. It's what makes this lean pork loin luscious.

2 large garlic cloves, minced
1½ teaspoons sea salt, or to taste
1 teaspoon crushed dried rosemary
¾ teaspoon freshly ground black pepper, or to taste
½ teaspoon ground sage
1 (3½-pound) boneless center-cut pork loin roast,
trimmed
1 tablespoon unsalted butter
2 large Granny Smith or other tart apples, cored,
and very thinly sliced
1 large sweet onion, halved and thinly sliced
2 teaspoons apple cider vinegar
1 tablespoon chopped fresh sage
1 teaspoon Dijon mustard
1½ cups 100% unsweetened apple juice

1. Mix together the garlic, 1 teaspoon of the salt, the rosemary, pepper, and ground sage in a small bowl. Butterfly the pork by cutting it lengthwise with the knife parallel to the cutting surface, about 90 percent of the way through, then open up both sides of the pork and flatten. Rub half of the garlic mixture onto the cut sides of pork.

2. Preheat the oven to 325°F.

3. Melt the butter in a large skillet over medium-high heat. Add the apples, onion, vinegar, and ¼ teaspoon of the salt and sauté until the apples

continues on next page

are softened and onion is lightly caramelized, about 10 minutes. Remove from heat and stir in the fresh sage and mustard.

4. Spread the apple mixture evenly onto half of the cut side of roast. Close the halves and tie with kitchen twine or silicone bands about every 1½ inches or skewer shut.

5. Place the roast on a rack in a roasting pan. Pour the apple juice over the roast, rub the roast with remaining garlic mixture, and sprinkle with the remaining ¼ teaspoon salt.

6. Roast, uncovered, basting frequently with the drippings until desired doneness, about 1 hour 45 minutes to 2 hours for medium. Remove the roast from oven and let stand for 15 minutes to complete the cooking process. Adjust seasoning.

7. Slice as desired, drizzle with any remaining pan drippings, and serve.

Per serving: 240 calories, 8g total fat, 3g saturated fat, 0g trans fat, 85mg cholesterol, 420mg sodium, 14g total carbohydrate, 2g dietary fiber, 10g sugars, 26g protein

Flash-Fried Pork Loin Chops

Makes 4 servings: 1 chop each

This recipe uses my flash-frying technique. It involves quickly frying the breaded pork loin chops in very hot oil just to get the coating crisp, then completing the cooking in a hot oven. The best part, though . . . these pork chops are delicious.

4 (4-ounce) boneless pork loin chops
    (about ¾ inch thick)
¾ cup plain almond milk or unsweetened
    coconut milk beverage
1 large garlic clove, minced
1 teaspoon sea salt, or to taste
⅔ cup plain dry whole-wheat breadcrumbs
½ teaspoon freshly ground black pepper,
    or to taste
¼ teaspoon smoked paprika
2 cups grapeseed or peanut oil

1. Add the pork, almond milk, garlic, and ½ teaspoon of the salt to a medium bowl. Let marinate for 30 to 45 minutes, flipping over the chops halfway through to ensure even marinating.

2. Preheat the oven to 425°F.

3. Stir together the breadcrumbs, pepper, paprika, and the remaining ½ teaspoon salt in a large bowl. One at a time, remove a pork chop from the marinade, shake off the excess, and thoroughly coat the chop in the breadcrumb mixture. Discard leftover marinade.

4. Have ready an oven-safe cooling rack with a paper towel underneath. Heat the oil in a large skillet over high heat. Once hot (yet not smoking), add the pork chop and fry until the coating is browned, yet pork is not fully cooked, about 1 minute. For best results, make sure the pork is fully immersed in the oil so there's no need to flip each piece. Place each chop on the cooling rack to drain—and to help keep it crisp.

5. Keeping the pork on the rack, transfer the rack to a baking sheet and bake until the pork is cooked to medium doneness, about 6 minutes. Let stand for 5 minutes before serving. Adjust seasoning and serve.

Per serving: 230 calories, 10g total fat, 1.5g saturated fat, 0g trans fat, 60mg cholesterol, 430mg sodium, 10g total carbohydrate, 1g dietary fiber, 1g sugars, 23g protein

Caramelized Onion Salisbury Steak with Shiitake Gravy

Makes 4 servings: 1 (6-ounce) Salisbury steak with ¼ cup gravy each

When you're in the mood for a nostalgic comfort-food fix, give this especially tender Salisbury steak entrée a try. I gave it a modern makeover by way of whole-wheat ingredients, plenty of parsley, and freshly prepared onion soup plus woodsy shiitake gravy instead of canned condensed soup. You get the flavor memories of yesterday with today's smart sensibility.

1 tablespoon ketchup

2 teaspoons whole-wheat pastry flour

1 teaspoon Dijon mustard

1 teaspoon Worcestershire sauce

1½ cups Caramelized Red, White and Yellow Onion Soup (page 211) or other onion soup, chilled

1 pound lean ground beef sirloin

⅓ cup plain dry whole-wheat breadcrumbs

1 large egg, lightly beaten

¼ cup finely chopped fresh flat-leaf parsley

⅛ teaspoon sea salt, or to taste

⅛ teaspoon ground black pepper, or to taste

1 cup Shiitake Gravy (page 111) or other mushroom gravy

1. Stir together the ketchup, flour, mustard, and Worcestershire sauce in a small bowl until smooth. Stir in 1 cup of the soup. Set aside.

2. Mix together the remaining ½ cup soup, the beef, breadcrumbs, egg, 3 tablespoons of the parsley, the salt, and pepper. Form into 4 oval "burger-like" patties.

3. Heat a large nonstick skillet over medium-high heat. Add the patties and cook until brown, about 3 minutes per side. Pour the ketchup mixture over the patties, cover, reduce heat to low, and simmer until tender, about 18 minutes, stirring occasionally.

4. Stir in the gravy and cook while stirring until hot. Adjust seasoning.

5. Transfer the steaks to a platter and ladle the pan gravy over the steaks. Sprinkle with the remaining 1 tablespoon parsley, and serve.

Per serving: 260 calories, 8g total fat, 2.5g saturated fat, 0g trans fat, 115mg cholesterol, 650mg sodium, 15g total carbohydrate, 3g dietary fiber, 4g sugars, 29g protein

Oven-Fried Veal Parmigiana

Makes 4 servings: 1 cutlet with ¼ rounded cup sauce each

This parmigiana has the crispy goodness it deserves, as the veal is "oven-fried" with a flavorful, whole-grain coating, but the Italian cheese is still there to grab your taste buds' attention.

½ cup whole-wheat flour

¾ teaspoon sea salt, or to taste

2 large eggs

2 large garlic cloves, minced

¼ teaspoon ground cayenne (optional)

¾ cup plain dry whole-wheat breadcrumbs

4 (4-ounce) veal loin cutlets, pounded to ⅛-inch thickness

¼ teaspoon freshly ground black pepper, or to taste

2 tablespoons freshly grated Parmigiano-Reggiano or other Parmesan cheese

4 (¾-ounce) thin slices part-skim mozzarella cheese, cut into 3 slices each

1¼ cups Triple Tomato Marinara Sauce (page 101) or other marinara sauce, warm

1. Preheat the oven to 475°F.

2. Spread the flour on a plate; stir in ¼ teaspoon of the salt. Whisk together the eggs, 2 tablespoons cold water, the garlic, ¼ teaspoon of the salt, and the cayenne (if using) in an 8-inch round baking dish. Spread the breadcrumbs on another plate.

3. Season the veal with the remaining ¼ teaspoon salt and the black pepper. Lightly dredge the veal in the flour, dip into the egg mixture until fully moistened, and generously dredge in the breadcrumb mixture, shaking off excess mixture between each dipping.

4. Place the veal on a large parchment–paper lined baking tray. Lightly coat each side of the veal with cooking spray (preferably homemade, page xix). Bake until cooked through and crisp, about 9 minutes, flipping the veal about halfway through the baking process. Top each piece of veal with the Parmesan, then the mozzarella slices. Place under the broiler until the cheese is lightly browned, about 1 minute. Adjust seasoning.

5. Ladle the sauce onto individual plates, top with the veal, and serve immediately. Garnish with fresh basil and serve with whole-wheat pasta tossed with additional marinara sauce, if desired.

Per serving: 380 calories, 17g total fat, 7g saturated fat, 0g trans fat, 135mg cholesterol, 740mg sodium, 22g total carbohydrate, 4g dietary fiber, 3g sugars, 31g protein

Pinot Grigio Osso Buco

Makes 6 servings: 1 shank with about 1½ cups sauce each

This beautifully braised veal specialty of Milanese descent is a heart-warming and hearty one-dish wonder, ideal for nearly any special occasion. The slow-stewed meat is fall-off-the-bone tender. The rich broth and herb and spice notes may actually make you fall of your seat in flavor awe.

2 tablespoons + 2 teaspoons grapeseed or peanut oil

2 large white onions, finely chopped

1½ cups diced or thinly crosswise sliced carrots

1½ cups diced or thinly crosswise sliced celery

Juice and zest of ½ small lemon (1 tablespoon juice)

¾ teaspoon + ⅛ teaspoon sea salt, or to taste

4 large garlic cloves, minced

6 (8-ounce) lean veal shanks with bone and marrow (osso buco), about 1½ inches thick, tied around the middle with kitchen twine

½ cup whole-wheat pastry flour

1 (750-ml) bottle Pinot Grigio or other bright dry white wine

3½ cups low-sodium chicken broth or Chicken Stock (page 203), or to taste

1 (28-ounce) can plum or other whole tomatoes, crushed by hand

1 teaspoon dried thyme leaves

1 teaspoon freshly ground black pepper, or to taste

¼ teaspoon ground cinnamon

¼ cup finely chopped fresh flat-leaf parsley

1. Heat 2 teaspoons of the oil in a Dutch oven over medium-high heat. Add the onions, carrots, celery, lemon juice, and ⅛ teaspoon of the salt and sauté until vegetables begin to brown, about 10 minutes. Stir in the garlic and zest and sauté for 1 minute. Remove from heat.

2. Dredge the veal in the flour, shaking off any excess. Heat 1 tablespoon of the oil in a large skillet over medium-high heat. Add three of the veal shanks and sauté until golden brown, about 2½ minutes per side. Repeat with the remaining oil and veal. Add the veal on top of the vegetables in the Dutch oven.

3. Preheat the oven to 350°F.

4. Add the wine to the large skillet over medium-high heat and cook, stirring frequently, scraping up any browned bits, until the wine is slightly reduced, about 4 minutes. Drizzle over the veal and vegetables. Add the broth, tomatoes, thyme, pepper, cinnamon, and the remaining ¾ teaspoon salt to the Dutch oven. Add additional broth, if necessary, to cover the veal. Adjust seasoning.

5. Bring the veal and vegetable mixture to a boil over high heat. Remove from heat, cover, and roast in the oven for 1 hour 15 minutes. Remove cover and continue to roast until the veal is very tender, about 1 hour 15 minutes more. Adjust seasoning.

6. Transfer the veal to a platter. Ladle the sauce over the veal. Sprinkle with the parsley and serve.

Per serving: 450 calories, 11g total fat, 2g saturated fat, 0g trans fat, 150mg cholesterol, 795mg sodium, 24g total carbohydrate, 4g dietary fiber, 7g sugars, 38g protein

Cocoa-Dusted Lamb Loin

Makes 4 servings: 1 lamb chop with 3 tablespoons tzatziki each

You'll be intrigued by this roasted lamb loin that has an enticing seared appearance and a lovely, almost dessert-like scent from the cocoa and spice. Is the flavor anticipation getting to you yet? Well, then get roasting.

4 (5½-ounce) lamb loin chops on bone
    (about 2 inches thick)
2 teaspoons extra-virgin olive oil
¼ cup finely chopped fresh mint
1 tablespoon unsweetened cocoa powder
½ teaspoon ground cinnamon
½ teaspoon sea salt, or to taste
¾ cup Mint Tzatziki (page 95) or fat-free or low-fat
    plain Greek yogurt

1. Preheat the oven to 475°F.

2. Rub the lamb chops with the oil.

3. Combine the mint, cocoa, cinnamon, and salt in a small bowl. Rub both sides of each chop with the mint-cocoa mixture.

4. Place the lamb on a parchment paper–lined baking pan. Roast until medium-rare, about 10 minutes, or desired doneness. Remove from the oven and let stand at least 5 minutes before serving. Adjust seasoning and serve on the tzatziki.

Per serving: 190 calories, 10g total fat, 3g saturated fat, 0g trans fat, 60mg cholesterol, 410mg sodium, 3g total carbohydrate, 1g dietary fiber, 1g sugars, 22g protein

Tomato-Glazed Mini Meatloaves

Makes 4 servings: 2 loaves each

Enjoy luscious, inspired comfort food while keeping your calories in check. Here, the special accent from five-spice powder and hint of sweetness from apple butter enhances the combination of three different meats to make these uniquely succulent mini meatloaves.

6 ounces lean ground beef sirloin
5 ounces lean ground pork
5 ounces lean ground turkey or veal
1 medium red onion, minced
1 large garlic clove, minced
1 large egg, slightly beaten
⅓ cup old-fashioned oats
⅓ cup ketchup
3 tablespoons Pickled Jalapeño Mustard
    (page 127) or spicy brown mustard
2 tablespoons no-sugar-added apple butter
½ teaspoon finely chopped fresh oregano
    or ¼ teaspoon crushed dried oregano
½ teaspoon sea salt
½ teaspoon freshly ground black pepper
¼ teaspoon Chinese five-spice powder
    or ground cinnamon

1. Preheat the oven to 450°F.

2. Gently combine by hand the beef, pork, and turkey in a large bowl. Stir together in a small bowl the onion, garlic, egg, oats, 2 tablespoons of the ketchup, 2 tablespoons of the mustard, 1 tablespoon of the apple butter, the oregano, salt, pepper, and five-spice powder until combined. Add the onion mixture to the meat mixture and combine by hand until just combined.

3. Sculpt the meatloaf mixture into 8 football-shaped loaves, about 3½ ounces each. Place on a parchment paper–lined baking pan.

4. Stir together the remaining ketchup, mustard, and apple butter in a small bowl. Gently rub the ketchup mixture onto each meatloaf to lightly coat.

5. Bake until fully cooked, about 22 minutes. Let stand at least 5 minutes before serving.

Per serving: 230 calories, 7g total fat, 2g saturated fat, 0g trans fat, 105mg cholesterol, 540mg sodium, 17g total carbohydrate, 2g dietary fiber, 7g sugars, 26g protein

Roasted Bison Meatloaves

Makes 4 servings: 1 loaf with ½ cup spinach each

This rustic dish is all about delectableness. A bevy of veggies boosts body and flavor in the lean and trendy buffalo meat. And the cradle of steamy leafy greens completes it in savory style.

12 ounces ground grass-fed bison (buffalo) meat or lean ground grass-fed beef sirloin

1 medium red onion, minced or coarsely grated

½ cup coarsely grated zucchini or yellow squash

⅓ cup old-fashioned oats

1 large garlic clove, minced

1 large egg, lightly beaten

2 tablespoons ketchup

1 teaspoon aged balsamic vinegar

½ + ⅛ teaspoon sea salt, or to taste

½ teaspoon freshly ground black pepper, or to taste

¼ teaspoon ground cinnamon

⅛ teaspoon dried hot pepper flakes

2 cups steamed spinach or Balsamic Wilted Spinach Bed (page 450)

1. Preheat the oven to 425°F.

2. Thoroughly combine the meat, onion, zucchini, oats, garlic, egg, ketchup, vinegar, salt, black pepper, cinnamon, and hot pepper flakes in a large bowl by hand.

3. Form the meat mixture into 4 round loaves (about ¾ rounded cup each) and place onto a parchment paper–lined baking pan. Make a 1-inch long "X" about 1-inch deep in the center of each loaf

4. Bake until fully cooked, about 30 minutes. Let stand at least 5 minutes.

5. Arrange the spinach on individual plates or a platter, place meatloaves on top, and serve.

Per serving: 210 calories, 8g total fat, 3g saturated fat, 0g trans fat, 95mg cholesterol, 630mg sodium, 14g total carbohydrate, 4g dietary fiber, 3g sugars, 23g protein

Stir-Fried or Sautéed Poultry and Meat

Ginger Chicken, Broccoli, and Oyster Mushroom Stir-Fry

Makes 4 servings: 1 rounded cup each

My first introduction to Chinese food was a chicken and broccoli dish very similar to this one. Here I highlight the kicky flavors of soy sauce and garlic-chili sauce. The broccoli tenderizes just enough so the florets act like little sponges for the tasty sauce. And the abundance of veggies makes this one dish you can feel good about—especially when paired with brown rice or quinoa.

½ cup low-sodium chicken broth or Chicken Stock (page 203)

1 tablespoon + 2 teaspoons naturally brewed soy sauce, or to taste

1 tablespoon brown rice vinegar

1½ teaspoons Asian garlic-chili sauce

1 tablespoon cornstarch

12 ounces boneless skinless chicken breast, cut into ⅓-inch wide strips

⅛ teaspoon sea salt, or to taste

1 tablespoon peanut or canola oil

2 large garlic cloves, very thinly sliced

1 tablespoon freshly grated gingerroot

3 cups broccoli florets, cut into bite-size pieces

1 large sweet onion, quartered lengthwise, thinly sliced crosswise

3½ ounces fresh oyster mushrooms

¼ cup coarsely grated carrot

1. Whisk together the broth, soy sauce, vinegar, garlic-chili sauce, and cornstarch in a liquid measuring cup or small bowl until smooth. Set aside.

2. Season the chicken with the salt.

3. Heat the oil in a wok or large skillet over high heat. Carefully add the garlic, ginger, chicken, broccoli, onion, mushrooms, and carrot and stir-fry until the chicken is just cooked through and broccoli is crisp-tender, about 3½ minutes. Add the broth mixture and stir-fry until the sauce is thickened, about 1 minute. Adjust seasoning and serve.

Per serving: 200 calories, 6g total fat, 1g saturated fat, 0g trans fat, 45mg cholesterol, 630mg sodium, 16g total carbohydrate, 3g dietary fiber, 6g sugars, 21g protein

Garlic Chicken and Snow Pea Stir-Fry

Makes 4 servings: 1 cup each

For a stir-fry that's pleasingly mild, this recipe will delight with its aromatic touch of garlic and ginger shining though. The crisp textures from the snow peas and bok choy create a pleasantly crunchy finish. When served with Sticky Ginger Rice (page 478), it's a fully fragrant meal.

12 ounces boneless skinless chicken breast, cut into ¼-inch wide strips

¼ teaspoon sea salt, or to taste

1 tablespoon peanut or canola oil

2 teaspoons freshly grated gingerroot

1½ cups snow peas, trimmed

1 large sweet onion, quartered lengthwise, peeled, thinly sliced crosswise

1 cup thinly sliced bok choy or water chestnuts

¾ cup Cantonese Garlic Sauce (page 136), at room temperature

1. Season the chicken with the salt.

2. Heat the oil in a wok or large skillet over high heat. Carefully add the ginger, chicken, snow peas, onion, and bok choy and stir-fry until the chicken is just cooked through and snow peas are crisp-tender, about 3½ minutes. Add the garlic sauce and stir-fry until the sauce fully coats the chicken mixture, about 1 minute. Adjust seasoning and serve.

Per serving: 220 calories, 8g total fat, 1.5g saturated fat, 0g trans fat, 45mg cholesterol, 590mg sodium, 15g total carbohydrate, 2g dietary fiber, 10g sugars, 20g protein

Peppery Kung Pao Chicken

Makes 4 servings: 1 cup each

The lip-smacking combination of succulent chicken thigh, vibrant veggies, distinctive Asian flavors, and salty peanuts creates one enticing stir-fry.

½ cup low-sodium chicken broth or Chicken Stock (page 203)

1 tablespoon naturally brewed soy sauce

2 teaspoons brown rice vinegar

2 teaspoons Asian garlic-chili sauce

1 teaspoon toasted sesame oil

1 tablespoon cornstarch

2 teaspoons turbinado sugar

12 ounces boneless skinless chicken thighs, cut into ⅓-inch cubes

¼ teaspoon sea salt, or to taste

1 tablespoon peanut or canola oil

1 tablespoon freshly grated gingerroot

3 large garlic cloves, very thinly sliced

1 large red bell pepper, diced

1 large orange or yellow bell pepper, diced

1 cup thinly sliced bok choy or water chestnuts

3 scallions, green and white parts, sliced diagonally

3 tablespoons coarsely chopped salted dry-roasted peanuts

1. Whisk together the broth, soy sauce, vinegar, garlic-chili sauce, sesame oil, cornstarch, and sugar in a liquid measuring cup or small bowl until smooth. Set aside.

2. Season the chicken with the salt.

3. Heat the peanut oil in a wok or large skillet over high heat. Carefully add the chicken and ginger and stir-fry for 1½ minutes. Add the garlic, bell peppers, and bok choy and stir-fry until the chicken is cooked through, about 3 minutes. Add the broth mixture and scallions and stir-fry until the sauce is thickened, about 1 minute. Stir in the peanuts. Adjust seasoning and serve.

Per serving: 260 calories, 15g total fat, 3g saturated fat, 0g trans fat, 55mg cholesterol, 580mg sodium, 13g total carbohydrate, 3g dietary fiber, 6g sugars, 19g protein

Main Dishes: Poultry, Meat, and Game   **329**

Citrus Chicken Stir-Fry with Peppers and Pine Nuts

Makes 4 servings: 1 scant cup each

Fresh navel orange basically "melts" to create a citrusy and saucier-than-usual stir-fry. So whip out your wok to enjoy this memorable Asian chicken dish with glorious colors.

½ cup low-sodium chicken broth or Chicken Stock (page 203)

1 tablespoon naturally brewed soy sauce

2 teaspoons brown rice vinegar

2 teaspoons Asian garlic-chili sauce

1 teaspoon toasted sesame oil

1 tablespoon cornstarch

2 teaspoons turbinado sugar

12 ounces boneless skinless chicken breast, cut into small cubes

¼ teaspoon sea salt, or to taste

1 tablespoon peanut or canola oil

3 large garlic cloves, very thinly sliced

1 tablespoon grated unpeeled scrubbed gingerroot

1 large red bell pepper, diced

1 large navel orange, diced

4 scallions, green and white parts, sliced diagonally

3 tablespoons pine nuts, toasted

1. Whisk together the broth, soy sauce, vinegar, garlic-chili sauce, sesame oil, cornstarch, and sugar in a liquid measuring cup or small bowl until smooth. Set aside.

2. Season the chicken with the salt.

3. Heat the peanut oil in a wok or large skillet over high heat. Carefully add the garlic, ginger, and chicken, the bell pepper, and orange, and stir-fry until the chicken is just cooked through, about 3½ minutes. Add the broth mixture and scallions and stir-fry until the sauce is thickened, about 1 minute. Stir in the pine nuts. Adjust seasoning and serve.

Per serving: 240 calories, 11g total fat, 1.5g saturated fat, 0g trans fat, 45mg cholesterol, 550mg sodium, 15g total carbohydrate, 2g dietary fiber, 8g sugars, 20g protein

Szechuan Chicken and Asparagus

Makes 4 servings: 1 cup each

This has it all—sweet, savory, spicy, and salty!

1 large navel orange

½ cup low-sodium chicken broth or Chicken Stock (page 203)

1 tablespoon naturally brewed soy sauce

2 teaspoons brown rice vinegar

2 teaspoons Asian garlic-chili sauce

1 teaspoon toasted sesame oil

1 tablespoon cornstarch

2 teaspoons turbinado sugar

12 ounces boneless skinless chicken thighs, cut into ⅓-inch cubes

¼ teaspoon sea salt, or to taste

⅛ teaspoon ground Szechuan pepper or ¼ teaspoon dried hot pepper flakes, or to taste

1 tablespoon peanut or canola oil

3 large garlic cloves, very thinly sliced

1 tablespoon freshly grated gingerroot

12 medium asparagus spears, stems removed, and thinly sliced on the diagonal

3 scallions, green and white parts, sliced diagonally

1. Zest the orange; dice the flesh. Set aside.

2. Whisk together the broth, soy sauce, vinegar, garlic-chili sauce, sesame oil, cornstarch, and sugar in a small bowl until smooth. Set aside.

3. Season the chicken with the salt and pepper.

4. Heat the peanut oil in a wok or large skillet over high heat. Carefully add the garlic, ginger, chicken, asparagus, and diced orange, and stir-fry until the chicken is cooked through, about 4½ minutes. Add the broth mixture, 2 teaspoons of the orange zest, and the scallions and stir-fry until the sauce is thickened, about 1 minute. Adjust seasoning and serve.

Per serving: 230 calories, 11g total fat, 2.5g saturated fat, 0g trans fat, 55mg cholesterol, 550mg sodium, 14g total carbohydrate, 2g dietary fiber, 8g sugars, 18g protein

Mongolian Flank Steak Stir-Fry

Makes 4 servings: 1 cup each

You'll be especially enticed by this, as the little spoonful of turbinado sugar that's part of this bell pepper-packed recipe adds sweet intrigue and caramelization to the beef. Serve with soba noodles or quinoa and you've got a nutrient-rich, fully satisfying meal.

½ cup low-sodium beef broth

5 teaspoons naturally brewed soy sauce, or to taste

1 tablespoon Asian garlic-chili sauce

2 teaspoons brown rice vinegar

1 teaspoon toasted sesame oil

1 tablespoon cornstarch

12 ounces lean flank steak, cut into ¼-inch bite-size strips against the grain

2 teaspoons turbinado sugar

⅛ teaspoon sea salt, or to taste

1 tablespoon peanut or canola oil

3 large garlic cloves, minced

2 teaspoons freshly grated gingerroot

2 large red bell peppers, thinly sliced

6 scallions, green and white parts, sliced diagonally

1. Whisk together the broth, soy sauce, garlic-chili sauce, vinegar, sesame oil, and cornstarch in a liquid measuring cup or small bowl until smooth. Set aside.

2. Season the beef with the sugar and salt.

3. Heat the peanut oil in a wok or large skillet over high heat. Carefully add the garlic, ginger, and bell peppers and stir-fry for 30 seconds. Add the beef and stir-fry until browned, about 2 minutes. Add the broth mixture and scallions, and stir-fry until the sauce is thickened, about 1 minute. Adjust seasoning and serve.

Per serving: 250 calories, 12g total fat, 3g saturated fat, 0g trans fat, 60mg cholesterol, 620mg sodium, 13g total carbohydrate, 2g dietary fiber, 6g sugars, 21g protein

Cantonese Broccoli and Beef Tenderloin

Makes 4 servings: 1 rounded cup each

The pairing of beef and broccoli is a traditional and tasty one in a stir-fry. Add to the mix the delicious earthiness of wild mushrooms and savory sweetness of onion and you've got an unbelievably tasty dish. Complete the meal by serving it atop brown basmati rice.

12 ounces well-trimmed lean beef tenderloin or top loin steak, cut into ½-inch-wide strips

¼ teaspoon sea salt, or to taste

1 tablespoon peanut or canola oil

1 tablespoon freshly grated gingerroot

2½ cups broccoli or cauliflower florets or mixture, cut into bite-size pieces

1 large sweet onion, quartered lengthwise, thinly sliced crosswise

4 ounces fresh exotic mushroom pieces

¾ cup Cantonese Garlic Sauce, at room temperature (page 136)

1. Season the beef with the salt.

2. Heat the oil in a wok or large skillet over high heat. Carefully add the ginger, broccoli, and onion, and stir-fry until the broccoli is nearly crisp-tender, about 3 minutes. Add the beef and mushrooms and stir-fry until the beef is browned, about 2 minutes. Add the garlic sauce and stir-fry until the sauce fully coats the beef mixture, about 1 minute. Adjust seasoning and serve.

Per serving: 250 calories, 11g total fat, 3g saturated fat, 0g trans fat, 45mg cholesterol, 590mg sodium, 18g total carbohydrate, 3g dietary fiber, 9g sugars, 20g protein

Herb-Infused Steak Destiny

Makes 4 servings: 1 steak each

Here's a modern version of Steak Diane loaded with fresh herbs and just enough butter to provide a boost of richness. Enjoy the perfectly portioned twist on tradition.

2 teaspoons grapeseed or canola oil

4 (4-ounce) lean beef filet tips (about 1 inch thick)

¾ teaspoon sea salt, or to taste

¼ teaspoon freshly ground black pepper, or to taste

2 teaspoons unsalted butter

2 large shallots, minced

1 large garlic clove, minced

3 tablespoons chopped fresh chives

½ teaspoon chopped fresh thyme or oregano

½ teaspoon chopped fresh rosemary

Juice of 1 small lemon (2 tablespoons)

2 tablespoons 100% unsweetened apple juice

1 teaspoon Worcestershire sauce

1 teaspoon Dijon mustard

3 tablespoons finely chopped fresh flat-leaf parsley

1. Heat the oil in a large nonstick skillet over medium-high heat. Add the steaks, salt, and pepper to the skillet and cook until desired doneness, about 3 minutes per side for medium-rare. Transfer the steaks to a plate.

2. Melt the butter in the skillet over medium heat. Add the shallots and garlic and sauté for 1 minute. Add the chives, thyme, rosemary, lemon juice, apple juice, Worcestershire sauce, and mustard and sauté for 1 minute.

3. Add the steaks and residual juices to the skillet and cook while coating the steaks with the sauce, about 1 minute. Adjust seasoning.

4. Transfer the steaks to individual plates or a platter, sprinkle with the parsley, and serve.

Per serving: 210 calories, 11g total fat, 4g saturated fat, 0g trans fat, 65mg cholesterol, 530mg sodium, 6g total carbohydrate, 0g dietary fiber, 2g sugars, 23g protein

Meatballs Romano

Makes 6 servings: 3 meatballs each

This spicy meatball is definitely a winner. The steaminess created by the moist zucchini and the almond milk makes a softer, moister, and healthier meatball. The perfect pinches of prosciutto add mouthwatering magic.

⅔ cup plain dry whole-wheat breadcrumbs

1 small or ½ large red onion, grated

⅓ cup coarsely grated zucchini or
      summer yellow squash

¼ cup plain almond milk or light soy milk

⅓ cup finely chopped fresh basil

⅓ cup finely chopped fresh flat-leaf parsley

⅓ cup freshly grated Romano cheese

2 large eggs, lightly beaten

3 large garlic cloves, minced

8 ounces lean ground beef sirloin

6 ounces ground turkey (about 94% lean)
      or ground chicken breast

2 ounces thinly sliced prosciutto or country ham,
      finely chopped

¾ teaspoon dried hot pepper flakes, or to taste

½ teaspoon sea salt, or to taste

½ teaspoon freshly ground black pepper, or to taste

⅛ teaspoon freshly grated nutmeg

1 tablespoon extra-virgin olive oil

1. Stir together the breadcrumbs, onion, zucchini, and almond milk in a medium bowl. Let stand for at least 5 minutes to allow the breadcrumbs to become fully moistened.

2. Add the basil, parsley, cheese, eggs, and garlic and stir to combine. Add the beef, turkey, prosciutto, hot pepper flakes, salt, black pepper, and nutmeg and mix by hand until just evenly combined (do not overmix).

3. Form the mixture into 18 balls, about 2 rounded tablespoons each.

4. Preheat the oven to 400°F.

5. Heat 1½ teaspoons of the oil in a large nonstick skillet over medium heat. Add half the meatballs and sauté until well browned on all sides, about 10 minutes. Repeat with the remaining oil and meatballs.

6. Place the browned meatballs on a baking pan. Bake in the preheated oven until full cooked, about 15 minutes. Remove from oven; transfer to a bowl and serve.

Per serving: 210 calories, 10g total fat, 3g saturated fat, 0g trans fat, 110mg cholesterol, 590mg sodium, 9g total carbohydrate, 1g dietary fiber, 1g sugars, 21g protein

Papaya Pork

Makes 4 servings: 1½ cups each

Here's an interesting translation of sweet-n-sour pork. There's no need for breading and frying, as the pork is tossed with so many tantalizing flavors and textures. The tropical accent from papaya makes this stir-fry a true culinary joy. While it highlights the Hawaiian *kapoho,* a perfumey papaya with a sweet floral melon-like flavor, any other papaya will be tasty here, too. Pair it with Coconut-Spiked Basmati Rice (page 477), if you like.

½ cup low-sodium chicken broth or Chicken Stock
  (page 203)

1½ tablespoons naturally brewed soy sauce

1 tablespoon apple cider vinegar

1 tablespoon cornstarch

2 teaspoons turbinado sugar

12 ounces pork tenderloin, cut into ⅓-inch cubes

¼ teaspoon sea salt, or to taste

1 tablespoon peanut or canola oil

1 tablespoon freshly grated gingerroot

1 large red bell pepper, cut into ⅓-inch cubes

1 large green bell pepper, cut into ⅓-inch cubes

½ large sweet onion, diced

1 (16-ounce) Hawaiian kapoho or other papaya,
  peeled, seeded, and cut into ⅓-inch cubes

3 tablespoons coarsely chopped unsalted cashews
  (optional)

1. Whisk together the broth, soy sauce, vinegar, cornstarch, and sugar in a liquid measuring cup or small bowl until smooth. Set aside.

2. Season the pork with the salt.

3. Heat the oil in a wok or large skillet over high heat. Carefully add the pork, the ginger, bell peppers, and onion and stir-fry until the pork is just medium doneness, about 3 minutes. Add the broth mixture and papaya, and stir-fry until the sauce is thickened, about 1 minute. Adjust seasoning. Sprinkle with the cashews, if using, and serve.

Per serving: 210 calories, 6g total fat, 1.5g saturated fat, 0g trans fat, 55mg cholesterol, 560mg sodium, 20g total carbohydrate, 3g dietary fiber, 12g sugars, 20g protein

Petite Apricot Ham Steak

Makes 4 servings: 1 (2¼-ounce) wedge ham each

If a protein-rich entrée could actually taste like candy, this is it! This zesty apricot-glazed ham will hit the spot, naturally, as the best blend of savory and sweet. It's so flavorful, the petite portion is all you'll need. Savor it slowly with a fork and knife.

3 tablespoons 100% apricot preserves

1 tablespoon apple cider vinegar

2 teaspoons stone-ground mustard

¼ teaspoon finely chopped fresh rosemary
  or ⅛ teaspoon crushed dried rosemary

⅛ teaspoon ground cloves (optional)

1 (9-ounce) thick slice lean uncured ham,
  cut into 4 wedges

1. Add the preserves, vinegar, mustard, rosemary, and (if using) cloves to a large skillet over medium heat. Cook while stirring to bring to a boil. Add the ham wedges and sauté until the apricot mixture is thickened and caramelized, the ham is fully coated with the apricot mixture, and the ham is gently browned on both sides, about 2½ to 3 minutes per side.

2. Transfer the candied ham pieces to individual plates, and serve while warm.

Per serving: 110 calories, 2.5g total fat, 0.5g saturated fat, 0g trans fat, 25mg cholesterol, 730mg sodium, 13g total carbohydrate, 0g dietary fiber, 9g sugars, 10g protein

Lamb and Eggplant Stir-Fry

Makes 3 servings: about 1 cup each

Go for a change of taste at home and try out this lamb and eggplant stir-fry that's a sure pleaser. The lamb is big on savory flavor—and the sesame and scallion make it even more irresistible. Serve it over steamed quinoa or brown rice.

½ cup low-sodium beef broth

1 tablespoon + 1 teaspoon naturally brewed soy sauce, or to taste

1 tablespoon Asian garlic-chili sauce

2 teaspoons brown rice vinegar

1 teaspoon toasted sesame oil

1 tablespoon cornstarch

2 (7-ounce) lean lamb loin chops, bones removed, cut into ¼-inch wide strips

Pinch of sea salt, or to taste

1 tablespoon peanut or canola oil

1½ cups diced eggplant

2 large garlic cloves, minced

2 teaspoons freshly grated gingerroot

4 scallions, green and white parts, sliced diagonally

1 teaspoon sesame seeds, toasted

1. Whisk together the broth, soy sauce, garlic-chili sauce, vinegar, sesame oil, and cornstarch in a liquid measuring cup or small bowl until smooth. Set aside.

2. Season the lamb with the salt.

3. Heat the peanut oil in a wok or large skillet over high heat. Carefully add the eggplant and stir-fry until the eggplant is softened, about 2 minutes. Add the garlic, ginger, and lamb and stir-fry until the lamb is browned, about 1 minute. Add the broth mixture, the white part of the scallions, and half of the green part of the scallions and stir-fry until the sauce is thickened, about 1 minute. Adjust seasoning. Sprinkle with the sesame seeds and the remaining scallions and serve.

Per serving: 290 calories, 19g total fat, 6g saturated fat, 0g trans fat, 55mg cholesterol, 770mg sodium, 12g total carbohydrate, 2g dietary fiber, 3g sugars, 18g protein

Wok-Charred Turkish Lamb with Grape Tomatoes

Makes 4 servings: 1 cup each

Instead of soy sauce and sesame oil, you'll find lemon juice and olive oil provide an inspired bite in this stir-fry. The raisins and bursting grape tomatoes add a sweet counterbalance to the rich "stir-fried" lamb. Enjoy along with brown basmati rice, plain Greek yogurt, and a little hot chili pepper sauce for an inspired meal.

12 ounces boneless leg of lamb cutlets, cut against the grain into ¼-inch-wide strips

1½ teaspoons chopped fresh oregano

¾ teaspoon sea salt, or to taste

½ teaspoon freshly ground black pepper, or to taste

1½ teaspoons grapeseed or canola oil

⅓ cup coarsely grated carrot

2 large garlic cloves, minced

1½ cups grape tomatoes or small cherry tomatoes

4 scallions, green and white parts, sliced diagonally

2 tablespoons black seedless raisins or currants

2 teaspoons fresh lemon juice

1½ teaspoons extra-virgin olive oil

¼ cup chopped fresh flat-leaf parsley

1. Season the lamb with 1 teaspoon of the oregano, the salt, and pepper.

2. Heat the grapeseed oil in a wok or large skillet over high heat. Carefully add the carrot and garlic and sauté for 1 minute. Add the lamb, tomatoes, and scallions and sauté until the lamb is browned, about 1 minute. Add the raisins and lemon juice and sauté until the lamb is about medium doneness, about 1 minute. Adjust seasoning.

3. Transfer the lamb to a platter, drizzle with the olive oil, sprinkle with the parsley and remaining ½ teaspoon oregano, and serve.

Per serving: 180 calories, 9g total fat, 2g saturated fat, 0g trans fat, 50mg cholesterol, 490mg sodium, 9g total carbohydrate, 2g dietary fiber, 5g sugars, 16g protein

Slow-Cooked and Pressure-Cooked Poultry and Meat

Shiitake Chicken Cacciatore Ⓕ

Makes 4 servings: 1 chicken breast and 1¼ cups tomato-vegetable mixture each

This version of chicken cacciatore is prepared in a pressure-cooker; it doesn't need to spend hours stewing. Shiitake mushrooms and kalamata olives add an earthy tone to this otherwise Italian dish, making it globally inspired and extra tasty. Complete this nontraditional cacciatore by serving over whole-wheat couscous.

2 teaspoons extra-virgin olive oil

1 medium red onion, chopped

1 large green bell pepper, diced

½ cup Riesling or other white wine

½ teaspoon sea salt, or to taste

3 large garlic cloves, chopped

6 ounces fresh shiitake mushroom caps, sliced

1 ounce pitted Kalamata olives, quartered
    lengthwise

1 teaspoon finely chopped fresh rosemary
    or ½ teaspoon crushed dried rosemary

½ teaspoon freshly ground black pepper, or to taste

¼ teaspoon dried hot pepper flakes

4 (6-ounce) boneless skinless chicken breasts

2 cups canned crushed tomatoes

1 cup fresh grape tomatoes or halved cherry
    tomatoes

¼ cup freshly grated Parmigiano-Reggiano
    or other Parmesan cheese

¼ cup roughly chopped fresh flat-leaf parsley

1. Heat the oil in a pressure-cooker over medium heat. Add the onion, bell pepper, 1 tablespoon of the wine, and the salt and sauté until the onion is softened, about 8 minutes. Add the garlic and sauté for 1 minute.

2. Add the remaining wine, increase heat to high, and bring to a boil while stirring. Continue to stir while boiling for 1 minute. Stir in the mushrooms, olives, rosemary, black pepper, and hot pepper flakes. Place the chicken on top. Add the crushed and grape tomatoes.

3. Close the pressure-cooker lid and turn to the high-pressure setting. Once the pressure-cooker hisses, adjust the heat as necessary to maintain high pressure with very gentle hissing and cook for 10 minutes, or until stew-like and chicken is fully cooked. Carefully release the pressure and remove the lid. Sprinkle with or stir in the cheese and parsley. Adjust seasoning and serve immediately.

Per serving: 350 calories, 10g total fat, 2.5g saturated fat, 0g trans fat, 100mg cholesterol, 740mg sodium, 21g total carbohydrate, 5g dietary fiber, 4g sugars, 41g protein

Coq au Vin Cabernet

Makes 4 servings: 1 thigh and 1 cup vegetables with sauce each

Consider this a contemporary take on coq au vin, the French chicken and wine stew, that's now brimming with carrots. It's prepared much more quickly since it's cooked under pressure. But, just like the original, this recipe is rich tasting and satisfying and even saucier than when made in a traditional stew pot. It's lovely served over Soft Polenta (page 492).

4 (5-ounce) boneless skinless chicken thighs

¾ teaspoon sea salt, or to taste

½ teaspoon freshly ground black pepper, or to taste

2 teaspoons extra-virgin olive oil

1 medium red onion, chopped

1¼ cups Cabernet or other red wine

2 large garlic cloves, minced

3 tablespoons whole-wheat pastry flour

1½ cups baby carrots

1 cup sliced portabella mushroom caps

1½ teaspoons chopped fresh thyme
    or ¾ teaspoon dried thyme

1 cup low-sodium chicken broth or Chicken Stock
    (page 203)

1. Season the chicken with ½ teaspoon of the salt and the pepper.

2. Heat the oil in a pressure-cooker over medium heat. Add the chicken, meatiest side down, and cook until lightly browned, about 3 minutes. Transfer the chicken with tongs to a bowl.

3. To the remaining juices and oil in the pressure-cooker, add the onion, 1 tablespoon of the wine, and the remaining ¼ teaspoon salt and sauté over medium heat until softened, about 5 minutes. Add the garlic and sauté for 1 minute. Stir in the flour and cook while stirring for 1 minute. Add the carrots, mushrooms, and thyme. Place the chicken and any collected juices on top of the vegetables. Pour in the broth and remaining wine. Increase to medium-high heat.

4. Close the pressure-cooker lid and turn to the high-pressure setting. Once the pressure-cooker hisses, adjust the heat as necessary to maintain high pressure with very gentle hissing and cook for 8 minutes, or until stew-like and chicken is fully cooked. Carefully release the pressure and remove the lid. Adjust seasoning and serve immediately.

Per serving: 350 calories, 13g total fat, 3.5g saturated fat, 0g trans fat, 95mg cholesterol, 570mg sodium, 15g total carbohydrate, 3g dietary fiber, 4g sugars, 28g protein

Pulled Chicken Mole

Makes 6 servings: 1⅓ cups each

The earthy and somewhat exotic flavors of this slow-cooked chicken concoction are memorable thanks to the distinctive spices, dark chocolate, and ancho chiles. Turn it into an impressive meal by ladling it over Caramelized Vidalia Millet Pilaf (page 485) or other whole-grain pilaf.

2 teaspoons peanut or grapeseed oil

24 ounces bone-in skinless chicken breasts

2 teaspoons extra-virgin olive oil

1 large white onion, chopped

1 medium red bell pepper, chopped

2 teaspoons apple cider vinegar

1 teaspoon sea salt, or to taste

2 large garlic cloves, minced

2 tablespoons chili powder

1 teaspoon ground cumin

½ teaspoon freshly ground black pepper, or to taste

½ teaspoon ground cinnamon

1 (14.5-ounce) can diced tomatoes (with liquid)

2 stemmed seeded dried ancho chiles or roasted
    poblano peppers, chopped

1½ cups low-sodium chicken broth
    or Chicken Stock (page 203)

1¾ ounces bittersweet chocolate, chopped

2 tablespoons no-salt-added almond
    or peanut butter

2 tablespoons black seedless raisins

1 teaspoon grated orange zest

2 tablespoons roasted pumpkin seeds
    or chopped roasted pistachios

1. Heat the peanut oil in a wok, stockpot, or large skillet over medium-high heat. Add the chicken, meaty side down, and sauté until lightly browned, about 4 minutes. Transfer to a slow-cooker, meaty side up.

2. Heat the olive oil in the wok over medium heat. Add the onion, bell pepper, vinegar, and ¼ teaspoon of the salt and sauté until the onion is softened, about 8 minutes. Add the garlic, chili powder, cumin, black pepper, cinnamon, and the remaining ¾ teaspoon salt and sauté for 1 minute. Add the tomatoes with liquid, chiles, broth, chocolate, almond butter, raisins, and zest and stir until well combined and the chocolate is melted, about 5 minutes. Pour the mixture into the slow-cooker over the chicken.

3. Cover the slow-cooker, set to high, and cook until the chicken is fork-tender, about 2½ hours or on low for 5 hours.

4. Remove the chicken from the cooker. Turn the cooker down to the warm setting. Shred the chicken with two forks. Return the shredded chicken to the cooker, stirring to coat. Discard all of the chicken bones. When ready to serve, adjust seasoning.

5. Ladle the chicken mole into a large serving bowl, sprinkle with the pumpkin seeds, and serve.

Per serving: 280 calories, 13g total fat, 3.5g saturated fat, 0g trans fat, 50mg cholesterol, 650mg sodium, 21g total carbohydrate, 5g dietary fiber, 9g sugars, 23g protein

Sticky Lebanese Cinnamon Chicken and Rice

Makes 12 servings: 1 cup each

This chicken and rice entrée with its aromatic cinnamon accent is a comforting memory from my childhood. I've added my own home-style twists, including the sticky-textured slow-cooked approach, to recreate this crave-worthy dish.

3 cups brown basmati rice

1½ pounds boneless skinless chicken breasts, thinly sliced

2 tablespoons unsalted butter

2¾ teaspoons sea salt, or to taste

3 cinnamon sticks

2 bay leaves

¾ teaspoon freshly ground black or white pepper

5½ cups low-sodium chicken broth, Chicken Stock (page 203), or fresh cold water

1 tablespoon extra-virgin olive oil

2 large white onions, halved and thinly sliced

2 teaspoons white balsamic vinegar

½ teaspoon ground cinnamon, or to taste

½ cup chopped fresh flat-leaf parsley

½ cup sliced natural almonds or pine nuts, or a mixture, toasted

1. Add the rice, chicken, butter, 2½ teaspoons of the salt, the cinnamon sticks, bay leaves, pepper, and broth to a slow-cooker. Stir to combine. Cook, covered, on high for 3 hours. Remove lid and continue to slow-cook on high, stirring a few times, until the rice and chicken are fully cooked and liquid is absorbed, about 45 minutes.

2. Meanwhile, heat the oil in a large nonstick skillet over medium heat. Add the onions, vinegar, and remaining ¼ teaspoon salt, stir to coat, cover, and cook, stirring twice, until the onions are fully softened, about 15 minutes. Remove lid, increase heat to medium-high, and sauté until fully caramelized, about 12 to 15 minutes. Chill until ready to use.

3. After the 3 hours 45 minutes in the slow-cooker, remove just the cinnamon sticks and bay leaves and discard.

4. Stir the onions into the chicken-rice mixture. Continue to slow-cook, uncovered, until the onions are fully heated, about 10 minutes.

5. Spoon the chicken-rice mixture family-style onto a large platter, sprinkle with the cinnamon, parsley, and almonds, and serve.

Per serving: 270 calories, 8g total fat, 2g saturated fat, 0g trans fat, 35mg cholesterol, 600mg sodium, 35g total carbohydrate, 3g dietary fiber, 2g sugars, 17g protein

Beef Brisket with Squash

Makes 10 servings: 3 ounces beef with ¾ cup
vegetable-sauce mixture each

This fork-tender dish is best served when you're
in need of a holiday even though there may not
be one on the calendar—especially in spring
and summer. Pattypan squash and baby zucchini are seasonal then. The surprise addition of
beer here creates extra depth of flavor for super
party-friendly appeal.

1 (3-pound) trimmed flat-cut beef brisket,
    cut in half crosswise

1¾ teaspoons sea salt, or to taste

½ teaspoon freshly ground black pepper, or to taste

2 tablespoons grapeseed or canola oil

2 large red onions, halved, sliced

2 tablespoons aged balsamic vinegar

1 large garlic clove, chopped

1 (12-ounce) bottle light beer

2 cups low-sodium beef broth

1 (6-ounce) can tomato paste

1 pound small pattypan squash or baby zucchini

1. Rub the brisket with the 1¼ teaspoons of the
salt and the pepper.

2. Heat 2 teaspoons of the oil in a large skillet
over medium-high heat. Add one of the brisket
halves and sauté until browned, about 5 minutes
per side. Transfer to a plate. Repeat with another
2 teaspoons of the oil and remaining brisket.
Set aside.

3. Heat the remaining 2 teaspoons oil in the skillet
over medium-high heat. Add the onions, vinegar,
and the remaining ½ teaspoon salt and sauté until
the onions begin to caramelize, about 8 minutes.
Add the garlic and sauté for 1 minute. Stir in the
beer, broth, and tomato paste and cook while stirring until well combined.

4. Add the squash to a slow-cooker. Place the
brisket on top of the squash. Pour the onion mixture on top of the brisket.

5. Cover the slow-cooker, set to low, and cook
until the beef is fork-tender, about 6 hours. Adjust
seasoning.

6. Remove the brisket and thinly slice diagonally
against the grain.

7. Arrange the brisket on a platter, ladle the sauce
and vegetables over the brisket, and serve.

Per serving: 250 calories, 11g total fat, 3g saturated fat, 0g trans
fat, 60mg cholesterol, 490mg sodium, 9g total carbohydrate,
2g dietary fiber, 4g sugars, 25g protein

Poultry and Meat Pastas and One-Dish Meals

Asparagus Chicken Linguine

Makes 4 servings: 2 cups each

This asparagus-lover's meal will delight you. It's easy to prepare and has bright flavors.

1½ teaspoons sea salt, or to taste

10 ounces whole-wheat linguine or fettuccine

12 ounces boneless skinless chicken breast, thinly sliced crosswise into ¼-inch strips

16 medium spears asparagus, stems removed, sliced into ¼-inch-thick coins

1 small or ½ medium red onion, diced

3 large garlic cloves, thinly sliced

½ cup Enlightened Fresh Basil Pesto (page 117) or ¼ cup other basil pesto

2 tablespoons fresh grated Parmigiano-Reggiano or other Parmesan cheese (optional)

1 tablespoon pine nuts, toasted

1. Bring 2 quarts water to a boil in a large saucepan over high heat. Add 1 teaspoon of the salt and stir in the pasta, chicken, asparagus, onion, and garlic. Return to a boil. Reduce heat to medium and cook according to the pasta package directions, until the chicken and pasta are done.

2. Drain, reserving the cooking liquid. Return the pasta, chicken, vegetables, and the remaining ½ teaspoon salt to the dry pan and toss with the pesto. Add desired amount of the cooking liquid for desired consistency.

3. Transfer the mixture to a serving bowl, sprinkle with the cheese (if using) and pine nuts, and serve.

Per serving: 450 calories, 10g total fat, 1.5g saturated fat, 0g trans fat, 45mg cholesterol, 730mg sodium, 62g total carbohydrate, 11g dietary fiber, 5g sugars, 31g protein

Vodka Chicken Fettuccine

Makes 4 servings: 1½ cups each

This scrumptious whole-wheat fettuccine recipe is surprisingly simple to prepare. All it takes is two additions to a typical pasta and sauce recipe—sautéing chicken and sprinkling on some fresh herbs. But green tea sneaks in a surprise cooking liquid, if you wish.

2 teaspoons extra-virgin olive oil

10 ounces boneless skinless chicken breast, thinly sliced into ¼-inch strips

½ teaspoon finely chopped fresh rosemary or oregano, or to taste

¾ teaspoon sea salt, or to taste

¼ teaspoon freshly ground black or white pepper, or to taste

1½ cups 80-Proof Vodka Sauce (page 103) or tomato-based pasta sauce

¼ cup unsweetened green tea or water

10 ounces dry whole-wheat or other whole-grain fettuccine or linguine

3 tablespoons thinly sliced fresh basil leaves

1. Heat the oil in a large skillet or saucepan over medium heat. Add the chicken, rosemary, ½ teaspoon of the salt, and the pepper, and sauté until cooked through, about 8 minutes. Stir in the vodka sauce and tea, cover, and reduce heat to low to simmer.

2. Meanwhile, cook the pasta according to package directions. Drain the pasta, add to the skillet with the chicken and vodka sauce, sprinkle with remaining ¼ teaspoon salt and half of the basil, and toss to coat. Adjust seasoning.

3. Transfer the pasta mixture to a serving bowl or individual bowls, sprinkle with remaining basil, and serve.

Per serving: 400 calories, 7g total fat, 2g saturated fat, 0g trans fat, 45mg cholesterol, 660mg sodium, 57g total carbohydrate, 10g dietary fiber, 4g sugars, 26g protein

Grilled Chicken Fusilli Marinara Ⓕ

Makes 4 servings: 2 cups each

Tossing caramelized cauliflower florets and grilled chicken into tasty pasta adds depth of flavor and smoky satisfaction. Sprinkling in lemon zest provides fresh citrus appeal. All together, you've got a brilliant meal in a bowl.

1 tablespoon extra-virgin olive oil

10 ounces boneless skinless chicken thighs

½ teaspoon sea salt, or to taste

¼ teaspoon freshly ground black pepper, or to taste

3 cups cauliflower florets

1 teaspoon grated lemon zest

1½ cups Triple Tomato Marinara Sauce (page 101) or other marinara sauce

10 ounces dry whole-wheat or other whole-grain fusilli or other pasta shape

1. Prepare an indoor or outdoor grill.

2. Rub ½ tablespoon of the oil over the chicken thighs. Season with ¼ teaspoon of the salt and the pepper. Grill the chicken over direct high heat until done, about 5 minutes per side. Transfer to a cutting board and let stand.

3. Heat the remaining ½ tablespoon oil in a large skillet over medium-high heat. Add the cauliflower, zest, and the remaining ¼ teaspoon salt and sauté until caramelized, about 6 minutes. Stir in the marinara sauce, cover, reduce heat to low, and simmer for 10 minutes.

4. Meanwhile, cook the pasta according to package directions.

5. While the pasta is cooking, cut the grilled chicken into ⅓-inch-thick slices crosswise. Stir into the simmering cauliflower mixture. Cover and simmer until the chicken has absorbed some of the sauce, about 3 minutes.

6. Reserve ½ cup of the pasta cooking liquid. Drain the pasta, and add to the skillet with the chicken, cauliflower, and marinara sauce. Toss to coat, adding additional cooking liquid if required for desired consistency. Adjust seasoning.

7. Transfer the pasta mixture to a serving bowl or individual bowls, and serve.

Per serving: 430 calories, 11g total fat, 2.5g saturated fat, 0g trans fat, 45mg cholesterol, 600mg sodium, 61g total carbohydrate, 9g dietary fiber, 6g sugars, 26g protein

Chicken Fajita Bowl Ⓕ

Makes 4 servings: 2 cups each

Here's a Mexican-style twist on a quick Asian cooking technique. You'll be stir-frying chicken and vegetables in a wok. The rest is fajita-like, yet everything is served in a bowl with rice rather than in a tortilla. Dollop with guacamole for extra appeal but count the calories in accordingly. ¡Olé!

½ cup fat-free or low-fat plain Greek yogurt

Juice and zest of 1 lime (2 tablespoons juice)

2 cups cooked brown basmati rice

1 (15-ounce) can pinto beans, drained

2 scallions, green and white parts, thinly sliced

2 tablespoons chopped fresh cilantro

1 teaspoon sea salt, or to taste

1 tablespoon peanut or canola oil

1 medium white onion, halved and thinly sliced

1 small jalapeño pepper with seeds, thinly sliced

12 ounces boneless skinless chicken breasts, cut crosswise into 24 thin strips

1 large red bell pepper, thinly sliced

1 large green bell pepper, thinly sliced

1 medium zucchini, cut in matchstick-size strips

2 large garlic cloves, minced

½ cup Spicy Raw Tomatillo Salsa (page 114) or other salsa verde

1. Stir together the yogurt and the lime zest in a small bowl. Set aside.

2. Stir together the rice, beans, scallions, cilantro, 1 tablespoon of the lime juice, and ¼ teaspoon of the salt in a medium saucepan over low heat. Cover and keep warm, stirring as needed.

3. Heat the oil in a wok over high heat. Carefully add the onion, jalapeño, and ¼ teaspoon of the salt and sauté for 2 minutes. Add the chicken, bell peppers, zucchini, garlic, and the remaining 1 tablespoon lime juice and sauté until the chicken and vegetables are fully cooked, about 5 minutes. Add the remaining ½ teaspoon salt.

4. Stir 2 tablespoons of the tomatillo salsa into the rice-bean mixture, adjust seasoning, and spoon into a large serving bowl. Top with the chicken-vegetable mixture, and dollop with the lime yogurt. Serve with remaining salsa on the side.

Per serving: 370 calories, 7g total fat, 1.5g saturated fat, 0g trans fat, 45mg cholesterol, 790mg sodium, 49g total carbohydrate, 10g dietary fiber, 8g sugars, 29g protein

Lemon Chicken and Broccoli Casserole

Makes 6 servings: ⅙ of casserole (1⅓ cups) each

The Asiago cheese bubbling on top of this home-style recipe makes it seem extra rich. The wild mushrooms add intrigue. And the lemon creates fresh citrus flair. All slow-baked together with chicken, broccoli, and basmati rice, it's a satisfying "new-fashioned" delight.

1⅔ cup brown basmati rice

12 ounces boneless skinless chicken breasts, cut crosswise into 24 thin strips

2 cups finely chopped fresh broccoli florets and tender stems

1 cup thinly sliced fresh exotic mushrooms or crimini (baby bella) mushrooms

2 cups low-sodium chicken broth or Chicken Stock (page 203)

1 cup plain almond milk or light soy milk

1 tablespoon unsalted butter, melted

Juice and zest of 1 lemon (3 tablespoons juice)

1 tablespoon cornstarch

1¼ teaspoons sea salt, or to taste

¾ teaspoon freshly ground black pepper, or to taste

½ cup shredded Asiago cheese

1. Preheat the oven to 375°F.

2. Add the rice, chicken, broccoli, and mushrooms to a 2-quart baking dish or pan. Whisk together the broth, almond milk, butter, lemon juice and zest, cornstarch, salt, and pepper in a medium bowl or large liquid measuring cup and pour into the baking dish.

3. Bake for 1 hour 30 minutes, sprinkle with the cheese, return to oven, and bake until the rice is done and cheese is bubbly, about 15 minutes.

4. Remove from the oven and let stand for 10 minutes to complete the cooking process, and serve.

Per serving: 300 calories, 8g total fat, 3.5g saturated fat, 0g trans fat, 45mg cholesterol, 660mg sodium, 40g total carbohydrate, 3g dietary fiber, 3g sugars, 19g protein

Garlic Chicken Bucatini and Herbs ⓕ

Makes 2 servings: 1½ cups each

Here's a dish that's hearty, spicy, fresh, and fragrant—a superb combination that's fully satisfying, even for big eaters. If you're unfamiliar with bucatini, it's basically chubby spaghetti. Enjoy a bowl of it here as a slim and scrumptious supper.

2 teaspoons extra-virgin olive oil

3 large garlic cloves, thinly sliced

4½ ounces ground chicken or turkey

¼ teaspoon sea salt, or to taste

¼ teaspoon freshly ground black pepper, or to taste

⅛ teaspoon dried hot pepper flakes, or to taste

1 cup Triple Tomato Marinara Sauce (page 101) or other marinara sauce

¾ cup low-sodium chicken broth or Chicken Stock (page 203)

1 teaspoon finely chopped fresh sage, or to taste

½ teaspoon finely chopped fresh rosemary, or to taste

5 ounces whole-wheat or other whole-grain bucatini or linguine

¼ cup finely chopped fresh basil, or to taste

continues on next page

1. Heat the oil in a large skillet over medium heat. Add the garlic and sauté until the garlic is slightly softened and fully fragrant, about 2 minutes. Add the chicken, salt, black pepper, and hot pepper flakes and sauté until the chicken is cooked through and crumbled, about 2 minutes. Stir in the marinara sauce, broth, sage, and rosemary and bring to a boil over high heat. Partially cover, reduce heat to low, and simmer, stirring occasionally, until flavors are well combined and sauce has reached desired consistency, about 20 minutes.

2. Meanwhile, cook the pasta according to package directions. Drain the pasta.

3. Add the pasta to the skillet with the chicken marinara sauce along with 3 tablespoons of the basil and toss to coat, cooking over medium heat for about 1 minute. Adjust seasoning.

4. Transfer the pasta to a serving platter, sprinkle with the remaining basil, and serve.

Per serving: 440 calories, 12 total fat, 2.5 saturated fat, 0g trans fat, 40mg cholesterol, 680mg sodium, 62g total carbohydrate, 11g dietary fiber, 7g sugars, 24g protein

Tequila Turkey Pasta Ⓕ

Makes 5 servings: 2 cups each

Tequila! Now that's something worth celebrating in this tangy turkey and pasta dish of decidedly Southwestern flavor flamboyance. With its two types of peppers, generous handful of cilantro, and sharp finish of cheese, your taste buds will be captivated by this one-dish recipe.

12 ounces whole-grain spinach fusilli or other pasta shape

2 teaspoons unsalted butter

1½ tablespoon extra-virgin olive oil

10 ounces boneless skinless turkey breast, cut into ½-inch cubes

1 medium red onion, halved, diced

⅓ cup 80-proof tequila, such as 4 Copas

¾ teaspoon sea salt, or to taste

2 large garlic cloves, minced

1 small jalapeño pepper with seeds, minced

2 large yellow or orange bell peppers, cut into ⅓-inch cubes

1 recipe Creamy Lime Santa Fe Sauce, warm or room temperature (page 100)

¼ cup chopped fresh cilantro

½ teaspoon freshly ground black pepper, or to taste

2 tablespoons fresh grated Parmigiano-Reggiano or other Parmesan cheese

1. Cook the pasta according to package directions. Drain the pasta.

2. Meanwhile, melt the butter with the oil in a large deep skillet over medium heat. Add the turkey, onion, 1 tablespoon of the tequila, and ¼ teaspoon of the salt and sauté until the turkey is no longer pink on the outside, about 5 minutes; add the garlic and jalapeño and sauté for 3 minutes; and add the bell peppers, remaining tequila, and the remaining ½ teaspoon salt and sauté until the turkey is fully cooked, about 3 minutes. Add the cooked pasta and stir to coat. Add the Santa Fe Sauce, cilantro, and black pepper, stir to combine, and continue to cook for 1 minute. Adjust seasoning.

3. Transfer the pasta to a serving bowl or individual bowls, sprinkle with the cheese, and serve.

Per serving: 490 calories, 14g total fat, 6g saturated fat, 0g trans fat, 65mg cholesterol, 550mg sodium, 61g total carbohydrate, 7g dietary fiber, 5g sugars, 27g protein

Fennel-Turkey Spaghetti Bolognese Ⓕ

Makes 4 servings: 1½ cups each

If you've planned in advance, this is a perfect pasta recipe to prepare when you have the Fennel Turkey Pasta Sauce on hand. What make this spaghetti dish brilliant are the sharp culinary notes from the feta and the fresh citrusy twist from the orange zest.

10 ounces whole-wheat or other whole-grain spaghetti

2⅔ cups Fennel Turkey Pasta Sauce (page 102)

3 tablespoons crumbled feta cheese

1 teaspoon grated orange zest

1. Cook the pasta according to package directions. Drain the pasta.

2. Return the pasta to the dry pot over medium heat, add the sauce and toss to coat, cooking for 1 minute. Adjust seasoning.

3. Transfer the pasta to a serving platter, sprinkle with the cheese and zest, and serve.

Per serving: 350 calories, 4.5g total fat, 1.5g saturated fat, 0g trans fat, 20mg cholesterol, 400mg sodium, 59g total carbohydrate, 11g dietary fiber, 6g sugars, 22g protein

Turkey Sausage Lasagna

Makes 12 servings: 1 (3 × 3¼-inch) portion each

Believe it! This triple-cheese lasagna falls into the good-for-you category. One of the tricks is that cauliflower adds a lot of body but not a lot of calories. And it's the just-right amount of turkey sausage along with layers of tomato flavors that takes this lasagna over the top taste-wise.

8 ounces whole-wheat or other whole-grain lasagna noodles

1 teaspoon extra-virgin olive oil

8 ounces mild or spicy Italian turkey sausage, removed from casings and crumbled

1 small or ½ large red onion, finely chopped

1 large egg

1½ cups finely chopped cauliflower florets and tender stems

24 ounces part-skim ricotta cheese

1½ cups shredded part-skim mozzarella cheese

4 ounces crumbled soft goat cheese

⅓ cup finely chopped fresh basil

Juice of ½ small lemon (1 tablespoon)

1 teaspoon fresh oregano

¾ teaspoon sea salt, or to taste

½ teaspoon freshly ground black pepper, or to taste

3 cups Triple Tomato Marinara Sauce (page 101) or other tomato-based pasta sauce

1 cup thinly sliced cherry tomatoes

1. Fill a large bowl with the hot water. Add the noodles and allow them to sit in the water for 20 minutes. Drain.

2. Meanwhile, heat the oil in a large skillet over medium heat. Add the sausage and onion and sauté until the sausage is well done and onion is fully softened, about 10 minutes. Set aside in a small bowl.

3. Preheat the oven to 350°F.

4. Whisk the egg in a large bowl. Add the cauliflower, ricotta, ½ cup of the mozzarella, the goat cheese, basil, lemon juice, oregano, salt, and pepper and stir until well combined. Set aside.

5. Stir together the marinara sauce and cherry tomatoes in a medium bowl or large liquid measuring cup.

6. Spread one-third of the tomato sauce mixture in a 9 × 13-inch baking dish. Then layer as follows: half of the noodles, half of the cauliflower mixture, half of the sausage mixture, one-third of the tomato sauce mixture, half of the noodles, half of the cauliflower mixture, half of the sausage mixture, and one-third of the tomato sauce mixture. Sprinkle with the remaining 1 cup mozzarella.

7. Bake until the lasagna is fully cooked and cheese is fully browned, about 1 hour 15 minutes. Remove from oven and let stand for 10 minutes to complete the cooking process.

8. Cut into 12 squares. Garnish with additional fresh basil, if desired, and serve.

Per serving: 280 calories, 12g total fat, 6g saturated fat, 0g trans fat, 60mg cholesterol, 620mg sodium, 22g total carbohydrate, 4g dietary fiber, 4g sugars, 20g protein

Tijuana Turkey "Lasagna" Verde

Makes 4 servings: 1 wedge (¼ pie) each

A bit of lusciousness is a good thing for keeping you happy while following a healthful eating plan. The calories are still kept in check in this layered Mexican-flavored dish by using tangy fat-free Greek yogurt, lean turkey, and a generous amount of fresh tomatoes. You'll enjoy every zesty, bubbly, cheesy bite.

2 teaspoons grapeseed or peanut oil

10½ ounces ground turkey (about 94% lean)

½ teaspoon sea salt, or to taste

½ cup Roasted Green Tomato Salsa (page 114) or other salsa verde

⅓ cup + 1 tablespoon chopped fresh cilantro

⅔ cup fat-free or low-fat plain Greek yogurt

¼ cup sour cream

2 teaspoons fresh lime juice

1½ teaspoons cornstarch

4 (6-inch) stone-ground corn tortillas, halved

2 cups cherry tomatoes, halved, or grape tomatoes

1¼ cups shredded pepper Jack or Monterey Jack cheese

1. Preheat the oven to 425°F.

2. Heat the oil in a large skillet over medium-high heat. Add the turkey and salt and sauté until the turkey is crumbled and brown, about 5 minutes. Stir in the salsa and ⅓ cup of the cilantro. Set aside.

3. Whisk together the yogurt, sour cream, lime juice, and cornstarch in a small bowl. Set aside.

4. Arrange in a 9-inch deep-sided pie dish the following: 4 pieces of the tortillas, half of the yogurt mixture, half of the turkey mixture, half of the tomatoes (round side up), and half of the cheese. Repeat.

5. Bake in the oven until the layered mixture is hot and bubbly, cheese is fully melted and lightly browned, and tomatoes are fully roasted and gently caramelized, about 35 minutes. Remove from the oven and let stand at least 10 minutes before slicing.

6. Cut the round "lasagna" into four wedges, sprinkle with the remaining 1 tablespoon cilantro, and serve.

Per serving: 390 calories, 23g total fat, 9g saturated fat, 0g trans fat, 95mg cholesterol, 610mg sodium, 19g total carbohydrate, 2g dietary fiber, 5g sugars, 29g protein

Fresh Spaghetti and Meatballs Ⓕ

Makes 4 servings: 1¼ cups pasta and 3 meatballs each

Fresh pasta is paired here with two wonderful dishes from this book, bringing a fresher twist on classic spaghetti and meatballs. Enjoy with a simple salad or seasonal veggies and you've got a classic family-friendly meal.

2 cups Fresh Marinara (page 101), Triple Tomato Marinara (page 101), or other marinara sauce

12 Meatballs Romano (page 332) or other meatballs

14 ounces fresh or 10 ounces whole-wheat or other whole-grain spaghetti

2 tablespoons thinly sliced or chopped fresh basil leaves

1. Bring the sauce to a simmer in a medium saucepan over medium heat. Stir in the meatballs, cover, reduce heat to low, and simmer until the meatballs are fully heated through, about 10 minutes, stirring gently occasionally.

2. Meanwhile, cook the pasta according to package directions. Drain the pasta, reserving 1 cup cooking liquid. Return the pasta to the saucepan, and toss with half of the sauce. Toss with desired amount of reserved cooking liquid, if necessary. Adjust seasoning.

3. Divide the pasta among four plates or bowls. Top each with the meatballs and remaining sauce, sprinkle with the basil, and serve.

Per serving: 495 calories, 13g total fat, 3.5g saturated fat, 0g trans fat, 110mg cholesterol, 770mg sodium, 67g total carbohydrate, 11g dietary fiber, 7g sugars, 33g protein

Main Dishes: Fish and Shellfish

Roasted Fish

Nut-Crusted Barramundi
with Papaya Puree

Cornmeal-Breaded
Catfish Bites

Prosciutto-Wrapped
Roasted Cod

Roasted Scrod with
Caramelized Onions

Creole Panko-Crusted
Tilapia Sticks

Black and White Sesame
Salmon

Vegetable-Stuffed Trout

Skillet-Cooked and Poached Fish

Cilantro-Mint Chutney
Seared Halibut

Blackened Margarita Catfish

Buttery Tarragon
Seared Arctic Char

Melon Mahi Mahi

Salmon Piccata

Salmon with Ginger-Scallion
Chutney

Salmon with Lemon-Dill
Yogurt

Herb Tangerine-Poached
Lemon Sole

Grilled and Broiled Fish

Greek Striped Bass

Bloody Mary Grilled Bass

Grilled Calamari over
Balsamic Spinach

Tuscan-Grilled Pacific Halibut

Southern Trout
with Spicy Beans

Grilled Tuna with Fruit Salsa

Citrus Tuna Ceviche

Dominican Tilapia Mangu

Shellfish

Tandoori Shrimp

Garlic Grilled Shrimp

Spicy Greek-style Shrimp

Shrimp Jambalaya

Sea Salt and Pepper Scallops

Pan-Seared Sea Scallops

Mediterranean Mussels

Mussels à la Marinière

Roasted Artichoke–Stuffed
Mussels

Fish and Shellfish Pastas and Noodles

Pesto Couscous with Shrimp

Clams Oreganata Linguine

Sardine Bruschetta-Style Pasta

Scallop Orecchiette
with Broccoli Raab

Vietnamese Soba Spot Prawns

Shrimp Pad Thai Noodles

Sun-Dried Tomato Pesto
Pasta with Tuna

Summer Squash and Shrimp
Farfalle

Seafood is a scrumptious part of any cuisine.

Because it reels in plenty of nutrition for the calories it provides, it can also be an especially important part of low-calorie eating.

Fish is an excellent source of high-quality protein. Many varieties are rich in omega-3 fatty acids, such as salmon, mackerel, herring, sardines, albacore tuna, and lake trout. Omega-3s are essential for human health. These good-for-you fats are known for their beneficial role in reducing inflammation, reducing risk of heart disease, and promoting overall health.

The American Heart Association recommends eating two servings of fish (especially omega-3-rich fish) a week. A serving is considered 3½ ounces cooked, or about ¾ cup of flaked fish. If you're only eating one serving a week now, shoot for two. (If you or others in your family are not fish eaters, rest assured there are omega-3s in eggs and many plant-based foods, like soybeans, walnuts, and canola oil, too.

FISH CAUTION

Some fish do carry high levels of environmental pollutants, such as mercury, PCBs, and dioxins, and may have harmful effects when they're eaten frequently. The U.S. Food and Drug Administration (FDA) advises children and pregnant women to enjoy no more than 12 ounces per week of a variety of low-mercury fish and shellfish, such as shrimp, salmon, pollock, and catfish, and to avoid high-mercury fish, such as shark, swordfish, king mackerel, and tilefish. Here are a couple tips. Eat a variety of fish to help minimize potentially adverse effects due to contaminants. And check fish consumption advisories on the U.S. Environmental Protection Agency's (EPA) Web site: http://water.epa.gov/scitech/swguidance/fishshellfish/fishadvisories/index.cfm.

When you're eating in a healthful way, I think it's important to consider "health" in a larger sense—which includes how our food choices impact the health of our environment and vice versa. Therefore, when you're focusing on ocean-friendly cuisine, it's important to be aware of potential issues, such as environmental contaminants. (See "Fish Caution," below, for more information.) I suggest being thoughtful when you select which fish and shellfish to prepare; some seafood populations are overfished and/or otherwise considered an ecologically poor pick. Luckily, there's the Monterey Bay Aquarium's Seafood Watch to help you enjoy the best picks most often. (See "Eco-Fish," page 347, for more.) Ultimately, the positives of fish and shellfish consumption do outweigh the negatives. So simply enjoy the delish fish dishes in *1,000 Low-Calorie Recipes*. The fish and shellfish I suggest using in these recipes keeps in mind the best choices for your health as well as the health of the aquatic population.

The chapter starts by sharing recipes for fish in three different cooking technique-based sections: roasted, skillet cooked, and poached, then grilled and broiled. Next you'll find the main shrimp, shellfish and mussel recipes. The chapter concludes with combined fish and shellfish in pasta and noodle dishes—some of which can be complete meals!

Roasted fish dishes offer something for everyone, such as family-friendly Creole Panko-Crusted Tilapia Sticks (page 350). You can bake these kicked-up fish sticks in a jiffy in the toaster oven, too, and kids love them. The scrumptious skillet dishes offer an array of high-flavored options, including Melon Mahi Mahi (page 353) and Salmon with Ginger-Scallion Chutney (page 354). And fresh from the grill or the broiler are special dishes with accompaniments included, like the Grilled Calamari over Balsamic Spinach (page 356) and Dominican Tilapia Mangu (page 359).

The shrimp, shellfish, and mussel dishes offer something for those who like straightforward tastes, including Garlic Grilled Shrimp (page 360), perfectly accented with garlic, or who prefer recipes with more complexity, such as the Spicy Greek-Style Shrimp (page 360), which has tomato, lemon, feta, garlic, hot pepper flakes, and more. For the grand taste finale, you'll find seafood pasta and noodle dishes that will provide calorie-friendly, comforting bites with great taste, including the Shrimp Pad Thai Noodles (page 368) and the Sun-Dried Tomato Pesto Pasta with Tuna (page 368).

Before serving, add a desired garnish to any of these entrées for extra appeal. The best bets are fresh herbs, like fresh basil and tarragon. Look for herbs already used in the recipe (or that are planned into the entire meal), and simply add a little more for garnish on top. No herbs in the recipe? Consider a pinch of citrus zest, like lemon, especially if the citrus juice is already used in the recipe.

Calorie range in this chapter: 110 to 460 calories.

Low-calorie pick: Sea Salt and Pepper Scallops, 110 calories (page 361).

ECO-FISH

By purchasing fish that's caught or farmed using environmentally friendly practices, you're supporting healthy oceans. The eco-best fish and shellfish (which are abundant, well managed, and caught or farmed in environmentally friendly ways) found in this *1,000 Low-Calorie Recipes* chapter include:

FISH/SHELLFISH	RECOMMENDED	FISH/SHELLFISH	RECOMMENDED
Arctic char	Farmed	Sardines (Pacific, canned)	U.S. wild
Barramundi	U.S. farmed	Scallops	Farmed off-bottom
Catfish	U.S. farmed	Scallops (sea)	Mexico/Baja California Sur (diver-caught)
Clams (Littleneck)	Farmed		
Cod (Pacific)	U.S. wild (bottom longline)	Shrimp (Pink)	Oregon wild
		Spot prawn	British Columbia wild
Cod/Scrod (Atlantic)	Icelandic/Northeast Arctic wild (hook and line)	Squid (Atlantic)	U.S. wild (trawl)
Halibut (Pacific)	U.S. wild	Striped bass	U.S. farmed and wild
Mahi mahi (Atlantic)	U.S. wild (troll/pole)	Tilapia	U.S. farmed
Mussels	Farmed	Trout (Rainbow)	U.S. farmed
Salmon (Coho)	Alaska wild and U.S. farmed (in tank)	Tuna (Albacore, canned)	U.S. wild (troll/pole)
Salmon (Sockeye)	Alaska wild	Tuna (Yellowfin)	U.S. wild (troll/pole)

Go to http://www.montereybayaquarium.org/cr/seafoodwatch.aspx for a complete listing. There you'll also find a list of "Super Green" fish, which are considered good-for-you, good-for-the-oceans choices since they're low in pollutants and are good sources of Omega-3s.

Main Dishes: Fish and Shellfish **347**

Roasted Fish

Nut-Crusted Barramundi with Papaya Puree

Makes 4 servings: 1 filet each with ¼ cup puree

Originally from Australia, barramundi is now easily accessible and farmed in the United States. The combination of the nuttiness of the macadamia nuts and the sweet tang of the papaya puree adds vibrancy to the flavor of the dish, while the slight crunch of the panko breadcrumbs perfectly contrasts with the delicate texture of the fish.

4 (6-ounce) barramundi or wild turbot fillets

¾ teaspoon sea salt, or to taste

2 large eggs

¾ cup whole-wheat panko breadcrumbs

⅓ cup macadamia nuts, very finely chopped

1½ teaspoons black sesame seeds

1 cup Papaya Puree (page 131), warm
    or at room temperature

¼ cup minced fresh chives or 2 tablespoons
    chopped fresh cilantro

1. Preheat the oven to 450°F.

2. Season the fillets with ½ teaspoon of the salt. Set aside.

3. Whisk together the eggs and 2 tablespoons cold water in a medium bowl. Mix together the panko, nuts, and sesame seeds on a plate. Dip each fillet into the egg wash, then dredge in the nut mixture to completely coat, pressing the nut mixture onto each fillet to adhere. Place coated fillets onto a large parchment paper–lined baking sheet.

4. Spray both sides of the fillets with cooking spray (preferably homemade, page xix) and sprinkle with remaining ¼ teaspoon salt.

5. Roast the fillets until cooked through and the coating is golden, about 8 minutes. Adjust seasoning.

6. Smear the papaya puree onto each of four individual plates using the back of a spoon, arrange the fillets on top, sprinkle with the chives, and serve.

Per serving: 380 calories, 15g total fat, 2.5g saturated fat, 0g trans fat, 185mg cholesterol, 700mg sodium, 18g total carbohydrate, 4g dietary fiber, 4g sugars, 43g protein

Cornmeal-Breaded Catfish Bites

Makes 8 servings: 4 pieces each

If you have a hankering for zesty flavors, the mix of spices in these catfish bites will hit the spot. The unique flash-frying cooking technique creates a lightly crisped coating over the catfish cubes. For extra tang, serve with Fresh Tartar Sauce (page 129).

3 (8-ounce) farm-raised catfish fillets,
    cut into 1½-inch cubes (about 32 cubes)

¾ teaspoon sea salt, or to taste

½ teaspoon freshly ground black pepper, or to taste

¼ cup plain almond milk or light soy milk

1 tablespoon spicy brown mustard

2 large garlic cloves, minced

¼ teaspoon smoked paprika (optional)

¼ teaspoon ground cayenne, or to taste

½ cup whole-wheat flour

¼ cup yellow whole-grain medium-grind cornmeal

2 cups peanut or canola oil

1. Season the fillets with ¼ teaspoon each of the salt and black pepper. Set aside.

2. Whisk together the almond milk, mustard, garlic, paprika (if using), cayenne, ¼ teaspoon of the salt, and the remaining ¼ teaspoon black pepper in a medium bowl. Add the fish pieces and toss to coat. Let stand to marinate for 30 to 45 minutes.

3. Preheat the oven to 475°F.

4. Stir together the flour, cornmeal, and the remaining ¼ teaspoon salt in a medium bowl. Transfer the fish pieces to the flour-cornmeal mixture, 3 or 4 at a time, and gently toss to coat. Transfer to a plate and repeat with remaining pieces.

5. Heat the oil in a large skillet over high heat. Add the fish pieces in batches (about 8 at a time) and fry until the coating is just golden brown, about 15 seconds per side. Place each piece onto a rack to drain.

6. Spread the fish pieces in a large baking pan, allowing space between each piece. Roast in the oven until the fish is fully cooked, about 5 minutes. Transfer the bites to a platter and serve.

Per serving: 170 calories, 10g total fat, 2g saturated fat, 0g trans fat, 45mg cholesterol, 290mg sodium, 5g total carbohydrate, 1g dietary fiber, 0g sugars, 14g protein

Prosciutto-Wrapped Roasted Cod

Makes 4 servings: 1 fillet each

Stock up on omega-3s while adding a little meat-lovers delight into the mix. Be careful not to overcook the thin prosciutto or it will toughen; it should only yield a slight crisp. It adds flavor pizzazz to the mild flavor of the cod.

4 (6-ounce) wild cod fillets, patted dry

1 tablespoon extra-virgin olive oil

Juice of ½ small lemon (1 tablespoon)

¼ teaspoon freshly ground black pepper, or to taste

⅛ teaspoon sea salt, or to taste

2 tablespoons finely chopped fresh basil

2 teaspoons finely chopped fresh tarragon

4 (½-ounce) thin slices prosciutto or country ham

1. Preheat the oven to 450°F.

2. Rub each of the fillets with the oil, drizzle with the lemon juice, season with the pepper and salt, and sprinkle with the basil and tarragon. Wrap the prosciutto around each fillet.

3. Place into a baking pan and roast in the oven until the cod is cooked through and the ham is slightly crisp, about 10 minutes, and serve.

Per serving: 200 calories, 6g total fat, 1g saturated fat, 0g trans fat, 85mg cholesterol, 540mg sodium, 1g total carbohydrate, 0g dietary fiber, 0g sugars, 34g protein

Roasted Scrod with Caramelized Onion

Makes 4 servings: 1 fillet plus onion each

Scrod describes a smaller, younger cod fish and maintains the same mild taste. The pungent garlic and vivid sweet paprika sprinkled over the flaky flesh add wonderful flavor and color. The caramelized onions layered on top not only make a great decoration but are a fantastic flavor addition to the dish.

4 (6-ounce) wild cod (scrod) fillets

4 teaspoons extra-virgin olive oil

Juice of ½ small lemon (1 tablespoon)

1 garlic clove, minced

1 teaspoon finely chopped fresh thyme

¾ teaspoon sea salt, or to taste

¼ teaspoon sweet paprika

1 medium red onion, halved and very thinly sliced

1. Preheat the oven to 400°F.

2. Rub the fillets with 2 teaspoons of the oil, drizzle with ½ tablespoon of the lemon juice, and sprinkle with the garlic, thyme, ½ teaspoon of the salt, and the paprika.

3. Heat the remaining 2 teaspoons oil in a large nonstick skillet over medium heat. Add the onion and the remaining ½ tablespoon lemon juice and ¼ teaspoon salt and sauté until softened and beginning to caramelize, about 12 to 15 minutes.

4. Transfer the onion to a large parchment paper–lined baking pan. Position the fish on top of the onion. Roast until the fish is firm and flakes easily, about 10 minutes.

5. Transfer the cod to individual plates, top with the onion, and serve immediately. Garnish with additional fresh thyme, if desired.

Per serving: 190 calories, 6g total fat, 1g saturated fat, 0g trans fat, 75mg cholesterol, 530mg sodium, 3g total carbohydrate, 1g dietary fiber, 1g sugars, 31g protein

Creole Panko-Crusted Tilapia Sticks

Makes 6 serving: 4 sticks each

Here's a fresh take on an American classic, the fish stick. Not only for kids (although they'll love it!), this recipe revitalizes the common fish favorite by coating flaky tilapia strips in panko breadcrumbs to give it a distinctive crispness. Make your own Creole seasoning (page 31) to spice things up and dip them in Fresh Tartar Sauce (page 129) for added enjoyment.

¼ cup whole-wheat pastry flour

½ teaspoon sea salt, or to taste

1 large egg, lightly beaten

¼ cup plain almond milk or light soy milk

Juice of 1 small lemon (2 tablespoons)

2 teaspoons unsalted butter, melted

1¼ cups whole-wheat panko breadcrumbs

1½ teaspoons Creole seasoning (page 31),
    or to taste

½ teaspoon freshly ground black pepper, or to taste

3 (8-ounce) tilapia or halibut fillets, cut into
    3½ × 1-inch strips (about 24 strips)

1. Preheat the oven to 475°F.

2. Mix together the flour and ¼ teaspoon of the salt in a shallow dish. Whisk together the egg, almond milk, lemon juice, and butter in a second shallow dish. Stir together the panko, Creole seasoning, the remaining ¼ teaspoon salt, and the pepper in a third shallow dish.

3. Dredge each strip of fish in the flour, dip it in the egg mixture (shake off excess), and dredge in the panko mixture to fully coat. Place into a baking pan. Lightly coat both sides of the breaded fish with cooking spray (preferably homemade, page xix).

4. Bake until the fish is cooked through and the coating is golden brown and crisp, about 8 minutes. Adjust seasoning and serve.

Per serving: 210 calories, 4.5g total fat, 2g saturated fat, 0g trans fat, 90mg cholesterol, 310mg sodium, 15g total carbohydrate, 2g dietary fiber, 1g sugars, 27g protein

Black and White Sesame Salmon

Makes 4 servings: 1 fillet with 1 tablespoon sauce each

The black and white sesame seeds embedded in the tender fillets bring more than just flavor to this Asian-inspired dish. The seeds add a hearty crunch, while the sweet citrus of the blood orange-shallot sauce is a unique way to enhance the beautiful, tender salmon.

4 (5-ounce) wild sockeye Alaskan salmon fillets
    with skin

½ teaspoon toasted sesame oil

1 teaspoon freshly grated gingerroot

2 teaspoons naturally brewed soy sauce

1 tablespoon black sesame seeds

1 tablespoon white sesame seeds

¼ teaspoon sea salt, or to taste

¼ cup Blood Orange–Shallot Sauce (page 137),
    or to taste

1. Preheat the oven to 400°F.

2. Place the salmon fillets on a parchment paper–lined baking sheet, skin side down. Rub the top of each with the oil and ginger, and drizzle with the soy sauce.

3. Mix together the black and white sesame seeds on a small plate. Firmly dip the oil-rubbed side of each fillet into the seeds and place again on the baking sheet, skin side down. Sprinkle with the salt.

4. Roast until opaque in the center, about 8 minutes.

5. Drizzle the sauce onto each of four plates, place the salmon on top of the sauce, and serve.

Per serving: 290 calories, 16g total fat, 2.5g saturated fat, 0g trans fat, 90mg cholesterol, 410mg sodium, 2g total carbohydrate, 1g dietary fiber, 1g sugars, 32g protein

Vegetable-Stuffed Trout

Makes 4 servings: ½ trout plus vegetables each

Here, vegetables are infused with Asian-style flavor, which adds zing to the otherwise mild rainbow trout. The bright colors of the fresh spring vegetables and the trout will create a farmers' market–inspired plate.

2 (12-ounce) whole rainbow trout, cleaned, boned, and butterflied

¼ teaspoon sea salt, or to taste

¼ teaspoon freshly ground black pepper, or to taste

2 medium yellow summer squash, quartered lengthwise and cut crosswise into ¼-inch slices

12 medium asparagus spears, ends trimmed and cut crosswise or diagonally into ¼-inch pieces

¼ cup thinly sliced fresh morels

1 large shallot, minced

1 tablespoon freshly grated gingerroot

2 large garlic cloves, minced

1 tablespoon naturally brewed soy sauce

2 teaspoons toasted sesame oil

⅛ teaspoon dried hot pepper flakes or to taste

2 tablespoons chopped fresh cilantro

1. Preheat the oven to 400°F.

2. Open both trout up like a book and place skin side down on a parchment paper–lined baking sheet. Season with the salt and pepper.

3. Mix together the squash, asparagus, morels, shallot, ginger, garlic, soy sauce, oil, and hot pepper flakes. Sprinkle the vegetable mixture evenly over both of the trout.

4. Roast until the fish is opaque in center and the vegetables are tender, about 20 minutes. Adjust seasoning.

5. Cut each stuffed trout in half, sprinkle with the cilantro, and serve. If desired, serve with additional soy sauce on the side.

Per serving: 250 calories, 10g total fat, 2.5g saturated fat, 0g trans fat, 90mg cholesterol, 450mg sodium, 8g total carbohydrate, 2g dietary fiber, 3g sugars, 33g protein

Skillet-Cooked and Poached Fish

Cilantro-Mint Chutney Seared Halibut

Makes 4 servings: 1 fillet with 1 tablespoon chutney each

The cilantro-mint chutney and flaky halibut combine to give you the perfect balance of textures. To top it off, the fresh flavors of the aromatic herbs infuse into the seared halibut for a taste that's too good to resist!

4 (4½-ounce) halibut fillets (about 1 inch thick), patted dry

¼ teaspoon freshly ground black pepper, or to taste

Pinch of sea salt, or to taste

2 teaspoons grapeseed or canola oil

¼ cup Cilantro-Mint Chutney (page 120)

1. Season the fillets with the pepper and salt.

2. Heat 1 teaspoon of the oil in a large nonstick skillet over medium-high heat. Add 2 of the fillets and sear until the bottom sides of fillets are lightly browned, about 2½ minutes. Flip over, spread each with 1 tablespoon of the chutney, and cook just until flaky, about 2 minutes. Repeat with the remaining oil, halibut, and chutney.

3. Adjust seasoning, and serve.

Per serving: 180 calories, 6g total fat, 0.5g saturated fat, 0g trans fat, 45mg cholesterol, 230mg sodium, 2g total carbohydrate, 0g dietary fiber, 1g sugars, 30g protein

Blackened Margarita Catfish

Makes 4 servings: 1 filet with ½ tablespoon sauce each

Bring some Mexican spirit into your own home with this simple recipe. The vivid flavors of the margarita serving sauce drizzled atop the fillet of blackened catfish garnished with a squeeze of fresh lime juice will have your taste buds dancing. This meal is a sure cause for celebration.

4 (6-ounce) farm-raised catfish fillets
½ cup + 2 tablespoons Margarita Serving Sauce
     (page 138), at room temperature
¼ teaspoon sea salt, or to taste
¼ teaspoon freshly ground black pepper, or to taste
4 lime wedges

1. Place the catfish fillets in a medium bowl with ½ cup of the sauce and toss to coat. Let marinate for 30 to 45 minutes.

2. Heat a large nonstick skillet over medium-high heat. Remove 2 fillets from the marinade, letting excess marinade drip back into the bowl, and add to the dry pan. Sauté until just blackened and fully cooked, about 3 minutes per side. Remove to a plate and cover with aluminum foil to keep warm. Repeat with the remaining fillets. Discard any remaining marinade. Season all the fillets with the salt and pepper.

3. Arrange the fillets on a platter or individual plates, drizzle with the remaining 2 tablespoons sauce, and serve with the lime wedges.

Per serving: 150 calories, 8g total fat, 1.5g saturated fat, 0g trans fat, 40mg cholesterol, 260mg sodium, 4g total carbohydrate, 0g dietary fiber, 3g sugars, 13g protein

Buttery Tarragon Seared Arctic Char

Makes 4 servings: 1 fillet each

Arctic char is similar to salmon or trout, but its delicate and milder taste make it even more appealing for those who aren't big fish fans. Plus, you have another great fish choice with an abundance of Omega-3s. This is a simple dish to dive into often.

Juice and zest of 1 Meyer lemon or small lemon
     (2 tablespoons juice)
2 tablespoons finely chopped fresh tarragon
1 tablespoon unsalted butter, melted
¾ teaspoon sea salt, or to taste
¼ teaspoon freshly ground black pepper, or to taste
¼ teaspoon ground cayenne
4 (6-ounce) farm-raised Arctic char fillets with skin
2 teaspoons grapeseed or canola oil

1. Stir together the lemon juice, 1 tablespoon of the tarragon, the butter, salt, black pepper, and cayenne in a small bowl. Rub or brush the lemon mixture on the flesh side only of each fillet.

2. Heat 1 teaspoon of the oil in a large nonstick skillet over medium-high heat. Add 2 of the fillets skin side down and sauté until the fish is cooked through and flakes easily, about 4 minutes per side. Remove to a plate and cover with aluminum foil to keep warm. Repeat with the remaining 1 teaspoon oil and 2 fillets. Adjust seasoning.

3. Transfer the fillets to a platter, sprinkle with the remaining tablespoon tarragon and desired amount of lemon zest, and serve.

Per serving: 270 calories, 12g total fat, 2g saturated fat, 0g trans fat, 10mg cholesterol, 520mg sodium, 1g total carbohydrate, 0g dietary fiber, 0g sugars, 38g protein

Melon Mahi Mahi

Makes 4 servings: 1 fillet with ¼ cup salsa each

Pair the mahi mahi with my memorable melon salsa for a delightful twist. The subtle sweetness of the melon salsa contrasts with the rich savoriness of the pan-seared mahi mahi to create a sweet and savory meal great for any night of the week.

1½ teaspoons smoked paprika

1 teaspoon dried thyme or oregano

½ teaspoon sea salt, or to taste

½ teaspoon freshly ground black pepper, or to taste

⅛ teaspoon ground cayenne

4 (5-ounce) wild mahi mahi fillets (about ½ inch thick)

1 tablespoon grapeseed or canola oil

1 garlic clove, minced

1 cup Sweet-n-Savory Melon Salsa (page 116)

1. Mix together the paprika, thyme, salt, black pepper, and cayenne in a small bowl. Sprinkle, then rub the seasoning onto both sides of the fillets.

2. Heat ½ tablespoon of the oil in a large skillet over high heat. Add 2 of the fillets and sauté until the fish is deeply browned, about 3 minutes per side, adding half of the garlic to the skillet the last 30 seconds of sautéing. Repeat with the remaining ½ tablespoon oil, 2 fillets, and remaining garlic. (Alternatively, prepare one batch by using a griddle.) Adjust seasoning.

3. Transfer the fish to a platter or individual plates, top with the salsa, and serve.

Per serving: 170 calories, 4.5g total fat, 0.5g saturated fat, 0g trans fat, 105mg cholesterol, 490mg sodium, 5g total carbohydrate, 1g dietary fiber, 3g sugars, 27g protein

Salmon Piccata

Makes 2 servings: 1 fillet each

The wild Alaskan Coho salmon is a sustainable fish, and is worth the splurge if possible. The freshly prepared piccata sauce packs a powerful punch. Pour it on top of the salmon to make a quick dish that'll intrigue your taste buds.

2 (5½-ounce) skinless wild Alaskan Coho or other salmon fillets

¼ teaspoon sea salt, or to taste

¼ teaspoon freshly ground black pepper, or to taste

1 tablespoon whole-wheat pastry flour

4 teaspoons unsalted butter

⅓ cup low-sodium vegetable broth or Vegetable Stock (page 203)

Juice and zest of ½ small lemon (1 tablespoon juice)

2 teaspoons tiny drained capers

⅛ teaspoon dried hot pepper flakes, or to taste (optional)

1. Season the salmon with salt and black pepper and coat both sides with the flour.

2. Melt 1 tablespoon of the butter in a large nonstick skillet over medium-high heat. Add the salmon and cook until brown and just opaque in the center, about 4 minutes per side. Transfer the salmon to a platter.

3. Add the broth, lemon juice, capers, hot pepper flakes (if using), and the remaining teaspoon butter to the skillet and bring to a boil for 1 minute.

4. Pour the sauce over the salmon, sprinkle with desired amount of the zest, and serve.

Per serving: 270 calories, 13g total fat, 6g saturated fat, 0g trans fat, 90mg cholesterol, 470mg sodium, 4g total carbohydrate, 1g dietary fiber, 1g sugars, 31g protein

Salmon with Ginger-Scallion Chutney

Makes 2 servings: 1 fillet each

The zesty chutney-style topping is a delicious accompaniment to the flavors of the seared salmon. The scallions, ginger, and sesame oil combine to provide substance and eye appeal, too. Add the hot pepper flakes if you like a kick.

2 (5-ounce) freshwater farmed salmon fillets
    with skin (about 1 inch thick)

¼ teaspoon sea salt, or to taste

¼ teaspoon freshly ground black pepper

1 tablespoon whole-wheat pastry flour

2 teaspoons grapeseed or canola oil

1 teaspoon toasted sesame oil

2 teaspoons freshly grated ginger

2 scallions, green and white parts, minced

⅓ cup low-sodium vegetable broth
    or Vegetable Stock (page 203)

⅛ teaspoon dried hot pepper flakes, or to taste
    (optional)

1. Season the salmon with salt and black pepper and coat both sides with the flour.

2. Heat the grapeseed oil in a large nonstick skillet over medium-high heat. Add the salmon and cook until brown and just opaque in the center, about 4 minutes per side. Transfer the salmon to a platter.

3. Heat the sesame oil in the skillet over medium heat. Add the ginger and white parts of the scallions and sauté for 30 seconds. Add the broth, the green parts of the scallions, and the hot pepper flakes (if using) and bring to a boil for 1 minute.

4. Top the salmon with the ginger-scallion mixture, and serve.

Per serving: 350 calories, 23g total fat, 4g saturated fat, 0g trans fat, 80mg cholesterol, 390mg sodium, 5g total carbohydrate, 1g dietary fiber, 1g sugars, 29g protein

Salmon with Lemon-Dill Yogurt

Makes 4 servings: 1 fillet with about 2½ tablespoon sauce each

Dress up petite salmon fillets with some home-made lemon-dill yogurt sauce. The savory sauce is creamy and light, yet a fresh and flavorful delight. Drizzled on top of the fillets, it's a Greek-inspired addition, creating a lovely fish dish.

2 (8-ounce) wild Alaskan salmon fillets with skin,
    halved

¾ teaspoon sea salt, or to taste

½ teaspoon freshly ground black pepper, or to taste

1 cup low-sodium vegetable broth
    or Vegetable Stock (page 203)

½ cup Sauvignon Blanc or other white wine

1 large shallot, very thinly sliced

4 fresh dill sprigs

⅔ cup Lemon-Dill Yogurt Sauce (page 137)

1. Season the salmon with salt and pepper. Set aside.

2. Add the broth, wine, shallot, and dill to a large nonstick skillet over medium heat and bring to a simmer. Add the fillets, skin side down, and cover the skillet. Cook until the salmon is just opaque in the center, about 5 to 6 minutes.

3. Transfer the salmon to a platter or individual plates. Using a slotted spoon, arrange the shallot and dill around the salmon. Top the salmon with the yogurt sauce and serve.

Per serving: 240 calories, 10g total fat, 1.5g saturated fat, 0g trans fat, 0mg cholesterol, 650mg sodium, 5g total carbohydrate, 1g dietary fiber, 2g sugars, 26g protein

Herb Tangerine-Poached Lemon Sole

Makes 2 servings: 1 fillet each

Few ingredients pair more naturally than seafood and citrus, so you're sure to love the tangerine and mildly sweet wild lemon sole combination. The clean burst of flavors in the dish will refresh and revitalize your soul.

1 (10-ounce) wild lemon sole or Pacific halibut fillet, cut in half lengthwise

¼ teaspoon sea salt, or to taste

¼ teaspoon freshly ground black or white pepper, or to taste

Juice and zest of 1 large tangerine or small orange (¼ cup juice)

⅓ cup Sauvignon Blanc or other dry white wine

½ teaspoon crushed dried tarragon

½ cup low-sodium vegetable broth or Vegetable Stock (page 203)

1 teaspoon unsalted butter

1 teaspoon chopped fresh tarragon or ¼ teaspoon finely chopped fresh rosemary

1. Season the fillets with the salt and pepper. Set aside.

2. Bring the tangerine juice and zest, wine, and dried tarragon to a boil in a large skillet over high heat. When the liquid is nearly evaporated, add the broth and bring to a boil. Reduce heat to medium-low, add the fillets, cover, and gently simmer until just cooked through, about 8 minutes.

3. Gently transfer the sole to a platter or individual plates.

4. Bring the poaching liquid to a boil over high heat and let boil for about 1 minute. Stir in the butter and adjust seasoning.

5. Top the sole with the sauce, sprinkle with the fresh tarragon, and serve.

Per serving: 170 calories, 4.5g total fat, 2g saturated fat, 0g trans fat, 60mg cholesterol, 680mg sodium, 10g total carbohydrate, 2g dietary fiber, 7g sugars, 16g protein

Grilled and Broiled Fish

Greek Striped Bass

Makes 4 servings: 1 fillet each

Broil your fish for a fast method of cooking. Then do as the Greeks do and serve it with some of this Mediterranean country's most delicious foods—creamy yogurt, tangy feta, and fresh lemon.

4 (6-ounce) wild striped bass (rockfish) fillets with skin

1 tablespoon extra-virgin olive oil

½ teaspoon sea salt, or to taste

¼ cup fat-free or low-fat plain Greek yogurt

¼ cup crumbled feta cheese

2 scallions, green and white parts, minced

1 large garlic clove, minced

¼ teaspoon freshly ground black pepper, or to taste

1 teaspoon chopped fresh dill or basil, or to taste

1 small lemon, cut into wedges

1. Preheat the broiler.

2. Rub the fillets with the oil, sprinkle with ¼ teaspoon of the salt, and place in a baking pan, skin side down.

3. Stir together the yogurt, cheese, scallions, garlic, pepper, and the remaining ¼ teaspoon salt, and spread on the fillets.

4. Broil the fillets, on one side only, about 6 inches from the heat source, until the fish flakes easily and is browned, about 7 minutes. Adjust seasoning.

5. Transfer the fish to a platter or individual plates, sprinkle with dill, and serve with the lemon wedges.

Per serving: 210 calories, 9g total fat, 2.5g saturated fat, 0g trans fat, 125mg cholesterol, 500mg sodium, 2g total carbohydrate, 0g dietary fiber, 1g sugars, 29g protein

Bloody Mary Grilled Bass

Makes 4 servings: 1 fillet each

Here, cocktail-inspired vinaigrette will intoxicate you with flavor. Pair its tangy tomato goodness with the flavorful, flaky, and meaty striped bass, and enjoy a night of friends, fun, and food. Your taste buds will be buzzing with delight.

4 (5-ounce) wild striped bass (rockfish) fillets
    with skin (about ⅔ inch thick each)
½ cup Bloody Mary Vinaigrette (page 145)
¼ teaspoon freshly ground black pepper, or to taste
⅛ teaspoon sea salt, or to taste
2 tablespoons chopped fresh flat-leaf parsley
    or tarragon
½ teaspoon grated lemon zest

1. Make a few slits through the skin of each fillet. Add the fillets and vinaigrette to a 9 × 13-inch or similar-size dish. Let marinate for about 30 to 45 minutes, turning the fillets over halfway through the marinating time.

2. Prepare an outdoor or indoor grill.

3. Grill the fillets over direct medium-high heat until the fish easily flakes, about 5 minutes per side. Discard any remaining marinade. Add the pepper and salt.

4. Transfer the fish to a platter or individual plates, sprinkle with the parsley and lemon zest, and serve.

Per serving: 160 calories, 4.5g total fat, 1g saturated fat, 0g trans fat, 115mg cholesterol, 210mg sodium, 2g total carbohydrate, 0g dietary fiber, 1g sugars, 26g protein

Grilled Calamari over Balsamic Spinach F

Makes 4 servings: 5 whole squid with ½ cup spinach each

Move over fried calamari. Grilled calamari is the more nutritious option. It's incredibly tasty, too. The pairing with spinach makes it a memorable entrée. But if you still desire crunch, sprinkle with the pine nuts.

20 calamari, cleaned, bodies lightly scored with
    "X"s, and patted dry (1½ pounds)
1 tablespoon extra-virgin olive oil
½ teaspoon sea salt, or to taste
¼ teaspoon freshly ground black pepper, or to taste
⅛ teaspoon dried hot pepper flakes, or to taste
1 recipe Balsamic Wilted Spinach (page 450),
    warm, or 2 cups steamed greens of choice
2 tablespoons pine nuts, toasted (optional)

1. Prepare an outdoor or indoor grill, or a grill pan.

2. Gently toss together the squid, oil, salt, black pepper, and hot pepper flakes in a medium bowl.

3. Grill the calamari (in batches, if necessary) over direct high heat until lightly charred or grill marks just form, about 1 minute per side. Adjust seasoning.

4. Arrange the spinach on a platter. Top with the grilled calamari, sprinkle with the pine nuts (if using), and serve.

Per serving: 260 calories, 8g total fat, 1.5g saturated fat, 0g trans fat, 395mg cholesterol, 690mg sodium, 19g total carbohydrate, 5g dietary fiber, 1g sugars, 29g protein

Tuscan-Grilled Pacific Halibut

Makes 4 servings: 1 steak each

Enjoy the natural flavor of the fish grilled and simply prepared with fresh herbs and served with lemon. Simple can be sensational.

4 (5-ounce) Pacific halibut steaks, about ¾ inch thick

1 tablespoon extra-virgin olive oil

1 small lemon, half juiced and half cut into wedges

1 large garlic clove, minced

½ teaspoon sea salt, or to taste

¼ teaspoon freshly ground black pepper, or to taste

3 tablespoons chopped fresh basil

1 tablespoon chopped fresh flat-leaf parsley

¼ teaspoon dried hot pepper flakes, or to taste

1. Rub the fish with the oil, lemon juice, and garlic. Add the salt and black pepper. Let stand for 15 to 30 minutes.

2. Prepare an outdoor or indoor grill, or a grill pan.

3. Grill the steaks over direct medium-high heat until the fish easily flakes and is just opaque in the center, about 4 minutes per side. Adjust seasoning.

4. Transfer the steaks to a platter or individual plates, sprinkle with the basil, parsley, and hot pepper flakes, and serve with the lemon wedges.

Per serving: 190 calories, 7g total fat, 1g saturated fat, 0g trans fat, 45mg cholesterol, 370mg sodium, 1g total carbohydrate, 0g dietary fiber, 0g sugars, 30g protein

Southern Trout with Spicy Beans Ⓕ

Makes 4 servings: 1 trout and ½ cup warm bean salad each

Creole food is sometimes known as heat with flavor. Grilling the fish and dressing it with this special seasoning makes it the main focus of the plate. But a bean side is included here, too, that might try to steal the spotlight. Together, they make a full meal with plenty of appeal.

2½ tablespoons extra-virgin olive oil

⅓ cup minced Vidalia or other sweet onion

2 tablespoons white balsamic vinegar

½ teaspoon Creole seasoning (page 31)

¾ teaspoon sea salt, or to taste

¼ teaspoon freshly ground black pepper, or to taste

1 (15-ounce) can kidney or white beans, drained

1 tablespoon finely chopped fresh flat-leaf parsley

1 teaspoon grated lemon zest, or to taste

4 (10-ounce) cleaned boned butterflied farm-raised rainbow trout, head removed, if desired

1½ cups packed fresh baby spinach

1. Prepare an outdoor or indoor grill.

2. Whisk together the oil, onion, vinegar, Creole seasoning, ½ teaspoon of the salt, and the pepper in a small bowl. Set aside.

3. Stir together the beans, parsley, lemon zest, and 2 tablespoons of the vinaigrette in a medium skillet. Place the skillet on the edge of grill to warm through.

4. Spray the skin side of the trout with cooking spray (preferably homemade, page xix). Brush about 1½ to 2 tablespoons of the vinaigrette over the flesh side of the trout.

5. Grill the trout, flesh side down, until brown, about 2 minutes. Turn trout over; grill until cooked through, about 2 minutes. Sprinkle with the remaining ¼ teaspoon salt.

6. Transfer the trout to individual plates. Stir the spinach into the warm beans, spoon onto plates next to or onto the trout. Spoon the remaining vinaigrette over the trout and beans, and serve.

Per serving: 440 calories, 19g total fat, 4g saturated fat, 0g trans fat, 125mg cholesterol, 740mg sodium, 18g total carbohydrate, 5g dietary fiber, 3g sugars, 35g protein

Grilled Tuna with Fruit Salsa

Makes 4 servings: 1 steak with ½ cup salsa each

This is a sweet-n-savory take on simple grilled tuna steaks to put some zest on your plate. The fresh melon salsa makes it extra special.

4 (5-ounce) wild yellowfin tuna steaks
    (about ¾ inch thick)

1 tablespoon grapeseed or peanut oil

1 serrano pepper with some seeds, minced

¾ teaspoon sea salt, or to taste

½ teaspoon grated lime zest

2 cups Sweet-n-Savory Melon Salsa (page 116)
    or other fruit salsa

1. Prepare an outdoor or indoor grill.

2. Rub the steaks with the oil. Sprinkle with the serrano, salt, and lime zest and firmly press with a spatula to assure ingredients adhere to the tuna.

3. Grill the steaks over direct high heat until medium-rare and grill marks form, about 2 minutes per side. Adjust seasoning.

4. Transfer to a platter or individual plates, top with the salsa, and serve.

Per serving: 220 calories, 5g total fat, 0.5g saturated fat, 0g trans fat, 65mg cholesterol, 640mg sodium, 8g total carbohydrate, 1g dietary fiber, 6g sugars, 34g protein

Citrus Tuna Ceviche

Makes 4 servings: 1 cup each

Get expert flavor with minimal cooking when you make this stunning dish. In ceviche, the acid of the citrus fruits "cooks" the fish to perfection. The citrus flavors infuse through the fish to heighten its fresh flavor. The presentation in martini glasses makes it dazzling enough to be a showcase appetizer, too.

2 (6-ounce) fresh sushi-grade wild yellowfin tuna
    fish fillets (about ½ inch thick)

¾ teaspoon sea salt, or to taste

¼ teaspoon freshly ground black pepper, or to taste

⅓ cup fresh-squeezed white or pink grapefruit juice

Juice of 1½ limes (3 tablespoons)

1½ teaspoons mild honey or agave nectar

1 medium-large beefsteak tomato, pulp removed
    and chopped

½ cup chopped red onion

1 small jalapeño pepper with some seeds, minced

2 teaspoons extra-virgin olive oil

1 Hass avocado, pitted, peeled, and diced

3 tablespoons chopped fresh cilantro

¼ cup fat-free or low-fat plain Greek yogurt

2 tablespoons sliced natural almonds, toasted

1. Lightly coat the tuna with cooking spray (preferably homemade, page xix) and season with ½ teaspoon of the salt and the pepper. Place a large nonstick skillet over medium-high heat until hot. Add the tuna and sear about 45 seconds per side. Remove from heat. Let stand for at least 5 minutes. Cut the tuna into ½-inch cubes.

2. Whisk together the grapefruit juice, 2 tablespoons of the lime juice, and the honey in a medium bowl. Add the seared tuna and toss to fully coat. Cover and chill, tossing occasionally, about 3 to 4 hours, to allow the tuna to gently "cook."

3. Strain the fish and discard the marinade. Place the ceviche in a large bowl. Add the tomato, onion, jalapeño, oil, and the remaining 1 tablespoon lime juice and remaining ¼ teaspoon salt and toss until combined. Add the avocado and cilantro and gently toss. Adjust seasoning.

4. Transfer to four martini glasses or festive dishes, top each with 1 tablespoon of the yogurt and ½ tablespoon of the almonds, and serve.

Per serving: 230 calories, 10g total fat, 1.5g saturated fat, 0g trans fat, 35mg cholesterol, 490mg sodium, 13g total carbohydrate, 4g dietary fiber, 5g sugars, 24g protein

Dominican Tilapia Mangu

Makes 4 servings: 1 fillet with ½ cup mangu each

Enjoy a grilling experience anytime—without firing up the barbecue. Using a panini grill to cook your fish is faster and the result is scrumptious, with similar appealing grill marks. Accompany the tilapia with my mashed sweet plantains with frizzled leeks, a sweeter version of traditional Dominican mangu, for a filling and mouthwatering main dish.

4 (6-ounce) farm-raised tilapia fillets

1 tablespoon peanut or canola oil

1 small serrano pepper, finely minced

½ teaspoon sea salt, or to taste

¼ teaspoon freshly ground black pepper, or to taste

1 teaspoon grated lime zest

2 cups Mashed Plantains with Frizzled Leeks
   (page 458)

1. Preheat a panini grill.

2. Rub or brush the tilapia with the oil. Sprinkle with the serrano, salt, and black pepper.

3. Cook in the panini grill, in batches, on medium-high heat until cooked through and grill marks form, about 4 minutes. Gently remove from the panini grill.

4. Sprinkle with the lime zest. Serve on top of the mashed plantains garnishing with the frizzled leeks.

Per serving: 380 calories, 10g total fat, 2.5g saturated fat, 0g trans fat, 90mg cholesterol, 690mg sodium, 43g total carbohydrate, 4g dietary fiber, 19g sugars, 36g protein

Shellfish

Tandoori Shrimp

Makes 2 servings: 8 extra-jumbo shrimp (2 skewers with 4 shrimp) each

Attention shrimp lovers! This recipe showcases big flavors. Allow the marinade to seep into the shrimp; the blend of fragrant spices imparts a zesty, earthy flavor with Indian essence.

16 extra-jumbo shrimp, peeled and deveined

Juice of ½ small lemon (1 tablespoon)

¼ cup fat-free or low-fat plain Greek yogurt

¼ cup grated red onion

1 tablespoon tahini (sesame seed paste)

3 large garlic cloves, minced

2 teaspoons freshly grated gingerroot

¾ teaspoon garam masala

¼ teaspoon ground turmeric

¼ teaspoon sea salt, or to taste

1. Place the shrimp in a shallow baking dish. Drizzle with the lemon juice, toss, and let stand for 15 minutes.

2. Whisk together the yogurt, onion, tahini, garlic, ginger, garam masala, turmeric, and salt in a small bowl. Add the yogurt mixture to the lemon-marinated shrimp, toss, and marinate for 30 minutes (no more than 45 minutes).

3. Prepare an outdoor or indoor grill.

4. Thread 4 shrimp each onto four large water-soaked bamboo or reusable skewers, so that they lay flat on the grill. Grill the skewers over direct medium-high heat until cooked through and lightly charred, about 4½ to 5 minutes per side, and serve.

Per serving: 140 calories, 5g total fat, 0.5g saturated fat, 0g trans fat, 95mg cholesterol, 720mg sodium, 9g total carbohydrate, 1g dietary fiber, 3g sugars, 15g protein

Garlic Grilled Shrimp

Makes 4 servings: about 7 shrimp each

Here's "fast food" that's good for you. This garlic grilled shrimp is simple, quick, and 100 percent delicious, making it a perfect pick for a hassle-free cookout. Turn it into a spectacular meal by serving with Soba with Greens and Nectarine (page 300).

1 pound extra-large shrimp, peeled, leaving tail
    and adjoining first segment attached,
    and deveined (about 28 shrimp)
1 tablespoon grapeseed or canola oil
1 tablespoon low-sodium vegetable broth
    or Vegetable Stock (page 203)
2 large garlic cloves, minced
½ teaspoon sea salt, or to taste
¼ teaspoon freshly ground black pepper, or to taste
¼ teaspoon dried hot pepper flakes, or to taste

1. Thread the shrimp onto reusable or water-soaked bamboo skewers, so that they lay flat.

2. Prepare an outdoor or indoor grill.

3. Whisk together the oil, broth, garlic, salt, black pepper, and hot pepper flakes, then brush on skewered shrimp until well coated.

4. Grill shrimp (in batches, if necessary), turning only as needed, until lightly charred and just cooked through, about 6 minutes. Adjust seasoning and serve.

Per serving: 150 calories, 5g total fat, 0.5g saturated fat, 0g trans fat, 170mg cholesterol, 460mg sodium, 2g total carbohydrate, 0g dietary fiber, 0g sugars, 23g protein

Spicy Greek-Style Shrimp

Makes 6 servings: ⅙ casserole (5 shrimp) each

Impress guests with this Greek entrée. This spicy shrimp dish is prepared in a pan on the stovetop that then goes into the oven to be broiled to caramelized perfection. From there, you can serve it directly from the pan. It has so much color and Mediterranean flavor appeal you'll be impressed it was this simple to prepare. Serve it over Wild Rice Pilaf (page 479); it's the ideal companion.

1 tablespoon extra-virgin olive oil
1 large or 2 small yellow onions, diced
¼ cup Pinot Grigio or other white wine
1 large red bell pepper, cut into ½-inch cubes
1 large yellow summer squash, quartered
    lengthwise and cut crosswise into ½-inch slices
4 large garlic cloves, thinly sliced
⅛ teaspoon sea salt, or to taste
1 (14.5-ounce) can no-salt-added diced tomatoes
    (with liquid)
2½ tablespoons chopped fresh oregano
1 bay leaf
¼ teaspoon freshly ground black pepper, or to taste
¼ teaspoon dried hot pepper flakes, or to taste
⅔ cup crumbled feta cheese
30 extra-large shrimp, peeled, deveined,
    and tails removed
Juice of ½ lemon (1½ tablespoons)

1. Preheat the broiler.

2. Heat the oil in an extra-large oven-safe sauté pan or casserole dish over medium heat. Add the onion and 1 tablespoon of the wine and sauté until softened, about 6 minutes. Add the bell pepper, squash, garlic, salt, and the remaining 3 tablespoons wine and cook, stirring often, until the squash is tender, about 6 to 8 minutes.

3. Add the tomatoes with liquid, 1½ tablespoons of the oregano, the bay leaf, black pepper, and hot pepper flakes, cover, and simmer until the mixture resembles a chunky tomato sauce, about 10 minutes. Remove from heat. Remove the bay leaf. Stir in 3 tablespoons of the cheese. Adjust seasoning.

4. Layer the shrimp on top of the tomato mixture. Sprinkle evenly with the remaining cheese.

5. Place about 6 inches under the broiler heat. Broil until the shrimp is cooked through. Remove from the broiler and let stand for 5 minutes.

6. Sprinkle with the lemon juice and the remaining 1 tablespoon oregano and serve.

Per serving: 190 calories, 7g total fat, 3g saturated fat, 0g trans fat, 135mg cholesterol, 790mg sodium, 12g total carbohydrate, 2g dietary fiber, 6g sugars, 17g protein

Shrimp Jambalaya

Makes 10 servings: 1 cup each

This seafood jambalaya is delicious in any season. The warmth and richness of the stew-like entrée (and the cayenne pepper!) will keep you comforted during the cold months. The array of vegetables and fresh herbs will have you feeling delightfully satisfied in the warm months. It's ideal for a gathering of family or friends.

1 tablespoon extra-virgin olive oil

1 large white onion, diced

1 large green bell pepper, chopped

1 large red bell pepper, chopped

2 large celery stalks, diced

2 large garlic cloves, thinly sliced

2 teaspoons red wine vinegar, or to taste

5 ounces lean smoked ham, diced

1 bay leaf

1 teaspoon ground cayenne, or to taste

¼ teaspoon smoked paprika, or to taste

1 (28-ounce) can diced tomatoes (with liquid)

1 (8-ounce) can no-salt-added tomato sauce

1½ cups low-sodium vegetable broth
    or Vegetable Stock (page 203)

¾ teaspoon sea salt, or to taste

¾ cup long-grain brown rice, uncooked

1 pound medium shrimp, shelled and deveined

3 tablespoons finely chopped fresh flat-leaf
    parsley, or to taste

1 teaspoon finely chopped fresh thyme, or to taste

1. Heat the oil in a Dutch oven over medium heat. Add the onion, bell peppers, celery, garlic, and vinegar and sauté until the onion is softened, about 10 minutes. Add the ham, bay leaf, cayenne, and paprika and cook, while stirring occasionally, until the bell peppers are softened about 5 minutes. Add the diced tomatoes with liquid, tomato sauce, broth, and salt. Continue to cook, while stirring occasionally, for 5 minutes.

2. Stir in the rice, increase heat to high, and bring to a boil. Reduce heat to low, cover, and cook until the rice is nearly cooked, about 45 minutes.

3. Uncover, stir in the shrimp, parsley, and thyme and cook, stirring occasionally, until the shrimp and rice are cooked, about 5 minutes.

4. Remove the bay leaf, adjust seasoning, and serve.

Per serving: 160 calories, 3g total fat, 0.5g saturated fat, 0g trans fat, 65mg cholesterol, 795mg sodium, 22g total carbohydrate, 3g dietary fiber, 6g sugars, 11g protein

Sea Salt and Pepper Scallops

Makes 4 servings: 4 large scallops each

It doesn't get much simpler than this. The secret is making sure you use fresh scallops and high-quality ingredients. The calorie count for this entrée is especially low; so serve with a large side dish or toss into a pasta entrée, like Luscious Lemony Linguine (page 291) or Spring Pea Risotto (page 303), for a one-dish meal.

16 large sea scallops, side muscles removed,
    rinsed, and patted dry (1 pound)

1 tablespoon extra-virgin olive oil

¼ teaspoon sea salt, or to taste

¼ teaspoon freshly ground black pepper, or to taste

1. Preheat a grill pan.

2. Add the scallops, oil, salt, and pepper to a medium bowl and toss to coat.

3. Cook over medium-high heat until golden brown and just cooked through, about 2 to 2½ minutes per side. Adjust seasoning and serve immediately.

Per serving: 110 calories, 4g total fat, 0.5g saturated fat, 0g trans fat, 25mg cholesterol, 590mg sodium, 4g total carbohydrate, 0g dietary fiber, 0g sugars, 14g protein

Pan-Seared Scallops

Makes 4 servings: 4 scallops each

These pan-seared sea scallops are like candy for adults—and kids! The sweet and savory flavors that are seared into the scallops provide indulgence without the guilt. You can enjoy them as a petite entrée, snack, or perched atop a pasta dish, like Scallop Orecchiette with Broccoli Raab (page 366).

16 large sea scallops, side muscles removed, rinsed, and patted dry (1 pound)

¼ teaspoon sea salt, or to taste

¼ teaspoon freshly ground black pepper, or to taste

⅛ teaspoon dried hot pepper flakes, or to taste

¼ teaspoon finely grated lemon zest

2 teaspoons unsalted butter

2 teaspoons grapeseed or peanut oil

1. Sprinkle the scallops with the salt, black pepper, hot pepper flakes, and half the zest. Set aside.

2. Melt the butter with the oil in an extra large skillet over high heat. Once it begins to slightly smoke, add the scallops. Cook until a golden brown crust forms on the scallops, about 1½ minutes per side. Sprinkle with the remaining zest, adjust seasoning, and serve immediately.

Per serving: 120 calories, 5g total fat, 1.5g saturated fat, 0g trans fat, 30mg cholesterol, 590mg sodium, 4g total carbohydrate, 0g dietary fiber, 0g sugars, 14g protein

Mediterranean Mussels

Makes 6 servings: 2⅔ cups mussels + broth

The combination of ouzo and fennel are flavor standouts in this recipe. After enjoying every bite of the mussels, enjoy dipping a piece of whole-grain Italian bread into the broth to sop up its deliciousness. And for an intriguing twist on texture and taste, try the Fennel Relish (see page 363) and use 1 cup of it in place of the tomato and olives.

2 tablespoons extra-virgin olive oil

4 leeks (white and pale green parts only), halved lengthwise, sliced crosswise and well rinsed

2 cups thinly sliced fennel bulb halves

1 large red onion, quartered lengthwise and thinly sliced crosswise

4 large garlic cloves, thinly sliced

⅓ cup ouzo or other anise-flavored liqueur

6 fresh oregano sprigs + 1½ tablespoons finely chopped fresh oregano

¼ teaspoon freshly ground black pepper, or to taste

¾ cup Pinot Grigio or other white wine

Zest and juice from 1 navel orange (reserve the peels)

3 pounds mussels, well scrubbed and debearded

1 large plum or medium vine-ripened tomato, pulp removed and diced

8 Kalamata olives, pitted and very thinly sliced crosswise

1. Heat the oil in a stockpot over medium heat. Add the leeks, fennel, onion, garlic, and 1 tablespoon of the ouzo and sauté until the leeks and onion are softened, about 8 minutes. Add the oregano sprigs, 1 tablespoon of the chopped oregano, and the pepper and sauté for another minute.

2. Add the wine, orange juice and peels, mussels, and the remaining ouzo, cover with tight-fitting lid, increase heat to high, and steam until the mussels open, about 6 minutes, stirring once during cooking to ensure mussels cook evenly. Discard the orange peels and any unopened mussels. Adjust seasoning.

3. Transfer the mussels to individual bowls, sprinkle with the tomato and olives, and ladle the cooking liquid (about ⅓ cup each) over top. Sprinkle with the remaining ½ tablespoon oregano, and serve immediately.

Per serving: 375 calories, 11g total fat, 2g saturated fat, 0g trans fat, 65mg cholesterol, 760mg sodium, 27g total carbohydrate, 3g dietary fiber, 6g sugars, 29g protein

FENNEL RELISH

Stir together 1 cup finely diced fennel bulb, 3 tablespoons minced red onion, 2 minced large garlic cloves, 8 chopped pitted Kalamata olives, ⅓ cup diced seeded plum tomato or quartered grape tomatoes, 1 or 2 tablespoons fresh-squeezed orange juice, 1 teaspoon grated orange zest, 2 tablespoons finely chopped fresh flat-leaf parsley, 1 teaspoon finely chopped fresh oregano, ¼ teaspoon freshly ground black pepper, and ⅛ teaspoon sea salt in a medium bowl. Cover and chill in the refrigerator for at least 2 hours. Adjust seasoning. Makes about 1¾ cups.

Mussels à la Marinière

Makes 6 servings: 2⅔ cups mussels + broth each

This simple recipe allows the freshness of the mussels to shine, enhanced by light citrus, herb, and garlic accents.

1 tablespoon extra-virgin olive oil
4 large shallots, thinly sliced
4 large garlic cloves, very thinly sliced
8 thyme sprigs + 1 tablespoon thyme leaves
Zest and juice of 1 lemon (3 tablespoons juice; reserve the peels)
1 cup Pinot Grigio or other dry white wine
3½ pounds mussels, well scrubbed and debearded
2 teaspoons unsalted butter
1 teaspoon Dijon mustard

1. Heat the oil in a stockpot over medium heat. Add the shallots and sauté until softened, about 3 minutes. Add the garlic and sauté for 30 seconds.

2. Add the thyme sprigs, lemon juice and peels, wine, and mussels. Cover with a tight-fitting lid, increase heat to high, and steam until the mussels open, about 6 minutes, stirring once during cooking to ensure mussels cook evenly.

3. Transfer the mussels with a slotted spoon to a large bowl; set aside. Discard thyme sprigs, lemon peels, and any unopened mussels.

4. Reduce the heat of the broth to medium-high. Whisk in the butter and mustard until fully incorporated into the broth. Continue to cook to concentrate flavors, about 2 minutes. Remove from heat and gently pour the mussels along with any accumulated juices back into the broth and stir to combine. Adjust seasoning.

5. Ladle into individual bowls, garnish with the thyme leaves and lemon zest, and serve immediately.

Per serving: 320 calories, 10g total fat, 2.5g saturated fat, 0g trans fat, 75mg cholesterol, 780mg sodium, 17g total carbohydrate, 0g dietary fiber, 1g sugars, 32g protein

Roasted Artichoke–Stuffed Mussels

Makes 6 servings: 11 to 12 stuffed mussels each

Combine the fresh flavor of mussels with a roasted artichoke stuffing to create a little piece of heaven in a shell. The salty Romano cheese accent makes these mussels pop with flavor. Squeezing on the lemon juice before enjoying each succulent bite balances and brightens all the flavors.

¾ cup plain dry whole-wheat breadcrumbs

¼ cup freshly grated Pecorino Romano cheese
    or Parmesan cheese

8 ounces frozen artichoke hearts, thawed,
    finely diced, and patted dry

⅓ cup + 1 tablespoon finely chopped fresh mint

Juice of 1 small lemon (2 tablespoons)
    + 1 lemon cut into wedges

1½ tablespoons extra-virgin olive oil

½ teaspoon freshly ground black pepper, or to taste

3 pounds mussels, well scrubbed and debearded

1. Preheat the oven to 450°F.

2. Stir together the breadcrumbs, cheese, artichoke hearts, ⅓ cup of the mint, the lemon juice, oil, and pepper in a small bowl; set aside.

3. Bring 1 cup water to a boil over high heat in a stockpot. Add the mussels, cover, and steam, shaking pot occasionally for until the mussels just open, about 4 minutes. Discard any unopened mussels.

4. Transfer the mussels to a large baking pan. Split mussels fully open by hand and discard empty shell halves. Top each with about 2 teaspoons of the breadcrumb mixture to lightly coat the mussel and fill the shell. Bake until the breadcrumb mixture is lightly browned, about 5 minutes. Preheat the broiler. Place under broiler and broil until the breadcrumb mixture is crisp and well browned, about 1½ to 2 minutes.

5. Adjust seasoning, sprinkle with the remaining 1 tablespoon mint, and serve with the lemon wedges. Squeeze each with the lemon before enjoying.

Per serving: 310 calories, 12g total fat, 2.5g saturated fat, 0g trans fat, 65mg cholesterol, 750mg sodium, 20g total carbohydrate, 3g dietary fiber, 1g sugars, 30g protein

Fish and Shellfish
Pastas and Noodles

Pesto Couscous
with Shrimp Ⓕ

Makes 4 servings: 1 cup couscous with 5 shrimp each

Create a delightful dish by placing garlicky grilled shrimp over a steaming plate of scrumptious pesto couscous. Freshen it up with fresh basil, pine nuts, and a squeeze of lemon. Give this tasty idea a try with other flavorful couscous or pasta dishes, too.

4 cups Swiss Chard Pesto Couscous, warm
    (page 476)

20 Garlic Grilled Shrimp, warm (page 360)

2 teaspoons chopped fresh basil or flat-leaf
    parsley

2 teaspoons pine nuts, toasted

4 lemon wedges

1. Onto each of four separate plates, spoon 1 cup of the couscous.

2. Top each with 5 shrimp.

3. Sprinkle with the basil and pine nuts, and serve with the lemon wedges.

Per serving: 380 calories, 13g total fat, 1.5g saturated fat, 0g trans fat, 130mg cholesterol, 700mg sodium, 42g total carbohydrate, 7g dietary fiber, 2g sugars, 26g protein

Clams Oreganata Linguine Ⓕ

Makes 6 servings: 2⅓ cups each (including clam shells)

Here's a stellar-looking dish full of Italian appeal. It's brimming with all of the right flavors—from savory to sweet and herbal to heat—making it a fully satisfying meal.

1½ tablespoons extra-virgin olive oil

1 large Spanish onion, diced

1 cup Chardonnay or other dry white wine

3 large garlic cloves, thinly sliced

1 pound white button mushrooms, stems removed and sliced

1½ teaspoons sea salt, or to taste

2 pounds 12 ounces littleneck clams (about 30), scrubbed

¼ teaspoon dried hot pepper flakes, or to taste

1 pound whole-grain spinach or other whole-grain linguine

2 heads roasted garlic (see right)

⅓ cup chopped fresh flat-leaf parsley

3 tablespoons finely chopped fresh oregano

1½ tablespoons unsalted butter

¼ teaspoon freshly ground black pepper, or to taste

1 teaspoon grated lemon zest

3 lemons, halved

1. Heat the oil in an extra-large deep skillet or stockpot over medium heat. Add the onion and 2 tablespoons of the wine and sauté until softened, about 8 minutes. Add the garlic slices and sauté for 1 minute. Add the mushrooms and ½ teaspoon of the salt and sauté until the mushrooms are softened, about 6 minutes.

2. Add the clams, hot pepper flakes, and the remaining wine, increase heat to high, cover, and steam until the clams open, about 8 minutes. Discard any unopened clams.

3. Meanwhile, cook the pasta 2 minutes less than indicated on package directions. Drain the pasta.

4. Transfer the drained pasta to the skillet with the clams over medium heat. Add the roasted garlic cloves, the parsley, 2 tablespoons of the oregano, the butter, black pepper, and the remaining 1 teaspoon salt. Toss to combine and continue cooking until sauce has thickened and nicely coats the pasta.

5. Transfer to a serving bowl and garnish with the remaining 1 tablespoon oregano and the lemon zest. Serve with the lemon halves.

Per serving: 460 calories, 10g total fat, 3g saturated fat, 0g trans fat, 30mg cholesterol, 630mg sodium, 70g total carbohydrate, 10g dietary fiber, 6g sugars, 22g protein

ROASTED GARLIC

Preheat the oven to 375°F. Cut off the top of each garlic head to just expose the cloves. Drizzle each with 1 teaspoon extra-virgin olive oil. Wrap each head in aluminum foil and roast until the cloves are softened and golden, about 30 minutes. Squeeze out the soft garlic cloves for use in recipes.

Sardine Bruschetta-Style Pasta Ⓕ

Makes 6 servings: 2 cups each

Consider sardines as small fish with big benefits. They're a notable source of vitamin B_{12}, calcium, high-quality protein, and heart-healthful omega-3s. They debut here as a flavor star in this hearty capellini recipe. The fresh arugula, basil, and oregano provide fragrance and freshness to complete this beautifully pleasing pasta dish.

3 large beefsteak or 4 medium vine-ripened
    tomatoes, pulp removed, diced

½ cup packed thinly sliced fresh basil leaves
    + ½ cup whole fresh basil leaves

3 large garlic cloves, minced

1½ tablespoons aged balsamic vinegar

2 tablespoons extra-virgin olive oil

1¼ teaspoons sea salt, or to taste

1 (4.375-ounce) can Pacific sardines in oil, drained

Juice and zest of 1 lemon (3 tablespoons juice)

1 teaspoon finely chopped fresh oregano

½ teaspoon freshly ground black pepper, or to taste

1 pound whole-wheat or other whole-grain
    capellini or spaghettini

2 cups packed baby arugula

1. Stir together the tomatoes, sliced basil, garlic, vinegar, 1 tablespoon of the oil, and ¾ teaspoon of the salt in a medium bowl. Set aside for at least 30 minutes.

2. Combine the sardines, lemon juice, oregano, and black pepper in a small bowl. Let marinate for at least 30 minutes.

3. Break apart the marinated sardines with a fork into bite-size pieces. Add the sardines to the tomato mixture and gently stir. Adjust seasoning.

4. Cook the pasta according to package directions. Drain the pasta, reserving ½ cup of the cooking liquid. Transfer the pasta to a serving bowl.

5. Add the tomato-sardine mixture and desired amount of the reserved cooking liquid to the pasta and toss to combine. Add the arugula and the remaining 1 tablespoon oil and ½ teaspoon salt and toss to combine. Adjust seasoning.

6. Sprinkle with the desired amount of the lemon zest and the whole basil leaves. Serve with additional balsamic vinegar on the side.

Per serving: 370 calories, 9g total fat, 1.5g saturated fat, 0g trans fat, 10mg cholesterol, 590mg sodium, 63g total carbohydrate, 11g dietary fiber, 6g sugars, 16g protein

Scallop Orecchiette with Broccoli Raab Ⓕ

Makes 4 servings: 2 cups each

When you want pasta with lots of jazz, seared sweet scallops on top of orecchiette will do the trick. The orecchiette pasta, named for its cute ear-like shape, is an appealing option in place of spaghetti. The pleasant bitterness of broccoli raab is an ideal companion for mild and creamy beans. And the garlic, tomato, and Romano provide distinctive Italian flair in every satisfying bite.

1 tablespoon extra-virgin olive oil

2 large garlic cloves, minced

3 medium vine-ripened tomatoes, pulp removed,
    and chopped

1 teaspoon finely chopped fresh oregano

⅛ teaspoon dried hot pepper flakes

1 (15-ounce) can cannellini or other white beans,
    drained

¼ teaspoon sea salt, or to taste

½ teaspoon freshly ground pepper, or to taste

8 ounces whole-wheat orecchiette or
    other shaped pasta

12 ounces broccoli raab, cut into large bite-size
    pieces

12 Pan-Seared Sea Scallops (page 362)

2 tablespoons freshly grated Romano cheese

2 tablespoons pine nuts, toasted (optional)

1. Heat the oil in a large deep skillet over medium heat. Add the garlic and sauté for 1 minute. Add the tomatoes, oregano, and hot pepper flakes, cover, and simmer until a sauce-like consistency, about 6 minutes, stirring occasionally. Add the beans, salt, and black pepper, cover, turn the heat to low, and simmer while preparing the pasta.

2. Cook the pasta in boiling water in a large saucepan for 7 minutes. Stir in the broccoli raab and continue to cook until the pasta is al dente and broccoli raab is done, about 3 minutes. Drain the pasta and broccoli raab, reserving ½ cup of the cooking liquid.

3. Add the pasta and broccoli raab along with the scallops to the skillet with the simmering tomato-bean mixture and gently toss to coat. Add the reserved cooking liquid as needed for desired consistency. Adjust seasoning.

4. Divide the pasta and vegetable mixture among individual bowls, place the scallops on top, sprinkle with the cheese and pine nuts (if using), and serve.

Per serving: 410 calories, 6g total fat, 2g saturated fat, 0g trans fat, 25mg cholesterol, 780mg sodium, 66g total carbohydrate, 13g dietary fiber, 6g sugars, 29g protein

Vietnamese Soba Spot Prawns

Makes 6 servings: 1½ cups each

Soirée for six? This Asian-spiced soba noodle dish with the spotlight ingredient, the spot prawn, creates a sensational and satisfying entrée with festive appeal. Spot prawns are basically super-size shrimp with a white-spotted shell; they have a delicately sweet flavor. Though it's the gingery heat of the entire dish that'll be sure to give zing to everyone's palate and add pep to the dinner party.

3 tablespoons brown rice vinegar
Juice of 1 lime (2 tablespoons)
2 tablespoons honey or agave nectar
2 tablespoons naturally brewed soy sauce
1½ tablespoons freshly grated gingerroot
2 teaspoons Asian garlic-chili sauce
6 peeled cooked spot prawns or extra-jumbo shrimp
1 (12.8-ounce) package soba noodles
3 tablespoons toasted sesame oil
1 cup shredded green or napa cabbage
1 large red bell pepper, finely diced
3 scallions, green and white parts, thinly sliced on diagonal
¼ cup coarsely grated carrot
3 tablespoons chopped fresh cilantro or mixture of fresh cilantro, basil, and mint

1. Whisk together the vinegar, lime juice, honey, soy sauce, gingerroot, and garlic-chili sauce in a medium bowl. Add the prawns and stir to coat. Set aside to allow prawns to marinate.

2. Cook the noodles in simmering water until just al dente, or 1 minute less than suggested on package directions. Drain the noodles well (do not rinse) and place in a large bowl. Drizzle with the oil and toss to coat. Add the cabbage, bell pepper, scallions, carrot, and vinegar mixture (reserving the prawns) and toss again.

3. Top the noodles with the marinated prawns and the cilantro. Serve warm, at room temperature, or chilled.

Per serving: 330 calories, 8g total fat, 1g saturated fat, 0g trans fat, 10mg cholesterol, 450mg sodium, 57g total carbohydrate, 4g dietary fiber, 10g sugars, 9g protein

Shrimp Pad Thai Noodles Ⓕ

Makes 6 servings: about 1 cup each

Thai cuisine is known for its balance of spicy, salty, and sweet flavors. That combination is sure to satisfy the palate—including every bite of this comforting pad Thai noodle meal. Hint: Eden Organic and Annie Chun make brown rice noodles that you can find in the international section of the supermarket.

⅓ cup low-sodium vegetables broth
    or Vegetable Stock (page 203)

3 tablespoons naturally brewed soy sauce

1½ tablespoons honey or agave nectar

1½ teaspoons Thai hot chili sauce or other
    hot sauce

6 ounces flat brown rice noodles

1 tablespoon + 2 teaspoons unrefined peanut oil

6 ounces medium shrimp, peeled and deveined

1 (3-ounce) boneless skinless chicken thigh,
    cut into ½-inch cubes

2 large garlic cloves, thinly sliced or chopped

2 large eggs, lightly beaten

4 scallions, green and white parts, thinly sliced
    on a diagonal

1½ cups mung bean sprouts or shredded
    green cabbage

3 tablespoons coarsely chopped unsalted
    dry-roasted peanuts

Juice and zest of 1 lime (2 tablespoons juice)

2 tablespoons chopped fresh cilantro

1. Whisk together the broth, soy sauce, honey, and hot chili sauce in a small bowl. Set aside.

2. Bring a large saucepan of water to a boil, add the noodles, and remove from heat. Let the noodles steep according to package directions, about 5 minutes. Drain, rinse in cold water, and drain again. Transfer the noodles to a medium bowl and set aside.

3. Heat 1 tablespoon of the oil over medium heat in a wok or large, deep nonstick skillet. Add the shrimp, chicken, and garlic and sauté until cooked through, about 3 minutes.

4. Add the soaked noodles and cook while tossing for 1 minute. Increase to medium-high heat and add the soy sauce mixture and cook while tossing for 1 minute.

5. Push the noodles to the sides of the pan. Add the remaining 2 teaspoons oil. Add the eggs and scramble until done. Add the scallions and bean sprouts and sauté with the noodles and egg until the sprouts are softened, about 1 minute.

6. Sprinkle the peanuts and lime juice over the noodles and then toss to combine.

7. Transfer the noodles to a serving platter. Sprinkle with the cilantro and desired amount of the lime zest, and serve hot.

Per serving: 430 calories, 10g total fat, 2g saturated fat, 0g trans fat, 115mg cholesterol, 790mg sodium, 57g total carbohydrate, 12g dietary fiber, 5g sugars, 29g protein

Sun-Dried Tomato Pesto Pasta with Tuna Ⓕ

Makes 6 servings: 1⅓ cups each

This savory, satisfying, tuna-spiked pasta dish is simple to make. The fragrance of the pesto and basil delight the senses. But it's the flavors that will delight both kids and adults. For extra-special appeal, enjoy sprinkled with freshly grated Parmigiano-Reggiano cheese.

12 ounces whole-wheat spaghetti
    or other whole-grain pasta

7 ounces canned water-packed tuna,
    drained and flaked

¾ cup Sun-Dried Tomato Pesto (page 119)
    or other pesto

½ teaspoon sea salt, or to taste

2 tablespoons finely chopped fresh basil

2 tablespoons pine nuts, toasted

1. Cook the pasta according to package directions. Drain the pasta, reserving ½ cup of the cooking liquid. Return the pasta to the dry pan and toss with the tuna and pesto, adding cooking liquid as needed for desired consistency. Add the salt. Adjust seasoning.

2. Divide the pasta among individual plates or bowls, sprinkle with the basil and pine nuts, and serve.

Per serving: 350 calories, 12g total fat, 1.5g saturated fat, 0g trans fat, 10mg cholesterol, 510mg sodium, 45g total carbohydrate, 7g dietary fiber, 3g sugars, 19g protein

Summer Squash and Shrimp Farfalle Ⓕ

Makes 5 servings: 2 cups each

Here, fresh, fragrant, and satisfying ingredients marry in a refreshing culinary creation. The pops of sweet peas and summery squashes pair perfectly with the aromatic basil and oregano. Serve this shrimp farfalle dish on a warm summer night for a light dinner with true delight.

12 ounces whole-wheat farfalle

2 tablespoons extra-virgin olive oil

1 medium zucchini, cut into ½-inch slices

1 medium yellow squash, cut into ½-inch slices

1 large shallot, thinly sliced

12 ounces peeled deveined medium shrimp

½ cup fresh or frozen green peas, thawed

2 large garlic cloves, minced

Juice of 1 lemon (3 tablespoons)

½ teaspoon sea salt, or to taste

¼ teaspoon freshly ground black pepper, or to taste

¼ cup thinly sliced fresh basil leaves

1½ teaspoons finely chopped fresh oregano

3 tablespoons freshly grated Parmigiano-Reggiano or other Parmesan cheese

1. Cook the pasta according to package directions. Drain the pasta, reserving ½ cup of the cooking liquid. Toss the pasta with 1 tablespoon of the oil in the dry pan. Set aside.

2. Heat the remaining 1 tablespoon oil over medium heat in a large deep skillet. Add the zucchini, yellow squash, and shallot and sauté until the squash is nearly tender and shallot is caramelized, about 10 minutes. Add the shrimp, peas, and garlic and sauté until the shrimp is just cooked, about 3 minutes. Stir in the lemon juice, pasta, desired amount of the reserved cooking liquid, the salt, and pepper and cook while tossing until hot, about 1 minute. Adjust seasoning.

3. Transfer the pasta mixture to a large serving bowl. Add the basil, oregano, and cheese and gently toss to combine, and serve.

Per serving: 370 calories, 8g total fat, 1.5g saturated fat, 0g trans fat, 90mg cholesterol, 680mg sodium, 57g total carbohydrate, 7g dietary fiber, 4g sugars, 22g protein

Sandwiches, Burgers, Burritos, and More

Cool Sandwiches: Vegetarian

PB&A Sandwich

Vegetarian Gyro with Mint Tzatziki

Cucumber and Caramelized Onion Tea Sandwiches

PLT Sandwich with Avocado

Smoked Gouda-Artichoke Club Sandwich

Lemon Soybean Hummus Bagel Sandwich

Chick'n Salad on Rye

7-Veggie Sandwich on 7-Grain

Fresh Egg Salad Pita Sandwich

Cool Sandwiches: Poultry, Fish, and Meat

Rotisserie Tarragon Chicken Salad Sandwich

Turkey and Fig Salad on Toasted Muffin

Turkey, Mango, and Chipotle Lime–Dressed Greens on Naan

Sassy Lobster Roll

New-Age Hero with Herbal Tofunnaise

Peppercorn Beef and Brie on Bread Ends

Danish Beef Smørrebrød Sandwich

Italian-Style Submarine

Applewood-Smoked BLT Baguette

Ciabatta Provencale

Prosciutto and Provolone Ciabatta with Fig Jam

Warm Sandwiches: Vegetarian

Edamame Salad Shawarma

Roasted Veggie Roti

Eggplant Parmesan Sliders

Barbecued Seitan Sandwich

Philly Cheesesteak-less

Egg, Muenster, and Greens Grinder

Warm Sandwiches: Poultry, Fish, and Meat

Jerk Chicken Sandwich

Chicken-Arugula Hero

Chicken Shawarma

Tuna Salad Gruyère Melt Sandwich

Philly-Inspired Cheesesteak

Bell Pepper–Stuffed Turkey Sausage Sandwich

Pineapple-Serrano BBQ Pork Sandwich

Sloppy Jackies

Romano Meatball Open Sandwich Marinara

Panini and Toasties

Smoked Caprese Egg Panini

Goat Cheese and Piquillo Pepper Panini

Broccolini and Aged Cheddar Panini

Pesto, Tomato, and Mozzarella Panini

Cuban-Inspired Smoked Ham Baguette

Grilled Fontina and Fig Sandwich

Grilled Feta and Spinach Naan Sandwich

Peanut Butter and Grilled-Grape Toastie

Turkey, Cheese, and Tart Apple Toastie

Avocado, Basil, and Zucchini Toastie

Burgers and Dogs

Smoky Portabella and Cheese Burger

Grilled Vegan Veggie Burgers

Roasted Winter Veggie Burgers

Luscious Lentil and Cheese Burger

Vietnamese-Style Chicken Burger

Serbian Grilled Turkey Burger

Bodacious Bison Burger

Madras Naan Burger

Smokin' Salmon "Dog"

Moroccan "Burger-Dog"

Chi-Chi Chicken Hot Dog

Wraps

Fruit-n-Nut Energy Roti

Punjabi Spinach and Chickpea Wrap

Stuffed Vegetarian Banger Wrap

Pumpkin-Avocado Wrap with Refried Beans

Take-Away Thai Chicken Wrap

California Smoked Turkey Wrap

Tacos, Burritos, and Quesadillas

Southwestern Bean Soft Tacos

Turkey Tacos Monterey

Blackened Tilapia Tacos with Papaya

Santa Cruz Spinach and Black Bean Burrito

Tropical Rotisserie Chicken Burrito

Lebanese Grilled Lamb Burrito

Caprese Quesadilla

Papaya and Goat Cheese Quesadilla

Caramelized Pear, Roquefort, and Prosciutto Quesadilla

Veggie Enchilada Verde

My favorite sandwich as a kid was bologna and potato chips on white bread.

My tastes have definitely changed for the better since then, as my favorite sandwiches now consist of whole-grain breads, seasonal veggie-focused fillings, fresh herbs, and a bit of mayo with big flavors.

If prepared on whole-grain bread, a sandwich can be a truly healthful, satisfying entrée any time of the day. Occasionally it can become an entire meal, such as the Tropical Rotisserie Chicken Burrito (page 406). It provides a vehicle by which you can enjoy plenty of veggies, so you'll see many dishes here with breads piled high with crisp and colorful vegetables; they look hearty and inviting and are filling, too. If you're choosing a meat or poultry sandwich, make it a lean pick whenever you have the option. And do try to go organic when you can; it's an overall healthful bonus.

This chapter starts with cool sandwiches for every kind of taste—both vegetarian and with meats. They're the best choices for packed lunches, whether for school, the workplace, or a picnic. There's nothing but full taste here, including the PLT Sandwich with Avocado (page 374) and the Smoked Gouda–Artichoke Club Sandwich (page 375). The poultry, fish, and meat sandwiches each provide something that's a unique idea, such as the jasmine green tea used as part of the cooking liquid in the Turkey and Fig Salad on Toasted Muffin (page 378), and the celebration of the bread heels in Peppercorn Beef and Brie on Bread Ends (page 380).

If you prefer warm sandwiches, there are many intriguing options for you. You'll notice two versions of the popular Philly cheesesteak sandwich; one is actually vegetarian! There are some made-over versions of comforting classics, including Sloppy Jackies (page 390) and Romano Meatball Open Sandwich Marinara (page 390). The Sloppy Jackies filling incorporates veggies into the meat, along with extra heat and a splash of beer for flavor depth. The low-cal cuisine key to the meatball sandwich is to simply serve it without the bun top.

If you prefer your bread on the toastier side, some of the most memorable flavor combinations are in the Panini and Toasties section, including Broccolini and Aged Cheddar Panini (page 392) and Turkey, Cheese, and Tart Apple Toastie (page 395). Highly aromatic cheese is part of the trick to their deliciousness—and you need only a little for great taste. The Peanut Butter and Grilled-Grape Toastie (page 394) will put a smile on any kid's face, too.

The equally smile-worthy burgers, dogs, and wraps are next, which includes four different ways to enjoy a meat-free burger to ensure there's something to suit anyone, anytime. Whether it's the grilled portabella, grilled vegan, oven-roasted winter veggie, or broiled lentil burger, you'll definitely want to try one (or hopefully all!) of them. There are succulent chicken, turkey, bison, and beef burgers, too.

Finally, you will enjoy the Mexican-influenced tacos and burritos that highlight ingredients like buttery avocado, crunchy fresh corn, savory beans, zesty salsa, and more. There are three unique quesadillas that may capture your culinary creative side, too. When you start with whole-grain tortillas and pile on the produce, these picks are low-cal winners.

You'll be able to pair many of the recipes in this chapter with the great-tasting "mayos," tofunnaises, spreads, or sauces found in Chapter 3 to make them especially good for you. What's more, they'll make them extra delish!

Calorie range in this chapter: 190 to 470 calories.

Low-calorie pick: Danish Beef Smørrebrød Sandwich, 190 calories (page 381).

Cool Sandwiches: Vegetarian

PB&A Sandwich

Makes 1 serving: 1 sandwich each

This is like a peanut butter and jelly sandwich gone glam. Pistachio butter is the spread of choice here due to its appealing green color—and because the pistachio happens to be one of the lowest calorie nuts. Plus, an apricot is used instead of jam to add fresh flair—while saving about 80 calories.

2 tablespoons no-salt-added roasted or raw
    pistachio, almond, or cashew butter
1 ripe apricot, pitted, minced, and gently smashed
2 slices whole-grain bread, toasted

Spread the pistachio butter on one side of each toast slice. Sprinkle one of the slices with the apricot. Gently smash together, slice in half, and serve.

Per serving: 340 calories, 15g total fat, 2g saturated fat, 0g trans fat, 0mg cholesterol, 220mg sodium, 36g total carbohydrate, 8g dietary fiber, 7g sugars, 13g protein

Vegetarian Gyro with Mint Tzatziki

Makes 4 servings: 1 gyro (½ stuffed pita) each

One of my late-late night snacks during my college years used to be a gyro with lamb, beef, or chicken. I hope you enjoy this meat-free version—made with well-seasoned seitan in place of the usual gyro meat. It creates a substantial and savory sandwich to be enjoyed anytime.

2 teaspoons extra-virgin olive oil
1 (8-ounce) package seitan or other plant-based
    strips
1 teaspoon finely chopped fresh oregano
    or ½ teaspoon crushed dried oregano
½ teaspoon sweet paprika
½ teaspoon freshly ground black pepper, or to taste
⅛ teaspoon sea salt, or to taste
1½ teaspoons fresh lemon juice
1 cup Mint Tzatziki (page 95)
2 (8-inch) whole-grain pitas, halved and warm
1½ cups shredded romaine lettuce
½ small red onion, very thinly sliced
1 small green bell pepper, thinly sliced

1. Heat the oil in a large nonstick skillet over medium heat. Add the seitan, oregano, paprika, pepper, and salt and sauté until fully heated and lightly browned, about 8 minutes. Stir in the lemon juice.

2. Spoon half of the tzatziki into the pita halves. Top with the sautéed seitan, the lettuce, onion, and bell pepper. Top with the remaining tzatziki or serve it on the side.

Per serving: 240 calories, 6g total fat, 1g saturated fat, 0g trans fat, 0mg cholesterol, 640mg sodium, 28g total carbohydrate, 4g dietary fiber, 4g sugars, 22g protein

Cucumber and Caramelized-Onion Tea Sandwiches Ⓕ

Makes 4 servings: 3 "finger" sandwiches each

A British-style tea sandwich is a petite sandwich typically eaten at afternoon teatime—ideal to curb that slight hunger pang between lunch and dinner. I've taken these little darlings to the next level and incorporated delightfully fragrant jasmine green tea into the sandwiches. Sip a cup of green tea along with these, too, if you like.

1 medium or ½ extra-large sweet onion,
    halved and thinly sliced
1 cup freshly brewed unsweetened jasmine green
    tea or other green tea (made with 1 tea bag)
4 teaspoons unsalted butter, softened
½ teaspoon + ⅛ teaspoon sea salt, or to taste
½ large English cucumber, unpeeled and very
    thinly sliced crosswise (about 64 slices)
8 slices hearty whole-wheat or other whole-grain
    bread
3 tablespoons minced fresh chives
1 teaspoon finely chopped fresh dill
¼ teaspoon freshly ground black pepper, or to taste

1. Add the onion and tea to a large nonstick skillet over medium-high heat. Cook while stirring until the liquid is fully evaporated, about 12 minutes. Add 2 teaspoons of the butter and ⅛ teaspoon of the salt and sauté until the onion is caramelized, about 4 minutes. Set aside to cool. Chill in the refrigerator until ready to use.

2. Arrange the cucumber slices in a single layer on a large plate. Sprinkle with the remaining ½ teaspoon salt. Cover the cucumber slices with another plate. Weight the plate with condiment jars. Let stand in the refrigerator to allow cucumbers to soften, at least 2 hours. Drain the juices from the cucumber slices. Pat dry between layers of paper towels. Chill in the refrigerator between sheets of paper towels until ready to use.

3. Very lightly spread 1 side of each bread slice with the remaining 2 teaspoons butter. Top the buttered side of 4 of the slices with the chives, drained cucumber slices, caramelized onion, the dill, and pepper. Cover with the remaining bread slices, buttered side down. Trim the crusts from the sandwiches.

4. Cut each sandwich into 3 fingers each, with a bread knife, and serve.

Per serving: 200 calories, 6g total fat, 3g saturated fat, 0g trans fat, 10mg cholesterol, 520mg sodium, 29g total carbohydrate, 5g dietary fiber, 7g sugars, 8g protein

PLT Sandwich with Avocado Ⓕ

Makes 4 servings: 1 sandwich each

Move over BLT, there's a vegetarian knock-off in town. This PLT—roasted pepper, leafy green, and tomato—is fresher and more flavorful with peppery arugula, a tangy blue cheese spread, and a buttery addition of avocado . . . all for less than 300 calories.

½ cup Blue Cheese Tofunnaise (page 124)
    or other tofunnaise
8 slices whole-wheat sourdough bread, toasted
1 large roasted red bell pepper (page 27),
    sliced into 4 pieces
2 cups packed baby arugula, spinach,
    or other leafy green
1 Hass avocado, pitted, peeled, and sliced
1 large beefsteak or heirloom red or yellow
    tomato, thinly sliced
⅛ teaspoon sea salt, or to taste
⅛ teaspoon freshly ground black pepper, or to taste

1. Spread the tofunnaise on one side of each toast slice. Top 4 of the slices with the bell pepper, arugula, avocado, and tomato. Add the salt and black pepper. Firmly top with the remaining bread slices, tofunnaise side down.

2. Cut sandwiches in half diagonally, skewer with bamboo or reusable picks, if desired, and serve.

Per serving: 290 calories, 10g total fat, 2.5g saturated fat, 0g trans fat, 5mg cholesterol, 550mg sodium, 38g total carbohydrate, 9g dietary fiber, 7g sugars, 13g protein

Smoked Gouda-Artichoke Club Sandwich Ⓕ

Makes 3 servings: 1 sandwich each

The Gouda in this sandwich gives the smoky, salty flavor essence of bacon—so you'll only have calories from cheese, not both bacon and cheese! The onion provides distinct crispness. For extra deliciousness, if you have a few extra minutes, grill the artichoke hearts on skewers on a grill pan or grill before slicing and serving in the sandwich. Grill the bread, too, for another layer of flavor.

3 tablespoons Lemon-Caper "Mayo" (page 124)

6 slices hearty whole-grain bread, toasted

1 Hass avocado, pitted, peeled, and sliced

¼ teaspoon freshly ground black pepper, or to taste

⅛ teaspoon sea salt, or to taste

1 box (9 ounces) frozen artichoke hearts, thawed, patted dry and sliced

1 medium vine-ripened tomato, sliced

3 large slices red onion

3 ounces smoked Gouda cheese or smoked mozzarella cheese, thinly sliced

1½ cups packed watercress or arugula

1. Spread the "mayo" onto one side of all toast slices.

2. Layer onto 3 of the bread slices the avocado, pepper, salt, artichoke hearts, tomato, onion, cheese, and watercress.

3. Place remaining toast slices, "mayo" side down, firmly on top, cut diagonally in half with a bread knife, and serve.

Per serving: 410 calories, 22g total fat, 7g saturated fat, 0g trans fat, 35mg cholesterol, 700mg sodium, 38g total carbohydrate, 13g dietary fiber, 6g sugars, 19g protein

Lemon Soybean Hummus Bagel Sandwich Ⓕ

Makes 2 servings: 1 sandwich each

Every once in a while a bagel might be calling your name. Relish it topped with velvety hummus and fresh veggies. Do make sure you're using a 3-ounce bagel, not a 5-ounce bakery one. But if your bagel is big, just pinch out some of the doughy part to right-size it. Or split the large bagel into thirds instead of in half and save a section for later.

2 teaspoons fresh lemon juice

2 teaspoons extra-virgin olive oil

1½ cups packed baby arugula

⅓ cup very thinly sliced unpeeled English cucumber

¼ teaspoon freshly ground black pepper, or to taste

⅛ teaspoon sea salt, or to taste

½ cup Zesty Lemon Soybean Hummus (page 88) or other hummus

2 (3-ounce) whole-grain "everything" bagels or other whole-grain bagel, split, and lightly toasted

2 paper-thin slices large red onion, separated

1 medium vine-ripened tomato, cut into 4 thick slices or 8 thin slices

1. Whisk together the lemon juice and oil in a small bowl. Add the arugula, cucumber, pepper, and salt and toss to coat. Set aside.

2. Spread the hummus onto the bottom portion of each bagel. Top with the onion, tomato, and arugula salad, and the top portion of the bagels. Cut sandwiches in half, if desired.

Per serving: 370 calories, 15g total fat, 2g saturated fat, 0g trans fat, 0mg cholesterol, 530mg sodium, 52g total carbohydrate, 10g dietary fiber, 9g sugars, 16g protein

Chick'n Salad on Rye Ⓕ

Makes 4 sandwiches: 1 sandwich (with ¾ cup chick'n salad) each

Tofu is the new "chicken" in this refreshing sandwich on rye. It really is chameleon-like here as it bathes in a bevy of enticing ingredients and takes on their flavors. The array of textures from the crisp fennel, crunchy almonds, and luscious fig adds to the excitement. You can also serve the chick'n salad as a snack or hors d'oeuvre: mound it atop small round brown rice crackers and garnish with tarragon for an appetizing bite.

¼ cup Garlic "Mayo" (page 123) or other "mayo"

1 large fresh Black Mission fig, stem removed and finely diced, or ¼ cup thinly sliced red or black seedless grapes

¼ cup finely diced fresh fennel bulb or shaved raw artichoke

¼ cup minced red onion

1 tablespoon finely chopped fresh basil

1 tablespoon finely chopped fresh tarragon

1½ teaspoons fresh lemon juice

½ teaspoon freshly ground black pepper, or to taste

¼ teaspoon + ⅛ teaspoon sea salt, or to taste

¼ teaspoon hot Madras curry powder, or to taste

1 (14-ounce) package firm tofu, well-drained, and finely diced

3 tablespoons sliced natural almonds, toasted

8 slices rye bread

1. Stir together the "mayo," fig, fennel, onion, basil, tarragon, lemon juice, pepper, salt, and curry powder in a medium bowl until well combined. Stir in the tofu, cover, and chill in the refrigerator to allow flavors to blend, at least 1 hour. Adjust seasoning. Stir in the almonds.

2. Spread about ¾ cup each of the tofu mixture onto 4 of the bread slices, place the other slices on top, slice in half with a bread knife, and serve.

Per serving: 310 calories, 12g total fat, 1.5g saturated fat, 0g trans fat, 0mg cholesterol, 690mg sodium, 36g total carbohydrate, 6g dietary fiber, 6g sugars, 16g protein

7-Veggie Sandwich on 7-Grain Ⓕ

Makes 4 servings: 1 sandwich each

I guess this could be considered a lucky sandwich—with seven veggies on seven-grain bread. The fresh layers make it rather pretty—and pretty filling. Show off this star at a casual gathering or picnic.

1 (10-ounce) 7-grain whole-wheat or whole-grain ciabatta bread, split

½ cup Tuscan Basil White Bean Spread (page 126) or hummus mixed with fresh basil

1 teaspoon finely chopped fresh rosemary

½ teaspoon freshly ground black pepper, or to taste

¼ teaspoon sea salt, or to taste

2 large freshly roasted red or orange bell peppers (page 27), sliced into large pieces

1 small or ½ large zucchini, ends trimmed and thinly sliced lengthwise

3 ounces thinly sliced portobella mushroom caps

1½ cups packed baby arugula or wild greens

1 large beefsteak or heirloom yellow or red tomato, thinly sliced

1. Spread the cut surfaces of the bread loaf with the bean spread. Sprinkle with the rosemary, black pepper, and salt.

2. Layer the roasted peppers, zucchini, mushrooms, arugula, and tomato on the bottom portion of the bread loaf. Firmly place the top portion of the bread loaf on the vegetables, bean spread side down.

3. Secure the sandwich layers with bamboo skewers. Cut the sandwich into 4 pieces, and serve.

Per serving: 270 calories, 5g total fat, 1g saturated fat, 0g trans fat, 0mg cholesterol, 560mg sodium, 45g total carbohydrate, 10g dietary fiber, 11g sugars, 14g protein

Fresh Egg Salad
Pita Sandwich

Makes 4 servings: 1 stuffed pita half each

A good egg salad can totally hit the spot. You'll love the fresh flavor from herbs and arugula in this one. Plus, the naturally light "mayo" lightens the calories while it pleasantly heightens the taste. Stuffing it in a pita pocket adds a fun factor.

¼ cup Sassy "Mayo" (page 123)

2 teaspoons stone-ground mustard

1 large shallot, minced

1 scallion, green and white part, very thinly sliced

2 teaspoons finely chopped fresh dill
    or 1 teaspoon dried dill

2 teaspoons finely chopped fresh tarragon
    or 1 teaspoon dried tarragon

7 large hard-cooked eggs, chopped (right)

¼ teaspoon sea salt, or to taste

⅛ teaspoon ground cayenne, or to taste

1½ packed cups baby arugula

2 (8-inch) whole-grain pitas, halved

1. Stir together the "mayo," mustard, shallot, scallion, dill, and tarragon in a medium bowl until well combined. Fold or gently stir in the eggs, salt, and cayenne. Adjust seasoning.

2. Stuff each pita half with the arugula and egg salad, and serve.

Per serving: 270 calories, 14g total fat, 3.5g saturated fat, 0g trans fat, 330mg cholesterol, 560mg sodium, 22g total carbohydrate, 3g dietary fiber, 3g sugars, 16g protein

EASY WAY TO HARD-COOK EGGS

Ever hard-cook eggs and find the center has turned green? That's from overcooking them. Try this technique to keep the eggs tender and bright yellow while also cooking them to the right hard-boiled stage.

Place large eggs in a single layer in a large saucepan. Cover with fresh water, ½ inch above the eggs. Place over high heat. Just before it boils, cover and turn off the heat. (Remove from the burner if using an electric stove.) Let stand for 9 minutes. Pour off the water, cool to room temperature for 30 minutes, then chill in the refrigerator.

Cool Sandwiches: Poultry, Fish, and Meat

Tarragon Chicken Salad Sandwich

Makes 4 servings: 1 sandwich each

The mixture of real mayonnaise and non-fat Greek yogurt provides a naturally lower calorie dressing in this creamy chicken salad sandwich. And the fresh lemon juice, tarragon, and surprising addition of almond extract add amazing flavor.

3 tablespoons mayonnaise

3 tablespoons fat-free or low-fat plain Greek yogurt

Juice of ½ small lemon (1 tablespoon)

1 tablespoon finely chopped fresh tarragon

¼ teaspoon sea salt, or to taste

⅛ teaspoon freshly ground black pepper, or to taste

2 drops pure almond extract

12 ounces rotisserie or oven-roasted chicken breast, cubed and chilled (about 2 cups)

¼ cup minced sweet onion

2 tablespoons minced fennel bulb

8 slices whole-grain raisin-nut bread

1 cup packed fresh mixed field greens or mesclun (optional)

1. In a large bowl, combine the mayonnaise, yogurt, lemon juice, tarragon, salt, pepper, and almond extract. Stir in the chicken, onion, and fennel. Chill in the refrigerator until ready to serve. Adjust seasoning.

2. Spoon about ½ packed cup of chicken salad onto each of 4 slices of the bread. Add the greens (if using), top with remaining slices of bread and serve.

Per serving: 370 calories, 13g total fat, 2g saturated fat, 0g trans fat, 70mg cholesterol, 480mg sodium, 27g total carbohydrate, 4g dietary fiber, 6g sugars, 34g protein

Turkey and Fig Salad on Toasted Muffin Ⓕ

Makes 5 servings: 1 sandwich with ⅔ cup turkey salad each

There's something from every food group in this turkey salad sandwich—which makes it an ideal meal. Plus, it tastes sensational. The hits of fresh fig and poppy seeds are enchanting.

1 pound boneless skinless turkey tenderloin or breast, cut into ½-inch cubes

2 cups low-sodium vegetable broth or Vegetable Stock (page 203)

¾ teaspoon sea salt, or to taste

2 jasmine green tea bags

1 cup diced stemmed fresh Black Mission figs or ⅓ cup finely diced dried figs

⅔ cup shaved or minced fennel bulb or thinly sliced celery

1 large shallot, minced

¼ cup mayonnaise

2 tablespoons fat-free or low-fat plain Greek yogurt

2 teaspoons apple cider vinegar

½ teaspoon freshly ground black pepper, or to taste

⅓ cup pecan halves, toasted and coarsely chopped

2 teaspoons poppy seeds

5 escarole leaves

5 whole-grain English muffins, split and toasted

1. Add the turkey to a medium saucepan. Add the broth and ½ teaspoon of the salt. Place over medium-high heat. Bring just to a boil, reduce heat to medium-low, add the tea bags, cover, and cook until the turkey is just cooked through, about 8 minutes. Remove from heat, and let stand for further steeping, about 5 minutes. Drain the turkey and remove the tea bags. Set aside the turkey to slightly cool, about 15 minutes.

2. Gently combine the cooked turkey, the figs, fennel, shallot, mayonnaise, yogurt, vinegar, pepper, and the remaining ¼ teaspoon salt in a medium bowl. Chill in the refrigerator until ready to serve.

3. Stir in the pecans and poppy seeds. Adjust seasoning. Lay an escarole leaf on the bottom portion of the English muffin halves, top with the turkey mixture, place on the top English muffin halves, and serve.

Per serving: 420 calories, 17g total fat, 2g saturated fat, 0g trans fat, 40mg cholesterol, 750mg sodium, 41g total carbohydrate, 7g dietary fiber, 14g sugars, 30g protein

Turkey, Mango, and Chipotle Lime–Dressed Greens on Naan Ⓕ

Makes 4 servings: 1 sandwich each

This naan sandwich, made with Indian flatbread, is a one-dish wonder. It's like a fresh leafy salad, a smoky turkey sandwich, and a sweet side of fruit all wrapped in one. As a bonus, it's so good for you; it's an excellent source of vitamin C, beta-carotene, and calcium.

Juice of 1 lime (2 tablespoons)
1½ tablespoons mayonnaise
1 shallot, minced
½ teaspoon chipotle chili powder
⅛ teaspoon sea salt, or to taste
1 small mango, peeled, pitted, and thinly sliced
4 packed cups mesclun or other mixed baby greens
2 tablespoons finely chopped fresh cilantro leaves
4 (3-ounce) whole-grain naan (Indian flatbread)
    or Middle Eastern flatbreads
6 ounces thinly sliced deli smoked turkey breast

1. Whisk together the lime juice, mayonnaise, shallot, chili powder, and salt. Add the mango, mesclun, and cilantro and toss until well dressed.

2. Divide the turkey evenly among the flatbreads. Top with the dressed greens and mango. Adjust seasoning. Fold to eat.

Per serving: 390 calories, 12g total fat, 2g saturated fat, 0g trans fat, 20mg cholesterol, 720mg sodium, 53g total carbohydrate, 7g dietary fiber, 13g sugars, 18g protein

Sassy Lobster Roll

Makes 2 servings: 1 roll each

It is possible to have your lobster roll and eat it, too. The use of my Sassy "Mayo" helps make it thoroughly feasible to feast upon. And the freshly fragrant tarragon is what makes this lively sandwich thoroughly memorable.

1 (12-ounce) lobster tail
3 tablespoons Sassy "Mayo" (page 123)
2 teaspoons chopped fresh tarragon
¼ teaspoon freshly ground black pepper, or to taste
⅛ teaspoon sea salt, or to taste
2 teaspoons unsalted butter, softened
2 whole-wheat hot dog rolls, split and grilled
    or toasted
1 cup chopped frisée or sliced Boston lettuce

1. Bring several inches of water to a boil in a large, wide pot. Add the lobster tail, reduce heat to medium, and poach until the lobster meat is cooked through, about 6 minutes. Drain and set aside to cool. Press firmly on the back of the tail until it cracks. Cut through the tail shell on its underside and pull apart to release the meat. Tear or chop the lobster meat into bite-size pieces. Chill in the refrigerator in a well-sealed container until ready to use. (Makes about 6 ounces lobster meat; 1 cup.)

2. Add the chilled lobster meat, "mayo," tarragon, pepper, and salt to a medium bowl and stir to combine. Adjust seasoning.

3. Thinly spread the butter onto the cut surfaces of the grilled rolls. Fill with the lettuce and lobster mixture, and serve.

Per serving: 330 calories, 13g total fat, 4g saturated fat, 0g trans fat, 90mg cholesterol, 660mg sodium, 27g total carbohydrate, 4g dietary fiber, 5g sugars, 28g protein

New-Age Hero with Herbal Tofunnaise Ⓕ

Makes 2 servings: 1 sandwich each

Piled high with full-flavored ingredients, including salami and microgreens, this tall sandwich is deliciously designed for the superhero in all of us.

2 tablespoons Herbal Tofunnaise (page 125)

2 (2½-ounce) whole-grain sandwich rolls, split and lightly toasted or grilled

¼ teaspoon freshly ground black pepper, or to taste

2½ ounces thinly sliced deli roasted or herb roasted turkey breast

1 ounce thinly sliced Genoa salami

2 (¾-ounce) thin slices fresh or smoked mozzarella cheese

1 medium vine-ripened tomato, cut into 6 slices

½ packed cup microgreens or baby arugula

1. Spread the tofunnaise onto the cut surfaces of the rolls. Sprinkle with the pepper.

2. Layer the bottom portion of the rolls with the turkey, salami, cheese, tomato, and microgreens.

3. Cover with the top portion of the rolls, and serve.

Per serving: 330 calories, 10g total fat, 3.5g saturated fat, 0g trans fat, 35mg cholesterol, 770mg sodium, 38g total carbohydrate, 7g dietary fiber, 7g sugars, 22g protein

Peppercorn Beef and Brie on Bread Ends Ⓕ

Makes 4 servings: 1 sandwich each

Yes, "bread ends" are exactly what you think they are . . . the end pieces of the sliced loaf bread that sometimes get tossed out! Save these crusty slices in the freezer specifically for this recipe. They're ideal for heartier sandwich ingredients, like roast beef. When coupled with a sliver of decadently creamy brie and other distinctly flavored ingredients, you'll be creating a nutritional masterpiece filled with high-quality protein, iron, and zinc . . . and mouthwatering goodness.

¼ cup Creamy Peppercorn Dressing (page 150) or other sandwich spread

2 teaspoons freshly grated or prepared horseradish

8 (1-ounce) whole-grain bread crusts (ends) or slices

7 ounces thinly sliced or shaved extra-lean roast beef

¼ teaspoon freshly ground black pepper, or to taste

3 ounces very thinly sliced Brie or Paesanella cheese

4 thin slices large sweet or red onion, separated into rings

2 packed cups mizuna or baby arugula

1. Stir together the dressing and horseradish in a small bowl. Spread the dressing mixture on the cut side of each bread crust.

2. Place 4 of the bread "ends" on four plates. Top with the roast beef, pepper, cheese, onion, and mizuna. Cover with other bread "ends" to form a sandwich.

3. Secure each sandwich with a toothpick, if desired, and serve.

Per serving: 300 calories, 11g total fat, 5g saturated fat, 0g trans fat, 45mg cholesterol, 450mg sodium, 30g total carbohydrate, 5g dietary fiber, 5g sugars, 24g protein

Danish Beef Smørrebrød Sandwich

Makes 4 servings: 2 open-face sandwiches each

Smørrebrød is a Danish open-face sandwich that starts with buttered dark bread and is topped with meat, fish, or cold cuts and garnishes. This version of smørrebrød starts with a hearty piece of fresh rye bread, then it's spread with a zingy, buttery mixture, and topped with deli roast beef, radishes, and cornichons. Whatever your toppings, the resulting sandwich will look artfully crafted and appealing and the taste will be even better than it looks.

2 tablespoons fat-free or low-fat plain Greek yogurt

2 teaspoons unsalted butter, at room temperature

2 teaspoons minced fresh chives

2 teaspoons prepared horseradish

⅛ teaspoon sea salt, or to taste

8 (¾-ounce) very thin slices hearty rye or pumpernickel bread, such as rugbrød

7 ounces thinly sliced lean deli roast beef

3 radishes, shaved or very thinly sliced

6 cornichons, thinly sliced

¼ teaspoon freshly ground black pepper, or to taste

1. Stir together the yogurt, butter, chives, horseradish, and salt in a small bowl.

2. Spread the yogurt mixture on the entire top surface of each bread slice.

3. Arrange the roast beef, radishes, and cornichons on each bread slice. Sprinkle with the pepper, and serve open-face style.

Per serving: 190 calories, 4g total fat, 2.5g saturated fat, 0g trans fat, 30mg cholesterol, 620mg sodium, 24g total carbohydrate, 4g dietary fiber, 4g sugars, 15g protein

Italian-Style Submarine

Makes 8 servings: 1 sandwich each

So the truth is sometimes we want our sandwiches to have as much bread as the filling. It's okay to love carbs—if you choose them wisely. This smart whole-grain sandwich has every bit of traditional taste that you'd expect from an Italian sub.

¼ cup Balsamic-Basil "Mayo" (page 124)

1 (1-pound) loaf crusty whole-wheat Italian bread or ciabatta, split

1 tablespoon aged balsamic vinegar, or to taste

1 tablespoon chopped fresh oregano

3 tablespoons sliced or chopped pepperoncini or hot Italian peppers, or to taste

2½ cups packed mesclun or mixed baby greens

4 ounces deli smoked turkey breast

3 ounces thinly sliced country ham or prosciutto

3 ounces part-skim mozzarella cheese, thinly sliced

2 ounces provolone cheese, thinly sliced

½ teaspoon freshly ground black pepper, or to taste

1. Spread the "mayo" on the cut surface of the bottom bread portion. Drizzle the vinegar on the cut surface of the top bread portion.

2. Sprinkle the bottom bread half with the oregano, pepperoncini, and half the mesclun.

3. Arrange the turkey, ham, mozzarella, and provolone in alternating fashion. Top with the remaining mesclun and add the pepper. Cover with the top bread half. Press down firmly.

4. Slice into 8 sandwiches, secure with bamboo skewers, if desired, and serve.

Per serving: 270 calories, 10g total fat, 3.5g saturated fat, 0g trans fat, 25mg cholesterol, 780mg sodium, 31g total carbohydrate, 4g dietary fiber, 3g sugars, 16g protein

Applewood-Smoked BLT Baguette

Makes 5 servings: 1 sandwich each

Yes, you can relish a real BLT sandwich even when eating healthfully. It might surprise you to know that bacon isn't über-high in calories—just 50 calories a slice! Since it tips the sodium scale, I've kept the portion size slender here. The smoky roasted tomatoes highlight this enticing baguette sandwich.

6 slices applewood-smoked uncured bacon
2 medium vine-ripened tomatoes,
    cut into ¼-inch rounds
¼ teaspoon freshly ground black pepper, or to taste
¼ cup Cilantro-Jalapeño "Mayo" (page 124)
1 (8-ounce) whole-grain baguette, split
¾ cup thinly sliced Belgian endive or mixed salad greens
¼ cup thinly sliced red onion

1. Preheat the oven to 450°F.

2. Pan-fry the bacon according to package directions. Remove the crisp slices to a paper towel–lined plate to drain. Reserve the bacon grease in the pan.

3. Place the tomatoes on a parchment paper–lined baking sheet. Sprinkle with 1½ teaspoons of the reserved bacon grease and the pepper. Roast in the oven until the tomatoes are soft and blistered, about 20 minutes.

4. Spread the "mayo" on the cut surfaces of the baguette. Top the bottom portion with the endive, tomatoes, bacon, and the onion. Firmly cover with the baguette top, "mayo" side down.

5. Cut into 5 sandwiches, secure with bamboo skewers, if desired, and serve.

Per serving: 250 calories, 12g total fat, 4.5g saturated fat, 0g trans fat, 20mg cholesterol, 750mg sodium, 23g total carbohydrate, 4g dietary fiber, 5g sugars, 16g protein

Ciabatta Provencale

Makes 5 servings: 1 sandwich each

Don't you love it when your friends desperately try to figure out the "secret" ingredient that makes a recipe a standout? Here, fragrant cantaloupe holds your secret. Its mellow sweetness is a perfect flavor partner for the prosciutto and onion. Do share this not-so-secret tip: to make the sandwich seem larger, start with a bigger portion of ciabatta and pinch out some of the doughy bread inside to create an 8-ounce portion.

¼ cup Creamy Herbes de Provence Sandwich
    Spread (page 126)
1 (8-ounce) whole-grain ciabatta or whole-grain
    baguette, split
¼ teaspoon freshly ground black pepper, or to taste
1 cup packed fresh baby spinach
⅓ cup thinly sliced white or red onion
⅓ cup thinly sliced fresh cantaloupe pieces
2½ ounces thinly sliced prosciutto or country ham
4 ounces part-skim mozzarella cheese, sliced
¾ cup packed thinly sliced radicchio

1. Smear the sandwich spread on the cut surfaces of the ciabatta. Sprinkle with the pepper.

2. Layer the spinach, onion, cantaloupe, prosciutto, cheese, and radicchio onto the bottom portion of the ciabatta. Firmly cover with the bread top, sandwich spread side down.

3. Cut into 5 sandwiches, secure with bamboo skewers, if desired, and serve.

Per serving: 240 calories, 9g total fat, 3.5g saturated fat, 0g trans fat, 25mg cholesterol, 760mg sodium, 25g total carbohydrate, 4g dietary fiber, 4g sugars, 17g protein

Prosciutto and Provolone Ciabatta with Fig Jam Ⓕ

Makes 5 servings: 1 sandwich each

Instead of thinking only about low calorie, think high flavor—as with aged cheese and prosciutto. You won't need as much of the rich ingredients to get rich taste. Then pump up freshness—such as with fig fruit spread and baby arugula. All together, you'll have a sandwich that'll astound your taste buds!

½ cup Fresh Fig Fruit Spread (page 132)
    or 3 tablespoons 100% fig jam of choice
1 (8-ounce) whole-grain ciabatta or whole-grain
    baguette, split
¼ teaspoon freshly ground black pepper, or to taste
¼ cup very thinly sliced red onion
3 ounces very thinly sliced prosciutto
    or American country ham
2 ounces aged provolone cheese, very thinly sliced
1½ cups packed baby arugula

1. Smear the fig spread on both cut surfaces of the ciabatta. Season with the pepper.

2. Layer the onion, prosciutto, cheese, and arugula onto the bottom portion of the ciabatta. Firmly cover with the bread top, fig spread side down.

3. Cut into 5 sandwiches, secure with bamboo skewers, if desired, and serve.

Per serving: 230 calories, 7g total fat, 3g saturated fat, 0g trans fat, 20mg cholesterol, 790mg sodium, 29g total carbohydrate, 5g dietary fiber, 10g sugars, 14g protein

Warm Sandwiches: Vegetarian

Edamame Salad Shawarma Ⓕ

Makes 4 servings: 1 sandwich each

Middle Eastern shawarma is traditionally made with lamb or chicken. Here, edamame provides great body and taste while pickled turnip adds cuisine intrigue. The high-flavor tahini sauce connects it to tradition in a modern way.

1 medium vine-ripened tomato, pulp removed
    and diced
1 medium green bell pepper, finely diced
¼ cup finely diced white onion
¼ cup finely diced pickled turnip or dill pickles
3 tablespoons finely chopped fresh flat-leaf parsley
3 tablespoons finely chopped fresh cilantro
1 large garlic clove, minced
½ teaspoon ground cumin
1½ cups frozen shelled edamame
¼ teaspoon sea salt, or to taste
2 (8-inch) whole-grain pitas, halved and warm
¼ cup Harissa Lemon-Tahini Sauce (page 109),
    at room temperature

1. Gently stir together the tomato, bell pepper, onion, turnip, parsley, cilantro, garlic, and cumin in a medium bowl. Set aside.

2. Cook the frozen edamame in a large saucepan of boiling water until nearly tender, about 1 minute less than package directions suggest, about 4 minutes. Drain. (Do not rinse.)

3. Add the cooked edamame and the salt to the tomato mixture and gently stir. Adjust seasoning.

4. Stuff about 1 cup of the edamame mixture into each pita half, drizzle with 1 tablespoon of the sauce, and serve while warm.

Per serving: 230 calories, 7g total fat, 0.5g saturated fat, 0g trans fat, 0mg cholesterol, 380mg sodium, 31g total carbohydrate, 7g dietary fiber, 4g sugars, 11g protein

Roasted Veggie Roti Ⓕ

Makes 8 servings: 1 roti each

Roti is an unleavened thin Indian flatbread that can be rolled up with nearly any filling that you can imagine. Here it's filled with a flavorful mélange of roasted vegetables dressed with a fusion balsamic-basil "mayo." They go surprisingly well together.

12 ounces small baby carrots

2 large parsnips or rutabagas, peeled and
    cut into ½-inch rounds or cubes

12 ounces red potatoes, unpeeled, scrubbed,
    and cut into ½-inch cubes

1 large red onion, cut into 16 wedges

½ teaspoon sea salt, or to taste

¼ teaspoon hot Madras curry powder, or to taste

1 cup + 2 tablespoons Balsamic-Basil "Mayo"
    (page 124)

8 (7- to 8-inch) whole-wheat roti or other soft thin
    flatbread

¼ cup chopped fresh flat-leaf parsley

2 tablespoons thinly sliced fresh basil leaves

1. Preheat the oven to 425°F.

2. Toss together the carrots, parsnips, potatoes, onion, salt, curry powder, and 2 tablespoons of the "mayo" in a large bowl. Arrange the vegetables on 1 large or 2 medium parchment paper–lined baking pan(s). Roast while stirring periodically until the vegetables are tender and lightly caramelized, about 35 to 40 minutes. Adjust seasoning.

3. Heat the roti in the microwave until just warm, about 20 seconds.

4. Spread each roti with 2 tablespoons of the remaining "mayo." Spoon the vegetables onto the roti, sprinkle with the parsley and basil, and roll or fold in half. Serve while warm.

Per serving: 290 calories, 9g total fat, 2g saturated fat, 0g trans fat, 5mg cholesterol, 570mg sodium, 46g total carbohydrate, 7g dietary fiber, 8g sugars, 8g protein

Eggplant Parmesan Sliders Ⓕ

Makes 8 servings: 1 slider each

These veggie sliders are stacked high with savory Sicilian pleasure. What's more, they freeze surprisingly well when tightly wrapped and can be quickly reheated in the microwave oven anytime you need a "fast-food" fix.

1 large Italian eggplant (about 4-inch diameter
    at widest part)

¾ teaspoon sea salt, or to taste

⅔ cup stone-ground whole-wheat flour

¼ teaspoon freshly ground black pepper

2 large eggs

¾ cup plain dry whole-wheat breadcrumbs

⅓ cup grated Parmigiano-Reggiano, Pecorino
    Romano, or other Parmesan cheese

16 (¾-ounce) slices fresh mozzarella

8 (2-ounce) whole-grain rolls, split, lightly toasted

1 cup Fresh Sicilian Salsa (page 115)

1½ cups baby arugula (optional)

1. Cut the eggplant crosswise into ⅓-inch-thick rounds (16 slices). Sprinkle the eggplant slices with ½ teaspoon of the salt. Place in a colander over the sink. Let stand for 30 minutes.

2. Preheat the oven to 425°F.

3. Stir together the flour, remaining ¼ teaspoon salt, and the pepper in a shallow bowl. Lightly beat the eggs with 2 tablespoons cold water in a second shallow bowl. Stir together the breadcrumbs and Parmesan cheese in a third shallow bowl.

4. Working with 1 slice at a time, dredge the eggplant into the flour, shaking off excess, then dip into the egg mixture, letting excess drip off, and dredge in the breadcrumb-Parmesan mixture until evenly coated. Transfer the eggplant to two large baking sheets, spraying both sides of each eggplant slice with cooking spray (preferably homemade, page xix).

5. Bake until crisp, golden brown, and cooked through, about 25 minutes, rotating trays halfway through the cooking process. Top each with the mozzarella and bake until the cheese is melted and lightly browned, about 5 minutes. Adjust seasoning.

6. Place the eggplant slices and salsa in the rolls with the arugula, if using, and enjoy while warm.

Per serving: 370 calories, 16g total fat, 8g saturated fat, 0g trans fat, 70mg cholesterol, 600mg sodium, 37g total carbohydrate, 7g dietary fiber, 6g sugars, 19g protein

Barbecued Seitan Sandwich

Makes 4 servings: 1 sandwich each

This voluptuous vegan sandwich will make true veggie believers out of most meat eaters. Seitan gets its meaty texture from wheat gluten—so some call it "meat wheat." Pairing it with full-bodied, smoky barbecue sauce is an excellent preparation—even if you're a seitan first-timer.

2 teaspoons grapeseed or canola oil

8 ounces thinly sliced seitan or other plant-based strips, drained of any excess liquid

½ cup Ancho Chili Barbecue Sauce (page 105) or other barbecue sauce

4 (2-ounce) whole-grain sandwich rolls, split and toasted, or (8-inch) whole-wheat pita pockets

4 thin round slices large red onion, raw or grilled

12 bread and butter pickle chips or small pieces of pickled vegetables (optional)

1. Heat the oil in a large nonstick skillet over medium-high heat. Add the seitan and sauté until browned, about 5 minutes. Reduce heat to low, add the barbecue sauce, and sauté until the seitan absorbs the sauce, about 1 minute.

2. Spoon the barbecued seitan onto the bottom portion of the rolls, add the onion, pickles (if using), and roll tops, and serve immediately.

Per serving: 300 calories, 6g total fat, 0g saturated fat, 0g trans fat, 0mg cholesterol, 660mg sodium, 41g total carbohydrate, 3g dietary fiber, 5g sugars, 22g protein

Philly Cheesesteak-less Ⓕ

Makes 4 servings: 1 sandwich each

How can a cheesesteak sandwich really be called one when it's not stuffed with steak? When you mound it with notably meaty portabella mushrooms and other voluminous vegetables—and when you keep its cheese-laden gloriousness. This has a savory goodness of its own that you need to experience first-hand.

¼ cup Garlic "Mayo" (page 123) or other "mayo"

¼ teaspoon hot pepper sauce, or to taste

4 whole-wheat hamburger buns

5½ ounces provolone cheese, thinly sliced

1½ tablespoons grapeseed or canola oil

1 large Spanish or white onion, halved and thinly sliced

2 large green bell peppers, thinly sliced

6 ounces thinly sliced large portabella mushroom caps

2 teaspoons white balsamic vinegar

½ teaspoon freshly ground black pepper, to taste

¼ teaspoon sea salt, to taste

1. Preheat the broiler.

2. Stir together the "mayo" and hot pepper sauce in a small bowl until well combined. Set aside.

3. Split open the buns and top with the cheese. Place under the broiler until the buns are toasted and cheese is melted, about 1 minute.

4. Heat the oil in an extra-large skillet over medium-high heat. Add the onion, bell peppers, and mushrooms, cover, and cook (no need to stir) until the vegetables are slightly softened, about 8 minutes. Uncover, add the vinegar, black pepper, and salt, and sauté until the vegetables are fully softened and no excess liquid remains, about 10 minutes. Adjust seasoning.

5. Spread each bun with the mayonnaise mixture, fill with the vegetables, and enjoy immediately.

Per serving: 370 calories, 21g total fat, 8g saturated fat, 0g trans fat, 30mg cholesterol, 760mg sodium, 33g total carbohydrate, 6g dietary fiber, 9g sugars, 16g protein

Egg, Muenster, and Greens Grinder

Makes 1 serving: 1 sandwich each

This is one of my top recipes when I need something delicious—fast. The cheese is rich and buttery. The arugula is fresh and peppery. And the egg is the satisfying star. It's a comforting bite anytime.

1 whole-wheat or other whole-grain hamburger
    bun, split
1 thin (¾-ounce) slice muenster cheese, cut in half
½ teaspoon extra-virgin olive oil
1 large egg
Pinch of sea salt
Pinch of freshly ground black pepper
½ cup wild baby arugula leaves

1. Toast the bun halves. Top each with a piece of the cheese. Set aside.

2. Heat the oil in a small nonstick skillet over medium heat. Add the egg, break the yolk, and cook both sides of the egg to desired doneness. Add the salt and pepper.

3. Place the egg on the bottom portion of the bun. Top with the arugula and the bun top, and serve.

Per serving: 280 calories, 16g total fat, 6g saturated fat, 0g trans fat, 205mg cholesterol, 540mg sodium, 23g total carbohydrate, 3g dietary fiber, 4g sugars, 16g protein

Warm Sandwiches: Poultry, Fish, and Meat

Jerk Chicken Sandwich

Makes 4 servings: 1 sandwich each

Totally tropical! That's what this Caribbean sandwich is. Be sure to let the chicken marinate in the flavorful jerk rub for at least a few hours—or overnight—and it'll be totally tasty. Using chicken thighs makes this sandwich especially succulent. Using the fruity ketchup makes it irresistible.

4 (3½-ounce) boneless skinless chicken thighs
1½ tablespoons jerk seasoning rub (page 311),
    or to taste
⅓ cup Banana-Guava Ketchup (page 127)
4 (2-ounce) whole-grain sandwich rolls,
    split and grilled
2 cups packed mixed salad greens

1. Rub the chicken with the seasoning. Let flavors blend at least 4 hours or overnight, covered, in the refrigerator.

2. Prepare an outdoor or indoor grill.

3. Grill the chicken over direct medium-high heat until fully cooked and nicely charred, turning the chicken only as needed, about 5 minutes per side. Transfer to a plate and let stand for at least 5 minutes to complete the cooking process.

4. Spread the ketchup onto the cut surfaces of the rolls. Place the chicken onto the bottom roll portions. Top with the greens and roll tops, and serve.

Per serving: 320 calories, 10g total fat, 2.5g saturated fat, 0g trans fat, 65mg cholesterol, 680mg sodium, 35g total carbohydrate, 5g dietary fiber, 9g sugars, 23g protein

Chicken-Arugula Hero

Makes 4 servings: 1 sandwich each

Being creative with traditional dishes and recipes is an important way to make everyday eating appealing. That's how this Greek-accented take on a hero sandwich was invented. Feel free to invent your own version.

1 recipe Santorini Chicken Breast Skewers
   (page 308), warm
4 (2-ounce) whole-grain or onion sandwich rolls,
   split, toasted or grilled, warm
2 plum tomatoes or 12 cherry tomatoes, sliced
⅛ teaspoon sea salt, or to taste
⅛ teaspoon freshly ground black pepper, or to taste
2 packed cups baby arugula

1. Remove the chicken from the skewers.

2. On each roll bottom, arrange the tomatoes and season with the salt and pepper. Top with the chicken and arugula. Spread the accompanying the dip and capers (from the Santorini Chicken Breast Skewers recipe) on the cut side of the roll top. Firmly place the roll top, spread side down, onto the arugula, and serve.

Per serving: 370 calories, 12g total fat, 2.5g saturated fat, 0g trans fat, 50mg cholesterol, 720mg sodium, 38g total carbohydrate, 2g dietary fiber, 7g sugars, 28g protein

Chicken Shawarma Ⓕ

Makes 4 servings: 1 shawarma each

The fragrant spices of the chicken in this spring-time shawarma are a highlight—especially thanks to the spike of black pepper. Stuffed into a whole-grain pita, you'll find this recipe to be like a thoroughly modern Middle Eastern–style soft taco. You can also use whole-grain tortillas instead.

½ cup fat-free or low-fat plain Greek yogurt
Juice of ½ small lemon (1 tablespoon)
3 large garlic cloves, minced
1¼ teaspoons freshly ground black pepper,
   or to taste

¾ teaspoon sea salt, or to taste
½ teaspoon ground allspice
¼ teaspoon freshly grated nutmeg
¼ teaspoon ground cardamom or cloves (optional)
¼ teaspoon ground cinnamon
1 pound boneless skinless thin chicken breast
   cutlets, cut into long thin strips
2 (8-inch) whole-grain pitas, halved
½ cup grape tomatoes, halved lengthwise
½ cup diced unpeeled English cucumber
¼ cup finely chopped pickled beets, turnips,
   or green tomatoes
3 fresh ramps, bulbs and greens, very thinly sliced,
   or 1½ cups mixture fresh baby spinach and
   sliced scallions
½ cup Creamy Tahini Sauce (page 108)
   or fat-free plain Greek yogurt

1. Stir together the yogurt, lemon juice, garlic, 1 teaspoon of the pepper, the salt, allspice, nutmeg, cardamom (if using), and cinnamon in a medium bowl. Add the chicken and stir to coat. Set aside to marinate for 1 hour, stirring once during marinating. (Note: If longer than 1 hour, marinate covered in the refrigerator.)

2. Preheat the broiler.

3. Remove chicken from marinade and discard any excess marinade. Spread the chicken evenly in a single layer in a baking pan. Broil about 6 inches from the broiler heat for 4 minutes. Flip over the chicken pieces and broil until well done, about 3 minutes. Sprinkle with the remaining ¼ teaspoon pepper. Let stand for 5 minutes to allow juices to settle.

4. Stuff the chicken into the pita halves along with the tomatoes, cucumber, pickled beets, and ramps. Drizzle with the tahini sauce, and serve warm. If desired, serve with harissa or hot pepper sauce on the side.

Per serving: 340 calories, 12g total fat, 2g saturated fat, 0g trans fat, 65mg cholesterol, 780mg sodium, 29g total carbohydrate, 5g dietary fiber, 5g sugars, 32g protein

Tuna Salad Gruyère Melt Sandwich

Makes 4 servings: 1 sandwich with ¾ cup tuna salad each

Focusing more on what you can boost rather than reduce is a smart approach to healthful eating. So treasure tuna. Savor more veggies. Both are possible here. The full-sensory appeal makes this sandwich seem extra luscious.

1 (7-ounce) can water-packed solid yellowfin
    or albacore tuna, drained and separated
    into chunks
1 large celery stalk, thinly sliced crosswise
10 cherry tomatoes, thinly sliced
¼ cup finely diced red onion
3 tablespoons chopped fresh flat-leaf parsley
1 tablespoon finely chopped fresh tarragon
Juice of 1 lemon (3 tablespoons)
2 tablespoons mayonnaise
1 tablespoon spicy brown mustard
⅛ teaspoon sea salt, or to taste
⅛ teaspoon freshly ground black pepper, or to taste
8 slices whole-grain sourdough bread
1 large garlic clove, peeled, halved
4 ounces shredded Gruyère, Comté,
    or other Swiss cheese

1. Stir together the tuna, celery, tomatoes, onion, parsley, tarragon, lemon juice, mayonnaise, mustard, salt, and pepper in a medium bowl. Set aside.

2. Preheat the broiler.

3. Broil one side of the bread slices until lightly toasted, about 30 seconds. Rub the toasted side with the garlic. Flip slices over, sprinkle with the cheese, and broil until the cheese melts, about 30 seconds.

4. Top four of the cheesy toast slices with the tuna salad. Place the other toast slices on top, cheese side down, and serve immediately.

Per serving: 400 calories, 17g total fat, 6g saturated fat, 0g trans fat, 50mg cholesterol, 690mg sodium, 30g total carbohydrate, 4g dietary fiber, 6g sugars, 27g protein

Philly-Inspired Cheesesteak

Makes 8 servings: 1 sandwich each

This full-flavored and filling Philly-style sandwich is definitively refined with the fresh herb duet, layers of caramelized onions, and pleasantly pungent cheese. Plus, this recipe demonstrates how nearly anything can fit into your eating plan if it's "right sized."

1 tablespoon grapeseed or canola oil
1 medium white onion, halved and very thinly sliced
1 medium red onion, halved and very thinly sliced
2 teaspoons aged balsamic vinegar
¾ teaspoon sea salt, or to taste
14 ounces boneless New York strip steak (top loin),
    finely chopped or cut into extra-thin strips
½ teaspoon fresh thyme leaves
½ teaspoon freshly ground black pepper, or to taste
⅓ cup chopped fresh flat-leaf parsley
2 (10-ounce) whole-grain baguettes, cut into
    four portions each and split partway open
¼ cup Bourbon "Mayo" (page 123) or other "mayo"
    (optional)
4 ounces Taleggio, Robiola, or provolone cheese,
    thinly sliced

1. Heat the oil in a large nonstick skillet over medium-high heat. Add the onions, vinegar, and ¼ teaspoon of the salt and sauté until lightly caramelized, about 12 minutes. Add the steak, thyme, pepper, and the remaining ½ teaspoon salt and sauté until cooked through, about 2½ minutes. Stir in the parsley and adjust seasoning.

2. Spread the inside of each baguette piece with the "mayo" (if using). Add the cheese, stuff with the steak-onion mixture, and serve.

Per serving: 330 calories, 11g total fat, 4g saturated fat, 0g trans fat, 30mg cholesterol, 660mg sodium, 34g total carbohydrate, 6g dietary fiber, 6g sugars, 24g protein

Bell Pepper–Stuffed Turkey Sausage Sandwich

Makes 4 servings: 1 sandwich each

This zesty sausage sandwich is topped with a vivid array of bell peppers. It's served open-face to show those colors off in style. Enjoy with a fork and knife—which actually will slow down your eating . . . and increase your gastronomic gratification.

4 (3-ounce) cooked Italian turkey or other
    poultry sausage links
2 slices whole-grain bread, toasted and cut into
    two long halves each
3 cups Tri-Color Bell Pepper Sauté, warm
    (page 471)

1. Heat the sausage according to package directions until browned.

2. Serve each sausage on a toasted bread half, open-face style. Top with the bell pepper sauté, and serve.

Per serving: 220 calories, 10g total fat, 2.5g saturated fat, 0g trans fat, 65mg cholesterol, 760mg sodium, 14g total carbohydrate, 3g dietary fiber, 5g sugars, 18g protein

Pineapple-Serrano BBQ Pork Sandwich

Makes 4 servings: 1 sandwich each

Grilling pork tenderloin just until medium doneness, as is done here, keeps the lean meat juicy. Pairing it with a sweet and spicy barbecue sauce will make this a favorite of even hearty eaters.

14 ounces lean trimmed pork tenderloin
2 teaspoons extra-virgin olive oil
½ teaspoon freshly ground black pepper, or to taste
¼ teaspoon sea salt, or to taste
10 tablespoons Pineapple-Serrano Barbecue
    Sauce (page 105)
1 cup packed shredded red or green cabbage
    (optional)
4 (2-ounce) whole-grain sandwich rolls,
    split and lightly grilled or toasted

1. Prepare an outdoor or indoor grill.

2. Rub or brush the pork with the oil. Add the pepper and salt.

3. Transfer ¼ cup (4 tablespoons) of the barbecue sauce to a small bowl to use for basting. Pour the remaining sauce into a large skillet. Set aside.

4. Grill the pork over direct medium-high heat until medium-doneness and brown (meat thermometer inserted into center registers 140 to 145°F), turning only as needed with tongs, about 12 minutes. Brush the pork with the reserved ¼-cup barbecue sauce and continue to grill for 2 minutes. Transfer pork to a cutting board and let stand to complete the cooking process, about 10 minutes. Very thinly slice or shave the pork.

5. Heat the sauce that's in the skillet over medium heat. Add the pork and toss with the sauce until well coated. Adjust seasoning.

6. Divide the pork mixture and the cabbage (if using) among the rolls, and serve immediately.

Per serving: 310 calories, 7g total fat, 1.5g saturated fat, 0g trans fat, 50mg cholesterol, 560mg sodium, 37g total carbohydrate, 2g dietary fiber, 4g sugars, 24g protein

Sloppy Jackies Ⓕ

Makes 4 servings: 1 sandwich each

Yes, these sandwiches are sloppy indeed. So have a napkin ready and enjoy every messy bite of this meaty sandwich, which gets its unique flavor accent from beer and its intrigue from the sweet onion and cinnamon.

2 teaspoons extra-virgin olive oil
1 large sweet onion, chopped
1 small jalapeño pepper with seeds, minced
1 large green bell pepper, finely chopped
½ cup finely diced zucchini or green beans
½ cup light beer
½ teaspoon sea salt, or to taste
14 ounces lean ground beef sirloin
1 large garlic clove, minced
3 tablespoons low-sodium ketchup
2 tablespoons no-salt-added tomato paste
2 teaspoons Worcestershire sauce (optional)
¾ teaspoon finely chopped fresh oregano
    or ¼ teaspoon crushed dried oregano
¼ teaspoon ground cinnamon, or to taste
4 whole-grain hamburger buns or English muffins,
    split and lightly toasted

1. Heat the oil in a large skillet over medium heat. Add the onion, jalapeño, bell pepper, zucchini, 1 tablespoon of the beer, and ¼ teaspoon of the salt and sauté until the onion is softened, about 8 minutes. Add the beef and garlic and sauté over medium-high heat until the meat is cooked through, about 5 minutes. Add the remaining beer and sauté for 1 minute. Reduce heat to medium, add the ketchup, tomato paste, Worcestershire sauce (if using), oregano, cinnamon, and the remaining ¼ teaspoon salt, and simmer, uncovered, until saucy but runny, about 7 minutes. Adjust seasoning.

2. Spoon 1 cup mixture into each bun and serve immediately.

Per serving: 360 calories, 9g total fat, 2.5g saturated fat, 0g trans fat, 35mg cholesterol, 770mg sodium, 43g total carbohydrate, 6g dietary fiber, 14g sugars, 26g protein

Romano Meatball Open Sandwich Marinara

Makes 4 servings: 1 sandwich each

The Italian meatballs and sweet peppery marinara are so wildly flavorful. Adding a fresh cheese and tender arugula adds beautiful balance to this scrumptious open-face sandwich.

1¼ cups Bell Pepper Marinara (page 102)
    or other marinara sauce
8 Meatballs Romano (page 332) or other meatballs
2 whole-wheat hot dog buns, fully split in half
2 ounces fresh mozzarella cheese, finely chopped
1 cup packed baby arugula or torn arugula

1. Preheat the oven to 450°F.

2. Bring the sauce to a simmer in a medium saucepan over medium heat. Stir in the meatballs, cover, reduce heat to low, and simmer until fully heated through, about 10 minutes, stirring gently occasionally.

3. Meanwhile, place the 4 bun halves cut side up on a baking sheet. Sprinkle with the cheese and bake until the cheese is melted and buns are lightly toasted, about 6 to 7 minutes.

4. Remove the meatballs from the sauce; cut each meatball in half. Gently stir the meatball halves back into the sauce.

5. Top each bun half with four of the meatball halves and desired amount of the sauce. Sprinkle with the arugula, and serve immediately. Serve any remaining sauce on the side. Enjoy with a fork and knife.

Per serving: 270 calories, 12g total fat, 4.5g saturated fat, 0g trans fat, 85mg cholesterol, 650mg sodium, 22g total carbohydrate, 4g dietary fiber, 6g sugars, 20g protein

Panini and Toasties

Smoked Caprese Egg Panini

Makes 4 servings: 1 panini each

How can you enjoy the smoky flavor of bacon without actually eating it? Upgrade to smoked cheese. When delectably paired with fruity tomatoes and fresh basil, it's like an inspired Italian holiday for your taste buds. (Or go further and imagine you're enjoying this while on the island of Capri.) Paired with an egg, it's extra special and extra satisfying.

4 whole-grain English muffins, split

4 ounces smoked fresh mozzarella cheese, cut into 8 thin slices

4 (¼-inch) slices beefsteak tomato

1 teaspoon extra-virgin olive oil

4 large eggs

¼ teaspoon sea salt or smoked sea salt, or to taste

⅛ teaspoon freshly ground black pepper, or to taste

12 large fresh basil leaves

1. Arrange the muffin halves cut side up on a plate. Top all the halves with the cheese. Top 4 of the halves with the tomato, and set aside.

2. Heat the oil in a large nonstick skillet over medium heat. Add the eggs and cook until the bottom of the eggs are just firm, about 3 minutes. Flip over and cook until the yolks are soft, but not firm, about 1½ minutes. Add the salt and pepper.

3. Place an egg on top of each tomato. Cover with the remaining muffin halves, cheese side down.

4. Heat a panini grill to medium-high heat. Grill the sandwiches (in batches, if necessary) until toasted and the cheese is melted, about 4 minutes. Insert the basil leaves, and serve.

Per serving: 300 calories, 14g total fat, 6g saturated fat, 0g trans fat, 210mg cholesterol, 660mg sodium, 28g total carbohydrate, 5g dietary fiber, 6g sugars, 17g protein

Goat Cheese and Piquillo Pepper Panini Ⓕ

Makes 2 servings: 1 sandwich each

If I were to write a love song about a sandwich, this panino would be my inspiration! You'll be blissfully happy with this sweetheart of a sandwich that connects with your culinary soul, sourdough style.

1 garlic clove, halved

3 ounces soft goat cheese

1 scallion, green and white part, minced

1 tablespoon chopped fresh flat-leaf parsley

1 teaspoon finely chopped fresh mint or ½ teaspoon finely chopped fresh thyme

¼ teaspoon freshly ground black pepper

4 slices whole-wheat sourdough bread

4 ounces well-drained roasted piquillo, Peppadew, or red bell peppers

1. Mince half of the garlic clove. Reserve the other half.

2. Stir together the minced garlic, the goat cheese, scallion, parsley, mint, and black pepper until well combined. Spread the goat cheese mixture onto each of the bread slices. Top 2 of the bread slices with the piquillos, then the remaining bread slices, cheese side down. Lightly spray both sides of the sandwiches with cooking spray (preferably homemade, page xix).

3. Heat a panini grill to medium-high heat. Grill the sandwiches (in batches, if necessary) until golden brown and fully heated through, about 4 minutes.

4. Immediately rub the entire surface of the toasted bread with the cut end of the reserved garlic half, and serve immediately.

Per serving: 320 calories, 12g total fat, 6g saturated fat, 0g trans fat, 20mg cholesterol, 670mg sodium, 35g total carbohydrate, 5g dietary fiber, 6g sugars, 15g protein

Broccolini and Aged Cheddar Panini Ⓕ

Makes 2 servings: 1 sandwich each

This is not your ordinary grilled cheese. The broccolini makes a full-flavored companion for the sharp cheese. And the garlic aroma will tempt you even before you have that first bodacious bite.

10 ounces trimmed broccolini stalks with florets

4 slices whole-grain rye bread

2½ ounces aged or sharp Cheddar cheese, finely shredded

2 scallions, green and white parts, minced

1 tablespoon chopped fresh flat-leaf parsley

¾ teaspoon chopped fresh rosemary

¼ teaspoon freshly ground black pepper, or to taste

⅛ teaspoon dried hot pepper flakes, or to taste

½ teaspoon grated lemon zest

Pinch of sea salt

1 large garlic clove, peeled and halved

1. Steam the broccolini until just tender, about 5 minutes. Pat dry with a clean kitchen towel or paper towels.

2. Sprinkle the entire surface of 2 of the bread slices with the half of the cheese. Then sprinkle with the scallions, parsley, rosemary, black pepper, and hot pepper flakes. Top with the steamed broccolini, lemon zest, and salt. Then sprinkle with the remaining cheese. Top with the remaining bread slices. Lightly spray both sides of the sandwiches with cooking spray (preferably homemade, page xix).

3. Heat a panini grill to medium-high heat. Grill the sandwiches (in batches, if necessary) until golden brown and the cheese is melted, about 4 minutes. Immediately rub the entire surface of all the toasted bread with the cut end of the garlic, and serve immediately.

Per serving: 330 calories, 15g total fat, 8g saturated fat, 0g trans fat, 40mg cholesterol, 740mg sodium, 34g total carbohydrate, 8g dietary fiber, 3g sugars, 19g protein

Pesto, Tomato, and Mozzarella Panini Ⓕ

Makes 2 servings: 1 sandwich each

Heirloom tomatoes are truly full of culinary glory—all their shapes, sizes, and shades. So let them shine as a main ingredient in cuisine. This pesto-laced grilled cheese sandwich is a showcase of the tomato taste!

¾ cup shredded part-skim mozzarella cheese

4 slices whole-grain sourdough bread

1 large red, yellow, or other color heirloom tomato, cut into 8 slices

⅛ teaspoon freshly ground black pepper, or to taste

¼ cup Arugula Pesto (page 118)

1 large garlic clove, peeled and halved

1. Divide half the cheese between 2 of the bread slices. Top with the tomato slices, pepper, and the remaining cheese.

2. Spread the pesto on one side of the remaining bread slices. Place these slices, pesto side down, onto the cheese to form a sandwich. Lightly spray both sides of the sandwiches with cooking spray (preferably homemade, page xix).

3. Heat a panini grill to medium-high heat. Grill the sandwiches (in batches, if necessary) until golden brown and the cheese is melted, about 4 minutes.

4. Immediately rub the entire surface of all the toasted bread with the garlic halves, cut the paninis in half (if desired), and serve immediately.

Per serving: 390 calories, 17g total fat, 6g saturated fat, 0g trans fat, 30mg cholesterol, 700mg sodium, 36g total carbohydrate, 5g dietary fiber, 7g sugars, 19g protein

Cuban-Inspired Smoked Ham Baguette

Makes 4 servings: 1 sandwich each

This recipe is inspired by a traditional Cuban sandwich, with the classic combo of cheese, ham, and roasted pork. So if you can't be in the Caribbean, you can still enjoy this fresh twist on a classic.

1½ tablespoons stone-ground mustard, or to taste

1 (8-ounce) whole-grain baguette, split

3½ ounces French Comté or aged Swiss cheese, very thinly sliced

3½ ounces thinly sliced smoked ham or Virginia ham

4 ounces roasted pork sirloin or tenderloin, thinly sliced, chilled

4 dill pickle sandwich slices

1 cup packed wild baby arugula or other wild baby greens

1. Thinly spread the mustard on the cut surfaces of the baguette.

2. On the bottom portion of the baguette, place half the cheese, all the ham, pork, pickles, and the remaining cheese. Place the top of the baguette on top to form a sandwich, firmly pressing down. Slice into 4 (3-inch) sandwiches.

3. Heat a panini grill to medium-high heat. Grill the sandwiches (in batches, if necessary) until lightly toasted and the cheese is slightly melted, about 3½ minutes.

4. Stuff the sandwiches with the arugula and serve while warm.

Per serving: 340 calories, 14g total fat, 6g saturated fat, 0g trans fat, 65mg cholesterol, 790mg sodium, 25g total carbohydrate, 4g dietary fiber, 4g sugars, 28g protein

Grilled Fontina and Fig Sandwich Ⓕ

Makes 2 servings: 1 sandwich each

I don't know about you, but I find figs simply dreamy. I'm always a slight bit gloomy when fresh fig season is over, though dried figs are still a fine alternative. They are indeed the pleasantly sweet surprise in this savory grilled sandwich.

4 large slices whole-grain fruit-nut bread

2 ounces fontina cheese, thinly sliced, at room temperature

2 medium dried Black Mission or Calimyrna figs, very thinly sliced

¼ teaspoon finely chopped fresh thyme or rosemary or ⅛ teaspoon crushed dried thyme

⅛ teaspoon sea salt, or to taste

⅛ teaspoon freshly ground black pepper, or to taste

2 tablespoons part-skim ricotta cheese, at room temperature

1. Top 2 of the bread slices with the fontina cheese, figs, thyme, salt, and pepper.

2. Spread the ricotta on one side of the remaining bread slices. Place these slices, ricotta side down, on top of the other slices to form a sandwich.

3. Heat a large grill pan, griddle, or skillet over medium heat. Lightly spray both sides of the sandwiches with cooking spray (preferably home-made, page xix). Place the sandwiches on the grill pan; cook until the bread is toasted and cheese is melted, about 4½ to 5 minutes per side. Serve warm.

Per serving: 370 calories, 12g total fat, 6g saturated fat, 0g trans fat, 40mg cholesterol, 400mg sodium, 47g total carbohydrate, 10g dietary fiber, 29g sugars, 18g protein

Grilled Feta and Spinach Naan Sandwich Ⓕ

Makes 2 servings: 1 sandwich each

This naan sandwich is the tasty result of a spinach pizza recipe makeover. Piled with crisp baby spinach and sublimely accented with lemon zest, this is one you can't pass up.

⅓ cup finely crumbled feta cheese

¼ cup shredded part-skim mozzarella cheese

1 garlic clove, minced

½ teaspoon grated lemon zest

⅛ teaspoon freshly ground black pepper, or to taste

⅛ teaspoon dried hot pepper flakes

2 (3-ounce) whole-grain naan, halved

1½ cups packed fresh baby spinach

1. Stir together the feta, mozzarella, garlic, lemon zest, black pepper, and hot pepper flakes in a small bowl.

2. Lightly spray one side of each naan piece with cooking spray (preferably homemade, page xix). Place the sprayed side down on a cutting board. Evenly top all the naan pieces with the cheese mixture.

3. Heat a large grill pan, griddle, or skillet over medium heat. Place the cheese-topped naan on the pan and grill until the naan is toasted and mozzarella is melted, about 8 to 10 minutes. (Grill in batches, if necessary.)

4. Top two of the naan pieces with the spinach. Place the other naan pieces, cheese side down, on the spinach. Firmly press each to form a sandwich, and serve.

Per serving: 350 calories, 14g total fat, 7g saturated fat, 0g trans fat, 30mg cholesterol, 790mg sodium, 42g total carbohydrate, 6g dietary fiber, 5g sugars, 14g protein

Peanut Butter and Grilled-Grape Toastie Ⓕ

Makes 2 servings: 1 sandwich each

Move over grape jam; peanut butter has a cheekier mate, grilled grapes. Served in this toastie, they have equal appeal to kids and adults. Do also try this recipe with other seasonal fruit fresh and caramelized from the grill to find other playful combinations.

24 red or green seedless grapes

Pinch of sea salt

4 slices whole-wheat or other whole-grain bead

3 tablespoons creamy or chunky natural
    peanut butter

1. Prepare an outdoor or indoor grill.

2. Insert grapes onto reusable or water-soaked bamboo skewers. Grill over direct medium-high heat, flipping just once, until grill marks form on both sides, about 8 minutes. Sprinkle with the salt. Let cool slightly, then cut each grape in half lengthwise.

3. Grill or toast the bread slices. Immediately spread one side of each toast slice with a scant tablespoon peanut butter.

4. Top 2 of the slices with the grape halves, cut side down. Place the other toast slices, peanut butter side down, on the grapes, firmly press to form the sandwiches, and serve.

Per serving: 330 calories, 14g total fat, 2g saturated fat, 0g trans fat, 0mg cholesterol, 430mg sodium, 39g total carbohydrate, 6g dietary fiber, 14g sugars, 13g protein

Turkey, Cheese, and Tart Apple Toastie Ⓕ

Makes 4 servings: 1 sandwich each

This toastie uses generous amounts of crisp tart apple, pungent cheese, fragrant herbs, and sweet and savory turkey on fruit-and-nut studded bread. It's great tasting—and a great source of protein and fiber.

8 long slices whole-grain raisin-pecan
    or other fruit-nut bead

6 ounces Bavarian Limburger, Appenzeller,
    or Brie cheese, very thinly sliced and
    at room temperature

4 (1-ounce) slices honey- or maple-roasted
    deli turkey breast

½ teaspoon finely chopped fresh rosemary

1 medium Granny Smith, unpeeled, cored,
    and very thinly sliced

1. Toast or grill the bread slices. Immediately top all toast slices with the cheese.

2. Top 4 of the bread slices with the turkey, rosemary, and apple. Place the other toast slices cheese side down, on the apple, firmly press to form sandwiches, and serve.

Per serving: 330 calories, 13g total fat, 7g saturated fat, 0g trans fat, 50mg cholesterol, 720mg sodium, 34g total carbohydrate, 7g dietary fiber, 21g sugars, 21g protein

SLICED APPLE TIP

If you cut apple slices in advance, keep them submerged in acidulated water—2 to 3 cups cold water and juice of 1 small lemon (2 tablespoons)—to help prevent browning. Drain and pat dry before adding the slices to a sandwich or other preparation.

Avocado, Basil, and Zucchini Toastie Ⓕ

Makes 2 servings: 1 sandwich each

For a sandwich that's full of fresh flavor, this zucchini-laden toastie is one of my top picks in summertime. Usually I grill extra zucchini and other vegetables anytime the grill's going so I can prepare meals quickly for days afterward—like this fix, layered with creamy avocado and fresh basil.

4 slices whole-grain rye or sourdough bead

½ Hass avocado, pitted, peeled, and cubed

1 teaspoon white balsamic vinegar or
    fresh lemon juice

Pinch of sea salt, or to taste

8 large fresh basil leaves

1½ cups Garlic Zucchini Coins (page 467)
    or grilled zucchini slices, drained of
    excess liquid

1. Toast or grill the bread slices.

2. Mash together the avocado, vinegar, and salt in a small bowl. Spread the avocado mixture on one side of the toast slices.

3. Top 2 of the toast slices with the basil and zucchini. Place the other toast slices, avocado side down, on the zucchini, firmly press to form sandwiches, and serve.

Per serving: 260 calories, 10g total fat, 1.5g saturated fat, 0g trans fat, 0mg cholesterol, 770mg sodium, 37g total carbohydrate, 7g dietary fiber, 7g sugars, 8g protein

Burgers and Dogs

Smoky Portabella and Cheese Burger Ⓕ

Makes 4 servings: 1 cheeseburger each

One of the all-time best-tasting flavor combinations is mushroom, cheese, and avocado. That makes this one of the best-tasting meat-free burgers! It also makes it one of the most nutritious. An intriguing highlight is the bone-friendly vitamin D from portabellas. Mushrooms are the only food in the produce aisle that naturally provide it. And check out this burger's whopping amount of fiber!

1 Hass avocado, pitted and peeled

1½ teaspoons fresh lemon juice

¼ teaspoon sea salt, or to taste

8 slices whole-grain sprouted or seeded bread or 4 lightly grilled whole-grain sprouted sandwich rolls

4 thin slices large red onion

4 Smoky Mozzarella Grilled Portabellas (page 455), warm

1. Mash the avocado, lemon juice, and salt with a fork in a small bowl. Spread the avocado mixture on each of the bread slices.

2. Top 4 of the bread slices with the onion and mushrooms. Place the remaining bread slices on the mushrooms, avocado side down, and serve while warm.

Per serving: 360 calories, 17g total fat, 5g saturated fat, 0g trans fat, 15mg cholesterol, 600mg sodium, 38g total carbohydrate, 10g dietary fiber, 3g sugars, 16g protein

Grilled Veggie Burgers Ⓕ

Makes 4 servings: 1 burger each

This is one big bite. Luckily the burger patty is delicate so you can squash it slightly while savoring every mouthwatering morsel. Yep, it's vegan and mouthwatering!

2 teaspoons extra-virgin olive oil

1 cup finely chopped broccoli florets and tender stems

1 cup finely chopped cauliflower florets and tender stems

1 medium red onion, half minced and half thinly sliced

2 teaspoons aged balsamic vinegar

¾ teaspoon sea salt, or to taste

1 large garlic clove, minced

9 tablespoons Creamy Almond Hummus (page 88) or other hummus

2 teaspoons naturally brewed soy sauce

½ teaspoon freshly ground black pepper, or to taste

1 (14-ounce) package firm tofu, well drained, gently squeezed dry, and crumbled

1 cup plain dry whole-wheat breadcrumbs

1 medium carrot, grated

4 whole-wheat or whole-grain sesame hamburger buns, split and lightly grilled

4 slices large beefsteak tomato

2 cups packed mesclun or mixed salad greens

1. Heat the oil in a large nonstick skillet over medium heat. Add the broccoli, cauliflower, minced onion, vinegar, and ¼ teaspoon of the salt and sauté until the broccoli and cauliflower are tender, about 12 minutes. Stir in the garlic and sauté for 1 minute. Cover and set aside.

2. Add ⅓ cup of the hummus, the soy sauce, pepper, and the remaining ½ teaspoon salt to a large bowl and stir until combined. Stir in the tofu, breadcrumbs, and carrot until combined. Stir in the broccoli mixture and thoroughly combine with your hands.

3. Firmly form the mixture into 4 (1-inch-thick) patties, about 1 cup mixture each.

4. Prepare an outdoor or indoor grill, or a grill pan.

5. Grill the patties over direct medium-high heat until well browned and cooked through, about 5 to 6 minutes per side, flipping only once.

6. Place the patties into the buns with the tomato, sliced onion, mesclun, and the remaining hummus, and serve.

Per serving: 420 calories, 16g total fat, 1.5g saturated fat, 0g trans fat, 0mg cholesterol, 750mg sodium, 53g total carbohydrate, 11g dietary fiber, 8g sugars, 21g protein

Roasted Winter Veggie Burgers Ⓕ

Makes 8 servings: 1 burger each

Here's a homemade vegetarian burger recipe for you that takes advantage of a variety of wintertime veggies. The hummus and fresh touch of rosemary make these extra special.

2 teaspoons extra-virgin olive oil

1 large sweet potato unpeeled, scrubbed, and diced

1 medium red onion, half minced and half thinly sliced

2 teaspoons apple cider vinegar

1 teaspoon sea salt, or to taste

1 medium parsnip, grated

1 medium carrot, grated

1 large garlic clove, minced

1½ cups Sun-Dried Tomato Pesto Hummus (page 87) or other hummus

2 teaspoons finely chopped fresh rosemary

1 teaspoon freshly ground black pepper, or to taste

¼ teaspoon ground cayenne, or to taste

1 (14-ounce) package firm tofu, well drained, gently squeezed dry, and crumbled

1 cup plain dry whole-wheat breadcrumbs

4 whole-grain hamburger buns, split, or 8 whole-grain sandwich rounds (thins), toasted

2 cups shredded romaine lettuce

4 slices large beefsteak tomato (optional)

1. Heat the oil in a large nonstick skillet over medium heat. Add the sweet potato, minced onion, vinegar, and ¼ teaspoon of the salt and sauté until the sweet potato is nearly tender, about 15 minutes. Add the parsnip and carrot, cover, and cook, stirring occasionally, until all vegetables are tender, about 6 minutes. Stir in the garlic and sauté for 1 minute. Set aside, uncovered, to cool slightly.

2. Preheat the oven to 450°F.

3. Add 1 cup of the hummus, the rosemary, black pepper, cayenne, and the remaining ¾ teaspoon salt to a medium bowl and stir until combined. Stir in the tofu and breadcrumbs until combined. Stir in the sweet potato mixture and thoroughly combine with your hands.

4. Firmly form the mixture into 8 (4-inch-wide) patties, about ⅔ rounded cup mixture each.

5. Place the patties on a parchment paper–lined baking sheet. Roast until well browned and cooked through, about 8 minutes per side.

6. Place the patties into the buns with the lettuce, tomato (if using), sliced onion, and the remaining ½ cup hummus, and serve.

Per serving: 260 calories, 8g total fat, 1g saturated fat, 0g trans fat, 0mg cholesterol, 550mg sodium, 38g total carbohydrate, 7g dietary fiber, 7g sugars, 12g protein

Luscious Lentil and Cheese Burger Ⓕ

Makes 6 servings: 1 burger each

There's nothing quite like a real, fresh, substantial vegetable burger. In this case, it's made with seasoned lentils. It's scrumptious!

¾ cup dried lentils, rinsed and drained

1¾ cups low-sodium vegetable broth
or Vegetable Stock (page 203)

Juice and zest of 1 small lemon (2 tablespoons juice)

2 teaspoons extra-virgin olive oil

1 large white onion, half finely chopped and
half thinly sliced

¾ teaspoon sea salt, or to taste

10 ounces fresh baby spinach, chopped

2 large garlic cloves, minced

¼ teaspoon freshly ground black pepper, or to taste

⅛ teaspoon dried hot pepper flakes, or to taste

1 cup whole-wheat breadcrumbs

⅓ cup pine nuts, toasted and finely chopped

⅔ cup finely shredded extra-sharp Cheddar cheese
or vegan Cheddar alternative

6 whole-grain hamburger buns or whole-grain
sandwich rounds (thins), split, toasted

6 large slices beefsteak tomato or roasted red bell
pepper

2 tablespoons ketchup, or to taste

2 tablespoons Dijon mustard, or to taste

1. Bring the lentils and broth to a boil in a medium saucepan over high heat. Reduce heat to medium-low, partially cover, and simmer until the lentils are fully softened and liquid is absorbed, about 30 minutes. Transfer to a medium bowl with 1 table-spoon of the lemon juice, and mash well with a potato masher. Set aside.

2. Heat the oil in a large nonstick skillet over medium heat. Add the chopped onion, the remaining 1 tablespoon lemon juice, and ¼ teaspoon of the salt and sauté until softened, about 8 minutes. Add 8 ounces of the spinach, the garlic, the lemon zest, the black pepper, hot pepper flakes, and the remaining ½ teaspoon salt and sauté until no excess liquid remains, about 5 minutes.

3. Add the spinach mixture, the breadcrumbs, and pine nuts to the lentils and mix thoroughly. Cover, and chill for at least 1 hour.

4. Preheat the broiler.

5. Form mixture into 6 (¾-inch-thick) patties. Broil until golden brown, about 2 minutes per side. Top the patties with the cheese and broil for 30 seconds.

6. Place the patties into the buns with the tomato, sliced onion, remaining spinach, the ketchup, and mustard, and serve.

Per serving: 390 calories, 13g total fat, 3.5g saturated fat, 0g trans fat, 15mg cholesterol, 795mg sodium, 57g total carbohydrate, 10g dietary fiber, 7g sugars, 18g protein

Vietnamese-Style Chicken Burger Ⓕ

Makes 4 servings: 1 burger with ¼ cup papaya salsa each

The *bánh mì* sandwich from Vietnam is popular street fare. It was my inspiration for this zesty chicken burger.

1 pound ground chicken breast

¼ cup fat-free or low-fat plain Greek yogurt

2 teaspoons Asian garlic-chili sauce

2 teaspoons hoisin sauce

2 teaspoons freshly grated gingerroot

¼ teaspoon + ⅛ teaspoon sea salt, or to taste

2 tablespoons sesame seeds

1 tablespoon peanut or grapeseed oil

½ cup finely diced fresh papaya

½ cup finely diced radishes or daikon

¼ cup roughly chopped fresh cilantro

2 tablespoons chopped fresh mint or basil, or mixture

Juice of 1 lime (2 tablespoons)

4 whole-grain sandwich rounds (thins) or English muffins, split and toasted

1. Add the chicken, yogurt, garlic-chili sauce, hoisin sauce, ginger, and salt to a medium bowl. Mix by hand until just combined. Gently form the mixture into 4 (½-inch-thick) patties. Sprinkle the sesame seeds on both sides of the patties, firmly patting so they adhere well to the patties.

2. Heat 1½ teaspoons of the oil in a stick-resistant grill pan or large nonstick skillet over medium-high heat. Cook the patties until well done, about 5 minutes per side, flipping only once, adding the remaining oil when flipping the patties.

3. Meanwhile, gently stir together the papaya, radishes, cilantro, mint, and lime juice.

4. Place the patties into the sandwich rounds with the papaya mixture, and serve.

Per serving: 310 calories, 10g total fat, 1.5g saturated fat, 0g trans fat, 65mg cholesterol, 680mg sodium, 27g total carbohydrate, 7g dietary fiber, 5g sugars, 31g protein

Serbian Grilled Turkey Burger

Makes 4 servings: 1 burger each

Pljeskavica, also known as the Balkan burger, is a Serbian grilled patty of highly seasoned ground meat. This better-for-you version captures the essence of the original. Stuffed into a pita, it's an intriguing take on a turkey burger, with an array of flavors that will not disappoint.

1 pound ground turkey (about 94% lean)

1 small white onion, grated

3 tablespoons chopped fresh flat-leaf parsley

1½ tablespoons finely chopped fresh dill

1 teaspoon ground coriander

¾ teaspoon sea salt, or to taste

½ teaspoon freshly ground black pepper

¼ teaspoon ground cumin

1 large beefsteak tomato, diced

1 small or ½ large red onion, finely diced

2 (8-inch) whole-grain pitas, halved, warm

¼ cup chopped pickled green tomatoes or pickled peppers

1. Prepare an outdoor or indoor grill.

2. Add the turkey, onion, parsley, dill, coriander, salt, pepper, and cumin to a medium bowl and mix by hand until just combined. Gently form the mixture into 4 large, thin burgers about ½ inch thick.

3. Grill the burgers over medium-high heat until fully cooked through and golden brown, about 5 minutes per side.

4. Stuff the burgers into the pita halves with the beefsteak tomato, onion, and pickled tomatoes, and serve.

Per serving: 270 calories, 8g total fat, 2g saturated fat, 0g trans fat, 65mg cholesterol, 700mg sodium, 24g total carbohydrate, 4g dietary fiber, 3g sugars, 26g protein

Bodacious Bison Burger

Makes 4 servings: 1 burger each

If you haven't tried bison yet, a burger is the best way to sink your teeth into this nutritious, lean, and delicious red meat. You'll get the full taste of bison as it's meant to be enjoyed—seasoned simply with salt and pepper.

1 pound lean ground grass-fed bison

½ teaspoon sea salt, or to taste

½ teaspoon freshly ground black pepper, or to taste

4 whole-grain hamburger buns, grilled

2 tablespoons ketchup

1½ tablespoons Dijon mustard

4 thin slices large sweet onion

4 slices large beefsteak or red or purple heirloom tomato

12 large arugula leaves

1. Prepare an outdoor or indoor grill, or a grill pan.

2. Break up the bison meat into small pieces. Add the salt and pepper. Gently form into 4 (5-inch-wide) patties.

3. Grill the patties over direct medium-high heat until desired doneness, about 2 to 2½ minutes per side for medium, flipping only once, if possible. Adjust seasoning.

4. Place the patties in the buns with the ketchup, mustard, onion, tomato, and arugula, and serve.

Per serving: 320 calories, 10g total fat, 3.5g saturated fat, 0g trans fat, 60mg cholesterol, 770mg sodium, 30g total carbohydrate, 4g dietary fiber, 8g sugars, 28g protein

Madras Naan Burger

Makes 4 servings: 1 burger each

You'll take pleasure in the fragrant culinary appeal of India in this beef burger on naan. Yogurt raita makes a refreshing condiment companion.

1 pound lean ground beef or lamb sirloin

¼ cup grated red or white onion

1 tablespoon finely chopped fresh cilantro

1 teaspoon freshly grated gingerroot

¾ teaspoon hot Madras curry powder

¾ teaspoon sea salt

½ teaspoon freshly ground black pepper

2 (3-ounce) whole-wheat naan (Indian flatbread), quartered and lightly grilled

4 slices large beefsteak tomato

½ cup Cucumber Raita (page 97) or fat-free or low-fat plain Greek yogurt

1 cup packed mixed Asian or baby greens

1. Prepare an outdoor or indoor grill, or a grill pan.

2. Add the beef, onion, cilantro, ginger, curry powder, salt, and pepper to a medium bowl. Gently combine and form into 4 (4-inch-wide) patties.

3. Grill the patties over direct medium-high heat until desired doneness, about 2 to 2½ minutes per side for medium, flipping only once, if possible.

4. Place the patties on four of the naan pieces. Top with the tomato, raita, greens, and the remaining naan, and serve.

Per serving: 360 calories, 16g total fat, 6g saturated fat, 0g trans fat, 60mg cholesterol, 780mg sodium, 25g total carbohydrate, 4g dietary fiber, 4g sugars, 27g protein

Smokin' Salmon "Dog"

Makes 4 servings: 1 salmon dog each

If you're a hot dog devotee and a fish aficionado, this recipe is for you. The highlight is the kicked-up salmon—and, actually, all the other ingredients stuffed into the frankfurter bun. So be sure to use fresh ingredients and a fully ripe tomato.

1 (10-ounce) salmon fillet, skinned and cut into 4 bun-length strips

2 teaspoons grapeseed or canola oil

1 teaspoon Creole seasoning (page 31)

⅛ teaspoon sea salt, or to taste

¼ cup Zesty Lime Avocado Spread (page 125)

4 whole-wheat hot dog buns, split open most of way and lightly grilled

1 cup packed baby arugula

1 plum tomato, very thinly sliced crosswise

⅓ cup finely diced red onion

1. Prepare an outdoor or indoor grill, or a grill pan.

2. Rub the oil all over the salmon. Sprinkle the salmon with the Creole seasoning and salt. Grill the salmon over direct high heat until cooked through, about 2 minutes on the first side and 1 minute on the flip side.

3. Smear the avocado spread on the bottom half of each bun. Top with the arugula, tomato, salmon, and onion, and serve.

Per serving: 280 calories, 11g total fat, 1.5g saturated fat, 0g trans fat, 40mg cholesterol, 500mg sodium, 26g total carbohydrate, 5g dietary fiber, 5g sugars, 19g protein

Moroccan "Burger-Dog"

Makes 4 servings: 1 turkey "dog" each

Is it a hot dog or is it a turkey burger? It's both, sort of! You can feel good about eating the whole robust serving when it's stuffed in a portion-conscious frankfurter bun. It's remarkable taste-wise, too.

8 ounces ground turkey (about 94% lean)

⅓ cup minced or coarsely grated white onion

2 tablespoons ketchup

2 tablespoons minced pitted or sun-dried-tomato-stuffed green olives

2 tablespoons dried currants or minced black seedless raisins

½ teaspoon grated lemon zest

¼ teaspoon ground cumin

¼ teaspoon sea salt, or to taste

¼ teaspoon freshly ground black pepper, or to taste

⅛ teaspoon ground cinnamon

¼ cup Creamy Tahini Sauce (page 108) or hummus

4 whole-wheat hot dog buns, split open most of way and lightly grilled

4 curly endive or escarole leaves

1 plum tomato, thinly sliced crosswise

1. Prepare an outdoor or indoor grill, or a grill pan.

2. Add the turkey, onion, ketchup, olives, currants, zest, cumin, salt, pepper, and cinnamon to a medium bowl. Very gently combine by hand. Shape the mixture into 4 hot dog shapes in your hands, and place each directly onto the grill once formed. (Note: The mixture will be loose.)

3. Grill the "dogs" over direct medium heat until well done, about 12 minutes total, flipping only once, if possible.

4. Spread the sauce on the bottom half of each bun. Top evenly with the endive, tomato, and the "dogs," and serve.

Per serving: 280 calories, 11g total fat, 2.5g saturated fat, 0g trans fat, 45mg cholesterol, 580mg sodium, 31g total carbohydrate, 5g dietary fiber, 9g sugars, 16g protein

Chi-Chi Chicken Hot Dog 🄵

Makes 1 serving: 1 hot dog

For those times when you have a hankering for a hot dog, this poultry pick can satisfy more leanly than a regular dog. Hot dogs, by nature, are actually a perfectly portioned food, too. This smoky hot dog is dressed with purplish-hued relish and springy green avocado, making it a downright pretty dish!

¼ Hass avocado, pitted and peeled

¼ teaspoon fresh lemon juice, or to taste

Pinch of salt (optional)

1 whole-grain hot dog bun, split open most of way and fresh or lightly grilled

1 grilled or pan-cooked chicken hot dog

1½ tablespoons Pickled Red Onion–Jalapeño Relish (page 128)

1. Mash with a fork the avocado, lemon juice, and salt (if using) in a small bowl.

2. Spread the avocado mixture into the bun. Top with the grilled hot dog and the relish, and serve.

Per serving: 250 calories, 12g total fat, 2g saturated fat, 0g trans fat, 30mg cholesterol, 760mg sodium, 27g total carbohydrate, 6g dietary fiber, 5g sugars, 12g protein

Wraps

Fruit-n-Nut Energy Roti Ⓕ

Makes 1 serving: 1 roti each

Have you banned the bagel? The roti, which is an Indian flatbread, provides an interesting alternative. Spread with Neufchâtel and spiked with raisins, nuts, and cinnamon, this is a fast, filling, and full meal. It's ideal for breakfast on the run.

1 medium (7- to 8-inch) whole-wheat roti or tortilla
3 tablespoons Neufchâtel (light cream cheese),
    at room temperature
2 tablespoons black seedless raisins
    or other dried fruit pieces
1½ tablespoons chopped walnuts, toasted or raw
Pinch of ground cinnamon

1. Heat the roti in the microwave until just warm, about 20 seconds.

2. Spread the Neufchâtel on the entire surface of the roti. Sprinkle with the raisins, walnuts, and cinnamon.

3. Roll tightly, cut diagonally in half (if desired), and serve.

Per serving: 390 calories, 19g total fat, 7g saturated fat, 0g trans fat, 30mg cholesterol, 360mg sodium, 48g total carbohydrate, 6g dietary fiber, 15g sugars, 11g protein

Punjabi Spinach and Chickpea Wrap Ⓕ

Makes 1 serving: 1 wrap each

This wrap takes advantage of my Punjabi Spinach with Chickpeas recipe—especially good for the next day, when there's extras of it in the fridge. It's enjoyed burrito style here.

½ cup steamed whole-wheat couscous
    or sticky brown rice, warm
2 teaspoons chopped fresh cilantro

Pinch of sea salt
1 (10-inch) whole-wheat tortilla or wrap
½ cup Punjabi Spinach with Chickpeas (page 452),
    warm
1 lemon wedge

1. Stir together the couscous, cilantro, and salt in a small bowl.

2. Top the tortilla with the couscous and spinach mixtures. Roll tightly, folding in the sides, if desired. Cut diagonally in half, if desired, and serve warm or at room temperature with the lemon wedge.

Per serving: 340 calories, 5g total fat, 0g saturated fat, 0g trans fat, 0mg cholesterol, 640mg sodium, 61g total carbohydrate, 10g dietary fiber, 4g sugars, 12g protein

Stuffed Vegetarian Banger Wrap Ⓕ

Makes 4 servings: 1 wrap each

You'll get a thrill out of this vegetarian soft taco-style wrap—even if you're a confirmed carnivore. The recipe is full-flavored with fresh Southwestern flair. And the bangers (aka sausage) give it comfort flair. Consider it a savory treat indeed.

½ cup Avocado-Ranch Dipping Sauce (page 98)
4 (8-inch) whole-wheat tortillas or wraps
4 Vegetarian "Bangers" (page 266) or other
    vegetarian sausage, warm
3 cups shredded romaine lettuce
2 plum tomatoes, thinly sliced crosswise
2 scallions, green and white parts, minced
¼ teaspoon freshly ground black pepper, or to taste

1. Spread the sauce on the entire surface of the tortillas. Top with the bangers, lettuce, tomatoes, scallions, and pepper.

2. Roll tightly, cut diagonally in half and/or secure with a toothpick, and serve.

Per serving: 370 calories, 17g total fat, 2.5g saturated fat, 0g trans fat, 55mg cholesterol, 710mg sodium, 40g total carbohydrate, 6g dietary fiber, 6g sugars, 14g protein

Pumpkin-Avocado Wrap with Refried Beans ⓕ

Makes 1 serving: 1 wrap each

Pumpkin isn't just for serving at Halloween. You can make this wrap anytime using pure canned pumpkin. The wrap is loaded with beta-carotene from the pumpkin, folate from the avocado and lettuce, and fiber from the beans and tortilla. Multiply the ingredients by as many servings as you need so others can experience it, too.

¼ cup Spicy Un-fried Beans (page 487) or other vegetarian refried beans, warm

1 (8-inch) whole-wheat tortilla or wrap

¼ cup no-salt-added pumpkin puree or mashed baked sweet potato, warm

1 scallion, green and white part, thinly sliced

1 rounded tablespoon chopped fresh cilantro

¼ Hass avocado, pitted, peeled, and diced

1½ teaspoons fresh lime juice

Pinch of sea salt

¾ cup finely shredded romaine lettuce

1. Spread the beans over the entire surface of the tortilla. Spread the pumpkin on top of the beans.

2. Sprinkle the tortillas with the scallion and cilantro.

3. Gently stir together the avocado, lime juice, and salt. Sprinkle the avocado mixture over the tortilla.

4. Top with the lettuce.

5. Roll tightly, cut diagonally in half, and serve at room temperature.

Per serving: 280 calories, 9g total fat, 1g saturated fat, 0g trans fat, 0mg cholesterol, 610mg sodium, 41g total carbohydrate, 10g dietary fiber, 5g sugars, 9g protein

Take-Away Thai Chicken Wrap ⓕ

Makes 4 servings: 1 wrap each

Calorie-friendly food can be fun and flavorful. This Thai-inspired chicken-breast wrap has fresh nutty appeal. It'll be equally popular for kids' packed lunches or for adult luncheons.

4 (4-ounce) boneless skinless chicken breast cutlets

1½ teaspoons teriyaki sauce

⅛ teaspoon dried hot pepper flakes, or to taste

4 (10-inch) whole-wheat tortillas

6 tablespoons Gingery Peanut-Almond Sauce (page 108) or Thai peanut satay sauce

4 scallions, green and white parts, thinly sliced

1½ cups shredded or very thinly sliced red cabbage

1½ cups thinly sliced unpeeled English cucumber or mung bean sprouts

⅓ cup coarsely grated carrot

¼ cup chopped fresh cilantro

1. Place the chicken on a parchment paper–lined baking pan. Brush the chicken with the teriyaki sauce. Add the hot pepper flakes. Roast in a 375°F toaster oven (or preheated conventional oven) until well done, about 15 minutes. Remove from oven and let stand for at least 5 minutes to complete the cooking process. Cut the chicken into long thin strips.

2. Meanwhile, thinly spread the entire surface of each tortilla with 1½ tablespoons of the sauce. Top with the scallions, cabbage, cucumber, carrot, cilantro, and cooked chicken strips.

3. Roll tightly, cut diagonally in half or secure with a toothpick, and serve.

Per serving: 360 calories, 10g total fat, 1.5g saturated fat, 0g trans fat, 65mg cholesterol, 790mg sodium, 39g total carbohydrate, 5g dietary fiber, 9g sugars, 31g protein

California Smoked Turkey Wrap Ⓕ

Makes 4 servings: 1 wrap each

Here I began with the idea of a turkey sandwich. Then I went wild—in the culinary sense. I started with smoked turkey; paired it with a robust, slightly nutty, fairly funky cheese; switched up the bread and greens; and then finished it with a tangy sandwich spread. It's hard to imagine going back to a typical turkey sandwich again.

½ cup Zesty Lime Avocado Spread (page 125)

4 (9-inch) whole-grain wraps, flatbreads, or thin pitas

8 (½-ounce) slices deli smoked turkey breast

8 (½-ounce) thin slices Appenzeller or aged semisoft Swiss cheese

⅔ cup thinly sliced red onion

2 cups alfalfa or other sprouts

½ teaspoon freshly ground black pepper, or to taste

Smear 2 tablespoons of the avocado spread over the entire surface of each wrap. Top with the turkey, cheese, onion, and sprouts. Add the pepper. Roll or fold, and serve.

Per serving: 360 calories, 15g total fat, 6g saturated fat, 0g trans fat, 40mg cholesterol, 730mg sodium, 37g total carbohydrate, 6g dietary fiber, 5g sugars, 21g protein

Tacos, Burritos, and Quesadillas

Southwestern Bean Soft Tacos Ⓕ

Makes 1 serving: 2 soft tacos each

These soft tacos are 100 percent simple to prepare, family friendly, and *muy delicioso.* Multiply the recipe by as many as you need for family or fiesta.

2 (6-inch) soft whole-grain corn tortillas, warm

¾ cup packed mixed baby salad greens

½ cup Southwestern Pinto Beans, warm (page 487)

¼ cup shredded Monterey Jack or sharp Cheddar cheese

¼ cup Vine-Ripened Pico de Gallo (page 114) or other pico de gallo

Lay out the tortillas. Top with the greens, beans, cheese, and pico de gallo. Fold, and enjoy while warm.

Per serving: 350 calories, 13g total fat, 6g saturated fat, 0g trans fat, 25mg cholesterol, 630mg sodium, 44g total carbohydrate, 11g dietary fiber, 4g sugars, 16g protein

Turkey Tacos Monterey

Makes 4 servings: 2 tacos each

These kid- and adult-friendly tacos will likely remind you of the first taco you may have ever had—served in a crisp taco shell with a meaty filling. Here, the nicely spiced stuffing is made with wholesome turkey. And the shredded cheese has not been forgotten. At just 150 calories apiece, yes, you can have it all when it comes to these tasty tacos.

2 teaspoons peanut or canola oil

12 ounces ground turkey (about 94% lean)

¼ cup Roasted Green Tomato Salsa (page 114) or other salsa verde

Juice of ½ lime (1 tablespoon)

¼ teaspoon chili powder, or to taste

¼ teaspoon ground cumin, or to taste

¼ teaspoon sea salt, or to taste

¼ teaspoon freshly ground black pepper, or to taste

4 hard whole-grain corn taco shells or soft corn tortillas, warm

1 cup packed fresh baby spinach

⅓ cup shredded Monterey Jack cheese

16 grape tomatoes, halved lengthwise, or 8 cherry tomatoes, quartered lengthwise

2 tablespoons chopped fresh cilantro

1. Heat the oil in a large nonstick skillet over medium-high heat. Add the turkey and sauté until cooked through, slightly browned, and crumbled, about 5 minutes. Add the salsa, lime juice, chili powder, cumin, salt, and pepper and sauté until the salsa is absorbed by the turkey, about 2 minutes. Adjust seasoning.

2. Stuff each taco shell with the spinach, turkey mixture, the cheese, tomatoes, and cilantro. Serve while warm.

Per serving: 300 calories, 16g total fat, 5g saturated fat, 0g trans fat, 55mg cholesterol, 490mg sodium, 20g total carbohydrate, 2g dietary fiber, 2g sugars, 21g protein

Blackened Tilapia Tacos with Papaya Ⓕ

Makes 4 servings: 2 tacos each

These grilled fish tacos are best when the fish is absolutely fresh. Ask the market fishmonger what white fish fillets are freshest. Accessorized with somewhat exotic papaya and black bean salsa, these tacos will be visually impressive and satisfying.

2 (8-ounce) tilapia fillets

2 teaspoons extra-virgin olive oil

Juice and zest of ½ lime (1 tablespoon juice)

½ teaspoon sea salt, or to taste

½ teaspoon freshly ground black pepper, or to taste

½ teaspoon ground cumin

⅛ teaspoon chipotle or ancho chili powder (optional)

8 (6-inch) soft whole-grain corn tortillas, gently warmed on grill

2 cups shredded red or green cabbage or coleslaw mix

1 cup Black Bean Salsa (page 117)

1 cup finely diced papaya

1. Prepare an outdoor or indoor grill, or a grill pan.

2. Drizzle, then rub the fillets with a mixture of the oil and lime juice. Sprinkle, then rub with the salt, pepper, cumin, and chili powder (if using).

3. Grill the fillets over direct high heat until grill marks form and they begin to flake, about 3 minutes per side. Transfer to a platter and let stand for about 5 minutes to complete the cooking process. Shred the tilapia using a fork. Adjust seasoning.

4. Top each tortilla with the fish, cabbage, salsa, papaya, and desired amount of the lime zest. Fold, and serve immediately.

Per serving: 300 calories, 6g total fat, 1g saturated fat, 0g trans fat, 55mg cholesterol, 520mg sodium, 35g total carbohydrate, 6g dietary fiber, 6g sugars, 28g protein

Santa Cruz Spinach and Black Bean Burrito Ⓕ

Makes 4 servings: 1 burrito each

The model for this savory veggie-lover's recipe is a burrito I often enjoy at Taco Chulo in Williamsburg, Brooklyn. It's creamy from the avocado, with plenty of texture from the black beans. The standout is the spinach, whose flavors are balanced beautifully with heat and fresh lime.

4 (9-inch) whole-wheat tortillas, warm

1 (15-ounce) can black beans, drained

2 cups Creamed Spinach with Lemon (page 452)
    or steamed spinach, drained and warm

⅓ cup diced white onion

1 small jalapeño pepper with some seeds, minced

1 Hass avocado, pitted, peeled, and diced

Juice of 1 lime (2 tablespoons)

2 tablespoons chopped fresh cilantro

½ teaspoon sea salt, or to taste

½ cup Spicy Raw Tomatillo Salsa (page 114)
    or other salsa verde

1. Top each tortilla with the beans, spinach, onion, jalapeño, and avocado. Sprinkle with the lime juice, cilantro, and salt.

2. Roll up tightly, folding in the sides (if desired). Serve at room temperature with the salsa on the side.

Per serving: 350 calories, 10g total fat, 1g saturated fat, 0g trans fat, 0mg cholesterol, 710mg sodium, 53g total carbohydrate, 11g dietary fiber, 7g sugars, 13g protein

Tropical Rotisserie Chicken Burrito Ⓕ

Makes 4 servings: 1 burrito each

Here's a refreshing twist on a meal-sized burrito. It's a little more challenging to eat by hand (have a fork and knife handy), since you're not tucking in the tortilla sides. Besides, this chicken burrito looks grander with the bodacious confetti of ingredients bursting out.

4 (10-inch) whole-wheat tortillas

1 cup 3-Ingredient Guacamole (page 89)
    or other guacamole

2 cups shredded rotisserie chicken breast

1 (15-ounce) can black beans, drained

1 small mango, peeled, pitted, finely diced,
    and drained (¾ cup diced)

⅓ cup finely chopped red onion

¼ cup chopped fresh cilantro

¼ cup Roasted Green Tomato Salsa (page 114)
    or other salsa verde

2 cups mixed baby greens

1. Top each tortilla evenly with the guacamole, chicken, beans, mango, onion, cilantro, salsa, and greens.

2. Roll each up tightly, secure with a toothpick, and serve.

Per serving: 470 calories, 12g total fat, 1.5g saturated fat, 0g trans fat, 60mg cholesterol, 710mg sodium, 55g total carbohydrate, 11g dietary fiber, 11g sugars, 33g protein

Lebanese Grilled Lamb Burrito Ⓕ

Makes 1 serving: 1 burrito each

Here is a next-day creation using Lebanese Lamb and Fig Kebabs. It's somewhat shawarma-like, yet looks more like a burrito. And it's downright delicious. Who knew yesterday's eats could be such a treat?

1 serving Lebanese Lamb and Fig Kebabs
    (page 321), skewer removed and warm

1 tablespoon fat-free or low-fat plain Greek yogurt

½ teaspoon fresh lemon juice, or to taste

1 garlic clove, minced

¼ teaspoon freshly ground black pepper,
    or to taste

1 (8-inch) whole-wheat tortilla, warm

¼ cup thinly sliced cherry tomatoes or finely
    chopped vine-ripened tomato

¼ cup finely chopped unpeeled English cucumber

1. Thinly slice the lamb, onion, and fig from the Lebanese Lamb and Fig Kebabs recipe.

2. Stir together the yogurt, lemon juice, garlic, and pepper in a small bowl.

3. Top the tortilla, in order, with the lamb, onion, tomato, cucumber, and yogurt mixture. Adjust seasoning.

4. Roll up tightly, and serve warm or at room temperature with the fig on the side. (Alternatively, enjoy the fig mixed into a side dish that you serve along with the burrito, such as brown rice pilaf.)

Per serving: 330 calories, 9g total fat, 1.5g saturated fat, 0g trans fat, 45mg cholesterol, 600mg sodium, 40g total carbohydrate, 5g dietary fiber, 13g sugars, 21g protein

Caprese Quesadilla

Makes 1 serving: 4 wedges each

This is good ol' Italian-meets-Mexican fare—lip-smacking comforts of both popular cuisines. Fresh tomato salsa meets oozing mozzarella in a toasty tortilla. Does it get any better than this?

2 (8-inch) whole-wheat tortillas
⅓ cup shredded part-skim mozzarella cheese
¾ cup Raw Diced Tomato Basil Sauce (page 100), drained

1. Lay the tortillas on a large cutting board and lightly spray one side only of each with cooking spray (preferably homemade, page xix). Turn one of the tortillas over and top the entire surface with half the cheese. Sprinkle with half the sauce and the remaining cheese. Top with the remaining tortilla, sprayed side up. Firmly press the quesadilla with a spatula to compact the ingredients.

2. Cook in a large nonstick skillet over medium-high heat until toasted, about 1½ minutes per side. Cut into 4 wedges.

3. Arrange the quesadilla wedges on a plate. Top with, or serve on the side, the remaining sauce. Serve while warm.

Per serving: 460 calories, 18g total fat, 6g saturated fat, 0g trans fat, 30mg cholesterol, 795mg sodium, 50g total carbohydrate, 5g dietary fiber, 6g sugars, 21g protein

Papaya and Goat Cheese Quesadilla Ⓕ

Makes 8 servings: 2 wedges with ¼ cup salsa

This fresh main-dish quesadilla, with its generous amount of bean salsa, was loosely inspired by one I indulged in at Library Ale House in Santa Monica, California. Caution: This dish may be addictive!

8 (8-inch) whole-wheat tortillas
4 ounces soft goat cheese, finely crumbled
½ cup shredded part-skim mozzarella cheese
½ cup shredded dry Jack cheese
2 cups finely diced fresh papaya
2 scallions, green and white parts, minced
2 tablespoons chopped fresh cilantro
¼ teaspoon freshly ground black pepper, or to taste
2 cups Black Bean Salsa (page 117), drained of excess liquid
½ teaspoon grated lime zest

1. Lay the tortillas on a clean surface or large cutting board and lightly spray one side only of each with cooking spray (preferably homemade, page xix). Turn 4 of the tortillas over and sprinkle the entire surface with the half the cheeses. Sprinkle with the papaya, scallions, cilantro, pepper, and remaining cheeses. Top with the remaining 4 tortillas, sprayed side up. Firmly press each quesadilla with a spatula to compact the ingredients.

2. Cook quesadillas in batches in a large nonstick skillet over medium-high heat until well toasted, about 2 minutes per side. Cut each quesadilla into 4 wedges.

3. Arrange the quesadilla wedges on a platter or individual plates while warm. Top with the black bean salsa and lime zest, and serve.

Per serving: 310 calories, 10g total fat, 4g saturated fat, 0g trans fat, 15mg cholesterol, 460mg sodium, 40g total carbohydrate, 6g dietary fiber, 8g sugars, 14g protein

Caramelized Pear, Roquefort, and Prosciutto Quesadilla

Makes 4 servings: 2 wedges each

A flavor explosion! One bite of this sweet and savory quesadilla, and you'll be hooked. The caramelized pear, Roquefort, fresh herbs, and prosciutto marry harmoniously. And the balsamic reduction provides a high-flavored finale for this memorable treat.

1 large Bosc or other pear of choice, unpeeled, cored, and very thinly sliced

4 (8-inch) whole-wheat tortillas

⅓ cup finely crumbled Roquefort cheese or other blue cheese

1 ounce country ham or prosciutto, finely chopped

6 large fresh sage leaves, thinly sliced

6 large fresh basil leaves, thinly sliced

⅛ teaspoon freshly ground black pepper, or to taste

1 tablespoon Aged Balsamic Reduction (page 138), honey, or agave nectar

1. Preheat the broiler. Arrange the pear slices in a single layer on a baking sheet. Lightly coat with cooking spray (preferably homemade, page xix). Broil until cooked through and lightly caramelized, about 3 minutes.

2. Lay the tortillas on a large baking sheet. Lightly coat one side of each tortilla with cooking spray (preferably homemade). Turn 2 of the tortillas over. Divide half of the cheese evenly over entire surface of the turned-over tortillas. Top with the ham, sage, basil, and caramelized pears. Sprinkle with the remaining cheese and pepper. Top with the remaining 2 tortillas, sprayed sides up. Firmly press each quesadilla with a spatula to compact the ingredients.

3. Broil the quesadillas until toasted, about 45 seconds per side. (Alternatively, cook the quesadillas in a large nonstick skillet over medium-high heat, one at a time, about 1½ minutes per side.)

4. Cut each quesadilla into 4 wedges. Lightly drizzle with the balsamic reduction. Serve warm.

Per serving: 230 calories, 6g total fat, 2.5g saturated fat, 0g trans fat, 15mg cholesterol, 750mg sodium, 36g total carbohydrate, 5g dietary fiber, 10g sugars, 9g protein

Veggie Enchilada Verde

Makes 2 servings: 1 enchilada each

Enchiladas can be full of unneeded calories and unhealthful ingredients. But, not here. This whole-grain–based recipe boasts of corn, salsa, and just enough cheese to bring it together. It'll give you your enchilada fix simply, quickly, and without the excess. Make it a meal full of appeal with a side of refried beans.

⅔ cup shredded Monterey Jack cheese

2 (8-inch) whole-wheat tortillas

¾ cup Western Peppered Corn (page 448) or other freshly cooked vegetable, at room temperature

¼ cup Spicy Raw Tomatillo Salsa (page 114) or other salsa verde

1. Sprinkle half the cheese down the center of the tortillas. Top with the corn mixture, then the remaining cheese. Roll up tightly into long skinny rolls, without tucking in the edges. Place on a microwave-safe dish, seam side down. Top with the salsa.

2. Microwave on high until the corn mixture is hot and the cheese melts, about 75 seconds. Serve warm.

Per serving: 320 calories, 14g total fat, 7g saturated fat, 0g trans fat, 35mg cholesterol, 630mg sodium, 37g total carbohydrate, 5g dietary fiber, 7g sugars, 14g protein

Pizzas and Savory Pies

Pizza Dough

Whole-Wheat Pizza Dough

Spelt Pizza Dough with Flax

Summer Squash Pizza Crust

Thin-Crust Pizzas

Pizza Margherita

Crispy "Buffalo Wing" Squash Pizza

"BLT" Pizza

Hawaiian Luau Pizza

Pizza Huevos with Guacamole

Grilled Caesar Salad Pizza

Grilled Steak Pizza

Thai Turkey Pizza

Deep-Dish Pizzas

Peppery Eggplant Pan Pizza

Baby Spinach Pan Pizza

Superfood Veggie Stuffed Pizza

Barbecued Chicken Pizza

Caramelized Onion and Sausage Deep Dish

Contemporary Pizzas

Goat Cheese and Basil Naan Pizzette

Grilled Squash Pizzette

Heirloom Tomato "Carpaccio" Pizzette

Cinnamon-Spiced Meatball Pizzette

Pesto Chicken Pizzette

Pear and Blue Cheese Pizza

Roasted Cauliflower Pizza

Rosemary Fingerling Pizza

Feta and Fresh Greens Pitza

Mesclun and Gorgonzola Pitza

Hummus Pitza

Calzones, Pockets and Savory Mini Pies

Santorini Chicken Calzone

Prosciutto and Fig "Stromboli"

Ham and Gruyère "Egg Roll"

Caramelized Onion, Chard, and Cheese Pockets

Lemony Spinach Pockets

Lamb Fatayer

Green Spanakopita Pockets

Jackie's "Quiche"

Pizza can get a "junk food" reputation when it's topped with rich meats like pepperoni or extra cheese or it comes "deep-dish" style with a white dough crust that's practically fried.

But that label doesn't apply to anything you find in this chapter. Pizza can actually provide you with a balanced bite that's oh-so-good. In *1,000 Low-Calorie Recipes,* the crusts are made with whole grains and even veggies, too. Cheeses accent the top instead of smothering it. The toppings are plentiful, but are focused on fresh ingredients like produce and leaner meats. Plus, portions are just the right size.

One of my tips for savoring the joy of pizza—and to help keep you from overeating—is to try using a fork and knife whenever possible. It will slow down the eating process and allow you to enjoy each bite. Plus, it's actually easier for pizza that's served on the Summer Squash Pizza Crust (page 412), which has a tender texture, and stuffed pizzas, like Superfood Veggie-Stuffed Pizza (page 419), that are overflowing with veggies.

Three pizza dough recipes kick off this chapter. They are followed by various types of pizzas (aka pizza pies), including thin-crust, deep-dish, and contemporary pizzas. Thin-crust pizzas are either baked or grilled. For grilled pizzas, you can prepare them in your kitchen on a grill pan all-year round, if you prefer. For baked pizzas, you'll transfer the shaped pizza dough via parchment paper onto a preheated pizza stone or pizza pan. This way you'll get the crispest crust without having to use extra oil. For best results, place cooked pizza on a rack to keep it crisp as it sits.

Deep-dish pizzas include both pan style and stuffed versions. These recipes can all be made with a regular thin crust instead of a thick crust, if you prefer; simply use only 1 pound of dough instead of 1½ pounds. If you keep the serving size the same, you'll be cutting calories further.

Contemporary pizzas forgo the traditional idea of a thin- or thick-crust pizza and use other breads to make a "crust." Here they're served on whole-grain naan, lavash, tortillas, and pita. The pizzettes, which are on naan or lavash, include a wide range of flavor choices—from a mild goat cheese and basil combination to a cinnamon-spiced meatball pizzette. For the crispiest crust, place the topped pizzettes directly on the oven rack to bake. For a super-thin crust, some recipes use tortillas. If your tortillas or wraps are larger than the suggested size in the recipe, just trim them. The pita pizzas, which I call pitzas, include Hummus Pitza (page 426) that's fun for the whole family to make and eat.

Concluding this party-friendly chapter are calzones, pockets, and savory mini pies. Basically, the "pizza" toppings are wrapped in their crusts, forming portable meals. You'll see plenty of Middle Eastern, Mediterranean, and French influences here. Be sure to try Jackie's "Quiche" (page 431) and be creative with the ingredients, then name it after yourself instead of me.

Every dish here has fewer than 400 calories. But the best part of the recipes is that they taste great!

Calorie range in this chapter: 80 to 390 calories.

Low-calorie pick: Summer Squash Pizza Crust, 80 calories (page 412).

Pizza Dough

Whole-Wheat Pizza Dough

Makes 8 servings: Dough for 1 (14-inch) thin-crust pizza or 2 (8-inch) thick-crust pizzas

A whole-wheat dough that bakes into a tender, yet crisp crust. It's a better-for-you option than the refined white-flour version, yet equally versatile. Pick this dough for any pizza of your choosing.

1 tablespoon honey or agave nectar

1 cup warm (115°F) water

1 (¼-ounce) envelope active dry yeast

2¾ cups + ⅓ cup whole-wheat pastry flour

1 teaspoon sea salt

2 tablespoons extra-virgin olive oil

1. Stir the honey into the water in a small bowl or liquid measuring cup until smooth. Sprinkle with the yeast and stir gently until a smooth, beige color results. Let stand in a warm place until a thin foam layer forms on the surface, about 5 minutes. (If this does not happen, repeat step 1 with fresh yeast, as the yeast was not active.)

2. Combine 2¾ cups of the flour and the salt in a large mixing bowl. Make a well in the center and pour in the yeast mixture and 1½ tablespoons of the oil. Vigorously stir the flour into the well until a soft dough begins to form.

3. Turn the dough out onto a lightly floured surface (use only as much of the remaining ⅓ cup flour as necessary). Dust your hands with the flour and knead the dough until smooth and elastic, about 12 minutes, adding additional flour only as needed.

4. Shape the dough into a ball and place it into a bowl rubbed with the remaining ½ tablespoon oil, turning the dough in the bowl to lightly coat with the oil. Cover the bowl tightly and set aside to rise in a warm, draft-free place.

5. When the dough has doubled in size, after about 1 hour, punch it down with your fist to prevent over-rising. Shape the dough into a ball while pressing out the air bubbles. Use the dough within 2 hours. (Otherwise, punch the dough down again, turn it in an oiled bowl to coat again, cover the bowl, and chill in the refrigerator; bring to room temperature before use.)

Per serving: 170 calories, 4g total fat, 0.5g saturated fat, 0g trans fat, 0mg cholesterol, 290mg sodium, 29g total carbohydrate, 4g dietary fiber, 2g sugars, 5g protein

Spelt Pizza Dough with Flax

Makes 10 servings: Dough for 1 (14-inch) thin-crust pizza or 2 (8-inch) thick-crust pizzas

If you're looking for an intriguing whole-grain crust, here's one for you! It bakes into a heartier and richer-tasting crust than the usual all-purpose or typical wheat pizza dough. Pair it with highly flavored toppings.

1 tablespoon honey or agave nectar

1 cup warm (115°F) water

1 (¼-ounce) envelope active dry yeast

2¾ cups + ⅓ cup whole spelt or gluten-free whole-grain flour

3 tablespoons whole ground flaxseed meal

1 tablespoon whole flaxseeds

1 teaspoon sea salt

2 tablespoons extra-virgin olive oil

1. Stir the honey into the water in a small bowl or liquid measuring cup until smooth. Sprinkle with the yeast and stir gently until a smooth, beige color results. Let stand in a warm place until a thin foam layer forms on the surface, about 5 minutes. (If this does not happen, repeat step 1 with fresh yeast as the yeast was not active.)

2. Combine 2¾ cups of the flour, the flaxseed meal, flaxseeds, and salt in a large mixing bowl. Make a well in the center and pour in the yeast

continues on next page

mixture and 1½ tablespoons of the oil. Vigorously stir the flour into the well until a soft dough begins to form.

3. Turn the dough out onto a lightly floured surface (use only as much of the remaining ⅓ cup flour as necessary). Dust your hands with the flour and knead the dough until smooth and elastic, about 12 minutes, adding additional flour only as needed.

4. Shape the dough into a ball and place it into a bowl rubbed with the remaining ½ tablespoon oil, turning the dough in the bowl to lightly coat with the oil. Cover the bowl tightly and set aside to rise in a warm, draft-free place.

5. When the dough has doubled in size, after about 1 hour, punch it down with your fist to prevent over-rising. Shape the dough into a ball while pressing out the air bubbles. Use the dough within 2 hours. (Otherwise, punch the dough down again, turn it in an oiled bowl to coat again, cover the bowl, and chill in the refrigerator; bring to room temperature before use.)

Per serving: 180 calories, 5g total fat, 0.5 g saturated fat, 0g trans fat, 0mg cholesterol, 230mg sodium, 31g total carbohydrate, 4g dietary fiber, 3g sugars, 7g protein

Summer Squash Pizza Crust

Makes 8 servings: Crust for 1 (13-inch) pizza

You'll do a double take at this very different doughy delight. It's a parbaked crust that's almost like a zucchini pancake. It has a unique flavor, along with plenty of moistness. It's delicate, so plan to enjoy your pizza with a fork and knife.

4 cups coarsely grated zucchini or yellow summer squash
1 teaspoon sea salt, or to taste
2 large eggs, lightly beaten
2 teaspoons extra-virgin olive oil
⅔ cup whole-wheat pastry flour
¼ cup grated Parmigiano-Reggiano or other Parmesan cheese
2 tablespoons finely chopped fresh basil
1 large garlic clove, minced

1. Place the zucchini in a large colander (preferably lined with cheesecloth) and sprinkle with the salt. Let stand for 15 minutes. Transfer to a clean kitchen towel, roll up tightly, and squeeze out the excess liquid.

2. Preheat the oven to 375°F.

3. Add the zucchini, the eggs, and oil to a large bowl and stir to combine. Add the flour, cheese, basil, and garlic and stir to combine.

4. Spread the dough on a sheet of parchment paper placed on an extra-large cutting board. Pat into a 13-inch pizza crust. Transfer the crust with the parchment paper to a preheated 14-inch pizza stone or pizza pan. Bake until the crust is lightly browned on the bottom and firm on top, yet still moist (parbaked) in the center, about 30 to 35 minutes. Remove from oven and transfer the crust with parchment paper to a rack to cool.

5. The crust is now ready for topping and then being baked into a pizza. (If you don't plan to use it immediately, store tightly wrapped in the freezer for up to 1 month.)

Per serving: 80 calories, 3.5g total fat, 1g saturated fat, 0g trans fat, 50mg cholesterol, 280mg sodium, 9g total carbohydrate, 2g dietary fiber, 1g sugars, 4g protein

Thin-Crust Pizzas

Pizza Margherita

Makes 8 servings: 1 slice each

Though there are so many fanciful ways to top a crust, I have to admit, traditional tomato, mozzarella, and basil is still my favorite. You know what they say—sometimes less is more. Try this slightly tailored twist on the classic—on whole wheat.

1 recipe Whole-Wheat Pizza Dough (page 411)
    or 1½ pounds other whole-grain pizza dough

1 tablespoon extra-virgin olive oil

½ cup Triple Tomato Marinara Sauce (page 101)
    or other marinara sauce

8 ounces lightly salted fresh buffalo mozzarella
    cheese, thinly sliced

⅛ teaspoon sea salt, or to taste

8 large fresh basil leaves

1. Cut about a 14½-inch round piece of parchment paper and place on a large cutting board. (Note: Use your pizza stone or pan as a guide for cutting the paper.)

2. Place a 14-inch baking stone or pizza pan in the oven. Preheat the oven to 500°F.

3. Shape the pizza dough on the parchment paper into a 14-inch round thin crust. (Alternatively, roll out the dough and then carefully transfer to the parchment paper with the rolling pin.) Brush or rub the dough with 1½ teaspoons of the oil. Spread with the sauce, leaving about ½-inch rim. Top with the cheese.

4. Transfer the pizza with the parchment paper to the preheated pizza stone. Bake until the crust is cooked through, crisp, and brown and the cheese is melted, bubbly, and golden brown in spots, about 15 minutes.

5. Slide the pizza onto a cutting board. Sprinkle with salt. Top with the basil and drizzle with the remaining 1½ teaspoons oil. Slice into 8 pieces, and serve immediately.

Per serving: 270 calories, 13g total fat, 4.5g saturated fat, 0g trans fat, 25mg cholesterol, 380mg sodium, 30g total carbohydrate, 4g dietary fiber, 3g sugars, 10g protein

Crispy "Buffalo Wing" Squash Pizza Ⓕ

Makes 8 servings: 1 slice each

If you love chicken wings and pizza, this recipe channels these "pub grub" picks—with vegetarian panache. It's more healthful, too. Enjoy your pizza slice with a pint—with your mates. Drizzle with Rosemary Ranch-Style Dipping Sauce (page 48) for extra panache.

1 recipe Whole-Wheat Pizza Dough (page 411)
    or 1½ pounds other whole-wheat pizza dough

1½ teaspoons extra-virgin olive oil

½ cup shredded provolone cheese

2 large garlic cloves, thinly sliced

8 pieces "Buffalo Wing" Yellow Squash (page 63)
    or grilled or roasted yellow squash

3 ounces fresh buffalo mozzarella cheese,
    finely chopped

3 tablespoons crumbled Gorgonzola cheese

¼ cup coarsely grated carrots

¼ cup coarsely grated celery

2 tablespoons thinly sliced fresh basil leaves

2 teaspoons aged balsamic vinegar

Hot pepper sauce, to taste (optional)

1. Cut about a 14½-inch round piece of parchment paper and place on a large cutting board. (Note: Use your pizza stone or pan as a guide for cutting the paper.)

2. Place a 14-inch baking stone or pizza pan in the oven. Preheat the oven to 500°F.

3. Shape the pizza dough on the parchment paper into a 14-inch round thin crust. (Alternatively, roll out the dough and then carefully transfer to the parchment paper with the rolling pin.) Brush or rub the dough with the oil. Sprinkle with the provolone cheese and garlic.

4. Transfer the pizza with the parchment paper to the preheated pizza stone. Bake until the crust is golden brown, about 12 minutes. Top with the

continues on next page

squash and mozzarella and Gorgonzola cheese and bake until the crust is well browned, cooked through, and crisp and the cheeses are melted, about 3 minutes.

5. Slide the pizza onto a cutting board. Top with the carrots, celery, and basil. Sprinkle with the vinegar and hot pepper sauce (if using). Slice into 8 pieces, and serve immediately.

Per serving: 320 calories, 12g total fat, 5g saturated fat, 0g trans fat, 40mg cholesterol, 560mg sodium, 40g total carbohydrate, 5g dietary fiber, 4g sugars, 13g protein

BLT Pizza

Makes 8 servings: 1 slice each

Like a BLT sandwich? Then you'll love this pizza. The mixture of melted cheese, smoky bacon, juicy tomatoes, and pepper arugula is a mouthwatering flavor combination. The creamy "mayo" sinks into the crust and balances the greens while adding a pleasing garlicky accent. At less than 250 calories, grab a slice anytime—even for breakfast with a sunnyside-up egg on top.

1 recipe Whole-Wheat Pizza Dough (page 411) or 1½ pounds other whole-grain pizza dough

3 tablespoons Garlic "Mayo" (page 123)

1 cup shredded part-skim mozzarella cheese

1 large or 2 small plum tomatoes, cut into 12 slices crosswise

4 slices applewood-smoked uncured bacon, uncooked, chopped

¼ teaspoon freshly ground black pepper, or to taste

2 cups packed baby arugula, chilled

1. Cut about a 14½-inch round piece of parchment paper and place on a large cutting board. (Note: Use your pizza stone or pan as a guide for cutting the paper.)

2. Place a 14-inch baking stone or pizza pan in the oven. Preheat the oven to 500°F.

3. Shape the pizza dough on the parchment paper into a 14-inch round thin crust. (Alternatively, roll out the dough and then carefully transfer to the parchment paper with the rolling pin.) Brush or rub the dough with 1 tablespoon of the "mayo." Top with the cheese, tomatoes, and bacon.

4. Transfer the pizza with the parchment paper to the preheated pizza stone. Bake until the crust is cooked through, crisp, and brown, cheese is melted, and bacon is crisp, about 15 minutes.

5. Slide the pizza onto a cutting board. Sprinkle with the pepper. Slice into 8 pieces.

6. Quickly toss the arugula with the remaining 2 tablespoons "mayo," mound it onto the pizza, and serve immediately.

Per serving: 240 calories, 9g total fat, 2.5g saturated fat, 0g trans fat, 15mg cholesterol, 470mg sodium, 31g total carbohydrate, 4g dietary fiber, 3g sugars, 10g protein

Hawaiian Luau Pizza

Makes 8 servings: 1 slice each

Aloha! This attention-grabbing pizza pie will transport you to the Big Island. The pineapple topping creates tropical appeal and the waft of cinnamon adds a sweet-savory thrill. For extra flavor, try two cheeses—equal parts mozzarella and aged provolone.

1 recipe Whole-Wheat Pizza Dough (page 411) or 1½ pounds other whole-grain pizza dough

1½ teaspoons extra-virgin olive oil

⅛ teaspoon ground cinnamon, or to taste

½ cup Fresh Marinara (page 101) or other marinara sauce

1½ cups shredded part-skim mozzarella cheese

4 ounces Canadian-style bacon or lean baked ham, chopped

½ cup diced fresh pineapple, drained

1 small green bell pepper, diced

3 tablespoons minced red onion

3 tablespoons sliced natural almonds

1. Cut about a 14½-inch round piece of parchment paper and place on a large cutting board. (Note: Use your pizza stone or pan as a guide for cutting the paper.)

2. Place a 14-inch baking stone or pizza pan in the oven. Preheat the oven to 500°F.

3. Shape the pizza dough on the parchment paper into a 14-inch round thin crust. (Alternatively, roll out the dough and then carefully transfer to the parchment paper with the rolling pin.) Brush or rub the dough with the oil and dust with the cinnamon. Spread with the sauce, leaving about ½-inch rim. Top with the cheese, bacon, pineapple, pepper, onion, and almonds.

4. Transfer the pizza with the parchment paper to the preheated baking stone. Bake until the crust is cooked through, crisp, and brown, cheese is melted, and bell pepper is slightly caramelized, about 15 minutes.

5. Slide the pizza onto a cutting board. Slice into 8 pieces, and serve immediately.

Per serving: 270 calories, 11g total fat, 3g saturated fat, 0g trans fat, 20mg cholesterol, 580mg sodium, 33g total carbohydrate, 5g dietary fiber, 4g sugars, 13g protein

Pizza Huevos with Guacamole Ⓕ

Makes 10 servings: 1 slice each

It's a pizza that's an eye-opener for brunch. Its scrumptious scrambled-egg topping and chic, healthful spelt crust will intrigue. And if you really want to wow 'em, prepare the guacamole tableside; your guests can then add their own dollop atop each slice.

5 large eggs
2 tablespoons plain fat-free or low-fat Greek yogurt
¼ teaspoon + ⅛ teaspoon sea salt, or to taste
1½ teaspoons peanut or canola oil
½ cup thinly sliced fresh shiitake mushroom caps
½ cup drained canned no-salt-added black beans
3 tablespoons medium or spicy salsa or salsa verde
1 recipe Spelt Pizza Dough with Flax (page 411)
    or 1½ pounds other whole-grain pizza dough
¾ cup shredded extra-sharp Cheddar cheese

¾ cup shredded Monterey Jack cheese
12 cherry tomatoes, thinly sliced
2 tablespoons roughly chopped fresh cilantro
1 cup 3-Ingredient Guacamole (page 89)
    or other guacamole
1 lime, cut into 8 wedges

1. Whisk together the eggs, yogurt, and ¼ teaspoon of the salt in a medium bowl.

2. Heat the oil in a large nonstick skillet over medium heat. Add the egg mixture and mushrooms and stir until gently scrambled yet still slightly runny, about 3 minutes. Remove from heat and stir in the black beans and salsa. Transfer to a plate and set aside.

3. Cut about a 14½-inch round piece of parchment paper and place on a large cutting board. (Note: Use your pizza stone or pan as a guide for cutting the paper.)

4. Place a 14-inch baking stone or pizza pan in the oven. Preheat the oven to 500°F.

5. Shape the pizza dough on the parchment paper into a 14-inch round thin crust. (Alternatively, roll out the dough and then carefully transfer to the parchment paper with the rolling pin.) Thinly spread the dough with the scrambled-egg mixture, leaving about ½-inch rim. Top with the cheeses and cherry tomatoes. Sprinkle with the remaining ⅛ teaspoon salt.

6. Transfer the pizza with the parchment paper to the preheated pizza stone. Bake until the crust is cooked through, crisp, and brown, and the cheese is melted, bubbly, and golden brown in spots, about 15 minutes.

7. Slide the pizza onto a cutting board. Top with the cilantro. Slice into 10 pieces, and serve immediately with the guacamole and lime wedges.

Per serving: 330 calories, 16g total fat, 5g saturated fat, 0g trans fat, 110mg cholesterol, 570mg sodium, 37g total carbohydrate, 5g dietary fiber, 4g sugars, 16g protein

Grilled Caesar Salad Pizza Ⓕ

Makes 8 servings: 1 slice each

The fresh, grilled cheese-laced pizza with its puffy charred crust topped with a cool and crispy spiked Caesar salad is like a slice of epicurean heaven.

1 recipe Whole-Wheat Pizza Dough (page 411)
    or 1½ pounds other whole-grain pizza dough

2 teaspoons extra-virgin olive oil

3 ounces part-skim mozzarella cheese, grated or
    shredded (¾ cup)

1 ounce grated Parmigiano-Reggiano
    or other Parmesan cheese (¼ cup)

4 cups chopped or torn romaine lettuce, chilled

¼ cup "Caliente" Caesar Dijon Dressing (page 148)
    or other Caesar dressing

½ teaspoon freshly ground black pepper, or to taste

1. Prepare an outdoor or indoor grill, or a grill pan.

2. Shape the pizza dough into two 9-inch-round thin crusts. Brush or rub both sides of the dough with the oil.

3. Gently lay the dough on the grill grates over direct medium heat and grill for 5 minutes, then grill over medium-high heat until the bottom has well-defined, charred grill marks, about 5 minutes. Flip over, top each pizza immediately with the cheeses, cover, and grill over medium-high heat for 2 minutes; rotate so the crust forms cross-hatch grill marks, and continue to grill, covered, until the crust bottom is browned, dough is cooked through, and mozzarella cheese is melted, about 2 minutes more.

4. Transfer the pizzas to a cutting board. Slice into 4 pieces each.

5. Quickly toss the lettuce with half of the dressing in a medium bowl. Top the pizza slices with the salad, sprinkle with the pepper, and serve immediately with the remaining salad dressing on the side.

Per serving: 230 calories, 8g total fat, 2g saturated fat, 0g trans fat, 10mg cholesterol, 430mg sodium, 32g total carbohydrate, 5g dietary fiber, 3g sugars, 9g protein

Grilled Steak Pizza

Makes 8 servings: 1 piece each

This may be the most satisfying, best-tasting pizza ever! Need I say more?

1 (8-ounce) lean beef tenderloin steak
    (about 1 inch thick)

½ teaspoon freshly ground black pepper, or to taste

½ teaspoon rosemary, mushroom, or other
    naturally flavored sea salt, or to taste

1 recipe Whole-Wheat Pizza Dough (page 411)
    or 1½ pounds other whole-grain pizza dough

2 teaspoons extra-virgin olive oil

¾ cup shredded part-skim mozzarella cheese

3 tablespoons minced red onion

2 teaspoons white truffle oil

¼ cup chopped fresh flat-leaf parsley

1. Prepare an outdoor or indoor grill, or a grill pan.

2. Rub the beef with the pepper to completely coat. Grill the beef over direct high heat until charred on the outside and rare to medium-rare on the inside, about 2½ to 3 minutes per side. Let stand for at least 5 minutes. Slice into 16 or more thin strips. Sprinkle with ¼ teaspoon of the salt.

3. Shape the pizza dough into two 9-inch-round thin crusts. Brush or rub both sides of the dough with the olive oil.

4. Gently lay the dough on the grill grates over direct medium heat and grill for 5 minutes, then grill over medium-high heat until the bottom has well-defined, charred grill marks, about 5 minutes. Flip over, top each pizza immediately with the cheese, grilled beef, and the onion, cover, and grill over medium-high heat for 2 minutes; rotate so the crust forms cross-hatch grill marks, and continue to grill, covered, until the crust bottom is browned, dough is cooked through, and cheese is melted, about 2 minutes more.

5. Transfer the pizzas to a cutting board, drizzle with the truffle oil, and sprinkle with the remaining ¼ teaspoon salt. Slice into 4 pieces each. Sprinkle with the parsley, and serve immediately.

Per serving: 260 calories, 10g total fat, 2.5g saturated fat, 0g trans fat, 20mg cholesterol, 590mg sodium, 30g total carbohydrate, 4g dietary fiber, 2g sugars, 13g protein

Thai Turkey Pizza

Makes 8 servings: 1 slice each

Inspired by California Pizza Kitchen's classic Thai Chicken Pizza, the pizza crust with surprising squash provides a memorable foundation here for toothsome Thai toppings. Don't forget the peanuts! Then plan to eat it right away while the pizza is at its crispest.

1 recipe **Summer Squash Pizza Crust (page 412)**

1¼ **cups shredded part-skim mozzarella cheese**

8 **ounces boneless skinless turkey breast,**
    cut into about 24 thin slices

¾ **cup Peanut Sauce (page 108) or Asian peanut**
    satay sauce

2 **scallions, green and white parts, thinly sliced**
    on diagonal

½ **cup mung bean sprouts or thinly sliced**
    water chestnuts

⅓ **cup coarsely grated carrot**

3 **tablespoons roughly chopped fresh cilantro**

2 **tablespoons chopped lightly salted dry-roasted**
    peanuts

1. Place a 14-inch baking stone or pizza pan in the oven. Preheat the oven to 375°F.

2. Sprinkle the parbaked crust (on parchment paper) with half the cheese. Toss together the turkey, peanut sauce, and white parts of the scallions in a medium bowl, and scatter onto the crust. Sprinkle with the remaining cheese.

3. Transfer the pizza on the parchment paper to the preheated pizza stone. Bake until the crust edges are well browned, cheese is melted and golden brown, and turkey is well done, about 25 minutes.

4. Top with the green parts of the scallions, the bean sprouts, carrot, cilantro, and peanuts. Slide the pizza onto a cutting board, slice into 8 pieces, and serve immediately.

Per serving: 240 calories, 11g total fat, 3.5g saturated fat, 0g trans fat, 80mg cholesterol, 510mg sodium, 16g total carbohydrate, 3g dietary fiber, 5g sugars, 18g protein

Deep-Dish Pizzas

Peppery Eggplant Pan Pizza Ⓕ

Makes 8 servings: 1 slice each

You'll enjoy a thick bread-lover's crust with this eye-appealing pizza. And the clever mix of toppings will surprise and intrigue you—from the roasted eggplant to the piquant peppers to the pungent cheese.

1 recipe Whole-Wheat Pizza Dough (page 411) or 1½ pounds other whole-grain pizza dough

6 ounces Robiola, Taleggio or Pont l'Evêque cheese, thinly sliced or chopped

1 large orange bell pepper, diced

1 cup finely diced Asian or Italian eggplant, unpeeled

½ cup finely diced sweet onion

2 ounces Peppadew or banana peppers in brine, well drained, thinly sliced

1 large garlic clove, minced

1 tablespoon white truffle oil or extra-virgin olive oil

½ teaspoon sea salt, or to taste

½ cup shredded part-skim mozzarella cheese

3 tablespoons roughly chopped fresh flat-leaf parsley

1. Preheat the oven to 450°F. Coat two 8-inch round baking pans with cooking spray (preferably homemade, page xix).

2. Shape the pizza dough into 2 round crusts in the pans. Top with the Robiola cheese.

3. Toss together the bell pepper, eggplant, onion, Peppadews, garlic, oil, and salt in a medium bowl, and arrange on the pizzas and gently press the vegetable mixture into the crust to adhere. Sprinkle with the mozzarella cheese.

4. Bake until the crusts are golden brown, cheese is fully melted, and the vegetables are cooked through and lightly caramelized, about 25 minutes. If desired, place under the broiler for extra caramelization of the vegetables and cheese, about 1 minute.

5. Remove from the oven to a rack and let stand for at least 5 minutes. Transfer to a cutting board. Sprinkle with the parsley, slice into 4 pieces each, and serve immediately.

Per serving: 290 calories, 13g total fat, 5g saturated fat, 0g trans fat, 25mg cholesterol, 640mg sodium, 33g total carbohydrate, 5g dietary fiber, 4g sugars, 12g protein

Baby Spinach Pan Pizza

Makes 8 servings: 1 slice each

Pizza can be an ideal entrée that's "all inclusive"—including vegetables, like spinach. So eat this cheesy "good food"—and get some veggies, too.

1 recipe Whole-Wheat Pizza Dough (page 411) or 1½ pounds other whole-grain pizza dough

⅓ cup part-skim ricotta cheese

½ teaspoon sea salt, or to taste

3½ cups packed fresh baby spinach

Juice of ½ small lemon (1 tablespoon)

3 large garlic cloves, minced

¼ teaspoon dried hot pepper flakes, or to taste

½ cup shredded part-skim mozzarella cheese

¼ cup grated Parmigiano-Reggiano or other Parmesan or Romano cheese

½ cup shredded fontina cheese

1. Preheat the oven to 450°F. Coat two 8-inch round baking pans with cooking spray (preferably homemade, page xix).

2. Shape the pizza dough into 2 round crusts in the pans. Spread each with the ricotta cheese, leaving about ½-inch rim. Sprinkle with ¼ teaspoon of the salt.

3. Toss together the spinach, lemon juice, garlic, hot pepper flakes, and the remaining ¼ teaspoon salt. Top each crust with one-sixth of the spinach mixture, half the mozzarella cheese, one-sixth of the spinach mixture, half of the Parmesan cheese, one-sixth of the spinach mixture, and half of the fontina cheese.

4. Bake until the crusts are golden brown and the cheeses are fully melted and lightly browned, about 20 minutes.

5. Remove from the oven to a rack and let stand for at least 5 minutes. Transfer to a cutting board. Slice into 4 pieces each, and serve immediately.

Per serving: 250 calories, 10g total fat, 3.5g saturated fat, 0g trans fat, 20mg cholesterol, 610mg sodium, 32g total carbohydrate, 4g dietary fiber, 2g sugars, 11g protein

Superfood Veggie Stuffed Pizza Ⓕ

Makes 8 servings: 1 slice each

This stuffed pizza is a vegetable lover's dream. Served on a thick crust and accessorized with the perfect accent of cheeses, this pizza is an enjoyable way to eat your veggies.

1 recipe Whole-Wheat Pizza Dough (page 411)
   or 1½ pounds other whole-grain pizza dough
1 cup Triple Tomato Marinara Sauce (page 101)
   or other marinara sauce
1½ cups shredded part-skim mozzarella cheese
½ cup diced red bell pepper
½ cup diced broccoli florets
½ cup thinly sliced frozen artichoke hearts, thawed
½ cup thinly sliced fresh shiitake mushroom caps
   or cremini (baby bella) mushrooms
½ cup finely diced Asian or Italian eggplant
½ cup finely diced red onion
2 large garlic cloves, minced
1 tablespoon extra-virgin olive oil
¼ teaspoon sea salt, or to taste
⅓ cup crumbled soft goat cheese
1 teaspoon finely chopped fresh rosemary
3 tablespoons thinly sliced fresh basil leaves (optional)

1. Preheat the oven to 450°F. Coat two 8-inch round baking pans with cooking spray (preferably homemade, page xix).

2. Shape the pizza dough into 2 round crusts in the pans. Spread with the marinara sauce, leaving

about ½-inch rim. Top with 1 cup of the mozzarella cheese.

3. Toss together the bell pepper, broccoli, artichoke hearts, mushrooms, eggplant, onion, garlic, oil, and salt in a medium bowl, arrange onto the pizzas, and gently press the vegetable mixture into the crusts to adhere. Sprinkle with the remaining ½ cup mozzarella cheese, the goat cheese, and rosemary.

4. Bake until the crusts are golden brown, cheeses are fully melted, and the vegetables are softened, about 25 minutes.

5. Remove from the oven to a rack and let stand for at least 8 minutes. Transfer to a cutting board. Slice into 4 pieces each, sprinkle with the basil (if using), and serve immediately.

Per serving: 290 calories, 11g total fat, 4g saturated fat, 0g trans fat, 15mg cholesterol, 610mg sodium, 35g total carbohydrate, 6g dietary fiber, 5g sugars, 13g protein

Barbecued Chicken Pizza

Makes 8 servings: 1 slice each

For those times when you'd like to have it both ways, this slice is for you. There's no need to choose; it's cheese pizza and barbecued chicken co-habitating in perfect culinary harmony.

1 recipe Whole-Wheat Pizza Dough (page 411)
   or 1½ pounds other whole-grain pizza dough
¾ cup Ancho Chili Barbecue Sauce (page 105)
   or other barbecue sauce
¾ cup finely diced smoked fresh mozzarella cheese
¾ cup finely diced fresh mozzarella cheese
½ cup thinly sliced or finely diced red onion
6 ounces boneless skinless chicken breast, thinly sliced into strips or finely diced
⅓ cup finely diced red or orange bell pepper
2 tablespoons chopped fresh cilantro

1. Preheat the oven to 450°F. Coat two 8-inch round baking pans with cooking spray (preferably homemade, page xix).

continues on next page

2. Shape the pizza dough into 2 round crusts in the pans. Spread ¼ cup of the sauce on each crust, leaving about ½-inch rim. Top with the cheeses and onion.

3. Toss together the remaining ¼ cup sauce and the chicken in a small bowl, and arrange on the pizzas. Sprinkle with the bell pepper.

4. Bake until the crusts are golden brown, cheeses are fully melted, and the chicken is done, about 20 minutes.

5. Remove from the oven to a rack and let stand for at least 5 minutes. Transfer to a cutting board. Sprinkle with the cilantro, slice into 4 pieces each, and serve immediately.

Per serving: 280 calories, 11g total fat, 4g saturated fat, 0g trans fat, 30mg cholesterol, 400mg sodium, 34g total carbohydrate, 4g dietary fiber, 5g sugars, 13g protein

Caramelized Onion and Sausage Deep Dish Ⓕ

Makes 8 servings: 1 slice each

Here's my very own version of the famous Chicago-style pizza. Though still rather decadent, It's a bit more mod with the caramelized onions and a bit more healthful with turkey sausage, whole-wheat crust, and just-right amount of cheeses. It's more than a bit tasty!

2 tablespoons extra-virgin olive oil

2 large sweet onions, halved and thinly sliced

½ cup Chardonnay or other dry white wine

¼ teaspoon sea salt, or to taste

3 large garlic cloves, minced

6 ounces cooked hot or sweet Italian turkey or
    chicken sausage, cut into ⅓-inch-thick slices

1 medium orange or yellow bell pepper, diced

¼ cup chopped fresh flat-leaf parsley

1 teaspoon finely chopped fresh rosemary

1 recipe Whole-Wheat Pizza Dough (page 411)
    or 1½ pounds other whole-grain pizza dough

1 cup shredded fontina cheese

½ cup shredded part-skim mozzarella cheese

2 tablespoons freshly grated Pecorino Romano
    or other Romano cheese

1. Preheat the oven to 450°F. Coat two 8-inch round baking pans with cooking spray (preferably homemade, page xix).

2. Heat 1 tablespoon of the oil in a large nonstick skillet over medium heat. Add the onions, 1 table-spoon of the wine, and the salt, stir to coat, cover, and cook, stirring twice, until the onions are fully softened, about 15 minutes. Remove cover, increase heat to medium-high, and sauté until caramelized, about 7 to 10 minutes. Stir in the garlic and sausage, then stir in the remaining wine. Sauté until the wine is reduced but mixture is still moist, about 3 minutes. Stir in the bell pepper, half of the parsley, and the rosemary, and remove from heat.

3. Shape the pizza dough into 2 round crusts in the pans. Brush dough all over with the remaining 1 tablespoon oil. Top with the cheeses, then the onion-sausage mixture, leaving about ½-inch rim.

4. Bake until the crusts are golden brown, about 20 minutes.

5. Remove from the oven to a rack and let stand for at least 8 minutes. Transfer to a cutting board. Sprinkle with the remaining parsley, slice into 4 pieces each, and serve immediately.

Per serving: 360 calories, 16g total fat, 5g saturated fat, 0g trans fat, 40mg cholesterol, 680mg sodium, 38g total carbohydrate, 5g dietary fiber, 7g sugars, 16g protein

Contemporary Pizzas

Goat Cheese and Basil Naan Pizzette Ⓕ

Makes 4 servings: 2 pieces (½ pizzette) each

Whole-wheat naan (Indian flatbread) becomes an ideal platform for topping with lemony white beans, tangy soft goat cheese, mildly pungent red onion, and sweet-scented basil. It won't weigh you down; it will delight and satisfy.

1 (15-ounce) can no-salt-added cannellini
    or other white beans, drained
1 tablespoon extra-virgin olive oil
2 teaspoons fresh lemon juice
1 large garlic clove, minced
¼ teaspoon sea salt, or to taste
⅛ teaspoon freshly ground black pepper, or to taste
2 (3-ounce) whole-wheat naan or soft lavash
    flatbreads
⅓ cup very thinly sliced red onion
1 cup crumbled soft goat cheese
3 tablespoons thinly sliced fresh basil leaves
    or a handful of small whole fresh basil leaves

1. Preheat the oven to 450°F.

2. Add ¾ cup of the beans, the oil, lemon juice, garlic, ⅛ teaspoon of the salt, and the pepper to a food processor. Cover and puree. Spread the bean mixture on the naan like a pizza sauce. Sprinkle with the onion, the remaining beans, remaining ⅛ teaspoon salt, and the goat cheese.

3. Place the naan pizzas on a rack set on a large baking sheet or directly on an extra-large perforated pizza pan. Bake until the crust bottom is crisp and goat cheese is slightly browned, about 16 to 18 minutes.

4. Transfer to a cutting board and adjust seasoning. Sprinkle with the basil, cut each into 4 pieces, and serve.

Per serving: 320 calories, 14g total fat, 5g saturated fat, 0g trans fat, 15mg cholesterol, 490mg sodium, 36g total carbohydrate, 7g dietary fiber, 4g sugars, 14g protein

Grilled Squash Pizzette

Makes 4 servings: 1 large piece (½ pizzette) each

Make grilled summer squash the star of your pizzette. It grills quickly and creates a succulent-textured pizzette topping. A pinch of sharp aged Manchego and fresh herbs then complete this pizzette with style and fragrance.

1 medium yellow summer squash, cut into 12 slices
    on the diagonal
2 teaspoons extra-virgin olive oil
⅛ teaspoon sea salt, or to taste
2 (3-ounce) whole-wheat naan or soft lavash
    flatbreads
2 large garlic cloves, minced
½ cup shredded or finely diced 12-month aged
    Manchego or other aged sheep milk cheese
½ cup shredded part-skim mozzarella cheese
½ teaspoon finely chopped fresh oregano
3 tablespoons thinly sliced fresh basil leaves

1. Prepare an outdoor or indoor grill.

2. Brush the yellow squash slices with the oil. Sprinkle with the salt. Grill over direct medium-high heat until just cooked through and grill marks form, about 3½ to 4 minutes per side.

3. Sprinkle the naan with the garlic and Manchego cheese. Top with the grilled squash slices, the mozzarella cheese, and oregano.

4. Place the naan pizzas on a rack set on a large baking sheet or directly on an extra-large perforated pizza pan. Bake until the crust bottom is crisp and cheese is melted, about 16 to 18 minutes.

5. Transfer to a cutting board and adjust seasoning. Sprinkle with the basil, cut each in half, and serve.

Per serving: 250 calories, 13g total fat, 5g saturated fat, 0g trans fat, 20mg cholesterol, 540mg sodium, 25g total carbohydrate, 3g dietary fiber, 5g sugars, 11g protein

Heirloom Tomato "Carpaccio" Pizzette

Makes 4 servings: 1 piece each

If you still think "healthy pizza" is an oxymoron, you must try this flatbread pizzette. Any way you slice it, it's an excellent bite. The secret to its great taste is to use fully ripened tomatoes, which when sliced super-thin look like beef carpaccio.

2 (3½- to 4-ounce) soft whole-wheat lavash flatbreads

1 garlic clove, minced

3½ ounces fresh mozzarella cheese, thinly sliced (optional)

1 tablespoon extra-virgin olive oil

1 teaspoon fresh lemon juice

1 large heirloom tomato or 2 medium vine-ripened tomatoes, very thinly sliced

⅛ teaspoon sea salt, or to taste

⅛ teaspoon freshly ground black pepper, or to taste

2 tablespoons thinly sliced fresh basil leaves

1 tablespoon chopped fresh flat-leaf parsley

¼ teaspoon minced fresh rosemary

1 tablespoon pine nuts, toasted

1 teaspoon drained tiny capers (optional)

1. Preheat the oven to 450°F. Place a large baking sheet in the oven to heat.

2. Sprinkle the lavash with the garlic and cheese (if using).

3. Transfer the pizzettes to the heated baking sheet and bake until the crust is crisp and golden brown, about 10 to 12 minutes.

4. Meanwhile, whisk together the oil and lemon juice in a small bowl.

5. Remove the pizzettes from oven, place pan on rack, and immediately arrange the tomato slices, overlapping slightly, onto the entire surface of each pizzette. Drizzle with the lemon-oil mixture. Add the salt and pepper. Sprinkle with the basil, parsley, rosemary, pine nuts, and capers (if using).

6. Transfer the pizzettes to a cutting board, cut each in half, and serve.

Per serving: 190 calories, 6g total fat, 1g saturated fat, 0g trans fat, 0mg cholesterol, 340mg sodium, 30g total carbohydrate, 4g dietary fiber, 2g sugars, 6g protein

Cinnamon-Spiced Meatball Pizzette Ⓕ

Makes 4 servings: 1 piece each

Meatballs on pizza . . . good idea. Mediterranean-style cinnamon-spiced lamb meatballs on pizzette . . . great idea. Then top with ingredients to complement, including sharp feta cheese, fresh lemon juice, and creamy Greek yogurt—which makes every intriguing bite seem especially cheesy—and you'll get a grand pizzette.

2 (3½- to 4-ounce) soft whole-wheat lavash flatbreads or 4 (7-inch) whole-wheat pocketless pitas

½ cup shredded part-skim mozzarella cheese

¼ cup crumbled feta cheese

9 Cinnamon-Spiced Lamb Meatballs (page 81), cut into 4 slices each and chilled

⅓ cup fat-free or low-fat plain Greek yogurt

1 large garlic clove, minced

2 teaspoons fresh lemon juice

⅛ teaspoon freshly ground black pepper, or to taste

12 grape tomatoes or 6 cherry tomatoes, thinly sliced crosswise

3 tablespoons chopped fresh flat-leaf parsley

2 teaspoons pine nuts, toasted

Pinch of ground cinnamon (optional)

1. Preheat the oven to 450°F. Place a large baking sheet in the oven to heat.

2. Sprinkle the lavash with the cheeses. Top with the meatball slices.

3. Stir together the yogurt, garlic, lemon juice, and pepper in a small bowl. Drizzle the yogurt mixture over the meatballs using a fork. Sprinkle with the tomato slices.

4. Transfer the pizzettes to the heated baking sheet and bake until the crust is crisp and golden brown, meatball slices are hot, and cheese is melted, about 10 to 12 minutes.

5. Remove from oven and let sit on pan on rack for 5 minutes. Sprinkle with the parsley and pine nuts.

6. Transfer the pizzettes to a cutting board. Adjust seasoning and sprinkle with the ground cinnamon (if using). Cut each in half, and serve.

Per serving: 290 calories, 9g total fat, 4g saturated fat, 0g trans fat, 35mg cholesterol, 660mg sodium, 35g total carbohydrate, 5g dietary fiber, 3g sugars, 18g protein

Pesto Chicken Pizzette

Makes 4 servings: 1 piece each

When pesto meets chicken it makes for a flavorful match. But the real gems here are the sun-dried tomatoes. They deliver a pop of smokiness, crispness, and eye appeal that add to the overall satisfaction of this scrumptious pizzette.

4 ounces boneless skinless grilled or roasted chicken breast, diced and chilled

⅛ teaspoon sea salt, or to taste

½ cup Arugula Pesto (page 118)

2 (3-ounce) whole-wheat naan or soft lavash flatbreads

¼ cup very thinly sliced red onion

6 sun-dried tomato halves (rehydrate, if need), thinly sliced

½ cup shredded fontina cheese or chopped Taleggio cheese

1. Add the chicken to a medium bowl. Sprinkle with the salt and toss to combine. Add the pesto and stir to combine. Spread the chicken mixture onto the naan. Sprinkle with the onion, sun-dried tomatoes, and cheese.

2. Bake each pizzette directly on racks in a toaster oven at 450°F (bake separately, if necessary) or in a preheated oven until the crust bottom is browned and crisp, chicken is hot, and cheese is melted, about 9 minutes.

3. Transfer to a cutting board and adjust seasoning. Cut each in half, and serve.

Per serving: 320 calories, 16g total fat, 5g saturated fat, 0g trans fat, 45mg cholesterol, 620mg sodium, 24g total carbohydrate, 3g dietary fiber, 4g sugars, 19g protein

Red Pear and Blue Cheese Pizza Ⓕ

Makes 2 servings: 1 tortilla pizza (4 wedges) each

A dazzling duet of Gorgonzola and caramelized pear is on full flavor display here. Yum!

2 (9-inch) whole-wheat tortillas or wraps

¼ cup shredded fontina cheese

1 small or ½ large red Anjou or Starkrimson pear, cored and very thinly sliced

¼ cup very thinly sliced sweet onion

2 teaspoons extra-virgin olive oil

2 tablespoons crumbled Gorgonzola or other blue cheese

½ teaspoon finely chopped fresh rosemary, or to taste

¼ teaspoon freshly ground black pepper, or to taste

2 tablespoons thinly sliced fresh basil leaves

1. Preheat the oven to 400°F.

2. Lightly spray both sides of the tortillas with cooking spray (preferably homemade, page xix). Place the tortillas on a rack on a large baking sheet or directly on an extra-large perforated pizza pan. Top the entire surface of both tortillas with the fontina cheese, pear, and onion. Sprinkle with the oil, Gorgonzola cheese, rosemary, and pepper.

3. Bake until the tortillas are crisp and fully browned, pears are soft and lightly caramelized, and cheese is melted and golden brown, about 22 to 25 minutes.

4. Sprinkle with the basil; adjust seasoning. Cut into 4 wedges each, if desired, and serve immediately. (If not serving immediately, keep on baking rack or transfer to a cooling rack and serve at room temperature.)

Per serving: 350 calories, 15g total fat, 5g saturated fat, 0g trans fat, 25mg cholesterol, 680mg sodium, 46g total carbohydrate, 7g dietary fiber, 12g sugars, 12g protein

Roasted Cauliflower Pizza Ⓕ

Makes 2 servings: 1 tortilla pizza (4 wedges) each

A few years ago I attended a culinary event where roasted cauliflower pizza was being served. It wasn't expected to be the star, but it stole the show. Something magical happens when cauliflower is roasted and combines with nutty Gruyère. Try this generously topped, extra crispy pizza and you'll become a believer.

2 (9-inch) whole-wheat tortillas or wraps

2 cups Extra-Virgin Roasted Cauliflower, chilled (page 446)

⅓ cup shredded Gruyère or other aged Swiss cheese

1 tablespoon grated Pecorino Romano or Parmesan cheese

¼ teaspoon freshly ground black pepper, or to taste

1 scallion, green and white part, thinly sliced

15 unsalted dry-roasted pistachios, chopped

1. Preheat the oven to 400°F.

2. Lightly spray both sides of the tortillas with cooking spray (preferably homemade, page xix). Place the tortillas on a rack on a large baking sheet or directly onto an extra-large perforated pizza pan. Top the entire surface of both tortillas with the cauliflower, cheeses, pepper, and the white portion of the scallion.

3. Bake until the tortillas are crisp and fully browned and cheese is melted and golden browned, about 22 to 25 minutes.

4. Sprinkle with the green portion of the scallion and the pistachios; adjust seasoning. Cut into 4 wedges each, if desired, and serve immediately. (If not serving immediately, keep on baking rack or transfer to a cooling rack and serve at room temperature.)

Per serving: 370 calories, 18g total fat, 5g saturated fat, 0g trans fat, 25mg cholesterol, 700mg sodium, 42g total carbohydrate, 9g dietary fiber, 8g sugars, 16g protein

Rosemary Fingerling Pizza Ⓕ

Makes 2 servings: 1 tortilla pizza (4 wedges) each

Inspired by a potato pizza from the famed New York Sullivan Street Bakery, called "pizza patate," this tortilla pizza is half pizza, half hash browns, and wholly delectable.

2 (8½- to 9-inch) whole-wheat tortillas or wraps

1 cup Rosemary Potatoes and Leeks (page 461), chilled, thinly sliced crosswise

¼ cup shredded part-skim mozzarella cheese

¼ cup crumbled soft goat cheese

¼ cup finely diced red onion

½ teaspoon finely chopped fresh rosemary, or to taste

¼ teaspoon freshly ground black pepper, or to taste

1. Preheat the oven to 400°F.

2. Lightly spray both sides of the tortillas with cooking spray (preferably homemade, page xix). Place the tortillas on a rack on a large baking sheet or directly on an extra-large perforated pizza pan. Top the entire surface of both tortillas with the potatoes and leeks, cheeses, onion, rosemary, and pepper.

3. Bake until the tortillas are crisp and fully browned and cheese is melted and golden brown, about 22 to 25 minutes.

4. Adjust seasoning. Cut into 4 wedges each, if desired, and serve immediately. If not serving immediately, keep on baking rack or transfer to a cooling rack and serve at room temperature.

Per serving: 330 calories, 11g total fat, 4g saturated fat, 0g trans fat, 15mg cholesterol, 700mg sodium, 47g total carbohydrate, 6g dietary fiber, 6g sugars, 13g protein

Feta and Fresh Greens Pitza

Makes 2 servings: 2 pitza wedges each

Za'atar is a Middle Eastern herb and spice mixture featuring oregano as a key note. Adding a touch of it creates a hint of the exotic to anything it graces. Whip up this simple feta and leafy green pizza on pocketless pita when you're in the mood for something that's anything but ordinary.

1 (7-inch) whole-grain pocketless pita or flatbread

½ teaspoon extra-virgin olive oil

¼ cup shredded or finely diced part-skim mozzarella cheese

1 cup packed fresh baby spinach or chopped Swiss chard

2 teaspoons fresh lemon juice

¼ cup crumbled feta cheese

¼ teaspoon za'atar or crushed dried oregano, or to taste

⅛ teaspoon dried hot pepper flakes, or to taste

1. Preheat the oven to 400°F.

2. Place the pita on a baking sheet. Rub or brush the entire top surface of the pita with the oil. Top with the mozzarella cheese and spinach. Sprinkle with the lemon juice, feta cheese, za'atar, and hot pepper flakes.

3. Bake until the pita is crisp and brown and cheese is melted and lightly browned, about 18 minutes.

4. Transfer to a cutting board and adjust seasoning. Cut into quarters, and serve.

Per serving: 210 calories, 8g total fat, 4.5g saturated fat, 0g trans fat, 25mg cholesterol, 530mg sodium, 25g total carbohydrate, 4g dietary fiber, 1g sugars, 10g protein

Mesclun and Gorgonzola Pitza Ⓕ

Makes 2 servings: 1 whole topped pizza each

Leafy green salad makes a lovely companion to pizza. It can also make a superb topping. Or, try this pitza with other refreshing salad favorites, too. You can sprinkle it lightly with Parmesan instead of Gorgonzola, if you like. A complete and luscious lunch any way you serve or slice it.

2 (7-inch) whole-grain pocketless pitas or flatbreads

1 teaspoon pecan or extra-virgin olive oil

½ cup shredded or finely diced part-skim mozzarella cheese

3 tablespoons crumbled Gorgonzola or other blue cheese

2½ cups Jasmine Green Tea and Pear-Dressed Mesclun (page 155) or Bibb-n-Blue Chopped Salad (page 154)

1. Preheat the oven to 400°F.

2. Place the pitas on a baking sheet. Rub or brush the entire top surface of each pita with the oil. Sprinkle with the cheeses.

3. Bake until the pitas are crisp and brown and cheese is melted and lightly browned, about 18 minutes.

4. Transfer to a cutting board or plates, top each evenly with the salad, cut into quarters, if desired, and serve.

Per serving: 390 calories, 18g total fat, 6g saturated fat, 0g trans fat, 30mg cholesterol, 790mg sodium, 44g total carbohydrate, 7g dietary fiber, 6g sugars, 17g protein

Hummus Pitza Ⓕ

Makes 1 serving: 1 whole topped pitza each

The idea of reinventing hummus as a dreamy pizza topping came to me as a food-loving teenager. Today, I'm pleased to share this crispy crust slathered with a creamy sun-dried tomato-spiked hummus and topped with fresh, crispy cucumber and onion to bring you a taste of the Mediterranean in a pitza.

1 (7-inch) whole-grain pocketless pita or flatbread

½ teaspoon extra-virgin olive oil

6 tablespoons Sun-Dried Tomato Pesto Hummus (page 87) or other hummus

¼ cup thinly sliced Kirby or English cucumber

⅛ cup very thinly sliced or finely chopped red onion

1 tablespoon chopped fresh flat-leaf parsley or basil

1 tablespoon sun-dried tomato bits (optional)

1. Preheat the oven to 400°F.

2. Place the pita on a baking sheet. Rub or brush the entire top surface of the pita with the oil.

3. Bake until the pita is crisp and brown, about 18 minutes, flipping over the pita halfway through the baking process.

4. Transfer to a cutting board, spread with the hummus, and top with the cucumber, onion, parsley, and sun-dried tomatoes (if using). If desired, season with pepper, to taste. Cut into quarters, if desired, and serve.

Per serving: 380 calories, 17g total fat, 2.5g saturated fat, 0g trans fat, 0mg cholesterol, 720mg sodium, 49g total carbohydrate, 7g dietary fiber, 3g sugars, 11g protein

Calzones, Pockets, and Savory Mini Pies

Santorini Chicken Calzone Ⓕ

Makes 8 servings: 1 calzone each

On the Greek island of Santorini, you'll find cuisine highlights including bursting little tomatoes, the freshest of cheeses, grilled kebabs with tzatziki, and a sweet pastry called *melitinia*. These distinctive delights are reinterpreted here as a fresh-baked chicken and spinach savory "pastry." The result: divine!

2 teaspoons extra-virgin olive oil

1 large garlic clove, minced

5 cups packed fresh baby spinach

3 ounces shredded part-skim mozzarella cheese (¾ cup)

⅓ cup crumbled feta cheese

1 large egg, lightly beaten

½ teaspoon grated lemon zest

¼ teaspoon sea salt, or to taste

¼ teaspoon black pepper, or to taste

1 recipe Santorini Chicken Breast Skewers (page 308) or 10 ounces grilled chicken breast, chilled and diced

¾ cup grape tomatoes

1 recipe Whole-Wheat Pizza Dough (page 411) or 1½ pounds other whole-grain pizza dough

3 tablespoons stone-ground whole-wheat flour

1. Preheat the oven to 450°F.

2. Heat the oil in a large nonstick skillet over medium heat. Add the garlic and sauté for 1 minute. Add the spinach and sauté until wilted, about 3 minutes. Transfer to a fine-mesh strainer and firmly press to squeeze out excess liquid.

3. Stir together the mozzarella, feta, egg, lemon zest, salt, and pepper in a medium bowl until combined. Stir in the sautéed spinach, the chicken, and tomatoes.

4. Cut the dough into 8 pieces. Press by hand or roll out using a rolling pin 4 of the dough pieces into about 6-inch rounds on a lightly floured surface using the whole-wheat flour. Place about ⅓ rounded cup of the chicken mixture (draining of any excess liquid) in the center of each dough round. Fold the dough over the chicken mixture to form a semicircle. Do not overstuff. Press the edges together to seal with fork tongs.

5. Bake the 4 calzones on a parchment paper–lined baking sheet until puffed and lightly browned, about 18 minutes. Repeat with the remaining dough and chicken mixture, rolling and filling while the first calzone batch is baking

6. Remove from the oven, let stand for about 10 minutes, and serve warm.

Per serving: 350 calories, 14g total fat, 4g saturated fat, 0g trans fat, 60mg cholesterol, 740mg sodium, 38g total carbohydrate, 5g dietary fiber, 6g sugars, 21g protein

Prosciutto and Fig "Stromboli"

Makes 6 servings: 1 (6-inch) roll each

This "stromboli" is sure to please in every way. Each enticing bite provides sweetness from the fresh figs, savoriness and saltiness from the ham, flakiness from the phyllo, and creaminess from the russet potato and goat cheese. It's a sensational entrée, snack, or party app that will steal the spotlight.

1 baked large russet potato, chilled and diced

1 teaspoon finely chopped fresh rosemary

¼ teaspoon freshly ground black pepper, or to taste

6 whole-wheat or spelt phyllo sheets

1 cup crumbled soft mild goat cheese

4 ounces thinly sliced country ham or prosciutto, chopped

8 medium fresh Black Mission or other figs, stems removed and finely diced

1. Preheat the oven to 400°F.

2. Toss together the potato, rosemary, and pepper in a small bowl. Set aside.

3. Keep the phyllo sheets in a stack with the short end toward you. Coat the top phyllo sheet with cooking spray (preferably homemade, page xix). Fold the top sheet in half lengthwise, forming about a 6×17-inch double-layer sheet. Spray again. In order, sprinkle the entire surface of the 6×17-inch sheet with one-sixth each of the cheese, potato, ham, and figs. Gently pack mixture down, then tightly roll up, forming about a 6-inch log, without folding in the sides. Repeat with the remaining phyllo sheets and filling, spraying each sheet before filling.

4. Transfer, seam side down, to a parchment paper–lined baking sheet. Coat the rolls with cooking spray. Bake until golden brown, about 25 minutes, rotating tray halfway through the baking process. Cool on baking sheet on a rack for at least 10 minutes. Serve warm or at room temperature.

Per serving: 230 calories, 8g total fat, 3.5g saturated fat, 0g trans fat, 25mg cholesterol, 640mg sodium, 31g total carbohydrate, 3g dietary fiber, 12g sugars, 12g protein

Ham and Gruyère "Egg Roll"

Makes 8 servings: 1 (6-inch) roll each

These long slender rolls may resemble egg rolls, but taste nothing like them. When you nibble on these creamy potato, ham, and Gruyère delights wrapped in crispy baked phyllo flakiness, you will be so pleased. The addition of piquant cornichons and sweetly spiced nutmeg is a delightful ending.

1 baked large russet potato, chilled and finely diced

¼ teaspoon freshly ground black pepper, or to taste

¼ teaspoon freshly grated nutmeg

Pinch of sea salt, or to taste

8 whole-wheat or spelt phyllo sheets

6 ounces French bistro or baked Virginia ham, finely chopped

4 ounces Gruyère or other aged Swiss cheese, coarsely grated

¼ cup freshly grated Parmigiano-Reggiano or other Parmesan cheese

10 cornichons, minced

1. Preheat the oven to 400°F.

2. Toss together the potato with the pepper, nutmeg, and salt in a small bowl. Set aside.

3. Keep the phyllo sheets in a stack with the short end toward you. Coat the top phyllo sheet with cooking spray (preferably homemade, page xix). Fold the top sheet in half lengthwise, forming about a 6×17-inch double-layer sheet. Spoon about one-eighth each of the seasoned potato mixture, ham, Gruyère, Parmesan, and cornichons along the end closest to you and tightly roll up like a burrito, without folding in the sides, forming about a 6-inch log. Repeat with remaining phyllo sheets and filling, spraying each sheet before filling.

4. Transfer, seam side down, to a parchment paper–lined baking sheet. Coat with cooking spray. Bake until golden brown, about 25 minutes,

rotating tray halfway through the baking process. Cool on baking sheet on a rack for at least 10 minutes. Serve warm or at room temperature.

Per serving: 220 calories, 7g total fat, 3.5g saturated fat, 0g trans fat, 25mg cholesterol, 470mg sodium, 26g total carbohydrate, 2g dietary fiber, 3g sugars, 11g protein

Caramelized Onion, Chard, and Cheese Pockets

Makes 8 servings: 1 pocket each

These are better for you than frozen, boxed stuffed pockets. Better yet, they taste downright decadent. My favorite part is the savory specks of sun-dried tomato that create hits of bright flavor in every bite. Consider this grab-and-go grub for the gourmet.

2 teaspoons extra-virgin olive oil

2 extra-large sweet onions, thinly sliced

2 teaspoons aged balsamic vinegar or white balsamic vinegar

1 teaspoon sea salt, or to taste

5 ounces red Swiss chard, leaves and stems finely chopped

2 large garlic cloves, minced

1 teaspoon freshly ground black pepper, or to taste

1¼ cups crumbled soft goat cheese

12 sun-dried tomato halves (rehydrated), finely chopped

2 large eggs

3 tablespoons plain almond milk or light soy milk

8 (8-inch) whole-wheat tortillas

1 tablespoon unsalted butter, melted

1. Heat the oil in an extra-large deep skillet or Dutch oven over medium heat. Add the onions, vinegar, and ¼ teaspoon of the salt, cover, and cook until the onions are fully softened, about 20 minutes, stirring occasionally. Remove cover and increase heat to medium-high. Add the chard, garlic, pepper, and the remaining ¾ teaspoon salt and sauté until the onions are lightly caramelized, about 12 minutes. Remove from the heat and stir in the cheese and sun-dried tomatoes until well combined. Set aside.

2. Meanwhile, preheat the oven to 425°F. Whisk together the eggs and almond milk in a small bowl. Brush both sides of each tortilla with the egg mixture, using all the mixture. Alternatively, soak the tortillas in the egg mixture like French toast.

3. Working on a cutting board, place about ½ cup of the onion mixture in the center of each moistened tortilla. Tightly roll up like a burrito, folding in the sides, brushing the pockets with any residual egg mixture.

4. Bake on a parchment paper–lined baking sheet until the tortillas form a crust and are golden brown, about 20 minutes. Brush with the butter, and let stand for at least 5 minutes. Serve warm.

Per serving: 280 calories, 11g total fat, 4g saturated fat, 0g trans fat, 60mg cholesterol, 650mg sodium, 35g total carbohydrate, 4g dietary fiber, 9g sugars, 11g protein

Lemony Spinach Pockets Ⓕ

Makes 8 servings: 1 pocket each

I enjoy a Lebanese savory pie called *fatayer,* but seldom make it because the recipe traditionally requires fresh dough—and some free time. So to please my fatayer passion more quickly, I developed this recipe using tortillas. It's still fully satisfying with all of the flavors of the traditional Middle Eastern spinach pie.

1 medium yellow onion, finely chopped

2 large garlic cloves, minced

Juice and zest of 1 lemon (3 tablespoons juice)

1 teaspoon sea salt, or to taste

1 teaspoon freshly ground black pepper, or to taste

½ teaspoon ground cinnamon

30 ounces fresh spinach leaves and tender stems

2 large eggs

3 tablespoons plain almond milk or light soy milk

8 (8-inch) whole-wheat tortillas

1 tablespoon unsalted butter, melted, or extra-virgin olive oil

1. Add the onion, garlic, lemon juice, salt, pepper, and cinnamon to a Dutch oven over medium heat and stir to combine. Add the spinach, a couple handfuls at a time, until all spinach fits into the Dutch oven. Cover and steam for 5 minutes. Uncover and toss with tongs until all the spinach is wilted. Transfer the wilted spinach and onion to a medium bowl, leaving excess liquids in the Dutch oven. Adjust seasoning.

2. Meanwhile, preheat the oven to 425°F. Whisk together the eggs and almond milk in a small bowl. Brush both sides of each tortilla with the egg mixture, using all the mixture. Alternatively, soak the tortillas in the egg mixture like French toast.

3. Working on a cutting board, place ½ cup of the spinach mixture in the center of each moistened tortilla, again leaving excess liquids in the bowl. Tightly roll up like a burrito, folding in the sides. Arrange on a parchment paper–lined baking pan, seam side down.

4. Bake until the tortillas are golden brown, about 20 minutes. Immediately brush with the butter, sprinkle with the lemon zest, and serve warm.

Per serving: 210 calories, 6g total fat, 1.5g saturated fat, 0g trans fat, 50mg cholesterol, 570mg sodium, 28g total carbohydrate, 5g dietary fiber, 2g sugars, 9g protein

Lamb Fatayer 🄵

Makes 6 servings: 2 fatayer each

Here's a Lebanese doughy treat with meat. These petite savory pies with their memorable cinnamon accent may be better than dessert. If you're a lamb lover, bake a batch of these pastries made with fresh dough, and you'll see what I mean.

8 ounces lean ground lamb

1 small white or red onion, finely chopped

1 large garlic clove, minced

½ teaspoon ground cinnamon

¼ teaspoon + ⅛ teaspoon sea salt, or to taste

¼ teaspoon + ⅛ teaspoon freshly ground
  black pepper, or to taste

Juice of ½ small lemon (1 tablespoon)

1 pound whole-grain bread dough or pizza dough

3 tablespoons stone-ground whole-wheat flour

1. Add the lamb, onion, garlic, cinnamon, salt, and pepper to a large skillet over medium heat. Sauté until the lamb is just cooked through and onion is softened, about 8 to 10 minutes. Stir in the lemon juice. Chill.

2. Cut dough into 12 slices. Place onto a lightly floured surface using the whole-wheat flour.

3. Preheat the oven to 350°F.

4. One at a time, press the dough by hand or roll with a rolling pin into circles about 4½ inches diameter; place a heaping tablespoonful of the lamb mixture into the center of each dough circle; then fold and pinch corners of each dough circle together over the lamb filling to form a triangle. Do not overstuff. Place on a parchment paper–lined baking sheet and lightly coat with cooking spray (preferably homemade, page xix). Repeat with the remaining dough and lamb mixture.

5. Bake until golden brown, about 22 minutes. Remove from oven and let stand for about 10 minutes. Serve warm or at room temperature.

Per serving: 290 calories, 8g total fat, 2g saturated fat, 0g trans fat, 25mg cholesterol, 530mg sodium, 41g total carbohydrate, 7g dietary fiber, 5g sugars, 16g protein

Green Spanakopita Pockets 🄵

Makes 9 servings: 1 pocket each

Are you a fan of feta? Then stock up on these green Greek-style pockets. You can bake, then freeze, and simply reheat these handheld pies in the toaster oven or microwave as you need. They contain all the flavors of spanakopita in a neat entrée-size bundle. Try one with an egg on top for breakfast or any other time, too.

1 medium white onion, finely chopped

2 large garlic cloves, minced

Juice of 1 lemon (3 tablespoons)

1 teaspoon freshly ground black pepper, or to taste

¾ teaspoon sea salt, or to taste

¼ teaspoon dried hot pepper flakes, or to taste

⅛ teaspoon freshly grated nutmeg, or to taste

30 ounces fresh spinach leaves and tender stems

2 large eggs

3 tablespoons plain almond milk or light soy milk

9 (8-inch) whole-grain spinach or whole-wheat
  tortillas

1 rounded cup crumbled feta cheese

3 tablespoons chopped fresh mint or dill

1 tablespoon unsalted butter, melted

1. Add the onion, garlic, lemon juice, black pepper, salt, hot pepper flakes, and nutmeg to a Dutch oven over medium heat and stir to combine. Add the spinach, a couple handfuls at a time, until all spinach fits into the Dutch oven. Cover and steam for 5 minutes. Uncover and toss with tongs until all the spinach is wilted. Transfer the wilted spinach and onion to a medium bowl, leaving excess liquids in the Dutch oven. Adjust seasoning.

2. Meanwhile, preheat the oven to 425°F. Whisk together the eggs and almond milk in a small bowl. Brush both sides of each tortilla with the egg mixture, using all the mixture. Alternatively, soak the tortillas in the egg mixture like French toast.

3. Working on a cutting board, place 2 tablespoons of the feta, 1 teaspoon of the mint, and about ½ cup of the spinach mixture in the center of each moistened tortilla, again leaving excess liquids in the bowl. Tightly roll up like a burrito, folding in the sides. Arrange onto a parchment paper–lined baking pan, seam side down.

4. Bake until the tortillas are golden brown, about 20 minutes. Immediately brush with the butter and serve warm.

Per serving: 250 calories, 10g total fat, 4g saturated fat, 0g trans fat, 60mg cholesterol, 670mg sodium, 28g total carbohydrate, 4g dietary fiber, 3g sugars, 11g protein

Jackie's "Quiche"

Makes 8 servings: 1 hand pie each

If you're looking for a delicious, perfectly portioned bite, this recipe is a wonderfully savory surprise. And it's filled with my secret (until now!) combination of ingredients, including the Greek yogurt and Yukon gold potato for creaminess, trio of herbs for flair, plenty of onion, and a just-right amount of butter for richness. Feel free to vary and rename this dish.

7 large eggs

2 tablespoons fat-free or low-fat plain Greek yogurt

¾ teaspoon sea salt, or to taste

½ teaspoon freshly ground black pepper, or to taste

2 teaspoons extra-virgin olive oil

1 tablespoon + 2 teaspoons unsalted butter

1 medium-large red or white onion, finely chopped

1 medium zucchini, halved lengthwise and thinly sliced crosswise

1 medium Yukon Gold potato, unpeeled, scrubbed, and finely diced

¾ cup shredded provolone cheese

3 tablespoons thinly sliced fresh basil leaves

1 teaspoon finely chopped fresh rosemary

½ teaspoon finely chopped fresh oregano

3 tablespoons plain almond milk or light soy milk

8 (8-inch) whole-wheat tortillas

1. Whisk together 5 of the eggs with the yogurt, ½ teaspoon of the salt, and the pepper in a medium bowl or large liquid measuring cup. Set aside.

2. Heat the oil and 2 teaspoons of the butter in a large nonstick skillet over medium-high heat. Once the butter is melted, add the onion, zucchini, potato, and the remaining ¼ teaspoon salt and sauté until the onion, zucchini, and potato are all lightly caramelized, about 12 minutes.

3. Remove the skillet from the heat and immediately add the reserved egg-yogurt mixture. Scramble until the eggs are still slightly runny, about 30 seconds. (Do not fully cook.) Transfer to a large bowl and stir in the cheese, basil, ½ teaspoon of the rosemary, and the oregano.

4. Meanwhile, preheat the oven to 425°F. Whisk together the remaining 2 eggs and the almond milk in a small bowl. Brush both sides of each tortilla with the egg mixture, using all the mixture. Alternatively, soak the tortillas in the egg mixture like French toast.

5. Working on a cutting board, place about ½ cup of the egg-vegetable mixture in the center of each moistened tortilla. Fold the bottom portion of the tortilla over the filling, then fold the left and right side over the egg filling, then fold over to form a rectangular shape. Arrange onto a parchment paper–lined baking pan, seam side down. Flatten slightly by pressing with your hand or the back of a spatula.

6. Bake until the tortillas are golden brown, about 20 minutes.

7. Meanwhile, melt the remaining 1 tablespoon butter. Immediately brush the pies with the butter, sprinkle with the remaining ½ teaspoon rosemary, and serve warm.

Per serving: 300 calories, 14g total fat, 5g saturated fat, 0g trans fat, 180mg cholesterol, 500mg sodium, 28g total carbohydrate, 3g dietary fiber, 3g sugars, 14g protein

Sides

Vegetable Side Dishes

Warm Grilled Artichokes with Herb Dressing

Baked Artichoke Gratin

Artichoke Heart "Salsa"

Chilled Sesame Asparagus

Citrusy Grilled Asparagus

Salt and Pepper Asparagus

White Asparagus Romesco

Balsamic Roasted Beet Fries

Roasted Rosemary Beets

Beet, Goat Cheese, and Basil Napoleon

Wok Broccoli with Raisins

Broccoli Velvet

Steamed Broccoli with Zest

White Balsamic Broccolini

Cashew Brussels Sprouts

"Stir-fried" Brussels Sprouts

Brussels Sprouts Gruyère Gratin

Roasted Brussels Sprouts and Pearl Onions

Whipped Gingery Carrots

Buttery Baby Carrots

Roasted Dilly Carrots

Whipped Cauliflower

Extra-Virgin Roasted Cauliflower

Herbed Corn on the Cob

Creamed Sweet Corn

Western Peppered Corn

South African Cucumber Sambal

French Onion Haricots Verts

Hot Wok Beans

Mid-East Tomato-Stewed Beans

Leek and Goat Cheese Soufflé

Balsamic Wilted Spinach

Sweet-Spiced Spinach

Garlicky Creamed Spinach

Creamed Spinach with Lemon

Punjabi Spinach with Chickpeas

Garlic Leafy Greens

Strawberries, Chard, and Vidalia Sauté

Rosemary Red Cabbage Sauté

Chanterelle Ragout with Blue Cheese

Smoky Mozzarella Grilled Portabellas

Mushroom-Herb Sauté

Cayenne Onion Rings

Baked Vidalia Onions

Grilled Spicy Red Onion

Minty Petite Peas

Dill-Dressed English Peas

Wok-Seared Snow Peas

Mashed Plantains
with Frizzled Leeks

Marmalade Glazed
Grilled Plantain

Roasted Garlic
Plantain Cubes

Spicy Skinny Fries

Truffled Fries with Herbs

Yukon Steak Fries

Montreal-Inspired Poutine

Spiced Yam Fries

Rosemary Potatoes
and Leeks

Mashed Purple Potatoes

Fluffy Buttermilk Blues

Southern Sweet Smashers

Scalloped Potatoes
with Chives

Sweet Potato Casserole

Celery Root Mash

Thyme Turnip Gratin

Rutabaga Hash Browns

Autumn Parsnip Puree

Crisp Zucchini Stacks

Steam-Fried Zucchini Halves

Garlic Zucchini Coins

Squash on a Stick

Curry Apple Acorn Squash

Asiago Butternut Squash
Bake

Buttercup Squash Parmesan

Tomato-Basil Spaghetti
Squash

Roasted Grape Tomatoes

Moroccan Grilled Tomatoes

Pressure-Cooked Stewed
Tomatoes Oregano

Tri-Color Bell Pepper Sauté

Swiss Chard and Potato
Gratin

Colcannon-Style
Hash Browns

Berkshire Summer Succotash

Pinot Noir Lentils and Kale

Miso-Dressed Vegetables

Couscous and Rice

Confetti Saffron Couscous

Veggie Mélange Couscous

Spanish Goat Cheese
Couscous

Swiss Chard Pesto
Couscous

Coconut-Spiked
Basmati Rice

Saigon Cinnamon Pilaf

Mango Rice Pilaf

Minted Pine Nut Pilaf

Sticky Ginger Rice

Wild Rice Pilaf

Bloody Mary Wild Rice

Creamy Truffled Black Rice

Quinoa, Bulgur, and Other Whole-Grain Sides

Pomegranate and Citrus Quinoa Pilaf

Thai Lemongrass Quinoa Pilaf

"Trail Mix" Quinoa

Sunflower Red Quinoa

Jalapeño Tabbouleh

Sweet Potato Bulgur Pilaf

Thyme Onion Bulgur

Fusion Sesame Spaetzle

Minty Pea Farro

Creamy Amaranth with Chives

Caramelized Vidalia Millet Pilaf

Spaghetti a Cacio e Pepe

Beans

Garlicky White Beans on Roasted Tomato

Southwestern Pinto Beans

Spicy Un-fried Beans

Buttermilk Mashed Beans

Brooklyn Lager Baked Beans

Apple Cider Barbecue Beans

Lemony Dill-Dressed Garbanzos

Dal Masala with Cilantro

Cuban Beans with Lime

Heirloom Italian Bean and Kale Sauté

Polenta

Soft Polenta

Fresh Herbal Polenta

Baked Polenta with Swiss Chard

Goat Cheese Teff Polenta

Stuffings

Sage Whole-Grain Stuffing

Herb and Cranberry Stuffing

Turkey Sausage Stuffing

Breads and Corn Breads

Irish Soda Bread Rolls

Fresh Rosemary Focaccia

Seed-Crusted Whole-Grain Bread

Jalapeño-Jack Corn Bread

Autumn Corn Bread

The term "sides" in a way is a misnomer because vegetables and grains are as important, if not more important, as anything else you can eat.

One of the keys to eating healthfully is to make sure half of your plate is full of nutrient-rich produce, especially veggies. Also important is to select whole instead of refined grains and to incorporate beans and legumes into your meals. This chapter becomes your one-stop solution to help you do all of the above . . . deliciously.

The chapter begins with dozens of vegetable side dishes covering every popular vegetable in the produce aisle. Check out your local supermarket or farmers' market and see what's in season, then browse here to decide which recipes to prepare. By purchasing fresh, in-season produce, you'll make sure the side dish is at its nutritional and flavorful best.

You'll find several recipes where frozen vegetables can be used equally well as they are flash-frozen at their peak, providing plenty of nutrients and taste. Expand your produce repertoire by preparing some of the recipes using more adventuresome picks, like white asparagus, Broccolini, and purple Peruvian potatoes. Be sure to enjoy the more traditional picks prepared in nontraditional ways, like beets that are "roasted" in the microwave (it's so much quicker), Brussels sprouts that are stir-fried, and carrots whipped like mashed potatoes.

For calorie-friendly plates, you can also consider many of these side dishes as entrées. So if you're asked "What's for dinner?" your response might be "Berkshire Summer Succotash" (page 473), "Pinot Noir Lentils and Kale" (page 474), or "Crisp Zucchini Stacks" (page 466). You can pair those dishes with small amounts of protein-rich foods, like chicken, meat, fish, or tofu, to complete them.

This chapter also provides so many scrumptious ways to boost your whole-grain and bean intake, which will likewise boost your dietary fiber; that's important for overall good health and for providing meal satisfaction. According to the Academy of Nutrition and Dietetics, Americans on average get only about half of the fiber they need daily; enjoying recipes here (and throughout the cookbook) will easily help you boost your fiber intake. There are whole-wheat couscous dishes that can be made in a jiffy and rice dishes ranging from brown, to black, to wild. You can add excitement to your plate with whole grains, including quinoa, farro, and amaranth. Most are easier to fix than you might think, especially the quinoa and bulgur recipes, as quinoa cooks in less than 20 minutes and bulgur needs only to be rehydrated.

Nearly all the bean recipes can be prepared using canned beans for ease. I suggest using Eden Organic brand of beans since they provide a full range of no-salt-added varieties and use BPA-free cans. If you prefer, use dried beans that you'll soak and cook in advance for use in the recipes. (See "Preparing Dried Beans" on page 436.) But above all, include beans in your meal plan often. They're a nutrient-rich food that combines protein with fiber, which is especially helpful for that feeling of fullness when you're keeping calories in check.

Rounding out this chapter are polentas, stuffings, rolls, breads, and corn breads, which are prepared with whole grains. If your favorite market doesn't carry some of the whole-grain products suggested, you'll be able to find many of them online at www.bobsredmill.com. For the rolls and bread, be patient when adding the whole-grain flour so you don't wind up incorporating too much into the dough—especially since it provides a heartier texture. Then remember to keep portions reasonable using the serving sizes suggested, so you can enjoy them while maintaining a healthy weight.

Many of these recipes complement each other. Pair Creamy Truffled Black Rice (page 480) with Salt and Pepper Asparagus (page 439) or enjoy Moroccan Grilled Tomatoes (page 470) or Confetti Saffron Couscous (page 475) alongside Dal Masala with Cilantro (page 490), for instance. They'll create mouthwatering and fully satisfying vegetarian entrées. Think outside the norm and enjoy nearly any of these recipes simply as is for a sensationally satisfying snack. And, of course, pair any side dish here with an entrée of choice for a nutrient boost, overall meal balance, and extra appeal on you plate.

Calorie range in this chapter: 15 to 270 calories.

Low-calorie pick: South African Cucumber Sambal, 15 calories (page 448).

PREPARING DRIED BEANS

To replace dried beans for canned, determine how much dried beans is the quantity equivalent of their canned counterparts. One (15-ounce) can of drained beans is about 1⅔ cups cooked beans; 1 pound of dried beans (about 2 cups) makes about 5½ cups cooked beans. Then, determine which preparation method you'd like to use.

Try this no-salt-added way to prepare 1 pound dried beans:

Bring 10 cups water and the beans to a full boil for a couple minutes. Remove from heat, cover, and let stand for about 4 hours. Drain the soaking water. Then place the drained beans into a large stockpot, add hot water (about 6 cups) to cover the beans by about 1 inch. Though not necessary, this is where you can add seasonings of choice. Gently boil with lid slightly ajar until desired tenderness, about 1 hour 15 minutes. Now they're ready to use in recipes.

Vegetable Side Dishes

Warm Grilled Artichokes with Herb Dressing 🅕

Makes 4 servings: 4 pieces each

Artichokes are beautiful and satisfying when grilled, then slathered with a fresh herb vinaigrette. They're worth the little extra effort for their fiber and refreshing flavor.

Juice of 2 large lemons (½ cup)
4 large fresh artichokes
1 teaspoon sea salt, or to taste
3 tablespoons extra-virgin olive oil
2 tablespoons finely chopped fresh mint
2 tablespoons finely chopped fresh tarragon
2 tablespoons finely chopped fresh basil
1 large garlic clove, minced
½ teaspoon freshly ground black pepper, or to taste

1. Fill a large bowl with cold water and add 3 tablespoons of the lemon juice to make acidulated water.

2. Trim the stems of an artichoke, leaving about 1 inch. Snap off the outer 2 rows of leaves. Cut off the top third of the artichoke. Quarter the artichoke lengthwise. Cut out the choke and small prickly leaves using a paring knife. Place the artichoke into the acidulated water. Repeat with the remaining artichokes.

3. Bring a large saucepan of water to a boil. Add ½ teaspoon of the salt. Drain the artichokes, add to the water, and boil until crisp-tender, about 10 to 12 minutes. Drain well.

4. Prepare an outdoor or indoor grill.

5. Whisk together the oil, the remaining lemon juice, the mint, tarragon, basil, garlic, remaining ½ teaspoon salt, and the pepper in a medium bowl. Remove 3 tablespoons of the dressing to a small bowl and set aside. Add the artichokes to the dressing in the medium bowl and toss to fully coat. Grill over direct medium-high heat until lightly charred and tender, about 7 minutes, rotating as needed. Adjust seasoning.

6. Transfer the artichokes to a platter. Drizzle with the reserved dressing, and serve while warm.

Per serving: 250 calories, 11g total fat, 1.5g saturated fat, 0g trans fat, 0mg cholesterol, 730mg sodium, 36g total carbohydrate, 15g dietary fiber, 1g sugars, 11g protein

Baked Artichoke Gratin

Makes 8 servings: ⅛ of gratin (about ½ cup) each

Here's a madeover version of a cheesy artichoke dish with all of the comfort and great taste, yet without all of the calories. Oat flour and almond milk work wonders in place of heavy cream. Who knew a creamy gratin could be good for you?

2 (9-ounce) packages frozen artichoke hearts
1 teaspoon sea salt, or to taste
1 large egg
⅓ cup freshly grated Parmigiano-Reggiano or other Parmesan cheese
3 tablespoons unsalted butter
1 large shallot, minced
1 large garlic clove, minced
3 tablespoons whole oat or soy flour
1 cup plain almond milk or light soy milk
2 teaspoons Dijon mustard
¼ teaspoon freshly ground black pepper, or to taste
2 tablespoons whole-wheat panko breadcrumbs
⅛ teaspoon ground cayenne, or to taste

1. Cook the artichokes according to package directions. Drain and reserve 2 tablespoons of the cooking liquid.

2. Preheat the oven to 450°F.

3. Arrange the artichokes in a single layer in a 2-quart baking dish. Sprinkle with ¼ teaspoon of the salt. Set aside.

continues on next page

4. Lightly beat the egg in a medium bowl with a fork. Stir in half of the cheese until combined. Set aside.

5. Melt the butter in a small saucepan over medium heat. Add the shallot and garlic and cook while stirring for 1 minute. Stir in the flour and cook while stirring until bubbly, about 1½ minutes. Gradually whisk in the reserved cooking liquid, the almond milk, and mustard and continue to cook while whisking until a slightly thickened, creamy sauce forms, about 4 minutes. Add the black pepper and the remaining ¾ teaspoon salt and remove from heat.

6. Gradually whisk the creamy sauce mixture into the egg mixture until well combined. Pour the sauce evenly over the artichokes. Sprinkle with the panko and remaining cheese. Dust with the cayenne.

7. Bake the gratin until a golden brown crust forms on top, about 20 minutes.

8. Let stand for 5 minutes to complete the cooking process, and serve.

Per serving: 120 calories, 7g total fat, 3.5g saturated fat, 0g trans fat, 40mg cholesterol, 440mg sodium, 10g total carbohydrate, 4g dietary fiber, 2g sugars, 4g protein

Artichoke Heart "Salsa"

Makes 3 servings: ½ cup each

This quick, versatile, delightfully tangy side dish is part salsa and part salad and also makes a great topper for pasta, like Artichoke Heart Spaghettini Toss (page 289).

2 teaspoons extra-virgin olive oil

1½ teaspoons fresh lemon juice

¼ cup minced fresh chives

1 garlic clove, minced

¼ teaspoon sea salt, or to taste

¼ teaspoon freshly ground black pepper, or to taste

1 (9-ounce) package frozen artichoke hearts, slightly thawed and diced

2 tablespoons pine nuts, toasted

1. Whisk together the oil and lemon in a medium bowl. Stir in the chives, garlic, salt, and pepper. Set aside.

2. Cook the artichokes according to package directions. Drain well of excess liquid (if any).

3. Add the cooked artichokes to the mixture in the medium bowl and toss to coat. Adjust seasoning.

4. Add the pine nuts and serve while warm.

Per serving: 110 calories, 8g total fat, 0.5g saturated fat, 0g trans fat, 0mg cholesterol, 250mg sodium, 9g total carbohydrate, 5g dietary fiber, 0g sugars, 3g protein

Chilled Sesame Asparagus

Makes 4 servings: 6 spears each

Sesame and asparagus make wonderful flavor companions—especially when bathed together in Asian flavors. One simple tablespoon of toasted sesame oil goes a long way flavor-wise.

¼ teaspoon sea salt

24 medium asparagus spears, ends trimmed

1 tablespoon toasted sesame oil

1 tablespoon brown rice vinegar

2 teaspoons naturally brewed soy sauce

1 teaspoon honey or agave nectar

1½ teaspoons sesame seeds, toasted

1. Add 1 cup water to a large skillet and bring to a boil over high heat. Add the salt. Reduce heat to medium, add the asparagus, cover, and steam until crisp-tender, about 5 to 6 minutes. Plunge the asparagus into a bowl of ice water to stop the cooking process; drain well. Place the asparagus on a serving dish, cover, and chill in the refrigerator.

2. When ready to serve, whisk together the oil, vinegar, soy sauce, and honey. Uncover the asparagus. Sprinkle with the dressing and sesame seeds, and serve.

Per serving: 70 calories, 4g total fat, 0.5g saturated fat, 0g trans fat, 0mg cholesterol, 230mg sodium, 6g total carbohydrate, 2g dietary fiber, 4g sugars, 3g protein

Citrusy Grilled Asparagus

Makes 4 servings: 6 spears each

Here, grilled asparagus is paired with lemon and orange zest for a refreshing citrus twist. The nutmeg gives it a hint of sweet spiciness.

24 medium asparagus spears, ends trimmed

1 tablespoon extra-virgin olive oil

¾ teaspoon grated lemon zest, or to taste

¼ teaspoon sea salt, or to taste

¼ teaspoon freshly ground black pepper, or to taste

⅛ teaspoon freshly grated nutmeg

¾ teaspoon grated orange zest, or to taste

1. Preheat an outdoor or indoor grill, or a grill pan.

2. Place the asparagus in a 9×13-inch dish. Drizzle with the oil and sprinkle with the lemon zest, salt, pepper, and nutmeg, and toss with tongs to coat.

3. Place the asparagus spears directly on the grill and grill over direct medium-high heat until crisp-tender and grill marks form, about 4½ to 5 minutes total, turning the spears as needed. Adjust seasoning.

4. Transfer the asparagus to a platter, sprinkle with the orange zest, and serve immediately.

Per serving: 50 calories, 3.5g total fat, 0.5g saturated fat, 0g trans fat, 0mg cholesterol, 160mg sodium, 4g total carbohydrate, 2g dietary fiber, 1g sugars, 2g protein

Salt and Pepper Asparagus

Makes 4 servings: 6 spears each

When asparagus is abundant and seasonal, this simple roasted preparation lets its full glory shine. Experiment with various sea salts—or fleur de sel—to add elegance along with its simple wonderment.

24 medium asparagus spears, ends trimmed

1½ tablespoons extra-virgin olive oil

¼ teaspoon sea salt, or to taste

¼ teaspoon freshly ground black pepper, or to taste

1. Preheat the oven to 475°F.

2. Place the spears in a single layer on a baking sheet, drizzle with the oil, sprinkle with the salt and pepper, and toss with tongs to coat.

3. Roast the asparagus until crisp-tender or desired doneness, about 10 to 12 minutes, shaking the pan to rotate the asparagus halfway through the cooking time. Adjust seasoning.

4. Transfer the asparagus to a platter or individual plates, and serve. If desired, serve with lemon wedges.

Per serving: 70 calories, 5g total fat, 1g saturated fat, 0g trans fat, 0mg cholesterol, 160mg sodium, 4g total carbohydrate, 2g dietary fiber, 1g sugars, 2g protein

White Asparagus Romesco

Makes 4 servings: 6 spears each

White asparagus grow underground, which keeps them white. Their spears are chubbier and silkier than the green variety. When grilled and sauced with a tasty Romesco-style dip, they are unforgettable. But green asparagus are tasty here, too.

24 medium white asparagus spears, ends trimmed

1 tablespoon extra-virgin olive oil

¼ teaspoon sea salt, or to taste

¼ teaspoon freshly ground black pepper, or to taste

½ cup Romesco-Style Dip (page 94)

½ teaspoon grated lemon zest

1. Preheat an outdoor or indoor grill, or a grill pan.

2. Place the asparagus in a 9×13-inch dish or pan. Drizzle with the oil, sprinkle with the salt and pepper, and gently toss with tongs to coat.

3. Place the asparagus spears directly on the grill and grill over direct medium-high heat until crisp-tender and grill marks form, about 4½ to 5 minutes total, turning the spears as needed. Adjust seasoning.

4. Transfer the asparagus to a platter, top with the dip, sprinkle with the lemon zest, and serve immediately.

Per serving: 100 calories, 8g total fat, 1g saturated fat, 0g trans fat, 0mg cholesterol, 260mg sodium, 7g total carbohydrate, 3g dietary fiber, 3g sugars, 4g protein

Balsamic Roasted Beet Fries

Makes 4 servings: about 14 fries each

These look like fries, but have a garnet gem-like vividness. This is one way to get kids (and some adults!) to eat their beets. But when roasted, the somewhat misunderstood root vegetable is moist, slightly sweet, and marvelous. Serve these vivid sticks anywhere you normally might have the crispy potato version . . . without ketchup. Try them with a drizzle of balsamic vinegar.

2 medium beets

1 tablespoon extra-virgin olive oil

1½ teaspoons aged balsamic vinegar
    or white balsamic vinegar

¼ teaspoon sea salt, or to taste

1. Preheat the oven to 400°F.

2. Trim the greens from the beets, if still attached.

3. Wrap the beets in aluminum foil. Place in the oven and roast until cooked through and a knife can be inserted into the center of the beet, about 1 hour 30 minutes. Unwrap and let cool slightly, about 20 minutes.

4. Preheat the oven to 475°F.

5. Peel the beets and cut into thick fries, about 28 fries per beet. Place in a medium bowl, add the oil, vinegar, and salt, and gently toss to coat. Place the beet fries in a single layer on a parchment paper–lined large baking sheet. Roast the fries until well caramelized on their edges, about 25 minutes, flipping fries over halfway through roasting. Adjust seasoning.

6. Transfer the fries to a platter or individual bowls, and serve immediately.

Per serving: 80 calories, 3.5g total fat, 0.5g saturated fat, 0g trans fat, 0mg cholesterol, 230mg sodium, 11g total carbohydrate, 2g dietary fiber, 9g sugars, 2g protein

Quick Rosemary Beets

Makes 4 servings: ⅔ cup each

Roasting beets is ideal when you have the time. But cooking them in the microwave takes just minutes. Dressing them with flavor-enhancing vinaigrette, like in this recipe, will make them succulent.

2 large beets

1 tablespoon extra-virgin olive oil

2 teaspoons aged balsamic vinegar

½ teaspoon + ⅛ teaspoon sea salt, or to taste

½ teaspoon finely chopped fresh rosemary

1. Trim the greens from the beets, if still attached.

2. Place the beets in a large microwave-safe dish or bowl and cover with parchment paper. Microwave on high for 10 minutes, or until beets can be easily pierced with a paring knife, checking for doneness a couple times throughout the cooking process. (Do not overcook.) Let cool for about 20 minutes.

3. Peel the beets and cut into ½-inch dice. Place back into the microwave-safe dish or bowl, add the oil, vinegar, salt, and rosemary, and toss to coat. Cover again with parchment paper. Cook for 1 minute on high, or until steaming hot. Adjust seasoning.

4. Serve immediately as a side dish or enjoy chilled in a salad.

Per serving: 90 calories, 4g total fat, 0.5g saturated fat, 0g trans fat, 0mg cholesterol, 470mg sodium, 14g total carbohydrate, 3g dietary fiber, 11g sugars, 2g protein

Beet, Goat Cheese, and Basil Napoleon

Makes 4 servings: 1 Napoleon each

This stunning Napoleon multitasks as a side or starter. Whipping couscous with goat cheese makes the cheese layers of this roasted beet dish extra luscious and satisfying.

2 medium beets

1 cup cooked whole-wheat couscous, chilled

3½ ounces soft goat cheese, at room temperature

3 tablespoons finely chopped fresh basil
+ 4 small fresh basil sprigs

1½ tablespoons aged balsamic vinegar
or white balsamic vinegar

2 teaspoons extra-virgin olive oil

½ teaspoon sea salt, or to taste

¼ teaspoon freshly ground black pepper

1. Preheat the oven to 400°F.

2. Trim the greens from the beets, if still attached.

3. Wrap the beets in aluminum foil. Place in the oven and roast until cooked through and a knife can be inserted into the center of the beet, about 1 hour 30 minutes. Unwrap and let cool slightly, about 20 minutes.

4. Meanwhile add the couscous, goat cheese, chopped basil, 1 tablespoon of the vinegar, the oil, salt, and pepper to a medium bowl. Stir well using the back of a spoon into a smooth mixture. Form the mixture into 8 flattened disks about the same size as the beet slices, about 2 measuring tablespoons each. Set aside.

5. Peel the beets and cut into 6 round slices each. Let sit to further cool to room temperature, if necessary.

6. On 4 of the beet slices, place 1 goat cheese disk. Top each with another beet slice and remaining goat cheese disks. Top with remaining beet slices, drizzle with the remaining ½ tablespoon vinegar, and adjust seasoning.

7. Top each with a basil sprig, and serve as a side dish or appetizer at room temperature.

Per serving: 180 calories, 8g total fat, 4g saturated fat, 0g trans fat, 10mg cholesterol, 470mg sodium, 22g total carbohydrate, 4g dietary fiber, 10g sugars, 8g protein

Wok Broccoli with Raisins Ⓕ

Makes 3 servings: 1 rounded cup each

Using a wok helps to caramelize broccoli florets, making them more flavorful than if plainly steamed. They're extra delightful fragrantly spiced with ginger and sprinkled with sweet raisins and sunflower seeds.

½ cup unsweetened green tea or water

6 cups bite-size broccoli florets

1 tablespoon grapeseed oil

2 teaspoons freshly grated gingerroot

¼ teaspoon sea salt, or to taste

3 tablespoons black seedless raisins

1½ tablespoons lightly salted dry-roasted
sunflower seeds

1. Heat the tea in a wok or extra-large skillet over medium heat. Add the broccoli and cook while stirring until the tea has evaporated, about 6 minutes.

2. Increase heat to high, add the oil, ginger, and salt and stir-fry the broccoli until nearly crisp-tender, about 2 minutes. Add the raisins and sauté until the broccoli is crisp-tender and beginning to brown, about 1 minute.

3. Transfer the broccoli to a serving platter, sprinkle with the sunflower seeds, and serve.

Per serving: 140 calories, 7g total fat, 0.5g saturated fat, 0g trans fat, 0mg cholesterol, 250mg sodium, 17g total carbohydrate, 5g dietary fiber, 6g sugars, 5g protein

Broccoli Velvet

Makes 7 servings: ½ cup each

Potatoes aren't the only vegetable that can be served mashed. Here, flavorfully sautéed broccoli is blended into a refined, velvety puree. It's a brilliant accompaniment to roasted chicken and steamed brown rice.

2 teaspoons extra-virgin olive oil

1½ pounds broccoli florets and tender stems, finely chopped

2 large shallots, finely chopped

1 large garlic clove, minced

Juice of ½ small lemon (1 tablespoon)

¾ teaspoon sea salt, or to taste

¼ teaspoon freshly ground black pepper, or to taste

⅛ teaspoon ground cayenne

1 cup low-sodium vegetable broth or Vegetable Stock (page 203)

1 tablespoon tahini (sesame seed paste)

1. Heat the oil in an extra-large skillet over medium heat. Add the broccoli and shallots and sauté until the shallots are softened, about 5 minutes. Stir in the garlic, lemon juice, salt, black pepper, and cayenne and sauté for 1 minute.

2. Increase heat to medium-high, add the broth, cover, and cook until the broccoli is fully softened and liquid is nearly evaporated, about 10 minutes, stirring twice during cooking.

3. Transfer the mixture to a food processor along with the tahini. Cover and puree, scraping down sides of container as needed. Adjust seasoning.

4. Transfer the broccoli puree to a serving bowl or individual bowls, and serve while warm.

Per serving: 70 calories, 3g total fat, 0g saturated fat, 0g trans fat, 0mg cholesterol, 310mg sodium, 10g total carbohydrate, 3g dietary fiber, 2g sugars, 3g protein

Steamed Broccoli with Zest Ⓕ

Makes 2 servings: 1½ cups each

Is it possible to have a bodacious bite of broccoli? Just a fresh sprinkle of lemon zest and a pinch of nutmeg take simple steamed broccoli from plain to amazing.

10 ounces large bite-size broccoli florets

1½ teaspoons extra-virgin olive oil

½ teaspoon grated lemon zest

¼ teaspoon sea salt, or to taste

⅛ teaspoon freshly ground black pepper, or to taste

Pinch of freshly grated nutmeg

1. Steam the broccoli in a steamer rack placed over boiling water, covered, until crisp-tender, about 4 minutes.

2. Transfer the broccoli to a bowl, toss with the oil, lemon zest, salt, pepper, and nutmeg, and serve.

Per serving: 80 calories, 4g total fat, 0.5g saturated fat, 0g trans fat, 0mg cholesterol, 350mg sodium, 10g total carbohydrate, 5g dietary fiber, 2g sugars, 3g protein

White Balsamic Broccolini

Makes 2 servings: ½ of recipe each

For a pleasantly perky and peppery change of pace from traditional broccoli, bite into this crisp-tender Broccolini dish. The sweet and tangy dressing with a perfect hint of heat takes the slender green vegetable with its mini bud-like florets to extra-pleasurable flavor heights.

1 tablespoon white balsamic or champagne vinegar

1 tablespoon apricot 100% fruit jam

¼ teaspoon sea salt, or to taste

¼ teaspoon freshly ground black pepper, or to taste

⅛ teaspoon dried hot pepper flakes

2 teaspoons grapeseed oil or canola oil

12 ounces Broccolini, bottom 1 inch of stems trimmed

1 large shallot, minced

1 large garlic clove, minced

1. Whisk together the vinegar, jam, salt, black pepper, and hot pepper flakes in a small bowl or liquid measuring cup. Set aside.

2. Heat the oil in large skillet over high heat. Add the Broccolini and shallot and toss with tongs until the Broccolini is heated through and bright green, about 2 minutes. Add ¼ cup water and the garlic, and toss until the Broccolini is crisp-tender and shallot is caramelized, about 4 to 5 minutes. Remove from heat and immediately add the vinegar mixture, tossing until the Broccolini is coated, about 30 seconds. Adjust seasoning.

3. Transfer the Broccolini to a platter, and serve.

Per serving: 120 calories, 5g total fat, 0.5g saturated fat, 0g trans fat, 0mg cholesterol, 350mg sodium, 16g total carbohydrate, 4g dietary fiber, 7g sugars, 5g protein

Cashew Brussels Sprouts

Makes 4 servings: 1 cup each

This caramelized confetti-like preparation of Brussels sprouts along with cashews will captivate your taste buds. And if you're not so passionate about this cruciferous veggie, it will convert you.

¾ cup low-sodium vegetable broth
    or Vegetable Broth (page 203)
1½ teaspoons apple cider vinegar
1 pound Brussels sprouts, trimmed, halved,
    and cut lengthwise into ¼-inch-thick slices
2 large shallots, sliced
1 tablespoon grapeseed or canola oil
½ teaspoon sea salt, or to taste
¼ teaspoon freshly ground black pepper, or to taste
¼ cup unsalted dry-roasted cashews,
    coarsely chopped

1. Bring the broth and vinegar to a boil in a large nonstick skillet over medium-high heat. Add the Brussels sprouts and shallots. Cook while stirring until the shallots are softened and no liquid remains, about 6 minutes. Add the oil, salt, and pepper and sauté until the sprouts are crisp-tender

and lightly caramelized, about 4 to 5 minutes. Adjust seasoning.

2. Transfer to a serving bowl or individual plates, sprinkle with the cashews, and serve.

Per serving: 140 calories, 8g total fat, 1g saturated fat, 0g trans fat, 0mg cholesterol, 350mg sodium, 16g total carbohydrate, 4g dietary fiber, 4g sugars, 5g protein

"Stir-fried" Brussels Sprouts **F**

Makes 3 servings: 1 cup each

Brussels sprouts have a strong and exciting flavor, if cooked well. Here they're stir-fried with garlic, spices, and a splash of balsamic vinegar to bring out the best of their earthy taste.

1¼ cups low-sodium vegetable broth
    or Vegetable Stock (page 203)
1½ teaspoons aged balsamic vinegar
1 pound Brussels sprouts, trimmed and halved
2 teaspoons extra-virgin olive oil
2 large garlic cloves, thinly sliced
½ teaspoon finely chopped fresh marjoram
    or oregano (optional)
¼ teaspoon sea salt, or as needed
¼ teaspoon freshly ground black pepper,
    or as needed

1. Bring the broth and vinegar to a boil in a wok or large skillet over high heat. Add the Brussels sprouts and stir-fry until the liquid has reduced to a thick syrup and Brussels sprouts are nearly crisp-tender, about 8 minutes.

2. Reduce heat to medium, add the oil, garlic, marjoram (if using), salt, and pepper, and stir-fry until the spouts are crisp-tender, about 1 minute. Adjust seasoning.

3. Transfer to a serving bowl or individual plates, and serve.

Per serving: 90 calories, 4g total fat, 0.5g saturated fat, 0g trans fat, 0mg cholesterol, 290mg sodium, 13g total carbohydrate, 5g dietary fiber, 4g sugars, 4g protein

Brussels Sprouts Gruyère Gratin

Makes 8 servings: ¾ cup each

Brussels sprouts create a scrumptious, swanky gratin combining the distinctive flavors of the veggie with a nutty, creamy gratin sauce. Its rich tastes are highlighted by the extra-crisp topping thanks to panko breadcrumbs.

1½ tablespoons unsalted butter

2 large garlic cloves, minced

1½ tablespoons whole oat or soybean flour

2 cups plain almond milk or unsweetened
    sunflower beverage, at room temperature

1 teaspoon sea salt, or to taste

½ teaspoon freshly ground black pepper

¼ teaspoon freshly grated nutmeg

¼ teaspoon ground cayenne

1½ pounds Brussels sprouts, trimmed and quartered

1 cup shredded Gruyère or other aged Swiss cheese

3 tablespoons whole-wheat panko breadcrumbs

2 tablespoons freshly grated Parmigiano-Reggiano
    or other Parmesan cheese

1. Preheat the oven to 400°F.

2. Melt the butter in a small saucepan over medium heat. Add the garlic and sauté for 1 minute. Stir in the flour and cook while stirring constantly for 1 minute. Gradually whisk in the almond milk and continue to cook while whisking until steaming hot and just slightly thickened, about 8 minutes. Add the salt, black pepper, nutmeg, and cayenne.

3. Evenly arrange the Brussels sprouts in a 2-quart baking dish. Pour the sauce over the sprouts and evenly sprinkle with the Gruyère, panko, and Parmesan.

4. Bake until deep golden brown and bubbling and sprouts are tender, about 50 minutes.

5. Let stand for at least 8 minutes to complete the cooking process and allow liquids to settle, and serve.

Per serving: 140 calories, 8g total fat, 4.5g saturated fat, 0g trans fat, 20mg cholesterol, 410mg sodium, 10g total carbohydrate, 3g dietary fiber, 3g sugars, 7g protein

Roasted Brussels Sprouts and Pearl Onions

Makes 4 servings: 1 cup each

Tossed with pearl onions when roasting, this aromatic Brussels sprouts dish provides a double dose of caramelized allure. To ensure even roasting, just cut the largest Brussels sprouts in half lengthwise in advance.

1 pound Brussels sprouts, trimmed

12 ounces pearl onions, blanched and peeled

2½ tablespoons aged balsamic vinegar

1½ tablespoons extra-virgin olive oil

¾ teaspoon sea salt, or to taste

½ teaspoon freshly ground black pepper,
    or to taste

1. Preheat the oven to 425°F.

2. Mix together the Brussels sprouts, onions, vinegar, oil, salt, and pepper in a large bowl.

3. Transfer the vegetable mixture to a 9×13-inch baking pan and roast until the onions and sprouts are crisp and well caramelized outside and tender inside, about 35 minutes, shaking the pan a few times during roasting for even cooking. Remove from oven and let stand for 5 minutes to complete the cooking process.

4. Adjust seasoning, and serve.

Per serving: 150 calories, 6g total fat, 1g saturated fat, 0g trans fat, 0mg cholesterol, 480mg sodium, 23g total carbohydrate, 3g dietary fiber, 7g sugars, 4g protein

Whipped Gingery Carrots Ⓕ

Makes 6 servings: 1 cup each

Carrots are nutrient rich and can go from being a plain side to giving any dish rich color, flavor, and texture. The addition of cashews creates nutty intrigue; potatoes add extra creaminess. Prepared here into a zingy gingery puree, this comforting carrot side goes well with whole grains or roasted poultry.

2 teaspoons unsalted butter

1¼ pounds carrots, sliced, or 1 pound fresh baby carrots

2 large celery stalks, chopped

1 large sweet onion, sliced

2 tablespoons freshly grated gingerroot

¼ cup unsalted dry-roasted cashews

2 teaspoons apple cider vinegar

¾ teaspoon sea salt, or to taste

12 ounces Yukon Gold potatoes, unpeeled, scrubbed, and sliced

2 cups low-sodium vegetable broth or Vegetable Stock (page 203)

1 cup plain almond milk and unsweetened coconut milk beverage

¼ teaspoon freshly ground black or white pepper, or to taste

⅛ teaspoon ground cayenne, or to taste

3 tablespoons chopped fresh chives

1. Melt the butter in a Dutch oven or stockpot over medium heat. Add the carrots, celery, onion, ginger, cashews, vinegar, and ¼ teaspoon of the salt. Cover and sweat, stirring occasionally, until the onion is softened, about 10 minutes.

2. Add the potatoes, broth, almond milk, black pepper, cayenne, and the remaining ½ teaspoon salt and bring to a boil over high heat.

3. Reduce heat to medium-low, cover, and simmer until the potatoes and carrots are very tender, about 45 minutes.

4. Remove from heat. Blend until smooth using an immersion blender. (Or blend in batches in a blender or food processor, using the hot-fill line as a guide. Return to pot.)

5. Reduce heat to low, partially cover, and simmer until desired thickened consistency, about 15 minutes. Adjust seasoning.

6. Transfer the whipped carrots to a serving bowl, sprinkle with the chives, and serve.

Per serving: 150 calories, 4.5g total fat, 1.5g saturated fat, 0g trans fat, 5mg cholesterol, 450mg sodium, 25g total carbohydrate, 5g dietary fiber, 10g sugars, 3g protein

Buttery Baby Carrots

Makes 4 servings: ¾ cup each

The trick to using butter in this dish is to use just enough to make it luscious. Serve these lean and delicious babies with roasted chicken or grilled fish.

1 pound baby carrots

¼ cup low-sodium vegetable broth or Vegetable Stock (page 203)

2 teaspoons unsalted butter

1½ teaspoons turbinado sugar

½ teaspoon sea salt, or to taste

1. Add the carrots and broth to a large skillet over high heat. Once the broth sizzles, reduce heat to medium, cover, and steam the carrots until nearly crisp-tender, about 8 minutes. Remove cover.

2. Increase heat to high. Add the butter, sugar, and salt and sauté until the carrots are crisp-tender, about 3 minutes. Adjust seasoning, and serve.

Per serving: 60 calories, 2g total fat, 1g saturated fat, 0g trans fat, 5mg cholesterol, 390mg sodium, 11g total carbohydrate, 3g dietary fiber, 7g sugars, 1g protein

Roasted Dilly Carrots

Makes 4 servings: ¾ cup each

In my opinion, the best culinary accessory for carrots is fresh dill. The second best may be butter. Include both and these oven-roasted carrots become brilliant.

1 pound baby carrots

¼ cup low-sodium vegetable broth
    or Vegetable Stock (page 203)

2 teaspoons extra-virgin olive oil

½ teaspoon sea salt, or to taste

¼ teaspoon freshly ground white or black pepper,
    or to taste

1½ teaspoons unsalted butter, melted

1½ teaspoons finely chopped fresh dill

1 teaspoon aged red wine vinegar

1. Preheat the oven to 450°F.

2. Add the carrots, broth, oil, salt, and pepper to a 2-quart baking dish or shallow baking pan. Toss to coat and arrange the carrots in a single layer.

3. Roast in the oven until crisp-tender, about 30 minutes, stirring halfway through the cooking process.

4. Meanwhile stir together the butter, dill, and vinegar in a small bowl. Set aside.

5. Add the butter mixture to the carrots and toss to coat. Adjust seasoning.

6. Garnish with additional fresh dill, if desired, and serve.

Per serving: 70 calories, 4g total fat, 1.5g saturated fat, 0g trans fat, 5mg cholesterol, 390mg sodium, 10g total carbohydrate, 3g dietary fiber, 6g sugars, 1g protein

Whipped Cauliflower

Makes 4 servings: ¾ cup each

This whipped veggie dish looks like mashed potatoes. You can serve it exactly as you might the potatoes, too. But it's indeed made with cauliflower, providing a unique taste and fewer calories.

1 medium head cauliflower, cut into small florets
    (about 8 cups)

⅓ cup plain almond milk or light soy milk

1 tablespoon extra-virgin olive oil

1½ teaspoons unsalted butter or extra-virgin olive oil

1 large garlic clove, minced

½ teaspoon sea salt, or to taste

¼ teaspoon freshly ground black pepper, or to taste

2 tablespoons minced fresh chives

1. Bring a large saucepan of water to a boil over high heat. Add the cauliflower and boil until very tender, about 12 minutes. Drain the cauliflower and reserve ¼ cup of the cooking liquid.

2. Meanwhile, add the almond milk, oil, butter, garlic, salt, and pepper to a small saucepan and keep hot over medium-low heat.

3. Add the cooked cauliflower to a food processor. Add the almond milk mixture, cover, and puree. Add some of the reserved cooking liquid, if necessary, for desired consistency. Adjust seasoning.

4. Transfer to a serving bowl, sprinkle with the chives, and serve hot.

Per serving: 80 calories, 4.5g total fat, 1.5g saturated fat, 0g trans fat, 5mg cholesterol, 330mg sodium, 9g total carbohydrate, 4g dietary fiber, 4g sugars, 4g protein

Extra-Virgin Roasted Cauliflower

Makes 4 servings: 1 cup each

Just the simple process of roasting can turn a straightforward vegetable into a spectacular one. A little drizzle of extra-virgin olive oil and a sprinkle of sea salt, and it becomes a flavor spectacle. This roasted cauliflower is a true caramelized wonder. Show it off as a side—or in Roasted Cauliflower Pizza (page 424).

1 medium head cauliflower, cut into 1½-inch florets
    (about 8 cups)

1½ tablespoons extra-virgin olive oil

¼ teaspoon sea salt, or to taste

1. Preheat the oven to 450°F.

2. Add the cauliflower, oil, and salt to a large bowl and toss to coat.

3. Arrange the cauliflower in a single layer on a large baking sheet. Roast, stirring occasionally, until tender and caramelized, about 35 minutes. Adjust seasoning and serve.

Per serving: 90 calories, 6g total fat, 1g saturated fat, 0g trans fat, 0mg cholesterol, 170mg sodium, 8g total carbohydrate, 4g dietary fiber, 4g sugars, 4g protein

Herbed Corn on the Cob

Makes 4 servings: 1 cob each

Sometimes it's nice to glam up simple corn on the cob. Here a buttery spread with sweet and savory highlights from onion, balsamic vinegar, and fresh herbs provides lip-smacking satisfaction.

1½ tablespoons unsalted butter, at room temperature

¼ cup minced sweet onion

1 teaspoon white balsamic vinegar

¾ teaspoon sea salt, or to taste

¼ teaspoon freshly ground black pepper, or to taste

2 teaspoons minced fresh cilantro

¾ teaspoon minced fresh thyme or oregano

4 medium ears fresh corn, husks removed

1. Melt the butter in a large nonstick skillet over medium heat. Add the onion, vinegar, ¼ teaspoon of the salt, and the pepper and sauté until the onion is lightly caramelized, about 7 to 8 minutes. Stir in the cilantro and thyme. Transfer to a ramekin or small bowl and place in the refrigerator to cool and solidify.

2. Place a Dutch oven filled about halfway with water over high heat. Bring to a boil and add the remaining ½ teaspoon salt. Add the corn, cover, and cook until tender, about 5 minutes. Drain the corn.

3. Serve the corn while hot with the onion-herb mixture on the side.

Per serving: 130 calories, 6g total fat, 3g saturated fat, 0g trans fat, 10mg cholesterol, 450mg sodium, 20g total carbohydrate, 2g dietary fiber, 7g sugars, 4g protein

Creamed Sweet Corn

Makes 4 servings: about ½ cup each

There's no need for heavy cream or added sugar to enjoy a side dish of succulently creamy corn. Here, fat-free evaporated milk provides both creaminess and natural sweetness. Turmeric adds earthy appeal while making the corn seem extra-enticing from its rich golden accent.

2 teaspoons unsalted butter

1 large shallot, minced

1 tablespoon whole oat or soybean flour

¾ cup fat-free evaporated milk

1 (10-ounce) package frozen sweet yellow corn kernels, thawed

½ teaspoon sea salt, or to taste

¼ teaspoon freshly ground black or white pepper, or to taste

⅛ teaspoon ground turmeric, or to taste

2 tablespoons minced fresh chives

1. Melt the butter in a large skillet over medium heat. Add the shallot and sauté until softened, about 3 minutes. Stir in the flour and cook while stirring constantly for 1 minute. Gradually whisk in the milk and continue to cook while whisking until a slightly thickened mixture forms, about 2½ minutes. Add the corn, salt, pepper, and turmeric. Continue to cook while stirring until the corn is cooked through, about 5 minutes.

2. Remove from the heat, stir in half of the chives, and adjust seasoning.

3. Transfer to a serving bowl, sprinkle with the remaining chives, and serve while hot.

Per serving: 130 calories, 2.5g total fat, 1.5g saturated fat, 0g trans fat, 5mg cholesterol, 350mg sodium, 23g total carbohydrate, 2g dietary fiber, 8g sugars, 6g protein

Western Peppered Corn

Makes 4 servings: ¾ cup each

The sweet corn and bell pepper, sea salt, and jalapeño combine to provide sweet, salty, and spicy excitement. The medley of colorful and enticing ingredients will surely satisfy all of your senses.

2 teaspoons unsalted butter

1 small white or yellow onion, finely diced

1 medium red bell pepper, finely diced

1 small jalapeño pepper with some seeds, minced

1½ teaspoons apple cider vinegar

¼ teaspoon sea salt, or to taste

1 (10-ounce) package frozen sweet yellow corn kernels, thawed

2 tablespoons chopped fresh cilantro or flat-leaf parsley

1. Melt the butter in a large nonstick skillet over medium heat. Add the onion, bell pepper, jalapeño, vinegar, and salt and sauté until the onion is fully softened, about 8 minutes. Add the corn and sauté until the corn and bell pepper are tender, about 5 minutes.

2. Stir in the cilantro. Adjust seasoning.

3. Transfer the corn mixture to a bowl, and serve.

Per serving: 110 calories, 3g total fat, 1g saturated fat, 0g trans fat, 5mg cholesterol, 150mg sodium, 20g total carbohydrate, 3g dietary fiber, 5g sugars, 3g protein

South African Cucumber Sambal

Makes 5 servings: ¼ cup each

This South African–inspired sambal is basically a cucumber relish with a hint of "heat." It's versatile and thoroughly enjoyable, even refreshing, as a fresh chutney-like side dish, as a sandwich topper, or mixed into rice.

1 large English cucumber, unpeeled

½ teaspoon sea salt, or to taste

1 tablespoon apple cider vinegar

1 small garlic clove, minced

½ small jalapeño pepper with seeds, minced

1. Grate the cucumber on the large holes of a box grater into a large bowl. Sprinkle with the salt and let stand for 2 hours. Drain in a colander, pressing out the liquid.

2. Transfer the strained cucumber to a medium bowl. Add the vinegar, garlic, and jalapeño and stir well to combine. Cover and chill for at least 1 hour, and serve.

Per serving: 15 calories, 0g total fat, 0g saturated fat, 0g trans fat, 0mg cholesterol, 120mg sodium, 4g total carbohydrate, 0g dietary fiber, 1g sugars, 1g protein

French Onion Haricots Verts

Makes 6 servings: 1 ramekin each

Here's a light recipe to accompany any holiday meal—without giving up tradition. This green bean casserole-style dish served in individual ramekins offers an alternative to richer dishes like stuffing or mashed potatoes with gravy.

20 ounces frozen cut haricots verts or green beans

1½ tablespoons plain almond milk or light soy milk

1½ tablespoons whole oat or almond flour

2 cups Caramelized Red, White, and Yellow Onion Soup (page 211) or other French onion–style soup, at room temperature

1 teaspoon naturally brewed soy sauce

¼ teaspoon sea salt, or to taste

¼ teaspoon freshly ground black pepper

¼ cup sliced natural almonds, finely chopped

3 tablespoons whole-wheat panko breadcrumbs

6 tablespoons grated Asiago or dry Jack cheese (optional)

1. Preheat the oven to 425°F.

2. Divide the green beans among 6 ramekins or other small baking dishes (at least 1 cup capacity each).

3. Whisk together the almond milk and flour in a medium bowl or 4-cup liquid measuring cup. Stir in the soup, soy sauce, salt, and pepper until well combined.

4. Divide the soup mixture evenly atop the green beans. Evenly sprinkle with the almonds, panko, and cheese (if using). Place the dishes on a large baking sheet and bake until fully cooked and golden brown on top, about 30 minutes.

5. Let stand for at least 5 minutes. Adjust seasoning, and serve.

Per serving: 90 calories, 3g total fat, 0g saturated fat, 0g trans fat, 0mg cholesterol, 320mg sodium, 13g total carbohydrate, 4g dietary fiber, 4g sugars, 3g protein

Hot Wok Green Beans

Makes 4 servings: 1 cup each

A stir-fried veggie side dish is delish and easy to fix. The results here are crisp-tender green beans with extra-sesame Asian flavors.

1½ tablespoons naturally brewed soy sauce

1½ tablespoons toasted sesame oil

1 tablespoon honey or agave nectar

1 tablespoon brown rice vinegar

1 large garlic clove, minced

1 teaspoon freshly grated gingerroot

¼ teaspoon dried hot pepper flakes

1 pound green beans, trimmed

⅔ cup low-sodium vegetable broth
or Vegetable Stock (page 203)

1 small shallot, minced

2 teaspoons sesame seeds, toasted

1. Whisk together the soy sauce, oil, honey, vinegar, garlic, ginger, and hot pepper flakes in a liquid measuring cup or small bowl. Set aside.

2. Add the green beans, broth, and shallot to a wok or large skillet and set over high heat. Cook while tossing with tongs until the green beans are nearly crisp-tender and broth is fully reduced, about 7 to 8 minutes.

3. Add the soy sauce mixture and stir-fry until the beans are crisp-tender and the sauce reduces to lightly coat the beans, about 2 minutes.

4. Transfer the beans and any sauce remaining in the wok to a platter or large bowl. Sprinkle with the sesame seeds, and serve immediately.

Per serving: 130 calories, 6g total fat, 1g saturated fat, 0g trans fat, 0mg cholesterol, 370mg sodium, 16g total carbohydrate, 4g dietary fiber, 7g sugars, 3g protein

Mid-East Tomato-Stewed Beans Ⓕ

Makes 6 servings: 1 cup each

This aromatic, brothy Lebanese green bean and tomato dish, called *loubia b'zeit,* is one of those dishes that's as good on day one as it is on day two or three. The cinnamon and allspice add authenticity and make this side unforgettable.

1 tablespoon extra-virgin olive oil

1 large yellow onion, finely chopped

2 teaspoons aged red wine vinegar

¾ teaspoon sea salt, or to taste

1 large garlic clove, minced

1½ cups low-sodium vegetable broth
or Vegetable Stock (page 203)

1½ pounds green beans, trimmed

5 plum tomatoes, pulp removed and chopped

1 teaspoon honey or agave nectar

½ teaspoon ground cinnamon, or to taste

¼ teaspoon ground allspice, or to taste

1. Heat the oil in a Dutch oven or extra-large saucepan over medium heat. Add the onion, vinegar, and ¼ teaspoon of the salt and sauté until softened, about 8 minutes. Add the garlic and sauté for 1 minute.

2. Stir in the broth, beans, tomatoes, honey, cinnamon, allspice, and the remaining ½ teaspoon salt, cover, and simmer over medium-low heat until the beans are fully softened, about 45 minutes, stirring occasionally. Adjust seasoning.

3. Serve in bowls as a side dish.

Per serving: 90 calories, 3g total fat, 0g saturated fat, 0g trans fat, 0mg cholesterol, 330mg sodium, 15g total carbohydrate, 5g dietary fiber, 5g sugars, 3g protein

Leek and Goat Cheese Soufflé

Makes 6 servings: 1 soufflé each

You'll love this light, airy, and creamy soufflé. The blend of flavors—from Asiago, goat cheese, leeks, and thyme—creates a side dish worth slowly savoring.

2 teaspoons unsalted butter, at room temperature

⅓ cup freshly grated Asiago or Parmesan cheese

2 teaspoons extra-virgin olive oil

2 medium leeks, white and light green parts only, well rinsed and finely chopped

1 tablespoon chopped fresh thyme

1 large garlic clove, minced

¾ cup plain almond milk or light soy milk

2 teaspoons arrowroot powder

¾ teaspoon sea salt, or to taste

¼ teaspoon freshly ground white or black pepper, or to taste

⅛ teaspoon ground cayenne

⅛ teaspoon freshly grated nutmeg (optional)

3 ounces soft goat cheese

4 large egg whites

⅛ teaspoon cream of tartar

1. Very lightly rub 6 small (6-ounce) ramekins with 1 teaspoon of the butter, then sprinkle with 2 tablespoons of the Asiago cheese.

2. Melt the remaining 1 teaspoon butter with the oil in a large nonstick skillet over medium heat. Add the leeks and 2 teaspoons of the thyme and sauté until the leeks are softened, about 10 minutes. Add the garlic and sauté for 1 minute.

3. Preheat the oven to 475°F.

4. Add the leeks to a blender or food processor along with the almond milk, arrowroot, salt, white pepper, cayenne, and nutmeg (if using). Cover and blend until smooth. Pour into a small saucepan over medium heat. Simmer the leek mixture while stirring until thickened, about 4 minutes. Remove from heat and stir in the goat cheese and the remaining Asiago. Set aside to cool.

5. Place the egg whites in a mixing bowl with the cream of tartar and beat to form nearly stiff peaks. Whisk one-third of the egg whites into the leek mixture. Fold in remaining whites. Evenly fill the ramekins. Wipe around the inside lips of the dishes to form a cap. Sprinkle with the remaining 1 teaspoon thyme.

6. Place the filled ramekins in a large roasting pan. Add boiling water to the pan to reach about one-third of the way up the sides of the ramekins. Bake on the middle rack until the soufflés are puffed and golden brown, about 10 minutes.

7. Sprinkle with additional freshly grated nutmeg, if desired, and serve immediately.

Per serving: 120 calories, 8g total fat, 4g saturated fat, 0g trans fat, 15mg cholesterol, 470mg sodium, 7g total carbohydrate, 1g dietary fiber, 2g sugars, 7g protein

Balsamic Wilted Spinach

Makes 4 servings: ½ cup each

Steamed spinach is without doubt one of those side dish-friendly foods. It's delicious served on its own or as a bed for Roasted Buffalo Meatloaves (page 328) or Grilled Calamari over Balsamic Spinach (page 356).

2 teaspoons extra-virgin olive oil

2 large garlic cloves, minced

1 pound fresh baby spinach

1 tablespoon aged balsamic vinegar

½ teaspoon sea salt, or to taste

¼ teaspoon freshly ground black pepper, or to taste

1. Heat the oil in a large, deep skillet or Dutch oven over medium heat. Add the garlic and sauté until sizzling well, but not brown, about 1½ minutes.

2. Add the spinach to the skillet a couple handfuls at a time and toss with tongs until wilted, about 5½ to 6 minutes.

3. Sprinkle with the vinegar, salt, and pepper and continue to toss for 30 seconds. Adjust seasoning.

4. Transfer the spinach with tongs to a serving bowl or platter, leaving excess liquids in the skillet. Serve immediately with additional balsamic vinegar on the side, if desired.

Per serving: 70 calories, 2.5g total fat, 0g saturated fat, 0g trans fat, 0mg cholesterol, 470mg sodium, 13g total carbohydrate, 5g dietary fiber, 1g sugars, 3g protein

Sweet-Spiced Spinach

Makes 4 servings: ½ cup each

Want to play "dress up" with greens? The spinach here is simply sautéed, then accessorized with tart cherries, lemon zest, cinnamon, hot pepper flakes, and toasted pine nuts. Tasty!

2 teaspoons extra-virgin olive oil
1 large garlic clove, very thinly sliced
3 (5-ounce) packages fresh baby spinach
Juice and zest of 1 small lemon (2 tablespoons juice)
2 tablespoon dried tart cherries, finely chopped
½ teaspoon sea salt, or to taste
⅛ teaspoon freshly ground black pepper, or to taste
⅛ teaspoon ground cinnamon, or to taste
⅛ teaspoon dried hot pepper flakes, or to taste
1½ tablespoons pine nuts, toasted

1. Heat the oil in a large, deep skillet or Dutch oven over medium heat. Add the garlic and sauté until lightly caramelized, about 2 minutes. Transfer the garlic to a small plate and set aside.

2. Add the spinach a couple handfuls at a time to the skillet and toss with tongs until wilted, about 5½ to 6 minutes.

3. Add the lemon juice, dried cherries, salt, black pepper, cinnamon, and hot pepper flakes and continue to toss for 30 seconds. Adjust seasoning.

4. Transfer the spinach with tongs to a serving bowl or platter, leaving excess liquids in the skillet. Top with the sautéed garlic slices, the pine nuts, and desired amount of lemon zest. Enjoy immediately.

Per serving: 100 calories, 4.5g total fat, 0g saturated fat, 0g trans fat, 0mg cholesterol, 460mg sodium, 16g total carbohydrate, 6g dietary fiber, 3g sugars, 3g protein

Garlicky Creamed Spinach

Makes 4 servings: ¾ cup each

Comfort food can be calorie friendly. This creamy, sweetly spiced spinach side doesn't have cream, but you'd swear there was. Instead, it uses evaporated milk and oat flour to make a velvety, comforting sauce. The garlicky kiss completes it.

½ cup fat-free evaporated milk
1 tablespoon whole oat or soybean flour
¾ teaspoon sea salt, or to taste
½ teaspoon freshly ground black pepper, or to taste
¼ teaspoon freshly grated nutmeg
⅛ teaspoon ground cinnamon
⅛ teaspoon dried hot pepper flakes, or to taste
1 tablespoon + 1 teaspoon unsalted butter
2 large shallots, finely chopped
2 large garlic cloves, minced
20 ounces fresh spinach

1. Whisk together the milk, flour, salt, black pepper, nutmeg, cinnamon, and hot pepper flakes in a liquid measuring cup or small bowl. Set aside.

2. Melt the butter in a Dutch oven or large deep skillet over medium heat. Add the shallots and sauté until softened, about 5 minutes. Add the garlic and sauté for 1 minute.

3. Add the spinach a couple handfuls at a time and cook while tossing with tongs until all of the spinach is fully wilted, about 8 minutes.

4. Add the milk mixture and cook while tossing with tongs until the mixture is well incorporated with the spinach and thickened, about 2 minutes. Adjust seasoning. Serve immediately.

Per serving: 110 calories, 4.5g total fat, 2.5g saturated fat, 0g trans fat, 10mg cholesterol, 580mg sodium, 13g total carbohydrate, 4g dietary fiber, 4g sugars, 7g protein

Creamed Spinach with Lemon

Makes 2 servings: 1 cup each

There's no need to snip off any stems. This recipe uses the entire spinach leaf, stem and all. The lemon zest and creamy dairy goodness help balance the spinach stems' slight bitterness.

2 garlic cloves, very thinly sliced crosswise

10 ounces fresh spinach

2 teaspoons unsalted butter

2 teaspoons whole-grain oat or soybean flour

½ cup fat-free evaporated milk

¼ teaspoon sea salt, or to taste

⅛ teaspoon freshly ground black pepper, or to taste

⅛ teaspoon freshly grated nutmeg, or to taste

½ teaspoon grated lemon zest

1. Sprinkle the garlic into a large microwave-safe dish. Mound the spinach into the dish. Microwave on high until the spinach is gently wilted, about 1 minute 45 seconds. Set aside.

2. Melt the butter in a large saucepan over medium heat. Stir in the flour and cook while stirring for 1 minute. Stir in the milk, salt, pepper, and nutmeg and simmer, stirring constantly, until the mixture is thickened, about 3 minutes. With tongs, add the spinach and garlic to the sauce and toss until the spinach is well coated and steaming hot, about 45 seconds. Adjust seasoning.

3. Sprinkle with the lemon zest and serve.

Per serving: 130 calories, 5g total fat, 2.5g saturated fat, 0g trans fat, 15mg cholesterol, 480mg sodium, 15g total carbohydrate, 3g dietary fiber, 8g sugars, 9g protein

Punjabi Spinach with Chickpeas Ⓕ

Makes 6 servings: about 1 cup each

The alluring flavors of this hearty and healthful spinach dish are from the earthy Indian spices. And the chickpeas give it staying power thanks to their protein and fiber. Go beyond the side dish and enjoy this in Punjabi Spinach and Chickpea Wrap (page 402) or Punjabi Spinach Omelet (page 23), too.

2 teaspoons unrefined peanut or canola oil

2 large yellow onions, chopped

Juice of 1 small lemon (2 tablespoons)

½ teaspoon sea salt, or to taste

6 large garlic cloves, minced

1 tablespoon freshly grated gingerroot

1 serrano pepper with some seeds, minced

1 teaspoon ground turmeric

¾ teaspoon ground cumin

½ teaspoon ground coriander

1 (14.5-ounce) can diced tomatoes (with liquid)

1 (15-ounce) can chickpeas (garbanzo beans), drained

¼ teaspoon freshly ground black pepper, or to taste

20 ounces fresh baby spinach

⅓ cup fat-free or low-fat plain Greek yogurt (optional)

1. Heat the oil in a large stockpot over medium heat. Add the onions, 1 tablespoon of the lemon juice, and ¼ teaspoon of the salt and cook while stirring occasionally until lightly caramelized, about 30 minutes. Add the garlic, ginger, serrano, turmeric, cumin, and coriander and sauté for 1 minute.

2. Increase heat to medium-high. Add the tomatoes with liquid, chickpeas, black pepper, and the remaining ¼ teaspoon salt and add the spinach in batches. Simmer while stirring occasionally until the excess liquid has evaporated, about 15 minutes. Stir in the remaining 1 tablespoon lemon juice. Adjust seasoning.

3. Top with the yogurt (if using), and serve.

Per serving: 160 calories, 3g total fat, 0g saturated fat, 0g trans fat, 0mg cholesterol, 580mg sodium, 30g total carbohydrate, 9g dietary fiber, 6g sugars, 7g protein

Garlic Leafy Greens

Makes 3 servings: ¾ cup each

These dark leafy greens are satisfying "soul food" and are an easy way to round out any meal. If you ever have leftovers, they're scrumptious stuffed into omelets.

½ teaspoon sea salt, or to taste
1 pound collard greens or beet greens, stems and thick ribs removed, leaves cut into 1-inch strips
1 tablespoon extra-virgin olive oil
2 large garlic cloves, very thinly sliced crosswise
½ teaspoon freshly ground black pepper, or to taste
⅛ teaspoons dried hot pepper flakes, or to taste
1 small lemon, cut into 4 wedges

1. Bring a Dutch oven or large saucepan of water to a boil. Add ¼ teaspoon of the salt. Add the greens in two batches and cook until nearly tender (about 10 minutes for collard greens or 2 minutes for beet greens). Transfer the greens using tongs to a large bowl of ice water to stop the cooking process, about 30 seconds. Drain the greens through a strainer, pressing to remove excess liquid. Set aside.

2. Heat the oil in a large skillet over medium heat. Add the garlic and sauté until sizzling, yet not brown, about 1½ minutes. Add the cooked greens, the remaining ¼ teaspoon salt, the black pepper, and hot pepper flakes and sauté until the greens are tender, about 4 to 5 minutes. Adjust seasoning.

3. Serve immediately with the lemon wedges on the side.

Per serving: 90 calories, 5g total fat, 0.5g saturated fat, 0g trans fat, 0mg cholesterol, 310 mg sodium, 9g total carbohydrate, 4g dietary fiber, 1g sugars, 3g protein

Strawberries, Chard, and Vidalia Sauté

Makes 6 servings: 1 cup each

The balsamic-infused berries temper the bitterness of chard for a perfectly balanced bite that'll thrill your palate. It's a lovely spring side dish.

1 tablespoon + 1 teaspoon extra-virgin olive oil
1 large Vidalia or other sweet onion, finely chopped
1 tablespoon + 1 teaspoon aged balsamic vinegar
¾ teaspoon sea salt, or to taste
½ teaspoon freshly ground black pepper, or to taste
⅛ teaspoon ground cayenne
1½ pounds rainbow or red Swiss chard, leaves and stems cut into ½-inch strips
½ cup diced fresh strawberries

1. Heat the oil in a Dutch oven over medium heat. Add the onion, 1 teaspoon of the vinegar, the salt, black pepper, and cayenne and sauté until the onion is fully softened, about 10 minutes.

2. Add the chard stems and sauté until the onion is beginning to caramelize and stems are nearly al dente, about 10 minutes.

3. Stir in the chard leaves, cover, and cook until the leaves are fully wilted, stirring once, about 6 minutes.

4. Add the strawberries and the remaining 1 tablespoon vinegar and sauté until the vinegar is well distributed and strawberries are heated through, about 30 seconds. Adjust seasoning.

5. Serve immediately.

Per serving: 70 calories, 3.5g total fat, 0g saturated fat, 0g trans fat, 0mg cholesterol, 480mg sodium, 10g total carbohydrate, 3g dietary fiber, 5g sugars, 3g protein

Rosemary Red Cabbage Sauté Ⓕ

Makes 5 servings: 1 cup each

The red onion in this recipe caramelizes to provide sweetness, a perfect partner for the savory cabbage. The generous splash of cider vinegar and pinch of rosemary complete the bright, lively seasonings in this dish.

1 tablespoon extra-virgin olive oil

1 medium red onion, halved and very thinly sliced

4 teaspoons apple cider vinegar

¾ teaspoon sea salt, or to taste

½ head red cabbage, cored and thinly sliced

1 teaspoon unsalted butter or extra-virgin olive oil

½ teaspoon finely chopped fresh rosemary
   or ¼ teaspoon crushed dried rosemary

¼ teaspoon freshly ground black pepper, or to taste

⅛ teaspoon ground cayenne (optional)

1. Heat the oil in a nonstick Dutch oven over medium heat. Add the onion, 2 teaspoons of the vinegar, and ¼ teaspoon of the salt and sauté until softened, about 5 minutes. Add the cabbage, increase heat to medium-high, and sauté until the cabbage is crisp-tender, about 8 minutes. Stir in the remaining 2 teaspoons vinegar, the butter, rosemary, black pepper, cayenne (if using), and the remaining ½ teaspoon salt and sauté until just wilted, about 2 minutes. Adjust seasoning.

2. Serve the cabbage immediately.

Per serving: 90 calories, 4g total fat, 1g saturated fat, 0g trans fat, 0mg cholesterol, 390mg sodium, 15g total carbohydrate, 5g dietary fiber, 5g sugars, 3g protein

Chanterelle Ragout with Blue Cheese Ⓕ

Makes 4 servings: ½ rounded cup each

There's nothing quite like the nutty, gently peppery flavor and slightly sweet, delicately earthy aroma of fresh chanterelles, as in this dish. If you can't find chanterelles, use any fresh in-season mushroom. And don't forget the blue cheese; its tanginess provides a memorable flavor counterbalance.

¼ cup low-sodium vegetable broth
   or Vegetable Stock (page 203)

1 tablespoon unsalted butter

1 pound fresh chanterelle or mixed stemmed
   exotic mushrooms, cut into ⅓-inch slices

3 large garlic cloves, minced

¼ cup chopped fresh flat-leaf parsley

1 teaspoon finely chopped fresh rosemary

¾ teaspoon sea salt

½ teaspoon freshly ground black pepper, or to taste

1 tablespoon aged red wine vinegar

2 tablespoons finely crumbled blue cheese

1. Bring the broth and butter to a boil in a large skillet over high heat. Add the mushrooms and sauté until softened, about 4 minutes. Add the garlic, parsley, rosemary, salt, and pepper and sauté until the garlic is fragrant, about 1 minute. Add the vinegar and sauté until the vinegar is well distributed, about 30 seconds. Adjust seasoning.

2. Transfer to a serving dish, sprinkle with the cheese, and serve. If desired, garnish with additional fresh parsley or rosemary.

Per serving: 90 calories, 4.5g total fat, 2.5g saturated fat, 0g trans fat, 10mg cholesterol, 520mg sodium, 9g total carbohydrate, 5g dietary fiber, 2g sugars, 3g protein

Smoky Mozzarella Grilled Portobellas

Makes 4 servings: 1 mushroom cap each

Mushrooms are nutritional standouts, especially due to their vitamin D. With their deep flavor and a hearty meat texture, these portobellas are delicious when grilled and topped with smoky cheese! The delights are culinary standouts as is or in Smoky Portobella and Cheese Burger (page 396).

4 large portobella mushroom caps, stems removed
    and dark gills scraped out
1 tablespoon + 1 teaspoon extra-virgin olive oil
1 large garlic clove, minced
1 teaspoon minced fresh thyme
¼ teaspoon sea salt, or to taste
¼ teaspoon freshly ground black pepper, or to taste
4 (¾-ounce) thin slices smoked mozzarella,
    provolone, or Gouda cheese
3 tablespoons finely chopped fresh flat-leaf parsley

1. Place the mushroom caps on a large dish and dab both sides of the caps with the oil using a silicone pastry brush. Sprinkle the gill side with the garlic, thyme, salt, and pepper. Let stand, gill side up, for 30 to 45 minutes.

2. Prepare an outdoor or indoor grill.

3. Grill the mushroom caps, gill side down, over direct medium-high heat until lightly charred, about 5 minutes. Gently flip over, and grill for 2 minutes. Top with the cheese, and grill until mushrooms are tender and cheese is melted, about 2 to 3 minutes.

4. Adjust seasoning, sprinkle with the parsley, and serve.

Per serving: 140 calories, 11g total fat, 4.5g saturated fat, 0g trans fat, 15mg cholesterol, 300mg sodium, 5g total carbohydrate, 1g dietary fiber, 2g sugars, 7g protein

Mushroom-Herb Sauté

Makes 3 servings: ½ cup each

The wild mushrooms in this recipe cook briefly to maintain their intoxicating aroma and taste. The splendid freshness from the mélange of herbs is the key—so do use all four of the herbs, if you can, or use an equivalent mix of your favorite herbs.

2 teaspoons extra-virgin olive oil
1 large shallot, chopped
2 tablespoons low-sodium vegetable broth
    or Vegetable Stock (page 203)
1 teaspoon unsalted butter or extra-virgin olive oil
10 ounces sliced stemmed fresh mixed wild
    mushrooms, such as maitake, oyster,
    and beech
¼ teaspoon + ⅛ teaspoon sea salt, or to taste
¼ teaspoon freshly ground black pepper
1 large garlic clove, minced
3 tablespoons chopped fresh flat-leaf parsley
1 tablespoon chopped fresh basil
1 tablespoon chopped fresh chives
2 teaspoons chopped fresh mint

1. Heat the oil in a large skillet over medium heat. Add the shallot and sauté until it is softened and begins to caramelize, about 5 minutes. Stir in the broth and butter and cook until the butter is melted, about 30 seconds. Add the mushrooms, salt, and pepper and sauté until all of the mushrooms are cooked through and just tender, about 6 minutes. Add the garlic and sauté until fragrant, about 1 minute. Remove from heat.

2. Stir in the parsley, basil, chives, and mint. Adjust seasoning, and serve immediately.

Per serving: 80 calories, 4.5g total fat, 1.5g saturated fat, 0g trans fat, 5mg cholesterol, 300mg sodium, 10g total carbohydrate, 3g dietary fiber, 3g sugars, 2g protein

Cayenne Onion Rings

Makes 4 servings: 5 large onion rings each

These well-crisped and golden brown rings, featuring a flavor kick from cayenne, have a luscious, slightly sweet juiciness from the onion on the inside. The distinctive contrast will make these onions rings memorable.

½ cup whole-wheat pastry flour

1 cup plain almond milk or light soy milk

1 large egg

1 large garlic clove, minced

¾ teaspoon salt

½ teaspoon freshly ground black pepper

1 cup plain dry whole-wheat breadcrumbs

½ teaspoon ground cayenne

1 large sweet onion, peeled, cut into ½-inch rings and separated

1. Add the flour to a shallow bowl and set aside. Whisk together the almond milk, egg, garlic, ½ teaspoon of the salt, and the black pepper in another shallow bowl and set aside. Stir together the breadcrumbs and cayenne in another shallow bowl and set aside.

2. Preheat the oven to 475°F.

3. Using only the 20 largest onion rings, dip each to fully coat in the flour, then almond milk mixture, then the breadcrumb mixture, gently shaking off excess between each mixture so that the breadcrumb mixture remains as dry as possible.

4. Arrange the coated onion rings on two large baking sheets. Spray the rings with cooking spray (preferably homemade, page xix) and bake both trays of onion rings until the coating is fully crisped and golden brown, about 20 minutes.

5. Sprinkle with the remaining ¼ teaspoon salt, and serve in stacks.

Per serving: 160 calories, 5g total fat, 0g saturated fat, 0g trans fat, 25mg cholesterol, 320mg sodium, 26g total carbohydrate, 2g dietary fiber, 4g sugars, 3g protein

Baked Vidalia Onions

Makes 2 servings: 1 onion each

This showstopping sweet onion and rosemary side dish will be a highlight at any meal. It's an ideal pairing with roasted chicken.

2 large Vidalia or other sweet onions

1 tablespoon aged balsamic vinegar

½ teaspoon finely chopped fresh rosemary or thyme

¼ teaspoon sea salt, or to taste

¼ teaspoon freshly ground black pepper, or to taste

1. Preheat the oven to 400°F.

2. Cut out the core of the onions in a cone-like fashion. Score the tops of each onion three times, halfway down, creating 6 partial wedges while the onion remains whole. Place each onion on a sheet of aluminum foil. Into the center of each onion place the vinegar, rosemary, salt, and pepper. Completely wrap the onions in the foil.

3. Roast until fully softened, about 1 hour. Remove from the oven, and let stand for 5 minutes.

4. Carefully open, and serve in the foil with the edges peeled down.

Per serving: 110 calories, 0g total fat, 0g saturated fat, 0g trans fat, 0mg cholesterol, 320mg sodium, 27g total carbohydrate, 3g dietary fiber, 18g sugars, 3g protein

Grilled Spicy Red Onions

Makes 4 servings: 2 rounds each

Grilling onions brings out all of their sweet and savory highlights. These thick red onion rounds with Louisiana flair and enticing grill marks are a full-flavored and healthful alternative to fried onion rings.

2 large red onions

1½ tablespoons peanut or canola oil

¾ teaspoon Creole seasoning, or to taste (page 31)

½ teaspoon sea salt, or to taste

½ teaspoon freshly ground black pepper, or to taste

1. Prepare an outdoor or indoor grill.

2. Cut each onion into 6 slices crosswise, then peel. You'll use the 4 center slices from each onion for grilling; use the end slices for another purpose. Do not separate the onion rounds into rings.

3. Lightly brush or rub both sides of the rounds with the oil and sprinkle with the Creole seasoning, salt, and pepper.

4. Grill the onion rounds over direct medium-high heat until deep grill marks form and the onions are crisp-tender, about 4 to 5 minutes per side.

5. Adjust seasoning, and serve.

Per serving: 80 calories, 5g total fat, 1g saturated fat, 0g trans fat, 0mg cholesterol, 390mg sodium, 7g total carbohydrate, 1g dietary fiber, 3g sugars, 1g protein

Minty Petite Peas

Makes 6 servings: ½ cup each

Lively green peas, scallions, and mint unite for one good-looking, great-tasting, and very green dish.

2 teaspoons extra-virgin olive oil

2 scallions, green and white parts, thinly sliced

1 pound frozen petite peas, thawed

1 tablespoon finely chopped fresh mint

½ teaspoon finely chopped fresh rosemary (optional)

¼ teaspoon sea salt, or to taste

1. Heat the oil in a large nonstick skillet over medium heat. Add the white parts of the scallions and sauté until fully softened, about 3 minutes. Stir in the peas, green parts of the scallions, the mint, and rosemary (if using), cover, and cook until the peas are steaming hot and tender, about 3 minutes, shaking the skillet a few times during cooking.

2. Sprinkle with the salt. Adjust seasoning. Garnish with small sprigs of fresh mint, if desired, and serve.

Per serving: 70 calories, 2g total fat, 0g saturated fat, 0g trans fat, 0mg cholesterol, 150mg sodium, 10g total carbohydrate, 4g dietary fiber, 3g sugars, 4g protein

Dill-Dressed English Peas

Makes 3 servings: ½ cup each

Vivid green peas with snappy crispness are paired with fresh dill and lemon. It's a simple, fresh taste of spring.

1½ teaspoons extra-virgin olive oil

1 large shallot, minced

8 ounces fresh English green peas

2 teaspoons chopped fresh dill

1 teaspoon fresh lemon juice

⅛ teaspoon sea salt, or to taste

1. Heat the oil in a large nonstick skillet over medium heat. Add the shallot and sauté until lightly caramelized, about 5 minutes. Stir in the peas and dill, cover, and cook until the peas are just cooked through, about 3½ to 4 minutes, shaking the skillet a few times during cooking.

2. Sprinkle with the lemon juice and salt. Adjust seasoning and serve.

Per serving: 90 calories, 2.5g total fat, 0g saturated fat, 0g trans fat, 0mg cholesterol, 100mg sodium, 13g total carbohydrate, 4g dietary fiber, 5g sugars, 4g protein

Wok-Seared Snow Peas

Makes 2 servings: 1 cup each

This Asian-style preparation, with a touch of soy sauce and sesame oil, makes the crispy snow peas most interesting. Cooking them first in broth means you don't need excess oil for proper prep.

3 tablespoons low-sodium vegetable broth
   or Vegetable Stock (page 203)

1½ teaspoon naturally brewed soy sauce

8 ounces snow peas, ends trimmed

1½ teaspoons toasted sesame oil

1 garlic clove, thinly sliced

1. Bring the broth and soy sauce to a boil in a wok or large skillet over high heat. Add the snow peas and sauté until the liquid is evaporated and the snow peas are nearly crisp-tender, about 3½ minutes.

2. Add the oil and garlic and stir-fry until the snow peas are crisp-tender, about 30 seconds.

3. Transfer to a platter and serve.

Per serving: 80 calories, 3.5g total fat, 0.5g saturated fat, 0g trans fat, 0mg cholesterol, 250mg sodium, 9g total carbohydrate, 3g dietary fiber, 4g sugars, 4g protein

Mashed Plantains with Frizzled Leeks

Makes 8 servings: ½ cup each

Mangu is a Dominican side dish traditionally made with green plantains. This recipe is a sweeter take on it. If you prefer a not-so-sweet side, use green instead of yellow plantains—and boil a little longer. First, do remember that plantain peel is tougher than banana peel, so cut off the ends, score the skin down to the fruit, then peel.

4 large fully ripened yellow plantains, peeled and
   cut into 1-inch pieces

1 tablespoon peanut or canola oil

4 medium leeks, white and light green parts only,
   well rinsed and very thinly sliced crosswise

1 teaspoon sea salt, or to taste

¼ cup plain almond milk or unsweetened coconut
   milk beverage, warm

2 teaspoons unsalted butter

Juice of ½ lime (1 tablespoon)

1. Bring a large saucepan of water to a boil. Add the plantains and boil until fully softened and a rich yellow color, about 10 minutes. Drain and transfer to a medium bowl.

2. Meanwhile, heat the oil in a large skillet over medium-high heat. Add the leeks and ¼ teaspoon of the salt and sauté until well caramelized, about 8 minutes. Set aside.

3. Add the almond milk, butter, lime juice, and the remaining ¾ teaspoon salt to the plantains and mash with a potato masher or large fork until nearly smooth or desired consistency. Adjust seasoning.

4. Transfer to a serving bowl, sprinkle with the leeks, and serve. Enjoy like mashed sweet potatoes.

Per serving: 190 calories, 3.5g total fat, 1g saturated fat, 0g trans fat, 5mg cholesterol, 310mg sodium, 42g total carbohydrate, 3g dietary fiber, 19g sugars, 2g protein

Marmalade-Glazed Grilled Plantain Ⓢ

Makes 4 servings: 1 half each

Try this exciting taste of Caribbean-style street food. You grill it with the plantain peel on and then eat it directly out of the peel. You're allowed to enjoy it with a fork.

1½ tablespoons orange marmalade

1½ tablespoons unsalted butter, at room
   temperature

¼ teaspoon sea salt, or to taste

⅛ teaspoon ground cayenne

2 large fully ripened plantains, unpeeled and
   cut in half lengthwise

1 lime, cut into wedges

1. Prepare an outdoor or indoor grill.

2. Stir together the marmalade, butter, salt, and cayenne. Thinly spread half the marmalade mixture over the cut sides of the plantains.

3. Grill the plantain halves, cut surface up, over direct medium-high heat until the flesh is heated through, about 6 to 7 minutes. Turn the plantain halves over and grill until grill marks are well formed on the cut surface, about 2 to 3 minutes. Spread the remaining marmalade mixture onto the cut surface of the plantains. Adjust seasoning.

4. Serve warm with the lime wedges.

Per serving: 190 calories, 4.5g total fat, 3g saturated fat, 0g trans fat, 10mg cholesterol, 150mg sodium, 41g total carbohydrate, 3g dietary fiber, 21g sugars, 2g protein

Roasted Garlic Plantain Cubes

Makes 2 servings: 4 to 5 cubes each

The plantain is basically a cooking banana—just not as sweet and thicker skinned. Because of its starchy texture, nearly anything you can do with a potato or other root vegetables you can do with a plantain. This recipe is like roasted baby potatoes, just softer and sweeter. The hint of cinnamon adds a lovely touch of sweet spice.

1 large fully ripened yellow plantain, peeled and cut on slight diagonal into 1-inch cubes
1 teaspoon peanut or canola oil
1 garlic clove, minced
⅛ teaspoon sea salt, or to taste
Pinch of ground cinnamon

1. Preheat the oven to 425°F.

2. Add the plantain to a bowl. Sprinkle with the oil, garlic, salt, and cinnamon, cover, and gently toss to coat.

3. Arrange the plantain cubes in a single layer on a parchment paper–lined baking sheet. Roast, turning as needed, until golden brown, about 20 minutes.

4. Serve immediately.

Per serving: 170 calories, 2.5g total fat, 0.5g saturated fat, 0g trans fat, 0mg cholesterol, 150mg sodium, 39g total carbohydrate, 3g dietary fiber, 18g sugars, 2g protein

Spicy Skinny Fries

Makes 4 servings: about 20 fries each

These crisp oven-baked russet fries are for those that like it "hot!" They're tossed in just enough oil and baked in a super-hot oven to crisp the potatoes just right. A high-flavored spice mixture that gives them extra appeal in every bite. Pair them with a condiment of choice or turn into an even more comforting side dish in Montreal-Inspired Poutine (page 460), if you wish.

3 medium russet potatoes, unpeeled and scrubbed
1½ tablespoons peanut or canola oil
1 teaspoon paprika
1 teaspoon garlic powder
½ teaspoon sea salt, or to taste
¼ teaspoon ground cayenne, or to taste

1. Preheat the oven to 475°F.

2. Cut each potato into 4 slices lengthwise and then cut each of the 4 slices into 6 to 7 lengthwise slices, making 24 to 28 strips each. Add the potato strips to a large bowl with a lid. Add the oil, cover, and toss to coat.

3. Mix together the paprika, garlic powder, salt, and cayenne in a small bowl. Sprinkle on the potatoes, cover, and toss to coat.

4. Arrange the fries closely together (without touching) in a single layer on a parchment paper–lined large baking sheet. Bake until crispy on the outside and tender on the inside, about 30 minutes, rotating the tray halfway through the cooking process.

5. Serve in individual bowls or parchment paper cones.

Per serving: 150 calories, 5g total fat, 1g saturated fat, 0g trans fat, 0mg cholesterol, 300mg sodium, 24g total carbohydrate, 2g dietary fiber, 1g sugars, 3g protein

Truffled Fries with Herbs

Makes 4 servings: about 20 fries each

You may have already succumbed to decadent versions of these in restaurants. Inspired by the lovely ingredients and aromas of Provence, these baked fries (frites) are just as irresistible but not as detrimental to your eating plan. If you don't have fines herbes or herbes de Provence, try a mixture of ½ teaspoon each dried tarragon, chervil, chives, and parsley. But, do splurge on a little bottle of truffle oil; it's key to the fries' enticing aroma and flavor. Dip these frites into Garlic "Mayo" (page 123) and the savory seduction is complete.

3 medium russet potatoes, unpeeled and scrubbed

1½ tablespoons white truffle oil

2 teaspoon dried fines herbes or herbes de Provence

½ teaspoon sea salt or truffle salt, or to taste

1½ tablespoons freshly grated Parmigiano-Reggiano or other Parmesan cheese

1. Preheat the oven to 475°F.

2. Cut each potato into 4 slices lengthwise and then cut each of the 4 slices into 6 to 7 lengthwise slices, making 24 to 28 strips each. Add the potato strips to a large bowl with a lid. Add the oil, cover, and toss to coat.

3. Mix together the fines herbes and salt in a small bowl. Sprinkle on the potatoes, cover, and toss to coat.

4. Arrange the fries close together (without touching) in a single layer on a parchment paper–lined large baking sheet. Bake until crispy on the outside and tender on the inside, about 30 minutes, rotating the tray halfway through the cooking process.

5. Serve in individual bowls or parchment paper cones and sprinkle with the cheese.

Per serving: 160 calories, 6g total fat, 1g saturated fat, 0g trans fat, 0mg cholesterol, 330mg sodium, 23g total carbohydrate, 2g dietary fiber, 1g sugars, 3g protein

Yukon Steak Fries

Makes 3 servings: 8 large fries each

These big baked potato-like fries will wow you with their buttery texture and hint of Greek flair from the mint and lemon zest. Enjoy these fork-ready fries as is or with your condiment of choice on the side.

2 large Yukon Gold potatoes, unpeeled and scrubbed

1½ tablespoons peanut or canola oil

1 tablespoon finely chopped fresh mint

1 teaspoon finely chopped fresh rosemary

½ teaspoon grated lemon zest

¼ teaspoon + ⅛ teaspoon sea salt, or to taste

1. Preheat the oven to 400°F.

2. Cut each potato into 3 slices lengthwise and then cut each of the 3 slices into 4 lengthwise slices, making 12 strips each. Add the potato strips to a large bowl with a lid. Add the oil, cover, and toss to coat.

3. Mix together the mint, rosemary, lemon zest, and salt in a small bowl. Sprinkle on the potatoes, cover, and toss to coat.

4. Arrange the fries in a single layer on a parchment paper–lined baking sheet. Bake until crispy on the outside and tender on the inside, about 35 to 40 minutes, turning fries once halfway through the cooking process.

5. Serve in individual bowls or parchment paper cones.

Per serving: 170 calories, 7g total fat, 1g saturated fat, 0g trans fat, 0mg cholesterol, 320mg sodium, 24g total carbohydrate, 3g dietary fiber, 2g sugars, 3g protein

Montreal-Inspired Poutine

Makes 4 servings: about 20 fries each

A smart way of eating includes occasional indulgences! The calories in this classic French-Canadian comfort food dish, *poutine,* are substantial because it's basically a mound of fries, cheese, and gravy. Luckily, you can enjoy a special kind of culinary pleasure with this madeover recipe using flavorful crispy baked fries, a luscious yet calorie-friendly gravy, and an accent of "squeaky" cheese.

1 recipe Spicy Skinny Fries (page 459), hot

½ cup Home-style Chicken Gravy (page 113) or other gravy, hot

3 ounces fresh cheese curds or farmer cheese, chopped

1. Arrange the fries on a platter, drizzle with the gravy, sprinkle with the cheese curds, and serve.

2. Enjoy with a fork.

Per serving: 230 calories, 11g total fat, 4.5g saturated fat, 0g trans fat, 20mg cholesterol, 630mg sodium, 27g total carbohydrate, 2g dietary fiber, 2g sugars, 6g protein

Spiced Yam Fries

Makes 4 servings: 9 to 10 fries each

The velvety texture of these special fries is the best part—or is it the flavor? Or both? The bright orange color and lovely hit of spice are tempting.

2 medium garnet sweet potatoes (red yams), unpeeled and scrubbed

1½ tablespoons unrefined peanut or canola oil

½ teaspoon Chinese five-spice powder, or to taste

½ teaspoon sea salt, or to taste

1. Preheat the oven to 425°F.

2. Cut the potatoes to make 36 to 40 total strips. Add the potato strips to a large bowl. Add the oil and toss to coat.

3. Mix together the five-spice powder and salt in a small bowl. Sprinkle onto the potato slices and gently toss to coat.

4. Arrange the fries in a single layer on a parchment paper–lined large baking sheet. Bake until slightly browned on the outside and tender on the inside, about 40 minutes, turning fries once halfway through the cooking process. Adjust seasoning.

5. Serve in individual bowls or parchment paper cones.

Per serving: 160 calories, 5g total fat, 1g saturated fat, 0g trans fat, 0mg cholesterol, 360mg sodium, 26g total carbohydrate, 4g dietary fiber, 5g sugars, 2g protein

Rosemary Potatoes and Leeks

Makes 5 servings: 1 cup each

Roasted fingerling potatoes are a comforting taste delight. Add fragrant, pine-like rosemary and they're an aromatic delight. Add a flavorful accent of caramelized leeks and they will become a flat-out favorite.

1½ pounds fingerling potatoes, unpeeled and scrubbed

1½ tablespoons extra-virgin olive oil

1½ teaspoons finely chopped fresh rosemary

½ teaspoon sea salt, or to taste

1 large leek, white and pale green parts only, well rinsed, halved lengthwise, and thinly sliced crosswise

3 large garlic cloves, minced

1. Preheat the oven to 400°F.

2. Toss together the potatoes, 1 tablespoon of the oil, the rosemary, and ¼ teaspoon of the salt in a large bowl. Arrange the potatoes in a single layer on a large baking sheet. Roast for 15 minutes.

3. Stir in the leek and roast for 15 minutes.

4. Combine the garlic with the remaining ½ tablespoon oil in a small bowl. Stir the garlic mixture into the roasted potatoes. Roast until the potatoes are tender and leek is lightly caramelized, about 15 minutes. Sprinkle with the remaining ¼ teaspoon salt.

5. Serve immediately.

Per serving: 150 calories, 4.5g total fat, 0.5g saturated fat, 0g trans fat, 0mg cholesterol, 260mg sodium, 26g total carbohydrate, 3g dietary fiber, 3g sugars, 3g protein

Mashed Purple Potatoes

Makes 5 servings: ¾ cup each

Here, purple Peruvian potatoes create drama with their distinct, rich color. Mash them as usual—along with fragrant roasted garlic and high-flavor truffle oil—and you'll get a memorable recipe that's hard to resist. Roasting the garlic mellows its bite so do use all the cloves.

1 small head garlic

1 teaspoon extra-virgin olive oil or white truffle oil

1½ pounds purple Peruvian or baby creamer potatoes, unpeeled and scrubbed

2 teaspoons unsalted butter, at room temperature

1½ teaspoons white truffle oil or extra-virgin olive oil

⅓ cup plain almond milk or light soy milk, warm

¾ teaspoon sea salt, or to taste

¼ teaspoon freshly ground white or black pepper, or to taste

1. Preheat the oven to 375°F. Cut off the top of the garlic head to just expose the cloves. Drizzle with the extra-virgin olive oil. Wrap in aluminum foil and roast until the cloves are softened and golden, about 30 minutes.

2. Meanwhile, cut the potatoes into ½-inch-thick slices. Place the potatoes in a large saucepan, cover with cold water, and bring to a boil over high heat. Reduce the heat to medium-low and simmer uncovered until the potatoes are very soft, about 15 minutes. Drain, reserving ½ cup of the cooking liquid.

3. Mash the potatoes with the butter until no large lumps remain. Squeeze the roasted garlic cloves from their skins onto the potatoes and mash.

4. Whisk the truffle oil into the almond milk. Add the milk mixture, the salt, and pepper to the potatoes and mash until fluffy, adding the reserved cooking liquid by the tablespoon, if necessary, until desired consistency is reached. Adjust seasoning. Serve hot.

Per serving: 140 calories, 4.5g total fat, 1.5g saturated fat, 0g trans fat, 5mg cholesterol, 380mg sodium, 24g total carbohydrate, 3g dietary fiber, 2g sugars, 3g protein

Fluffy Buttermilk Blues

Makes 5 servings: ⅔ cup each

Buttermilk gives these mashers rich tang and super creaminess. The lovely lavender-like hue created by the blue potatoes will be the attention-getter and make them seem richer. But it's okay to use Yukon Golds if you can't find blue potatoes. They're deliciously comforting either way.

1½ pounds All Blue, Adirondack Blue, or other blue potatoes, unpeeled and scrubbed

2 teaspoons unsalted butter, at room temperature, or extra-virgin olive oil

⅔ cup low-fat buttermilk or plain almond milk, warm

¾ teaspoon sea salt, or to taste

¼ teaspoon freshly ground black pepper, or to taste

1. Cut the potatoes into 1-inch cubes. Place the potato cubes in a large saucepan, cover with cold water, and bring to a boil over high heat. Reduce the heat to medium-low and simmer until the potatoes are very soft, about 18 minutes. Drain.

2. Mash the potatoes with the butter until no large lumps remain. Add the buttermilk, salt, and pepper to the potatoes and mash or beat with an electric mixer until fluffy. Adjust seasoning. Serve hot.

Per serving: 120 calories, 2g total fat, 1g saturated fat, 0g trans fat, 5mg cholesterol, 410mg sodium, 23g total carbohydrate, 2g dietary fiber, 3g sugars, 4g protein

Southern Sweet Smashers

Makes 6 servings: ½ cup each

This mashed white sweet potato dish has it all—sweetness, savoriness, creaminess, nuttiness, and butteriness—all with a surprising shot of bourbon for flavor depth to boot. If unable to find the white variety, regular sweet potatoes are tasty here, too. Use a little less maple syrup if you make the swap.

1½ pounds white sweet potatoes, unpeeled and scrubbed

¼ cup 80-proof bourbon

1 tablespoon pure maple syrup

2 teaspoons unsalted butter

½ teaspoon sea salt, or to taste

¼ teaspoon pure vanilla extract

2 tablespoons chopped dry-roasted pecans

1. Cut the potatoes into 1-inch cubes. Place the potato cubes in a large saucepan, cover with cold water, and bring to a boil over high heat. Reduce the heat to medium-low and simmer uncovered until the potatoes are very soft, about 12 minutes. Drain.

2. Meanwhile, add the bourbon, maple syrup, butter, salt, and vanilla extract to a small saucepan and stir to combine. Bring to a boil over high heat, stirring occasionally, and let boil for 30 seconds. Remove from heat and cover to keep warm.

3. Mash the potatoes with the warm bourbon mixture until fluffy. Adjust seasoning.

4. Transfer to a serving bowl, sprinkle with the pecans, and serve.

Per serving: 130 calories, 3g total fat, 1g saturated fat, 0g trans fat, 5mg cholesterol, 240mg sodium, 19g total carbohydrate, 3g dietary fiber, 6g sugars, 2g protein

Scalloped Potatoes with Chives

Makes 12 servings: about 1 cup each

The contrasting combination of a creamy potato filling and crisp browned topping will make this dish a memorable family favorite. The almond milk keeps it light. The chives heighten the freshness. And the Comté, a complex French cheese, makes it especially comforting with its slightly nutty, deep butterscotch-like taste.

4 cups plain almond or light soy milk, cold

2 pounds russet potatoes, unpeeled, scrubbed, and very thinly sliced crosswise

2 large garlic cloves, minced

1½ teaspoons sea salt

3 tablespoons arrowroot powder

1½ cups shredded Comté or aged Swiss cheese

⅓ cup chopped fresh chives

¾ cup whole-wheat panko breadcrumbs

3 tablespoons freshly grated Parmigiano-Reggiano or other Parmesan cheese

1. Preheat the oven to 425°F.

2. Add 3¾ cups of the almond milk, the potatoes, garlic, and salt to a Dutch oven or large saucepan. Bring to a simmer over medium-high heat. (Do not boil.) Reduce heat to medium-low and simmer for 12 minutes, gently stirring once. (Potatoes will still be slightly crisp.)

3. Dilute the arrowroot powder in the remaining ¼ cup almond milk. Add the arrowroot mixture to the simmering potato mixture.

4. Remove from heat. Working quickly using tongs, transfer the potatoes and arrange in overlapping layers into a 9 ×13-inch baking pan.

5. Stir the Comté cheese and chives into the remaining milk in the Dutch oven until the cheese melts, scraping the bottom to ensure it's well mixed, and pour evenly over the potatoes.

6. Combine the panko with the Parmesan cheese and scatter evenly over the potatoes.

7. Bake until the potatoes are tender and the top is crisp and brown, about 35 minutes.

8. Let stand for at least 15 minutes to complete the cooking process and allow liquids to settle.

9. Divide into 12 portions and serve.

Per serving: 180 calories, 6g total fat, 3g saturated fat, 0g trans fat, 15mg cholesterol, 420mg sodium, 24g total carbohydrate, 3g dietary fiber, 3g sugars, 8g protein

Sweet Potato Casserole

Makes 6 servings: 1 ramekin each

This redo of the classic holiday-friendly casserole has all the flavor with fewer calories—all served in a perfectly portioned ramekin. The arrowroot and almond milk pairing creates calorie-friendly creaminess; the apple butter addition adds nutrient-rich sweetness.

1 cup plain almond milk or unsweetened coconut milk beverage

1½ tablespoons arrowroot powder

2 large eggs, lightly beaten

3 tablespoons turbinado sugar

1½ tablespoons no-sugar-added apple butter

1½ tablespoons unsalted butter, melted

¼ teaspoon pure vanilla extract

¼ teaspoon sea salt, or to taste

⅛ teaspoon ground cayenne (optional)

3 cups finely diced scrubbed unpeeled sweet potatoes

2 tablespoons finely chopped dry-roasted pecans

1. Preheat the oven to 325°F.

2. Whisk together the almond milk and arrowroot powder in a medium bowl until well combined. Add the eggs and whisk until well combined. Add the sugar, apple butter, butter, vanilla extract, salt, and cayenne (if using) and whisk until well combined.

3. Place 6 (6- to 8-ounce) ramekins or crème brûlée–type individual baking dishes onto a large baking sheet. Place ½ cup of the sweet potatoes into each ramekin. Pour the milk mixture evenly over the sweet potatoes.

4. Bake for 15 minutes. Sprinkle with the pecans and bake until the sweet potatoes are very tender and the top of the each casserole is well caramelized, about 45 minutes.

5. Let stand for about 10 minutes before serving to allow the liquids to settle, and serve warm.

Per serving: 170 calories, 7g total fat, 2.5g saturated fat, 0g trans fat, 70mg cholesterol, 180mg sodium, 24g total carbohydrate, 2g dietary fiber, 11g sugars, 4g protein

Celery Root Mash

Makes 5 servings: ½ cup each

Celery root, also called celeriac, is a knobby root vegetable with a rough skin, so use a knife to peel it and discover its inner beauty. This microwave-prepared mashed celery root recipe has an intriguing texture and a savory taste along with a hint of sweetness provided by the celery root itself. Accented with freshly grated nutmeg along with a just-right buttery richness, this is an intriguing alternative to mashed potatoes.

1 large celery root, peeled and cut into ¼-inch slices

⅓ cup plain almond milk or light soy milk

2 teaspoons unsalted butter, at room temperature

3 tablespoons minced fresh chives

½ teaspoon sea salt, or to taste

¼ teaspoon freshly ground white or black pepper, or to taste

⅛ teaspoon freshly grated nutmeg

1. Place the celery root into a large microwave-safe dish with the almond milk. Cover loosely with parchment paper and cook in the microwave on high for 8 minutes or until the celery root is tender.

2. Mash the celery root with the butter to desired consistency. Stir in the chives, salt, pepper, and nutmeg, and serve.

Per serving: 90 calories, 2.5g total fat, 1.5g saturated fat, 0g trans fat, 5mg cholesterol, 470mg sodium, 17g total carbohydrate, 3g dietary fiber, 3g sugars, 3g protein

Thyme Turnip Gratin

Makes 6 servings: ⅙ of the gratin

Turnips gratin-style is one of the tastiest preparations for the root vegetable. Baked with sharp Asiago cheese and fresh thyme, this will make you a turnip convert for good.

3 medium turnips

2 tablespoons arrowroot powder

⅞ cup plain almond milk or light soy milk

2 teaspoons unsalted butter

2 teaspoons finely chopped fresh thyme

¾ teaspoon sea salt, or to taste

¼ teaspoon ground sage

¼ teaspoon freshly ground black pepper, or to taste

⅛ teaspoon ground cayenne (optional)

½ cup shredded Asiago or blend of Italian cheeses

1. Preheat the oven to 425°F.

2. Peel the turnips, cut in half lengthwise, then cut crosswise into very thin slices. Arrange the turnips in overlapping layers in a 2-quart baking dish.

3. Whisk the arrowroot powder with ¼ cup of the almond milk in a small saucepan until smooth. Place over low heat, add the remaining almond milk, the butter, thyme, salt, sage, black pepper, and cayenne (if using), and whisk until the butter is melted and mixture is just thickened.

4. Pour the milk mixture evenly over the turnips, spreading the top with a spatula to ensure even coverage, if necessary. Sprinkle with the cheese.

5. Bake until the turnips are tender and the cheese is well browned and bubbly, about 40 minutes.

6. Let stand about 10 minutes before serving to allow the liquids to settle. Garnish with additional fresh thyme sprigs, if desired.

Per serving: 100 calories, 5g total fat, 2.5g saturated fat, 0g trans fat, 10mg cholesterol, 480mg sodium, 11g total carbohydrate, 2g dietary fiber, 5g sugars, 3g protein

Rutabaga Hash Browns

Makes 6 servings: 1 cup each

These rutabaga hash browns make a scrumptious side. The sweet earthiness from the rutabaga, caramelized sweetness from the onion, and hit of spiciness from the jalapeño make this a delicious dish to serve any time of the day.

1 medium rutabaga, peeled and cut into ⅓-inch cubes

1 large sweet onion, finely chopped

1 small jalapeño pepper with seeds, halved lengthwise and thinly sliced crosswise

1½ cups low-sodium vegetable broth or Vegetable Stock (page 203)

¾ teaspoon sea salt, or to taste

1 tablespoon extra-virgin olive oil

1 tablespoon unsalted butter

2 teaspoons apple cider vinegar

¼ cup chopped fresh flat-leaf parsley

1. Add the rutabaga, onion, jalapeño, broth, and ¼ teaspoon of the salt to an extra-large nonstick skillet. Place over medium-high heat, cover, and cook until the rutabaga is nearly al dente, about 15 minutes, stirring a few times.

2. Add the oil, butter, vinegar, and the remaining ½ teaspoon salt and cook, uncovered, stirring occasionally, until the liquid is fully reduced and rutabaga is tender and caramelized as desired, about 15 minutes. Adjust seasoning. Stir in the parsley.

3. Transfer to a platter and serve.

Per serving: 120 calories, 4.5g total fat, 1.5g saturated fat, 0g trans fat, 5mg cholesterol, 360mg sodium, 18g total carbohydrate, 5g dietary fiber, 12g sugars, 2g protein

Autumn Parsnip Puree

Makes 5 servings: ½ cup each

Parsnip is a slightly sweet root vegetable, but it's the addition of the sweet Anjou pear and intriguing hint of pumpkin pie spice that make this puree rather dessert-like. (It's wonderful paired with very rich or spicy foods.) The rosemary and cayenne add a savory note. If you don't have pumpkin pie spice, use cinnamon or a mixture of cinnamon, ginger, and nutmeg.

1 pound parsnips, cut crosswise into ½-inch slices

1 tablespoon unsalted butter

½ cup low-sodium vegetable broth
    or Vegetable Stock (page 203)

1 large Anjou or other pear, peeled, cored,
    quartered lengthwise, and sliced crosswise
    into ½-inch slices

1 large sprig fresh rosemary + ¼ teaspoon minced
    fresh rosemary

¾ teaspoon sea salt, or to taste

½ teaspoon freshly ground black pepper, or to taste

¼ teaspoon pumpkin pie spice, or to taste

⅛ teaspoon ground cayenne, or to taste

1. Add the parsnips, butter, broth, pear, and rosemary sprig to a large saucepan over medium-low heat. Cover and simmer until the parsnips are fork-tender, about 30 minutes. Remove the rosemary sprig.

2. Mash the parsnips until desired consistency. Alternatively, if you desire a smoother consistency, blend in a food processor until pureed. Add the salt, black pepper, pumpkin pie spice, and cayenne. Adjust seasoning.

3. Transfer to a serving bowl, sprinkle with the minced rosemary, and serve while warm.

Per serving: 110 calories, 2.5g total fat, 1.5g saturated fat, 0g trans fat, 5mg cholesterol, 370mg sodium, 22g total carbohydrate, 4g dietary fiber, 10g sugars, 1g protein

Crisp Zucchini Stacks

Makes 4 servings: 4 zucchini slices with ¼ cup marinara each

Drizzled with marinara and lightly adorned with fresh basil, these crisp zucchini superstars are ready for the red carpet—or at least your dinner plate. Enjoy as a generous side or notable entrée.

1 cup low-fat buttermilk

3 large garlic cloves, minced

¾ teaspoon sea salt, or to taste

¾ teaspoon freshly ground black pepper, or to taste

1 cup stone-ground whole-wheat flour

2 large eggs

1⅓ cups whole-wheat panko breadcrumbs

4 medium zucchini, cut into 4 lengthwise slices each

1½ tablespoons freshly grated extra-aged
    goat cheese or Pecorino Romano

1 cup Bell Pepper Marinara (page 102) or other
    marinara sauce, warm

2 tablespoons thinly sliced fresh basil leaves

1. Preheat the oven to 400°F.

2. Whisk together the buttermilk, garlic, and ½ teaspoon of the salt and ½ teaspoon of the pepper in a shallow dish. In a second dish, add the flour. In a third dish, whisk the eggs with 2 tablespoons cold water. In a fourth dish, add the panko.

3. Dip each zucchini slice into the buttermilk mixture, then the flour, the egg mixture, and the panko, gently shaking off excess between each.

4. Place the coated zucchini slices on a large baking sheet. Lightly coat with cooking spray (preferably homemade, page xix). Bake until the zucchini are cooked through and the coating is crisp and browned, about 30 minutes. Sprinkle with the remaining ¼ teaspoon salt and ¼ teaspoon pepper and the goat cheese. Adjust seasoning.

5. Arrange the zucchini in stacks or fanned out on individual plates, 4 per stack. Drizzle with the marinara, sprinkle with the basil, and serve.

Per serving: 270 calories, 6g total fat, 1.5g saturated fat, 0g trans fat, 95mg cholesterol, 560mg sodium, 42g total carbohydrate, 8g dietary fiber, 9g sugars, 14g protein

Steam-Fried Zucchini Halves

Makes 1 serving: 1 cup each

Steam-frying is a combination of frying in a minimal amount of oil and steaming by trapping in moisture with a lid. So you get the browning and rich caramelization without adding extra calories from excess oil. Plus, it's simple as it takes less than 5 minutes to whip up this savory, three-ingredient side.

1 teaspoon extra-virgin olive oil

1 medium zucchini, cut in half lengthwise and
    cut crosswise into ¼-inch slices

⅛ teaspoon sea salt, or to taste

1. Heat a large nonstick skillet over medium-high heat. Drizzle in the oil.

2. Add the zucchini in a single layer, sprinkle with the salt, cover, and steam-fry until cooked through and well caramelized, about 4½ minutes, stirring once halfway through cooking.

3. Adjust seasoning, and serve.

Per serving: 60 calories, 5g total fat, 1g saturated fat, 0g trans fat, 0mg cholesterol, 300mg sodium, 4g total carbohydrate, 1g dietary fiber, 3g sugars, 2g protein

Garlic Zucchini Coins

Makes 4 servings: ¾ cup each

Simmering before sautéing allows much less oil to be used. Try it here in this tasty preparation of zucchini—that's made especially tasty with the addition of lemon, garlic, and oregano. You can also use yellow summer squash in place of the zucchini.

½ cup low-sodium vegetable broth or
    Vegetable Stock (page 203)

1½ teaspoons fresh lemon juice

2 large garlic cloves, minced

½ teaspoon sea salt, or to taste

2 large or 3 medium zucchini, cut crosswise into
    ¼-inch coins

2 teaspoons extra-virgin olive oil

1 teaspoon chopped fresh oregano

¼ teaspoon freshly ground black pepper, or to taste
    (optional)

1. Add the broth, lemon juice, garlic, and salt to a wok or extra-large nonstick skillet and bring to a boil over medium-high heat. Add the zucchini and cook while stirring until the liquid is evaporated and zucchini is cooked through, about 8 minutes.

2. Add the oil, oregano, and pepper (if using) and sauté for 30 seconds. Adjust seasoning. Serve warm or at room temperature.

Per serving: 50 calories, 3g total fat, 0g saturated fat, 0g trans fat, 0mg cholesterol, 320mg sodium, 6g total carbohydrate, 2g dietary fiber, 4g sugars, 2g protein

Squash on a Stick

Makes 4 servings: 1 squash on a stick each

Serving food on a stick adds a fun factor. This simple preparation is an innovative way to cook this often abundant summer veggie, yellow summer squash. Try it dipped into Sun-Dried Tomato Pesto Hummus (page 87) for added fun.

4 medium yellow summer squash

1 teaspoon extra-virgin olive oil

½ teaspoon freshly ground black pepper, or to taste

¼ teaspoon sea salt, or to taste

1. Prepare an outdoor or indoor grill.

2. Rub or brush the whole squash to lightly but completely coat with the oil. Season with the pepper and salt.

3. Grill the squash over direct medium-high heat until crisp-tender and grill marks form on all sides, about 12 to 15 total minutes. Adjust seasoning.

4. Insert a craft stick or two long bamboo skewers into each grilled squash, and serve. Enjoy warm or at room temperature.

Per serving: 40 calories, 1.5g total fat, 0g saturated fat, 0g trans fat, 0mg cholesterol, 150mg sodium, 7g total carbohydrate, 2g dietary fiber, 4g sugars, 2g protein

Curry Apple-Acorn Squash Ⓕ

Makes 4 servings: ½ squash each

Acorn squash is roasted here with sweet, savory, salty, and spicy components. Eat it straight from its peel with a little extra glaze alongside. It's 160 calories of pure indulgence.

2 medium acorn squashes
⅓ cup no-sugar-added apple butter
1 tablespoon mango chutney
1 tablespoon apple cider vinegar
2 teaspoons hot Madras curry powder or other curry powder
2 teaspoons unsalted butter, melted
½ teaspoon sea salt, or to taste

1. Preheat the oven to 400°F.

2. Halve the squash lengthwise and scoop out the seeds.

3. Arrange the squash, cut side up, on two baking pans. Wrap in aluminum foil. Roast until the squash is nearly tender, about 30 minutes.

4. Meanwhile, stir together the apple butter, chutney, vinegar, curry powder, butter, and salt until well combined.

5. Remove the foil. Brush the cut side of the squash with about one-third of the curry-apple mixture, and roast for 10 minutes. Brush with another one-third of the mixture and roast until the squash is fully tender, about 10 minutes. Adjust seasoning.

6. Serve the squash halves warm, as is, or sliced with remaining curry-apple mixture on the side.

Per serving: 160 calories, 2.5g total fat, 1.5g saturated fat, 0g trans fat, 5mg cholesterol, 300mg sodium, 37g total carbohydrate, 5g dietary fiber, 14g sugars, 2g protein

Asiago Butternut Squash Bake Ⓕ

Makes 4 servings: 1 cup each

Here's a comforting gratin-style dish that's golden brown and crispy on top and sweetly moist in the middle. The natural sweetness of the butternut squash and onion are the main flavor features. But its double dose of high-flavored cheese takes the taste to another level—and it's still good for you. Try other winter squash in this recipe, too.

1 medium butternut squash, peeled, seeded, and cut into ½-inch cubes
1 large sweet onion, halved and thinly sliced
1 tablespoon extra-virgin olive oil
⅔ cup plain almond milk or light soy milk
2 teaspoons arrowroot powder
1 large egg
1 teaspoon finely chopped fresh thyme
½ teaspoon sea salt, or to taste
¼ teaspoon freshly ground black pepper, or to taste
¼ teaspoon ground cayenne
⅓ cup shredded Italian-style fontina cheese
⅓ cup whole-wheat panko breadcrumbs
⅓ cup freshly grated Asiago or extra-aged goat cheese

1. Preheat the oven to 425°F.

2. Stir together the squash, onion, and oil in a 2-quart baking dish. Roast until the squash is crisp-tender and the onion is fully softened, about 25 minutes.

3. Meanwhile, whisk together the almond milk and arrowroot powder until well combined. Add the egg, thyme, salt, black pepper, and ⅛ teaspoon of the cayenne and whisk until well combined. Set aside.

4. Stir the squash-onion mixture. Sprinkle with the fontina cheese and evenly pour in the milk mixture. Sprinkle the top with the panko, Asiago cheese,

and the remaining ⅛ teaspoon cayenne. Roast until the squash is tender and the Asiago coating is crisp and golden brown, about 20 minutes.

5. Let stand 10 minutes to complete the cooking process, and serve.

Per serving: 240 calories, 12g total fat, 4.5g saturated fat, 0g trans fat, 65mg cholesterol, 530mg sodium, 27g total carbohydrate, 6g dietary fiber, 8g sugars, 9g protein

Buttercup Squash Parmesan ⓕ

Makes 4 servings: 1 cup each

Are your taste buds ready for culinary bliss? This caramelized winter squash recipe is an explosion of deliciousness thanks to the combination of tender squash, fresh herbs, and toasted nutty cheesy topping.

1 medium buttercup or butternut squash, peeled, seeded, and cut into ¾-inch cubes
2 cups low-sodium vegetable broth or Vegetable Stock (page 203)
2 teaspoons unsalted butter
2 teaspoons extra-virgin olive oil
¾ teaspoon sea salt, or to taste
¼ teaspoon freshly ground black pepper, or to taste
2 large shallots, minced
1 large garlic clove, minced
2 tablespoons minced fresh chives
2 tablespoons chopped fresh flat-leaf parsley
2 tablespoons freshly grated Parmigiano-Reggiano or other Parmesan cheese
2 tablespoons finely chopped toasted walnuts

1. Place the squash in a small saucepan with the broth. Add water, if necessary, to cover the squash. Place over medium heat, cover, and simmer until crisp-tender, about 20 minutes. Drain the squash.

2. Melt the butter with the oil in a large nonstick skillet over medium-high heat. Add the squash, the salt, and pepper, and sauté until the squash is just tender and lightly caramelized, about

12 minutes. Add the shallots and sauté for 2 minutes. Add the garlic and sauté for 1 minute. Remove from heat and stir in the chives and parsley. Adjust seasoning.

3. Transfer to a serving platter, sprinkle with the cheese and walnuts, and serve.

Per serving: 170 calories, 8g total fat, 2.5g saturated fat, 0g trans fat, 5mg cholesterol, 560mg sodium, 25g total carbohydrate, 7g dietary fiber, 5g sugars, 4g protein

Tomato-Basil Spaghetti Squash

Makes 4 servings: 1½ cups each

Spaghetti squash transforms into extra-tasty "spaghetti." Here its pasta-esque quality creates a fully satisfying yet rather slim side dish with true Italian attitude.

1 medium spaghetti squash
3 cups Raw Diced Tomato Basil Sauce (page 100), drained, at room temperature, or 1 cup marinara sauce, heated
1 tablespoon thinly sliced fresh basil leaves
⅛ teaspoon sea salt, or to taste
⅛ teaspoon freshly ground black pepper, or to taste

1. Pierce the squash all over with a small paring knife. Microwave the squash on high for 8 minutes in a microwave-safe dish. Carefully turn the squash over and cook until the squash gives slightly to pressure, about 8 minutes more. Let the squash stand for 5 minutes to complete the cooking process.

2. Carefully halve the squash lengthwise and remove the seeds along with any dry white strands attached to the seeds. Working quickly, scrape the squash flesh into a serving bowl using a fork, separating the strands as you go.

3. Toss with the sauce, basil, salt, and pepper. Adjust seasoning. Serve while warm.

Per serving: 140 calories, 5g total fat, 1g saturated fat, 0g trans fat, 0mg cholesterol, 270mg sodium, 25g total carbohydrate, 2g dietary fiber, 3g sugars, 3g protein

Roasted Grape Tomatoes

Makes 3 servings: ½ cup each

Grape tomatoes are tiny treasures bursting with flavor. So imagine what they'll taste like when freshly roasted with garlic and olive oil. Roast them in the toaster oven, if you prefer. Then savor as a side dish for any meal, including breakfast, or toss with fresh basil and pasta for a divine dinner.

1 pint grape tomatoes

2 teaspoons extra-virgin olive oil

2 tablespoons low-sodium vegetable broth
    or Vegetable Stock (page 203)

1 teaspoon aged balsamic vinegar

¼ teaspoon sea salt, or to taste

2 large garlic cloves, very thinly sliced

1. Preheat the oven to 400°F.

2. Place the tomatoes in a baking pan. Drizzle with the oil and toss to coat, arranging the tomatoes in a single layer. Add the broth, vinegar, and ⅛ teaspoon of the salt. Loosely cover with aluminum foil to help prevent splattering.

3. Roast the tomatoes for 18 minutes, shaking the tray halfway through the roasting. Stir the garlic into the tomatoes and roast until the tomatoes are fully cooked and slightly shriveled and the garlic is fully softened, about 5 minutes. Sprinkle with the remaining ⅛ teaspoon salt and let stand for 5 minutes on the tray before serving.

4. Transfer the tomatoes to a serving bowl, and enjoy while warm.

Per serving: 35 calories, 2.5g total fat, 0g saturated fat, 0g trans fat, 0mg cholesterol, 150mg sodium, 4g total carbohydrate, 1g dietary fiber, 2g sugars, 1g protein

Moroccan Grilled Tomatoes

Makes 4 servings: 8 cherry tomatoes each

The earthy spices and fresh cilantro paired with juicy sweet cherry tomatoes, and grilled to smoky, savory perfection, make this side unforgettable.

1 tablespoon extra-virgin olive oil

2 teaspoons aged red wine vinegar or
    fresh lemon juice

2 large garlic cloves, minced

1 teaspoon ground cumin

½ teaspoon sea salt, or to taste

½ teaspoon ground coriander

⅛ teaspoon ground allspice

32 cherry tomatoes

2 tablespoons chopped fresh cilantro
    or flat-leaf parsley

1. Prepare an indoor or outdoor grill.

2. Whisk together the oil, vinegar, garlic, cumin, salt, coriander, and allspice in a large bowl. Add the tomatoes and toss to coat. Secure the tomatoes on 8 (8-inch) reusable or water-soaked bamboo skewers.

3. Position the skewers on the grill, immediately brushing with any remaining marinade. Grill over direct medium-high heat until cooked through and grill marks form, about 6 to 7 minutes total, turning only as needed. Adjust seasoning.

4. Transfer to a platter or individual plates, sprinkle with the cilantro, and serve warm, at room temperature, or chilled.

Per serving: 60 calories, 4g total fat, 0.5g saturated fat, 0g trans fat, 0mg cholesterol, 300mg sodium, 6g total carbohydrate, 2g dietary fiber, 4g sugars, 1g protein

Pressure-Cooked Stewed Tomatoes Oregano

Makes 4 servings: 1 tomato with about ½ cup onion broth each

A pressure-cooker is the secret in this dish. It works in fast and mystifying ways, transforming fresh tomatoes into this voluptuous vegetable side with a savory, garlicky broth. It's stew-like with an herb and spice kick for extra flavor.

1 tablespoon extra-virgin olive oil
1 medium red onion, finely chopped
2 teaspoons aged red wine vinegar
½ teaspoon + ⅛ teaspoon sea salt, or to taste
3 large garlic cloves, minced
4 medium vine-ripened tomatoes
1 cup low-sodium vegetable broth or
    Vegetable Stock (page 203)
1 tablespoon chopped fresh oregano
¼ teaspoon dried hot pepper flakes, or to taste
⅛ teaspoon ground cinnamon (optional)

1. Heat the oil in an uncovered pressure-cooker on medium heat. Add the onion, vinegar, and ¼ teaspoon of the salt and sauté until the onion is softened, about 5 minutes. Add the garlic and sauté until fragrant, about 1 minute.

2. Add the tomatoes, broth, oregano, hot pepper flakes, cinnamon (if using), and ¼ teaspoon of the salt and increase heat to medium-high. Close the pressure-cooker lid and turn to the high-pressure setting.

3. Once the pressure-cooker hisses, adjust the heat as necessary to maintain high pressure with gentle hissing, and cook for 7 minutes. Turn off the heat and gradually release the pressure-cooker lid.

4. Sprinkle with the remaining ⅛ teaspoon salt, and adjust seasoning.

5. Arrange the tomatoes on a lipped serving platter or into individual bowls. Drizzle with the remaining onion broth from the pressure-cooker, and serve.

Per serving: 70 calories, 4g total fat, 0.5g saturated fat, 0g trans fat, 0mg cholesterol, 410mg sodium, 9g total carbohydrate, 2g dietary fiber, 5g sugars, 2g protein

Tri-Color Bell Pepper Sauté

Makes 4 servings: 1 cup each

Here the vivid array of colors and slightly sweet flavors create a dish of bell peppery delight. Cooked in a wok, its preparation becomes an easy delight. Enjoy as a side or as a dazzling topping for Bell Pepper–Stuffed Turkey Sausage Sandwich (page 389).

1 tablespoon extra-virgin olive oil
1 medium red onion, halved, thinly sliced
2 teaspoons white balsamic vinegar
½ teaspoon sea salt, or to taste
3 large bell peppers, various colors, thinly sliced
¼ teaspoon freshly ground black pepper, or to taste
1 teaspoon finely chopped fresh oregano
    or ½ teaspoon crushed dried oregano

1. Heat the oil in a wok or extra-large nonstick skillet over medium heat. Add the onion, vinegar, and ¼ teaspoon of the salt and sauté until softened, about 8 minutes. Stir in the bell peppers, increase heat to medium-high and sauté for 5 minutes.

2. Add the black pepper, oregano, and the remaining ¼ teaspoon salt, and continue to sauté until the onions and peppers are lightly caramelized, about 5 minutes. Adjust seasoning. Serve while warm.

Per serving: 80 calories, 4g total fat, 0.5g saturated fat, 0g trans fat, 0mg cholesterol, 300mg sodium, 10g total carbohydrate, 3g dietary fiber, 6g sugars, 1g protein

Swiss Chard and Potato Gratin

Makes 12 servings: 1 (3 × 3¼-inch) portion each

Here's a home-style potato gratin that's made fresher, more flavorful, and better for you by adding spring onion, chard, and chives. The grated nutmeg and several garlic cloves provide an extra dose of flavor. The synergy of using two cheeses with contrasting flavor profiles makes this springtime comfort food seem extra cheesy. Don't rush and serve this too fast—it's important to let it rest after baking.

14 ounces red Swiss chard, leaves torn into large bite-size pieces and stems thinly sliced

4 cups plain almond milk or light soy milk, cold

2 pounds russet potatoes, unpeeled, scrubbed, and very thinly sliced crosswise

3 large garlic cloves, minced

1½ teaspoons sea salt, or to taste

⅛ teaspoon freshly grated nutmeg

¼ cup arrowroot powder

1¼ cups shredded Gruyère, Appenzeller, or aged Swiss cheese (5 ounces)

1 red spring onion, red and green part, or 2 scallions, green and white parts, very thinly sliced crosswise

¾ cup whole-wheat panko breadcrumbs

3 tablespoons freshly grated extra-aged goat cheese or Pecorino Romano cheese

1 tablespoon white or black truffle oil or extra-virgin olive oil

1 tablespoon minced fresh chives

1. Steam the chard in a covered saucepan over medium-low heat. Squeeze dry through a mesh strainer.

2. Preheat the oven to 425°F.

3. Arrange the steamed chard on the bottom of a 9 × 13-inch baking pan. Set aside.

4. Add 3¾ cups of the almond milk, the potatoes, garlic, salt, and nutmeg to a Dutch oven or large saucepan. Bring to a simmer over medium-high heat.

(Do not boil.) Reduce heat to medium-low and simmer for 12 minutes, gently stirring once. (Potatoes will still be underdone.)

5. Dilute the arrowroot powder in the remaining ¼ cup almond milk. Add the arrowroot mixture to the simmering potato mixture.

6. Remove from heat. Working quickly using tongs, transfer the potatoes and arrange evenly in overlapping layers over the chard.

7. Stir the Gruyère cheese and spring onion into the remaining milk in the saucepan until the cheese melts, scraping the bottom to ensure it's well mixed, and pour evenly over the potatoes.

8. Combine the panko and goat cheese and scatter evenly over the potatoes. Drizzle with 1½ teaspoons of the truffle oil.

9. Bake until the potatoes are tender and the top is crisp and golden brown, about 35 minutes. Sprinkle with the chives and drizzle with the remaining 1½ teaspoons truffle oil.

10. Let stand on a rack for about 20 minutes to complete the cooking process and allow liquids to settle. Divide into 12 portions, and serve.

Per serving: 180 calories, 7g total fat, 2.5g saturated fat, 0g trans fat, 15mg cholesterol, 460mg sodium, 24g total carbohydrate, 2g dietary fiber, 3g sugars, 7g protein

Colcannon-Style Hash Browns

Makes 4 servings: 1 cup each

Here's a twist on the dreamy Irish dish, colcannon. Served like hash browns, it derives extra flavor from the caramelization of the potato rather than by relying on lots of butter.

1 tablespoon unsalted butter

2 teaspoons extra-virgin olive oil

1 pound baby Dutch yellow creamer potatoes, unpeeled, scrubbed, and cut into ⅓-inch coins

1 small or ½ large red onion, chopped

2 teaspoons apple cider vinegar

¾ teaspoon sea salt, or to taste

12 ounces finely shredded napa cabbage

⅓ cup plain almond milk or light soy milk

2½ ounces Canadian-style bacon or baked Virginia ham, finely diced (optional)

3 scallions, green and white parts, minced

2 large garlic cloves, minced

¼ teaspoon freshly ground black pepper, or to taste

¼ cup chopped fresh flat-leaf parsley

1. Melt the butter with the oil in a large nonstick skillet over medium-high heat. Add the potatoes, onion, vinegar, and ¼ teaspoon of the salt and stir to combine. Top with the cabbage. (Don't worry if the skillet is very full; it will cook down.) Cover and cook until the onion and cabbage are softened and potatoes are lightly caramelized, about 15 minutes, stirring a few times during cooking to ensure even doneness.

2. Uncover and add the almond milk, scraping up any browned bits from the bottom of the skillet, and sauté until the potatoes are fully cooked through, about 3 minutes.

3. Add the Canadian bacon (if using), scallions, garlic, pepper, and the remaining ½ teaspoon salt, and sauté until the hash browns are done, about 2 minutes.

4. Adjust seasoning. Stir in or sprinkle with the parsley, and serve immediately from the skillet.

Per serving: 160 calories, 6g total fat, 2g saturated fat, 0g trans fat, 10mg cholesterol, 480mg sodium, 24g total carbohydrate, 4g dietary fiber, 3g sugars, 4g protein

Berkshire Summer Succotash Ⓕ

Makes 5 servings: 1 cup each

Yes, you can eat right and eat bacon. Here, Berkshire bacon adorns fresh corn, peppers, squash, and lima beans. Berkshire bacon comes from a heritage-breed pig that's pasture raised. When bacon is this good, you need only a bit for unbelievable taste. But if you prefer to forgo it, simply sauté with 2 tablespoons extra-virgin olive oil in its place.

3 thick slices Berkshire bacon, cut crosswise into ⅓-inch-wide slices

1 medium red onion, diced

1 pound fresh lima beans in pods, shelled, or 10 ounces frozen lima beans, thawed

1½ cups fresh or frozen yellow corn kernels, thawed (from 3 ears of corn)

1 medium green bell pepper, diced

1 medium yellow summer squash, diced

¾ cup plain almond milk or light soy milk

¾ teaspoon sea salt, or to taste

¾ teaspoon freshly ground black pepper, or to taste

12 grape tomatoes, quartered lengthwise

2 teaspoons apple cider vinegar

3 tablespoons finely chopped fresh cilantro or chives

1. Sauté the bacon in a large skillet over medium heat until fully browned and crisp, about 8 minutes. Transfer the bacon with a slotted spoon to paper towels to drain.

2. Add the onion to the residual bacon fat in the skillet and sauté for 1 minute. Add the lima beans, corn, bell pepper, and squash and sauté until heated through, about 4 minutes.

3. Add the almond milk, salt, and black pepper, increase heat to medium-high, and cook uncovered while stirring occasionally until the vegetables are tender and liquid is fully reduced yet vegetable mixture is still moist, about 15 minutes.

4. Immediately stir in the tomatoes and vinegar, and adjust seasoning.

5. Transfer to a serving bowl, sprinkle with the cilantro and crisp bacon pieces, and serve.

Per serving: 220 calories, 9g total fat, 2.5g saturated fat, 0g trans fat, 10mg cholesterol, 690mg sodium, 29g total carbohydrate, 6g dietary fiber, 7g sugars, 9g protein

Pinot Noir Lentils and Kale

Makes 5 servings: ½ cup each

Pinot Noir brings elegance to the lovely little lentil here along with a generous accent of kale and a finishing touch of fresh oregano. Sip a glass of Pinot Noir along with the meal when this fine dining-worthy dish is served.

1 tablespoon extra-virgin olive oil

1 medium red or white onion, halved, thinly sliced

⅓ cup Pinot Noir or other red wine

¾ teaspoon sea salt, or to taste

2 large garlic cloves, minced

½ cup dried lentils, rinsed and drained

1½ cups low-sodium vegetable broth or Vegetable Stock (page 203)

3 cups thinly sliced kale leaves

2 teaspoons chopped fresh oregano

1. Heat the oil in a large skillet over medium heat. Add the onion, 1 tablespoon of the wine, and ¼ teaspoon of the salt and sauté until softened, about 5 minutes. Add the garlic and sauté for 1 minute. Add the lentils, broth, and ¼ teaspoon of the salt, and simmer over medium-low heat, covered, until the lentils are just tender, about 25 minutes.

2. Increase heat to medium high. Add the remaining wine, the kale, oregano, and the remaining ¼ teaspoon salt and sauté until the kale is tender, about 5 minutes. Adjust seasoning.

3. Transfer to a serving dish, and serve.

Per serving: 140 calories, 3.5g total fat, 0g saturated fat, 0g trans fat, 0mg cholesterol, 410mg sodium, 19g total carbohydrate, 4g dietary fiber, 2g sugars, 7g protein

Miso-Dressed Vegetables

Makes 6 servings: about 1 cup each

Miso dressing isn't just for salads. Here it's slathered over an array of hearty roasted root vegetables, creating an uncommonly tasty side dish with a lovely Asian flair. Be playful and make this recipe with other veggies, like celery root, beets, or purple potatoes, too.

1 tablespoon grapeseed or canola oil

2 teaspoons toasted sesame oil

2 large parsnips, cut crosswise into ¾-inch pieces

1 medium sweet potato, unpeeled, scrubbed, and cut lengthwise in half, and cut crosswise into 1-inch pieces

1 large turnip, peeled, cut crosswise into 1-inch pieces, and then cut into wedges

1 large purple carrot, cut crosswise into ¾-inch-thick pieces, or 8 ounces whole baby carrots

1 tablespoon naturally brewed soy sauce

1 large leek, white and pale green parts only, well rinsed, cut lengthwise in half, and then cut crosswise into 1-inch pieces

1½ tablespoons white miso

1 tablespoon low-sodium vegetable broth or Vegetable Stock (page 203)

2 large garlic cloves, minced

1½ teaspoons honey or agave nectar

1. Preheat the oven to 400°F.

2. Add the grapeseed and sesame oils to a large bowl. Add the parsnips, sweet potato, turnip, and carrot and toss to coat. Drizzle with the soy sauce and toss to coat.

3. Transfer the vegetables to a parchment paper–lined large baking sheet and roast for 30 minutes. Stir in the leeks and roast for 20 minutes.

4. Stir together the miso, broth, garlic, and honey in a small bowl. Brush onto the vegetables and stir. Roast until all the vegetables are tender and caramelized, about 20 minutes more. Serve while warm.

Per serving: 150 calories, 4.5g total fat, 0.5g saturated fat, 0g trans fat, 0mg cholesterol, 370mg sodium, 26g total carbohydrate, 5g dietary fiber, 9g sugars, 3g protein

Couscous and Rice

Confetti Saffron Couscous Ⓕ

Makes 6 servings: ⅔ cup each

The scallions, dried plum, toasted almonds, and fresh cilantro are like perky pieces of confetti speckled through this warm side of saffron-scented couscous. Its mixture of contrasting tastes and textures is celebration worthy.

2 teaspoons grapeseed or canola oil

1 large garlic clove, minced

4 scallions, green and white parts, thinly sliced

1⅔ cups low-sodium vegetable broth or Vegetable Stock (page 203)

½ teaspoon sea salt, or to taste

Pinch of crushed saffron threads

1 cup whole-wheat couscous

3 tablespoons finely chopped dried plums, Black Mission figs, or tart cherries

3 tablespoons sliced almonds, toasted, or unsalted dry-roasted pistachios

2 tablespoons chopped fresh cilantro

1. Heat the oil in a small saucepan over medium heat. Add the garlic and white part of the scallions and sauté until the scallions are softened, about 2 minutes. Increase heat to high, add the broth, salt, and saffron and bring to a boil.

2. Stir in the couscous, dried plums, and the green part of the scallions. Immediately cover and remove from heat. Let stand for 7 minutes, covered, to finish the cooking process. Uncover, stir in the almonds and cilantro, and adjust seasoning.

3. Serve warm.

Per serving: 160 calories, 3.5g total fat, 0g saturated fat, 0g trans fat, 0mg cholesterol, 230mg sodium, 30g total carbohydrate, 5g dietary fiber, 3g sugars, 6g protein

Veggie Mélange Couscous

Makes 8 servings: ⅔ cup each

Throwing a party? Then you'll want to throw this colorful couscous dish together. It's ideal for a last-minute gathering as it's a cinch to make in a pinch. The fresh oregano stirred in at the end lends perfect aromatic appeal.

1 tablespoon extra-virgin olive oil

1 large garlic clove, minced

1½ cups low-sodium vegetable broth or Vegetable Stock (page 203)

1 medium red bell pepper, finely diced

1 small zucchini, diced, or ½ cup thinly sliced green beans

½ cup fresh or frozen peas, thawed

¼ cup coarsely grated carrot or finely diced yellow squash

¾ teaspoon sea salt, or to taste

½ teaspoon minced fresh rosemary

1 cup whole-wheat couscous

1 tablespoon finely chopped fresh oregano

1. Heat the oil in a small saucepan over medium heat. Add the garlic and sauté until fragrant, about 1½ minutes. (Do not brown garlic.) Increase heat to high, add the broth, bell pepper, zucchini, peas, carrot, salt, and rosemary, and bring to a boil.

2. Stir in the couscous. Immediately cover and remove from heat. Let stand for 7 minutes, covered, to finish the cooking process. Uncover, stir in the oregano, and adjust seasoning.

3. Serve warm.

Per serving: 120 calories, 2g total fat, 0g saturated fat, 0g trans fat, 0mg cholesterol, 250mg sodium, 22g total carbohydrate, 4g dietary fiber, 2g sugars, 4g protein

Spanish Goat Cheese Couscous

Makes 7 servings: ⅔ cup each

A richly flavored concoction of vibrant sun-dried tomatoes, piquant capers, and tangy goat cheese creates flavor drama in this whole-wheat couscous dish. It looks dramatic, too.

1 tablespoon extra-virgin olive oil

2 large garlic cloves, minced

4 scallions, green and white parts, thinly sliced

1½ cups low-sodium vegetable broth or
    Vegetable Stock (page 203)

½ teaspoon sea salt, or to taste

½ teaspoon freshly ground black pepper, or to taste

1 cup whole-wheat couscous

6 sun-dried tomato halves, finely chopped
    (do not rehydrate)

2 teaspoons tiny capers, drained

3 tablespoons chopped fresh flat-leaf parsley

2 ounces crumbled soft goat cheese

1. Heat the oil in a small saucepan over medium heat. Add the garlic and white part of the scallions and sauté until the scallions are softened, about 2 minutes. Increase heat to high, add the broth, salt, and pepper, and bring to a boil.

2. Stir in the couscous, sun-dried tomatoes, capers, and the green part of the scallions. Immediately cover and remove from heat. Let stand for 7 minutes, covered, to finish the cooking process. Uncover, and adjust seasoning.

3. Transfer to a platter or large bowl, sprinkle with the parsley and cheese, and serve warm.

Per serving: 150 calories, 4g total fat, 1.5g saturated fat, 0g trans fat, 5mg cholesterol, 290mg sodium, 24g total carbohydrate, 4g dietary fiber, 2g sugars, 6g protein

Swiss Chard Pesto Couscous Ⓕ

Makes 6 servings: ⅔ cup each

Make couscous. Add pesto. That's it. So simple, yet so incredibly yum! Want more? Transform it into a marvelous main dish, in Pesto Couscous with Shrimp (page 364).

1½ cups low-sodium vegetable broth or
    Vegetable Stock (page 203)

¼ teaspoon sea salt, or to taste

1 cup whole-wheat couscous

½ cup Swiss Chard Pesto (page 118)
    or other pesto

1. Bring the broth and salt to a boil in a small saucepan over medium heat. Stir in the couscous. Immediately cover and remove from heat. Let stand for 7 minutes, covered, to finish the cooking process.

2. Uncover, stir in 6 tablespoons of the pesto while fluffing with a fork, and adjust seasoning. Top each serving with a 1-teaspoon dollop of the remaining pesto. Serve warm.

Per serving: 170 calories, 5g total fat, 0.5g saturated fat, 0g trans fat, 0mg cholesterol, 230mg sodium, 26g total carbohydrate, 5g dietary fiber, 1g sugars, 6g protein

Coconut-Spiked Basmati Rice

Makes 6 servings: ½ cup each

There are ways for the flavor of coconut to go a long, long way without overdoing it on calories. Layer the flavors by using a combination of shredded coconut, pure coconut extract, and coconut oil. Here it transforms rice into a versatile, tropical savory side that goes well with tofu, chicken, pork, or beef.

2 teaspoons coconut or grapeseed oil

1 medium sweet onion, finely chopped

2 teaspoons brown rice vinegar

½ teaspoon sea salt, or to taste

1 cup brown basmati rice

1⅞ cups low-sodium vegetable broth or Vegetable Stock (page 203)

3 tablespoons shredded unsweetened coconut

¼ teaspoon pure coconut extract

1 tablespoon minced fresh chives

1. Heat the oil in a large saucepan over medium-high heat. Add the onion, vinegar, and ¼ teaspoon of the salt, cover, and cook until the onion begins to caramelize, about 4 minutes, stirring twice. Add the rice and sauté for 1 minute. Add the broth, coconut, coconut extract, and the remaining ¼ teaspoon salt and bring to a boil over high heat.

2. Reduce heat to low, cover, and simmer until the liquid is absorbed and rice is tender, about 45 minutes. Remove from heat and let stand covered for 5 to 10 minutes to complete the cooking process. Fluff the rice with a fork. Adjust seasoning.

3. Transfer to a serving dish, sprinkle with or stir in the chives, and serve.

Per serving: 140 calories, 4.5g total fat, 3g saturated fat, 0g trans fat, 0mg cholesterol, 240mg sodium, 24g total carbohydrate, 2g dietary fiber, 3g sugars, 2g protein

Saigon Cinnamon Brown Rice Pilaf

Makes 6 servings: ½ cup each

Brown basmati rice is a whole grain that's lightly fragrant and nutty. The distinct freshness of cilantro, sweet spice of cinnamon, and crunchiness of toasted almonds mingle to turn the already lovely rice into an exciting and fairly exotic pilaf.

2 teaspoons grapeseed or canola oil

1 large white onion, finely chopped

2 teaspoons apple cider vinegar

½ teaspoon sea salt, or to taste

1 cup brown basmati rice

1⅞ cups low-sodium vegetable broth or Vegetable Stock (page 203)

¾ teaspoon ground Saigon cinnamon or other ground cinnamon

1 tablespoon finely chopped fresh cilantro or flat-leaf parsley

2 tablespoons sliced natural almonds or pine nuts, toasted

1. Heat the oil in a large saucepan over medium-high heat. Add the onion, vinegar, and ¼ teaspoon of the salt and sauté until the onion is lightly caramelized, about 6 minutes. Add the rice and sauté for 1 minute. Add the broth, cinnamon, and the remaining ¼ teaspoon salt and bring to a boil over high heat.

2. Reduce heat to low, cover, and simmer until the liquid is absorbed and rice is tender, about 45 minutes. Remove from heat and let stand covered for 5 to 10 minutes to complete the cooking process. Fluff the rice with a fork. Adjust seasoning.

3. Transfer to a serving dish, sprinkle with or stir in the cilantro and almonds, and serve.

Per serving: 130 calories, 3.5g total fat, 0g saturated fat, 0g trans fat, 0mg cholesterol, 240mg sodium, 25g total carbohydrate, 2g dietary fiber, 2g sugars, 3g protein

Mango Rice Pilaf

Makes 5 servings: ½ cup each

You'll be mad for the sweet bits of mango in every mouthful of this pilaf, also accented with mint and almonds. This recipe uses Ataulfo (Champagne) mango—which is exceptionally fruity with a creamy, string-free flesh. It's also smaller than other mangoes. Look for its golden yellow skin in spring or fall or use what is available to you.

2 teaspoons grapeseed or coconut oil

2 large shallots, finely chopped

1 cup brown basmati rice

1⅔ cups low-sodium vegetable broth or
    Vegetable Stock (page 203)

½ teaspoon pure coconut extract

½ teaspoon sea salt, or to taste

¼ teaspoon ground cumin

⅛ teaspoon saffron threads

1 fresh Ataulfo (Champagne) mango, pitted and
    diced, or ¾ cup diced fresh mango of choice

3 tablespoons chopped fresh mint or cilantro

2 tablespoons sliced natural almonds, toasted,
    or chopped macadamia nuts

1. Heat the oil in a large saucepan over medium-high heat. Add the shallots and sauté until they begin to caramelize, about 3 minutes. Add the rice and sauté for 1 minute. Add the broth, coconut extract, salt, cumin, saffron, and half of the mango and bring to a boil over high heat.

2. Reduce heat to low, cover, and simmer until the liquid is absorbed and rice is tender, about 45 minutes. Remove from heat and let stand covered for 5 to 10 minutes to complete the cooking process.

3. Immediately add the remaining mango while stirring well and fluffing the rice with a fork. Adjust seasoning.

4. Transfer to a serving dish, sprinkle with the mint and almonds, and serve.

Per serving: 180 calories, 4.5g total fat, 0g saturated fat, 0g trans fat, 0mg cholesterol, 280mg sodium, 33g total carbohydrate, 3g dietary fiber, 5g sugars, 4g protein

Minted Pine Nut Pilaf

Makes 5 servings: ½ cup each

This pilaf will please anyone who loves mint. The fragrance and flavor will be sure to please. It deliciously complements Greek entrées, such as Vegetable Souvlaki (page 266) and Tzatziki Shish Kebabs (page 59).

2 teaspoons extra-virgin olive oil

6 scallions, white and green parts, thinly sliced

1 cup brown basmati rice

1⅞ cups low-sodium vegetable broth or
    Vegetable Stock (page 203)

Juice of ½ small lemon (1 tablespoon)

½ teaspoon sea salt, or to taste

¼ cup chopped fresh mint

2 tablespoons pine nuts, toasted

1. Heat the oil in a large saucepan over medium heat. Add the white part of the scallions and sauté until lightly caramelized, about 3 minutes. Add the rice and sauté for 1 minute. Add the broth, lemon juice, and salt, and bring to a boil over high heat.

2. Stir in the green part of the scallions, reduce heat to low, cover, and simmer until the liquid is absorbed and rice is tender, about 45 minutes. Remove from heat and let stand covered for 5 to 10 minutes to complete the cooking process. Fluff the rice with a fork.

3. Stir in half the mint and half the pine nuts. Adjust seasoning.

4. Transfer to a serving dish, sprinkle with the remaining mint and pine nuts, and serve.

Per serving: 160 calories, 5g total fat, 0g saturated fat, 0g trans fat, 0mg cholesterol, 290mg sodium, 28g total carbohydrate, 3g dietary fiber, 2g sugars, 3g protein

Sticky Ginger Rice Ⓢ

Makes 6 servings: ½ cup each

Here's a gingery rice recipe where you can forgo the fluffy and intentionally aim for sticky! The short-grain rice kernel is ideal for this result.

Have fun with the presentation, too—form it using a culinary ring mold or measuring cup.

1 cup short-grain brown rice

2⅔ cups low-sodium vegetable broth or Vegetable Stock (page 203)

1 tablespoon freshly grated gingerroot

2 teaspoons turbinado sugar

½ teaspoon sea salt, or to taste (optional)

1. Add the rice, broth, ginger, sugar, and salt (if using) to a large saucepan and bring to a boil over high heat.

2. Reduce heat to low, cover, and simmer until the liquid is absorbed and rice is tender and sticky, about 50 minutes. Remove from heat and let stand covered for 10 minutes to complete the cooking process. Adjust seasoning.

3. Transfer to a bowl or individual bowls, and serve.

Per serving: 130 calories, 1g total fat, 0g saturated fat, 0g trans fat, 0mg cholesterol, 65mg sodium, 29g total carbohydrate, 3g dietary fiber, 3g sugars, 2g protein

Wild Rice Pilaf

Makes 6 servings: about ⅔ cup each

Another name for wild rice is "Indian rice." That's because this rice is really an ancient grass—and it's traditionally harvested by American Indians. You'll enjoy the nutty taste of this wonderfully chewy pilaf.

1 tablespoon extra-virgin olive oil

1 small diced yellow onion

1 cup wild rice

1 bay leaf

2 cups low-sodium vegetable broth or Vegetable Stock (page 203)

¼ teaspoon sea salt, or to taste

1. Heat the oil in a medium saucepan over medium heat. Add the onion and sauté until softened, about 5 minutes.

2. Add the rice, bay leaf, broth, and salt and bring to a boil over high heat.

3. Cover, reduce heat to low, and simmer until the liquid is absorbed and rice kernels are puffed open, about 45 to 50 minutes. Remove from heat and let stand covered for about 10 minutes to complete the cooking process. Fluff the rice with a fork. Remove the bay leaf.

4. Adjust seasoning, and serve.

Per serving: 140 calories, 2.5g total fat, 0g saturated fat, 0g trans fat, 0mg cholesterol, 150mg sodium, 25g total carbohydrate, 2g dietary fiber, 2g sugars, 4g protein

Bloody Mary Wild Rice

Makes 6 servings: about ⅔ cup each

You won't actually taste the spirits splashed into this wild rice dish; it becomes part of the "broth" and simply provides a backdrop of flavor. Along with the Bloody Mary essence, butter adds a lovely hint of richness and the chives, freshness.

1 cup wild rice

⅓ cup finely diced celery

1½ cups low-sodium vegetable broth or Vegetable Stock (page 203)

¾ cup Jamaican Bloody Mary Shots (page 558) or spicy vegetable juice

½ cup tomato juice

½ teaspoon sea salt, or to taste

1½ teaspoons unsalted butter or extra-virgin olive oil

¼ cup minced fresh chives

1. Add the wild rice, celery, broth, Bloody Mary, tomato juice, and salt to a medium saucepan and bring to a boil over high heat.

2. Cover, reduce heat to low, and simmer until the liquid is absorbed and rice kernels are puffed open, about 45 to 50 minutes. Remove from heat and let stand covered for about 10 minutes to complete the cooking process.

3. Stir in the butter until melted. Stir in the chives. Adjust seasoning.

4. Transfer to a bowl or individual bowls, and serve.

Per serving: 170 calories, 1.5g total fat, 0g saturated fat, 0g trans fat, 0mg cholesterol, 300mg sodium, 289 total carbohydrate, 3g dietary fiber, 3g sugars, 5g protein

Creamy Truffled Black Rice

Makes 5 servings: ½ cup each

The black rice in this dramatic side dish is labeled "forbidden" because at one point in history it was only allowed to be eaten by Chinese nobility. Not to worry, it's 100 percent permissible in this exotic and, yes . . . black-hued side dish. You may need to order forbidden rice online if you can't find it locally, but it's worth it, especially if you like or already eat rice often. It will be a new ingredient to try that you will wish you had tried sooner. The truffled goat cheese makes this dish creamy and exceptionally aromatic.

1 cup forbidden black rice

⅔ cup finely chopped fennel bulb

1¾ cups low-sodium vegetable broth,
Vegetable Stock (page 203), or water

½ teaspoon truffle sea salt or sea salt, or to taste

½ cup crumbled semisoft goat cheese with
truffles, rind removed, or soft goat cheese

1. Add the rice, fennel, broth, and salt to a small saucepan. Bring to a boil over high heat. Reduce heat to low, cover, and cook until the rice is al dente, about 30 minutes. Remove from heat and stir in the goat cheese.

2. Garnish with fresh fennel fronds, if desired, and serve immediately.

Per serving: 170 calories, 3.5g total fat, 1.5g saturated fat, 0g trans fat, 5mg cholesterol, 330mg sodium, 29g total carbohydrate, 2g dietary fiber, 1g sugars, 6g protein

Quinoa, Bulgur, and Other Whole-Grain Sides

Pomegranate and Citrus Quinoa Pilaf

Makes 7 servings: ½ cup each

This warm and cozy side dish is made with quinoa that's simmered in a citrusy, gingery broth. Then, for bonus culinary points, it's studded with pink pomegranate seeds (arils) and flecks of fresh herbs to make it visually appealing and uniquely refreshing.

1 tablespoon extra-virgin olive oil

1 large red onion, finely chopped

Juice of ½ small lemon (1 tablespoon)

½ teaspoon sea salt, or to taste

2 teaspoons freshly grated gingerroot

1 cup quinoa, rinsed and well drained

1 cup low-sodium vegetable broth or
Vegetable Stock (page 203)

⅞ cup fresh-squeezed orange juice

⅓ cup fresh pomegranate seeds

3 tablespoons finely chopped fresh basil

2 tablespoons finely chopped fresh mint

1. Heat the oil in a medium or large saucepan over medium heat. Add the onion, lemon juice, and ¼ teaspoon of the salt and sauté until the onion is softened and just beginning to caramelize, about 10 minutes. Add the ginger and sauté for 1 minute.

2. Add the quinoa, broth, orange juice, and the remaining ¼ teaspoon salt and bring to a boil over high heat. Cover, reduce heat to low, and cook until the quinoa is al dente and the broth is absorbed, about 18 minutes, while only partially covering during the final 5 minutes. Adjust seasoning.

3. Stir in the pomegranate seeds, basil, and mint, and serve.

Per serving: 140 calories, 3.5g total fat, 0g saturated fat, 0g trans fat, 0mg cholesterol, 190mg sodium, 23g total carbohydrate, 3g dietary fiber, 6g sugars, 4g protein

Thai Lemongrass Quinoa Pilaf

Makes 7 servings: ½ cup each

Quinoa is actually a seed that counts as a whole grain. It's the star of this pilaf—no rice required. Here, it unites with bright Thai flavors and creates a really unexpected, really good dish.

1 tablespoon extra-virgin olive oil

1 medium white onion, finely chopped

1 tablespoon freshly grated lemongrass

Juice of ½ lime (1 tablespoon)

½ teaspoon sea salt, or to taste

2 teaspoons freshly grated gingerroot

¼ teaspoon ground coriander

¼ teaspoon ground cumin

1 cup quinoa, rinsed and well drained

1⅞ cups low-sodium vegetable broth or
    Vegetable Stock (page 203)

2 tablespoons finely chopped fresh cilantro

2 tablespoons finely chopped fresh mint

1. Heat the oil in a medium or large saucepan over medium heat. Add the onion, lemongrass, lime juice, and ¼ teaspoon of salt and sauté until the onion is softened and just beginning to caramelize, about 8 minutes. Add the ginger, coriander, and cumin and sauté for 1 minute.

2. Add the quinoa, broth, and the remaining ¼ teaspoon salt and bring to a boil over high heat. Cover,

reduce heat to low, and cook until the quinoa is al dente and the broth is absorbed, about 18 minutes, while only partially covering during the final 5 minutes. Adjust seasoning.

3. Stir in the cilantro and mint, and serve.

Per serving: 120 calories, 3.5g total fat, 0g saturated fat, 0g trans fat, 0mg cholesterol, 210mg sodium, 18g total carbohydrate, 2g dietary fiber, 2g sugars, 4g protein

"Trail Mix" Quinoa

Makes 8 servings: ½ cup each

Some consider quinoa a superfood because it's a complete protein. Combine it with dried fruits and nuts (which is this recipe's "trail mix"), and it's completely super.

1 tablespoon extra-virgin olive oil

1 large shallot, minced

1 cup quinoa, rinsed and well drained

⅓ cup dried tart cherries, dried cranberries,
    or other pieces dried fruit of choice

2 cups low-sodium vegetable broth or
    Vegetable Stock (page 203)

½ teaspoon sea salt, or to taste

⅓ cup lightly salted mixed nuts

1. Heat the oil in a medium or large saucepan over medium heat. Add the shallot and sauté until softened and just beginning to caramelize, about 5 minutes.

2. Add the quinoa, dried cherries, broth, and salt and bring to a boil over high heat. Cover, reduce heat to low, and cook until the quinoa is al dente and the broth is absorbed, about 18 minutes, while only partially covering during the final 5 minutes. Adjust seasoning. Stir in the nuts, and serve.

Per serving: 150 calories, 6g total fat, 1g saturated fat, 0g trans fat, 0mg cholesterol, 220mg sodium, 21g total carbohydrate, 4g dietary fiber, 4g sugars, 4g protein

Sunflower Red Quinoa Ⓕ

Makes 4 servings: ½ cup each

Combine deep, vivid red quinoa with fresh springy green chives and parsley, zingy lemon zest, and crunchy sunflower seeds and you've got something to appeal to all of your senses.

⅔ cup red quinoa, rinsed and well drained

1½ cups low-sodium vegetable broth, Vegetable Stock (page 203), or water

2 tablespoons lightly salted dry-roasted sunflower seeds

½ teaspoon sea salt, or to taste

2 tablespoons minced fresh chives

1½ teaspoons grated lemon zest

2 tablespoons finely chopped fresh flat-leaf parsley

1. Add the quinoa, broth, 1 tablespoon of the sunflower seeds, and the salt to a small or medium saucepan. Bring to a boil over high heat. Cover, reduce heat to low, and cook until the quinoa is al dente and the broth is absorbed, about 18 minutes, and only partially covered during the final 5 minutes.

2. Stir in the chives and half the lemon zest. Adjust seasoning. Transfer to a bowl. Sprinkle with the parsley, the remaining 1 tablespoon sunflower seeds, and remaining lemon zest, and serve.

Per serving: 150 calories, 4.5g total fat, 0g saturated fat, 0g trans fat, 0mg cholesterol, 370mg sodium, 21g total carbohydrate, 8g dietary fiber, 2g sugars, 6g protein

Jalapeño Tabbouleh Ⓕ

Makes 7 servings: ¾ cup each

Sometimes just a little "heat" can give new life to a traditional dish. The jalapeño actually becomes the highlight of this nontraditional tabbouleh salad . . . like fireworks for the palate. You can of course leave it out for a beautifully mild version.

1 cup medium (#2) bulgur wheat

½ large English cucumber, unpeeled and finely diced

12 cherry tomatoes, thinly sliced

2 scallions, green and white parts, minced

1 jalapeño pepper with seeds, half minced and half very thinly sliced crosswise

⅓ cup chopped flat-leaf parsley

3 tablespoon finely chopped fresh mint

1 large garlic clove, minced

3 tablespoons extra-virgin olive oil

Juice and zest of 1 lemon (3 tablespoons juice)

¾ teaspoon sea salt, or to taste

½ teaspoon freshly ground black pepper, or to taste

1. Place the bulgur in a medium bowl and completely cover with about 1 cup fresh cool water. Allow to stand for 1 hour. Drain any remaining liquid.

2. Place the soaked bulgur in a large serving bowl along with the cucumber, tomatoes, scallions, minced jalapeño, parsley, mint, and garlic. Stir to combine.

3. Stir in the oil, lemon juice, salt, and black pepper.

4. Top with the sliced jalapeño and desired amount of lemon zest. Serve at cool room temperature.

Per serving: 140 calories, 6g total fat, 1g saturated fat, 0g trans fat, 0mg cholesterol, 260mg sodium, 19g total carbohydrate, 5g dietary fiber, 2g sugars, 3g protein

Sweet Potato Bulgur Pilaf 🄵

Makes 5 servings: 1 cup each

This pilaf has an appealing contrast of textures from the moist and chewy pilaf and the crunchy toasted almonds. Plus, there's sweet taste intrigue from the sweet potato and apricots along with spice thrill from the cayenne and cinnamon.

1 tablespoon extra-virgin olive oil

1 medium sweet potato, unpeeled, scrubbed, and coarsely grated

1 large shallot, thinly sliced

⅛ teaspoon ground cayenne, or to taste

⅛ teaspoon cinnamon, or to taste

1 cup medium (#2) or fine (#1) bulgur wheat

¼ cup very thinly sliced dried unsulfured apricots

1¾ cups low-sodium vegetable broth or Vegetable Stock (page 203)

¾ teaspoon sea salt, or to taste

½ teaspoon freshly ground black pepper, or to taste

¼ cup sliced natural almonds, toasted

1. Heat the oil in a medium saucepan over medium heat. Add the sweet potato and shallot and sauté until the sweet potato is crisp-tender and shallot is softened, about 6 minutes. Add the cayenne and cinnamon and sauté for 1 minute.

2. Add the bulgur, apricots, broth, salt, and black pepper and bring to a boil over high heat. Cover, turn off the heat, and let stand until the bulgur is tender, fully cooked, and liquid is absorbed, about 20 minutes.

3. Adjust seasoning. Stir in half the almonds.

4. Transfer to a serving bowl, sprinkle with the remaining almonds, and serve.

Per serving: 170 calories, 2.5g total fat, 0g saturated fat, 0g trans fat, 0mg cholesterol, 410mg sodium, 35g total carbohydrate, 8g dietary fiber, 7g sugars, 5g protein

Thyme Onion Bulgur 🄵

Makes 3 servings: ⅔ cup each

If you've got onion soup on hand, then you can be just minutes away from a simple side. The onion soup transforms into a fragrant, satisfying pilaf using bulgur wheat. The fresh thyme on top finishes the dish with herbal fragrance.

⅔ cup medium (#2) or fine (#1) bulgur wheat

2 cups Caramelized Red, White, and Yellow Onion Soup with Fresh Thyme (page 211) or other onion soup

¾ teaspoon chopped fresh thyme

1. Add the bulgur and soup to a small saucepan. Bring to a boil over high heat while stirring occasionally. Cover, reduce heat to low, and simmer until the bulgur is tender and liquid is absorbed, about 15 minutes. Adjust seasoning.

2. Sprinkle with the thyme, and serve.

Per serving: 140 calories, 1.5g total fat, 0g saturated fat, 0g trans fat, 0mg cholesterol, 330mg sodium, 28g total carbohydrate, 7g dietary fiber, 2g sugars, 4g protein

Fusion Sesame Spaetzle

Makes 8 servings: ¾ cup each

Try this unforgettable culinary fusion. German essence comes from spaetzle and apple butter. Asian flair comes from the rest. And actually, baby corn is notable in both cuisines.

3 tablespoons seasoned brown rice vinegar

2 tablespoons naturally brewed soy sauce

1½ tablespoons no-sugar-added apple butter

1 tablespoon freshly grated gingerroot

2 teaspoons Asian garlic-chili sauce, or to taste

1 (9-ounce) package whole-grain spaetzle or
    (10-ounce) package whole spelt noodles

1 tablespoon toasted sesame oil

6 ounces steamed fresh or canned drained
    baby corn, thinly sliced on diagonal
    (about 1¼ cups sliced)

¾ cup snow peas, trimmed and thinly sliced
    on diagonal

½ cup coarsely grated daikon or carrot or mixture

2 scallions, green and white parts, thinly sliced
    on diagonal

3 tablespoons chopped fresh cilantro

1 teaspoon black sesame seeds

1 teaspoon white sesame seeds

1. Whisk together the vinegar, soy sauce, apple butter, ginger, and garlic-chili sauce in a small bowl or liquid measuring cup. Set aside.

2. Prepare the spaetzle according to package directions, drain well (do not rinse), and transfer to a large bowl. Drizzle with the oil and toss to coat. Add the vinegar mixture and toss to coat.

3. Add the baby corn, snow peas, daikon, scallions, and 2 tablespoons of the cilantro and toss until combined.

4. Transfer to a platter, sprinkle with the black and white sesame seeds and the remaining 1 tablespoon cilantro, and serve warm or at room temperature.

Per serving: 180 calories, 3.5g total fat, 0.5g saturated fat, 0g trans fat, 35mg cholesterol, 390mg sodium, 29g total carbohydrate, 3g dietary fiber, 2g sugars, 6g protein

Minty Pea Farro

Makes 12 servings: ½ cup each

Farro, an ancient grain that's chewy, rich, and nutty, will bring modern appeal to any meal. This salad, with its charming inclusion of fresh mint and peas, will be a hit at your next gathering.

2 cups whole farro, rinsed and drained

1 (32-ounce) carton low-sodium vegetable broth
    or 4 cups Vegetable Stock (page 203)

1¼ teaspoons sea salt, or to taste

3 tablespoons extra-virgin olive oil

1 small or ½ large red onion, diced

Juice of 1 small lemon (2 tablespoons)

3 large garlic cloves, minced

1½ cups fresh or frozen peas, thawed

2 tablespoons chopped fresh mint

1 teaspoon freshly ground black pepper, or to taste

1. Add the farro, broth, and ½ teaspoon of the salt to a medium saucepan. Bring to a boil over high heat. Reduce the heat to medium-low, cover, and simmer until the farro is desired tenderness, about 40 minutes (or about 30 minutes for semi-pearled farro).

2. Meanwhile, add the oil to a large skillet over medium heat. Add the onion, 1 tablespoon of the lemon juice, and the remaining ¾ teaspoon salt and sauté until softened and lightly caramelized, about 8 minutes. Add the garlic and peas and sauté until the peas are cooked through, about 3 minutes. Set aside.

3. Drain the farro, add it to the pea mixture in the skillet, and stir over medium-high heat until the mixture is well combined, about 1 minute. Stir in the remaining 1 tablespoon lemon juice, the mint, and pepper. Adjust seasoning.

4. Transfer to a serving dish, and serve warm.

Per serving: 150 calories, 4.5g total fat, 0.5g saturated fat, 0g trans fat, 0mg cholesterol, 300mg sodium, 25g total carbohydrate, 4g dietary fiber, 3g sugars, 4g protein

Creamy Amaranth with Chives

Makes 7 servings: ½ cup each

Amaranth is a tiny iron-rich grain—or what some call a "pseudo-grain" since it's technically a seed. Here it becomes a hearty, highly textured bowl of "grits" with malty sweet flavor that's nicely contrasted by the sharp Romano and fresh chives.

3 cups low-sodium vegetable broth or Vegetable Stock (page 203)
¾ cup fat-free evaporated milk
2 teaspoons unsalted butter
¾ teaspoon sea salt, or to taste
¼ teaspoon freshly ground white or black pepper, or to taste
1 cup whole-grain amaranth
3 tablespoons minced fresh chives
1 tablespoon freshly grated Romano cheese

1. Add the broth, milk, butter, salt, and pepper to a medium saucepan, place over medium heat, and bring to a simmer.

2. Whisk in the amaranth. Reduce heat to low, cover, and cook for 25 minutes.

3. Uncover and cook while stirring occasionally until desired thickened consistency, about 45 minutes. Remove from heat. Let stand uncovered for 5 minutes to complete the cooking process. (Note: The mixture will not keep thickening like grits after removing from heat.) Stir in 2 tablespoons of the chives, and adjust seasoning.

4. Transfer to individual bowls, sprinkle with the cheese and the remaining 1 tablespoon chives, and serve while hot.

Per serving: 140 calories, 3.5g total fat, 1.5g saturated fat, 0g trans fat, 5mg cholesterol, 350mg sodium, 23g total carbohydrate, 2g dietary fiber, 4g sugars, 6g protein

Caramelized Vidalia Millet Pilaf Ⓕ

Makes 4 servings: 1 cup each

The chewy texture of millet makes a full-bodied pilaf yet has an extremely mild flavor. The flavors of the woodsy mushrooms, caramelized onion, pungent cinnamon, and bright orange zest are this recipe's highlights.

1 tablespoon grapeseed or peanut oil
1 large Vidalia or other sweet onion, chopped fine
2 teaspoons apple cider vinegar
¾ teaspoon sea salt, or to taste
1 medium green bell pepper, chopped
½ cup finely chopped fresh shiitake mushrooms caps
1 cup millet
2 cups low-sodium vegetable broth or Vegetable Stock (page 203)
½ teaspoon ground cinnamon
1 teaspoon grated orange zest, or to taste
2 teaspoons chopped fresh oregano

1. Heat the oil in a large skillet or saucepan over medium-high heat. Add the onion, vinegar, and ¼ teaspoon of the salt and sauté until lightly caramelized, about 12 minutes. Add the bell pepper, mushrooms, and millet and cook while stirring until the millet begins to turn golden and pop, about 3 minutes.

2. Add the broth, cinnamon, ½ teaspoon of the orange zest, and the remaining ½ teaspoon salt and bring to a boil over high heat. Reduce heat to low, cover, and simmer until the liquid is absorbed and millet is tender, about 18 minutes. Remove from heat and let stand covered for 5 minutes to complete the cooking process. Fluff with a fork and adjust seasoning.

3. Transfer the mixture to a medium serving bowl, stir in or sprinkle with the oregano and the remaining ½ teaspoon orange zest, and serve.

Per serving: 260 calories, 6g total fat, 0.5g saturated fat, 0g trans fat, 0mg cholesterol, 520mg sodium, 47g total carbohydrate, 6g dietary fiber, 7g sugars, 7g protein

Spaghetti a Cacio e Pepe
Ⓢ Ⓕ

Makes 4 servings: ¾ cup each

Like simple? You'll love this. It's a spaghetti dish made with Pecorino Romano and freshly crushed black pepper—that's it! Starting with spinach spaghetti instead of plain pasta, this is one of the tastiest 3-ingredient dishes you'll make. Enjoy as a generous side or light entree.

2 teaspoons whole black peppercorns

8 ounces whole-wheat spinach spaghetti or other whole-grain spaghetti

½ cup extra finely grated Pecorino Romano or Parmigiano-Reggiano cheese

1. Toast the peppercorns in a small skillet over medium-high heat until fragrant and peppercorns begin to "pop," about 2½ minutes. Coarsely crush the peppercorns using a mortar and pestle or by pulsing a few times in a coffee grinder.

2. Cook the pasta according to package directions. Drain the pasta quickly, reserving 1 cup cooking liquid.

3. Add the pasta to a warm bowl along with ½ cup of the reserved liquid and ⅓ cup of the cheese; toss quickly using tongs, sprinkling with additional liquid while tossing, if needed.

4. Divide the pasta among four salad plates, sprinkle with the remaining cheese and pepper, and serve immediately.

Per serving: 260 calories, 4.5g total fat, 2.5g saturated fat, 0g trans fat, 15mg cholesterol, 170mg sodium, 44g total carbohydrate, 7g dietary fiber, 2g sugars, 13g protein

Beans

Garlicky White Beans on Roasted Tomato Ⓕ

Makes 4 servings: 2 topped tomato halves each

There's no need to be sneaky. Beans are the star atop deliciously roasted tomatoes.

4 medium vine-ripened tomatoes, halved crosswise

1½ tablespoons extra-virgin olive oil

½ teaspoon sea salt, or to taste

½ teaspoon freshly ground black pepper, or to taste

1 tablespoon white balsamic vinegar

2 large garlic cloves, minced

1 (15-ounce) can cannellini or other white beans, drained

2 tablespoons finely diced red onion

1 tablespoon thinly sliced fresh basil

1 teaspoon finely chopped fresh sage (optional)

1. Preheat the oven to 475°F.

2. Place the tomatoes in a baking dish, cut side up. Very lightly rub or brush the cut surface of the tomato halves with ½ tablespoon of the oil. Sprinkle with ¼ teaspoon of the salt and ¼ teaspoon of the pepper. Roast until the tomatoes are cooked through and begin to caramelize on the bottom, about 20 minutes.

3. Meanwhile, whisk together the remaining 1 tablespoon oil with the vinegar, garlic, and the remaining ¼ teaspoon salt and ¼ teaspoon pepper in a small bowl. Add the beans, onion, basil, and sage (if using) and stir to coat. Adjust seasoning.

4. Arrange 2 tomato halves per plate, top each half with about 3 tablespoons of the bean mixture, and serve at room temperature.

Per serving: 160 calories, 6g total fat, 1g saturated fat, 0g trans fat, 0mg cholesterol, 410mg sodium, 22g total carbohydrate, 7g dietary fiber, 6g sugars, 7g protein

Southwestern Pinto Beans

Makes 3 servings: ½ cup each

These stewed beans seriously taste like they've been slow-cooked for hours . . . but they take just a few minutes. The recipe is an ideal side dish to complement any Mexican-style entrée. They're also scrumptious when stuffed into a burrito or taco, as in Southwestern Bean Soft Tacos (page 404)—or even an omelet.

2 teaspoons peanut or canola oil

1 large garlic clove, minced

1 jalapeño pepper with some seeds, minced

⅛ teaspoon ground cumin, or to taste

⅛ teaspoon ground chipotle or other chili powder, or to taste

1 (15-ounce) can pinto, red kidney, or black beans, drained

¼ cup low-sodium vegetable broth or Vegetable Stock (page 203)

¼ teaspoon sea salt, or to taste

¼ cup roughly chopped fresh cilantro

2 teaspoons fresh lime juice

1. Heat the oil in a small saucepan over medium-high heat. Add the garlic, jalapeño, cumin, and chipotle. Cook, while stirring, for 30 seconds.

2. Add the beans, broth, and salt. Cook, stirring occasionally, until only a small amount of liquid remains, about 3½ to 4 minutes.

3. Remove from heat. Stir in the cilantro and lime juice. Adjust seasoning. Transfer to a bowl, and serve hot or at room temperature.

Per serving: 140 calories, 3g total fat, 0.5g saturated fat, 0g trans fat, 0mg cholesterol, 350mg sodium, 22g total carbohydrate, 8g dietary fiber, 2g sugars, 7g protein

Spicy Un-fried Beans

Makes 5 servings: ¼ cup each

If you're not really fond of the refried beans that you find in a can, and you don't want the unfriendly fat that's found in some restaurant-style refried beans, then whip up this kicked-up un-fried dish. It has a smoother texture and is an easier version of *frijoles refritos*. Savor as a side or in Pumpkin-Avocado Wrap with Refried Beans (page 402) or Layered Baja Bean Dip (page 93).

1 recipe Southwestern Pinto Beans (page 487)

½ teaspoon fresh oregano leaves

⅛ teaspoon sea salt, or to taste

Pinch of ground cayenne

2 tablespoons low-sodium vegetable broth or Vegetable Stock (page 203; optional)

1. Add the beans, oregano, salt, and cayenne to a food processor. Cover and blend until smooth, adding broth (if using) by the teaspoon for a thinner consistency, if desired.

2. Adjust seasoning. Heat in the microwave or serve at room temperature.

Per serving: 80 calories, 2g total fat, 0g saturated fat, 0g trans fat, 0mg cholesterol, 270mg sodium, 13g total carbohydrate, 5g dietary fiber, 1g sugars, 4g protein

Buttermilk Mashed Beans Ⓕ

Makes 3 servings: ⅓ rounded cup each

Inspired by mashed potatoes, this black bean side dish is satisfying, and offers a boost of fiber and protein. The rosemary and buttermilk addition makes this dish a nice change from the ordinary.

2 teaspoons unsalted butter or extra-virgin olive oil
1 small garlic clove, minced
1 (15-ounce) can no-salt-added black, pinto, or Great Northern beans, drained
¼ cup low-fat buttermilk or plain almond milk
1 teaspoon finely chopped fresh rosemary
¼ teaspoon sea salt, or to taste
¼ teaspoon freshly ground black pepper, or to taste
2 tablespoons low-sodium vegetable broth or Vegetable Stock (page 203), or to taste
1 tablespoon minced fresh chives

1. Melt the butter in a medium saucepan over medium heat. Add the garlic and sauté for 1 minute. Add the beans, buttermilk, rosemary, salt, and pepper and cook while stirring until the liquid is nearly evaporated, about 6 minutes. Remove from heat.

2. Add the broth and mash with a potato masher to desired consistency, adding additional broth, if desired. Stir in the chives and adjust seasoning.

3. Transfer to a serving bowl and serve warm.

Per serving: 140 calories, 3g total fat, 1.5g saturated fat, 0g trans fat, 10mg cholesterol, 240mg sodium, 21g total carbohydrate, 7g dietary fiber, 1g sugars, 8g protein

Brooklyn Lager Baked Beans Ⓕ

Makes 8 servings: ¾ cup each

These baked beans are pungent and spicy with aromatic flavor and a hint of natural sweetness. Though the best part for beer fans . . . they've been baked with lager until luscious.

2 teaspoons unrefined peanut or grapeseed oil
1 large sweet onion, finely chopped
1 small jalapeño pepper with seeds, minced
½ cup Brooklyn lager or beer of choice
⅛ teaspoon sea salt, or to taste
3 (15-ounce) cans Great Northern beans, drained
¾ cup Home-Style Barbecue Sauce (page 104) or other barbecue sauce
2 tablespoons no-sugar-added apple butter
1½ tablespoons honey mustard
1 tablespoon vegetarian Worcestershire sauce
1½ teaspoons naturally brewed soy sauce
2 tablespoons chopped fresh cilantro or flat-leaf parsley

1. Preheat the oven to 400°F.

2. Heat the oil in a large oven-safe skillet or saucepan over medium-high heat. Add the onion, jalapeño, 1 tablespoon of the beer, and the salt and sauté until the onion is lightly caramelized, about 8 minutes. Add the remaining beer, the beans, barbecue sauce, apple butter, mustard, Worcestershire sauce, and soy sauce and stir to combine.

3. Bake uncovered until thickened and bubbly, about 15 minutes, stirring once halfway through the baking process. Let stand for at least 5 minutes to complete the cooking process.

4. Transfer to a large bowl, sprinkle with the cilantro, and serve.

Per serving: 160 calories, 1g total fat, 0g saturated fat, 0g trans fat, 0mg cholesterol, 320mg sodium, 28g total carbohydrate, 8g dietary fiber, 5g sugars, 9g protein

Apple Cider Barbecue Beans Ⓢ Ⓕ

Makes 10 servings: ½ cup each

These slow-cooked beans are on the savory side. So if you do desire sweeter baked beans, simply stir in a little more apple butter at the end of the cooking process. Sweet or savory, the splash of bourbon adds just the right depth of flavor.

2 teaspoons unrefined peanut or grapeseed oil

1 large sweet onion, finely chopped

1 small jalapeño pepper with seeds, minced

2 teaspoons apple cider vinegar

¾ teaspoon sea salt, or to taste

3 (15-ounce) cans no-salt-added Great Northern beans or mixture of no-salt-added Great Northern, red kidney, and butter beans, drained

1 cup Apple Cider Barbecue Sauce (page 106) or other barbecue sauce

½ cup low-sodium vegetable broth or Vegetable Stock (page 203)

¼ cup no-sugar-added apple butter, or to taste

3 tablespoons bourbon

1½ teaspoons naturally brewed soy sauce

½ teaspoon crushed dried rosemary

½ teaspoon dried thyme (optional)

1. Heat the oil in a large nonstick skillet or sauce-pan over medium-high heat. Add the onion, jala-peño, vinegar, and salt and sauté until the onion is lightly caramelized, about 8 minutes.

2. Transfer the onion mixture to a slow-cooker on the high setting. Add the beans, barbecue sauce, broth, apple butter, bourbon, soy sauce, rosemary, and thyme (if using) and stir to combine.

3. Cover and let cook for 2 hours on the high set-ting for 4 hours on the low setting.

4. Transfer to a large bowl, and serve.

Per serving: 150 calories, 2g total fat, 0g saturated fat, 0g trans fat, 0mg cholesterol, 310mg sodium, 26g total carbohydrate, 9g dietary fiber, 6g sugars, 5g protein

Lemony Dill-Dressed Garbanzos Ⓕ

Makes 6 servings: ⅔ cup each

Explore the goodness of garbanzos such as in this cool lemony bean dish with its fresh herbal accent. It's a satisfying and refreshing side ideal at lunchtime.

2 (15-ounce) cans chickpeas (garbanzo beans), drained

1 serving Lemon-Dill Yogurt Sauce (page 137)

¾ cup finely diced unpeeled English cucumber

½ cup finely diced red onion

2 tablespoons finely chopped fresh mint

2 large garlic clove, minced

½ teaspoon sea salt, or to taste

4 fresh dill or mint sprigs (optional)

4 lemon wedges

1. Stir together the chickpeas, yogurt sauce, cucumber, onion, mint, garlic, and salt in a serving bowl. Cover and chill in the refrigerator for at least 2 hours to allow flavors to mingle. Stir and adjust seasoning.

2. Top with the dill (if using) and serve at room temperature with the lemon wedges.

Per serving: 140 calories, 3g total fat, 0g saturated fat, 0g trans fat, 0mg cholesterol, 380mg sodium, 23g total carbohydrate, 6g dietary fiber, 4g sugars, 8g protein

Dal Masala with Cilantro

Makes 8 servings: ⅔ cup each

Dal is an Indian dish made with legumes such as lentils or, in this recipe, yellow split peas. Masala refers to a fragrant mixture of Indian spices. Simmered together and pureed, it's a velvety, savory treat. Serve it along with brown basmati rice or whole-wheat naan . . . and make it often.

1½ cups dried yellow split peas, rinsed
1 (32-ounce) carton low-sodium vegetable broth or 4 cups Vegetable Stock (page 203)
2 teaspoons extra-virgin olive oil
1 large white onion, finely chopped
2 teaspoons white balsamic vinegar
1 teaspoon sea salt, or to taste
1 large garlic clove, minced
½ teaspoon ground cumin
¼ teaspoon ground turmeric
¼ teaspoon ground cayenne
¼ cup roughly chopped fresh cilantro

1. Add the split peas to a bowl, cover with simmering water, and let stand for 1 hour to slightly soften. Drain.

2. Add the soaked split peas and broth to a large saucepan. Bring to a boil over high heat. Partially cover, reduce heat to medium-low, and simmer until fully softened, about 45 minutes.

3. Meanwhile, heat the oil in a large nonstick skillet over medium high heat. Add the onion, vinegar, and ¼ teaspoon of the salt and sauté until lightly caramelized, about 10 minutes. Add the garlic, cumin, turmeric, and cayenne and sauté for 1 minute. Set aside.

4. Remove the split peas from the heat and puree until desired consistency using an immersion blender. Or vigorously mix with a whisk if prefer a chunkier dal.

5. Place over medium heat, add the onion mixture and the remaining ¾ teaspoon salt, and stir until fully heated and well combined. Adjust seasoning.

6. Transfer to individual bowls, sprinkle with the cilantro, and serve.

Per serving: 150 calories, 2g total fat, 0g saturated fat, 0g trans fat, 0mg cholesterol, 360mg sodium, 25g total carbohydrate, 11g dietary fiber, 3g sugars, 8g protein

Cuban Beans with Lime

Makes 6 servings: about 1 cup each

This hearty, stew-like dish is exceptionally full of flavor and tang. Sautéing mainly in lime juice brings this bell pepper and bean recipe to life along with the spices and touch of fruity jam. Consider using any leftovers in place of the bean recipe in Southwestern Beans and Rice (page 274).

2 teaspoons peanut or canola olive oil
1 large red onion, finely diced
1 medium red bell pepper, finely chopped
1 medium green bell pepper, finely chopped
Juice and zest of 1 lime (2 tablespoons juice)
½ teaspoon sea salt, or to taste
2 large garlic cloves, minced
2 (15-ounce) cans black beans, drained
1¼ cups low-sodium vegetable broth or Vegetable Stock (page 203)
¼ cup tomato paste
2 tablespoons 100% mango, papaya, or peach jam

1 teaspoon chopped fresh oregano

½ teaspoon black pepper

¼ teaspoon ground cumin

⅛ teaspoon ground cayenne or smoked paprika

2 tablespoons chopped fresh cilantro (optional)

1. Heat the oil in a large saucepan over medium-high heat. Add the onion, bell peppers, 1 tablespoon of the lime juice, and ¼ teaspoon of the salt and sauté until the onion is fully softened and begins to caramelize, about 10 minutes. Add the garlic and sauté for 1 minute.

2. Add remaining 1 tablespoon lime juice, the beans, broth, tomato paste, mango jam, oregano, black pepper, cumin, cayenne, and the remaining ¼ teaspoon salt. Bring to a boil over high heat. Reduce heat to medium-low and simmer until the mixture has thickened to desired consistency, about 12 minutes, stirring occasionally. Adjust seasoning.

3. Transfer the beans to a serving dish or bowl, sprinkle with the lime zest and cilantro (if using), and serve hot as a side dish.

Per serving: 170 calories, 1.5g total fat, 0g saturated fat, 0g trans fat, 0mg cholesterol, 390mg sodium, 32g total carbohydrate, 7g dietary fiber, 11g sugars, 8g protein

Heirloom Italian Bean and Kale Sauté Ⓕ

Makes 6 servings: ½ cup each

Using a captivating variety of beans creates so much interest, especially when their sauté partners are a variety of fully flavored ingredients, including kale, garlic, and rosemary. Make this with any three favorite beans, if you wish. Look for heirloom dried beans at local Italian markets, or on line at www.republicofbeans.com.

2 tablespoons extra virgin olive oil

1 medium white onion, finely diced

⅓ cup finely diced fennel bulb or celery

⅓ cup finely diced carrot

2 cups roughly chopped kale

1 tablespoon aged red wine vinegar

½ teaspoon sea salt, or to taste

2 cups cooked (page 436) or drained canned no-salt-added heirloom Italian beans, such as Zolfini, Ghiareto, Borlotti and/or Pavoni

2 large garlic cloves, minced

½ teaspoon finely chopped fresh rosemary

1 teaspoon grated lemon zest

¼ teaspoon freshly ground black pepper, or to taste

1. Heat the oil in a large nonstick skillet over medium-high heat. Add the onion, fennel, carrot, kale, vinegar, and ¼ teaspoon of the salt and sauté until the onion is fully softened, carrot is crisp-tender, and kale is tender, about 8 minutes.

2. Reduce heat to medium, add the beans, garlic, rosemary, lemon zest, pepper, and the remaining ¼ teaspoon salt, and sauté until well combined and fully cooked, about 3 minutes. Adjust seasoning. Transfer to a serving bowl, and enjoy warm.

Per serving: 130 calories, 6g total fat, 0.5g saturated fat, 0g trans fat, 0mg cholesterol, 240mg sodium, 17g total carbohydrate, 5g dietary fiber, 2g sugars, 5g protein

Polenta

Soft Polenta

Makes 5 servings: ¾ cup each

This polenta is creamy thanks to the Neufchâtel cream cheese and has great texture since you're starting with medium-grind cornmeal. The sprinkling of tangy Parmesan and black pepper adds flavor pizazz. And the fact that it's only 100 calories will inspire you. Serve with Coq Au Vin Cabernet (page 336) for a mouthwatering meal.

2 cups low-sodium vegetable broth or
    Vegetable Stock (page 203)
¾ teaspoon sea salt, or to taste
1 cup whole-grain medium-grind yellow cornmeal
    (not quick-cooking polenta)
2 teaspoons Neufchâtel (light cream cheese),
    at room temperature
2 teaspoons grated Parmigiano-Reggiano
    or other Parmesan cheese
¼ teaspoon freshly ground black pepper

1. Bring the broth and 2 cups of water to a boil in a large saucepan over high heat. Add the salt.

2. Reduce heat to medium. Slowly add the cornmeal while continuously whisking. Continue to cook while whisking until well combined, about 1 minute.

3. Cover, reduce heat to low, and simmer until desired consistency, about 40 minutes, carefully stirring well with a long-handled spoon several times while scraping the pan during the cooking process. Stir in the Neufchâtel until well combined. Adjust seasoning.

4. Transfer to a serving bowl, sprinkle with the Parmesan cheese and pepper, and serve warm.

Per serving: 100 calories, 1.5g total fat, 0.5g saturated fat, 0g trans fat, 0mg cholesterol, 430mg sodium, 20g total carbohydrate, 2g dietary fiber, 1g sugars, 2g protein

Fresh Herb Polenta

Makes 5 servings: ¾ cup each

This comfort food is like a flavor symphony with its fresh mixture of four herbs—sage, thyme, rosemary, and parsley. They're worked into the polenta in three enticing ways—simmered with the cornmeal to infuse it, stirred in after simmering for another flavor layer, and sprinkled on for eye appeal and fragrance. Pinot Grigio Osso Bucco (page 326) is an ideal culinary companion.

2 cups low-sodium vegetable broth or
    Vegetable Stock (page 203)
¾ teaspoon sea salt, or to taste
1 cup whole-grain medium-grind yellow cornmeal
    (not quick-cooking polenta)
1 teaspoon finely chopped fresh sage
½ teaspoon fresh thyme leaves
¼ teaspoon finely chopped fresh rosemary
2 teaspoons Neufchâtel (light cream cheese),
    at room temperature
3 tablespoons chopped fresh flat-leaf parsley
2 teaspoons freshly grated Parmigiano-Reggiano
    or other Parmesan cheese
¼ teaspoon freshly ground black pepper

1. Bring the broth and 2 cups of water to a boil in a large saucepan over high heat. Add the salt.

2. Reduce heat to medium. Slowly add the cornmeal while continuously whisking. Add half each of the sage, thyme, and rosemary and continue to cook while whisking until well combined, about 1 minute.

3. Cover, reduce heat to low, and simmer until desired consistency, about 40 minutes, carefully stirring well with a long-handled spoon several times while scraping the pan during the cooking process. Stir in the Neufchâtel, 2 tablespoons of the parsley, and the remaining sage, thyme, and rosemary until well combined. Adjust seasoning.

4. Transfer to a serving bowl, sprinkle with the Parmesan cheese, pepper, and the remaining 1 tablespoon parsley, and serve warm.

Per serving: 100 calories, 1.5g total fat, 0.5g saturated fat, 0g trans fat, 0mg cholesterol, 430mg sodium, 20g total carbohydrate, 2g dietary fiber, 1g sugars, 3g protein

Baked Polenta with Swiss Chard

Makes 8 servings: 1 (2-inch) square each

If you were to dream up a comfort food with nostalgia and a perfect touch of richness, this may be it. It's a creamy, cheesy, casserole-style polenta stuffed with aromatic garlicky leafy greens and baked to a fork-friendly, yet moist texture.

2 teaspoons extra-virgin olive oil

5 large garlic cloves, minced

6 cups packed chopped rainbow Swiss chard, stems and leaves separated

2 teaspoons white balsamic vinegar

¾ teaspoon sea salt, or to taste

⅛ teaspoon dried hot pepper flakes, or to taste

2½ cups plain almond milk or light soy milk

¾ cup low-sodium vegetable broth or Vegetable Stock (page 203)

1 cup stone-ground corn grits (polenta)

2 teaspoons unsalted butter

¾ cup shredded aged provolone cheese

3 tablespoons freshly grated Pecorino Romano or other Romano cheese

¼ cup sour cream

2 tablespoons finely chopped fresh chives or scallions

1. Heat the oil in a large skillet over medium heat. Add the garlic and sauté for 1 minute. Add the chard stems and vinegar, cover, and steam for 2 minutes. Uncover and add the chard leaves. Cover, and steam until the leaves are wilted, about 4 minutes, stirring twice during steaming. Uncover and set aside to slightly cool. Drain the chard well through a fine-mesh strainer, pressing to remove excess liquid. Transfer to a medium bowl and add ¼ teaspoon of the salt and the hot pepper flakes.

2. Preheat the oven to 425°F. Lightly coat an 8-inch square baking pan with cooking spray (preferably homemade, page xix).

3. Bring the almond milk, broth, and the remaining ½ teaspoon salt just to a boil in a medium saucepan over high heat. Reduce heat to low, slowly add the grits while continuously whisking. Continue to cook and whisk the polenta until a slightly thickened consistency forms, about 3 minutes. Remove from heat and whisk in the butter, provolone, and 2 tablespoons of the Romano cheese until well combined. Adjust seasoning.

4. Working quickly, spread half of the polenta in the baking dish, evenly top with the drained chard, thinly and evenly spread with the sour cream, sprinkle with the chives, evenly spread with the remaining polenta, and sprinkle with the remaining 1 tablespoon Romano cheese.

5. Bake until golden brown and crisp on top yet still moist on the inside, about 30 minutes. Let stand for 10 to 15 minutes. Cut into 8 squares and serve warm.

Per serving: 170 calories, 9g total fat, 4g saturated fat, 0g trans fat, 15mg cholesterol, 500mg sodium, 17g total carbohydrate, 2g dietary fiber, 3g sugars, 6g protein

Goat Cheese Teff Polenta

Makes 9 servings: 1 (2⅔-inch square) piece each

Teff is a tiny, ancient gluten-free grain that's packed with nutrition. By turning the slightly nutty grain with its molasses-like appeal into polenta, you create a nutritious dish any way you stack or slice it. It's especially scrumptious layered here with creamy, tangy goat cheese, fresh basil, and vine-ripened tomatoes.

1½ tablespoons extra-virgin olive oil

1 medium white onion, finely chopped

1½ tablespoons aged balsamic or red wine vinegar

¾ teaspoon sea salt, or to taste

2 or 3 large garlic cloves, minced

⅔ cup teff

2 cups low-sodium vegetable broth or
    Vegetable Stock (page 203)

⅓ cup crumbled soft goat cheese

½ cup thinly sliced fresh basil leaves

2 medium vine-ripened tomatoes, thinly sliced
    and patted very dry

1. Heat the oil in a medium skillet or saucepan over medium heat. Add the onion, ½ tablespoon of the vinegar, and ¼ teaspoon of the salt and sauté until softened, about 8 minutes. Add the garlic and sauté for 1 minute. Stir in the teff, broth, and the remaining ½ teaspoon salt and cook while stirring for 2 minutes.

2. Cover and simmer until the broth is absorbed, the teff is tender, and the mixture is fully thickened and polenta-like, about 35 minutes, stirring occasionally. Adjust seasoning.

3. Spread half of the teff mixture in a parchment paper–lined 8-inch square baking pan. Top with the goat cheese, half the basil, and half of the tomatoes. Top and spread with remaining teff mixture. Let it stand until firm, at least 30 minutes. Slice into 9 pieces. (Note: This won't be as firm as traditional polenta.)

4. Place each piece on a serving plate, top with the remaining tomato and basil, drizzle with the remaining tablespoon vinegar, and serve at room temperature.

Per serving: 140 calories, 4g total fat, 1.5g saturated fat, 0g trans fat, 5mg cholesterol, 250mg sodium, 22g total carbohydrate, 3g dietary fiber, 3g sugars, 5g protein

Stuffings

Sage Whole-Grain Stuffing

Makes 8 servings: ⅔ cup each

Thankfully, stuffing can be made delicious by using just a couple tablespoons of butter (not a couple of sticks!) and focusing on generous amounts of fresh and dried herbs, especially pungent and perfumey sage. That's what makes this skillet stuffing special.

2½ tablespoons unsalted butter

2 large leeks, white and light green parts only, sliced lengthwise, well rinsed, and thinly sliced crosswise

½ cup coarsely grated carrot

1 large celery stalk, finely diced

2¾ cups low-sodium vegetable broth or Vegetable Stock (page 203)

¼ cup chopped fresh flat-leaf parsley

1½ tablespoons thinly sliced fresh sage leaves

2 teaspoons chopped fresh thyme

1 teaspoon finely chopped fresh rosemary

1 teaspoon ground sage, or to taste

1 teaspoon sea salt, or to taste

½ teaspoon freshly ground black pepper, or to taste

10 ounces day-old crusty whole-grain bread, cut into bite-size pieces

1. Melt the butter in a large, deep nonstick skillet over medium-high heat. Add the leeks, carrot, and celery and sauté until the leeks are fully softened and begin to caramelize, about 10 minutes.

2. Increase heat to high and add 2½ cups of the broth, the parsley, fresh sage, thyme, rosemary, ground sage, salt, and pepper. Stir to combine and bring to a boil. Stir in the bread until well combined.

3. Reduce heat to medium-low, firmly press and flatten the stuffing into the skillet, cover, and cook until the bottom of the stuffing is fully browned, about 10 to 12 minutes.

4. Meanwhile, heat the remaining ¼ cup broth.

5. Drizzle the stuffing with the remaining broth. Serve from the skillet or transfer to a bowl, and serve.

Per serving: 160 calories, 5g total fat, 2.5g saturated fat, 0g trans fat, 10mg cholesterol, 520mg sodium, 22g total carbohydrate, 4g dietary fiber, 4g sugars, 6g protein

Herb and Cranberry Stuffing Ⓕ

Makes 8 servings: 1 cup each

Apple juice is used as part of the broth to provide natural sweetness to balance this savory stuffing. But it's the distinctive herbal aroma along with the sweet-tart pops of cranberry found in each bite of this oven-baked stuffing that are the highlights.

12 ounces day-old crusty whole-grain bread, finely chopped

3 tablespoons unsalted butter

2 medium leeks, white and light green parts only, thinly sliced and well rinsed

1 medium red onion, finely diced

¾ cup finely diced celery

½ cup coarsely grated carrot

2 cups low-sodium vegetable broth or Vegetable Stock (page 203)

½ cup 100% unsweetened apple juice

¼ cup dried sweetened cranberries or chopped dried plums

¼ cup chopped fresh flat-leaf parsley

1½ tablespoons chopped fresh sage

2 teaspoons chopped fresh thyme

1 teaspoon finely chopped fresh rosemary

1 teaspoon ground sage, or to taste

1 teaspoon sea salt, or to taste

½ teaspoon freshly ground black pepper, or to taste

1 large egg, lightly beaten

1. Preheat the oven to 425°F.

2. Place the bread in a large mixing bowl. Set aside.

3. Melt the butter in a large, deep skillet over medium heat. Add the leeks, onion, celery, and carrot and sauté until the leeks and onion are fully softened and carrot is crisp-tender, about 10 minutes.

4. Increase heat to high, add the broth, apple juice, dried cranberries, parsley, fresh sage, thyme, rosemary, ground sage, salt, and pepper, and bring to a boil. Remove from heat.

5. Stir the broth mixture into the bread until well combined. Stir in the egg.

6. Arrange the bread mixture evenly in a 9×13-inch baking dish. Cover with aluminum foil and bake for 18 minutes. Uncover and bake until desired doneness and crisp on top, about 18 minutes.

7. Remove from oven and let stand for 10 minutes to complete the cooking process. Serve warm.

Per serving: 200 calories, 7g total fat, 3.5g saturated fat, 0g trans fat, 35mg cholesterol, 530mg sodium, 29g total carbohydrate, 5g dietary fiber, 9g sugars, 7g protein

Turkey Sausage Stuffing

Makes 12 servings: 1 cup each

Roasted grapes are like ritzy gems studded throughout this stuffing. The pairing of the sweet grapes with spicy turkey sausage may knock your socks off.

12 ounces spicy bulk turkey sausage

1 (32-ounce) carton low-sodium chicken broth or 4 cups Chicken Stock (page 203)

1 cup red seedless grapes, quartered lengthwise

3 tablespoons unsalted butter

¾ teaspoon sea salt, or to taste

½ teaspoon ground sage

1 tablespoon extra-virgin olive oil

1 large red onion, chopped

5 celery stalks, thinly sliced on a diagonal

2 large cloves garlic, minced

3 tablespoons finely chopped fresh sage

12 ounces day-old crusty whole-grain bread, cut into bite-size pieces

1. Add the sausage to a large nonstick skillet over medium-high heat and sauté until cooked through, crumbled, and brown, about 6 minutes. Transfer the sausage to a 9 × 13-inch baking dish.

2. Preheat the oven to 425°F.

3. Add the broth, grapes, butter, salt, and ground sage to a large saucepan over medium-low heat, cover, and simmer, about 15 minutes.

4. Meanwhile, heat the oil in the large nonstick skillet over medium heat. Add the onion, celery, garlic, and fresh sage and sauté until the onion is fully softened, about 15 minutes. Transfer the onion mixture to a large bowl along with the bread and toss to combine.

5. Arrange the bread mixture evenly in the baking dish on top of the sausage. Drizzle the broth mixture over the bread mixture and press into dish. (Note: The grapes should remain on top of the stuffing.) Cover with aluminum foil and bake for 18 minutes. Uncover and bake until desired doneness and crisp on top, about 18 minutes.

6. Remove from the oven and let stand for 10 minutes to complete the cooking process. Serve warm.

Per serving: 190 calories, 8g total fat, 2.5g saturated fat, 0g trans fat, 0mg cholesterol, 500mg sodium, 19g total carbohydrate, 3g dietary fiber, 5g sugars, 10g protein

Breads and Corn Breads

Irish Soda Bread Rolls

Makes 12 servings: 1 roll each

Enjoy this healthful twist on the traditional bread that hails from Ireland. Calorie-friendly almond milk, whole-wheat pastry flour, and no-sugar-added applesauce are the nutrient-rich keys to this new creation.

3¾ cups whole-wheat pastry flour

1 teaspoon baking soda

¾ teaspoon sea salt

¼ cup black seedless raisins, finely chopped

1 teaspoon caraway seeds

1½ cups plain almond milk or light soy milk

2 teaspoons fresh lemon juice

2 tablespoons no-sugar-added applesauce

1. Preheat the oven to 400°F.

2. Combine 3½ cups of the flour, the baking soda, salt, raisins, and caraway seeds in a large bowl. Add the almond milk and lemon juice and stir to combine. Turn out onto a floured surface (use only as much of the ¼ cup remaining flour as needed) and knead the dough into a ball. Cut into 12 equal portions. Form each portion into a ball.

3. Place the dough balls on a parchment paper–lined baking sheet. Cut an "X" in the top of each. Lightly brush the top of each roll with the applesauce. Bake until lightly browned, about 30 minutes. Serve warm or at room temperature.

Per serving: 160 calories, 1g total fat, 0g saturated fat, 0g trans fat, 0mg cholesterol, 270mg sodium, 33g total carbohydrate, 5g dietary fiber, 3g sugars, 4g protein

Fresh Rosemary Focaccia 🅕

Makes 15 servings: 1 (3⅓- × 2¾-inch) piece each

Focaccia is a flat, pizza-like baked Italian bread. This heartier and healthier version is moist from the addition of potato and fully flavored with generous use of fresh rosemary and a kick of hot pepper flakes. Pair it with stews, soups, or saucy tomato dishes to soak up their goodness.

2 cups warm (115°F) water

1½ teaspoons honey or agave nectar

1 (¼-ounce) package active dry yeast

4¼ cups whole-wheat pastry flour

1 large garlic clove, minced

1½ teaspoons sea salt

¼ teaspoon dried hot pepper flakes

3 tablespoons extra-virgin olive oil

1 medium Yukon Gold potato, unpeeled, scrubbed, and finely diced

1 tablespoon roughly chopped fresh rosemary

1 teaspoon coarsely grated lemon zest

1. Add the water and honey to a large bowl, sprinkle with the yeast, and gently stir. Let stand until the yeast fully dissolves, about 10 minutes.

2. Add 3¾ cups of the flour, the garlic, 1 teaspoon of the salt, and the hot pepper flakes to the yeast mixture. Stir until a sticky dough forms. Turn the dough out onto a floured surface (use ¼ cup of the remaining flour, or as needed) and knead until the dough is smooth and springy, about 8 minutes.

3. Rub ½ tablespoon of the oil to coat the inside of a large bowl. Add the dough, turning it to coat. Cover and let rise in warm area until doubled in size, about 1 hour.

4. Punch the dough down. Toss the potato with the remaining ¼ cup of flour, and add to the dough. Knead into a ball while ensuring the potato is well distributed, and return to the bowl. Cover and let rise again for 20 minutes.

5. Punch down the dough and transfer to a parchment paper–lined large baking sheet. Press and form by hand into about a 10×14-inch rectangle. Sprinkle with the rosemary, zest, and remaining oil. Let the dough rise again for 20 minutes.

6. Preheat the oven to 450°F.

7. Make indentations into the dough by poking with your finger a couple dozen times. Bake until the top is crisp and browned, about 25 to 30 minutes.

8. Cut the focaccia into 15 pieces, and serve warm or at room temperature.

Per serving: 160 calories, 3.5g total fat, 0g saturated fat, 0g trans fat, 0mg cholesterol, 230mg sodium, 29g total carbohydrate, 5g dietary fiber, 1g sugars, 4g protein

Seed-Crusted Whole-Grain Bread

Makes 40 servings: 1 slice each

Making bread from scratch is incredibly satisfying take pleasure in preparing this whole-grain bread recipe adorned with a trio of seeds. It will provide you with bread slices for days, so simply freeze whatever you don't need now.

2¾ cups plain almond milk or light soy milk

2 tablespoons extra-virgin olive oil

1 tablespoon + 1½ teaspoons honey
    or agave nectar

1 tablespoon unsulfured molasses

1 tablespoon sea salt

⅓ cup (115°F) warm water

1 (¼-ounce) envelope active dry yeast

6 cups stone-ground whole-wheat flour
    or other whole-grain flour

2 tablespoons white or black sesame seeds

2 tablespoons sunflower seeds

2 tablespoons flaxseeds or poppy seeds

1. Bring the almond milk, oil, 1 ta[...] honey, the molasses, and salt to a [...] boil) in a medium saucepan over m[...] Remove from heat and let cool do[...]

2. Meanwhile, add the water and r[...] spoons honey to a large bowl, sprinkle with the yeast, and gently stir. Let stand until the yeast fully dissolves, about 10 minutes.

3. When the milk mixture's temperature is between 100 to 115°F stir it into the yeast mixture until combined.

4. Gradually stir in 5¾ cups of the flour, 1 cup at a time, and combine by hand until a soft dough begins to form.

5. Turn the dough out onto a floured surface (use the ¼ cup remaining flour) and knead until the dough is smooth and springy, about 8 minutes. (Note: If the mixture is too sticky, add additional flour, about 2 teaspoons at a time, if necessary.)

6. Shape the dough into 2 long loaves (about 10 inches each) on a parchment paper–lined large baking sheet. Sprinkle and firmly press the seeds into the entire top surface of each loaf so that they adhere. Let rise in a warm place until the loaves nearly doubled in size, about 30 to 35 minutes. Meanwhile, preheat the oven to 375°F.

7. Bake the loaves until done, about 45 to 50 minutes. Remove from oven and let stand for 10 minutes to complete the cooking process. Slice each loaf into 20 slices when ready to serve.

Per serving: 90 calories, 2g total fat, 0g saturated fat, 0g trans fat, 0mg cholesterol, 190mg sodium, 16g total carbohydrate, 3g dietary fiber, 2g sugars, 3g protein

Jalapeño-Jack Corn Bread

Makes 21 servings: 1 piece each

For a bite that'll excite, this cheesy corn bread marries a great texture with "heat" and a hint of sweet. If you have some calories to spare, a drizzle of honey or a smear of butter on top is delicious.

1 cup whole-grain medium-grind yellow cornmeal

1 cup whole-wheat pastry flour or other whole-grain flour

4 teaspoons baking powder

½ teaspoon sea salt

1 cup plain almond milk or light soy milk

3 large eggs

¼ cup turbinado sugar

1 small jalapeño pepper with seeds, minced

¼ cup unsalted butter, melted

1¼ cups fresh or frozen corn kernels, thawed

1 medium poblano pepper, roasted, charred skin removed, and finely diced

½ cup shredded extra-sharp Cheddar cheese

½ cup shredded Monterey Jack cheese

1. Preheat the oven to 375°F. Line the bottom of a 9 × 13-inch baking pan with parchment paper.

2. Whisk together the cornmeal, flour, baking powder, and salt in a medium bowl; set aside.

3. Whisk together the almond milk, eggs, sugar, and jalapeño in a large bowl. Add the butter and whisk until combined.

4. Add the cornmeal mixture and vigorously stir until well combined. Stir in the corn, poblano, and cheeses until evenly combined.

5. Pour the batter into the prepared pan and evenly spread. Bake until an inserted toothpick comes out clean, about 35 minutes. Remove pan to rack to cool for at least 20 minutes to complete the baking process.

6. Cut around the edges of the corn bread, slice into 21 pieces, and serve warm or at room temperature.

Per serving: 110 calories, 5g total fat, 2.5g saturated fat, 0g trans fat, 40mg cholesterol, 200mg sodium, 14g total carbohydrate, 1.5g dietary fiber, 3g sugars, 4g protein

Autumn Corn Bread

Makes 21 servings: 1 piece each

This corn bread seems too darn good to be good for you. The bits of sweet potato, red onion, and rosemary make it a savory and slightly sweet treat with exactly 100 calories a piece.

1 cup whole-grain medium-grind yellow cornmeal

1 cup whole-wheat pastry flour or other whole-grain flour

4 teaspoons baking powder

½ teaspoon sea salt

1 cup plain almond milk or light soy milk

3 large eggs

¼ cup turbinado sugar

½ teaspoon finely chopped fresh rosemary or ¼ teaspoon dried rosemary

¼ cup unsalted butter, melted

2 cups finely diced sweet potato, butternut squash, or rutabaga, or a mixture

1 small red onion, finely diced

1. Preheat the oven to 375°F. Line the bottom of a 9 × 13-inch baking pan with parchment paper.

2. Whisk together the cornmeal, flour, baking powder, and salt in a medium bowl; set aside.

3. Whisk together the almond milk, eggs, sugar, and rosemary in a large bowl. Add the butter and whisk until combined.

4. Add the cornmeal mixture and vigorously stir until well combined. Stir in the sweet potato and onion until evenly combined.

5. Pour the batter into the prepared pan and evenly spread. Bake until an inserted toothpick comes out clean, about 35 minutes. Remove pan to rack to cool for at least 20 minutes to complete the baking process.

6. Cut around the edges of the corn bread, slice into 21 pieces, and serve warm or at room temperature.

Per serving: 100 calories, 3.5g total fat, 1.5g saturated fat, 0g trans fat, 30mg cholesterol, 170mg sodium, 15g total carbohydrate, 2g dietary fiber, 3g sugars, 2g protein

Desserts, Muffins, and Sweet Toppings

Cakes and Cupcakes

Devil's Food Cake

Angelic Cake

Pomegranate Angelic Cake

Pound-less Cake

Lemon Pound-less Cake

Blueberry Bundt Cake

Springtime Strawberry-Rhubarb Angel Food Shortcake

Blackberry Mousse Almond Crumb Cake

Hint-of-Mint Snack Cake

Double Chocolate Mini Cupcakes

Mini Red Velvet Cupcakes

Cookies

100-Calorie Dark Chocolate Chip Cookies

Cocoa Meringue Cookies

Apricot Oatmeal Cookies

Crisp Lace Cookies

Almond Cookies

Orange Pistachio Cookies

Brownies and Bars

Fudgy Superfood Brownies

Raspberry Brownie-Style Fudge

Fleur de Sel Brownie Rounds

"Energy Bar" Brownies

Macadamia Nut Blondie Bars

Zesty Lemon Bars

Pies, Cobblers, and Cheesecakes

Petite Pumpkin Pie

Banana Pecan "Pie"

Mississippi Mud Pie Parfait

Bing Cherry Cobbler

New York–Style Peachy Cheesecake

Citrus Cheesecake Squares

Fruit Desserts

Fudge-Drizzled Strawberries

Bittersweet Chocolate–
Dressed Banana

Semisweet Chocolate
Dipped Figs

White Chocolate
and Pistachio-Dipped Apple

Almond Zabaglione
with Berries

Citrus-Pomegranate
Compote

Fruit Mélange in Melon Bowl

Grilled White Nectarines

Grilled Summer Fruit Sundae

Berry-Papaya Popsicles

Banana-Berry Pops

Frozen Grape "Pops"

Mango Mint Parfait

Puddings, Mousses, Fondues, and Other Desserts

French Vanilla Pudding

Cocoa Velvet Mousse

White Chocolate Fondue

Silky Banana "Fondue"

Spicy Campfire S'Mores

Cookie Dough "Truffles"

Peppermint Frozen Dessert

Frozen Dessert Sandwich

Muffins and Quick Breads

Apple Streusel Mini-Muffins

Pumpkin Mini-Muffins

Tropical Carrot Cake Muffins

Fruity Blueberry Muffins

Rainforest Chocolate Muffins

Mom's Banana Bread

Double Squash Bread

Glazes, Frostings, Syrups, and Other Sweet Toppings

Mango Coulis

Cilantro and Pomegranate
Syrups

Rhubarb-Strawberry
Compote

Angel Frosting

Hint-of-Mint
Vanilla Buttercream Icing

Silken Icing

Fluffy Chocolate Yogurt
Frosting

Basil-Strawberry Sauce

Fresh Blueberry Crème
Sauce

Chantilly Vanilla Yogurt

In *1,000 Low-Calorie Recipes*, the focus of desserts is on deliciousness.

When developing the recipes, my aim was to find a place of just-right sweetness without going overboard. They are sweets, after all. But they showcase nutrient-rich ingredients, too. So please enjoy these desserts as part of your healthful eating plan.

The flour of choice is a whole-grain pick: whole-wheat pastry flour. It can be used exactly like all-purpose white flour, but it has the health-promoting benefits of the whole grain, including satisfying fiber. Gluten-free options, including garbanzo bean (chickpea), almond, tapioca, and quinoa flour, can be used in place of the wheat flour when needed.

I use turbinado sugar instead of white granulated sugar for a more natural product and more caramel-like flavor. (Coconut palm sugar is not as easy to find but is another natural sugar option. Consider replacing part of the turbinado sugar in these recipes with it, in equal amounts, since it may have less impact on blood sugar.) If it works better for a recipe, you'll see honey, which is about as pure as you can get for a sweetener. For those who want to create vegan recipes, agave nectar can be used in place of honey.

Also, if you need to be extra conscientious of calories, you can replace part of the sugar with zero-calorie stevia. Check the package for instructions. I suggest replacing no more than half of the sugar with it since too much stevia in a recipe can result in a slightly bitter taste, plus you'll lose the baking qualities provided by sugar. (See page xxxv for more details.)

Fruit is used plentifully as the main focus of many recipes here—in creative ways. What's more, fruit is used as part of the "sugar" in some cases,

especially apple butter, which provides sweetness, antioxidants, and a hint of fruity pleasure.

Of course, no sweets chapter would be complete without chocolate . . . real chocolate. This chapter in *1,000 Low-Calorie Recipes* is no exception. In fact, there's a chocolaty recipe in every section of it, including Cookies, Fruit Desserts, and Muffins and Quick Breads. Eating chocolate might be associated with a reduction in the risk of developing heart disease—tasty news, indeed.

One of my favorite tricks in this chapter is to heighten flavors in a calorie-free way with pure extracts. We all know and love vanilla extract. But there are so many other extracts from which to choose . . . coconut, coffee, lemon, orange, and yes, chocolate. For instance, chocolate extract can make a baked goodie seem extra chocolaty without overdoing the more devilish ingredients. It's the best of both the culinary and calorie-friendly worlds.

But do remember that even though there are plenty of better-for-you ingredients used throughout the recipes in this chapter, they still are considered treats. So plan them in you eating routine when you know you're meeting nutrient needs otherwise—and have "room" for the calories. Luckily, nothing here is over 300 calories!

This delicious chapter starts off with cakes and cupcakes—a chocolate cake is very first, of course. There are cute mini cupcakes, too, which are your best bets for a perfectly portioned bite. Cookies come next. Every single cookie serving is exactly 100 calories! The only thing that's better: you can actually have six of the Cocoa Meringue Cookies (page 514) for those 100.

There are a dozen recipes that fall within the categories of brownies, bars, pies, cobblers, and cheesecakes. Pies have been "redefined" as something other than traditional pies, such as combining a banana bread and pecan pie recipe to create a new kind of "pie," as well as serving a mud pie in parfait-style using Greek yogurt. If you're a fan of muffins and quick breads, you'll find a bevy of options here chock full of veggies and fruits, including pumpkin, carrot, and summer squash.

The fruit dessert recipes are bountiful, including chocolate-dipped delights. You'll also find velvety pudding, mousse, fondue, and some extra fun recipes, like Spicy Campfire S'Mores (page 531) and Cookie Dough "Truffles" (page 531). Plus, you'll find anything sweet that you can spread or drizzle, including frostings, syrups, and a coulis. The Fluffy Chocolate Yogurt Frosting (page 539) is made with Greek yogurt; it's a must-try!

And one final note about desserts: Please don't think you have to label them rewards for "good" eating behavior. Again, the best way to think about dessert is to plan ahead and consider it part of your healthful eating repertoire—and just enjoy them.

Calorie range in this chapter: 15 to 300 calories.

Low-calorie picks: Silken Icing, 15 calories (page 539), Basil-Strawberry Sauce, 15 calories (page 540), or Fresh Blueberry Crème Sauce, 15 calories (page 540).

Cakes and Cupcakes

Devil's Food Cake S

Makes 20 servings: 1 (2¼ by 2⅔-inch) piece each

This is a pure, rich, moist chocolate-lover's delight. Using a 9×13-inch pan lets you use less frosting than a layer cake. You'll still get to enjoy frosting, but in a calorie-friendlier way since it's just on the top. For added fun, forgo the usual frosting and top as you choose, such as with dollops of organic marshmallow crème.

1¾ cups whole-wheat pastry flour

1¼ teaspoons baking soda

½ teaspoon sea salt

¾ cup unsweetened cocoa powder

1 teaspoon instant coffee powder

¾ cup plain almond milk or unsweetened coconut
    milk beverage

⅓ cup fat-free or low-fat plain Greek yogurt

3 tablespoons no-sugar-added apple butter

1½ teaspoons pure vanilla extract

5 tablespoons unsalted butter, at room temperature

2 tablespoons canola or peanut oil

¾ cup packed dark brown sugar

¾ cup turbinado sugar

4 large eggs

1 recipe Angel Frosting (page 538)

1. Preheat the oven to 350°F. Line the bottom of a 9×13-inch stick-resistant baking pan with parchment paper.

2. Sift together the flour, baking soda, and salt in a medium bowl. Set aside.

3. Bring 1 cup water to a boil in a small saucepan over high heat. Remove from heat and whisk in the cocoa powder and instant coffee until combined. Whisk in the almond milk, yogurt, apple butter, and vanilla extract until smooth. Set aside.

4. Blend together the butter, oil, and sugars in a large bowl with an electric mixer until well combined. Add the eggs, beating well after each addition. Blend in half of the flour mixture, then half of the cocoa mixture, and repeat.

5. Pour the batter evenly into the prepared baking pan. Bake until a toothpick inserted into the center of the cake comes out clean, about 40 minutes. Cool the cake in the pan on a rack.

6. When the cake is cool, cut around the edges of the pan. Spread the top of the cake with the frosting when it's in the pan. Cut into 20 pieces, and serve.

Per serving: 210 calories, 7g total fat, 3g saturated fat, 0g trans fat, 45mg cholesterol, 180mg sodium, 36g total carbohydrate, 3g dietary fiber, 26g sugars, 3g protein

Angelic Cake Ⓢ

Makes 12 servings: 1 slice each

This cake isn't as "white" as angel food cake typically is, but it's sure angelic, with zero fat and a light bounce from the whipped egg whites. Pair this with some of summer's berry bounty.

⅞ cup whole-grain pastry flour

1⅓ cups superfine sugar

¼ teaspoon sea salt

10 large egg whites, at room temperature

1 teaspoon cream of tartar

1¼ teaspoons pure vanilla extract

¼ teaspoon pure almond extract

¼ teaspoon pure lemon extract or 1 teaspoon
     finely grated lemon zest

1. Preheat the oven to 350°F.

2. Sift together well the flour, ⅓ cup of the sugar, and the salt in a medium bowl.

3. Beat together the egg whites with an electric mixer with whisk attachment on medium speed in a large bowl until fully frothy, about 1 minute. Add the cream of tartar, increase speed to high, and beat until soft peaks form, about 1 minute 15 seconds. Add all the extracts and slowly add the remaining 1 cup sugar, beating until stiff peaks form, about 4 minutes.

4. About ¼ cup at a time, gently fold the flour mixture into the egg mixture just until combined.

5. Transfer the angel food cake batter to an ungreased 10-inch angel food cake (tube) pan with 4-inch-high sides and removable bottom, smoothing the top. Gently tap the pan on the counter or run a dinner knife through the batter to eliminate large air pockets.

6. Bake until a light golden brown, springy to the touch, and a toothpick inserted into the center comes out clean, about 40 to 45 minutes.

7. Let the cake cool inverted in the pan on a rack. When cool, remove from the pan by running a thin, flexible knife around the outside and inside edges of the cake. Remove the outer portion of the pan and then run your knife under the bottom of the cake to release. Invert to release the cake from the tube, and invert again onto a serving plate.

8. Cut the cake into 12 slices, and serve.

Per serving: 140 calories, 0g total fat, 0g saturated fat, 0g trans fat, 0mg cholesterol, 95mg sodium, 29g total carbohydrate, 1g dietary fiber, 23g sugars, 4g protein

Pomegranate Angelic Cake Ⓢ

Makes 1 serving: 1 slice

Just as deep red lipstick can complete an outfit, the fresh ruby pomegranate arils (they're the juicy seeds) add a whole new dimension to this dessert. Crunchy, and both sweet and tart, these beauties are the ultimate complement to the dainty Angelic Cake.

1 slice Angelic Cake (page 506) or other
     angel food cake

1 tablespoon fresh pomegranate seeds (arils)

2 teaspoons Cilantro and Pomegranate Syrups
     (page 538)

½ teaspoon fresh cilantro leaves or
     1 sprig fresh cilantro

Place the cake on a dessert plate. Sprinkle with the pomegranate arils, lightly drizzle with the syrups (1 teaspoon of the cilantro and 1 teaspoon of the pomegranate syrup), garnish with the cilantro, and serve.

Per serving: 170 calories, 0g total fat, 0g saturated fat, 0g trans fat, 0mg cholesterol, 120mg sodium, 38g total carbohydrate, 2g dietary fiber, 30g sugars, 4g protein

Pound-less Cake Ⓢ

Makes 14 servings: 1 slice each

Originally, pound cake was made with a pound of each main ingredient: flour, sugar, butter, and eggs. Not here! That's a good thing, as this version is a moist and sweet treat that won't make you gain a pound. It has some real butter in it so it still tastes rich. Make it memorable by adorning your slice with vanilla Greek yogurt and a burst of fresh berries.

2 cups whole-wheat pastry flour

½ teaspoon baking powder

¼ teaspoon sea salt

**½ cup plain almond milk or unsweetened coconut
   milk beverage, at room temperature**

½ cup fat-free or low-fat plain Greek yogurt

2 tablespoons no-sugar-added apple butter

6 tablespoons unsalted butter, at room temperature

1¼ cups turbinado sugar

3 large eggs, at room temperature

1¼ teaspoons pure vanilla extract

**¼ teaspoon pure lemon extract or 1 teaspoon
   finely grated lemon zest**

1. Preheat the oven to 350°F. Line the bottom of a 9 × 5-inch stick-resistant loaf pan with parchment paper. Coat the pan with cooking spray (preferably homemade, page xix).

2. Sift or whisk together the flour, baking powder, and salt in a medium bowl. Set aside.

3. Whisk together the almond milk, yogurt, and apple butter in a small bowl. Set aside.

4. Beat together the butter and sugar with an electric mixer in a large bowl at medium speed until well blended, about 2 minutes. Add the eggs, beating well after each addition, then beat in the extracts. On low speed, beat in half of the flour mixture and half of the milk mixture until just combined, and repeat.

5. Transfer the batter to the loaf pan, smoothing the top. Gently tap the pan on the counter to eliminate large air pockets. Bake until light golden brown and a toothpick inserted into the center comes out clean, about 1 hour 10 minutes.

6. Cool the cake in the pan on a rack for 30 minutes, then invert onto rack and cool completely.

7. Cut the loaf into 14 slices, like a loaf of bread, and serve.

Per serving: 200 calories, 7g total fat, 3.5g saturated fat, 0g trans fat, 55mg cholesterol, 85mg sodium, 32g total carbohydrate, 2g dietary fiber, 19g sugars, 4g protein

Lemon Pound-less Cake Ⓢ

Makes 14 servings: 1 slice each

Luscious lemon cake, extra moist, with real lemon slices on top! There are so many secret ingredients in this cake that make it taste so scrumptious: apple butter, crunchy sweet turbinado sugar, almond milk, and creamy smooth yogurt. Love its sweet lemony goodness—pure and simple. Or serve with Basil-Strawberry Sauce (page 540) for extra fruity appeal.

2 cups whole-wheat pastry flour

½ teaspoon ground ginger (optional)

½ teaspoon baking powder

¼ teaspoon sea salt

½ cup plain almond milk or unsweetened coconut milk beverage, at room temperature

½ cup plain fat-free or low-fat Greek yogurt

2 tablespoons no-sugar-added apple butter

5 tablespoons unsalted butter, at room temperature

1¼ cups turbinado sugar

3 large eggs, at room temperature

1 teaspoon pure vanilla extract

½ teaspoon pure lemon extract or 2 teaspoons finely grated lemon zest

5 very thin lemon slices, each cut into 4 pieces

1. Preheat the oven to 350°F. Line the bottom of a stick-resistant 9 × 5-inch loaf pan with parchment paper. Coat the pan with cooking spray (preferably homemade, page xix).

2. Sift or whisk together the flour, ginger (if using), baking powder, and salt in a medium bowl. Set aside.

3. Whisk together the milk, yogurt, and apple butter in a small bowl. Set aside.

4. Beat together the butter and sugar with an electric mixer in a large bowl at medium speed until well blended, about 2 minutes. Add the eggs, beating well after each addition, then beat in the extracts. On low speed, beat in half of the flour

mixture and half of the milk mixture until just combined, and repeat.

5. Transfer the batter to the loaf pan, smoothing the top. Gently tap the pan on the counter to eliminate large air pockets. Arrange the lemon pieces on top of the loaf. Bake until light golden brown and a toothpick inserted into the center comes out with crumbs adhering, about 1 hour 10 minutes.

6. Cool the cake in the pan on a rack for 30 minutes, then invert onto rack and cool completely.

7. Cut the loaf into 14 slices, and serve.

Per serving: 190 calories, 6g total fat, 3g saturated fat, 0g trans fat, 50mg cholesterol, 85mg sodium, 32g total carbohydrate, 2g dietary fiber, 19g sugars, 4g protein

Blueberry Bundt Cake Ⓢ

Makes 16 servings: 1 slice each

Here's a memorably modern way to enjoy an old-fashioned Bundt cake. The fresh vivid blueberries and creamy lavender-colored blueberry sauce create a wholesome and delicious burst of sweet fruity flavor. The antioxidants from the blueberries are a health and beauty bonus.

2¾ cups whole-wheat pastry flour

½ teaspoon ground ginger

1 teaspoon baking powder

½ teaspoon baking soda

½ teaspoon sea salt

1 cup plain almond milk or unsweetened coconut milk beverage

½ cup plain fat-free or low-fat Greek yogurt

3 tablespoons no-sugar-added apple butter

6 tablespoons unsalted butter, at room temperature

1¼ cups turbinado sugar

4 large eggs

Juice and zest of ½ small lemon (1 tablespoon juice)

1 teaspoon pure vanilla extract

¼ teaspoon pure almond extract

12 ounces fresh blueberries

1 recipe Fresh Blueberry Crème Sauce (page 540)

1. Preheat the oven to 350°F.

2. Sift or whisk together the flour, ginger, baking powder, baking soda, and salt in a medium bowl. Set aside.

3. Whisk together the almond milk, yogurt, and apple butter in a small bowl. Set aside.

4. Beat together the butter and sugar with an electric mixer at medium speed in a large bowl until well combined. Add the eggs, beating well after each addition, then beat in the lemon juice, lemon zest, and extracts. Reduce the speed to low, beat in half of the flour mixture and half of the almond milk mixture until just combined, and repeat. Fold in half of the blueberries.

5. Transfer the batter to a stick-resistant Bundt (9½-inch fluted) cake pan, smoothing the top. Gently tap the pan on the counter to eliminate large air pockets.

6. Bake until light golden brown and a toothpick inserted into the center comes out clean, about 55 minutes to 1 hour. Cool in the pan 1 hour, then invert onto a rack and cool completely, about 1 hour.

7. Cut the Bundt cake into 16 slices. Drizzle with the blueberry sauce, garnish with remaining fresh blueberries, and serve.

Per serving: 230 calories, 6g total fat, 3g saturated fat, 0g trans fat, 60mg cholesterol, 180mg sodium, 39g total carbohydrate, 4g dietary fiber, 20g sugars, 5g protein

Springtime Strawberry-Rhubarb Angel Food Shortcake Ⓢ

Makes 1 servings: 1 shortcake

Angel food cake instead of a buttery biscuit, and frozen dessert instead of whipped cream, helps keep the calories in check here compared to your typical strawberry shortcake. And the rhubarb adds a unique taste twist. You'll be able to serve yourself a substantial portion. Go ahead—plan for this indulgence.

1 slice Angelic Cake (page 506) or other
    angel food cake
⅓ cup Rhubarb-Strawberry Compote (page 538)
2 tablespoons frozen vanilla yogurt or soy
    or rice frozen dessert (25-calorie portion)
¼ teaspoon grated orange zest, or to taste
1 piece crystallized ginger (optional)

Place the slice of cake on a dessert plate. Top with the compote and the scoop of frozen dessert. Sprinkle with the orange zest, top with the ginger (if using), and serve immediately.

Per serving: 270 calories, 0g total fat, 0g saturated fat, 0g trans fat, 0mg cholesterol, 110mg sodium, 63g total carbohydrate, 2g dietary fiber, 53g sugars, 5g protein

Blackberry Mousse Almond Crumb Cake

Makes 10 servings: 1 wedge each

This dreamy crumb cake is dotted with fresh berries and studded with crunchy almonds, all nestled in a bed of creamy mousse and a moist, yet flaky crust. Not only is it delicious to eat, it looks beautifully impressive on the plate—a real showstopper.

1 cup whole-wheat pastry flour

⅓ cup turbinado sugar

⅛ teaspoon sea salt

5 tablespoons cold unsalted butter, cut into small pieces

4 ounces Neufchâtel (light cream cheese), at room temperature

⅓ cup seedless blackberry jam or preserves

⅔ cup fat-free or low-fat plain Greek yogurt

2 teaspoons honey or agave nectar

1½ teaspoons pure vanilla extract

½ teaspoon pure almond extract

1 large egg

½ teaspoon baking powder

¼ teaspoon baking soda

6 ounces fresh blackberries

2 tablespoons sliced blanched almonds

1. Preheat the oven to 350°F. Line the bottom of an 8-inch round baking pan with parchment paper.

2. Sift or whisk together the flour, sugar, and salt in a large bowl. Cut in the butter with a pastry blender or potato masher until crumbly. Remove ½ cup of the mixture and set aside.

3. Blend the Neufchâtel and jam with an electric mixer in a medium bowl at low speed until light and fluffy. Set aside.

4. Whisk together the yogurt, honey, extracts, egg, baking powder, and baking soda in a small bowl until evenly combined.

5. Add the yogurt mixture to the crumbly flour mixture in the large bowl and beat with an electric mixer on medium speed until well blended. Pour the mixture into the baking pan.

6. Spread the Neufchâtel-jam mixture evenly over the batter. Sprinkle with the blackberries, almonds, and reserved ½ cup crumbly flour mixture.

7. Bake until the edges are lightly browned and center is nearly set, about 1 hour. Cool in the pan on a rack. (Note: When cooling, the cake will deflate slightly.) Transfer to the refrigerator until well chilled, at least 3 hours.

8. Cut into 10 wedges, and serve.

Per serving: 210 calories, 10g total fat, 5g saturated fat, 0g trans fat, 40mg cholesterol, 135mg sodium, 27g total carbohydrate, 3g dietary fiber, 16g sugars, 5g protein

Hint-of-Mint Snack Cake

Makes 20 servings: 1 piece each

Minty fresh coolness and va-va vanilla come together to create this moist fancy-free snack cake draped with a buttercream icing. Delicious!

1⅓ cups whole-wheat pastry flour

1 teaspoon baking powder

½ teaspoon baking soda

¾ teaspoon sea salt

5 tablespoons unsalted butter, at room temperature

1 cup turbinado sugar

3 large eggs

2 tablespoons fat-free or low-fat plain Greek yogurt

1½ teaspoons pure vanilla extract

¼ teaspoon pure peppermint extract

5 ounces plain almond milk, unsweetened coconut milk beverage, or light soy milk

½ cup + 2 tablespoons Hint-of-Mint Vanilla Buttercream Icing (page 539)

20 tiny fresh mint sprigs

1. Preheat the oven to 350°F. Line the bottom of a 9×13-inch baking pan with parchment paper. Set aside.

2. Sift or whisk together the flour, baking powder, baking soda, and salt in a medium bowl. Set aside.

3. Beat together the butter and sugar with an electric mixer at medium speed in a large bowl until well combined. Add the eggs, yogurt, and extracts, beating well until combined. Reduce the speed to low, beat in half of the flour mixture and half of the almond milk until just combined, and repeat.

4. Pour the batter evenly into the baking pan. Bake until golden, springy to the touch, and a toothpick inserted into the center of the cake comes out clean, about 30 minutes. Cool completely in the pan on a rack.

5. Cut the cake into 20 pieces. Drizzle or dollop the icing onto the center of each piece, allowing the icing to run slightly down the edges. Insert a mint sprig on top of each piece, and serve.

Per serving: 130 calories, 4.5g total fat, 2.5g saturated fat, 0g trans fat, 35mg cholesterol, 170mg sodium, 22g total carbohydrate, 1g dietary fiber, 16g sugars, 2g protein

Double Chocolate Mini Cupcakes Ⓢ

Makes 32 servings: 2 mini-cupcakes each

At only 80 calories a pop, these ooey-gooey rich and chocolaty cupcakes make a guilt-free after-dinner treat. The pinch of cayenne pepper is subtle and complements the deep chocolaty sweetness. Want a bigger cupcake? Spoon ¼ cup batter into lined standard cupcake pans and bake 20 minutes to make two dozen.

2 cups whole-wheat pastry flour
2 teaspoons baking powder
½ teaspoon sea salt
⅛ teaspoon ground cinnamon
⅛ teaspoon ground cayenne
6 ounces semisweet baking chocolate, chopped

2 ounces unsweetened baking chocolate, chopped
5 tablespoons unsalted butter, at room temperature
1½ cups firmly packed dark brown sugar
3 large eggs
2 teaspoons pure vanilla extract
1⅔ cups plain almond milk or unsweetened coconut milk beverage
1 recipe Fluffy Chocolate Yogurt Frosting (page 539)

1. Line 64 cups of mini muffin tins with mini cupcake liners. Set aside.

2. Sift or whisk together the flour, baking powder, salt, cinnamon, and cayenne in a medium bowl. Set aside.

3. Melt the chocolates in a small saucepan over low heat, stirring occasionally until smooth. Set aside.

4. Preheat the oven to 375°F.

5. Beat together the butter and brown sugar with an electric mixer on medium speed in a large bowl until well combined. Add the eggs, beating well after each addition. Stir in the melted chocolates and vanilla extract.

6. Reduce the speed to low, beat in half of the flour mixture and half of the almond milk until just combined, and repeat. Spoon the batter evenly (1½ tablespoons each) into each mini-muffin cup.

7. Bake (in batches, if necessary) until springy to the touch, about 15 to 17 minutes.

8. Cool in the pans on wire racks for about 15 minutes. Remove the cupcakes from the pans and cool completely on wire racks.

9. Spread the cooled cupcakes with 1 slightly rounded teaspoon of the frosting each, and serve.

Per serving: 160 calories, 7g total fat, 4g saturated fat, 0g trans fat, 20mg cholesterol, 95mg sodium, 23g total carbohydrate, 2g dietary fiber, 14g sugars, 3g protein

Mini Red Velvet Cupcakes

Makes 14 servings: 3 mini-cupcakes each

Instead of artificial red food coloring, these cupcakes get their name by this addition of seedless red raspberry jam. If you prefer, use strawberry, cherry, red currant, or rhubarb jam instead. The artful drizzle of Silken Icing adds the perfect sweet topping to reinvent this classic cake.

1¾ cups whole-wheat pastry flour

3½ tablespoons unsweetened cocoa powder

1 teaspoon baking soda

1 teaspoon baking powder

½ teaspoon sea salt

1 cup low-fat buttermilk

3 tablespoons seedless red raspberry jam

1 teaspoon white vinegar

1¼ teaspoons pure vanilla extract

1¼ cups turbinado sugar

6 tablespoons unsalted butter, room temperature

2 large eggs

⅔ cup Silken Icing (page 539)

1. Line 42 cups of mini muffin tins with mini cupcake liners. Set aside.

2. Preheat the oven to 375°F.

3. Sift or whisk together the flour, cocoa powder, baking soda, baking powder, and salt into a medium bowl. Set aside.

4. Whisk together the buttermilk, jam, vinegar, and vanilla extract in a small bowl to blend. Set aside.

5. Beat together the sugar and butter with an electric mixer on medium speed in a large bowl until creamy. Add the eggs, beating well after each addition.

6. Reduce the speed to low, beat in one-third of the flour mixture and one-third of the milk mixture until just combined, and repeat twice. Pour the batter evenly into each mini-muffin cup.

7. Bake until a toothpick inserted in the center comes out clean, about 15 minutes. Cool in the pans on wire racks for about 15 minutes. Remove the cupcakes from the pans and cool completely on wire racks.

8. Splatter or drizzle each of the cooled cupcakes with ¾ teaspoon of the icing each, and serve.

Per serving: 160 calories, 5g total fat, 3g saturated fat, 0g trans fat, 30mg cholesterol, 190mg sodium, 26g total carbohydrate, 2g dietary fiber, 16g sugars, 3g protein

Cookies

100-Calorie Dark Chocolate Chip Cookies

Makes 24 servings: 1 cookie each

Move over "100-calorie packs." There's a real fresh-baked chocolate chip cookie in town. It will help keep your body—and taste buds—happy. It's baked in an energy-saving, eco-friendlier way, too. You might be surprised to see spices in this cookie, but they add flavor depth and intrigue.

1 cup stone-ground whole-wheat flour

1 teaspoon baking soda

½ teaspoon sea salt

¼ teaspoon ground cinnamon

⅛ teaspoon ground cayenne

⅛ teaspoon ground ginger (optional)

¼ cup unrefined peanut or canola oil

1 cup turbinado sugar

1 large egg, lightly beaten

3 tablespoons no-sugar-added apple butter

1¾ teaspoons pure vanilla extract

¼ teaspoon pure chocolate extract

⅓ cup old-fashioned oats

⅔ cup semisweet chocolate chips

1. Combine the flour, baking soda, salt, cinnamon, cayenne, and ginger (if using) in a medium bowl. Set aside.

2. Stir together the oil and sugar in a large bowl until combined. Stir in the egg, apple butter, and vanilla extract, and chocolate extract (if using) until smooth.

3. Stir the flour mixture into the oil-sugar mixture until thoroughly combined. Stir in the oats, then the chocolate chips until just combined.

4. Line two large baking sheets with parchment paper. Drop the dough by rounded tablespoons onto the sheets, 12 cookies each.

5. Place in the oven, then turn the heat to 375°F (do not preheat oven). Bake until they just spread out to cookie shape, yet are still undercooked to the touch, 10 to 12 minutes. As quickly as possible (so you don't let out too much heat), open the oven and swap the trays—move the tray on the top rack to the bottom and bottom rack to the top. Close the oven, then turn the oven off and let the cookies continue baking in the off oven until desired brownness and crispness, about 7 to 9 minutes. Remove from the oven and let cool completely on the baking sheets on racks.

Per serving: 100 calories, 4g total fat, 1.5g saturated fat, 0g trans fat, 10mg cholesterol, 105mg sodium, 17g total carbohydrate, 1g dietary fiber, 11g sugars, 1g protein

Cocoa Meringue Cookies Ⓢ

Makes 7 servings: 6 cookies each

Craving a chocolate cookie that won't weigh you down? How about one that literally melts in your mouth? That's exactly what you get with these crisp, airy, and chocolaty cloud-like cookies. You can revel in being able to enjoy 6 cookies for a serving!

3 tablespoons unsweetened cocoa powder

⅔ cup powdered sugar

1½ teaspoons cornstarch

4 large egg whites (about ½ cup)

⅓ cup superfine sugar

1 teaspoon pure vanilla extract

1. Preheat the oven to 275°F.

2. Sift together cocoa, powdered sugar, and cornstarch in a medium bowl.

3. Beat together the egg whites at medium speed with an electric mixer in a large bowl until soft peaks form.

4. Gradually add the superfine sugar and continue beating until the sugar is dissolved and the whites are stiff and glossy, about 2 minutes. Add the vanilla extract and mix well. Gently fold in the cocoa mixture until evenly combined.

5. Drop the batter by heaping teaspoon onto two parchment paper–lined baking sheets to make 42 meringue drops. Bake until the cookies are nearly firm to the touch, about 1 hour, gently rotating and switching pan positions halfway through the baking time.

6. Turn off the oven and keep the cookies in the oven for 2 hours. Then cool cookies completely on baking sheets on racks. Store cookies in an airtight container.

Per serving: 100 calories, 0g total fat, 0g saturated fat, 0g trans fat, 0mg cholesterol, 30mg sodium, 22g total carbohydrate, 1g dietary fiber, 21g sugars, 3g protein

Apricot Oatmeal Cookies

Makes 18 servings: 1 cookie each

Here's a twist on oatmeal raisin cookies for a refreshing taste update. The dried apricot addition will make you smile but also try figs (a favorite of mine) or other dried fruits. There are so many delicious dried fruits available, such as apples, dates, plums, mangoes, and more.

1 cup old-fashioned oats

¾ cup whole-wheat pastry flour

1½ teaspoons baking powder

¾ teaspoon sea salt

¼ teaspoon ground cinnamon

¾ cup turbinado sugar

¼ cup unsalted butter, room temperature

3 tablespoons no-sugar-added applesauce

1 large egg

1½ teaspoons pure vanilla extract

⅓ cup finely chopped sun-dried or unsulfured Turkish apricots or dried figs

1. Preheat the oven to 350°F.

2. Stir together the oats, flour, baking powder, salt, and cinnamon in a medium bowl until combined.

3. Blend together the sugar and butter with an electric mixer at medium speed in a large bowl until well combined. Add the applesauce, egg, and vanilla extract and blend until smooth.

4. Reduce speed to low, add the oat mixture, and blend until just combined. Stir in the apricots.

5. Onto two parchment paper–lined baking sheets, drop batter by rounded tablespoon (2 tablespoons batter each), about 2 inches apart. Bake until rich golden brown, about 25 minutes, rotating trays halfway through baking. Remove from oven and let cool completely on the baking sheets on racks.

Per serving: 100 calories, 3g total fat, 2g saturated fat, 0g trans fat, 15mg cholesterol, 140mg sodium, 17g total carbohydrate, 1g dietary fiber, 10g sugars, 1g protein

Crisp Lace Cookies

Makes 16 servings: 1 cookie each

Enjoy this divine cookie as is—my preferred way! Or consider it as your canvas for whatever suits your fancy. Crumble on top of Greek yogurt. Or be creative and slather with chocolate-hazelnut spread or frozen yogurt to make an impressive open-face cookie sandwich.

1 cup old-fashioned oats

¼ cup whole-wheat pastry flour

1½ teaspoon baking powder

½ teaspoon + ⅛ teaspoon sea salt

⅛ teaspoon ground cinnamon

¼ cup unsalted butter, at room temperature

¾ cup turbinado sugar

1 large egg

3 tablespoons no-sugar-added apple butter

1¼ teaspoons pure vanilla extract

1. Preheat the oven to 325°F.

2. Mix together the oats, flour, baking powder, salt, and cinnamon in a medium bowl until thoroughly combined.

3. Blend together the butter and sugar with an electric mixer on medium speed in a large bowl until well combined. Add the egg, apple butter, and vanilla extract and blend until combined. Add the oat mixture and blend until well combined.

4. Drop the batter by rounded tablespoon, at least 2 inches apart, onto parchment paper–lined baking sheets.

5. Bake until rich golden brown, about 28 minutes, rotating trays halfway through baking. Cool the cookies on baking sheets for 10 minutes. Peel the cookies off the parchment paper with your fingers and let cookies cool completely on racks.

Per serving: 100 calories, 4g total fat, 2g saturated fat, 0g trans fat, 0mg cholesterol, 140mg sodium, 16g total carbohydrate, 1g dietary fiber, 10g sugars, 1g protein

Almond Cookies

Makes 30 servings: 1 large cookie each

These cookies bake up so beautifully into large bites of sweet nutty goodness. The chewy bites are a taste of culinary heaven for almond lovers. They have the lovely nut included in three ways—as almond flour, pure extract, and sliced.

1¾ cups whole-wheat pastry flour

⅓ cup finely ground almond flour

1 teaspoon baking soda

1 teaspoon sea salt

7 tablespoons unsalted butter, at room temperature

1¼ cups turbinado sugar

1 teaspoon pure vanilla extract

½ teaspoon pure almond extract

¼ cup no-sugar-added apple butter

3 tablespoons fat-free or low-fat plain Greek yogurt

2 large eggs

⅓ cup sliced natural almonds

1. Preheat the oven to 350°F.

2. Whisk together the flours, baking soda, and salt in a medium bowl. Set aside.

3. Add the butter, sugar, and extracts to a large bowl and blend with an electric mixer on medium speed until well combined. Add the apple butter, yogurt, and eggs and beat until well combined. Gradually add the flour mixture and beat on low speed until creamy. Gently stir in the nuts.

4. Drop by rounded tablespoon onto four parchment paper–lined baking sheets to make 30 large cookies. If desired, gently press onto the top of each cookie 2 almond slices before baking.

5. Bake in batches (two sheets at a time) until rich golden brown, about 22 minutes, rotating trays halfway through baking. Cool on baking sheets for 5 minutes. Transfer the cookies to racks to cool.

Per serving: 100 calories, 4g total fat, 2g saturated fat, 0g trans fat, 20mg cholesterol, 125mg sodium, 15g total carbohydrate, 1g dietary fiber, 9g sugars, 2g protein

Orange Pistachio Cookies

Makes 30 servings: 2 cookies each

These standout petite and chewy cookies are so appealing, with refreshing brightness from the orange zest and crunchiness of the green pistachios. I added some finely chopped rosemary for intrigue. You can use lavender or thyme, for a mysteriously wonderful taste, and other nuts, too, like almonds or walnuts.

2 cups whole-wheat pastry flour

1 teaspoon baking soda

¾ teaspoon sea salt

7 tablespoons unsalted butter, at room temperature

1¼ cups turbinado sugar

1½ teaspoons finely grated orange zest, or to taste

1 teaspoon pure vanilla extract

¼ teaspoon pure almond extract

½ teaspoon minced fresh rosemary

3 tablespoons no-sugar-added apple butter

3 tablespoons fat-free or low-fat plain Greek yogurt

2 large eggs

½ cup lightly salted roasted pistachios, chopped

1. Preheat the oven to 375°F.

2. Whisk together the flour, baking soda, and salt in a medium bowl. Set aside.

3. Add the butter, sugar, orange zest, extracts, and rosemary to a large bowl and blend with an electric mixer on medium speed until well combined. Add the apple butter, yogurt, and eggs and beat until well combined. Gradually add the flour mixture and beat on low speed until creamy. Stir in the pistachios.

4. Drop by rounded tablespoon onto four parchment paper–lined baking sheets to make 60 small cookies. If desired, gently press onto the top of each cookie a pistachio before baking.

5. Bake in batches (two sheets at a time) until rich golden brown, about 15 minutes, rotating trays halfway through baking. Cool on baking sheets for 5 minutes. Transfer the cookies to racks to cool.

Per serving: 100 calories, 4g total fat, 2g saturated fat, 0g trans fat, 20mg cholesterol, 115mg sodium, 15g total carbohydrate, 1g dietary fiber, 9g sugars, 2g protein

Brownies and Bars

Fudgy Superfood Brownies Ⓢ

Makes 25 servings: 1 brownie each

These are the perfect bite when you want something chocolatey but you don't want to break your calorie bank. The surprising beans, creamy tofu, and "hot" wasabi powder unite to create a super-fudgy, seriously tasty, 100-calorie superfood brownie. If you've never tried spicy sweets, be adventurous—the wasabi or cayenne add a hint of intrigue, but leave it out, if you like.

½ cup drained canned no-salt-added black beans

5 tablespoons no-sugar-added applesauce or apricot-applesauce

¼ cup silken tofu, well drained

1¼ teaspoons pure vanilla extract

1½ cups turbinado sugar

¼ cup canola or peanut oil

¼ teaspoon sea salt

3 ounces unsweetened baking chocolate, chopped

⅓ cup unsweetened cocoa powder

¾ teaspoon wasabi powder or ¼ teaspoon ground cayenne, or to taste

⅔ cup whole-wheat pastry flour

1. Line the bottom of a 6½ × 8½-inch or similar size stick-resistant toaster oven pan with parchment paper. Set aside.

2. Add the beans, 3 tablespoons of the applesauce, the tofu, and vanilla extract to a food processor. Cover and puree. Set aside.

3. Stir together the sugar, oil, the remaining 2 tablespoons applesauce, and the salt in a large microwave-safe bowl. Cook in the microwave on high for 2½ minutes, stirring once halfway through the cooking time (mixture will be fully bubbling). Carefully remove the very hot mixture from the microwave.

4. Stir in the chocolate, cocoa, and wasabi powder until the chocolate is melted.

5. Stir the bean mixture into the chocolate mixture until well combined. Stir in the flour until just combined.

6. Pour the batter into the prepared pan. Bake in the toaster oven at 375°F or standard preheated oven until springy to the touch, about 20 minutes. Remove from the oven. Cool completely in the pan on a rack. When cool, cut into 25 rectangular pieces, and serve.

Per serving: 100 calories, 4.5g total fat, 1.5g saturated fat, 0g trans fat, 0mg cholesterol, 25mg sodium, 17g total carbohydrate, 2g dietary fiber, 12g sugars, 1g protein

Raspberry Brownie-Style Fudge Ⓢ

Makes 20 servings: 1 piece each

This recipe is like an extra, extra fudgy brownie. That's why I call it brownie-style fudge. And that's what makes these yummy morsels seem extra decadent. The combination of chocolate and raspberry is special, too.

2 large eggs

2 teaspoons pure vanilla extract

⅛ teaspoon pure peppermint extract (optional)

1½ cups turbinado sugar

⅓ cup canola oil

½ teaspoon sea salt

¼ cup unsweetened cocoa powder

3 ounces unsweetened baking chocolate, chopped

⅔ cup whole-wheat pastry flour

¾ cup fresh or frozen raspberries, thawed

1. Line the bottom and the sides of an 8-inch square baking pan with parchment paper. Then lightly coat the pan with cooking spray (preferably homemade, page xix). Set aside.

2. Preheat the oven to 350°F.

3. Add the eggs, vanilla extract, peppermint extract (if using), and 1 tablespoon water to a small bowl or liquid measuring cup and whisk until well combined. Set aside.

4. Add the sugar, oil, salt, and 2 tablespoons water to a large, microwave-safe bowl and stir to combine. Cook in the microwave on high for 2½ minutes, stirring once halfway through the cooking time (mixture will be fully bubbling). Carefully remove the very hot mixture from the microwave.

5. Gently stir the cocoa and chocolate into the sugar mixture until the chocolate is melted. Gradually and vigorously stir in the egg mixture until well incorporated. Stir in the flour until the batter is smooth.

6. Immediately spread the batter in the baking pan. Sprinkle with the raspberries and slightly stir the raspberries into the batter. Bake until springy to the touch around the edges, about 30 minutes. (Note: The brownies will slightly firm up upon chilling.) Cool completely in the pan on a rack, then chill in the refrigerator for at least 2 hours or overnight. Cut into 20 bars, and serve.

Per serving: 140 calories, 7g total fat, 2g saturated fat, 0g trans fat, 20mg cholesterol, 65mg sodium, 20g total carbohydrate, 2g dietary fiber, 15g sugars, 2g protein

Fleur de Sel Brownie Rounds Ⓢ

Makes 12 servings: 1 brownie round each

Fancy flaky sea salt . . . it enhances the intense chocolate flavor of this brownie! Paired with good-quality cocoa and espresso powders, you've got yourself a chocolate dessert that'll take your taste buds on a sweet and salty ride. Or, better yet, plan for a little extra indulgence and top with a scoop of light mint or French vanilla frozen yogurt.

2 large eggs

1¼ teaspoons pure vanilla extract

⅓ cup unsweetened cocoa powder

1 teaspoon instant espresso powder

1½ cups turbinado sugar

3 tablespoons canola or peanut oil

3 tablespoons no-sugar-added applesauce

½ teaspoon fleur de sel, or to taste

3 ounces unsweetened baking chocolate, chopped

⅔ cup whole-wheat pastry flour

1. Preheat the oven to 400°F. Set aside one 12-cup or two 6-cup silicone or cooking spray–coated nonstick muffin trays. Alternatively, place 12 silicone nonstick reusable muffin liners into a 12-cup muffin tray. Do not use paper muffin liners; the brownies will stick to the wrappers.

2. Whisk together with a fork the eggs and vanilla extract in a medium bowl until combined. Add the cocoa and espresso powders and whisk until a smooth pudding-like texture results. Set aside.

3. Stir together the sugar, oil, applesauce, and ¼ teaspoon of the fleur de sel in a large microwave-safe bowl. Cook in the microwave oven on high for 2½ minutes, stirring once midway through the cooking time (mixture will be fully bubbling). Carefully remove the very hot mixture from the microwave.

4. Immediately stir the chocolate into the hot mixture with a fork until the chocolate is just melted. Stir in the reserved egg-cocoa mixture until well combined. Stir in the flour until just combined. (Note: The mixture will not be silky smooth.)

5. Spoon the batter into the muffin cups, filling about halfway, about 2 rounded or 3 level tablespoons each. Sprinkle with the remaining ¼ teaspoon fleur de sel using your fingers.

6. Bake until the brownies are springy to the touch, about 15 minutes. Remove from the oven. Cool the brownies completely in the pan on a rack, and serve.

Per serving: 200 calories, 8g total fat, 3g saturated fat, 0g trans fat, 30mg cholesterol, 95mg sodium, 33g total carbohydrate, 3g dietary fiber, 25g sugars, 3g protein

"Energy Bar" Brownies

Makes 15 servings: 1 piece each

"Energy" is another name for calories. These super-moist, fluffy, brownie-like bars are meant to give you energy, but in delicious, just-right-size bites. Along with liquids, they're an ideal nibble right after a workout. You'll be able to replace energy within your muscles, plus they provide potassium to help replenish lost electrolytes. For extra energy and crunch, sprinkle with chopped nuts before baking.

3 ounces dried plums (about 10)

1 small or ½ large fully ripened banana

1 small or ½ large Hass avocado, pitted and peeled

3 large eggs

4 large egg whites

2½ ounces unsweetened baking chocolate, chopped

⅔ cup turbinado sugar

3 tablespoons unsweetened cocoa powder

1 teaspoon sea salt

⅓ cup old-fashioned oats

1½ teaspoons pure vanilla extract

⅓ cup whole-wheat pastry flour

1. Preheat the oven to 350°F. Line the bottom of an 8-inch square baking pan with parchment paper. Then lightly coat the pan with cooking spray (preferably homemade, page xix). Set aside.

2. Add the dried plums, banana, avocado, and eggs to a food processor. Cover and puree until paste-like. Add the egg whites and puree just until incorporated. Set aside.

3. Place the chocolate into a heatproof bowl. Place the bowl over a saucepan with simmering water. Stir only as needed, just until chocolate is melted.

4. Meanwhile add the plum-banana mixture, sugar, cocoa, and salt to a large bowl. Stir vigorously until thoroughly combined. Stir in the oats. Stir in the melted chocolate and vanilla until evenly distributed. Stir in the flour just until incorporated.

5. Spread the batter evenly in the pan. Bake until springy to the touch about 2 inches from the edges, about 35 minutes.

6. Cool completely on a rack. Cut into 15 bars. Enjoy at room temperature, warm, or chilled.

Per serving: 130 calories, 5g total fat, 2g saturated fat, 0g trans fat, 35mg cholesterol, 190mg sodium, 19g total carbohydrate, 3g dietary fiber, 11g sugars, 4g protein

Macadamia Nut Blondie Bars Ⓢ

Makes 16 servings: 1 blondie each

The Blondie! This white chocolate-macadamia-studded dessert bar has a cake-like texture and extra volume, which is produced partly with the use of baking soda. It's extra satisfying and simply scrumptious.

¾ cup firmly packed dark brown sugar

¼ cup unsalted butter, melted

¼ cup no-sugar-added apple butter

1 large egg

1¼ teaspoons pure vanilla extract

1 cup whole-wheat pastry flour

½ teaspoon baking soda

⅛ teaspoon sea salt

¼ cup chopped white chocolate

¼ cup chopped unsalted macadamia nuts

1. Preheat the oven to 350°F. Line the bottom of an 8-inch square baking pan with parchment paper. Lightly coat the pan with cooking spray (preferably homemade, page xix).

2. Whisk together the sugar, butter, and apple butter in a medium bowl. Add the egg and vanilla extract and whisk until well combined. Add the flour, baking soda, and salt, stirring until just combined. Add the chocolate and 3 tablespoons of the nuts and stir until evenly combined.

3. Pour into the prepared pan and spread evenly. Lightly sprinkle with the remaining 1 tablespoon macadamia nuts.

4. Bake until a toothpick inserted into the center of the blondies comes out clean, about 25 minutes. Allow to cool in the pan on a rack. Cut around the edges of the pan to loosen the blondies from the side of the pan. Cut into squares, and serve.

Per serving: 130 calories, 6g total fat, 3g saturated fat, 0g trans fat, 20mg cholesterol, 65mg sodium, 19g total carbohydrate, 1g dietary fiber, 13g sugars, 2g protein

Desserts, Muffins, and Sweet Toppings   **519**

Zesty Lemon Bars Ⓢ

Makes 24 servings: 1 bar each

These luscious lemony bars contain much less butter compared to most similar bar recipes, but still leave you with a deep, rich, golden-yellow sweet-tart treat. The sweet secret: a mashed banana in the shortbread cookie-style crust. You'd never know it unless you whipped these up yourself.

3 lemons

2 cups sifted whole-wheat pastry flour

¾ cup + 1 tablespoon powdered sugar

6 tablespoons unsalted butter, melted

1 small or ½ large fully ripened banana, mashed

4 large eggs

1¼ cups turbinado sugar

⅛ teaspoon sea salt

1. Preheat the oven to 350°F. Line the bottom of a 9 × 13-inch baking pan with parchment paper.

2. Finely grate the zest from one of the lemons. Set aside.

3. Juice all the lemons. Reserve ½ cup of the juice; set aside.

4. Whisk together 1¾ cups of the flour and ¾ cup of the powdered sugar in a medium bowl. Add the butter, banana, and lemon zest and stir until well combined. Press the mixture into the bottom of the prepared pan. Bake until golden brown around the edges, about 20 minutes.

5. Meanwhile, whisk together the eggs in a large bowl for 1 minute.

6. Stir together the sugar, salt, and the remaining ¼ cup flour in a medium bowl until well mixed.

7. Add the sugar mixture to the eggs and whisk to combine. Add the lemon juice and whisk to combine.

8. Pour the lemon mixture over the warm bars and return to the oven.

9. Bake until the bars are set, about 25 minutes. Cool completely in the pan on a rack, then chill.

10. Cut around the edges of the pan and cut into 24 bars. Just before serving, dust with the remaining tablespoon powdered sugar through a fine-mesh strainer or sifter, and serve.

Per serving: 130 calories, 4g total fat, 2g saturated fat, 0g trans fat, 40mg cholesterol, 25mg sodium, 23g total carbohydrate, 1g dietary fiber, 15g sugars, 2g protein

Pies, Cobblers, and Cheesecakes

Petite Pumpkin Pie

Makes 16 servings: 1 mini-pie each

Delicious dessert for less than 100 calories? Believe it. This personal-size pumpkin pie has tender, moist, flan-like appeal. The sweet Greek yogurt topping makes these mini pleasures seem rather decadent.

½ cup whole-grain graham cracker crumbs

¾ cup turbinado sugar

1 tablespoon cornstarch

1¼ teaspoons ground cinnamon

½ teaspoon ground ginger

½ teaspoon sea salt

Pinch of ground cloves

2 large eggs

1 (15-ounce) can no-salt-added 100% pure pumpkin puree

12 ounces fat-free evaporated milk

½ cup fat-free or low-fat plain Greek yogurt

1 teaspoon mild honey or agave nectar

⅛ teaspoon pure vanilla extract

1. Preheat the oven to 350°F. Spray each of 16 cups of two silicone or nonstick muffin trays with cooking spray (preferably homemade, page xix). Sprinkle ½ tablespoon of the graham cracker crumbs into the bottom of each cup. Set aside.

2. Stir together the sugar, cornstarch, 1 teaspoon of the cinnamon, the ginger, salt, and cloves in a small bowl. Set aside.

3. Whisk the eggs in a large bowl. Stir in the pumpkin until well combined. Stir in the sugar mixture until well combined. Whisk in the milk until well combined.

4. Divide the mixture evenly among the 16 muffin cups, about ¼ cup each. Bake both trays until a knife inserted near the center comes out clean, about 33 to 35 minutes. Cool in the muffin trays on racks for about 30 minutes. Chill in the refrigerator for at least 1 hour.

5. Meanwhile, whisk together the yogurt, honey, and vanilla extract.

6. When ready to serve, carefully remove each pie from the tray. Top each with the yogurt mixture, sprinkle with the remaining ¼ teaspoon cinnamon, and serve.

Per serving: 90 calories, 1.5g total fat, 0g saturated fat, 0g trans fat, 25mg cholesterol, 125mg sodium, 17g total carbohydrate, 1g dietary fiber, 14g sugars, 4g protein

Banana Pecan "Pie"

Makes 12 servings: 1 wedge each

This is irresistible! It's banana bread meets pecan pie—rich flavors accented with crunchy nuts, all baked in a pie pan. Try it warm with a scoop of vanilla frozen yogurt for a really special treat.

⅓ cup finely chopped pecans + 12 pecan halves

1¼ cups whole-wheat pastry flour

1 teaspoon baking soda

¼ teaspoon sea salt

2 tablespoons peanut or canola oil

2 tablespoons unsalted butter, melted

⅔ cup turbinado sugar

2 large eggs

3 large fully ripened bananas, mashed

1 ounce 80-proof bourbon

1½ teaspoons pure vanilla extract

1. Lightly coat a nonstick 9-inch pie pan with cooking spray (preferably homemade, page xix). Sprinkle the chopped pecans evenly into the pan. Preheat the oven to 350°F.

continues on next page

2. Whisk or sift together the flour, baking soda, and salt in a medium bowl. Set aside.

3. Whisk together the oil, butter, and sugar in a large mixing bowl until combined. Add the eggs and whisk until well combined. Add the bananas, bourbon, and vanilla extract and whisk until well combined. Add the flour mixture and stir until just combined.

4. Pour the batter into the pan. Very lightly press the pecan halves onto batter, like they're numbers on a clock. Bake until the center is springy to the touch, about 35 minutes. Cool in the pan on a rack.

5. Slice into 12 pie-like wedges. Chill in the refrigerator or freezer.

Per serving: 210 calories, 9g total fat, 2g saturated fat, 0g trans fat, 35mg cholesterol, 170mg sodium, 29g total carbohydrate, 3g dietary fiber, 15g sugars, 3g protein

Mississippi Mud Pie Parfait Ⓢ

Makes 2 servings: 1 parfait each

Kids and adults will adore this inspired dessert that has the flavor essence of Mississippi mud pie, but it's served parfait style with dreamy yogurt (and without the calorie excess). As a bonus, each pleasurable chocolaty parfait supplies 25 percent of the daily value for calcium.

5 ounces fat-free or low-fat chocolate Greek yogurt
½ cup chocolate graham cracker pieces
5 ounces fat-free or low-fat vanilla Greek yogurt
1½ tablespoons chopped pecans
1½ tablespoons semisweet chocolate chips

1. Evenly layer the chocolate yogurt, graham cracker pieces, then vanilla yogurt into two dessert glasses or old-fashioned cocktail glasses.

2. Sprinkle with the pecans and chocolate chips. Serve immediately.

Per serving: 290 calories, 9g total fat, 1.5g saturated fat, 0g trans fat, 0mg cholesterol, 130mg sodium, 39g total carbohydrate, 2g dietary fiber, 29g sugars, 15 g protein

Bing Cherry Cobbler Ⓢ

Makes 10 servings: 1 wedge (¹⁄₁₀ of 9-inch pan) each

Take glorious advantage of Bing cherries when they're in season in June and July. Here, the sweet cherry filling is creamy and saucy. The cobbler topping is crisp and cookie-like. It's like two desserts in one.

3 cups Bing cherries, pitted
1 tablespoon cornstarch
1 cup whole-wheat pastry flour
1¼ cups turbinado sugar
1 teaspoon baking powder
¼ teaspoon ground cinnamon
¼ teaspoon sea salt
3 tablespoons cold unsalted butter, cut into small pieces
½ cup plain almond milk or unsweetened coconut milk beverage

1. Lightly coat a 9-inch round or 8-inch deep round baking pan with cooking spray (preferably homemade, page xix). Preheat the oven to 375°F.

2. Place the cherries in the bottom of the baking pan.

3. Whisk together the cornstarch and ¾ cup boiling water in a small bowl until smooth. Pour the mixture over the cherries.

4. Stir together the flour, sugar, baking powder, cinnamon, and salt in a medium bowl. Add the butter and cut it in with a pastry blender until crumbly. Add the almond milk and stir with a fork until just combined. Drop the dough topping by tablespoonfuls onto the cherry mixture.

5. Place the baking pan on a large baking sheet to allow for any spillover during baking. Bake until the topping is crisp and golden brown, about 40 to 45 minutes. Let stand for about 15 minutes. Serve while warm.

Per serving: 200 calories, 4.5g total fat, 2.5g saturated fat, 0g trans fat, 10mg cholesterol, 115mg sodium, 42g total carbohydrate, 3g dietary fiber, 30g sugars, 2g protein

New York–Style Peachy Cheesecake Ⓢ

Makes 8 servings: 1 wedge each

A typical slice of cheesecake can have up to 700 calories . . . sometimes more! But it is possible to make a cheesecake that's luscious as well as light. You'll be delightfully surprised by a slice of this fresh peach-topped cheesecake that's lightened with Neufchâtel and accented with pure almond extract.

10 ounces Neufchâtel (light cream cheese), at room temperature

¼ cup turbinado sugar

1 teaspoon pure vanilla extract

¼ teaspoon pure almond extract

1 large egg

2 large egg whites

1 (9-inch) ready-to-use graham cracker pie crust

2 teaspoons fresh lemon juice

1 teaspoon honey or agave nectar

⅛ teaspoon ground cinnamon

⅛ teaspoon sea salt

2 ripe peaches, halved, pitted and thinly sliced

1. Preheat the oven to 325°F.

2. Blend together the Neufchâtel, sugar, and extracts in a large bowl with electric mixer on medium speed until smooth. Add the egg and egg whites and blend until smooth. Pour into the crust. Bake until the center is nearly set, about 30 minutes.

3. Cool in the pan on a rack. Transfer to the refrigerator until well chilled, at least 3 hours.

4. Meanwhile, whisk together the lemon juice, honey, cinnamon, and salt in a medium bowl. Add the peach slices and toss until well combined. Cover and chill.

5. Cut the cheesecake into 8 wedges. Transfer each slice onto an individual plate, top with the peach mixture, and serve.

Per serving: 250 calories, 14g total fat, 7g saturated fat, 0g trans fat, 50mg cholesterol, 240mg sodium, 26g total carbohydrate, 1g dietary fiber, 18g sugars, 6g protein

Citrus Cheesecake Squares

Makes 9 servings: 1 square each

This simple square-shaped cheesecake is one that you'll want to make again and again. It's elegant scrumptiousness served on a tender graham cracker crust—and a beautiful blending of velvety, tangy, creamy, and citrusy.

4½ full sheets whole-grain graham crackers, broken neatly in half (9 squares)

10 ounces Neufchâtel (light cream cheese), at room temperature

¼ cup turbinado sugar

Juice and zest of ½ small lemon (1 tablespoon juice)

Juice of ½ lime (1 tablespoon)

1 teaspoon pure vanilla extract

1 large egg

2 large egg whites

1. Preheat the oven to 325°F. Lightly coat an 8-inch square baking pan with cooking spray (preferably homemade, page xix).

2. Line the bottom of the pan with a single layer of the graham cracker squares.

3. Blend together the Neufchâtel, sugar, lemon and lime juices, and vanilla extract with an electric mixer on medium speed in a large bowl until smooth. Add the egg and egg whites and blend until smooth.

4. Pour evenly onto the graham crackers. Sprinkle with the lemon zest. Bake until the center is nearly set, about 27 minutes.

5. Cool in the pan on a rack. Transfer to the refrigerator until well chilled, at least 3 hours.

6. Cut the cheesecake into 9 squares, and serve.

Per serving: 150 calories, 9g total fat, 4.5g saturated fat, 0g trans fat, 45mg cholesterol, 160mg sodium, 12g total carbohydrate, 0g dietary fiber, 9g sugars, 5g protein

Fruit Desserts

Fudge-Drizzled Strawberries Ⓢ

Makes 4 servings: 3 large strawberries

This is quite possibly the perfect 100-calorie dessert! Make sure you select the best berries. Try local sources or farmers' markets.

⅓ cup plain almond milk or unsweetened coconut milk beverage
2 tablespoons mild honey or agave nectar
½ teaspoon pure vanilla extract
1 ounce unsweetened chocolate, finely chopped
12 extra-large whole fresh strawberries
Pinch of fleur de sel (optional)

1. Add the almond milk, honey, and vanilla to a small saucepan and stir until combined. Place over medium heat, add the chocolate, and cook while stirring until the sauce is bubbling fully, about 4 minutes. Continue to cook while stirring constantly until the sauce is silky smooth and slightly thickened, about 1 more minute.

2. Place the strawberries in bowls. Immediately drizzle the fudge sauce over the strawberries, sprinkle with the fleur de sel (if using), and enjoy.

Per serving: 100 calories, 4g total fat, 2.5g saturated fat, 0g trans fat, 0mg cholesterol, 15mg sodium, 18g total carbohydrate, 3g dietary fiber, 13g sugars, 2g protein

Bittersweet Chocolate–Dressed Banana Ⓢ

Makes 4 servings: 1 banana each

There's no need to douse the banana in chocolate; drizzling it is just as tasty . . . and it's prettier. It'll bring out the splatter artiste in everyone. It's fun to make with kids, too. Served frozen, it's extra yummy.

4 small (6-inch) bananas
2 ounces bittersweet (about 70% cacao) chocolate, chopped

1. Carefully insert a craft stick or thick bamboo skewer lengthwise into the center of each peeled banana. Place the bananas on a parchment paper–lined baking sheet. Place the baking sheet in the freezer while preparing the chocolate.

2. Slowly melt half of the chocolate in a double boiler over hot water or in a microwave on high for about 60 seconds. Remove from the heat and stir until completely melted. Using a fork or spoon, drizzle or splatter the chocolate onto the entire exposed surface of each banana. Place the bananas back into the freezer and freeze until the chocolate is solidly crisp, at least 15 minutes.

3. Melt the remaining chocolate. Remove the bananas from the freezer and flip on the other side, uncoated side up. Drizzle or splatter the chocolate onto the bananas.

4. Place the bananas back into the freezer, freeze until the chocolate is solidly crisp and banana is frozen, at least 1 hour, and serve frozen.

Per serving: 170 calories, 6g total fat, 3.5g saturated fat, 0g trans fat, 0mg cholesterol, 34mg sodium, 30g total carbohydrate, 3g dietary fiber, 17g sugars, 2g protein

Semisweet Chocolate–Dipped Figs Ⓢ

Makes 8 servings: 1 large fig each

Fresh figs are a unique fruit that deserves to be showcased as often as possible when in season. And when paired with dark chocolate, fresh figs transform into a divine dessert that's stunning.

8 large fresh Brown Turkey, Black Mission, Calimyrna, or other figs, with stems

3 ounces semisweet chocolate, chopped

⅛ teaspoon fleur de sel or coarse sea salt, or to taste

1. Place the figs on a parchment paper–lined baking sheet. Chill in the refrigerator until cool.

2. Slowly melt the chocolate in a double boiler over hot water or in the microwave on high for about 75 seconds, stirring halfway through the heating time. Remove from the heat and stir until completely melted and warm. Pour the chocolate into a teacup.

3. Holding the fig by the stem, working very quickly, dunk each into the chocolate to coat about two-thirds of the way up to the stem, allowing the excess to drip back into the teacup, and place back onto the baking sheet. Immediately sprinkle each fig with a pinch of the fleur de sel after dipping. Chill in the refrigerator until the chocolate is set.

4. Serve at room temperature.

Per serving: 110 calories, 4g total fat, 2.5g saturated fat, 0g trans fat, 0mg cholesterol, 30mg sodium, 18g total carbohydrate, 2g dietary fiber, 15g sugars, 1g protein

White Chocolate and Pistachio-Dipped Apple Ⓢ

Makes 4 servings: 3 apple wedges each

Here a sweet-tart apple meets white chocolate and roasted pistachios—simple and satisfying anytime. For added pleasure, immediately stir together any remaining melted white chocolate and chopped pistachios and dollop onto the parchment paper to create candy pieces—or "bark."

1 large Granny Smith or other sweet-tart apple, chilled, cored, and cut into 12 wedges

Juice of 1 small lemon (2 tablespoons)

3 ounces white chocolate, chopped, or white chocolate chips

¼ cup chopped lightly salted dry-roasted pistachios

1. Place the apple wedges into a medium bowl. Add cold water (2 to 3 cups) to cover the apple wedges and add the lemon juice. Let sit for 15 to 20 minutes. Drain and pat dry using a clean kitchen towel.

2. Place the apple wedges on a parchment paper–lined baking sheet.

3. Meanwhile, slowly melt the chocolate in a double boiler over hot water or in the microwave on high for about 75 seconds, stirring halfway through the heating time. Remove from the heat and stir until completely melted and warm. Pour the chocolate into a teacup.

4. Working quickly, dunk each apple wedge into the chocolate to coat about halfway up, allowing the excess to drip back into the teacup, and place back onto the baking sheet. Sprinkle the chocolate-dipped portion with the pistachios. Chill in the refrigerator until the chocolate is set.

5. Serve at room temperature.

Per serving: 180 calories, 10g total fat, 5g saturated fat, 0g trans fat, 0mg cholesterol, 50mg sodium, 24g total carbohydrate, 2g dietary fiber, 20g sugars, 3g protein

Almond Zabaglione with Berries Ⓢ

Makes 4 servings: ½ cup berries with 3 tablespoons zabaglione

Zabaglione is an Italian dessert that's typically made with egg yolks, sugar, and sweet wine. My version uses pomegranate juice instead of wine. The velvety delight is deceptively sinful. It's whipped with a whisk into airy custard. Paired with fresh berries and almonds, it's an elegant and dreamy dessert.

4 large egg yolks
3 tablespoons turbinado sugar
¼ teaspoon pure almond extract
3 tablespoons 100% pomegranate or berry juice
2 cups small strawberries or blueberries,
    or a mixture, chilled
2 tablespoons sliced natural almonds, toasted

1. Bring a saucepan with a few inches of water to a simmer over medium-low heat.

2. Combine the egg yolks and sugar in a stainless or glass heat-resistant bowl and whisk until foamy. Set the bowl over the simmering water (the bowl should not touch the water) and continue to whisk constantly. Add the almond extract and gradually add the juice while continuing to whisk. Reduce heat to low to maintain a slow simmer, if necessary. Do not let egg mixture boil. Continue to whisk vigorously until the egg mixture is very thick and custard-like, about 5 minutes.

3. Spoon 1½ cups of the berries into dessert dishes, top with the zabaglione, add the remaining berries, sprinkle with the almonds, and serve at room temperature.

Per serving: 140 calories, 6g total fat, 2g saturated fat, 0g trans fat, 185mg cholesterol, 10mg sodium, 18g total carbohydrate, 2g dietary fiber, 15g sugars, 4g protein

Citrus-Pomegranate Compote Ⓢ

Makes 2 servings: 1 cup

The citrus fruits pop with sweet-tangy delight. The pomegranate arils are sweet-tart gems with crunchy and juicy, fruity goodness. Toss with a ginger "pop" reduction, and wow your palate.

½ cup ginger ale (preferably made with fresh ginger)
1 red or pink grapefruit, segmented
1 blood or red navel orange, segmented
1 navel orange, segmented
½ cup fresh pomegranate seeds (arils)

1. Add the ginger ale to a small saucepan. Bring to a boil over high heat. Reduce heat to medium and simmer uncovered until reduced to about 2 tablespoons, about 8 minutes. Pour into a small bowl and chill in the refrigerator.

2. Add the grapefruit, blood orange, and navel orange segments to a medium bowl.

3. Gently stir in the pomegranate arils and ginger ale reduction. Let sit for at least 15 minutes, and gently stir again.

4. Divide the fruit evenly among dessert glasses, and serve.

Per serving: 170 calories, 0.5g total fat, 0g saturated fat, 0g trans fat, 0mg cholesterol, 10mg sodium, 42g total carbohydrate, 6g dietary fiber, 23g sugars, 2g protein

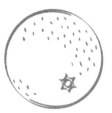

Fruit Mélange in Melon Bowl Ⓢ

Makes 5 servings: 1 cup each

To enjoy the best of the best, simply hit the farmers' market and pick four fruits—any fruits. Discover your personal favorite combination for every season. Try one of my favorite fruit mixtures, showcased here in a cantaloupe "bowl" for drama and deserty appeal.

½ cantaloupe, seeded
1 cup green seedless grapes
1 cup quartered lengthwise fresh strawberries
1 cup cubed fresh pineapple
3 tablespoons chilled ginger ale or sparkling wine
1½ teaspoons finely chopped fresh mint or basil (optional)

1. Using a melon baller, remove most of the cantaloupe flesh from the rind (about 2 cups). Reserve the rind, slicing a very thin piece off of the bottom, if necessary, to allow it to stand.

2. Add the cantaloupe balls, grapes, strawberries, and pineapple to a large bowl. Drizzle with the ginger ale and sprinkle with the mint (if using). Gently toss.

3. Mound the fruit salad into the reserved cantaloupe rind, and serve.

Per serving: 80 calories, 0g total fat, 0g saturated fat, 0g trans fat, 0mg cholesterol, 15mg sodium, 19g total carbohydrate, 2g dietary fiber, 16g sugars, 1g protein

Grilled White Nectarines Ⓢ

Makes 2 servings: 2 nectarine halves each

Simply by grilling for a few minutes, these white nectarines go from fruity to succulently sweet and from pretty to goodness-gracious gorgeous. Savor alongside of Blackened Cajun Duck Breast (page 311) or serve in decadent-style in Grilled Summer Fruit Sundae (page 527). While you're at it, try grilling other fruits as well—peaches, plums, bananas all work well.

2 medium ripe white or yellow nectarines
1 teaspoon unsalted butter, melted, or grapeseed oil
Pinch of fleur de sel or other sea salt (optional)

1. Remove the nectarine stems. Slice nectarines in half, twist, and remove pit.

2. Prepare an outdoor or indoor grill.

3. Lightly brush the butter over the cut side of each nectarine half. Grill the halves over medium-high heat, cut side down, until grill marks just form, about 3 minutes. Rotate halves a quarter turn, and grill until warmed through and (cross hatch) grill marks form, about 1 minute. Sprinkle with the fleur de sel (if using), and serve.

Per serving: 80 calories, 2.5g total fat, 1.5g saturated fat, 0g trans fat, 5mg cholesterol, 0mg sodium, 15g total carbohydrate, 2g dietary fiber, 11g sugars, 2g protein

Grilled Summer Fruit Sundae Ⓢ

Makes 4 servings: 1 sundae each

If you're stuck on sundaes, this is a taste treasure with crunchy nuts, creamy vanilla, and juicy fruit.

1 recipe Grilled White Nectarines (page 527) or 2 cups grilled summer fruit cubes of choice
1 cup fat-free or low-fat vanilla frozen yogurt or frozen dessert
1½ tablespoons sliced natural almonds, toasted
4 sprigs fresh mint (optional)

1. Place each grilled nectarine half on a small plate, cut side up.

2. Top with the frozen yogurt, almonds, and mint (if using), and serve.

Per serving: 100 calories, 2.5g total fat, 0.5g saturated fat, 0g trans fat, 5mg cholesterol, 35mg sodium, 18g total carbohydrate, 1g dietary fiber, 15g sugars, 3g protein

Berry-Papaya Popsicles ⓢ

Makes 6 servings: 1 popsicle each

The beautifully vivid layers and naturally sweet flavors of the real fruit in this frozen pop create simple brilliance—three fruits; that's it. It proves that there's no need for artificial sweeteners when going for a low-cal treat.

1 cup fresh or frozen chopped papaya, thawed or mango
1 cup fresh or frozen sliced strawberries, thawed
1 cup fresh or frozen blueberries, thawed

1. Add the papaya to a blender. Cover and puree until silky smooth. Transfer to a liquid measuring cup. Add about 2 tablespoons of the papaya puree to the bottom of each popsicle mold and freeze until well chilled, but not frozen, about 10 minutes. (The popsicle molds should be about one-third filled.)

2. Meanwhile, puree the strawberries. Pour about 2 tablespoons of the strawberry puree into each popsicle mold over the papaya layer. Freeze until well chilled, but not frozen, about 15 minutes.

3. Meanwhile, puree the blueberries. Pour about 2 tablespoons of the blueberry puree into each popsicle mold on the strawberry layer. Insert the popsicle sticks, tap the molds to ensure the purees adhere to the sticks, and freeze until the molds are completely solid, at least 4 hours or overnight.

4. Enjoy while frozen.

Per serving: 30 calories, 0g total fat, 0g saturated fat, 0g trans fat, 0mg cholesterol, 0mg sodium, 8g total carbohydrate, 2g dietary fiber, 5g sugars, 0g protein

Banana-Berry Pops ⓢ

Makes 5 servings: 1 pop each

A creamy and decadent treat, this pop gets its lovely lavender-like color from blueberries. It's decadent, as there's white chocolate in the "fondue" of what will be a fresh-from-the-freezer favorite.

1 recipe Silky Banana "Fondue" (page 530), chilled
⅓ cup fresh blueberries

1. Add the "fondue" and blueberries to a blender. Cover and puree on low speed until smooth, about 1 minute.

2. Transfer to a liquid measuring cup. Pour about ½ cup into each popsicle mold, insert the sticks, and freeze until the molds are completely solid, at least 4 hours, or overnight.

3. Enjoy while frozen.

Per serving: 200 calories, 9g total fat, 5g saturated fat, 0g trans fat, 10mg cholesterol, 30mg sodium, 25g total carbohydrate, 1g dietary fiber, 21g sugars, 5g protein

Frozen Grape "Pops" ⓢ

Makes 4 servings: 2 pops each

Frozen grapes are a popular treat, especially if you want a light and refreshing dessert. Freezing a colorful string of them on a stick adds a fun factor. These popsicle-style grape skewers are only 20 calories a pop.

24 large green seedless grapes
24 large red seedless grapes

1. Insert 6 grapes (single color or alternating colors) onto each of 8 (8-inch or longer) bamboo skewers or lollipop sticks.

2. Place in a single layer on a baking sheet. Cover and freeze for at least 3 hours, or overnight.

3. Enjoy immediately from the freezer on the sticks.

Per serving: 40 calories, 0g total fat, 0g saturated fat, 0g trans fat, 0mg cholesterol, 0mg sodium, 11g total carbohydrate, 1g dietary fiber, 9g sugars, 0g protein

Mango Mint Parfait Ⓢ

Makes 4 servings: 1 parfait each

Enjoy this mango lover's dish of joy whenever you wish. It's like an upside down sundae. The luscious, vitamin C–rich fruit is the main ingredient and the cute scoops of frozen dessert along with the crunchy granola are the toppings.

3 cups diced fresh mango

2 tablespoons chopped fresh mint

1 teaspoon honey or agave nectar

1 cup low-fat vanilla frozen rice or soy dessert or frozen yogurt

½ cup Pure Maple Cinnamon Granola (page 6) or other granola

1 teaspoon grated lime or lemon zest

1. Toss together the mango, mint, and honey in a medium bowl.

2. Scoop the frozen dessert into 12 or 16 small balls. Layer or arrange the mango mixture, the granola, and frozen dessert as desired into four parfait, sundae, or other dessert glasses.

3. Sprinkle with the lime zest, and serve immediately.

Per serving: 190 calories, 2.5g total fat, 0g saturated fat, 0g trans fat, 0mg cholesterol, 35mg sodium, 38g total carbohydrate, 4g dietary fiber, 30g sugars, 5g protein

Puddings, Mousses, Fondues, and Other Desserts

French Vanilla Pudding

Makes 4 servings: ½ cup each

Just the word "pudding" puts a smile on my face. This silky vanilla pudding is lovely and smile-worthy on its own. You can also pair this treat with any fresh fruit you fancy; it becomes one of those sweet pleasures that you'll hope never ends.

⅓ cup turbinado sugar

3 tablespoons cornstarch

¼ teaspoon sea salt

2 cups plain almond milk or unsweetened coconut milk beverage

1¼ teaspoons pure vanilla extract

2 teaspoons unsalted butter

1. Stir together the sugar, cornstarch, and salt in a small bowl. Set aside.

2. Add the almond milk to a medium saucepan. Place over medium heat and cook, stirring occasionally, until the milk comes to a simmer and bubbles form near the edges. (Do not boil.)

3. Very gradually pour the sugar mixture into the simmering milk, whisking continuously until the sugar is fully dissolved and the mixture thickens enough to coat the back of a spoon, about 2½ minutes.

4. Remove the mixture from the heat and whisk in the vanilla extract and butter. Once the butter melts, pour the mixture through a fine-mesh strainer (to collect any lumps) into individual ramekins or serving dishes and chill in the refrigerator for at least 3 hours.

5. Serve chilled.

Per serving: 130 calories, 3g total fat, 1g saturated fat, 0g trans fat, 5mg cholesterol, 220mg sodium, 25g total carbohydrate, 0g dietary fiber, 19g sugars, 1g protein

Cocoa Velvet Mousse

Makes 4 servings: ⅓ cup each

You'll be overjoyed by this dessert's velvety, buttery texture. You'll be mesmerized by its sinfully rich, uniquely chocolaty taste. You'll be intrigued that avocados are the secret to its creamy richness. And you'll be charmed with every silky serving by way of spoon—or strawberries.

2 fully ripened Hass avocados, pitted, peeled, and cubed

2 tablespoons unsweetened cocoa powder

2 tablespoons honey or agave nectar

¾ teaspoon pure chocolate extract, or to taste

½ teaspoon pure vanilla extract

¼ teaspoon sea salt

1. Add the avocados, cocoa powder, honey, extracts, and salt to a food processor. Cover and puree until velvety smooth, about 3 to 4 minutes, scraping down the sides a few times to ensure all ingredients are well incorporated.

2. Transfer to a serving bowl or four champagne flutes and chill for at least 1 hour, and serve.

Per serving: 160 calories, 11g total fat, 1.5g saturated fat, 0g trans fat, 0mg cholesterol, 150mg sodium, 16g total carbohydrate, 6g dietary fiber, 9g sugars, 2g protein

White Chocolate Fondue

Makes 6 servings: ⅓ cup each

Fondue is fun no matter what you dip into it, including fresh seasonal fruits or whole-grain pretzel chips. Taste it with my favorite: fresh raspberries on bamboo skewers. The white chocolate creates decadence. The tofu and almond milk keep it delightful—with the emphasis on "light."

10 ounces silken tofu, well drained

3 tablespoons plain almond milk or unsweetened coconut milk beverage

1 tablespoon honey or agave nectar

1½ teaspoons pure vanilla extract

⅛ teaspoon pure almond extract

4 ounces white chocolate, chopped

1. Add the tofu, almond milk, honey, and extracts to a blender. Cover and puree on low speed until smooth, about 1 minute.

2. Pour the tofu mixture and white chocolate into a medium saucepan. Place over medium heat and cook while stirring until the chocolate is melted and mixture is steaming hot, about 4 to 5 minutes. (Do not boil.)

3. Serve immediately, fondue style.

Per serving: 150 calories, 7g total fat, 4g saturated fat, 0g trans fat, 5mg cholesterol, 25mg sodium, 15g total carbohydrate, 0g dietary fiber, 14g sugars, 3g protein

Silky Banana "Fondue" ⓢ

Makes 7 servings: ⅓ cup each

You can serve this traditionally as fondue along with juicy strawberries. But this recipe is so versatile; you can also drizzle it over cake, like Devil's Food Cake (page 505), sip it from a spoon chilled as a soup, or freeze it into the luscious Banana-Berry Pops (page 528).

10 ounces silken tofu, well drained

1 medium-large banana, broken into 4 pieces

¼ cup plain almond milk or unsweetened coconut milk beverage

1 tablespoon honey or agave nectar

1½ teaspoons pure vanilla extract

⅛ teaspoon pure almond or coconut extract

4 ounces white chocolate, chopped

1. Add the tofu, banana, almond milk, honey, and extracts to a blender. Cover and puree on low speed until smooth, about 1 minute.

2. Pour the tofu-banana mixture and white chocolate into a medium saucepan. Place over medium heat and cook while stirring until the chocolate is melted and mixture is steaming hot, about 5 minutes. (Do not boil.)

3. Serve immediately, fondue style.

Per serving: 140 calories, 6g total fat, 3.5g saturated fat, 0g trans fat, 5mg cholesterol, 25mg sodium, 17g total carbohydrate, 0g dietary fiber, 14g sugars, 3g protein

Spicy Campfire S'Mores Ⓢ

Makes 6 servings: 1 s'more each

S'mores—oh, the campfire memories! Here's a twist on tradition—the rich spice in the dark chocolate makes it adult-friendly, but the gooey marshmallow certainly speaks to the kid in you. Just one is the perfect amount to satisfy your sweet tooth—and your comfort-food tooth. Choose the spice or flavor you prefer—ginger or orange, for example, or if you are a traditionalist, just use your favorite plain dark chocolate.

6 full sheets whole-grain graham crackers, neatly broken in half
1 (2½-ounce) spicy bittersweet or other dark chocolate bar, evenly broken into 6 pieces
6 large all-natural marshmallows

1. Place the graham cracker halves on a cutting board or platter. Top 6 of the crackers with the chocolate.

2. Skewer the marshmallows onto two long metal skewers, leaving a space between each marshmallow. Gently toast over an open flame or hot grill to desired brownness, rotating during the toasting.

3. Place a toasted marshmallow onto each piece of chocolate, then immediately top with the remaining crackers, pressing firmly to create a sandwich. If the chocolate is not properly melted, heat the (microwave-safe) platter of s'mores in the microwave until the chocolate just melts, about 10 to 15 seconds.

4. Enjoy once the chocolate is melted.

Per serving: 150 calories, 6g total fat, 3g saturated fat, 0g trans fat, 0mg cholesterol, 75mg sodium, 22g total carbohydrate, 1g dietary fiber, 12g sugars, 2g protein

Cookie Dough "Truffles" Ⓢ

Makes 24 servings: 1 truffle each

There's no baking required of this upscale cookie dough. It's served like a truffle, and for just 80 calories. The dusting of spiced cocoa powder adds a dark chocolaty essence to this inspired treat.

½ cup old-fashioned oats
1 cup whole-wheat pastry flour
½ teaspoon sea salt
⅛ teaspoon ground cinnamon
1½ cups turbinado sugar
⅓ cup + 1 tablespoon plain almond milk or unsweetened coconut milk beverage
1 tablespoon unsalted butter or canola oil
1 tablespoon unrefined peanut or canola oil
1 teaspoon pure vanilla extract
¼ cup unsweetened cocoa powder
Pinch of ground cayenne or wasabi powder

1. Add the oats to a food processor. Cover and pulse to a finer texture, as desired.

2. Whisk to combine the oats, the flour, salt, and cinnamon in a small bowl. Set aside.

3. Add the sugar and almond milk to a small saucepan. Place over low heat, stirring occasionally, until the sugar is dissolved and the mixture becomes syrupy, about 20 minutes. Remove from the heat and whisk in the butter, oil, and vanilla extract until the butter is melted and mixture is well combined.

4. Transfer the syrupy mixture to a medium bowl. Add the flour mixture and stir until well combined. Let stand at room temperature until just firm enough to form a ball, about 30 minutes, stirring a couple times while cooling. Mixture will become firmer upon cooling.

5. Form the mixture by hand into 24 balls, about 1 slightly rounded tablespoon each, and place on a sheet of parchment paper. Wipe hands clean regularly with a water-moistened towel during the truffle making.

6. Sift the cocoa powder and cayenne through a fine-mesh strainer into a small bowl. Gently roll each ball of cookie dough into the cocoa until coated. Freeze until ready to serve. If desired, roll each again in any remaining cocoa before serving. Serve chilled or at room temperature.

Per serving: 80 calories, 1.5g total fat, 0.5g saturated fat, 0g trans fat, 0mg cholesterol, 50mg sodium, 18g total carbohydrate, 1g dietary fiber, 12g sugars, 1g protein

Peppermint Frozen Dessert

Makes 2 servings: 1 cup each

A real treat! This is like creamy Italian ice with a burst of refreshing mint—for only 100 calories a full cup. If you favor the classic pairing of chocolate and mint, simply add 2 tablespoons unsweetened cocoa powder to this recipe and you've got chocolate-mint bliss.

1½ cups plain almond milk

1½ tablespoons honey or agave nectar

1¼ teaspoons pure vanilla extract

¼ teaspoon pure peppermint extract

1½ teaspoons minced fresh mint

1. Add all ingredients to the container end of an ice cream "ball" or other ice cream maker. Follow manufacturer's instructions for preparation of the frozen dessert.

2. Scoop into 1-cup portions, garnish with fresh mint sprigs, if desired, and enjoy immediately. Or freeze and enjoy at your leisure.

Per serving: 100 calories, 2g total fat, 0g saturated fat, 0g trans fat, 0mg cholesterol, 110mg sodium, 19g total carbohydrate, 0g dietary fiber, 18g sugars, 1g protein

Frozen Dessert Sandwich Ⓢ

Makes 4 servings: 1 sandwich each

Not everything yummy has to be complicated. Pound cake is used in place of a more traditional cookie and a creamy dairy-free dessert is sandwiched in between. It's a simple and scrumptious dessert when you have the calories to spend on something rather luscious. Actually, you may need to enjoy with a fork since this is so grand.

1 (11-ounce) frozen pound cake, flavor of choice, or 1 recipe Pound-Less Cake (page 507), frozen

1 cup dairy-free frozen dessert, flavor of choice

1. Let the pound cake sit at room temperature until just slightly thawed, about 5 minutes.

2. Cut the frozen cake crosswise into 8 slices.

3. Using a dry ¼ cup measure, scoop out each portion of frozen dessert and using clean hands gently form into the same shape as the cake.

4. Place each portion of frozen dessert on top of four of the slices, then firmly top with the remaining cake slices. Wrap with parchment paper or foil and immediately freeze until ready to serve.

Per serving: 300 calories, 9g total fat, 0g saturated fat, 0g trans fat, 0mg cholesterol, 250mg sodium, 50g total carbohydrate, 2g dietary fiber, 27g sugars, 4g protein

Muffins and Quick Breads

Apple Streusel Mini-Muffins Ⓢ

Makes 12 servings: 2 mini muffins each

You don't have to choose between a pie and a muffin. You can enjoy the best of both. These bites of happiness have all of the rich, real, and comforting apple flavor along with the crust-like appeal of an apple pie.

½ cup granola cereal without fruit or Pure Maple Cinnamon Granola (page 6)

⅓ cup no-sugar-added apple butter

1 cup whole-wheat pastry flour

1½ teaspoons baking powder

½ teaspoon ground cinnamon

¼ teaspoon sea salt

⅛ teaspoon ground cardamom

3 tablespoons unsalted butter

3 tablespoons turbinado sugar

1 large egg, beaten

½ teaspoon pure vanilla extract

1 large Granny Smith apple, cored and finely diced

¼ cup hazelnuts or walnuts, toasted and chopped

1. Add the granola to a food processor. Cover and pulse until nicely crumbled. Do not process too finely or into a powder. Transfer to a small bowl. Stir in 2 tablespoons of the apple butter. Set aside.

2. Preheat the oven to 400°F. Place mini-muffin liners into 24 cups of a mini-muffin tray. Or lightly coat 24 cups of a mini-muffin tray with cooking spray (preferably homemade, page xix).

3. Sift or whisk together the flour, baking powder, cinnamon, salt, and cardamom in a medium bowl. Set aside.

4. Melt the butter in a small saucepan over medium heat. Add the remaining apple butter and the sugar and continue to stir until the sugar is dissolved. Remove the pan from the heat and vigorously whisk in the egg, about a tablespoon at a time, and vanilla extract until smooth.

5. Pour the warm butter mixture into the flour mixture in the medium bowl and stir until just combined. Add the diced apple and hazelnuts and stir until evenly combined. Set aside.

6. Divide the batter among the muffin cups, 1½ measuring tablespoons each. Top each with the reserved granola mixture, gently spreading to coat the surface.

7. Bake until the streusel topping is golden brown and the muffin is springy to the touch, about 18 minutes. Let cool for 5 minutes in the pan. Transfer the muffins to a wire rack to cool. Serve at room temperature.

Per serving: 130 calories, 5g total fat, 2g saturated fat, 0g trans fat, 25mg cholesterol, 115mg sodium, 20g total carbohydrate, 3g dietary fiber, 8g sugars, 3g protein

Pumpkin Mini-Muffins

Makes 14 servings: 3 mini muffins each

Oh, joy! These bites have all of the holiday-inspired nostalgia of old-fashioned pumpkin pie.

1¾ cups whole-wheat pastry flour

2 teaspoons baking powder

¼ teaspoon baking soda

¼ teaspoon sea salt

1 (15-ounce) can no-salt-added 100% pure
    pumpkin puree

1¼ teaspoons ground cinnamon

1 teaspoon ground ginger

⅛ teaspoon ground nutmeg

⅛ teaspoon ground allspice or cloves

¾ cup turbinado sugar

¼ cup no-sugar-added apple butter

¼ cup peanut or canola oil

2 large eggs, lightly beaten

1. Preheat the oven to 425°F. Place mini-muffin liners into 42 cups of mini-muffin trays. Or lightly coat 42 cups of mini-muffin trays with cooking spray (preferably homemade, page xix).

2. Whisk together the flour, baking powder, baking soda, and salt in a medium bowl. Set aside.

3. Add the pumpkin, cinnamon, ginger, nutmeg, and allspice to a medium saucepan. Cook over medium heat while stirring until thickened, about 6 minutes. Transfer the pumpkin mixture to a large bowl. Whisk in the sugar, apple butter, and oil until well combined. Gradually add the eggs while whisking continuously. Stir in the flour mixture until just combined.

4. Divide the batter among the muffin cups, about 1½ tablespoons each.

5. Bake the muffins until springy to the touch, about 12 minutes. Let cool for 5 minutes in the pan. Transfer the muffins to a wire rack to cool. Serve at room temperature.

Per serving: 100 calories, 4.5g total fat, 1g saturated fat, 0g trans fat, 25mg cholesterol, 150mg sodium, 15g total carbohydrate, 1g dietary fiber, 13g sugars, 1g protein

Tropical Carrot Cake Muffins

Makes 12 servings: 1 muffin each

Here you can have comforting carrot cake essence, but in a muffin—a full-size one.

1½ cups whole-wheat pastry flour

1¼ teaspoons baking powder

1 teaspoon baking soda

1½ teaspoons ground cinnamon

¼ teaspoon ground ginger

⅛ teaspoon freshly ground nutmeg (optional)

½ cup turbinado sugar

2 large eggs

2 tablespoons walnut or peanut oil

3 ounces plain almond milk or light soy milk

1½ teaspoons pure vanilla extract

¼ teaspoon pure almond extract

1½ cups coarsely grated carrots

⅔ cup finely diced fresh pineapple

1 teaspoon finely grated orange zest

2 tablespoons unsalted roasted pistachios,
    coarsely chopped

1. Preheat the oven to 350°F. Place muffin liners into 12 cups of a muffin tray.

2. Whisk together the flour, baking powder, baking soda, cinnamon, ginger, nutmeg (if using), and sugar in a large bowl. Set aside.

3. Whisk together the eggs, oil, almond milk, and extracts in a small bowl. Set aside.

4. Stir together the carrots, pineapple, and zest in a medium bowl. Stir in the egg mixture until well combined. Stir in the flour mixture until just combined.

5. Divide the mixture among the 12 muffin cups, about ¼ cup each. Sprinkle with the pistachios and gently press onto the batter to adhere.

6. Bake until the muffins are browned and springy to the touch, about 25 minutes. Let cool for 10 minutes in the pan. Transfer the muffins to a wire rack to cool. Serve at room temperature.

Per serving: 150 calories, 4g total fat, 0.5g saturated fat, 0g trans fat, 30mg cholesterol, 280mg sodium, 27g total carbohydrate, 3g dietary fiber, 14g sugars, 3g protein

Fruity Blueberry Muffins

Makes 12 servings: 1 muffin each

If you like your muffins to taste more like cupcakes, then whip up a batch of these winners.

1⅔ cups whole-wheat pastry flour

1½ teaspoon baking powder

¾ teaspoon sea salt

1 cup plain almond milk or light soy milk

2 tablespoons unsalted butter, melted

1 large egg

½ teaspoon grated lemon zest

1 teaspoon pure vanilla extract

½ teaspoon pure almond extract

¾ cup turbinado sugar

1 cup fresh blueberries

1 large white nectarine or peach, pitted and finely diced

1. Preheat the oven to 375°F. Place muffin liners into 12 cups of a muffin tray. Or lightly coat 12 cups of a muffin tray with cooking spray (preferably homemade, page xix).

2. Sift or whisk together the flour, baking powder, and salt in a medium bowl. Set aside.

3. Whisk together the almond milk and butter in a large bowl until well blended. Whisk in the egg, zest, and extracts until combined. Whisk in the sugar until well combined.

4. Stir the flour mixture into the milk mixture until just combined. Fold in the blueberries and nectarine.

5. Divide the batter among 12 muffin cups, about ⅓ cup batter per cup.

6. Bake until firm and springy to the touch, about 25 minutes. Let cool for 10 minutes in the pan. Transfer the muffins to a wire rack to cool. Serve at room temperature.

Per serving: 150 calories, 3g total fat, 1.5g saturated fat, 0g trans fat, 20mg cholesterol, 220mg sodium, 29g total carbohydrate, 3g dietary fiber, 15g sugars, 3g protein

Rainforest Chocolate Muffins

Makes 12 servings: 1 muffin each

Start with chocolate and add a rainforest twist with banana, pure coconut extract, and Brazil nuts—this muffin will capture your culinary spirit.

1⅔ cups whole-wheat pastry flour

½ cup unsweetened cocoa powder

1½ teaspoons baking powder

½ teaspoon baking soda

½ teaspoon sea salt

7 ounces plain almond milk or unsweetened coconut milk beverage

2 tablespoons canola oil

2 large eggs

1 extra-large or 2 small fully ripened bananas, mashed

1 teaspoon pure vanilla extract

¾ teaspoon pure coconut extract

¾ cup + 2 teaspoons turbinado sugar

⅓ cup Brazil nuts, toasted and chopped

1 tablespoon chopped unsalted pistachios

1. Preheat the oven to 375°F. Place muffin liners into 12 cups of a muffin tray. Or lightly coat 12 cups of a muffin tray with cooking spray (preferably homemade, page xix).

2. Sift or whisk together the flour, cocoa powder, baking powder, baking soda, and salt in a medium bowl. Set aside.

3. Whisk together the almond milk and oil in a large bowl until well blended. Whisk in the eggs until well blended. Whisk in the banana and extracts until combined. Whisk in the sugar until well combined.

4. Stir the flour mixture into the milk mixture until just combined. Gently stir in the Brazil nuts.

5. Divide the batter among 12 muffin cups, about ⅓ cup batter per muffin cup. Sprinkle with the pistachios.

continues on next page

6. Bake until firm and springy to the touch, about 20 minutes. Let cool for 10 minutes in the pan. Transfer the muffins to a wire rack to cool. Serve at room temperature.

Per serving: 190 calories, 7g total fat, 1.5g saturated fat, 0g trans fat, 30mg cholesterol, 230mg sodium, 32g total carbohydrate, 4g dietary fiber, 15g sugars, 4g protein

Mom's Banana Bread

Makes 20 servings: 1 slice each

I've kept the essence of my mother's classic banana bread recipe, then added an extra banana and a hint of walnut oil in place of half of the butter. It makes this treat nuttier, moister, and naturally sweeter. Plus, I boosted whole-grain goodness with whole-wheat flour and a surprise crunchy accent of millet. Dare I say it's better than mom's classic?

1¾ cups whole-wheat pastry flour

1 teaspoon baking soda

½ teaspoon sea salt

½ teaspoon cream of tartar

1 cup turbinado sugar

3 tablespoons unsalted butter, melted

2 teaspoons unrefined or roasted walnut
    or unrefined peanut oil

2 large eggs

4 large fully-ripened bananas, mashed

1½ teaspoons pure vanilla extract

⅓ cup hulled millet

¼ cup walnuts, toasted and chopped

1. Preheat the oven to 350°F. Lightly coat a 9×5-inch loaf pan with cooking spray (preferably homemade, page xix). Dust with 1 tablespoon of the flour.

2. Sift or whisk together the remaining flour, the baking soda, salt, and cream of tartar in a medium bowl. Set aside.

3. Blend together the sugar, butter, and walnut oil with an electric mixer on low speed in a large bowl until combined. Add the eggs and blend well. Add the flour mixture and blend until just combined. Add the bananas and vanilla extract and blend until just combined.

4. Stir in the millet and walnuts until evenly combined.

5. Pour the batter into the loaf pan. Bake until browned, set, and a toothpick inserted in the center comes out clean, about 1 hour 10 minutes. Let cool completely in the pan on a wire rack. Cut into 20 slices and serve at room temperature, chilled, or semi-frozen.

Per serving: 150 calories, 4g total fat, 1.5g saturated fat, 0g trans fat, 25mg cholesterol, 130mg sodium, 27g total carbohydrate, 3g dietary fiber, 13g sugars, 3g protein

Double Squash Bread Ⓢ

Makes 24 servings: 1 slice each

My culinary assistant says that this "zucchini" bread recipe is the best she's ever tasted! The secret is using two kinds of summer squash and sneaking in pure almond extract. Enjoy some—then share the rest.

1⅓ cups whole-wheat pastry flour
½ teaspoon sea salt
½ teaspoon baking powder
½ teaspoon baking soda
1½ teaspoons ground cinnamon
2 large eggs
⅓ cup peanut or canola oil
¾ cup turbinado sugar
2 tablespoons no-sugar-added apple butter
1¼ teaspoons pure vanilla extract
¼ teaspoon pure almond extract
½ teaspoon grated lemon zest
¾ cup coarsely grated zucchini
½ cup coarsely grated yellow squash
¼ cup walnuts or pecans, toasted, chopped

1. Preheat the oven to 350°F. Lightly coat a 9×5-inch loaf pan with cooking spray (preferably home-made, page xix). Dust with 1 tablespoon of the flour.

2. Sift or whisk together the remaining flour, the salt, baking powder, baking soda, and cinnamon in a medium bowl.

3. Beat together the eggs, oil, sugar, apple butter, extracts, and zest with an electric mixer on medium speed in a large bowl. Add the flour mixture and beat well on low speed until just combined. Stir in the zucchini, yellow squash, and nuts until well combined. Pour the batter into the loaf pan.

4. Bake until a toothpick inserted in the center comes out clean, about 50 minutes. Cool in the pan on a wire rack for 20 minutes. Remove the bread from the pan, and completely cool. Cut into 24 slices and serve at room temperature.

Per serving: 100 calories, 5g total fat, 0g saturated fat, 0g trans fat, 15mg cholesterol, 90mg sodium, 12g total carbohydrate, 1g dietary fiber, 7g sugars, 1g protein

Glazes, Frostings, Syrups, and Other Sweet Toppings

Mango Coulis

Makes 6 servings: 2 rounded tablespoons each

This delightful syrup has only 30 calories—much less than traditional maple syrup. So if you're a little heavy handed with your drizzling, no worries here. This fruity coulis goes great with pancakes or waffles, including Mini-Pancakes with Mango Coulis (page 9). Serve it cool as a dessert topping, too.

1 mango, peeled, pitted, and cubed
¼ cup 100% unsweetened apple or pineapple juice
1½ teaspoons pure maple syrup
¼ teaspoon sea salt, or to taste

1. Add the mango, apple juice, maple syrup, and salt to a food processor. Cover and puree.

2. Add to a small saucepan, heat gently over warm heat, and serve.

Per serving: 30 calories, 0g total fat, 0g saturated fat, 0g trans fat, 0mg cholesterol, 100mg sodium, 8g total carbohydrate, 1g dietary fiber, 7g sugars, 0g protein

Cilantro and Pomegranate Syrups Ⓢ

Makes 12 servings: 2 teaspoons (1 teaspoon of each syrup) each

Tangy and herbal meets fruity and sweet. A small drizzle of each—red and green—is all you need to transform a cake from plain to pizzazzy, especially in Pomegranate Angelic Cake (page 506).

¼ cup honey or agave nectar

Juice of 1 small lemon (2 tablespoons)

1 teaspoon minced fresh cilantro

⅛ teaspoon sea salt

2 tablespoons 100% pomegranate juice

1. Stir together 2 tablespoons of the honey, the lemon juice, cilantro, and half of the salt in a small bowl until well combined.

2. Stir together the remaining 2 tablespoons honey, the pomegranate juice, and the remaining salt in another small bowl until well combined.

3. Serve both of the syrups drizzled over cake or other dessert.

Per serving: 25 calories, 0g total fat, 0g saturated fat, 0g trans fat, 0mg cholesterol, 25mg sodium, 6g total carbohydrate, 0g dietary fiber, 6g sugars, 0g protein

Rhubarb-Strawberry Compote Ⓢ

Makes 7 servings: ⅓ cup compote each

Whether a strawberry or rhubarb aficionado, you'll become a devotee of this warm or cool springtime compote. Enjoy atop a slice of angel food cake, scoop of low-fat frozen dessert, or other light dessert of choice. It's the star of Springtime Strawberry-Rhubarb Angel Food Shortcake (page 509).

⅔ cup turbinado or demerara sugar

3 tablespoons strawberry, raspberry, or other 100% fruit spread

1½ teaspoons Valencia orange zest

2 (12-inch) stalks fresh rhubarb, sliced into ⅓-inch pieces

2 cups sliced fresh strawberries

¾ teaspoon aged balsamic vinegar, or to taste

1. Bring the sugar, fruit spread, 3 tablespoons water, and 1 teaspoon of the orange zest to a boil in a medium saucepan over medium-high heat. Stir in the rhubarb and cook while stirring for 2 minutes. Cover, reduce heat to low, and simmer until the rhubarb is softened, about 6 minutes.

2. Let stand uncovered at room temperature until slightly cooled, about 20 minutes.

3. Stir in the strawberries and vinegar, and serve warm or chilled. Sprinkle with the remaining ½ teaspoon orange zest and serve.

Per serving: 110 calories, 0g total fat, 0g saturated fat, 0g trans fat, 0mg cholesterol, 0mg sodium, 28g total carbohydrate, 1g dietary fiber, 26g sugars, 0g protein

Angel Frosting

Makes 20 servings: 1 scant tablespoon each

This white buttercream-style frosting can be considered at least a little better for you than traditional buttercream frosting. It has just a bit of butter, yet it's still velvety rich tasting. It's the topping of choice for Devil's Food Cake (page 505).

1¾ cups powdered sugar

1½ tablespoons plain almond milk or unsweetened coconut milk beverage, at room temperature

1 tablespoon fat-free or low-fat plain Greek yogurt

1 tablespoon unsalted butter, at room temperature

½ teaspoon pure vanilla extract

⅛ teaspoon sea salt

1. Blend together the powdered sugar, 1 tablespoon of the almond milk, the yogurt, butter, vanilla extract, and salt in a medium bowl with an electric mixer until combined. Add the remaining ½ tablespoon almond milk, if needed, and blend until desired smooth and fluffy frosting consistency is reached.

2. Thinly spread onto a cooled 9×13-inch cake.

Per serving: 45 calories, 0.5g total fat, 0g saturated fat, 0g trans fat, 0mg cholesterol, 15mg sodium, 11g total carbohydrate, 0g dietary fiber, 10g sugars, 0g protein

Hint-of-Mint Vanilla Buttercream Icing ⓢ

Makes 30 servings: 1½ teaspoons each

Drizzle this icing rather than spread it to use a little rather than a lot. It has just enough butter to make it seem decadent, plus a lovely note of peppermint, adding special brightness to anything you drape it over, namely Hint-of-Mint Snack Cake (page 510).

1½ cups powdered sugar

1½ tablespoons unsalted butter, softened

2½ tablespoons plain almond milk or unsweetened coconut milk beverage, at room temperature

¼ teaspoon pure vanilla extract

¼ teaspoon pure peppermint extract

⅛ teaspoon sea salt

1. Blend together the powdered sugar, butter, 1 tablespoon of the almond milk, the extracts, and salt in a medium bowl with an electric mixer until combined. Add the remaining almond milk, ½ tablespoon at a time, as needed, and blend until the desired smooth icing consistency is reached.

2. Drizzle or very thinly spread onto a cooled 9 × 13-inch cake.

Per serving: 30 calories, 0.5g total fat, 0g saturated fat, 0g trans fat, 0mg cholesterol, 10mg sodium, 6g total carbohydrate, 0g dietary fiber, 6g sugars, 0g protein

Silken Icing ⓢ

Makes 36 servings: 2¼ teaspoons each

This tangy tofu-based icing is an ideal option in place of a richer, sweeter cream cheese-based frosting. It'll delight as it's drizzled or splattered expressively over cake or cupcakes, like Mini Red Velvet Cupcakes (page 512).

1 (16-ounce) package silken tofu, well drained

Juice and zest of 1 lemon

3 tablespoons honey or agave nectar

1½ teaspoons pure vanilla extract

Place all the ingredients in a blender or food processor. Cover and puree until smooth. Chill well and serve.

Per serving: 15 calories, 0g total fat, 0g saturated fat, 0g trans fat, 0mg cholesterol, 0mg sodium, 2g total carbohydrate, 0g dietary fiber, 2g sugars, 1g protein

Fluffy Chocolate Yogurt Frosting ⓢ

Makes 32 servings: 2 rounded teaspoons each

Greek yogurt as the creamy base of this tangy, chocolaty frosting is true love. It can be finicky if you don't frost fast, though. So if it is getting too firm during use, gently warm the frosting in the microwave for a few seconds to loosen it. This frosting is delicious on Double Chocolate Mini Cupcakes (page 511).

6 ounces high-quality semisweet baking chocolate

¾ teaspoon instant espresso coffee powder

1 cup fat-free or low-fat plain Greek yogurt, at room temperature

¼ teaspoon pure chocolate extract

⅛ teaspoon pure vanilla extract

⅛ teaspoon sea salt

1. Place the chocolate in a heatproof medium bowl. Place the bowl over a saucepan with simmering water. Stir only as needed, just until chocolate is melted.

2. Remove the bowl from heat, stir in the espresso powder, and let the chocolate cool down slightly to a warm room temperature, about 15 minutes.

3. Meanwhile stir together the yogurt, extracts, and salt in a small bowl.

4. Fold the yogurt mixture into the chocolate, about ⅓ cup at a time, until smooth.

5. Use immediately.

Per serving: 35 calories, 2g total fat, 1.5g saturated fat, 0g trans fat, 0mg cholesterol, 10mg sodium, 3g total carbohydrate, 0g dietary fiber, 2g sugars, 1g protein

Basil-Strawberry Sauce ⓢ

Makes 8 servings: 2 tablespoons each

The sweet and lovely fragrance that wafts from this sauce is captivating. Enjoy it with Lemon Pound-less Cake (page 507). You might just want to turn the herbal strawberry delight into a cool soup or cocktail, so you can indulge rather than use it for drizzling.

1½ cups sliced fresh strawberries

1½ teaspoons honey or agave nectar

1½ teaspoons white balsamic vinegar, aged balsamic vinegar, or fresh lemon juice

1 teaspoon minced fresh basil

1. Add the strawberries, honey, and vinegar to a food processor. Cover and blend until smooth. Stir in the basil.

2. Lightly drizzle the sauce over dessert of choice and serve.

Per serving: 15 calories, 0g total fat, 0g saturated fat, 0g trans fat, 0mg cholesterol, 0mg sodium, 4g total carbohydrate, 1g dietary fiber, 3g sugars, 0g protein

Fresh Blueberry Crème Sauce ⓢ

Makes 16 servings: 1½ tablespoons each

This dessert sauce will impress you with its creamy, fruity sweet, and intriguing mix of ingredients. You'll be surprised to find that white beans create its unique creaminess without compromising flavor. The highlight is the lovely lavender color that the blueberries contribute. And it's indeed a key appeal of Blueberry Bundt Cake (page 508).

4 ounces silken tofu, well drained

¾ cup fresh blueberries

⅓ cup drained canned no-salt-added cannellini or other white beans

1 tablespoon + 2 teaspoons fresh lemon juice

2 teaspoons mild honey or agave nectar

1. Add the tofu, blueberries, beans, lemon juice, and honey to a blender. Cover and puree until smooth and the consistency of a smoothie. Transfer to a covered container and refrigerate until well chilled.

2. Drizzle over cake of choice and enjoy.

Per serving: 15 calories, 0g total fat, 0g saturated fat, 0g trans fat, 0mg cholesterol, 0mg sodium, 3g total carbohydrate, 0.5g dietary fiber, 1g sugars, 1g protein

Chantilly Vanilla Yogurt ⓢ

Makes 6 servings: 2 tablespoons each

Who needs whipped cream when you can have Chantilly Vanilla Yogurt? It's a sweet that's a real treat—especially since it has only 25 calories for a heaping dollop. The recipe easily doubles for a crowd.

¾ cup fat-free or low-fat plain Greek yogurt

2½ teaspoons honey or agave nectar

¾ teaspoon pure vanilla extract

2 to 3 drops rose water (optional)

1. Add the yogurt, honey, vanilla extract, and rose water (if using) to a small bowl. Stir until just combined. Chill in the refrigerator.

2. Enjoy with waffles, pancakes, or as a topping for a sweet dessert.

Per serving: 25 calories, 0g total fat, 0g saturated fat, 0g trans fat, 0mg cholesterol, 10mg sodium, 4g total carbohydrate, 0g dietary fiber, 4g sugars, 3g protein

Beverages, Smoothies, and Mocktails

Fruit and Vegetable Drinks

Homemade Citrus Soda

Strawberry Basil Lemonade

Minty Melon Cooler

Gingered Carrot Juice

Spa H_2O

Roasted Veggie Juice Smoothie

Hot Spiced Apple Cider

Non-Dairy Smoothies, Shakes, and Floats

All-American Apple Pie Smoothie

Bing Cherry–Vanilla Smoothie

Banana-Nut Smoothie

Berry Good Smoothie

Chocolate Soy Milkshake-tini

Freshly Squeezed Orange Float

Root Beer Flute Float

Dairy Smoothies and Shakes

Blueberry Pie Smoothie

Pretty in Pink Smoothie

Tropical Pineapple Shake

Semisweet Cocoa Shake

Mango Lassi

White Peach Melba Lassi

Tea and Coffee Beverages

Iced Ginger Spa Tea

Raspberry Mint Iced Tea

Blended Iced Mocha

Espresso Frothy

Iced Chai Tea Frothy

Hot Chocolate au Lait

Pumpkin Spice Coffee

Mocktails

Shirley Temple Party Punch

Virgin Mary

Green Grasshopper

Fresh-Squeezed Citrus "007"

The focus of this refreshing chapter is beverages with benefits—such as vitamins, minerals, and fiber.

Some beverages, like those rich in vegetables or fruits, can become a beneficial part of a nutritious eating plan to help ensure that you are getting what you need. Check out the tasty Roasted Veggie Juice Smoothie (page 544), which provides an array of plant-based nutrients, including over half of the daily requirement for vitamin C. Other drinks can simply be thought of as low-calorie, tasty thirst quenchers, like the uplifting Spa H_2O (page 544), which is a nice change from just water. And there are a handful of others that are geared more for pleasure, such as the oh-so-chocolaty Semisweet Cocoa Shake (page 549), which counts as a combination of a "dairy" group plus dessert. It's best to be enjoyed after a workout, for instance, to replenish energy supplies. All of these beverages can add variety to your eating plan, which will help you follow a healthful lifestyle long term. Of course, remember to count all of your liquid calories as part of your total daily intake. Keep a close eye on the serving sizes that you sip, too.

This quenching chapter begins with fruit and vegetable drinks. These are the most refreshing picks of the chapter. There's something unique about each of them, like the zingy fresh ginger in the Gingered Carrot Juice (page 544) and the fruit and herb infusion in Strawberry Basil Lemonade (page 543). If you're a fan of soda, try the Homemade Citrus Soda (page 543) that's part real fruit juice and part seltzer water for fewer calories than a regular soda. And if you prefer something to warm you up, there's a steamy apple cider that's loaded with sweet spices—and antioxidants.

Creamy refreshers are next, including smoothies, shakes, floats, and lassis. You have nondairy and dairy choices. A variety of fresh fruit is whirled into nearly all of them. The remaining two have chocolate! For extra appeal, a few of the fruity recipes taste like dessert—without the excess calories, such as the All-American Apple Pie Smoothie (page 545), which is a velvety mixture of Granny Smith apple, vanilla frozen dessert, almond milk, and cinnamon, then sprinkled with graham cracker crumbs. No pie crust required for this drinkable sweet.

There are both chilled and hot tea and coffee beverages. By blending Espresso Frothy, Raspberry Mint Iced Tea, or Iced Chai Tea Frothy (pages 550–551), you'll enjoy special effervescence any time of day.

The chapter ends with select "mocktails"— beverages that mimic cocktails but don't contain alcohol so the whole family can enjoy them. Or prepare them along with their spirit-containing versions so there's a choice of both. If you're looking for an immune-boosting lift, go for the fruity Fresh-Squeezed Citrus "007" (page 553) or tomato-based Virgin Mary (page 553); they're both loaded with antioxidants, including vitamin C. If you need to boost your calcium intake, go for the Green Grasshopper (page 553).

Calorie range in this chapter: 5 to 200 calories.

Low calorie pick: Spa H_2O, 5 calories (page 544).

Fruit and Vegetable Drinks

Homemade Citrus Soda ⓢ

Makes 2 servings: 1 cup each

Ahh, refreshing! Here's a soda with just the right touch of tart sweetness and fizziness. It provides 30 fewer calories than a typical cup of soda. Plus, it can count as one of your fruit servings.

¾ cup fresh-squeezed orange juice
½ cup fresh-squeezed pink or red grapefruit juice
¾ cup seltzer water or club soda

1. Stir together the orange juice and grapefruit juice in a large liquid measuring cup. Slowly add the seltzer water and gently stir.

2. Pour over ice in tall glasses or old-fashioned cocktail glasses and serve.

Per serving: 70 calories, 0g total fat, 0g saturated fat, 0g trans fat, 0mg cholesterol, 0mg sodium, 15g total carbohydrate, 0g dietary fiber, 8g sugars, 1g protein

Strawberry Basil Lemonade ⓢ

Makes 4 servings: 1 cup each

Need something refreshing but prefer it with a touch of sweetness? This lemonade is a super-light delight. Much of the sweetness is derived naturally from strawberries. Its pleasant pink color and fresh herbal flair create intrigue, too. Make it in the morning and enjoy sipping the servings throughout the day.

1 cup sliced or quartered fresh strawberries
Juice of 2 lemons (6 tablespoons)
1 tablespoon honey or agave nectar
3 fresh basil leaves, finely chopped

1. Add the strawberries, lemon juice, honey, and ½ cup cold water to a blender. Cover and puree until smooth. Pour the strawberry mixture into a pitcher. Add the basil and 2⅓ cups cold water and stir until well combined.

2. Pour over ice in tall glasses and serve.

Per serving: 35 calories, 0g total fat, 0g saturated fat, 0g trans fat, 0mg cholesterol, 0mg sodium, 9g total carbohydrate, 1g dietary fiber, 7g sugars, 0g protein

Minty Melon Cooler

Makes 1 serving: 1 cup

Sometimes it's enjoyable to drink your fruit rather than eat it. This watermelon and cantaloupe cooler will enable you to do that in a purely refreshing way—and the pretty peach color is irresistible. You can serve this cooler in a small bowl and slurp with a spoon as a cool fruit soup, too.

⅔ cup seedless watermelon cubes
⅔ cup cantaloupe cubes
2 fresh mint leaves
¾ teaspoon fresh lemon juice
½ teaspoon fresh lime juice
Pinch of sea salt
4 teaspoons unsweetened white tea or water, chilled

1. Add the watermelon cubes, cantaloupe cubes, mint, lemon and lime juices, salt, and tea to a blender. Cover and puree until smooth.

2. Pour over ice in a tall glass and serve.

Per serving: 70 calories, 0g total fat, 0g saturated fat, 0g trans fat, 0mg cholesterol, 115mg sodium, 17g total carbohydrate, 1g dietary fiber, 14g sugars, 2g protein

Gingered Carrot Juice

Makes 1 serving: 1 cup

There's truly no easier way to get your vegetables than by pouring them into a glass and sipping away. Freshly pressed carrot juice is one of the tastiest—and prettiest—options with its vivid orange hue. Here, the added zing from the ginger makes an already appetizing carrot beverage that much tastier.

1 cup 100% pure pressed carrot juice
½ teaspoon fresh lemon juice
½ teaspoon freshly grated gingerroot, or to taste

1. Stir together all the ingredients in a liquid measuring cup. Cover and chill for at least 2 hours.

2. Stir, pour over ice, if desired, and enjoy.

Per serving: 70 calories, 0g total fat, 0g saturated fat, 0g trans fat, 0mg cholesterol, 150mg sodium, 14g total carbohydrate, 0g dietary fiber, 0g sugars, 2g protein

Spa H₂0 ⓢ

Makes 4 servings: 1⅓ cups each

Each sip of this fragrant water seems to have some mystical properties—you'll feel like you've been to a rejuvenating spa even if you're just at home. After satisfying your thirst, you can snack on the cucumber slices and nibble on the mint as a breath freshener, too.

¼ English cucumber, thinly sliced
1 small lemon, thinly sliced
1 lime, thinly sliced
8 fresh mint sprigs

1. Add 4 cups cold filtered water, the cucumber, lemon, lime, and 4 of the mint sprigs to a large water pitcher. Stir well to combine.

2. Chill for at least 2 hours. Serve over ice (made with filtered water) in water goblets or tall pilsner glasses. Garnish with the remaining mint.

Per serving: 5 calories, 0g total fat, 0g saturated fat, 0g trans fat, 0mg cholesterol, 0mg sodium, 2g total carbohydrate, 0g dietary fiber, 1g sugars, 0g protein

Roasted Veggie Juice Smoothie

Makes 4 servings: 1 cup each

This tastes nothing like traditional vegetable juice. The veggies are roasted, which adds a layer of caramelized, smoky goodness. Serve it as a savory smoothie—or enjoy as a refreshing, cool soup. It's thick, velvety-smooth, and delicious.

1 pint grape tomatoes
1 medium zucchini, cut crosswise into ⅓-inch slices
1 large sweet onion, peeled, cut into large dice
1 Cubanelle pepper, roughly chopped
2 teaspoons extra-virgin olive oil
½ teaspoon sea salt, or to taste
¼ teaspoon freshly ground black pepper, or to taste
2 cups low-sodium vegetable broth or Vegetable Stock (page 203), chilled
Juice of ½ small lemon (1 tablespoon)

1. Preheat the oven to 400°F.

2. Toss together the tomatoes, zucchini, onion, Cubanelle, oil, salt, and black pepper in a large bowl. Arrange the vegetables in a single layer in two parchment–paper lined baking pans.

3. Roast until the vegetables are fully cooked and caramelized, about 45 minutes, stirring the vegetables and rotating the pans halfway through the roasting process. Remove from heat and let cool for 1 hour. Or chill in a covered container in the refrigerator until ready to use.

4. Place the cool roasted vegetables into a blender along with 1 cup of the broth. Cover and puree until velvety smooth.

5. Pour into a large pitcher along with the remaining 1 cup broth and the lemon juice. Alternatively, if using a large-capacity blender, puree all ingredients in the blender. Stir, and adjust seasoning. Pour into tall skinny glasses over ice and serve.

Per serving: 80 calories, 2.5g total fat, 0g saturated fat, 0g trans fat, 0mg cholesterol, 380mg sodium, 13g total carbohydrate, 3g dietary fiber, 9g sugars, 2g protein

Hot Spiced Apple Cider Ⓢ

Makes 4 servings: ¾ cup each

Nothing says autumn more than fresh-brewed apple cider, especially when it's steamy and spiced up. It's a lovely change of pace and taste from a typical cup of brewed coffee. And it's much healthier than some of the calorie-laden coffee-house concoctions.

¼ teaspoon whole cloves
⅛ teaspoon whole allspice (optional)
1 small cinnamon stick
⅛ teaspoon sea salt
½ mandarin orange or ¼ small navel orange, unpeeled, cut into 3 wedges
3 cups freshly pressed apple cider
2 teaspoons fresh lemon juice
1½ teaspoons pure maple syrup
Pinch of freshly grated nutmeg

1. Place a filter in the basket of a coffee maker. Add the cloves, allspice (if using), cinnamon stick, salt, and orange wedges.

2. Stir together the cider and lemon juice. Pour into the coffee pot where the water normally goes, then brew.

3. Stir the maple syrup into the brewed cider. Pour the cider into four tea or coffee cups. Sprinkle each with a dash of nutmeg, and serve hot. If desired, serve a cinnamon stick in each cup of cider.

Per serving: 100 calories, 0g total fat, 0g saturated fat, 0g trans fat, 0mg cholesterol, 90mg sodium, 26g total carbohydrate, 0g dietary fiber, 23g sugars, 0g protein

Non-Dairy Smoothies, Shakes, and Floats

All-American Apple Pie Smoothie Ⓢ

Makes 3 servings: 1 cup each

All of the wondrous flavors of a real apple pie go into this inspired, kid- and adult-friendly smoothie. It's like a home-baked pie and a creamy milkshake in one. Made with the crisp, juicy, tart, and versatile Granny Smith apple that's in season all-year-round means you can enjoy this pie smoothie any time you wish.

1 large Granny Smith apple, unpeeled, cored, and diced
1½ cups almond-, soy-, or coconut milk-based vanilla frozen dessert
½ cup plain almond milk or light soy milk, well chilled
¼ teaspoon ground cinnamon
2 teaspoons whole-grain graham cracker crumbs

1. Arrange the apple in a single layer on a large microwave-safe plate. Microwave on high until slightly softened, about 1½ minutes. Let cool completely at room temperature.

2. Add the apple, the frozen dessert, almond milk, and cinnamon to a blender. Cover and blend until smooth.

3. Pour into two chilled glasses. Sprinkle each smoothie with the graham cracker crumbs and serve.

Per serving: 170 calories, 2.5g total fat, 0g saturated fat, 0g trans fat, 0mg cholesterol, 160mg sodium, 37g total carbohydrate, 4g dietary fiber, 19g sugars, 3g protein

Bing Cherry–Vanilla Smoothie Ⓢ

Makes 3 servings: ¾ cup each

If your favorite color is purple, then you've gotta swirl up this smoothie. Its rich lavender color is something only nature can concoct. Sip on this in June or July when cherries are seasonal and plentiful. Or make it with frozen cherries to enjoy year-round.

1 cup fresh or thawed frozen Bing cherries, pitted

1½ cups almond-, soy-, or coconut milk-based vanilla frozen dessert

½ cup plain almond milk or light soy milk, well chilled

1 teaspoon fresh lemon juice

⅛ teaspoon pure vanilla extract

1. Add all the ingredients to a blender. Cover and blend well until smooth.

2. Pour into three chilled glasses, and serve.

Per serving: 150 calories, 2g total fat, 0g saturated fat, 0g trans fat, 0mg cholesterol, 150mg sodium, 34g total carbohydrate, 3g dietary fiber, 17g sugars, 3g protein

Banana-Nut Smoothie Ⓢ

Makes 3 servings: 1 scant cup each

Just finished your workout or back from an active family outing? It's a perfect time to enjoy this family-friendly fruit smoothie. It's rich, so you won't need a lot to feel satisfied. Serve it with a cinnamon stick, or with a straw to sip all its goodness.

2 medium fully ripened bananas, sliced

1⅓ cups plain almond milk or unsweetened sunflower beverage, well chilled

1 tablespoon + 1 teaspoon no-salt-added creamy natural peanut or almond butter

1½ teaspoons mild honey or agave nectar

¼ teaspoon pure vanilla extract

⅛ teaspoon pure almond or walnut extract

Pinch of ground cinnamon (optional)

1. Arrange the banana slices in a single layer on a tray or plate, cover, and freeze for at least 1 hour or overnight.

2. Add the frozen bananas, the almond milk, peanut butter, honey, and extracts to a blender. Cover and blend until smooth.

3. Pour into chilled glasses. Top with a dash of the cinnamon (if using), and serve.

Per serving: 150 calories, 5g total fat, 1g saturated fat, 0g trans fat, 0mg cholesterol, 65mg sodium, 26g total carbohydrate, 3g dietary fiber, 16g sugars, 3g protein

Berry Good Smoothie Ⓢ

Makes 1 serving: 1 cup

Take a bevy of super-chilled "superfood" fruits and whirl them in a blender. You'll get a 100 percent pure fruit smoothie with a beautiful burgundy hue to boot. It tastes super, too.

¼ cup fresh blackberries

¼ cup fresh blueberries

¼ cup sliced fresh strawberries

⅓ cup 100% unsweetened apple juice, chilled

¼ cup 100% pomegranate juice, chilled

1. Arrange the blackberries, blueberries, and sliced strawberries in a single layer on a parchment paper–lined tray, cover, and freeze for at least 1 hour or overnight.

2. Add the frozen berries and the juices to a blender. Cover and blend until smooth.

3. Pour into a chilled glass, and serve.

Per serving: 120 calories, 0.5g total fat, 0g saturated fat, 0g trans fat, 0mg cholesterol, 10mg sodium, 30g total carbohydrate, 4g dietary fiber, 23g sugars, 1g protein

Chocolate Soy Milkshake-tini Ⓢ

Makes 1 serving: about ⅔ cup each

Wow, this is mighty-thick and rich—in a very good way. You actually won't need that much of this dairy-free delight to fully satisfy your sweet tooth. By serving it in a martini glass, you want to sip this chocolaty treat rather than gulp it, too.

⅔ cup soy-milk based or other non-dairy chocolate frozen dessert

2 tablespoons plain light soy milk or almond milk, well chilled, or to taste

½ teaspoon unsweetened cocoa powder

Couple drops of pure vanilla extract

½ teaspoon shaved semi-sweet dark chocolate (optional)

1. Add the frozen dessert, soy milk, cocoa powder, and vanilla extract to a blender. Cover and blend until smooth. Add additional soy milk by the teaspoon, if necessary, for proper blending.

2. Pour into a chilled martini glass or other medium-size beverage glass. Sprinkle with the shaved chocolate (if using), and serve.

Per serving: 180 calories, 5g total fat, 0.5g saturated fat, 0g trans fat, 0mg cholesterol, 80mg sodium, 32g total carbohydrate, 2g dietary fiber, 19g sugars, 4g protein

Freshly Squeezed Orange Float Ⓢ

Makes 1 serving: 1¼ cup

Make this a treat for yourself. Your taste buds will be tickled by this orange creamsicle-inspired float.

¾ cup fresh-squeezed orange juice, chilled

¼ cup seltzer water or natural orange flavor seltzer water, chilled

¼ cup scoop almond-, soy-, or coconut milk-based vanilla frozen dessert

¼ teaspoon grated orange zest

1. Pour the orange juice into a chilled glass. Add the seltzer water and gently stir.

2. Top with the scoop of frozen dessert, sprinkle with the orange zest, and serve.

Per serving: 140 calories, 1g total fat, 0g saturated fat, 0g trans fat, 0mg cholesterol, 65mg sodium, 31g total carbohydrate, 1g dietary fiber, 20g sugars, 2g protein

Root Beer Flute Float Ⓢ

Makes 1 serving: about ⅔ cup

I have such fond memories of my family's trips to the drive-in root beer stand for a root beer float treat when I was a kid. This brand-new, bubbly, sweet, and fizzy float served in a champagne flute is my modern take on the old-fashioned treasure. For a still slimmer version, make this with a stevia-sweetened natural diet ginger root beer.

⅓ cup natural root beer soda

¼ cup almond-, soy-, or coconut milk-based vanilla frozen dessert

Gently pour the root beer into a chilled champagne flute or glass. Top with two (2 tablespoon) scoops of the frozen dessert, and serve.

Per serving: 90 calories, 1g total fat, 0g saturated fat, 0g trans fat, 0mg cholesterol, 75mg sodium, 22g total carbohydrate, 1g dietary fiber, 15g sugars, 1g protein

Dairy Smoothies and Shakes

Blueberry Pie Smoothie

Makes 3 servings: 1 cup each

Here's a smoothie that's equally delightful for kids and adults. It's pure eye candy. Its vivid deep purple is stunning. The cookie crumbs on top are tempting. The taste is like pure blueberry pie-in-a-glass.

2¾ cups fresh or frozen blueberries

¾ cup plain almond milk or unsweetened coconut milk beverage, well chilled

½ cup fat-free or low-fat plain Greek yogurt

1½ teaspoons mild honey or agave nectar

½ teaspoon pure vanilla extract

½ teaspoon grated lemon zest

2 teaspoons natural vanilla wafer cookie or graham cracker crumbs

Pinch of ground cinnamon

1. If using fresh berries, freeze the blueberries for at least 1 hour or overnight.

2. Add the frozen berries, the almond milk, yogurt, honey, vanilla extract, and lemon zest to a blender. Cover and blend until smooth.

3. Pour into chilled glasses. Sprinkle the top of each smoothie with the graham cracker crumbs and dash of cinnamon, and serve.

Per serving: 130 calories, 1g total fat, 0g saturated fat, 0g trans fat, 0mg cholesterol, 60mg sodium, 27g total carbohydrate, 3g dietary fiber, 20g sugars, 5g protein

Pretty in Pink Smoothie

Makes 3 servings: 1 cup each

Here's a great way to enjoy a treat after dinner that's only 100 calories; I highly recommend it!

2 cups sliced fresh strawberries + 3 whole fresh strawberries

1 cup plain almond milk or unsweetened coconut milk beverage, well chilled

1 medium fully ripened banana, sliced

⅓ cup fat-free or low-fat plain Greek yogurt

½ teaspoon pure vanilla extract

1. Arrange the sliced strawberries in a single layer on a tray or plate, cover, and freeze for at least 1 hour or overnight.

2. Add the frozen sliced strawberries, the almond milk, banana, yogurt, and vanilla extract to a blender. Cover and blend until smooth.

3. Pour into chilled glasses. Garnish the rim of each glass with a whole strawberry, and serve.

Per serving: 100 calories, 1.5g total fat, 0g saturated fat, 0g trans fat, 0mg cholesterol, 60mg sodium, 20g total carbohydrate, 3g dietary fiber, 3g sugars, 4g protein

Tropical Pineapple Shake

Makes 2 servings: about 1 cup each

One summer day my fridge was overstocked with pineapple. So I asked my intern, Courtney, to help me create a tropical beverage out of it. Here it is!

2 cups diced fresh pineapple + 2 pineapple wedges (optional)

½ cup fat-free or low-fat vanilla frozen yogurt

½ cup fresh-squeezed orange juice, chilled

1. Add the diced pineapple, frozen yogurt, and juice to a blender. Cover and blend until smooth.

2. Pour into chilled glasses, and serve. Garnish the glass rims with a fresh pineapple wedge (if using).

Per serving: 160 calories, 0g total fat, 0g saturated fat, 0g trans fat, 0mg cholesterol, 0mg sodium, 35g total carbohydrate, 2g dietary fiber, 31g sugars, 3g protein

Semisweet Cocoa Shake Ⓢ

Makes 2 servings: 1 cup each

This is like heaven in a glass for chocolate shake devotees. You may feel like you're drinking something devilish. But no worries, the 200 delectable calories here are rather angelic compared to the 450 (or significantly more!) calories of a regular-size drive-thru shake.

2 tablespoons unsweetened cocoa powder

1¾ cups fat-free or low-fat vanilla frozen yogurt

½ cup plain almond milk or unsweetened coconut milk beverage, well chilled

1. Add all the ingredients to a blender. Cover and blend until smooth.

2. Pour into two chilled glasses and serve.

Per serving: 200 calories, 1.5g total fat, 0g saturated fat, 0g trans fat, 0mg cholesterol, 150mg sodium, 40g total carbohydrate, 2g dietary fiber, 35g sugars, 8g protein

Mango Lassi Ⓢ

Makes 3 servings: 1 cup each

The lassi is to India as perhaps the smoothie is to America. Here's a creamy mango interpretation of the thick, yet light Indian yogurt beverage.

1¾ cups fresh mango cubes, well chilled

1 cup fat-free or low-fat plain Greek yogurt

½ cup plain almond milk or unsweetened coconut milk beverage, well chilled

2 teaspoons fresh lemon juice

1 teaspoon mild honey or agave nectar

Pinch of ground cardamom (optional)

1. Add the mango, yogurt, almond milk, lemon juice, and honey to a blender. Cover and blend until smooth.

2. Pour into two chilled glasses, top with a dash of cardamom (if using), and serve.

Per serving: 120 calories, 1g total fat, 0g saturated fat, 0g trans fat, 0mg cholesterol, 55mg sodium, 21g total carbohydrate, 2g dietary fiber, 19g sugars, 8g protein

White Peach Melba Lassi Ⓢ

Makes 2 servings: 1⅓ cup each

The traditional Melba dessert involves sweet poached peach halves topped with vanilla ice cream, raspberry sauce, and often whipped cream and sliced almonds. This creamy peach Melba-inspired lassi whirls together similar components into a rich-tasting drink that's protein-rich, too. Use other peaches, if you like.

1 cup fat-free or low-fat plain Greek yogurt

1 large or 2 small white peaches, pitted, sliced, and chilled

½ cup plain almond milk or unsweetened sunflower beverage, well chilled

1 tablespoon 100% raspberry jam or fruit spread

2 small fresh mint sprigs (optional)

1. Add the yogurt, peach slices, and almond milk to a blender. Cover and blend until smooth.

2. Pour into two chilled glasses and top with the jam. Garnish with fresh mint sprigs, if using, and serve.

Per serving: 120 calories, 1g total fat, 0g saturated fat, 0g trans fat, 0mg cholesterol, 80mg sodium, 17g total carbohydrate, 2g dietary fiber, 15g sugars, 11g protein

Tea and Coffee Beverages

Iced Ginger Spa Tea Ⓢ

2 servings: 1 cup each

This tea has only a slight hint of sweetness, so the fresh fragrances of the ginger and cucumber shine. It's refreshing served before or after a yoga session. It's thirst quenching after outdoor activities, too. For a still skinnier tea, prepare this with stevia-sweetened natural diet ginger ale.

⅞ cup green tea, jasmine green tea, or ginger peach green tea (made with 1 tea bag), well chilled

⅓ cup sliced or diced unpeeled English cucumber

1 cup natural ginger ale (preferably made with fresh ginger), well chilled

2 lime wedges

1. Add the tea and cucumber to a blender. Cover and puree.

2. Pour the tea mixture into a large liquid measuring cup. Slowly add the ginger ale and gently stir to combine.

3. Pour over ice in tall glasses. Squirt with the lime wedges. Top each with a lime or cucumber slice, if desired, and serve.

Per serving: 45 calories, 0g total fat, 0g saturated fat, 0g trans fat, 0mg cholesterol, 10mg sodium, 12g total carbohydrate, 0g dietary fiber, 11g sugars, 0g protein

Raspberry Mint Iced Tea Ⓢ

2 servings: 1¼ cups each

The deep pink and sweet-tartness of the raspberry sparkles here. The ginger ale adds an interesting hint of sweetness—and gives the tea cool frothy appeal. Plus, it's an excellent source of vitamin C and health-promoting antioxidants naturally found in tea! So, sip away as you chill out . . . for only 50 calories. Make this even calorie-friendlier with stevia-sweetened natural diet ginger ale.

1½ cups English Breakfast or other black tea (made with 1 tea bag), well chilled

1 cup fresh raspberries

6 large fresh mint leaves + 2 fresh mint sprigs

½ cup natural ginger ale (preferably made with fresh ginger), well chilled

1. Add the tea, raspberries, and mint leaves to a blender. Cover and puree.

2. Pour the tea mixture through a fine-mesh strainer to catch seeds (using the back of a spoon while straining to assist) into a large liquid measuring cup. Slowly add the ginger ale and gently stir to combine.

3. Pour over ice in tall glasses. Garnish each with a sprig of the mint, if desired, and serve.

Per serving: 50 calories, 0g total fat, 0g saturated fat, 0g trans fat, 0mg cholesterol, 0mg sodium, 12g total carbohydrate, 3g dietary fiber, 8g sugars, 1g protein

Blended Iced Mocha Ⓢ

Makes 1 serving: 1½ cups

Mocha is the magical flavor fusion of chocolate and coffee. You'll get a jolt from this large frothy and refreshing mocha beverage. Enjoy it as a delicious snack—or as dessert.

⅔ cup fat-free or low-fat chocolate frozen yogurt

⅓ cup espresso or strong black coffee, well chilled

3 tablespoons plain almond milk or unsweetened coconut milk beverage, well chilled

1 teaspoon unsweetened cocoa powder

1 teaspoon mild honey or agave nectar

⅛ teaspoon pure vanilla extract

1. Add 2 large ice cubes to a blender. Cover and crush.

2. Add the frozen yogurt, espresso, almond milk, cocoa powder, honey, and vanilla extract. Cover and puree.

3. Pour into a tall chilled glass or to-go cup.

Per serving: 170 calories, 0.5g total fat, 0g saturated fat, 0g trans fat, 0mg cholesterol, 115mg sodium, 35g total carbohydrate, 1g dietary fiber, 32g sugars, 6g protein

Espresso Frothy

Makes 1 serving: about 1 cup

Espresso is a strong and dark Italian-roast coffee. This is a frothy and light Greek-style chilled coffee beverage. It's an ideal way to enjoy your espresso on a warm and steamy day.

⅓ cup plain almond milk or unsweetened coconut milk beverage, well chilled

¼ cup espresso or strong black coffee, chilled

¼ cup fat-free or low-fat plain Greek yogurt

1½ teaspoons mild honey or agave nectar

⅛ teaspoon pure vanilla extract

1. Add 2 large ice cubes to a blender. Cover and crush.

2. Add the almond milk, espresso, yogurt, honey, and vanilla extract. Cover and puree on high speed until smooth and frothy.

3. Pour into a chilled glass or to-go cup.

Per serving: 80 calories, 1g total fat, 0g saturated fat, 0g trans fat, 0mg cholesterol, 75mg sodium, 14g total carbohydrate, 0g dietary fiber, 13g sugars, 6g protein

Iced Chai Tea Frothy

Makes 1 serving: 1½ cups

The result of pureeing together the ingredients in this recipe is spectacular. The foamy top and spicy aroma will be incredibly enticing.

⅔ cup plain almond milk or unsweetened sunflower beverage, well chilled

½ cup freshly brewed chai tea, well chilled

2 teaspoons mild honey or agave nectar

¼ teaspoon ground cinnamon

Pinch of ground cardamom

1. Add 2 large ice cubes to a blender. Cover and crush.

2. Add the almond milk, tea, honey, and cinnamon. Cover and blend on high speed until smooth and frothy.

3. Pour into a chilled glass or to-go cup and sprinkle with the cardamom.

Per serving: 80 calories, 2g total fat, 0g saturated fat, 0g trans fat, 0mg cholesterol, 95mg sodium, 17g total carbohydrate, 1g dietary fiber, 16g sugars, 1g protein

Hot Chocolate au Lait Ⓢ

Makes 4 servings: about 1 cup each

I use dairy milk instead of a plant-based version here as it simply makes the tastiest hot chocolate. The pure chocolate extract provides extra chocolaty goodness without unnecessary calories.

3¾ cups fat-free or low-fat milk

2 ounces high-quality semisweet or Mexican chocolate, chopped

⅛ teaspoon sea salt

1 tablespoon mild honey or agave nectar

½ teaspoon pure chocolate extract

⅛ teaspoon ground cinnamon, or to taste (optional)

1. Heat 1 cup of the milk in a medium saucepan over medium heat until barely simmering. Add the chocolate and salt and stir until the chocolate is fully melted.

2. Whisk in the remaining 2¾ cups milk, the honey, and chocolate extract, heating until the mixture is simmering and smooth. Whisk in the cinnamon (if using) and serve.

Per serving: 170 calories, 4.5g total fat, 2.5g saturated fat, 0g trans fat, 5mg cholesterol, 170mg sodium, 24g total carbohydrate, 1g dietary fiber, 23g sugars, 9g protein

Pumpkin Spice Coffee Ⓢ

Makes 1 serving: about 1 cup

Here's an intriguing coffee recipe for fall or wintertime. You'll think you are enjoying a slice of pumpkin pie when sipping this fresh-brewed cup o' joe.

¾ cup freshly brewed black coffee, hot

3 tablespoons plain almond milk or unsweetened coconut milk beverage

1 teaspoon mild honey or agave nectar

¼ teaspoon + pinch pumpkin pie seasoning

1. Into the hot coffee stir the almond milk, honey, and ¼ teaspoon of the pumpkin pie seasoning until combined.

2. Top with the pinch of pumpkin pie seasoning, and serve.

Per serving: 35 calories, 0.5g total fat, 0g saturated fat, 0g trans fat, 0mg cholesterol, 35mg sodium, 8g total carbohydrate, 1g dietary fiber, 7g sugars, 1g protein

---

DIET SODA

There are regular sodas used sparingly in this cookbook and they keep the recipes 100% natural and tasty. The nutrition analyses in *1,000 Low-Calorie Recipes* are based on these sweet choices when they're in the ingredient lists. But if you prefer, replace regular soda with 0-calorie soda in any of the recipes. I recommend choosing one that contains no artificial colors, flavors, or preservatives, and is made with naturally derived sweetener, such as stevia, which is an herb. This zero-calorie sweetener is extracted from the stevia leaf and has no effect on blood sugar levels. One soda brand with this sweetener is Zevia 100% Natural Diet Soda. But one note: Research is not clear about the benefit of drinking diet soda in efforts to lose weight or reduce risk of diabetes. Some studies find that 0-calorie sugar substitutes may help with a short-term loss of weight; others don't find a clear connection.

Mocktails

Shirley Temple Party Punch Ⓢ

Makes 12 servings: ½ cup each

Instead of traditional grenadine syrup—which is made from pomegranates but is über-sweet, 100% pomegranate juice is the key ingredient in this punch. To keep it light and refreshing, seltzer water is splashed in. To make it even lighter, use stevia-sweetened natural diet ginger ale. To keep it real and fun, fresh cherry-mint ice cubes are plopped into the punch.

12 fresh mint leaves

12 fresh Bing cherries with stems

1½ cups 100% pomegranate juice, well chilled

2½ cups seltzer water or club soda, well chilled

3 cups natural ginger ale (preferably made with fresh ginger), well chilled

1½ teaspoons freshly grated gingerroot, or to taste

1. Fill each section of an ice cube tray (with 12 compartments) with a mint leaf and a cherry (allowing stem to stick out) and top with filtered tap water. Freeze overnight to form ice with a cherry in the middle.

2. Fill a pitcher with the pomegranate juice. Slow add the seltzer water and ginger ale. Gently stir.

3. Pour into punch cups or white wine glasses. Add a pinch of the ginger and a cherry-mint ice cube to each cup, and serve.

Per serving: 45 calories, 0g total fat, 0g saturated fat, 0g trans fat, 0mg cholesterol, 5mg sodium, 11g total carbohydrate, 0g dietary fiber, 10g sugars, 0g protein

Virgin Mary

Makes 1 serving: ⅔ cup

You'll love this Virgin Mary made with kicked-up tomato juice—no spirits are needed to give this alcohol-free eye-opener spirit.

5 ounces tomato juice (low sodium, if desired)

½ teaspoon fresh lemon juice

⅛ teaspoon vegetarian Worcestershire sauce

⅛ teaspoon red or green hot pepper sauce, or to taste

⅛ teaspoon freshly ground black pepper, or to taste

1 celery stalk

1. Add the tomato juice, lemon juice, Worcestershire sauce, hot sauce, and black pepper to a liquid measuring cup and stir well.

2. Pour into a tall skinny glass and fill with ice. Garnish with the celery and an additional pinch of black pepper, if desired, and serve

Per serving: 35 calories, 0g total fat, 0g saturated fat, 0g trans fat, 0mg cholesterol, 450mg sodium, 8g total carbohydrate, 1g dietary fiber, 6g sugars, 1g protein

Green Grasshopper Ⓢ

Makes 1 serving: 1 cup

The tiny flecks of fresh mint floating in this creamy beverage add tingle and intrigue. Serve this splendid sipper as dessert . . . a delicious happy ending after dinner, indeed.

¾ cup fat-free or low-fat vanilla frozen yogurt

¼ cup plain almond milk or unsweetened coconut milk beverage, well chilled

2½ tablespoons fat-free or low-fat plain Greek yogurt

¾ teaspoon mild honey or agave nectar

1 teaspoon finely chopped fresh mint

⅛ teaspoon pure vanilla extract

2 drops pure peppermint extract, or to taste

1 or 2 drops pure chocolate extract, or to taste (optional)

1. Add all the ingredients to a blender. Cover and blend until smooth.

2. Pour into a chilled martini or whiskey glass. Garnish the top with additional fresh mint, if desired, and serve.

Per serving: 200 calories, 0.5g total fat, 0g saturated fat, 0g trans fat, 0mg cholesterol, 150mg sodium, 38g total carbohydrate, 0g dietary fiber, 36g sugars, 9g protein

Fresh-Squeezed Citrus "007" Ⓢ

Makes 1 serving: 1 cup

A "007" cocktail is typically made with lemon-lime soda, orange juice, and vodka. But here I've freshened it up by using seltzer water along with fresh lemon and lime juices—and no added sugars. Plus, I've given it an extra flavor punch with orange zest . . . no vodka required.

¾ cup fresh-squeezed orange juice, chilled

1 teaspoon fresh lemon juice

1 teaspoon fresh lime juice

¼ teaspoon grated orange zest

¼ cup seltzer water or club soda

1. Add the orange, lemon, and lime juices and orange zest to a 2-cup liquid measuring cup. Slowly add the seltzer water, and gently stir.

2. Fill a tall chilled highball glass with crushed ice. Pour over the ice and serve immediately.

Per serving: 90 calories, 0g total fat, 0g saturated fat, 0g trans fat, 0mg cholesterol, 0mg sodium, 20g total carbohydrate, 0g dietary fiber, 16g sugars, 1g protein

Cocktails

Vodka

Zesty Vodka Collins

Fresh Basil Fresca

Orange Jackie

Georgia Peach Mule

Merry Cranberry Cosmopolitan

Jamaican Bloody Mary Shots

Middle Eastern Bloody Mary

Chocolate Mint
Vodka Almond-tini

Thai Carrot Vodka Martini

Gin

Herbal Lemon Gin Martini

Muddled Cucumber
Gin Martini

Seedless Watermelon Gin Fizz

Gin Berry Fizz

Fresh-Squeezed Gin Gimlet

Seasonal Pimm's Cup

Rum

All-Year-Round Mojito

Itoo Mojito

Fresh Gingered Strawberry
Daiquiri

Frozen Peaches and "Cream"
Daiquiri

Light Jamaican Breeze

Tropical Rum Frozen Cocktail

Tequila

Mango Margarita Smoothie

Spicy Green Margarita

Bloody Maria

Papaya Sipper

Citrus Tequila Sunrise

Garden Tequila Cocktail

Whiskey/Bourbon/ Brandy

Half Irish Coffee

Egg Nog Amandine

Fresh Mint Julep Bouquet

Mixed Spirits and Other Cocktails

Pink Grapefruit Teaser

Long Island Earl Grey
Iced Tea

"Big Apple" Manhattan

Bubbly Raspberry
Ginger Vodka

Natural Peanut Butter Cup

Wine and Sparkling Wine Beverages

Summer Sangria

Blood Orange Mimosa

Sweet Cherry-Apricot
Mimosa

(S) = Low-Sodium   (F) = Fiber-Rich

I approach consuming alcoholic beverages the same way I approach eating—enjoy it and do it mindfully as part of a healthy lifestyle.

So, that means you can drink a beer, enjoy a glass of wine, or sip a cocktail with your meal—at least from time to time. When consumed in moderation, which is one drink a day for women or two drinks a day for men, it can be a healthful part of an eating plan. Convincing evidence shows that it's associated with a reduced risk of heart disease. One drink is defined as a 12-ounce beer, 5-ounce glass of wine, or 1½-ounce 80-proof distilled spirit. These standard-size drinks actually contain the same amount of alcohol. Of course, there are some occasions to steer clear of alcohol, such as when you're pregnant, on certain medications, under the legal drinking age, or planning to drive.

Need more facts? A U.S. Centers for Disease Control and Prevention study confirms that moderate alcohol consumption is one of four healthy lifestyle behaviors that help people live longer. In addition to moderate alcohol consumption, the other lifestyle behaviors include having never smoked, eating a healthful diet, and getting regular physical activity. Please do keep this all in mind when pleasantly sipping your way through this chapter . . . in moderation. Though healthful, remember the calories from drinks still count.

So know that you can feel good about enjoying cocktails—and especially good about the pleasures of those in *1,000 Low-Calorie Recipes*. I focus on the "good" part of most recipes with the inclusion of fresh nutrient-rich ingredients, like fruits, vegetables, and herbs. Plus I keep the serving sizes just right to help you keep calories in check. In fact, every beverage here provides 200 or fewer calories!

The chapter is arranged by types of alcohol: vodka, gin, rum, tequila, whiskey, bourbon, and brandy. To these bases, I add a variety of fresh juices, herbs, and other innovative "mixers" to keep things interesting. The balance of the chapter is rounded out by mixed spirits, other cocktails, and wine beverages.

I mainly include fresh twists on classics, which range from the mild to wonderfully wild. Some of the most dramatic are the Thai Carrot Vodka Martini (page 559), Middle Eastern Bloody Mary (page 558), and Garden Tequila Cocktail (page 566): the martini actually tastes like Thai cuisine—so it's slightly sweet and slightly savory with a touch of "heat"; the Bloody Mary incorporates hummus, creating a velvety creaminess and amazing flavor intrigue; and the tequila drink is a sweet, salty, and smoky concoction that's a blended mixture of vegetables, tequila (of course!), lime juice, and smoked sea salt, creating a gorgeous orange color. And some cocktail recipes are show-offs, including the Fresh Mint Julep Bouquet (page 567), which is actually topped with a "bouquet" of fresh mint.

Calorie range in this chapter: 40 to 200 calories.

Low-calorie pick: Jamaican Bloody Mary Shots, 40 calories (page 558).

Vodka

Zesty Vodka Collins Ⓢ

Makes 1 serving: 1 (6-fluid-ounce) drink

Tart, tangy, and refreshing . . . like glistening lemonade for cocktail enthusiasts.

1½ ounces 80-proof vodka
Juice and zest of ½ small lemon (1 tablespoon juice)
1 teaspoon honey or agave nectar
½ cup seltzer water or club soda
1 lemon slice (optional)

1. Add the vodka, lemon juice and zest, and honey to a tall glass and stir until the honey dissolves. Fill the glass with ice, add the seltzer, and gently stir.

2. Garnish with the lemon slice (if using), and serve.

Per serving: 120 calories, 0g total fat, 0g saturated fat, 0g trans fat, 0mg cholesterol, 0mg sodium, 7g total carbohydrate, 0g dietary fiber, 6g sugars, 0g protein

GREEN SPIRITS

Choosing organic vodka is one way to green your martinis. But choosing locally produced spirits that may not be organic can be a sustainable habit, too. Since spirits have grown in popularity, so have the available brands. You might have a high-quality one produced more locally than you realize, if you haven't checked lately. Give these a shot: Hanger One Vodka (California), Skyy Vodka (California), Teton Glacier Potato Vodka (Idaho), Blue Ice Organic Wheat Vodka (Idaho), Hamptons Vodka (New York), LiV Vodka (New York), Tito's Handmade Vodka (Texas), and Vermont Spirits Gold Vodka (Vermont).

Fresh Basil Fresca Ⓢ

Makes 1 serving: 1 (4½-fluid-ounce) drink

A shiny, happy cocktail awaits. This shimmering vodka drink will have you breathing in its fresh fragrance while smiling. Then you'll be sipping in its citrus and basil goodness while beaming.

2 large fresh basil leaves, muddled or finely chopped
1½ ounces 80-proof vodka
1 ounce fresh-squeezed red or pink grapefruit juice
1 teaspoon fresh lime juice
½ teaspoon mild honey or agave nectar
1 ounce seltzer water or club soda
1 small fresh basil sprig (optional)

1. Add the basil leaves, vodka, grapefruit juice, lime juice, and honey to a shaker container. Whisk or cover and shake until the honey dissolves. Fill with ice, cover, and shake well.

2. Strain into a chilled martini glass, top with the seltzer, garnish with the basil sprig (if using), and serve.

Per serving: 120 calories, 0g total fat, 0g saturated fat, 0g trans fat, 0mg cholesterol, 0mg sodium, 6g total carbohydrate, 0g dietary fiber, 3g sugars, 0g protein

Orange Jackie Ⓢ

Makes 1 serving: 1 (9-fluid-ounce) drink

This is my kind of cocktail—a little sweet, a little savory, and a little spicy—which is why I named it after myself! It's one of those beverages that you actually feel really good about drinking. But be careful, it's also one of those drinks that you may forget is alcoholic. So savor every sip . . . slowly.

1½ ounces 80-proof cucumber vodka

¼ cup 100% pure pressed carrot juice

¼ cup fresh-squeezed orange juice

¼ cup chopped unpeeled English cucumber
    + 1 slice English cucumber

2 teaspoons no-sugar-added apple butter

1 teaspoon freshly grated gingerroot

1. Add the vodka, carrot juice, orange juice, chopped cucumber, apple butter, and ginger to a blender with 2 large ice cubes. Cover and blend until smooth and frothy.

2. Pour over ice into a tall chilled glass, garnish with the cucumber slice, and serve.

Per serving: 160 calories, 0g total fat, 0g saturated fat, 0g trans fat, 0mg cholesterol, 40mg sodium, 15g total carbohydrate, 1g dietary fiber, 9g sugars, 1g protein

Georgia Peach Mule Ⓢ

Makes 1 serving: 1 (3-fluid-ounce) drink

The fresh ginger shines in this refreshing peachy cocktail, ideal for summertime sipping. Choose whatever peaches are local to you. It's sure to provide a glass of juicy sweet excitement.

3 very thin slices fresh gingerroot

¼ cup finely chopped fresh peeled fully ripened
    peach or nectarine

1 ounce 80-proof vodka

1 teaspoon fresh lime juice

1½ ounces ginger beer, such as Fentimans
    Botanically Brewed Ginger Beer

½ ounce seltzer water or club soda

1 slice fresh peach or nectarine (optional)

1. Muddle together the ginger and peach in a shaker container. Add the vodka and lime juice. Cover and shake well.

2. Strain into a chilled glass filled with ice, add the ginger beer and seltzer, garnish with the peach slice (if using), and serve.

Per serving: 100 calories, 0g total fat, 0g saturated fat, 0g trans fat, 0mg cholesterol, 0mg sodium, 8g total carbohydrate, 0.5g dietary fiber, 7g sugars, 0g protein

Merry Cranberry Cosmopolitan Ⓢ

Makes 1 serving: 1 (4-fluid-ounce) drink

The Cosmo was made famous by "Sex and the City." But you'll have the opportunity to make this saucy cranberry version famous—at least among your family or friends. It's frothy, festive, and fragrant. In fact, this merrymaking cocktail even smells like the holidays!

1 ounce 80-proof lemon vodka

1 ounce seltzer water

½ ounce 30-proof triple sec

2 tablespoons Seasonal Cranberry Sauce
    (page 130) or 1½ tablespoons canned
    whole berry cranberry sauce, chilled

2 teaspoons fresh lime juice

¼ teaspoon minced fresh rosemary
    + 1 fresh rosemary sprig

1. Add the vodka, seltzer, triple sec, cranberry sauce, lime juice, and minced rosemary to a blender. Cover and puree.

2. Pour into a chilled martini glass, garnish with the rosemary sprig, and serve.

Per serving: 130 calories, 0g total fat, 0g saturated fat, 0g trans fat, 0mg cholesterol, 20mg sodium, 17g total carbohydrate, 1g dietary fiber, 15g sugars, 0g protein

Jamaican Bloody Mary Shots

Makes 4 servings: 1 (1½-fluid-ounce) shot each

I dare ya! This is literally a "hot" shot. It packs some heat from the Jamaican pepper. So cut back on the pepper for a less spicy version if you want to tame the heat. And if you want to further tempt your taste buds, enjoy it in cuisine: Bloody Mary Wild Rice (page 479).

3½ ounces tomato juice, chilled

¼ cup 80-proof vodka, chilled

½ small Jamaican or serrano pepper, without seeds, stem removed

1 small garlic clove, chopped

½ teaspoon fresh lemon juice or apple cider vinegar

¼ teaspoon freshly grated horseradish

⅛ teaspoon vegetarian Worcestershire sauce

⅛ teaspoon freshly ground black pepper

4 slender celery strips

1. Add the tomato juice, vodka, Jamaican pepper, garlic, lemon juice, horseradish, Worcestershire sauce, and black pepper to a blender with 1 large ice cube.

2. Cover and puree. Adjust ingredients to taste, if desired.

3. Pour into four shot or dessert wine glasses. Top each glass with a celery strip, and serve.

Per serving: 40 calories, 0g total fat, 0g saturated fat, 0g trans fat, 0mg cholesterol, 75mg sodium, 2g total carbohydrate, 0g dietary fiber, 1g sugars, 0g protein

Middle Eastern Bloody Mary

Makes 2 servings: 1 (5-fluid-ounce) drink each

Get ready to be intrigued. This Bloody Mary-esque drink is made with hummus, creating a creamy, earthy orange hue. If you enjoy hummus (which is made with chickpeas), you've gotta give this inspired drink a sip. You actually may be tempted to dip a piece of pita into it. I won't stop you.

5 ounces tomato juice, chilled

1½ ounces 80-proof lemon vodka, chilled

¼ cup Tahini Chickpea Hummus (page 87) or other hummus

1 teaspoon chopped fresh mint or flat-leaf parsley

¼ teaspoon harissa sauce or ⅛ teaspoon hot pepper sauce, or to taste

⅛ teaspoon freshly ground black pepper

2 lemon slices

1. Add the tomato juice, vodka, hummus, mint, harissa, and black pepper to a blender with 2 large ice cubes. Cover and puree.

2. Pour into two short cocktail glasses, garnish each with the lemon slice, and serve.

Per serving: 120 calories, 2.5g total fat, 0g saturated fat, 0g trans fat, 0mg cholesterol, 300mg sodium, 10g total carbohydrate, 2g dietary fiber, 3g sugars, 4g protein

Chocolate Mint Vodka Almond-tini Ⓢ

Makes 1 serving: 1 (5-fluid-ounce) drink

I've gone a little lighter than usual on the vodka in this martini-style cocktail to keep calories in check, but I've chosen vanilla vodka to keep it richly flavored. Then I married it with my favorite dessert flavor combo: chocolate mint. That makes this sexy sipper better than dessert to me!

2 teaspoons mild honey or agave nectar

2 teaspoons unsweetened cocoa powder

3½ ounces plain almond milk or unsweetened coconut milk beverage

1 ounce 80-proof vanilla vodka

2 or 3 drops pure peppermint extract

1 fresh mint leaf (optional)

1. Rub the rim of a martini glass with about ¼ teaspoon of the honey. Measure the cocoa into a small dish and dip the rim of the glass into the cocoa to coat.

2. Add the almond milk and the remaining 1¾ teaspoons honey to a shaker container. Whisk or cover and shake until the honey dissolves. Fill with ice and add the vodka, peppermint extract, and remaining cocoa to the container. Cover and shake vigorously.

3. Strain into the prepared glass, top with the mint leaf (if using), and serve.

Per serving: 140 calories, 1.5g total fat, 0g saturated fat, 0g trans fat, 0mg cholesterol, 65mg sodium, 17g total carbohydrate, 1g dietary fiber, 14g sugars, 1g protein

Thai Carrot Vodka Martini Ⓢ

Makes 1 serving: 1 (4½-fluid-ounce) drink

Here's a must-try martini—especially if you're into cocktail exploration. This is a unique and savory cocktail with a hint of heat and sweet that pairs perfectly with the distinct flavors of Asian dishes. It's just as appetizing when its Thai-inspired glory is sipped all its own, too.

2½ ounces 100% pure pressed carrot juice

1½ ounces 80-proof cucumber or green tea vodka

½ teaspoon fresh lime juice

¼ teaspoon freshly grated gingerroot

⅛ teaspoon red curry paste

¼ teaspoon minced scallion, green part only

1. Add the carrot juice, vodka, lime juice, ginger, and curry paste to a shaker container filled with ice. Cover and shake well.

2. Strain into a chilled martini glass, garnish with the scallion, and serve.

Per serving: 120 calories, 0g total fat, 0g saturated fat, 0g trans fat, 0mg cholesterol, 70mg sodium, 5g total carbohydrate, 0g dietary fiber, 0g sugars, 1g protein

COCKTAIL CALORIES

Need to be extra-calorie conscious? Simply reduce the amount of the spirit by ½ ounce (1 tablespoon) in any of the cocktails. You'll be cutting 30 calories by doing this for any 80-proof spirit. By reducing the vodka by ½ ounce in this Thai Carrot Martini, for instance, it'll become a 90-calorie cocktail. If you drink cocktails regularly, every 30-calorie reduction will add up!

Also, be sure to start with 80-proof spirits instead of aiming for 100. This is one of those cases where 80 beats 100! For every increment of 10 that you go up, consider it an extra 10 calories for a 1½-ounce shot:

1 shot (80-proof) vodka = 100 cals

1 shot (90-proof) vodka = 110 cals

1 shot (100-proof) vodka = 120 cals

Gin

Herbal Lemon Gin Martini Ⓢ

Makes 1 serving: 1 (3-fluid-ounce) drink

For those who find a straight-up gin martini a bit too hard to handle, this lighter, lemony version may provide a smoother experience. But if you can handle the gin, simply add less of the tea or none at all. Either way, it'll still be a straight 100 calories.

1 teaspoon extra-dry vermouth

1½ ounces 80-proof gin or herbal lemon-infused gin (page 560)

½ teaspoon fresh lemon juice

2 tablespoons unsweetened white tea or water, chilled

1 fresh lemon slice

1 fresh thyme sprig

1. Add the vermouth to a chilled martini glass. Swirl it around until all inside surfaces are coated.

2. Add the gin, lemon juice, and tea to a shaker container filled with ice. Cover and shake well.

3. Strain into the martini glass. Top with the lemon slice and thyme sprig, and serve.

Per serving: 100 calories, 0g total fat, 0g saturated fat, 0g trans fat, 0mg cholesterol, 0mg sodium, 1g total carbohydrate, 0g dietary fiber, 0g sugars, 0g protein

Muddled Cucumber Gin Martini Ⓢ

Makes 1 serving: 1 (3-fluid-ounce) drink

What a freshly fragrant martini this is. You'll get a bright herbal scent from the mint, a garden-fresh essence from the cucumber, and a beautiful floral note from the rose water. All together, it's an aromatic pleasure.

¼ cup finely chopped English cucumber without skin

6 fresh mint leaves

1½ ounces 80-proof gin

¼ teaspoon mild honey or agave nectar

⅛ teaspoon rose water

1 tablespoon unsweetened green tea or water, chilled

1 slice English cucumber or fresh mint sprig (optional)

1. Muddle the cucumber and mint in the bottom of a shaker container. Add the gin, honey, rose water, and tea and stir until the honey dissolves. Fill with ice, cover, and shake well.

2. Pour into a chilled martini glass, garnish with the cucumber slice, and serve.

Per serving: 110 calories, 0g total fat, 0g saturated fat, 0g trans fat, 0mg cholesterol, 0mg sodium, 2g total carbohydrate, 0g dietary fiber, 2g sugars, 0g protein

TO MAKE HERBAL LEMON-INFUSED GIN

Place 8 ounces 80-proof gin, 5 thin slices lemon, and 5 sprigs fresh thyme (first rub between your fingers to awaken the fragrant essential oils) in a covered container, and let mixture stand for at least 24 hours (and up to a week) in the refrigerator, stirring occasionally. Strain the infused gin into a fresh container or bottle before using. Makes 8 ounces.

Seedless Watermelon Gin Fizz Ⓢ

Makes 1 serving: 1 (8½-fluid-ounce) drink

If you enjoy your drinks light on the alcohol and heavy on the refreshing, this fizz and you are made for each other. Your eyes (and heart) will be filled with delight by the vivid watermelon pink color of this spirited summery sipper. Bonus: it counts as a fruit serving, too.

1 cup chopped seedless watermelon

1½ ounces seltzer water or club soda

1 ounce 80-proof gin

1½ teaspoons fresh lemon juice

1 teaspoon fresh lime juice

½ teaspoon mild honey or agave nectar

1 small wedge watermelon or 1 lime slice (optional)

1. Add the watermelon, seltzer, gin, lemon juice, lime juice, and honey to a blender. Cover and puree.

2. Pour into a tall chilled glass filled with ice, garnish with the watermelon wedge (if using), and serve immediately.

Per serving: 120 calories, 0g total fat, 0g saturated fat, 0g trans fat, 0mg cholesterol, 0mg sodium, 16g total carbohydrate, 1g dietary fiber, 13g sugars, 1g protein

Gin Berry Fizz Ⓢ

Makes 1 serving: 1 (4-fluid-ounce) drink

If there were a beauty contest for cocktails, this pretty little gin fizz would win the crown. It's light on the gin and overflowing with fresh berry goodness. And it's fuchsia!

¼ cup chopped or sliced fresh strawberries

¼ cup fresh raspberries

¼ cup fresh blueberries

1 teaspoon raspberry or strawberry 100% fruit jam or ½ teaspoon mild honey

6 fresh mint leaves

1 ounce 80-proof gin

1 tablespoon fresh lemon juice

¼ cup seltzer water or club soda

1 large strawberry (optional)

1. Muddle the strawberries, raspberries, blueberries, jam, and mint in the bottom of a shaker container. Fill with ice and add the gin and lemon juice. Cover and shake well.

2. Strain into a chilled glass filled with ice, add the seltzer, and gently stir; garnish with the strawberry (if using), and serve.

Per serving: 100 calories, 0g total fat, 0g saturated fat, 0g trans fat, 0mg cholesterol, 0mg sodium, 9g total carbohydrate, 2g dietary fiber, 6g sugars, 1g protein

Fresh-Squeezed Gin Gimlet Ⓢ

Makes 1 serving: 1 (3-fluid-ounce) drink

Cocktail connoisseurs, my apologies for not making this drink in the traditional sense. But for those looking for a fresh take on tradition, I hope you'll agree that no apology is required for this fresh-squeezed gimlet. Shake, sip, and enjoy its goodness.

1½ ounces 80-proof gin

2 teaspoons fresh lime juice

1 teaspoon mild honey or agave nectar

1 tablespoon unsweetened green tea or water, chilled

1 lime slice

1. Add the gin, lime juice, honey, and tea to a shaker container. Whisk or cover and shake until the honey dissolves. Fill with ice, cover, and shake well.

2. Strain into a chilled martini glass (or pour into a lowball cocktail glass along with ice), garnish with the lime slice, and serve.

Per serving: 120 calories, 0g total fat, 0g saturated fat, 0g trans fat, 0mg cholesterol, 0mg sodium, 7g total carbohydrate, 0g dietary fiber, 6g sugars, 0g protein

Seasonal Pimm's Cup ⑤

Makes 1 serving: 1 (6½-fluid-ounce) drink plus produce

One of the most important components of a healthy diet is plenty of vegetables and fruits. So why not add produce to a cocktail? Actually, do plan to eat the fruits and veggies in this English-inspired beverage—during or after enjoyment of your rather thirst-quenching Pimm's cup. It's like a drink and an appetizer in one. And if you need to be extra calorie conscious, stir up a "Slim Pimm" by using a stevia-sweetened natural diet ginger ale.

1½ ounces Pimm's No. 1

3 ounces natural ginger ale (preferably made with fresh ginger)

2 ounces seltzer water or club soda

¼ cup thinly sliced fresh seasonal fruit, such as strawberry, peach, pear, or fig

1 slice lemon and/or orange

3 thin slices English cucumber

1 fresh mint sprig

1. Add the Pimm's, ginger ale, seltzer, and seasonal fruit to a chilled pilsner or other tall glass and gently stir.

2. Add a few ice cubes and the lemon and cucumber and gently stir.

3. Add extra ice to fill the glass.

4. Top with the mint sprig, and serve.

Per serving: 120 calories, 0g total fat, 0g saturated fat, 0g trans fat, 0mg cholesterol, 5mg sodium, 14g total carbohydrate, 1g dietary fiber, 10g sugars, 0g protein

Rum

All-Year-Round Mojito ⑤

Makes 1 serving: 1 (6-fluid-ounce) drink

Grow your own mint indoors on a sunny windowsill so you can muddle up this delicious beverage—with just enough sweetness—whenever you wish. It's especially agreeable paired with some spicy dancing. Salsa or cha-cha-cha anyone?

8 fresh mint leaves + 1 fresh mint sprig

1½ teaspoons fresh lime juice

1½ ounces 80-proof golden rum

2 teaspoons mild honey or agave nectar

½ cup seltzer water or club soda

1. Muddle the mint leaves and lime juice in a tall glass.

2. Add the rum and honey, and stir until the honey dissolves. Add ice (preferably crushed) and stir well. Add the seltzer, and gently stir.

3. Garnish with the mint sprig, and serve.

Per serving: 140 calories, 0g total fat, 0g saturated fat, 0g trans fat, 0mg cholesterol, 0mg sodium, 12g total carbohydrate, 0g dietary fiber, 12g sugars, 0g protein

Itoo Mojito ⑤

Makes 1 serving: 1 (6-fluid-ounce) drink

Although the mojito is traditionally considered a Cuban drink, I've given it even more international flair. My mother's roots are in a beautiful region of Lebanon near a hilltop village called Aitou—or Itoo. She often shared with me inspired tastes of the local cuisine, which was memorably rich in cinnamon, lemon, and mint. Those are the fragrant flavors that influenced this twist on a mojito.

8 fresh mint leaves + 1 fresh mint sprig

2 teaspoons fresh lemon juice

1½ ounces 80-proof spiced rum

2 teaspoons local honey or agave nectar

⅛ teaspoon ground cinnamon

½ cup seltzer water or club soda

1. Muddle the mint leaves and lemon juice in a tall glass.

2. Add the rum, honey, and cinnamon and stir until the honey dissolves. Add ice (preferably crushed), and stir well. Add the seltzer, and gently stir.

3. Garnish with the mint sprig, and serve.

Per serving: 140 calories, 0g total fat, 0g saturated fat, 0g trans fat, 0mg cholesterol, 0mg sodium, 13g total carbohydrate, 0g dietary fiber, 12g sugars, 0g protein

Fresh Gingered Strawberry Daiquiri Ⓢ

Makes 1 serving: 1 (10-fluid-ounce) drink

The coupling of fresh strawberries and ginger is a sweet and zingy one. Enjoy this punchy pink drink as a frozen-style daiquiri, too; simply use frozen strawberries. Enjoy a slimmer version by using a stevia-sweetened natural diet ginger.

¼ cup natural ginger ale (preferably made with fresh ginger)

5 large whole fresh strawberries

1½ ounces 80-proof golden rum

2 teaspoons fresh lime juice

½ teaspoon freshly grated gingerroot, or to taste

1. Add the ginger ale, 4 large ice cubes, 4 of the strawberries, the rum, lime juice, and ginger to a blender. Cover and puree.

2. Pour into a chilled daiquiri or other large beverage glass. Garnish with the remaining strawberry, and serve.

Per serving: 150 calories, 0g total fat, 0g saturated fat, 0g trans fat, 0mg cholesterol, 5mg sodium, 13g total carbohydrate, 2g dietary fiber, 10g sugars, 1g protein

Frozen Peaches and "Cream" Daiquiri Ⓢ

Makes 1 serving: 1 (8-fluid ounce) drink

Wow! This frozen daiquiri is tangy, peachy, and extra creamy. It's like sweet comfort in a glass. It's 100 calories less than a typical frozen daiquiri!

¼ cup + 1 teaspoon fat-free or low-fat plain Greek yogurt

½ cup diced fresh peaches, frozen

1½ ounces 80-proof golden rum

1 teaspoon fresh lemon juice

½ teaspoon mild honey or agave nectar

⅛ teaspoon pure vanilla extract

⅛ teaspoon pure almond extract

1. Add ¼ cup of the yogurt, ½ cup ice, the peaches, rum, lemon juice, honey, and extracts to a blender. Cover and puree.

2. Pour into a chilled martini, daiquiri, or other beverage glass. Top with the remaining 1 teaspoon yogurt, and serve immediately.

Per serving: 170 calories, 0g total fat, 0g saturated fat, 0g trans fat, 0mg cholesterol, 25mg sodium, 13g total carbohydrate, 1g dietary fiber, 12g sugars, 6g protein

Light Jamaican Breeze Ⓢ

Makes 1 serving: 1 (6½-fluid-ounce) drink

I've got a perky cocktail for you. Take a sip. But before you do, have a look. You'll first get a kick out of the lovely fuchsia color. Then you'll get a kick out of the tropical essence. It'll remind you of why you love pineapple—the fruit of hospitality.

3 thin slices fresh gingerroot

1½ ounces 80-proof white rum

2½ ounces 100% pineapple juice

1 ounce 100% cranberry or pomegranate juice

1½ ounces seltzer water or club soda

1 small pineapple wedge (optional)

1. Muddle the ginger and ½ ounce (1 tablespoon) of the rum in the bottom of a shaker container. Fill with ice and add the remaining 1 ounce rum, the pineapple juice, and cranberry juice. Cover and shake well.

2. Strain into a chilled glass with ice, add the seltzer, and stir. Garnish with the pineapple wedge (if using), and serve.

Per serving: 150 calories, 0g total fat, 0g saturated fat, 0g trans fat, 0mg cholesterol, 0mg sodium, 14g total carbohydrate, 0g dietary fiber, 13g sugars, 0g protein

Tropical Rum Frozen Cocktail Ⓢ

Makes 2 servings: 1 (11-fluid-ounce) drink each

I developed this as an afternoon cocktail . . . like one you'll sip as you hang out poolside or at the beach. Think of it as a gently spiked fruit smoothie. Its beachy appeal will win over any fruit aficionado's body—and soul.

1½ ounces 80-proof)light rum

10 large fresh strawberries, sliced and frozen

1 small or ½ large banana, sliced and frozen

½ cup diced fresh pineapple

½ cup low-fat vanilla frozen yogurt or non-dairy frozen dessert

¼ cup plain unsweetened coconut milk beverage or almond milk, well chilled

¼ teaspoon pure coconut extract, or to taste

2 whole strawberries or small pineapple wedges for garnish (optional)

1. Add the rum and strawberries to a blender. Cover and puree until smooth.

2. Pour into two tall glasses, such as pilsner glasses.

3. Add the banana, pineapple, frozen yogurt, coconut milk beverage, and coconut extract to a blender. Cover and puree until smooth.

4. Slowly pour the banana mixture over the strawberry mixture in the glasses, garnish each glass with a strawberry or pineapple wedge, if desired, and serve.

Per serving: 200 calories, 1g total fat, 0.5g saturated fat, 0g trans fat, 0mg cholesterol, 35mg sodium, 34g total carbohydrate, 4g dietary fiber, 24g sugars, 4g protein

Tequila

Mango Margarita Smoothie

Makes 1 serving: 1 (6-fluid-ounce) drink

Here's a sunny sipper for you. This spiked smoothie with its gorgeous golden-orange color has a thick velvety creaminess that you can't get anywhere except from a luscious mango. The mouth-feel—and taste—of this tequila cocktail is simply marvelous. Try it with 4 Copas tequila, which is made in a "green" distillery, meaning no chemicals are used.

1 ounce 80-proof reposado or gold tequila

½ ounce 30-proof triple sec or Cointreau

½ cup chopped fresh mango

2 teaspoons fresh lime juice

Pinch of sea salt

1 lime slice or long wedge fresh mango (optional)

1. Add the tequila, triple sec, mango, lime juice, salt, and 2 large ice cubes to a blender. Cover and puree well.

2. Pour into a chilled old-fashioned cocktail glass, garnish with the lime slice or mango wedge (if using), and serve.

Per serving: 140 calories, 0g total fat, 0g saturated fat, 0g trans fat, 0mg cholesterol, 160mg sodium, 19g total carbohydrate, 1g dietary fiber, 17g sugars, 1g protein

Spicy Green Margarita Ⓢ

Makes 1 serving: 1 (5-fluid-ounce) drink

This hits all the right spicy notes. But no worries if you're more of a "medium" instead of a "hot" spice fan; the roasted poblano is relatively mild while adding flavor depth, plus the hint of honey balances the spicier heat of the serrano. On top of that, this veggie drink has texture to add intrigue.

1 ounce 80-proof añejo, reposado, or gold tequila

½ ounce 30-proof triple sec or Cointreau

1 freshly roasted poblano pepper (page 27)

1 small serrano or ½ jalapeño pepper,
    with or without some seeds, chopped

2 teaspoons fresh lime juice

1 teaspoon honey or agave nectar

1 pepperoncini (optional)

1. Add the tequila, triple sec, poblano, serrano, lime juice, honey, and 2 large ice cubes to a blender. Cover and puree well.

2. Pour into a chilled old-fashioned cocktail glass, garnish with the pepperoncini (if using), and serve.

Per serving: 130 calories, 0g total fat, 0g saturated fat, 0g trans fat, 0mg cholesterol, 0mg sodium, 16g total carbohydrate, 1g dietary fiber, 14g sugars, 1g protein

Bloody Maria

Makes 1 serving: 1 (6½-fluid-ounce) drink

Replace vodka with tequila and you get a Bloody Maria instead of a Bloody Mary. Pair it with your favorite Mexican-style meal and you've got a fiesta caliente. ¡Olé!

½ cup tomato juice

1½ ounces 80-proof reposado or gold tequila

1 small serrano or ½ jalapeño pepper with
    some seeds, chopped

1 small garlic clove, chopped

1 teaspoon fresh lime juice

½ teaspoon freshly grated horseradish

⅛ teaspoon vegetarian Worcestershire sauce

⅛ teaspoon freshly ground black pepper

1 celery stalk or long jicama stick

1. Add the tomato juice, tequila, serrano, garlic, lime juice, horseradish, Worcestershire sauce, and black pepper to a shaker container filled with ice. Cover and shake well.

2. Strain into a tall chilled glass filled with ice, and serve with the celery.

Per serving: 130 calories, 0g total fat, 0g saturated fat, 0g trans fat, 0mg cholesterol, 380mg sodium, 8g total carbohydrate, 1g dietary fiber, 5g sugars, 2g protein

Papaya Sipper

Makes 1 serving: 1 (4-fluid-ounce) drink

Tequila is a tempter. Papaya is a temptress. Together they create an "M"-rated sexy and downright taste-tempting cocktail . . . for mature palates only.

¼ cup papaya or apricot nectar

1½ ounces 80-proof reposado or gold tequila

Pinch of sea salt

1 lime wedge

1. Add the papaya nectar, tequila, and salt to a shaker container filled with ice. Cover and shake well.

2. Strain into a chilled whiskey snifter or other small glass, garnish with the lime wedge, and serve. (The lime is to be squirted onto the beverage before sipping.)

Per serving: 130 calories, 0g total fat, 0g saturated fat, 0g trans fat, 0mg cholesterol, 160mg sodium, 9g total carbohydrate, 0g dietary fiber, 9g sugars, 0g protein

Citrus Tequila Sunrise

Makes 1 serving: 1 (8½-fluid-ounce) drink

This is one of those refreshing cocktails that can be easily sipped in the morning hours . . . at sunrise, in fact. It's rich in citrus rather than alcohol. Serve it at your next hangover-free brunch.

1 ounce 80-proof reposado or gold tequila

¼ cup fresh-squeezed pink or red grapefruit juice

1 ounce seltzer water or club soda

½ cup fresh-squeezed orange juice

½ ounce black raspberry liqueur, such as
    Chambord, or pomegranate liqueur

1 orange slice (optional)

1. Add the tequila, grapefruit juice, seltzer, and orange juice to a tall glass filled with ice.

2. Gently pour the liqueur down the inside of the glass, allowing it to sink to the bottom, garnish with the orange slice (if using), and serve.

Per serving: 200 calories, 0g total fat, 0g saturated fat, 0g trans fat, 0mg cholesterol, 10mg sodium, 24g total carbohydrate, 0g dietary fiber, 16g sugars, 1g protein

Garden Tequila Cocktail

Makes 1 serving: 1 (12-fluid-ounce) drink

Earthy folks will embrace this frothy cocktail. It has a pumpkin-orange color and lovely sweet, salty, and smoky overtones. It's full of vegetables, after all. But I bet many a beer connoisseur will embrace this unique cocktail, too. Serve it in a pilsner glass to woo them.

½ cup 100% pure pressed carrot juice

⅓ cup chopped unpeeled English cucumber
    + 1 English cucumber slice

⅓ cup chopped freshly roasted red bell pepper
    (page 27)

1½ ounces 80-proof reposado or gold tequila

1 teaspoon fresh lime juice

⅛ teaspoon smoked sea salt

1. Add the carrot juice, chopped cucumber, bell pepper, tequila, lime juice, salt, and 2 large ice cubes to a blender. Cover and puree until smooth and frothy.

2. Pour into a pilsner or other tall chilled glass, garnish with the cucumber slice, and serve.

Per serving: 150 calories, 0g total fat, 0g saturated fat, 0g trans fat, 0mg cholesterol, 320mg sodium, 12g total carbohydrate, 1g dietary fiber, 2g sugars, 2g protein

Whiskey/Bourbon/ Brandy

Half Irish Coffee

Makes 2 servings: 1 (7½-fluid-ounce) drink each

The combination of fat-free evaporated milk and a dollop of frozen yogurt provides delicious velvety creaminess without the excess calories . . . which is one of the reasons I call this a half Irish coffee. The other is because I'm half Irish. Sláinte!

1 ounce 80-proof Irish whiskey

1 double espresso, steaming hot (¾ cup)

1½ teaspoons mild honey or agave nectar

1 cup (8 ounces) fat-free evaporated milk, warm

2 mini-scoops (1 measuring tablespoon each)
    fat-free vanilla frozen yogurt

Pinch of unsweetened cocoa powder, ground
    cinnamon, or pumpkin pie spice (optional)

1. Preheat two heat-proof beverage glasses with hot water.

2. Stir together the whiskey, espresso, and honey in a 2-cup or larger, heat-proof liquid measuring cup. Add the evaporated milk and gently stir.

3. Pour the hot water out of the heat-proof beverage glasses. Pour the coffee beverage into each glass.

4. Top with the frozen yogurt, add the cocoa (if using), and serve immediately.

Per serving: 160 calories, 0g total fat, 0g saturated fat, 0g trans fat, 5mg cholesterol, 170mg sodium, 21g total carbohydrate, 0g dietary fiber, 21g sugars, 11g protein

Egg Nog Amandine Ⓢ

Makes 13 servings: 1 (4-fluid-ounce) drink each

Traditional egg nog pours close to 200 calories per ½ cup serving; this slender version tastes equally divine. Its slim secret is simply almond milk. This lively nog will be a hit at a holiday gathering, but plan ahead, as it needs at least four hours to chill.

5 large eggs

¼ cup turbinado sugar

¼ teaspoon sea salt

1 quart plain almond milk or unsweetened coconut milk beverage

1 teaspoon pure vanilla extract

¼ teaspoon pure almond extract

8 ounces 80-proof brandy

4 ounces 80-proof light rum

4 ounces 100% peach or apricot nectar

⅛ teaspoon freshly grated nutmeg, or to taste

1. Whisk together the eggs, sugar, and salt in a large saucepan. Stir in 2 cups of the almond milk. Simmer over low heat, stirring constantly, until the sugar is dissolved and mixture is steaming and slightly thickened, about 20 minutes. Remove from the heat. (Note: If you start to notice any egg scrambling during simmering, remove from the heat; it's ready.)

2. Stir in the remaining 2 cups almond milk and the extracts. Cover and chill in the refrigerator, at least 4 hours or overnight.

3. Just before serving, strain through a fine-mesh strainer into a punch-style bowl or glass pitcher and add the brandy, rum and nectar. Stir.

4. Ladle or pour into individual punch cups, sprinkle with the nutmeg, and serve.

Per serving: 120 calories, 2.5g total fat, 0.5g saturated fat, 0g trans fat, 70mg cholesterol, 120mg sodium, 8g total carbohydrate, 0g dietary fiber, 7g sugars, 3g protein

Fresh Mint Julep Bouquet Ⓢ

Makes 1 serving: 1 (2½-fluid-ounce) drink

My addition to this traditional Southern cocktail is ginger. It's the presentation that may just be the highlight of this potent sip of pleasure. There's a bouquet of mint served atop the julep, like a floral bouquet. A delight for the senses.

10 fresh mint leaves + 1 large sprig or several smaller sprigs fresh mint

2 teaspoons turbinado sugar

½ teaspoon freshly grated gingerroot

1½ ounces 80-proof bourbon or dark rum

1. Muddle the mint leaves with the sugar and ginger in a cocktail shaker. Fill with ice (preferably crushed or shaved), add the bourbon, and shake vigorously.

2. Pour the entire contents, including the ice, into an old-fashioned cocktail glass. Top with the mint sprig like it's a floral bouquet, and serve.

Per serving: 130 calories, 0g total fat, 0g saturated fat, 0g trans fat, 0mg cholesterol, 0mg sodium, 8g total carbohydrate, 0g dietary fiber, 8g sugars, 0g protein

Mixed Spirits and Other Cocktails

Pink Grapefruit Teaser ⓢ

Makes 1 serving: 1 (7½-fluid-ounce) drink

Salt the glass rim here; it provides a fancy front to this twist on a Salty Dog. The sweet and salty contrast along with the ginger-grapefruit pairing results in a palate pleaser with a punch. And for a slimmer "Trim Teaser," use a stevia-sweetened natural diet ginger ale.

1 ounce 80-proof blanco ("white") tequila

½ ounce 80-proof vodka

½ cup fresh-squeezed pink grapefruit juice

¼ cup natural ginger ale (preferably made with fresh ginger)

Pinch of sea salt

1 lime wedge

1. Pour the tequila and vodka into a chilled glass over 2 large ice cubes. (Use a coarse sea salt-rimmed glass, if preferred.)

2. Add the grapefruit juice, ginger ale, and salt and stir.

3. Garnish with the lime wedge, and serve.

Per serving: 170 calories, 0g total fat, 0g saturated fat, 0g trans fat, 0mg cholesterol, 150mg sodium, 18g total carbohydrate, 0g dietary fiber, 5g sugars, 1g protein

Long Island Earl Grey Iced Tea ⓢ

Makes 2 servings: 1 (6½-fluid-ounce) drink each

There's no actual iced tea in a traditional Long Island Iced Tea cocktail, so I decided to add it, truly making it a tea drink. I use bergamot-scented Earl Grey in place of the standard cola for a refreshing finish.

½ cup unsweetened Earl Grey tea
(made with 2 tea bags), chilled

1 tablespoon mild honey or agave nectar

¾ ounce 80-proof vodka

¾ ounce 80-proof gin

¾ ounce 80-proof light rum

¾ ounce 80-proof blanco ("white") tequila

½ ounce 30-proof triple sec

Juice of 1 small lemon (2 tablespoons)

3 ounces seltzer water or club soda

2 lemon wedges

1. Add the iced tea and honey to a cocktail shaker. Whisk or cover and shake until the honey dissolves. Fill with ice and add the vodka, gin, rum, tequila, triple sec, and lemon juice. Cover and shake well.

2. Pour the entire contents, with the ice, into two chilled tall or old-fashioned cocktail glasses. Add the seltzer, and stir.

3. Garnish with lemon wedges, and serve.

Per serving: 140 calories, 0g total fat, 0g saturated fat, 0g trans fat, 0mg cholesterol, 0mg sodium, 13g total carbohydrate, 0g dietary fiber, 12g sugars, 0g protein

"Big Apple" Manhattan Ⓢ

Makes 1 serving: 1 (4-fluid ounce) drink

This whiskey drink was inspired by the nickname for New York City. I created this sweet-tart fruit version of the Manhattan with a Granny Smith apple. Plunk in a cinnamon stick and you've got a glass of cool autumn contentment.

¼ cup finely chopped peeled Granny Smith apple

¼ cup unsweetened apple or white grape juice

1 ounce 80-proof rye whiskey

½ ounce extra-dry vermouth

Dash of Angostura bitters

1 cinnamon stick (optional)

1. Add the apple, apple juice, whiskey, vermouth, bitters, and 1 large ice cube to a blender. Cover and puree.

2. Strain through a fine-mesh strainer into a chilled martini glass, add the cinnamon stick (if using), and serve.

Per serving: 130 calories, 0g total fat, 0g saturated fat, 0g trans fat, 0mg cholesterol, 0mg sodium, 13g total carbohydrate, 0.5g dietary fiber, 9g sugars, 0g protein

Bubbly Raspberry Ginger Vodka Ⓢ

Makes 1 serving: 1 (4½-fluid-ounce) drink

Girls' night? Be sure to add this Champagne-splashed vodka cocktail to the party plan. Then pucker up to this pretty pink beverage with its spotlight on fresh raspberry and ginger. Or pucker up to an even skinnier version by using a stevia-sweetened natural diet ginger ale. Either way, it'll be sure to have you all feeling perky.

8 fresh or thawed frozen raspberries

3 very thin slices fresh gingerroot

1 ounce 80-proof vodka

1 ounce Champagne or sparkling white wine

2 ounces natural ginger ale (preferably made with fresh ginger)

1 fresh mint leaf (optional)

1. Muddle 7 of the raspberries with the ginger in a shaker container. Add the vodka and 3 large ice cubes, cover, shake well, and strain into a chilled martini glass.

2. Add the Champagne and ginger ale, top with the remaining raspberry and the mint leaf (if using), and serve.

Per serving: 110 calories, 0g total fat, 0g saturated fat, 0g trans fat, 0mg cholesterol, 0mg sodium, 8g total carbohydrate, 1g dietary fiber, 6g sugars, 0g protein

Natural Peanut Butter Cup Ⓢ

Makes 3 servings: 1 (3½-fluid ounce) drink

Enjoy this chocolate-covered peanut butter–inspired beverage in place of dessert. Velvety smooth and exceptionally rich tasting, this sweet cocktail is one to be sipped and savored slowly.

1¼ cups fat-free or low-fat vanilla frozen yogurt (100 calories per ½-cup serving)

1 ounce seltzer water or club soda

1 ounce 80-proof dark rum

½ ounce 80-proof vanilla vodka

1½ tablespoons no-salt-added creamy natural peanut butter

¼ teaspoon pure chocolate extract, or to taste

¼ teaspoon unsweetened cocoa powder

1. Add the frozen yogurt, seltzer, rum, vodka, peanut butter, chocolate extract, and ⅛ teaspoon of the cocoa powder to a blender. Cover and blend until smooth.

2. Pour into three whiskey snifters, champagne flutes, or juice glasses, dust the top of each with the remaining ⅛ teaspoon cocoa powder, and serve.

Per serving: 160 calories, 4g total fat, 1g saturated fat, 0g trans fat, 0mg cholesterol, 60mg sodium, 18g total carbohydrate, 1g dietary fiber, 17g sugars, 5g protein

Wine and Sparkling Wine Beverages

Summer Sangria Ⓢ

Makes 13 servings: 1 (6-fluid-ounce) drink + fruit

Serving a pitcher of sangria is a sure sign of a party in the making. Overloaded with fresh fruit, you and your party guests can have your drink and eat it, too. It'll be refreshing, filling, and, of course, festive.

2 bottles Spanish dry white wine or Sauvignon Blanc

4 ounces 80-proof brandy

4 ounces unsweetened white grape or apple juice

2 ounces 80-proof Cointreau

2 yellow nectarines, pitted and sliced

1 cup white seedless grapes

2 white or yellow peaches, pitted and sliced

1 lemon, unpeeled and thinly sliced

16 ounces seltzer water or club soda

13 fresh mint sprigs

1. Stir together the wine, brandy, grape juice, Cointreau, nectarines, grapes, peaches, and lemon in a large pitcher until combined. Chill in the refrigerator for up to 24 hours.

2. Add the seltzer and mint sprigs, and serve immediately.

Per serving: 160 calories, 0g total fat, 0g saturated fat, 0g trans fat, 0mg cholesterol, 0mg sodium, 13g total carbohydrate, 1g dietary fiber, 8g sugars, 1g protein

Blood Orange Mimosa Ⓢ

Makes 1 serving: 1 (3-fluid-ounce) drink

Apparently there's no such thing as perfect. But this fresh-squeezed mimosa begs to differ. It's a perfect beverage for sipping at brunch—even for those who are watching their calories.

1½ ounces Champagne or sparkling white wine, well chilled

1½ ounces fresh-squeezed blood orange or red navel juice, well chilled

Pour the Champagne into a champagne flute. Add the juice, and serve.

Per serving: 45 calories, 0g total fat, 0g saturated fat, 0g trans fat, 0mg cholesterol, 0mg sodium, 5g total carbohydrate, 0g dietary fiber, 3g sugars, 0g protein

Sweet Cherry-Apricot Mimosa Ⓢ

Makes 2 servings: 1 (3-fluid-ounce) drink each

It's June or July and you'd like to place mimosa on your personal menu? This version is a must-try. Bing cherries are in season—and create an incredible companion for Champagne. Cheers!

3 fresh or thawed frozen Bing cherries, pitted

2 ounces apricot nectar, well chilled

2 ounces Champagne or sparkling white wine, well chilled

1 ounce seltzer water or club soda, well chilled

1. Add the cherries and apricot nectar to a blender. Cover and puree until smooth and only tiny flecks of cherry skin remain. Pour the puree into champagne flutes.

2. Pour the Champagne and seltzer into the flutes, and serve.

Per serving: 45 calories, 0g total fat, 0g saturated fat, 0g trans fat, 0mg cholesterol, 0mg sodium, 7g total carbohydrate, 0g dietary fiber, 6g sugars, 0g protein

Appendices

Equivalence Charts

WEIGHTS AND MEASURES EQUIVALENCIES

MEASUREMENT	EQUALS
3 teaspoons	1 tablespoon (½ fluid ounce)
½ tablespoon	1½ teaspoons
2 tablespoons	⅛ cup (1 fluid ounce)
4 tablespoons	¼ cup (2 fluid ounces)
5⅓ tablespoons	⅓ cup; 5 tablespoons + 1 teaspoon
8 tablespoons	½ cup (4 fluid ounces)
10⅔ tablespoons	⅔ cup; 10 tablespoons + 2 teaspoons
12 tablespoons	¾ cup (6 fluid ounces)
16 tablespoons	1 cup (8 fluid ounces)
2 cups	1 pint (16 fluid ounces)
2 pints	1 quart; 4 cups (32 fluid ounces)
4 quarts	1 gallon; 8 pints; 16 cups (128 fluid ounces)

METRIC CONVERSION CHART

MEASUREMENT	CONVERT TO	MULTIPLY BY
ounces	grams	28.35
pounds	kilograms	0.45
teaspoons	milliliters	5
tablespoons	milliliters	15
fluid ounces	milliliters	30
cups	liters	0.24
pints	liters	0.47
quarts	liters	0.95

METRIC WEIGHTS AND MEASURES EQUIVALENCIES

OUNCES	GRAMS
0.035 ounce	1 gram
½ ounce	15 grams
1 ounce	28 grams
2 ounces	57 grams
4 ounces	115 grams
6 ounces	170 grams
8 ounces (½ pound)	225 grams
12 ounces	340 grams
16 ounces (1 pound)	450 grams
2.2 pounds	1 kilogram

TEMPERATURE CONVERSION CHART

DEGREES FARENHEIT (°F)	DEGREES CELSIUS (°C)
212	100
275	135
300	150
325	165
350	175
375	190
400	205
425	220
450	230
475	245
500	260

Recommended Safe Cooking Temperatures

It's best to use a food thermometer to determine these recommended minimum internal temperatures of foods.

FOOD	DEGREES FAHRENHEIT (°F)
Ground meat and meat mixtures	
Beef, pork, veal, lamb	160
Turkey, chicken	165
Fresh beef, veal, lamb	
Steaks, roasts, chops	145
Poultry	
Chicken and turkey, whole	165
Poultry breasts, roasts	165
Poultry thighs, wings	165
Duck and goose	165
Stuffing (cooked alone or in bird)	165
Fresh pork	145
Ham	
Fresh (raw)	145
Pre-cooked (to reheat)	140
Eggs and egg dishes	
Eggs	Cook until yolk and white are firm.
Egg dishes	160
Seafood	
Fish	145
	Cook fish until it is opaque (milky white) and flakes with a fork.
Shellfish	
Shrimp, lobster, scallops	Cook until the flesh of shrimp and lobster are an opaque color. Scallops should be opaque and firm.
Clams, mussels, oysters	Cook until their shells open. This means that they are done. Throw away any that were already open before cooking as well as ones that did not open after cooking.
Casseroles and reheated leftovers	165

Source: FoodSafety.gov

Resources

There's an enormous amount of information available about diet and healthful eating. To help you filter through all of the good and the bad, below is a selected list of some of the most useful resources.

Healthy Weight

Academy of Nutrition and Dietetics: Registered Dietitian Finder
http://www.eatright.org/programs/rdfinder

Calorie Control Council
http://www.caloriecontrol.org

The National Weight Loss Registry
http://www.nwcr.ws

Oldways: The Mediterranean Diet
http://www.oldwayspt.org/mediterraneandiet

WebMD Food & Fitness Planner
http://www.webmd.com/diet/food-fitness-planner

Weight Management (a practice group of the Academy of Nutrition and Dietetics): News
http://wmdpg.org/category/news/

Weight Watchers
http://www.weightwatchers.com

Diet and Weight Loss Apps

DietPoint
http://www.diet2goapp.com

FoodScanner
http://dailyburn.com/foodscanner

Lose It!
http://www.loseit.com

Tap & Track—Calorie Tracker
http://www.tapandtrack.com

WeightBot
http://tapbots.com/software/weightbot

Weight Watchers Mobile (including PointsPlus Calculators and iPad Kitchen Companion)
http://www.weightwatchers.com/templates/
marketing/marketing_utool_1col.
aspx?pageid=1191351

Diet and Nutrition Books

Eat Right When Time Is Tight
by Patricia Bannan, MS, RD. NorLightsPress, 2010.
http://patriciabannan.com

Your Inner Skinny
by Joy Bauer. HarperCollins, 2010.
http://www.joybauer.com

The Flexitarian Diet
by Dawn Jackson Blatner, RD, LDN. McGraw-Hill, 2009.
http://www.dawnjacksonblatner.com

The Calorie King®: Calorie, Fat and Carbohydrate Counter
by Allan Borushek, RD. Family Health Publications, 2011.
http://www.calorieking.com

***American Dietetic Association Complete Food and Nutrition Guide,* 4th Edition**
by Roberta Larson Duyff, MS, RD, FADA, CFCS. Wiley, 2012.
http://www.duyff.com

The Biggest Loser—6 Weeks to a Healthier You: Lose Weight and Get Healthy for Life
by Cheryl Forberg, RD, Melissa Roberson, Lisa Wheeler. Rodale, 2010.
http://www.cherylforberg.com

The Small Change Diet: 10 Steps to a Thinner, Healthier You
by Keri Gans, MS, RD, CDN. Gallery Books, 2011.
http://kerigansnutrition.com

Go Green Get Lean
by Kate Geagan, MS, RD. Rodale, 2009.
http://kategeagan.com

The DASH Diet Action Plan
by Marla Heller, MS, RD. Grand Central Life
& Style, 2011.
http://dashdiet.org

The Mediterranean Diet: Health & Science
by Richard Hoffman and Mariette Gerber.
Wiley-Blackwell, 2011.
http://www.wiley.com/WileyCDA/WileyTitle/
productCd-1444330020.html

*S.A.S.S! Yourself Slim: Conquer Cravings,
Drop Pounds and Lose Inches*
by Cynthia Sass, MPH, MA, RD, CSSD.
HarperOne, 2012.
http://www.cynthiasass.com

Small Changes, Big Results
by Ellie Krieger, MS, RD. Clarkson Potter, 2012.
http://elliekrieger.com

The Calorie Counter for Dummies
by Rosanne Rust, MS, RD, LDN and Meri
Raffetto, RD, LDN. Wiley, 2010.
http://www.rustnutrition.com
http://www.reallivingnutrition.com

*Eat Out, Eat Right: The Guide to Healthier
Restaurant Eating,* 3rd Edition
by Hope S. Warshaw, MMSc, RD, CDE. Surrey
Books, 2008.
http://www.hopewarshaw.com

Nutrition & Health

Academy of Nutrition and Dietetics
http://www.eatright.org

American Cancer Society
http://www.cancer.org

American Diabetes Association
http://www.diabetes.org

American Heart Association
http://www.americanheart.org

DASH Eating Plan
http://www.nhlbi.nih.gov/health/dci/Diseases/
dash/dash_what.html

The Dietary Guidelines for Americans
http://www.dietaryguidelines.gov

National Fiber Council
http://www.nationalfibercouncil.org

**International Food Information Council:
Food Insight**
http://www.foodinsight.org

MyPlate
http://www.choosemyplate.gov

**The Partnership for Food Safety Education/
Fight Bac!**
http://www.fightbac.org

Produce for Better Health Foundation
http://www.fruitsandveggiesmorematters.org

Sharecare
http://www.sharecare.com

WebMD
http://www.webmd.com

Foods/Ingredients

Annie's
dressings, condiments, snack foods
http://www.annies.com

Amy's Kitchen
canned beans, salsa, frozen cakes
http://www.amys.com

Applegate Farms
sliced cheeses, deli meats, sausage, hot dogs,
bacon
http://www.applegatefarms.com

Arrowhead Mills
whole grains, whole-grain flours, pie crust,
dry beans, lentils, seeds, nut butters
http://www.arrowheadmills.com

Bionaturae
pasta, olive oil, fruit spread, fruit nectars
http://www.bionaturae.com/products.html

Birds Eye
frozen vegetables
http://www.birdseye.com

Bob's Red Mill
whole grains, whole-grain flours, dried beans,
lentils, seeds
http://www.bobsredmill.com

Cascadian Farm
frozen produce, fruit spreads, granola
http://cascadianfarm.com

Chobani
Greek yogurt
http://www.chobani.com

Coleman Natural
poultry and pork products
http://www.colemannatural.com

DeBoles
pasta
http://www.deboles.com

Del Monte Fresh Produce
fresh whole and cut fruits and vegetables
http://www.freshdelmonte.com

Earthbound Farm
salad greens, vegetables, herbs, fruits
http://www.ebfarm.com

Earth's Best
applesauce, graham crackers
http://www.earthsbest.com

Eden Foods
canned beans, dried fruits, fruit sauces and
butters, fruit juices, vinegars, tomato products
http://www.edenfoods.com

Falksalt
flaked sea salts
http://www.falksalt.com

The Fillo Factory
whole-wheat and spelt phyllo dough
http://www.fillofactory.com

4 Copas Tequila
certified organic tequila
http://4copas.com

Fresh Ginger, Ginger Ale by Bruce Cost
ginger ale
http://www.freshgingerale.com

Garden of Eatin'
tortilla chips, whole-wheat tortillas, taco shells
http://www.gardenofeatin.com

Good Health Natural Foods
popcorn
http://www.goodhealthnaturalfoods.com

Hain Pure Foods
turbinado and other sugars, oils, sea salt
http://www.hainpurefoods.com

Heritage Foods
poultry, pork, beef, lamb, bison, tuna
http://heritagefoodsusa.com

Horizon
milk, butter, eggs, sour cream, cheese
http://www.horizondairy.com

Ian's Natural Foods
whole-wheat panko, frozen chicken nuggets
http://www.iansnaturalfoods.com

Imagine Foods
low-sodium broths
http://www.imaginefoods.com

Kashi
whole-grain cereals, crackers
http://www.kashi.com

Mary's Gone Crackers
whole-grain crackers
http://www.marysgonecrackers.com

McCormick
dried herbs and spices
http://www.mccormick.com

Muir Glen
tomato products
http://www.muirglen.com

Nature's Path
whole-grain cereals, sprouted whole-grain bread
http://www.naturespath.com

Nielsen-Massey Vanillas
pure flavor extracts
http://www.nielsenmassey.com

Oikos
Greek yogurt
http://www.stonyfield.com/products/oikos

Organic Prarie
meat, poultry, ham, bacon
http://www.organicprairie.com

Organic Valley
milk, cream, butter, cottage cheese, sour cream, eggs, soy milk
http://www.organicvalley.coop

Pacific Natural Foods
low-sodium broths, soy milk, almond milk, other plant-based milk beverages
http://www.pacificfoods.com

Pom Wonderful
pomegranates, fresh arils, juice
http://www.pomwonderful.com

Red Jacket Orchards
fresh fruits, fruit juices and nectars
http://www.redjacketorchards.com

Rudi's Organic Bakery
whole-grain breads, buns, rolls, tortillas, wraps, bagels, English muffins, sandwich thins (flatz)
http://www.rudisbakery.com

Santa Cruz Organic
fruit juices, sauces, spreads, peanut butter
http://www.scojuice.com

Silk
soy milk, almond milk
http://silksoymilk.com

Simply Organic
spices, pure flavor extracts
http://www.simplyorganicfoods.com

Soy Dream
plant-based milk beverages and frozen desserts
http://www.tastethedream.com

Spectrum
oils and vinegars
http://www.spectrumorganics.com

Stonyfield Farm
yogurt and frozen yogurt
http://www.stonyfield.com

Sunsweet
dried fruits
http://www.sunsweet.com

Westbrae Natural
condiments, pasta, miso
http://www.westbrae.com

Wild Harvest
salsas, frozen produce
http://wildharvestorganic.com

Wonderful Pistachios
shelled and in-shell pistachios
http://getcrackin.com

Plant-Based Info

Apples: U.S. Apple Association
http://www.usapple.org

Almonds: Almond Board of California
http://www.almondboard.com

Asparagus: California Asparagus Commission
http://www.calasparagus.com

Avocados: California Avocado Commission
http://www.avocado.org

Avocados: Hass Avocado Board
http://www.avocadocentral.com

Avocados: Avocados from Mexico
www.avocadosfrommexico.com

Beans: California Dry Bean Board
http://calbeans.org

Beans: U.S. Dry Bean Council
http://www.beansforhealth.org

Beer: National Beer Wholesalers of America
http://nbwa.org/about/all-about-brew/
beer-pairings

Blackberries: Oregon Raspberry & Blackberry Commission
http://www.oregon-berries.com

Blueberries: U.S. Highbush Blueberry Council
http://www.blueberrycouncil.com

Cherries: California Cherry Marketing and Research Board
http://www.calcherry.com

Cherries: Cherry Marketing Institute
http://www.choosecherries.com

Citrus: Florida Department of Citrus
http://www.floridajuice.com

Cranberries: Cranberry Marketing Committee
http://www.uscranberries.com

Dry Peas, Lentils & Chickpeas: USA Dry Pea & Lentil Council
http://www.pea-lentil.com

Figs: California Fig Advisory Board
http://www.californiafigs.com

Grapes: California Table Grape Commission
http://www.tablegrape.com

Grains/Wheat: Kansas Wheat Commission
http://www.kswheat.com

Grains/Wheat: Wheat Foods Council
http://www.wheatfoods.org

Honey: National Honey Board
http://www.honey.com

Kiwifruit: California Kiwifruit Commission
http://www.kiwifruit.org

Maple Syrup: Maine Maple Producers Association
http://www.mainemapleproducers.com

Mushrooms: The Mushroom Council
http://mushroominfo.com

Nuts: International Tree Nut Council
http://www.nuthealth.org

Oil, Canola: Canola Council of Canada
http://canolainfo.org

Oil, Olive: California Olive Oil Council
http://www.cooc.com

Oil, Olive: Foods from Spain
http://www.oliveoilfromspain.com

Onions: National Onion Association
http://www.onions-usa.org

Pasta: National Pasta Association
http://www.ilovepasta.org

Peanuts: The Peanut Institute
http://www.peanut-institute.org

Peanut Butter: Southern Peanut Growers
http://www.peanutbutterlovers.com

Pears: Pear Bureau Northwest
http://www.usapears.com

Pecans: National Pecan Shellers Association
http://www.ilovepecans.org

Pistachios: Pistachio Health
http://www.pistachiohealth.com

Potato: United States Potato Board
http://www.healthypotato.com

Prunes: California Dried Plum Board
http://www.californiadriedplums.org

Raisins: California Raisin Marketing Board
http://www.calraisins.org

Raspberries: Washington Red Raspberry Commission
http://www.red-raspberry.org

Rice: USA Rice Federation
http://www.riceinfo.com

Soy: United Soybean Board
http://unitedsoybean.org

Spirits: Distilled Spirits Council of the United States
http://www.discus.org

Strawberries: California Strawberry Commission
http://www.calstrawberry.com

Sweet Potato: The United States Sweet Potato Council
http://www.sweetpotatousa.org

Tea: The Tea Association of the USA, the Tea Council of the USA, and the Specialty Tea Institute
http://www.teausa.org

Tomatoes: Florida Tomato Committee
http://www.floridatomatoes.org

Tomato Products: Tomato Products Wellness Council
http://www.tomatowellness.com

Vinegar: The Vinegar Institute
http://www.versatilevinegar.org

Walnuts: California Walnut Commission
http://www.walnut.org

Whole Grains: The Whole Grains Council
http://www.wholegrainscouncil.org

Wine: Wine Market Council
http://www.americanwinesociety.org

Media

Cooking Light
http://www.cookinglight.com

Fitness
http://www.fitnessmagazine.com

Food Network: Healthy Eating
http://www.foodnetwork.com/healthy-eating

Health
http://www.health.com

Kiwi
http://www.kiwimagonline.com

Natural Health
http://www.naturalhealthmag.com

Prevention
http://www.prevention.com

Men's Health
http://www.menshealth.com

WebMD
http://www.webmd.com

Equipment

Blenders (Food & Beverage):
Waring PRO or Vitamix
http://www.waringproducts.com
http://www.vitamix.com

Blenders (Immersion): Cuisinart
http://www.cuisinart.com

Citrus Reamers: Norpro
http://www.norpro.com

Coffee Grinder: Krups
http://www.krups.com

Cookware/Pans (PFOA-free Nonstick):
Scanpan
http://www.scanpan.com

Cookware/Pans (Stainless): All-Clad
http://www.all-clad.com

Cookware/Pans (Cast Iron):
Lodge or Le Creuset
http://lodgemfg.com
http://www.lecreuset.com

Cutting Boards: Architec
http://www.architecproducts.com

Food Processors: KitchenAid
http://www.kitchenaid.com

Grater/Zesters: Microplane
http://microplane.com

Kitchen Scales: EatSmart
http://www.eatsmartproducts.com

Knives: Wüsthof
http://www.wusthof.com

Measuring Utensils: All-Clad
http://www.all-clad.com

Oil Sprayers: Misto (Pfaltzgraff)
http://www.pfaltzgraff.com

Panini Grills: De'Longhi or Breville
http://www.shopdelonghi.com
https://www.brevilleusa.com

Peelers: OXO
http://www.oxo.com

Prep Equipment & Mixing Bowls: Pyrex
http://www.pyrex.com

Silicone Brushes: Le Creuset
http://www.lecreuset.com

Timers (Kitchen, Digital): Presto
http://www.gopresto.com

Whisks: Norpro
http://www.norpro.com

Woks: Town Food Service
http://townfood.com

Farmers' Markets and CSAs

Biodynamic Farming and Gardening
Association
http://www.biodynamics.com/csa.html

Farm Locator
http://newfarm.org/farmlocator/index.php

Local Harvest
http://www.localharvest.org

National Sustainable Agriculture Information
Service
https://attra.ncat.org/attra-pub/local_food/
search.php

USDA Farmers' Market Search
http://apps.ams.usda.gov/FarmersMarkets

Sustainable, Organic and "Green" Resources

The Daily Green
http://www.thedailygreen.com

Eat Well Guide
http://www.eatwellguide.org

Environmental Defense Fund
http://www.edf.org

Environmental Working Group (EWG)
http://www.ewg.org

EWG's Shopper's Guide to Pesticides in Produce
http://www.ewg.org/foodnews

Greenopia
http://www.greenopia.com

Hunger & Environmental Nutrition (a practice group of the Academy of Nutrition and Dietetics)
http://www.hendpg.com

Marine Stewardship Council
http://www.msc.org

Monterey Bay Aquarium Seafood Watch
http://www.mbayaq.org/cr/seafoodwatch.asp

Natural Resources Defense Council
http://www.nrdc.org

Organic Consumers Association
http://www.organicconsumers.org

Slow Food USA
http://www.slowfoodusa.org

Sustainable Table
http://www.sustainabletable.org

TreeHugger
http://www.treehugger.com

USDA Agricultural Marketing Service– National Organic Program
http://ams.usda.gov/nop

Vegetarian Resources

Vegetarian Nutrition (a dietetic practice group)
http://vegetariannutrition.net

Vegetarian Resource Group (VRG)
http://www.vrg.org

Dining

Green Restaurant Association's Dine Green
http://dinegreen.com/customers/default.asp

Happy Cow
http://www.happycow.net

Healthy Dining
http://healthydiningfinder.com

Culinary Information

Food & Culinary Professionals (a dietetic practice group)
http://www.foodculinaryprofs.org

The Institute of Culinary Education (cooking school)
http://iceculinary.com

ROUXBE (online cooking school)
http://rouxbe.com

Also, please check out my other cookbooks, *Big Green Cookbook* and *The All-Natural Diabetes Cookbook* and my website for more recipes that fit into your healthful lifestyle.

http://jackienewgent.com

Index